The Editor

MICHAEL GORRA is the Mary Augusta Jordan Professor of English at Smith College and the author of *Portrait of a Novel: Henry James and the Making of an American Masterpiece*, a finalist for the Pulitzer Prize in biography. He has received fellowships from the Guggenheim Foundation and twice from the National Endowment for the Humanities, including a Public Scholar Award, along with the Balakian Award from the National Book Critics Circle for his work as a reviewer. His other books include *The English Novel at Mid-Century; After Empire: Scott, Naipaul, Rushdie;* and *The Bells in Their Silence: Travels through Germany;* as well as the Norton Critical Editions of William Faulkner's *The Sound and the Fury* and *As I Lay Dying*.

D1158657

NORTON CRITICAL EDITIONS
AMERICAN REALISM & REFORM

For a complete list of Norton Critical Editions, visit
wwnorton.com/nortoncriticals

A NORTON CRITICAL EDITION

Henry James
THE PORTRAIT OF A LADY

AN AUTHORITATIVE TEXT
BACKGROUNDS AND CONTEXTS
CRITICISM

Edited by

MICHAEL GORRA
SMITH COLLEGE

W · W · NORTON & COMPANY · *New York* · *London*

W. W. Norton & Company has been independent since its founding in 1923, when William Warder Norton and Mary D. Herter Norton first published lectures delivered at the People's Institute, the adult education division of New York City's Cooper Union. The firm soon expanded its program beyond the Institute, publishing books by celebrated academics from America and abroad. By midcentury, the two major pillars of Norton's publishing program—trade books and college texts—were firmly established. In the 1950s, the Norton family transferred control of the company to its employees, and today—with a staff of four hundred and a comparable number of trade, college, and professional titles published each year—W. W. Norton & Company stands as the largest and oldest publishing house owned wholly by its employees.

Copyright © 2018 by W. W. Norton & Company, Inc.

All rights reserved
Printed in the United States of America
First Edition

Composition by Westchester Publishing Services
Manufacturing by LSC Communications
Production supervisor: Liz Marotta

Library of Congress Cataloging-in-Publication Data

Names: James, Henry, 1843–1916, author. | Gorra, Michael Edward, editor.
Title: The portrait of a lady : an authoritative text, backgrounds and contexts
    criticism / Henry James ; edited by Michael Gorra.
Description: First edition. | New York : W. W. Norton & Company, 2018. |
    Series: A Norton critical edition | Includes bibliographical references.
Identifiers: LCCN 2017017112 | ISBN 9780393938531 (pbk.)
Subjects: LCSH: James, Henry, 1843–1916. Portrait of a lady. | Young
    women—Fiction. | Americans—Italy—Fiction. | Inheritance and
    succession—Fiction. | Married people—Fiction. | Triangles (Interpersonal
    relations)—Fiction. | Italy—Fiction. | Psychological fiction. | Love stories.
Classification: LCC PS2116 .P6 2018 | DDC 813/.4—dc23
LC record available at https://lccn.loc.gov/2017017112

ISBN: 978-0-393-93853-1 (pbk.)

W. W. Norton & Company, Inc., 500 Fifth Avenue, New York, NY 10110
wwnorton.com

W. W. Norton & Company Ltd., 15 Carlisle Street, London W1D 3BS

1 2 3 4 5 6 7 8 9 0

Contents

Introduction

The Portrait of a Lady was Henry James's first true success: the novel in which, after a long and careful apprenticeship, he at last allowed his imagination full stretch. It told the story of a girl named Isabel Archer, who at twenty claims that she's fond of her freedom but who stands just the same, after the death of her spendthrift father, on the verge of marriage to a New England mill-owner. Then she suffers a fairy-tale rescue at the hands of an aunt. Taken to Europe and furnished with an unexpected inheritance, Isabel finds what looks like an ever-expanding field in which to exercise her own sense of independence. At first. For she will soon make the mistake of her young life, and her mixture of "curiosity and fastidiousness" (45),[1] brittle intelligence, and inflated confidence, would make her an easy mark for the reader's criticism if she were not, as James wrote, meant to awaken our sense of tenderness instead.

As a young man James had made fun of the idea of the Great American Novel, but greatness had always been on his mind, and the *Portrait* was the book from which, as he told a friend, he "would pretend to date."[2] And for us today it appears to look backward and forward at once, offering a Janus-faced lens on the history of the novel itself. It provides the link between George Eliot and Virginia Woolf, the bridge across which Victorian fiction stepped over into modernism. James used his heroine to crystallize one of his period's central concerns, that of what George Eliot herself had described as the "delicate vessels"[3] of female experience. Isabel's chronicle touched the limits of what could and couldn't be said about sex in the Anglo-American fiction of the period, and James also flouted the conventions of his era by risking an ending that was both unhappy and open; the novel's final pages leave Isabel's fate more unsettled than ever. Moreover, the *Portrait* challenged its readers' assumptions about the nature of fictional events. In James's hands the drama of the interior life took on the thrill that other writers might find in "the surprise of a caravan or the identification of a pirate" (13), and the result was the most searching account of the moment-by-moment flow of consciousness that any novelist had yet attempted.

But the book looks two ways in another sense as well, not temporally but spatially. In 1888 James told his brother, the Harvard philosopher William James, that he wanted to make it impossible for his readers to know whether he was "an American writing about England or an Englishman writing about America."[4] Sometimes he managed the trick and sometimes

---

1. Page numbers in parentheses refer to this Norton Critical Edition.
2. Letter to Thomas Sergeant Perry, in Virginia Harlow, *Thomas Sergeant Perry* (Durham: Duke University Press, 1950), p. 305.
3. George Eliot, *Daniel Deronda*, ch. 11.
4. *Henry James Letters III*, ed. Leon Edel (Cambridge: The Belknap Press, 1980), p. 244.

he didn't, but one mark of his overall success lies in the different contexts within which his work is now read. That's especially true of *The Portrait of a Lady*. It appears as often in discussions of the Victorian novel as it does in those of American literature, and rightfully so. For its richly suggestive picture of what it is to be an American depends, paradoxically, on the way it uses both its European setting and the thematics of European fiction—the marriage plot, the novel of adultery—to mount a critique of the guiding assumptions of American identity itself.

There's much, too much, to say about the *Portrait* and its author, and his story has been told many times, in his own memoirs and in those of his friends, and by a series of skilled biographers. There's the strange childhood in a remarkable and yet smothering family, in which he and his siblings were ferried back and forth across the ocean in accordance with their father's whims; there's the prolonged period of invalidism and passivity in early manhood, while his younger brothers were fighting in the Civil War. He started to publish not long before the war's conclusion, and at the end of the 1860s he began to travel, to make at last an independent life. James discovered himself in Europe, in England and France, and especially Italy, and in doing so he also discovered his first great subject in the lives of Americans abroad. In 1875 he left his native land behind and settled for a year in Paris before moving to London, where he would make his home. "I have made my choice," he wrote in 1881, when after finishing the *Portrait* he returned for a few months to America, and what he had chosen was "the old world—my choice, my need, my life" (432).

Henry James had a long career, some fifty years from start to finish, and it contained failures as well as successes. It's a complicated tale, and anyone grappling with it should ask what was at stake in James's choices. So let's look closely at a moment in *The Portrait of a Lady* itself. When Isabel first arrives in England, she stays at a house on the Thames called Gardencourt, one owned by her uncle, Daniel Touchett, an elderly American banker who has made his career in Britain. There she both receives and refuses a proposal from a charming, bashful Englishman who has the misfortune of being "a territorial, a political, a social magnate" (78). Isabel has hoped that Gardencourt would show her a lord, but she turns down this one because as Lord Warburton he seems to her less a person than a personage, because she cannot separate him from all the things and traditions that cluster around him.

Before long, Isabel's uncle falls gravely ill, and she's getting used to the idea of his probable death when she hears an unexpected ripple of music from Gardencourt's vast drawing room. The pianist plays with unusual skill, and Isabel is immediately intrigued by the fact that this new guest, though an American, should so much resemble a Frenchwoman. In fact, her name is French. "I'm Madame Merle," she says, as though "referring to a person of tolerably distinct identity" (126). The two women spend the next weeks in each other's company, and Isabel's admiration of her new friend grows by the day. Madame Merle is tall and fair and widowed, and something over forty. She works elaborate morsels of embroidery, she plays and paints, and though Gardencourt is hushed by sickness, she stays on because Isabel's Aunt Touchett wants her to: a welcome guest who knows just when to leave, and where to go next.

Isabel soon recognizes that she's under the older woman's influence, that at moments, indeed, she wants to be like her. Still, she does see that Madame Merle has a fault. She is "too perfectly the social animal" (137), and Isabel admits to herself that she cannot conceive of this supple creature in isolation, cannot imagine her inner life. And she's troubled as well by the fact that her kind and amusing cousin Ralph doesn't like her. He says that he was long ago in love with Madame Merle, but he does not like her. Isabel's two friends do, however, agree about one thing. They are each interested in her future, and yet that interest takes different forms. Ralph wants to see what the young woman does with herself, to see the kind of life she will fashion. Madame Merle, however, says that she wants "to see what life makes" (135) of Isabel, and emphasizes the shaping force of the world around her. The difference is crucial, and points to a talk the two women have as they wait in that great house for the old man's death.

The older woman admits to being ambitious, but she calls her own unrealized dreams "preposterous" (143). Isabel answers that she herself has already known that kind of success. She has seen a childhood fantasy come true, though she has to blush at the accuracy with which her friend defines and discounts it. A young man on his knees? We have all had that, Madame Merle says, and if "yours was a paragon . . . why didn't you fly with him to his castle in the Apennines?" (144). The location is nicely chosen. Hawthorne gave his readers such a mountain refuge in *The Marble Faun* (1860), and Anne Radcliffe had earlier used that setting in her 1794 Gothic romance *The Mysteries of Udolpho*. Madame Merle's words imply that Isabel's dream is above all a literary one, and tired. They remind the girl of the conventional plot she has rejected in rejecting Lord Warburton, and they also suggest her lingering naïveté, in a way that makes her prickly. He has no such castle, she says, and besides, "I don't care anything about his house" (144).

Isabel's friend finds that sentiment crude, and the conversation that follows stands as one of the most probing moments in all of James's work. He gives us here an understated examination of the very nature of the self, of the American self in particular, and the passage needs to be quoted at length. "When you have lived as long as I," Madame Merle says,

> "you'll see that every human being has his shell and that you must take the shell into account. By the shell I mean the whole envelope of circumstances. There's no such thing as an isolated man or woman; we're each of us made up of some cluster of appurtenances. What shall we call our 'self'? Where does it begin? Where does it end? It overflows into everything that belongs to us—and then it flows back again. I know a large part of myself is in the clothes I choose to wear. I've a great respect for *things*! One's self—for other people—is one's expression of one's self; and one's house, one's furniture, one's garments, the books one reads, the company one keeps—these things are all expressive." (144)

A great respect for *things*. The phrase links her to Balzac, in whose world sexual desire is but a shadow of the lust for material goods, and whose great hero, as James himself wrote, is the 20-franc piece. And Isabel replies:

> "I think just the other way. I don't know whether I succeed in expressing myself, but I know that nothing else expresses me. Nothing that

belongs to me is any measure of me; everything's on the contrary a limit, a barrier, and a perfectly arbitrary one. Certainly the clothes which, as you say, I choose to wear, don't express me; and heaven forbid they should . . . [They] may express the dressmaker, but they don't express me." (144)

For one thing, it's not in fact her choice to wear them, though Madame Merle puts a stop to that line of reasoning by asking if she'd prefer to go naked.

Early in *Anna Karenina*, Tolstoy writes that his heroine's beauty lies in the way that she seems to stand apart from her clothes. "What she wore was never seen on her,"[5] and even the most luxurious dress becomes an unnoticeable frame for the self. So it is for Isabel—or rather, that's how she wants it to be. The passage I've quoted comes a few pages after we learn something that she herself does not yet know: her uncle plans to leave her a staggering fortune. So we read her words with a certain irony, knowing that whether or not her wardrobe expresses her, she's soon going to have a bigger one. Still, this argument looks like a fair fight. We can't easily reject either woman's position, and while the balance does finally tip, we're not happy about it. We'd prefer to side with Isabel—with youth—and her ideal remains necessary, the ideal of some unified and autonomous self, independent of and anterior to its social circumstances. Madame Merle suggests, in contrast, that the self is socially determined and not entirely separable from the world around it. The things that surround us not only express that self, but they also serve to shape it. Our possessions represent us—they provide the shell within which the self is bound and through which other people know it.

Madame Merle speaks for the kind of self that Isabel had rejected in rejecting Lord Warburton: the self as defined by its appurtenances, by a trailing penumbra of houses and history; the self as both person and personage. She speaks for age, for the things our young woman will need another twenty years to learn, and she also speaks as a "lady," the social category to which both women belong and whose shaping force is so completely naturalized that Isabel can't even see it. But above all she speaks for Europe. And Isabel is the voice of American exceptionalism, a woman who sings of herself, and only herself; who believes her possessions are arbitrary, a limit imposed on her freedom; and who cannot accept the idea of merging that self in some other identity. She likes instead to see herself as a version of what the critic R. W. B. Lewis called the "American Adam," heroine "of a new adventure, an individual emancipated from history, happily bereft of ancestry, untouched and undefiled by the usual inheritance of family and race."[6] Isabel is an orphan, and even as her Aunt Touchett pays the bills, she describes the girl as being her own mistress, someone who wants, as James tells us, "to leave the past behind her" (33). The paradox is that she finds her clean start in coming to Europe, to an ancient land in which she appears newborn. Yet her very desire to discard the past tells us that she has one. No "lady" is without a social inheritance; no one with a sudden fortune of family money is quite so pleasantly bereft.

---

5. In the Pevear and Volokhonsky translation (New York: Viking Penguin, 2001), p. 79.
6. R. W. B. Lewis, *The American Adam* (Chicago: U of Chicago P, 1955), p. 5.

James historicized such ambitions in his 1879 study of Hawthorne, writing that the idea of "the supremacy of the individual to himself . . . must have had a great charm for people whose society seemed bare of other amusements."[7] The words come from his account of Hawthorne's relations with New England's reforming class in general and Emerson in particular, and this moment in the novel is indeed often read in terms of Emerson. Many critics cite a line from "The Transcendentalist," in which Emerson writes that "you think me the child of my circumstances. I make my circumstances," and suggests that the thought "which is called I" has the power to mold the world into the form of its own desire.[8] Though in truth, there's nothing easier than to find Emersonian tags for Isabel's self-conception. We may pluck a line from "Self-Reliance," in which Emerson describes the human soul as defined by a continuous process of *becoming*, "self-sufficing . . . self-relying," and goes on to treat one's possessions as a form of accident, scorning a world in which people measure each other by what one has rather than what one is. We may look at "History," in which he tells us that the self is greater than all geography; history matters only because it allows us to make metaphors for our souls. But we also need to remember that the *Portrait* itself is larger than Isabel's own consciousness. It knows from the start some things that she will only gradually discover, and we must remember too that James thought Emerson's own great weakness was his "ripe unconsciousness of evil."[9]

Isabel believes in her own autonomy, her own enabling isolation: a belief, and a dream, that all her later experience will challenge, as she learns what the Old World always has to teach; a folly at whose cost she will purchase wisdom. For in the words of John Adams, "there is no special providence for Americans, their nature is the same with that of others."[1] The same, except in ideology, in our fixed belief that we aren't; a belief that makes us the perpetual victims of our born-again innocence, lost one year and renewed the next. James asks us here to define our relation to the world outside, to the life beyond our borders. Do we need it? Can we stand alone? The stakes in this delicate talk about clothes are enormous, and his characters' words address not only the nature and limits of the individual self but also that of our country's relation to other lands; the relation that James's own expatriation had put into question. And that account of the limits of self-sufficiency is what, above all, gives *The Portrait of a Lady* its place among the greatest of great American novels.

James began his concerted effort on the novel in Florence during the spring of 1880, where in a hotel room overlooking the Arno he "took up, and worked over, an old beginning made long ago" (432). He wrote through the spring, and then returned to London and a visit from his brother William; wrote through a series of stays in coastal towns and country houses, and then in the new year took himself to the south once more, stopping eventually in Venice and lingering there through June until he had "finished, or virtually finished, my novel" (434). He put the final touches on it

---

7. Henry James, *Literary Criticism I: Essays, American and English Writers* (New York: Library of America, 1984), p. 383.
8. The essays quoted here each form a chapter of Emerson's *Essays: First Series* (1841).
9. *Literary Criticism I*, p. 254.
1. Quoted in Gordon Wood, *Revolutionary Characters* (New York: Penguin, 2006), p. 181.

in London in the summer of 1881, but by that time much of it was already in print. The novel had begun its serial run the previous year, appearing in Britain's *Macmillan's Magazine* from October 1880 through November 1881, and in Boston's *Atlantic Monthly* from November 1880 to December 1881. The American magazine typically came out two weeks before its cover date, in the middle of the preceding month, and so the lag between British and U.S. publication was brief. James sent each month's copy to Macmillan's printer, the firm of Clay and Taylor, which returned two sets of proof sheets for him to correct. One of them went back to Macmillan, the other crossed the ocean to Houghton Mifflin, the *Atlantic*'s publisher. Neither the novel's manuscript nor those proofs survive. Many nineteenth-century magazines were illustrated, and James's *Washington Square*, with drawings by George du Maurier, had just completed its course in the British *Cornhill* when the *Portrait* began its run. But neither *Macmillan's* nor the *Atlantic* had pictures, and the author preferred it that way.[2]

James often told his friends not to read his work in the magazines but to wait for the finished book. It would, he said, be far more effective in that form: he didn't conceive of each installment as a dramatic unit in its own right, but worked instead with an eye to its overall shape. *The Portrait of a Lady* may have been serialized, but it was not a serial novel, not in the way that Dickens's books were, with their monthly denouements, or even George Eliot's *Middlemarch*. Still, it's interesting to note what's included in each part, as well as James's decision, in two places, to change the chapter-breaks. For the first four months the chapter structure of the serial version and the finished book are identical, and run as follows:

I: Ch. 1 to 5
II: 6 to 10
III: 11 to 14
IV: 15 to 18

But chapter 20 in the serialized version was extremely long, and in preparing the book version James decided to split it in two. The serial version of part V includes just chapters 19 and 20; in the finished book that corresponds to chapters 19–21.

For the following months the first pair of figures designates the chapter numbers as the novel ran in the magazines, the second as the chapters appeared—and appear—in the book:

VI: 21–24; 22–25
VII: 25–28; 26–29
VIII: 29–34; 30–35
IX: 35–38; 36–39
X: 39–42; 40–43
XI: 43–46; 44–47 (half)

2. In preparing these notes on the novel's textual and publication history I have consulted and drawn upon the following: *Henry James: Novels 1881–1886*, ed. William T. Stafford (New York: Library of America, 1985); Adrian Poole, "Dying Before the End: The Reader in *The Portrait of a Lady*," *The Yearbook of English Studies*, vol. 26; Philip Horne, *Henry James and Revision* (Oxford: The Clarendon Press, 1990); and David J. Supino, *Henry James: A Bibliographical Catalogue of a Collection of Editions to 1921*, 2nd edition, revised (Liverpool University Press, 2006, 2014).

One surprise here is that the novel's famous and in many ways climactic chapter 42 (41 in the serial), which in his preface James singled out as the best thing in the book, does *not* conclude a magazine installment. At this point James altered his chapter-breaks once more, combining the serial's brief chapters 46 and 47 into a single long chapter for the book version. Part XII accordingly began with what became the second half of the book's chapter 47, and ran on through 49. That once more synchronized the chapter numbering of the monthly installments and the finished volume, and the last parts went as follows:

XIII: 50 to 52
XIV: 53 to 55

James was correcting proofs for the book edition of the novel well before it completed its serial run; those chapter-breaks aside, he made only minor changes between the two.

Clay and Taylor once more set type, from which molds were made for stereographic plates that were then shipped to Boston. After that the type was leaded out—more space inserted between the lines—to make it fill the three volumes that were the British standard for new novels. Macmillan released the novel in October 1881, in an edition of 750 copies. The first volume ended with chapter 19; the second with chapter 39. Houghton Mifflin published the novel in a single volume that November, but with a date of 1882 on its title page; the first printing was of 1,520 copies.

That version of the novel is often read today—it's in print in several editions, and can also be found in many older library copies. This Norton Critical Edition, however, uses the text as James revised it for what is called the New York Edition of his Novels and Tales. In 1904 he returned to America for his first visit in more than twenty years. He saw the places where he'd grown up, he gave lectures and gossiped with old friends, and he was both fascinated and appalled by the way the country had changed. When he went home to England he brought with him a mind of gathered impressions that he began to turn into a travel book called *The American Scene*. But in America he had also matured another plan, arranging with the help of his agent, J. B. Pinker, for the publication by Scribner's of a definitive edition of his work, one that he decided to name after the city of his birth. That edition was to be "selective as well as collective; I want to quietly disown a few things."[3] Some of those things were masterpieces, like *Washington Square* or *The Bostonians*. The ones that made his cut were to have their surfaces rubbed over, their style brought into line with that of his later work, and to each of them he planned to add a "frank critical"[4] preface; prefaces, and especially that to the *Portrait*, that now stand among the most idiosyncratic and greatest of his achievements.

James's revisions were often heavy, on this novel in particular, and fortunately the sheets on which he worked do survive and can be seen at Harvard's Houghton Library. The issues raised by James's revisions have become one of the major scholarly questions about his work, and this Norton Critical Edition devotes a separate section to them. For now it's enough

---

3. Letter to J. B. Pinker, June 6, 1905. Unpublished; MS held at Yale's Beinecke Library.
4. *Henry James Letters IV*, ed. Leon Edel (Cambridge; The Belknap Press, 1984), p. 367.

to note that James reworked the novel in the late spring and summer of 1906, sending in his last batch of copy on August 1; the preface followed a few weeks later. Scribner's published the novel as volumes 3 and 4 of the New York Edition in December 1907 and January 1908, respectively; the volume break came after chapter 27 and has no structural importance whatever. The print-run was 1,500 copies, and James overcame his aversion to illustration just enough to allow for the inclusion in each volume of a frontispiece, more evocative than representative, by the young American photographer Alvin Langdon Coburn.

This volume replaces an earlier Norton Critical Edition of *The Portrait of a Lady*, first edited by Robert D. Bamberg in 1975, with a second edition appearing in 1995. That's the book from which I myself first learned my way around this novel and from which I've taught, and over the years it has given me a great deal of pleasure and instruction alike. Some of the material included here is inevitably the same; much of it is not. I've written headnotes for each of the four sections of secondary material, and the text of the novel itself has been newly and fully annotated; my thanks to the editors of the earlier editions I consulted in preparing those annotations: William T. Stafford (Library of America), Roger Luckhurst (Oxford World's Classics), and Philip Horne (Penguin Classics). All my work on Henry James is indebted to Bob Weil, my wonderful editor at Liveright and the publisher of my earlier *Portrait of a Novel*. In preparing this Norton Critical Edition I benefitted from the work of my able and dedicated research assistant, Marie Wilken. Michael Anesko kindly helped me with the pasted-up pages of James's revisions for the New York Edition, and has patiently answered my questions for many years now. So too has Philip Horne; my deepest thanks to each of them. Charlotte Mitchell clarified an obscure reference in one of the novel's first reviews; and at W. W. Norton, Carol Bemis, aided by Rachel Goodman, has been the most patient of editors.

The Text of
THE PORTRAIT OF A LADY

Preface to the New York Edition
(1908)

"The Portrait of a Lady" was, like "Roderick Hudson," begun in Florence, during three months spent there in the spring of 1879.[1] Like "Roderick" and like "The American," it had been designed for publication in "The Atlantic Monthly," where it began to appear in 1880. It differed from its two predecessors, however, in finding a course also open to it, from month to month, in "Macmillan's Magazine"; which was to be for me one of the last occasions of simultaneous "serialisation" in the two countries that the changing conditions of literary intercourse between England and the United States had up to then left unaltered.[2] It is a long novel, and I was long in writing it; I remember being again much occupied with it, the following year, during a stay of several weeks made in Venice. I had rooms on Riva Schiavoni, at the top of a house near the passage leading off to San Zaccaria;[3] the waterside life, the wondrous lagoon spread before me, and the ceaseless human chatter of Venice came in at my windows, to which I seem to myself to have been constantly driven, in the fruitless fidget of composition, as if to see whether, out in the blue channel, the ship of some right suggestion, of some better phrase, of the next happy twist of my subject, the next true touch for my canvas, mightn't come into sight. But I recall vividly enough that the response most elicited, in general, to these restless appeals was the rather grim admonition that romantic and historic sites, such as the land of Italy abounds in, offer the artist a questionable aid to concentration when they themselves are not to be the subject of it. They are too rich in their own life and too charged with their own meanings merely to help him out with a lame phrase; they draw him away from his small question to their own greater ones; so that, after a little, he feels, while thus yearning toward them in his difficulty, as if he were asking an army of glorious veterans to help him to arrest a peddler who has given him the wrong change.

There are pages of the book which, in the reading over, have seemed to make me see again the bristling curve of the wide Riva, the large colour-spots of the balconied houses and the repeated undulation of the little hunchbacked bridges, marked by the rise and drop again, with the wave, of foreshortened clicking pedestrians. The Venetian footfall and the Venetian cry—all talk there, wherever uttered, having the pitch of a call across the water—come in once more at the window, renewing one's old impression

---

1. In fact James visited Florence in the spring of 1880.
2. For further details of the novel's publication, see pp. xi–xiv of this Norton Critical Edition.
3. For an account of James's Venetian stay, see pp. 433–35 of this Norton Critical Edition.

of the delighted senses and the divided, frustrated mind. How can places that speak *in general* so to the imagination not give it, at the moment, the particular thing it wants? I recollect again and again, in beautiful places, dropping into that wonderment. The real truth is, I think, that they express, under this appeal, only too much—more than, in the given case, one has use for; so that one finds one's self working less congruously, after all, so far as the surrounding picture is concerned, than in presence of the moderate and the neutral, to which we may lend something of the light of our vision. Such a place as Venice is too proud for such charities; Venice doesn't borrow, she but all magnificently gives. We profit by that enormously, but to do so we must either be quite off duty or be on it in her service alone. Such, and so rueful, are these reminiscences; though on the whole, no doubt, one's book, and one's "literary effort" at large, were to be the better for them. Strangely fertilising, in the long run, does a wasted effort of attention often prove. It all depends on *how* the attention has been cheated, has been squandered. There are high-handed insolent frauds, and there are insidious sneaking ones. And there is, I fear, even on the most designing artist's part, always witless enough good faith, always anxious enough desire, to fail to guard him against their deceits.

Trying to recover here, for recognition, the germ of my idea, I see that it must have consisted not at all in any conceit of a "plot," nefarious name, in any flash, upon the fancy, of a set of relations, or in any one of those situations that, by a logic of their own, immediately fall, for the fabulist, into movement, into a march or a rush, a patter of quick steps; but altogether in the sense of a single character, the character and aspect of a particular engaging young woman, to which all the usual elements of a "subject," certainly of a setting, were to need to be super-added. Quite as interesting as the young woman herself, at her best, do I find, I must again repeat, this projection of memory upon the whole matter of the growth, in one's imagination, of some such apology for a motive. These are the fascinations of the fabulist's art, these lurking forces of expansion, these necessities of upspringing in the seed, these beautiful determinations, on the part of the idea entertained, to grow as tall as possible, to push into the light and the air and thickly flower there; and, quite as much, these fine possibilities of recovering, from some good standpoint on the ground gained, the intimate history of the business—of retracing and reconstructing its steps and stages. I have always fondly remembered a remark that I heard fall years ago from the lips of Ivan Turgenieff[4] in regard to his own experience of the usual origin of the fictive picture. It began for him almost always with the vision of some person or persons, who hovered before him, soliciting him, as the active or passive figure, interesting him and appealing to him just as they were and by what they were. He saw them, in that fashion, as *disponibles*,[5] saw them subject to the chances, the complications of existence, and saw them vividly, but then had to find for them the right relations, those that would most bring them out; to imagine, to invent

4. Russian novelist (1818–1883) who wrote *A Sportsman's Sketches* (1852) and *Fathers and Sons* (1862) and spent much of his later life in Paris. James met him soon after moving to Paris in 1875, and wrote admiringly of him in both his criticism and his letters. His conception of the relation between what, in "The Art of Fiction" (1884), James would call "character" and "incident" was crucial not only to *The Portrait of a Lady* itself but also to James's entire aesthetic.
5. Available (French).

and select and piece together the situations most useful and favourable to the sense of the creatures themselves, the complications they would be most likely to produce and to feel.

"To arrive at these things is to arrive at my 'story,'" he said, "and that's the way I look for it. The result is that I'm often accused of not having 'story' enough. I seem to myself to have as much as I need—to show my people, to exhibit their relations with each other; for that is all my measure. If I watch them long enough I see them come together, I see them *placed*, I see them engaged in this or that act and in this or that difficulty. How they look and move and speak and behave, always in the setting I have found for them, is my account of them—of which I dare say, alas, *que cela manqué souvent d'architecture.*[6] But I would rather, I think, have too little architecture than too much—when there's danger of its interfering with my measure of the truth. The French of course like more of it than I give—having by their own genius such a hand for it; and indeed one must give all one can. As for the origin of one's wind-blown germs themselves, who shall say, as you ask, where *they* come from? We have to go too far back, too far behind, to say. Isn't it all we can say that they come from every quarter of heaven, that they are *there* at almost any turn of the road? They accumulate, and we are always picking them over, selecting among them. They are the breath of life—by which I mean that life, in its own way, breathes them upon us. They are so, in a manner prescribed and imposed—floated into our minds by the current of life. That reduces to imbecility the vain critic's quarrel, so often, with one's subject, when he hasn't the wit to accept it. Will he point out then which other it should properly have been?—his office being, essentially *to* point out. *Il en serait bien embarrassé.*[7] Ah, when he points out what I've done or failed to do with it, that's another matter: there he's on his ground. I give him up my 'architecture,'" my distinguished friend concluded, "as much as he will."

So this beautiful genius, and I recall with comfort the gratitude I drew from his reference to the intensity of suggestion that may reside in the stray figure, the unattached character, the image *en disponibilité.*[8] It gave me higher warrant than I seemed then to have met for just that blest habit of one's own imagination, the trick of investing some conceived or encountered individual, some brace or group of individuals, with the germinal property and authority. I was myself so much more antecedently conscious of my figures than of their setting—a too preliminary, a preferential interest in which struck me as in general such a putting of the cart before the horse. I might envy, though I couldn't emulate, the imaginative writer so constituted as to see his fable first and to make out its agents afterwards: I could think so little of any fable that didn't need its agents positively to launch it; I could think so little of any situation that didn't depend for its interest on the nature of the persons situated, and thereby on their way of taking it. There are methods of so-called presentation, I believe—among novelists who have appeared to flourish—that offer the situation as indifferent to that support; but I have not lost the sense of the value for me, at the time, of the admirable Russian's testimony to my not needing, all

6. That it often lacks structure (French).
7. He'd find it rather awkward (French).
8. Free-floating image (French).

superstitiously, to try and perform any such gymnastic. Other echoes from the same source linger with me, I confess, as unfadingly—if it be not all indeed one much-embracing echo. It was impossible after that not to read, for one's uses, high lucidity into the tormented and disfigured and bemuddled question of the objective value, and even quite into that of the critical appreciation, of "subject" in the novel.

One had had from an early time, for that matter, the instinct of the right estimate of such values and of its reducing to the inane the dull dispute over the "immoral" subject and the moral. Recognising so promptly the one measure of the worth of a given subject, the question about it that, rightly answered, disposes of all others—is it valid, in a word, is it genuine, is it sincere, the result of some direct impression or perception of life?—I had found small edification, mostly, in a critical pretension that had neglected from the first all delimitation of ground and all definition of terms. The air of my earlier time shows, to memory, as darkened, all round, with that vanity—unless the difference to-day be just in one's own final impatience, the lapse of one's attention. There is, I think, no more nutritive or suggestive truth in this connexion than that of the perfect dependence of the "moral" sense of a work of art on the amount of felt life concerned in producing it. The question comes back thus, obviously, to the kind and the degree of the artist's prime sensibility, which is the soil out of which his subject springs. The quality and capacity of that soil, its ability to "grow" with due freshness and straightness any vision of life, represents, strongly or weakly, the projected morality. That element is but another name for the more or less close connexion of the subject with some mark made on the intelligence, with some sincere experience. By which, at the same time, of course, one is far from contending that this enveloping air of the artist's humanity—which gives the last touch to the worth of the work—is not a widely and wondrously varying element; being on one occasion a rich and magnificent medium and on another a comparatively poor and ungenerous one. Here we get exactly the high price of the novel as a literary form—its power not only, while preserving that form with closeness, to range through all the differences of the individual relation to its general subject-matter, all the varieties of outlook on life, of disposition to reflect and project, created by conditions that are never the same from man to man (or, so far as that goes, from man to woman), but positively to appear more true to its character in proportion as it strains, or tends to burst, with a latent extravagnce, its mould.

The house of fiction has in short not one window, but a million—a number of possible windows not to be reckoned, rather; every one of which has been pierced, or is still pierceable, in its vast front, by the need of the individual vision and by the pressure of the individual will. These apertures, of dissimilar shape and size, hang so, all together, over the human scene that we might have expected of them a greater sameness of report than we find. They are but windows at the best, mere holes in a dead wall, disconnected, perched aloft; they are not hinged doors opening straight upon life. But they have this mark of their own that at each of them stands a figure with a pair of eyes, or at least with a field-glass, which forms, again and again, for observation, a unique instrument, insuring to the person making use of it an impression distinct from every other. He and his neighbours are watching the same show, but one seeing more where the other sees less, one seeing black where the other sees white, one seeing big where the other sees small, one seeing coarse where the other sees fine. And so on, and so on; there is fortunately no saying on what, for the particular pair of eyes, the window may *not* open; "fortunately" by reason, precisely, of this incalculability of range. The spreading field, the human scene, is the "choice of subject"; the pierced aperture, either broad or balconied or slit-like and low-browed, is the "literary form"; but they are, singly or together, as nothing without the posted presence of the watcher—without, in other words, the consciousness of the artist. Tell me what the artist is, and I will tell you of what he has *been* conscious. Thereby I shall express to you at once his boundless freedom and his "moral" reference.

All this is a long way round, however, for my word about my dim first move toward "The Portrait," which was exactly my grasp of a single character—an acquisition I had made, moreover, after a fashion not here to be retraced. Enough that I was, as seemed to me, in complete possession of it, that I had been so for a long time, that this had made it familiar and yet had not blurred its charm, and that, all urgently, all tormentingly, I saw it in motion and, so to speak, in transit. This amounts to saying that I saw it as bent upon its fate—some fate or other; *which*, among the possibilities, being precisely the question. Thus I had my vivid individual—vivid, so strangely, in spite of being still at large, not confined by the conditions, not engaged in the tangle, to which we look for much of the impress that constitutes an identity. If the apparition was still all to be placed how came it to be vivid?—since we puzzle such quantities out, mostly, just by the business of placing them. One could answer such a question beautifully, doubtless, if one could do so subtle, if not so monstrous, a thing as to write the history of the growth of one's imagination. One would describe then what, at a given time, had extraordinarily happened to it, and one would so, for instance, be in a position to tell, with an approach to clearness, how, under favour of occasion, it had been able to take over (take over straight from life) such and such a constituted, animated figure or form. The figure has to that extent, as you see, *been* placed—placed in the imagination that detains it, preserves, protects, enjoys it, conscious of its presence in the dusky, crowded, heterogeneous back-shop of the mind very much as a wary dealer in precious odds and ends, competent to make an "advance" on rare objects confided to him, is conscious of the rare little "piece" left in deposit by the reduced, mysterious lady of title or the speculative amateur, and which is already there to disclose its merit afresh as soon as a key shall have clicked in a cupboard-door.

That may be, I recognise, a somewhat superfine analogy for the particular "value" I here speak of, the image of the young feminine nature that I had had for so considerable a time all curiously at my disposal; but it appears to fond memory quite to fit the fact—with the recall, in addition, of my pious desire but to place my treasure right. I quite remind myself thus of the dealer resigned not to "realise," resigned to keeping the precious object locked up indefinitely rather than commit it, at no matter what price, to vulgar hands. For there *are* dealers in these forms and figures and treasures capable of that refinement. The point is, however, that this single small corner-stone, the conception of a certain young woman affronting her destiny, had begun with being all my outfit for the large building of "The Portrait of a Lady." It came to be a square and spacious house—or has at least seemed so to me in this going over it again; but, such as it is, it had to be put up round my young woman while she stood there in perfect isolation. That is to me, artistically speaking, the circumstance of interest; for I have lost myself once more, I confess, in the curiosity of analysing the structure. By what process of logical accretion was this slight "personality," the mere slim shade of an intelligent but presumptuous girl, to find itself endowed with the high attributes of a Subject?— and indeed by what thinness, at the best, would such a subject not be vitiated? Millions of presumptuous girls, intelligent or not intelligent, daily affront their destiny, and what is it open to their destiny to *be*, at the most, that we should make an ado about it? The novel is of its very nature an "ado," an ado about something, and the larger the form it takes the greater of course the ado. Therefore, consciously, that was what one was in for— for positively organising an ado about Isabel Archer.

One looked it well in the face, I seem to remember, this extravagance; and with the effect precisely of recognising the charm of the problem. Challenge any such problem with any intelligence, and you immediately see how full it is of substance; the wonder being, all the while, as we look at the world, how absolutely, how inordinately, the Isabel Archers, and even much smaller female fry, insist on mattering. George Eliot has admirably noted it—"In these frail vessels is borne onward through the ages the treasure of human affection." In "Romeo and Juliet" Juliet has to be important, just as, in "Adam Bede" and "The Mill on the Floss" and "Middlemarch" and "Daniel Deronda," Hetty Sorrel and Maggie Tulliver and Rosamond Vincy and Gwendolen Harleth have to be; with that much of firm ground, that much of bracing air, at the disposal all the while of their feet and their lungs.[9] They are typical, none the less, of a class difficult, in the individual case, to make a centre of interest; so difficult in fact that many an expert painter, as for instance Dickens and Walter Scott, as for instance even, in the main, so subtle a hand as that of R. L. Stevenson, has preferred to leave the task unattempted. There are in fact writers as to whom we make out that their refuge from this is to assume it to be not worth their attempting; by which pusillanimity in truth their honour is scantly saved. It is never an attestation of a value, or even of our imperfect sense of one, it is never a tribute to any truth at all, that we shall represent that value badly. It never makes up, artistically, for an artist's dim feeling about a thing that he shall "do" the thing as ill as possible. There are better ways than that, the best of all of which is to begin with less stupidity.

It may be answered meanwhile, in regard to Shakespeare's and to George Eliot's testimony, that their concession to the "importance" of their Juliets and Cleopatras and Portias (even with Portia as the very type and model of the young person intelligent and presumptuous) and to that of their Hettys and Maggies and Rosamonds and Gwendolens, suffers the abatement that these slimnesses are, when figuring as the main props of the theme, never suffered to be sole ministers of its appeal, but have their inadequacy

---

9. George Eliot, pen name of Mary Ann Evans (1819–1880); of all English novelists the one James most admired. His parallelism suggests the novels in which these different female characters appear: *Adam Bede* (1859), *The Mill on the Floss* (1860), *Middlemarch* (1871–72), and *Daniel Deronda* (1876). At the same time, and working from memory, he misquotes a line from chapter 11 of that last novel; George Eliot had actually written "In these delicate vessels is borne onward through the ages the treasure of human affections."

eked out with comic relief and underplots, as the playwrights say, when not with murders and battles and the great mutations of the world. If they are shown as "mattering" as much as they could possibly pretend to, the proof of it is in a hundred other persons, made of much stouter stuff, and each involved moreover in a hundred relations which matter to *them* concomitantly with that one. Cleopatra matters, beyond bounds, to Antony, but his colleagues, his antagonists, the state of Rome and the impending battle also prodigiously matter; Portia matters to Antonio, and to Shylock, and to the Prince of Morocco, to the fifty aspiring princes, but for these gentry there are other lively concerns; for Antonio, notably, there are Shylock and Bassanio and his lost ventures and the extremity of his predicament. This extremity indeed, by the same token, matters to Portia—though its doing so becomes of interest all by the fact that Portia matters to *us*. That she does so, at any rate, and that almost everything comes round to it again, supports my contention as to this fine example of the value recognised in the mere young thing. (I say "mere" young thing because I guess that even Shakespeare, preoccupied mainly though he may have been with the passions of princes, would scarce have pretended to found the best of his appeal for her on her high social position.) It is an example exactly of the deep difficulty braved—the difficulty of making George Eliot's "frail vessel," if not the all-in-all for our attention, at least the clearest of the call.

Now to see deep difficulty braved is at any time, for the really addicted artist, to feel almost even as a pang the beautiful incentive, and to feel it verily in such sort as to wish the danger intensified. The difficulty most worth tackling can only be for him, in these conditions, the greatest the case permits of. So I remember feeling here (in presence, always, that is, of the particular uncertainty of my ground), that there would be one way better than another—oh, ever so much better than any other!—of making it fight out its battle. The frail vessel, that charged with George Eliot's "treasure," and thereby of such importance to those who curiously approach it, has likewise possibilities of importance to itself, possibilities which permit of treatment and in fact peculiarly require it from the moment they are considered at all. There is always the escape from any close account of the weak agent of such spells by using as a bridge for evasion, for retreat and fight, the view of her relation to those surrounding her. Make it predominantly a view of *their* relation and the trick is played: you give the general sense of her effect, and you give it, so far as the raising on it of a superstructure goes, with the maximum of ease. Well, I recall perfectly how little, in my now quite established connexion, the maximum of ease appealed to me, and how I seemed to get rid of it by an honest transposition of the weights in the two scales. "Place the centre of the subject in the young woman's own consciousness," I said to myself, "and you get as interesting and as beautiful a difficulty as you could wish. Stick to *that*— for the centre; put the heaviest weight into *that* scale, which will be so largely the scale of her relation to herself. Make her only interested enough, at the same time, in the things that are not herself, and this relation needn't fear to be too limited. Place meanwhile in the other scale the lighter weight (which is usually the one that tips the balance of interest): press least hard, in short, on the consciousness of your heroine's satellites, especially the male; make it an interest contributive only to the greater one. See, at all events, what can be done in this way. What better field could there be for a due ingenuity? The girl hovers, inextinguishable, as a charming creature, and the job will be to translate her into the highest terms of that formula, and as nearly as possible moreover into *all* of them. To depend upon her and her little concerns wholly to see you through will necessitate, remember, your really 'doing' her."

So far I reasoned, and it took nothing less than that technical rigour, I now easily see, to inspire me with the right confidence for erecting on such a plot of ground the neat and careful and proportioned pile of bricks that arches over it and that was thus to form, constructionally speaking, a literary monument. Such is the aspect that to-day "The Portrait" wears for me: a structure reared with an "architectural" competence, as Turgenieff would have said, that makes it, to the author's own sense, the most proportioned of his productions after "The Ambassadors"—which was to follow it so many years later and which has, no doubt, a superior roundness.[1] On one thing I was determined; that, though I should clearly have to pile brick upon brick for the creation of an interest, I would leave no pretext for saying that anything is out of line, scale or perspective. I would build large—in fine embossed vaults and painted arches, as who should say, and yet never let it appear that the chequered pavement, the ground under the reader's feet, fails to stretch at every point to the base of the walls. That precautionary spirit, on re-perusal of the book, is the old note that most touches me: it testifies so, for my own ear, to the anxiety of my provision for the reader's amusement. I felt, in view of the possible limitations of my subject, that no such provision could be excessive, and the development of the latter was simply the general form of that earnest quest. And I find indeed that this is the only account I can give myself of the evolution of the fable: it is all under the head thus named that I conceive the needful accretion as having taken place, the right complications as having started. It was naturally of the essence that the young woman should be herself complex; that was rudimentary—or was at any rate the light in which Isabel Archer had originally dawned. It went, however, but a certain way, and other lights, contending, conflicting lights, and of as many different colours, if possible, as the rockets, the Roman candles and Catherine-wheels of a "pyrotechnic display," would be employable to attest that she was. I had, no doubt, a groping instinct for the right complications, since I am quite unable to track the footsteps of those that constitute, as the case stands, the general situation exhibited. They are there, for what they are worth, and as numerous as might be; but my memory, I confess, is a blank as to how and whence they came.

I seem to myself to have waked up one morning in possession of them—of Ralph Touchett and his parents, of Madame Merle, of Gilbert Osmond and his daughter and his sister, of Lord Warburton, Caspar Goodwood and Miss Stackpole, the definite array of contributions to Isabel Archer's history. I recognised them, I knew them, they were the numbered pieces of my puzzle, the concrete terms of my "plot." It was as if they had simply, by an impulse of their own, floated into my ken, and all in response to my primary question: "Well, what will she *do*?" Their answer seemed to be that if I would trust them they would show me; on which, with an urgent

---

1. *The Ambassadors* (1903) was James's favorite among his own works; in his New York Edition preface he described it as "frankly, quite the best, 'all round,' of all my productions."

appeal to them to make it at least as interesting as they could, I trusted them. They were like the group of attendants and entertainers who come down by train when people in the country give a party; they represented the contract for carrying the party on. That was an excellent relation with them—a possible one even with so broken a reed (from her slightness of cohesion) as Henrietta Stackpole. It is a familiar truth to the novelist, at the strenuous hour, that, as certain elements in any work are of the essence, so others are only of the form; that as this or that character, this or that disposition of the material, belongs to the subject directly, so to speak, so this or that other belongs to it but indirectly—belongs intimately to the treatment. This is a truth, however, of which he rarely gets the benefit—since it could be assured to him, really, but by criticism based upon perception, criticism which is too little of this world. He must not think of benefits, moreover, I freely recognise, for that way dishonour lies: he has, that is, but one to think of—the benefit, whatever it may be, involved in his having cast a spell upon the simpler, the very simplest, forms of attention. This is all he is entitled to; he is entitled to nothing, he is bound to admit, that can come to him, from the reader, as a result on the latter's part of any act of reflexion or discrimination. He may *enjoy* this finer tribute—that is another affair, but on condition only of taking it as a gratuity "thrown in," a mere miraculous windfall, the fruit of a tree he may not pretend to have shaken. Against reflexion, against discrimination, in his interest, all earth and air conspire; wherefore it is that, as I say, he must in many a case have schooled himself, from the first, to work but for a "living wage." The living wage is the reader's grant of the least possible quantity of attention required for consciousness of a "spell." The occasional charming "tip" is an act of his intelligence over and beyond this, a golden apple, for the writer's lap, straight from the wind-stirred tree. The artist may of course, in wanton moods, dream of some Paradise (for art) where the direct appeal to the intelligence might be legalised; for to such extravagances as these his yearning mind can scarce hope ever completely to close itself. The most he can do is to remember they *are* extravagances.

All of which is perhaps but a gracefully devious way of saying that Henrietta Stackpole was a good example, in "The Portrait," of the truth to which I just adverted—as good an example as I could name were it not that Maria Gostrey, in "The Ambassadors," then in the bosom of time, may be mentioned as a better. Each of these persons is but wheels to the coach; neither belongs to the body of that vehicle, or is for a moment accommodated with a seat inside. There the subject alone is ensconced, in the form of its "hero and heroine," and the privileged high officials, say, who ride with the king and queen. There are reasons why one would have liked this to be felt, as in general one would like almost anything to be felt, in one's work, that one has one's self contributively felt. We have seen, however, how idle is that pretension, which I should be sorry to make too much of. Maria Gostrey and Miss Stackpole then are cases, each, of the light *ficelle*,[2]

---

2. The word has several meanings in French: a piece of string or thread; a loaf of bread shaped like a baguette but thinner; and even a horse too weak to pull a carriage. Its primary meaning in the nineteenth century came from the theater: a bit of stage business, a piece of trickery or manipulation, in which indeed a hidden string might be useful. James uses it to indicate a secondary character, one who serves to tell us about the book's "agents" but without becoming a source of interest in her own right.

not of the true agent; they may run beside the coach "for all they are worth," they may cling to it till they are out of breath (as poor Miss Stackpole all so visibly does), but neither, all the while, so much as gets her foot on the step, neither ceases for a moment to tread the dusty road. Put it even that they are like the fishwives who helped to bring back to Paris from Versailles, on that most ominous day of the first half of the French Revolution, the carriage of the royal family. The only thing is that I may well be asked, I acknowledge, why then, in the present fiction, I have suffered Henrietta (of whom we have indubitably too much) so officiously, so strangely, so almost inexplicably, to pervade. I will presently say what I can for that anomaly—and in the most conciliatory fashion.

A point I wish still more to make is that if my relation of confidence with the actors in my drama, who *were*, unlike Miss Stackpole, true agents, was an excellent one to have arrived at, there still remained my relation with the reader, which was another affair altogether and as to which I felt no one to be trusted but myself. That solicitude was to be accordingly expressed in the artful patience with which, as I have said, I piled brick upon brick. The bricks, for the whole counting-over—putting for bricks little touches and inventions and enhancements by the way—affect me in truth as well-nigh innumerable and as ever so scrupulously fitted together and packed-in. It is an effect of detail, of the minutest; though, if one were in this connexion to say all, one would express the hope that the general, the ampler air of the modest monument still survives. I do at least seem to catch the key to a part of this abundance of small anxious, ingenious illustration as I recollect putting my finger, in my young woman's interest, on the most obvious of her predicates. "What will she 'do'? Why, the first thing she'll do will be to come to Europe; which in fact will form, and all inevitably, no small part of her principal adventure. Coming to Europe is even for the 'frail vessels,' in this wonderful age, a mild adventure; but what is truer than that on one side—the side of their independence of flood and field, of the moving accident, of battle and murder and sudden death—her adventures are to be mild? Without her sense of them, her sense *for* them, as one may say, they are next to nothing at all; but isn't the beauty and the difficulty just in showing their mystic conversion by that sense, conversion into the stuff of drama or, even more delightful word still, of 'story'?" It was all as clear, my contention, as a silver bell. Two very good instances, I think, of this effect of conversion, two cases of the rare chemistry, are the pages in which Isabel, coming into the drawing-room at Gardencourt, coming in from a wet walk or whatever, that rainy afternoon, finds Madame Merle in possession of the place, Madame Merle seated, all absorbed but all serene, at the piano, and deeply recognises, in the striking of such an hour, in the presence there, among the gathering shades, of this personage, of whom a moment before she had never so much as heard, a turning-point in her life. It is dreadful to have too much, for any artistic demonstration, to dot one's i's and insist on one's intentions, and I am not eager to do it now; but the question here was that of producing the maximum of intensity with the minimum of strain.

The interest was to be raised to its pitch and yet the elements to be kept in their key; so that, should the whole thing duly impress, I might show what an "exciting" inward life may do for the person leading it even while it remains perfectly normal. And I cannot think of a more consistent application of that ideal unless it be in the long statement, just beyond the middle of the book, of my young woman's extraordinary meditative vigil on the occasion that was to become for her such a landmark. Reduced to its essence, it is but the vigil of searching criticism; but it throws the action further forward than twenty "incidents" might have done. It was designed to have all the vivacity of incident and all the economy of picture. She sits up, by her dying fire, far into the night, under the spell of recognitions on which she finds the last sharpness suddenly wait. It is a representation simply of her motionlessly *seeing*, and an attempt withal to make the mere still lucidity of her act as "interesting" as the surprise of a caravan or the identification of a pirate. It represents, for that matter, one of the identifications dear to the novelist, and even indispensable to him; but it all goes on without her being approached by another person and without her leaving her chair. It is obviously the best thing in the book, but it is only a supreme illustration of the general plan. As to Henrietta, my apology for whom I just left incomplete, she exemplifies, I fear, in her superabundance, not an element of my plan, but only an excess of my zeal. So early was to begin my tendency to *overtreat*, rather than undertreat (when there was choice or danger) my subject. (Many members of my craft, I gather, are far from agreeing with me, but I have always held overtreating the minor disservice.) "Treating" that of "The Portrait" amounted to never forgetting, by any lapse, that the thing was under a special obligation to be amusing. There was the danger of the noted "thinness"—which was to be averted, tooth and nail, by cultivation of the lively. That is at least how I see it today. Henrietta must have been at that time a part of my wonderful notion of the lively. And then there was another matter. I had, within the few preceding years, come to live in London, and the "international" light lay, in those days, to my sense, thick and rich upon the scene. It was the light in which so much of the picture hung. But that *is* another matter. There is really too much to say.

HENRY JAMES.

The Portrait of a Lady

Volume I

Chapter I

Under certain circumstances there are few hours in life more agreeable than the hour dedicated to the ceremony known as afternoon tea. There are circumstances in which, whether you partake of the tea or not—some people of course never do,—the situation is in itself delightful. Those that I have in mind in beginning to unfold this simple history offered an admirable setting to an innocent pastime. The implements of the little feast had been disposed upon the lawn of an old English country-house, in what I should call the perfect middle of a splendid summer afternoon. Part of the afternoon had waned, but much of it was left, and what was left was of the finest and rarest quality. Real dusk would not arrive for many hours; but the flood of summer light had begun to ebb, the air had grown mellow, the shadows were long upon the smooth, dense turf. They lengthened slowly, however, and the scene expressed that sense of leisure still to come which is perhaps the chief source of one's enjoyment of such a scene at such an hour. From five o'clock to eight is on certain occasions a little eternity; but on such an occasion as this the interval could be only an eternity of pleasure. The persons concerned in it were taking their pleasure quietly, and they were not of the sex which is supposed to furnish the regular votaries of the ceremony I have mentioned. The shadows on the perfect lawn were straight and angular; they were the shadows of an old man sitting in a deep wicker-chair near the low table on which the tea had been served, and of two younger men strolling to and fro, in desultory talk, in front of him. The old man had his cup in his hand; it was an unusually large cup, of a different pattern from the rest of the set and painted in brilliant colours. He disposed of its contents with much circumspection, holding it for a long time close to his chin, with his face turned to the house. His companions had either finished their tea or were indifferent to their privilege; they smoked cigarettes as they continued to stroll. One of them, from time to time, as he passed, looked with a certain attention at the elder man, who, unconscious of observation, rested his eyes upon the rich red front of his dwelling. The house that rose beyond the lawn was a structure to repay such consideration and was the most characteristic object in the peculiarly English picture I have attempted to sketch.

It stood upon a low hill, above the river—the river being the Thames at some forty miles from London.[1] A long gabled front of red brick, with the

---

1. James's model here is Hardwick House, near Whitchurch-on-Thames in Oxfordshire, the home of Charles Day Rose, a banker and Liberal MP to whom the novelist was distantly related. In 1906 James asked Alvin Langdon Coburn to take a photograph of the building; it served as the frontispiece for the first volume of the novel in the New York Edition; see p. 417 of this Norton Critical Edition.

complexion of which time and the weather had played all sorts of pictorial tricks, only, however, to improve and refine it, presented to the lawn its patches of ivy, its clustered chimneys, its windows smothered in creepers. The house had a name and a history; the old gentleman taking his tea would have been delighted to tell you these things: how it had been built under Edward the Sixth, had offered a night's hospitality to the great Elizabeth (whose august person had extended itself upon a huge, magnificent and terribly angular bed which still formed the principal honour of the sleeping apartments), had been a good deal bruised and defaced in Cromwell's wars, and then, under the Restoration, repaired and much enlarged; and how, finally, after having been remodelled and disfigured in the eighteenth century, it had passed into the careful keeping of a shrewd American banker, who had bought it originally because (owing to circumstances too complicated to set forth) it was offered at a great bargain: bought it with much grumbling at its ugliness, its antiquity, its incommodity, and who now, at the end of twenty years, had become conscious of a real aesthetic passion for it, so that he knew all its points and would tell you just where to stand to see them in combination and just the hour when the shadows of its various protuberances—which fell so softly upon the warm, weary brickwork—were of the right measure. Besides this, as I have said, he could have counted off most of the successive owners and occupants, several of whom were known to general fame; doing so, however, with an undemonstrative conviction that the latest phase of its destiny was not the least honourable. The front of the house overlooking that portion of the lawn with which we are concerned was not the entrance-front; this was in quite another quarter. Privacy here reigned supreme, and the wide carpet of turf that covered the level hill-top seemed but the extension of a luxurious interior. The great still oaks and beeches flung down a shade as dense as that of velvet curtains; and the place was furnished, like a room, with cushioned seats, with rich-coloured rugs, with the books and papers that lay upon the grass. The river was at some distance; where the ground began to slope the lawn, properly speaking, ceased. But it was none the less a charming walk down to the water.

The old gentleman at the tea-table, who had come from America thirty years before, had brought with him, at the top of his baggage, his American physiognomy; and he had not only brought it with him, but he had kept it in the best order, so that, if necessary, he might have taken it back to his own country with perfect confidence. At present, obviously, nevertheless, he was not likely to displace himself; his journeys were over and he was taking the rest that precedes the great rest. He had a narrow, clean-shaven face, with features evenly distributed and an expression of placid acuteness. It was evidently a face in which the range of representation was not large, so that the air of contented shrewdness was all the more of a merit. It seemed to tell that he had been successful in life, yet it seemed to tell also that his success had not been exclusive and invidious, but had had much of the inoffensiveness of failure. He had certainly had a great experience of men, but there was an almost rustic simplicity in the faint smile that played upon his lean, spacious cheek and lighted up his humorous eye as he at last slowly and carefully deposited his big tea-cup upon the table. He was neatly dressed, in well-brushed black; but a shawl was folded upon his knees, and his feet were encased in thick, embroidered slippers. A beautiful collie dog lay upon the grass near his chair, watching the master's face almost as tenderly as the master took in the still more magisterial physiognomy of the house; and a little bristling, bustling terrier bestowed a desultory attendance upon the other gentlemen.

One of these was a remarkably well-made man of five-and-thirty, with a face as English as that of the old gentleman I have just sketched was something else; a noticeably handsome face, fresh-coloured, fair and frank, with firm, straight features, a lively grey eye and the rich adornment of a chestnut beard. This person had a certain fortunate, brilliant exceptional look—the air of a happy temperament fertilised by a high civilisation—which would have made almost any observer envy him at a venture. He was booted and spurred, as if he had dismounted from a long ride; he wore a white hat, which looked too large for him; he held his two hands behind him, and in one of them—a large white, well-shaped fist—was crumpled a pair of soiled dog-skin gloves.

His companion, measuring the length of the lawn beside him, was a person of quite a different pattern, who, although he might have excited grave curiosity, would not, like the other, have provoked you to wish yourself, almost blindly, in his place. Tall, lean, loosely and feebly put together, he had an ugly, sickly, witty, charming face, furnished, but by no means decorated, with a straggling moustache and whisker. He looked clever and ill—a combination by no means felicitous; and he wore a brown velvet jacket. He carried his hands in his pockets, and there was something in the way he did it that showed the habit was inveterate. His gait had a shambling, wandering quality; he was not very firm on his legs. As I have said, whenever he passed the old man in the chair he rested his eyes upon him; and at this moment, with their faces brought into relation, you would easily have seen they were father and son. The father caught his son's eye at last and gave him a mild, responsive smile.

"I'm getting on very well," he said.

"Have you drunk your tea?" asked the son.

"Yes, and enjoyed it."

"Shall I give you some more?"

The old man considered, placidly. "Well, I guess I'll wait and see." He had, in speaking, the American tone.

"Are you cold?" the son enquired.

The father slowly rubbed his legs. "Well, I don't know. I can't tell till I feel."

"Perhaps some one might feel for you," said the younger man, laughing.

"Oh, I hope some one will always feel for me! Don't you feel for me, Lord Warburton?"

"Oh, yes, immensely," said the gentleman addressed as Lord Warburton, promptly. "I'm bound to say you look wonderfully comfortable."

"Well, I suppose I am, in most respects." And the old man looked down at his green shawl and smoothed it over his knees. "The fact is I've been comfortable so many years that I suppose I've got so used to it I don't know it."

"Yes, that's the bore of comfort," said Lord Warburton. "We only know when we're uncomfortable."

"It strikes me we're rather particular," his companion remarked.

"Oh yes, there's no doubt we're particular," Lord Warburton murmured. And then the three men remained silent a while; the two younger ones standing looking down at the other, who presently asked for more tea. "I should think you would be very unhappy with that shawl," Lord Warburton resumed while his companion filled the old man's cup again.

"Oh no, he must have the shawl!" cried the gentleman in the velvet coat. "Don't put such ideas as that into his head."

"It belongs to my wife," said the old man simply.

"Oh, if it's for sentimental reasons—" And Lord Warburton made a gesture of apology.

"I suppose I must give it to her when she comes," the old man went on.

"You'll please to do nothing of the kind. You'll keep it to cover your poor old legs."

"Well, you mustn't abuse my legs," said the old man. "I guess they are as good as yours."

"Oh, you're perfectly free to abuse mine," his son replied, giving him his tea.

"Well, we're two lame ducks; I don't think there's much difference."

"I'm much obliged to you for calling me a duck. How's your tea?"

"Well, it's rather hot."

"That's intended to be a merit."

"Ah, there's a great deal of merit," murmured the old man kindly. "He's a very good nurse, Lord Warburton."

"Isn't he a bit clumsy?" asked his lordship.

"Oh no, he's not clumsy—considering that he's an invalid himself. He's a very good nurse—for a sick-nurse. I call him my sick-nurse because he's sick himself."

"Oh, come, daddy!" the ugly young man exclaimed.

"Well, you are; I wish you weren't. But I suppose you can't help it."

"I might try: that's an idea," said the young man.

"Were you ever sick, Lord Warburton?" his father asked.

Lord Warburton considered a moment. "Yes, sir, once, in the Persian Gulf."

"He's making light of you, daddy," said the other young man. "That's a sort of joke."

"Well, there seem to be so many sorts now," daddy replied, serenely. "You don't look as if you had been sick, any way, Lord Warburton."

"He's sick of life; he was just telling me so; going on fearfully about it," said Lord Warburton's friend.

"Is that true, sir?" asked the old man gravely.

"If it is, your son gave me no consolation. He's a wretched fellow to talk to—a regular cynic. He doesn't seem to believe in anything."

"That's another sort of joke," said the person accused of cynicism.

"It's because his health is so poor," his father explained to Lord Warburton. "It affects his mind and colours his way of looking at things; he seems to feel as if he had never had a chance. But it's almost entirely theoretical, you know; it doesn't seem to affect his spirits. I've hardly ever seen him when he wasn't cheerful—about as he is at present. He often cheers me up."

The young man so described looked at Lord Warburton and laughed. "Is it a glowing eulogy or an accusation of levity? Should you like me to carry out my theories, daddy?"

"By Jove, we should see some queer things!" cried Lord Warburton.

"I hope you haven't taken up that sort of tone," said the old man.

"Warburton's tone is worse than mine; he pretends to be bored. I'm not in the least bored; I find life only too interesting."

"Ah, *too* interesting; you shouldn't allow it to be that, you know!"

"I'm never bored when I come here," said Lord Warburton. "One gets such uncommonly good talk."

"Is that another sort of joke?" asked the old man. "You've no excuse for being bored anywhere. When I was your age I had never heard of such a thing."

"You must have developed very late."

"No, I developed very quick; that was just the reason. When I was twenty years old I was very highly developed indeed. I was working tooth and nail. You wouldn't be bored if you had something to do; but all you young men are too idle. You think too much of your pleasure. You're too fastidious, and too indolent, and too rich."

"Oh, I say," cried Lord Warburton, "you're hardly the person to accuse a fellow-creature of being too rich!"

"Do you mean because I'm a banker?" asked the old man.

"Because of that, if you like; and because you have—haven't you?—such unlimited means."

"He isn't very rich," the other young man mercifully pleaded. "He has given away an immense deal of money."

"Well, I suppose it was his own," said Lord Warburton; "and in that case could there be a better proof of wealth? Let not a public benefactor talk of one's being too fond of pleasure."

"Daddy's very fond of pleasure—of other people's."

The old man shook his head. "I don't pretend to have contributed anything to the amusement of my contemporaries."

"My dear father, you're too modest!"

"That's a kind of joke, sir," said Lord Warburton.

"You young men have too many jokes. When there are no jokes you've nothing left."

"Fortunately there are always more jokes," the ugly young man remarked.

"I don't believe it—I believe things are getting more serious. You young men will find that out."

"The increasing seriousness of things, then—that's the great opportunity of jokes."

"They'll have to be grim jokes," said the old man. "I'm convinced there will be great changes; and not all for the better."

"I quite agree with you, sir," Lord Warburton declared. "I'm very sure there will be great changes, and that all sorts of queer things will happen. That's why I find so much difficulty in applying your advice; you know you told me the other day that I ought to 'take hold' of something. One hesitates to take hold of a thing that may the next moment be knocked sky-high."

"You ought to take hold of a pretty woman," said his companion. "He's trying hard to fall in love," he added, by way of explanation, to his father.

"The pretty women themselves may be sent flying!" Lord Warburton exclaimed.

"No, no, they'll be firm," the old man rejoined; "they'll not be affected by the social and political changes I just referred to."

"You mean they won't be abolished? Very well, then, I'll lay hands on one as soon as possible and tie her round my neck as a life-preserver."

"The ladies will save us," said the old man; "that is the best of them will—for I make a difference between them. Make up to a good one and marry her, and your life will become much more interesting."

A momentary silence marked perhaps on the part of his auditors a sense of the magnanimity of this speech, for it was a secret neither for his son nor for his visitor that his own experiment in matrimony had not been a happy one. As he said, however, he made a difference; and these words may have been intended as a confession of personal error; though of course it was not in place for either of his companions to remark that apparently the lady of his choice had not been one of the best.

"If I marry an interesting woman I shall be interested: is that what you say?" Lord Warburton asked. "I'm not at all keen about marrying—your son misrepresented me; but there's no knowing what an interesting woman might do with me."

"I should like to see your idea of an interesting woman," said his friend.

"My dear fellow, you can't see ideas—especially such highly ethereal ones as mine. If I could only see it myself—that would be a great step in advance."

"Well, you may fall in love with whomsoever you please; but you mustn't fall in love with my niece," said the old man.

His son broke into a laugh. "He'll think you mean that as a provocation! My dear father, you've lived with the English for thirty years, and you've picked up a good many of the things they say. But you've never learned the things they don't say!"

"I say what I please," the old man returned with all his serenity.

"I haven't the honour of knowing your niece," Lord Warburton said. "I think it's the first time I've heard of her."

"She's a niece of my wife's; Mrs. Touchett brings her to England."

Then young Mr. Touchett explained. "My mother, you know, has been spending the winter in America, and we're expecting her back. She writes that she has discovered a niece and that she has invited her to come out with her."

"I see—very kind of her," said Lord Warburton. "Is the young lady interesting?"

"We hardly know more about her than you; my mother has not gone into details. She chiefly communicates with us by means of telegrams, and her telegrams are rather inscrutable. They say women don't know how to write them, but my mother has thoroughly mastered the art of condensation. 'Tired America, hot weather awful, return England with niece, first steamer decent cabin.' That's the sort of message we get from her—that was the last that came. But there had been another before, which I think contained the first mention of the niece. 'Changed hotel, very bad, impudent clerk, address here. Taken sister's girl, died last year, go to Europe, two sisters, quite independent.' Over that my father and I have scarcely stopped puzzling; it seems to admit of so many interpretations."

"There's one thing very clear in it," said the old man; "she has given the hotel-clerk a dressing."

"I'm not sure even of that, since he has driven her from the field. We thought at first that the sister mentioned might be the sister of the clerk;

but the subsequent mention of a niece seems to prove that the allusion is to one of my aunts. Then there was a question as to whose the two other sisters were; they are probably two of my late aunt's daughters. But who's 'quite independent,' and in what sense is the term used?—that point's not yet settled. Does the expression apply more particularly to the young lady my mother has adopted, or does it characterise her sisters equally?—and is it used in a moral or in a financial sense? Does it mean that they've been left well off, or that they wish to be under no obligations? or does it simply mean that they're fond of their own way?"

"Whatever else it means, it's pretty sure to mean that," Mr. Touchett remarked.

"You'll see for yourself," said Lord Warburton. "When does Mrs. Touchett arrive?"

"We're quite in the dark; as soon as she can find a decent cabin. She may be waiting for it yet; on the other hand she may already have disembarked in England."

"In that case she would probably have telegraphed to you."

"She never telegraphs when you would expect it—only when you don't," said the old man. "She likes to drop on me suddenly; she thinks she'll find me doing something wrong. She has never done so yet, but she's not discouraged."

"It's her share in the family trait, the independence she speaks of." Her son's appreciation of the matter was more favourable. "Whatever the high spirit of those young ladies may be, her own is a match for it. She likes to do everything for herself and has no belief in any one's power to help her. She thinks me of no more use than a postage-stamp without gum, and she would never forgive me if I should presume to go to Liverpool to meet her."

"Will you at least let me know when your cousin arrives?" Lord Warburton asked.

"Only on the condition I've mentioned—that you don't fall in love with her!" Mr. Touchett replied.

"That strikes me as hard. Don't you think me good enough?"

"I think you too good—because I shouldn't like her to marry you. She hasn't come here to look for a husband, I hope; so many young ladies are doing that, as if there were no good ones at home. Then she's probably engaged; American girls are usually engaged, I believe. Moreover I'm not sure, after all, that you'd be a remarkable husband."

"Very likely she's engaged; I've known a good many American girls, and they always were; but I could never see that it made any difference, upon my word! As for my being a good husband," Mr. Touchett's visitor pursued, "I'm not sure of that either. One can but try!"

"Try as much as you please, but don't try on my niece," smiled the old man, whose opposition to the idea was broadly humorous.

"Ah, well," said Lord Warburton with a humour broader still, "perhaps, after all, she's not worth trying on!"

Chapter II

While this exchange of pleasantries took place between the two Ralph Touchett wandered away a little, with his usual slouching gait, his hands in his pockets and his little rowdyish terrier at his heels. His face was turned toward the house, but his eyes were bent musingly on the lawn; so that he had been an object of observation to a person who had just made her appearance in the ample doorway for some moments before he perceived her. His attention was called to her by the conduct of his dog, who had suddenly darted forward with a little volley of shrill barks, in which the note of welcome, however, was more sensible than that of defiance. The person in question was a young lady, who seemed immediately to interpret the greeting of the small beast. He advanced with great rapidity and stood at her feet, looking up and barking hard; whereupon, without hesitation, she stooped and caught him in her hands, holding him face to face while he continued his quick chatter. His master now had had time to follow and to see that Bunchie's new friend was a tall girl in a black dress, who at first sight looked pretty. She was bare-headed, as if she were staying in the house—a fact which conveyed perplexity to the son of its master, conscious of that immunity from visitors which had for some time been rendered necessary by the latter's ill-health. Meantime the two other gentlemen had also taken note of the new-comer.

"Dear me, who's that strange woman?" Mr. Touchett had asked.

"Perhaps it's Mrs. Touchett's niece—the independent young lady," Lord Warburton suggested. "I think she must be, from the way she handles the dog."

The collie, too, had now allowed his attention to be diverted, and he trotted toward the young lady in the doorway, slowly setting his tail in motion as he went.

"But where's my wife then?" murmured the old man.

"I suppose the young lady has left her somewhere: that's a part of the independence."

The girl spoke to Ralph, smiling, while she still held up the terrier. "Is this your little dog, sir?"

"He was mine a moment ago; but you've suddenly acquired a remarkable air of property in him."

"Couldn't we share him?" asked the girl. "He's such a perfect little darling."

Ralph looked at her a moment, she was unexpectedly pretty. "You may have him altogether," he then replied.

The young lady seemed to have a great deal of confidence, both in herself and in others; but this abrupt generosity made her blush. "I ought to tell you that I'm probably your cousin," she brought out, putting down the dog. "And here's another!" she added quickly, as the collie came up.

"Probably?" the young man exclaimed, laughing. "I supposed it was quite settled! Have you arrived with my mother?"

"Yes, half an hour ago."

"And has she deposited you and departed again?"

"No, she went straight to her room, and she told me that, if I should see you, I was to say to you that you must come to her there at a quarter to seven."

The young man looked at his watch. "Thank you very much; I shall be punctual." And then he looked at his cousin. "You're very welcome here. I'm delighted to see you."

She was looking at everything, with an eye that denoted clear perception— at her companion, at the two dogs, at the two gentlemen under the trees, at the beautiful scene that surrounded her. "I've never seen anything so lovely as this place. I've been all over the house; it's too enchanting."

"I'm sorry you should have been here so long without our knowing it."

"Your mother told me that in England people arrived very quietly; so I thought it was all right. Is one of those gentlemen your father?"

"Yes, the elder one—the one sitting down," said Ralph.

The girl gave a laugh. "I don't suppose it's the other. Who's the other?"

"He is a friend of ours—Lord Warburton."

"Oh, I hoped there would be a lord; it's just like a novel!" And then, "Oh you adorable creature!" she suddenly cried, stooping down and picking up the small dog again.

She remained standing where they had met, making no offer to advance or to speak to Mr. Touchett, and while she lingered so near the threshold, slim and charming, her interlocutor wondered if she expected the old man to come and pay her his respects. American girls were used to a great deal of deference, and it had been intimated that this one had a high spirit. Indeed Ralph could see that in her face.

"Won't you come and make acquaintance with my father?" he nevertheless ventured to ask. "He's old and infirm—he doesn't leave his chair."

"Ah, poor man, I'm very sorry!" the girl exclaimed, immediately moving forward. "I got the impression from your mother that he was rather— rather intensely active."

Ralph Touchett was silent a moment. "She hasn't seen him for a year."

"Well, he has a lovely place to sit. Come along, little hound."

"It's a dear old place," said the young man, looking sidewise at his neighbour.

"What's his name?" she asked, her attention having again reverted to the terrier.

"My father's name?"

"Yes," said the young lady with amusement; "but don't tell him I asked you."

They had come by this time to where old Mr. Touchett was sitting, and he slowly got up from his chair to introduce himself.

"My mother has arrived," said Ralph, "and this is Miss Archer."

The old man placed his two hands on her shoulders, looked at her a moment with extreme benevolence and then gallantly kissed her. "It's a great pleasure to me to see you here; but I wish you had given us a chance to receive you."

"Oh, we were received," said he girl. "There were about a dozen servants in the hall. And there was an old woman curtseying at the gate."

"We can do better than that—if we have notice!" And the old man stood there smiling, rubbing his hands and slowly shaking his head at her. "But Mrs. Touchett doesn't like receptions."

"She went straight to her room."

"Yes—and locked herself in. She always does that. Well, I suppose I shall see her next week." And Mrs. Touchett's husband slowly resumed his former posture.

"Before that," said Miss Archer. "She's coming down to dinner—at eight o'clock. Don't you forget a quarter to seven," she added, turning with a smile to Ralph.

"What's to happen at a quarter to seven?"

"I'm to see my mother," said Ralph.

"Ah, happy boy!" the old man commented. "You must sit down—you must have some tea," he observed to his wife's niece.

"They gave me some tea in my room the moment I got there," this young lady answered. "I'm sorry you're out of health," she added, resting her eyes upon her venerable host.

"Oh, I'm an old man, my dear; it's time for me to be old. But I shall be the better for having you here."

She had been looking all round her again—at the lawn, the great trees, the reedy, silvery Thames, the beautiful old house; and while engaged in this survey she had made room in it for her companions; a comprehensiveness of observation easily conceivable on the part of a young woman who was evidently both intelligent and excited. She had seated herself and had put away the little dog; her white hands, in her lap, were folded upon her black dress; her head was erect, her eye lighted, her flexible figure turned itself easily this way and that, in sympathy with the alertness with which she evidently caught impressions. Her impressions were numerous, and they were all reflected in a clear, still smile. "I've never seen anything so beautiful as this."

"It's looking very well," said Mr. Touchett. "I know the way it strikes you. I've been through all that. But you're very beautiful yourself," he added with a politeness by no means crudely jocular and with the happy consciousness that his advanced age gave him the privilege of saying such things—even to young persons who might possibly take alarm at them.

What degree of alarm this young person took need not be exactly measured; she instantly rose, however, with a blush which was not a refutation. "Oh yes, of course I'm lovely!" she returned with a quick laugh. "How old is your house? Is it Elizabethan?"

"It's early Tudor," said Ralph Touchett.

She turned toward him, watching his face. "Early Tudor? How very delightful! And I suppose there are a great many others."

"There are many much better ones."

"Don't say that, my son!" the old man protested. "There's nothing better than this."

"I've got a very good one; I think in some respects it's rather better," said Lord Warburton, who as yet had not spoken, but who had kept an attentive eye upon Miss Archer. He slightly inclined himself, smiling; he had an excellent manner with women. The girl appreciated it in an instant; she had not forgotten that this was Lord Warburton. "I should like very much to show it to you," he added.

"Don't believe him," cried the old man; "don't look at it! It's a wretched old barrack—not to be compared with this."

"I don't know—I can't judge," said the girl, smiling at Lord Warburton.

In this discussion Ralph Touchett took no interest whatever; he stood with his hands in his pockets, looking greatly as if he should like to renew his conversation with his new-found cousin. "Are you very fond of dogs?" he enquired by way of beginning. He seemed to recognise that it was an awkward beginning for a clever man.

"Very fond of them indeed."

"You must keep the terrier, you know," he went on, still awkwardly.

"I'll keep him while I'm here, with pleasure."

"That will be for a long time, I hope."

"You're very kind. I hardly know. My aunt must settle that."

"I'll settle it with her—at a quarter to seven." And Ralph looked at his watch again.

"I'm glad to be here at all," said the girl.

"I don't believe you allow things to be settled for you."

"Oh yes; if they're settled as I like them."

"I shall settle this as I like it," said Ralph. "It's most unaccountable that we should never have known you."

"I was there—you had only to come and see me."

"There? Where do you mean?"

"In the United States: in New York and Albany and other American places."

"I've been there—all over, but I never saw you. I can't make it out."

Miss Archer just hesitated. "It was because there had been some disagreement between your mother and my father, after my mother's death, which took place when I was a child. In consequence of it we never expected to see you."

"Ah, but I don't embrace all my mother's quarrels—heaven forbid!" the young man cried. "You've lately lost your father?" he went on more gravely.

"Yes; more than a year ago. After that my aunt was very kind to me; she came to see me and proposed that I should come with her to Europe."

"I see," said Ralph. "She has adopted you."

"Adopted me?" The girl stared, and her blush came back to her, together with a momentary look of pain which gave her interlocutor some alarm. He had underestimated the effect of his words. Lord Warburton, who appeared constantly desirous of a nearer view of Miss Archer, strolled toward the two cousins at the moment, and as he did so she rested her wider eyes on him. "Oh no; she has not adopted me. I'm not a candidate for adoption."

"I beg a thousand pardons," Ralph murmured. "I meant—I meant—" He hardly knew what he meant.

"You meant she has taken me up. Yes; she likes to take people up. She has been very kind to me; but," she added with a certain visible eagerness of desire to be explicit, "I'm very fond of my liberty."

"Are you talking about Mrs. Touchett?" the old man called out from his chair. "Come here, my dear, and tell me about her. I'm always thankful for information."

The girl hesitated again, smiling. "She's really very benevolent," she answered; after which she went over to her uncle, whose mirth was excited by her words.

Lord Warburton was left standing with Ralph Touchett, to whom in a moment he said: "You wished a while ago to see my idea of an interesting woman. There it is!"

Chapter III

Mrs. Touchett was certainly a person of many oddities, of which her behaviour on returning to her husband's house after many months was a noticeable specimen. She had her own way of doing all that she did, and this is the simplest description of a character which, although by no means without liberal motions, rarely succeeded in giving an impression of suavity.

Mrs. Touchett might do a great deal of good, but she never pleased. This way of her own, of which she was so fond, was not intrinsically offensive—it was just unmistakeably distinguished from the ways of others. The edges of her conduct were so very clear-cut that for susceptible persons it sometimes had a knife-like effect. That hard fineness came out in her deportment during the first hours of her return from America, under circumstances in which it might have seemed that her first act would have been to exchange greetings with her husband and son. Mrs. Touchett, for reasons which she deemed excellent, always retired on such occasions into impenetrable seclusion, postponing the more sentimental ceremony until she had repaired the disorder of dress with a completeness which had the less reason to be of high importance as neither beauty nor vanity were concerned in it. She was a plain-faced old woman, without graces and without any great elegance, but with an extreme respect for her own motives. She was usually prepared to explain these—when the explanation was asked as a favour; and in such a case they proved totally different from those that had been attributed to her. She was virtually separated from her husband, but she appeared to perceive nothing irregular in the situation. It had become clear, at an early stage of their community, that they should never desire the same thing at the same moment, and this appearance had prompted her to rescue disagreement from the vulgar realm of accident. She did what she could to erect it into a law—a much more edifying aspect of it—by going to live in Florence, where she bought a house and established herself; and by leaving her husband to take care of the English branch of his bank. This arrangement greatly pleased her; it was so felicitously definite. It struck her husband in the same light, in a foggy square in London, where it was at times the most definite fact he discerned; but he would have preferred that such unnatural things should have a greater vagueness. To agree to disagree had cost him an effort; he was ready to agree to almost anything but that, and saw no reason why either assent or dissent should be so terribly consistent. Mrs. Touchett indulged in no regrets nor speculations, and usually came once a year to spend a month with her husband, a period during which she apparently took pains to convince him that she had adopted the right system. She was not fond of the English style of life, and had three or four reasons for it to which she currently alluded; they bore upon minor points of that ancient order, but for Mrs. Touchett they amply justified non-residence. She detested bread-sauce, which, as she said, looked like a poultice and tasted like soap; she objected to the consumption of beer by her maidservants; and she affirmed that the British laundress (Mrs. Touchett was very particular about the appearance of her linen) was not a mistress of her art. At fixed intervals she paid a visit to her own country; but this last had been longer than any of its predecessors.

She had taken up her niece—there was little doubt of that. One wet afternoon, some four months earlier than the occurrence lately narrated, this young lady had been seated alone with a book. To say she was so occupied is to say that her solitude did not press upon her; for her love of knowledge had a fertilising quality and her imagination was strong. There was at this time, however, a want of fresh taste in her situation which the arrival of an unexpected visitor did much to correct. The visitor had not been announced; the girl heard her at last walking about the adjoining room. It was in an old house at Albany, a large, square, double house, with a notice of sale in the windows of one of the lower apartments.[1] There were two entrances, one of which had long been out of use but had never been removed. They were exactly alike—large white doors, with an arched frame and wide side-lights, perched upon little "stoops" of red stone, which descended sidewise to the brick pavement of the street. The two houses together formed a single dwelling, the party-wall having been removed and the rooms placed in communication. These rooms, above-stairs, were extremely numerous, and were painted all over exactly alike, in a yellowish white which had grown sallow with time. On the third floor there was a sort of arched passage, connecting the two sides of the house, which Isabel and her sisters used in their childhood to call the tunnel and which, though it was short and well-lighted, always seemed to the girl to be strange and lonely, especially on winter afternoons. She had been in the house, at different periods, as a child; in those days her grandmother lived there. Then there had been an absence of ten years, followed by a return to Albany before her father's death. Her grandmother, old Mrs. Archer, had exercised, chiefly within the limits of the family, a large hospitality in the early period, and the little girls often spent weeks under her roof—weeks of which Isabel had the happiest memory. The manner of life was different from that of her own home—larger, more plentiful, practically more festal; the discipline of the nursery was delightfully vague and the opportunity of listening to the conversation of one's elders (which with Isabel was a highly-valued pleasure) almost unbounded. There was a constant coming and going; her grandmother's sons and daughters and their children appeared to be in the enjoyment of standing invitations to arrive and remain, so that the house offered to a certain extent the appearance of a bustling provincial inn kept by a gentle old landlady who sighed a great deal and never presented a bill. Isabel of course knew nothing about bills; but even as a child she thought her grandmother's home romantic. There was a covered piazza behind it, furnished with a swing which was a source of tremulous interest; and beyond this was a long garden, sloping down to the stable and containing peach-trees of barely credible familiarity. Isabel had stayed with her grandmother at various seasons, but somehow all her visits had a flavour of peaches. On the other side, across the street, was an old house that was called the Dutch House—a peculiar structure dating from the earliest colonial time, composed of bricks that had been painted yellow, crowned with a gable that was pointed out to strangers, defended by a rickety wooden paling and standing sidewise to the street. It was occupied by a primary school for children of both sexes, kept or rather let go, by a demonstrative lady of whom Isabel's chief recollection was that her hair was fastened with strange bedroomy combs at the temples and that she was the widow of some one of consequence. The little girl had been offered the opportunity of laying a foundation of knowledge in this establishment; but having spent a single day in it, she had protested against its laws and had been allowed to stay at home, where, in the September days, when the windows of the Dutch House were open, she used to

1. The description of the Albany house corresponds, down to the "peach-trees" and the "Dutch House" across the street, to that of James's paternal grandmother, Catharine Barber James. See the first chapter of *A Small Boy and Others* (1913).

hear the hum of childish voices repeating the multiplication-table—an incident in which the elation of liberty and the pain of exclusion were indistinguishably mingled. The foundation of her knowledge was really laid in the idleness of her grandmother's house, where, as most of the other inmates were not reading people, she had uncontrolled use of a library full of books with frontispieces, which she used to climb upon a chair to take down. When she had found one to her taste—she was guided in the selection chiefly by the frontispiece—she carried it into a mysterious apartment which lay beyond the library and which was called, traditionally, no one knew why, the office. Whose office it had been and at what period it had flourished, she never learned; it was enough for her that it contained an echo and a pleasant musty smell and that it was a chamber of disgrace for old pieces of furniture whose infirmities were not always apparent (so that the disgrace seemed unmerited and rendered them victims of injustice) and with which, in the manner of children, she had established relations almost human, certainly dramatic. There was an old haircloth sofa in especial, to which she had confided a hundred childish sorrows. The place owed much of its mysterious melancholy to the fact that it was properly entered from the second door of the house, the door that had been condemned, and that it was secured by bolts which a particularly slender little girl found it impossible to slide. She knew that this silent, motionless portal opened into the street; if the sidelights had not been filled with green paper she might have looked out upon the little brown stoop and the well-worn brick pavement. But she had no wish to look out, for this would have interfered with her theory that there was a strange, unseen place on the other side—a place which became to the child's imagination, according to its different moods, a region of delight or of terror.

It was in the "office" still that Isabel was sitting on that melancholy afternoon of early spring which I have just mentioned. At this time she might have had the whole house to choose from, and the room she had selected was the most depressed of its scenes. She had never opened the bolted door nor removed the green paper (renewed by other hands) from its side-lights; she had never assured herself that the vulgar street lay beyond. A crude, cold rain fell heavily; the spring-time was indeed an appeal—and it seemed a cynical, insincere appeal—to patience. Isabel, however, gave as little heed as possible to cosmic treacheries; she kept her eyes on her book and tried to fix her mind. It had lately occurred to her that her mind was a good deal of a vagabond, and she had spent much ingenuity in training it to a military step and teaching it to advance, to halt, to retreat, to perform even more complicated manoeuvres, at the word of command. Just now she had given it marching orders and it had been trudging over the sandy plains of a history of German Thought. Suddenly she became aware of a step very different from her own intellectual pace; she listened a little and perceived that some one was moving in the library, which communicated with the office. It struck her first as the step of a person from whom she was looking for a visit, then almost immediately announced itself as the tread of a woman and a stranger—her possible visitor being neither. It had an inquisitive, experimental quality which suggested that it would not stop short of the threshold of the office; and in fact the doorway of this apartment was presently occupied by a lady who paused there and looked very hard at our heroine. She was a plain, elderly woman, dressed in a comprehensive waterproof mantle; she had a face with a good deal of rather violent point. "Oh," she began, "is that where you usually sit?" She looked about at the heterogeneous chairs and tables. "Not when I have visitors," said Isabel, getting up to receive the intruder. She directed their course back to the library while the visitor continued to look about her. "You seem to have plenty of other rooms; they're in rather better condition. But everything's immensely worn."

"Have you come to look at the house?" Isabel asked. "The servant will show it to you."

"Send her away; I don't want to buy it. She has probably gone to look for you and is wandering about upstairs; she didn't seem at all intelligent. You had better tell her it's no matter." And then, since the girl stood there hesitating and wondering, this unexpected critic said to her abruptly: "I suppose you're one of the daughters?"

Isabel thought she had very strange manners. "It depends upon whose daughters you mean."

"The late Mr. Archer's—and my poor sister's."

"Ah," said Isabel slowly, "you must be our crazy Aunt Lydia!"

"Is that what your father told you to call me? I'm your Aunt Lydia, but I'm not at all crazy: I haven't a delusion! And which of the daughters are you?"

"I'm the youngest of the three, and my name's Isabel."

"Yes; the others are Lilian and Edith. And are you the prettiest?"

"I haven't the least idea," said the girl.

"I think you must be." And in this way the aunt and the niece made friends. The aunt had quarrelled years before with her brother-in-law, after the death of her sister, taking him to task for the manner in which he brought up his three girls. Being a high-tempered man he had requested her to mind her own business, and she had taken him at his word. For many years she held no communication with him and after his death had addressed not a word to his daughters, who had been bred in that disrespectful view of her which we have just seen Isabel betray. Mrs. Touchett's behaviour was, as usual, perfectly deliberate. She intended to go to America to look after her investments (with which her husband, in spite of his great financial position, had nothing to do) and would take advantage of this opportunity to enquire into the condition of her nieces. There was no need of writing, for she should attach no importance to any account of them she should elicit by letter; she believed, always, in seeing for one's self. Isabel found, however, that she knew a good deal about them, and knew about the marriage of the two elder girls; knew that their poor father had left very little money, but that the house in Albany, which had passed into his hands, was to be sold for their benefit; knew, finally, that Edmund Ludlow, Lilian's husband, had taken upon himself to attend to this matter, in consideration of which the young couple, who had come to Albany during Mr. Archer's illness, were remaining there for the present and, as well as Isabel herself, occupying the old place.

"How much money do you expect for it?" Mrs. Touchett asked of her companion, who had brought her to sit in the front parlour, which she had inspected without enthusiasm.

"I haven't the least idea," said the girl.

"That's the second time you have said that to me," her aunt rejoined. "And yet you don't look at all stupid."

"I'm not stupid; but I don't know anything about money."

"Yes, that's the way you were brought up—as if you were to inherit a million. What have you in point of fact inherited?"

"I really can't tell you. You must ask Edmund and Lilian; they'll be back in half an hour."

"In Florence we should call it a very bad house," said Mrs. Touchett; "but here, I dare say, it will bring a high price. It ought to make a considerable sum for each of you. In addition to that you *must* have something else; it's most extraordinary your not knowing. The position's of value, and they'll probably pull it down and make a row of shops. I wonder you don't do that yourself; you might let the shops to great advantage."

Isabel stared; the idea of letting shops was new to her. "I hope they won't pull it down," she said; "I'm extremely fond of it."

"I don't see what makes you fond of it; your father died here."

"Yes; but I don't dislike it for that," the girl rather strangely returned. "I like places in which things have happened—even if they're sad things. A great many people have died here; the place has been full of life."

"Is that what you call being full of life?"

"I mean full of experience—of people's feelings and sorrows. And not of their sorrows only, for I've been very happy here as a child."

"You should go to Florence if you like houses in which things have happened—especially deaths. I live in an old palace in which three people have been murdered; three that were known and I don't know how many more besides."

"In an old palace?" Isabel repeated.

"Yes, my dear; a very different affair from this. This is very bourgeois."

Isabel felt some emotion, for she had always thought highly of her grandmother's house. But the emotion was of a kind which led her to say: "I should like very much to go to Florence."

"Well, if you'll be very good, and do everything I tell you I'll take you there," Mrs. Touchett declared.

Our young woman's emotion deepened; she flushed a little and smiled at her aunt in silence. "Do everything you tell me? I don't think I can promise that."

"No, you don't look like a person of that sort. You're fond of your own way; but it's not for me to blame you."

"And yet, to go to Florence," the girl exclaimed in a moment, "I'd promise almost anything!"

Edmund and Lilian were slow to return, and Mrs. Touchett had an hour's uninterrupted talk with her niece, who found her a strange and interesting figure: a figure essentially—almost the first she had ever met. She was as eccentric as Isabel had always supposed; and hitherto, whenever the girl had heard people described as eccentric, she had thought of them as offensive or alarming. The term had always suggested to her something grotesque and even sinister. But her aunt made it a matter of high but easy irony, or comedy, and led her to ask herself if the common tone, which was all she had known, had ever been as interesting. No one certainly had on any occasion so held her as this little thin-lipped, bright-eyed, foreign-looking woman, who retrieved an insignificant appearance by a distinguished manner and, sitting there in a well-worn waterproof, talked with striking familiarity of the courts of Europe. There was nothing flighty about Mrs. Touchett, but she recognised no social superiors, and, judging the great ones of the earth in a way that spoke of this, enjoyed the consciousness of making an impression on a candid and susceptible mind. Isabel at first had answered a good many questions, and it was from her answers apparently that Mrs. Touchett derived a high opinion of her intelligence. But after this she had asked a good many, and her aunt's answers, whatever turn they took, struck her as food for deep reflexion. Mrs. Touchett waited for the return of her other niece as long as she thought reasonable, but as at six o'clock Mrs. Ludlow had not come in she prepared to take her departure.

"Your sister must be a great gossip. Is she accustomed to staying out so many hours?"

"You've been out almost as long as she," Isabel replied; "she can have left the house but a short time before you came in."

Mrs. Touchett looked at the girl without resentment; she appeared to enjoy a bold retort and to be disposed to be gracious. "Perhaps she hasn't had so good an excuse as I. Tell her at any rate that she must come and see me this evening at that horrid hotel. She may bring her husband if she likes, but she needn't bring you. I shall see plenty of you later."

Chapter IV

Mrs. Ludlow was the eldest of the three sisters, and was usually thought the most sensible; the classification being in general that Lilian was the practical one, Edith the beauty and Isabel the "intellectual" superior. Mrs. Keyes, the second of the group, was the wife of an officer of the United States Engineers, and as our history is not further concerned with her it will suffice that she was indeed very pretty and that she formed the ornament of those various military stations, chiefly in the unfashionable West, to which, to her deep chagrin, her husband was successively relegated. Lilian had married a New York lawyer, a young man with a loud voice and an enthusiasm for his profession; the match was not brilliant, any more than Edith's, but Lilian had occasionally been spoken of as a young woman who might be thankful to marry at all—she was so much plainer than her sisters. She was, however, very happy, and now, as the mother of two peremptory little boys and the mistress of a wedge of brown stone violently driven into Fifty-third Street,[1] seemed to exult in her condition as in a bold escape. She was short and solid, and her claim to figure was questioned, but she was conceded presence, though not majesty; she had moreover, as people said, improved since her marriage, and the two things in life of which she was most distinctly conscious were her husband's force in argument and her sister Isabel's originality. "I've never kept up with Isabel—it would have taken all my time," she had often remarked; in spite of which, however, she held her rather wistfully in sight; watching her as a motherly spaniel might watch a free greyhound. "I want

1. The novel's first edition describes Lilian's house more simply as one that "presented a narrowness of new brown stone to Fifty-third Street," making James's revision here stand as a nice example of the New York Edition's greater metaphoric power.

to see her safely married—that's what I want to see," she frequently noted to her husband.

"Well, I must say I should have no particular desire to marry her," Edmund Ludlow was accustomed to answer in an extremely audible tone. "I know you say that for argument; you always take the opposite ground. I don't see what you've against her except that she's so original."

"Well, I don't like originals; I like translations," Mr. Ludlow had more than once replied. "Isabel's written in a foreign tongue. I can't make her out. She ought to marry an Armenian or a Portuguese."

"That's just what I'm afraid she'll do!" cried Lilian, who thought Isabel capable of anything.

She listened with great interest to the girl's account of Mrs. Touchett's appearance and in the evening prepared to comply with their aunt's commands. Of what Isabel then said no report has remained, but her sister's words had doubtless prompted a word spoken to her husband as the two were making ready for their visit. "I do hope immensely she'll do something handsome for Isabel; she has evidently taken a great fancy to her."

"What is it you wish her to do?" Edmund Ludlow asked. "Make her a big present?"

"No indeed; nothing of the sort. But take an interest in her—sympathise with her. She's evidently just the sort of person to appreciate her. She has lived so much in foreign society; she told Isabel all about it. You know you've always thought Isabel rather foreign."

"You want her to give her a little foreign sympathy, eh? Don't you think she gets enough at home?"

"Well, she ought to go abroad," said Mrs. Ludlow. "She's just the person to go abroad."

"And you want the old lady to take her, is that it?"

"She has offered to take her—she's dying to have Isabel go. But what I want her to do when she gets her there is to give her all the advantages. I'm sure all we've got to do," said Mrs. Ludlow, "is to give her a chance."

"A chance for what?"

"A chance to develop."

"Oh Moses!" Edmund Ludlow exclaimed. "I hope she isn't going to develop any more!"

"If I were not sure you only said that for argument I should feel very badly," his wife replied. "But you know you love her."

"*Do* you know I love you?" the young man said, jocosely, to Isabel a little later, while he brushed his hat.

"I'm sure I don't care whether you do or not!" exclaimed the girl; whose voice and smile, however, were less haughty than her words.

"Oh, she feels so grand since Mrs. Touchett's visit," said her sister.

But Isabel challenged this assertion with a good deal of seriousness. "You must not say that, Lily. I don't feel grand at all."

"I'm sure there's no harm," said the conciliatory Lily.

"Ah, but there's nothing in Mrs. Touchett's visit to make one feel grand."

"Oh," exclaimed Ludlow, "she's grander than ever!"

"Whenever I feel grand," said the girl, "it will be for a better reason."

Whether she felt grand or no, she at any rate felt different, felt as if something had happened to her. Left to herself for the evening she sat a while under the lamp, her hands empty, her usual avocations unheeded. Then she rose and moved about the room, and from one room to another, preferring the places where the vague lamplight expired. She was restless and even agitated; at moments she trembled a little. The importance of what had happened was out of proportion to its appearance; there had really been a change in her life. What it would bring with it was as yet extremely indefinite; but Isabel was in a situation that gave a value to any change. She had a desire to leave the past behind her and, as she said to herself, to begin afresh. This desire indeed was not a birth of the present occasion; it was as familiar as the sound of the rain upon the window and it had led to her beginning afresh a great many times. She closed her eyes as she sat in one of the dusky corners of the quiet parlour; but it was not with a desire for dozing forgetfulness. It was on the contrary because she felt too wide-eyed and wished to check the sense of seeing too many things at once. Her imagination was by habit ridiculously active; when the door was not open it jumped out of the window. She was not accustomed indeed to keep it behind bolts; and at important moments, when she would have been thankful to make use of her judgement alone, she paid the penalty of having given undue encouragement to the faculty of seeing without judging. At present, with her sense that the note of change had been struck, came gradually a host of images of the things she was leaving behind her. The years and hours of her life came back to her, and for a long time, in a stillness broken only by the ticking of the big bronze clock, she passed them in review. It had been a very happy life and she had been a very fortunate person—this was the truth that seemed to emerge most vividly. She had had the best of everything, and in a world in which the circumstances of so many people made them unenviable it was an advantage never to have known anything particularly unpleasant. It appeared to Isabel that the unpleasant had been even too absent from her knowledge, for she had gathered from her acquaintance with literature that it was often a source of interest and even of instruction. Her father had kept it away from her—her handsome, much-loved father, who always had such an aversion to it. It was a great felicity to have been his daughter; Isabel rose even to pride in her parentage. Since his death she had seemed to see him as turning his braver side to his children and as not having managed to ignore the ugly quite so much in practice as in aspiration. But this only made her tenderness for him greater; it was scarcely even painful to have to suppose him too generous, too good-natured, too indifferent to sordid considerations. Many persons had held that he carried this indifference too far, especially the large number of those to whom he owed money. Of their opinions Isabel was never very definitely informed; but it may interest the reader to know that, while they had recognised in the late Mr. Archer a remarkably handsome head and a very taking manner (indeed, as one of them had said, he was always taking something), they had declared that he was making a very poor use of his life. He had squandered a substantial fortune, he had been deplorably convivial, he was known to have gambled freely. A few very harsh critics went so far as to say that he had not even brought up his daughters. They had had no regular education and no permanent home: they had been at once spoiled and neglected; they had lived with nursemaids and governesses (usually very bad ones) or had been sent to superficial schools, kept by the French, from which, at the end of a month, they had been removed in tears. This view of the matter would have excited Isabel's indignation, for to her own sense her opportunities had been large. Even when her father had left his daughters for three months at Neufchatel with a French *bonne*[2] who had eloped with a Russian nobleman staying at the same hotel—even in this irregular situation (an incident of the girl's eleventh year) she had been neither frightened nor ashamed, but had thought it a romantic episode in a liberal education. Her father had a large way of looking at life, of which his restlessness and even his occasional incoherency of conduct had been only a proof. He wished his daughters, even as children, to see as much of the world as possible; and it was for this purpose that, before Isabel was fourteen, he had transported them three times across the Atlantic, giving them on each occasion, however, but a few months' view of the subject proposed: a course which had whetted our heroine's curiosity without enabling her to satisfy it. She ought to have been a partisan of her father, for she was the member of his trio who most "made up" to him for the disagreeables he didn't mention. In his last days his general willingness to take leave of a world in which the difficulty of doing as one liked appeared to increase as one grew older had been sensibly modified by the pain of separation from his clever, his superior, his remarkable girl. Later, when the journeys to Europe ceased, he still had shown his children all sorts of indulgence, and if he had been troubled about money-matters nothing disturbed their irreflective consciousness of many possessions. Isabel, though she danced very well, had not the recollection of having been in New York a successful member of the choreographic circle; her sister Edith was, as every one said, so very much more fetching. Edith was so striking an example of success that Isabel could have no illusions as to what constituted this advantage, or as to the limits of her own power to frisk and jump and shriek—above all with rightness of effect. Nineteen persons out of twenty (including the younger sister herself) pronounced Edith infinitely the prettier of the two; but the twentieth, besides reversing this judgement, had the entertainment of thinking all the others aesthetic vulgarians. Isabel had in the depths of her nature an even more unquenchable desire to please than Edith; but the depths of this young lady's nature were a very out-of-the-way place, between which and the surface communication was interrupted by a dozen capricious forces. She saw the young men who came in large numbers to see her sister; but as a general thing they were afraid of her; they had a belief that some special preparation was required for talking with her. Her reputation of reading a great deal hung about her like the cloudy envelope of a goddess in an epic; it was supposed to engender difficult questions and to keep the conversation at a low temperature. The poor girl liked to be thought clever, but she hated to be thought bookish; she used to read in secret and, though her memory was excellent, to abstain from showy reference. She had a great desire for knowledge, but she really preferred almost any source of information to the printed page; she had an immense curiosity about life and was constantly staring and wondering. She carried within herself a great fund of life, and her deepest enjoyment was to feel the continuity

2. A maidservant or nurse. *Neufchâtel*: A lakeside resort in the French-speaking part of Switzerland; Isabel's rackety education resembles that received by James and his siblings during their family travels in Europe in 1855–58 and 1859–60.

between the movements of her own soul and the agitations of the world. For this reason she was fond of seeing great crowds and large stretches of country, of reading about revolutions and wars, of looking at historical pictures—a class of efforts as to which she had often committed the conscious solecism of forgiving them much bad painting for the sake of the subject. While the Civil War went on she was still a very young girl; but she passed months of this long period in a state of almost passionate excitement, in which she felt herself at times (to her extreme confusion) stirred almost indiscriminately by the valour of either army. Of course the circumspection of suspicious swains had never gone the length of making her a social proscript; for the number of those whose hearts, as they approached her, beat only just fast enough to remind them they had heads as well, had kept her unacquainted with the supreme disciplines of her sex and age. She had had everything a girl could have: kindness, admiration, bonbons, bouquets, the sense of exclusion from none of the privileges of the world she lived in, abundant opportunity for dancing, plenty of new dresses, the London *Spectator*, the latest publications, the music of Gounod, the poetry of Browning, the prose of George Eliot.[3]

These things now, as memory played over them, resolved themselves into a multitude of scenes and figures. Forgotten things came back to her; many others, which she had lately thought of great moment, dropped out of sight. The result was kaleidoscopic, but the movement of the instrument was checked at last by the servant's coming in with the name of a gentleman. The name of the gentleman was Caspar Goodwood; he was a straight young man from Boston, who had known Miss Archer for the last twelvemonth and who, thinking her the most beautiful young woman of her time, had pronounced the time, according to the rule I have hinted at, a foolish period of history. He sometimes wrote to her and had within a week or two written from New York. She had thought it very possible he would come in—had indeed all the rainy day been vaguely expecting him. Now that she learned he was there, nevertheless, she felt no eagerness to receive him. He was the finest young man she had ever seen, was indeed quite a splendid young man; he inspired her with a sentiment of high, of rare respect. She had never felt equally moved to it by any other person. He was supposed by the world in general to wish to marry her, but this of course was between themselves. It at least may be affirmed that he had travelled from New York to Albany expressly to see her; having learned in the former city, where he was spending a few days and where he had hoped to find her, that she was still at the State capital. Isabel delayed for some minutes to go to him; she moved about the room with a new sense of complications. But at last she presented herself and found him standing near the lamp. He was tall, strong and somewhat stiff; he was also lean and brown. He was not romantically, he was much rather obscurely, handsome; but his physiognomy had an air of requesting your attention, which it rewarded according to the charm you found in blue eyes of remarkable

---

3. The *Spectator,* founded in 1828 and still going, was and is a conservative weekly journal of opinion; see its review of *The Portrait of a Lady* on pp. 449–51 of this Norton Critical Edition. Charles Gounod (1818–1893) is best known for his 1859 opera *Faust*; Robert Browning (1812–1889) became a friend of James's in London and the subject of several of the novelist's critical essays; no Victorian novelist was more important to James than George Eliot (1819–1880). The first edition omits these three proper names and merely notes that Isabel has had "a glimpse of contemporary aesthetics."

fixedness, the eyes of a complexion other than his own, and a jaw of the somewhat angular mould which is supposed to bespeak resolution. Isabel said to herself that it bespoke resolution to-night; in spite of which, in half an hour, Caspar Goodwood, who had arrived hopeful as well as resolute, took his way back to his lodging with the feeling of a man defeated. He was not, it may be added, a man weakly to accept defeat.

Chapter V

Ralph Touchett was a philosopher, but nevertheless he knocked at his mother's door (at a quarter to seven) with a good deal of eagerness. Even philosophers have their preferences, and it must be admitted that of his progenitors his father ministered most to his sense of the sweetness of fil-ial dependence. His father, as he had often said to himself, was the more motherly; his mother, on the other hand, was paternal, and even, accord-ing to the slang of the day, gubernatorial. She was nevertheless very fond of her only child and had always insisted on his spending three months of the year with her. Ralph rendered perfect justice to her affection and knew that in her thoughts and her thoroughly arranged and servanted life his turn always came after the other nearest subjects of her solicitude, the various punctualities of performance of the workers of her will. He found her completely dressed for dinner, but she embraced her boy with her gloved hands and made him sit on the sofa beside her. She enquired scrupu-lously about her husband's health and about the young man's own, and, receiving no very brilliant account of either, remarked that she was more than ever convinced of her wisdom in not exposing herself to the English climate. In this case she also might have given way. Ralph smiled at the idea of his mother's giving way, but made no point of reminding her that his own infirmity was not the result of the English climate, from which he absented himself for a considerable part of each year.

He had been a very small boy when his father, Daniel Tracy Touchett, a native of Rutland,[1] in the State of Vermont, came to England as subor-dinate partner in a banking-house where some ten years later he gained preponderant control. Daniel Touchett saw before him a life-long residence in his adopted country, of which, from the first, he took a simple, sane and accommodating view. But, as he said to himself, he had no intention of disamericanising, nor had he a desire to teach his only son any such subtle art. It had been for himself so very soluble a problem to live in England assimilated yet unconverted that it seemed to him equally simple his lawful heir should after his death carry on the grey old bank in the white American light. He was at pains to intensify this light, however, by sending the boy home for his education. Ralph spent several terms at an American school and took a degree at an American university, after which, as he struck his father on his return as even redundantly native, he was placed for some three years in residence at Oxford. Oxford swallowed up Harvard, and Ralph became at last English enough. His outward confor-mity to the manners that surrounded him was none the less the mask of a mind that greatly enjoyed its independence, on which nothing long

---

1. The original home of James's cousins, the Temples; Mary "Minny" Temple (1845–1870), who died young from tuberculosis, is the acknowledged model for Isabel. See pp. 425–28 of this Norton Critical Edition.

imposed itself, and which, naturally inclined to adventure and irony, indulged in a boundless liberty of appreciation. He began with being a young man of promise; at Oxford he distinguished himself, to his father's ineffable satisfaction, and the people about him said it was a thousand pities so clever a fellow should be shut out from a career. He might have had a career by returning to his own country (though this point is shrouded in uncertainty) and even if Mr. Touchett had been willing to part with him (which was not the case) it would have gone hard with him to put a watery waste permanently between himself and the old man whom he regarded as his best friend. Ralph was not only fond of his father, he admired him— he enjoyed the opportunity of observing him. Daniel Touchett, to his perception, was a man of genius, and though he himself had no aptitude for the banking mystery he made a point of learning enough of it to measure the great figure his father had played. It was not this, however, he mainly relished; it was the fine ivory surface, polished as by the English air, that the old man had opposed to possibilities of penetration. Daniel Touchett had been neither at Harvard nor at Oxford, and it was his own fault if he had placed in his son's hands the key to modern criticism. Ralph, whose head was full of ideas which his father had never guessed, had a high esteem for the latter's originality. Americans, rightly or wrongly, are commended for the ease with which they adapt themselves to foreign conditions; but Mr. Touchett had made of the very limits of his pliancy half the ground of his general success. He had retained in their freshness most of his marks of primary pressure; his tone, as his son always noted with pleasure, was that of the more luxuriant part of New England. At the end of his life he had become, on his own ground, as mellow as he was rich; he combined consummate shrewdness with the disposition superficially to fraternise, and his "social position," on which he had never wasted a care, had the firm perfection of an unthumbed fruit. It was perhaps his want of imagination and of what is called the historic consciousness; but to many of the impressions usually made by English life upon the cultivated stranger his sense was completely closed. There were certain differences he had never perceived, certain habits he had never formed, certain obscurities he had never sounded. As regards these latter, on the day he *had* sounded them his son would have thought less well of him.

Ralph, on leaving Oxford, had spent a couple of years in travelling; after which he had found himself perched on a high stool in his father's bank. The responsibility and honour of such positions is not, I believe, measured by the height of the stool, which depends upon other considerations: Ralph, indeed, who had very long legs, was fond of standing, and even of walking about, at his work. To this exercise, however, he was obliged to devote but a limited period, for at the end of some eighteen months he had become aware of his being seriously out of health. He had caught a violent cold, which fixed itself on his lungs and threw them into dire confusion. He had to give up work and apply, to the letter, the sorry injunction to take care of himself. At first he slighted the task; it appeared to him it was not himself in the least he was taking care of, but an uninteresting and uninterested person with whom he had nothing in common. This person, however, improved on acquaintance, and Ralph grew at last to have a certain grudging tolerance, even an undemonstrative respect, for him. Misfortune makes strange bedfellows, and our young man, feeling that he had something at stake in the matter—it usually struck him as his reputation for ordinary wit—devoted to his graceless charge an amount of attention of which note was duly taken and which had at least the effect of keeping the poor fellow alive. One of his lungs began to heal, the other promised to follow its example, and he was assured he might outweather a dozen winters if he would betake himself to those climates in which consumptives chiefly congregate. As he had grown extremely fond of London, he cursed the flatness of exile: but at the same time that he cursed he conformed, and gradually, when he found his sensitive organ grateful even for grim favours, he conferred them with a lighter hand. He wintered abroad, as the phrase is; basked in the sun, stopped at home when the wind blew, went to bed when it rained, and once or twice, when it had snowed over-night, almost never got up again.

A secret hoard of indifference—like a thick cake a fond old nurse might have slipped into his first school outfit—came to his aid and helped to reconcile him to sacrifice; since at the best he was too ill for aught but that arduous game. As he said to himself, there was really nothing he had wanted very much to do, so that he had at least not renounced the field of valour. At present, however, the fragrance of forbidden fruit seemed occasionally to float past him and remind him that the finest of pleasures is the rush of action. Living as he now lived was like reading a good book in a poor translation—a meagre entertainment for a young man who felt that he might have been an excellent linguist. He had good winters and poor winters, and while the former lasted he was sometimes the sport of a vision of virtual recovery. But this vision was dispelled some three years before the occurrence of the incidents with which this history opens: he had on that occasion remained later than usual in England and had been overtaken by bad weather before reaching Algiers. He arrived more dead than alive and lay there for several weeks between life and death. His convalescence was a miracle, but the first use he made of it was to assure himself that such miracles happen but once. He said to himself that his hour was in sight and that it behoved him to keep his eyes upon it, yet that it was also open to him to spend the interval as agreeably as might be consistent with such a preoccupation. With the prospect of losing them the simple use of his faculties became an exquisite pleasure; it seemed to him the joys of contemplation had never been sounded. He was far from the time when he had found it hard that he should be obliged to give up the idea of distinguishing himself; an idea none the less importunate for being vague and none the less delightful for having had to struggle in the same breast with bursts of inspiring self-criticism. His friends at present judged him more cheerful, and attributed it to a theory, over which they shook their heads knowingly, that he would recover his health. His serenity was but the array of wild flowers niched in his ruin.

It was very probably this sweet-tasting property of the observed thing in itself that was mainly concerned in Ralph's quickly-stirred interest in the advent of a young lady who was evidently not insipid. If he was consideringly disposed, something told him, here was occupation enough for a succession of days. It may be added, in summary fashion, that the imagination of loving—as distinguished from that of being loved—had still a place in his reduced sketch. He had only forbidden himself the riot of expression. However, he shouldn't inspire his cousin with a passion, nor would she be able, even should she try, to help him to one. "And now tell me about the young lady," he said to his mother. "What do you mean to do with her?"

Mrs. Touchett was prompt. "I mean to ask your father to invite her to stay three or four weeks at Gardencourt."

"You needn't stand on any such ceremony as that," said Ralph. "My father will ask her as a matter of course."

"I don't know about that. She's my niece; she's not his."

"Good Lord, dear mother; what a sense of property! That's all the more reason for his asking her. But after that—I mean after three months (for it's absurd asking the poor girl to remain but for three or four paltry weeks)—what do you mean to do with her?"

"I mean to take her to Paris. I mean to get her clothing."

"Ah yes, that's of course. But independently of that?"

"I shall invite her to spend the autumn with me in Florence."

"You don't rise above detail, dear mother," said Ralph. "I should like to know what you mean to do with her in a general way."

"My duty!" Mrs. Touchett declared. "I suppose you pity her very much," she added.

"No, I don't think I pity her. She doesn't strike me as inviting compassion. I think I envy her. Before being sure, however, give me a hint of where you see your duty."

"In showing her four European countries—I shall leave her the choice of two of them—and in giving her the opportunity of perfecting herself in French, which she already knows very well."

Ralph frowned a little. "That sounds rather dry—even allowing her the choice of two of the countries."

"If it's dry," said his mother with a laugh, "you can leave Isabel alone to water it! She is as good as a summer rain, any day."

"Do you mean she's a gifted being?"

"I don't know whether she's a gifted being, but she's a clever girl—with a strong will and a high temper. She has no idea of being bored."

"I can imagine that," said Ralph; and then he added abruptly: "How do you two get on?"

"Do you mean by that that I'm a bore? I don't think she finds me one. Some girls might, I know; but Isabel's too clever for that. I think I greatly amuse her. We get on because I understand her; I know the sort of girl she is. She's very frank, and I'm very frank: we know just what to expect of each other."

"Ah, dear mother," Ralph exclaimed, "one always knows what to expect of you! You've never surprised me but once, and that's to-day—in presenting me with a pretty cousin whose existence I had never suspected."

"Do you think her so very pretty?"

"Very pretty indeed; but I don't insist upon that. It's her general air of being some one in particular that strikes me. Who is this rare creature, and what is she? Where did you find her, and how did you make her acquaintance?"

"I found her in an old house at Albany, sitting in a dreary room on a rainy day, reading a heavy book and boring herself to death. She didn't know she was bored, but when I left her no doubt of it she seemed very grateful for the service. You may say I shouldn't have enlightened her—I should have let her alone. There's a good deal in that, but I acted conscientiously; I thought she was meant for something better. It occurred to me that it would be a kindness to take her about and introduce her to the world. She thinks she knows a great deal of it—like most American girls; but like most American girls she's ridiculously mistaken. If you want to know, I thought she would do me credit. I like to be well thought of, and for a woman of my age there's no greater convenience, in some ways, than an attractive niece. You know I had seen nothing of my sister's children for years; I disapproved entirely of the father. But I always meant to do something for them when he should have gone to his reward. I ascertained where they were to be found and, without any preliminaries, went and introduced myself. There are two others of them, both of whom are married; but I saw only the elder, who has, by the way, a very uncivil husband. The wife, whose name is Lily, jumped at the idea of my taking an interest in Isabel; she said it was just what her sister needed—that some one should take an interest in her. She spoke of her as you might speak of some young person of genius—in want of encouragement and patronage. It may be that Isabel's a genius; but in that case I've not yet learned her special line. Mrs. Ludlow was especially keen about my taking her to Europe; they all regard Europe over there as a land of emigration, of rescue, a refuge for their superfluous population. Isabel herself seemed very glad to come, and the thing was easily arranged. There was a little difficulty about the money-question, as she seemed averse to being under pecuniary obligations. But she has a small income and she supposes herself to be travelling at her own expense."

Ralph had listened attentively to this judicious report, by which his interest in the subject of it was not impaired. "Ah, if she's a genius," he said, "we must find out her special line. Is it by chance for flirting?"

"I don't think so. You may suspect that at first, but you'll be wrong. You won't, I think, in any way, be easily right about her."

"Warburton's wrong then!" Ralph rejoicingly exclaimed. "He flatters himself he has made that discovery."

His mother shook her head. "Lord Warburton won't understand her. He needn't try."

"He's very intelligent," said Ralph; "but it's right he should be puzzled once in a while."

"Isabel will enjoy puzzling a lord," Mrs. Touchett remarked.

Her son frowned a little. "What does she know about lords?"

"Nothing at all: that will puzzle him all the more."

Ralph greeted these words with a laugh and looked out of the window. Then, "Are you not going down to see my father?" he asked.

"At a quarter to eight," said Mrs. Touchett.

Her son looked at his watch. "You've another quarter of an hour then. Tell me some more about Isabel." After which, as Mrs. Touchett declined his invitation, declaring that he must find out for himself, "Well," he pursued, "she'll certainly do you credit. But won't she also give you trouble?"

"I hope not; but if she does I shall not shrink from it. I never do that."

"She strikes me as very natural," said Ralph.

"Natural people are not the most trouble."

"No," said Ralph; "you yourself are a proof of that. You're extremely natural, and I'm sure you have never troubled any one. It *takes* trouble to do that. But tell me this; it just occurs to me. Is Isabel capable of making herself disagreeable?"

"Ah," cried his mother, "you ask too many questions! Find that out for yourself."

His questions, however, were not exhausted. "All this time," he said, "you've not told me what you intend to do with her."

"Do with her? You talk as if she were a yard of calico. I shall do absolutely nothing with her, and she herself will do everything she chooses. She gave me notice of that."

"What you meant then, in your telegram, was that her character's independent."

"I never know what I mean in my telegrams—especially those I send from America. Clearness is too expensive. Come down to your father."

"It's not yet a quarter to eight," said Ralph.

"I must allow for his impatience," Mrs. Touchett answered. Ralph knew what to think of his father's impatience; but, making no rejoinder, he offered his mother his arm. This put it in his power, as they descended together, to stop her a moment on the middle landing of the staircase—the broad, low, wide-armed staircase of time-blackened oak which was one of the most striking features of Gardencourt. "You've no plan of marrying her?" he smiled.

"Marrying her? I should be sorry to play her such a trick! But apart from that, she's perfectly able to marry herself. She has every facility."

"Do you mean to say she has a husband picked out?"

"I don't know about a husband, but there's a young man in Boston—!"

Ralph went on; he had no desire to hear about the young man in Boston. "As my father says, they're always engaged!"

His mother had told him that he must satisfy his curiosity at the source, and it soon became evident he should not want for occasion. He had a good deal of talk with his young kinswoman when the two had been left together in the drawing-room. Lord Warburton, who had ridden over from his own house, some ten miles distant, remounted and took his departure before dinner; and an hour after this meal was ended Mr. and Mrs. Touchett, who appeared to have quite emptied the measure of their forms, withdrew, under the valid pretext of fatigue, to their respective apartments. The young man spent an hour with his cousin; though she had been travelling half the day she appeared in no degree spent. She was really tired; she knew it, and knew she should pay for it on the morrow; but it was her habit at this period to carry exhaustion to the furthest point and confess to it only when dissimulation broke down. A fine hypocrisy was for the present possible; she was interested; she was, as she said to herself, floated. She asked Ralph to show her the pictures; there were a great many in the house, most of them of his own choosing. The best were arranged in an oaken gallery, of charming proportions, which had a sitting-room at either end of it and which in the evening was usually lighted. The light was insufficient to show the pictures to advantage, and the visit might have stood over to the morrow. This suggestion Ralph had ventured to make; but Isabel looked disappointed—smiling still, however—and said: "If you please I should like to see them just a little." She was eager, she knew she was eager and now seemed so; she couldn't help it. "She doesn't take suggestions," Ralph said to himself; but he said it without irritation; her pressure amused and even pleased him. The lamps were on brackets, at intervals, and if the light was imperfect it was genial. It fell upon the vague squares of rich colour and on the faded gilding of heavy frames; it made a sheen on the polished floor of the gallery. Ralph took a candlestick and moved about, pointing out the things he liked; Isabel, inclining to one picture after another, indulged in little exclamations and murmurs. She was evidently a judge; she had a natural taste; he was struck with that. She took a candlestick herself and held it slowly here and there; she lifted it high, and as she did so he found himself pausing in the middle of the place and bending his eyes much less upon the pictures than on her presence. He lost nothing, in truth, by these wandering glances, for she was better worth looking at than most works of art. She was undeniably spare, and ponderably light, and proveably tall; when people had wished to distinguish her from the other two Miss Archers they had always called her the willowy one. Her hair, which was dark even to blackness, had been an object of envy to many women; her light grey eyes, a little too firm perhaps in her graver moments, had an enchanting range of concession. They walked slowly up one side of the gallery and down the other, and then she said: "Well, now I know more than I did when I began!"

"You apparently have a great passion for knowledge," her cousin returned.

"I think I have; most girls are horridly ignorant."

"You strike me as different from most girls."

"Ah, some of them *would*—but the way they're talked to!" murmured Isabel, who preferred not to dilate just yet on herself. Then in a moment, to change the subject, "Please tell me—isn't there a ghost?" she went on.

"A ghost?"

"A castle-spectre, a thing that appears. We call them ghosts in America."

"So we do here, when we see them."

"You do see them then? You ought to, in this romantic old house."

"It's not a romantic old house," said Ralph. "You'll be disappointed if you count on that. It's a dismally prosaic one; there's no romance here but what you may have brought with you."

"I've brought a great deal; but it seems to me I've brought it to the right place."

"To keep it out of harm, certainly; nothing will ever happen to it here, between my father and me."

Isabel looked at him a moment. "Is there never any one here but your father and you?"

"My mother, of course."

"Oh, I know your mother; she's not romantic. Haven't you other people?"

"Very few."

"I'm sorry for that; I like so much to see people," said Isabel.

"Oh, we'll invite all the county to amuse you," said Ralph.

"Now you're making fun of me," the girl answered rather gravely. "Who was the gentleman on the lawn when I arrived?"

"A county neighbour; he doesn't come very often."

"I'm sorry for that; I liked him," said Isabel.

"Why, it seemed to me that you barely spoke to him," Ralph objected.

"Never mind, I like him all the same. I like your father too, immensely."

"You can't do better than that. He's the dearest of the dear."

"I'm so sorry he is ill," said Isabel.

"You must help me to nurse him; you ought to be a good nurse."

"I don't think I am; I've been told I'm not; I'm said to have too many theories. But you haven't told me about the ghost," she added.

Ralph, however, gave no heed to this observation. "You like my father and you like Lord Warburton. I infer also that you like my mother."

"I like your mother very much, because—because—" And Isabel found herself attempting to assign a reason for her affection for Mrs. Touchett.

"Ah, we never know why!" said her companion, laughing.

"I always know why," the girl answered. "It's because she doesn't expect one to like her. She doesn't care whether one does or not."

"So you adore her—out of perversity? Well, I take greatly after my mother," said Ralph.

"I don't believe you do at all. You wish people to like you, and you try to make them do it."

"Good heavens, how you see through one!" he cried with a dismay that was not altogether jocular.

"But I like you all the same," his cousin went on. "The way to clinch the matter will be to show me the ghost."

Ralph shook his head sadly. "I might show it to you, but you'd never see it. The privilege isn't given to every one; it's not enviable. It has never been seen by a young, happy, innocent person like you. You must have suffered first, have suffered greatly, have gained some miserable knowledge. In that way your eyes are opened to it. I saw it long ago," said Ralph.

"I told you just now I'm very fond of knowledge," Isabel answered.

"Yes, of happy knowledge—of pleasant knowledge. But you haven't suffered, and you're not made to suffer. I hope you'll never see the ghost!"

She had listened to him attentively, with a smile on her lips, but with a certain gravity in her eyes. Charming as he found her, she had struck him as rather presumptuous—indeed it was a part of her charm; and he wondered what she would say. "I'm not afraid, you know," she said: which seemed quite presumptuous enough.

"You're not afraid of suffering?"

"Yes, I'm afraid of suffering. But I'm not afraid of ghosts. And I think people suffer too easily," she added.

"I don't believe *you* do," said Ralph, looking at her with his hands in his pockets.

"I don't think that's a fault," she answered. "It's not absolutely necessary to suffer; we were not made for that."

"You were not, certainly."

"I'm not speaking of myself." And she wandered off a little.

"No, it isn't a fault," said her cousin. "It's a merit to be strong."

"Only, if you don't suffer they call you hard," Isabel remarked.

They passed out of the smaller drawing-room, into which they had returned from the gallery, and paused in the hall, at the foot of the staircase. Here Ralph presented his companion with her bed-room candle, which he had taken from a niche. "Never mind what they call you. When you do suffer they call you an idiot. The great point's to be as happy as possible."

She looked at him a little; she had taken her candle and placed her foot on the oaken stair. "Well," she said, "that's what I came to Europe for, to be as happy as possible. Good-night."

"Good-night! I wish you all success, and shall be very glad to contribute to it!"

She turned away, and he watched her as she slowly ascended. Then, with his hands always in his pockets, he went back to the empty drawing-room.

Chapter VI

Isabel Archer was a young person of many theories; her imagination was remarkably active. It had been her fortune to possess a finer mind than most of the persons among whom her lot was cast; to have a larger perception of surrounding facts and to care for knowledge that was tinged with the unfamiliar. It is true that among her contemporaries she passed for a young woman of extraordinary profundity; for these excellent people never withheld their admiration from a reach of intellect of which they themselves were not conscious, and spoke of Isabel as a prodigy of learning, a creature reported to have read the classic authors—in translations. Her paternal aunt, Mrs. Varian, once spread the rumour that Isabel was writing a book—Mrs. Varian having a reverence for books, and averred that the girl would distinguish herself in print. Mrs. Varian thought highly of literature, for which she entertained that esteem that is connected with a sense of privation. Her own large house, remarkable for its assortment of mosaic tables and decorated ceilings, was unfurnished with a library, and in the way of printed volumes contained nothing but half a dozen novels in paper on a shelf in the apartment of one of the Miss Varians. Practically, Mrs. Varian's acquaintance with literature was confined to *The New York Interviewer*; as she very justly said, after you had read the *Interviewer* you had lost all faith in culture. Her tendency, with this, was rather to keep the *Interviewer* out of the way of her daughters; she was determined to bring them up properly, and they read nothing at all. Her impression with regard to Isabel's labours was quite illusory; the girl had never attempted to write a book and had no desire for the laurels of authorship. She had no talent for expression and too little of the consciousness of genius; she only had a general idea that people were right when they treated her as if she were rather superior. Whether or no she were superior, people were right in admiring her if they thought her so; for it seemed to her often that her mind moved more quickly than theirs, and this encouraged an impatience that might easily be confounded with superiority. It may be affirmed without delay that Isabel was probably very liable to the sin of self-esteem; she often surveyed with complacency the field of her own nature; she was in the habit of taking for granted, on scanty evidence, that she was right; she treated herself to occasions of homage. Meanwhile her errors and delusions were frequently such as a biographer interested in preserving the dignity of his subject must shrink from specifying. Her thoughts were a tangle of vague outlines which had never been corrected by the judgement of people speaking with authority. In matters of opinion she had had her own way, and it had led her into a thousand ridiculous zig-zags. At moments she discovered she was grotesquely wrong, and then she treated herself to a week of passionate humility. After this she held her head higher than ever again; for it was of no use, she had an unquenchable desire to think well of herself. She had a theory that it was only under this provision life was worth living; that one should be one of the best, should be conscious of a fine organisation (she couldn't help knowing her organisation was fine), should move in a realm of light, of natural wisdom, of happy impulse, of inspiration gracefully chronic. It was almost as unnecessary to cultivate doubt of one's self as to cultivate doubt of one's best friend: one should try to be one's own best friend and to give one's self, in this manner, distinguished company. The girl had a certain nobleness of imagination which rendered her a good many services and played her a great many tricks. She spent half her time in thinking of beauty and bravery and magnanimity; she had a fixed determination to regard the world as a place of brightness, of free expansion, of irresistible action: she held it must be detestable to be afraid or ashamed. She had an infinite hope that she should never do anything wrong. She had resented so strongly, after discovering them, her mere errors of feeling (the discovery always made her tremble as if she had escaped from a trap which might have caught her and smothered her) that the chance of inflicting a sensible injury upon another person, presented only as a contingency, caused her at moments to hold her breath. That always struck her as the worst thing that could happen to her. On the whole, reflectively, she was in no uncertainty about the things that were wrong. She had no love of their look, but when she fixed them hard she recognised them. It was wrong to be mean, to be jealous, to be false, to be cruel; she had seen very little of the evil of the world, but she had seen women who lied and who tried to hurt each other. Seeing such things had quickened her high spirit; it seemed indecent not to scorn them. Of course the danger of a high spirit was the danger of inconsistency—the danger of keeping up the flag after the place has surrendered; a sort of behaviour so crooked as to be almost a dishonour to the flag. But Isabel, who knew little of the sorts of artillery to which young women are exposed, flattered herself that such contradictions would never be noted in her own conduct. Her life should always be in harmony with the most pleasing impression she should produce; she would be what she appeared, and she would appear what she was. Sometimes she went so far as to wish that she might find herself some day in a difficult position, so that she should have the pleasure of being as heroic as the occasion demanded. Altogether, with her meagre knowledge, her inflated ideals, her confidence at once innocent and dogmatic, her temper at once exacting and indulgent, her mixture of curiosity and fastidiousness, of vivacity and indifference, her desire to look very well and to be if possible even better, her determination to see, to try, to know, her combination of the delicate, desultory, flame-like spirit and the eager and personal creature of conditions: she would be an easy victim of scientific criticism if she were not intended to awaken on the reader's part an impulse more tender and more purely expectant.

It was one of her theories that Isabel Archer was very fortunate in being independent, and that she ought to make some very enlightened use of that state. She never called it the state of solitude, much less of singleness; she thought such descriptions weak, and, besides, her sister Lily constantly urged her to come and abide. She had a friend whose acquaintance she had made shortly before her father's death, who offered so high an example of useful activity that Isabel always thought of her as a model. Henrietta Stackpole had the advantage of an admired ability; she was thoroughly launched in journalism, and her letters to the *Interviewer*, from

Washington, Newport, the White Mountains and other places, were universally quoted. Isabel pronounced them with confidence "ephemeral," but she esteemed the courage, energy and good-humour of the writer, who, without parents and without property, had adopted three of the children of an infirm and widowed sister and was paying their school-bills out of the proceeds of her literary labour. Henrietta was in the van of progress and had clear-cut views on most subjects; her cherished desire had long been to come to Europe and write a series of letters to the *Interviewer* from the radical point of view—an enterprise the less difficult as she knew perfectly in advance what her opinions would be and to how many objections most European institutions lay open. When she heard that Isabel was coming she wished to start at once; thinking, naturally, that it would be delightful the two should travel together. She had been obliged, however, to postpone this enterprise. She thought Isabel a glorious creature, and had spoken of her covertly in some of her letters, though she never mentioned the fact to her friend, who would not have taken pleasure in it and was not a regular student of the *Interviewer*. Henrietta, for Isabel, was chiefly a proof that a woman might suffice to herself and be happy. Her resources were of the obvious kind; but even if one had not the journalistic talent and a genius for guessing, as Henrietta said, what the public was going to want, one was not therefore to conclude that one had no vocation, no beneficent aptitude of any sort, and resign one's self to being frivolous and hollow. Isabel was stoutly determined not to be hollow. If one should wait with the right patience one would find some happy work to one's hand. Of course, among her theories, this young lady was not without a collection of views on the subject of marriage. The first on the list was a conviction of the vulgarity of thinking too much of it. From lapsing into eagerness on this point she earnestly prayed she might be delivered; she held that a woman ought to be able to live to herself, in the absence of exceptional flimsiness, and that it was perfectly possible to be happy without the society of a more or less coarse-minded person of another sex. The girl's prayer was very sufficiently answered; something pure and proud that there was in her—something cold and dry an unappreciated suitor with a taste for analysis might have called it—had hitherto kept her from any great vanity of conjecture on the article of possible husbands. Few of the men she saw seemed worth a ruinous expenditure, and it made her smile to think that one of them should present himself as an incentive to hope and a reward of patience. Deep in her soul—it was the deepest thing there—lay a belief that if a certain light should dawn she could give herself completely; but this image, on the whole, was too formidable to be attractive. Isabel's thoughts hovered about it, but they seldom rested on it long; after a little it ended in alarms. It often seemed to her that she thought too much about herself; you could have made her colour, any day in the year, by calling her a rank egoist. She was always planning out her development, desiring her perfection, observing her progress. Her nature had, in her conceit, a certain garden-like quality, a suggestion of perfume and murmuring boughs, of shady bowers and lengthening vistas, which made her feel that introspection was, after all, an exercise in the open air, and that a visit to the recesses of one's spirit was harmless when one returned from it with a lapful of roses. But she was often reminded that there were other gardens in the world than those of her remarkable soul, and that there were moreover a great many places which were not gardens at all—only dusky pestiferous tracts, planted thick with ugliness and misery. In the current of that repaid curiosity on which she had lately been floating, which had conveyed her to this beautiful old England and might carry her much further still, she often checked herself with the thought of the thousands of people who were less happy than herself—a thought which for the moment made her fine, full consciousness appear a kind of immodesty. What should one do with the misery of the world in a scheme of the agreeable for one's self? It must be confessed that this question never held her long. She was too young, too impatient to live, too unacquainted with pain. She always returned to her theory that a young woman whom after all every one thought clever should begin by getting a general impression of life. This impression was necessary to prevent mistakes, and after it should be secured she might make the unfortunate condition of others a subject of special attention.

England was a revelation to her, and she found herself as diverted as a child at a pantomime. In her infantine excursions to Europe she had seen only the Continent, and seen it from the nursery window; Paris, not London, was her father's Mecca, and into many of his interests there his children had naturally not entered. The images of that time moreover had grown faint and remote, and the old-world quality in everything that she now saw had all the charm of strangeness. Her uncle's house seemed a picture made real; no refinement of the agreeable was lost upon Isabel; the rich perfection of Gardencourt at once revealed a world and gratified a need. The large, low rooms, with brown ceilings and dusky corners, the deep embrasures and curious casements, the quiet light on dark, polished panels, the deep greenness outside, that seemed always peeping in, the sense of well-ordered privacy in the centre of a "property"—a place where sounds were felicitously accidental, where the tread was muffled by the earth itself and in the thick mild air all friction dropped out of contact and all shrillness out of talk—these things were much to the taste of our young lady, whose taste played a considerable part in her emotions. She formed a fast friendship with her uncle, and often sat by his chair when he had had it moved out to the lawn. He passed hours in the open air, sitting with folded hands like a placid, homely household god, a god of service, who had done his work and received his wages and was trying to grow used to weeks and months made up only of off-days. Isabel amused him more than she suspected—the effect she produced upon people was often different from what she supposed—and he frequently gave himself the pleasure of making her chatter. It was by this term that he qualified her conversation, which had much of the "point" observable in that of the young ladies of her country, to whom the ear of the world is more directly presented than to their sisters in other lands. Like the mass of American girls Isabel had been encouraged to express herself; her remarks had been attended to; she had been expected to have emotions and opinions. Many of her opinions had doubtless but a slender value, many of her emotions passed away in the utterance; but they had left a trace in giving her the habit of seeming at least to feel and think, and in imparting moreover to her words when she was really moved that prompt vividness which so many people had regarded as a sign of superiority. Mr. Touchett used to think that she reminded him of his wife when his wife was in her teens. It was because she was fresh and natural and quick to understand, to speak—so many characteristics of her niece—that he had fallen in love with Mrs. Touchett. He never expressed this analogy to the girl herself, however; for if Mrs. Touchett had once been like Isabel, Isabel was not at all like Mrs. Touchett. The old man was full of kindness for her; it was a long time, as he said, since they had had any young life in the house; and our rustling, quickly-moving, clear-voiced heroine was as agreeable to his sense as the sound of flowing water. He wanted to do something for her and wished she would ask it of him. She would ask nothing but questions; it is true that of these she asked a quantity. Her uncle had a great fund of answers, though her pressure sometimes came in forms that puzzled him. She questioned him immensely about England, about the British constitution, the English character, the state of politics, the manners and customs of the royal family, the peculiarities of the aristocracy, the way of living and thinking of his neighbours; and in begging to be enlightened on these points she usually enquired whether they corresponded with the descriptions in the books. The old man always looked at her a little with his fine dry smile while he smoothed down the shawl spread across his legs.

"The books?" he once said: "well, I don't know much about the books. You must ask Ralph about that. I've always ascertained for myself—got my information in the natural form. I never asked many questions even; I just kept quiet and took notice. Of course I've had very good opportunities—better than what a young lady would naturally have. I'm of an inquisitive disposition, though you mightn't think it if you were to watch me: however much you might watch me I should be watching you more. I've been watching these people for upwards of thirty-five years, and I don't hesitate to say that I've acquired considerable information. It's a very fine country on the whole—finer perhaps than what we give it credit for on the other side. There are several improvements I should like to see introduced; but the necessity of them doesn't seem to be generally felt as yet. When the necessity of a thing is generally felt they usually manage to accomplish it; but they seem to feel pretty comfortable about waiting till then. I certainly feel more at home among them than I expected to when I first came over; I suppose it's because I've had a considerable degree of success. When you're successful you naturally feel more at home."

"Do you suppose that if I'm successful I shall feel at home?" Isabel asked.

"I should think it very probable, and you certainly will be successful. They like American young ladies very much over here; they show them a great deal of kindness. But you mustn't feel too much at home, you know."

"Oh, I'm by no means sure it will *satisfy* me," Isabel judicially emphasised. "I like the place very much, but I'm not sure I shall like the people."

"The people are very good people; especially if you like them."

"I've no doubt they're good," Isabel rejoined; "but are they pleasant in society? They won't rob me nor beat me; but will they make themselves agreeable to me? That's what I like people to do. I don't hesitate to say so, because I always appreciate it. I don't believe they're very nice to girls; they're not nice to them in the novels."

"I don't know about the novels." said Mr. Touchett. "I believe the novels have a great deal of ability, but I don't suppose they're very accurate. We once had a lady who wrote novels staying here; she was a friend of Ralph's and he asked her down. She was very positive, quite up to everything; but she was not the sort of person you could depend on for evidence. Too free a fancy—I suppose that was it. She afterwards published a work of fiction in which she was understood to have given a representation—something in the nature of a caricature, as you might say—of my unworthy self. I didn't read it, but Ralph just handed me the book with the principal passages marked. It was understood to be a description of my conversation; American peculiarities, nasal twang, Yankee notions, stars and stripes. Well, it was not at all accurate; she couldn't have listened very attentively. I had no objection to her giving a report of my conversation, if she liked; but I didn't like the idea that she hadn't taken the trouble to listen to it. Of course I talk like an American—I can't talk like a Hottentot. However I talk, I've made them understand me pretty well over here. But I don't talk like the old gentleman in that lady's novel. He wasn't an American; we wouldn't have him over there at any price. I just mention that fact to show you that they're not always accurate. Of course, as I've no daughters, and as Mrs. Touchett resides in Florence, I haven't had much chance to notice about the young ladies. It sometimes appears as if the young women in the lower class were not very well treated; but I guess their position is better in the upper and even to some extent in the middle."

"Gracious," Isabel exclaimed; "how many classes have they? About fifty, I suppose."

"Well, I don't know that I ever counted them. I never took much notice of the classes: That's the advantage of being an American here; you don't belong to any class."

"I hope so," said Isabel. "Imagine one's belonging to an English class!"

"Well, I guess some of them are pretty comfortable—especially towards the top. But for me there are only two classes: the people I trust and the people I don't. Of those two, my dear Isabel, you belong to the first."

"I'm much obliged to you," said the girl quickly. Her way of taking compliments seemed sometimes rather dry; she got rid of them as rapidly as possible. But as regards this she was sometimes misjudged; she was thought insensible to them, whereas in fact she was simply unwilling to show how infinitely they pleased her. To show that was to show too much. "I'm sure the English are very conventional," she added.

"They've got everything pretty well fixed," Mr. Touchett admitted. "It's all settled beforehand—they don't leave it to the last moment."

"I don't like to have everything settled beforehand," said the girl. "I like more unexpectedness."

Her uncle seemed amused at her distinctness of preference. "Well, it's settled beforehand that you'll have great success," he rejoined. "I suppose you'll like that."

"I shall not have success if they're too stupidly conventional. I'm not in the least stupidly conventional. I'm just the contrary. That's what they won't like."

"No, no you're all wrong," said the old man. "You can't tell what they'll like. They're very inconsistent; that's their principal interest."

"Ah well," said Isabel, standing before her uncle with her hands clasped about the belt of her black dress and looking up and down the lawn—"that will suit me perfectly!"

Chapter VII

The two amused themselves, time and again, with talking of the attitude of the British public as if the young lady had been in a position to appeal to it; but in fact the British public remained for the present profoundly indifferent to Miss Isabel Archer, whose fortune had dropped her, as her cousin said, into the dullest house in England. Her gouty uncle received very little company, and Mrs. Touchett, not having cultivated relations with her husband's neighbours, was not warranted in expecting visits from them. She had, however, a peculiar taste; she liked to receive cards.[1] For what is usually called social intercourse she had very little relish; but nothing pleased her more than to find her hall-table whitened with oblong morsels of symbolic pasteboard. She flattered herself that she was a very just woman, and had mastered the sovereign truth that nothing in this world is got for nothing. She had played no social part as mistress of Gardencourt, and it was not to be supposed that, in the surrounding country, a minute account should be kept of her comings and goings. But it is by no means certain that she did not feel it to be wrong that so little notice was taken of them and that her failure (really very gratuitous) to make herself important in the neighbourhood had not much to do with the acrimony of her allusions to her husband's adopted country. Isabel presently found herself in the singular situation of defending the British constitution against her aunt; Mrs. Touchettt having formed the habit of sticking pins into this venerable instrument. Isabel always felt an impulse to pull out the pins; not that she imagined they inflicted any damage on the tough old parchment, but because it seemed to her her aunt might make better use of her sharpness. She was very critical herself—it was incidental to her age, her sex and her nationality; but she was very sentimental as well, and there was something in Mrs. Touchett's dryness that set her own moral fountains flowing.

"Now what's your point of view?" she asked of her aunt. "When you criticise everything here you should have a point of view. Yours doesn't seem to be American—you thought everything over there so disagreeable. When I criticise I have mine; it's thoroughly American!"

"My dear young lady," said Mrs. Touchett, "there are as many points of view in the world as there are people of sense to take them. You may say that doesn't make them very numerous! American? Never in the world; that's shockingly narrow. My point of view, thank God, is personal!"

Isabel thought this a better answer than she admitted; it was a tolerable description of her own manner of judging, but it would not have sounded well for her to say so. On the lips of a person less advanced in life and less enlightened by experience than Mrs. Touchett such a declaration would savour of immodesty, even of arrogance. She risked it nevertheless in talking with Ralph, with whom she talked a great deal and with whom her conversation was of a sort that gave a large licence to extravagance. Her cousin used, as the phrase is, to chaff her; he very soon established with her a reputation for treating everything as a joke, and he was not a man to neglect the privileges such a reputation conferred. She accused

---

1. Calling cards engraved with the owner's name and sometimes his or her address; often left in lieu of an actual visit.

him of an odious want of seriousness, of laughing at all things, beginning with himself. Such slender faculty of reverence as he possessed centred wholly upon his father; for the rest, he exercised his wit indifferently upon his father's son, this gentleman's weak lungs, his useless life, his fantastic mother, his friends (Lord Warburton in especial), his adopted, and his native country, his charming new-found cousin. "I keep a band of music in my ante-room," he said once to her. "It has orders to play without stopping; it renders me two excellent services. It keeps the sounds of the world from reaching the private apartments, and it makes the world think that dancing's going on within." It was dance-music indeed that you usually heard when you came within ear-shot of Ralph's band; the liveliest waltzes seemed to float upon the air. Isabel often found herself irritated by this perpetual fiddling; she would have liked to pass through the ante-room, as her cousin called it, and enter the private apartments. It mattered little that he had assured her they were a very dismal place; she would have been glad to undertake to sweep them and set them in order. It was but half-hospitality to let her remain outside; to punish him for which Isabel administered innumerable taps with the ferule of her straight young wit. It must be said that her wit was exercised to a large extent in self-defence, for her cousin amused himself with calling her "Columbia"[2] and accusing her of a patriotism so heated that it scorched. He drew a caricature of her in which she was represented as a very pretty young woman dressed, on the lines of the prevailing fashion, in the folds of the national banner. Isabel's chief dread in life at this period of her development was that she should appear narrow-minded; what she feared next afterwards was that she should really be so. But she nevertheless made no scruple of abounding in her cousin's sense and pretending to sigh for the charms of her native land. She would be as American as it pleased him to regard her, and if he chose to laugh at her she would give him plenty of occupation. She defended England against his mother, but when Ralph sang its praises on purpose, as she said, to work her up, she found herself able to differ from him on a variety of points. In fact, the quality of this small ripe country seemed as sweet to her as the taste of an October pear; and her satisfaction was at the root of the good spirits which enabled her to take her cousin's chaff and return it in kind. If her good-humour flagged at moments it was not because she thought herself ill-used, but because she suddenly felt sorry for Ralph. It seemed to her he was talking as a blind and had little heart in what he said.

"I don't know what's the matter with you," she observed to him once; "but I suspect you're a great humbug."

"That's your privilege," Ralph answered, who had not been used to being so crudely addressed.

"I don't know what you care for; I don't think you care for anything. You don't really care for England when you praise it; you don't care for America even when you pretend to abuse it."

"I care for nothing but you, dear cousin," said Ralph.

"If I could believe even that, I should be very glad."

"Ah well, I should hope so!" the young man exclaimed.

---

2. As in "District of Columbia." A poetic name for, and female personification of, the United States.

Isabel might have believed it and not have been far from the truth. He thought a great deal about her; she was constantly present to his mind. At a time when his thoughts had been a good deal of a burden to him her sudden arrival, which promised nothing and was an open-handed gift of fate, had refreshed and quickened them, given them wings and something to fly for. Poor Ralph had been for many weeks steeped in melancholy; his outlook, habitually sombre, lay under the shadow of a deeper cloud. He had grown anxious about his father, whose gout, hitherto confined to his legs, had begun to ascend into regions more vital. The old man had been gravely ill in the spring, and the doctors had whispered to Ralph that another attack would be less easy to deal with. Just now he appeared disburdened of pain, but Ralph could not rid himself of a suspicion that this was a subterfuge of the enemy, who was waiting to take him off his guard. If the manoeuvre should succeed there would be little hope of any great resistance. Ralph had always taken for granted that his father would survive him—that his own name would be the first grimly called. The father and son had been close companions, and the idea of being left alone with the remnant of a tasteless life on his hands was not gratifying to the young man, who had always and tacitly counted upon his elder's help in making the best of a poor business. At the prospect of losing his great motive Ralph lost indeed his one inspiration. If they might die at the same time it would be all very well; but without the encouragement of his father's society he should barely have patience to await his own turn. He had not the incentive of feeling that he was indispensable to his mother; it was a rule with his mother to have no regrets. He bethought himself of course that it had been a small kindness to his father to wish that, of the two, the active rather than the passive party should know the felt wound; he remembered that the old man had always treated his own forecast of an early end as a clever fallacy, which he should be delighted to discredit so far as he might by dying first. But of the two triumphs, that of refuting a sophistical son and that of holding on a while longer to a state of being which, with all abatements, he enjoyed, Ralph deemed it no sin to hope the latter might be vouchsafed to Mr. Touchett.

These were nice questions, but Isabel's arrival put a stop to his puzzling over them. It even suggested there might be a compensation for the intolerable ennui of surviving his genial sire. He wondered whether he were harbouring "love" for this spontaneous young woman from Albany; but he judged that on the whole he was not. After he had known her for a week he quite made up his mind to this, and every day he felt a little more sure. Lord Warburton had been right about her; she was a really interesting little figure. Ralph wondered how their neighbour had found it out so soon; and then he said it was only another proof of his friend's high abilities, which he had always greatly admired. If his cousin were to be nothing more than an entertainment to him, Ralph was conscious she was an entertainment of a high order. "A character like that," he said to himself—"a real little passionate force to see at play is the finest thing in nature. It's finer than the finest work of art—than a Greek bas-relief, than a great Titian,[3] than a Gothic cathedral. It's very pleasant to be so well

---

3. Tiziano Vecelli (ca. 1488/90–1576), Venetian painter famed for his use of color; one of James's favorites.

treated where one had least looked for it. I had never been more blue, more bored, than for a week before she came; I had never expected less that anything pleasant would happen. Suddenly I receive a Titian, by the post, to hang on my wall—a Greek bas-relief to stick over my chimney-piece. The key of a beautiful edifice is thrust into my hand, and I'm told to walk in and admire. My poor boy, you've been sadly ungrateful, and now you had better keep very quiet and never grumble again." The sentiment of these reflexions was very just; but it was not exactly true that Ralph Touchett had had a key put into his hand. His cousin was a very brilliant girl, who would take, as he said, a good deal of knowing; but she needed the knowing, and his attitude with regard to her, though it was contemplative and critical, was not judicial. He surveyed the edifice from the outside and admired it greatly; he looked in at the windows and received an impression of proportions equally fair. But he felt that he saw it only by glimpses and that he had not yet stood under the roof. The door was fastened, and though he had keys in his pocket he had a conviction that none of them would fit. She was intelligent and generous; it was a fine free nature; but what was she going to do with herself? This question was irregular, for with most women one had no occasion to ask it. Most women did with themselves nothing at all; they waited, in attitudes more or less gracefully passive, for a man to come that way and furnish them with a destiny. Isabel's originality was that she gave one an impression of having intentions of her own. "Whenever she executes them," said Ralph "may I be there to see!"

It devolved upon him of course to do the honours of the place. Mr. Touchett was confined to his chair, and his wife's position was that of rather a grim visitor; so that in the line of conduct that opened itself to Ralph duty and inclination were harmoniously mixed. He was not a great walker, but he strolled about the grounds with his cousin—a pastime for which the weather remained favourable with a persistency not allowed for in Isabel's somewhat lugubrious prevision of the climate; and in the long afternoons, of which the length was but the measure of her gratified eagerness, they took a boat on the river, the dear little river, as Isabel called it, where the opposite shore seemed still a part of the foreground of the landscape; or drove over the country in a phaeton[4]—a low, capacious, thick-wheeled phaeton formerly much used by Mr. Touchett, but which he had now ceased to enjoy. Isabel enjoyed it largely and, handling the reins in a manner which approved itself to the groom as "knowing," was never weary of driving her uncle's capital horses through winding lanes and byways full of the rural incidents she had confidently expected to find; past cottages thatched and timbered, past ale-houses latticed and sanded, past patches of ancient common and glimpses of empty parks, between hedgerows made thick by mid-summer. When they reached home they usually found tea had been served on the lawn and that Mrs. Touchett had not shrunk from the extremity of handing her husband his cup. But the two for the most part sat silent; the old man with his head back and his eyes closed, his wife occupied with her knitting and wearing that appearance of rare profundity with which some ladies consider the movement of their needles.

4. A four-wheeled open carriage.

One day, however, a visitor had arrived. The two young persons, after spending an hour on the river, strolled back to the house and perceived Lord Warburton sitting under the trees and engaged in conversation, of which even at a distance the desultory character was appreciable, with Mrs. Touchett. He had driven over from his own place with a portmanteau and had asked, as the father and son often invited him to do, for a dinner and a lodging. Isabel, seeing him for half an hour on the day of her arrival, had discovered in this brief space that she liked him; he had indeed rather sharply registered himself on her fine sense and she had thought of him several times. She had hoped she should see him again—hoped too that she should see a few others. Gardencourt was not dull; the place itself was sovereign, her uncle was more and more a sort of golden grandfather, and Ralph was unlike any cousin she had ever encountered—her idea of cousins having tended to gloom. Then her impressions were still so fresh and so quickly renewed that there was as yet hardly a hint of vacancy in the view. But Isabel had need to remind herself that she was interested in human nature and that her foremost hope in coming abroad had been that she should see a great many people. When Ralph said to her, as he had done several times, "I wonder you find this endurable; you ought to see some of the neighbours and some of our friends, because we have really got a few, though you would never suppose it"—when he offered to invite what he called a "lot of people" and make her acquainted with English society, she encouraged the hospitable impulse and promised in advance to hurl herself into the fray. Little, however, for the present, had come of his offers, and it may be confided to the reader that if the young man delayed to carry them out it was because he found the labour of providing for his companion by no means so severe as to require extraneous help. Isabel had spoken to him very often about "specimens;" it was a word that played a considerable part in her vocabulary; she had given him to understand that she wished to see English society illustrated by eminent cases.

"Well now, there's a specimen," he said to her as they walked up from the riverside and he recognised Lord Warburton.

"A specimen of what?" asked the girl.

"A specimen of an English gentleman."

"Do you mean they're all like him?"

"Oh no; they're not all like him."

"He's a favourable specimen then," said Isabel; "because I'm sure he's nice."

"Yes, he's very nice. And he's very fortunate."

The fortunate Lord Warburton exchanged a handshake with our heroine and hoped she was very well. "But I needn't ask that," he said, "since you've been handling the oars."

"I've been rowing a little," Isabel answered; "but how should you know it?"

"Oh, I know *he* doesn't row; he's too lazy," said his lordship, indicating Ralph Touchett with a laugh.

"He has a good excuse for his laziness," Isabel rejoined, lowering her voice a little.

"Ah, he has a good excuse for everything!" cried Lord Warburton, still with his sonorous mirth.

"My excuse for not rowing is that my cousin rows so well," said Ralph.
"She does everything well. She touches nothing that she doesn't adorn!"
"It makes one want to be touched, Miss Archer," Lord Warburton declared.

"Be touched in the right sense and you'll never look the worse for it," said Isabel, who, if it pleased her to hear it said that her accomplishments were numerous, was happily able to reflect that such complacency was not the indication of a feeble mind, inasmuch as there were several things in which she excelled. Her desire to think well of herself had at least the element of humility that it always needed to be supported by proof.

Lord Warburton not only spent the night at Gardencourt, but he was persuaded to remain over the second day; and when the second day was ended he determined to postpone his departure till the morrow. During this period he addressed many of his remarks to Isabel, who accepted this evidence of his esteem with a very good grace. She found herself liking him extremely; the first impression he had made on her had had weight, but at the end of an evening spent in his society she scarce fell short of seeing him—though quite without luridity—as a hero of romance. She retired to rest with a sense of good fortune, with a quickened consciousness of possible felicities. "It's very nice to know two such charming people as those," she said, meaning by "those" her cousin and her cousin's friend. It must be added moreover that an incident had occurred which might have seemed to put her good-humour to the test. Mr. Touchett went to bed at half-past nine o'clock, but his wife remained in the drawing-room with the other members of the party. She prolonged her vigil for something less than an hour, and then, rising, observed to Isabel that it was time they should bid the gentlemen good-night. Isabel had as yet no desire to go to bed; the occasion wore, to her sense, a festive character, and feasts were not in the habit of terminating so early. So, without further thought, she replied, very simply—

"Need I go, dear aunt? I'll come up in half an hour."

"It's impossible I should wait for you," Mrs. Touchett answered.

"Ah, you needn't wait! Ralph will light my candle," Isabel gaily engaged.

"I'll light your candle; do let me light your candle, Miss Archer!" Lord Warburton exclaimed. "Only I beg it shall not be before midnight."

Mrs. Touchett fixed her bright little eyes upon him a moment and transferred them coldly to her niece. "You can't stay alone with the gentlemen. You're not—you're not at your blest Albany, my dear."

Isabel rose, blushing. "I wish I were," she said.

"Oh, I say, mother!" Ralph broke out.

"My dear Mrs. Touchett!" Lord Warburton murmured.

"I didn't make your country, my lord," Mrs. Touchett said majestically. "I must take it as I find it."

"Can't I stay with my own cousin?" Isabel enquired.

"I'm not aware that Lord Warburton is your cousin."

"Perhaps I had better go to bed!" the visitor suggested. "That will arrange it."

Mrs. Touchett gave a little look of despair and sat down again. "Oh, if it's necessary I'll stay up till midnight."

Ralph meanwhile handed Isabel her candlestick. He had been watching her; it had seemed to him her temper was involved—an accident that might be interesting. But if he had expected anything of a flare he was disappointed, for the girl simply laughed a little, nodded good-night and withdrew accompanied by her aunt. For himself he was annoyed at his mother, though he thought she was right. Above-stairs the two ladies separated at Mrs. Touchett's door. Isabel had said nothing on her way up.

"Of course you're vexed at my interfering with you," said Mrs. Touchett.

Isabel considered. "I'm not vexed, but I'm surprised—and a good deal mystified. Wasn't it proper I should remain in the drawing-room?"

"Not in the least. Young girls here—in decent houses—don't sit alone with the gentlemen late at night."

"You were very right to tell me then," said Isabel. "I don't understand it, but I'm very glad to know it."

"I shall always tell you," her aunt answered, "whenever I see you taking what seems to me too much liberty."

"Pray do; but I don't say I shall always think your remonstrance just."

"Very likely not. You're too fond of your own ways."

"Yes, I think I'm very fond of them. But I always want to know the things one shouldn't do."

"So as to do them?" asked her aunt.

"So as to choose," said Isabel.

Chapter VIII

As she was devoted to romantic effects Lord Warburton ventured to express a hope that she would come some day and see his house, a very curious old place. He extracted from Mrs. Touchett a promise that she would bring her niece to Lockleigh, and Ralph signified his willingness to attend the ladies if his father should be able to spare him. Lord Warburton assured our heroine that in the mean time his sisters would come and see her. She knew something about his sisters, having sounded him, during the hours they spent together while he was at Gardencourt, on many points connected with his family. When Isabel was interested she asked a great many questions, and as her companion was a copious talker she urged him on this occasion by no means in vain. He told her he had four sisters and two brothers and had lost both his parents. The brothers and sisters were very good people—"not particularly clever, you know," he said, "but very decent and pleasant;" and he was so good as to hope Miss Archer might know them well. One of the brothers was in the Church, settled in the family living, that of Lockleigh, which was a heavy, sprawling parish, and was an excellent fellow in spite of his thinking differently from himself on every conceivable topic. And then Lord Warburton mentioned some of the opinions held by his brother, which were opinions Isabel had often heard expressed and that she supposed to be entertained by a considerable portion of the human family. Many of them indeed she supposed she had held herself, till he assured her she was quite mistaken, that it was really impossible, that she had doubtless imagined she entertained them, but that she might depend that, if she thought them over a little, she would find there was nothing in them. When she answered that she had already thought several of the questions involved over very attentively he declared that she was only another example of what he had often been struck with—the fact that, of all the people in the world, the

Americans were the most grossly superstitious. They were rank Tories and bigots, every one of them; there were no conservatives like American conservatives. Her uncle and her cousin were there to prove it; nothing could be more mediæval than many of their views; they had ideas that people in England nowadays were ashamed to confess to; and they had the impudence moreover, said his lordship, laughing, to pretend they knew more about the needs and dangers of this poor stupid old England than he who was born in it and owned a considerable slice of it—the more shame to him! From all of which Isabel gathered that Lord Warburton was a nobleman of the newest pattern, a reformer, a radical, a contemner of ancient ways. His other brother, who was in the army in India, was rather wild and pig-headed and had not been of much use as yet but to make debts for Warburton to pay—one of the most precious privileges of an elder brother. "I don't think I shall pay any more," said her friend; "he lives a monstrous deal better than I do, enjoys unheard of luxuries and thinks himself a much finer gentleman than I. As I'm a consistent radical I go in only for equality; I don't go in for the superiority of the younger brothers." Two of his four sisters, the second and fourth, were married, one of them having done very well, as they said, the other only so-so. The husband of the elder, Lord Haycock, was a very good fellow, but unfortunately a horrid Tory; and his wife, like all good English wives, was worse than her husband. The other had espoused a smallish squire in Norfolk and, though married but the other day, had already five children. This information and much more Lord Warburton imparted to his young American listener, taking pains to make many things clear and to lay bare to her apprehension the peculiarities of English life. Isabel was often amused at his explicitness and at the small allowance he seemed to make either for her own experience or for her imagination. "He thinks I'm a barbarian," she said, "and that I've never seen forks and spoons;" and she used to ask him artless questions for the pleasure of hearing him answer seriously. Then when he had fallen into the trap, "It's a pity you can't see me in my war-paint and feathers," she remarked; "if I had known how kind you are to the poor savages I would have brought over my native costume!" Lord Warburton had travelled through the United States and knew much more about them than Isabel; he was so good as to say that America was the most charming country in the world, but his recollections of it appeared to encourage the idea that Americans in England would need to have a great many things explained to them. "If I had only had you to explain things to me in America!" he said. "I was rather puzzled in your country; in fact I was quite bewildered, and the trouble was that the explanations only puzzled me more. You know I think they often gave me the wrong ones on purpose; they're rather clever about that over there. But when I explain you can trust me; about what I tell you there's no mistake." There was no mistake at least about his being very intelligent and cultivated and knowing almost everything in the world. Although he gave the most interesting and thrilling glimpses Isabel felt he never did it to exhibit himself, and though he had had rare chances and had tumbled in, as she put it, for high prizes, he was as far as possible from making a merit of it. He had enjoyed the best things of life, but they had not spoiled his sense of proportion. His quality was a mixture of the effect of rich experience—oh, so easily come by!—with a modesty at times almost boyish; the sweet and

wholesome savour of which—it was as agreeable as something tasted—
lost nothing from the addition of a tone of responsible kindness.

"I like your specimen English gentleman very much," Isabel said to
Ralph after Lord Warburton had gone.

"I like him too—I love him well," Ralph returned. "But I pity him more."

Isabel looked at him askance. "Why, that seems to me his only fault—
that one can't pity him a little. He appears to have everything, to know
everything, to *be* everything."

"Oh, he's in a bad way!" Ralph insisted.

"I suppose you don't mean in health?"

"No, as to that he's detestably sound. What I mean is that he's a man
with a great position who's playing all sorts of tricks with it. He doesn't
take himself seriously."

"Does he regard himself as a joke?"

"Much worse; he regards himself as an imposition—as an abuse."

"Well, perhaps he is," said Isabel.

"Perhaps he is—though on the whole I don't think so. But in that case
what's more pitiable than a sentient, self-conscious abuse planted by other
hands, deeply rooted but aching with a sense of its injustice? For me, in
his place, I could be as solemn as a statue of Buddha. He occupies a position that appeals to my imagination. Great responsibilities, great opportunities, great consideration, great wealth, great power, a natural share in
the public affairs of a great country. But he's all in a muddle about himself,
his position, his power, and indeed about everything in the world. He's
the victim of a critical age; he has ceased to believe in himself and he
doesn't know what to believe in. When I attempt to tell him (because if
I were he I know very well what I should believe in) he calls me a pam-
pered bigot. I believe he seriously thinks me an awful Philistine; he says
I don't understand my time. I understand it certainly better than he, who
can neither abolish himself as a nuisance nor maintain himself as an
institution."

"He doesn't look very wretched," Isabel observed.

"Possibly not; though, being a man of a good deal of charming taste, I
think he often has uncomfortable hours. But what is it to say of a being of
his opportunities that he's not miserable? Besides, I believe he is."

"I don't," said Isabel.

"Well," her cousin rejoined, "if he isn't he ought to be!"

In the afternoon she spent an hour with her uncle on the lawn, where
the old man sat, as usual, with his shawl over his legs and his large cup of
diluted tea in his hands. In the course of conversation he asked her what
she thought of their late visitor.

Isabel was prompt. "I think he's charming."

"He's a nice person," said Mr. Touchett, "but I don't recommend you to
fall in love with him."

"I shall not do it then; I shall never fall in love but on your recommendation. Moreover," Isabel added, "my cousin gives me rather a sad account
of Lord Warburton."

"Oh, indeed? I don't know what there may be to say, but you must
remember that Ralph *must* talk."

"He thinks your friend's too subversive—or not subversive enough! I
don't quite understand which," said Isabel.

The old man shook his head slowly, smiled and put down his cup. "I don't know which either. He goes very far, but it's quite possible he doesn't go far enough. He seems to want to do away with a good many things, but he seems to want to remain himself. I suppose that's natural, but it's rather inconsistent."

"Oh, I hope he'll remain himself," said Isabel. "If he were to be done away with his friends would miss him sadly."

"Well," said the old man, "I guess he'll stay and amuse his friends. I should certainly miss him very much here at Gardencourt. He always amuses me when he comes over, and I think he amuses himself as well. There's a considerable number like him, round in society; they're very fashionable just now. I don't know what they're trying to do—whether they're trying to get up a revolution. I hope at any rate they'll put it off till after I'm gone. You see they want to disestablish[1] everything; but I'm a pretty big landowner here, and I don't want to be disestablished. I wouldn't have come over if I had thought they were going to behave like that," Mr. Touchett went on with expanding hilarity. "I came over because I thought England was a safe country. I call it a regular fraud if they are going to introduce any considerable changes; there'll be a large number disappointed in that case."

"Oh, I do hope they'll make a revolution!" Isabel exclaimed. "I should delight in seeing a revolution."

"Let me see," said her uncle, with a humorous intention; "I forget whether you're on the side of the old or on the side of the new. I've heard you take such opposite views."

"I'm on the side of both. I guess I'm a little on the side of everything. In a revolution—after it was well begun—I think I should be a high, proud loyalist. One sympathises more with them, and they've a chance to behave so exquisitely. I mean so picturesquely."

"I don't know that I understand what you mean by behaving picturesquely, but it seems to me that you do that always, my dear."

"Oh, you lovely man, if I could believe that!" the girl interrupted.

"I'm afraid, after all, you won't have the pleasure of going gracefully to the guillotine here just now," Mr. Touchett went on. "If you want to see a big outbreak you must pay us a long visit. You see, when you come to the point it wouldn't suit them to be taken at their word."

"Of whom are you speaking?"

"Well, I mean Lord Warburton and his friends—the radicals of the upper class. Of course I only know the way it strikes me. They talk about the changes, but I don't think they quite realise. You and I, you know, we know what it is to have lived under democratic institutions: I always thought them very comfortable, but I was used to them from the first. And then I ain't a lord; you're a lady, my dear, but I ain't a lord. Now over here I don't think it quite comes home to them. It's a matter of every day and every hour, and I don't think many of them would find it as pleasant as what they've got. Of course if they want to try, it's their own business; but I expect they won't try very hard."

1. The term usually refers to the idea of severing the official relation between the Church of England—the "established" Church—and the British state, but Mr. Touchett extends it to the disruption of the inherited social structure as a whole.

"Don't you think they're sincere?" Isabel asked.

"Well, they want to *feel* earnest," Mr. Touchett allowed; "but it seems as if they took it out in theories mostly. Their radical views are a kind of amusement; they've got to have some amusement, and they might have coarser tastes than that. You see they're very luxurious, and these progressive ideas are about their biggest luxury. They make them feel moral and yet don't damage their position. They think a great deal of their position; don't let one of them ever persuade you he doesn't, for if you were to proceed on that basis you'd be pulled up very short."

Isabel followed her uncle's argument, which he unfolded with his quaint distinctness, most attentively, and though she was unacquainted with the British aristocracy she found it in harmony with her general impressions of human nature. But she felt moved to put in a protest on Lord Warburton's behalf. "I don't believe Lord Warburton's a humbug; I don't care what the others are. I should like to see Lord Warburton put to the test."

"Heaven deliver me from my friends!" Mr. Touchett answered. "Lord Warburton's a very amiable young man—a very fine young man. He has a hundred thousand a year. He owns fifty thousand acres of the soil of this little island and ever so many other things besides. He has half a dozen houses to live in. He has a seat in Parliament as I have one at my own dinner-table. He has elegant tastes—cares for literature, for art, for science, for charming young ladies. The most elegant is his taste for the new views. It affords him a great deal of pleasure—more perhaps than anything else, except the young ladies. His old house over there—what does he call it, Lockleigh?—is very attractive; but I don't think it's as pleasant as this. That doesn't matter, however—he has so many others. His views don't hurt any one as far as I can see; they certainly don't hurt himself. And if there were to be a revolution he would come off very easily. They wouldn't touch him, they'd leave him as he is: he's too much liked."

"Ah, he couldn't be a martyr even if he wished!" Isabel sighed. "That's a very poor position."

"He'll never be a martyr unless you make him one," said the old man.

Isabel shook her head; there might have been something laughable in the fact that she did it with a touch of melancholy. "I shall never make any one a martyr."

"You'll never be one, I hope."

"I hope not. But you don't pity Lord Warburton then as Ralph does?"

Her uncle looked at her a while with genial acuteness. "Yes, I do, after all!"

Chapter IX

The two Misses Molyneux, this nobleman's sisters, came presently to call upon her, and Isabel took a fancy to the young ladies, who appeared to her to show a most original stamp. It is true that when she described them to her cousin by that term he declared that no epithet could be less applicable than this to the two Misses Molyneux, since there were fifty thousand young women in England who exactly resembled them. Deprived of this advantage, however, Isabel's visitors retained that of an extreme sweetness and shyness of demeanour, and of having, as she thought, eyes like the balanced basins, the circles of "ornamental water," set, in parterres, among the geraniums.

"They're not morbid, at any rate, whatever they are," our heroine said to herself; and she deemed this a great charm, for two or three of the friends of her girlhood had been regrettably open to the charge (they would have been so nice without it), to say nothing of Isabel's having occasionally suspected it as a tendency of her own. The Misses Molyneux were not in their first youth, but they had bright, fresh complexions and something of the smile of childhood. Yes, their eyes, which Isabel admired, were round, quiet and contented, and their figures, also of a generous roundness, were encased in sealskin jackets. Their friendliness was great, so great that they were almost embarrassed to show it; they seemed somewhat afraid of the young lady from the other side of the world and rather looked than spoke their good wishes. But they made it clear to her that they hoped she would come to luncheon at Lockleigh, where they lived with their brother, and then they might see her very, very often. They wondered if she wouldn't come over some day and sleep: they were expecting some people on the twenty-ninth, so perhaps she would come while the people were there.

"I'm afraid it isn't any one very remarkable," said the elder sister; "but I dare say you'll take us as you find us."

"I shall find you delightful; I think you're enchanting just as you are," replied Isabel, who often praised profusely.

Her visitors flushed, and her cousin told her, after they were gone, that if she said such things to those poor girls they would think she was in some wild, free manner practising on them: he was sure it was the first time they had been called enchanting.

"I can't help it," Isabel answered. "I think it's lovely to be so quiet and reasonable and satisfied. I should like to be like that."

"Heaven forbid!" cried Ralph with ardour.

"I mean to try and imitate them," said Isabel. "I want very much to see them at home."

She had this pleasure a few days later, when, with Ralph and his mother, she drove over to Lockleigh. She found the Misses Molyneux sitting in a vast drawing-room (she perceived afterwards it was one of several) in a wilderness of faded chintz; they were dressed on this occasion in black velveteen. Isabel liked them even better at home than she had done at Gardencourt, and was more than ever struck with the fact that they were not morbid. It had seemed to her before that if they had a fault it was a want of play of mind; but she presently saw they were capable of deep emotion. Before luncheon she was alone with them for some time, on one side of the room, while Lord Warburton, at a distance, talked to Mrs. Touchett.

"Is it true your brother's such a great radical?" Isabel asked. She knew it was true, but we have seen that her interest in human nature was keen, and she had a desire to draw the Misses Molyneux out.

"Oh dear, yes; he's immensely advanced," said Mildred, the younger sister.

"At the same time Warburton's very reasonable," Miss Molyneux observed.

Isabel watched him a moment at the other side of the room; he was clearly trying hard to make himself agreeable to Mrs. Touchett. Ralph had met the frank advances of one of the dogs before the fire that the temperature of an English August, in the ancient expanses, had not made an impertinence. "Do you suppose your brother's sincere?" Isabel enquired with a smile.

"Oh, he must be, you know!" Mildred exclaimed quickly, while the elder sister gazed at our heroine in silence.

"Do you think he would stand the test?"

"The test?"

"I mean for instance having to give up all this."

"Having to give up Lockleigh?" said Miss Molyneux, finding her voice.

"Yes, and the other places; what are they called?"

The two sisters exchanged an almost frightened glance. "Do you mean—do you mean on account of the expense?" the younger one asked.

"I dare say he might let one or two of his houses," said the other.

"Let them for nothing?" Isabel demanded.

"I can't fancy his giving up his property," said Miss Molyneux.

"Ah, I'm afraid he is an impostor!" Isabel returned. "Don't you think it's a false position?"

Her companions, evidently, had lost themselves. "My brother's position?" Miss Molyneux enquired.

"It's thought a very good position," said the younger sister. "It's the first position in this part of the county."

"I dare say you think me very irreverent," Isabel took occasion to remark. "I suppose you revere your brother and are rather afraid of him."

"Of course one looks up to one's brother," said Miss Molyneux simply.

"If you do that he must be very good—because you, evidently, are beautifully good."

"He's most kind. It will never be known, the good he does."

"His ability is known," Mildred added; "every one thinks it's immense."

"Oh, I can see that," said Isabel. "But if I were he I should wish to fight to the death: I mean for the heritage of the past. I should hold it tight."

"I think one ought to be liberal," Mildred argued gently. "We've always been so, even from the earliest times."

"Ah well," said Isabel, "you've made a great success of it; I don't wonder you like it. I see you're very fond of crewels."

When Lord Warburton showed her the house, after luncheon, it seemed to her a matter of course that it should be a noble picture. Within, it had been a good deal modernised—some of its best points had lost their purity; but as they saw it from the gardens, a stout grey pile, of the softest, deepest, most weather-fretted hue, rising from a broad, still moat, it affected the young visitor as a castle in a legend. The day was cool and rather lustreless; the first note of autumn had been struck, and the watery sunshine rested on the walls in blurred and desultory gleams, washing them, as it were, in places tenderly chosen, where the ache of antiquity was keenest. Her host's brother, the Vicar, had come to luncheon, and Isabel had had five minutes' talk with him—time enough to institute a search for a rich ecclesiasticism and give it up as vain. The marks of the Vicar of Lockleigh were a big, athletic figure, a candid, natural countenance, a capacious appetite and a tendency to indiscriminate laughter. Isabel learned afterwards from her cousin that before taking orders he had been a mighty wrestler and that he was still, on occasion—in the privacy of the family circle as it were—quite capable of flooring his man. Isabel liked him—she was in the mood for liking everything; but her imagination was a good deal taxed to think of him as a source of spiritual aid. The whole party, on leaving lunch, went to walk in the grounds; but Lord Warburton exercised some ingenuity in engaging his least familiar guest in a stroll apart from the others.

"I wish you to see the place properly, seriously," he said. "You can't do so if your attention is distracted by irrelevant gossip." His own conversation (though he told Isabel a good deal about the house, which had a very curious history) was not purely archæological; he reverted at intervals to matters more personal—matters personal to the young lady as well as to himself. But at last, after a pause of some duration, returning for a moment to their ostensible theme, "Ah, well," he said, "I'm very glad indeed you like the old barrack. I wish you could see more of it—that you could stay here a while. My sisters have taken an immense fancy to you—if that would be any inducement."

"There's no want to inducements," Isabel answered; "but I'm afraid I can't make engagements. I'm quite in my aunt's hands."

"Ah, pardon me if I say I don't exactly believe that. I'm pretty sure you can do whatever you want."

"I'm sorry if I make that impression on you; I don't think it's a nice impression to make."

"It has the merit of permitting me to hope." And Lord Warburton paused a moment.

"To hope what?"

"That in future I may see you often."

"Ah," said Isabel, "to enjoy that pleasure I needn't be so terribly emancipated."

"Doubtless not; and yet, at the same time, I don't think your uncle likes me."

"You're very much mistaken. I've heard him speak very highly of you."

"I'm glad you have talked about me," said Lord Warburton. "But, I nevertheless don't think he'd like me to keep coming to Gardencourt."

"I can't answer for my uncle's tastes," the girl rejoined, "though I ought as far as possible to take them into account. But for myself I shall be very glad to see you."

"Now that's what I like to hear you say. I'm charmed when you say that."

"You're easily charmed, my lord," said Isabel.

"No, I'm not easily charmed!" And then he stopped a moment. "But you've charmed me, Miss Archer."

These words were uttered with an indefinable sound which startled the girl; it struck her as the prelude to something grave: she had heard the sound before and she recognised it. She had no wish, however, that for the moment such a prelude should have a sequel, and she said as gaily as possible and as quickly as an appreciable degree of agitation would allow her: "I'm afraid there's no prospect of my being able to come here again."

"Never?" said Lord Warburton.

"I won't say 'never'; I should feel very melodramatic."

"May I come and see you then some day next week?"

"Most assuredly. What is there to prevent it?"

"Nothing tangible. But with you I never feel safe. I've a sort of sense that you're always summing people up."

"You don't of necessity lose by that."

"It's very kind of you to say so; but, even if I gain, stern justice is not what I most love. Is Mrs. Touchett going to take you abroad?"

"I hope so."

"Is England not good enough for you?"

"That's a very Machiavellian speech; it doesn't deserve an answer. I want to see as many countries as I can."

"Then you'll go on judging, I suppose."

"Enjoying, I hope, too."

"Yes, that's what you enjoy most; I can't make out what you're up to," said Lord Warburton. "You strike me as having mysterious purposes—vast designs."

"You're so good as to have a theory about me which I don't at all fill out. Is there anything mysterious in a purpose entertained and executed every year, in the most public manner, by fifty thousand of my fellow-countrymen—the purpose of improving one's mind by foreign travel?"

"You can't improve your mind, Miss Archer," her companion declared. "It's already a most formidable instrument. It looks down on us all; it despises us."

"Despises you? You're making fun of me," said Isabel seriously.

"Well, you think us 'quaint'—that's the same thing. I won't be thought 'quaint,' to begin with; I'm not so in the least. I protest."

"That protest is one of the quaintest things I've ever heard," Isabel answered with a smile.

Lord Warburton was briefly silent. "You judge only from the outside—you don't care," he said presently. "You only care to amuse yourself." The note she had heard in his voice a moment before reappeared, and mixed with it now was an audible strain of bitterness—a bitterness so abrupt and inconsequent that the girl was afraid she had hurt him. She had often heard that the English are a highly eccentric people, and she had even read in some ingenious author that they are at bottom the most romantic of races. Was Lord Warburton suddenly turning romantic—was he going to make her a scene, in his own house, only the third time they had met? She was reassured quickly enough by her sense of his great good manners, which was not impaired by the fact that he had already touched the furthest limit of good taste in expressing his admiration of a young lady who had confided in his hospitality. She was right in trusting to his good manners, for he presently went on, laughing a little and without a trace of the accent that had discomposed her: "I don't mean of course that you amuse yourself with trifles. You select great materials; the foibles, the afflictions of human nature, the peculiarities of nations!"

"As regards that," said Isabel, "I should find in my own nation entertainment for a lifetime. But we've a long drive, and my aunt will soon wish to start." She turned back toward the others and Lord Warburton walked beside her in silence. But before they reached the others, "I shall come and see you next week," he said.

She had received an appreciable shock, but as it died away she felt that she couldn't pretend to herself that it was altogether a painful one. Nevertheless she made answer to his declaration, coldly enough, "Just as you please." And her coldness was not the calculation of her effect—a game she played in a much smaller degree than would have seemed probable to many critics. It came from a certain fear.

Chapter X

The day after her visit to Lockleigh she received a note from her friend Miss Stackpole—a note of which the envelope, exhibiting in conjunction the postmark of Liverpool and the neat calligraphy of the quick-fingered Henrietta, caused her some liveliness of emotion. "Here I am, my lovely friend," Miss Stackpole wrote; "I managed to get off at last. I decided only the night before I left New York—the *Interviewer* having come round to my figure. I put a few things into a bag, like a veteran journalist, and came down to the steamer in a street-car. Where are you and where can we meet? I suppose you're visiting at some castle or other and have already acquired the correct accent. Perhaps even you have married a lord; I almost hope you have, for I want some introductions to the first people and shall count on you for a few. The *Interviewer* wants some light on the nobility. My first impressions (of the people at large) are not rose-coloured; but I wish to talk them over with you, and you know that, whatever I am, at least I'm not superficial. I've also something very particular to tell you. Do appoint a meeting as quickly as you can; come to London (I should like so much to visit the sights with you) or else let me come to you, *wherever you are*. I will do so with pleasure; for you know everything interests me and I wish to see as much as possible of the inner life."

Isabel judged best not to show this letter to her uncle; but she acquainted him with its purport, and, as she expected, he begged her instantly to assure Miss Stackpole, in his name, that he should be delighted to receive her at Gardencourt. "Though she's a literary lady," he said, "I suppose that, being an American, she won't show me up, as that other one did. She has seen others like me."

"She has seen no other so delightful!" Isabel answered; but she was not altogether at ease about Henrietta's reproductive instincts, which belonged to that side of her friend's character which she regarded with least complacency. She wrote to Miss Stackpole, however, that she would be very welcome under Mr. Touchett's roof; and this alert young woman lost no time in announcing her prompt approach. She had gone up to London, and it was from that centre that she took the train for the station nearest to Gardencourt, where Isabel and Ralph were in waiting to receive her.

"Shall I love her or shall I hate her?" Ralph asked while they moved along the platform.

"Whichever you do will matter very little to her," said Isabel. "She doesn't care a straw what men think of her."

"As a man I'm bound to dislike her then. She must be a kind of monster. Is she very ugly?"

"No, she's decidedly pretty."

"A female interviewer—a reporter in petticoats? I'm very curious to see her," Ralph conceded.

"It's very easy to laugh at her but it is not easy to be as brave as she."

"I should think not; crimes of violence and attacks on the person require more or less pluck. Do you suppose she'll interview *me*?"

"Never in the world. She'll not think you of enough importance."

"You'll see," said Ralph. "She'll send a description of us all, including Bunchie, to her newspaper."

"I shall ask her not to," Isabel answered.

"You think she's capable of it then?"

"Perfectly."

"And yet you've made her your bosom-friend?"

"I've not made her my bosom-friend; but I like her in spite of her faults."

"Ah well," said Ralph, "I'm afraid I shall dislike her in spite of her merits."

"You'll probably fall in love with her at the end of three days."

"And have my love-letters published in the *Interviewer*? Never!" cried the young man.

The train presently arrived, and Miss Stackpole, promptly descending, proved, as Isabel had promised, quite delicately, even though rather provincially, fair. She was a neat, plump person, of medium stature, with a round face, a small mouth, a delicate complexion, a bunch of light brown ringlets at the back of her head and a peculiarly open, surprised-looking eye. The most striking point in her appearance was the remarkable fixedness of this organ, which rested without impudence or defiance, but as if in conscientious exercise of a natural right, upon every object it happened to encounter. It rested in this manner upon Ralph himself, a little arrested by Miss Stackpole's gracious and comfortable aspect, which hinted that it wouldn't be so easy as he had assumed to disapprove of her. She rustled, she shimmered, in fresh, dove-coloured draperies, and Ralph saw at a glance that she was as crisp and new and comprehensive as a first issue before the folding. From top to toe she had probably no misprint. She spoke in a clear, high voice—a voice not rich but loud; yet after she had taken her place with her companions in Mr. Touchett's carriage she struck him as not all in the large type, the type of horrid "headings," that he had expected. She answered the enquiries made to her by Isabel, however, and in which the young man ventured to join, with copious lucidity; and later, in the library at Gardencourt, when she had made the acquaintance of Mr. Touchett (his wife not having thought it necessary to appear) did more to give the measure of her confidence in her powers.

"Well, I should like to know whether you consider yourselves American or English," she broke out. "If once I knew I could talk to you accordingly."

"Talk to us anyhow and we shall be thankful," Ralph liberally answered.

She fixed her eyes on him, and there was something in their character that reminded him of large polished buttons—buttons that might have fixed the elastic loops of some tense receptacle: he seemed to see the reflection of surrounding objects on the pupil. The expression of a button is not usually deemed human, but there was something in Miss Stackpole's gaze that made him, as a very modest man, feel vaguely embarrassed—less inviolate, more dishonoured, than he liked. This sensation, it must be added, after he had spent a day or two in her company, sensibly diminished, though it never wholly lapsed. "I don't suppose that you're going to undertake to persuade me that *you're* an American," she said.

"To please you I'll be an Englishman, I'll be a Turk!"

"Well, if you can change about that way you're very welcome," Miss Stackpole returned.

"I'm sure you understand everything and that differences of nationality are no barrier to you," Ralph went on.

Miss Stackpole gazed at him still. "Do you mean the foreign languages?"

"The languages are nothing. I mean the spirit—the genius."

"I'm not sure that I understand you," said the correspondent of the *Interviewer*; "but I expect I shall before I leave."

"He's what's called a cosmopolite," Isabel suggested.

"That means he's a little of everything and not much of any. I must say I think patriotism is like charity—it begins at home."

"Ah, but where does home begin, Miss Stackpole?" Ralph enquired.

"I don't know where it begins, but I know where it ends. It ended a long time before I got here."

"Don't you like it over here?" asked Mr. Touchett with his aged, innocent voice.

"Well, sir, I haven't quite made up my mind what ground I shall take. I feel a good deal cramped. I felt it on the journey from Liverpool to London."

"Perhaps you were in a crowded carriage," Ralph suggested.

"Yes, but it was crowded with friends—a party of Americans whose acquaintance I had made upon the steamer; a lovely group from Little Rock, Arkansas. In spite of that I felt cramped—I felt something pressing upon me; I couldn't tell what it was. I felt at the very commencement as if I were not going to accord with the atmosphere. But I suppose I shall make my own atmosphere. That's the true way—then you can breathe. Your surroundings seem very attractive."

"Ah, we too are a lovely group!" said Ralph. "Wait a little and you'll see."

Miss Stackpole showed every disposition to wait and evidently was prepared to make a considerable stay at Gardencourt. She occupied herself in the mornings with literary labour; but in spite of this Isabel spent many hours with her friend, who, once her daily task performed, deprecated, in fact defied, isolation. Isabel speedily found occasion to desire her to desist from celebrating the charms of their common sojourn in print, having discovered, on the second morning of Miss Stackpole's visit, that she was engaged on a letter to the *Interviewer*, of which the title, in her exquisitely neat and legible hand (exactly that of the copybooks which our heroine remembered at school) was "Americans and Tudors—Glimpses of Gardencourt."[1] Miss Stackpole, with the best conscience in the world, offered to read her letter to Isabel, who immediately put in her protest.

"I don't think you ought to do that. I don't think you ought to describe the place."

Henrietta gazed at her as usual. "Why, it's just what the people want, and it's a lovely place."

"It's too lovely to be put in the newspapers, and it's not what my uncle wants."

"Don't you believe that!" cried Henrietta. "They're always delighted afterwards."

---

1. James wrote a few such travel letters during his own first years in Britain, though he was discreet enough to omit the names of the houses he described. See, for example, his 1877 "Abbeys and Castles," first written for *Lippincott's Magazine*, in *English Hours* (1905).

"My uncle won't be delighted—nor my cousin either. They'll consider it a breach of hospitality."

Miss Stackpole showed no sense of confusion; she simply wiped her pen, very neatly, upon an elegant little implement which she kept for the purpose, and put away her manuscript. "Of course if you don't approve I won't do it; but I sacrifice a beautiful subject."

"There are plenty of other subjects, there are subjects all round you. We'll take some drives; I'll show you some charming scenery."

"Scenery's not my department; I always need a human interest. You know I'm deeply human, Isabel; I always was," Miss Stackpole rejoined. "I was going to bring in your cousin—the alienated American. There's a great demand just now for the alienated American, and your cousin's a beautiful specimen. I should have handled him severely."

"He would have died of it!" Isabel exclaimed. "Not of the severity, but of the publicity."

"Well, I should have liked to kill him a little. And I should have delighted to do your uncle, who seems to me a much nobler type—the American faithful still. He's a grand old man; I don't see how he can object to my paying him honour."

Isabel looked at her companion in much wonderment; it struck her as strange that a nature in which she found so much to esteem should break down so in spots. "My poor Henrietta," she said, "you've no sense of privacy."

Henrietta coloured deeply, and for a moment her brilliant eyes were suffused, while Isabel found her more than ever inconsequent. "You do me great injustice," said Miss Stackpole with dignity. "I've never written a word about myself!"

"I'm very sure of that; but it seems to me one should be modest for others also!"

"Ah, that's very good!" cried Henrietta, seizing her pen again. "Just let me make a note of it and I'll put it in somewhere." She was a thoroughly good-natured woman, and half an hour later she was in as cheerful a mood as should have been looked for in a newspaper-lady in want of matter. "I've promised to do the social side," she said to Isabel; "and how can I do it unless I get ideas? If I can't describe this place don't you know some place I *can* describe?" Isabel promised she would bethink herself, and the next day, in conversation with her friend, she happened to mention her visit to Lord Warburton's ancient house. "Ah, you must take me there—that's just the place for me!" Miss Stackpole cried. "I must get a glimpse of the nobility."

"I can't take you," said Isabel; "but Lord Warburton's coming here, and you'll have a chance to see him and observe him. Only if you intend to repeat his conversation I shall certainly give him warning."

"Don't do that," her companion pleaded; "I want him to be natural."

"An Englishman's never so natural as when he's holding his tongue," Isabel declared.

It was not apparent, at the end of three days, that her cousin had, according to her prophecy, lost his heart to their visitor, though he had spent a good deal of time in her society. They strolled about the park together and sat under the trees, and in the afternoon, when it was delightful to float along the Thames, Miss Stackpole occupied a place in the boat in which hitherto Ralph had had but a single companion. Her presence proved somehow less irreducible to soft particles than Ralph had expected in the natural perturbation of his sense of the perfect solubility of that of his cousin; for the correspondent of the *Interviewer* prompted mirth in him, and he had long since decided that the *crescendo* of mirth should be the flower of his declining days. Henrietta, on her side, failed a little to justify Isabel's declaration with regard to her indifference to masculine opinion; for poor Ralph appeared to have presented himself to her as an irritating problem, which it would be almost immoral not to work out.

"What does he do for a living?" she asked of Isabel the evening of her arrival. "Does he go round all day with his hands in his pockets?"

"He does nothing," smiled Isabel; "he's a gentleman of large leisure."

"Well, I call that a shame—when I have to work like a car-conductor," Miss Stackpole replied. "I should like to show him up."

"He's in wretched health; he's quite unfit for work," Isabel urged.

"Pshaw! don't you believe it. I work when I'm sick," cried her friend. Later, when she stepped into the boat on joining the water-party, she remarked to Ralph that she supposed he hated her and would like to drown her.

"Ah no," said Ralph, "I keep my victims for a slower torture. And you'd be such an interesting one!"

"Well, you do torture me; I may say that. But I shock all your prejudices; that's one comfort."

"My prejudices? I haven't a prejudice to bless myself with. There's intellectual poverty for you."

"The more shame to you; I've some delicious ones. Of course I spoil your flirtation, or whatever it is you call it, with your cousin, but I don't care for that, as I render her the service of drawing you out. She'll see how thin you are."

"Ah, do draw me out!" Ralph exclaimed. "So few people will take the trouble."

Miss Stackpole, in this undertaking, appeared to shrink from no effort; resorting largely, whenever the opportunity offered, to the natural expedient of interrogation. On the following day the weather was bad, and in the afternoon the young man, by way of providing indoor amusement, offered to show her the pictures. Henrietta strolled through the long gallery in his society, while he pointed out its principal ornaments and mentioned the painters and subjects. Miss Stackpole looked at the pictures in perfect silence, committing herself to no opinion, and Ralph was gratified by the fact that she delivered herself of none of the little ready-made ejaculations of delight of which the visitors to Gardencourt were so frequently lavish. This young lady indeed, to do her justice, was but little addicted to the use of conventional terms; there was something earnest and inventive in her tone, which at times, in its strained deliberation, suggested a person of high culture speaking a foreign language. Ralph Touchett subsequently learned that she had at one time officiated as art-critic to a journal of the other world; but she appeared, in spite of this fact, to carry in her pocket none of the small change of admiration. Suddenly, just after he had called her attention to a charming Constable,[2] she turned and looked at him as if he himself had been a picture.

2. John Constable (1776–1837), English painter known for his landscapes and pictures of country life; now valued in particular for his studies of cloud formations.

"Do you always spend your time like this?" she demanded.

"I seldom spend it so agreeably."

"Well, you know what I mean—without any regular occupation."

"Ah," said Ralph, "I'm the idlest man living."

Miss Stackpole directed her gaze to the Constable again, and Ralph bespoke her attention for a small Lancret[3] hanging near it, which represented a gentleman in a pink doublet and hose and a ruff, leaning against the pedestal of the statue of a nymph in a garden and playing the guitar to two ladies seated on the grass. "That's my ideal of a regular occupation," he said.

Miss Stackpole turned to him again, and, though her eyes had rested upon the picture, he saw she had missed the subject. She was thinking of something much more serious. "I don't see how you can reconcile it to your conscience."

"My dear lady, I *have* no conscience!"

"Well, I advise you to cultivate one. You'll need it the next time you go to America."

"I shall probably never go again."

"Are you ashamed to show yourself?"

Ralph meditated with a mild smile. "I suppose that if one has no conscience one has no shame."

"Well, you've got plenty of assurance," Henrietta declared. "Do you consider it right to give up your country?"

"Ah, one doesn't give up one's country any more than one gives up one's grandmother. They're both antecedent to choice—elements of one's composition that are not to be eliminated."

"I suppose that means that you've tried and been worsted. What do they think of you over here?"

"They delight in me."

"That's because you truckle to them."

"Ah, set it down a little to my natural charm!" Ralph sighed.

"I don't know anything about your natural charm. If you've got any charm it's quite unnatural. It's wholly acquired—or at least you've tried hard to acquire it, living over here. I don't say you've succeeded. It's a charm that I don't appreciate, anyway. Make yourself useful in some way, and then we'll talk about it."

"Well, now, tell me what I shall do," said Ralph.

"Go right home, to begin with."

"Yes, I see. And then?"

"Take right hold of something."

"Well, now, what sort of thing?"

"Anything you please, so long as you take hold. Some new idea, some big work."

"Is it very difficult to take hold?" Ralph enquired.

"Not if you put your heart into it."

"Ah, my heart," said Ralph. "If it depends upon my heart—!"

"Haven't you got a heart?"

"I had one a few days ago, but I've lost it since."

---

3. Nicholas Lancret (1690–1743), French painter whose work mixes the pastoral and the theatrical. The 1881 edition has Ralph take down a more valuable Watteau, whom Lancret resembled.

"You're not serious," Miss Stackpole remarked; "that's what's the matter with you." But for all this, in a day or two, she again permitted him to fix her attention and on the later occasion assigned a different cause to her mysterious perversity. "I know what's the matter with you, Mr. Touchett," she said. "You think you're too good to get married."

"I thought so till I knew you, Miss Stackpole." Ralph answered; "and then I suddenly changed my mind."

"Oh pshaw!" Henrietta groaned.

"Then it seemed to me," said Ralph, "that I was not good enough."

"It would improve you. Besides, it's your duty."

"Ah," cried the young man, "one has so many duties! Is that a duty too?"

"Of course it is—did you never know that before? It's every one's duty to get married."

Ralph meditated a moment; he was disappointed. There was something in Miss Stackpole he had begun to like; it seemed to him that if she was not a charming woman she was at least a very good "sort." She was wanting in distinction, but, as Isabel had said, she was brave: she went into cages, she flourished lashes, like a spangled lion-tamer. He had not supposed her to be capable of vulgar arts, but these last words struck him as a false note. When a marriageable young woman urges matrimony on an unencumbered young man the most obvious explanation of her conduct is not the altruistic impulse.

"Ah, well now, there's a good deal to be said about that," Ralph rejoined.

"There may be, but that's the principal thing. I must say I think it looks very exclusive, going round all alone, as if you thought no woman was good enough for you. Do you think you're better than any one else in the world? In America it's usual for people to marry."

"If it's my duty," Ralph asked, "is it not, by analogy, yours as well?"

Miss Stackpole's ocular surfaces unwinkingly caught the sun. "Have you the fond hope of finding a flaw in my reasoning? Of course I've as good a right to marry as any one else."

"Well then," said Ralph, "I won't say it vexes me to see you single. It delights me rather."

"You're not serious yet. You never will be."

"Shall you not believe me to be so on the day I tell you I desire to give up the practice of going round alone?"

Miss Stackpole looked at him for a moment in a manner which seemed to announce a reply that might technically be called encouraging. But to his great surprise this expression suddenly resolved itself into an appearance of alarm and even of resentment. "No, not even then," she answered dryly. After which she walked away.

"I've not conceived a passion for your friend," Ralph said that evening to Isabel. "though we talked some time this morning about it."

"And you said something she didn't like," the girl replied.

Ralph stared. "Has she complained of me?"

"She told me she thinks there's something very low in the tone of Europeans towards women."

"Does she call me a European?"

"One of the worst. She told me you had said to her something that an American never would have said. But she didn't repeat it."

Ralph treated himself to a luxury of laughter. "She's an extraordinary combination. Did she think I was making love to her?"

"No; I believe even Americans do that. But she apparently thought you mistook the intention of something she had said, and put an unkind construction on it."

"I thought she was proposing marriage to me and I accepted her. Was that unkind?"

Isabel smiled. "It was unkind to *me*. I don't want you to marry."

"My dear cousin, what's one to do among you all?" Ralph demanded. "Miss Stackpole tells me it's my bounden duty, and that it's hers, in general, to see I do mine!"

"She has a great sense of duty," said Isabel gravely. "She has indeed, and it's the motive of everything she says. That's what I like her for. She thinks it's unworthy of you to keep so many things to yourself. That's what she wanted to express. If you thought she was trying to—to attract you, you were very wrong."

"It's true it was an odd way, but I did think she was trying to attract me. Forgive my depravity."

"You're very conceited. She had no interested views, and never supposed you would think she had."

"One must be very modest then to talk with such women," Ralph said humbly. "But it's a very strange type. She's too personal—considering that she expects other people not to be. She walks in without knocking at the door."

"Yes," Isabel admitted, "she doesn't sufficiently recognize the existence of knockers; and indeed I'm not sure that she doesn't think them rather a pretentious ornament. She thinks one's door should stand ajar. But I persist in liking her."

"I persist in thinking her too familiar," Ralph rejoined, naturally somewhat uncomfortable under the sense of having been doubly deceived in Miss Stackpole.

"Well," said Isabel, smiling, "I'm afraid it's because she's rather vulgar that I like her."

"She would be flattered by your reason!"

"If I should tell her I wouldn't express it in that way. I should say it's because there's something of the 'people' in her."

"What do you know about the people? and what does she, for that matter?"

"She knows a great deal, and I know enough to feel that she's a kind of emanation of the great democracy—of the continent, the country, the nation. I don't say that she sums it all up, that would be too much to ask of her. But she suggests it; she vividly figures it."

"You like her then for patriotic reasons. I'm afraid it is on those very grounds I object to her."

"Ah," said Isabel with a kind of joyous sigh, "I like so many things! If a thing strikes me with a certain intensity I accept it. I don't want to swagger, but I suppose I'm rather versatile. I like people to be totally different from Henrietta—in the style of Lord Warburton's sisters for instance. So long as I look at the Misses Molyneux they seem to me to answer a kind of ideal. Then Henrietta presents herself, and I'm straightway convinced by *her*; not so much in respect to herself as in respect to what masses behind her."

"Ah, you mean the back view of her," Ralph suggested.

"What she says is true," his cousin answered; "you'll never be serious. I like the great country stretching away beyond the rivers and across the prairies, blooming and smiling and spreading till it stops at the green Pacific! A strong, sweet, fresh odour seems to rise from it, and Henrietta—pardon my simile—has something of that odour in her garments."

Isabel blushed a little as she concluded this speech, and the blush, together with the momentary ardour she had thrown into it, was so becoming to her that Ralph stood smiling at her for a moment after she had ceased speaking. "I'm not sure the Pacific's so green as that," he said; "but you're a young woman of imagination. Henrietta, however, does smell of the Future—it almost knocks one down!"

Chapter XI

He took a resolve after this not to misinterpret her words even when Miss Stackpole appeared to strike the personal note most strongly. He bethought himself that persons, in her view, were simple and homogeneous organisms, and that he, for his own part, was too perverted a representative of the nature of man to have a right to deal with her in strict reciprocity. He carried out his resolve with a great deal of tact, and the young lady found in renewed contact with him no obstacle to the exercise of her genius for unshrinking enquiry, the general application of her confidence. Her situation at Gardencourt therefore, appreciated as we have seen her to be by Isabel and full of appreciation herself of that free play of intelligence which, to her sense, rendered Isabel's character a sister-spirit, and of the easy venerableness of Mr. Touchett, whose noble tone, as she said, met with her full approval—her situation at Gardencourt would have been perfectly comfortable had she not conceived an irresistible mistrust of the little lady for whom she had at first supposed herself obliged to "allow" as mistress of the house. She presently discovered, in truth, that this obligation was of the lightest and that Mrs. Touchett cared very little how Miss Stackpole behaved. Mrs. Touchett had defined her to Isabel as both an adventuress and a bore—adventuresses usually giving one more of a thrill; she had expressed some surprise at her niece's having selected such a friend, yet had immediately added that she knew Isabel's friends were her own affair and that she had never undertaken to like them all or to restrict the girl to those she liked.

"If you could see none but the people I like, my dear, you'd have a very small society," Mrs. Touchett frankly admitted; "and I don't think I like any man or woman well enough to recommend them to you. When it comes to recommending it's a serious affair. I don't like Miss Stackpole—everything about her displeases me; she talks so much too loud and looks at one as if one wanted to look at *her*—which one doesn't. I'm sure she has lived all her life in a boarding-house, and I detest the manners and the liberties of such places. If you ask me if I prefer my own manners, which you doubtless think very bad, I'll tell you that I prefer them immensely. Miss Stackpole knows I detest boarding-house civilisation, and she detests me for detesting it, because she thinks it the highest in the world. She'd like Gardencourt a great deal better if it were a boarding-house. For me, I find it almost too much of one! We shall never get on together therefore, and there's no use trying."

Mrs. Touchett was right in guessing that Henrietta disapproved of her, but she had not quite put her finger on the reason. A day or two after Miss Stackpole's arrival she had made some invidious reflexions on American hotels, which excited a vein of counter-argument on the part of the correspondent of the *Interviewer*, who in the exercise of her profession had acquainted herself, in the western world, with every form of caravansary. Henrietta expressed the opinion that American hotels were the best in the world, and Mrs. Touchett, fresh from a renewed struggle with them, recorded a conviction that they were the worst. Ralph, with his experimental geniality, suggested, by way of healing the breach, that the truth lay between the two extremes and that the establishments in question ought to be described as fair middling. This contribution to the discussion, however, Miss Stackpole rejected with scorn. Middling indeed! If they were not the best in the world they were the worst, but there was nothing middling about an American hotel.

"We judge from different points of view, evidently," said Mrs. Touchett. "I like to be treated as an individual; you like to be treated as a 'party.'"

"I don't know what you mean," Henrietta replied. "I like to be treated as an American lady."

"Poor American ladies!" cried Mrs. Touchett with a laugh. "They're the slaves of slaves."

"They're the companions of freemen," Henrietta retorted.

"They're the companions of their servants—the Irish chambermaid and the negro waiter. They share their work."

"Do you call the domestics in an American household 'slaves'?" Miss Stackpole enquired. "If that's the way you desire to treat them, no wonder you don't like America."

"If you've not good servants you're miserable," Mrs. Touchett serenely said. "They're very bad in America, but I've five perfect ones in Florence."

"I don't see what you want with five," Henrietta couldn't help observing. "I don't think I should like to see five persons surrounding me in that menial position."

"I like them in that position better than in some others," proclaimed Mrs. Touchett with much meaning.

"Should you like me better if I were your butler, dear?" her husband asked.

"I don't think I should: you wouldn't at all have the *tenue*."[1]

"The companions of freemen—I like that, Miss Stackpole," said Ralph. "It's a beautiful description."

"When I said freemen I didn't mean you, sir!"

And this was the only reward that Ralph got for his compliment. Miss Stackpole was baffled; she evidently thought there was something treasonable in Mrs. Touchett's appreciation of a class which she privately judged to be a mysterious survival of feudalism. It was perhaps because her mind was oppressed with this image that she suffered some days to elapse before

1. Deportment, bearing; the proper gravity of manner (French).

she took occasion to say to Isabel: "My dear friend, "I wonder if you're growing faithless."

"Faithless? Faithless to you, Henrietta?"

"No, that would be a great pain; but it's not that."

"Faithless to my country then?"

"Ah, that I hope will never be. When I wrote to you from Liverpool I said I had something particular to tell you. You've never asked me what it is. Is it because you've suspected?"

"Suspected what? As a rule I don't think I suspect," said Isabel. "I remember now that phrase in your letter, but I confess I had forgotten it. What have you to tell me?"

Henrietta looked disappointed, and her steady gaze betrayed it. "You don't ask that right—as if you thought it important. You're changed—you're thinking of other things."

"Tell me what you mean, and I'll think of that."

"Will you really think of it? That's what I wish to be sure of."

"I've not much control of my thoughts, but I'll do my best," said Isabel. Henrietta gazed at her, in silence, for a period which tried Isabel's patience, so that our heroine added at last: "Do you mean that you're going to be married?"

"Not till I've seen Europe!" said Miss Stackpole. "What are you laughing at?" she went on. "What I mean is that Mr. Goodwood came out in the steamer with me."

"Ah!" Isabel responded.

"You say *that* right. I had a good deal of talk with him; he has come after you."

"Did he tell you so?"

"No, he told me nothing; that's how I knew it," said Henrietta cleverly. "He said very little about you, but I spoke of you a good deal."

Isabel waited. At the mention of Mr. Goodwood's name she had turned a little pale. "I'm very sorry you did that," she observed at last.

"It was a pleasure to me, and I liked the way he listened. I could have talked a long time to such a listener; he was so quiet, so intense; he drank it all in."

"What did you say about me?" Isabel asked.

"I said you were on the whole the finest creature I know."

"I'm very sorry for that. He thinks too well of me already; he oughtn't to be encouraged."

"He's dying for a little encouragement. I see his face now, and his earnest absorbed look while I talked. I never saw an ugly man look so handsome."

"He's very simple-minded," said Isabel. "And he's not so ugly."

"There's nothing so simplifying as a grand passion."

"It's not a grand passion; I'm very sure it's not that."

"You don't say that as if you were sure."

Isabel gave rather a cold smile. "I shall say it better to Mr. Goodwood himself."

"He'll soon give you a chance," said Henrietta. Isabel offered no answer to this assertion, which her companion made with an air of great confidence. "He'll find you changed," the latter pursued. "You've been affected by your new surroundings."

"Very likely. I'm affected by everything."

"By everything but Mr. Goodwood!" Miss Stackpole exclaimed with a slightly harsh hilarity.

Isabel failed even to smile back and in a moment she said: "Did he ask you to speak to me?"

"Not in so many words. But his eyes asked it—and his handshake, when he bade me good-bye."

"Thank you for doing so." And Isabel turned away.

"Yes, you're changed; you've got new ideas over here," her friend continued.

"I hope so," said Isabel; "one should get as many new ideas as possible."

"Yes; but they shouldn't interfere with the old ones when the old ones have been the right ones."

Isabel turned about again. "If you mean that I had any idea with regard to Mr. Goodwood—!" But she faltered before her friend's implacable glitter.

"My dear child, you certainly encouraged him."

Isabel made for the moment as if to deny this charge; instead of which, however, she presently answered: "It's very true. I did encourage him." And then she asked if her companion had learned from Mr. Goodwood what he intended to do. It was a concession to her curiosity, for she disliked discussing the subject and found Henrietta wanting in delicacy.

"I asked him, and he said he meant to do nothing," Miss Stackpole answered. "But I don't believe that; he's not a man to do nothing. He is a man of high, bold action. Whatever happens to him he'll always do something, and whatever he does will always be right."

"I quite believe that." Henrietta might be wanting in delicacy, but it touched the girl, all the same, to hear this declaration.

"Ah, you *do* care for him!" her visitor rang out.

"Whatever he does will always be right," Isabel repeated. "When a man's of that infallible mould what does it matter to him what one feels?"

"It may not matter to him, but it matters to one's self."

"Ah, what it matters to me—that's not what we're discussing," said Isabel with a cold smile.

This time her companion was grave. "Well, I don't care; you *have* changed. You're not the girl you were a few short weeks ago, and Mr. Goodwood will see it. I expect him here any day."

"I hope he'll hate me then," said Isabel.

"I believe you hope it about as much as I believe him capable of it."

To this observation our heroine made no return; she was absorbed in the alarm given her by Henrietta's intimation that Caspar Goodwood would present himself at Gardencourt. She pretended to herself, however, that she thought the event impossible, and, later, she communicated her disbelief to her friend. For the next forty-eight hours, nevertheless, she stood prepared to hear the young man's name announced. The feeling pressed upon her; it made the air sultry, as if there were to be a change of weather; and the weather, socially speaking, had been so agreeable during Isabel's stay at Gardencourt that any change would be for the worse. Her suspense indeed was dissipated the second day. She had walked into the park in company with the sociable Bunchie, and after strolling about for some time, in a manner at once listless and restless, had seated herself on a garden-bench, within sight of the house, beneath a spreading beech, where, in a white dress ornamented with black ribbons, she formed among the flickering shadows a graceful and harmonious image. She entertained herself for some moments with talking to the little terrier, as to whom the proposal of an ownership divided with her cousin had been applied as impartially as possible—as impartially as Bunchie's own somewhat fickle and inconstant sympathies would allow. But she was notified for the first time, on this occasion, of the finite character of Bunchie's intellect; hitherto she had been mainly struck with its extent. It seemed to her at last that she would do well to take a book; formerly, when heavy-hearted, she had been able, with the help of some well-chosen volume, to transfer the seat of consciousness to the organ of pure reason. Of late, it was not to be denied, literature had seemed a fading light, and even after she had reminded herself that her uncle's library was provided with a complete set of those authors which no gentleman's collection should be without, she sat motionless and empty-handed, her eyes bent on the cool green turf of the lawn. Her meditations were presently interrupted by the arrival of a servant who handed her a letter. The letter bore the London postmark and was addressed in a hand she knew—that came into her vision, already so held by him, with the vividness of the writer's voice or his face. This document proved short and may be given entire.

MY DEAR MISS ARCHER—I don't know whether you will have heard of my coming to England, but even if you have not it will scarcely be a surprise to you. You will remember that when you gave me my dismissal at Albany, three months ago, I did not accept it. I protested against it. You in fact appeared to accept my protest and to admit that I had the right on my side. I had come to see you with the hope that you would let me bring you over to my conviction; my reasons for entertaining this hope had been of the best. But you disappointed it; I found you changed, and you were able to give me no reason for the change. You admitted that you were unreasonable, and it was the only concession you would make; but it was a very cheap one, because that's not your character. No, you are not, and you never will be, arbitrary or capricious. Therefore it is that I believe you will let me see you again. You told me that I'm not disagreeable to you, and I believe it; for I don't see why that should be. I shall always think of you; I shall never think of any one else. I came to England simply because you are here; I couldn't stay at home after you had gone: I hated the country because you were not in it. If I like this country at present it is only because it holds you. I have been to England before, but have never enjoyed it much. May I not come and see you for half an hour? This at present is the dearest wish of yours faithfully

CASPAR GOODWOOD.

Isabel read this missive with such deep attention that she had not perceived an approaching tread on the soft grass. Looking up, however, as she mechanically folded it she saw Lord Warburton standing before her.

Chapter XII

She put the letter into her pocket and offered her visitor a smile of welcome, exhibiting no trace of discomposure and half surprised at her coolness.

"They told me you were out here," said Lord Warburton; "and as there was no one in the drawing-room and it's really you that I wish to see, I came out with no more ado."

Isabel had got up; she felt a wish, for the moment, that he should not sit down beside her. "I was just going indoors."

"Please don't do that; it's much jollier here; I've ridden over from Lockleigh; it's a lovely day." His smile was peculiarly friendly and pleasing, and his whole person seemed to emit that radiance of good-feeling and good fare which had formed the charm of the girl's first impression of him. It surrounded him like a zone of fine June weather.

"We'll walk about a little then," said Isabel, who could not divest herself of the sense of an intention on the part of her visitor and who wished both to elude the intention and to satisfy her curiosity about it. It had flashed upon her vision once before, and it had given her on that occasion, as we know, a certain alarm. This alarm was composed of several elements, not all of which were disagreeable; she had indeed spent some days in analysing them and had succeeded in separating the pleasant part of the idea of Lord Warburton's "making up" to her from the painful. It may appear to some readers that the young lady was both precipitate and unduly fastidious; but the latter of these facts, if the charge be true, may serve to exonerate her from the discredit of the former. She was not eager to convince herself that a territorial magnate, as she had heard Lord Warburton called, was smitten with her charms; the fact of a declaration from such a source carrying with it really more questions than it would answer. She had received a strong impression of his being a "personage," and she had occupied herself in examining the image so conveyed. At the risk of adding to the evidence of her self-sufficiency it must be said that there had been moments when this possibility of admiration by a personage represented to her an aggression almost to the degree of an affront, quite to the degree of an inconvenience. She had never yet known a personage; there had been no personages, in this sense, in her life; there were probably none such at all in her native land. When she had thought of individual eminence she had thought of it on the basis of character and wit—of what one might like in a gentleman's mind and in his talk. She herself was a character—she couldn't help being aware of that; and hitherto her visions of a completed consciousness had concerned themselves largely with moral images—things as to which the question would be whether they pleased her sublime soul. Lord Warburton loomed up before her, largely and brightly, as a collection of attributes and powers which were not to be measured by this simple rule, but which demanded a different sort of appreciation—an appreciation that the girl, with her habit of judging quickly and freely, felt she lacked patience to bestow. He appeared to demand of her something that no one else, as it were, had presumed to do. What she felt was that a territorial, a political, a social magnate had conceived the design of drawing her into the system in which he rather invidiously lived and moved. A certain instinct, not imperious, but persuasive, told her to resist—murmured to her that virtually she had a system and an orbit of her own. It told her other things besides—things which both contradicted and confirmed each other; that a girl might do much worse than trust herself to such a man and that it would be very interesting to see something of his system from his own point of view; that on the other hand, however, there was evidently a great deal of it which she should regard only as a complication of every hour, and that even in the whole there was something stiff and stupid which would make it a burden. Furthermore there was a young man lately come from America who had no system at all, but who had a character of which it was useless for her to try to persuade herself that the impression on her mind had been light. The letter she carried in her pocket all sufficiently reminded her of the contrary. Smile not, however, I venture to repeat, at this simple young woman from Albany who debated whether she should accept an English peer before he had offered himself and who was disposed to believe that on the whole she could do better. She was a person of great good faith, and if there was a great deal of folly in her wisdom those who judge her severely may have the satisfaction of finding that, later, she became consistently wise only at the cost of an amount of folly which will constitute almost a direct appeal to charity.

Lord Warburton seemed quite ready to walk, to sit or to do anything that Isabel should propose, and he gave her this assurance with his usual air of being particularly pleased to exercise a social virtue. But he was, nevertheless, not in command of his emotions, and as he strolled beside her for a moment, in silence, looking at her without letting her know it, there was something embarrassed in his glance and his misdirected laughter. Yes, assuredly—as we have touched on the point, we may return to it for a moment again—the English are the most romantic people in the world and Lord Warburton was about to give an example of it. He was about to take a step which would astonish all his friends and displease a great many of them, and which had superficially nothing to recommend it. The young lady who trod the turf beside him had come from a queer country across the sea which he knew a good deal about; her antecedents, her associations were very vague to his mind except in so far as they were generic, and in this sense they showed as distinct and unimportant. Miss Archer had neither a fortune nor the sort of beauty that justifies a man to the multitude, and he calculated that he had spent about twenty-six hours in her company. He had summed up all this—the perversity of the impulse, which had declined to avail itself of the most liberal opportunities to subside, and the judgement of mankind, as exemplified particularly in the more quickly-judging half of it: he had looked these things well in the face and then had dismissed them from his thoughts. He cared no more for them than for the rosebud in his buttonhole. It is the good fortune of a man who for the greater part of a lifetime has abstained without effort from making himself disagreeable to his friends, that when the need comes for such a course it is not discredited by irritating associations.

"I hope you had a pleasant ride," said Isabel, who observed her companion's hesitancy.

"It would have been pleasant if for nothing else than that it brought me here."

"Are you so fond of Gardencourt?" the girl asked, more and more sure that he meant to make some appeal to her; wishing not to challenge him if he hesitated, and yet to keep all the quietness of her reason if he proceeded. It suddenly came upon her that her situation was one which a few weeks ago she would have deemed deeply romantic: the park of an old English country-house, with the foreground embellished by a "great" (as she supposed) nobleman in the act of making love to a young lady who, on careful inspection, should be found to present remarkable analogies with herself. But if she was now the heroine of the situation she succeeded scarcely the less in looking at it from the outside.

"I care nothing for Gardencourt," said her companion. "I care only for you."

"You've known me too short a time to have a right to say that, and I can't believe you're serious."

These words of Isabel's were not perfectly sincere, for she had no doubt whatever that he himself was. They were simply a tribute to the fact, of which she was perfectly aware, that those he had just uttered would have excited surprise on the part of a vulgar world. And, moreover, if anything beside the sense she had already acquired that Lord Warburton was not a loose thinker had been needed to convince her, the tone in which he replied would quite have served the purpose.

"One's right in such a matter is not measured by the time, Miss Archer; it's measured by the feeling itself. If I were to wait three months it would make no difference; I shall not be more sure of what I mean than I am to-day. Of course I've seen you very little, but my impression dates from the very first hour we met. I lost no time, I fell in love with you then. It was at first sight, as the novels say; I know now that's not a fancy-phrase, and I shall think better of novels for evermore. Those two days I spent here settled it; I don't know whether you suspected I was doing so, but I paid—mentally speaking I mean—the greatest possible attention to you. Nothing you said, nothing you did, was lost upon me. When you came to Lockleigh the other day—or rather when you went away—I was perfectly sure. Nevertheless I made up my mind to think it over and to question myself narrowly. I've done so; all these days I've done nothing else. I don't make mistakes about such things; I'm a very judicious animal. I don't go off easily, but when I'm touched, it's for life. It's for life, Miss Archer, it's for life." Lord Warburton repeated in the kindest, tenderest, pleasantest voice Isabel had ever heard, and looking at her with eyes charged with the light of a passion that had sifted itself clear of the baser parts of emotion—the heat, the violence, the unreason—and that burned as steadily as a lamp in a windless place.

By tacit consent, as he talked, they had walked more and more slowly, and at last they stopped and he took her hand. "Ah, Lord Warburton, how little you know me!" Isabel said very gently. Gently too she drew her hand away.

"Don't taunt me with that; that I don't know you better makes me unhappy enough already; it's all my loss. But that's what I want, and it seems to me I'm taking the best way. If you'll be my wife, then I shall know you, and when I tell you all the good I think of you you'll not be able to say it's from ignorance."

"If you know me little I know you even less," said Isabel.

"You mean that, unlike yourself, I may not improve on acquaintance? Ah, of course that's very possible. But think, to speak to you as I do, how determined I must be to try and give satisfaction! You do like me rather, don't you?"

"I like you very much, Lord Warburton," she answered; and at this moment she liked him immensely.

"I thank you for saying that; it shows you don't regard me as a stranger. I really believe I've filled all the other relations of life very creditably, and I don't see why I shouldn't fill this one—in which I offer myself to you—seeing that I care so much more about it. Ask the people who know me well; I've friends who'll speak for me."

"I don't need the recommendation of your friends," said Isabel.

"Ah now, that's delightful of you. You believe in me yourself."

"Completely," Isabel declared. She quite glowed there, inwardly, with the pleasure of feeling she did.

The light in her companion's eyes turned into a smile, and he gave a long exhalation of joy. "If you're mistaken, Miss Archer, let me lose all I possess!"

She wondered whether he meant this for a reminder that he was rich, and, on the instant, felt sure that he didn't. He was thinking that, as he would have said himself; and indeed he might safely leave it to the memory of any interlocutor, especially of one to whom he was offering his hand. Isabel had prayed that she might not be agitated, and her mind was tranquil enough, even while she listened and asked herself what it was best she should say, to indulge in this incidental criticism. What she should say, had she asked herself? Her foremost wish was to say something if possible not less kind than what he had said to her. His words had carried perfect conviction with them; she felt she did, all so mysteriously, matter to him. "I thank you more than I can say for your offer," she returned at last. "It does me great honour."

"Ah, don't say that!" he broke out. "I was afraid you'd say something like that. I don't see what you've to do with that sort of thing. I don't see why you should thank me—it's I who ought to thank you for listening to me: a man you know so little coming down on you with such a thumper! Of course it's a great question; I must tell you that I'd rather ask it than have it to answer myself. But the way you've listened—or at least your having listened at all—gives me some hope."

"Don't hope too much," Isabel said.

"Oh Miss Archer!" her companion murmured, smiling again, in his seriousness, as if such a warning might perhaps be taken but as the play of high spirits, the exuberance of elation.

"Should you be greatly surprised if I were to beg you not to hope at all?" Isabel asked.

"Surprised? I don't know what you mean by surprise. It wouldn't be that; it would be a feeling very much worse."

Isabel walked on again; she was silent for some minutes. "I'm very sure that, highly as I already think of you, my opinion of you, if I should know you well, would only rise. But I'm by no means sure that you wouldn't be disappointed. And I say that not in the least out of conventional modesty; it's perfectly sincere."

"I'm willing to risk it, Miss Archer," her companion replied.

"It's a great question, as you say. It's a very difficult question."

"I don't expect you of course to answer it outright. Think it over as long as may be necessary. If I can gain by waiting I'll gladly wait a long time. Only remember that in the end my dearest happiness depends on your answer."

"I should be very sorry to keep you in suspense," said Isabel.

"Oh, don't mind. I'd much rather have a good answer six months hence than a bad one to-day."

"But it's very probable that even six months hence I shouldn't be able to give you one that you'd think good."

"Why not, since you really like me?"

"Ah, you must never doubt that," said Isabel.

"Well then, I don't see what more you ask!"

"It's not what I ask; it's what I can give. I don't think I should suit you; I really don't think I should."

"You needn't worry about that. That's my affair. You needn't be a better royalist than the king."

"It's not only that," said Isabel; "but I'm not sure I wish to marry any one."

"Very likely you don't. I've no doubt a great many women begin that way," said his lordship, who, be it averred, did not in the least believe in the axiom he thus beguiled his anxiety by uttering. "But they're frequently persuaded."

"Ah, that's because they want to be!" And Isabel lightly laughed.

Her suitor's countenance fell, and he looked at her for a while in silence. "I'm afraid it's my being an Englishman that makes you hesitate," he said presently. "I know your uncle thinks you ought to marry in your own country."

Isabel listened to this assertion with some interest; it had never occurred to her that Mr. Touchett was likely to discuss her matrimonial prospects with Lord Warburton. "Has he told you that?"

"I remember his making the remark. He spoke perhaps of Americans generally."

"He appears himself to have found it very pleasant to live in England." Isabel spoke in a manner that might have seemed a little perverse, but which expressed both her constant perception of her uncle's outward felicity and her general disposition to elude any obligation to take a restricted view.

It gave her companion hope, and he immediately cried with warmth: "Ah, my dear Miss Archer, old England's a very good sort of country, you know! And it will be still better when we've furbished it up a little."

"Oh, don't furbish it, Lord Warburton; leave it alone. I like it this way."

"Well then, if you like it, I'm more and more unable to see your objection to what I propose."

"I'm afraid I can't make you understand."

"You ought at least to try. I've a fair intelligence. Are you afraid—afraid of the climate? We can easily live elsewhere, you know. You can pick out your climate, the whole world over."

These words were uttered with a breadth of candour that was like the embrace of strong arms—that was like the fragrance straight in her face, and by his clean, breathing lips, of she knew not what strange gardens, what charged airs. She would have given her little finger at that moment to feel strongly and simply the impulse to answer: "Lord Warburton, it's impossible for me to do better in this wonderful world, I think, than commit myself, very gratefully, to your loyalty." But though she was lost in admiration of her opportunity she managed to move back into the deepest shade of it, even as some wild, caught creature in a vast cage. The "splendid" security so offered her was *not* the greatest she could conceive. What

she finally bethought herself of saying was something very different—
something that deferred the need of really facing her crisis. "Don't think
me unkind if I ask you to say no more about this to-day."

"Certainly, certainly!" her companion cried. "I wouldn't bore you for the
world."

"You've given me a great deal to think about, and I promise you to do it
justice."

"That's all I ask of you, of course—and that you'll remember how absolutely my happiness is in your hands."

Isabel listened with extreme respect to this admonition, but she said
after a minute: "I must tell you that what I shall think about is some way
of letting you know that what you ask is impossible—letting you know it
without making you miserable."

"There's no way to do that, Miss Archer. I won't say that if you refuse
me you'll kill me; I shall not die of it. But I shall do worse; I shall live to
no purpose."

"You'll live to marry a better woman than I."

"Don't say that, please," said Lord Warburton very gravely. "That's fair
to neither one of us."

"To marry a worse one then."

"If there are better women than you I prefer the bad ones. That's all I
can say," he went on with the same earnestness. "There's no accounting
for tastes."

His gravity made her feel equally grave, and she showed it by again
requesting him to drop the subject for the present. "I'll speak to you
myself—very soon. Perhaps I shall write to you."

"At your convenience, yes," he replied. "Whatever time you take, it must
seem to me long, and I suppose I must make the best of that."

"I shall not keep you in suspense; I only want to collect my mind a little."

He gave a melancholy sigh and stood looking at her a moment, with his
hands behind him, giving short nervous shakes to his hunting-crop. "Do
you know I'm very much afraid of it—of that remarkable mind of yours?"

Our heroine's biographer can scarcely tell why, but the question made
her start and brought a conscious blush to her cheek. She returned his
look a moment, and then with a note in her voice that might almost have
appealed to his compassion, "So am I, my lord!" she oddly exclaimed.

His compassion was not stirred, however; all he possessed of the faculty
of pity was needed at home. "Ah! be merciful, be merciful," he murmured.

"I think you had better go," said Isabel. "I'll write to you."

"Very good; but whatever you write I'll come and see you, you know."
And then he stood reflecting, his eyes fixed on the observant countenance
of Bunchie, who had the air of having understood all that had been said
and of pretending to carry off the indiscretion by a simulated fit of curiosity as to the roots of an ancient oak. "There's one thing more," he went
on. "You know, if you don't like Lockleigh—if you think it's damp or
anything of that sort—you need never go within fifty miles of it. It's not
damp, by the way; I've had the house thoroughly examined; it's perfectly
safe and right. But if you shouldn't fancy it you needn't dream of living in
it. There's no difficulty whatever about that; there are plenty of houses. I
thought I'd just mention it; some people don't like a moat, you know.
Good-bye."

"I adore a moat," said Isabel. "Good-bye."

He held out his hand, and she gave him hers a moment—a moment long enough for him to bend his handsome bared head and kiss it. Then, still agitating, in his mastered emotion, his implement of the chase, he walked rapidly away. He was evidently much upset.

Isabel herself was upset, but she had not been affected as she would have imagined. What she felt was not a great responsibility, a great difficulty of choice; it appeared to her there had been no choice in the question. She couldn't marry Lord Warburton; the idea failed to support any enlightened prejudice in favour of the free exploration of life that she had hitherto entertained or was now capable of entertaining. She must write this to him, she must convince him, and that duty was comparatively simple. But what disturbed her, in the sense that it struck her with wonderment, was this very fact that it cost her so little to refuse a magnificent "chance." With whatever qualifications one would, Lord Warburton had offered her a great opportunity; the situation might have discomforts, might contain oppressive, might contain narrowing elements, might prove really but a stupefying anodyne; but she did her sex no injustice in believing that nineteen women out of twenty would have accommodated themselves to it without a pang. Why then upon her also should it not irresistibly impose itself? Who was she, what was she, that she should hold herself superior? What view of life, what design upon fate, what conception of happiness, had she that pretended to be larger than these large, these fabulous occasions? If she wouldn't do such a thing as that then she must do great things, she must do something greater. Poor Isabel found ground to remind herself from time to time that she must not be too proud, and nothing could be more sincere than her prayer to be delivered from such a danger: the isolation and loneliness of pride had for her mind the horror of a desert place. If it had been pride that interfered with her accepting Lord Warburton such a *bêtise*[1] was singularly misplaced; and she was so conscious of liking him that she ventured to assure herself it was the very softness, and the fine intelligence, of sympathy. She liked him too much to marry him, that was the truth; something assured her there was a fallacy somewhere in the glowing logic of the proposition—as he saw it— even though she mightn't put her very finest finger-point on it; and to inflict upon a man who offered so much a wife with a tendency to criticise would be a peculiarly discreditable act. She had promised him she would consider his question, and when, after he had left her, she wandered back to the bench where he had found her and lost herself in meditation, it might have seemed that she was keeping her vow. But this was not the case; she was wondering if she were not a cold, hard, priggish person, and, on her at last getting up and going rather quickly back to the house, felt, as she had said to her friend, really frightened at herself.

Chapter XIII

It was this feeling and not the wish to ask advice—she had no desire whatever for that—that led her to speak to her uncle of what had taken place. She wished to speak to some one; she should feel more natural, more

1. Folly (French).

human, and her uncle, for this purpose, presented himself in a more attractive light than either her aunt or her friend Henrietta. Her cousin of course was a possible confidant; but she would have had to do herself violence to air this special secret to Ralph. So the next day, after breakfast, she sought her occasion. Her uncle never left his apartment till the afternoon, but he received his cronies, as he said, in his dressing-room. Isabel had quite taken her place in the class so designated, which, for the rest, included the old man's son, his physician, his personal servant, and even Miss Stackpole. Mrs. Touchett did not figure in the list, and this was an obstacle the less to Isabel's finding her host alone. He sat in a complicated mechanical chair, at the open window of his room, looking westward over the park and the river, with his newspapers and letters piled up beside him, his toilet freshly and minutely made, and his smooth, speculative face composed to benevolent expectation.

She approached her point directly. "I think I ought to let you know that Lord Warburton has asked me to marry him. I suppose I ought to tell my aunt; but it seems best to tell you first."

The old man expressed no surprise, but thanked her for the confidence she showed him. "Do you mind telling me whether you accepted him?" he then enquired.

"I've not answered him definitely yet; I've taken a little time to think of it, because that seems more respectful. But I shall not accept him."

Mr. Touchett made no comment upon this; he had the air of thinking that, whatever interest he might take in the matter from the point of view of sociability, he had no active voice in it. "Well, I told you you'd be a success over here. Americans are highly appreciated."

"Very highly indeed," said Isabel. "But at the cost of seeming both tasteless and ungrateful, I don't think I can marry Lord Warburton."

"Well," her uncle went on, "of course an old man can't judge for a young lady. I'm glad you didn't ask me before you made up your mind. I suppose I ought to tell you," he added slowly, but as if it were not of much consequence, "that I've known all about it these three days."

"About Lord Warburton's state of mind?"

"About his intentions, as they say here. He wrote me a very pleasant letter, telling me all about them. Should you like to see his letter?" the old man obligingly asked.

"Thank you; I don't think I care about that. But I'm glad he wrote to you; it was right that he should, and he would be certain to do what was right."

"Ah well, I guess you do like him!" Mr. Touchett declared. "You needn't pretend you don't."

"I like him extremely; I'm very free to admit that. But I don't wish to marry any one just now."

"You think some one may come along whom you may like better. Well, that's very likely," said Mr. Touchett, who appeared to wish to show his kindness to the girl by easing off her decision, as it were, and finding cheerful reasons for it.

"I don't care if I don't meet any one else. I like Lord Warburton quite well enough." She fell into that appearance of a sudden change of point of view with which she sometimes startled and even displeased her interlocutors.

Her uncle, however, seemed proof against either of these impressions. "He's a very fine man," he resumed in a tone which might have passed for that of encouragement. "His letter was one of the pleasantest I've received for some weeks. I suppose one of the reasons I liked it was that it was all about you; that is all except the part that was about himself. I suppose he told you all that."

"He would have told me everything I wished to ask him," Isabel said.

"But you didn't feel curious?"

"My curiosity would have been idle—once I had determined to decline his offer."

"You didn't find it sufficiently attractive?" Mr. Touchett enquired.

She was silent a little. "I suppose it was that," she presently admitted. "But I don't know why."

"Fortunately ladies are not obliged to give reasons," said her uncle. "There's a great deal that's attractive about such an idea; but I don't see why the English should want to entice us away from our native land. I know that we try to attract them over there, but that's because our population is insufficient. Here, you know, they're rather crowded. However, I presume there's room for charming young ladies everywhere."

"There seems to have been room here for you," said Isabel, whose eyes had been wandering over the large pleasure-spaces of the park.

Mr. Touchett gave a shrewd, conscious smile. "There's room everywhere, my dear, if you'll pay for it. I sometimes think I've paid too much for this. Perhaps you also might have to pay too much."

"Perhaps I might," the girl replied.

That suggestion gave her something more definite to rest on than she had found in her own thoughts, and the fact of this association of her uncle's mild acuteness with her dilemma seemed to prove that she was concerned with the natural and reasonable emotions of life and not altogether a victim to intellectual eagerness and vague ambitions—ambitions reaching beyond Lord Warburton's beautiful appeal, reaching to something indefinable and possibly not commendable. In so far as the indefinable had an influence upon Isabel's behaviour at this juncture, it was not the conception, even unformulated, of a union with Caspar Goodwood; for however she might have resisted conquest at her English suitor's large quiet hands she was at least as far removed from the disposition to let the young man from Boston take positive possession of her. The sentiment in which she sought refuge after reading his letter was a critical view of his having come abroad; for it was part of the influence he had upon her that he seemed to deprive her of the sense of freedom. There was a disagreeably strong push, a kind of hardness of presence, in his way of rising before her. She had been haunted at moments by the image, by the danger, of his disapproval and had wondered—a consideration she had never paid in equal degree to any one else—whether he would like what she did. The difficulty was that more than any man she had ever known, more than poor Lord Warburton (she had begun now to give his lordship the benefit of this epithet), Caspar Goodwood expressed for her an energy—and she had already felt it as a power—that was of his very nature. It was in no degree a matter of his "advantages"—it was a matter of the spirit that sat in his clear-burning eyes like some tireless watcher at a window. She might like it or not, but he insisted, ever, with his whole weight and force: even in one's usual contact with him one had to reckon with that. The idea of a diminished liberty was particularly disagreeable to her at present, since she had just given a sort of personal accent to her independence by looking so straight at Lord Warburton's big bribe and yet turning away from it. Sometimes Caspar Goodwood had seemed to range himself on the side of her destiny, to be the stubbornest fact she knew; she said to herself at such moments that she might evade him for a time, but that she must make terms with him at last—terms which would be certain to be favourable to himself. Her impulse had been to avail herself of the things that helped her to resist such an obligation; and this impulse had been much concerned in her eager acceptance of her aunt's invitation, which had come to her at an hour when she expected from day to day to see Mr. Goodwood and when she was glad to have an answer ready for something she was sure he would say to her. When she had told him at Albany, on the evening of Mrs. Touchett's visit, that she couldn't then discuss difficult questions, dazzled as she was by the great immediate opening of her aunt's offer of "Europe," he declared that this was no answer at all; and it was now to obtain a better one that he was following her across the sea. To say to herself that he was a kind of grim fate was well enough for a fanciful young woman who was able to take much for granted in him; but the reader has a right to a nearer and a clearer view.

He was the son of a proprietor of well-known cotton-mills in Massachusetts—a gentleman who had accumulated a considerable fortune in the exercise of this industry. Caspar at present managed the works, and with a judgement and a temper which, in spite of keen competition and languid years, had kept their prosperity from dwindling. He had received the better part of his education at Harvard College, where, however, he had gained renown rather as a gymnast and an oarsman than as a gleaner of more dispersed knowledge. Later on he had learned that the finer intelligence too could vault and pull and strain—might even, breaking the record, treat itself to rare exploits. He had thus discovered in himself a sharp eye for the mystery of mechanics, and had invented an improvement in the cotton-spinning process which was now largely used and was known by his name. You might have seen it in the newspapers in connection with this fruitful contrivance; assurance of which he had given to Isabel by showing her in the columns of the New York *Interviewer* an exhaustive article on the Goodwood patent—an article not prepared by Miss Stackpole, friendly as she had proved herself to his more sentimental interests. There were intricate, bristling things he rejoiced in; he liked to organise, to contend, to administer; he could make people work his will, believe in him, march before him and justify him. This was the art, as they said, of managing men—which rested, in him, further, on a bold though brooding ambition. It struck those who knew him well that he might do greater things than carry on a cotton-factory; there was nothing cottony about Caspar Goodwood, and his friends took for granted that he would somehow and somewhere write himself in bigger letters. But it was as if something large and confused, something dark and ugly, would have to call upon him: he was not after all in harmony with mere smug peace and greed and gain, an order of things of which the vital breath was ubiquitous advertisement. It pleased Isabel to believe that he might have ridden, on a plunging steed, the whirlwind of a great war—a war like the Civil strife that had overdarkened her conscious childhood and his ripening youth.

She liked at any rate this idea of his being by character and in fact a mover of men—liked it much better than some other points in his nature and aspect. She cared nothing for his cotton-mill—the Goodwood patent left her imagination absolutely cold. She wished him no ounce less of his manhood, but she sometimes thought he would be rather nicer if he looked, for instance, a little differently. His jaw was too square and set and his figure too straight and stiff: these things suggested a want of easy consonance with the deeper rhythms of life. Then she viewed with reserve a habit he had of dressing always in the same manner; it was not apparently that he wore the same clothes continually, for, on the contrary, his garments had a way of looking rather too new. But they all seemed of the same piece; the figure, the stuff, was so drearily usual. She had reminded herself more than once that this was a frivolous objection to a person of his importance; and then she had amended the rebuke by saying that it would be a frivolous objection only if she were in love with him. She was not in love with him and therefore might criticise his small defects as well as his great—which latter consisted in the collective reproach of his being too serious, or, rather, not of his being so, since one could never be, but certainly of his seeming so. He showed his appetites and designs too simply and artlessly; when one was alone with him he talked too much about the same subject, and when other people were present he talked too little about anything. And yet he was of supremely strong, clean make—which was so much: she saw the different fitted parts of him as she had seen, in museums and portraits, the different fitted parts of armoured warriors—in plates of steel handsomely inlaid with gold. It was very strange: where, ever, was any tangible link between her impression and her act? Caspar Goodwood had never corresponded to her idea of a delightful person, and she supposed that this was why he left her so harshly critical. When, however, Lord Warburton, who not only did correspond with it, but gave an extension to the term, appealed to her approval, she found herself still unsatisfied. It was certainly strange.

The sense of her incoherence was not a help to answering Mr. Goodwood's letter, and Isabel determined to leave it a while unhonoured. If he had determined to persecute her he must take the consequences; foremost among which was his being left to perceive how little it charmed her that he should come down to Gardencourt. She was already liable to the incursions of one suitor at this place, and though it might be pleasant to be appreciated in opposite quarters there was a kind of grossness in entertaining two such passionate pleaders at once, even in a case where the entertainment should consist of dismissing them. She made no reply to Mr. Goodwood; but at the end of three days she wrote to Lord Warburton, and the letter belongs to our history.

DEAR LORD WARBURTON—A great deal of earnest thought has not led me to change my mind about the suggestion you were so kind as to make me the other day. I am not, I am really and truly not, able to regard you in the light of a companion for life; or to think of your home—your various homes—as the settled seat of my existence. These things cannot be reasoned about, and I very earnestly entreat you not to return to the subject we discussed so exhaustively. We see our lives from our own point of view;

that is the privilege of the weakest and humblest of us; and I shall never be able to see mine in the manner you proposed. Kindly let this suffice you, and do me the justice to believe that I have given your proposal the deeply respectful consideration it deserves. It is with this very great regard that I remain sincerely yours,

ISABEL ARCHER.

While the author of this missive was making up her mind to despatch it Henrietta Stackpole formed a resolve which was accompanied by no demur. She invited Ralph Touchett to take a walk with her in the garden, and when he had assented with that alacrity which seemed constantly to testify to his high expectations, she informed him that she had a favour to ask of him. It may be admitted that at this information the young man flinched; for we know that Miss Stackpole had struck him as apt to push an advantage. The alarm was unreasoned, however; for he was clear about the area of her indiscretion as little as advised of its vertical depth, and he made a very civil profession of the desire to serve her. He was afraid of her and presently told her so. "When you look at me in a certain way my knees knock together, my faculties desert me; I'm filled with trepidation and I ask only for strength to execute your commands. You've an address that I've never encountered in any woman."

"Well," Henrietta replied good-humouredly, "if I had not known before that you were trying somehow to abash me I should know it now. Of course I'm easy game—I was brought up with such different customs and ideas. I'm not used to your arbitrary standards, and I've never been spoken to in America as you have spoken to me. If a gentleman conversing with me over there were to speak to me like that I shouldn't know what to make of it. We take everything more naturally over there, and, after all, we're a great deal more simple. I admit that; I'm very simple myself. Of course if you choose to laugh at me for it you're very welcome; but I think on the whole I would rather be myself than you. I'm quite content to be myself; I don't want to change. There are plenty of people that appreciate me just as I am. It's true they're nice fresh free-born Americans!" Henrietta had lately taken up the tone of helpless innocence and large concession. "I want you to assist me a little," she went on. "I don't care in the least whether I amuse you while you do so; or, rather, I'm perfectly willing your amusement should be your reward. I want you to help me about Isabel."

"Has she injured you?" Ralph asked.

"If she had I shouldn't mind, and I should never tell you. What I'm afraid of is that she'll injure herself."

"I think that's very possible," said Ralph.

His companion stopped in the garden-walk, fixing on him perhaps the very gaze that unnerved him. "That too would amuse you, I suppose. The way you do say things! I never heard any one so indifferent."

"To Isabel? Ah, not that!"

"Well, you're not in love with her, I hope."

"How can that be, when I'm in love with Another?"

"You're in love with yourself, that's the Other!" Miss Stackpole declared. "Much good may it do you! But if you wish to be serious once in your life here's a chance; and if you really care for your cousin here's an opportunity to prove it. I don't expect you to understand her; that's too much to ask. But you needn't do that to grant my favour. I'll supply the necessary intelligence."

"I shall enjoy that immensely!" Ralph exclaimed. "I'll be Caliban and you shall be Ariel."

"You're not at all like Caliban, because you're sophisticated, and Caliban was not. But I'm not talking about imaginary characters; I'm talking about Isabel. Isabel's intensely real. What I wish to tell you is that I find her fearfully changed."

"Since you came, do you mean?"

"Since I came and before I came. She's not the same as she once so beautifully was."

"As she was in America?"

"Yes, in America. I suppose you know she comes from there. She can't help it, but she does."

"Do you want to change her back again?"

"Of course I do, and I want you to help me."

"Ah," said Ralph, "I'm only Caliban; I'm not Prospero."[1]

"You were Prospero enough to make her what she has become. You've acted on Isabel Archer since she came here, Mr. Touchett."

"I, my dear Miss Stackpole? Never in the world. Isabel Archer has acted on me—yes; she acts on every one. But I've been absolutely passive."

"You're too passive then. You had better stir yourself and be careful. Isabel's changing every day; she's drifting away—right out to sea. I've watched her and I can see it. She's not the bright American girl she was. She's taking different views, a different colour, and turning away from her old ideals. I want to save those ideals, Mr. Touchett, and that's where you come in."

"Not surely as an ideal?"

"Well, I hope not," Henrietta replied promptly. "I've got a fear in my heart that she's going to marry one of these fell Europeans, and I want to prevent it."

"Ah, I see," cried Ralph; "and to prevent it you want me to step in and marry her?"

"Not quite; that remedy would be as bad as the disease, for you're the typical, the fell European from whom I wish to rescue her. No; I wish you to take an interest in another person—a young man to whom she once gave great encouragement and whom she now doesn't seem to think good enough. He's a thoroughly grand man and a very dear friend of mine, and I wish very much you would invite him to pay a visit here."

Ralph was much puzzled by this appeal, and it is perhaps not to the credit of his purity of mind that he failed to look at it at first in the simplest light. It wore, to his eyes, a tortuous air, and his fault was that he was not quite sure that anything in the world could really be as candid as this request of Miss Stackpole's appeared. That a young woman should demand that a gentleman whom she described as her very dear friend should be furnished with an opportunity to make himself agreeable to another young woman, a young woman whose attention had wandered and whose charms were greater—this was an anomaly which for the moment

---

1. Caliban, Ariel, and Prospero are all characters in Shakespeare's *The Tempest* (1611); the first two are servants held in bondage on a tropical island by the wizard Prospero. Caliban is presented as a misshapen and savage native inhabitant, and Ariel as an otherworldly sprite.

challenged all his ingenuity of interpretation. To read between the lines was easier than to follow the text, and to suppose that Miss Stackpole wished the gentleman invited to Gardencourt on her own account was the sign not so much of a vulgar as of an embarrassed mind. Even from this venial act of vulgarity, however, Ralph was saved, and saved by a force that I can only speak of as inspiration. With no more outward light on the subject than he already possessed he suddenly acquired the conviction that it would be a sovereign injustice to the correspondent of the *Interviewer* to assign a dishonourable motive to any act of hers. This conviction passed into his mind with extreme rapidity; it was perhaps kindled by the pure radiance of the young lady's imperturbable gaze. He returned this challenge a moment, consciously, resisting an inclination to frown as one frowns in the presence of larger luminaries. "Who's the gentleman you speak of?"

"Mr. Caspar Goodwood—of Boston. He has been extremely attentive to Isabel—just as devoted to her as he can live. He has followed her out here and he's at present in London. I don't know his address, but I guess I can obtain it."

"I've never heard of him," said Ralph.

"Well, I suppose you haven't heard of every one. I don't believe he has ever heard of you; but that's no reason why Isabel shouldn't marry him."

Ralph gave a mild ambiguous laugh. "What a rage you have for marrying people! Do you remember how you wanted to marry *me* the other day?"

"I've got over that. You don't know how to take such ideas. Mr. Goodwood does, however; and that's what I like about him. He's a splendid man and a perfect gentleman, and Isabel knows it."

"Is she very fond of him?"

"If she isn't she ought to be. He's simply wrapped up in her."

"And you wish me to ask him here," said Ralph reflectively.

"It would be an act of true hospitality."

"Caspar Goodwood," Ralph continued—"it's rather a striking name."

"I don't care anything about his name. It might be Ezekiel Jenkins, and I should say the same. He's the only man I have ever seen whom I think worthy of Isabel."

"You're a very devoted friend," said Ralph.

"Of course I am. If you say that to pour scorn on me I don't care."

"I don't say it to pour scorn on you; I'm very much struck with it."

"You're more satiric than ever, but I advise you not to laugh at Mr. Goodwood."

"I assure you I'm very serious; you ought to understand that," said Ralph.

In a moment his companion understood it. "I believe you are; now you're too serious."

"You're difficult to please."

"Oh, you're very serious indeed. You won't invite Mr. Goodwood."

"I don't know," said Ralph. "I'm capable of strange things. Tell me a little about Mr. Goodwood. What's he like?"

"He's just the opposite of you. He's at the head of a cotton-factory; a very fine one."

"Has he pleasant manners?" asked Ralph.

"Splendid manners—in the American style."

"Would he be an agreeable member of our little circle?"

"I don't think he'd care much about our little circle. He'd concentrate on Isabel."

"And how would my cousin like that?"

"Very possibly not at all. But it will be good for her. It will call back her thoughts."

"Call them back—from where?"

"From foreign parts and other unnatural places. Three months ago she gave Mr. Goodwood every reason to suppose he was acceptable to her, and it's not worthy of Isabel to go back on a real friend simply because she has changed the scene. I've changed the scene too, and the effect of it has been to make me care more for my old associations than ever. It's my belief that the sooner Isabel changes it back again the better. I know her well enough to know that she would never be truly happy over here, and I wish her to form some strong American tie that will act as a preservative."

"Aren't you perhaps a little too much in a hurry?" Ralph enquired. "Don't you think you ought to give her more of a chance in poor old England?"

"A chance to ruin her bright young life? One's never too much in a hurry to save a precious human creature from drowning."

"As I understand it then," said Ralph, "you wish me to push Mr. Goodwood overboard after her. Do you know," he added, "that I've never heard her mention his name?"

Henrietta gave a brilliant smile. "I'm delighted to hear that; it proves how much she thinks of him."

Ralph appeared to allow that there was a good deal in this, and he surrendered to thought while his companion watched him askance. "If I should invite Mr. Goodwood," he finally said, "it would be to quarrel with him."

"Don't do that; he'd prove the better man."

"You certainly are doing your best to make me hate him! I really don't think I can ask him. I should be afraid of being rude to him."

"It's just as you please," Henrietta returned. "I had no idea you were in love with her yourself."

"Do you really believe that?" the young man asked with lifted eyebrows.

"That's the most natural speech I've ever heard you make! Of course I believe it," Miss Stackpole ingeniously said.

"Well," Ralph concluded, "to prove to you that you're wrong I'll invite him. It must be of course as a friend of yours."

"It will not be as a friend of mine that he'll come; and it will not be to prove to me that I'm wrong that you'll ask him—but to prove it to yourself!"

These last words of Miss Stackpole's (on which the two presently separated) contained an amount of truth which Ralph Touchett was obliged to recognise; but it so far took the edge from too sharp a recognition that, in spite of his suspecting it would be rather more indiscreet to keep than to break his promise, he wrote Mr. Goodwood a note of six lines, expressing the pleasure it would give Mr. Touchett the elder that he should join a little party at Gardencourt, of which Miss Stackpole was a valued member. Having sent his letter (to the care of a banker whom Henrietta suggested) he waited in some suspense. He had heard this fresh formidable figure named for the first time; for when his mother had mentioned on her arrival that there was a story about the girl's having an "admirer" at home, the idea had seemed deficient in reality and he had taken no pains to ask questions the answers to which would involve only the vague or the disagreeable. Now, however, the native admiration of which his cousin was the object had become more concrete; it took the form of a young man who had followed her to London, who was interested in a cotton-mill and had manners in the most splendid of the American styles. Ralph had two theories about this intervener. Either his passion was a sentimental fiction of Miss Stackpole's (there was always a sort of tacit understanding among women, born of the solidarity of the sex, that they should discover or invent lovers for each other), in which case he was not to be feared and would probably not accept the invitation; or else he would accept the invitation and in this event prove himself a creature too irrational to demand further consideration. The latter clause of Ralph's argument might have seemed incoherent; but it embodied his conviction that if Mr. Goodwood were interested in Isabel in the serious manner described by Miss Stackpole he would not care to present himself at Gardencourt on a summons from the latter lady. "On this supposition," said Ralph, "he must regard her as a thorn on the stem of his rose; as an intercessor he must find her wanting in tact."

Two days after he had sent his invitation he received a very short note from Caspar Goodwood, thanking him for it, regretting that other engagements made a visit to Gardencourt impossible and presenting many compliments to Miss Stackpole. Ralph handed the note to Henrietta, who, when she had read it, exclaimed: "Well, I never have heard of anything so stiff!"

"I'm afraid he doesn't care so much about my cousin as you suppose," Ralph observed.

"No, it's not that; it's some subtler motive. His nature's very deep. But I'm determined to fathom it, and I shall write to him to know what he means."

His refusal of Ralph's overtures was vaguely disconcerting; from the moment he declined to come to Gardencourt our friend began to think him of importance. He asked himself what it signified to him whether Isabel's admirers should be desperadoes or laggards; they were not rivals of his and were perfectly welcome to act out their genius. Nevertheless he felt much curiosity as to the result of Miss Stackpole's promised enquiry into the causes of Mr. Goodwood's stiffness—a curiosity for the present ungratified, inasmuch as when he asked her three days later if she had written to London she was obliged to confess she had written in vain. Mr. Goodwood had not replied.

"I suppose he's thinking it over," she said; "he thinks everything over; he's not *really* at all impetuous. But I'm accustomed to having my letters answered the same day." She presently proposed to Isabel, at all events, that they should make an excursion to London together. "If I must tell the truth," she observed, "I'm not seeing much at this place, and I shouldn't think you were either. I've not even seen that aristocrat—what's his name?— Lord Washburton. He seems to let you severely alone."

"Lord Warburton's coming to-morrow, I happen to know," replied her friend, who had received a note from the master of Lockleigh in answer to her own letter. "You'll have every opportunity of turning him inside out."

"Well, he may do for one letter, but what's one letter when you want to write fifty? I've described all the scenery in this vicinity and raved about all the old women and donkeys. You may say what you please, scenery doesn't make a vital letter. I must go back to London and get some impressions of real life. I was there but three days before I came away, and that's hardly time to get in touch."

As Isabel, on her journey from New York to Gardencourt, had seen even less of the British capital than this, it appeared a happy suggestion of Henrietta's that the two should go thither on a visit of pleasure. The idea struck Isabel as charming; she was curious of the thick detail of London, which had always loomed large and rich to her. They turned over their schemes together and indulged in visions of romantic hours. They would stay at some picturesque old inn—one of the inns described by Dickens— and drive over the town in those delightful hansoms.[2] Henrietta was a literary woman, and the great advantage of being a literary woman was that you could go everywhere and do everything. They would dine at a coffee-house and go afterwards to the play; they would frequent the Abbey and the British Museum and find out where Doctor Johnson had lived, and Goldsmith and Addison.[3] Isabel grew eager and presently unveiled the bright vision to Ralph, who burst into a fit of laughter which scarce expressed the sympathy she had desired.

"It's a delightful plan," he said. "I advise you to go to the Duke's Head in Covent Garden,[4] an easy, informal, old-fashioned place, and I'll have you put down at my club."

"Do you mean it's improper?" Isabel asked. "Dear me, isn't anything proper here? With Henrietta surely I may go anywhere; she isn't hampered in that way. She has travelled over the whole American continent and can at least find her way about this minute island."

"Ah then," said Ralph, "let me take advantage of her protection to go up to town as well. I may never have a chance to travel so safely!"

Chapter XIV

Miss Stackpole would have prepared to start immediately; but Isabel, as we have seen, had been notified that Lord Warburton would come again to Gardencourt, and she believed it her duty to remain there and see him. For four or five days he had made no response to her letter; then he had written, very briefly, to say he would come to luncheon two days later. There was something in these delays and postponements that touched the girl and renewed her sense of his desire to be considerate and patient, not to appear to urge her too grossly; a consideration the more studied that she was so sure he "really liked" her. Isabel told her uncle she had written to him, mentioning also his intention of coming; and the old man, in consequence, left his room earlier than usual and made his appearance at the two o'clock repast. This was by no means an act of vigilance on his part, but the fruit of a benevolent belief that his being of the company might help to cover any conjoined straying away in case Isabel should give their

2. Hansom cabs were two-wheeled vehicles and typically carried two passengers, with the driver on a raised seat behind.
3. Samuel Johnson (1709–1784), Oliver Goldsmith (1730–1774), and Joseph Addison (1672–1719), eighteenth-century writers especially associated with London.
4. Ralph is joking. Covent Garden was the site of both London's biggest market and one of its most important theaters, but it was also a noted haunt for prostitutes, and its hotels were unsuitable for ladies. In the 1881 edition Ralph suggests that they go to the Tavistock Hotel which was—like his club—for men only.

noble visitor another hearing. That personage drove over from Lockleigh and brought the elder of his sisters with him, a measure presumably dictated by reflexions of the same order as Mr. Touchett's. The two visitors were introduced to Miss Stackpole, who, at luncheon, occupied a seat adjoining Lord Warburton's. Isabel, who was nervous and had no relish for the prospect of again arguing the question he had so prematurely opened, could not help admiring his good-humoured self-possession, which quite disguised the symptoms of that preoccupation with her presence it was natural she should suppose him to feel. He neither looked at her nor spoke to her, and the only sign of his emotion was that he avoided meeting her eyes. He had plenty of talk for the others, however, and he appeared to eat his luncheon with discrimination and appetite. Miss Molyneux, who had a smooth, nun-like forehead and wore a large silver cross suspended from her neck, was evidently preoccupied with Henrietta Stackpole, upon whom her eyes constantly rested in a manner suggesting a conflict between deep alienation and yearning wonder. Of the two ladies from Lockleigh she was the one Isabel had liked best; there was such a world of hereditary quiet in her. Isabel was sure moreover that her mild forehead and silver cross referred to some weird Anglican mystery—some delightful reinstitution perhaps of the quaint office of the canoness. She wondered what Miss Molyneux would think of her if she knew Miss Archer had refused her brother; and then she felt sure that Miss Molyneux would never know—that Lord Warburton never told her such things. He was fond of her and kind to her, but on the whole he told her little. Such, at least, was Isabel's theory; when, at table, she was not occupied in conversation she was usually occupied in forming theories about her neighbours. According to Isabel, if Miss Molyneux should ever learn what had passed between Miss Archer and Lord Warburton she would probably be shocked at such a girl's failure to rise; or no, rather (this was our heroine's last position) she would impute to the young American but a due consciousness of inequality.

Whatever Isabel might have made of her opportunities, at all events, Henrietta Stackpole was by no means disposed to neglect those in which she now found herself immersed. "Do you know you're the first lord I've ever seen?" she said very promptly to her neighbour. "I suppose you think I'm awfully benighted."

"You've escaped seeing some very ugly men," Lord Warburton answered, looking a trifle absently about the table.

"Are they very ugly? They try to make us believe in America that they're all handsome and magnificent and that they wear wonderful robes and crowns."

"Ah, the robes and crowns are gone out of fashion," said Lord Warburton, "like your tomahawks and revolvers."

"I'm sorry for that; I think an aristocracy ought to be splendid," Henrietta declared. "If it's not that, what is it?"

"Oh, you know, it isn't much, at the best," her neighbour allowed. "Won't you have a potato?"

"I don't care much for these European potatoes. I shouldn't know you from an ordinary American gentleman."

"Do talk to me as if I *were* one," said Lord Warburton. "I don't see how you manage to get on without potatoes; you must find so few things to eat over here."

Henrietta was silent a little; there was a chance he was not sincere. "I've had hardly any appetite since I've been here," she went on at last; "so it doesn't much matter. I don't approve of *you*, you know; I feel as if I ought to tell you that."

"Don't approve of me?"

"Yes; I don't suppose any one ever said such a thing to you before, did they? I don't approve of lords as an institution. I think the world has got beyond them—far beyond."

"Oh, so do I. I don't approve of myself in the least. Sometimes it comes over me—how I should object to myself if I were not myself, don't you know? But that's rather good, by the way—not to be vainglorious."

"Why don't you give it up then?" Miss Stackpole enquired.

"Give up—a—?" asked Lord Warburton, meeting her harsh inflexion with a very mellow one.

"Give up being a lord."

"Oh, I'm so little of one! One would really forget all about it if you wretched Americans were not constantly reminding one. However, I do think of giving it up, the little there is left of it, one of these days."

"I should like to see you do it!" Henrietta exclaimed rather grimly.

"I'll invite you to the ceremony; we'll have a supper and a dance."

"Well," said Miss Stackpole, "I like to see all sides. I don't approve of a privileged class, but I like to hear what they have to say for themselves."

"Mighty little, as you see!"

"I should like to draw you out a little more," Henrietta continued. "But you're always looking away. You're afraid of meeting my eye. I see you want to escape me."

"No, I'm only looking for those despised potatoes."

"Please explain about that young lady—your sister—then. I don't understand about her. Is she a Lady?"[1]

"She's a capital good girl."

"I don't like the way you say that—as if you wanted to change the subject. Is her position inferior to yours?"

"We neither of us have any position to speak of; but she's better off than I, because she has none of the bother."

"Yes, she doesn't look as if she had much bother. I wish I had as little bother as that. You do produce quiet people over here, whatever else you may do."

"Ah, you see one takes life easily, on the whole," said Lord Warburton. "And then you know we're very dull. Ah, we can be dull when we try!"

"I should advise you to try something else. I shouldn't know what to talk to your sister about; she looks so different. Is that silver cross a badge?"

"A badge?"

"A sign of rank."

Lord Warburton's glance had wandered a good deal, but at this it met the gaze of his neighbour. "Oh yes," he answered in a moment; "the women go in for those things. The silver cross is worn by the eldest daughters of Viscounts." Which was his harmless revenge for having occasionally had

---

1. A courtesy title given to the daughters of earls, marquesses, and dukes in the English peerage that precedes their first name; e.g., "Lady Barbarina," the title of James's 1884 short story. Warburton holds a lower title, that of viscount, and his sisters are therefore simply known as "Miss"; Molyneux is their family name.

his credulity too easily engaged in America. After luncheon he proposed to Isabel to come into the gallery and look at the pictures; and though she knew he had seen the pictures twenty times she complied without criticising this pretext. Her conscience now was very easy; ever since she sent him her letter she had felt particularly light of spirit. He walked slowly to the end of the gallery, staring at its contents and saying nothing; and then he suddenly broke out: "I hoped you wouldn't write to me that way."

"It was the only way, Lord Warburton," said the girl. "Do try and believe that."

"If I could believe it of course I should let you alone. But we can't believe by willing it; and I confess I don't understand. I could understand your disliking me; that I could understand well. But that you should admit you do—"

"What have I admitted?" Isabel interrupted, turning slightly pale.

"That you think me a good fellow; isn't that it?" She said nothing, and he went on: "You don't seem to have any reason, and that gives me a sense of injustice."

"I have a reason, Lord Warburton." She said it in a tone that made his heart contract.

"I should like very much to know it."

"I'll tell you some day when there's more to show for it."

"Excuse my saying that in the mean time I must doubt of it."

"You make me very unhappy," said Isabel.

"I'm not sorry for that; it may help you to know how I feel. Will you kindly answer me a question?" Isabel made no audible assent, but he apparently saw in her eyes something that gave him courage to go on: "Do you prefer some one else?"

"That's a question I'd rather not answer."

"Ah, you *do* then!" her suitor murmured with bitterness.

The bitterness touched her, and she cried out: "You're mistaken! I don't."

He sat down on a bench, unceremoniously, doggedly, like a man in trouble; leaning his elbows on his knees and staring at the floor. "I can't even be glad of that," he said at last, throwing himself back against the wall; "for that would be an excuse."

She raised her eyebrows in surprise. "An excuse? Must I excuse myself?"

He paid, however, no answer to the question. Another idea had come into his head. "Is it my political opinions? Do you think I go too far?"

"I can't object to your political opinions, because I don't understand them."

"You don't care what I think!" he cried, getting up. "It's all the same to you."

Isabel walked to the other side of the gallery and stood there showing him her charming back, her light slim figure, the length of her white neck as she bent her head, and the density of her dark braids. She stopped in front of a small picture as if for the purpose of examining it; and there was something so young and free in her movement that her very pliancy seemed to mock at him. Her eyes, however, saw nothing; they had suddenly been suffused with tears. In a moment he followed her, and by this time she had brushed her tears away; but when she turned round her face was pale and the expression of her eyes strange. "That reason that I wouldn't tell you—I'll tell it you after all. It's that I can't escape my fate."

"Your fate?"

"I should try to escape it if I were to marry you."

"I don't understand. Why should not *that* be your fate as well as anything else?"

"Because it's not," said Isabel femininely. "I know it's not. It's not my fate to give up—I know it can't be."

Poor Lord Warburton stared, an interrogative point in either eye. "Do you call marrying *me* giving up?"

"Not in the usual sense. It's getting—getting—getting a great deal. But it's giving up other chances."

"Other chances for what?"

"I don't mean chances to marry," said Isabel, her colour quickly coming back to her. And then she stopped, looking down with a deep frown, as if it were hopeless to attempt to make her meaning clear.

"I don't think it presumptuous in me to suggest that you'll gain more than you'll lose," her companion observed.

"I can't escape unhappiness," said Isabel. "In marrying you I shall be trying to."

"I don't know whether you'd try to, but you certainly would: that I must in candour admit!" he exclaimed with an anxious laugh.

"I mustn't—I can't!" cried the girl.

"Well, if you're bent on being miserable I don't see why you should make *me* so. Whatever charms a life of misery may have for you, it has none for me."

"I'm not bent on a life of misery," said Isabel. "I've always been intensely determined to be happy, and I've often believed I should be. I've told people that; you can ask them. But it comes over me every now and then that I can never be happy in any extraordinary way; not by turning away, by separating myself."

"By separating yourself from what?"

"From life. From the usual chances and dangers, from what most people know and suffer."

Lord Warburton broke into a smile that almost denoted hope. "Why, my dear Miss Archer," he began to explain with the most considerate eagerness, "I don't offer you any exoneration from life or from any chances or dangers whatever. I wish I could; depend upon it I would! For what do you take me, pray? Heaven help me, I'm not the Emperor of China! All I offer you is the chance of taking the common lot in a comfortable sort of way. The common lot? Why, I'm devoted to the common lot! Strike an alliance with me, and I promise you that you shall have plenty of it. You shall separate from nothing whatever—not even from your friend Miss Stackpole."

"She'd never approve of it," said Isabel, trying to smile and take advantage of this side-issue; despising herself too, not a little, for doing so.

"Are we speaking of Miss Stackpole?" his lordship asked impatiently. "I never saw a person judge things on such theoretic grounds."

"Now I suppose you're speaking of me," said Isabel with humility; and she turned away again, for she saw Miss Molyneux enter the gallery, accompanied by Henrietta and by Ralph.

Lord Warburton's sister addressed him with a certain timidity and reminded him she ought to return home in time for tea, as she was expecting company to partake of it. He made no answer—apparently not having heard her; he was preoccupied, and with good reason. Miss Molyneux— as if he had been Royalty—stood like a lady-in-waiting.

"Well, I never, Miss Molyneux!" said Henrietta Stackpole. "If I wanted to go he'd have to go. If I wanted my brother to do a thing he'd have to do it."

"Oh, Warburton does everything one wants," Miss Molyneux answered with a quick, shy laugh. "How very many pictures you have!" she went on, turning to Ralph.

"They look a good many, because they're all put together," said Ralph. "But it's really a bad way."

"Oh, I think it's so nice. I wish we had a gallery at Lockleigh. I'm so very fond of pictures," Miss Molyneux went on, persistently, to Ralph, as if she were afraid Miss Stackpole would address her again. Henrietta appeared at once to fascinate and to frighten her.

"Ah yes, pictures are very convenient," said Ralph, who appeared to know better what style of reflexion was acceptable to her.

"They're so very pleasant when it rains," the young lady continued. "It has rained of late so very often."

"I'm sorry you're going away, Lord Warburton," said Henrietta. "I wanted to get a great deal more out of you."

"I'm not going away," Lord Warburton answered.

"Your sister says you must. In America the gentlemen obey the ladies."

"I'm afraid we have some people to tea," said Miss Molyneux, looking at her brother.

"Very good, my dear. We'll go."

"I hoped you would resist!" Henrietta exclaimed. "I wanted to see what Miss Molyneux would do."

"I never do anything," said this young lady.

"I suppose in your position it's sufficient for you to exist!" Miss Stack-pole returned. "I should like very much to see you at home."

"You must come to Lockleigh again," said Miss Molyneux, very sweetly, to Isabel, ignoring this remark of Isabel's friend.

Isabel looked into her quiet eyes a moment, and for that moment seemed to see in their grey depths the reflexion of everything she had rejected in rejecting Lord Warburton—the peace, the kindness, the honour, the possessions, a deep security and a great exclusion. She kissed Miss Molyneux and then she said: "I'm afraid I can never come again."

"Never again?"

"I'm afraid I'm going away."

"Oh, I'm so very sorry," said Miss Molyneux. "I think that's so very wrong of you."

Lord Warburton watched this little passage; then he turned away and stared at a picture. Ralph, leaning against the rail before the picture with his hands in his pockets, had for the moment been watching him.

"I should like to see you at home," said Henrietta, whom Lord Warburton found beside him. "I should like an hour's talk with you; there are a great many questions I wish to ask you."

"I shall be delighted to see you," the proprietor of Lockleigh answered; "but I'm certain not to be able to answer many of your questions. When will you come?"

"Whenever Miss Archer will take me. We're thinking of going to London, but we'll go and see you first. I'm determined to get some satisfaction out of you."

"If it depends upon Miss Archer I'm afraid you won't get much. She won't come to Lockleigh; she doesn't like the place."

"She told me it was lovely!" said Henrietta.

Lord Warburton hesitated. "She won't come, all the same. You had better come alone," he added.

Henrietta straightened herself, and her large eyes expanded. "Would you make that remark to an English lady?" she enquired with soft asperity.

Lord Warburton stared. "Yes, if I liked her enough."

"You'd be careful not to like her enough. If Miss Archer won't visit your place again it's because she doesn't want to take me. I know what she thinks of me, and I suppose you think the same—that I oughtn't to bring in individuals." Lord Warburton was at a loss; he had not been made acquainted with Miss Stackpole's professional character and failed to catch her allusion. "Miss Archer has been warning you!" she therefore went on.

"Warning me?"

"Isn't that why she came off alone with you here—to put you on your guard?"

"Oh dear, no," said Lord Warburton brazenly; "our talk had no such solemn character as that."

"Well, you've been on your guard—intensely. I suppose it's natural to you; that's just what I wanted to observe. And so, too, Miss Molyneux—she wouldn't commit herself. *You* have been warned, anyway," Henrietta continued, addressing this young lady; "but for you it wasn't necessary."

"I hope not," said Miss Molyneux vaguely.

"Miss Stackpole takes notes," Ralph soothingly explained. "She's a great satirist; she sees through us all and she works us up."

"Well, I must say I never have had such a collection of bad material!" Henrietta declared, looking from Isabel to Lord Warburton and from this nobleman to his sister and to Ralph. "There's something the matter with you all; you're as dismal as if you had got a bad cable."

"You do see through us, Miss Stackpole," said Ralph in a low tone, giving her a little intelligent nod as he led the party out of the gallery. "There's something the matter with us all."

Isabel came behind these two; Miss Molyneux, who decidedly liked her immensely, had taken her arm, to walk beside her over the polished floor. Lord Warburton strolled on the other side with his hands behind him and his eyes lowered. For some moments he said nothing; and then, "Is it true you're going to London?" he asked.

"I believe it has been arranged."

"And when shall you come back?"

"In a few days; but probably for a very short time. I'm going to Paris with my aunt."

"When, then, shall I see you again?"

"Not for a good while," said Isabel. "But some day or other, I hope."

"Do you really hope it?"

"Very much."

He went a few steps in silence; then he stopped and put out his hand. "Good-bye."

"Good-bye," said Isabel.

Miss Molyneux kissed her again, and she let the two depart. After it, without rejoining Henrietta and Ralph, she retreated to her own room; in which apartment, before dinner, she was found by Mrs. Touchett, who had stopped on her way to the saloon. "I may as well tell you," said that lady, "that your uncle has informed me of your relations with Lord Warburton."

Isabel considered. "Relations? They're hardly relations. That's the strange part of it: he has seen me but three or four times."

"Why did you tell your uncle rather than me?" Mrs. Touchett dispassionately asked.

Again the girl hesitated. "Because he knows Lord Warburton better."

"Yes, but I know you better."

"I'm not sure of that," said Isabel, smiling.

"Neither am I, after all; especially when you give me that rather conceited look. One would think you were awfully pleased with yourself and had carried off a prize! I suppose that when you refuse an offer like Lord Warburton's it's because you expect to do something better."

"Ah, my uncle didn't say that!" cried Isabel, smiling still.

Chapter XV

It had been arranged that the two young ladies should proceed to London under Ralph's escort, though Mrs. Touchett looked with little favour on the plan. It was just the sort of plan, she said, that Miss Stackpole would be sure to suggest, and she enquired if the correspondent of the *Interviewer* was to take the party to stay at her favourite boarding-house.

"I don't care where she takes us to stay, so long as there's local colour," said Isabel. "That's what we're going to London for."

"I suppose that after a girl has refused an English lord she may do anything," her aunt rejoined. "After that one needn't stand on trifles."

"Should you have liked me to marry Lord Warburton?" Isabel enquired.

"Of course I should."

"I thought you disliked the English so much."

"So I do; but it's all the greater reason for making use of them."

"Is that your idea of marriage?" And Isabel ventured to add that her aunt appeared to her to have made very little use of Mr. Touchett.

"Your uncle's not an English nobleman," said Mrs. Touchett, "though even if he had been I should still probably have taken up my residence in Florence."

"Do you think Lord Warburton could make me any better than I am?" the girl asked with some animation. "I don't mean I'm too good to improve. I mean—I mean that I don't love Lord Warburton enough to marry him."

"You did right to refuse him then," said Mrs. Touchett in her smallest, sparest voice. "Only, the next great offer you get, I hope you'll manage to come up to your standard."

"We had better wait till the offer comes before we talk about it. I hope very much I may have no more offers for the present. They upset me completely."

"You probably won't be troubled with them if you adopt permanently the Bohemian manner of life. However, I've promised Ralph not to criticise."

"I'll do whatever Ralph says is right," Isabel returned. "I've unbounded confidence in Ralph."

"His mother's much obliged to you!" this lady dryly laughed.

"It seems to me indeed she ought to feel it!" Isabel irrepressibly answered.

Ralph had assured her that there would be no violation of decency in their paying a visit—the little party of three—to the sights of the metropolis; but Mrs. Touchett took a different view. Like many ladies of her country who had lived a long time in Europe, she had completely lost her native tact on such points, and in her reaction, not in itself deplorable, against the liberty allowed to young persons beyond the seas, had fallen into gratuitous and exaggerated scruples. Ralph accompanied their visitors to town and established them at a quiet inn in a street that ran at right angles to Piccadilly. His first idea had been to take them to his father's house in Winchester Square, a large, dull mansion which at this period of the year was shrouded in silence and brown holland; but he bethought himself that, the cook being at Gardencourt, there was no one in the house to get them their meals, and Pratt's Hotel[1] accordingly became their resting-place. Ralph, on his side, found quarters in Winchester Square, having a "den" there of which he was very fond and being familiar with deeper fears than that of a cold kitchen. He availed himself largely indeed of the resources of Pratt's Hotel, beginning his day with an early visit to his fellow travellers, who had Mr. Pratt in person, in a large bulging white waistcoat, to remove their dish-covers. Ralph turned up, as he said, after breakfast, and the little party made out a scheme of entertainment for the day. As London wears in the month of September a face blank but for its smears of prior service, the young man, who occasionally took an apologetic tone, was obliged to remind his companion, to Miss Stackpole's high derision, that there wasn't a creature in town.

"I suppose you mean the aristocracy are absent," Henrietta answered; "but I don't think you could have a better proof that if they were absent altogether they wouldn't be missed. It seems to me the place is about as full as it can be. There's no one here, of course, but three or four millions of people. What is it you call them—the lower-middle class? They're only the population of London, and that's of no consequence."

Ralph declared that for him the aristocracy left no void that Miss Stackpole herself didn't fill, and that a more contented man was nowhere at that moment to be found. In this he spoke the truth, for the stale September days, in the huge half-empty town, had a charm wrapped in them as a coloured gem might be wrapped in a dusty cloth. When he went home at night to the empty house in Winchester Square, after a chain of hours with his comparatively ardent friends, he wandered into the big dusky dining-room, where the candle he took from the hall-table, after letting himself in, constituted the only illumination. The square was still, the house was still; when he raised one of the windows of the dining-room to

---

1. Winchester Square is a fictional location, as is Pratt's Hotel. James's own flat at the time he wrote *The Portrait of a Lady* was in Bolton Street, which "ran at right angles" to the fashionable Piccadilly. *Brown Holland*: a coarse linen fabric, often used to cover furniture in shuttered houses.

let in the air he heard the slow creak of the boots of a lone constable. His own step, in the empty place, seemed loud and sonorous; some of the carpets had been raised, and whenever he moved he roused a melancholy echo. He sat down in one of the armchairs; the big dark dining table twinkled here and there in the small candle-light; the pictures on the wall, all of them very brown, looked vague and incoherent. There was a ghostly presence as of dinners long since digested, of table-talk that had lost its actuality. This hint of the supernatural perhaps had something to do with the fact that his imagination took a flight and that he remained in his chair a long time beyond the hour at which he should have been in bed; doing nothing, not even reading the evening paper. I say he did nothing, and I maintain the phrase in the face of the fact that he thought at these moments of Isabel. To think of Isabel could only be for him an idle pursuit, leading to nothing and profiting little to any one. His cousin had not yet seemed to him so charming as during these days spent in sounding, tourist-fashion, the deeps and shallows of the metropolitan element. Isabel was full of premises, conclusions, emotions; if she had come in search of local colour she found it everywhere. She asked more questions than he could answer, and launched brave theories, as to historic cause and social effect, that he was equally unable to accept or to refute. The party went more than once to the British Museum and to that brighter palace of art[2] which reclaims for antique variety so large an area of a monotonous suburb; they spent a morning in the Abbey and went on a penny-steamer to the Tower; they looked at pictures both in public and private collections and sat on various occasions beneath the great trees in Kensington Gardens. Henrietta proved an indestructible sight-seer and a more lenient judge than Ralph had ventured to hope. She had indeed many disappointments, and London at large suffered from her vivid remembrance of the strong points of the American civic idea; but she made the best of its dingy dignities and only heaved an occasional sigh and uttered a desultory "Well!" which led no further and lost itself in retrospect. The truth was that, as she said herself, she was not in her element. "I've not a sympathy with inanimate objects," she remarked to Isabel at the National Gallery; and she continued to suffer from the meagreness of the glimpse that had as yet been vouchsafed to her of the inner life. Landscapes by Turner[3] and Assyrian bulls were a poor substitute for the literary dinner-parties at which she had hoped to meet the genius and renown of Great Britain.

"Where are your public men, where are your men and women of intellect?" she enquired of Ralph, standing in the middle of Trafalgar Square as if she had supposed this to be a place where she would naturally meet a few. "That's one of them on the top of the column, you say—Lord Nelson?[4] Was he a lord too? Wasn't he high enough, that they had to stick

2. The Crystal Palace, first built for the Great Exhibition of 1851 in Hyde Park, and then relocated to Sydenham, southeast of the city's center.
3. The paragraph provides an inventory of the tourist's London, from Westminster Abbey and the Tower of London to the National Gallery in Trafalgar Square and the Assyrian sculptures in the British Museum. J. M. W. Turner (1775–1851), British painter especially known for his atmospheric land- and seascapes.
4. Admiral Horatio Lord Nelson (1758–1805), British naval hero and victor over the French at the Battle of Trafalgar, where he himself was killed. His statue stands atop a column in the London square named for his victory.

him a hundred feet in the air? That's the past—I don't care about the past; I want to see some of the leading minds of the present. I won't say of the future, because I don't believe much in your future." Poor Ralph had few leading minds among his acquaintance and rarely enjoyed the pleasure of button-holing a celebrity; a state of things which appeared to Miss Stackpole to indicate a deplorable want of enterprise. "If I were on the other side I should call," she said, "and tell the gentleman, whoever he might be, that I had heard a great deal about him and had come to see for myself. But I gather from what you say that this is not the custom here. You seem to have plenty of meaningless customs, but none of those that would help along. We *are* in advance, certainly. I suppose I shall have to give up the social side altogether;" and Henrietta, though she went about with her guide-book and pencil and wrote a letter to the *Interviewer* about the Tower (in which she described the execution of Lady Jane Grey),[5] had a sad sense of falling below her mission.

The incident that had preceded Isabel's departure from Gardencourt left a painful trace in our young woman's mind: when she felt again in her face, as from a recurrent wave, the cold breath of her last suitor's surprise, she could only muffle her head till the air cleared. She could not have done less than what she did; this was certainly true. But her necessity, all the same, had been as graceless as some physical act in a strained attitude, and she felt no desire to take credit for her conduct. Mixed with this imperfect pride, nevertheless, was a feeling of freedom which in itself was sweet and which, as she wandered through the great city with her ill-matched companions, occasionally throbbed into odd demonstrations. When she walked in Kensington Gardens she stopped the children (mainly of the poorer sort) whom she saw playing on the grass; she asked them their names and gave them sixpence and, when they were pretty, kissed them. Ralph noticed these quaint charities; he noticed everything she did. One afternoon, that his companions might pass the time, he invited them to tea in Winchester Square, and he had the house set in order as much as possible for their visit. There was another guest to meet them, an amiable bachelor, an old friend of Ralph's who happened to be in town and for whom prompt commerce with Miss Stackpole appeared to have neither difficulty nor dread. Mr. Bantling, a stout, sleek, smiling man of forty, wonderfully dressed, universally informed and incoherently amused, laughed immoderately at everything Henrietta said, gave her several cups of tea, examined in her society the *bric-à-brac*, of which Ralph had a considerable collection, and afterwards, when the host proposed they should go out into the square and pretend it was a *fête-champétre*,[6] walked round the limited enclosure several times with her and, at a dozen turns of their talk, bounded responsive—as with a positive passion for argument—to her remarks upon the inner life.

"Oh, I see; I dare say you found it very quiet at Gardencourt. Naturally there's not much going on there when there's such a lot of illness about. Touchett's very bad, you know; the doctors have forbidden his being in

5. The Protestant Lady Jane Grey (1536/7–1554) was a puppet queen of England for nine days in the religious and political chaos after the death of Edward VI; she was executed for treason by her cousin, the Catholic Queen Mary.
6. A picnic or garden; in stylized form a frequent subject for painters such as Watteau or Lancret.

England at all, and he has only come back to take care of his father. The old man, I believe, has half a dozen things the matter with him. They call it gout, but to my certain knowledge he has organic disease so developed that you may depend upon it he'll go, some day soon, quite quickly. Of course that sort of thing makes a dreadfully dull house; I wonder they have people when they can do so little for them. Then I believe Mr. Touchett's always squabbling with his wife; she lives away from her husband, you know, in that extraordinary American way of yours. If you want a house where there's always something going on, I recommend you to go down and stay with my sister, Lady Pensil, in Bedfordshire. I'll write her to-morrow and I'm sure she'll be delighted to ask you. I know just what you want—you want a house where they go in for theatricals and picnics and that sort of thing. My sister's just that sort of woman; she's always getting up something or other and she's always glad to have the sort of people who help her. I'm sure she'll ask you down by return of post: she's tremendously fond of distinguished people and writers. She writes herself, you know; but I haven't read everything she has written. It's usually poetry, and I don't go in much for poetry—unless it's Byron.[7] I suppose you think a great deal of Byron in America," Mr. Bantling continued, expanding in the stimulating air of Miss Stackpole's attention, bringing up his sequences promptly and changing his topic with an easy turn of hand. Yet he none the less gracefully kept in sight of the idea, dazzling to Henrietta, of her going to stay with Lady Pensil in Bedfordshire. "I understand what you want; you want to see some genuine English sport. The Touchetts aren't English at all, you know; they have their own habits, their own language, their own food—some odd religion even, I believe, of their own. The old man thinks it's wicked to hunt, I'm told. You must get down to my sister's in time for the theatricals, and I'm sure she'll be glad to give you a part. I'm sure you act well; I know you're very clever. My sister's forty years old and has seven children, but she's going to play the principal part. Plain as she is she makes up awfully well—I *will* say for her. Of course you needn't act if you don't want to."

In this manner Mr. Bantling delivered himself while they strolled over the grass in Winchester Square, which, although it had been peppered by the London soot, invited the tread to linger. Henrietta thought her blooming, easy-voiced bachelor, with his impressibility to feminine merit and his splendid range of suggestion, a very agreeable man, and she valued the opportunity he offered her. "I don't know but I *would* go, if your sister should ask me. I think it would be my duty. What do you call her name?"

"Pensil. It's an odd name, but it isn't a bad one."

"I think one name's as good as another. But what's her rank?"

"Oh, she's a baron's wife; a convenient sort of rank. You're fine enough and you're not too fine."

"I don't know but what she'd be too fine for me. What do you call the place she lives in—Bedfordshire?"

"She lives away in the northern corner of it. It's a tiresome country, but I dare say you won't mind it. I'll try and run down while you're there."

---

7. George Gordon, Lord Byron (1788–1824), Romantic poet known also for his scandalous sex life, and for his death while fighting for Greek independence from the Ottoman Empire. His works include *Childe Harold's Pilgrimage* (1812–18) and *Don Juan* (1818–24).

All this was very pleasant to Miss Stackpole, and she was sorry to be obliged to separate from Lady Pensil's obliging brother. But it happened that she had met the day before, in Piccadilly, some friends whom she had not seen for a year: the Miss Climbers, two ladies from Wilmington, Delaware, who had been travelling on the Continent and were now preparing to re-embark. Henrietta had had a long interview with them on the Piccadilly pavement, and though the three ladies all talked at once they had not exhausted their store. It had been agreed therefore that Henrietta should come and dine with them in their lodgings in Jermyn Street[8] at six o'clock on the morrow, and she now bethought herself of this engagement. She prepared to start for Jermyn Street, taking leave first of Ralph Touchett and Isabel, who, seated on garden chairs in another part of the enclosure, were occupied—if the term may be used—with an exchange of amenities less pointed than the practical colloquy of Miss Stackpole and Mr. Bantling. When it had been settled between Isabel and her friend that they should be reunited at some reputable hour at Pratt's Hotel, Ralph remarked that the latter must have a cab. She couldn't walk all the way to Jermyn Street.

"I suppose you mean it's improper for me to walk alone!" Henrietta exclaimed. "Merciful powers, have I come to this?"

"There's not the slightest need of your walking alone," Mr. Bantling gaily interposed. "I should be greatly pleased to go with you."

"I simply meant that you'd be late for dinner," Ralph returned. "Those poor ladies may easily believe that we refuse, at the last, to spare you."

"You had better have a hansom, Henrietta," said Isabel.

"I'll get you a hansom if you'll trust me," Mr. Bantling went on. "We might walk a little till we meet one."

"I don't see why I shouldn't trust him, do *you?*" Henrietta enquired of Isabel.

"I don't see what Mr. Bantling could do to you," Isabel obligingly answered; "but, if you like, we'll walk with you till you find your cab."

"Never mind; we'll go alone. Come on, Mr. Bantling, and take care you get me a good one."

Mr. Bantling promised to do his best, and the two took their departure, leaving the girl and her cousin together in the square, over which a clear September twilight had now begun to gather. It was perfectly still; the wide quadrangle of dusky houses showed lights in none of the windows, where the shutters and blinds were closed; the pavements were a vacant expanse, and, putting aside two small children from a neighbouring slum, who, attracted by symptoms of abnormal animation in the interior, poked their faces between the rusty rails of the enclosure, the most vivid object within sight was the big red pillar-post on the southeast corner.

"Henrietta will ask him to get into the cab and go with her to Jermyn Street," Ralph observed. He always spoke of Miss Stackpole as Henrietta.

"Very possibly," said his companion.

"Or rather, no, she won't," he went on. "But Bantling will ask leave to get in."

"Very likely again. I'm very glad they're such good friends."

8. A fashionable shopping street—both historically and currently—parallel to and just south of Piccadilly.

"She has made a conquest. He thinks her a brilliant woman. It may go far," said Ralph.

Isabel was briefly silent. "I call Henrietta a very brilliant woman, but I don't think it will go far. They would never really know each other. He has not the least idea what she really is, and she has no just comprehension of Mr. Bantling."

"There's no more usual basis of union than a mutual misunderstanding. But it ought not to be so difficult to understand Bob Bantling," Ralph added. "He is a very simple organism."

"Yes, but Henrietta's a simpler one still. And, pray, what am I to do?" Isabel asked, looking about her through the fading light, in which the limited land-scape-gardening of the square took on a large and effective appearance. "I don't imagine that you'll propose that you and I, for our amusement, shall drive about London in a hansom."

"There's no reason we shouldn't stay here—if you don't dislike it. It's very warm; there will be half an hour yet before dark; and if you permit it I'll light a cigarette."

"You may do what you please," said Isabel, "if you'll amuse me till seven o'clock. I propose at that hour to go back and partake of a simple and solitary repast—two poached eggs and a muffin—at Pratt's Hotel."

"Mayn't I dine with you?" Ralph asked.

"No, you'll dine at your club."

They had wandered back to their chairs in the centre of the square again, and Ralph had lighted his cigarette. It would have given him extreme pleasure to be present in person at the modest little feast she had sketched; but in default of this he liked even being forbidden. For the moment, however, he liked immensely being alone with her, in the thickening dusk, in the centre of the multitudinous town; it made her seem to depend upon him and to be in his power. This power he could exert but vaguely; the best exercise of it was to accept her decisions submissively—which indeed there was already an emotion in doing. "Why won't you let me dine with you?" he demanded after a pause.

"Because I don't care for it."

"I suppose you're tired of me."

"I shall be an hour hence. You see I have the gift of foreknowledge."

"Oh, I shall be delightful meanwhile," said Ralph. But he said nothing more, and as she made no rejoinder they sat some time in a stillness which seemed to contradict his promise of entertainment. It seemed to him she was preoccupied, and he wondered what she was thinking about; there were two or three very possible subjects. At last he spoke again. "Is your objection to my society this evening caused by your expectation of another visitor?"

She turned her head with a glance of her clear, fair eyes. "Another visitor? What visitor should I have?"

He had none to suggest; which made his question seem to himself silly as well as brutal. "You've a great many friends that I don't know. You've a whole past from which I was perversely excluded."

"You were reserved for my future. You must remember that my past is over there across the water. There's none of it here in London."

"Very good, then, since your future is seated beside you. Capital thing to have your future so handy." And Ralph lighted another cigarette and reflected that Isabel probably meant she had received news that Mr. Caspar Goodwood had crossed to Paris. After he had lighted his cigarette he puffed it a while, and then he resumed. "I promised just now to be very amusing; but you see I don't come up to the mark, and the fact is there's a good deal of temerity in one's undertaking to amuse a person like you. What do you care for my feeble attempts? You've grand ideas—you've a high standard in such matters. I ought at least to bring in a band of music or a company of mountebanks."

"One mountebank's enough, and you do very well. Pray go on, and in another ten minutes I shall begin to laugh."

"I assure you I'm very serious," said Ralph. "You do really ask a great deal."

"I don't know what you mean. I ask nothing!"

"You accept nothing," said Ralph. She coloured, and now suddenly it seemed to her that she guessed his meaning. But why should he speak to her of such things? He hesitated a little and then he continued: "There's something I should like very much to say to you. It's a question I wish to ask. It seems to me I've a right to ask it, because I've a kind of interest in the answer."

"Ask what you will," Isabel replied gently, "and I'll try to satisfy you."

"Well then, I hope you won't mind my saying that Warburton has told me of something that has passed between you."

Isabel suppressed a start; she sat looking at her open fan. "Very good; I suppose it was natural he should tell you."

"I have his leave to let you know he has done so. He has some hope still," said Ralph.

"Still?"

"He had it a few days ago."

"I don't believe he has any now," said the girl.

"I'm very sorry for him then; he's such an honest man."

"Pray, did he ask you to talk to me?"

"No, not that. But he told me because he couldn't help it. We're old friends, and he was greatly disappointed. He sent me a line asking me to come and see him, and I drove over to Lockleigh the day before he and his sister lunched with us. He was very heavy-hearted; he had just got a letter from you."

"Did he show you the letter?" asked Isabel with momentary loftiness.

"By no means. But he told me it was a neat refusal. I was very sorry for him," Ralph repeated.

For some moments Isabel said nothing; then at last, "Do you know how often he had seen me?" she enquired. "Five or six times."

"That's to your glory."

"It's not for that I say it."

"What then do you say it for? Not to prove that poor Warburton's state of mind's superficial, because I'm pretty sure you don't think that."

Isabel certainly was unable to say she thought it; but presently she said something else. "If you've not been requested by Lord Warburton to argue with me, then you're doing it disinterestedly—or for the love of argument."

"I've no wish to argue with you at all. I only wish to leave you alone. I'm simply greatly interested in your own sentiments."

"I'm greatly obliged to you!" cried Isabel with a slightly nervous laugh. "Of course you mean that I'm meddling in what doesn't concern me. But why shouldn't I speak to you of this matter without annoying you or embarrassing myself? What's the use of being your cousin if I can't have a few privileges? What's the use of adoring you without hope of a reward if I can't have a few compensations? What's the use of being ill and disabled and restricted to mere spectatorship at the game of life if I really can't see the show when I've paid so much for my ticket? Tell me this," Ralph went on while she listened to him with quickened attention. "What had you in mind when you refused Lord Warburton?"

"What had I in mind?"

"What was the logic—the view of your situation—that dictated so remarkable an act?"

"I didn't wish to marry him—if that's logic."

"No, that's not logic—and I knew that before. It's really nothing, you know. What was it you *said* to yourself? You certainly said more than that."

Isabel reflected a moment, then answered with a question of her own. "Why do you call it a remarkable act? That's what your mother thinks too."

"Warburton's such a thorough good sort; as a man, I consider he has hardly a fault. And then he's what they call here no end of a swell. He has immense possessions, and his wife would be thought a superior being. He unites the intrinsic and the extrinsic advantages."

Isabel watched her cousin to see how far he would go. "I refused him because he was too perfect then. I'm not perfect myself, and he's too good for me. Besides, his perfection would irritate me."

"That's ingenious rather than candid," said Ralph. "As a fact you think nothing in the world too perfect for you."

"Do you think I'm so good?"

"No, but you're exacting, all the same, without the excuse of thinking yourself good. Nineteen women out of twenty, however, even of the most exacting sort, would have managed to do with Warburton. Perhaps you don't know how he has been stalked."

"I don't wish to know. But it seems to me," said Isabel, "that one day when we talked of him you mentioned odd things in him."

Ralph smokingly considered. "I hope that what I said then had no weight with you; for they were not faults, the things I spoke of: they were simply peculiarities of his position. If I had known he wished to marry you I'd never have alluded to them. I think I said that as regards that position he was rather a sceptic. It would have been in your power to make him a believer."

"I think not. I don't understand the matter, and I'm not conscious of any mission of that sort. You're evidently disappointed." Isabel added, looking at her cousin with rueful gentleness. "You'd have liked me to make such a marriage."

"Not in the least. I'm absolutely without a wish on the subject. I don't pretend to advise you, and I content myself with watching you—with the deepest interest."

She gave rather a conscious sigh. "I wish I could be as interesting to myself as I am to you!"

"There you're not candid again; you're extremely interesting to yourself. Do you know, however," said Ralph, "that if you've really given Warburton his final answer I'm rather glad it has been what it was. I don't mean I'm glad for you, and still less of course for him. I'm glad for myself."

"Are *you* thinking of proposing to me?"

"By no means. From the point of view I speak of that would be fatal; I should kill the goose that supplies me with the material of my inimitable omelettes. I use that animal as the symbol of my insane illusions. What I mean is that I shall have the thrill of seeing what a young lady does who won't marry Lord Warburton."

"That's what your mother counts upon too," said Isabel.

"Ah, there will be plenty of spectators! We shall hang on the rest of your career. I shall not see all of it, but I shall probably see the most interesting years. Of course if you were to marry our friend you'd still have a career—a very decent, in fact a very brilliant one. But relatively speaking it would be a little prosaic. It would be definitely marked out in advance; it would be wanting in the unexpected. You know I'm extremely fond of the unexpected, and now that you've kept the game in your hands I depend on your giving us some grand example of it."

"I don't understand you very well," said Isabel, "but I do so well enough to be able to say that if you look for grand examples of anything from me I shall disappoint you."

"You'll do so only by disappointing yourself—and that will go hard with you!"

To this she made no direct reply; there was an amount of truth in it that would bear consideration. At last she said abruptly: "I don't see what harm there is in my wishing not to tie myself. I don't want to begin life by marrying. There are other things a woman can do."

"There's nothing she can do so well. But you're of course so many-sided."

"If one's two-sided it's enough," said Isabel.

"You're the most charming of polygons!" her companion broke out. At a glance from his companion, however, he became grave, and to prove it went on: "You want to see life—you'll be hanged if you don't, as the young men say."

"I don't think I want to see it as the young men want to see it. But I do want to look about me."

"You want to drain the cup of experience."

"No, I don't wish to touch the cup of experience. It's a poisoned drink! I only want to see for myself."

"You want to see, but not to feel," Ralph remarked.

"I don't think that if one's a sentient being one can make the distinction. I'm a good deal like Henrietta. The other day when I asked her if she wished to marry she said: 'Not till I've seen Europe!' I too don't wish to marry till I've seen Europe."

"You evidently expect a crowned head will be struck with you."

"No, that would be worse than marrying Lord Warburton. But it's getting very dark," Isabel continued, "and I must go home." She rose from her place, but Ralph only sat still and looked at her. As he remained there she stopped, and they exchanged a gaze that was full on either side, but especially on Ralph's, of utterances too vague for words.

"You've answered my question," he said at last. "You've told me what I wanted. I'm greatly obliged to you."

"It seems to me I've told you very little."

"You've told me the great thing: that the world interests you and that you want to throw yourself into it."

Her silvery eyes shone a moment in the dusk. "I never said that."

"I think you meant it. Don't repudiate it. It's so fine!"

"I don't know what you're trying to fasten upon me, for I'm not in the least an adventurous spirit. Women are not like men."

Ralph slowly rose from his seat and they walked together to the gate of the square. "No," he said; "women rarely boast of their courage. Men do so with a certain frequency."

"Men have it to boast of!"

"Women have it too. You've a great deal."

"Enough to go home in a cab to Pratt's Hotel, but not more."

Ralph unlocked the gate, and after they had passed out he fastened it. "We'll find your cab," he said; and as they turned toward a neighbouring street in which this quest might avail he asked her again if he mightn't see her safely to the inn.

"By no means," she answered; "you're very tired; you must go home and go to bed."

The cab was found, and he helped her into it, standing a moment at the door. "When people forget I'm a poor creature I'm often incommoded," he said. "But it's worse when they remember it!"

Chapter XVI

She had had no hidden motive in wishing him not to take her home; it simply struck her that for some days past she had consumed an inordinate quantity of his time, and the independent spirit of the American girl whom extravagance of aid places in an attitude that she ends by finding "affected" had made her decide that for these few hours she must suffice to herself. She had moreover a great fondness for intervals of solitude, which since her arrival in England had been but meagrely met. It was a luxury she could always command at home and she had wittingly missed it. That evening, however, an incident occurred which—had there been a critic to note it—would have taken all colour from the theory that the wish to be quite by herself had caused her to dispense with her cousin's attendance. Seated toward nine o'clock in the dim illumination of Pratt's Hotel and trying with the aid of two tall candles to lose herself in a volume she had brought from Gardencourt, she succeeded only to the extent of reading other words than those printed on the page—words that Ralph had spoken to her that afternoon. Suddenly the well-muffled knuckle of the waiter was applied to the door, which presently gave way to his exhibition, even as a glorious trophy, of the card of a visitor. When this memento had offered to her fixed sight the name of Mr. Caspar Goodwood she let the man stand before her without signifying her wishes.

"Shall I show the gentleman up, ma'am?" he asked with a slightly encouraging inflexion.

Isabel hesitated still and while she hesitated glanced at the mirror. "He may come in," she said at last; and waited for him not so much smoothing her hair as girding her spirit.

Caspar Goodwood was accordingly the next moment shaking hands with her, but saying nothing till the servant had left the room. "Why didn't you answer my letter?" he then asked in a quick, full, slightly peremptory tone—the tone of a man whose questions were habitually pointed and who was capable of much insistence.

She answered by a ready question, "How did you know I was here?"

"Miss Stackpole let me know," said Caspar Goodwood. "She told me you would probably be at home alone this evening and would be willing to see me."

"Where did she see you—to tell you that?"

"She didn't see me; she wrote to me."

Isabel was silent; neither had sat down; they stood there with an air of defiance, or at least of contention. "Henrietta never told me she was writing to you," she said at last. "This is not kind of her."

"Is it so disagreeable to you to see me?" asked the young man.

"I didn't expect it. I don't like such surprises."

"But you knew I was in town; it was natural we should meet."

"Do you call this meeting? I hoped I shouldn't see you. In so big a place as London it seemed very possible."

"It was apparently repugnant to you even to write to me," her visitor went on.

Isabel made no reply; the sense of Henrietta Stackpole's treachery, as she momentarily qualified it, was strong within her. "Henrietta's certainly not a model of all the delicacies!" she exclaimed with bitterness. "It was a great liberty to take."

"I suppose I'm not a model either—of those virtues or of any others. The fault's mine as much as hers."

As Isabel looked at him it seemed to her that his jaw had never been more square. This might have displeased her, but she took a different turn. "No, it's not your fault so much as hers. What you've done was inevitable, I suppose, for *you*."

"It was indeed!" cried Caspar Goodwood with a voluntary laugh. "And now that I've come, at any rate, mayn't I stay?"

"You may sit down, certainly."

She went back to her chair again, while her visitor took the first place that offered, in the manner of a man accustomed to pay little thought to that sort of furtherance. "I've been hoping every day for an answer to my letter. You might have written me a few lines."

"It wasn't the trouble of writing that prevented me; I could as easily have written you four pages as one. But my silence was an intention," Isabel said. "I thought it the best thing."

He sat with eyes fixed on hers while she spoke; then he lowered them and attached them to a spot in the carpet as if he were making a strong effort to say nothing but what he ought. He was a strong man in the wrong, and he was acute enough to see that an uncompromising exhibition of his strength would only throw the falsity of his position into relief. Isabel was not incapable of tasting any advantage of position over a person of this quality, and though little desirous to flaunt it in his face she could enjoy being able to say "You know you oughtn't to have written to me yourself!" and to say it with an air of triumph.

Caspar Goodwood raised his eyes to her own again; they seemed to shine through a vizard of a helmet. He had a strong sense of justice and was ready any day in the year—over and above this—to argue the question of his rights. "You said you hoped never to hear from me again; I know that. But I never accepted any such rule as my own. I warned you that you should hear very soon."

"I didn't say I hoped *never* to hear from you," said Isabel.

"Not for five years then; for ten years; twenty years. It's the same thing."

"Do you find it so? It seems to me there's a great difference. I can imagine that at the end of ten years we might have a very pleasant correspondence. I shall have matured my epistolary style."

She looked away while she spoke these words, knowing them of so much less earnest a cast than the countenance of her listener. Her eyes, however, at last came back to him, just as he said very irrelevantly: "Are you enjoying your visit to your uncle?"

"Very much indeed." She dropped, but then she broke out. "What good do you expect to get by insisting?"

"The good of not losing you."

"You've no right to talk of losing what's not yours. And even from your own point of view," Isabel added, "You ought to know when to let one alone."

"I disgust you very much," said Caspar Goodwood gloomily; not as if to provoke her to compassion for a man conscious of this blighting fact, but as if to set it well before himself, so that he might endeavour to act with his eyes on it.

"Yes, you don't at all delight me, you don't fit in, not in any way, just now, and the worst is that your putting it to the proof in this manner is quite unnecessary." It wasn't certainly as if his nature had been soft, so that pin-pricks would draw blood from it; and from the first of her acquaintance with him, and of her having to defend herself against a certain air that he had of knowing better what was good for her than she knew herself, she had recognised the fact that perfect frankness was her best weapon. To attempt to spare his sensibility or to escape from him edgewise, as one might do from a man who had barred the way less sturdily— this, in dealing with Caspar Goodwood, who would grasp at everything of every sort that one might give him, was wasted agility. It was not that he had not susceptibilities, but his passive surface, as well as his active, was large and hard, and he might always be trusted to dress his wounds, so far as they required it, himself. She came back, even for her measure of possible pangs and aches in him, to her old sense that he was naturally plated and steeled, armed essentially for aggression.

"I can't reconcile myself to that," he simply said. There was a dangerous liberality about it; for she felt how open it was to him to make the point that he had not always disgusted her.

"I can't reconcile myself to it either, and it's not the state of things that ought to exist between us. If you'd only try to banish me from your mind for a few months we should be on good terms again."

"I see. If I should cease to think of you at all for a prescribed time, I should find I could keep it up indefinitely."

"Indefinitely is more than I ask. It's more even than I should like."

"You know that what you ask is impossible," said the young man, taking his adjective for granted in a manner she found irritating.

"Aren't you capable of making a calculated effort?" she demanded. "You're strong for everything else; why shouldn't you be strong for that?"

"An effort calculated for what?" And then as she hung fire, "I'm capable of nothing with regard to you," he went on, "but just of being infernally in love with you. If one's strong one loves only the more strongly."

"There's a good deal in that;" and indeed our young lady felt the force of it—felt it thrown off, into the vast of truth and poetry, as practically a bait to her imagination. But she promptly came round. "Think of me or not, as you find most possible; only leave me alone."

"Until when?"

"Well, for a year or two."

"Which do you mean? Between one year and two there's all the difference in the world."

"Call it two then," said Isabel with a studied effect of eagerness.

"And what shall I gain by that?" her friend asked with no sign of wincing.

"You'll have obliged me greatly."

"And what will be my reward?"

"Do you need a reward for an act of generosity?"

"Yes, when it involves a great sacrifice."

"There's no generosity without some sacrifice. Men don't understand such things. If you make the sacrifice you'll have all my admiration."

"I don't care a cent for your admiration—not one straw, with nothing to show for it. When will you marry me? That's the only question."

"Never—if you go on making me feel only as I feel at present."

"What do I gain then by not trying to make you feel otherwise?"

"You'll gain quite as much as by worrying me to death!" Caspar Goodwood bent his eyes again and gazed a while into the crown of his hat. A deep flush overspread his face; she could see her sharpness had at last penetrated. This immediately had a value—classic, romantic, redeeming, what did she know?—for her; "the strong man in pain" was one of the categories of the human appeal, little charm as he might exert in the given case. "Why do you make me say such things to you?" she cried in a trembling voice. "I only want to be gentle—to be thoroughly kind. It's not delightful to me to feel people care for me and yet to have to try and reason them out of it. I think others also ought to be considerate; we have each to judge for ourselves. I know you're considerate, as much as you can be; you've good reasons for what you do. But I really don't want to marry, or to talk about it at all now. I shall probably never do it—no, never. I've a perfect right to feel that way, and it's no kindness to a woman to press her so hard, to urge her against her will. If I give you pain I can only say I'm very sorry. It's not my fault; I can't marry you simply to please you. I won't say that I shall always remain your friend, because when women say that, in these situations, it passes, I believe, for a sort of mockery. But try me some day."

Caspar Goodwood, during this speech, had kept his eyes fixed upon the name of his hatter, and it was not until some time after she had ceased speaking that he raised them. When he did so the sight of a rosy, lovely eagerness in Isabel's face threw some confusion into his attempt to analyse her words. "I'll go home—I'll go to-morrow—I'll leave you alone," he brought out at last. "Only," he heavily said, "I hate to lose sight of you!"

"Never fear. I shall do no harm."

"You'll marry some one else, as sure as I sit here," Caspar Goodwood declared.

"Do you think that a generous charge?"

"Why not? Plenty of men will try to make you."

"I told you just now that I don't wish to marry and that I almost certainly never shall."

"I know you did, and I like your 'almost certainly'! I put no faith in what you say."

"Thank you very much. Do you accuse me of lying to shake you off? You say very delicate things."

"Why should I not say that? You've given me no pledge of anything at all."

"No, that's all that would be wanting!"

"You may perhaps even believe you're safe—from wishing to be. But you're not," the young man went on as if preparing himself for the worst.

"Very well then. We'll put it that I'm not safe. Have it as you please."

"I don't know, however," said Caspar Goodwood, "that my keeping you in sight would prevent it."

"Don't you indeed? I'm after all very much afraid of you. Do you think I'm so very easily pleased?" she asked suddenly, changing her tone.

"No—I don't; I shall try to console myself with that. But there are a certain number of very dazzling men in the world, no doubt; and if there were only one it would be enough. The most dazzling of all will make straight for you. You'll be sure to take no one who isn't dazzling."

"If you mean by dazzling brilliantly clever," Isabel said—"and I can't imagine what else you mean—I don't need the aid of a clever man to teach me how to live. I can find it out for myself."

"Find out how to live alone? I wish that, when you have, you'd teach *me!*"

She looked at him a moment; then with a quick smile, "Oh, *you* ought to marry!" she said.

He might be pardoned if for an instant this exclamation seemed to him to sound the infernal note, and it is not on record that her motive for discharging such a shaft had been of the clearest. He oughtn't to stride about lean and hungry, however—she certainly felt *that* for him. "God forgive you!" he murmured between his teeth as he turned away.

Her accent had put her slightly in the wrong, and after a moment she felt the need to right herself. The easiest way to do it was to place him where she had been. "You do me great injustice—you say what you don't know!" she broke out. "I shouldn't be an easy victim—I've proved it."

"Oh, to me, perfectly."

"I've proved it to others as well." And she paused a moment. "I refused a proposal of marriage last week; what they call—no doubt—a dazzling one."

"I'm very glad to hear it," said the young man gravely.

"It was a proposal many girls would have accepted; it had everything to recommend it." Isabel had not proposed to herself to tell this story, but, now she had begun, the satisfaction of speaking it out and doing herself justice took possession of her. "I was offered a great position and a great fortune—by a person whom I like extremely."

Caspar watched her with intense interest. "Is he an Englishman?"

"He's an English nobleman," said Isabel.

Her visitor received this announcement at first in silence, but at last said: "I'm glad he's disappointed."

"Well then, as you have companions in misfortune, make the best of it."

"I don't call him a companion," said Caspar grimly.

"Why not—since I declined his offer absolutely?"

"That doesn't make him my companion. Besides, he's an Englishman."

"And pray isn't an Englishman a human being?" Isabel asked.

"Oh, those people? They're not of *my* humanity, and I don't care what becomes of them."

"You're very angry," said the girl. "We've discussed this matter quite enough."

"Oh yes, I'm very angry. I plead guilty to that!"

She turned away from him, walked to the open window and stood a moment looking into the dusky void of the street, where a turbid gaslight alone represented social animation. For some time neither of these young persons spoke; Caspar lingered near the chimney-piece with eyes gloomily attached. She had virtually requested him to go—he knew that; but at the risk of making himself odious he kept his ground. She was too nursed a need to be easily renounced, and he had crossed the sea all to wring from her some scrap of a vow. Presently she left the window and stood again before him. "You do me very little justice—after my telling you what I told you just now. I'm sorry I told you—since it matters so little to you."

"Ah," cried the young man, "if you were thinking of *me* when you did it!" And then he paused with the fear that she might contradict so happy a thought.

"I was thinking of you a little," said Isabel.

"A little? I don't understand. If the knowledge of what I feel for you had any weight with you at all, calling it a 'little' is a poor account of it."

Isabel shook her head as if to carry off a blunder. "I've refused a most kind, noble gentleman. Make the most of that."

"I thank you then," said Caspar Goodwood gravely. "I thank you immensely."

"And now you had better go home."

"May I not see you again?" he asked.

"I think it's better not. You'll be sure to talk of this, and you see it leads to nothing."

"I promise you not to say a word that will annoy you."

Isabel reflected and then answered: "I return in a day or two to my uncle's, and I can't propose to you to come there. It would be too inconsistent."

Caspar Goodwood, on his side, considered. "You must do me justice too. I received an invitation to your uncle's more than a week ago, and I declined it."

She betrayed surprise. "From whom was your invitation?"

"From Mr. Ralph Touchett, whom I suppose to be your cousin. I declined it because I had not your authorisation to accept it. The suggestion that Mr. Touchett should invite me appeared to have come from Miss Stackpole."

"It certainly never did from me. Henrietta really goes very far," Isabel added.

"Don't be too hard on her—that touches *me*."

"No; if you declined you did quite right, and I thank you for it." And she gave a little shudder of dismay at the thought that Lord Warburton and Mr. Goodwood might have met at Gardencourt: it would have been so awkward for Lord Warburton.

"When you leave your uncle where do you go?" her companion asked.

"I go abroad with my aunt—to Florence and other places."

The serenity of this announcement struck a chill to the young man's heart; he seemed to see her whirled away into circles from which he was inexorably excluded. Nevertheless he went on quickly with his questions. "And when shall you come back to America?"

"Perhaps not for a long time. I'm very happy here."

"Do you mean to give up your country?"

"Don't be an infant!"

"Well, you'll be out of my sight indeed!" said Caspar Goodwood.

"I don't know," she answered rather grandly. "The world—with all these places so arranged and so touching each other—comes to strike one as rather small."

"It's a sight too big for *me*!" Caspar exclaimed with a simplicity our young lady might have found touching if her face had not been set against concessions.

This attitude was part of a system, a theory, that she had lately embraced, and to be thorough she said after a moment: "Don't think me unkind if I say it's just *that*—being out of your sight—that I like. If you were in the same place I should feel you were watching me, and I don't like that—I like my liberty too much. If there's a thing in the world I'm fond of," she went on with a slight recurrence of grandeur, "it's my personal independence."

But whatever there might be of the too superior in this speech moved Caspar Goodwood's admiration; there was nothing he winced at in the large air of it. He had never supposed she hadn't wings and the need of beautiful free movements—he wasn't, with his own long arms and strides, afraid of any force in her. Isabel's words, if they had been meant to shock him, failed of the mark and only made him smile with the sense that here was common ground. "Who would wish less to curtail your liberty than I? What can give me greater pleasure than to see you perfectly independent—doing whatever you like? It's to make you independent that I want to marry you."

"That's a beautiful sophism," said the girl with a smile more beautiful still.

"An unmarried woman—a girl of your age—isn't independent. There are all sorts of things she can't do. She's hampered at every step."

"That's as she looks at the question." Isabel answered with much spirit. "I'm not in my first youth—I can do what I choose—I belong quite to the independent class. I've neither father nor mother; I'm poor and of a serious disposition; I'm not pretty. I therefore am not bound to be timid and conventional; indeed I can't afford such luxuries. Besides, I try to judge things for myself; to judge wrong, I think, is more honourable than not to judge at all. I don't wish to be a mere sheep in the flock; I wish to choose my fate and know something of human affairs beyond what other people think it compatible with propriety to tell me." She paused a moment, but not long enough for her companion to reply. He was apparently on the point of doing so when she went on: "Let me say this to you, Mr. Good-wood. You're so kind as to speak of being afraid of my marrying. If you should hear a rumour that I'm on the point of doing so—girls are liable to have such things said about them—remember what I have told you about my love of liberty and venture to doubt it."

There was something passionately positive in the tone in which she gave him this advice, and he saw a shining candour in her eyes that helped him to believe her. On the whole he felt reassured, and you might have per-ceived it by the manner in which he said, quite eagerly: "You want simply to travel for two years? I'm quite willing to wait two years, and you may do what you like in the interval. If that's all you want, pray say so. I don't want you to be conventional; do I strike you as conventional myself? Do you want to improve your mind? Your mind's quite good enough for me; but if it interests you to wander about a while and see different countries I shall be delighted to help you in any way in my power."

"You're very generous; that's nothing new to me. The best way to help me will be to put as many hundred miles of sea between us as possible."

"One would think you were going to commit some atrocity!" said Cas-par Goodwood.

"Perhaps I am. I wish to be free even to do that if the fancy takes me."

"Well then," he said slowly, "I'll go home." And he put out his hand, try-ing to look contented and confident.

Isabel's confidence in him, however, was greater than any he could feel in her. Not that he thought her capable of committing an atrocity; but, turn it over as he would, there was something ominous in the way she reserved her option. As she took his hand she felt a great respect for him; she knew how much he cared for her and she thought him magnanimous. They stood so for a moment, looking at each other, united by a hand-clasp which was not merely passive on her side. "That's right," she said very kindly, almost tenderly. "You'll lose nothing by being a reasonable man."

"But I'll come back, wherever you are, two years hence," he returned with characteristic grimness.

We have seen that our young lady was inconsequent, and at this she suddenly changed her note. "Ah, remember, I promise nothing—absolutely nothing!" Then more softly, as if to help him to leave her: "And remember too that I shall not be an easy victim!"

"You'll get very sick of your independence."

"Perhaps I shall; it's even very probable. When that day comes I shall be very glad to see you."

She had laid her hand on the knob of the door that led into her room, and she waited a moment to see whether her visitor would not take his departure. But he appeared unable to move; there was still an immense unwillingness in his attitude and a sore remonstrance in his eyes. "I must leave you now," said Isabel; and she opened the door and passed into the other room.

The apartment was dark, but the darkness was tempered by a vague radiance sent up through the window from the court of the hotel, and Isa-bel could make out the masses of the furniture, the dim shining of the mirror and the looming of the big four-posted bed. She stood still a moment, listening, and at last she heard Caspar Goodwood walk out of the sitting-room and close the door behind him. She stood still a little longer, and then, by an irresistible impulse, dropped on her knees before her bed and hid her face in her arms.

Chapter XVII

She was not praying; she was trembling—trembling all over. Vibration was easy to her, was in fact too constant with her, and she found herself now humming like a smitten harp. She only asked, however, to put on the cover, to case herself again in brown holland, but she wished to resist her excitement, and the attitude of devotion, which she kept for some time, seemed to help her to be still. She intensely rejoiced that Caspar Goodwood was gone; there was something in having thus got rid of him that was like the payment, for a stamped receipt, of some debt too long on her mind. As she felt the glad relief she bowed her head a little lower; the sense was there, throbbing in her heart; it was part of her emotion, but it was a thing to be ashamed of—it was profane and out of place. It was not for some ten minutes that she rose from her knees, and even when she came back to the sitting-room her tremor had not quite subsided. It had had, verily, two causes: part of it was to be accounted for by her long discussion with Mr. Goodwood, but it might be feared that the rest was simply the enjoyment she found in the exercise of her power. She sat down in the same chair again and took up her book, but without going through the form of opening the volume. She leaned back, with that low, soft, aspiring murmur with which she often uttered her response to accidents of which the brighter side was not superficially obvious, and yielded to the satisfaction of having refused two ardent suitors in a fortnight. That love of liberty of which she had given Caspar Goodwood so bold a sketch was as yet almost exclusively theoretic; she had not been able to indulge it on a large scale. But it appeared to her she had done something; she had tasted of the delight, if not of battle, at least of victory; she had done what was truest to her plan. In the glow of this consciousness the image of Mr. Goodwood taking his sad walk homeward through the dingy town presented itself with a certain reproachful force; so that, as at the same moment the door of the room was opened, she rose with an apprehension that he had come back. But it was only Henrietta Stackpole returning from her dinner.

Miss Stackpole immediately saw that our young lady had been "through" something, and indeed the discovery demanded no great penetration. She went straight up to her friend, who received her without a greeting. Isabel's elation in having sent Caspar Goodwood back to America presupposed her being in a manner glad he had come to see her; but at the same time she perfectly remembered Henrietta had had no right to set a trap for her. "Has he been here, dear?" the latter yearningly asked.

Isabel turned away and for some moments answered nothing. "You acted very wrongly," she declared at last.

"I acted for the best. I only hope you acted as well."

"You're not the judge. I can't trust you," said Isabel.

This declaration was unflattering, but Henrietta was much too unselfish to heed the charge it conveyed; she cared only for what it intimated with regard to her friend. "Isabel Archer," she observed with equal abruptness and solemnity, "if you marry one of these people I'll never speak to you again!"

"Before making so terrible a threat you had better wait till I'm asked," Isabel replied. Never having said a word to Miss Stackpole about Lord Warburton's overtures, she had now no impulse whatever to justify herself to Henrietta by telling her that she had refused that nobleman.

"Oh, you'll be asked quick enough, once you get off on the Continent. Annie Climber was asked three times in Italy—poor plain little Annie."

"Well, if Annie Climber wasn't captured why should I be?"

"I don't believe Annie was pressed; but you'll be."

"That's a flattering conviction," said Isabel without alarm.

"I don't flatter you, Isabel, I tell you the truth!" cried her friend. "I hope you don't mean to tell me that you didn't give Mr. Goodwood some hope."

"I don't see why I should tell you anything; as I said to you just now, I can't trust you. But since you're so much interested in Mr. Goodwood I won't conceal from you that he returns immediately to America."

"You don't mean to say you've sent him off?" Henrietta almost shrieked.

"I asked him to leave me alone; and I ask you the same, Henrietta." Miss Stackpole glittered for an instant with dismay, and then passed to the mirror over the chimney-piece and took off her bonnet. "I hope you've enjoyed your dinner," Isabel went on.

But her companion was not to be diverted by frivolous propositions. "Do you know where you're going, Isabel Archer?"

"Just now I'm going to bed," said Isabel with persistent frivolity.

"Do you know where you're drifting?" Henrietta pursued, holding out her bonnet delicately.

"No, I haven't the least idea, and I find it very pleasant not to know. A swift carriage, of a dark night, rattling with four horses over roads that one can't see—that's my idea of happiness."

"Mr. Goodwood certainly didn't teach you to say such things as that—like the heroine of an immoral novel,"[1] said Miss Stackpole. "You're drifting to some great mistake."

Isabel was irritated by her friend's interference, yet she still tried to think what truth this declaration could represent. She could think of nothing that diverted her from saying: "You must be very fond of me, Henrietta, to be willing to be so aggressive."

"I love you intensely, Isabel," said Miss Stackpole with feeling.

"Well, if you love me intensely let me as intensely alone. I asked that of Mr. Goodwood, and I must also ask it of you."

"Take care you're not let alone too much."

"That's what Mr. Goodwood said to me. I told him I must take the risks."

"You're a creature of risks—you make me shudder!" cried Henrietta. "When does Mr. Goodwood return to America?"

"I don't know—he didn't tell me."

"Perhaps you didn't enquire," said Henrietta with the note of righteous irony.

---

1. Isabel's account of this imaginary carriage ride is in fact a close paraphrase of a sentence in book II, chapter XII, of Gustave Flaubert's *Madame Bovary* (1857), that epitome of nineteenth-century immorality; in Eleanor Marx's 1886 translation, Emma Bovary dreams that to "the gallop of four horses she was carried away for a week towards a new land, whence they would return no more."

"I gave him too little satisfaction to have the right to ask questions of him."

This assertion seemed to Miss Stackpole for a moment to bid defiance to comment; but at last she exclaimed: "Well, Isabel, if I didn't know you I might think you were heartless!"

"Take care," said Isabel; "you're spoiling me."

"I'm afraid I've done that already. I hope, at least," Miss Stackpole added, "that he may cross with Annie Climber!"

Isabel learned from her the next morning that she had determined not to return to Gardencourt (where old Mr. Touchett had promised her a renewed welcome), but to await in London the arrival of the invitation that Mr. Bantling had promised her from his sister Lady Pensil. Miss Stackpole related very freely her conversation with Ralph Touchett's sociable friend and declared to Isabel that she really believed she had now got hold of something that would lead to something. On the receipt of Lady Pensil's letter—Mr. Bantling had virtually guaranteed the arrival of this document—she would immediately depart for Bedfordshire, and if Isabel cared to look out for her impressions in the *Interviewer* she would certainly find them. Henrietta was evidently going to see something of the inner life this time.

"Do you know where you're drifting, Henrietta Stackpole?" Isabel asked, imitating the tone in which her friend had spoken the night before.

"I'm drifting to a big position—that of the Queen of American Journalism. If my next letter isn't copied all over the West I'll swallow my penwiper!"

She had arranged with her friend Miss Annie Climber, the young lady of the continental offers, that they should go together to make those purchases which were to constitute Miss Climber's farewell to a hemisphere in which she at least had been appreciated; and she presently repaired to Jermyn Street to pick up her companion. Shortly after her departure Ralph Touchett was announced, and as soon as he came in Isabel saw he had something on his mind. He very soon took his cousin into his confidence. He had received from his mother a telegram to the effect that his father had had a sharp attack of his old malady, that she was much alarmed and that she begged he would instantly return to Gardencourt. On this occasion at least Mrs. Touchett's devotion to the electric wire was not open to criticism.

"I've judged it best to see the great doctor, Sir Matthew Hope, first," Ralph said; "by great good luck he's in town. He's to see me at half-past twelve, and I shall make sure of his coming down to Gardencourt—which he will do the more readily as he has already seen my father several times, both there and in London. There's an express at two-forty-five, which I shall take; and you'll come back with me or remain here a few days longer, exactly as you prefer."

"I shall certainly go with you," Isabel returned. "I don't suppose I can be of any use to my uncle, but if he's ill I shall like to be near him."

"I think you're fond of him," said Ralph with a certain shy pleasure in his face. "You appreciate him, which all the world hasn't done. The quality's too fine."

"I quite adore him," Isabel after a moment said.

"That's very well. After his son he's your greatest admirer."

She welcomed this assurance, but she gave secretly a small sigh of relief at the thought that Mr. Touchett was one of those admirers who couldn't propose to marry her. This, however, was not what she spoke; she went on to inform Ralph that there were other reasons for her not remaining in London. She was tired of it and wished to leave it; and then Henrietta was going away—going to stay in Bedfordshire.

"In Bedfordshire?"

"With Lady Pensil, the sister of Mr. Bantling, who has answered for an invitation."

Ralph was feeling anxious, but at this he broke into a laugh. Suddenly, none the less, his gravity returned. "Bantling's a man of courage. But if the invitation should get lost on the way?"

"I thought the British post-office was impeccable."

"The good Homer sometimes nods,"[2] said Ralph. "However," he went on more brightly, "the good Bantling never does, and, whatever happens, he'll take care of Henrietta."

Ralph went to keep his appointment with Sir Mathew Hope, and Isabel made her arrangements for quitting Pratt's Hotel. Her uncle's danger touched her nearly, and while she stood before her open trunk, looking about her vaguely for what she should put into it, the tears suddenly rose to her eyes. It was perhaps for this reason that when Ralph came back at two o'clock to take her to the station she was not yet ready. He found Miss Stackpole, however, in the sitting-room, where she had just risen from her luncheon, and this lady immediately expressed her regret at his father's illness.

"He's a grand old man," she said; "he's faithful to the last. If it's really to be the last—pardon my alluding to it, but you must often have thought of the possibility—I'm sorry that I shall not be at Gardencourt."

"You'll amuse yourself much more in Bedfordshire."

"I shall be sorry to amuse myself at such a time," said Henrietta with much propriety. But she immediately added: "I should like so to commemorate the closing scene."

"My father may live a long time," said Ralph simply. Then, adverting to topics more cheerful, he interrogated Miss Stackpole as to her own future.

Now that Ralph was in trouble she addressed him in a tone of larger allowance and told him that she was much indebted to him for having made her acquainted with Mr. Bantling. "He has told me just the things I want to know," she said; "all the society-items and all about the royal family. I can't make out that what he tells me about the royal family is much to their credit; but he says that's only my peculiar way of looking at it. Well, all I want is that he should give me the facts; I can put them together quick enough, once I've got them." And she added that Mr. Bantling had been so good as to promise to come and take her out that afternoon.

"To take you where?" Ralph ventured to enquire.

"To Buckingham Palace. He's going to show me over it, so that I may get some idea how they live."

"Ah," said Ralph, "we leave you in good hands. The first thing we shall hear is that you're invited to Windsor Castle."

"If they ask me, I shall certainly go. Once I get started I'm not afraid. But for all that," Henrietta added in a moment, "I'm not satisfied; I'm not at peace about Isabel."

---

2. From Horace (65–8 B.C.E.), *Ars Poetica*, 1359; "even the best make mistakes."

"What is her last misdemeanour?"

"Well, I've told you before, and I suppose there's no harm in my going on. I always finish a subject that I take up. Mr. Goodwood was here last night."

Ralph opened his eyes; he even blushed a little—his blush being the sign of an emotion somewhat acute. He remembered that Isabel, in separating from him in Winchester Square, had repudiated his suggestion that her motive in doing so was the expectation of a visitor at Pratt's Hotel, and it was a new pang to him to have to suspect her of duplicity. On the other hand, he quickly said to himself, what concern was it of his that she should have made an appointment with a lover? Had it not been thought graceful in every age that young ladies should make a mystery of such appointments? Ralph gave Miss Stackpole a diplomatic answer. "I should have thought that, with the views you expressed to me the other day, this would satisfy you perfectly."

"That he should come to see her? That was very well, as far as it went. It was a little plot of mine; I let him know that we were in London, and when it had been arranged that I should spend the evening out I sent him a word—the word we just utter to the 'wise.' I hoped he would find her alone; I won't pretend I didn't hope that you'd be out of the way. He came to see her, but he might as well have stayed away."

"Isabel was cruel?"—and Ralph's face lighted with the relief of his cousin's not having shown duplicity.

"I don't exactly know what passed between them. But she gave him no satisfaction—she sent him back to America."

"Poor Mr. Goodwood!" Ralph sighed.

"Her only idea seems to be to get rid of him," Henrietta went on.

"Poor Mr. Goodwood!" Ralph repeated. The exclamation, it must be confessed, was automatic; it failed exactly to express his thoughts, which were taking another line.

"You don't say that as if you felt it. I don't believe you care."

"Ah," said Ralph, "you must remember that I don't know this interesting young man—that I've never seen him."

"Well, I shall see him, and I shall tell him not to give up. If I didn't believe Isabel would come round," Miss Stackpole added—"well, I'd give up myself. I mean I'd give *her* up!"

Chapter XVIII

It had occurred to Ralph that, in the conditions, Isabel's parting with her friend might be of a slightly embarrassed nature, and he went down to the door of the hotel in advance of his cousin, who, after a slight delay, followed with the traces of an unaccepted remonstrance, as he thought, in her eyes. The two made the journey to Gardencourt in almost unbroken silence, and the servant who met them at the station had no better news to give them of Mr. Touchett—a fact which caused Ralph to congratulate himself afresh on Sir Matthew Hope's having promised to come down in the five o'clock train and spend the night. Mrs. Touchett, he learned, on reaching home, had been constantly with the old man and was with him at that moment; and this fact made Ralph say to himself that, after all, what his mother wanted was just easy occasion. The finer natures were those that shone at the larger times. Isabel went to her own room, noting throughout the house that perceptible hush which precedes a crisis. At the end of an hour, however, she came downstairs in search of her aunt, whom she wished to ask about Mr. Touchett. She went into the library, but Mrs. Touchett was not there, and as the weather, which had been damp and chill, was now altogether spoiled, it was not probable she had gone for her usual walk in the grounds. Isabel was on the point of ringing to send a question to her room, when this purpose quickly yielded to an unexpected sound—the sound of low music proceeding apparently from the saloon. She knew her aunt never touched the piano, and the musician was therefore probably Ralph, who played for his own amusement. That he should have resorted to this recreation at the present time indicated apparently that his anxiety about his father had been relieved; so that the girl took her way, almost with restored cheer, toward the source of the harmony. The drawing-room at Gardencourt was an apartment of great distances, and, as the piano was placed at the end of it furthest removed from the door at which she entered, her arrival was not noticed by the person seated before the instrument. This person was neither Ralph nor his mother; it was a lady whom Isabel immediately saw to be a stranger to herself, though her back was presented to the door. This back—an ample and well-dressed one—Isabel viewed for some moments with surprise. The lady was of course a visitor who had arrived during her absence and who had not been mentioned by either of the servants—one of them her aunt's maid—of whom she had had speech since her return. Isabel had already learned, however, with what treasures of reserve the function of receiving orders may be accompanied, and she was particularly conscious of having been treated with dryness by her aunt's maid, through whose hands she had slipped perhaps a little too mistrustfully and with an effect of plumage but the more lustrous. The advent of a guest was in itself far from disconcerting; she had not yet divested herself of a young faith that each new aquaintance would exert some momentous influence on her life. By the time she had made these reflexions she became aware that the lady at the piano played remarkably well. She was playing something of Schubert's—Isabel knew not what, but recognised Schubert[1]— and she touched the piano with a discretion of her own. It showed skill, it showed feeling; Isabel sat down noiselessly on the nearest chair and waited till the end of the piece. When it was finished she felt a strong desire to thank the player, and rose from her seat to do so, while at the same time the stranger turned quickly round, as if but just aware of her presence.

"That's very beautiful, and your playing makes it more beautiful still," said Isabel with all the young radiance with which she usually uttered a truthful rapture.

"You don't think I disturbed Mr. Touchett then?" the musician answered as sweetly as this compliment deserved. "The house is so large and his room so far away that I thought I might venture, especially as I played just—just *du bout des doigts*."[2]

1. The 1881 edition gives the composer as Beethoven, but to the period's taste Franz Schubert (1797–1828) is indeed more in keeping with this character and her gift for the social arts.
2. With the tips of my fingers (French).

"She's a Frenchwoman," Isabel said to herself; "she says that as if she were French." And this supposition made the visitor more interesting to our speculative heroine. "I hope my uncle's doing well," Isabel added. "I should think that to hear such lovely music as that would really make him feel better."

The lady smiled and discriminated. "I'm afraid there are moments in life when even Schubert has nothing to say to us. We must admit, however, that they are our worst."

"I'm not in that state now then," said Isabel. "On the contrary I should be so glad if you would play something more."

"If it will give you pleasure—delighted." And this obliging person took her place again and struck a few chords, while Isabel sat down nearer the instrument. Suddenly the new-comer stopped with her hands on the keys, half-turning and looking over her shoulder. She was forty years old and not pretty, though her expression charmed. "Pardon me," she said; "but are you the niece—the young American?"

"I'm my aunt's niece," Isabel replied with simplicity.

The lady at the piano sat still a moment longer, casting her air of interest over her shoulder. "That's very well; we're compatriots." And then she began to play.

"Ah then she's not French," Isabel murmured; and as the opposite supposition had made her romantic it might have seemed that this revelation would have marked a drop. But such was not the fact; rarer even than to be French seemed it to be American on such interesting terms.

The lady played in the same manner as before, softly and solemnly, and while she played the shadows deepened in the room. The autumn twilight gathered in, and from her place Isabel could see the rain, which had now begun in earnest, washing the cold-looking lawn and the wind shaking the great trees. At last, when the music had ceased, her companion got up and, coming nearer with a smile, before Isabel had time to thank her again, said: "I'm very glad you've come back; I've heard a great deal about you."

Isabel thought her a very attractive person, but nevertheless spoke with a certain abruptness in reply to this speech. "From whom have you heard about me?"

The stranger hesitated a single moment and then, "From your uncle," she answered. "I've been here three days, and the first day he let me come and pay him a visit in his room. Then he talked constantly of you."

"As you didn't know me that must rather have bored you."

"It made me want to know you. All the more that since then—your aunt being so much with Mr. Touchett—I've been quite alone and have got rather tired of my own society. I've not chosen a good moment for my visit."

A servant had come in with lamps and was presently followed by another bearing the tea-tray. On the appearance of this repast Mrs. Touchett had apparently been notified, for she now arrived and addressed herself to the tea-pot. Her greeting to her niece did not differ materially from her manner of raising the lid of this receptacle in order to glance at the contents: in neither act was it becoming to make a show of avidity. Questioned about her husband she was unable to say he was better; but the local doctor was with him, and much light was expected from this gentleman's consultation with Sir Matthew Hope.

"I suppose you two ladies have made acquaintance," she pursued. "If you haven't I recommend you to do so; for so long as we continue—Ralph and I—to cluster about Mr. Touchett's bed you're not likely to have much society but each other."

"I know nothing about you but that you're a great musician," Isabel said to the visitor.

"There's a good deal more than that to know," Mrs. Touchett affirmed in her little dry tone.

"A very little of it, I am sure, will content Miss Archer!" the lady exclaimed with a light laugh. "I'm an old friend of your aunt's. I've lived much in Florence. I'm Madame Merle." She made this last announcement as if she were referring to a person of tolerably distinct identity. For Isabel, however, it represented little; she could only continue to feel that Madame Merle had as charming a manner as any she had ever encountered.

"She's not a foreigner in spite of her name," said Mrs. Touchett. "She was born—I always forget where you were born."

"It's hardly worth while then I should tell you."

"On the contrary," said Mrs. Touchett, who rarely missed a logical point; "if I remembered your telling me would be quite superfluous."

Madame Merle glanced at Isabel with a sort of world-wide smile, a thing that over-reached frontiers. "I was born under the shadow of the national banner."

"She's too fond of mystery," said Mrs. Touchett; "that's her great fault."

"Ah," exclaimed Madame Merle, "I've great faults, but I don't think that's one of them; it certainly isn't the greatest. I came into the world in the Brooklyn navy-yard. My father was a high officer in the United States Navy, and had a post—a post of responsibility—in that establishment at the time. I suppose I ought to love the sea, but I hate it. That's why I don't return to America. I love the land; the great thing is to love something."

Isabel, as a dispassionate witness, had not been struck with the force of Mrs. Touchett's characterisation of her visitor, who had an expressive, communicative, responsive face, by no means of the sort which, to Isabel's mind, suggested a secretive disposition. It was a face that told of an amplitude of nature and of quick and free motions and, though it had no regular beauty, was in the highest degree engaging and attaching. Madame Merle was a tall, fair, smooth woman; everything in her person was round and replete, though without those accumulations which suggest heaviness. Her features were thick but in perfect proportion and harmony, and her complexion had a healthy clearness. Her grey eyes were small but full of light and incapable of stupidity—incapable, according to some people, even of tears; she had a liberal, full-rimmed mouth which when she smiled drew itself upward to the left side in a manner that most people thought very odd, some very affected and a few very graceful. Isabel inclined to range herself in the last category. Madame Merle had thick, fair hair, arranged somehow "classically" and as if she were a Bust, Isabel judged—a

Juno or a Niobe;[3] and large white hands, of a perfect shape, a shape so perfect that their possessor, preferring to leave them unadorned, wore no jewelled rings. Isabel had taken her at first, as we have seen, for a Frenchwoman; but extended observation might have ranked her as a German—a German of high degree, perhaps an Austrian, a baroness, a countess, a princess. It would never have been supposed she had come into the world in Brooklyn—though one could doubtless not have carried through any argument that the air of distinction marking her in so eminent a degree was inconsistent with such a birth. It was true that the national banner had floated immediately over her cradle, and the breezy freedom of the stars and stripes might have shed an influence upon the attitude she there took towards life. And yet she had evidently nothing of the fluttered, flapping quality of a morsel of bunting in the wind; her manner expressed the repose and confidence which come from a large experience. Experience, however, had not quenched her youth; it had simply made her sympathetic and supple. She was in a word a woman of strong impulses kept in admirable order. This commended itself to Isabel as an ideal combination.

The girl made these reflexions while the three ladies sat at their tea, but that ceremony was interrupted before long by the arrival of the great doctor from London, who had been immediately ushered into the drawing-room. Mrs. Touchett took him off to the library for a private talk; and then Madame Merle and Isabel parted, to meet again at dinner. The idea of seeing more of this interesting woman did much to mitigate Isabel's sense of the sadness now settling on Gardencourt.

When she came into the drawing-room before dinner she found the place empty; but in the course of a moment Ralph arrived. His anxiety about his father had been lightened; Sir Matthew Hope's view of his condition was less depressed than his own had been. The doctor recommended that the nurse alone should remain with the old man for the next three or four hours; so that Ralph, his mother and the great physician himself were free to dine at table. Mrs. Touchett and Sir Matthew appeared; Madame Merle was the last.

Before she came Isabel spoke of her to Ralph, who was standing before the fireplace. "Pray who is this Madame Merle?"

"The cleverest woman I know, not excepting yourself," said Ralph.

"I thought she seemed very pleasant."

"I was sure you'd think her very pleasant."

"Is that why you invited her?"

"I didn't invite her, and when we came back from London I didn't know she was here. No one invited her. She's a friend of my mother's, and just after you and I went to town my mother got a note from her. She had arrived in England (she usually lives abroad, though she has first and last spent a good deal of time here), and asked leave to come down for a few days. She's a woman who can make such proposals with perfect confidence; she's so welcome wherever she goes. And with my mother there could be no question of hesitating; she's the one person in the world whom my mother very much admires. If she were not herself (which she after all

3. Common subjects for classical sculpture; Niobe was a Greek queen who wept for her dead children until she turned to stone.

much prefers), she would like to be Madame Merle. It would indeed be a great change."

"Well, she's very charming," said Isabel. "And she plays beautifully."

"She does everything beautifully. She's complete."

Isabel looked at her cousin a moment. "You don't like her."

"On the contrary, I was once in love with her."

"And she didn't care for you, and that's why you don't like her."

"How can we have discussed such things? Monsieur Merle was then living."

"Is he dead now?"

"So she says."

"Don't you believe her?"

"Yes, because the statement agrees with the probabilities. The husband of Madame Merle would be likely to pass away."

Isabel gazed at her cousin again. "I don't know what you mean. You mean something—that you don't mean. What was Monsieur Merle?"

"The husband of Madame."

"You're very odious. Has she any children?"

"Not the least little child—fortunately."

"Fortunately?"

"I mean fortunately for the child. She'd be sure to spoil it."

Isabel was apparently on the point of assuring her cousin for the third time that he was odious; but the discussion was interrupted by the arrival of the lady who was the topic of it. She came rustling in quickly, apologising for being late, fastening a bracelet, dressed in dark blue satin, which exposed a white bosom that was ineffectually covered by a curious silver necklace. Ralph offered her his arm with the exaggerated alertness of a man who was no longer a lover.

Even if this had still been his condition, however, Ralph had other things to think about. The great doctor spent the night at Gardencourt and, returning to London on the morrow, after another consultation with Mr. Touchett's own medical adviser, concurred in Ralph's desire that he should see the patient again on the day following. On the day following Sir Matthew Hope reappeared at Gardencourt, and now took a less encouraging view of the old man, who had grown worse in the twenty-four hours. His feebleness was extreme, and to his son, who constantly sat by his bedside, it often seemed that his end must be at hand. The local doctor, a very sagacious man, in whom Ralph had secretly more confidence than in his distinguished colleague, was constantly in attendance, and Sir Matthew Hope came back several times. Mr. Touchett was much of the time unconscious; he slept a great deal; he rarely spoke. Isabel had a great desire to be useful to him and was allowed to watch with him at hours when his other attendants (of whom Mrs. Touchett was not the least regular) went to take rest. He never seemed to know her, and she always said to herself "Suppose he should die while I'm sitting here;" an idea which excited her and kept her awake. Once he opened his eyes for a while and fixed them upon her intelligently, but when she went to him, hoping he would recognise her, he closed them and relapsed into stupor. The day after this, however, he revived for a longer time; but on this occasion Ralph only was with him. The old man began to talk, much to his son's satisfaction, who assured him that they should presently have him sitting up.

"No, my boy," said Mr. Touchett, "not unless you bury me in a sitting posture, as some of the ancients—was it the ancients?—used to do."

"Ah, daddy, don't talk about that," Ralph murmured. "You mustn't deny that you're getting better."

"There will be no need of my denying it if you don't say it," the old man answered. "Why should we prevaricate just at the last? We never prevaricated before. I've got to die some time, and it's better to die when one's sick than when one's well. I'm very sick—as sick as I shall ever be. I hope you don't want to prove that I shall ever be worse than this? That would be too bad. You don't? Well then."

Having made this excellent point he became quiet; but the next time that Ralph was with him he again addressed himself to conversation. The nurse had gone to her supper and Ralph was alone in charge, having just relieved Mrs. Touchett, who had been on guard since dinner. The room was lighted only by the flickering fire, which of late had become necessary, and Ralph's tall shadow was projected over wall and ceiling with an outline constantly varying but always grotesque.

"Who's that with me—is it my son?" the old man asked.

"Yes, it's your son, daddy."

"And is there no one else?"

"No one else."

Mr. Touchett said nothing for a while; and then, "I want to talk a little," he went on.

"Won't it tire you?" Ralph demurred.

"It won't matter if it does. I shall have a long rest. I want to talk about *you*."

Ralph had drawn nearer to the bed; he sat leaning forward with his hand on his father's. "You had better select a brighter topic."

"You were always bright; I used to be proud of your brightness. I should like so much to think you'd do something."

"If you leave us," said Ralph, "I shall do nothing but miss you."

"That's just what I don't want; it's what I want to talk about. You must get a new interest."

"I don't want a new interest, daddy. I have more old ones than I know what to do with."

The old man lay there looking at his son; his face was the face of the dying, but his eyes were the eyes of Daniel Touchett. He seemed to be reckoning over Ralph's interests. "Of course you have your mother," he said at last. "You'll take care of her."

"My mother will always take care of herself," Ralph returned.

"Well," said his father, "perhaps as she grows older she'll need a little help."

"I shall not see that. She'll outlive me."

"Very likely she will; but that's no reason—!" Mr. Touchett let his phrase die away in a helpless but not quite querulous sigh and remained silent again.

"Don't trouble yourself about us," said his son. "My mother and I get on very well together, you know."

"You get on by always being apart; that's not natural."

"If you leave us we shall probably see more of each other."

"Well," the old man observed with wandering irrelevance, "it can't be said that my death will make much difference in your mother's life."

"It will probably make more than you think."

"Well, she'll have more money," said Mr. Touchett. "I've left her a good wife's portion, just as if she had been a good wife."

"She has been one, daddy, according to her own theory. She has never troubled you."

"Ah, some troubles are pleasant," Mr. Touchett murmured. "Those you've given me for instance. But your mother has been less—less—what shall I call it? less out of the way since I've been ill. I presume she knows I've noticed it."

"I shall certainly tell her so; I'm glad you mention it."

"It won't make any difference to her; she doesn't do it to please me. She does it to please—to please—" And he lay a while trying to think why she did it. "She does it because it suits her. But that's not what I want to talk about," he added. "It's about *you*. You'll be very well off."

"Yes," said Ralph, "I know that. But I hope you've not forgotten the talk we had a year ago—when I told you exactly what money I should need and begged you to make some good use of the rest."

"Yes, yes, I remember. I made a new will—in a few days. I suppose it was the first time such a thing had happened—a young man trying to get a will made against him."

"It is not against me," said Ralph. "It would be against me to have a large property to take care of. It's impossible for a man in my state of health to spend much money, and enough is as good as a feast."

"Well, you'll have enough—and something over. There will be more than enough for one—there will be enough for two."

"That's too much," said Ralph.

"Ah, don't say that. The best thing you can do, when I'm gone, will be to marry."

Ralph had foreseen what his father was coming to, and this suggestion was by no means fresh. It had long been Mr. Touchett's most ingenious way of taking the cheerful view of his son's possible duration. Ralph had usually treated it facetiously; but present circumstances proscribed the facetious. He simply fell back in his chair and returned his father's appealing gaze.

"If I, with a wife who hasn't been very fond of me, have had a very happy life," said the old man, carrying his ingenuity further still, "what a life mightn't you have if you should marry a person different from Mrs. Touchett. There are more different from her than there are like her." Ralph still said nothing; and after a pause his father resumed softly: "What do you think of your cousin?"

At this Ralph started, meeting the question with a strained smile. "Do I understand you to propose that I should marry Isabel?"

"Well, that's what it comes to in the end. Don't you like Isabel?"

"Yes, very much." And Ralph got up from his chair and wandered over to the fire. He stood before it an instant and then he stooped and stirred it mechanically. "I like Isabel very much," he repeated.

"Well," said his father, "I know she likes you. She has told me how much she likes you."

"Did she remark that she would like to marry me?"

"No, but she can't have anything against you. And she's the most charming young lady I've ever seen. And she would be good to you. I have thought a great deal about it."

"So have I," said Ralph, coming back to the bedside again. "I don't mind telling you that."

"You *are* in love with her, then? I should think you would be. It's as if she came over on purpose."

"No, I'm not in love with her; but I should be if—if certain things were different."

"Ah, things are always different from what they might be," said the old man. "If you wait for them to change you'll never do anything. I don't know whether you know," he went on; "but I suppose there's no harm in my alluding to it at such an hour as this: there was some one wanted to marry Isabel the other day, and she wouldn't have him."

"I know she refused Warburton: he told me himself."

"Well, that proves there's a chance for somebody else."

"Somebody else took his chance the other day in London—and got nothing by it."

"Was it you?" Mr. Touchett eagerly asked.

"No, it was an older friend; a poor gentleman who came over from America to see about it."

"Well, I'm sorry for him, whoever he was. But it only proves what I say—that the way's open to you."

"If it is, dear father, it's all the greater pity that I'm unable to tread it. I haven't many convictions; but I have three or four that I hold strongly. One is that people, on the whole, had better not marry their cousins. Another is that people in an advanced stage of pulmonary disorder had better not marry at all."

The old man raised his weak hand and moved it to and fro before his face. "What do you mean by that? You look at things in a way that would make everything wrong. What sort of cousin is a cousin that you had never seen for more than twenty years of her life? We're all each other's cousins, and if we stopped at that the human race would die out. It's just the same with your bad lung. You're a great deal better than you used to be. All you want is to lead a natural life. It is a great deal more natural to marry a pretty young lady that you're in love with than it is to remain single on false principles."

"I'm not in love with Isabel," said Ralph.

"You said just now that you would be if you didn't think it wrong. I want to prove to you that it isn't wrong."

"It will only tire you, dear daddy," said Ralph, who marvelled at his father's tenacity and at his finding strength to insist. "Then where shall we all be?"

"Where shall you be if I don't provide for you? You won't have anything to do with the bank, and you won't have me to take care of. You say you've so many interests; but I can't make them out."

Ralph leaned back in his chair with folded arms; his eyes were fixed for some time in meditation. At last, with the air of a man fairly mustering courage, "I take a great interest in my cousin," he said, "but not the sort of interest you desire. I shall not live many years; but I hope I shall live long enough to see what she does with herself. She's entirely independent of me; I can exercise very little influence upon her life. But I should like to do something for her."

"What should you like to do?"

"I should like to put a little wind in her sails."

"What do you mean by that?"

"I should like to put it into her power to do some of the things she wants. She wants to see the world for instance. I should like to put money in her purse."

"Ah, I'm glad you've thought of that," said the old man. "But I've thought of it too. I've left her a legacy—five thousand pounds."

"That's capital; it's very kind of you. But I should like to do a little more."

Something of that veiled acuteness with which it had been on Daniel Touchett's part the habit of a lifetime to listen to a financial proposition still lingered in the face in which the invalid had not obliterated the man of business. "I shall be happy to consider it," he said softly.

"Isabel's poor then. My mother tells me that she has but a few hundred dollars a year. I should like to make her rich."

"What do you mean by rich?"

"I call people rich when they're able to meet the requirements of their imagination. Isabel has a great deal of imagination."

"So have you, my son," said Mr. Touchett, listening very attentively but a little confusedly.

"You tell me I shall have money enough for two. What I want is that you should kindly relieve me of my superfluity and make it over to Isabel. Divide my inheritance into two equal halves and give her the second."

"To do what she likes with?"

"Absolutely what she likes."

"And without an equivalent?"

"What equivalent could there be?"

"The one I've already mentioned."

"Her marrying—some one or other? It's just to do away with anything of that sort that I make my suggestion. If she has an easy income she'll never have to marry for a support. That's what I want cannily to prevent. She wishes to be free, and your bequest will make her free."

"Well, you seem to have thought it out," said Mr. Touchett. "But I don't see why you appeal to me. The money will be yours, and you can easily give it to her yourself."

Ralph openly stared. "Ah, dear father, I can't offer Isabel money!"

The old man gave a groan. "Don't tell me you're not in love with her! Do you want me to have the credit of it?"

"Entirely. I should like it simply to be a clause in your will, without the slightest reference to me."

"Do you want me to make a new will then?"

"A few words will do it; you can attend to it the next time you feel a little lively."

"You must telegraph to Mr. Hilary then. I'll do nothing without my solicitor."

"You shall see Mr. Hilary to-morrow."

"He'll think we've quarrelled, you and I," said the old man.

"Very probably; I shall like him to think it," said Ralph, smiling; "and, to carry out the idea, I give you notice that I shall be very sharp, quite horrid and strange, with you."

The humour of this appeared to touch his father, who lay a little while taking it in. "I'll do anything you like," Mr. Touchett said at last; "but I'm not sure it's right. You say you want to put wind in her sails; but aren't you afraid of putting too much?"

"I should like to see her going before the breeze!" Ralph answered.

"You speak as if it were for your mere amusement."

"So it is, a good deal."

"Well, I don't think I understand," said Mr. Touchett with a sigh. "Young men are very different from what I was. When I cared for a girl—when I was young—I wanted to do more than look at her. You've scruples that I shouldn't have had, and you've ideas that I shouldn't have had either. You say Isabel wants to be free, and that her being rich will keep her from marrying for money. Do you think that she's a girl to do that?"

"By no means. But she has less money than she has ever had before. Her father then gave her everything, because he used to spend his capital. She has nothing but the crumbs of that feast to live on, and she doesn't really know how meagre they are—she has yet to learn it. My mother has told me all about it. Isabel will learn it when she's really thrown upon the world, and it would be very painful to me to think of her coming to the consciousness of a lot of wants she should be unable to satisfy."

"I've left her five thousand pounds. She can satisfy a good many wants with that."

"She can indeed. But she would probably spend it in two or three years."

"You think she'd be extravagant then?"

"Most certainly," said Ralph, smiling serenely.

Poor Mr. Touchett's acuteness was rapidly giving place to pure confusion. "It would merely be a question of time then, her spending the larger sum?"

"No—though at first I think she'd plunge into that pretty freely: she'd probably make over a part of it to each of her sisters. But after that she'd come to her senses, remember she has still a lifetime before her, and live within her means."

"Well, you *have* worked it out," said the old man helplessly. "You do take an interest in her, certainly."

"You can't consistently say I go too far. You wished me to go further."

"Well, I don't know," Mr. Touchett answered. "I don't think I enter into your spirit. It seems to me immoral."

"Immoral, dear daddy?"

"Well, I don't know that it's right to make everything so easy for a person."

"It surely depends upon the person. When the person's good, your making things easy is all to the credit of virtue. To facilitate the execution of good impulses, what can be a nobler act?"

This was a little difficult to follow, and Mr. Touchett considered it for awhile. At last he said: "Isabel's a sweet young thing; but do you think she's so good as that?"

"She's as good as her best opportunities," Ralph returned.

"Well," Mr. Touchett declared, "she ought to get a great many opportunities for sixty thousand pounds."[4]

"I've no doubt she will."

---

4. Chapter 20 gives the figure as £70,000. In James's lifetime the pound was valued at around $4.85, making Isabel's inheritance worth $300,000 or more. Adjusted for inflation the sum comes to well over $6,000,000 in today's dollars, but its purchasing power at the time was far greater.

"Of course I'll do what you want," said the old man. "I only want to understand it a little."

"Well, dear daddy, don't you understand it now?" his son caressingly asked. "If you don't we won't take any more trouble about it. We'll leave it alone."

Mr. Touchett lay a long time still. Ralph supposed he had given up the attempt to follow. But at last, quite lucidly, he began again. "Tell me this first. Doesn't it occur to you that a young lady with sixty thousand pounds may fall a victim to the fortune-hunters?"

"She'll hardly fall a victim to more than one."

"Well, one's too many."

"Decidedly. That's a risk, and it has entered into my calculation. I think it's appreciable, but I think it's small, and I'm prepared to take it."

Poor Mr Touchett's acuteness had passed into perplexity, and his perplexity now passed into admiration. "Well, you *have* gone into it!" he repeated. "But I don't see what good you're to get of it."

Ralph leaned over his father's pillows and gently smoothed them; he was aware their talk had been unduly prolonged. "I shall get just the good I said a few moments ago I wished to put into Isabel's reach—that of having met the requirements of my imagination. But it's scandalous, the way I've taken advantage of you!"

Chapter XIX

As Mrs. Touchett had foretold, Isabel and Madame Merle were thrown much together during the illness of their host, so that if they had not become intimate it would have been almost a breach of good manners. Their manners were of the best, but in addition to this they happened to please each other. It is perhaps too much to say that they swore an eternal friendship, but tacitly at least they called the future to witness. Isabel did so with a perfectly good conscience, though she would have hesitated to admit she was intimate with her new friend in the high sense she privately attached to this term. She often wondered indeed if she ever had been, or ever could be, intimate with any one. She had an ideal of friendship as well as of several other sentiments, which it failed to seem to her in this case—it had not seemed to her in other cases—that the actual completely expressed. But she often reminded herself that there were essential reasons why one's ideal could never become concrete. It was a thing to believe in, not to see—a matter of faith, not of experience. Experience, however, might supply us with very creditable imitations of it, and the part of wisdom was to make the best of these. Certainly, on the whole, Isabel had never encountered a more agreeable and interesting figure than Madame Merle; she had never met a person having less of that fault which is the principal obstacle to friendship—the air of reproducing the more tiresome, the stale, the too-familiar parts of one's own character. The gates of the girl's confidence were opened wider than they had ever been; she said things to this amiable auditress that she had not yet said to any one. Sometimes she took alarm at her candour: it was as if she had given to a comparative stranger the key to her cabinet of jewels. These spiritual gems were the only ones of any magnitude that Isabel possessed, but there was all the greater reason for their being carefully guarded. Afterwards, however, she always remembered that one should never regret a generous error and that if Madame Merle had not the merits she attributed to her, so much the worse for Madame Merle. There was no doubt she had great merits— she was charming, sympathetic, intelligent, cultivated. More than this (for it had not been Isabel's ill-fortune to go through life without meeting in her own sex several persons of whom no less could fairly be said), she was rare, superior and preëminent. There are many amiable people in the world, and Madame Merle was far from being vulgarly good-natured and restlessly witty. She knew how to think—an accomplishment rare in women; and she had thought to very good purpose. Of course, too, she knew how to feel; Isabel couldn't have spent a week with her without being sure of that. This was indeed Madame Merle's great talent, her most perfect gift. Life had told upon her; she had felt it strongly, and it was part of the satis-faction to be taken in her society that when the girl talked of what she was pleased to call serious matters this lady understood her so easily and quickly. Emotion, it is true, had become with her rather historic; she made no secret of the fact that the fount of passion, thanks to having been rather violently tapped at one period, didn't flow quite so freely as of yore. She proposed moreover, as well as expected, to cease feeling; she freely admitted that of old she had been a little mad, and now she pretended to be perfectly sane.

"I judge more than I used to," she said to Isabel, "but it seems to me one has earned the right. One can't judge till one's forty; before that we're too eager, too hard, too cruel, and in addition much too ignorant. I'm sorry for you; it will be a long time before you're forty. But every gain's a loss of some kind; I often think that after forty one *can't* really feel. The fresh-ness, the quickness have certainly gone. You'll keep them longer than most people; it will be a great satisfaction to me to see you some years hence. I want to see what life makes of you. One thing's certain—it can't spoil you. It may pull you about horribly, but I defy it to break you up."

Isabel received this assurance as a young soldier, still panting from a slight skirmish in which he has come off with honour, might receive a pat on the shoulder from his colonel. Like such a recognition of merit it seemed to come with authority. How could the lightest word do less on the part of a person who was prepared to say, of almost everything Isabel told her, "Oh, I've been in that, my dear; it passes, like everything else." On many of her interlocutors Madame Merle might have produced an irritating effect; it was disconcertingly difficult to surprise her. But Isabel, though by no means incapable of desiring to be effective, had not at present this impulse. She was too sincere, too interested in her judicious companion. And then moreover Madame Merle never said such things in the tone of triumph or of boastfulness; they dropped from her like cold confessions.

A period of bad weather had settled upon Gardencourt; the days grew shorter and there was an end to the pretty tea-parties on the lawn. But our young woman had long indoor conversations with her fellow visitor, and in spite of the rain the two ladies often sallied forth for a walk, equipped with the defensive apparatus which the English climate and the English genius have between them brought to such perfection. Madame Merle liked almost everything, including the English rain. "There's always a little of it and never too much at once," she said; "and it never wets you and it always smells good." She declared that in England the pleasures of smell were great—that in this inimitable island there was a certain mixture of fog and beer and soot which, however odd it might sound, was the national aroma, and was most agreeable to the nostril; and she used to lift the sleeve of her British overcoat and bury her nose in it, inhaling the clear, fine scent of the wool. Poor Ralph Touchett, as soon as the autumn had begun to define itself, became almost a prisoner; in bad weather he was unable to step out of the house, and he used sometimes to stand at one of the windows with his hands in his pockets and, from a countenance half-rueful, half-critical, watch Isabel and Madame Merle as they walked down the avenue under a pair of umbrellas. The roads about Gardencourt were so firm, even in the worst weather, that the two ladies always came back with a healthy glow in their cheeks, looking at the soles of their neat, stout boots and declaring that their walk had done them inexpressible good. Before luncheon, always, Madame Merle was engaged; Isabel admired and envied her rigid possession of her morning. Our heroine had always passed for a person of resources and had taken a certain pride in being one; but she wandered, as by the wrong side of the wall of a private garden, round the enclosed talents, accomplishments, aptitudes of Madame Merle. She found herself desiring to emulate them, and in twenty such ways this lady presented herself as a model. "I should like awfully to be *so!*" Isabel secretly exclaimed, more than once, as one after another of her friend's fine aspects caught the light, and before long she knew that she had learned a lesson from a high authority. It took no great time indeed for her to feel herself, as the phrase is, under an influence. "What's the harm," she wondered, "so long as it's a good one? The more one's under a good influence the better. The only thing is to see our steps as we take them—to understand them as we go. That, no doubt, I shall always do. I needn't be afraid of becoming too pliable; isn't it my fault that I'm not pliable enough?" It is said that imitation is the sincerest flattery; and if Isabel was sometimes moved to gape at her friend aspiringly and despairingly it was not so much because she desired herself to shine as because she wished to hold up the lamp for Madame Merle. She liked her extremely, but was even more dazzled than attracted. She sometimes asked herself what Henrietta Stackpole would say to her thinking so much of this perverted product of their common soil, and had a conviction that it would be severely judged. Henrietta would not at all subscribe to Madame Merle; for reasons she could not have defined this truth came home to the girl. On the other hand she was equally sure that, should the occasion offer, her new friend would strike off some happy view of her old: Madame Merle was too humorous, too observant, not to do justice to Henrietta, and on becoming acquainted with her would probably give the measure of a tact which Miss Stackpole couldn't hope to emulate. She appeared to have in her experience a touchstone for everything, and somewhere in the capacious pocket of her genial memory she would find the key to Henrietta's value. "That's the great thing," Isabel solemnly pondered; "that's the supreme good fortune: to be in a better position for appreciating people than they are for appreciating you." And she added that such, when one considered it, was simply the essence of the aristocratic situation. In this light, if in none other, one should aim at the aristocratic situation.

I may not count over all the links in the chain which led Isabel to think of Madame Merle's situation as aristocratic—a view of it never expressed in any reference made to it by that lady herself. She had known great things and great people, but she had never played a great part. She was one of the small ones of the earth; she had not been born to honours; she knew the world too well to nourish fatuous illusions on the article of her own place in it. She had encountered many of the fortunate few and was perfectly aware of those points at which their fortune differed from hers. But if by her informed measure she was no figure for a high scene, she had yet to Isabel's imagination a sort of greatness. To be so cultivated and civilised, so wise and so easy, and still make so light of it—that was really to be a great lady, especially when one so carried and presented one's self. It was as if somehow she had all society under contribution, and all the arts and graces it practised—or was the effect rather that of charming uses found *for* her, even from a distance, subtle service rendered by her to a clamorous world wherever she might be? After breakfast she wrote a succession of letters, as those arriving for her appeared innumerable: her correspondence was a source of surprise to Isabel when they sometimes walked together to the village post-office to deposit Madame Merle's offering to the mail. She knew more people, as she told Isabel, than she knew what to do with, and something was always turning up to be written about. Of painting she was devotedly fond, and made no more of brushing in a sketch than of pulling off her gloves. At Gardencourt she was perpetually taking advantage of an hour's sunshine to go out with a camp-stool and a box of water-colours. That she was a brave musician we have already perceived, and it was evidence of the fact that when she seated herself at the piano, as she always did in the evening, her listeners resigned themselves without a murmur to losing the grace of her talk. Isabel, since she had known her, felt ashamed of her own facility, which she now looked upon as basely inferior; and indeed, though she had been thought rather a prodigy at home, the loss to society when, in taking her place upon the music-stool, she turned her back to the room, was usually deemed greater than the gain. When Madame Merle was neither writing, nor painting, nor touching the piano, she was usually employed upon wonderful tasks of rich embroidery, cushions, curtains, decorations for the chimney-piece; an art in which her bold, free invention was as noted as the agility of her needle. She was never idle, for when engaged in none of the ways I have mentioned she was either reading (she appeared to Isabel to read "everything important"), or walking out, or playing patience with the cards, or talking with her fellow inmates. And with all this she had always the social quality, was never rudely absent and yet never too seated. She laid down her pastimes as easily as she took them up; she worked and talked at the same time, and appeared to impute scant worth to anything she did. She gave away her sketches and tapestries; she rose from the piano or remained there, according to the convenience of her auditors, which she always unerringly divined. She was in short the most comfortable, profitable, amenable person to live with. If for Isabel she had a fault it was that she was not natural; by which the girl meant, not that she was either affected or pretentious, since from these vulgar vices no woman could have been more exempt, but that her nature had been too much overlaid by custom and her angles too much rubbed away. She had become too flexible, too useful, was too ripe and too final. She was in a word too perfectly the social animal that man and woman are supposed to have been intended to be; and she had rid herself of every remnant of that tonic wildness which we may assume to have belonged even to the most amiable persons in the ages before country-house life was the fashion. Isabel found it difficult to think of her in any detachment or privacy, she existed only in her relations, direct or indirect, with her fellow mortals. One might wonder what commerce she could possibly hold with her own spirit. One always ended, however, by feeling that a charming surface doesn't necessarily prove one superficial; this was an illusion in which, in one's youth, one had but just escaped being nourished. Madame Merle was not superficial—not she. She was deep, and her nature spoke none the less in her behaviour because it spoke a conventional tongue. "What's language at all but a convention?" said Isabel. "She has the good taste not to pretend, like some people I've met, to express herself by original signs."

"I'm afraid you've suffered much," she once found occasion to say to her friend in response to some allusion that had appeared to reach far.

"What makes you think that?" Madame Merle asked with the amused smile of a person seated at a game of guesses. "I hope I haven't too much the droop of the misunderstood."

"No; but you sometimes say things that I think people who have always been happy wouldn't have found out."

"I haven't always been happy," said Madame Merle, smiling still, but with a mock gravity, as if she were telling a child a secret. "Such a wonderful thing!"

But Isabel rose to the irony. "A great many people give me the impression of never having for a moment felt anything."

"It's very true; there are many more iron pots certainly than porcelain. But you may depend on it that every one bears some mark; even the hardest iron pots have a little bruise, a little hole somewhere. I flatter myself that I'm rather stout, but if I must tell you the truth I've been shockingly chipped and cracked. I do very well for service yet, because I've been cleverly mended; and I try to remain in the cupboard—the quiet, dusky cupboard where there's an odour of stale spices—as much as I can. But when I've to come out and into a strong light—then, my dear, I'm a horror!"

I know not whether it was on this occasion or on some other that when the conversation had taken the turn I have just indicated she said to Isabel that she would some day a tale unfold.[1] Isabel assured her she should delight to listen to one, and reminded her more than once of this engagement. Madame Merle, however, begged repeatedly for a respite, and at last frankly told her young companion that they must wait till they knew each other better. This would be sure to happen; a long friendship so visibly lay before them. Isabel assented, but at the same time enquired if she mightn't be trusted—if she appeared capable of a betrayal of confidence.

"It's not that I'm afraid of your repeating what I say," her fellow visitor answered; "I'm afraid, on the contrary, of your taking it too much to yourself. You'd judge me too harshly; you're of the cruel age." She preferred for the present to talk to Isabel of Isabel, and exhibited the greatest interest in our heroine's history, sentiments, opinions, prospects. She made her chatter and listened to her chatter with infinite good nature. This flattered and quickened the girl, who was struck with all the distinguished people her friend had known and with her having lived, as Mrs. Touchett said, in

1. "I could a tale unfold whose lightest word / Would harrow up thy soul": *Hamlet* I.v.15.

the best company in Europe. Isabel thought the better of herself for enjoying the favour of a person who had so large a field of comparison; and it was perhaps partly to gratify the sense of profiting by comparison that she often appealed to these stores of reminiscence. Madame Merle had been a dweller in many lands and had social ties in a dozen different countries. "I don't pretend to be educated," she would say, "but I think I know my Europe;" and she spoke one day of going to Sweden to stay with an old friend, and another of proceeding to Malta to follow up a new acquaintance. With England, where she had often dwelt, she was thoroughly familiar, and for Isabel's benefit threw a great deal of light upon the customs of the country and the character of the people, who "after all," as she was fond of saying, were the most convenient in the world to live with.

"You mustn't think it strange her remaining here at such a time as this, when Mr. Touchett's passing away," that gentleman's wife remarked to her niece. "She is incapable of a mistake; she's the most tactful woman I know. It's a favour to me that she stays; she's putting off a lot of visits at great houses," said Mrs. Touchett, who never forgot that when she herself was in England her social value sank two or three degrees in the scale. "She has her pick of places; she's not in want of a shelter. But I've asked her to put in this time because I wish you to know her. I think it will be a good thing for you. Serena Merle hasn't a fault."

"If I didn't already like her very much that description might alarm me," Isabel returned.

"She's never the least little bit 'off.' I've brought you out here and I wish to do the best for you. Your sister Lily told me she hoped I would give you plenty of opportunities. I give you one in putting you in relation with Madame Merle. She's one of the most brilliant women in Europe."

"I like her better than I like your description of her," Isabel persisted in saying.

"Do you flatter yourself that you'll ever feel her open to criticism? I hope you'll let me know when you do."

"That will be cruel—to you," said Isabel.

"You needn't mind me. You won't discover a fault in her."

"Perhaps not. But I dare say I shan't miss it."

"She knows absolutely everything on earth there is to know," said Mrs. Touchett.

Isabel after this observed to their companion that she hoped she knew Mrs. Touchett considered she hadn't a speck on her perfection. On which "I'm obliged to you," Madame Merle replied, "but I'm afraid your aunt imagines, or at least alludes to, no aberrations that the clock-face doesn't register."

"So that you mean you've a wild side that's unknown to her?"

"Ah no, I fear my darkest sides are my tamest. I mean that having no faults, for your aunt, means that one's never late for dinner—that is for *her* dinner. I was not late, by the way, the other day, when you came back from London; the clock was just at eight when I came into the drawing-room: it was the rest of you that were before the time. It means that one answers a letter the day one gets it and that when one comes to stay with her one doesn't bring too much luggage and is careful not to be taken ill. For Mrs. Touchett those things constitute virtue; it's a blessing to be able to reduce it to its elements."

Madame Merle's own conversation, it will be perceived, was enriched with bold, free touches of criticism, which, even when they had a restrictive effect, never struck Isabel as ill-natured. It couldn't occur to the girl for instance that Mrs. Touchett's accomplished guest was abusing her; and this for very good reasons. In the first place Isabel rose eagerly to the sense of her shades; in the second Madame Merle implied that there was a great deal more to say; and it was clear in the third that for a person to speak to one without ceremony of one's near relations was an agreeable sign of that person's intimacy with one's self. These signs of deep communion multiplied as the days elapsed, and there was none of which Isabel was more sensible than of her companion's preference for making Miss Archer herself a topic. Though she referred frequently to the incidents of her own career she never lingered upon them; she was as little of a gross egotist as she was of a flat gossip.

"I'm old and stale and faded," she said more than once; "I'm of no more interest than last week's newspaper. You're young and fresh and of to-day; you've the great thing—you've actuality. I once had it—we all have it for an hour. You, however, will have it for longer. Let us talk about you then; you can say nothing I shall not care to hear. It's a sign that I'm growing old—that I like to talk with younger people. I think it's a very pretty compensation. If we can't have youth within us we can have it outside, and I really think we see it and feel it better that way. Of course we must be in sympathy with it—that I shall always be. I don't know that I shall ever be ill-natured with old people—I hope not; there are certainly some old people I adore. But I shall never be anything but abject with the young; they touch me and appeal to me too much. I give you *carte blanche*[2] then; you can even be impertinent if you like; I shall let it pass and horribly spoil you. I speak as if I were a hundred years old, you say? Well, I am, if you please; I was born before the French Revolution. Ah, my dear, *je viens de loin*;[3] I belong to the old, old world. But it's not of that I want to talk; I want to talk about the new. You must tell me more about America; you never tell me enough. Here I've been since I was brought here as a helpless child, and it's ridiculous, or rather it's scandalous, how little I know about that splendid, dreadful, funny country—surely the greatest and drollest of them all. There are a great many of us like that in these parts, and I must say I think we're a wretched set of people. You should live in your own land; whatever it may be you have your natural place there. If we're not good Americans we're certainly poor Europeans; we've no natural place here. We're mere parasites, crawling over the surface; we haven't our feet in the soil. At least one can know it and not have illusions. A woman perhaps can get on; a woman, it seems to me, has no natural place anywhere; wherever she finds herself she has to remain on the surface and, more or less, to crawl. You protest, my dear? you're horrified? you declare you'll never crawl? It's very true that I don't see you crawling; you stand more upright than a good many poor creatures. Very good; on the whole, I don't think you'll crawl. But the men, the Americans; *je vous demande un peu*,[4] what do they make of it over here? I don't envy them trying to arrange

2. A free hand (French).
3. I go back a long ways (French).
4. I only ask you (French).

themselves. Look at poor Ralph Touchett; what sort of a figure do you call that? Fortunately he has a consumption; I say fortunately, because it gives him something to do. His consumption's his *carrière*; it's a kind of position. You can say: 'Oh, Mr. Touchett, he takes care of his lungs, he knows a great deal about climates.' But without that who would he be, what would he represent? 'Mr. Ralph Touchett: an American who lives in Europe.' That signifies absolutely nothing—it's impossible anything should signify less. 'He's very cultivated,' they say: 'he has a very pretty collection of old snuff-boxes.' The collection is all that's wanted to make it pitiful. I'm tired of the sound of the word; I think it's grotesque. With the poor old father it's different; he has his identity, and it's rather a massive one. He represents a great financial house, and that, in our day, is as good as anything else. For an American, at any rate, that will do very well. But I persist in thinking your cousin very lucky to have a chronic malady so long as he doesn't die of it. It's much better than the snuff-boxes. If he weren't ill, you say, he'd do something?—he'd take his father's place in the house. My poor child, I doubt it; I don't think he's at all fond of the house. However, you know him better than I, though I used to know him rather well, and he may have the benefit of the doubt. The worst case, I think, is a friend of mine, a countryman of ours, who lives in Italy (where he also was brought before he knew better), and who is one of the most delightful men I know. Some day you must know him. I'll bring you together and then you'll see what I mean. He's Gilbert Osmond—he lives in Italy; that's all one can say about him or make of him. He's exceedingly clever, a man made to be distinguished; but, as I tell you, you exhaust the description when you say he's Mr. Osmond who lives *tout bêtement*[5] in Italy. No career, no name, no position, no fortune, no past, no future, no anything. Oh yes, he paints, if you please—paints in water-colours; like me, only better than I. His painting's pretty bad; on the whole I'm rather glad of that. Fortunately he's very indolent, so indolent that it amounts to a sort of position. He can say, "Oh, I do nothing; I'm too deadly lazy. You can do nothing to-day unless you get up at five o'clock in the morning.' In that way he becomes a sort of exception; you feel he might do something if he'd only rise early. He never speaks of his painting—to people at large; he's too clever for that. But he has a little girl—a dear little girl; he does speak of *her*. He's devoted to her, and if it were a career to be an excellent father he'd be very distinguished. But I'm afraid that's no better than the snuff-boxes; perhaps not even so good. Tell me what they do in America," pursued Madame Merle, who, it must be observed parenthetically, did not deliver herself all at once of these reflexions, which are presented in a cluster for the convenience of the reader. She talked of Florence, where Mr. Osmond lived and where Mrs. Touchett occupied a mediæval palace; she talked of Rome, where she herself had a little *pied-à-terre* with some rather good old damask. She talked of places, of people and even, as the phrase is, of "subjects"; and from time to time she talked of their kind old host and of the prospect of his recovery. From the first she had thought this prospect small, and Isabel had been struck with the positive, discriminating, competent way in which she took the measure of his remainder of life. One evening she announced definitely that he wouldn't live.

5. Quite simply, foolishly (French).

"Sir Matthew Hope told me so as plainly as was proper," she said; "standing there, near the fire, before dinner. He makes himself very agreeable, the great doctor. I don't mean his saying that has anything to do with it. But he says such things with great tact. I had told him I felt ill at my ease, staying here at such a time; it seemed to me so indiscreet—it wasn't as if I could nurse. 'You must remain, you must remain,' he answered; 'your office will come later.' Wasn't that a very delicate way of saying both that poor Mr. Touchett would go and that I might be of some use as a consoler? In fact, however, I shall not be of the slightest use. You aunt will console herself; she, and she alone, knows just how much consolation she'll require. It would be a very delicate matter for another person to undertake to administer the dose. With your cousin it will be different; he'll miss his father immensely. But I should never presume to condole with Mr. Ralph; we're not on those terms." Madame Merle had alluded more than once to some undefined incongruity in her relations with Ralph Touchett; so Isabel took this occasion of asking her if they were not good friends.

"Perfectly, but he doesn't like me."

"What have you done to him?"

"Nothing whatever. But one has no need of a reason for that."

"For not liking you? I think one has need of a very good reason."

"You're very kind. Be sure you have one ready for the day you begin."

"Begin to dislike you? I shall never begin."

"I hope not; because if you do you'll never end. That's the way with your cousin; he doesn't get over it. It's an antipathy of nature—if I can call it that when it's all on his side. I've nothing whatever against him and don't bear him the least little grudge for not doing me justice. Justice is all I want. However, one feels that he's a gentleman and would never say anything underhand about one. *Cartes sur table*,"[6] Madame Merle subjoined in a moment, "I'm not afraid of him."

"I hope not indeed," said Isabel, who added something about his being the kindest creature living. She remembered, however, that on her first asking him about Madame Merle he had answered her in a manner which this lady might have thought injurious without being explicit. There was something between them, Isabel said to herself, but she said nothing more than this. If it were something of importance it should inspire respect; if it were not it was not worth her curiosity. With all her love of knowledge she had a natural shrinking from raising curtains and looking into unlighted corners. The love of knowledge coexisted in her mind with the finest capacity for ignorance.

But Madame Merle sometimes said things that startled her, made her raise her clear eyebrows at the time and think of the words afterwards. "I'd give a great deal to be your age again," she broke out once with a bitterness which, though diluted in her customary amplitude of ease, was imperfectly disguised by it. "If I could only begin again—if I could have my life before me!"

"Your life's before you yet," Isabel answered gently, for she was vaguely awe-struck.

"No, the best part's gone, and gone for nothing."

6. Cards on the table (French).

"Surely not for nothing," said Isabel.

"Why not—what have I got? Neither husband, nor child, nor fortune, nor position, nor the traces of a beauty that I never had."

"You have many friends, dear lady."

"I'm not so sure!" cried Madame Merle.

"Ah, you're wrong. You have memories, graces, talents—"

But Madame Merle interrupted her. "What have my talents brought me? Nothing but the need of using them still, to get through the hours, the years, to cheat myself with some pretence of movement, of unconsciousness. As for my graces and memories the less said about them the better. You'll be my friend till you find a better use for your friendship."

"It will be for you to see that I don't then," said Isabel.

"Yes; I would make an effort to keep you." And her companion looked at her gravely. "When I say I should like to be your age I mean with your qualities—frank, generous, sincere like you. In that case I should have made something better of my life."

"What should you have liked to do that you've not done?"

Madame Merle took a sheet of music—she was seated at the piano and had abruptly wheeled about on the stool when she first spoke—and mechanically turned the leaves. "I'm very ambitious!" she at last replied.

"And your ambitions have not been satisfied? They must have been great."

"They *were* great. I should make myself ridiculous by talking of them."

Isabel wondered what they could have been—whether Madame Merle had aspired to wear a crown. "I don't know what your idea of success may be, but you seem to me to have been successful. To me indeed you're a vivid image of success."

Madame Merle tossed away the music with a smile. "What's *your* idea of success?"

"You evidently think it must be a very tame one. It's to see some dream of one's youth come true."

"Ah," Madame Merle exclaimed, "that I've never seen! But my dreams were so great—so preposterous. Heaven forgive me, I'm dreaming now!" And she turned back to the piano and began grandly to play. On the morrow she said to Isabel that her definition of success had been very pretty, yet frightfully sad. Measured in that way, who had ever succeeded? The dreams of one's youth, why they were enchanting, they were divine! Who had ever seen such things come to pass?

"I myself—a few of them," Isabel ventured to answer.

"Already? They must have been dreams of yesterday."

"I began to dream very young," Isabel smiled.

"Ah, if you mean the aspirations of your childhood—that of having a pink sash and a doll that could close her eyes."

"No, I don't mean that."

"Or a young man with a fine moustache going down on his knees to you."

"No, nor that either," Isabel declared with still more emphasis.

Madame Merle appeared to note this eagerness. "I suspect that's what you do mean. We've all had the young man with the moustache. He's the inevitable young man; he doesn't count."

Isabel was silent a little but then spoke with extreme and characteristic inconsequence. "Why shouldn't he count? There are young men and young men."

"And yours was a paragon—is that what you mean?" asked her friend with a laugh. "If you've had the identical young man you dreamed of, then that was success, and I congratulate you with all my heart. Only in that case why didn't you fly with him to his castle in the Apennines?"

"He has no castle in the Apennines."[7]

"What has he? An ugly brick house in Fortieth Street? Don't tell me that; I refuse to recognise that as an ideal."

"I don't care anything about his house," said Isabel.

"That's very crude of you. When you've lived as long as I you'll see that every human being has his shell and that you must take the shell into account. By the shell I mean the whole envelope of circumstances. There's no such thing as an isolated man or woman; we're each of us made up of some cluster of appurtenances. What shall we call our 'self'? Where does it begin? where does it end? It overflows into everything that belongs to us—and then it flows back again. I know a large part of myself is in the clothes I choose to wear. I've a great respect for *things*! One's self—for other people—is one's expression of one's self; and one's house, one's furniture, one's garments, the books one reads, the company one keeps—these things are all expressive."

This was very metaphysical; not more so, however, than several observations Madame Merle had already made. Isabel was fond of metaphysics, but was unable to accompany her friend into this bold analysis of the human personality. "I don't agree with you. I think just the other way. I don't know whether I succeed in expressing myself, but I know that nothing else expresses me. Nothing that belongs to me is any measure of me; everything's on the contrary a limit, a barrier, and a perfectly arbitrary one. Certainly the clothes which, as you say, I choose to wear, don't express me; and heaven forbid they should!"

"You dress very well," Madame Merle lightly interposed.

"Possibly; but I don't care to be judged by that. My clothes may express the dressmaker, but they don't express me. To begin with it's not my own choice that I wear them; they're imposed upon me by society."

"Should you prefer to go without them?" Madame Merle enquired in a tone which virtually terminated the discussion.

I am bound to confess, though it may cast some discredit on the sketch I have given of the youthful loyalty practised by our heroine toward this accomplished woman, that Isabel had said nothing whatever to her about Lord Warburton and had been equally reticent on the subject of Caspar Goodwood. She had not, however, concealed the fact that she had had opportunities of marrying and had even let her friend know of how advantageous a kind they had been. Lord Warburton had left Lockleigh and was gone to Scotland, taking his sisters with him; and though he had written to Ralph more than once to ask about Mr. Touchett's health the girl was not liable to the embarrassment of such enquiries as, had he still been in the neighbourhood, he would probably have felt bound to make in person. He had excellent ways, but she felt sure that if he had come to Gardencourt he would have seen Madame Merle, and that if he had seen her he would have liked her and betrayed to her that he was in love with her

---

7. A conventional setting for Romantic or Gothic fiction; Nathaniel Hawthorne (1804–1864) gives such a castle to one of his characters in *The Marble Faun* (1860).

young friend. It so happened that during this lady's previous visits to Gardencourt—each of them much shorter than the present—he had either not been at Lockleigh or had not called at Mr. Touchett's. Therefore, though she knew him by name as the great man of that county, she had no cause to suspect him as a suitor of Mrs. Touchett's freshly-imported niece.

"You've plenty of time," she had said to Isabel in return for the mutilated confidences which our young woman made her and which didn't pretend to be perfect, though we have seen that at moments the girl had compunctions at having said so much. "I'm glad you've done nothing yet—that you have it still to do. It's a very good thing for a girl to have refused a few good offers—so long of course as they are not the best she's likely to have. Pardon me if my tone seems horribly corrupt; one must take the worldly view sometimes. Only don't keep on refusing for the sake of refusing. It's a pleasant exercise of power; but accepting's after all an exercise of power as well. There's always the danger of refusing once too often. It was not the one I fell into—I didn't refuse often enough. You're an exquisite creature, and I should like to see you married to a prime minister. But speaking strictly, you know, you're not what is technically called a *parti*.[8] You're extremely good-looking and extremely clever; in yourself you're quite exceptional. You appear to have the vaguest ideas about your earthly possessions; but from what I can make out you're not embarrassed with an income. I wish you had a little money."

"I wish I had!" said Isabel, simply, apparently forgetting for the moment that her poverty had been a venial fault for two gallant gentlemen.

In spite of Sir Matthew Hope's benevolent recommendation Madame Merle did not remain to the end, as the issue of poor Mr. Touchett's malady had now come frankly to be designated. She was under pledges to other people which had at last to be redeemed, and she left Gardencourt with the understanding that she should in any event see Mrs. Touchett there again, or else in town, before quitting England. Her parting with Isabel was even more like the beginning of a friendship than their meeting had been. "I'm going to six places in succession, but I shall see no one I like so well as you. They'll all be old friends, however; one doesn't make new friends at my age. I've made a great exception for you. You must remember that and must think as well of me as possible. You must reward me by believing in me."

By way of answer Isabel kissed her, and, though some women kiss with facility, there are kisses and kisses, and this embrace was satisfactory to Madame Merle. Our young lady, after this, was much alone; she saw her aunt and cousin only at meals, and discovered that of the hours during which Mrs. Touchett was invisible only a minor portion was now devoted to nursing her husband. She spent the rest in her own apartments, to which access was not allowed even to her niece, apparently occupied there with mysterious and inscrutable exercises. At table she was grave and silent; but her solemnity was not an attitude—Isabel could see it was a conviction. She wondered if her aunt repented of having taken her own way so much; but there was no visible evidence of this—no tears, no sighs, no exaggeration of a zeal always to its own sense adequate. Mrs. Touchett

---

8. A good match (French).

seemed simply to feel the need of thinking things over and summing them up; she had a little moral account-book—with columns unerringly ruled and a sharp steel clasp—which she kept with exemplary neatness. Uttered reflection had with her ever, at any rate, a practical ring. "If I had foreseen this I'd not have proposed your coming abroad now," she said to Isabel after Madame Merle had left the house. "I'd have waited and sent for you next year."

"So that perhaps I should never have known my uncle? It's a great happiness to me to have come now."

"That's very well. But it was not that you might know your uncle that I brought you to Europe." A perfectly veracious speech; but, as Isabel thought, not as perfectly timed. She had leisure to think of this and other matters. She took a solitary walk every day and spent vague hours in turning over books in the library. Among the subjects that engaged her attention were the adventures of her friend Miss Stackpole, with whom she was in regular correspondence. Isabel liked her friend's private epistolary style better than her public; that is she felt her public letters would have been excellent if they had not been printed. Henrietta's career, however, was not so successful as might have been wished even in the interest of her private felicity; that view of the inner life of Great Britain which she was so eager to take appeared to dance before her like an *ignis fatuus*.[9] The invitation from Lady Pensil, for mysterious reasons, had never arrived; and poor Mr. Bantling himself, with all his friendly ingenuity, had been unable to explain so grave a dereliction on the part of a missive that had obviously been sent. He had evidently taken Henrietta's affairs much to heart, and believed that he owed her a set-off to this illusory visit to Bedfordshire. "He says he should think I would go to the Continent," Henrietta wrote; "and as he thinks of going there himself I suppose his advice is sincere. He wants to know why I don't take a view of French life; and it's a fact that I want very much to see the new Republic. Mr. Bantling doesn't care much about the Republic, but he thinks of going over to Paris anyway. I must say he's quite as attentive as I could wish, and at least I shall have seen one polite Englishman. I keep telling Mr. Bantling that he ought to have been an American, and you should see how that pleases him. Whenever I say so he always breaks out with the same exclamation—'Ah, but really, come now!'" A few days later she wrote that she had decided to go to Paris at the end of the week and that Mr. Bantling had promised to see her off—perhaps even would go as far as Dover with her. She would wait in Paris till Isabel should arrive, Henrietta added; speaking quite as if Isabel were to start on her continental journey alone and making no allusion to Mrs. Touchett. Bearing in mind his interest in their late companion, our heroine communicated several passages from this correspondence to Ralph, who followed with an emotion akin to suspense the career of the representative of the *Interviewer*.

"It seems to me she's doing very well," he said, "going over to Paris with an ex-Lancer! If she wants something to write about she has only to describe that episode."

"It's not conventional, certainly," Isabel answered; "but if you mean that—as far as Henrietta is concerned—it's not perfectly innocent, you're very much mistaken. You'll never understand Henrietta."

9. Will-o'-the-wisp (Latin).

"Pardon me, I understand her perfectly. I didn't at all at first, but now I've the point of view. I'm afraid, however, that Bantling hasn't; he may have some surprises. Oh, I understand Henrietta as well as if I had made her!"

Isabel was by no means sure of this, but she abstained from expressing further doubt, for she was disposed in these days to extend a great charity to her cousin. One afternoon less than a week after Madame Merle's departure she was seated in the library with a volume to which her attention was not fastened. She had placed herself in a deep window-bench, from which she looked out into the dull, damp park; and as the library stood at right angles to the entrance-front of the house she could see the doctor's brougham, which had been waiting for the last two hours before the door. She was struck with his remaining so long, but at last she saw him appear in the portico, stand a moment slowly drawing on his gloves and looking at the knees of his horse, and then get into the vehicle and roll away. Isabel kept her place for half an hour; there was a great stillness in the house. It was so great that when she at last heard a soft, slow step on the deep carpet of the room she was almost startled by the sound. She turned quickly away from the window and saw Ralph Touchett standing there with his hands still in his pockets, but with a face absolutely void of its usual latent smile. She got up and her movement and glance were a question.

"It's all over," said Ralph.

"Do you mean that my uncle——?" And Isabel stopped.

"My dear father died an hour ago."

"Ah, my poor Ralph!" she gently wailed, putting out her two hands to him.

Chapter XX

Some fortnight after this Madame Merle drove up in a hansom cab to the house in Winchester Square. As she descended from her vehicle she observed, suspended between the dining-room windows, a large, neat, wooden tablet, on whose fresh black ground were inscribed in white paint the words—"This noble freehold mansion to be sold"; with the name of the agent to whom application should be made. "They certainly lose no time," said the visitor as, after sounding the big brass knocker, she waited to be admitted; "it's a practical country!" And within the house, as she ascended to the drawing-room, she perceived numerous signs of abdication; pictures removed from the walls and placed upon sofas, windows undraped and floors laid bare. Mrs. Touchett presently received her and intimated in a few words that condolences might be taken for granted.

"I know what you're going to say—he was a very good man. But I know it better than any one, because I gave him more chance to show it. In that I think I was a good wife." Mrs. Touchett added that at the end her husband apparently recognised this fact. "He has treated me most liberally," she said; "I won't say more liberally than I expected, because I didn't expect. You know that as a general thing I don't expect. But he chose, I presume, to recognise the fact that though I lived much abroad and mingled—you may say freely—in foreign life, I never exhibited the smallest preference for any one else."

"For any one but yourself," Madame Merle mentally observed; but the reflexion was perfectly inaudible.

"I never sacrificed my husband to another," Mrs. Touchett continued with her stout curtness.

"Oh no," thought Madame Merle; "you never did anything for another!"

There was a certain cynicism in these mute comments which demands an explanation; the more so as they are not in accord either with the view—somewhat superficial perhaps—that we have hitherto enjoyed of Madame Merle's character or with the literal facts of Mrs. Touchett's history; the more so, too, as Madame Merle had a well-founded conviction that her friend's last remark was not in the least to be construed as a side-thrust at herself. The truth is that the moment she had crossed the threshold she received an impression that Mr. Touchett's death had had subtle consequences and that these consequences had been profitable to a little circle of persons among whom she was not numbered. Of course it was an event which would naturally have consequences; her imagination had more than once rested upon this fact during her stay at Gardencourt. But it had been one thing to foresee such a matter mentally and another to stand among its massive records. The idea of a distribution of property—she would almost have said of spoils—just now pressed upon her senses and irritated her with a sense of exclusion. I am far from wishing to picture her as one of the hungry mouths or envious hearts of the general herd, but we have already learned of her having desires that had never been satisfied. If she had been questioned, she would of course have admitted—with a fine proud smile—that she had not the faintest claim to a share in Mr. Touchett's relics. "There was never anything in the world between us," she would have said. "There was never that, poor man!"—with a fillip of her thumb and her third finger. I hasten to add, moreover, that if she couldn't at the present moment keep from quite perversely yearning she was careful not to betray herself. She had after all as much sympathy for Mrs. Touchett's gains as for her losses.

"He has left me this house," the newly-made widow said; "but of course I shall not live in it; I've a much better one in Florence. The will was opened only three days since, but I've already offered the house for sale. I've also a share in the bank; but I don't yet understand if I'm obliged to leave it there. If not I shall certainly take it out. Ralph, of course, has Gardencourt; but I'm not sure that he'll have means to keep up the place. He's naturally left very well off, but his father has given away an immense deal of money; there are bequests to a string of third cousins in Vermont. Ralph, however, is very fond of Gardencourt and would be quite capable of living there—in summer—with a maid-of-all-work and a gardener's boy. There's one remarkable clause in my husband's will," Mrs. Touchett added. "He has left my niece a fortune."

"A fortune!" Madame Merle softly repeated.

"Isabel steps into something like seventy thousand pounds."

Madame Merle's hands were clasped in her lap; at this she raised them, still clasped, and held them a moment against her bosom while her eyes, a little dilated, fixed themselves on those of her friend. "Ah," she cried, "the clever creature!"

Mrs. Touchett gave her a quick look. "What do you mean by that?"

For an instant Madame Merle's colour rose and she dropped her eyes. "It certainly is clever to achieve such results—without an effort!"

"There assuredly was no effort. Don't call it an achievement."

Madame Merle was seldom guilty of the awkwardness of retracting what she had said; her wisdom was shown rather in maintaining it and placing it in a favourable light. "My dear friend, Isabel would certainly not have had seventy thousand pounds left her if she had not been the most charming girl in the world. Her charm includes great cleverness."

"She never dreamed, I'm sure, of my husband's doing anything for her; and I never dreamed of it either, for he never spoke to me of his intention," Mrs. Touchett said. "She had no claim upon him whatever; it was no great recommendation to him that she was my niece. Whatever she achieved she achieved unconsciously."

"Ah," rejoined Madame Merle, "those are the greatest strokes!"

Mrs. Touchett reserved her opinion. "The girl's fortunate; I don't deny that. But for the present she's simply stupefied."

"Do you mean that she doesn't know what to do with the money?"

"That, I think, she has hardly considered. She doesn't know what to think about the matter at all. It has been as if a big gun were suddenly fired off behind her; she's feeling herself to see if she be hurt. It's but three days since she received a visit from the principal executor, who came in person, very gallantly, to notify her. He told me afterwards that when he had made his little speech she suddenly burst into tears. The money's to remain in the affairs of the bank,[1] and she's to draw the interest."

Madame Merle shook her head with a wise and now quite benignant smile. "How very delicious! After she has done that two or three times she'll get used to it." Then after a silence, "What does your son think of it." she abruptly asked.

"He left England before the will was read—used up by his fatigue and anxiety and hurrying off to the south. He's on his way to the Riviera and I've not yet heard from him. But it's not likely he'll ever object to anything done by his father."

"Didn't you say his own share had been cut down?"

"Only at his wish. I know that he urged his father to do something for the people in America. He's not in the least addicted to looking after number one."

"It depends upon whom he regards as number one!" said Madame Merle. And she remained thoughtful a moment, her eyes bent on the floor. "Am I not to see your happy niece?" she asked at last as she raised them.

"You may see her; but you'll not be struck with her being happy. She has looked as solemn, these three days, as a Cimabue Madonna!"[2] And Mrs. Touchett rang for a servant.

Isabel came in shortly after the footman had been sent to call her; and Madame Merle thought, as she appeared, that Mrs. Touchett's comparison had its force. The girl was pale and grave—an effect not mitigated by her deeper mourning; but the smile of her brightest moments came into her face as she saw Madame Merle, who went forward, laid her hand on our heroine's shoulder and, after looking at her a moment, kissed her as if

1. Isabel's fortune remains as part of the bank's working capital, which gives her a significantly higher rate of return than the 3 or 4 percent per annum that most safe investments earned in the period, possibly as much as 8 percent.
2. Cimabue was a Florentine religious painter and mosaicist (ca. 1240–1302?) who worked in a Byzantine style; said to have been Giotto's teacher.

she were returning the kiss she had received from her at Gardencourt. This was the only allusion the visitor, in her great good taste, made for the present to her young friend's inheritance.

Mrs. Touchett had no purpose of awaiting in London the sale of her house. After selecting from among its furniture the objects she wished to transport to her other abode, she left the rest of its contents to be disposed of by the auctioneer and took her departure for the Continent. She was of course accompanied on this journey by her niece, who now had plenty of leisure to measure and weigh and otherwise handle the windfall on which Madame Merle had covertly congratulated her. Isabel thought very often of the fact of her accession of means, looking at it in a dozen different lights; but we shall not now attempt to follow her train of thought or to explain exactly why her new consciousness was at first oppressive. This failure to rise to immediate joy was indeed but brief; the girl presently made up her mind that to be rich was a virtue because it was to be able to *do*, and that to do could only be sweet. It was the graceful contrary of the stupid side of weakness—especially the feminine variety. To be weak was, for a delicate young person, rather graceful, but, after all, as Isabel said to herself, there was a larger grace than that. Just now, it is true, there was not much to do—once she had sent off a cheque to Lily and another to poor Edith; but she was thankful for the quiet months which her mourning robes and her aunt's fresh widowhood compelled them to spend together. The acquisition of power made her serious; she scrutinised her power with a kind of tender ferocity, but was not eager to exercise it. She began to do so during a stay of some weeks which she eventually made with her aunt in Paris, though in ways that will inevitably present themselves as trivial. They were the ways most naturally imposed in a city in which the shops are the admiration of the world, and that were prescribed unreservedly by the guidance of Mrs. Touchett, who took a rigidly practical view of the transformation of her niece from a poor girl to a rich one. "Now that you're a young woman of fortune you must know how to play the part—I mean to play it well," she said to Isabel once for all; and she added that the girl's first duty was to have everything handsome. "You don't know how to take care of your things, but you must learn," she went on; this was Isabel's second duty. Isabel submitted, but for the present her imagination was not kindled; she longed for opportunities, but these were not the opportunities she meant.

Mrs. Touchett rarely changed her plans, and, having intended before her husband's death to spend a part of the winter in Paris, saw no reason to deprive herself—still less to deprive her companion—of this advantage. Though they would live in great retirement she might still present her niece, informally, to the little circle of her fellow countrymen dwelling upon the skirts of the Champs Elysées.[3] With many of these amiable colonists Mrs. Touchett was intimate; she shared their expatriation, their convictions, their pastimes, their ennui. Isabel saw them arrive with a good deal of assiduity at her aunt's hotel, and pronounced on them with a trenchancy doubtless to be accounted for by the temporary exaltation of her sense of human duty. She made up her mind that their lives were, though

---

3. A fashionable boulevard in the west of Paris, lined for part of its length with parks, and with the Arc de Triomphe as its focal point.

luxurious, inane, and incurred some disfavour by expressing this view on bright Sunday afternoons, when the American absentees were engaged in calling on each other. Though her listeners passed for people kept exemplarily genial by their cooks and dressmakers, two or three of them thought her cleverness, which was generally admitted, inferior to that of the new theatrical pieces. "You all live here this way, but what does it lead to?" she was pleased to ask. "It doesn't seem to lead to anything, and I should think you'd get very tired of it."

Mrs. Touchett thought the question worthy of Henrietta Stackpole. The two ladies had found Henrietta in Paris, and Isabel constantly saw her; so that Mrs. Touchett had some reason for saying to herself that if her niece were not clever enough to originate almost anything, she might be suspected of having borrowed that style of remark from her journalistic friend. The first occasion on which Isabel had spoken was that of a visit paid by the two ladies to Mrs. Luce, an old friend of Mrs. Touchett's and the only person in Paris she now went to see. Mrs. Luce had been living in Paris since the days of Louis Philippe;[4] she used to say jocosely that she was one of the generation of 1830—a joke of which the point was not always taken. When it failed Mrs. Luce used to explain—"Oh yes, I'm one of the romantics;" her French had never become quite perfect. She was always at home on Sunday afternoons and surrounded by sympathetic compatriots, usually the same. In fact she was at home at all times, and reproduced with wondrous truth in her well-cushioned little corner of the brilliant city, the domestic tone of her native Baltimore. This reduced Mr. Luce, her worthy husband, a tall, lean, grizzled, well-brushed gentleman who wore a gold eye-glass and carried his hat a little too much on the back of his head, to mere platonic praise of the "distractions" of Paris—they were his great word—since you would never have guessed from what cares he escaped to them. One of them was that he went every day to the American banker's, where he found a post-office that was almost as sociable and colloquial an institution as in an American country town. He passed an hour (in fine weather) in a chair in Champs Elysées, and he dined uncommonly well at his own table, seated above a waxed floor which it was Mrs. Luce's happiness to believe had a finer polish than any other in the French capital. Occasionally he dined with a friend or two at the Café Anglais,[5] where his talent for ordering a dinner was a source of felicity to his companions and an object of admiration even to the headwaiter of the establishment. These were his only known pastimes, but they had beguiled his hours for upwards of half a century, and they doubtless justified his frequent declaration that there was no place like Paris. In no other place, on these terms, could Mr. Luce flatter himself that he was enjoying life. There was nothing like Paris, but it must be confessed that Mr. Luce thought less highly of this scene of his dissipations than in earlier days. In the list of his resources his political reflections should not be omitted, for they were doubtless the animating principle of many hours that superficially seemed vacant. Like many of his fellow colonists Mr. Luce was a high—or rather a deep—conservative, and gave no countenance to the

---

4. The last Bourbon ruler (1773–1850) of France, a constitutional monarch who reigned from the Revolution of 1830 to that of 1848, when the short-lived Second Republic was established.
5. Then regarded as the city's finest restaurant, on the Boulevard des Italiens.

government lately established in France.[6] He had no faith in its duration and would assure you from year to year that its end was close at hand. "They want to be kept down, sir, to be kept down; nothing but the strong hand— the iron heel—will do for them," he would frequently say of the French people; and his ideal of a fine showy clever rule was that of the superseded Empire. "Paris is much less attractive than in the days of the Emperor; *he* knew how to make a city pleasant," Mr. Luce had often remarked to Mrs. Touchett, who was quite of his own way of thinking and wished to know what one had crossed that odious Atlantic for but to get away from republics.

"Why, madam, sitting in the Champs Elysées, opposite to the Palace of Industry, I've seen the court-carriages from the Tuileries pass up and down as many as seven times a day. I remember one occasion when they went as high as nine. What do you see now? It's no use talking, the style's all gone. Napoleon knew what the French people want, and there'll be a dark cloud over Paris, *our* Paris, till they get the Empire back again."

Among Mrs. Luce's visitors on Sunday afternoons was a young man with whom Isabel had had a good deal of conversation and whom she found full of valuable knowledge. Mr. Edward Rosier—Ned Rosier as he was called—was native to New York and had been brought up in Paris, living there under the eye of his father who, as it happened, had been an early and intimate friend of the late Mr. Archer. Edward Rosier remembered Isabel as a little girl; it had been his father who came to the rescue of the small Archers at the inn at Neufchâtel (he was travelling that way with the boy and had stopped at the hotel by chance), after their *bonne* had gone off with the Russian prince and when Mr. Archer's whereabouts remained for some days a mystery. Isabel remembered perfectly the neat little male child whose hair smelt of a delicious cosmetic and who had a *bonne* all his own, warranted to lose sight of him under no provocation. Isabel took a walk with the pair beside the lake and thought little Edward as pretty as an angel—a comparison by no means conventional in her mind, for she had a very definite conception of a type of features which she supposed to be angelic and which her new friend perfectly illustrated. A small pink face surmounted by a blue velvet bonnet and set off by a stiff embroidered collar had become the countenance of her childish dreams; and she had firmly believed for some time afterwards that the heavenly hosts conversed among themselves in a queer little dialect of French-English, expressing the properest sentiments, as when Edward told her that he was "defended"[7] by his *bonne* to go near the edge of the lake, and that one must always obey to one's *bonne*. Ned Rosier's English had improved; at least it exhibited in a less degree the French variation. His father was dead and his *bonne* dismissed, but the young man still conformed to the spirit of their teaching—he never went to the edge of the lake. There was still something agreeable to the nostrils about him and something not offensive to nobler organs. He was a very gentle and gracious youth, with what are called cultivated tastes—an acquaintance with old china, with good wine, with the bindings of books, with the *Almanach*

---

6. The Third Republic, which after the Franco-Prussian War of 1870–71 succeeded the deposed Second Empire (1852–1870) of Napoleon III.
7. From *défendre*, to forbid; the young Ned thinks as much in French as in English.

de Gotha,[8] with the best shops, the best hotels, the hours of railway-trains. He could order a dinner almost as well as Mr. Luce, and it was probable that as his experience accumulated he would be a worthy successor to that gentleman, whose rather grim politics he also advocated in a soft and innocent voice. He had some charming rooms in Paris, decorated with old Spanish altar-lace, the envy of his female friends, who declared that his chimney-piece was better draped than the high shoulders of many a duchess. He usually, however, spent a part of every winter at Pau,[9] and had once passed a couple of months in the United States.

He took a great interest in Isabel and remembered perfectly the walk at Neufchâtel, when she would persist in going so near the edge. He seemed to recognise this same tendency in the subversive enquiry that I quoted a moment ago, and set himself to answer our heroine's question with greater urbanity than it perhaps deserved. "What does it lead to, Miss Archer? Why Paris leads everywhere. You can't go anywhere unless you come here first. Every one that comes to Europe has got to pass through. You don't mean it in that sense so much? You mean what good it does you? Well, how can you penetrate futurity? How can you tell what lies ahead? If it's a pleasant road I don't care where it leads. I like the road, Miss Archer; I like the dear old asphalte. You can't get tired of it—you can't if you try. You think you would, but you wouldn't; there's always something new and fresh. Take the Hôtel Drouot,[1] now; they sometimes have three and four sales a week. Where can you get such things as you can here? In spite of all they say I maintain they're cheaper too, if you know the right places. I know plenty of places, but I keep them to myself. I'll tell you, if you like, as a particular favour; only you mustn't tell any one else. Don't you go anywhere without asking me first; I want you to promise me that. As a general thing avoid the Boulevards; there's very little to be done on the Boulevards. Speaking conscientiously—*sans blague*[2]—I don't believe any one knows Paris better than I. You and Mrs. Touchett must come and breakfast with me some day, and I'll show you my things; *je ne vous dis que ça!*[3] There has been a great deal of talk about London of late; it's the fashion to cry up London. But there's nothing in it—you can't do anything in London. No Louis Quinze—nothing of the First Empire; nothing but their eternal Queen Anne.[4] It's good for one's bed-room, Queen Anne—for one's washing-room; but it isn't proper for a *salon*.[5] Do I spend my life at the auctioneer's?" Mr. Rosier pursued in answer to another question of Isabel's. "Oh no; I haven't the means. I wish I had. You think I'm a mere trifler; I can tell by the expression of your face—you've got a wonderfully expressive face. I hope you don't mind my saying that; I mean it as a kind of warning. You think I ought to do something, and so do I, so long as you leave it vague. But when you come to the point you see you have to stop. I can't go home and be a shopkeeper. You think I'm very well fitted? Ah,

8. A handbook showing the genealogy and interrelations of the various European royal and aristocratic families.
9. A resort town in Pyrenees, in the southwest of France.
1. Paris' main auction house, an equivalent of Sotheby's or Christie's, on the rue Dryout in the city's 9th Arrondissement (see p. 396, n.1).
2. No kidding (French).
3. That's all I'm saying! (French).
4. Styles of furniture and decorative arts identified with the reigns of France's Louis XV (1715–1774), Napoleon (1804–1815), and England's Anne (1702–1714).
5. Drawing room (French).

Miss Archer, you overrate me. I can buy very well, but I can't sell; you should see when I sometimes try to get rid of my things. It takes much more ability to make other people buy than to buy yourself. When I think how clever they must be, the people who make *me* buy! Ah no; I couldn't be a shopkeeper. I can't be a doctor; it's a repulsive business. I can't be a clergyman; I haven't got convictions. And then I can't pronounce the names right in the Bible. They're very difficult, in the Old Testament particularly. I can't be a lawyer; I don't understand—how do you call it?—the American *procédure*. Is there anything else? There's nothing for a gentleman in America. I should like to be a diplomatist; but American diplomacy— that's not for gentlemen either. I'm sure if you had seen the last min—"

Henrietta Stackpole, who was often with her friend when Mr. Rosier, coming to pay his compliments late in the afternoon, expressed himself after the fashion I have sketched, usually interrupted the young man at this point and read him a lecture on the duties of the American citizen. She thought him most unnatural; he was worse than poor Ralph Touchett. Henrietta, however, was at this time more than ever addicted to fine criticism, for her conscience had been freshly alarmed as regards Isabel. She had not congratulated this young lady on her augmentations and begged to be excused from doing so.

"If Mr. Touchett had consulted me about leaving you the money," she frankly asserted, "I'd have said to him 'Never!'"

"I see," Isabel had answered. "You think it will prove a curse in disguise. Perhaps it will."

"Leave it to some one you care less for—that's what I should have said."

"To yourself for instance?" Isabel suggested jocosely. And then, "Do you really believe it will ruin me?" she asked in quite another tone.

"I hope it won't ruin you; but it will certainly confirm your dangerous tendencies."

"Do you mean the love of luxury—of extravagance?"

"No, no," said Henrietta; "I mean your exposure on the moral side. I approve of luxury; I think we ought to be as elegant as possible. Look at the luxury of our western cities; I've seen nothing over here to compare with it. I hope you'll never become grossly sensual; but I'm not afraid of that. The peril for you is that you live too much in the world of your own dreams. You're not enough in contact with reality—with the toiling, striving, suffering, I may even say sinning, world that surrounds you. You're too fastidious; you've too many graceful illusions. Your newly-acquired thousands will shut you up more and more to the society of a few selfish and heartless people who will be interested in keeping them up."

Isabel's eyes expanded as she gazed at this lurid scene. "What are my illusions?" she asked. "I try so hard not to have any."

"Well," said Henrietta, "you think you can lead a romantic life, that you can live by pleasing yourself and pleasing others. You'll find you're mistaken. Whatever life you lead you must put your soul in it—to make any sort of success of it; and from the moment you do that it ceases to be romance, I assure you: it becomes grim reality! And you can't always please yourself; you must sometimes please other people. That, I admit, you're very ready to do; but there's another thing that's still more important— you must often displease others. You must always be ready for that—you must never shrink from it. That doesn't suit you at all—you're too fond of admiration, you like to be thought well of. You think we can escape disagreeable duties by taking romantic views—that's your great illusion, my dear. But we can't. You must be prepared on many occasions in life to please no one at all—not even yourself."

Isabel shook her head sadly; she looked troubled and frightened. "This, for you, Henrietta," she said, "must be one of those occasions!"

It was certainly true that Miss Stackpole, during her visit to Paris, which had been professionally more remunerative than her English sojourn, had not been living in the world of dreams. Mr. Bantling, who had now returned to England, was her companion for the first four weeks of her stay; and about Mr. Bantling there was nothing dreamy. Isabel learned from her friend that the two had led a life of great personal intimacy and that this had been a peculiar advantage to Henrietta, owing to the gentleman's remarkable knowledge of Paris. He had explained everything, shown her everything, been her constant guide and interpreter. They had breakfasted together, dined together, gone to the theatre together, supped together, really in a manner quite lived together. He was a true friend, Henrietta more than once assured our heroine; and she had never supposed that she could like any Englishman so well. Isabel could not have told you why, but she found something that ministered to mirth in the alliance the correspondent of the *Interviewer* had struck with Lady Pensil's brother; her amusement moreover subsisted in face of the fact that she thought it a credit to each of them. Isabel couldn't rid herself of a suspicion that they were playing somehow at cross-purposes—that the simplicity of each had been entrapped. But this simplicity was on either side none the less honourable. It was as graceful on Henrietta's part to believe that Mr. Bantling took an interest in the diffusion of lively journalism and in consolidating the position of lady-correspondents as it was on the part of his companion to suppose that the cause of the *Interviewer*—a periodical of which he never formed a very definite conception—was, if subtly analysed (a task to which Mr. Bantling felt himself quite equal), but the cause of Miss Stackpole's need of demonstrative affection. Each of these groping celibates supplied at any rate a want of which the other was impatiently conscious. Mr. Bantling, who was of rather a slow and a discursive habit, relished a prompt, keen, positive woman, who charmed him by the influence of a shining, challenging eye and a kind of bandbox freshness, and who kindled a perception of raciness in a mind to which the usual fare of life seemed unsalted. Henrietta, on the other hand, enjoyed the society of a gentleman who appeared somehow, in his way, made, by expensive, roundabout, almost "quaint" processes, for her use, and whose leisured state, though generally indefensible, was a decided boon to a breathless mate, and who was furnished with an easy, traditional, though by no means exhaustive, answer to almost any social or practical question that could come up. She often found Mr. Bantling's answers very convenient, and in the press of catching the American post would largely and showily address them to publicity. It was to be feared that she was indeed drifting toward those abysses of sophistication as to which Isabel, wishing for a good-humoured retort, had warned her. There might be danger in store for Isabel; but it was scarcely to be hoped that Miss Stackpole, on her side, would find permanent rest in any adoption of the views of a class pledged to all the old abuses. Isabel continued to warn her good-humouredly;

Lady Pensil's obliging brother was sometimes, on our heroine's lips, an object of irreverent and facetious allusion. Nothing, however, could exceed Henrietta's amiability on this point; she used to abound in the sense of Isabel's irony and to enumerate with elation the hours she had spent with this perfect man of the world—a term that had ceased to make with her, as previously, for opprobrium. Then, a few moments later, she would forget that they had been talking jocosely and would mention with impulsive earnestness some expedition she had enjoyed in his company. She would say: "Oh, I know all about Versailles; I went there with Mr. Bantling. I was bound to see it thoroughly—I warned him when we went out there that I was thorough: so we spent three days at the hotel and wandered all over the place. It was lovely weather—a kind of Indian summer, only not so good. We just lived in that park. Oh yes; you can't tell me anything about Versailles." Henrietta appeared to have made arrangements to meet her gallant friend during the spring in Italy.

Chapter XXI

Mrs. Touchett, before arriving in Paris, had fixed the day for her departure and by the middle of February had begun to travel southward. She interrupted her journey to pay a visit to her son, who at San Remo,[1] on the Italian shore of the Mediterranean, had been spending a dull, bright winter beneath a slow-moving white umbrella. Isabel went with her aunt as a matter of course, though Mrs. Touchett, with homely, customary logic, had laid before her a pair of alternatives.

"Now, of course, you're completely your own mistress and are as free as the bird on the bough. I don't mean you were not so before, but you're at present on a different footing—property erects a kind of barrier. You can do a great many things if you're rich which would be severely criticised if you were poor. You can go and come, you can travel alone, you can have your own establishment: I mean of course if you'll take a companion—some decayed gentlewoman, with a darned cashmere and dyed hair, who paints on velvet. You don't think you'd like that? Of course you can do as you please; I only want you to understand how much you're at liberty. You might take Miss Stackpole as your *dame de compagnie*;[2] she'd keep people off very well. I think, however, that it's a great deal better you should remain with me, in spite of there being no obligation. It's better for several reasons, quite apart from your liking it. I shouldn't think you'd like it, but I recommend you to make the sacrifice. Of course whatever novelty there may have been at first in my society has quite passed away, and you see me as I am—a dull, obstinate, narrow-minded old woman."

"I don't think you're at all dull," Isabel had replied to this.

"But you do think I'm obstinate and narrow-minded? I told you so!" said Mrs. Touchett with much elation at being justified.

Isabel remained for the present with her aunt, because, in spite of eccentric impulses, she had a great regard for what was usually deemed decent, and a young gentlewoman without visible relations had always struck her as a flower without foliage. It was true that Mrs. Touchett's conversation

---

1. A resort town on the Italian Riviera; James spent several weeks there in the winter of 1881 while working on *The Portrait of a Lady*.
2. Companion (French).

had never again appeared so brilliant as that first afternoon in Albany, when she sat in her damp water-proof and sketched the opportunities that Europe would offer to a young person of taste. This, however, was in a great measure the girl's own fault; she had got a glimpse of her aunt's experience, and her imagination constantly anticipated the judgements and emotions of a woman who had very little of the same faculty. Apart from this, Mrs. Touchett had a great merit; she was as honest as a pair of compasses. There was a comfort in her stiffness and firmness; you knew exactly where to find her and were never liable to chance encounters and concussions. On her own ground she was perfectly present, but was never over-inquisitive as regards the territory of her neighbour. Isabel came at last to have a kind of undemonstrable pity for her; there seemed something so dreary in the condition of a person whose nature had, as it were, so little surface—offered so limited a face to the accretions of human contact. Nothing tender, nothing sympathetic, had ever had a chance to fasten upon it—no wind-sown blossom, no familiar softening moss. Her offered, her passive extent, in other words, was about that of a knife-edge. Isabel had reason to believe none the less that as she advanced in life she made more of those concessions to the sense of something obscurely distinct from convenience—more of them than she independently exacted. She was learning to sacrifice consistency to considerations of that inferior order for which the excuse must be found in the particular case. It was not to the credit of her absolute rectitude that she should have gone the longest way round to Florence in order to spend a few weeks with her invalid son; since in former years it had been one of her most definite convictions that when Ralph wished to see her he was at liberty to remember that Palazzo Crescentini contained a large apartment known as the quarter of the signorino.

"I want to ask you something," Isabel said to this young man the day after her arrival at San Remo—"something I've thought more than once of asking you by letter, but that I've hesitated on the whole to write about. Face to face, nevertheless, my question seems easy enough. Did you know your father intended to leave me so much money?"

Ralph stretched his legs a little further than usual and gazed a little more fixedly at the Mediterranean. "What does it matter, my dear Isabel, whether I knew? My father was very obstinate."

"So," said the girl, "you did know."

"Yes; he told me. We even talked it over a little."

"What did he do it for?" asked Isabel abruptly.

"Why, as a kind of compliment."

"A compliment on what?"

"On your so beautifully existing."

"He liked me too much," she presently declared.

"That's a way we all have."

"If I believed that I should be very unhappy. Fortunately I don't believe it. I want to be treated with justice; I want nothing but that."

"Very good. But you must remember that justice to a lovely being is after all a florid sort of sentiment."

"I'm not a lovely being. How can you say that, at the very moment when I'm asking such odious questions? I must seem to you delicate!"

"You seem to me troubled," said Ralph.

"I am troubled."

"About what?"

For a moment she answered nothing; then she broke out: "Do you think it good for me suddenly to be made so rich? Henrietta doesn't."

"Oh, hang Henrietta!" said Ralph coarsely. "If you ask *me* I'm delighted at it."

"Is that why your father did it—for your amusement?"

"I differ with Miss Stackpole," Ralph went on more gravely. "I think it very good for you to have means."

Isabel looked at him with serious eyes. "I wonder whether you know what's good for me—or whether you care."

"If I know depend upon it I care. Shall I tell you what it is? Not to torment yourself."

"Not to torment you, I suppose you mean."

"You can't do that; I'm proof. Take things more easily. Don't ask yourself so much whether this or that is good for you. Don't question your conscience so much—it will get out of tune like a strummed piano. Keep it for great occasions. Don't try so much to form your character—it's like trying to pull open a tight, tender young rose. Live as you like best, and your character will take care of itself. Most things are good for you; the exceptions are very rare, and a comfortable income's not one of them." Ralph paused, smiling; Isabel had listened quickly. "You've too much power of thought—above all too much conscience," Ralph added. "It's out of all reason, the number of things you think wrong. Put back your watch. Diet your fever. Spread your wings; rise above the ground. It's never wrong to do that."

She had listened eagerly, as I say; and it was her nature to understand quickly. "I wonder if you appreciate what you say. If you do, you take a great responsibility."

"You frighten me a little, but I think I'm right," said Ralph, persisting in cheer.

"All the same what you say is very true," Isabel pursued. "You could say nothing more true. I'm absorbed in myself—I look at life too much as a doctor's prescription. Why indeed should we perpetually be thinking whether things are good for us, as if we were patients lying in a hospital? Why should I be so afraid of not doing right? As if it mattered to the world whether I do right or wrong!"

"You're a capital person to advise," said Ralph; "you take the wind out of *my* sails!"

She looked at him as if she had not heard him—though she was following out the train of reflexion which he himself had kindled. "I try to care more about the world than about myself—but I always come back to myself. It's because I'm afraid." She stopped; her voice had trembled a little. "Yes, I'm afraid; I can't tell you. A large fortune means freedom, and I'm afraid of that. It's such a fine thing, and one should make such a good use of it. If one shouldn't one would be ashamed. And one must keep thinking; it's a constant effort. I'm not sure it's not a greater happiness to be powerless."

"For weak people I've no doubt it's a greater happiness. For weak people the effort not to be contemptible must be great."

"And how do you know I'm not weak?" Isabel asked.

"Ah," Ralph answered with a flush that the girl noticed, "if you are I'm awfully sold!"

The charm of the Mediterranean coast only deepened for our heroine on acquaintance, for it was the threshold of Italy, the gate of admirations. Italy, as yet imperfectly seen and felt, stretched before her as a land of promise, a land in which a love of the beautiful might be comforted by endless knowledge. Whenever she strolled upon the shore with her cousin—and she was the companion of his daily walk—she looked across the sea, with longing eyes, to where she knew that Genoa lay. She was glad to pause, however, on the edge of this larger adventure; there was such a thrill even in the preliminary hovering. It affected her moreover as a peaceful interlude, as a hush of the drum and fife in a career which she had little warrant as yet for regarding as agitated, but which nevertheless she was constantly picturing to herself by the light of her hopes, her fears, her fancies, her ambitions, her predilections, and which reflected these subjective accidents in a manner sufficiently dramatic. Madame Merle had predicted to Mrs. Touchett that after their young friend had put her hand into her pocket half a dozen times she would be reconciled to the idea that it had been filled by a munificent uncle; and the event justified, as it had so often justified before, that lady's perspicacity. Ralph Touchett had praised his cousin for being morally inflammable, that is for being quick to take a hint that was meant as good advice. His advice had perhaps helped the matter; she had at any rate before leaving San Remo grown used to feeling rich. The consciousness in question found a proper place in rather a dense little group of ideas that she had about herself, and often it was by no means the least agreeable. It took perpetually for granted a thousand good intentions. She lost herself in a maze of visions; the fine things to be done by a rich, independent, generous girl who took a large human view of occasions and obligations were sublime in the mass. Her fortune therefore became to her mind a part of her better self; it gave her importance, gave her even, to her own imagination, a certain ideal beauty. What it did for her in the imagination of others is another affair, and on this point we must also touch in time. The visions I have just spoken of were mixed with other debates. Isabel liked better to think of the future than of the past; but at times, as she listened to the murmur of the Mediterranean waves, her glance took a backward flight. It rested upon two figures which, in spite of increasing distance, were still sufficiently salient; they were recognisable without difficulty as those of Caspar Goodwood and Lord Warburton. It was strange how quickly these images of energy had fallen into the background of our young lady's life. It was in her disposition at all times to lose faith in the reality of absent things; she could summon back her faith, in case of need, with an effort, but the effort was often painful even when the reality had been pleasant. The past was apt to look dead and its revival rather to show the livid light of a judgement-day. The girl moreover was not prone to take for granted that she herself lived in the mind of others—she had not the fatuity to believe she left indelible traces. She was capable of being wounded by the discovery that she had been forgotten; but of all liberties the one she herself found sweetest was the liberty to forget. She had not given her last shilling, sentimentally speaking, either to Caspar Goodwood or to Lord Warburton, and yet couldn't but feel them appreciably in debt to her. She had of course reminded herself that she was to hear from Mr. Goodwood again; but this was not to be for another year and a half, and in that time a great many things might happen. She had indeed failed to say to herself that her American suitor might find some other girl more comfortable to woo; because, though it was certain many other girls would prove so, she had not the smallest belief that this merit would attract him. But she reflected that she herself might know the humiliation of change, might really, for that matter, come to the end of the things that were not Caspar (even though there appeared so many of them), and find rest in those very elements of his presence which struck her now as impediments to the finer respiration. It was conceivable that these impediments should some day prove a sort of blessing in disguise—a clear and quiet harbour enclosed by a brave granite breakwater. But that day could only come in its order, and she couldn't wait for it with folded hands. That Lord Warburton should continue to cherish her image seemed to her more than a noble humility or an enlightened pride ought to wish to reckon with. She had so definitely undertaken to preserve no record of what had passed between them that a corresponding effort on his own part would be eminently just. This was not, as it may seem, merely a theory tinged with sarcasm. Isabel candidly believed that his lordship would, in the usual phrase, get over his disappointment. He had been deeply affected—this she believed, and she was still capable of deriving pleasure from the belief; but it was absurd that a man both so intelligent and so honourably dealt with should cultivate a scar out of proportion to any wound. Englishmen liked moreover to be comfortable, said Isabel, and there could be little comfort for Lord Warburton, in the long run, in brooding over a self-sufficient American girl who had been but a casual acquaintance. She flattered herself that, should she hear from one day to another that he had married some young woman of his own country who had done more to deserve him, she should receive the news without a pang even of surprise. It would have proved that he believed she was firm—which was what she wished to seem to him. That alone was grateful to her pride.

Chapter XXII

On one of the first days of May, some six months after old Mr. Touchett's death, a small group that might have been described by a painter as composing well was gathered in one of the many rooms of an ancient villa crowning an olive-muffled hill outside of the Roman gate of Florence.[1] The villa was a long, rather blank-looking structure, with the far-projecting roof which Tuscany loves and which, on the hills that encircle Florence, when considered from a distance, makes so harmonious a rectangle with the straight, dark, definite cypresses that usually rise in groups of three or four beside it. The house had a front upon a little grassy, empty, rural piazza which occupied a part of the hill-top; and this front, pierced with a few windows in irregular relations and furnished with a stone bench lengthily

1. The Porta Romana is at the southern end of the Boboli Gardens, on the southern side of the Arno, the river that divides the city. The villa has been identified as the Villa Castellani, on the hill of Bellosguardo; James's family friends, Frank Boott and his daughter Elizabeth, kept an apartment there. See the selection from "Recent Florence" in this Norton Critical Edition, p. 437. James's description here is exact to the place.

adjusted to the base of the structure and useful as a lounging-place to one or two persons wearing more or less of that air of undervalued merit which in Italy, for some reason or other, always gracefully invests any one who confidently assumes a perfectly passive attitude—this antique, solid, weather-worn, yet imposing front had a somewhat incommunicative character. It was the mask, not the face of the house. It had heavy lids, but no eyes; the house in reality looked another way—looked off behind, into splendid openness and the range of the afternoon light. In that quarter the villa overhung the slope of its hill and the long valley of the Arno, hazy with Italian colour. It had a narrow garden, in the manner of a terrace, productive chiefly of tangles of wild roses and other old stone benches, mossy and sun-warmed. The parapet of the terrace was just the height to lean upon, and beneath it the ground declined into the vagueness of olive-crops and vineyards. It is not, however, with the outside of the place that we are concerned; on this bright morning of ripened spring its tenants had reason to prefer the shady side of the wall. The windows of the ground-floor, as you saw them from the piazza, were, in their noble proportions, extremely architectural; but their function seemed less to offer communication with the world than to defy the world to look in. They were massively cross-barred, and placed at such a height that curiosity, even on tiptoe, expired before it reached them. In an apartment lighted by a row of three of these jealous apertures—one of the several distinct apartments into which the villa was divided and which were mainly occupied by foreigners of random race long resident in Florence—a gentleman was seated in company with a young girl and two good sisters from a religious house. The room was, however, less sombre than our indications may have represented, for it had a wide, high door, which now stood open into the tangled garden behind; and the tall iron lattices admitted on occasion more than enough of the Italian sunshine. It was moreover a seat of ease, indeed of luxury, telling of arrangements subtly studied and refinements frankly proclaimed, and containing a variety of those faded hangings of damask and tapestry, those chests and cabinets of carved and time-polished oak, those angular specimens of pictorial art in frames as pedantically primitive, those perverse-looking relics of mediæval brass and pottery, of which Italy has long been the not quite exhausted storehouse. These things kept terms with articles of modern furniture in which large allowance had been made for a lounging generation; it was to be noticed that all the chairs were deep and well padded and that much space was occupied by a writing-table of which the ingenious perfection bore the stamp of London and the nineteenth century. There were books in profusion and magazines and newspapers, and a few small, odd, elaborate pictures, chiefly in water-colour. One of these productions stood on a drawing-room easel before which, at the moment we begin to be concerned with her, the young girl I have mentioned had placed herself. She was looking at the picture in silence.

Silence—absolute silence—had not fallen upon her companions; but their talk had an appearance of embarrassed continuity. The two good sisters had not settled themselves in their respective chairs; their attitude expressed a final reserve and their faces showed the glaze of prudence. They were plain, ample, mild-featured women, with a kind of business-like modesty to which the impersonal aspect of their stiffened linen and of the serge that draped them as if nailed on frames gave an advantage. One of them, a person of a certain age, in spectacles, with a fresh complexion and a full cheek, had a more discriminating manner than her colleague, as well as the responsibility of their errand, which apparently related to the young girl. This object of interest wore her hat—an ornament of extreme simplicity and not at variance with her plain muslin gown, too short for her years, though it must already have been "let out." The gentleman who might have been supposed to be entertaining the two nuns was perhaps conscious of the difficulties of his function, it being in its way as arduous to converse with the very meek as with the very mighty. At the same time he was clearly much occupied with their quiet charge, and while she turned her back to him his eyes rested gravely on her slim, small figure. He was a man of forty, with a high but well-shaped head, on which the hair, still dense, but prematurely grizzled, had been cropped close. He had a fine, narrow, extremely modelled and composed face, of which the only fault was just this effect of its running a trifle too much to points; an appearance to which the shape of the beard contributed not a little. This beard, cut in the manner of the portraits of the sixteenth century and surmounted by a fair moustache, of which the ends had a romantic upward flourish, gave its wearer a foreign, traditionary look and suggested that he was a gentleman who studied style. His conscious, curious eyes, however, eyes at once vague and penetrating, intelligent and hard, expressive of the observer as well as of the dreamer, would have assured you that he studied it only within well-chosen limits, and that in so far as he sought it he found it. You would have been much at a loss to determine his original clime and country; he had none of the superficial signs that usually render the answer to this question an insipidly easy one. If he had English blood in his veins it had probably received some French or Italian commixture; but he suggested, fine gold coin as he was, no stamp nor emblem of the common mintage that provides for general circulation; he was the elegant complicated medal struck off for a special occasion. He had a light, lean, rather languid-looking figure, and was apparently neither tall nor short. He was dressed as a man dresses who takes little other trouble about it than to have no vulgar things.

"Well, my dear, what do you think of it?" he asked of the young girl. He used the Italian tongue, and used it with perfect ease; but this would not have convinced you he was Italian.

The child turned her head earnestly to one side and the other. "It's very pretty, papa. Did you make it yourself?"

"Certainly I made it. Don't you think I'm clever?"

"Yes, papa, very clever; I also have learned to make pictures." And she turned round and showed a small, fair face painted with a fixed and intensely sweet smile.

"You should have brought me a specimen of your powers."

"I've brought a great many; they're in my trunk."

"She draws very—very carefully," the elder of the nuns remarked, speaking in French.

"I'm glad to hear it. Is it you who have instructed her?"

"Happily no," said the good sister, blushing a little. "Ce n'est pas ma partie.[2] I teach nothing. I leave that to those who are wiser. We've an

2. That's not what I do (French).

excellent drawing-master, Mr.—Mr.—what is his name?" she asked of her companion.

Her companion looked about at the carpet. "It's a German name," she said in Italian, as if it needed to be translated.

"Yes," the other went on, "he's a German, and we've had him many years."

The young girl, who was not heeding the conversation, had wandered away to the open door of the large room and stood looking into the garden. "And you, my sister, are French," said the gentleman.

"Yes, sir," the visitor gently replied. "I speak to the pupils in my own tongue. I know no other. But we have sisters of other countries—English, German, Irish. They all speak their proper language."

The gentleman gave a smile. "Has my daughter been under the care of one of the Irish ladies?" And then, as he saw that his visitors suspected a joke, though failing to understand it, "You're very complete," he instantly added.

"Oh, yes, we're complete. We've everything, and everything's of the best."

"We have gymnastics," the Italian sister ventured to remark. "But not dangerous."

"I hope not. Is that *your* branch?" A question which provoked much candid hilarity on the part of the two ladies; on the subsidence of which their entertainer, glancing at his daughter, remarked that she had grown.

"Yes, but I think she has finished. She'll remain—not big," said the French sister.

"I'm not sorry. I prefer women like books—very good and not too long. But I know," the gentleman said, "no particular reason why my child should be short."

The nun gave a temperate shrug, as if to intimate that such things might be beyond our knowledge. "She's in very good health; that's the best thing."

"Yes, she looks sound." And the young girl's father watched her a moment. "What do you see in the garden?" he asked in French.

"I see many flowers," she replied in a sweet, small voice and with an accent as good as his own.

"Yes, but not many good ones. However, such as they are, go out and gather some for *ces dames*."

The child turned to with her smile heightened by pleasure. "May I, truly?"

"Ah, when I tell you," said her father.

The girl glanced at the elder of the nuns. "May I, truly, *ma mère*?"

"Obey monsieur your father, my child," said the sister, blushing again.

The child, satisfied with this authorisation, descended from the threshold and was presently lost to sight. "You don't spoil them," said her father gaily.

"For everything they must ask leave. That's our system. Leave is freely granted, but they must ask it."

"Oh, I don't quarrel with your system; I've no doubt it's excellent. I sent you my daughter to see what you'd make of her. I had faith."

"One must have faith," the sister blandly rejoined, gazing through her spectacles.

"Well, has my faith been rewarded? What have you made of her?"

The sister dropped her eyes a moment. "A good Christian, monsieur."

Her host dropped his eyes as well; but it was probable that the movement had in each case a different spring. "Yes, and what else?"

He watched the lady from the convent, probably thinking she would say that a good Christian was everything; but for all her simplicity she was not so crude as that. "A charming young lady—a real little woman—a daughter in whom you will have nothing but contentment."

"She seems to me very *gentille*,"[3] said the father. "She's really pretty."

"She's perfect. She has no faults."

"She never had any as a child, and I'm glad you have given her none."

"We love her too much," said the spectacled sister with dignity. "And as for faults, how can we give what we have not? *Le couvent n'est pas comme le monde, monsieur.*[4] She's our daughter, as you may say. We've had her since she was so small."

"Of all those we shall lose this year she's the one we shall miss most," the younger woman murmured deferentially.

"Ah, yes, we shall talk long of her," said the other. "We shall hold her up to the new ones." And at this the good sister appeared to find her spectacles dim; while her companion, after fumbling a moment, presently drew forth a pocket-handkerchief of durable texture.

"It's not certain you'll lose her; nothing's settled yet," their host rejoined quickly; not as if to anticipate their tears, but in the tone of a man saying what was most agreeable to himself.

"We should be very happy to believe that. Fifteen is very young to leave us."

"Oh," exclaimed the gentleman with more vivacity than he had yet used, "it is not I who wish to take her away. I wish you could keep her always!"

"Ah, monsieur," said the elder sister, smiling and getting up, "good as she is, she's made for the world. *Le monde y gagnera.*"[5]

"If all the good people were hidden away in convents how would the world get on?" her companion softly enquired, rising also.

This was a question of a wider bearing than the good woman apparently supposed; and the lady in spectacles took a harmonising view by saying comfortably: "Fortunately there are good people everywhere."

"If you're going there will be two less here," her host remarked gallantly.

For this extravagant sally his simple visitors had no answer, and they simply looked at each other in decent deprecation; but their confusion was speedily covered by the return of the young girl with two large bunches of roses—one of them all white, the other red.

"I give you your choice, mamman Catherine," said the child. "It's only the colour that's different, mamman Justine; there are just as many roses in one bunch as in the other."

The two sisters turned to each other, smiling and hesitating, with "Which will you take?" and "No, it's for you to choose."

"I'll take the red, thank you," said mother Catherine in the spectacles. "I'm so red myself. They'll comfort us on our way back to Rome."

"Ah, they won't last," cried the young girl. "I wish I could give you something that would last!"

"You've given us a good memory of yourself, my daughter. That will last!"

---

3. Nice, well-mannered (French).
4. The convent is not like the world, sir (French).
5. The world will gain by it (French).

"I wish nuns could wear pretty things. I would give you my blue beads," the child went on.

"And do you go back to Rome to-night?" her father enquired.

"Yes, we take the train again. We've so much to do *là-bas*."[6]

"Are you not tired?"

"We are never tired."

"Ah, my sister, sometimes," murmured the junior votaress.

"Not to-day, at any rate. We have rested too well here. *Que Dieu vous garde, ma fille.*"[7]

Their host, while they exchanged kisses with his daughter, went forward to open the door through which they were to pass; but as he did so he gave a slight exclamation, and stood looking beyond. The door opened into a vaulted ante-chamber, as high as a chapel and paved with red tiles; and into this ante-chamber a lady had just been admitted by a servant, a lad in shabby livery, who was now ushering her toward the apartment in which our friends were grouped. The gentleman at the door, after dropping his exclamation, remained silent; in silence too the lady advanced. He gave her no further audible greeting and offered her no hand, but stood aside to let her pass into the saloon. At the threshold she hesitated. "Is there any one?" she asked.

"Some one you may see."

She went in and found herself confronted with the two nuns and their pupil, who was coming forward, between them, with a hand in the arm of each. At the sight of the new visitor they all paused, and the lady, who had also stopped, stood looking at them. The young girl gave a little soft cry: "Ah, Madame Merle!"

The visitor had been slightly startled, but her manner the next instant was none the less gracious. "Yes, it's Madame Merle, come to welcome you home." And she held out two hands to the girl, who immediately came up to her, presenting her forehead to be kissed. Madame Merle saluted this portion of her charming little person and then stood smiling at the two nuns. They acknowledged her smile with a decent obeisance, but permitted themselves no direct scrutiny of this imposing, brilliant woman, who seemed to bring in with her something of the radiance of the outer world.

"These ladies have brought my daughter home, and now they return to the convent," the gentleman explained.

"Ah, you go back to Rome? I've lately come from there. It's very lovely now," said Madame Merle.

The good sisters, standing with their hands folded into their sleeves, accepted this statement uncritically; and the master of the house asked his new visitor how long it was since she had left Rome. "She came to see me at the convent," said the young girl before the lady addressed had time to reply.

"I've been more than once, Pansy," Madame Merle declared. "Am I not your great friend in Rome?"

"I remember the last time best," said Pansy, "because you told me I should come away."

"Did you tell her that?" the child's father asked.

6. There (French).
7. God protect you, my child (French).

"I hardly remember. I told her what I thought would please her. I've been in Florence a week. I hoped you would come to see me."

"I should have done so if I had known you were there. One doesn't know such things by inspiration—though I suppose one ought. You had better sit down."

These two speeches were made in a particular tone of voice—a tone half-lowered and carefully quiet, but as from habit rather than from any definite need. Madame Merle looked about her, choosing her seat. "You're going to the door with these women? Let me of course not interrupt the ceremony. *Je vous salue, mesdames*,"[8] she added, in French, to the nuns, as if to dismiss them.

"This lady's a great friend of ours; you will have seen her at the convent," said their entertainer. "We've much faith in her judgement, and she'll help me to decide whether my daughter shall return to you at the end of the holidays."

"I hope you'll decide in our favour, madame," the sister in spectacles ventured to remark.

"That's Mr. Osmond's pleasantry; I decide nothing," said Madame Merle, but also as in pleasantry. "I believe you've a very good school, but Miss Osmond's friends must remember that she's very naturally meant for the world."

"That's what I've told monsieur," sister Catherine answered. "It's precisely to fit her for the world," she murmured, glancing at Pansy, who stood, at a little distance, attentive to Madame Merle's elegant apparel.

"Do you hear that, Pansy? You're very naturally meant for the world," said Pansy's father.

The child fixed him an instant with her pure young eyes. "Am I not meant for you, papa?"

Papa gave a quick, light laugh. "That doesn't prevent it! I'm of the world, Pansy."

"Kindly permit us to retire," said sister Catherine. "Be good and wise and happy in any case, my daughter."

"I shall certainly come back and see you," Pansy returned, recommencing her embraces, which were presently interrupted by Madame Merle.

"Stay with me, dear child," she said, "while your father takes the good ladies to the door."

Pansy stared, disappointed, yet not protesting. She was evidently impregnated with the idea of submission, which was due to any one who took the tone of authority; and she was a passive spectator of the operation of her fate. "May I not see mamman Catherine get into the carriage?" she nevertheless asked very gently.

"It would please me better if you'd remain with me," said Madame Merle, while Mr. Osmond and his companions, who had bowed low again to the other visitor, passed into the ante-chamber.

"Oh yes, I'll stay," Pansy answered; and she stood near Madame Merle, surrendering her little hand, which this lady took. She stared out of the window; her eyes had filled with tears.

"I'm glad they've taught you to obey," said Madame Merle. "That's what good little girls should do."

---

8. I greet you, ladies; the phrase plays on the French of the Ave Maria, "Je vous salue, Marie."

"Oh yes, I obey very well," cried Pansy with soft eagerness, almost with boastfulness, as if she had been speaking of her piano-playing. And then she gave a faint, just audible sigh.

Madame Merle, holding her hand, drew it across her own fine palm and looked at it. The gaze was critical, but it found nothing to deprecate; the child's small hand was delicate and fair. "I hope they always see that you wear gloves," she said in a moment. "Little girls usually dislike them."

"I used to dislike them, but I like them now," the child made answer.

"Very good, I'll make you a present of a dozen."

"I thank you very much. What colours will they be?" Pansy demanded with interest.

Madame Merle meditated. "Useful colours."

"But very pretty?"

"Are you very fond of pretty things?"

"Yes; but—but not too fond," said Pansy with a trace of asceticism.

"Well, they won't be too pretty," Madame Merle returned with a laugh. She took the child's other hand and drew her nearer; after which, looking at her a moment, "Shall you miss mother Catherine?" she went on.

"Yes—when I think of her."

"Try then not to think of her. Perhaps some day," added Madame Merle, "you'll have another mother."

"I don't think that's necessary," Pansy said, repeating her little soft conciliatory sigh. "I had more than thirty mothers at the convent."

Her father's step sounded again in the ante-chamber, and Madame Merle got up, releasing the child. Mr. Osmond came in and closed the door; then, without looking at Madame Merle, he pushed one or two chairs back into their places. His visitor waited a moment for him to speak, watching him as he moved about. Then at last she said: "I hoped you'd have come to Rome. I thought it possible you'd have wished yourself to fetch Pansy away."

"That was a natural supposition; but I'm afraid it's not the first time I've acted in defiance of your calculations."

"Yes," said Madame Merle, "I think you very perverse."

Mr. Osmond busied himself for a moment in the room—there was plenty of space in it to move about—in the fashion of a man mechanically seeking pretexts for not giving an attention which may be embarrassing. Presently, however, he had exhausted his pretexts; there was nothing left for him—unless he took up a book—but to stand with his hands behind him looking at Pansy. "Why didn't you come and see the last of mamman Catherine?" he asked of her abruptly in French.

Pansy hesitated a moment, glancing at Madame Merle. "I asked her to stay with me," said this lady, who had seated herself again in another place.

"Ah, that was better," Osmond conceded. With which he dropped into a chair and sat looking at Madame Merle; bent forward a little, his elbows on the edge of the arms and his hands interlocked.

"She's going to give me some gloves," said Pansy.

"You needn't tell that to every one, my dear," Madame Merle observed.

"You're very kind to her," said Osmond. "She's supposed to have everything she needs."

"I should think she had had enough of the nuns."

"If we're going to discuss that matter she had better go out of the room."

"Let her stay," said Madame Merle. "We'll talk of something else."

"If you like I won't listen," Pansy suggested with an appearance of candour which imposed conviction.

"You may listen, charming child, because you won't understand," her father replied. The child sat down, deferentially, near the open door, within sight of the garden, into which she directed her innocent, wistful eyes; and Mr. Osmond went on irrelevantly, addressing himself to his other companion. "You're looking particularly well."

"I think I always look the same," said Madame Merle.

"You always *are* the same. You don't vary. You're a wonderful woman."

"Yes, I think I am."

"You sometimes change your mind, however. You told me on your return from England that you wouldn't leave Rome again for the present."

"I'm pleased that you remember so well what I say. That was my intention. But I've come to Florence to meet some friends who have lately arrived and as to whose movements I was at that time uncertain."

"That reason's characteristic. You're always doing something for your friends."

Madame Merle smiled straight at her host. "It's less characteristic than your comment upon it—which is perfectly insincere. I don't, however, make a crime of that," she added, "because if you don't believe what you say there's no reason *why* you should. I don't ruin myself for my friends; I don't deserve your praise. I care greatly for myself."

"Exactly; but yourself includes so many other selves—so much of every one else and of everything. I never knew a person whose life touched so many other lives."

"What do you call one's life?" asked Madame Merle. "One's appearance, one's movements, one's engagements, one's society?"

"I call *your* life your ambitions," said Osmond.

Madame Merle looked a moment at Pansy. "I wonder if she understands that," she murmured.

"You see she can't stay with us!" And Pansy's father gave rather a joyless smile. "Go into the garden, *mignonne*,[9] and pluck a flower or two for Madame Merle," he went on in French.

"That's just what I wanted to do," Pansy exclaimed, rising with promptness and noiselessly departing. Her father followed her to the open door, stood a moment watching her, and then came back, but remained standing, or rather strolling to and fro, as if to cultivate a sense of freedom which in another attitude might be wanting.

"My ambitions are principally for you," said Madame Merle, looking up at him with a certain courage.

"That comes back to what I say. I'm part of your life—I and a thousand others. You're not selfish—I can't admit that. If you were selfish, what should I be? What epithet would properly describe me?"

"You're indolent. For me that's your worst fault."

"I'm afraid it's really my best."

"You don't care," said Madame Merle gravely.

"No; I don't think I care much. What sort of a fault do you call that? My indolence, at any rate, was one of the reasons I didn't go to Rome. But it was only one of them."

9. An endearment (French).

"It's not of importance—to me at least—that you didn't go; though I should have been glad to see you. I'm glad you're not in Rome now—which you might be, would probably be, if you had gone there a month ago. There's something I should like you to do at present in Florence."

"Please remember my indolence," said Osmond.

"I do remember it; but I beg you to forget it. In that way you'll have both the virtue and the reward. This is not a great labour, and it may prove a real interest. How long is it since you made a new acquaintance?"

"I don't think I've made any since I made yours."

"It's time then you should make another. There's a friend of mine I want you to know."

Mr. Osmond, in his walk, had gone back to the open door again and was looking at his daughter as she moved about in the intense sunshine. "What good will it do me?" he asked with a sort of genial crudity.

Madame Merle waited. "It will amuse you." There was nothing crude in this rejoinder; it had been thoroughly well considered.

"If you say that, you know, I believe it," said Osmond, coming toward her. "There are some points in which my confidence in you is complete. I'm perfectly aware, for instance, that you know good society from bad."

"Society is all bad."

"Pardon me. That isn't—the knowledge I impute to you—a common sort of wisdom. You've gained it in the right way—experimentally; you've compared an immense number of more or less impossible people with each other."

"Well, I invite you to profit by my knowledge."

"To profit? Are you very sure that I shall?"

"It's what I hope. It will depend on yourself. If I could only induce you to make an effort!"

"Ah, there you are! I knew something tiresome was coming. What in the world—that's likely to turn up here—is worth an effort."

Madame Merle flushed as with a wounded intention. "Don't be foolish, Osmond. No one knows better than you what *is* worth an effort. Haven't *I* seen you in old days?"

"I recognise some things. But they're none of them probable in this poor life."

"It's the effort that makes them probable," said Madame Merle.

"There's something in that. Who then is your friend?"

"The person I came to Florence to see. She's a niece of Mrs. Touchett, whom you'll not have forgotten."

"A niece? The word niece suggests youth and ignorance. I see what you're coming to."

"Yes, she's young—twenty-three years old. She's a great friend of mine. I met her for the first time in England, several months ago, and we struck up a grand alliance. I like her immensely, and I do what I don't do every day—I admire her. You'll do the same."

"Not if I can help it."

"Precisely. But you won't be able to help it."

"Is she beautiful, clever, rich, splendid, universally intelligent and unprecedentedly virtuous? It's only on those conditions that I care to make her acquaintance. You know I asked you some time ago never to speak to me of a creature who shouldn't correspond to that description. I know plenty of dingy people; I don't want to know any more."

"Miss Archer isn't dingy; she's as bright as the morning. She corresponds to your description; it's for that I wish you to know her. She fills all your requirements."

"More or less, of course."

"No; quite literally. She's beautiful, accomplished, generous and, for an American, well-born. She's also very clever and very amiable, and she has a handsome fortune."

Mr. Osmond listened to this in silence, appearing to turn it over in his mind with his eyes on his informant. "What do you want to do with her?" he asked at last.

"What you see. Put her in your way."

"Isn't she meant for something better than that?"

"I don't pretend to know what people are meant for," said Madame Merle. "I only know what I can do with them."

"I'm sorry for Miss Archer!" Osmond declared.

Madame Merle got up. "If that's a beginning of interest in her I take note of it."

The two stood there face to face; she settled her mantilla, looking down at it as she did so. "You're looking very well," Osmond repeated still less relevantly than before. "You have some idea. You're never so well as when you've got an idea; they're always becoming to you."

In the manner and tone of these two persons, on first meeting at any juncture, and especially when they met in the presence of others, was something indirect and circumspect, as if they had approached each other obliquely and addressed each other by implication. The effect of each appeared to be to intensify to an appreciable degree the self-consciousness of the other. Madame Merle of course carried off any embarrassment better than her friend; but even Madame Merle had not on this occasion the form she would have liked to have—the perfect self-possession she would have wished to wear for her host. The point to be made is, however, that at a certain moment the element between them, whatever it was, always levelled itself and left them more closely face to face than either ever was with any one else. This was what had happened now. They stood there knowing each other well and each on the whole willing to accept the satisfaction of knowing as a compensation for the inconvenience—whatever it might be—of being known. "I wish very much you were not so heartless," Madame Merle quietly said. "It has always been against you, and it will be against you now."

"I'm not so heartless as you think. Every now and then something touches me—as for instance your saying just now that your ambitions are for me. I don't understand it; I don't see how or why they should be. But it touches me, all the same."

"You'll probably understand it even less as time goes on. There are some things you'll never understand. There's no particular need you should."

"You, after all, are the most remarkable of women," said Osmond. "You have more in you than almost any one. I don't see why you think Mrs. Touchett's niece should matter very much to me, when—when—" But he paused a moment.

"When I myself have mattered so little?"

"That of course is not what I meant to say. When I've known and appreciated such a woman as you."

"Isabel Archer's better than I," said Madame Merle.

Her companion gave a laugh. "How little you must think of her to say that!"

"Do you suppose I'm capable of jealousy? Please answer me that."

"With regard to me? No; on the whole I don't."

"Come and see me then, two days hence. I'm staying at Mrs. Touchett's—Palazzo Crescentini—and the girl will be there."

"Why didn't you ask me that at first simply, without speaking of the girl?" said Osmond. "You could have had her there at any rate."

Madame Merle looked at him in the manner of a woman whom no question he could ever put would find unprepared. "Do you wish to know why? Because I've spoken of you to her."

Osmond frowned and turned away. "I'd rather not know that." Then in a moment he pointed out the easel supporting the little water-colour drawing. "Have you seen what's there—my last?"

Madame Merle drew near and considered. "Is it the Venetian Alps—one of your last year's sketches?"

"Yes—but how you guess everything!"

She looked a moment longer, then turned away. "You know I don't care for your drawings."

"I know it, yet I'm always surprised at it. They're really so much better than most people's."

"That may very well be. But as the only thing you do—well, it's so little. I should have liked you to do so many other things: those were my ambitions."

"Yes; you've told me many times—things that were impossible."

"Things that were impossible," said Madame Merle. And then in quite a different tone: "In itself your little picture's very good." She looked about the room—at the old cabinets, pictures, tapestries, surfaces of faded silk. "Your rooms at least are perfect. I'm struck with that afresh whenever I come back; I know none better anywhere. You understand this sort of thing as nobody anywhere does. You've such adorable taste."

"I'm sick of my adorable taste," said Gilbert Osmond.

"You must nevertheless let Miss Archer come and see it. I've told her about it."

"I don't object to showing my things—when people are not idiots."

"You do it delightfully. As cicerone[1] of your museum you appear to particular advantage."

Mr. Osmond, in return for this compliment, simply looked at once colder and more attentive. "Did you say she was rich?"

"She has seventy thousand pounds."

"*En écus bien comptés?*"[2]

"There's no doubt whatever about her fortune. I've seen it, as I may say."

"Satisfactory woman!—I mean *you*. And if I go to see her shall I see the mother?"

"The mother? She has none—nor father either."

1. Guide.
2. Hard cash? Literally: In carefully counted money? (French).

"The aunt then—whom did you say?—Mrs. Touchett."

"I can easily keep her out of the way."

"I don't object to her," said Osmond; "I rather like Mrs. Touchett. She has a sort of old-fashioned character that's passing away—a vivid identity. But that long jackanapes the son—is he about the place?"

"He's there, but he won't trouble you."

"He's a good deal of a donkey."

"I think you're mistaken. He's a very clever man. But he's not fond of being about when I'm there, because he doesn't like me."

"What could be more asinine than that? Did you say she has looks?" Osmond went on.

"Yes; but I won't say it again, lest you should be disappointed in them. Come and make a beginning; that's all I ask of you."

"A beginning of what?"

Madame Merle was silent a little. "I want you of course to marry her."

"The beginning of the end? Well, I'll see for myself. Have you told her that?"

"For what do you take me? She's not so coarse a piece of machinery—nor am I."

"Really," said Osmond after some meditation, "I don't understand your ambitions."

"I think you'll understand this one after you've seen Miss Archer. Suspend your judgement." Madam Merle, as she spoke, had drawn near the open door of the garden, where she stood a moment looking out. "Pansy has really grown pretty," she presently added.

"So it seemed to me."

"But she has had enough of the convent."

"I don't know," said Osmond. "I like what they've made of her. It's very charming."

"That's not the convent. It's the child's nature."

"It's the combination, I think. She's as pure as a pearl."

"Why doesn't she come back with my flowers then?" Madame Merle asked. "She's not in a hurry."

"We'll go and get them."

"She doesn't like me," the visitor murmured us she raised her parasol and they passed into the garden.

Chapter XXIII

Madame Merle, who had come to Florence on Mrs. Touchett's arrival at the invitation of this lady—Mrs. Touchett offering her for a month the hospitality of Palazzo Crescentini—the judicious Madame Merle spoke to Isabel afresh about Gilbert Osmond and expressed the hope she might know him; making, however, no such point of the matter as we have seen her do in recommending the girl herself to Mr. Osmond's attention. The reason of this was perhaps that Isabel offered no resistance whatever to Madame Merle's proposal. In Italy, as in England, the lady had a multitude of friends, both among the natives of the country and its heterogeneous visitors. She had mentioned to Isabel most of the people the girl would find it well to "meet"—of course, she said, Isabel could know whomever in the wide world she would—and had placed Mr. Osmond near the top of the list. He was an old friend of her own; she had known him these dozen years; he was one of the cleverest and most agreeable men—well, in Europe simply. He was altogether above the respectable average; quite another affair. He wasn't a professional charmer—far from it, and the effect he produced depended a good deal on the state of his nerves and his spirits. When not in the right mood he could fall as low as any one, saved only by his looking at such hours rather like a demoralised prince in exile. But if he cared or was interested or rightly challenged—just exactly rightly it had to be—then one felt his cleverness and his distinction. Those qualities didn't depend, in him, as in so many people, on his not committing or exposing himself. He had his perversities—which indeed Isabel would find to be the case with all the men really worth knowing—and didn't cause his light to shine equally for all persons. Madame Merle, however, thought she could undertake that for Isabel he would be brilliant. He was easily bored, too easily, and dull people always put him out; but a quick and cultivated girl like Isabel would give him a stimulus which was too absent from his life. At any rate he was a person not to miss. One shouldn't attempt to live in Italy without making a friend of Gilbert Osmond, who knew more about the country than any one except two or three German professors. And if they had more knowledge than he it was he who had most perception and taste—being artistic through and through. Isabel remembered that her friend had spoken of him during their plunge, at Gardencourt, into the deeps of talk, and wondered a little what was the nature of the tie binding these superior spirits. She felt that Madame Merle's ties always somehow had histories, and such an impression was part of the interest created by this inordinate woman. As regards her relations with Mr. Osmond, however, she hinted at nothing but a long-established calm friendship. Isabel said she should be happy to know a person who had enjoyed so high a confidence for so many years. "You ought to see a great many men," Madame Merle remarked; "you ought to see as many as possible, so as to get used to them."

"Used to them?" Isabel repeated with that solemn stare which sometimes seemed to proclaim her deficient in the sense of comedy. "Why, I'm not afraid of them—I'm as used to them as the cook to the butcher-boys."

"Used to them, I mean, so as to despise them. That's what one comes to with most of them. You'll pick out, for your society, the few whom you don't despise."

This was a note of cynicism that Madame Merle didn't often allow herself to sound; but Isabel was not alarmed, for she had never supposed that as one saw more of the world the sentiment of respect became the most active of one's emotions. It was excited, none the less, by the beautiful city of Florence, which pleased her not less than Madame Merle had promised; and if her unassisted perception had not been able to gauge its charms she had clever companions as priests to the mystery. She was in no want indeed of aesthetic illumination, for Ralph found it a joy that renewed his own early passion to act as cicerone to his eager young kinswoman. Madame Merle remained at home; she had seen the treasures of Florence again and again and had always something else to do. But she talked of all things with remarkable vividness of memory—she recalled the right-hand corner of the large Perugino and the position of the hands of the Saint Elizabeth in the picture next to it.[1] She had her opinions as to the character of many famous works of art, differing often from Ralph with great sharpness and defending her interpretations with as much ingenuity as good-humour. Isabel listened to the discussions taking place between the two with a sense that she might derive much benefit from them and that they were among the advantages she couldn't have enjoyed for instance in Albany. In the clear May mornings before the formal breakfast— this repast at Mrs. Touchett's was served at twelve o'clock—she wandered with her cousin through the narrow and sombre Florentine streets, resting a while in the thicker dusk of some historic church or the vaulted chambers of some dispeopled convent. She went to the galleries and palaces; she looked at the pictures and statues that had hitherto been great names to her, and exchanged for a knowledge which was sometimes a limitation a presentiment which proved usually to have been a blank. She performed all those acts of mental prostration in which, on a first visit to Italy, youth and enthusiasm so freely indulge; she felt her heart beat in the presence of immortal genius and knew the sweetness of rising tears in eyes to which faded fresco and darkened marble grew dim. But the return, every day, was even pleasanter than the going forth; the return into the wide, monumental court of the great house in which Mrs. Touchett, many years before, had established herself, and into the high, cool rooms where the carven rafters and pompous frescoes of the sixteenth century looked down on the familiar commodities of the age of advertisement. Mrs. Touchett inhabited an historic building in a narrow street whose very name recalled the strife of mediæval factions;[2] and found compensation for the darkness of her frontage in the modicity of her rent and the brightness of a garden where nature itself looked as archaic as the rugged architecture of the palace and which cleared and scented the rooms in regular use. To live in such a place was, for Isabel, to hold to her ear all day a shell of the sea of the past. This vague eternal rumour kept her imagination awake.

Gilbert Osmond came to see Madame Merle, who presented him to the young lady lurking at the other side of the room. Isabel took on this occasion little part in the talk; she scarcely even smiled when the others turned to her invitingly; she sat there as if she had been at the play and had paid even a large sum for her place. Mrs. Touchett was not present, and these two had it, for the effect of brilliancy, all their own way. They talked of the Florentine, the Roman, the cosmopolite world, and might have been distinguished performers figuring for a charity. It all had the rich readiness that would have come from rehearsal. Madame Merle appealed to her as if she had been on the stage, but she could ignore any learnt cue without spoiling the scene—though of course she thus put dreadfully in the wrong the friend who had told Mr. Osmond she could be depended on. This was no matter for once; even if more had been involved she could have made no attempt to shine. There was something in the visitor that

---

1. Madame Merle is remembering the layout of the rooms in the Uffizi, Florence's grandest picture gallery. Perugino (ca. 1146/50–1523); the painting mentioned here is a Madonna and Child.
2. The Via Ghibellina, a long and mostly straight street in the center of the city. Thirteenth-century Florence was riven by a rivalry between the Guelphs, who supported the pope, and the Ghibellines, partisans of the Holy Roman Emperors in their long struggle for mastery in Italy.

checked her and held her in suspense—made it more important she should get an impression of him than that she should produce one herself. Besides, she had little skill in producing an impression which she knew to be expected: nothing could be happier, in general, than to seem dazzling, but she had a perverse unwillingness to glitter by arrangement. Mr. Osmond, to do him justice, had a well-bred air of expecting nothing, a quiet ease that covered everything, even the first show of his own wit. This was the more grateful as his face, his head, was sensitive; he was not handsome, but he was fine, as fine as one of the drawings in the long gallery above the bridge of the Uffizi. And his very voice was fine—the more strangely that, with its clearness, it yet somehow wasn't sweet. This had had really to do with making her abstain from interference. His utterance was the vibration of glass, and if she had put out her finger she might have changed the pitch and spoiled the concert. Yet before he went she had to speak.

"Madame Merle," he said, "consents to come up to my hill-top some day next week and drink tea in my garden. It would give me much pleasure if you would come with her. It's thought rather pretty—there's what they call a general view. My daughter too would be so glad—or rather, for she's too young to have strong emotions, I should be so glad—so very glad." And Mr. Osmond paused with a slight air of embarrassment, leaving his sentence unfinished. "I should be so happy if you could know my daughter," he went on a moment afterwards.

Isabel replied that she should be delighted to see Miss Osmond and that if Madame Merle would show her the way to the hill-top she should be very grateful. Upon this assurance the visitor took his leave; after which Isabel fully expected her friend would scold her for having been so stupid. But to her surprise that lady, who indeed never fell into the mere matter-of-course, said to her in a few moments: "You were charming, my dear; you were just as one would have wished you. You're never disappointing."

A rebuke might possibly have been irritating, though it is much more probable that Isabel would have taken it in good part; but, strange to say, the words that Madame Merle actually used caused her the first feeling of displeasure she had known this ally to excite. "That's more than I intended," she answered coldly. "I'm under no obligation that I know of to charm Mr. Osmond."

Madame Merle perceptibly flushed, but we know it was not her habit to retract. "My dear child, I didn't speak for him, poor man; I spoke for yourself. It's not of course a question as to his liking you; it matters little whether he likes you or not! But I thought you liked *him*."

"I did," said Isabel honestly. "But I don't see what that matters either."

"Everything that concerns you matters to me," Madame Merle returned with her weary nobleness; "especially when at the same time another old friend's concerned."

Whatever Isabel's obligations may have been to Mr. Osmond, it must be admitted that she found them sufficient to lead her to put to Ralph sundry questions about him. She thought Ralph's judgements distorted by his trials, but she flattered herself she had learned to make allowance for that.

"Do I know him?" said her cousin. "Oh, yes, I 'know' him; not well, but on the whole enough. I've never cultivated his society, and he apparently has never found mine indispensable to his happiness. Who is he, what is he? He's a vague, unexplained American who has been living these thirty years, or less, in Italy. Why do I call him unexplained? Only as a cover for my ignorance; I don't know his antecedents, his family, his origin. For all I do know he may be a prince in disguise; he rather looks like one, by the way—like a prince who has abdicated in a fit of fastidiousness and has been in a state of disgust ever since. He used to live in Rome; but of late years he has taken up his abode here; I remember hearing him say that Rome has grown vulgar. He has a great dread of vulgarity; that's his special line; he hasn't any other that I know of. He lives on his income, which I suspect of not being vulgarly large. He's a poor but honest gentleman— that's what he calls himself. He married young and lost his wife, and I believe he has a daughter. He also has a sister, who's married to some small Count or other, of these parts; I remember meeting her of old. She's nicer than he, I should think, but rather impossible. I remember there used to be some stories about her. I don't think I recommend you to know her. But why don't you ask Madame Merle about these people? She knows them all much better than I."

"I ask you because I want your opinion as well as hers," said Isabel.

"A fig for my opinion! If you fall in love with Mr. Osmond what will you care for that?"

"Not much, probably. But meanwhile it has a certain importance. The more information one has about one's dangers the better."

"I don't agree to that—it may make them dangers. We know too much about people in these days; we hear too much. Our ears, our minds, our mouths, are stuffed with personalities. Don't mind anything any one tells you about any one else. Judge every one and everything for yourself."

"That's what I try to do," said Isabel; "but when you do that people call you conceited."

"You're not to mind them—that's precisely my argument; not to mind what they say about yourself any more than what they say about your friend or your enemy."

Isabel considered. "I think you're right; but there are some things I can't help minding: for instance when my friend's attacked or when I myself am praised."

"Of course you're always at liberty to judge the critic. Judge people as critics, however," Ralph added, "and you'll condemn them all!"

"I shall see Mr. Osmond for myself," said Isabel. "I've promised to pay him a visit."

"To pay him a visit?"

"To go and see his view, his pictures, his daughter—I don't know exactly what. Madame Merle's to take me; she tells me a great many ladies call on him."

"Ah, with Madame Merle you may go anywhere, *de confiance*,"[3] said Ralph. "She knows none but the best people."

Isabel said no more about Mr. Osmond, but she presently remarked to her cousin that she was not satisfied with his tone about Madame Merle. "It seems to me you insinuate things about her. I don't know what you mean, but if you've any grounds for disliking her I think you should either mention them frankly or else say nothing at all."

3. With confidence (French).

Ralph, however, resented this charge with more apparent earnestness than he commonly used. "I speak of Madame Merle exactly as I speak *to* her: with an even exaggerated respect."

"Exaggerated, precisely. That's what I complain of."

"I do so because Madame Merle's merits are exaggerated."

"By whom, pray? By me? If so I do her a poor service."

"No, no; by herself."

"Ah, I protest!" Isabel earnestly cried. "If ever there was a woman who made small claims—"

"You put your finger on it," Ralph interrupted. "Her modesty's exaggerated. She has no business with small claims—she has a perfect right to make large ones."

"Her merits are large then. You contradict yourself."

"Her merits are immense," said Ralph. "She's indescribably blameless; a pathless desert of virtue; the only woman I know who never gives one a chance."

"A chance for what?"

"Well, say to call her a fool! She's the only woman I know who has but that one little fault."

Isabel turned away with impatience. "I don't understand you; you're too paradoxical for my plain mind."

"Let me explain. When I say she exaggerates I don't mean it in the vulgar sense—that she boasts, overstates, gives too fine an account of herself. I mean literally that she pushes the search for perfection too far—that her merits are in themselves overstrained. She's too good, too kind, too clever, too learned, too accomplished, too everything. She's too complete, in a word. I confess to you that she acts on my nerves and that I feel about her a good deal as that intensely human Athenian felt about Aristides the Just."[4]

Isabel looked hard at her cousin; but the mocking spirit, if it lurked in his words, failed on this occasion to peep from his face. "Do you wish Madame Merle to be banished?"

"By no means. She's much too good company. I delight in Madame Merle," said Ralph Touchett simply.

"You're very odious, sir!" Isabel exclaimed. And then she asked him if he knew anything that was not to the honour of her brilliant friend.

"Nothing whatever. Don't you see that's just what I mean? On the character of every one else you may find some little black speck; if I were to take half an hour to it, some day, I've no doubt I should be able to find one on yours. For my own, of course, I'm spotted like a leopard. But on Madame Merle's nothing, nothing, nothing!"

"That's just what I think!" said Isabel with a toss of her head. "That is why I like her so much."

"She's a capital person for you to know. Since you wish to see the world you couldn't have a better guide."

"I suppose you mean by that that she's worldly?"

"Worldly? No," said Ralph, "she's the great round world itself!"

---

4. An Athenian statesman and general, Aristides (530–468 B.C.) was so well known for his probity that he was called "the Just"; the nickname led at least one citizen to vote in favor of banishing him simply because he was tired of hearing his fellows refer to him as "the Just."

It had certainly not, as Isabel for the moment took it into her head to believe, been a refinement of malice in him to say that he delighted in Madame Merle. Ralph Touchett took his refreshment wherever he could find it, and he would not have forgiven himself if he had been left wholly unbeguiled by such a mistress of the social art. There are deep-lying sympathies and antipathies, and it may have been that, in spite of the administered justice she enjoyed at his hands, her absence from his mother's house would not have made life barren to him. But Ralph Touchett had learned more or less inscrutably to attend, and there could have been nothing so "sustained" to attend to as the general performance of Madame Merle. He tasted her in sips, he let her stand, with an opportuneness she herself could not have surpassed. There were moments when he felt almost sorry for her; and these, oddly enough, were the moments when his kindness was least demonstrative. He was sure she had been yearningly ambitious and that what she had visibly accomplished was far below her secret measure. She had got herself into perfect training, but had won none of the prizes. She was always plain Madame Merle, the widow of a Swiss *négociant*,[5] with a small income and a large acquaintance, who stayed with people a great deal and was almost as universally "liked" as some new volume of smooth twaddle. The contrast between this position and any one of some half-dozen others that he supposed to have at various moments engaged her hope had an element of the tragical. His mother thought he got on beautifully with their genial guest; to Mrs. Touchett's sense two persons who dealt so largely in too-ingenious theories of conduct—that is of their own—would have much in common. He had given due consideration to Isabel's intimacy with her eminent friend, having long since made up his mind that he could not, without opposition, keep his cousin to himself; and he made the best of it, as he had done of worse things. He believed it would take care of itself; it wouldn't last forever. Neither of these two superior persons knew the other as well as she supposed, and when each had made an important discovery or two there would be, if not a rupture, at least a relaxation. Meanwhile he was quite willing to admit that the conversation of the elder lady was an advantage to the younger, who had a great deal to learn and would doubtless learn it better from Madame Merle than from some other instructors of the young. It was not probable that Isabel would be injured.

Chapter XXIV

It would certainly have been hard to see what injury could arise to her from the visit she presently paid to Mr. Osmond's hill-top. Nothing could have been more charming than this occasion—a soft afternoon in the full maturity of the Tuscan spring. The companions drove out of the Roman Gate, beneath the enormous blank superstructure which crowns the fine clear arch of that portal and makes it nakedly impressive, and wound between high-walled lanes into which the wealth of blossoming orchards overdrooped and flung a fragrance, until they reached the small superurban piazza, of crooked shape, where the long brown wall of the villa

5. Merchant, broker, businessman.

occupied in part by Mr. Osmond formed a principal, or at least a very imposing, object. Isabel went with her friend through a wide, high court, where a clear shadow rested below and a pair of light-arched galleries, facing each other above, caught the upper sunshine upon their slim columns and the flowering plants in which they were dressed. There was something grave and strong in the place; it looked somehow as if, once you were in, you would need an act of energy to get out. For Isabel, however, there was of course as yet no thought of getting out, but only of advancing. Mr. Osmond met her in the cold ante-chamber—it was cold even in the month of May—and ushered her, with her conductress, into the apartment to which we have already been introduced. Madame Merle was in front, and while Isabel lingered a little, talking with him, she went forward familiarly and greeted two persons who were seated in the saloon. One of these was little Pansy, on whom she bestowed a kiss; the other was a lady whom Mr. Osmond indicated to Isabel as his sister, the Countess Gemini. "And that's my little girl," he said, "who has just come out of her convent."

Pansy had on a scant white dress, and her fair hair was neatly arranged in a net; she wore her small shoes tied sandal-fashion about her ankles. She made Isabel a little conventional curtsey and then came to be kissed. The Countess Gemini simply nodded without getting up: Isabel could see she was a woman of high fashion. She was thin and dark and not at all pretty, having features that suggested some tropical bird—a long beak-like nose, small, quickly-moving eyes and a mouth and chin that receded extremely. Her expression, however, thanks to various intensities of emphasis and wonder, of horror and joy, was not inhuman, and, as regards her appearance, it was plain she understood herself and made the most of her points. Her attire, voluminous and delicate, bristling with elegance, had the look of shimmering plumage, and her attitudes were as light and sudden as those of a creature who perched upon twigs. She had a great deal of manner; Isabel, who had never known any one with so much manner, immediately classed her as the most affected of women. She remembered that Ralph had not recommended her as an acquaintance; but she was ready to acknowledge that to a casual view the Countess Gemini revealed no depths. Her demonstrations suggested the violent waving of some flag of general truce—white silk with fluttering streamers.

"You'll believe I'm glad to see you when I tell you it's only because I knew you were to be here that I came myself. I don't come and see my brother—I make him come and see me. This hill of his is impossible—I don't see what possesses him. Really, Osmond, you'll be the ruin of my horses some day, and if it hurts them you'll have to give me another pair. I heard them wheezing to-day; I assure you I did. It's very disagreeable to hear one's horses wheezing when one's sitting in the carriage; it sounds too as if they weren't what they should be. But I've always had good horses; whatever else I may have lacked I've always managed that. My husband doesn't know much, but I think he knows a horse. In general Italians don't, but my husband goes in, according to his poor light, for everything English. My horses are English—so it's all the greater pity they should be ruined. I must tell you," she went on, directly addressing Isabel, "that Osmond doesn't often invite me; I don't think he likes to have me. It was quite my own idea, coming to-day. I like to see new people, and I'm sure you're very new. But don't sit there; that chair's not what it looks. There are some very good seats here, but there are also some horrors."

These remarks were delivered with a series of little jerks and pecks, of roulades of shrillness, and in an accent that was as some fond recall of good English, or rather of good American, in adversity.

"I don't like to have you, my dear?" said her brother. "I'm sure you're invaluable."

"I don't see any horrors anywhere," Isabel returned, looking about her. "Everything seems to me beautiful and precious."

"I've a few good things," Mr. Osmond allowed; "indeed I've nothing very bad. But I've not what I should have liked."

He stood there a little awkwardly, smiling and glancing about; his manner was an odd mixture of the detached and the involved. He seemed to hint that nothing but the right "values" was of any consequence. Isabel made a rapid induction; perfect simplicity was not the badge of his family. Even the little girl from the convent, who, in her prim white dress, with her small submissive face and her hands locked before her, stood there as if she were about to partake of her first communion, even Mr. Osmond's diminutive daughter had a kind of finish that was not entirely artless.

"You'd have liked a few things from the Uffizi and the Pitti[1]—that's what you'd have liked," said Madame Merle.

"Poor Osmond, with his old curtains and crucifixes!" the Countess Gemini exclaimed; she appeared to call her brother only by his family-name. Her ejaculation had no particular object; she smiled at Isabel as she made it and looked at her from head to foot.

Her brother had not heard her; he seemed to be thinking what he could say to Isabel. "Won't you have some tea?—you must be very tired," he at last bethought himself of remarking.

"No indeed, I'm not tired; what have I done to tire me?" Isabel felt a certain need of being very direct, of pretending to nothing; there was something in the air, in her general impression of things—she could hardly have said what it was—that deprived her of all disposition to put herself forward. The place, the occasion, the combination of people, signified more than lay on the surface; she would try to understand—she would not simply utter graceful platitudes. Poor Isabel was doubtless not aware that many women would have uttered graceful platitudes to cover the working of their observation. It must be confessed that her pride was a trifle alarmed. A man she had heard spoken of in terms that excited interest and who was evidently capable of distinguishing himself, had invited her, a young lady not lavish of her favours, to come to his house. Now that she had done so the burden of the entertainment rested naturally on his wit. Isabel was not rendered less observant, and for the moment, we judge, she was not rendered more indulgent, by perceiving that Mr. Osmond carried his burden less complacently than might have been expected. "What a fool I was to have let myself so needlessly in—!" she could fancy his exclaiming to himself.

"You'll be tired when you go home, if he shows you all his bibelots and gives you a lecture on each," said the Countess Gemini.

1. The Pitti Palace was the former seat of Florence's ducal rulers; in James's day, as in ours, a museum.

"I'm not afraid of that; but if I'm tired I shall at least have learned something."

"Very little, I suspect. But my sister's dreadfully afraid of learning anything," said Mr. Osmond.

"Oh, I confess to that; I don't want to know anything more—I know too much already. The more you know the more unhappy you are."

"You should not undervalue knowledge before Pansy, who has not finished her education," Madame Merle interposed with a smile.

"Pansy will never know any harm," said the child's father. "Pansy's a little convent-flower."

"Oh, the convents, the convents!" cried the Countess with a flutter of her ruffles. "Speak to me of the convents! You may learn anything there; I'm a convent-flower myself. I don't pretend to be good, but the nuns do. Don't you see what I mean?" she went on, appealing to Isabel.

Isabel was not sure she saw, and she answered that she was very bad at following arguments. The Countess then declared that she herself detested arguments, but that this was her brother's taste—he would always discuss. "For me," she said, "one should like a thing or one shouldn't; one can't like everything, of course. But one shouldn't attempt to reason it out—you never know where it may lead you. There are some very good feelings that may have bad reasons, don't you know? And then there are very bad feelings, sometimes, that have good reasons. Don't you see what I mean? I don't care anything about reasons, but I know what I like."

"Ah, that's the great thing," said Isabel, smiling and suspecting that her acquaintance with this lightly-flitting personage would not lead to intellectual repose. If the Countess objected to argument Isabel at this moment had as little taste for it, and she put out her hand to Pansy with a pleasant sense that such a gesture committed her to nothing that would admit of a divergence of views. Gilbert Osmond apparently took a rather hopeless view of his sister's tone; he turned the conversation to another topic. He presently sat down on the other side of his daughter, who had shyly brushed Isabel's fingers with her own; but he ended by drawing her out of her chair and making her stand between his knees, leaning against him while he passed his arm round her slimness. The child fixed her eyes on Isabel with a still, disinterested gaze which seemed void of an intention, yet conscious of an attraction. Mr. Osmond talked of many things; Madame Merle had said he could be agreeable when he chose, and to-day, after a little, he appeared not only to have chosen but to have determined. Madame Merle and the Countess Gemini sat a little apart, conversing in the effortless manner of persons who knew each other well enough to take their ease; but every now and then Isabel heard the Countess, at something said by her companion, plunge into the latter's lucidity as a poodle splashes after a thrown stick. It was as if Madame Merle were seeing how far she would go. Mr. Osmond talked of Florence, of Italy, of the pleasure of living in that country and of the abatements to the pleasure. There were both satisfactions and drawbacks; the drawbacks were numerous; strangers were too apt to see such a world as all romantic. It met the case soothingly for the human, for the social failure—by which he meant the people who couldn't "realise," as they said, on their sensibility: they could keep it about them there, in their poverty, without ridicule, as you might keep an heirloom or an inconvenient entailed place that brought you in nothing. Thus there were advantages in living in the country which contained the greatest sum of beauty. Certain impressions you could get only there. Others, favourable to life, you never got, and you got some that were very bad. But from time to time you got one of a quality that made up for everything. Italy, all the same, had spoiled a great many people; he was even fatuous enough to believe at times that he himself might have been a better man if he had spent less of his life there. It made one idle and dilettantish and second-rate; it had no discipline for the character, didn't cultivate in you, otherwise expressed, the successful social and other "cheek" that flourished in Paris and London. "We're sweetly provincial," said Mr. Osmond, "and I'm perfectly aware that I myself am as rusty as a key that has no lock to fit it. It polishes me up a little to talk with you—not that I venture to pretend I can turn that very complicated lock I suspect your intellect of being! But you'll be going away before I've seen you three times, and I shall perhaps never see you after that. That's what it is to live in a country that people come to. When they're disagreeable here it's bad enough; when they're agreeable it's still worse. As soon as you like them they're off again! I've been deceived too often; I've ceased to form attachments, to permit myself to feel attractions. You mean to stay—to settle? That would be really comfortable. Ah yes, your aunt's a sort of guarantee; I believe she may be depended on. Oh, she's an old Florentine; I mean literally an old one; not a modern outsider. She's a contemporary of the Medici; she must have been present at the burning of Savonarola, and I'm not sure she didn't throw a handful of chips into the flame. Her face is very much like some faces in the early pictures; little, dry, definite faces that must have had a good deal of expression, but almost always the same one. Indeed I can show you her portrait in a fresco of Ghirlandaio's.[2] I hope you don't object to my speaking that way of your aunt, eh? I've an idea you don't. Perhaps you think that's even worse. I assure you there's no want of respect in it, to either of you. You know I'm a particular admirer of Mrs. Touchett."

While Isabel's host exerted himself to entertain her in this somewhat confidential fashion she looked occasionally at Madame Merle, who met her eyes with an inattentive smile in which, on this occasion, there was no infelicitous intimation that our heroine appeared to advantage. Madame Merle eventually proposed to the Countess Gemini that they should go into the garden, and the Countess, rising and shaking out her feathers, began to rustle toward the door. "Poor Miss Archer!" she exclaimed, surveying the other group with expressive compassion. "She has been brought quite into the family."

"Miss Archer can certainly have nothing but sympathy for a family to which you belong," Mr. Osmond answered, with a laugh which, though it had something of a mocking ring, had also a finer patience.

"I don't know what you mean by that! I'm sure she'll see no harm in me but what you tell her. I'm better than he says, Miss Archer," the Countess went on. "I'm only rather an idiot and a bore. Is that all he has said? Ah

---

2. Various branches of the Medici family dominated Florentine politics from the fifteenth to the eighteenth centuries. Girolama Savonarola (1452–1498) was a charismatic Dominican priest who in effect ruled the city from 1494–98 when the Medici were in temporary exile; he was famous for burning humanist books, but on the Medicis' return to power was himself burned at the stake. Domenico Ghirlandaio (1449–1494), a Florentine painter of great delicacy and the teacher of Michelangelo.

then, you keep him in good-humour. Has he opened on one of his favourite subjects? I give you notice that there are two or three that he treats *à fond*.[3] In that case you had better take off your bonnet."

"I don't think I know what Mr. Osmond's favourite subjects are," said Isabel, who had risen to her feet.

The Countess assumed for an instant an attitude of intense meditation, pressing one of her hands, with the finger-tips gathered together, to her forehead. "I'll tell you in a moment. One's Machiavelli; the other's Vittoria Colonna; the next is Metastasio."[4]

"Ah, with me," said Madame Merle, passing her arm into the Countess Gemini's as if to guide her course to the garden, "Mr. Osmond's never so historical."

"Oh you," the Countess answered as they moved away, "you yourself are Machiavelli—you yourself are Vittoria Colonna!"

"We shall hear next that poor Madame Merle is Metastasio!" Gilbert Osmond resignedly sighed.

Isabel had got up on the assumption that they too were to go into the garden; but her host stood there with no apparent inclination to leave the room, his hands in the pockets of his jacket and his daughter, who had now locked her arm into one of his own, clinging to him and looking up while her eyes moved from his own face to Isabel's. Isabel waited, with a certain unuttered contentedness, to have her movements directed; she liked Mr. Osmond's talk, his company: she had what always gave her a very private thrill, the consciousness of a new relation. Through the open doors of the great room she saw Madame Merle and the Countess stroll across the fine grass of the garden; then she turned, and her eyes wandered over the things scattered about her. The understanding had been that Mr. Osmond should show her his treasures; his pictures and cabinets all looked like treasures. Isabel after a moment went toward one of the pictures to see it better; but just as she had done so he said to her abruptly: "Miss Archer, what do you think of my sister?"

She faced him with some surprise. "Ah, don't ask me that—I've seen your sister too little."

"Yes, you've seen her very little; but you must have observed that there is not a great deal of her to see. What do you think of our family tone?" he went on with his cool smile. "I should like to know how it strikes a fresh, unprejudiced mind. I know what you're going to say—you've had almost no observation of it. Of course this is only a glimpse. But just take notice, in future, if you have a chance. I sometimes think we've got into a rather bad way, living off here among things and people not our own, without responsibilities or attachments, with nothing to hold us together or keep us up; marrying foreigners, forming artificial tastes, playing tricks with our natural mission. Let me add, though, that I say that much more for myself than for my sister. She's a very honest lady—more so than she seems. She's rather unhappy, and as she's not of a serious turn she doesn't tend to show it tragically: she shows it comically instead. She has got a horrid

3. Exhaustively; literally: down to the bottom (French).
4. Niccolò Machiavelli (1469–1527), best known for *The Prince*, an always-controversial but foundational work of political theory. Vittoria Colonna (1490–1547), aristocrat and poet, in Osmond's day a recherché taste but now canonical. Pietro Metastasio (1698–1782), Rococo poet and librettist whose works were set to music by Handel and Mozart.

husband, though I'm not sure she makes the best of him. Of course, however, a horrid husband's an awkward thing. Madame Merle gives her
excellent advice, but it's a good deal like giving a child a dictionary to learn
a language with. He can look out the words, but he can't put them together.
My sister needs a grammar, but unfortunately she's not grammatical. Pardon
my troubling you with these details; my sister was very right in saying
you've been taken into the family. Let me take down that picture; you
want more light."

He took down the picture, carried it toward the window, related some
curious facts about it. She looked at the other works of art, and he gave
her such further information as might appear most acceptable to a young
lady making a call on a summer afternoon. His pictures, his medallions
and tapestries were interesting; but after a while Isabel felt the owner
much more so, and independently of them, thickly as they seemed to
overhang him. He resembled no one she had ever seen; most of the
people she knew might be divided into groups of half a dozen specimens.
There were one or two exceptions to this; she could think for instance of
no group that would contain her aunt Lydia. There were other people
who were, relatively speaking, original—original, as one might say, by
courtesy—such as Mr. Goodwood, as her cousin Ralph, as Henrietta
Stackpole, as Lord Warburton, as Madame Merle. But in essentials, when
one came to look at them, these individuals belonged to types already present to her mind. Her mind contained no class offering a natural place to
Mr. Osmond—he was a specimen apart. It was not that she recognised
all these truths at the hour, but they were falling into order before her.
For the moment she only said to herself that this "new relation" would perhaps prove her very most distinguished. Madame Merle had had that
note of rarity, but what quite other power it immediately gained when
sounded by a man! It was not so much what he said and did, but rather
what he withheld, that marked him for her as by one of those signs of the
highly curious that he was showing her on the underside of old plates and
in the corner of sixteenth-century drawings: he indulged in no striking
deflections from common usage, he was an original without being an
eccentric. She had never met a person of so fine a grain. The peculiarity
was physical, to begin with, and it extended to impalpabilities. His dense,
delicate hair, his overdrawn, retouched features, his clear complexion, ripe
without being coarse, the very evenness of the growth of his beard, and
that light, smooth slenderness of structure which made the movement of a
single one of his fingers produce the effect of an expressive gesture—these
personal points struck our sensitive young woman as signs of quality, of
intensity, somehow as promises of interest. He was certainly fastidious and
critical; he was probably irritable. His sensibility had governed him—
possibly governed him too much; it had made him impatient of vulgar troubles and had led him to live by himself, in a sorted, sifted, arranged world,
thinking about art and beauty and history. He had consulted his taste in
everything—his taste alone perhaps, as a sick man consciously incurable
consults at last only his lawyer: that was what made him so different from
every one else. Ralph had something of this same quality, this appearance
of thinking that life was a matter of connoisseurship; but in Ralph it was
an anomaly, a kind of humorous excrescence, whereas in Mr. Osmond it
was the keynote, and everything was in harmony with it. She was certainly

far from understanding him completely; his meaning was not at all times obvious. It was hard to see what he meant for instance by speaking of his provincial side—which was exactly the side she would have taken him most to lack. Was it a harmless paradox, intended to puzzle her? or was it the last refinement of high culture? She trusted she should learn in time; it would be very interesting to learn. If it was provincial to have that harmony, what then was the finish of the capital? And she could put this question in spite of so feeling her host a shy personage; since such shyness as his—the shyness of ticklish nerves and fine perceptions—was perfectly consistent with the best breeding. Indeed it was almost a proof of standards and touchstones other than the vulgar: he must be so sure the vulgar would be first on the ground. He wasn't a man of easy assurance, who chatted and gossiped with the fluency of a superficial nature; he was critical of himself as well as of others, and, exacting a good deal of others, to think them agreeable, probably took a rather ironical view of what he himself offered: a proof into the bargain that he was not grossly conceited. If he had not been shy he wouldn't have effected that gradual, subtle, successful conversion of it to which she owed both what pleased her in him and what mystified her. If he had suddenly asked her what she thought of the Countess Gemini, that was doubtless a proof that he was interested in her; it could scarcely be as a help to knowledge of his own sister. That he should be so interested showed an enquiring mind; but it was a little singular he should sacrifice his fraternal feeling to his curiosity. This was the most eccentric thing he had done.

There were two other rooms, beyond the one in which she had been received, equally full of romantic objects, and in these apartments Isabel spent a quarter of an hour. Everything was in the last degree curious and precious, and Mr. Osmond continued to be the kindest of ciceroni as he led her from one fine piece to another and still held his little girl by the hand. His kindness almost surprised our young friend, who wondered why he should take so much trouble for her; and she was oppressed at last with the accumulation of beauty and knowledge to which she found herself introduced. There was enough for the present; she had ceased to attend to what he said; she listened to him with attentive eyes, but was not thinking of what he told her. He probably thought her quicker, cleverer in every way, more prepared, than she was. Madame Merle would have pleasantly exaggerated; which was a pity, because in the end he would be sure to find out, and then perhaps even her real intelligence wouldn't reconcile him to his mistake. A part of Isabel's fatigue came from the effort to appear as intelligent as she believed Madame Merle had described her, and from the fear (very unusual with her) of exposing—not her ignorance; for that she cared comparatively little—but her possible grossness of perception. It would have annoyed her to express a liking for something he, in his superior enlightenment, would think she oughtn't to like; or to pass by something at which the truly initiated mind would arrest itself. She had no wish to fall into that grotesqueness—in which she had seen women (and it was a warning) serenely, yet ignobly, flounder. She was very careful therefore as to what she said, as to what she noticed or failed to notice; more careful than she had ever been before.

They came back into the first of the rooms, where the tea had been served; but as the two other ladies were still on the terrace, and as Isabel had not yet been made acquainted with the view, the paramount distinction of the place, Mr. Osmond directed her steps into the garden without more delay. Madame Merle and the Countess had had chairs brought out, and as the afternoon was lovely the Countess proposed they should take their tea in the open air. Pansy therefore was sent to bid the servant bring out the preparations. The sun had got low, the golden light took a deeper tone, and on the mountains and the plain that stretched beneath them the masses of purple shadow glowed as richly as the places that were still exposed. The scene had an extraordinary charm. The air was almost solemnly still, and the large expanse of the landscape, with its gardenlike culture and nobleness of outline, its teeming valley and delicately-fretted hills, its peculiarly human-looking touches of habitation, lay there in splendid harmony and classic grace. "You seem so well pleased that I think you can be trusted to come back," Osmond said as he led his companion to one of the angles of the terrace.

"I shall certainly come back," she returned, "in spite of what you say about its being bad to live in Italy. What was that you said about one's natural mission? I wonder if I should forsake my natural mission if I were to settle in Florence."

"A woman's natural mission is to be where she's most appreciated."

"The point's to find out where that is."

"Very true—she often wastes a great deal of time in the enquiry. People ought to make it very plain to her."

"Such a matter would have to be made very plain to me," smiled Isabel.

"I'm glad, at any rate, to hear you talk of settling. Madame Merle had given me an idea that you were of a rather roving disposition. I thought she spoke of your having some plan of going round the world."

"I'm rather ashamed of my plans; I make a new one every day."

"I don't see why you should be ashamed; it's the greatest of pleasures."

"It seems frivolous, I think," said Isabel. "One ought to choose something very deliberately, and be faithful to that."

"By that rule then, I've not been frivolous."

"Have you never made plans?"

"Yes, I made one years ago, and I'm acting on it to-day."

"It must have been a very pleasant one," Isabel permitted herself to observe.

"It was very simple. It was to be as quiet as possible."

"As quiet?" the girl repeated.

"Not to worry—not to strive nor struggle. To resign myself. To be content with little." He spoke these sentences slowly, with short pauses between, and his intelligent regard was fixed on his visitor's with the conscious air of a man who has brought himself to confess something.

"Do you call that simple?" she asked with mild irony.

"Yes, because it's negative."

"Has your life been negative?"

"Call it affirmative if you like. Only it has affirmed my indifference. Mind you, not my natural indifference—I *had* none. But my studied, my wilful renunciation."

She scarcely understood him; it seemed a question whether he were joking or not. Why should a man who struck her as having a great fund of reserve suddenly bring himself to be so confidential? This was his affair, however, and his confidences were interesting. "I don't see why you should have renounced," she said in a moment.

"Because I could do nothing. I had no prospects, I was poor, and I was not a man of genius. I had no talents even; I took my measure early in life. I was simply the most fastidious young gentleman living. There were two or three people in the world I envied—the Emperor of Russia, for instance, and the Sultan of Turkey! There were even moments when I envied the Pope of Rome—for the consideration he enjoys. I should have been delighted to be considered to that extent; but since that couldn't be I didn't care for anything less, and I made up my mind not to go in for honours. The leanest gentleman can always consider himself, and fortunately I *was*, though lean, a gentleman. I could do nothing in Italy—I couldn't even be an Italian patriot.[5] To do that I should have had to get out of the country; and I was too fond of it to leave it, to say nothing of my being too well satisfied with it, on the whole, as it then was, to wish it altered. So I've passed a great many years here on that quiet plan I spoke of. I've not been at all unhappy. I don't mean to say I've cared for nothing; but the things I've cared for have been definite—limited. The events of my life have been absolutely unperceived by any one save myself; getting an old silver crucifix at a bargain (I've never bought anything dear, of course), or discovering, as I once did, a sketch by Correggio[6] on a panel daubed over by some inspired idiot."

This would have been rather a dry account of Mr. Osmond's career if Isabel had fully believed it; but her imagination supplied the human element which she was sure had not been wanting. His life had been mingled with other lives more than he admitted; naturally she couldn't expect him to enter into this. For the present she abstained from provoking further revelations; to intimate that he had not told her everything would be more familiar and less considerate than she now desired to be—would in fact be uproariously vulgar. He had certainly told her quite enough. It was her present inclination, however, to express a measured sympathy for the success with which he had preserved his independence. "That's a very pleasant life," she said, "to renounce everything but Correggio!"

"Oh, I've made in my way a good thing of it. Don't imagine I'm whining about it. It's one's own fault if one isn't happy."

This was large; she kept down to something smaller. "Have you lived here always?"

"No, not always. I lived a long time at Naples, and many years in Rome. But I've been here a good while. Perhaps I shall have to change, however; to do something else. I've no longer myself to think of. My daughter's growing up and may very possibly not care so much for the Correggios and crucifixes as I. I shall have to do what's best for Pansy."

"Yes, do that," said Isabel. "She's such a dear little girl."

"Ah," cried Gilbert Osmond beautifully, "she's a little saint of heaven! She is my great happiness!"

---

5. For much of the nineteenth century Italy was divided into several small states, including the Kingdom of the Two Sicilies and the Grand Duchy of Tuscany; some of them were under Austrian control. The movement for unification was known as the Risorgimento or Resurgence, and many of its leaders spent long periods in exile before the final unification of the country in 1870, when the Papal States at last acceded to the new kingdom.
6. Antonio Allegri da Correggio (ca. 1494–1534), painter based in Parma, where his best work remains.

Chapter XXV

While this sufficiently intimate colloquy (prolonged for some time after we cease to follow it) went forward Madame Merle and her companion, breaking a silence of some duration, had begun to exchange remarks. They were sitting in an attitude of unexpressed expectancy; an attitude especially marked on the part of the Countess Gemini, who, being of a more nervous temperament than her friend, practised with less success the art of disguising impatience. What these ladies were waiting for would not have been apparent and was perhaps not very definite to their own minds. Madame Merle waited for Osmond to release their young friend from her *tête-à-tête*, and the Countess waited because Madame Merle did. The Countess, moreover, by waiting, found the time ripe for one of her pretty perversities. She might have desired for some minutes to place it. Her brother wandered with Isabel to the end of the garden, to which point her eyes followed them.

"My dear," she then observed to her companion, "you'll excuse me if I don't congratulate you!"

"Very willingly, for I don't in the least know why you should."

"Haven't you a little plan that you think rather well of?" And the Countess nodded at the sequestered couple.

Madame Merle's eyes took the same direction; then she looked serenely at her neighbour. "You know I never understand you very well," she smiled.

"No one can understand better than you when you wish. I see that just now you *don't* wish."

"You say things to me that no one else does," said Madame Merle gravely, yet without bitterness.

"You mean things you don't like? Doesn't Osmond sometimes say such things?"

"What your brother says has a point."

"Yes, a poisoned one sometimes. If you mean that I'm not so clever as he you mustn't think I shall suffer from your sense of our difference. But it will be much better that you should understand me."

"Why so?" asked Madame Merle. "To what will it conduce?"

"If I don't approve of your plan you ought to know it in order to appreciate the danger of my interfering with it."

Madame Merle looked as if she were ready to admit that there might be something in this; but in a moment she said quietly: "You think me more calculating than I am."

"It's not your calculating I think ill of; it's your calculating wrong. You've done so in this case."

"You must have made extensive calculations yourself to discover that."

"No, I've not had time. I've seen the girl but this once," said the Countess, "and the conviction has suddenly come to me. I like her very much."

"So do I," Madame Merle mentioned.

"You've a strange way of showing it."

"Surely I've given her the advantage of making your acquaintance."

"That indeed," piped the Countess, "is perhaps the best thing that could happen to her!"

Madame Merle said nothing for some time. The Countess's manner was odious, was really low; but it was an old story, and with her eyes upon the violet slope of Monte Morello[1] she gave herself up to reflection. "My dear lady," she finally resumed, "I advise you not to agitate yourself. The matter you allude to concerns three persons much stronger of purpose than yourself."

"Three persons? You and Osmond of course. But is Miss Archer also very strong of purpose?"

"Quite as much so as we."

"Ah then," said the Countess radiantly, "if I convince her it's her interest to resist you she'll do so successfully!"

"Resist us? Why do you express yourself so coarsely? She's not exposed to compulsion or deception."

"I'm not sure of that. You're capable of anything, you and Osmond. I don't mean Osmond by himself, and I don't mean you by yourself. But together you're dangerous—like some chemical combination."

"You had better leave us alone then," smiled Madame Merle.

"I don't mean to touch you—but I shall talk to that girl."

"My poor Amy," Madame Merle murmured, "I don't see what has got into your head."

"I take an interest in her—that's what has got into my head. I like her."

Madame Merle hesitated a moment. "I don't think she likes you."

The Countess's bright little eyes expanded and her face was set in a grimace. "Ah, you *are* dangerous—even by yourself!"

"If you want her to like you don't abuse your brother to her," said Madame Merle.

"I don't suppose you pretend she has fallen in love with him in two interviews."

Madame Merle looked a moment at Isabel and at the master of the house. He was leaning against the parapet, facing her, his arms folded; and she at present was evidently not lost in the mere impersonal view, persistently as she gazed at it. As Madame Merle watched her she lowered her eyes; she was listening, possibly with a certain embarrassment, while she pressed the point of her parasol into the path. Madame Merle rose from her chair. "Yes, I think so!" she pronounced.

The shabby footboy, summoned by Pansy—he might, tarnished as to livery and quaint as to type, have issued from some stray sketch of old-time manners, been "put in" by the brush of a Longhi or a Goya[2]—had come out with a small table and placed it on the grass, and then had gone back and fetched the tea-tray; after which he had again disappeared, to return with a couple of chairs. Pansy had watched these proceedings with the deepest interest, standing with her small hands folded together upon the front of her scanty frock; but she had not presumed to offer assistance. When the tea-table had been arranged, however, she gently approached her aunt.

"Do you think papa would object to my making the tea?"

The Countess looked at her with a deliberately critical gaze and without answering her question, "My poor niece," she said, "is that your best frock?"

1. A mountain to the city's northwest.
2. Pietro Longhi (1701–1785), Venetian painter, and Francisco José de Goya (1746–1828) Spanish painter and engraver; each of them was known for scenes of contemporary life.

"Ah no," Pansy answered, "it's just a little *toilette*[3] for common occasions."

"Do you call it a common occasion when I come to see you?—to say nothing of Madame Merle and the pretty lady yonder."

Pansy reflected a moment, turning gravely from one of the persons mentioned to the other. Then her face broke into its perfect smile. "I have a pretty dress, but even that one's very simple. Why should I expose it beside your beautiful things?"

"Because it's the prettiest you have; for me you must always wear the prettiest. Please put it on the next time. It seems to me they don't dress you so well as they might."

The child sparingly stroked down her antiquated skirt. "It's a good little dress to make tea—don't you think? Don't you believe papa would allow me?"

"Impossible for me to say, my child," said the Countess. "For me, your father's ideas are unfathomable. Madame Merle understands them better. Ask *her*."

Madame Merle smiled with her usual grace. "It's a weighty question—let me think. It seems to me it would please your father to see a careful little daughter making his tea. It's the proper duty of the daughter of the house—when she grows up."

"So it seems to me, Madame Merle!" Pansy cried. "You shall see how well I'll make it. A spoonful for each." And she began to busy herself at the table.

"Two spoonfuls for me," said the Countess, who, with Madame Merle, remained for some moments watching her. "Listen to me, Pansy," the Countess resumed at last. "I should like to know what you think of your visitor."

"Ah, she's not mine—she's papa's," Pansy objected.

"Miss Archer came to see you as well," said Madame Merle.

"I'm very happy to hear that. She has been very polite to me."

"Do you like her then?" the Countess asked.

"She's charming—charming," Pansy repeated in her little neat conversational tone. "She pleases me thoroughly."

"And how do you think she pleases your father?"

"Ah really, Countess!" murmured Madame Merle dissuasively. "Go and call them to tea," she went on to the child.

"You'll see if they don't like it!" Pansy declared; and departed to summon the others, who had still lingered at the end of the terrace.

"If Miss Archer's to become her mother it's surely interesting to know if the child likes her," said the Countess.

"If your brother marries again it won't be for Pansy's sake," Madame Merle replied. "She'll soon be sixteen, and after that she'll begin to need a husband rather than a stepmother."

"And will you provide the husband as well?"

"I shall certainly take an interest in her marrying fortunately. I imagine you'll do the same."

"Indeed I shan't!" cried the Countess. "Why should I, of all women, set such a price on a husband?"

3. Dress.

"You didn't marry fortunately; that's what I'm speaking of. When I say a husband I mean a good one."

"There are no good ones. Osmond won't be a good one."

Madame Merle closed her eyes a moment. "You're irritated just now; I don't know why," she presently said. "I don't think you'll really object either to your brother's or to your niece's marrying, when the time comes for them to do so; and as regards Pansy I'm confident that we shall some day have the pleasure of looking for a husband for her together. Your large acquaintance will be a great help."

"Yes, I'm irritated," the Countess answered. "You often irritate me. Your own coolness is fabulous. You're a strange woman."

"It's much better that we should always act together," Madame Merle went on.

"Do you mean that as a threat?" asked the Countess rising.

Madame Merle shook her head as for quiet amusement. "No indeed, you've not my coolness!"

Isabel and Mr. Osmond were now slowly coming toward them and Isabel had taken Pansy by the hand. "Do you pretend to believe he'd make her happy?" the Countess demanded.

"If he should marry Miss Archer I suppose he'd behave like a gentleman."

The Countess jerked herself into a succession of attitudes. "Do you mean as most gentlemen behave? That would be much to be thankful for! Of course Osmond's a gentleman; his own sister needn't be reminded of that. But does he think he can marry any girl he happens to pick out? Osmond's a gentleman, of course; but I must say I've *never*, no, no, never, seen any one of Osmond's pretensions! What they're all founded on is more than I can say. I'm his own sister; I might be supposed to know. Who is he, if you please? What has he ever done? If there had been anything particularly grand in his origin—if he were made of some superior clay—I presume I should have got some inkling of it. If there had been any great honours or splendours in the family I should certainly have made the most of them: they would have been quite in my line. But there's nothing, nothing, nothing. One's parents were charming people of course; but so were yours, I've no doubt. Every one's a charming person now-a-days. Even I'm a charming person; don't laugh, it has literally been said. As for Osmond, he has always appeared to believe that he's descended from the gods."

"You may say what you please," said Madame Merle, who had listened to this quick outbreak none the less attentively, we may believe, because her eye wandered away from the speaker and her hands busied themselves with adjusting the knots of ribbon on her dress. "You Osmonds are a fine race—your blood must flow from some very pure source. Your brother, like an intelligent man, has had the conviction of it if he has not had the proofs. You're modest about it, but you yourself are extremely distinguished. What do you say about your niece? The child's a little princess. Nevertheless," Madame Merle added, "it won't be an easy matter for Osmond to marry Miss Archer. Yet he can try."

"I hope she'll refuse him. It will take him down a little."

"We mustn't forget that he is one of the cleverest of men."

"I've heard you say that before, but I haven't yet discovered what he has done."

"What he has done? He has done nothing that has had to be undone. And he has known how to wait."

"To wait for Miss Archer's money? How much of it is there?"

"That's not what I mean," said Madame Merle. "Miss Archer has seventy thousand pounds."

"Well, it's a pity she's so charming," the Countess declared. "To be sacrificed, any girl would do. She needn't be superior."

"If she weren't superior your brother would never look at her. He must have the best."

"Yes," returned the Countess as they went forward a little to meet the others, "he's very hard to satisfy. That makes me tremble for her happiness!"

Chapter XXVI

Gilbert Osmond came to see Isabel again; that is he came to Palazzo Crescentini. He had other friends there as well, and to Mrs. Touchett and Madame Merle he was always impartially civil; but the former of these ladies noted the fact that in the course of a fortnight he called five times, and compared it with another fact that she found no difficulty in remembering. Two visits a year had hitherto constituted his regular tribute to Mrs. Touchett's worth, and she had never observed him select for such visits those moments, of almost periodical recurrence, when Madame Merle was under her roof. It was not for Madame Merle that he came; these two were old friends and he never put himself out for her. He was not fond of Ralph—Ralph had told her so—and it was not supposable that Mr. Osmond had suddenly taken a fancy to her son. Ralph was imperturbable—Ralph had a kind of loose-fitting urbanity that wrapped him about like an ill-made overcoat, but of which he never divested himself; he thought Mr. Osmond very good company and was willing at any time to look at him in the light of hospitality. But he didn't flatter himself that the desire to repair a past injustice was the motive of their visitor's calls; he read the situation more clearly. Isabel was the attraction, and in all conscience a sufficient one. Osmond was a critic, a student of the exquisite, and it was natural he should be curious of so rare an apparition. So when his mother observed to him that it was plain what Mr. Osmond was thinking of, Ralph replied that he was quite of her opinion. Mrs. Touchett had from far back found a place on her scant list for this gentleman, though wondering dimly by what art and what process—so negative and so wise as they were—he had everywhere effectively imposed himself. As he had never been an importunate visitor he had had no chance to be offensive, and he was recommended to her by his appearance of being as well able to do without her as she was to do without him—a quality that always, oddly enough, affected her as providing ground for a relation with her. It gave her no satisfaction, however, to think that he had taken it into his head to marry her niece. Such an alliance, on Isabel's part, would have an air of almost morbid perversity. Mrs. Touchett easily remembered that the girl had refused an English peer; and that a young lady with whom Lord Warburton had not successfully wrestled should content herself with an obscure American dilettante, a middle-aged widower with an uncanny child and an ambiguous income, this answered to nothing in Mrs. Touchett's conception of success. She took, it will be observed, not the sentimental, but the political, view of matrimony—a view which has always had much to recommend it. "I trust she won't have the folly to listen to him," she said to her son; to which Ralph replied that Isabel's listening was one thing and Isabel's answering quite another. He knew she had listened to several parties, as his father would have said, but had made them listen in return; and he found much entertainment in the idea that in these few months of his knowing her he should observe a fresh suitor at her gate. She had wanted to see life, and fortune was serving her to her taste; a succession of fine gentlemen going down on their knees to her would do as well as anything else. Ralph looked forward to a fourth, a fifth, a tenth besieger; he had no conviction she would stop at a third. She would keep the gate ajar and open a parley; she would certainly not allow number three to come in. He expressed this view, somewhat after this fashion, to his mother, who looked at him as if he had been dancing a jig. He had such a fanciful, pictorial way of saying things that he might as well address her in the deaf-mute's alphabet.

"I don't think I know what you mean," she said; "you use too many figures of speech; I could never understand allegories. The two words in the language I most respect are Yes and No. If Isabel wants to marry Mr. Osmond she'll do so in spite of all your comparisons. Let her alone to find a fine one herself for anything she undertakes. I know very little about the young man in America; I don't think she spends much of her time in thinking of him, and I suspect he has got tired of waiting for her. There's nothing in life to prevent her marrying Mr. Osmond if she only looks at him in a certain way. That's all very well; no one approves more than I of one's pleasing one's self. But she takes her pleasure in such odd things; she's capable of marrying Mr. Osmond for the beauty of his opinions or for his autograph of Michael Angelo. She wants to be disinterested: as if she were the only person who's in danger of not being so! Will *he* be so disinterested when he has the spending of her money? That was her idea before your father's death, and it has acquired new charms for her since. She ought to marry some one of whose disinterestedness she shall herself be sure; and there would be no such proof of that as his having a fortune of his own."

"My dear mother, I'm not afraid," Ralph answered. "She's making fools of us all. She'll please herself, of course; but she'll do so by studying human nature at close quarters and yet retaining her liberty. She has started on an exploring expedition, and I don't think she'll change her course, at the outset, at a signal from Gilbert Osmond. She may have slackened speed for an hour, but before we know it she'll be steaming away again. Excuse another metaphor."

Mrs. Touchett excused it perhaps, but was not so much reassured as to withhold from Madame Merle the expression of her fears. "You who know everything," she said, "you must know this: whether that curious creature's really making love to my niece."

"Gilbert Osmond?" Madame Merle widened her clear eyes and, with a full intelligence, "Heaven help us," she exclaimed, "that's an idea!"

"Hadn't it occurred to you?"

"You make me feel an idiot, but I confess it hadn't. I wonder," she added, "if it has occurred to Isabel."

"Oh, I shall now ask her," said Mrs. Touchett.

Madame Merle reflected. "Don't put it into her head. The thing would be to ask Mr. Osmond."

"I can't do that," said Mrs. Touchett. "I won't have him enquire of me—as he perfectly may with that air of his, given Isabel's situation—what business it is of mine."

"I'll ask him myself," Madame Merle bravely declared.

"But what business—for *him*—is it of yours?"

"It's being none whatever is just why I can afford to speak. It's so much less my business than any one's else that he can put me off with anything he chooses. But it will be by the way he does this that I shall know."

"Pray let me hear then," said Mrs. Touchett, "of the fruits of your penetration. If I can't speak to him, however, at least I can speak to Isabel."

Her companion sounded at this the note of warning. "Don't be too quick with her. Don't inflame her imagination."

"I never did anything in life to any one's imagination. But I'm always sure of her doing something—well, not of *my* kind."

"No, you wouldn't like this," Madame Merle observed without the point of interrogation.

"Why in the world should I, pray? Mr. Osmond has nothing the least solid to offer."

Again Madame Merle was silent while her thoughtful smile drew up her mouth even more charmingly than usual toward the left corner. "Let us distinguish. Gilbert Osmond's certainly not the first comer. He's a man who in favourable conditions might very well make a great impression. He has made a great impression, to my knowledge, more than once."

"Don't tell me about his probably quite cold-blooded love-affairs; they're nothing to me!" Mrs. Touchett cried. "What you say's precisely why I wish he would cease his visits. He has nothing in the world that I know of but a dozen or two of early masters and a more or less pert little daughter."

"The early masters are now worth a good deal of money," said Madame Merle, "and the daughter's a very young and very innocent and very harmless person."

"In other words she's an insipid little chit. Is that what you mean? Having no fortune she can't hope to marry as they marry here; so that Isabel will have to furnish her either with a maintenance or with a dowry."

"Isabel probably wouldn't object to being kind to her. I think she likes the poor child."

"Another reason then for Mr. Osmond's stopping at home! Otherwise, a week hence, we shall have my niece arriving at the conviction that her mission in life's to prove that a stepmother may sacrifice herself—and that, to prove it, she must first become one."

"She would make a charming stepmother," smiled Madame Merle; "but I quite agree with you that she had better not decide upon her mission too hastily. Changing the form of one's mission's almost as difficult as changing the shape of one's nose: there they are, each, in the middle of one's face and one's character—one has to begin too far back. But I'll investigate and report to you."

All this went on quite over Isabel's head; she had no suspicions that her relations with Mr. Osmond were being discussed. Madame Merle had said nothing to put her on her guard; she alluded no more pointedly to him than to the other gentlemen of Florence, native and foreign, who now arrived in considerable numbers to pay their respects to Miss Archer's aunt. Isabel thought him interesting—she came back to that; she liked so to think of him. She had carried away an image from her visit to his hill-top which her subsequent knowledge of him did nothing to efface and which put on for her a particular harmony with other supposed and divined things, histories within histories: the image of a quiet, clever, sensitive, distinguished man, strolling on a moss-grown terrace above the sweet Val d'Arno and holding by the hand a little girl whose bell-like clearness gave a new grace to childhood. The picture had no flourishes, but she liked its lowness of tone and the atmosphere of summer twilight that pervaded it. It spoke of the kind of personal issue that touched her most nearly; of the choice between objects, subjects, contacts—what might she call them?— of a thin and those of a rich association; of a lonely, studious life in a lovely land; of an old sorrow that sometimes ached to-day; of a feeling of pride that was perhaps exaggerated, but that had an element of nobleness; of a care for beauty and perfection so natural and so cultivated together that the career appeared to stretch beneath it in the disposed vistas and with the ranges of steps and terraces and fountains of a formal Italian garden— allowing only for and places freshened by the natural dews of a quaint half-anxious, half-helpless fatherhood. At Palazzo Crescentini Mr. Osmond's manner remained the same; diffident at first—oh self-conscious beyond doubt! and full of the effort (visible only to a sympathetic eye) to over-come this disadvantage; an effort which usually resulted in a great deal of easy, lively, very positive, rather aggressive, always suggestive talk. Mr. Osmond's talk was not injured by the indication of an eagerness to shine; Isabel found no difficulty in believing that a person was sincere who had so many of the signs of strong conviction—as for instance an explicit and graceful appreciation of anything that might be said on his own side of the question, said perhaps by Miss Archer in especial. What continued to please this young woman was that while he talked so for amusement he didn't talk, as she had heard people, for "effect." He uttered his ideas as if, odd as they often appeared, he were used to them and had lived with them; old polished knobs and heads and handles, of precious substance, that could be fitted if necessary to new walking-sticks—not switches plucked in destitution from the common tree and then too elegantly waved about. One day be brought his small daughter with him, and she rejoiced to renew acquaintance with the child, who, as she presented her forehead to be kissed by every member of the circle, reminded her vividly of an *ingénue*—in a French play. Isabel had never seen a little person of this pattern; American girls were very different— different too were the maidens of England. Pansy was so formed and finished for her tiny place in the world, and yet in imagination, as one could see, so innocent and infantine. She sat on the sofa by Isabel; she wore a small grenadine mantle and a pair of the useful gloves that Madame Merle had given her—little grey gloves with a single button. She was like a sheet of blank paper—the ideal *jeune fille* of foreign fiction. Isabel hoped that so fair and smooth a page would be covered with an edifying text.

The Countess Gemini also came to call upon her, but the Countess was quite another affair. She was by no means a blank sheet; she had been written over in a variety of hands, and Mrs. Touchett, who felt by no means honoured by her visit, pronounced that a number of unmistakeable blots were to be seen upon her surface. The Countess gave rise indeed to some discussion between the mistress of the house and the visitor from Rome, in which Madame Merle (who was not such a fool as to irritate people by always agreeing with them) availed herself felicitously enough of that large license of dissent which her hostess permitted as freely as she practised it. Mrs. Touchett had declared it a piece of audacity that this highly compromised character should have presented herself at such a time of day at the door of a house in which she was esteemed so little as she must long have known herself to be at Palazzo Crescentini. Isabel had been made acquainted with the estimate prevailing under that roof: it represented Mr. Osmond's sister as a lady who had so mismanaged her improprieties that they had ceased to hang together at all—which was at the least what one asked of such matters—and had become the mere floating fragments of a wrecked renown, incommoding social circulation. She had been married by her mother—a more administrative person, with an appreciation of foreign titles which the daughter, to do her justice, had probably by this time thrown off—to an Italian nobleman who had perhaps given her some excuse for attempting to quench the consciousness of outrage. The Countess, however, had consoled herself outrageously, and the list of her excuses had now lost itself in the labyrinth of her adventures. Mrs. Touchett had never consented to receive her, though the Countess had made overtures of old. Florence was not an austere city; but, as Mrs. Touchett said, she had to draw the line somewhere.

Madame Merle defended the luckless lady with a great deal of zeal and wit. She couldn't see why Mrs. Touchett should make a scapegoat of a woman who had really done no harm, who had only done good in the wrong way. One must certainly draw the line, but while one was about it one should draw it straight: it was a very crooked chalk-mark that would exclude the Countess Gemini. In that case Mrs. Touchett had better shut up her house; this perhaps would be the best course so long as she remained in Florence. One must be fair and not make arbitrary differences: the Countess had doubtless been imprudent, she had not been so clever as other women. She was a good creature, not clever at all; but since when had that been a ground of exclusion from the best society? For ever so long now one had heard nothing about her, and there could be no better proof of her having renounced the error of her ways than her desire to become a member of Mrs. Touchett's circle. Isabel could contribute nothing to this interesting dispute, not even a patient attention; she contented herself with having given a friendly welcome to the unfortunate lady, who, whatever her defects, had at least the merit of being Mr. Osmond's sister. As she liked the brother Isabel thought it proper to try and like the sister: in spite of the growing complexity of things she was still capable of these primitive sequences. She had not received the happiest impression of the Countess on meeting her at the villa, but was thankful for an opportunity to repair the accident. Had not Mr. Osmond remarked that she was a respectable person? To have proceeded from Gilbert Osmond this was a crude proposition, but Madame Merle bestowed upon it a certain improving polish. She told Isabel more about the poor Countess than Mr. Osmond had done, and related the history of her marriage and its consequences. The Count was a member of an ancient Tuscan family, but of such small estate that he had been glad to accept Amy Osmond, in spite of the questionable beauty which had yet not hampered her career, with the modest dowry her mother was able to offer—a sum about equivalent to that which had already formed her brother's share of their patrimony. Count Gemini since then, however, had inherited money, and now they were well enough off, as Italians went, though Amy was horribly extravagant. The Count was a low-lived brute; he had given his wife every pretext. She had no children; she had lost three within a year of their birth. Her mother, who had bristled with pretensions to elegant learning and published descriptive poems and corresponded on Italian subjects with the English weekly journals, her mother had died three years after the Countess's marriage, the father, lost in the grey American dawn of the situation, but reputed originally rich and wild, having died much earlier. One could see this in Gilbert Osmond, Madame Merle held—see that he had been brought up by a woman; though, to do him justice, one would suppose it had been by a more sensible woman than the American Corinne,[1] as Mrs. Osmond had liked to be called. She had brought her children to Italy after her husband's death, and Mrs. Touchett remembered her during the year that followed her arrival. She thought her a horrible snob; but this was an irregularity of judgment on Mrs. Touchett's part, for she, like Mrs. Osmond, approved of political marriages. The Countess was very good company and not really the featherhead she seemed; all one had to do with her was to observe the simple condition of not believing a word she said. Madame Merle had always made the best of her for her brother's sake; he appreciated any kindness shown to Amy, because (if it had to be confessed for him) he rather felt she let down their common name. Naturally he couldn't like her style, her shrillness, her egotism, her violations of taste and above all of truth: she acted badly on his nerves, she was not *his* sort of woman. What was his sort of woman? Oh, the very opposite of the Countess, a woman to whom the truth should be habitually sacred. Isabel was unable to estimate the number of times her visitor had, in half an hour, profaned it: the Countess indeed had given her an impression of rather silly sincerity. She had talked almost exclusively about herself; how much she should like to know Miss Archer; how thankful she should be for a real friend; how base the people in Florence were; how tired she was of the place; how much she should like to live somewhere else—in Paris, in London, in Washington; how impossible it was to get anything nice to wear in Italy except a little old lace; how dear the world was growing everywhere; what a life of suffering and privation she had led. Madame Merle listened with interest to Isabel's account of this passage, but she had not needed it to feel exempt from anxiety. On the whole she was not afraid of the Countess, and she could afford to do what was altogether best—not to appear so.

Isabel had meanwhile another visitor, whom it was not, even behind her back, so easy a matter to patronise. Henrietta Stackpole, who had left Paris after Mrs. Touchett's departure for San Remo and had worked her way down, as she said, through the cities of North Italy, reached the banks of the Arno about the middle of May. Madame Merle surveyed her with a single glance, took her in from head to foot, and after a pang of despair

---

1. *Corinne, or Italy* (1807), novel in French by Germaine de Staël (1766–1817), a central text of European Romanticism that celebrates the beauties of Italy and whose title character establishes a model for the life of the woman writer.

determined to endure her. She determined indeed to delight in her. She mightn't be inhaled as a rose, but she might be grasped as a nettle. Madame Merle genially squeezed her into insignificance, and Isabel felt that in foreseeing this liberality she had done justice to her friend's intelligence. Henrietta's arrival had been announced by Mr. Bantling, who, coming down from Nice while she was at Venice, and expecting to find her in Florence, which she had not yet reached, called at Palazzo Crescentini to express his disappointment. Henrietta's own advent occurred two days later and produced in Mr. Bantling an emotion amply accounted for by the fact that he had not seen her since the termination of the episode at Versailles. The humorous view of his situation was generally taken, but it was uttered only by Ralph Touchett, who, in the privacy of his own apartment, when Bantling smoked a cigar there, indulged in goodness knew what strong comedy on the subject of the all-judging one and her British backer. This gentleman took the joke in perfectly good part and candidly confessed that he regarded the affair as a positive intellectual adventure. He liked Miss Stackpole extremely; he thought she had a wonderful head on her shoulders, and found great comfort in the society of a woman who was not perpetually thinking about what would be said and how what she did, how what *they* did—and they had done things—would look. Miss Stackpole never cared how anything looked, and, if she didn't care, pray why should he? But his curiosity had been roused; he wanted awfully to see if she ever *would* care. He was prepared to go as far as she—he didn't see why he should break down first.

Henrietta showed no signs of breaking down. Her prospects had brightened on her leaving England, and she was now in the full enjoyment of her copious resources. She had indeed been obliged to sacrifice her hopes with regard to the inner life; the social question, on the Continent, bristled with difficulties even more numerous than those she had encountered in England. But on the Continent there was the outer life, which was palpable and visible at every turn, and more easily convertible to literary uses than the customs of those opaque islanders. Out of doors in foreign lands, as she ingeniously remarked, one seemed to see the right side of the tapestry; out of doors in England one seemed to see the wrong side, which gave one no notion of the figure. The admission costs her historian a pang, but Henrietta, despairing of more occult things, was now paying much attention to the outer life. She had been studying it for two months at Venice, from which city she sent to the *Interviewer* a conscientious account of the gondolas, the Piazza, the Bridge of Sighs, the pigeons and the young boatman who chanted Tasso.[2] The *Interviewer* was perhaps disappointed, but Henrietta was at least seeing Europe. Her present purpose was to get down to Rome before the malaria[3] should come on—she apparently supposed that it began on a fixed day; and with this design she was to spend at present but few days in Florence. Mr. Bantling was to go with her to Rome, and she pointed out to Isabel that as he had been there

---

2. Torquato Tasso (1544–1595), Italian poet best known for his epic *Jerusalem Delivered* (1581). Venetian gondoliers were famous for chanting his lines, a custom that by this time was no longer a folk practice but rather a show put on for tourists.

3. Malaria or mal'aria (Italian), bad air, was a summer health hazard in Rome, and the disease that kills the title character in James's "Daisy Miller" (1878). It was thought to be caused by "miasma" from the Roman marshes but is in fact spread by mosquitoes.

before, as he was a military man and as he had had a classical education—
he had been bred at Eton, where they study nothing but Latin and Whyte-
Melville,[4] said Miss Stackpole—he would be a most useful companion in
the city of the Cæsars. At this juncture Ralph had the happy idea of proposing to Isabel that she also, under his own escort, should make a pilgrimage to Rome. She expected to pass a portion of the next winter there—that
was very well; but meantime there was no harm in surveying the field.
There were ten days left of the beautiful month of May—the most precious month of all to the true Rome-lover. Isabel would become a Rome-
lover; that was a foregone conclusion. She was provided with a trusty
companion of her own sex, whose society, thanks to the fact of other calls
on this lady's attention, would probably not be oppressive. Madame Merle
would remain with Mrs. Touchett; she had left Rome for the summer and
wouldn't care to return. She professed herself delighted to be left at peace
in Florence; she had locked up her apartment and sent her cook home to
Palestrina.[5] She urged Isabel, however, to assent to Ralph's proposal, and
assured her that a good introduction to Rome was not a thing to be
despised. Isabel in truth needed no urging, and the party of four arranged
its little journey. Mrs. Touchett, on this occasion, had resigned herself to
the absence of a duenna;[6] we have seen that she now inclined to the
belief that her niece should stand alone. One of Isabel's preparations
consisted of her seeing Gilbert Osmond before she started and mentioning her intention to him.

"I should like to be in Rome with you," he commented. "I should like to
see you on that wonderful ground."

She scarcely faltered. "You might come then."

"But you'll have a lot of people with you."

"Ah," Isabel admitted, "of course I shall not be alone."

For a moment he said nothing more. "You'll like it," he went on at last.
"They've spoiled it, but you'll rave about it."

"Ought I to dislike it because, poor old dear—the Niobe[7] of Nations,
you know—it has been spoiled?" she asked.

"No, I think not. It has been spoiled so often," he smiled. "If I were to
go, what should I do with my little girl?"

"Can't you leave her at the villa?"

"I don't know that I like that—though there's a very good old woman
who looks after her. I can't afford a governess."

"Bring her with you then," said Isabel promptly.

Mr. Osmond looked grave. "She has been in Rome all winter, at her convent; and she's too young to make journeys of pleasure."

"You don't like bringing her forward?" Isabel enquired.

"No, I think young girls should be kept out of the world."

"I was brought up on a different system."

"You? Oh, with you it succeeded, because you—you were exceptional."

---

4. George John Whyte-Melville (1821–1878), British army officer and novelist who wrote mostly
   about foxhunting.
5. A town near Rome.
6. Chaperone (Italian).
7. In Greek mythology, the archetype of the bereaved mother (see p.127, n.3); the particular allusion here is to a description of Rome in Byron's *Childe Harold's Pilgrimage*: "The Niobe of
   Nations, there she stands / Childless and crownless, in her voiceless woe" (canto IV, stanza 79).

"I don't see why," said Isabel, who, however, was not sure there was not some truth in the speech.

Mr. Osmond didn't explain; he simply went on: "If I thought it would make her resemble you to join a social group in Rome I'd take her there to-morrow."

"Don't make her resemble me," said Isabel. "Keep her like herself."

"I might send her to my sister," Mr. Osmond observed. He had almost the air of asking advice; he seemed to like to talk over his domestic matters with Miss Archer.

"Yes," she concurred; "I think that wouldn't do much towards making her resemble me!"

After she had left Florence Gilbert Osmond met Madame Merle at the Countess Gemini's. There were other people present; the Countess's drawing-room was usually well filled, and the talk had been general, but after a while Osmond left his place and came and sat on an ottoman half-behind, half-beside Madame Merle's chair. "She wants me to go to Rome with her," he remarked in a low voice.

"To go with her?"

"To be there while she's there. She proposed it."

"I suppose you mean that you proposed it and she assented."

"Of course I gave her a chance. But she's encouraging—she's very encouraging."

"I rejoice to hear it—but don't cry victory too soon. Of course you'll go to Rome."

"Ah," said Osmond, "it makes one work, this idea of yours!"

"Don't pretend you don't enjoy it—you're very ungrateful. You've not been so well occupied these many years."

"The way you take it's beautiful," said Osmond. "I ought to be grateful for that."

"Not too much so, however," Madame Merle answered. She talked with her usual smile, leaning back in her chair and looking round the room. "You've made a very good impression, and I've seen for myself that you've received one. You've not come to Mrs. Touchett's seven times to oblige me."

"The girl's not disagreeable," Osmond quietly conceded.

Madame Merle dropped her eye on him a moment, during which her lips closed with a certain firmness. "Is that all you can find to say about that fine creature?"

"All? Isn't it enough? Of how many people have you heard me say more?"

She made no answer to this, but still presented her talkative grace to the room. "You're unfathomable," she murmured at last. "I'm frightened at the abyss into which I shall have cast her."

He took it almost gaily. "You can't draw back—you've gone too far."

"Very good; but you must do the rest yourself."

"I shall do it," said Gilbert Osmond.

Madame Merle remained silent and he changed his place again; but when she rose to go he also took leave. Mrs. Touchett's victoria[8] was awaiting her guest in the court, and after he had helped his friend into it he stood there detaining her. "You're very indiscreet," she said rather wearily; "you shouldn't have moved when I did."

---

8. A low-slung four-wheeled carriage, with a raised seat for the driver in front.

He had taken off his hat; he passed his hand over his forehead. "I always forget; I'm out of the habit."

"You're quite unfathomable," she repeated, glancing up at the windows of the house, a modern structure in the new part of the town.

He paid no heed to this remark, but spoke in his own sense. "She's really very charming. I've scarcely known any one more graceful."

"It does me good to hear you say that. The better you like her the better for me."

"I like her very much. She's all you described her, and into the bargain capable, I feel, of great devotion. She has only one fault."

"What's that?"

"Too many ideas."

"I warned you she was clever."

"Fortunately they're very bad ones," said Osmond.

"Why is that fortunate?"

"*Dame*,[9] if they must be sacrificed!"

Madame Merle leaned back, looking straight before her; then she spoke to the coachman. But her friend again detained her. "If I go to Rome what shall I do with Pansy?"

"I'll go and see her," said Madame Merle.

Chapter XXVII

I may not attempt to report in its fulness our young woman's response to the deep appeal of Rome, to analyse her feelings as she trod the pavement of the Forum or to number her pulsations as she crossed the threshold of Saint Peter's. It is enough to say that her impression was such as might have been expected of a person of her freshness and her eagerness. She had always been fond of history, and here was history in the stones of the street and the atoms of the sunshine. She had an imagination that kindled at the mention of great deeds, and wherever she turned some great deed had been acted. These things strongly moved her, but moved her all inwardly. It seemed to her companions that she talked less than usual, and Ralph Touchett, when he appeared to be looking listlessly and awkwardly over her head, was really dropping on her an intensity of observation. By her own measure she was very happy; she would even have been willing to take these hours for the happiest she was ever to know. The sense of the terrible human past was heavy to her, but that of something altogether contemporary would suddenly give it wings that it could wave in the blue. Her consciousness was so mixed that she scarcely knew where the different parts of it would lead her, and she went about in a repressed ecstasy of contemplation, seeing often in the things she looked at a great deal more than was there, and yet not seeing many of the items enumerated in her Murray.[1] Rome, as Ralph said, confessed to the psychological moment. The herd of reëchoing tourists had departed and most of the solemn places had relapsed into solemnity. The sky was a blaze of blue, and the plash of

9. Indeed (French); an interjection.
1. The London publishing house of John Murray produced a series of authoritative "Handbooks" to major European countries and cities; along with the competing series published by Karl Baedeker of Cologne, they were the most important tourist's guidebooks of the nineteenth century, and remain useful historical resources today. Isabel's itinerary here—Saint Peter's, the Forum, the Capitol—includes what were, both then and now, the most popular of standard sites.

the fountains in their mossy niches had lost its chill and doubled its music. On the corners of the warm, bright streets one stumbled on bundles of flowers. Our friends had gone one afternoon—it was the third of their stay—to look at the latest excavations in the Forum, these labours having been for some time previous largely extended. They had descended from the modern street to the level of the Sacred Way, along which they wandered with a reverence of step which was not the same on the part of each. Henrietta Stackpole was struck with the fact that ancient Rome had been paved a good deal like New York, and even found an analogy between the deep chariot-ruts traceable in the antique street and the overjangled iron grooves which express the intensity of American life. The sun had begun to sink, the air was a golden haze, and the long shadows of broken column and vague pedestal leaned across the field of ruin. Henrietta wandered away with Mr. Bantling, whom it was apparently delightful to her to hear speak of Julius Caesar as a "cheeky old boy," and Ralph addressed such elucidations as he was prepared to offer to the attentive ear of our heroine. One of the humble archæologists who hover about the place had put himself at the disposal of the two, and repeated his lesson with a fluency which the decline of the season had done nothing to impair. A process of digging was on view in a remote corner of the Forum, and he presently remarked that if it should please the *signori* to go and watch it a little they might see something of interest. The proposal commended itself more to Ralph than to Isabel, weary with much wandering; so that she admonished her companion to satisfy his curiosity while she patiently awaited his return. The hour and the place were much to her taste—she should enjoy being briefly alone. Ralph accordingly went off with the cicerone while Isabel sat down on a prostrate column near the foundations of the Capitol. She wanted a short solitude, but she was not long to enjoy it. Keen as was her interest in the rugged relics of the Roman past that lay scattered about her and in which the corrosion of centuries had still left so much of individual life, her thoughts, after resting a while on these things, had wandered, by a concatenation of stages it might require some subtlety to trace, to regions and objects charged with a more active appeal. From the Roman past to Isabel Archer's future was a long stride, but her imagination had taken it in a single flight and now hovered in slow circles over the nearer and richer field. She was so absorbed in her thoughts, as she bent her eyes upon a row of cracked but not dislocated slabs covering the ground at her feet, that she had not heard the sound of approaching footsteps before a shadow was thrown across the line of her vision. She looked up and saw a gentleman—a gentleman who was not Ralph come back to say that the excavations were a bore. This personage was startled as she was startled; he stood there baring his head to her perceptibly pale surprise.

"Lord Warburton!" Isabel exclaimed as she rose.

"I had no idea it was you. I turned that corner and came upon you."

She looked about her to explain. "I'm alone, but my companions have just left me. My cousin's gone to look at the work over there."

"Ah yes; I see." And Lord Warburton's eyes wandered vaguely in the direction she had indicated. He stood firmly before her now; he had recovered his balance and seemed to wish to show it, though very kindly. "Don't let me disturb you," he went on, looking at her dejected pillar. "I'm afraid you're tired."

"Yes, I'm rather tired." She hesitated a moment, but sat down again. "Don't let me interrupt *you*," she added.

"Oh dear, I'm quite alone, I've nothing on earth to do. I had no idea you were in Rome. I've just come from the East. I'm only passing through."

"You've been making a long journey," said Isabel, who had learned from Ralph that Lord Warburton was absent from England.

"Yes, I came abroad for six months—soon after I saw you last. I've been in Turkey and Asia Minor; I came the other day from Athens." He managed not to be awkward, but he wasn't easy, and after a longer look at the girl he came down to nature. "Do you wish me to leave you, or will you let me stay a little?"

She took it all humanely. "I don't wish you to leave me, Lord Warburton: I'm very glad to see you."

"Thank you for saying that. May I sit down?"

The fluted shaft on which she had taken her seat would have afforded a resting-place to several persons, and there was plenty of room even for a highly-developed Englishman. This fine specimen of that great class seated himself near our young lady, and in the course of five minutes he had asked her several questions, taken rather at random and to which, as he put some of them twice over, he apparently somewhat missed catching the answer; had given her too some information about himself which was not wasted upon her calmer feminine sense. He repeated more than once that he had not expected to meet her, and it was evident that the encounter touched him in a way that would have made preparation advisable. He began abruptly to pass from the impunity of things to their solemnity, and from their being delightful to their being impossible. He was splendidly sunburnt; even his multitudinous beard had been burnished by the fire of Asia. He was dressed in the loose-fitting, heterogeneous garments in which the English traveller in foreign lands is wont to consult his comfort and affirm his nationality; and with his pleasant steady eyes, his bronzed complexion, fresh beneath its seasoning, his manly figure, his minimising manner and his general air of being a gentleman and an explorer, he was such a representative of the British race as need not in any clime have been disavowed by those who have a kindness for it. Isabel noted these things and was glad she had always liked him. He had kept, evidently in spite of shocks, every one of his merits—properties these partaking of the essence of great decent houses, as one might put it; resembling their innermost fixtures and ornaments, not subject to vulgar shifting and removable only by some whole break-up. They talked of the matters naturally in order; her uncle's death, Ralph's state of health, the way she had passed her winter, her visit to Rome, her return to Florence, her plans for the summer, the hotel she was staying at; and then of Lord Warburton's own adventures, movements, intentions, impressions and present domicile. At last there was a silence, and it said so much more than either had said that it scarce needed his final words. "I've written to you several times."

"Written to me? I've never had your letters."

"I never sent them. I burned them up."

"Ah," laughed Isabel, "it was better that you should do that than I!"

"I thought you wouldn't care for them," he went on with a simplicity that touched her. "It seemed to me that after all I had no right to trouble you with letters."

"I should have been very glad to have news of you. You know how I hoped that—that—" But she stopped; there would be such a flatness in the utterance of her thought.

"I know what you're going to say. You hoped we should always remain good friends." This formula, as Lord Warburton uttered it, was certainly flat enough; but then he was interested in making it appear so.

She found herself reduced simply to "Please don't talk of all that"; a speech which hardly struck her as improvement on the other.

"It's a small consolation to allow me!" her companion exclaimed with force.

"I can't pretend to console you," said the girl, who, all still as she sat there, threw herself back with a sort of inward triumph on the answer that had satisfied him so little six months before. He was pleasant, he was powerful, he was gallant; there was no better man than he. But her answer remained.

"It's very well you don't try to console me; it wouldn't be in your power," she heard him say through the medium of her strange elation.

"I hoped we should meet again, because I had no fear you would attempt to make me feel I had wronged you. But when you do that—the pain's greater than the pleasure." And she got up with a small conscious majesty, looking for her companions.

"I don't want to make you feel that; of course I can't say that. I only just want you to know one or two things—in fairness to myself, as it were. I won't return to the subject again. I felt very strongly what I expressed to you last year; I couldn't think of anything else. I tried to forget—energetically, systematically. I tried to take an interest in somebody else. I tell you this because I want you to know I did my duty. I didn't succeed. It was for the same purpose I went abroad—as far away as possible. They say travelling distracts the mind, but it didn't distract mine. I've thought of you perpetually, ever since I last saw you. I'm exactly the same. I love you just as much, and everything I said to you then is just as true. This instant at which I speak to you shows me again exactly how, to my great misfortune, you just insuperably *charm* me. There—I can't say less. I don't mean, however, to insist; it's only for a moment. I may add that when I came upon you a few minutes since, without the smallest idea of seeing you, I was, upon my honour, in the very act of wishing I knew where you were." He had recovered his self-control, and while he spoke it became complete. He might have been addressing a small committee—making all quietly and clearly a statement of importance; aided by an occasional look at a paper of notes concealed in his hat, which he had not again put on. And the committee, assuredly, would have felt the point proved.

"I've often thought of you, Lord Warburton," Isabel answered. "You may be sure I shall always do that." And she added in a tone of which she tried to keep up the kindness and keep down the meaning: "There's no harm in that on either side."

They walked along together, and she was prompt to ask about his sisters and request him to let them know she had done so. He made for the moment no further reference to their great question, but dipped again into shallower and safer waters. But he wished to know when she was to leave Rome, and on her mentioning the limit of her stay declared he was glad it was still so distant.

"Why do you say that if you yourself are only passing through?" she enquired with some anxiety.

"Ah, when I said I was passing through I didn't mean that one would treat Rome as if it were Clapham Junction.[2] To pass through Rome is to stop a week or two."

"Say frankly that you mean to stay as long as I do!"

His flushed smile, for a little, seemed to sound her. "You won't like that. You're afraid you'll see too much of me."

"It doesn't matter what I like. I certainly can't expect you to leave this delightful place on my account. But I confess I'm afraid of you."

"Afraid I'll begin again? I promise to be very careful."

They had gradually stopped and they stood a moment face to face. "Poor Lord Warburton!" she said with a compassion intended to be good for both of them.

"Poor Lord Warburton indeed! But I'll be careful."

"You may be unhappy, but you shall not make *me* so. That I can't allow."

"If I believed I could make you unhappy I think I should try it.' At this she walked in advance and he also proceeded. "I'll never say a word to displease you."

"Very good. If you do, our friendship's at an end."

"Perhaps some day—after a while—you'll give me leave."

"Give you leave to make me unhappy?"

He hesitated. "To tell you again—" But he checked himself. "I'll keep it down. I'll keep it down always."

Ralph Touchett had been joined in his visit to the excavation by Miss Stackpole and her attendant, and these three now emerged from among the mounds of earth and stone collected round the aperture and came into sight of Isabel and her companion. Poor Ralph hailed his friend with joy qualified by wonder, and Henrietta exclaimed in a high voice, "Gracious, there's that lord!" Ralph and his English neighbour greeted with the austerity with which, after long separations, English neighbours greet, and Miss Stackpole rested her large intellectual gaze upon the sunburnt traveller. But she soon established her relation to the crisis. "I don't suppose you remember me, sir."

"Indeed I do remember you," said Lord Warburton. "I asked you to come and see me, and you never came."

"I don't go everywhere I'm asked," Miss Stackpole answered coldly.

"Ah well, I won't ask you again," laughed the master of Lockleigh.

"If you do I'll go; so be sure!"

Lord Warburton, for all his hilarity, seemed sure enough. Mr. Bantling had stood by without claiming a recognition, but he now took occasion to nod to his lordship, who answered him with a friendly "Oh, you here, Bantling?" and a handshake.

"Well," said Henrietta, "I didn't know you knew him!"

"I guess you don't know every one I know," Mr. Bantling rejoined facetiously.

"I thought that when an Englishman knew a lord he always told you."

"Ah, I'm afraid Bantling was ashamed of me," Lord Warburton laughed again. Isabel took pleasure in that note; she gave a small sigh of relief as they kept their course homeward.

---

2. A railway interchange south of the Thames in London; one of the busiest stations in Europe.

The next day was Sunday; she spent her morning over two long letters—one to her sister Lily, the other to Madame Merle; but in neither of these epistles did she mention the fact that a rejected suitor had threatened her with another appeal. Of a Sunday afternoon all good Romans (and the best Romans are often the northern barbarians) follow the custom of going to vespers at Saint Peter's; and it had been agreed among our friends that they would drive together to the great church. After lunch, an hour before the carriage came, Lord Warburton presented himself at the Hôtel de Paris[3] and paid a visit to the two ladies, Ralph Touchett and Mr. Bantling having gone out together. The visitor seemed to have wished to give Isabel a proof of his intention to keep the promise made her the evening before; he was both discreet and frank—not even dumbly importunate or remotely intense. He thus left her to judge what a mere good friend he could be. He talked about his travels, about Persia, about Turkey, and when Miss Stackpole asked him whether it would "pay" for her to visit those countries assured her they offered a great field to female enterprise. Isabel did him justice, but she wondered what his purpose was and what he expected to gain even by proving the superior strain of his sincerity. If he expected to melt her by showing what a good fellow he was, he might spare himself the trouble. She knew the superior strain of everything about him, and nothing he could now do was required to light the view. Moreover his being in Rome at all affected her as a complication of the wrong sort—she liked so complications of the right. Nevertheless, when, on bringing his call to a close, he said he too should be at Saint Peter's and should look out for her and her friends, she was obliged to reply that he must follow his convenience.

In the church, as she strolled over its tesselated acres, he was the first person she encountered. She had not been one of the superior tourists who are "disappointed" in Saint Peter's and find it smaller than its fame; the first time she passed beneath the huge leathern curtain that strains and bangs at the entrance, the first time she found herself beneath the far-arching dome and saw the light drizzle down through the air thickened with incense and with the reflections of marble and gilt, of mosaic and bronze, her conception of greatness rose and dizzily rose. After this it never lacked space to soar. She gazed and wondered like a child or a peasant, she paid her silent tribute to the seated sublime. Lord Warburton walked beside her and talked of Saint Sophia[4] of Constantinople; she feared for instance that he would end by calling attention to his exemplary conduct. The service had not yet begun, but at Saint Peter's there is much to observe, and as there is something almost profane in the vastness of the place, which seems meant as much for physical as for spiritual exercise, the different figures and groups, the mingled worshippers and spectators, may follow their various intentions without conflict or scandal. In that splendid immensity individual indiscretion carries but a short distance. Isabel and her companions, however, were guilty of none; for though Henrietta was obliged in candour

---

3. In the via San Sebastianello near the Spanish Steps; the Baedeker for 1879 lists it as "suitable for families." James himself preferred the larger Roma in the Corso.
4. Now the Hagia Sophia in Istanbul. It was built as the grandest of Byzantine churches, was converted into a mosque when the city fell to the Ottomans in 1453, and is today a museum.

to declare that Michael Angelo's dome[5] suffered by comparison with that of the Capitol at Washington, she addressed her protest chiefly to Mr. Bantling's ear and reserved it in its more accentuated form for the columns of the *Interviewer.* Isabel made the circuit of the church with his lordship, and as they drew near the choir on the left of the entrance the voices of the Pope's singers were borne to them over the heads of the large number of persons clustered outside the doors. They paused a while on the skirts of this crowd, composed in equal measure of Roman cockneys and inquisitive strangers, and while they stood there the sacred concert went forward. Ralph, with Henrietta and Mr. Bantling, was apparently within, where Isabel, looking beyond the dense group in front of her, saw the afternoon light, silvered by clouds of incense that seemed to mingle with the splendid chant, slope through the embossed recesses of high windows. After a while the singing stopped and then Lord Warburton seemed disposed to move off with her. Isabel could only accompany him; whereupon she found herself confronted with Gilbert Osmond, who appeared to have been standing at a short distance behind her. He now approached with all the forms—he appeared to have multiplied them on this occasion to suit the place.

"So you decided to come?" she said as she put out her hand.

"Yes, I came last night and called this afternoon at your hotel. They told me you had come here, and I looked about for you."

"The others are inside," she decided to say.

"I didn't come for the others," he promptly returned.

She looked away; Lord Warburton was watching them; perhaps he had heard this. Suddenly she remembered it to be just what he had said to her the morning he came to Gardencourt to ask her to marry him. Mr. Osmond's words had brought the colour to her cheek, and this reminiscence had not the effect of dispelling it. She repaired any betrayal by mentioning to each companion the name of the other, and fortunately at this moment Mr. Bantling emerged from the choir, cleaving the crowd with British valour and followed by Miss Stackpole and Ralph Touchett. I say fortunately, but this is perhaps a superficial view of the matter; since on perceiving the gentleman from Florence Ralph Touchett appeared to take the case as not committing him to joy. He didn't hang back, however, from civility, and presently observed to Isabel, with due benevolence, that she would soon have all her friends about her. Miss Stackpole had met Mr. Osmond in Florence, but she had already found occasion to say to Isabel that she liked him no better than her other admirers—than Mr. Touchett and Lord Warburton, and even than little Mr. Rosier in Paris. "I don't know what it's in you," she had been pleased to remark, "but for a nice girl you do attract the most unnatural people. Mr. Goodwood's the only one I've any respect for, and he's just the one you don't appreciate."

"What's your opinion of Saint Peter's?" Mr. Osmond was meanwhile enquiring of our young lady.

"It's very large and very bright," she contented herself with replying.

"It's too large; it makes one feel like an atom."

---

5. Michelangelo Buonarotti (1475–1564) was put in charge of the rebuilding of Saint Peter's in 1547; his design for the dome, not completed until 1590, was one of the last great works of his life.

"Isn't that the right way to feel in the greatest of human temples?" she asked with rather a liking for her phrase.

"I suppose it's the right way to feel everywhere, when one *is* nobody. But I like it in a church as little as anywhere else."

"You ought indeed to be a Pope!" Isabel exclaimed, remembering something he had referred to in Florence.

"Ah, I should have enjoyed that!" said Gilbert Osmond.

Lord Warburton meanwhile had joined Ralph Touchett, and the two strolled away together. "Who's the fellow speaking to Miss Archer?" his lordship demanded.

"His name's Gilbert Osmond—he lives in Florence," Ralph said.

"What is he besides?"

"Nothing at all. Oh yes, he's an American; but one forgets that—he's so little of one."

"Has he known Miss Archer long?"

"Three or four weeks."

"Does she like him?"

"She's trying to find out."

"And will she?"

"Find out—?" Ralph asked.

"Will she like him?"

"Do you mean will she accept him?"

"Yes," said Lord Warburton after an instant; "I suppose that's what I horribly mean."

"Perhaps not if one does nothing to prevent it," Ralph replied.

His lordship stared a moment, but apprehended. "Then we must be perfectly quiet?"

"As quiet as the grave. And only on the chance!" Ralph added.

"The chance she may?"

"The chance she may not?"

Lord Warburton took this at first in silence, but he spoke again. "Is he awfully clever?"

"Awfully," said Ralph.

His companion thought. "And what else?"

"What more do you want?" Ralph groaned.

"Do you mean what more does *she*?"

Ralph took him by the arm to turn him: they had to rejoin the others. "She wants nothing that *we* can give her."

"Ah well, if she won't have You—!" said his lordship handsomely as they went.

Volume II

Chapter XXVIII

On the morrow, in the evening, Lord Warburton went again to see his friends at their hotel, and at this establishment he learned that they had gone to the opera. He drove to the opera with the idea of paying them a visit in their box after the easy Italian fashion; and when he had obtained his admittance—it was one of the secondary theatres—looked about the large, bare, ill-lighted house. An act had just terminated and he was at liberty to pursue his quest. After scanning two or three tiers of boxes he perceived in one of the largest of these receptacles a lady whom he easily recognised. Miss Archer was seated facing the stage and partly screened by the curtain of the box; and beside her, leaning back in his chair, was Mr. Gilbert Osmond. They appeared to have the place to themselves, and Warburton supposed their companions had taken advantage of the recess to enjoy the relative coolness of the lobby. He stood a while with his eyes on the interesting pair; he asked himself if he should go up and interrupt the harmony. At last he judged that Isabel had seen him, and this accident determined him. There should be no marked holding off. He took his way to the upper regions and on the staircase met Ralph Touchett slowly descending, his hat at the inclination of ennui and his hands where they usually were.

"I saw you below a moment since and was going down to you. I feel lonely and want company," was Ralph's greeting.

"You've some that's very good which you've yet deserted."

"Do you mean my cousin? Oh, she has a visitor and doesn't want me. Then Miss Stackpole and Bantling have gone out to a café to eat an ice—Miss Stackpole delights in an ice. I didn't think *they* wanted me either. The opera's very bad; the women look like laundresses and sing like peacocks. I feel very low."

"You had better go home," Lord Warburton said without affectation.

"And leave my young lady in this sad place? Ah no, I must watch over her."

"She seems to have plenty of friends."

"Yes, that's why I must watch," said Ralph with the same large mock-melancholy.

"If she doesn't want you it's probable she doesn't want me."

"No, you're different. Go to the box and stay there while I walk about."

Lord Warburton went to the box, where Isabel's welcome was as to a friend so honourably old that he vaguely asked himself what queer temporal province she was annexing. He exchanged greetings with Mr. Osmond, to whom he had been introduced the day before and who, after he came in, sat blandly apart and silent, as if repudiating competence in the subjects of allusion now probable. It struck her second visitor that Miss Archer had, in operatic conditions, a radiance, even a slight exaltation; as she was, however, at all times a keenly-glancing, quickly-moving, completely animated young woman, he may have been mistaken on this point. Her talk with him moreover pointed to presence of mind; it expressed a kindness so ingenious and deliberate as to indicate that she was in undisturbed possession of her faculties. Poor Lord Warburton had moments of bewilderment. She had discouraged him, formally, as much as a woman could; what business had she then with such arts and such felicities, above all with such tones of reparation—preparation? Her voice had tricks of sweetness, but why play them on *him*? The others came back; the bare, familiar, trivial opera began again. The box was large, and there was room for him to remain if he would sit a little behind and in the dark. He did so for half an hour, while Mr. Osmond remained in front, leaning forward, his elbows on his knees, just behind Isabel. Lord Warburton heard nothing, and from his gloomy corner saw nothing but the clear profile of this young lady defined against the dim illumination of the house.

When there was another interval no one moved. Mr. Osmond talked to Isabel, and Lord Warburton kept his corner. He did so but for a short time, however; after which he got up and bade good-night to the ladies. Isabel said nothing to detain him, but it didn't prevent his being puzzled again. Why should she mark so one of his values—quite the wrong one—when she would have nothing to do with another, which was quite the right? He was angry with himself for being puzzled, and then angry for being angry. Verdi's[1] music did little to comfort him, and he left the theatre and walked homeward, without knowing his way, through the tortuous, tragic streets of Rome, where heavier sorrows than his had been carried under the stars.

"What's the character of that gentleman?" Osmond asked of Isabel after he had retired.

"Irreproachable—don't you see it?"

"He owns about half England; that's his character," Henrietta remarked. "That's what they call a free country!"

"Ah, he's a great proprietor? Happy man!" said Gilbert Osmond.

"Do you call that happiness—the ownership of wretched human beings?" cried Miss Stackpole. "He owns his tenants and has thousands of them. It's pleasant to own something, but inanimate objects are enough for me. I don't insist on flesh and blood and minds and consciences."

"It seems to me you own a human being or two," Mr. Bantling suggested jocosely. "I wonder if Warburton orders his tenants about as you do me."

"Lord Warburton's a great radical," Isabel said. "He has very advanced opinions."

"He has very advanced stone walls. His park's enclosed by a gigantic iron fence, some thirty miles round," Henrietta announced for the information of Mr. Osmond. "I should like him to converse with a few of our Boston radicals."

"Don't they approve of iron fences?" asked Mr. Bantling.

"Only to shut up wicked conservatives. I always feel as if I were talking to *you* over something with a neat top-finish of broken glass."

"Do you know him well, this unreformed reformer?" Osmond went on, questioning Isabel.

"Well enough for all the use I have for him."

"And how much of a use is that?"

"Well, I like to like him."

"'Liking to like'—why, it makes a passion!" said Osmond.

"No"—she considered—"keep that for liking to *dislike*."

"Do you wish to provoke me then," Osmond laughed, "to a passion for *him*?"

She said nothing for a moment, but then met the light question with a disproportionate gravity. "No, Mr. Osmond; I don't think I should ever dare to provoke you. Lord Warburton, at any rate," she more easily added, "is a very nice man."

"Of great ability?" her friend enquired.

"Of excellent ability, and as good as he looks."

---

1. Giuseppe Verdi (1813–1901), composer of *Aida* (1871), among many other staples of the operatic repertoire.

"As good as he's good-looking do you mean? He's very good-looking. How detestably fortunate!—to be a great English magnate, to be clever and handsome into the bargain, and, by way of finishing off, to enjoy your high favour! That's a man I could envy."

Isabel considered him with interest. "You seem to me to be always envying some one. Yesterday it was the Pope; to-day it's poor Lord Warburton."

"My envy's not dangerous; it wouldn't hurt a mouse. I don't want to destroy the people—I only want to *be* them. You see it would destroy only myself."

"You'd like to be the Pope?" said Isabel.

"I should love it—but I should have gone in for it earlier. But why"—Osmond reverted—"do you speak of your friend as poor?"

"Women—when they are very, very good—sometimes pity men after they've hurt them; that's their great way of showing kindness," said Ralph, joining in the conversation for the first time and with a cynicism so transparently ingenious as to be virtually innocent.

"Pray, have I hurt Lord Warburton?" Isabel asked, raising her eyebrows as if the idea were perfectly fresh.

"It serves him right if you have," said Henrietta while the curtain rose for the ballet.

Isabel saw no more of her attributive victim for the next twenty-four hours, but on the second day after the visit to the opera she encountered him in the gallery of the Capitol, where he stood before the lion of the collection, the statue of the Dying Gladiator.[2] She had come in with her companions, among whom, on this occasion again, Gilbert Osmond had his place, and the party, having ascended the staircase, entered the first and finest of the rooms. Lord Warburton addressed her alertly enough, but said in a moment that he was leaving the gallery. "And I'm leaving Rome," he added. "I must bid you good-bye." Isabel, inconsequently enough, was now sorry to hear it. This was perhaps because she had ceased to be afraid of his renewing his suit; she was thinking of something else. She was on the point of naming her regret, but she checked herself and simply wished him a happy journey; which made him look at her rather unlightedly. "I'm afraid you'll think me very 'volatile.' I told you the other day I wanted so much to stop."

"Oh no; you could easily change your mind."

"That's what I have done."

"*Bon voyage* then."

"You're in a great hurry to get rid of me," said his lordship quite dismally.

"Not in the least. But I hate partings."

"You don't care what I do," he went on pitifully.

Isabel looked at him a moment. "Ah," she said, "you're not keeping your promise!"

He coloured like a boy of fifteen. "If I'm not, then it's because I can't; and that's why I'm going."

---

2. Also known as "The Dying Gaul," and in Victorian times one of the most admired works of antiquity, in the Capitoline Museum on top of the most important of Rome's ancient hills. Hawthorne's *The Marble Faun* (1860) begins in the room that houses it, along with the other statues upon which Isabel will look later in the chapter.

"Good-bye then."

"Good-bye." He lingered still, however. "When shall I see you again?"

Isabel hesitated, but soon, as if she had had a happy inspiration: "Some day after you're married."

"That will never be. It will be after you are."

"That will do as well," she smiled.

"Yes, quite as well. Good-bye."

They shook hands, and he left her alone in the glorious room, among the shining antique marbles. She sat down in the centre of the circle of these presences, regarding them vaguely, resting her eyes on their beautiful blank faces; listening, as it were, to their eternal silence. It is impossible, in Rome at least, to look long at a great company of Greek sculptures without feeling the effect of their noble quietude; which, as with a high door closed for the ceremony, slowly drops on the spirit the large white mantle of peace. I say in Rome especially, because the Roman air is an exquisite medium for such impressions. The golden sunshine mingles with them, the deep stillness of the past, so vivid yet, though it is nothing but a void full of names, seems to throw a solemn spell upon them. The blinds were partly closed in the windows of the Capitol, and a clear, warm shadow rested on the figures and made them more mildly human. Isabel sat there a long time, under the charm of their motionless grace, wondering to what, of their experience, their absent eyes were open, and how, to our ears, their alien lips would sound. The dark red walls of the room threw them into relief: the polished marble floor reflected their beauty. She had seen them all before, but her enjoyment repeated itself, and it was all the greater because she was glad again, for the time, to be alone. At last, however, her attention lapsed, drawn off by a deeper tide of life. An occasional tourist came in, stopped and stared a moment at the Dying Gladiator, and then passed out of the other door, creaking over the smooth pavement. At the end of half an hour Gilbert Osmond reappeared, apparently in advance of his companions. He strolled toward her slowly, with his hands behind him and his usual enquiring, yet not quite appealing smile. "I'm surprised to find you alone, I thought you had company."

"So I have—the best." And she glanced at the Antinous and the Faun.

"Do you call them better company than an English peer?"

"Ah, my English peer left me some time ago." She got up, speaking with intention a little dryly.

Mr. Osmond noted her dryness, which contributed for him to the interest of his question. "I'm afraid that what I heard the other evening is true: you're rather cruel to that nobleman."

Isabel looked a moment at the vanquished Gladiator. "It's not true. I'm scrupulously kind."

"That's exactly what I mean!" Gilbert Osmond returned, and with such happy hilarity that his joke needs to be explained. We know that he was fond of originals, of rarities, of the superior and the exquisite; and now that he had seen Lord Warburton, whom he thought a very fine example of his race and order, he perceived a new attraction in the idea of taking to himself a young lady who had qualified herself to figure in his collection of choice objects by declining so noble a hand. Gilbert Osmond had a high appreciation of this particular patriciate; not so much for its distinction, which he thought easily surpassable, as for its solid actuality. He had never forgiven his star for not appointing him to an English dukedom, and he could measure the unexpectedness of such conduct as Isabel's. It would be proper that the woman he might marry should have done something of that sort.

Chapter XXIX

Ralph Touchett, in talk with his excellent friend, had rather markedly qualified, as we know, his recognition of Gilbert Osmond's personal merits; but he might really have felt himself illiberal in the light of that gentleman's conduct during the rest of the visit to Rome. Osmond spent a portion of each day with Isabel and her companions, and ended by affecting them as the easiest of men to live with. Who wouldn't have seen that he could command, as it were, both tact and gaiety?—which perhaps was exactly why Ralph had made his old-time look of superficial sociability a reproach to him. Even Isabel's invidious kinsman was obliged to admit that he was just now a delightful associate. His good-humour was imperturbable, his knowledge of the right fact, his production of the right word, as convenient as the friendly flicker of a match for your cigarette. Clearly he was amused—as amused as a man could be who was so little ever surprised, and that made him almost applausive. It was not that his spirits were visibly high—he would never, in the concert of pleasure, touch the big drum by so much as a knuckle: he had a mortal dislike to the high, ragged note, to what he called random ravings. He thought Miss Archer sometimes of too precipitate a readiness. It was pity she had that fault, because if she had not had it she would really have had none; she would have been as smooth to his general need of her as handled ivory to the palm. If he was not personally loud, however, he was deep, and during these closing days of the Roman May he knew a complacency that matched with slow irregular walks under the pines of the Villa Borghese,[1] among the small sweet meadow-flowers and the mossy marbles. He was pleased with everything; he had never before been pleased with so many things at once. Old impressions, old enjoyments, renewed themselves; one evening, going home to his room at the inn, he wrote down a little sonnet to which he prefixed the title of "Rome Revisited." A day or two later he showed this piece of correct and ingenious verse to Isabel, explaining to her that it was an Italian fashion to commemorate the occasions of life by a tribute to the muse.

He took his pleasures in general singly; he was too often—he would have admitted that—too sorely aware of something wrong, something ugly; the fertilising dew of a conceivable felicity too seldom descended on his spirit. But at present he was happy—happier than he had perhaps ever been in his life, and the feeling had a large foundation. This was simply the sense of success—the most agreeable emotion of the human heart. Osmond had never had too much of it; in this respect he had the irritation of satiety, as he knew perfectly well and often reminded himself. "Ah no, I've not been spoiled; certainly I've not been spoiled," he used inwardly to repeat. "If I do succeed before I die I shall thoroughly have earned it." He was too apt to reason as if "earning" this boon consisted above all of covertly aching

---

1. A large landscape park along the top of the Pincian hill; a fashionable and elegant place in which to be seen, whether on foot or in a carriage. The Galleria Borghese, in the villa from which the park takes its name, contains one of the city's finest collections of statues and paintings.

for it and might be confined to that exercise. Absolutely void of it, also, his career had not been; he might indeed have suggested to a spectator here and there that he was resting on vague laurels. But his triumphs were, some of them, now too old; others had been too easy. The present one had been less arduous than might have been expected, but had been easy—that is had been rapid—only because he had made an altogether exceptional effort, a greater effort than he had believed it in him to make. The desire to have something or other to show for his "parts"—to show somehow or other—had been the dream of his youth; but as the years went on the conditions attached to any marked proof of rarity had affected him more and more as gross and detestable; like the swallowing of mugs of beer to advertise what one could "stand." If an anonymous drawing on a museum wall had been conscious and watchful it might have known this peculiar pleasure of being at last and all of a sudden identified—as from the hand of a great master—by the so high and so unnoticed fact of style. His "style" was what the girl had discovered with a little help; and now, beside herself enjoying it, she should publish it to the world without his having any of the trouble. She should do the thing *for* him, and he would not have waited in vain.

Shortly before the time fixed in advance for her departure this young lady received from Mrs. Touchett a telegram running as follows: "Leave Florence 4th June for Bellaggio,[2] and take you if you have not other views. But can't wait if you dawdle in Rome."

The dawdling in Rome was very pleasant, but Isabel had different views, and she let her aunt know she would immediately join her. She told Gilbert Osmond that she had done so, and he replied that, spending many of his summers as well as his winters in Italy, he himself would loiter a little longer in the cool shadow of Saint Peter's. He would not return to Florence for ten days more, and in that time she would have started for Bellaggio. It might be months in this case before he should see her again. This exchange took place in the large decorated sitting-room occupied by our friends at the hotel; it was late in the evening, and Ralph Touchett was to take his cousin back to Florence on the morrow. Osmond had found the girl alone; Miss Stackpole had contracted a friendship with a delightful American family on the fourth floor and had mounted the interminable staircase to pay them a visit. Henrietta contracted friendships, in travelling, with great freedom, and had formed in railway-carriages several that were among her most valued ties. Ralph was making arrangements for the morrow's journey, and Isabel sat alone in a wilderness of yellow upholstery. The chairs and sofas were orange; the walls and windows were draped in purple and gilt. The mirrors, the pictures, had great flamboyant frames; the ceiling was deeply vaulted and painted over with naked muses and cherubs. For Osmond the place was ugly to distress; the false colours, the sham splendour were like vulgar, bragging, lying talk. Isabel had taken in hand a volume of Ampère,[3] presented, on their arrival in Rome, by Ralph; but though she held it in her lap with her finger vaguely kept in the place she was not impatient to pursue her study. A lamp covered with

2. A resort town on Lake Como, north of Milan and near the Swiss border.
3. Jean-Jacques Ampère (1800–1864), French author of a four-volume history of Rome; his father André-Marie Ampère (1775–1836) was the scientist after whom the unit of electric current was named.

a drooping veil of pink tissue-paper burned on the table beside her and diffused a strange pale rosiness over the scene.

"You say you'll come back; but who knows?" Gilbert Osmond said. "I think you're much more likely to start on your voyage round the world. You're under no obligation to come back; you can do exactly what you choose; you can roam through space."

"Well, Italy's a part of space," Isabel answered. "I can take it on the way."

"On the way round the world? No, don't do that. Don't put us in a parenthesis—give us a chapter to ourselves. I don't want to see you on your travels. I'd rather see you when they're over, I should like to see you when you're tired and satiated," Osmond added in a moment. "I shall prefer you in that state."

Isabel, with her eyes bent, fingered the pages of M. Ampère. "You turn things into ridicule without seeming to do it, though not, I think, without intending it. You've no respect for my travels—you think them ridiculous."

"Where do you find that?"

She went on in the same tone, fretting the edge of her book with the paper-knife. "You see my ignorance, my blunders, the way I wander about as if the world belonged to me, simply because—because it has been put into my power to do so. You don't think a woman ought to do that. You think it bold and ungraceful."

"I think it beautiful," said Osmond. "You know my opinions—I've treated you to enough of them. Don't you remember my telling you that one ought to make one's life a work of art? You looked rather shocked at first; but then I told you that it was exactly what you seemed to me to be trying to do with your own."

She looked up from her book. "What you despise most in the world is bad, is stupid art."

"Possibly. But yours seem to me very clear and very good."

"If I were to go to Japan next winter you would laugh at me," she went on.

Osmond gave a smile—a keen one, but not a laugh, for the tone of their conversation was not jocose. Isabel had in fact her solemnity; he had seen it before. "You have an imagination that startles one!"

"That's exactly what I say. You think such an idea absurd."

"I would give my little finger to go to Japan; it's one of the countries I want most to see. Can't you believe that, with my taste for old lacquer?"

"I haven't a taste for old lacquer to excuse me," said Isabel.

"You've a better excuse—the means of going. You're quite wrong in your theory that I laugh at you. I don't know what has put it into your head."

"It wouldn't be remarkable if you did think it ridiculous that I should have the means to travel when you've not; for you know everything, and I know nothing."

"The more reason why you should travel and learn," smiled Osmond. "Besides," he added as if it were a point to be made, "I don't know everything."

Isabel was not struck with the oddity of his saying this gravely; she was thinking that the pleasantest incident of her life—so it pleased her to qualify these too few days in Rome, which she might musingly have likened to the figure of some small princess of one of the ages of dress overmuffled in a mantle of state and dragging a train that it took pages or historians to hold up—that this felicity was coming to an end. That most of the interest of the time had been owing to Mr. Osmond was a reflexion she was not just now at pains to make; she had already done the point abundant justice. But she said to herself that if there were a danger they should never meet again, perhaps after all it would be as well. Happy things don't repeat themselves, and her adventure wore already the changed, the seaward face of some romantic island from which, after feasting on purple grapes, she was putting off while the breeze rose. She might come back to Italy and find him different—this strange man who pleased her just as he was; and it would be better not to come than run the risk of that. But if she was not to come the greater the pity that the chapter was closed; she felt for a moment a pang that touched the source of tears. The sensation kept her silent, and Gilbert Osmond was silent too; he was looking at her. "Go everywhere," he said at last, in a low, kind voice; "do everything; get everything out of life. Be happy—be triumphant."

"What do you mean by being triumphant?"

"Well, doing what you like."

"To triumph, then, it seems to me, is to fail! Doing all the vain things one likes is often very tiresome."

"Exactly," said Osmond with his quiet quickness. "As I intimated just now, you'll be tired some day." He paused a moment and then he went on: "I don't know whether I had better not wait till then for something I want to say to you."

"Ah, I can't advise you without knowing what it is. But I'm horrid when I'm tired," Isabel added with due inconsequence.

"I don't believe that. You're angry, sometimes—that I can believe, though I've never seen it. But I'm sure you're never 'cross.'"

"Not even when I lose my temper?"

"You don't lose it—you find it, and that must be beautiful." Osmond spoke with a noble earnestness. "They must be great moments to see."

"If I could only find it now!" Isabel nervously cried.

"I'm not afraid; I should fold my arms and admire you. I'm speaking very seriously." He leaned forward, a hand on each knee; for some moments he bent his eyes on the floor. "What I wish to say to you," he went on at last, looking up, "is that I find I'm in love with you."

She instantly rose. "Ah, keep that till I *am* tired!"

"Tired of hearing it from others?" He sat there raising his eyes to her. "No, you may heed it now or never, as you please. But after all I must say it now." She had turned away, but in the movement she had stopped herself and dropped her gaze upon him. The two remained a while in this situation, exchanging a long look—the large, conscious look of the critical hours of life. Then he got up and came near her, deeply respectful, as if he were afraid he had been too familiar. "I'm absolutely in love with you."

He had repeated the announcement in a tone of almost impersonal discretion, like a man who expected very little from it but who spoke for his own needed relief. The tears came into her eyes: this time they obeyed the sharpness of the pang that suggested to her somehow the slipping of a fine bolt—backward, forward, she couldn't have said which. The words he had uttered made him, as he stood there, beautiful and generous, invested him as with the golden air of early autumn; but, morally speaking, she retreated before them—facing him still—as she had retreated in the other cases before a like encounter. "Oh don't say that, please," she answered with an intensity that expressed the dread of having, in this case too, to choose and decide. What made her dread great was precisely the force which, as it would seem, ought to have banished all dread—the sense of something within herself, deep down, that she supposed to be inspired and trustful passion. It was there like a large sum stored in a bank—which there was a terror in having to begin to spend. If she touched it, it would all come out.

"I haven't the idea that it will matter much to you," said Osmond. "I've too little to offer you. What I have—it's enough for me; but it's not enough for you. I've neither fortune, nor fame, nor extrinsic advantages of any kind. So I offer nothing. I only tell you because I think it can't offend you, and some day or other it may give you pleasure. It gives me pleasure, I assure you," he went on, standing there before her, considerately inclined to her, turning his hat, which he had taken up, slowly round with a movement which had all the decent tremor of awkwardness and none of its oddity, and presenting to her his firm, refined, slightly ravaged face. "It gives me no pain, because it's perfectly simple. For me you'll always be the most important woman in the world."

Isabel looked at herself in this character—looked intently, thinking she filled it with a certain grace. But what she said was not an expression of any such complacency. "You don't offend me; but you ought to remember that, without being offended, one may be incommoded, troubled." "Incommoded:" she heard herself saying that, and it struck her as a ridiculous word. But it was what stupidly came to her.

"I remember perfectly. Of course you're surprised and startled. But if it's nothing but that, it will pass away. And it will perhaps leave something that I may not be ashamed of."

"I don't know what it may leave. You see at all events that I'm not overwhelmed," said Isabel with rather a pale smile. "I'm not too troubled to think. And I think that I'm glad we're separating—that I leave Rome to-morrow."

"Of course I don't agree with you there."

"I don't at all *know* you," she added abruptly; and then she coloured as she heard herself saying what she had said almost a year before to Lord Warburton.

"If you were not going away you'd know me better."

"I shall do that some other time."

"I hope so. I'm very easy to know."

"No, no," she emphatically answered—"there you're not sincere. You're not easy to know; no one could be less so."

"Well," he laughed, "I said that because I know myself. It may be a boast, but I do."

"Very likely; but you're very wise."

"So are you, Miss Archer!" Osmond exclaimed.

"I don't feel so just now. Still, I'm wise enough to think you had better go. Good-night."

"God bless you!" said Gilbert Osmond, taking the hand which she failed to surrender. After which he added: "If we meet again you'll find me as you leave me. If we don't I shall be so all the same."

"Thank you very much. Good-bye."

There was something quietly firm about Isabel's visitor; he might go of his own movement, but wouldn't be dismissed. "There's one thing more. I haven't asked anything of you—not even a thought in the future; you must do me that justice. But there's a little service I should like to ask. I shall not return home for several days; Rome's delightful, and it's a good place for a man in my state of mind. Oh, I know you're sorry to leave it; but you're right to do what your aunt wishes."

"She doesn't even wish it!" Isabel broke out strangely.

Osmond was apparently on the point of saying something that would match these words, but he changed his mind and rejoined simply: "Ah well, it's proper you should go with her, very proper. Do everything that's proper; I go in for that. Excuse my being so patronising. You say you don't know me, but when you do you'll discover what a worship I have for propriety."

"You're not conventional?" Isabel gravely asked.

"I like the way you utter that word! No, I'm not conventional: I'm convention itself. You don't understand that?" And he paused a moment, smiling. "I should like to explain it." Then with a sudden, quick, bright naturalness, "Do come back again," he pleaded. "There are so many things we might talk about."

She stood there with lowered eyes. "What service did you speak of just now?"

"Go and see my little daughter before you leave Florence. She's alone at the villa; I decided not to send her to my sister, who hasn't at all my ideas. Tell her she must love her poor father very much," said Gilbert Osmond gently.

"It will be a great pleasure to me to go," Isabel answered. "I'll tell her what you say. Once more good-bye."

On this he took a rapid, respectful leave. When he had gone she stood a moment looking about her and seated herself slowly and with an air of deliberation. She sat there till her companions came back, with folded hands, gazing at the ugly carpet. Her agitation—for it had not diminished—was very still, very deep. What had happened was something that for a week past her imagination had been going forward to meet; but here, when it came, she stopped—that sublime principle somehow broke down. The working of this young lady's spirit was strange, and I can only give it to you as I see it, not hoping to make it seem altogether natural. Her imagination, as I say, now hung back: there was a last vague space it couldn't cross—a dusky, uncertain tract which looked ambiguous and even slightly treacherous, like a moorland seen in the winter twilight. But she was to cross it yet.

Chapter XXX

She returned on the morrow to Florence, under her cousin's escort, and Ralph Touchett, though usually restive under railway discipline, thought very well of the successive hours passed in the train that hurried his companion away from the city now distinguished by Gilbert Osmond's preference—hours that were to form the first stage in a larger scheme of travel. Miss Stackpole had remained behind; she was planning a little trip to Naples, to be carried out with Mr. Bantling's aid. Isabel was to have three days in Florence before the 4th of June, the date of Mrs. Touchett's departure, and she determined to devote the last of these to her promise to call on Pansy Osmond. Her plan, however, seemed for a moment likely to modify itself in deference to an idea of Madame Merle's. This lady was still at Casa Touchett; but she too was on the point of leaving Florence, her next station being an ancient castle in the mountains of Tuscany, the residence of a noble family of that country, whose acquaintance (she had known them, as she said, "forever") seemed to Isabel, in the light of certain photographs of their immense crenellated dwelling which her friend was able to show her, a precious privilege. She mentioned to this fortunate woman that Mr. Osmond had asked her to take a look at his daughter, but didn't mention that he had also made her a declaration of love.

"Ah, comme cela se trouve!"[1] Madame Merle exclaimed. "I myself have been thinking it would be a kindness to pay the child a little visit before I go off."

"We can go together then," Isabel reasonably said: "reasonably" because the proposal was not uttered in the spirit of enthusiasm. She had prefigured her small pilgrimage as made in solitude; she should like it better so. She was nevertheless prepared to sacrifice this mystic sentiment to her great consideration for her friend.

That personage finely meditated. "After all, why should we both go; having, each of us, so much to do during these last hours?"

"Very good; I can easily go alone."

"I don't know about your going alone—to the house of a handsome bachelor. He has been married—but so long ago!"

Isabel stared. "When Mr. Osmond's away what does it matter?"

"They don't know he's away, you see."

"They? Whom do you mean?"

"Every one. But perhaps it doesn't signify."

"If you were going why shouldn't I?" Isabel asked.

"Because I'm an old frump and you're a beautiful young woman."

"Granting all that, you've not promised."

"How much you think of your promises!" said the elder woman in mild mockery.

"I think a great deal of my promises. Does that surprise you?"

"You're right," Madame Merle audibly reflected. "I really think you wish to be kind to the child."

"I wish very much to be kind to her."

"Go and see her then; no one will be the wiser. And tell her I'd have come if you hadn't. Or rather," Madame Merle added, "don't tell her. She won't care."

As Isabel drove, in the publicity of an open vehicle, along the winding way which led to Mr. Osmond's hill-top, she wondered what her friend had meant by no one's being the wiser. Once in while, at large intervals, this lady, whose voyaging discretion, as a general thing, was rather of the open sea than of the risky channel, dropped a remark of ambiguous quality, struck a note that sounded false. What cared Isabel Archer for the vulgar judgements of obscure people? and did Madame Merle suppose that she was capable of doing a thing at all if it had to be sneakingly done? Of course not: she must have meant something else—something which in the press of the hours that preceded her departure she had not had time to explain. Isabel would return to this some day; there were sorts of things as to which she liked to be clear. She heard Pansy strumming at the piano

1. So that's how it is! (French).

in another place as she herself was ushered into Mr. Osmond's drawing-room; the little girl was "practising," and Isabel was pleased to think she performed this duty with rigour. She immediately came in, smoothing down her frock, and did the honours of her father's house with a wide-eyed earnestness of courtesy. Isabel sat there half an hour, and Pansy rose to the occasion as the small, winged fairy in the pantomime soars by the aid of the dissimulated wire—not chattering, but conversing, and show-ing the same respectful interest in Isabel's affairs that Isabel was so good as to take in hers. Isabel wondered at her; she had never had so directly presented to her nose the white flower of cultivated sweetness. How well the child had been taught, said our admiring young woman; how prettily she had been directed and fashioned; and yet how simple, how natural, how inno-cent she had been kept! Isabel was fond, ever, of the question of character and quality, of sounding, as who should say, the deep personal mystery, and it had pleased her, up to this time, to be in doubt as to whether this tender slip were not really all-knowing. Was the extremity of her candour but the perfection of self-consciousness? Was it put on to please her father's visitor, or was it the direct expression of an unspotted nature? The hour that Isabel spent in Mr. Osmond's beautiful empty, dusky rooms—the windows had been half-darkened, to keep out the heat, and here and there, through an easy crevice, the splendid summer day peeped in, lighting a gleam of faded colour or tarnished gilt in the rich gloom—her interview with the daughter of the house, I say, effectually settled this question. Pansy was really a blank page, a pure white surface, successfully kept so; she had neither art, nor guile, nor temper, nor talent—only two or three small exquisite instincts: for knowing a friend, for avoiding a mistake, for taking care of an old toy or a new frock. Yet to be so tender was to be touching withal, and she could be felt as an easy victim of fate. She would have no will, no power to resist, no sense of her own importance; she would easily be mystified, easily crushed: her force would be all in knowing when and where to cling. She moved about the place with her visitor, who had asked leave to walk through the other rooms again, where Pansy gave her judgement on several works of art. She spoke of her prospects, her occupations, her father's intentions; she was not egotistical, but felt the propriety of supplying the information so distin-gushed a guest would naturally expect.

"Please tell me," she said, "did papa, in Rome, go to see Madame Cath-erine? He told me he would if he had time. Perhaps he had not time. Papa likes a great deal of time. He wished to speak about my education; it isn't finished yet, you know. I don't know what they can do with me more; but it appears it's far from finished. Papa told me one day he thought he would finish it himself; for the last year or two, at the convent, the masters that teach the tall girls are so very dear. Papa's not rich, and I should be very sorry if he were to pay much money for me, because I don't think I'm worth it. I don't learn quickly enough, and I have no memory. For what I'm told, yes—especially when it's pleasant; but not for what I learn in a book. There was a young girl who was my best friend, and they took her away from the convent, when she was fourteen, to make—how do you say it in English?—to make a *dot*.[2] You don't say it in English? I hope it isn't wrong; I only mean they wished to keep the money to marry her. I don't know whether

2. Dowry (French).

it is for that that papa wishes to keep the money—to marry *me*. It costs so much to marry!" Pansy went on with a sigh; "I think papa might make that economy. At any rate I'm too young to think about it yet, and I don't care for any gentleman; I mean for any but him. If he were not my papa I should like to marry him; I would rather be his daughter than the wife of—of some strange person. I miss him very much, but not so much as you might think, for I've been so much away from him. Papa has always been principally for holidays. I miss Madame Catherine almost more; but you must not tell him that. You shall not see him again? I'm very sorry, and he'll be sorry too. Of every one who comes here I like you the best. That's not a great compliment, for there are not many people. It was very kind of you to come to-day—so far from your house; for I'm really as yet only a child. Oh, yes, I've only the occupations of a child. When did *you* give them up, the occupations of a child? I should like to know how old you are, but I don't know whether it's right to ask. At the convent they told us that we must never ask the age. I don't like to do anything that's not expected; it looks as if one had not been properly taught. I myself—I should never like to be taken by surprise. Papa left directions for everything. I go to bed very early. When the sun goes off that side I go into the garden. Papa left strict orders that I was not to get scorched. I always enjoy the view; the mountains are so graceful. In Rome, from the convent, we saw nothing but roofs and bell-towers. I practise three hours. I don't play very well. You play yourself? I wish very much you'd play something for me; papa has the idea that I should hear good music. Madame Merle has played for me several times; that's what I like best about Madame Merle; she has great facility. I shall never have facility. And I've no voice—just a small sound like the squeak of a slate-pencil making flourishes."

Isabel gratified this respectful wish, drew off her gloves and sat down to the piano, while Pansy, standing beside her, watched her white hands move quickly over the keys. When she stopped she kissed the child good-bye, held her close, looked at her long. "Be very good," she said; "give pleasure to your father."

"I think that's what I live for," Pansy answered. "He has not much pleasure; he's rather a sad man."

Isabel listened to this assertion with an interest which she felt it almost a torment to be obliged to conceal. It was her pride that obliged her, and a certain sense of decency; there were still other things in her head which she felt a strong impulse, instantly checked, to say to Pansy about her father; there were things it would have given her pleasure to hear the child, to make the child, say. But she no sooner became conscious of these things than her imagination was hushed with horror at the idea of taking advantage of the little girl—it was of this she would have accused herself—and of exhaling into that air where he might still have a subtle sense for it any breath of her charmed state. She had come—she had come; but she had stayed only an hour. She rose quickly from the music-stool; even then, however, she lingered a moment, still holding her small companion, drawing the child's sweet slimness closer and looking down at her almost in envy. She was obliged to confess it to herself—she would have taken a passionate pleasure in talking of Gilbert Osmond to this innocent, diminutive creature who was so near him. But she said no other word; she only kissed Pansy once again. They went together through the vestibule, to the door that opened on the court; and there her young hostess stopped, look-ing rather wistfully beyond. "I may go no further. I've promised papa not to pass this door."

"You're right to obey him; he'll never ask you anything unreasonable."

"I shall always obey him. But when will you come again?"

"Not for a long time, I'm afraid."

"As soon as you can, I hope. I'm only a little girl," said Pansy, "but I shall always expect you." And the small figure stood in the high, dark doorway, watching Isabel cross the clear, grey court and disappear into the bright-ness beyond the big *portone*,[3] which gave a wider dazzle as it opened.

Chapter XXXI

Isabel came back to Florence, but only after several months; an interval sufficiently replete with incident. It is not, however, during this interval that we are closely concerned with her; our attention is engaged again on a certain day in the late spring-time, shortly after her return to Palazzo Crescentini and a year from the date of the incidents just narrated. She was alone on this occasion, in one of the smaller of the numerous rooms devoted by Mrs. Touchett to social uses, and there was that in her expres-sion and attitude which would have suggested that she was expecting a visitor. The tall window was open, and though its green shutters were partly drawn the bright air of the garden had come in through a broad inter-stice and filled the room with warmth and perfume. Our young woman stood near it for some time, her hands clasped behind her; she gazed abroad with the vagueness of unrest. Too troubled for attention she moved in a vain circle. Yet it could not be in her thought to catch a glimpse of her visitor before he should pass into the house, since the entrance to the palace was not through the garden, in which stillness and privacy always reigned. She wished rather to forestall his arrival by a process of conjecture, and to judge by the expression of her face this attempt gave her plenty to do. Grave she found herself, and positively more weighted, as by the experience of the lapse of the year she had spent in seeing the world. She had ranged, she would have said, through space and surveyed much of mankind, and was therefore now, in her own eyes, a very differ-ent person from the frivolous young woman from Albany who had begun to take the measure of Europe on the lawn at Gardencourt a couple of years before. She flattered herself she had harvested wisdom and learned a great deal more of life than this light-minded creature had even suspected. If her thoughts just now had inclined themselves to retrospect, instead of fluttering their wings nervously about the present, they would have evoked a multitude of interesting pictures. These pictures would have been both landscapes and figure-pieces; the latter, however, would have been the more numerous. With several of the images that might have been projected on such a field we are already acquainted. There would be for instance the conciliatory Lily, our heroine's sister and Edmund Ludlow's wife, who had come out from New York to spend five months with her relative. She had left her husband behind her, but had brought her children, to whom Isabel now played with equal munificence and tenderness the part of

3. Doorway (Italian).

maiden-aunt. Mr. Ludlow, toward the last, had been able to snatch a few weeks from his forensic triumphs and, crossing the ocean with extreme rapidity, had spent a month with the two ladies in Paris before taking his wife home. The little Ludlows had not yet, even from the American point of view, reached the proper tourist-age; so that while her sister was with her Isabel had confined her movements to a narrow circle. Lily and the babies had joined her in Switzerland in the month of July, and they had spent a summer of fine weather in an Alpine valley where the flowers were thick in the meadows and the shade of great chestnuts made a resting-place for such upward wanderings as might be undertaken by ladies and children on warm afternoons. They had afterwards reached the French capital, which was worshipped, and with costly ceremonies, by Lily, but thought of as noisily vacant by Isabel, who in these days made use of her memory of Rome as she might have done, in a hot and crowded room, of a phial of something pungent hidden in her handkerchief.

Mrs. Ludlow sacrificed, as I say, to Paris, yet had doubts and wonderments not allayed at that altar; and after her husband had joined her found further chagrin in his failure to throw himself into these speculations. They all had Isabel for subject; but Edmund Ludlow, as he had always done before, declined to be surprised, or distressed, or mystified, or elated, at anything his sister-in-law might have done or have failed to do. Mrs. Ludlow's mental motions were sufficiently various. At one moment she thought it would be so natural for that young woman to come home and take a house in New York—the Rossiters', for instance, which had an elegant conservatory and was just round the corner from her own; at another she couldn't conceal her surprise at the girl's not marrying some member of one of the great aristocracies. On the whole, as I have said, she had fallen from high communion with the probabilities. She had taken more satisfaction in Isabel's accession of fortune than if the money had been left to herself; it had seemed to her to offer just the proper setting for her sister's slightly meagre, but scarce the less eminent figure. Isabel had developed less, however, than Lily had thought likely—development, to Lily's understanding, being somehow mysteriously connected with morning-calls and evening-parties. Intellectually, doubtless, she had made immense strides; but she appeared to have achieved few of those social conquests of which Mrs. Ludlow had expected to admire the trophies. Lily's conception of such achievements was extremely vague; but this was exactly what she had expected of Isabel—to give it form and body. Isabel could have done as well as she had done in New York; and Mrs. Ludlow appealed to her husband to know whether there was any privilege she enjoyed in Europe which the society of that city might not offer her. We know ourselves that Isabel had made conquests—whether inferior or not to those she might have effected in her native land it would be a delicate matter to decide; and it is not altogether with a feeling of complacency that I again mention that she had not rendered these honourable victories public. She had not told her sister the history of Lord Warburton, nor had she given her a hint of Mr. Osmond's state of mind; and she had had no better reason for her silence than that she didn't wish to speak. It was more romantic to say nothing, and, drinking deep, in secret, of romance, she was as little disposed to ask poor Lily's advice as she would have been to close that rare volume forever. But Lily knew nothing of these discriminations, and could only pronounce her sister's

career a strange anti-climax—an impression confirmed by the fact that Isabel's silence about Mr. Osmond, for instance, was in direct proportion to
the frequency with which he occupied her thoughts. As this happened very
often it sometimes appeared to Mrs. Ludlow that she had lost her courage.
So uncanny a result of so exhilarating an incident as inheriting a fortune
was of course perplexing to the cheerful Lily; it added to her general sense
that Isabel was not at all like other people.

Our young lady's courage, however, might have been taken as reaching
its height after her relations had gone home. She could imagine braver
things than spending the winter in Paris—Paris had sides by which it so
resembled New York, Paris was like smart, neat prose—and her close correspondence with Madame Merle did much to stimulate such flights. She
had never had a keener sense of freedom, of the absolute boldness and
wantonness of liberty, than when she turned away from the platform at
the Euston Station one of the last days of November, after the departure of
the train that was to convey poor Lily, her husband and her children to
their ship at Liverpool.[1] It had been good for her to regale; she was very conscious of that; she was very observant, as we know, of what was good for
her, and her effort was constantly to find something that was good
enough. To profit by the present advantage till the latest moment she had
made the journey from Paris with the unenvied travellers. She would have
accompanied them to Liverpool as well, only Edmund Ludlow had asked
her, as a favour, not to do so; it made Lily so fidgety and she asked such
impossible questions. Isabel watched the train move away; she kissed her
hand to the elder of her small nephews, a demonstrative child who leaned
dangerously far out of the window of the carriage and made separation
an occasion of violent hilarity, and then she walked back into the foggy
London street. The world lay before her—she could do whatever she
chose.[2] There was a deep thrill in it all, but for the present her choice was
tolerably discreet; she chose simply to walk back from Euston Square to
her hotel. The early dusk of a November afternoon had already closed in;
the street-lamps, in the thick, brown air, looked weak and red; our heroine was unattended and Euston Square was a long way from Piccadilly.
But Isabel performed the journey with a positive enjoyment of its dangers
and lost her way almost on purpose, in order to get more sensations, so
that she was disappointed when an obliging policeman easily set her right
again.[3] She was so fond of the spectacle of human life that she enjoyed
even the aspect of gathering dusk in the London streets—the moving
crowds, the hurrying cabs, the lighted shops, the flaring stalls, the dark,
shining dampness of everything. That evening, at her hotel, she wrote to
Madame Merle that she should start in a day or two for Rome. She made
her way down to Rome without touching at Florence—having gone first
to Venice and then proceeded southward by Ancona.[4] She accomplished

---

1. Just north of Bloomsbury, Euston station was the London terminus of the London and North
   Western Railway from which travelers would depart for Liverpool, the major port city for American
   shipping.
2. An allusion to the conclusion of Milton's *Paradise Lost* (1667); as Adam and Eve leave Paradise,
   "The world was all before them, where to chose / Their place of rest." James will pick up on
   those lines again at the very end of the novel.
3. It was then regarded as daring for women of Isabel's class to walk alone through the city; see
   Judith Walkowitz, *City of Dreadful Delight* (1992).
4. An Adriatic seaport.

this journey without other assistance than that of her servant, for her natural protectors were not now on the ground. Ralph Touchett was spending the winter at Corfu,[5] and Miss Stackpole, in the September previous, had been recalled to America by a telegram from the *Interviewer*. This journal offered its brilliant correspondent a fresher field for her genius than the mouldering cities of Europe, and Henrietta was cheered on her way by a promise from Mr. Bantling that he would soon come over to see her. Isabel wrote to Mrs. Touchett to apologise for not presenting herself just yet in Florence, and her aunt replied characteristically enough. Apologies, Mrs. Touchett intimated, were of no more use to her than bubbles, and she herself never dealt in such articles. One either did the thing or one didn't, and what one "would" have done belonged to the sphere of the irrelevant, like the idea of a future life or of the origin of things. Her letter was frank, but (a rare case with Mrs. Touchett) not so frank as it pretended. She easily forgave her niece for not stopping at Florence, because she took it for a sign that Gilbert Osmond was less in question there than formerly. She watched of course to see if he would now find a pretext for going to Rome, and derived some comfort from learning that he had not been guilty of an absence.

Isabel, on her side, had not been a fortnight in Rome before she proposed to Madame Merle that they should make a little pilgrimage to the East. Madame Merle remarked that her friend was restless, but she added that she herself had always been consumed with the desire to visit Athens and Constantinople. The two ladies accordingly embarked on this expedition, and spent three months in Greece, in Turkey, in Egypt. Isabel found much to interest her in these countries, though Madame Merle continued to remark that even among the most classic sites, the scenes most calculated to suggest repose and reflexion, a certain incoherence prevailed in her. Isabel travelled rapidly and recklessly; she was like a thirsty person draining cup after cup. Madame Merle meanwhile, as lady-in-waiting to a princess circulating *incognita*, panted a little in her rear. It was on Isabel's invitation she had come, and she imparted all due dignity to the girl's uncountenanced state. She played her part with the tact that might have been expected of her, effacing herself and accepting the position of a companion whose expenses were profusely paid. The situation, however, had no hardships, and people who met this reserved though striking pair on their travels would not have been able to tell you which was patroness and which client. To say that Madame Merle improved on acquaintance states meagrely the impression she made on her friend, who had found her from the first so ample and so easy. At the end of an intimacy of three months Isabel felt she knew her better; her character had revealed itself, and the admirable woman had also at last redeemed her promise of relating her history from her own point of view—a consummation the more desirable as Isabel had already heard it related from the point of view of others. This history was so sad a one (in so far as it concerned the late M. Merle, a positive adventurer, she might say, though originally so plausible, who had taken advantage, years before, of her youth and of an inexperience in which doubtless those who knew her only now would find it difficult to

5. A Greek island in the Ionian sea, and a warm-weather resort; under Venetian rule for centuries, it was administered by the British from 1814–64.

believe); it abounded so in startling and lamentable incidents that her companion wondered a person so *éprouvée*[6] could have kept so much of her
freshness, her interest in life. Into this freshness of Madame Merle's she
obtained a considerable insight; she seemed to see it as professional, as
slightly mechanical, carried about in its case like the fiddle of the virtu-
oso, or blanketed and bridled like the "favourite" of the jockey. She liked
her as much as ever, but there was a corner of the curtain that never was
lifted; it was as if she had remained after all something of a public performer, condemned to emerge only in character and in costume. She had
once said that she came from a distance, that she belonged to the "old, old"
world, and Isabel never lost the impression that she was the product of a
different moral or social clime from her own, that she had grown up under
other stars.

She believed then that at bottom she had a different morality. Of course
the morality of civilised persons has always much in common; but our
young woman had a sense in her of values gone wrong or, as they said at
the shops, marked down. She considered, with the presumption of youth,
that a morality differing from her own must be inferior to it; and this conviction was an aid to detecting an occasional flash of cruelty, an occasional lapse from candour, in the conversation of a person who had raised
delicate kindness to an art and whose pride was too high for the narrow
ways of deception. Her conception of human motives might, in certain
lights, have been acquired at the court of some kingdom in decadence,
and there were several in her list of which our heroine had not even heard.
She had not heard of everything, that was very plain; and there were evidently things in the world of which it was not advantageous to hear. She
had once or twice had a positive scare; since it so affected her to have to
exclaim, of her friend, "Heaven forgive her, she doesn't understand me!"
Absurd as it may seem this discovery operated as a shock, left her with a
vague dismay in which there was even an element of foreboding. The dismay of course subsided, in the light of some sudden proof of Madame
Merle's remarkable intelligence; but it stood for a high-water-mark in the
ebb and flow of confidence. Madame Merle had once declared her belief
that when a friendship ceases to grow it immediately begins to decline—
there being no point of equilibrium between liking more and liking less.
A stationary affection, in other words, was impossible—It must move one
way or the other. However that might be, the girl had in these days a thousand uses for her sense of the romantic, which was more active than it
had ever been. I do not allude to the impulse it received as she gazed at the
Pyramids in the course of an excursion from Cairo, or as she stood among
the broken columns of the Acropolis and fixed her eyes upon the point
designated to her as the Strait of Salamis;[7] deep and memorable as these
emotions had remained. She came back by the last of March from Egypt and
Greece and made another stay in Rome. A few days after her arrival Gilbert Osmond descended from Florence and remained three weeks, during which the fact of her being with his old friend Madame Merle, in whose
house she had gone to lodge, made it virtually inevitable that he should see
her every day. When the last of April came she wrote to Mrs. Touchett that

6. Tested and tried (French).
7. The site of a battle in 480 B.C.E. between the Athenian and Persian navies.

she should now rejoice to accept an invitation given long before, and went to pay a visit to Palazzo Crescentini, Madame Merle on this occasion remaining in Rome. She found her aunt alone; her cousin was still at Corfu. Ralph, however, was expected in Florence from day to day, and Isabel, who had not seen him for upwards of a year, was prepared to give him the most affectionate welcome.

Chapter XXXII

It was not of him, nevertheless, that she was thinking while she stood at the window near which we found her a while ago, and it was not of any of the matters I have rapidly sketched. She was not turned to the past, but to the immediate, impending hour. She had reason to expect a scene, and she was not fond of scenes. She was not asking herself what she should say to her visitor; this question had already been answered. What he would say to her—that was the interesting issue. It could be nothing in the least soothing—she had warrant for this, and the conviction doubtless showed in the cloud on her brow. For the rest, however, all clearness reigned in her; she had put away her mourning and she walked in no small shimmering splendour. She only felt older—ever so much, and as if she were "worth more" for it, like some curious piece in an antiquary's collection. She was not at any rate left indefinitely to her apprehensions, for a servant at last stood before her with a card on his tray. "Let the gentleman come in," she said, and continued to gaze out of the window after the footman had retired. It was only when she had heard the door close behind the person who presently entered that she looked round.

Caspar Goodwood stood there—stood and received a moment, from head to foot, the bright, dry gaze with which she rather withheld than offered a greeting. Whether his sense of maturity had kept pace with Isabel's we shall perhaps presently ascertain; let me say meanwhile that to her critical glance he showed nothing of the injury of time. Straight, strong and hard, there was nothing in his appearance that spoke positively either of youth or of age; if he had neither innocence nor weakness, so he had no practical philosophy. His jaw showed the same voluntary cast as in earlier days; but a crisis like the present had in it of course something grim. He had the air of a man who had travelled hard; he said nothing at first, as if he had been out of breath. This gave Isabel time to make a reflexion: "Poor fellow, what great things he's capable of, and what a pity he should waste so dreadfully his splendid force! What a pity too that one can't satisfy everybody!" It gave her time to do more—to say at the end of a minute: "I can't tell you how I hoped you wouldn't come!"

"I've no doubt of that." And he looked about him for a seat. Not only had he come, but he meant to settle.

"You must be very tired," said Isabel, seating herself, and generously, as she thought, to give him his opportunity.

"No, I'm not at all tired. Did you ever know me to be tired?"

"Never; I wish I had! When did you arrive?"

"Last night, very late; in a kind of snail-train they call the express. These Italian trains go at about the rate of an American funeral."

"That's in keeping—you must have felt as if you were coming to bury me!" And she forced a smile of encouragement to an easy view of their situation. She had reasoned the matter well out, making it perfectly clear that she broke no faith and falsified no contract; but for all this she was afraid of her visitor. She was ashamed of her fear; but she was devoutly thankful there was nothing else to be ashamed of. He looked at her with his stiff insistence, an insistence in which there was such a want of tact; especially when the dull dark beam in his eye rested on her as a physical weight.

"No, I didn't feel that; I couldn't think of you as dead. I wish I could!" he candidly declared.

"I thank you immensely."

"I'd rather think of you as dead than as married to another man."

"That's very selfish of you!" she returned with the ardour of a real conviction. "If you're not happy yourself others have yet a right to be."

"Very likely it's selfish; but I don't in the least mind your saying so. I don't mind anything you can say now—I don't feel it. The cruellest things you could think of would be mere pin-pricks. After what you've done I shall never feel anything—I mean anything but that. That I shall feel all my life."

Mr. Goodwood made these detached assertions with dry deliberateness, in his hard, slow American tone, which flung no atmospheric colour over propositions intrinsically crude. The tone made Isabel angry rather than touched her; but her anger perhaps was fortunate, inasmuch as it gave her a further reason for controlling herself. It was under the pressure of this control that she became, after a little, irrelevant. "When did you leave New York?"

He threw up his head as if calculating. "Seventeen days ago."

"You must have travelled fast in spite of your slow trains."

"I came as fast as I could. I'd have come five days ago if I had been able."

"It wouldn't have made any difference, Mr. Goodwood," she coldly smiled.

"Not to you—no. But to me."

"You gain nothing that I see."

"That's for me to judge!"

"Of course. To me it seems that you only torment yourself." And then, to change the subject, she asked him if he had seen Henrietta Stackpole. He looked as if he had not come from Boston to Florence to talk of Henrietta Stackpole; but he answered, distinctly enough, that this young lady had been with him just before he left America. "She came to see you?" Isabel then demanded.

"Yes, she was in Boston, and she called at my office. It was the day I had got your letter."

"Did you tell her?" Isabel asked with a certain anxiety.

"Oh, no," said Caspar Goodwood simply; "I didn't want to do that. She'll hear it quick enough; she hears everything."

"I shall write to her, and then she'll write to me and scold me," Isabel declared, trying to smile again.

Caspar, however, remained sternly grave. "I guess she'll come right out," he said.

"On purpose to scold me?"

"I don't know. She seemed to think she had not seen Europe thoroughly."

"I'm glad you tell me that," Isabel said. "I must prepare for her."

Mr. Goodwood fixed his eyes for a moment on the floor; then at last, raising them, "Does she know Mr. Osmond?" he enquired.

"A little. And she doesn't like him. But of course I don't marry to please Henrietta," she added. It would have been better for poor Caspar if she had tried a little more to gratify Miss Stackpole; but he didn't say so; he only asked, presently, when her marriage would take place. To which she made answer that she didn't know yet. "I can only say it will be soon. I've told no one but yourself and one other person—an old friend of Mr. Osmond's."

"Is it a marriage your friends won't like?" he demanded.

"I really haven't an idea. As I say, I don't marry for my friends."

He went on, making no exclamation, no comment, only asking questions, doing it quite without delicacy. "Who and what then is Mr. Gilbert Osmond?"

"Who and what? Nobody and nothing but a very good and very honourable man. He's not in business," said Isabel. "He's not rich; he's not known for anything in particular."

She disliked Mr. Goodwood's questions, but she said to herself that she owed it to him to satisfy him as far as possible. The satisfaction poor Caspar exhibited was, however, small; he sat very upright, gazing at her. "Where does he come from? Where does he belong?"

She had never been so little pleased with the way he said "belawng." "He comes from nowhere. He has spent most of his life in Italy."

"You said in your letter he was American. Hasn't he a native place?"

"Yes, but he has forgotten it. He left it as a small boy."

"Has he never gone back?"

"Why should he go back?" Isabel asked, flushing all defensively. "He has no profession."

"He might have gone back for his pleasure. Doesn't he like the United States?"

"He doesn't know them. Then he's very quiet and very simple—he contents himself with Italy."

"With Italy and with you," said Mr. Goodwood with gloomy plainness and no appearance of trying to make an epigram. "What has he ever done?" he added abruptly.

"That I should marry him? Nothing at all," Isabel replied while her patience helped itself by turning a little to hardness. "If he had done great things would you forgive me any better? Give me up, Mr. Goodwood; I'm marrying a perfect nonentity. Don't try to take an interest in him. You can't."

"I can't appreciate him; that's what you mean. And you don't mean in the least that he's a perfect nonentity. You think he's grand, you think he's great, though no one else thinks so."

Isabel's colour deepened; she felt this really acute of her companion, and it was certainly a proof of the aid that passion might render perceptions she had never taken for fine. "Why do you always come back to what others think? I can't discuss Mr. Osmond with you."

"Of course not," said Caspar reasonably. And he sat there with his air of stiff helplessness, as if not only this were true, but there were nothing else that they might discuss.

"You see how little you gain," she accordingly broke out—"how little comfort or satisfaction I can give you."

"I didn't expect you to give me much."

"I don't understand then why you came."

"I came because I wanted to see you once more—even just as you are."

"I appreciate that; but if you had waited a while, sooner or later we should have been sure to meet, and our meeting would have been pleasanter for each of us than this."

"Waited till after you're married? That's just what I didn't want to do. You'll be different then."

"Not very. I shall still be a great friend of yours. You'll see."

"That will make it all the worse," said Mr. Goodwood grimly.

"Ah, you're unaccommodating! I can't promise to dislike you in order to help you to resign yourself."

"I shouldn't care if you did!"

Isabel got up with a movement of repressed impatience and walked to the window, where she remained a moment looking out. When she turned round her visitor was still motionless in his place. She came toward him again and stopped, resting her hand on the back of the chair she had just quitted. "Do you mean you came simply to look at me? That's better for you perhaps than for me."

"I wished to hear the sound of your voice," he said.

"You've heard it, and you see it says nothing very sweet."

"It gives me pleasure, all the same." And with this he got up.

She had felt pain and displeasure on receiving early that day the news he was in Florence and by her leave would come within an hour to see her. She had been vexed and distressed, though she had sent back word by his messenger that he might come when he would. She had not been better pleased when she saw him; his being there at all was so full of heavy implications. It implied things she could never assent to—rights, reproaches, remonstrance, rebuke, the expectation of making her change her purpose. These things, however, if implied, had not been expressed; and now our young lady, strangely enough, began to resent her visitor's remarkable self-control. There was a dumb misery about him that irritated her; there was a manly staying of his hand that made her heart beat faster. She felt her agitation rising, and she said to herself that she was angry in the way a woman is angry when she has been in the wrong. She was not in the wrong; she had fortunately not that bitterness to swallow; but, all the same, she wished he would denounce her a little. She had wished his visit would be short; it had no purpose, no propriety; yet now that he seemed to be turning away she felt a sudden horror of his leaving her without uttering a word that would give her an opportunity to defend herself more than she had done in writing to him a month before, in a few carefully chosen words, to announce her engagement. If she were not in the wrong, however, why should she desire to defend herself? It was an excess of generosity on Isabel's part to desire that Mr. Goodwood should be angry. And if he had not meanwhile held himself hard it might have made him so to hear the tone in which she suddenly exclaimed, as if she were accusing him of having accused her: "I've not deceived you! I was perfectly free!"

"Yes, I know that," said Caspar.

"I gave you full warning that I'd do as I chose."

"You said you'd probably never marry, and you said it with such a manner that I pretty well believed it."

She considered this an instant. "No one can be more surprised than myself at my present intention."

"You told me that if I heard you were engaged I was not to believe it," Caspar went on. "I heard it twenty days ago from yourself, but I remembered what you had said. I thought there might be some mistake, and that's partly why I came."

"If you wish me to repeat it by word of mouth, that's soon done. There's no mistake whatever."

"I saw that as soon as I came into the room."

"What good would it do you that I shouldn't marry?" she asked with a certain fierceness.

"I should like it better than this."

"You're very selfish, as I said before."

"I know that. I'm selfish as iron."

"Even iron sometimes melts! If you'll be reasonable I'll see you again."

"Don't you call me reasonable now?"

"I don't know what to say to you," she answered with sudden humility.

"I shan't trouble you for a long time," the young man went on. He made a step towards the door, but he stopped. "Another reason why I came was that I wanted to hear what you would say in explanation of your having changed your mind."

Her humbleness as suddenly deserted her. "In explanation? Do you think I'm bound to explain?"

He gave her one of his long dumb looks. "You were very positive. I did believe it."

"So did I. Do you think I could explain if I would?"

"No, I suppose not. Well," he added, "I've done what I wished. I've seen you."

"How little you make of these terrible journeys," she felt the poverty of her presently replying.

"If you're afraid I'm knocked up—in any such way as that—you may be at your ease about it." He turned away, this time in earnest, and no hand-shake, no sign of parting, was exchanged between them. At the door he stopped with his hand on the knob. "I shall leave Florence to-morrow," he said without a quaver.

"I'm delighted to hear it!" she answered passionately. Five minutes after he had gone out she burst into tears.

Chapter XXXIII

Her fit of weeping, however, was soon smothered, and the signs of it had vanished when, an hour later, she broke the news to her aunt. I use this expression because she had been sure Mrs. Touchett would not be pleased; Isabel had only waited to tell her till she had seen Mr. Goodwood. She had an odd impression that it would not be honourable to make the fact public before she should have heard what Mr. Goodwood would say about it. He had said rather less than she expected, and she now had a somewhat angry sense of having lost time. But she would lose no more; she waited till Mrs. Touchett came into the drawing-room before the mid-day breakfast, and then she began. "Aunt Lydia, I've something to tell you."

Mrs. Touchett gave a little jump and looked at her almost fiercely. "You needn't tell me; I know what it is."

"I don't know how you know."

"The same way that I know when the window's open—by feeling a draught. You're going to marry that man."

"What man do you mean?" Isabel enquired with great dignity.

"Madame Merle's friend—Mr. Osmond."

"I don't know why you call him Madame Merle's friend. Is that the principal thing he's known by?"

"If he's not her friend he ought to be—after what she has done for him!" cried Mrs. Touchett. "I shouldn't have expected it of her; I'm disappointed."

"If you mean that Madame Merle has had anything to do with my engagement you're greatly mistaken," Isabel declared with a sort of ardent coldness.

"You mean that your attractions were sufficient, without the gentleman's having had to be lashed up? You're quite right. They're immense, your attractions, and he would never have presumed to think of you if she hadn't put him up to it. He has a very good opinion of himself, but he was not a man to take trouble. Madame Merle took the trouble *for* him."

"He has taken a great deal for himself!" cried Isabel with a voluntary laugh.

Mrs. Touchett gave a sharp nod. "I think he must, after all, to have made you like him so much."

"I thought he even pleased *you*."

"He did, at one time; and that's why I'm angry with him."

"Be angry with me, not with him," said the girl.

"Oh, I'm always angry with you; that's no satisfaction! Was it for this that you refused Lord Warburton?"

"Please don't go back to that. Why shouldn't I like Mr. Osmond, since others have done so?"

"Others, at their wildest moments, never wanted to marry him. There's nothing *of* him," Mrs. Touchett explained.

"Then he can't hurt me," said Isabel.

"Do you think you're going to be happy? No one's happy, in such doings, you should know."

"I shall set the fashion then. What does one marry for?"

"What *you* will marry for, heaven only knows. People usually marry as they go into partnership—to set up a house. But in your partnership you'll bring everything."

"Is it that Mr. Osmond isn't rich? Is that what you're talking about?" Isabel asked.

"He has no money; he has no name; he has no importance. I value such things and I have the courage to say it; I think they're very precious. Many other people think the same, and they show it. But they give some other reason."

Isabel hesitated a little. "I think I value everything that's valuable. I care very much for money, and that's why I wish Mr. Osmond to have a little."

"Give it to him then; but marry some one else."

"His name's good enough for me," the girl went on. "It's a very pretty name. Have I such a fine one myself?"

"All the more reason you should improve on it. There are only a dozen American names. Do you marry him out of charity?"

"It was my duty to tell you, Aunt Lydia, but I don't think it's my duty to explain to you. Even if it were I shouldn't be able. So please don't remonstrate; in talking about it you have me at a disadvantage. I can't talk about it."

"I don't remonstrate, I simply answer you: I must give some sign of intelligence. I saw it coming, and I said nothing. I never meddle."

"You never do, and I'm greatly obliged to you. You've been very considerate."

"It was not considerate—it was convenient," said Mrs. Touchett. "But I shall talk to Madame Merle."

"I don't see why you keep bringing her in. She has been a very good friend to me."

"Possibly; but she has been a poor one to me."

"What has she done to you?"

"She has deceived me. She had as good as promised me to prevent your engagement."

"She couldn't have prevented it."

"She can do anything; that's what I've always liked her for. I knew she could play any part; but I understood that she played them one by one. I didn't understand that she would play two at the same time."

"I don't know what part she may have played to you," Isabel said; "that's between yourselves. To me she has been honest and kind and devoted."

"Devoted, of course; she wished you to marry her candidate. She told me she was watching you only in order to interpose."

"She said that to please you," the girl answered; conscious, however, of the inadequacy of the explanation.

"To please me by deceiving me? She knows me better. Am I pleased to-day?"

"I don't think you're ever much pleased," Isabel was obliged to reply. "If Madame Merle knew you would learn the truth what had she to gain by insincerity?"

"She gained time, as you see. While I waited for her to interfere you were marching away, and she was really beating the drum."

"That's very well. But by your own admission you saw I was marching, and even if she had given the alarm you wouldn't have tried to stop me."

"No, but some one else would."

"Whom do you mean?" Isabel asked, looking very hard at her aunt.

Mrs. Touchett's little bright eyes, active as they usually were, sustained her gaze rather than returned it. "Would you have listened to Ralph?"

"Not if he had abused Mr. Osmond."

"Ralph doesn't abuse people; you know that perfectly. He cares very much for you."

"I know he does," said Isabel; "and I shall feel the value of it now, for he knows that whatever I do I do with reason."

"He never believed you would do this. I told him you were capable of it, and he argued the other way."

"He did it for the sake of argument," the girl smiled. "You don't accuse him of having deceived you; why should you accuse Madame Merle?"

"He never pretended he'd prevent it."

"I'm glad of that!" cried Isabel gaily. "I wish very much," she presently added, "that when he comes you'd tell him first of my engagement."

"Of course I'll mention it," said Mrs. Touchett. "I shall say nothing more to you about it, but I give you notice I shall talk to others."

"That's as you please. I only meant that it's rather better the announcement should come from you than from me."

"I quite agree with you; it's much more proper!" And on this the aunt and the niece went to breakfast, where Mrs. Touchett, as good as her word, made no allusion to Gilbert Osmond. After an interval of silence, however, she asked her companion from whom she had received a visit an hour before.

"From an old friend—an American gentleman," Isabel said with a colour in her cheek.

"An American gentleman of course. It's only an American gentleman who calls at ten o'clock in the morning."

"It was half-past ten; he was in a great hurry; he goes away this evening."

"Couldn't he have come yesterday, at the usual time?"

"He only arrived last night."

"He spends but twenty-four hours in Florence?" Mrs. Touchett cried. "He's an American gentleman truly."

"He is indeed," said Isabel, thinking with perverse admiration of what Caspar Goodwood had done for her.

Two days afterward Ralph arrived; but though Isabel was sure that Mrs. Touchett had lost no time in imparting to him the great fact, he showed at first no open knowledge of it. Their prompted talk was naturally of his health; Isabel had many questions to ask about Corfu. She had been shocked by his appearance when he came into the room; she had forgotten how ill he looked. In spite of Corfu he looked very ill to-day, and she wondered if he were really worse or if she were simply disaccustomed to living with an invalid. Poor Ralph made no nearer approach to conventional beauty as he advanced in life, and the now apparently complete loss of his health had done little to mitigate the natural oddity of his person. Blighted and battered, but still responsive and still ironic, his face was like a lighted lantern patched with paper and unsteadily held; his thin whisker languished upon a lean cheek; the exorbitant curve of his nose defined itself more sharply. Lean he was altogether, lean and long and loose-jointed; an accidental cohesion of relaxed angles. His brown velvet jacket had become perennial; his hands had fixed themselves in his pockets; he shambled and stumbled and shuffled in a manner that denoted great physical helplessness. It was perhaps this whimsical gait that helped to mark his character more than ever as that of the humorous invalid—the invalid for whom even his own disabilities are part of the general joke. They might well indeed with Ralph have been the chief cause of the want of seriousness marking his view of a world in which the reason for his own continued presence was past finding out. Isabel had grown fond of his ugliness; his awkwardness had become dear to her. They had been sweetened by association; they struck her as the very terms on which it had been given him to be charming. He was so charming that her sense of his being ill had hitherto had a sort of comfort in it; the state of his health had seemed not a limitation, but a kind of intellectual advantage; it absolved him from all professional and official emotions and left him the luxury of being exclusively personal. The personality so resulting was delightful; he had remained proof against the staleness of disease; he had had to consent to be deplorably ill, yet had somehow escaped being formally sick. Such had been the girl's impression of her cousin; and when she had pitied him it was only on reflection. As she reflected a good deal she had allowed him a certain amount of compassion; but she always had a dread of wasting that essence—a precious article, worth more to the giver than to any one else. Now, however, it took no great sensibility to feel that poor Ralph's tenure of life was less elastic than it should be. He was a bright, free, generous spirit, he had all the illumination of wisdom and none of its pedantry, and yet he was distressfully dying.

Isabel noted afresh that life was certainly hard for some people, and she felt a delicate glow of shame as she thought how easy it now promised to become for herself. She was prepared to learn that Ralph was not pleased with her engagement; but she was not prepared, in spite of her affection for him, to let this fact spoil the situation. She was not even prepared, or so she thought, to resent his want of sympathy; for it would be his privilege—it would be indeed his natural line—to find fault with any step she might take toward marriage. One's cousin always pretended to hate one's husband; that was traditional, classical; it was part of one's cousin's always pretending to adore one. Ralph was nothing if not critical; and though she would certainly, other things being equal, have been as glad to marry to please him as to please any one, it would be absurd to regard as important that her choice should square with his views. What were his views after all? He had pretended to believe she had better have married Lord Warburton; but this was only because she had refused that excellent man. If she had accepted him Ralph would certainly have taken another tone; he always took the opposite. You could criticise any marriage; it was the essence of a marriage to be open to criticism. How well she herself, should she only give her mind to it, might criticise this union of her own! She had other employment, however, and Ralph was welcome to relieve her of the care. Isabel was prepared to be most patient and most indulgent. He must have seen that, and this made it the more odd he should say nothing. After three days had elapsed without his speaking our young woman wearied of waiting; dislike it as he would, he might at least go through the form. We, who know more about poor Ralph than his cousin, may easily believe that during the hours that followed his arrival at Palazzo Crescentini he had privately gone through many forms. His mother had literally greeted him with the great news, which had been even more sensibly chilling than Mrs. Touchett's maternal kiss. Ralph was shocked and humiliated; his calculations had been false and the person in the world in whom he was most interested was lost. He drifted about the house like a rudderless vessel in a rocky stream, or sat in the garden of the palace on a great cane chair, his long legs extended, his head thrown back and his hat pulled over his eyes. He felt cold about the heart; he had never liked anything less. What could he do, what could he say? If the girl were irreclaimable could he pretend to like it? To attempt to reclaim her was permissible only if the attempt should succeed. To try to persuade her of anything sordid or sinister in the man to whose deep art she had succumbed would be decently discreet only in the event of her being persuaded. Otherwise he should simply have damned himself. It cost him an equal effort to speak his thought and to dissemble; he could neither assent with sincerity nor protest with hope. Meanwhile he knew—or rather he supposed—that the affianced pair were daily renewing their mutual vows. Osmond at this moment showed himself little at Palazzo Crescentini; but Isabel met him every day elsewhere, as she was free to do after their engagement had been made public. She had taken a carriage by the month, so as not to be indebted to her aunt for the means of pursuing a course of which Mrs. Touchett disapproved, and she drove in the morning to the Cascine.[1] This suburban wilderness, during the early hours, was void of all intruders, and our young lady, joined by her lover in its quietest part, strolled with him a while through the grey Italian shade and listened to the nightingales.

Chapter XXXIV

One morning, on her return from her drive, some half-hour before luncheon, she quitted her vehicle in the court of the palace and, instead of ascending the great staircase, crossed the court, passed beneath another archway and entered the garden. A sweeter spot at this moment could not have been imagined. The stillness of noontide hung over it, and the warm shade, enclosed and still, made bowers like spacious caves. Ralph was sitting there in the clear gloom, at the base of a statue of Terpsichore[1]—a dancing nymph with taper fingers and inflated draperies in the manner of Bernini;[2] the extreme relaxation of his attitude suggested at first to Isabel that he was asleep. Her light footstep on the grass had not roused him, and before turning away she stood for a moment looking at him. During this instant he opened his eyes; upon which she sat down on a rustic chair that matched with his own. Though in her irritation she had accused him of indifference she was not blind to the fact that he had visibly had something to brood over. But she had explained his air of absence partly by the languor of his increased weakness, partly by worries connected with the property inherited from his father—the fruit of eccentric arrangements of which Mrs. Touchett disapproved and which, as she had told Isabel, now encountered opposition from the other partners in the bank. He ought to have gone to England, his mother said, instead of coming to Florence; he had not been there for months, and took no more interest in the bank than in the state of Patagonia.[3]

"I'm sorry I waked you," Isabel said; "you look too tired."

"I feel too tired. But I was not asleep. I was thinking of you."

"Are you tired of that?"

"Very much so. It leads to nothing. The road's long and I never arrive."

1. A large and elegant park along the Arno, downriver from the city's center; named after the Medici dairy farm, or *cascio*, that once occupied the site.
1. One of the Nine Muses in classical mythology; the goddess of dance.
2. Gianlorenzo Bernini (1598–1680), the greatest of the Baroque sculptors and architects; responsible for the external colonnade of Saint Peter's as well as many of Rome's fountains.
3. The southernmost region of South America, Patagonia is windswept, underpopulated, often freezing, and desolate. Used proverbially here to suggest something as far away from Europe as possible.

"What do you wish to arrive at?" she put to him, closing her parasol.

"At the point of expressing to myself properly what I think of your engagement."

"Don't think too much of it," she lightly returned.

"Do you mean that it's none of my business?"

"Beyond a certain point, yes."

"That's the point I want to fix. I had an idea you may have found me wanting in good manners. I've never congratulated you."

"Of course I've noticed that. I wondered why you were silent."

"There have been a good many reasons. I'll tell you now," Ralph said. He pulled off his hat and laid it on the ground; then he sat looking at her. He leaned back under the protection of Bernini, his head against his marble pedestal, his arms dropped on either side of him, his hands laid upon the rests of his wide chair. He looked awkward, uncomfortable; he hesitated long. Isabel said nothing; when people were embarrassed she was usually sorry for them, but she was determined not to help Ralph to utter a word that should not be to the honour of her high decision. "I think I've hardly got over my surprise," he went on at last. "You were the last person I expected to see caught."

"I don't know why you call it caught."

"Because you're going to be put into a cage."

"If I like my cage, that needn't trouble you," she answered.

"That's what I wonder at; that's what I've been thinking of."

"If you've been thinking you may imagine how I've thought! I'm satisfied that I'm doing well."

"You must have changed immensely. A year ago you valued your liberty beyond everything. You wanted only to see life."

"I've seen it," said Isabel. "It doesn't look to me now, I admit, such an inviting expanse."

"I don't pretend it is; only I had an idea that you took a genial view of it and wanted to survey the whole field."

"I've seen that one can't do anything so general. One must choose a corner and cultivate that."

"That's what I think. And one must choose as good a corner as possible. I had no idea, all winter, while I read your delightful letters, that you were choosing. You said nothing about it, and your silence put me off my guard."

"It was not a matter I was likely to write to you about. Besides, I knew nothing of the future. It has all come lately. If you had been on your guard, however," Isabel asked, "what would you have done?"

"I should have said 'Wait a little longer.'"

"Wait for what?"

"Well, for a little more light," said Ralph with rather an absurd smile, while his hands found their way into his pockets.

"Where should my light have come from? From you?"

"I might have struck a spark or two."

Isabel had drawn off her gloves; she smoothed them out as they lay upon her knee. The mildness of this movement was accidental, for her expression was not conciliatory. "You're beating about the bush, Ralph. You wish to say you don't like Mr. Osmond, and yet you're afraid."

"'Willing to wound and yet afraid to strike'?[4] I'm willing to wound *him*, yes—but not to wound you. I'm afraid of you, not of him. If you marry him it won't be a fortunate way for me to have spoken."

"*If* I marry him! Have you had any expectation of dissuading me?"

"Of course that seems to you too fatuous."

"No," said Isabel after a little; "it seems to me too touching."

"That's the same thing. It makes me so ridiculous that you pity me."

She stroked out her long gloves again. "I know you've a great affection for me. I can't get rid of that."

"For heaven's sake don't try. Keep that well in sight. It will convince you how intensely I want you to do well."

"And how little you trust me!"

There was a moment's silence; the warm noontide seemed to listen. "I trust you, but I don't trust him," said Ralph.

She raised her eyes and gave him a wide, deep look. "You've said it now, and I'm glad you've made it so clear. But you'll suffer by it."

"Not if you're just."

"I'm very just," said Isabel. "What better proof of it can there be than that I'm not angry with you? I don't know what's the matter with me, but I'm not. I was when you began, but it has passed away. Perhaps I ought to be angry, but Mr. Osmond wouldn't think so. He wants me to know everything; that's what I like him for. You've nothing to gain, I know that. I've never been so nice to you, as a girl, that you should have much reason for wishing me to remain one. You give very good advice; you've often done so. No, I'm very quiet; I've always believed in your wisdom," she went on, boasting of her quietness, yet speaking with a kind of contained exaltation. It was her passionate desire to be just; it touched Ralph to the heart, affected him like a caress from a creature he had injured. He wished to interrupt, to reassure her; for a moment he was absurdly inconsistent; he would have retracted what he had said. But she gave him no chance; she went on, having caught a glimpse, as she thought, of the heroic line and desiring to advance in that direction. "I see you've some special idea; I should like very much to hear it. I'm sure it's disinterested; I feel that. It seems a strange thing to argue about, and of course I ought to tell you definitely that if you expect to dissuade me you may give it up. You'll not move me an inch; it's too late. As you say, I'm caught. Certainly it won't be pleasant for you to remember this, but your pain will be in your own thoughts. I shall never reproach you."

"I don't think you ever will," said Ralph. "It's not in the least the sort of marriage I thought you'd make."

"What sort of marriage was that, pray?"

"Well, I can hardly say. I hadn't exactly a positive view of it, but I had a negative. I didn't think you'd decide for—well, for *that* type."

"What's the matter with Mr. Osmond's type, if it be one? His being so independent, so individual, is what I most see in him," the girl declared. "What do you know against him? You know him scarcely at all."

"Yes," Ralph said, "I know him very little, and I confess I haven't facts and items to prove him a villain. But all the same I can't help feeling that you're running a grave risk."

4. Ralph's quotation comes from Alexander Pope (1688–1744), the "Epistle to Dr. Arbuthnot" (1734), l. 203.

"Marriage is always a grave risk, and his risk's as grave as mine."

"That's his affair! If he's afraid, let him back out. I wish to God he would."

Isabel reclined in her chair, folding her arms and gazing a while at her cousin. "I don't think I understand you," she said at last coldly. "I don't know what you're talking about."

"I believed you'd marry a man of more importance."

Cold, I say, her tone had been, but at this a colour like a flame leaped into her face. "Of more importance to whom? It seems to me enough that one's husband should be of importance to one's self!"

Ralph blushed as well; his attitude embarrassed him. Physically speaking he proceeded to change it; he straightened himself, then leaned forward, resting a hand on each knee. He fixed his eyes on the ground; he had an air of the most respectful deliberation. "I'll tell you in a moment what I mean," he presently said. He felt agitated, intensely eager; now that he had opened the discussion he wished to discharge his mind. But he wished also to be superlatively gentle.

Isabel waited a little—then she went on with majesty. "In everything that makes one care for people Mr. Osmond is pre-eminent. There may be nobler natures, but I've never had the pleasure of meeting one. Mr. Osmond's is the finest I know; he's good enough for me, and interesting enough, and clever enough. I'm far more struck with what he has and what he represents than with what he may lack."

"I had treated myself to a charming vision of your future," Ralph observed without answering this; "I had amused myself with planning out a high destiny for you. There was to be nothing of this sort in it. You were not to come down so easily or so soon."

"Come down, you say?"

"Well, that renders my sense of what has happened to you. You seemed to me to be soaring far up in the blue—to be sailing in the bright light, over the heads of men. Suddenly some one tosses up a faded rosebud—a missile that should never have reached you—and straight you drop to the ground. It hurts me," said Ralph audaciously, "hurts me as if I had fallen myself!"

The look of pain and bewilderment deepened in his companion's face. "I don't understand you in the least," she repeated. "You say you amused yourself with a project for my career—I don't understand that. Don't amuse yourself too much, or I shall think you're doing it at my expense."

Ralph shook his head. "I'm not afraid of your not believing that I've had great ideas for you."

"What do you mean by my soaring and sailing?" she pursued. "I've never moved on a higher plane than I'm moving on now. There's nothing higher for a girl than to marry a—a person she likes," said poor Isabel, wandering into the didactic.

"It's your liking the person we speak of that I venture to criticise, my dear cousin. I should have said that the man for you would have been a more active, larger, freer sort of nature." Ralph hesitated, then added: "I can't get over the sense that Osmond is somehow—well, small." He had uttered the last word with no great assurance; he was afraid she would flash out again. But to his surprise she was quiet; she had the air of considering.

"Small?" She made it sound immense.

"I think he's narrow, selfish. He takes himself so seriously!"

"He has a great respect for himself; I don't blame him for that," said Isabel. "It makes one more sure to respect others."

Ralph for a moment felt almost reassured by her reasonable tone. "Yes, but everything is relative; one ought to feel one's relation to things—to others. I don't think Mr. Osmond does that."

"I've chiefly to do with his relation to me. In that he's excellent."

"He's the incarnation of taste," Ralph went on, thinking hard how he could best express Gilbert Osmond's sinister attributes without putting himself in the wrong by seeming to describe him coarsely. He wished to describe him impersonally, scientifically. "He judges and measures, approves and condemns, altogether by that."

"It's a happy thing then that his taste should be exquisite."

"It's exquisite, indeed, since it has led him to select you as his bride. But have you ever seen such a taste—a really exquisite one—ruffled?"

"I hope it may never be my fortune to fail to gratify my husband's."

At these words a sudden passion leaped to Ralph's lips. "Ah, that's wilful, that's unworthy of you! You were not meant to be measured in that way—you were meant for something better than to keep guard over the sensibilities of a sterile dilettante!"

Isabel rose quickly and he did the same, so that they stood for a moment looking at each other as if he had flung down a defiance or an insult. But "You go too far," she simply breathed.

"I've said what I had on my mind—and I've said it because I love you!"

Isabel turned pale: was he too on that tiresome list? She had a sudden wish to strike him off. "Ah then, you're not disinterested!"

"I love you, but I love without hope," said Ralph quickly, forcing a smile and feeling that in that last declaration he had expressed more than he intended.

Isabel moved away and stood looking into the sunny stillness of the garden; but after a little she turned back to him. "I'm afraid your talk then is the wildness of despair! I don't understand it—but it doesn't matter. I'm not arguing with you; it's impossible I should; I've only tried to listen to you. I'm much obliged to you for attempting to explain," she said gently, as if the anger with which she had just sprung up had already subsided. "It's very good of you to try to warn me, if you're really alarmed; but I won't promise to think of what you've said: I shall forget it as soon as possible. Try and forget it yourself; you've done your duty, and no man can do more. I can't explain to you what I feel, what I believe, and I wouldn't if I could." She paused a moment and then went on with an inconsequence that Ralph observed even in the midst of his eagerness to discover some symptom of concession. "I can't enter into your idea of Mr. Osmond; I can't do it justice, because I see him in quite another way. He's not important—no, he's not important; he's a man to whom importance is supremely indifferent. If that's what you mean when you call him 'small,' then he's as small as you please. I call that large—it's the largest thing I know. I won't pretend to argue with you about a person I'm going to marry," Isabel repeated. "I'm not in the least concerned to defend Mr. Osmond; he's not so weak as to need my defence. I should think it would seem strange even to yourself that I should talk of him so quietly and coldly, as if he were any one else. I wouldn't talk of him at all to any one but you; and you, after what you've said—I may just answer you once for all. Pray, would you wish me to make a mercenary marriage—what they call a marriage of ambition? I've only one ambition—to be free to follow out a good feeling. I had others once, but they've passed away. Do you complain of Mr. Osmond because he's not rich? That's just what I like him for. I've fortunately money enough; I've never felt so thankful for it as today. There have been moments when I should like to go and kneel down by your father's grave: he did perhaps a better thing than he knew when he put it into my power to marry a poor man—a man who has borne his poverty with such dignity, with such indifference. Mr. Osmond has never scrambled nor struggled—he has cared for no worldly prize. If that's to be narrow, if that's to be selfish, then it's very well. I'm not frightened by such words, I'm not even displeased; I'm only sorry that you should make a mistake. Others might have done so, but I'm surprised that *you* should. You might know a gentleman when you see one—you might know a fine mind. Mr. Osmond makes no mistakes! He knows everything, he understands everything, he has the kindest, gentlest, highest spirit. You've got hold of some false idea. It's a pity, but I can't help it; it regards you more than me." Isabel paused a moment, looking at her cousin with an eye illumined by a sentiment which contradicted the careful calmness of her manner—a mingled sentiment, to which the angry pain excited by his words and the wounded pride of having needed to justify a choice of which she felt only the nobleness and purity, equally contributed. Though she paused Ralph said nothing; he saw she had more to say. She was grand, but she was highly solicitous; she was indifferent, but she was all in a passion. "What sort of a person should you have liked me to marry?" she asked suddenly. "You talk about one's soaring and sailing, but if one marries at all one touches the earth. One has human feelings and needs, one has a heart in one's bosom, and one must marry a particular individual. Your mother has never forgiven me for not having come to a better understanding with Lord Warburton, and she's horrified at my contenting myself with a person who has none of his great advantages—no property, no title, no honours, no houses, nor lands, nor position, nor reputation, nor brilliant belongings of any sort. It's the total absence of all these things that pleases me. Mr. Osmond's simply a very lonely, a very cultivated and a very honest man—he's not a prodigious proprietor."

Ralph had listened with great attention, as if everything she said merited deep consideration; but in truth he was only half thinking of the things she said, he was for the rest simply accommodating himself to the weight of his total impression—the impression of her ardent good faith. She was wrong, but she believed; she was deluded, but she was dismally consistent. It was wonderfully characteristic of her that, having invented a fine theory about Gilbert Osmond, she loved him not for what he really possessed, but for his very poverties dressed out as honours. Ralph remembered what he had said to his father about wishing to put it into her power to meet the requirements of her imagination. He had done so, and the girl had taken full advantage of the luxury. Poor Ralph felt sick; he felt ashamed. Isabel had uttered her last words with a low solemnity of conviction which virtually terminated the discussion, and she closed it formally by turning away and walking back to the house. Ralph walked beside her, and they passed into the court together and reached the big staircase.

Here he stopped and Isabel paused, turning on him a face of elation—absolutely and perversely of gratitude. His opposition had made her own conception of her conduct clearer to her. "Shall you not come up to breakfast?" she asked.

"No; I want no breakfast; I'm not hungry."

"You ought to eat," said the girl; "you live on air."

"I do, very much, and I shall go back into the garden and take another mouthful. I came thus far simply to say this. I told you last year that if you were to get into trouble I should feel terribly sold. That's how I feel to-day."

"Do you think I'm in trouble?"

"One's in trouble when one's in error."

"Very well," said Isabel; "I shall never complain of my trouble to you!" And she moved up the staircase.

Ralph, standing there with his hands in his pockets, followed her with his eyes; then the lurking chill of the high-walled court struck him and made him shiver, so that he returned to the garden to breakfast on the Florentine sunshine.

Chapter XXXV

Isabel, when she strolled in the Cascine with her lover, felt no impulse to tell him how little he was approved at Palazzo Crescentini. The discreet opposition offered to her marriage by her aunt and her cousin made on the whole no great impression upon her; the moral of it was simply that they disliked Gilbert Osmond. This dislike was not alarming to Isabel; she scarcely even regretted it; for it served mainly to throw into higher relief the fact, in every way so honourable, that she married to please herself. One did other things to please other people; one did this for a more personal satisfaction; and Isabel's satisfaction was confirmed by her lover's admirable good conduct. Gilbert Osmond was in love, and he had never deserved less than during these still, bright days, each of them numbered, which preceded the fulfilment of his hopes, the harsh criticism passed upon him by Ralph Touchett. The chief impression produced on Isabel's spirit by this criticism was that the passion of love separated its victim terribly from every one but the loved object. She felt herself disjoined from every one she had ever known before—from her two sisters, who wrote to express a dutiful hope that she would be happy, and a surprise, somewhat more vague, at her not having chosen a consort who was the hero of a richer accumulation of anecdote; from Henrietta, who, she was sure, would come out, too late, on purpose to remonstrate; from Lord Warburton, who would certainly console himself, and from Caspar Goodwood, who perhaps would not; from her aunt, who had cold, shallow ideas about marriage, for which she was not sorry to display her contempt; and from Ralph, whose talk about having great views for her was surely but a whimsical cover for a personal disappointment. Ralph apparently wished her not to marry at all—that was what it really meant—because he was amused with the spectacle of her adventure as a single woman. His disappointment made him say angry things about the man she had preferred even to him: Isabel flattered herself that she believed Ralph had been angry. It was the more easy for her to believe this because, as I say, she had now little free or unemployed emotion for minor needs, and accepted as an incident, in fact quite as an ornament, of her lot the idea that to prefer Gilbert Osmond as she preferred him was perforce to break all other ties. She tasted of the sweets of this preference, and they made her conscious, almost with awe, of the invidious and remorseless tide of the charmed and possessed condition, great as was the traditional honour and imputed virtue of being in love. It was the tragic part of happiness; one's right was always made of the wrong of some one else.

The elation of success, which surely now flamed high in Osmond, emitted meanwhile very little smoke for so brilliant a blaze. Contentment, on his part, took no vulgar form; excitement, in the most self-conscious of men, was a kind of ecstasy of self-control. This disposition, however, made him an admirable lover; it gave him a constant view of the smitten and dedicated state. He never forgot himself, as I say; and so he never forgot to be graceful and tender, to wear the appearance—which presented indeed no difficulty—of stirred senses and deep intentions. He was immensely pleased with his young lady; Madame Merle had made him a present of incalculable value. What could be a finer thing to live with than a high spirit attuned to softness? For would not the softness be all for one's self, and the strenuousness for society, which admired the air of superiority? What could be a happier gift in a companion than a quick, fanciful mind which saved one repetitions and reflected one's thought on a polished, elegant surface? Osmond hated to see his thought reproduced literally—that made it look stale and stupid; he preferred it to be freshened in the reproduction even as "words" by music. His egotism had never taken the crude form of desiring a dull wife; this lady's intelligence was to be a silver plate, not an earthen one—a plate that he might heap up with ripe fruits, to which it would give a decorative value, so that talk might become for him a sort of served dessert. He found the silver quality in this perfection in Isabel; he could tap her imagination with his knuckle and make it ring. He knew perfectly, though he had not been told, that their union enjoyed little favour with the girl's relations; but he had always treated her so completely as an independent person that it hardly seemed necessary to express regret for the attitude of her family. Nevertheless, one morning, he made an abrupt allusion to it. "It's the difference in our fortune they don't like," he said. "They think I'm in love with your money."

"Are you speaking of my aunt—of my cousin?" Isabel asked. "How do you know what they think?"

"You've not told me they're pleased, and when I wrote to Mrs. Touchett the other day she never answered my note. If they had been delighted I should have had some sign of it, and the fact of my being poor and you rich is the most obvious explanation of their reserve. But of course when a poor man marries a rich girl he must be prepared for imputations. I don't mind them; I only care for one thing—for your not having the shadow of a doubt. I don't care what people of whom I ask nothing think—I'm not even capable perhaps of wanting to know. I've never so concerned myself, God forgive me, and why should I begin to-day, when I have taken to myself a compensation for everything? I won't pretend I'm sorry you're rich; I'm delighted. I delight in everything that's yours—whether it be money or virtue. Money's a horrid thing to follow, but a charming thing to meet. It seems to me, however, that I've sufficiently proved the limits of my itch for it: I never in my life tried to earn a penny, and I ought to be less sub-ject to suspicion than most of the people one sees grubbing and grabbing. I suppose it's their business to suspect—that of your family; it's proper on the whole they should. They'll like me better some day; so will you, for that matter. Meanwhile my business is not to make myself bad blood, but simply to be thankful for life and love." "It has made me better, loving you," he said on another occasion; "it has made me wiser and easier and—I won't pretend to deny—brighter and nicer and even stronger. I used to want a great many things before and to be angry I didn't have them. Theoreti-cally I was satisfied, as I once told you. I flattered myself I had limited my wants. But I was subject to irritation; I used to have morbid, sterile, hateful fits of hunger, of desire. Now I'm really satisfied, because I can't think of anything better. It's just as when one has been trying to spell out a book in the twilight and suddenly the lamp comes in. I had been putting out my eyes over the book of life and finding nothing to reward me for my pains; but now that I can read it properly I see it's a delightful story. My dear girl, I can't tell you how life seems to stretch there before us—what a long summer afternoon awaits us. It's the latter half of an Italian day—with a golden haze, and the shadows just lengthening, and that divine delicacy in the light, the air, the landscape, which I have loved all my life and which you love to-day. Upon my honour, I don't see why we shouldn't get on. We've got what we like—to say nothing of having each other. We've the faculty of admiration and several capital convictions. We're not stupid, we're not mean, we're not under bonds to any kind of igno-rance or dreariness. You're remarkably fresh, and I'm remarkably well-seasoned. We've my poor child to amuse us; we'll try and make up some little life for her. It's all soft and mellow—it has the Italian colouring."

They made a good many plans, but they left themselves also a good deal of latitude; it was a matter of course, however, that they should live for the present in Italy. It was in Italy that they had met, Italy had been a party to their first impressions of each other, and Italy should be a party to their happiness. Osmond had the attachment of old acquaintance and Isabel the stimulus of new, which seemed to assure her a future at a high level of consciousness of the beautiful. The desire for unlimited expansion had been succeeded in her soul by the sense that life was vacant without some private duty that might gather one's energies to a point. She had told Ralph she had "seen life" in a year or two and that she was already tired, not of the act of living, but of that of observing. What had become of all her ardours, her aspirations, her theories, her high estimate of her indepen-dence and her incipient conviction that she should never marry? These things had been absorbed in a more primitive need—a need the answer to which brushed away numberless questions, yet gratified infinite desires. It simplified the situation at a stroke, it came down from above like the light of the stars, and it needed no explanation. There was explanation enough in the fact that he was her lover, her own, and that she should be able to be of use to him. She could surrender to him with a kind of humil-ity, she could marry him with a kind of pride; she was not only taking, she was giving.

He brought Pansy with him two or three times to the Cascine—Pansy who was very little taller than a year before, and not much older. That she would always be a child was the conviction expressed by her father, who held her by the hand when she was in her sixteenth year and told her to go and play while he sat down a little with the pretty lady. Pansy wore a short dress and a long coat; her hat always seemed too big for her. She found pleasure in walking off, with quick, short steps, to the end of the alley, and then in walking back with a smile that seemed an appeal for approbation. Isabel approved in abundance, and the abundance had the personal touch that the child's affectionate nature craved. She watched her indications as if for herself also much depended on them—Pansy already so represented part of the service she could render, part of the responsibility she could face. Her father took so the childish view of her that he had not yet explained to her the new relation in which he stood to the elegant Miss Archer. "She doesn't know," he said to Isabel; "she doesn't guess; she thinks it perfectly natural that you and I should come and walk here together simply as good friends. There seems to me something enchantingly innocent in that; it's the way I like her to be. No, I'm not a failure, as I used to think; I've succeeded in two things. I'm to marry the woman I adore, and I've brought up my child, as I wished, in the old way."

He was very fond, in all things, of the "old way"; that had struck Isabel as one of his fine, quiet, sincere notes. "It occurs to me that you'll not know whether you've succeeded until you've told her," she said. "You must see how she takes your news. She may be horrified—she may be jealous."

"I'm not afraid of that; she's too fond of you on her own account. I should like to leave her in the dark a little longer—to see if it will come into her head that if we're not engaged we ought to be."

Isabel was impressed by Osmond's artistic, the plastic view, as it somehow appeared, of Pansy's innocence—her own appreciation of it being more anxiously moral. She was perhaps not the less pleased when he told her a few days later that he had communicated the fact to his daughter, who had made such a pretty little speech—"Oh, then I shall have a beautiful sister!" She was neither surprised nor alarmed; she had not cried, as he expected.

"Perhaps she had guessed it," said Isabel.

"Don't say that; I should be disgusted if I believed that. I thought it would be just a little shock; but the way she took it proves that her good manners are paramount. That's also what I wished. You shall see for yourself; to-morrow she shall make you her congratulations in person."

The meeting, on the morrow, took place at the Countess Gemini's, whither Pansy had been conducted by her father, who knew that Isabel was to come in the afternoon to return a visit made her by the Countess on learning that they were to become sisters-in-law. Calling at Casa Touchett the visitor had not found Isabel at home; but after our young woman had been ushered into the Countess's drawing-room Pansy arrived to say that her aunt would presently appear. Pansy was spending the day with that lady, who thought her of an age to begin to learn how to carry herself in company. It was Isabel's view that the little girl might have given lessons in deportment to her relative, and nothing could have justified this conviction more than the manner in which Pansy acquitted herself while they waited together for the Countess. Her father's decision, the year before, had finally been to send her back to the convent to receive the last graces, and Madame Catherine had evidently carried out her theory that Pansy was to be fitted for the great world.

"Papa has told me that you've kindly consented to marry him," said this excellent woman's pupil. "It's very delightful; I think you'll suit very well."

"You think I shall suit *you?*"

"You'll suit me beautifully; but what I mean is that you and papa will suit each other. You're both so quiet and so serious. You're not so quiet as he—or even as Madame Merle; but you're more quiet than many others. He should not for instance have a wife like my aunt. She's always in motion, in agitation—to-day especially; you'll see when she comes in. They told us at the convent it was wrong to judge our elders, but I suppose there's no harm if we judge them favourably. You'll be a delightful companion for papa."

"For you too, I hope," Isabel said.

"I speak first of him on purpose. I've told you already what I myself think of you; I liked you from the first. I admire you so much that I think it will be a good fortune to have you always before me. You'll be my model; I shall try to imitate you though I'm afraid it will be very feeble. I'm very glad for papa—he needed something more than me. Without you I don't see how he could have got it. You'll be my stepmother, but we mustn't use that word. They're always said to be cruel; but I don't think you'll ever so much as pinch or even push me. I'm not afraid at all."

"My good little Pansy," said Isabel gently, "I shall be ever so kind to you." A vague, inconsequent vision of her coming in some odd way to need it had intervened with the effect of a chill.

"Very well then, I've nothing to fear," the child returned with her note of prepared promptitude. What teaching she had had, it seemed to suggest—or what penalties for non-performance she dreaded!

Her description of her aunt had not been incorrect; the Countess Gemini was further than ever from having folded her wings. She entered the room with a flutter through the air and kissed Isabel first on the forehead and then on each cheek as if according to some ancient prescribed rite. She drew the visitor to a sofa and, looking at her with a variety of turns of the head, began to talk very much as if, seated brush in hand before an easel, she were applying a series of considered touches to a composition of figures already sketched in. "If you expect me to congratulate you I must beg you to excuse me. I don't suppose you care if I do or not; I believe you're supposed not to care—through being so clever—for all sorts of ordinary things. But I care myself if I tell fibs; I never tell them unless there's something rather good to be gained. I don't see what's to be gained with you—especially as you wouldn't believe me. I don't make professions any more than I make paper flowers or flouncey lampshades—I don't know how. My lampshades would be sure to take fire, my roses and my fibs to be larger than life. I'm very glad for my own sake that you're to marry Osmond; but I won't pretend I'm glad for yours. You're very brilliant—you know that's the way you're always spoken of; you're an heiress and very good-looking and original, not *banal*; so it's a good thing to have you in the family. Our family's very good, you know; Osmond will have told you that; and my mother was rather distinguished—she was called the American Corinne. But we're dreadfully fallen, I think, and perhaps you'll pick us up. I've great confidence in you; there are ever so many things I want to talk to you about. I never congratulate any girl on marrying; I think they ought to make it somehow not quite so awful a steel trap. I suppose Pansy oughtn't to hear all this; but that's what she has come to me for—to acquire the tone of society. There's no harm in her knowing what horrors she may be in for. When first I got an idea that my brother had designs on you I thought of writing to you, to recommend you, in the strongest terms, not to listen to him. Then I thought it would be disloyal, and I hate anything of that kind. Besides, as I say, I was enchanted for myself; and after all I'm very selfish. By the way, you won't respect me, not one little mite, and we shall never be intimate. I should like it, but you won't. Some day, all the same, we shall be better friends than you will believe at first. My husband will come and see you, though, as you probably know, he's on no sort of terms with Osmond. He's very fond of going to see pretty women, but I'm not afraid of you. In the first place I don't care what he does. In the second, you won't care a straw for him; he won't be a bit, at any time, your affair, and, stupid as he is, he'll see you're not his. Some day, if you can stand it, I'll tell you all about him. Do you think my niece ought to go out of the room? Pansy, go and practise a little in my boudoir."

"Let her stay, please," said Isabel. "I would rather hear nothing that Pansy may not!"

Chapter XXXVI

One afternoon of the autumn of 1876,[1] toward dusk, a young man of pleasing appearance rang at the door of a small apartment on the third floor of an old Roman house. On its being opened he enquired for Madame Merle; whereupon the servant, a neat, plain woman, with a French face and a lady's maid's manner, ushered him into a diminutive drawing-room and requested the favour of his name. "Mr. Edward Rosier," said the young man, who sat down to wait till his hostess should appear.

The reader will perhaps not have forgotten that Mr. Rosier was an ornament of the American circle in Paris, but it may also be remembered that he sometimes vanished from its horizon. He had spent a portion of several winters at Pau, and as he was a gentleman of constituted habits he might have continued for years to pay his annual visit to this charming resort. In the summer of 1876, however, an incident befell him which changed the current not only of his thoughts, but of his customary sequences. He passed a month in the Upper Engadine and encountered at Saint Moritz[2] a charming young girl. To this little person he began to pay, on the spot, particular attention: she struck him as exactly the household angel he had long been looking for. He was never precipitate, he was nothing if not discreet, so he forbore for the present to declare his passion; but it seemed to him when they parted—the young lady to go down into Italy and her admirer to proceed to Geneva, where he was under bonds to join other friends—that he should be romantically wretched if he were not to see her again. The simplest way to do so was to go in the autumn to Rome, where Miss Osmond was domiciled with her family. Mr. Rosier started on his pilgrimage to the Italian capital and reached it on the first of November. It was a pleasant

---

1. This is the only date given in the novel, but it is enough to allow one to work out the book's chronology. The novel begins in 1871, Isabel first goes to Italy in the spring of 1872, and she marries Osmond in 1873.
2. The Engadine Valley, made by the River Inn, lies in the southeastern corner of Switzerland; its upper portion is known for its lakes, and St. Moritz, now a ski center, is its most famous resort. In James's day it was a summer escape from the heat of Italy, and already overcrowded.

thing to do, but for the young man there was a strain of the heroic in the enterprise. He might expose himself, unseasoned, to the poison of the Roman air, which in November lay, notoriously, much in wait. Fortune, however, favours the brave; and this adventurer, who took three grains of quinine[3] a day, had at the end of a month no cause to deplore his temerity. He had made to a certain extent good use of his time; he had devoted it in vain to finding a flaw in Pansy Osmond's composition. She was admirably finished; she had had the last touch; she was really a consummate piece. He thought of her in amorous meditation a good deal as he might have thought of a Dresden-china shepherdess. Miss Osmond, indeed, in the bloom of her juvenility, had a hint of the rococo which Rosier, whose taste was predominantly for that manner, could not fail to appreciate. That he esteemed the productions of comparatively frivolous periods would have been apparent from the attention he bestowed upon Madame Merle's drawing-room, which, although furnished with specimens of every style, was especially rich in articles of the last two centuries. He had immediately put a glass into one eye and looked round; and then "By Jove, she has some jolly good things!" he had yearningly murmured. The room was small and densely filled with furniture; it gave an impression of faded silk and little statuettes which might totter if one moved. Rosier got up and wandered about with his careful tread, bending over the tables charged with knick-knacks and the cushions embossed with princely arms. When Madame Merle came in she found him standing before the fireplace with his nose very close to the great lace flounce attached to the damask cover of the mantel. He had lifted it delicately, as if he were smelling it.

"It's old Venetian," she said; "it's rather good."

"It's too good for this; you ought to wear it."

"They tell me you have some better in Paris, in the same situation."

"Ah, but I can't wear mine," smiled the visitor.

"I don't see why you shouldn't! I've better lace than that to wear."

His eyes wandered, lingeringly, round the room again. "You've some very good things."

"Yes, but I hate them."

"Do you want to get rid of them?" the young man quickly asked.

"No, it's good to have something to hate: one works it off!"

"I love my things," said Mr. Rosier as he sat there flushed with all his recognitions. "But it's not about them, nor about yours, that I came to talk to you." He paused a moment and then, with greater softness: "I care more for Miss Osmond than for all the *bibelots*[4] in Europe!"

Madame Merle opened wide eyes. "Did you come to tell me that?"

"I came to ask your advice."

She looked at him with a friendly frown, stroking her chin with her large white hand. "A man in love, you know, doesn't ask advice."

"Why not, if he's in a difficult position? That's often the case with a man in love. I've been in love before, and I know. But never so much as this time—really never so much. I should like particularly to know what you think of my prospects. I'm afraid that for Mr. Osmond I'm not—well, a real collector's piece."

"Do you wish me to intercede?" Madame Merle asked with her fine arms folded and her handsome mouth drawn up to the left.

"If you could say a good word for me I should be greatly obliged. There will be no use in my troubling Miss Osmond unless I have good reason to believe her father will consent."

"You're very considerate; that's in your favour. But you assume in rather an off-hand way that I think you a prize."

"You've been very kind to me," said the young man. "That's why I came."

"I'm always kind to people who have good Louis Quatorze.[5] It's very rare now, and there's no telling what one may get by it." With which the left-hand corner of Madame Merle's mouth gave expression to the joke.

But he looked, in spite of it, literally apprehensive and consistently strenuous. "Ah, I thought you liked me for myself!"

"I like you very much; but, if you please, we won't analyse. Pardon me if I seem patronising, but I think you a perfect little gentleman. I must tell you, however, that I've not the marrying of Pansy Osmond."

"I didn't suppose that. But you've seemed to me intimate with her family, and I thought you might have influence."

Madame Merle considered. "Whom do you call her family?"

"Why, her father; and—how do you say it in English?—her *belle-mère*."[6]

"Mr. Osmond's her father, certainly; but his wife can scarcely be termed a member of her family. Mrs. Osmond has nothing to do with marrying her."

"I'm sorry for that," said Rosier with an amiable sigh of good faith. "I think Mrs. Osmond would favour me."

"Very likely—if her husband doesn't."

He raised his eyebrows. "Does she take the opposite line from him?"

"In everything. They think quite differently."

"Well," said Rosier, "I'm sorry for that; but it's none of my business. She's very fond of Pansy."

"Yes, she's very fond of Pansy."

"And Pansy has a great affection for her. She has told me how she loves her as if she were her own mother."

"You must, after all, have had some very intimate talk with the poor child," said Madame Merle. "Have you declared your sentiments?"

"Never!" cried Rosier, lifting his neatly-gloved hand. "Never till I've assured myself of those of the parents."

"You always wait for that? You've excellent principles; you observe the proprieties."

"I think you're laughing at me," the young man murmured, dropping back in his chair and feeling his small moustache. "I didn't expect that of you, Madame Merle."

She shook her head calmly, like a person who saw things as she saw them. "You don't do me justice. I think your conduct in excellent taste and the best you could adopt. Yes, that's what I think."

"I wouldn't agitate her—only to agitate her; I love her too much for that," said Ned Rosier.

5. The style associated with the reign of France's Louis XIV (1634–1715).
6. Stepmother (French).

"I'm glad, after all, that you've told me," Madame Merle went on. "Leave it to me a little; I think I can help you."

"I said you were the person to come to!" her visitor cried with prompt elation.

"You were very clever," Madame Merle returned more dryly. "When I say I can help you I mean once assuming your cause to be good. Let us think a little if it is."

"I'm awfully decent, you know," said Rosier earnestly. "I won't say I've no faults, but I'll say I've no vices."

"All that's negative, and it always depends, also, on what people call vices. What's the positive side? What's the virtuous? What have you got besides your Spanish lace and your Dresden teacups?"

"I've a comfortable little fortune—about forty thousand francs a year.[7] With the talent I have for arranging, we can live beautifully on such an income."

"Beautifully, no. Sufficiently, yes. Even that depends on where you live."

"Well, in Paris. I would undertake it in Paris."

Madame Merle's mouth rose to the left. "It wouldn't be famous; you'd have to make use of the teacups, and they'd get broken."

"We don't want to be famous. If Miss Osmond should have everything pretty it would be enough. When one's as pretty as she one can afford— well, quite cheap *faience*.[8] She ought never to wear anything but muslin— without the sprig," said Rosier reflectively.

"Wouldn't you even allow her the sprig? She'd be much obliged to you at any rate for that theory."

"It's the correct one, I assure you; and I'm sure she'd enter into it. She understands all that; that's why I love her."

"She's a very good little girl, and most tidy—also extremely graceful. But her father, to the best of my belief, can give her nothing."

Rosier scarce demurred. "I don't in the least desire that he should. But I may remark, all the same, that he lives like a rich man."

"The money's his wife's; she brought him a large fortune."

"Mrs. Osmond then is very fond of her stepdaughter; she may do something."

"For a love-sick swain you have your eyes about you!" Madame Merle exclaimed with a laugh.

"I esteem a *dot* very much. I can do without it, but I esteem it."

"Mrs. Osmond," Madame Merle went on, "will probably prefer to keep her money for her own children."

"Her own children? Surely she has none."

"She may have yet. She had a poor little boy, who died two years ago, six months after his birth. Others therefore may come."

"I hope they will, if it will make her happy. She's a splendid woman."

Madame Merle failed to burst into speech. "Ah, about her there's much to be said. Splendid as you like! We've not exactly made out that you're a *parti*. The absence of vices is hardly a source of income."

"Pardon me, I think it may be," said Rosier quite lucidly.

---

7. In chapter 43 Warburton will give this figure as £1,600 a year.
8. Glazed earthernware (French).

"You'll be a touching couple, living on your innocence!"

"I think you underrate me."

"You're not so innocent as that? Seriously," said Madame Merle, "of course forty thousand francs a year and a nice character are a combination to be considered. I don't say it's to be jumped at, but there might be a worse offer. Mr. Osmond, however, will probably incline to believe he can do better."

"*He* can do so perhaps; but what can his daughter do? She can't do better than marry the man she loves. For she does, you know," Rosier added eagerly.

"She does—I know it."

"Ah," cried the young man, "I said you were the person to come to."

"But I don't know how *you* know it, if you haven't asked her," Madame Merle went on.

"In such a case there's no need of asking and telling; as you say, we're an innocent couple. How did *you* know it?"

"I who am not innocent? By being very crafty. Leave it to me; I'll find out for you."

Rosier got up and stood smoothing his hat. "You say that rather coldly. Don't simply find out how it is, but try to make it as it should be."

"I'll do my best. I'll try to make the most of your advantages."

"Thank you so very much. Meanwhile then I'll say a word to Mrs. Osmond."

"*Gardez-vous-en bien!*"[9] And Madame Merle was on her feet. "Don't set her going, or you'll spoil everything."

Rosier gazed into his hat; he wondered whether his hostess *had* been after all the right person to come to. "I don't think I understand you. I'm an old friend of Mrs. Osmond, and I think she would like me to succeed."

"Be an old friend as much as you like; the more old friends she has the better, for she doesn't get on very well with some of her new. But don't for the present try to make her take up the cudgels for you. Her husband may have other views, and, as a person who wishes her well, I advise you not to multiply points of difference between them."

Poor Rosier's face assumed an expression of alarm; a suit for the hand of Pansy Osmond was even a more complicated business than his taste for proper transitions had allowed. But the extreme good sense which he concealed under a surface suggesting that of a careful owner's "best set" came to his assistance. "I don't see that I'm bound to consider Mr. Osmond so very much!" he exclaimed.

"No, but you should consider *her*. You say you're an old friend. Would you make her suffer?"

"Not for the world."

"Then be very careful, and let the matter alone till I've taken a few soundings."

"Let the matter alone, dear Madame Merle? Remember that I'm in love."

"Oh, you won't burn up! Why did you come to me, if you're not to heed what I say?"

---

9. Take care not to! (French).

"You're very kind; I'll be very good," the young man promised. "But I'm afraid Mr. Osmond's pretty hard," he added in his mild voice as he went to the door.

Madame Merle gave a short laugh. "It has been said before. But his wife isn't easy either."

"Ah, she's a splendid woman!" Ned Rosier repeated, for departure.

He resolved that his conduct should be worthy of an aspirant who was already a model of discretion; but he saw nothing in any pledge he had given Madame Merle that made it improper he should keep himself in spirits by an occasional visit to Miss Osmond's home. He reflected constantly on what his adviser had said to him, and turned over in his mind the impression of her rather circumspect tone. He had gone to her *de confiance*, as they put it in Paris; but it was possible he had been precipitate. He found difficulty in thinking of himself as rash—he had incurred this reproach so rarely; but it certainly was true that he had known Madame Merle only for the last month, and that his thinking her a delightful woman was not, when one came to look into it, a reason for assuming that she would be eager to push Pansy Osmond into his arms, gracefully arranged as these members might be to receive her. She had indeed shown him benevolence, and she was a person of consideration among the girl's people, where she had a rather striking appearance (Rosier had more than once wondered how she managed it) of being intimate without being familiar. But possibly he had exaggerated these advantages. There was no particular reason why she should take trouble for him; a charming woman was charming to every one, and Rosier felt rather a fool when he thought of his having appealed to her on the ground that she had distinguished him. Very likely—though she had appeared to say it in joke—she was really only thinking of his *bibelots*. Had it come into her head that he might offer her two or three of the gems of his collection? If she would only help him to marry Miss Osmond he would present her with his whole museum. He could hardly say so to her outright; it would seem too gross a bribe. But he should like her to believe it.

It was with these thoughts that he went again to Mrs. Osmond's, Mrs. Osmond having an "evening"—she had taken the Thursday of each week—when his presence could be accounted for on general principles of civility. The object of Mr. Rosier's well-regulated affection dwelt in a high house in the very heart of Rome; a dark and massive structure overlooking a sunny *piazzetta* in the neighbourhood of the Farnese Palace.[1] In a palace, too, little Pansy lived—a palace by Roman measure, but a dungeon to poor Rosier's apprehensive mind. It seemed to him of evil omen that the young lady he wished to marry, and whose fastidious father he doubted of his ability to conciliate, should be immured in a kind of domestic fortress, a pile which bore a stern old Roman name, which smelt of historic deeds, of crime and craft and violence, which was mentioned in "Murray" and visited by tourists who looked, on a vague survey, disappointed and depressed, and which had frescoes by Caravaggio[2] in the *piano nobile* and a row of mutilated statues and dusty urns in the wide,

1. The sixteenth-century Farnese Palace, near the Campo di'Fiori, is now the French Embassy. *Piazzetta*: small square.
2. Michelangelo Merisi (1573–1610), known as Caravaggio, did not work in fresco, but his highly dramatic work, with its odd effects of light and shadow, is otherwise suitable for Isabel's life here.

nobly-arched loggia[3] overhanging the damp court where a fountain gushed out of a mossy niche. In a less preoccupied frame of mind he could have done justice to the Palazzo Roccanera;[4] he could have entered into the sentiment of Mrs. Osmond, who had once told him that on settling themselves in Rome she and her husband had chosen this habitation for the love of local colour. It had local colour enough, and though he knew less about architecture than about Limoges[5] enamels he could see that the proportions of the windows and even the details of the cornice had quite the grand air. But Rosier was haunted by the conviction that at picturesque periods young girls had been shut up there to keep them from their true loves, and then, under the threat of being thrown into convents, had been forced into unholy marriages. There was one point, however, to which he always did justice when once he found himself in Mrs. Osmond's warm, rich-looking reception-rooms, which were on the second floor. He acknowledged that these people were very strong in "good things." It was a taste of Osmond's own—not at all of hers; this she had told him the first time he came to the house, when, after asking himself for a quarter of an hour whether they had even better "French" than he in Paris, he was obliged on the spot to admit that they had, very much, and vanquished his envy, as a gentleman should, to the point of expressing to his hostess his pure admiration of her treasures. He learned from Mrs. Osmond that her husband had made a large collection before their marriage and that, though he had annexed a number of fine pieces within the last three years, he had achieved his greatest finds at a time when he had not the advantage of her advice. Rosier interpreted this information according to principles of his own. For "advice" read "cash," he said to himself; and the fact that Gilbert Osmond had landed his highest prizes during his impecunious season confirmed his most cherished doctrine—the doctrine that a collector may freely be poor if he be only patient. In general, when Rosier presented himself on a Thursday evening, his first recognition was for the walls of the saloon; there were three or four objects his eyes really yearned for. But after his talk with Madame Merle he felt the extreme seriousness of his position; and now, when he came in, he looked about for the daughter of the house with such eagerness as might be permitted a gentleman whose smile, as he crossed a threshold, always took everything comfortable for granted.

Chapter XXXVII

Pansy was not in the first of the rooms, a large apartment with a concave ceiling and walls covered with old red damask; it was here Mrs. Osmond usually sat—though she was not in her most customary place to-night— and that a circle of more especial intimates gathered about the fire. The room was flushed with subdued, diffused brightness; it contained the larger things and—almost always—an odour of flowers. Pansy on this occasion was presumably in the next of the series, the resort of younger

3. An arched, open gallery, here a kind of balcony. *Piano nobile*: main floor.
4. The Black Rock; a fictional name, but the description of the palace corresponds to the Palazzo Antici Mattei, built to designs by Carlo Maderno (1556–1629). The piazzetta outside contains a small fountain decorated with bronze tortoises that is usually attributed to Bernini.
5. Painted enamels of all kinds, from religious articles to snuffboxes, were produced in that French city; Rosier's connoisseurship here suggests his overrefinement.

visitors, where tea was served. Osmond stood before the chimney, leaning back with his hands behind him; he had one foot up and was warming the sole. Half a dozen persons, scattered near him, were talking together; but he was not in the conversation; his eyes had an expression, frequent with them, that seemed to represent them as engaged with objects more worth their while than the appearances actually thrust upon them. Rosier, coming in unannounced, failed to attract his attention; but the young man, who was very punctilious, though he was even exceptionally conscious that it was the wife, not the husband, he had come to see, went up to shake hands with him. Osmond put out his left hand, without changing his attitude.

"How d' ye do? My wife's somewhere about."

"Never fear; I shall find her," said Rosier cheerfully.

Osmond, however, took him in; he had never in his life felt himself so efficiently looked at. "Madame Merle has told him, and he doesn't like it," he privately reasoned. He had hoped Madame Merle would be there, but she was not in sight; perhaps she was in one of the other rooms or would come later. He had never especially delighted in Gilbert Osmond, having a fancy he gave himself airs. But Rosier was not quickly resentful, and where politeness was concerned had ever a strong need of being quite in the right. He looked round him and smiled, all without help, and then in a moment, "I saw a jolly good piece of Capo di Monte[1] to-day," he said.

Osmond answered nothing at first; but presently, while he warmed his boot-sole, "I don't care a fig for Capo di Monte!" he returned.

"I hope you're not losing your interest?"

"In old pots and plates? Yes, I'm losing my interest."

Rosier for an instant forgot the delicacy of his position. "You're not thinking of parting with a—a piece or two?"

"No, I'm not thinking of parting with anything at all, Mr. Rosier," said Osmond, with his eyes still on the eyes of his visitor.

"Ah, you want to keep, but not to add," Rosier remarked brightly.

"Exactly. I've nothing I wish to match."

Poor Rosier was aware he had blushed; he was distressed at his want of assurance. "Ah, well, I have!" was all he could murmur; and he knew his murmur was partly lost as he turned away. He took his course to the adjoining room and met Mrs. Osmond coming out of the deep doorway. She was dressed in black velvet; she looked high and splendid, as he had said, and yet oh so radiantly gentle! We know what Mr. Rosier thought of her and the terms in which, to Madame Merle, he had expressed his admiration. Like his appreciation of her dear little stepdaughter it was based partly on his eye for decorative character, his instinct for authenticity; but also on a sense for uncatalogued values, for that secret of a "lustre" beyond any recorded losing or rediscovering, which his devotion to brittle wares had still not disqualified him to recognise. Mrs. Osmond, at present, might well have gratified such tastes. The years had touched her only to enrich her; the flower of her youth had not faded, it only hung more quietly on its stem. She had lost something of that quick eagerness to which her husband had privately taken exception—she had more the air of being able

---

1. A make of porcelain, produced near Naples from the mid-eighteenth century on, often taking the form of rococo figurines or vases studded with china flowers.

to wait. Now, at all events, framed in the gilded doorway, she struck our young man as the picture of a gracious lady. "You see I'm very regular," he said. "But who should be if I'm not?"

"Yes, I've known you longer than any one here. But we mustn't indulge in tender reminiscences. I want to introduce you to a young lady."

"Ah, please, what young lady?" Rosier was immensely obliging; but this was not what he had come for.

"She sits there by the fire in pink and has no one to speak to."

Rosier hesitated a moment. "Can't Mr. Osmond speak to her? He's within six feet of her."

Mrs. Osmond also hesitated. "She's not very lively, and he doesn't like dull people."

"But she's good enough for me? Ah now, that's hard!"

"I only mean that you've ideas for two. And then you're so obliging."

"So is your husband."

"No, he's not—to me." And Mrs. Osmond vaguely smiled.

"That's a sign he should be doubly so to other women."

"So I tell him," she said, still smiling.

"You see I want some tea," Rosier went on, looking wistfully beyond.

"That's perfect. Go and give some to my young lady."

"Very good; but after that I'll abandon her to her fate. The simple truth is I'm dying to have a little talk with Miss Osmond."

"Ah," said Isabel, turning away, "I can't help you there!"

Five minutes later, while he handed a tea-cup to the damsel in pink, whom he had conducted into the other room, he wondered whether, in making to Mrs. Osmond the profession I have just quoted, he had broken the spirit of his promise to Madame Merle. Such a question was capable of occupying this young man's mind for a considerable time. At last, however, he became—comparatively speaking—reckless; he cared little what promises he might break. The fate to which he had threatened to abandon the damsel in pink proved to be none so terrible; for Pansy Osmond, who had given him the tea for his companion—Pansy was as fond as ever of making tea—presently came and talked to her. Into this mild colloquy Edward Rosier entered little; he sat by moodily, watching his small sweetheart. If we look at her now through his eyes we shall at first not see much to remind us of the obedient little girl who, at Florence, three years before, was sent to walk short distances in the Cascine while her father and Miss Archer talked together of matters sacred to elder people. But after a moment we shall perceive that if at nineteen Pansy has become a young lady she doesn't really fill out the part; that if she has grown very pretty she lacks in a deplorable degree the quality known and esteemed in the appearance of females as style; and that if she is dressed with great freshness she wears her smart attire with an undisguised appearance of saving it—very much as if it were lent her for the occasion. Edward Rosier, it would seem, would have been just the man to note these defects; and in point of fact there was not a quality of this young lady, of any sort, that he had not noted. Only he called her qualities by names of his own—some of which indeed were happy enough. "No, she's unique—she's absolutely unique," he used to say to himself; and you may be sure that not for an instant would he have admitted to you that she was wanting in style. Style? Why, she had the style of a little princess; if you couldn't see it you had no eye. It was not modern, it was not conscious, it would produce no impression in Broadway; the small, serious damsel, in her stiff little dress, only looked like an Infanta of Velasquez.[2] This was enough for Edward Rosier, who thought her delightfully old-fashioned. Her anxious eyes, her charming lips, her slip of a figure, were as touching as a childish prayer. He had now an acute desire to know just to what point she liked him—a desire which made him fidget as he sat in his chair. It made him feel hot, so that he had to pat his forehead with his handkerchief; he had never been so uncomfortable. She was such a perfect *jeune fille*, and one couldn't make of a *jeune fille* the enquiry requisite for throwing light on such a point. A *jeune fille* was what Rosier had always dreamed of—a *jeune fille* who should yet not be French, for he had felt that this nationality would complicate the question. He was sure Pansy had never looked at a newspaper and that, in the way of novels, if she had read Sir Walter Scott it was the very most.[3] An American *jeune fille*—what could be better than that? She would be frank and gay, and yet would not have walked alone, nor have received letters from men, nor have been taken to the theatre to see the comedy of manners. Rosier could not deny that, as the matter stood, it would be a breach of hospitality to appeal directly to this unsophisticated creature; but he was now in imminent danger of asking himself if hospitality were the most sacred thing in the world. Was not the sentiment that he entertained for Miss Osmond of infinitely greater importance? Of greater importance to him—yes; but not probably to the master of the house. There was one comfort; even if this gentleman had been placed on his guard by Madame Merle he would not have extended the warning to Pansy; it would not have been part of his policy to let her know that a prepossessing young man was in love with her. But he *was* in love with her, the prepossessing young man; and all these restrictions of circumstance had ended by irritating him. What had Gilbert Osmond meant by giving him two fingers of his left hand? If Osmond was rude, surely he himself might be bold. He felt extremely bold after the dull girl in so vain a disguise of rose-colour had responded to the call of her mother, who came in to say, with a significant simper at Rosier, that she must carry her off to other triumphs. The mother and daughter departed together, and now it depended only upon him that he should be virtually alone with Pansy. He had never been alone with her before; he had never been alone with a *jeune fille*. It was a great moment; poor Rosier began to pat his forehead again. There was another room beyond the one in which they stood—a small room that had been thrown open and lighted, but that, the company not being numerous, had remained empty all the evening. It was empty yet; it was upholstered in pale yellow; there were several lamps; through the open door it looked the very temple of authorised love. Rosier gazed a moment through this aperture; he was afraid that Pansy would run away, and felt almost capable of stretching out a hand to detain her. But she lingered where the other maiden had left them, making no motion

---

2. Diego de Velásquez (1599–1660), Spanish painter who did many portraits of the country's *infantas*, or princesses, during the reign of Philip IV, including *Las Meninas* (1656), which depicts Infanta Margaret Theresa.
3. Sir Walter Scott (1771–1832) was regarded as "safe" even by those few people in James's day who still thought that novels were dangerous things for an impressionable young girl (*jeune fille*) to read. Scott's works include *Waverley* (1814) and *Ivanhoe* (1820).

to join a knot of visitors on the far side of the room. For a little it occurred to him that she was frightened—too frightened perhaps to move; but a second glance assured him she was not, and he then reflected that she was too innocent indeed for that. After a supreme hesitation he asked her if he might go and look at the yellow room, which seemed so attractive yet so virginal. He had been there already with Osmond, to inspect the furniture, which was of the First French Empire,[4] and especially to admire the clock (which he didn't really admire), an immense classic structure of that period. He therefore felt that he had now begun to manœuvre.

"Certainly, you may go," said Pansy; "and if you like I'll show you." She was not in the least frightened.

"That's just what I hoped you'd say; you're so very kind," Rosier murmured.

They went in together; Rosier really thought the room very ugly, and it seemed cold. The same idea appeared to have struck Pansy. "It's not for winter evenings; it's more for summer," she said. "It's papa's taste; he has so much."

He had a good deal, Rosier thought; but some of it was very bad. He looked about him; he hardly knew what to say in such a situation. "Doesn't Mrs. Osmond care how her rooms are done? Has she no taste?" he asked.

"Oh yes, a great deal; but it's more for literature," said Pansy—"and for conversation. But papa cares also for those things. I think he knows everything."

Rosier was silent a little. "There's one thing I'm sure he knows!" he broke out presently. "He knows that when I come here it's, with all respect to him, with all respect to Mrs. Osmond, who's so charming—it's really," said the young man, "to see you!"

"To see me?" And Pansy raised her vaguely-troubled eyes.

"To see you; that's what I come for," Rosier repeated, feeling the intoxication of a rupture with authority.

Pansy stood looking at him, simply, intently, openly; a blush was not needed to make her face more modest. "I thought it was for that."

"And it was not disagreeable to you?"

"I couldn't tell; I didn't know. You never told me," said Pansy.

"I was afraid of offending you."

"You don't offend me," the young girl murmured, smiling as if an angel had kissed her.

"You like me then, Pansy?" Rosier asked very gently, feeling very happy.

"Yes—I like you."

They had walked to the chimney-piece where the big cold Empire clock was perched; they were well within the room and beyond observation from without. The tone in which she had said these four words seemed to him the very breath of nature, and his only answer could be to take her hand and hold it a moment. Then he raised it to his lips. She submitted, still with her pure, trusting smile, in which there was something ineffably passive. She liked him—she had liked him all the while; now anything might happen! She was ready—she had been ready always, waiting for him to speak. If he had not spoken she would have waited for ever; but when the

---

4. The Napoleonic First Empire (1804–15); its decorative arts were neoclassical in style, and sometimes massive.

word came she dropped like the peach from the shaken tree. Rosier felt that if he should draw her toward him and hold her to his heart she would submit without a murmur, would rest there without a question. It was true that this would be a rash experiment in a yellow Empire *salottino*.[5] She had known it was for her he came, and yet like what a perfect little lady she had carried it off!

"You're very dear to me," he murmured, trying to believe that there was after all such a thing as hospitality.

She looked a moment at her hand, where he had kissed it. "Did you say papa knows?"

"You told me just now he knows everything."

"I think you must make sure," said Pansy.

"Ah, my dear, when once I'm sure of *you*!" Rosier murmured in her ear; whereupon she turned back to the other rooms with a little air of consistency which seemed to imply that their appeal should be immediate.

The other rooms meanwhile had become conscious of the arrival of Madame Merle, who, wherever she went, produced an impression when she entered. How she did it the most attentive spectator could not have told you, for she neither spoke loud, nor laughed profusely, nor moved rapidly, nor dressed with splendour, nor appealed in any appreciable manner to the audience. Large, fair, smiling, serene, there was something in her very tranquillity that diffused itself, and when people looked round it was because of a sudden quiet. On this occasion she had done the quietest thing she could do; after embracing Mrs. Osmond, which was more striking, she had sat down on a small sofa to commune with the master of the house. There was a brief exchange of commonplaces between these two—they always paid, in public, a certain formal tribute to the commonplace—and then Madame Merle, whose eyes had been wandering, asked if little Mr. Rosier had come this evening.

"He came nearly an hour ago—but he has disappeared," Osmond said.

"And where's Pansy?"

"In the other room. There are several people there."

"He's probably among them," said Madame Merle.

"Do you wish to see him?" Osmond asked in a provokingly pointless tone.

Madame Merle looked at him a moment; she knew each of his tones to the eighth of a note. "Yes, I should like to say to him that I've told you what he wants, and that it interests you but feebly."

"Don't tell him that. He'll try to interest me more—which is exactly what I don't want. Tell him I hate his proposal."

"But you don't hate it."

"It doesn't signify; I don't love it. I let him see that, myself, this evening; I was rude to him on purpose. That sort of thing's a great bore. There's no hurry."

"I'll tell him that you'll take time and think it over."

"No, don't do that. He'll hang on."

"If I discourage him he'll do the same."

"Yes, but in the one case he'll try to talk and explain—which would be exceedingly tiresome. In the other he'll probably hold his tongue and go

5. A study or small room (Italian).

in for some deeper game. That will leave me quiet. I hate talking with a donkey."

"Is that what you call poor Mr. Rosier?"

"Oh, he's a nuisance—with his eternal majolica."[6]

Madame Merle dropped her eyes; she had a faint smile. "He's a gentleman, he has a charming temper; and, after all, an income of forty thousand francs!"

"It's misery—'genteel' misery," Osmond broke in. "It's not what I've dreamed of for Pansy."

"Very good then. He has promised me not to speak to her."

"Do you believe him?" Osmond asked absent-mindedly.

"Perfectly. Pansy has thought a great deal about him; but I don't suppose you consider that that matters."

"I don't consider it matters at all; but neither do I believe she has thought of him."

"That opinion's more convenient," said Madame Merle quietly.

"Has she told you she's in love with him?"

"For what do you take her? And for what do you take me?" Madame Merle added in a moment.

Osmond had raised his foot and was resting his slim ankle on the other knee; he clasped his ankle in his hand familiarly—his long, fine forefinger and thumb could make a ring for it—and gazed a while before him. "This kind of thing doesn't find me unprepared. It's what I educated her for. It was all for this—that when such a case should come up she should do what I prefer."

"I'm not afraid that she'll not do it."

"Well then, where's the hitch?"

"I don't see any. But, all the same, I recommend you not to get rid of Mr. Rosier. Keep him on hand; he may be useful."

"I can't keep him. Keep him yourself."

"Very good; I'll put him into a corner and allow him so much a day." Madame Merle had, for the most part, while they talked, been glancing about her; it was her habit in this situation, just as it was her habit to interpose a good many blank-looking pauses. A long drop followed the last words I have quoted; and before it had ended she saw Pansy come out of the adjoining room, followed by Edward Rosier. The girl advanced a few steps and then stopped and stood looking at Madame Merle and at her father.

"He has spoken to her," Madame Merle went on to Osmond.

Her companion never turned his head. "So much for your belief in his promises. He ought to be horse-whipped."

"He intends to confess, poor little man!"

Osmond got up; he had now taken a sharp look at his daughter. "It doesn't matter," he murmured, turning away.

Pansy after a moment came up to Madame Merle with her little manner of unfamiliar politeness. This lady's reception of her was not more intimate; she simply, as she rose from the sofa, gave her a friendly smile.

"You're very late," the young creature gently said.

"My dear child, I'm never later than I intend to be."

6. Brightly painted earthernware; *not* Capodimonte.

Madame Merle had not got up to be gracious to Pansy; she moved toward Edward Rosier. He came to meet her and, very quickly, as if to get it off his mind, "I've spoken to her!" he whispered.

"I know it, Mr. Rosier."

"Did she tell you?"

"Yes, she told me. Behave properly for the rest of the evening, and come and see me to-morrow at a quarter past five." She was severe, and in the manner in which she turned her back to him there was a degree of contempt which caused him to mutter a decent imprecation.

He had no intention of speaking to Osmond; it was neither the time nor the place. But he instinctively wandered toward Isabel, who sat talking with an old lady. He sat down on the other side of her; the old lady was Italian, and Rosier took for granted she understood no English. "You said just now you wouldn't help me," he began to Mrs. Osmond. "Perhaps you'll feel differently when you know—when you know—!"

Isabel met his hesitation. "When I know what?"

"That she's all right."

"What do you mean by that?"

"Well, that we've come to an understanding."

"She's all wrong," said Isabel. "It won't do."

Poor Rosier gazed at her half-pleadingly, half-angrily; a sudden flush testified to his sense of injury. "I've never been treated so," he said. "What is there against me, after all? That's not the way I'm usually considered. I could have married twenty times."

"It's a pity you didn't. I don't mean twenty times, but once, comfortably," Isabel added, smiling kindly. "You're not rich enough for Pansy."

"She doesn't care a straw for one's money."

"No, but her father does."

"Ah yes, he has proved that!" cried the young man.

Isabel got up, turning away from him, leaving her old lady without ceremony; and he occupied himself for the next ten minutes in pretending to look at Gilbert Osmond's collection of miniatures, which were neatly arranged on a series of small velvet screens. But he looked without seeing; his cheek burned; he was too full of his sense of injury. It was certain that he had never been treated that way before; he was not used to being thought not good enough. He knew how good he was, and if such a fallacy had not been so pernicious he could have laughed at it. He searched again for Pansy, but she had disappeared, and his main desire was now to get out of the house. Before doing so he spoke once more to Isabel; it was not agreeable to him to reflect that he had just said a rude thing to her— the only point that would now justify a low view of him.

"I referred to Mr. Osmond as I shouldn't have done, a while ago," he began. "But you must remember my situation."

"I don't remember what you said," she answered coldly.

"Ah, you're offended, and now you'll never help me."

She was silent an instant, and then with a change of tone: "It's not that I won't; I simply can't!" Her manner was almost passionate.

"If you *could*, just a little, I'd never again speak of your husband save as an angel."

"The inducement's great," said Isabel gravely—inscrutably, as he afterwards, to himself, called it; and she gave him, straight in the eyes, a look which was also inscrutable. It made him remember somehow that he had known her as a child; and yet it was keener than he liked, and he took himself off.

Chapter XXXVIII

He went to see Madame Merle on the morrow, and to his surprise she let him off rather easily. But she made him promise that he would stop there till something should have been decided. Mr. Osmond had had higher expectations; it was very true that as he had no intention of giving his daughter a portion such expectations were open to criticism or even, if one would, to ridicule. But she would advise Mr. Rosier not to take that tone; if he would possess his soul in patience he might arrive at his felicity. Mr. Osmond was not favourable to his suit, but it wouldn't be a miracle if he should gradually come round. Pansy would never defy her father, he might depend on that; so nothing was to be gained by precipitation. Mr. Osmond needed to accustom his mind to an offer of a sort that he had not hitherto entertained, and this result must come of itself—it was useless to try to force it. Rosier remarked that his own situation would be in the meanwhile the most uncomfortable in the world, and Madame Merle assured him that she felt for him. But, as she justly declared, one couldn't have everything one wanted; she had learned that lesson for herself. There would be no use in his writing to Gilbert Osmond, who had charged her to tell him as much. He wished the matter dropped for a few weeks and would himself write when he should have anything to communicate that it might please Mr. Rosier to hear.

"He doesn't like your having spoken to Pansy. Ah, he doesn't like it at all," said Madame Merle.

"I'm perfectly willing to give him a chance to tell me so!"

"If you do that he'll tell you more than you care to hear. Go to the house, for the next month, as little as possible, and leave the rest to me."

"As little as possible? Who's to measure the possibility?"

"Let me measure it. Go on Thursday evenings with the rest of the world, but don't go at all at odd times, and don't fret about Pansy. I'll see that she understands everything. She's a calm little nature; she'll take it quietly."

Edward Rosier fretted about Pansy a good deal, but he did as he was advised, and awaited another Thursday evening before returning to Palazzo Roccanera. There had been a party at dinner, so that though he went early the company was already tolerably numerous. Osmond, as usual, was in the first room, near the fire, staring straight at the door, so that, not to be distinctly uncivil, Rosier had to go and speak to him.

"I'm glad that you can take a hint," Pansy's father said, slightly closing his keen, conscious eyes.

"I take no hints. But I took a message, as I supposed it to be."

"You took it? Where did you take it?"

It seemed to poor Rosier he was being insulted, and he waited a moment, asking himself how much a true lover ought to submit to. "Madame Merle gave me, as I understood it, a message from you—to the effect that you declined to give me the opportunity I desire, the opportunity to explain my wishes to you." And he flattered himself he spoke rather sternly.

"I don't see what Madame Merle has to do with it. Why did you apply to Madame Merle?"

"I asked her for an opinion—for nothing more. I did so because she had seemed to me to know you very well."

"She doesn't know me so well as she thinks," said Osmond.

"I'm sorry for that, because she has given me some little ground for hope."

Osmond stared into the fire a moment. "I set a great price on my daughter."

"You can't set a higher one than I do. Don't I prove it by wishing to marry her?"

"I wish to marry her very well," Osmond went on with a dry impertinence which, in another mood, poor Rosier would have admired.

"Of course I pretend she'd marry well in marrying me. She couldn't marry a man who loves her more—or whom, I may venture to add, she loves more."

"I'm not bound to accept your theories as to whom my daughter loves"— Osmond looked up with a quick, cold smile.

"I'm not theorising. Your daughter has spoken."

"Not to me," Osmond continued, now bending forward a little and dropping his eyes to his boot-toes.

"I have her promise, sir!" cried Rosier with the sharpness of exasperation.

As their voices had been pitched very low before, such a note attracted some attention from the company. Osmond waited till this little movement had subsided; then he said, all undisturbed: "I think she has no recollection of having given it."

They had been standing with their faces to the fire, and after he had uttered these last words the master of the house turned round again to the room. Before Rosier had time to reply he perceived that a gentleman—a stranger—had just come in, unannounced, according to the Roman custom, and was about to present himself to his host. The latter smiled blandly, but somehow blankly; the visitor had a handsome face and a large, fair beard, and was evidently an Englishman.

"You apparently don't recognise me," he said with a smile that expressed more than Osmond's.

"Ah yes, now I do. I expected so little to see you."

Rosier departed and went in direct pursuit of Pansy. He sought her, as usual, in the neighbouring room, but he again encountered Mrs. Osmond in his path. He gave his hostess no greeting—he was too righteously indignant, but said to her crudely: "Your husband's awfully cold-blooded."

She gave the same mystical smile he had noticed before. "You can't expect every one to be as hot as yourself."

"I don't pretend to be cold, but I'm cool. What has he been doing to his daughter?"

"I've no idea."

"Don't you take any interest?" Rosier demanded with his sense that she too was irritating.

For a moment she answered nothing; then, "No!" she said abruptly and with a quickened light in her eyes which directly contradicted the word.

"Pardon me if I don't believe that. Where's Miss Osmond?"

"In the corner, making tea. Please leave her there."

Rosier instantly discovered his friend, who had been hidden by intervening groups. He watched her, but her own attention was entirely given to her occupation. "What on earth has he done to her?" he asked again imploringly. "He declares to me she has given me up."

"She has not given you up," Isabel said in a low tone and without looking at him.

"Ah, thank you for that! Now I'll leave her alone as long as you think proper!"

He had hardly spoken when he saw her change colour, and became aware that Osmond was coming toward her accompanied by the gentleman who had just entered. He judged the latter, in spite of the advantage of good looks and evident social experience, a little embarrassed. "Isabel," said her husband, "I bring you an old friend."

Mrs. Osmond's face, though it wore a smile, was, like her old friend's, not perfectly confident. "I'm very happy to see Lord Warburton," she said. Rosier turned away and, now that his talk with her had been interrupted, felt absolved from the little pledge he had just taken. He had a quick impression that Mrs. Osmond wouldn't notice what he did.

Isabel in fact, to do him justice, for some time quite ceased to observe him. She had been startled; she hardly knew if she felt a pleasure or a pain. Lord Warburton, however, now that he was face to face with her, was plainly quite sure of his own sense of the matter; though his grey eyes had still their fine original property of keeping recognition and attestation strictly sincere. He was "heavier" than of yore and looked older; he stood there very solidly and sensibly.

"I suppose you didn't expect to see me," he said; "I've but just arrived. Literally, I only got here this evening. You see I've lost no time in coming to pay you my respects. I knew you were at home on Thursdays."

"You see the fame of your Thursdays has spread to England," Osmond remarked to his wife.

"It's very kind of Lord Warburton to come so soon; we're greatly flattered," Isabel said.

"Ah well, it's better than stopping in one of those horrible inns," Osmond went on.

"The hotel seems very good; I think it's the same at which I saw you four years since. You know it was here in Rome that we first met; it's a long time ago. Do you remember where I bade you good-bye?" his lordship asked of his hostess. "It was in the Capitol, in the first room."

"I remember that myself," said Osmond. "I was there at the time."

"Yes, I remember you there. I was very sorry to leave Rome—so sorry that, somehow or other, it became almost a dismal memory, and I've never cared to come back till to-day. But I knew you were living here," her old friend went on to Isabel, "and I assure you I've often thought of you. It must be a charming place to live in," he added with a look, round him, at her established home, in which she might have caught the dim ghost of his old ruefulness.

"We should have been glad to see you at any time," Osmond observed with propriety.

"Thank you very much. I haven't been out of England since then. Till a month ago I really supposed my travels over."

"I've heard of you from time to time," said Isabel, who had already, with her rare capacity for such inward feats, taken the measure of what meeting him again meant for her.

"I hope you've heard no harm. My life has been a remarkably complete blank."

"Like the good reigns in history," Osmond suggested. He appeared to think his duties as a host now terminated—he had performed them so conscientiously. Nothing could have been more adequate, more nicely measured, than his courtesy to his wife's old friend. It was punctilious, it was explicit, it was everything but natural—a deficiency which Lord Warburton, who himself, had on the whole a good deal of nature, may be supposed to have perceived. "I'll leave you and Mrs. Osmond together," he added. "You have reminiscences into which I don't enter."

"I'm afraid you lose a good deal!" Lord Warburton called after him, as he moved away, in a tone which perhaps betrayed overmuch an appreciation of his generosity. Then the visitor turned on Isabel the deeper, the deepest, consciousness of his look, which gradually became more serious. "I'm really very glad to see you."

"It's very pleasant. You're very kind."

"Do you know that you're changed—a little?"

She just hesitated. "Yes—a good deal."

"I don't mean for the worse, of course; and yet how can I say for the better?"

"I think I shall have no scruple in saying that to *you*," she bravely returned.

"Ah well, for me—it's a long time. It would be a pity there shouldn't be something to show for it." They sat down and she asked him about his sisters, with other enquiries of a somewhat perfunctory kind. He answered her questions as if they interested him, and in a few moments she saw—or believed she saw—that he would press with less of his whole weight than of yore. Time had breathed upon his heart and, without chilling it, given it a relieved sense of having taken the air. Isabel felt her usual esteem for Time rise at a bound. Her friend's manner was certainly that of a contented man, one who would rather like people, or like her at least, to know him for such. "There's something I must tell you without more delay," he resumed. "I've brought Ralph Touchett with me."

"Brought him with you?" Isabel's surprise was great.

"He's at the hotel; he was too tired to come out and has gone to bed."

"I'll go to see him," she immediately said.

"That's exactly what I hoped you'd do. I had an idea you hadn't seen much of him since your marriage, that in fact your relations were a—a little more formal. That's why I hesitated—like an awkward Briton."

"I'm as fond of Ralph as ever," Isabel answered. "But why has he come to Rome?" The declaration was very gentle, the question a little sharp.

"Because he's very far gone, Mrs. Osmond."

"Rome then is no place for him. I heard from him that he had determined to give up his custom of wintering abroad and to remain in England, indoors, in what he called an artificial climate."

"Poor fellow, he doesn't succeed with the artificial! I went to see him three weeks ago, at Gardencourt, and found him thoroughly ill. He has been getting worse every year, and now he has no strength left. He smokes no more cigarettes! He had got up an artificial climate indeed; the house was as hot as Calcutta. Nevertheless he had suddenly taken it into his head to start for Sicily. I didn't believe in it—neither did the doctors, nor any of his friends. His mother, as I suppose you know, is in America, so there was no one to prevent him. He stuck to his idea that it would be the saving of him to spend the winter at Catania.[1] He said he could take servants and furniture, could make himself comfortable, but in point of fact he hasn't brought anything. I wanted him at least to go by sea, to save fatigue; but he said he hated the sea and wished to stop at Rome. After that, though I thought it all rubbish, I made up my mind to come with him. I'm acting as—what do you call it in America?—as a kind of moderator. Poor Ralph's very moderate now. We left England a fortnight ago, and he has been very bad on the way. He can't keep warm, and the further south we come the more he feels the cold. He has got rather a good man, but I'm afraid he's beyond human help. I wanted him to take with him some clever fellow— I mean some sharp young doctor; but he wouldn't hear of it. If you don't mind my saying so, I think it was a most extraordinary time for Mrs. Touchett to decide on going to America."

Isabel had listened eagerly; her face was full of pain and wonder. "My aunt does that at fixed periods and lets nothing turn her aside. When the date comes round she starts; I think she'd have started if Ralph had been dying."

"I sometimes think he *is* dying," Lord Warburton said.

Isabel sprang up. "I'll go to him then now."

He checked her; he was a little disconcerted at the quick effect of his words. "I don't mean I thought so to-night. On the contrary, to-day, in the train, he seemed particularly well; the idea of our reaching Rome—he's very fond of Rome, you know—gave him strength. An hour ago, when I bade him good-night, he told me he was very tired, but very happy. Go to him in the morning; that's all I mean. I didn't tell him I was coming here; I didn't decide to till after we had separated. Then I remembered he had told me you had an evening, and that it was this very Thursday. It occurred to me to come in and tell you he's here, and let you know you had perhaps better not wait for him to call. I think he said he hadn't written to you." There was no need of Isabel's declaring that she would act upon Lord Warburton's information; she looked, as she sat there, like a winged creature held back. "Let alone that I wanted to see you for myself," her visitor gallantly added.

"I don't understand Ralph's plan; it seems to me very wild," she said. "I was glad to think of him between those thick walls at Gardencourt."

"He was completely alone there; the thick walls were his only company."

"You went to see him; you've been extremely kind."

"Oh dear, I had nothing to do," said Lord Warburton.

"We hear, on the contrary, that you're doing great things. Every one speaks of you as a great statesman, and I'm perpetually seeing your name in the *Times*, which, by the way, doesn't appear to hold it in reverence. You're apparently as wild a radical as ever."

"I don't feel nearly so wild; you know the world has come round to me. Touchett and I have kept up a sort of parliamentary debate all the way

1. An ancient port on Sicily's east coast, at the foot of Mount Etna.

from London. I tell him he's the last of the Tories, and he calls me the King of the Goths[2]—says I have, down to the details of my personal appearance, every sign of the brute. So you see there's life in him yet."

Isabel had many questions to ask about Ralph, but she abstained from asking them all. She would see for herself on the morrow. She perceived that after a little Lord Warburton would tire of that subject—he had a conception of other possible topics. She was more and more able to say to herself that he had recovered, and, what is more to the point, she was able to say it without bitterness. He had been for her, of old, such an image of urgency, of insistence, of something to be resisted and reasoned with, that his reappearance at first menaced her with a new trouble. But she was now reassured; she could see he only wished to live with her on good terms, that she was to understand he had forgiven her and was incapable of the bad taste of making pointed allusions. This was not a form of revenge, of course; she had no suspicion of his wishing to punish her by an exhibition of disillusionment; she did him the justice to believe it had simply occurred to him that she would now take a good-natured interest in knowing he was resigned. It was the resignation of a healthy, manly nature, in which sentimental wounds could never fester. British politics had cured him; she had known they would. She gave an envious thought to the happier lot of men, who are always free to plunge into the healing waters of action. Lord Warburton of course spoke of the past, but he spoke of it without implications; he even went so far as to allude to their former meeting in Rome as a very jolly time. And he told her he had been immensely interested in hearing of her marriage and that it was a great pleasure for him to make Mr. Osmond's acquaintance—since he could hardly be said to have made it on the other occasion. He had not written to her at the time of that passage in her history, but he didn't apologise to her for this. The only thing he implied was that they were old friends, intimate friends. It was very much as an intimate friend that he said to her, suddenly, after a short pause which he had occupied in smiling, as he looked about him, like a person amused, at a provincial entertainment, by some innocent game of guesses—

"Well now, I suppose you're very happy and all that sort of thing?"

Isabel answered with a quick laugh; the tone of his remark struck her almost as the accent of comedy. "Do you suppose if I were not I'd tell you?"

"Well, I don't know. I don't see why not."

"I do then. Fortunately, however, I'm very happy."

"You've got an awfully good house."

"Yes, it's very pleasant. But that's not my merit—it's my husband's."

"You mean he has arranged it?"

"Yes, it was nothing when we came."

"He must be very clever."

"He has a genius for upholstery," said Isabel.

"There's a great rage for that sort of thing now. But you must have a taste of your own."

"I enjoy things when they're done, but I've no ideas. I can never propose anything."

---

2. I.e., someone bent on the destruction of all established order, as the Goths of late antiquity were long believed to have been. The edition of 1881 reads "head of the Communists."

"Do you mean you accept what others propose?"

"Very willingly, for the most part."

"That's a good thing to know. I shall propose to you something."

"It will be very kind. I must say, however, that I've in a few small ways a certain initiative. I should like for instance to introduce you to some of these people."

"Oh, please don't; I prefer sitting here. Unless it be to that young lady in the blue dress. She has a charming face."

"The one talking to the rosy young man? That's my husband's daughter."

"Lucky man, your husband. What a dear little maid!"

"You must make her acquaintance."

"In a moment—with pleasure. I like looking at her from here." He ceased to look at her, however, very soon; his eyes constantly reverted to Mrs. Osmond. "Do you know I was wrong just now in saying you had changed?" he presently went on. "You seem to me, after all, very much the same."

"And yet I find it a great change to be married," said Isabel with mild gaiety.

"It affects most people more than it has affected you. You see I haven't gone in for that."

"It rather surprises me."

"You ought to understand it, Mrs. Osmond. But I do want to marry," he added more simply.

"It ought to be very easy," Isabel said, rising—after which she reflected, with a pang perhaps too visible, that she was hardly the person to say this. It was perhaps because Lord Warburton divined the pang that he generously forbore to call her attention to her not having contributed then to the facility.

Edward Rosier had meanwhile seated himself on an ottoman beside Pansy's tea-table. He pretended at first to talk to her about trifles, and she asked him who was the new gentleman conversing with her stepmother.

"He's an English lord," said Rosier. "I don't know more."

"I wonder if he'll have some tea. The English are so fond of tea."

"Never mind that; I've something particular to say to you."

"Don't speak so loud—every one will hear," said Pansy.

"They won't hear if you continue to look that way; as if your only thought in life was the wish the kettle would boil."

"It has just been filled; the servants never know!"—and she sighed with the weight of her responsibility.

"Do you know what your father said to me just now? That you didn't mean what you said a week ago."

"I don't mean everything I say. How can a young girl do that? But I mean what I say to *you*."

"He told me you had forgotten me."

"Ah no, I don't forget," said Pansy, showing her pretty teeth in a fixed smile.

"Then everything's just the very same?"

"Ah no, not the very same. Papa has been terribly severe."

"What has he done to you?"

"He asked me what *you* had done to me, and I told him everything. Then he forbade me to marry you."

"You needn't mind that."

"Oh yes, I must indeed. I can't disobey papa."

"Not for one who loves you as I do, and whom you pretend to love?"

She raised the lid of the tea-pot, gazing into this vessel for a moment; then she dropped six words into its aromatic depths. "I love you just as much."

"What good will that do me?"

"Ah," said Pansy, raising her sweet, vague eyes, "I don't know that."

"You disappoint me," groaned poor Rosier.

She was silent a little; she handed a tea-cup to a servant. "Please don't talk any more."

"Is this to be all my satisfaction?"

"Papa said I was not to talk with you."

"Do you sacrifice me like that? Ah, it's too much!"

"I wish you'd wait a little," said the girl in a voice just distinct enough to betray a quaver.

"Of course I'll wait if you'll give me hope. But you take my life away."

"I'll not give you up—oh no!" Pansy went on.

"He'll try and make you marry some one else."

"I'll never do that."

"What then are we to wait for?"

She hesitated again. "I'll speak to Mrs. Osmond and she'll help us." It was in this manner that she for the most part designated her stepmother.

"She won't help us much. She's afraid."

"Afraid of what?"

"Of your father, I suppose."

Pansy shook her little head. "She's not afraid of any one. We must have patience."

"Ah, that's an awful word," Rosier groaned; he was deeply disconcerted. Oblivious of the customs of good society, he dropped his head into his hands and, supporting it with a melancholy grace, sat staring at the carpet. Presently he became aware of a good deal of movement about him and, as he looked up, saw Pansy making a curtsey—it was still her little curtsey of the convent—to the English lord whom Mrs. Osmond had introduced.

Chapter XXXIX

It will probably not surprise the reflective reader that Ralph Touchett should have seen less of his cousin since her marriage than he had done before that event—an event of which he took such a view as could hardly prove a confirmation of intimacy. He had uttered his thought, as we know, and after this had held his peace, Isabel not having invited him to resume a discussion which marked an era in their relations. That discussion had made a difference—the difference he feared rather than the one he hoped. It had not chilled the girl's zeal in carrying out her engagement, but it had come dangerously near to spoiling a friendship. No reference was ever again made between them to Ralph's opinion of Gilbert Osmond, and by surrounding this topic with a sacred silence they managed to preserve a semblance of reciprocal frankness. But there was a difference, as Ralph often said to himself—there was a difference. She had not forgiven him, she never would forgive him: that was all he had gained. She thought she had forgiven him; she believed she didn't care; and as she was both very generous and very proud these convictions represented a certain reality. But whether or no the event should justify him he would virtually have done her a wrong, and the wrong was of the sort that women remember best. As Osmond's wife she could never again be his friend. If in this character she should enjoy the felicity she expected, she would have nothing but contempt for the man who had attempted, in advance, to undermine a blessing so dear; and if on the other hand his warning should be justified the vow she had taken that he should never know it would lay upon her spirit such a burden as to make her hate him. So dismal had been, during the year that followed his cousin's marriage, Ralph's prevision of the future; and if his meditations appear morbid we must remember he was not in the bloom of health. He consoled himself as he might by behaving (as he deemed) beautifully, and was present at the ceremony by which Isabel was united to Mr. Osmond, and which was performed in Florence in the month of June. He learned from his mother that Isabel at first had thought of celebrating her nuptials in her native land, but that as simplicity was what she chiefly desired to secure she had finally decided, in spite of Osmond's professed willingness to make a journey of any length, that this characteristic would be best embodied in their being married by the nearest clergyman in the shortest time. The thing was done therefore at the little American chapel, on a very hot day, in the presence only of Mrs. Touchett and her son, of Pansy Osmond and the Countess Gemini. That severity in the proceedings of which I just spoke was in part the result of the absence of two persons who might have been looked for on the occasion and who would have lent it a certain richness. Madame Merle had been invited, but Madame Merle, who was unable to leave Rome, had written a gracious letter of excuses. Henrietta Stackpole had not been invited, as her departure from America, announced to Isabel by Mr. Goodwood, was in fact frustrated by the duties of her profession; but she had sent a letter, less gracious than Madame Merle's, intimating that, had she been able to cross the Atlantic, she would have been present not only as a witness but as a critic. Her return to Europe had taken place somewhat later, and she had effected a meeting with Isabel in the autumn, in Paris, when she had indulged—perhaps a trifle too freely—her critical genius. Poor Osmond, who was chiefly the subject of it, had protested so sharply that Henrietta was obliged to declare to Isabel that she had taken a step which put a barrier between them. "It isn't in the least that you've married—it is that you have married *him*," she had deemed it her duty to remark; agreeing, it will be seen, much more with Ralph Touchett than she suspected, though she had few of his hesitations and compunctions. Henrietta's second visit to Europe, however, was not apparently to have been made in vain; for just at the moment when Osmond had declared to Isabel that he really must object to that newspaper-woman, and Isabel had answered that it seemed to her he took Henrietta too hard, the good Mr. Bantling had appeared upon the scene and proposed that they should take a run down to Spain. Henrietta's letters from Spain had proved the most acceptable she had yet published, and there had been one in especial, dated from the

Alhambra[1] and entitled 'Moors and Moonlight,' which generally passed for her masterpiece. Isabel had been secretly disappointed at her husband's not seeing his way simply to take the poor girl for funny. She even wondered if his sense of fun, or of the funny—which would be his sense of humour, wouldn't it?—were by chance defective. Of course she herself looked at the matter as a person whose present happiness had nothing to grudge to Henrietta's violated conscience. Osmond had thought their alliance a kind of monstrosity; he couldn't imagine what they had in common. For him, Mr. Bantling's fellow tourist was simply the most vulgar of women, and he had also pronounced her the most abandoned. Against this latter clause of the verdict Isabel had appealed with an ardour that had made him wonder afresh at the oddity of some of his wife's tastes. Isabel could explain it only by saying that she liked to know people who were as different as possible from herself. "Why then don't you make the acquaintance of your washerwoman?" Osmond had enquired; to which Isabel had answered that she was afraid her washerwoman wouldn't care for her. Now Henrietta cared so much.

Ralph had seen nothing of her for the greater part of the two years that had followed her marriage; the winter that formed the beginning of her residence in Rome he had spent again at San Remo, where he had been joined in the spring by his mother, who afterwards had gone with him to England, to see what they were doing at the bank—an operation she couldn't induce him to perform. Ralph had taken a lease of his house at San Remo, a small villa which he had occupied still another winter; but late in the month of April of this second year he had come down to Rome. It was the first time since her marriage that he had stood face to face with Isabel; his desire to see her again was then of the keenest. She had written to him from time to time, but her letters told him nothing he wanted to know. He had asked his mother what she was making of her life, and his mother had simply answered that she supposed she was making the best of it. Mrs. Touchett had not the imagination that communes with the unseen, and she now pretended to no intimacy with her niece, whom she rarely encountered. This young woman appeared to be living in a sufficiently honourable way, but Mrs. Touchett still remained of the opinion that her marriage had been a shabby affair. It had given her no pleasure to think of Isabel's establishment, which she was sure was a very lame business. From time to time, in Florence, she rubbed against the Countess Gemini, doing her best always to minimise the contact; and the Countess reminded her of Osmond, who make her think of Isabel. The Countess was less talked of in these days; but Mrs. Touchett augured no good of that: it only proved how she had been talked of before. There was a more direct suggestion of Isabel in the person of Madame Merle; but Madame Merle's relations with Mrs. Touchett had undergone a perceptible change. Isabel's aunt had told her, without circumlocution, that she had played too ingenious a part; and Madame Merle, who never quarrelled with any one, who appeared to think no one worth it, and who had performed the miracle of living, more or less, for several years with Mrs. Touchett and

---

1. A thirteenth-century palace complex built by the Muslim rulers of Granada in the south of Spain. For American readers the site was popularized by Washington Irving's *Tales of the Alhambra* (1832), and Henrietta's title is a touristic cliché.

showing no symptom of irritation—Madame Merle now took a very high tone and declared that this was an accusation from which she couldn't stoop to defend herself. She added, however (without stooping), that her behaviour had been only too simple, that she had believed only what she saw, that she saw Isabel was not eager to marry and Osmond not eager to please (his repeated visits had been nothing; he was boring himself to death on his hill-top and he came merely for amusement). Isabel had kept her sentiments to herself, and her journey to Greece and Egypt had effectually thrown dust in her companion's eyes. Madame Merle accepted the event—she was unprepared to think of it as a scandal; but that she had played any part in it, double or single, was an imputation against which she proudly protested. It was doubtless in consequence of Mrs. Touchett's attitude, and of the injury it offered to habits consecrated by many charming seasons, that Madame Merle had, after this, chosen to pass many months in England, where her credit was quite unimpaired. Mrs. Touchett had done her a wrong; there are some things that can't be forgiven. But Madame Merle suffered in silence; there was always something exquisite in her dignity.

Ralph, as I say, had wished to see for himself; but while engaged in this pursuit he had yet felt afresh what a fool he had been to put the girl on her guard. He had played the wrong card, and now he had lost the game. He should see nothing, he should learn nothing; for him she would always wear a mask. His true line would have been to profess delight in her union, so that later, when, as Ralph phrased it, the bottom should fall out of it, she might have the pleasure of saying to him that he had been a goose. He would gladly have consented to pass for a goose in order to know Isabel's real situation. At present, however, she neither taunted him with his fallacies nor pretended that her own confidence was justified; if she wore a mask it completely covered her face. There was something fixed and mechanical in the serenity painted on it; this was not an expression, Ralph said—it was a representation, it was even an advertisement. She had lost her child; that was a sorrow, but it was a sorrow she scarcely spoke of; there was more to say about it than she could say to Ralph. It belonged to the past, moreover; it had occurred six months before and she had already laid aside the tokens of mourning. She appeared to be leading the life of the world; Ralph heard her spoken of as having a "charming position." He observed that she produced the impression of being peculiarly enviable, that it was supposed, among many people, to be a privilege even to know her. Her house was not open to every one, and she had an evening in the week to which people were not invited as a matter of course. She lived with a certain magnificence, but you needed to be a member of her circle to perceive it; for there was nothing to gape at, nothing to criticise, nothing even to admire, in the daily proceedings of Mr. and Mrs. Osmond. Ralph, in all this, recognised the hand of the master; for he knew that Isabel had no faculty for producing studied impressions. She struck him as having a great love of movement, of gaiety, of late hours, of long rides, of fatigue; an eagerness to be entertained, to be interested, even to be bored, to make acquaintances, to see people who were talked about, to explore the neighbourhood of Rome, to enter into relation with certain of the mustiest relics of its old society. In all this there was much less discrimination than in that desire for comprehensiveness of development on which he had been used to exercise his wit. There was a kind of violence in some of her impulses, of crudity in some of her experiments, which took him by surprise: it seemed to him that she even spoke faster, moved faster, breathed faster, than before her marriage. Certainly she had fallen into exaggerations—she who used to care so much for the pure truth; and whereas of old she had a great delight in good-humoured argument, in intellectual play (she never looked so charming as when in the genial heat of discussion she received a crushing blow full in the face and brushed it away as a feather), she appeared now to think there was nothing worth people's either differing about or agreeing upon. Of old she had been curious, and now she was indifferent, and yet in spite of her indifference her activity was greater than ever. Slender still, but lovelier than before, she had gained no great maturity of aspect; yet there was an amplitude and a brilliancy in her personal arrangements that gave a touch of insolence to her beauty. Poor human-hearted Isabel, what perversity had bitten her? Her light step drew a mass of drapery behind it; her intelligent head sustained a majesty of ornament. The free, keen girl had become quite another person; what he saw was the fine lady who was supposed to represent something. What did Isabel represent? Ralph asked himself; and he could only answer by saying that she represented Gilbert Osmond. "Good heavens, what a function," he then woefully exclaimed. He was lost in wonder at the mystery of things.

He recognised Osmond, as I say; he recognised him at every turn. He saw how he kept all things within limits; how he adjusted, regulated, animated their manner of life. Osmond was in his element; at last he had material to work with. He always had an eye to effect, and his effects were deeply calculated. They were produced by no vulgar means, but the motive was as vulgar as the art was great. To surround his interior with a sort of invidious sanctity, to tantalise society with a sense of exclusion, to make people believe his house was different from every other, to impart to the face that he presented to the world a cold originality—this was the ingenious effort of the personage to whom Isabel had attributed a superior morality. "He works with superior material," Ralph said to himself; "it's rich abundance compared with his former resources." Ralph was a clever man; but Ralph had never—to his own sense—been so clever as when he observed, *in petto,*[2] that under the guise of caring only for intrinsic values Osmond lived exclusively for the world. Far from being its master as he pretended to be, he was its very humble servant, and the degree of its attention was his only measure of success. He lived with his eye on it from morning till night, and the world was so stupid it never suspected the trick. Everything he did was *pose*—*pose* so subtly considered that if one were not on the lookout one mistook it for impulse. Ralph had never met a man who lived so much in the land of consideration. His tastes, his studies, his accomplishments, his collections, were all for a purpose. His life on his hill-top at Florence had been the conscious attitude of years. His solitude, his ennui, his love for his daughter, his good manners, his bad manners, were so many features of a mental image constantly present to him as a model of impertinence and mystification. His ambition was not to

2. To himself (Italian).

please the world, but to please himself by exciting the world's curiosity
and then declining to satisfy it. It had made him feel great, ever, to play
the world a trick. The thing he had done in his life most directly to please
himself was his marrying Miss Archer; though in this case indeed the gullible world was in a manner embodied in poor Isabel, who had been mystified to the top of her bent. Ralph of course found a fitness in being
consistent; he had embraced a creed, and as he had suffered for it he could
not in honour forsake it. I give this little sketch of its articles for what they
may at the time have been worth. It was certain that he was very skilful
in fitting the facts to his theory—even the fact that during the month he
spent in Rome at this period the husband of the woman he loved appeared
to regard him not in the least as an enemy.

For Gilbert Osmond Ralph had not now that importance. It was not that
he had the importance of a friend; it was rather that he had none at all.
He was Isabel's cousin and he was rather unpleasantly ill—it was on this
basis that Osmond treated with him. He made the proper enquiries, asked
about his health, about Mrs. Touchett, about his opinion of winter climates, whether he were comfortable at his hotel. He addressed him, on
the few occasions of their meeting, not a word that was not necessary; but
his manner had always the urbanity proper to conscious success in the
presence of conscious failure. For all this, Ralph had had, toward the end,
a sharp inward vision of Osmond's making it of small ease to his wife that
she should continue to receive Mr. Touchett. He was not jealous—he had
not that excuse; no one could be jealous of Ralph. But he made Isabel pay
for her old-time kindness, of which so much was still left; and as Ralph
had no idea of her paying too much, so when his suspicion had become
sharp, he had taken himself off. In doing so he had deprived Isabel of a
very interesting occupation: she had been constantly wondering what fine
principle was keeping him alive. She had decided that it was his love of
conversation; his conversation had been better than ever. He had given
up walking; he was no longer a humorous stroller. He sat all day in a
chair—almost any chair would serve, and was so dependent on what you
would do for him that, had not his talk been highly contemplative, you
might have thought he was blind. The reader already knows more about
him than Isabel was ever to know, and the reader may therefore be given
the key to the mystery. What kept Ralph alive was simply the fact that he
had not yet seen enough of the person in the world in whom he was most
interested: he was not yet satisfied. There was more to come; he couldn't
make up his mind to lose that. He wanted to see what she would make of
her husband—or what her husband would make of her. This was only the
first act of the drama, and he was determined to sit out the performance.
His determination had held good; it had kept him going some eighteen
months more, till the time of his return to Rome with Lord Warburton. It
had given him indeed such an air of intending to live indefinitely that
Mrs. Touchett, though more accessible to confusions of thought in the
matter of this strange, unremunerative—and unremunerated—son of hers
than she had ever been before, had, as we have learned, not scrupled to
embark for a distant land. If Ralph had been kept alive by suspense it was
with a good deal of the same emotion—the excitement of wondering in
what state she should find him—that Isabel mounted to his apartment the
day after Lord Warburton had notified her of his arrival in Rome.

She spent an hour with him; it was the first of several visits. Gilbert Osmond called on him punctually, and on their sending their carriage for him Ralph came more than once to Palazzo Roccanera. A fortnight elapsed, at the end of which Ralph announced to Lord Warburton that he thought after all he wouldn't go to Sicily. The two men had been dining together after a day spent by the latter in ranging about the Campagna.[3] They had left the table, and Warburton, before the chimney, was lighting a cigar, which he instantly removed from his lips.

"Won't go to Sicily? Where then will you go?"

"Well, I guess I won't go anywhere," said Ralph, from the sofa, all shamelessly.

"Do you mean you'll return to England?"

"Oh dear no; I'll stay in Rome."

"Rome won't do for you. Rome's not warm enough."

"It will have to do. I'll make it do. See how well I've been."

Lord Warburton looked at him a while, puffing a cigar and as if trying to see it. "You've been better than you were on the journey, certainly. I wonder how you lived through that. But I don't understand your condition. I recommend you to try Sicily."

"I can't try," said poor Ralph. "I've done trying. I can't move further. I can't face that journey. Fancy me between Scylla and Charybdis![4] I don't want to die on the Sicilian plains—to be snatched away, like Proserpine[5] in the same locality, to the Plutonian shades."

"What the deuce then did you come for?" his lordship enquired.

"Because the idea took me. I see it won't do. It really doesn't matter where I am now. I've exhausted all remedies, I've swallowed all climates. As I'm here I'll stay. I haven't a single cousin in Sicily—much less a married one."

"Your cousin's certainly an inducement. But what does the doctor say?"

"I haven't asked him, and I don't care a fig. If I die here Mrs. Osmond will bury me. But I shall not die here."

"I hope not." Lord Warburton continued to smoke reflectively. "Well, I must say," he resumed, "for myself I'm very glad you don't insist on Sicily. I had a horror of that journey."

"Ah, but for you it needn't have mattered. I had no idea of dragging you in my train."

"I certainly didn't mean to let you go alone."

"My dear Warburton, I never expected you to come further than this," Ralph cried.

"I should have gone with you and seen you settled," said Lord Warburton.

"You're a very good Christian. You're a very kind man."

"Then I should have come back here."

"And then you'd have gone to England."

3. The countryside around Rome, heavily marked with ancient ruins. James was fond of going over it on horseback; see the selection from his "Roman Rides" in this Norton Critical Edition, pp. 442–45.
4. In the *Odyssey*, Odysseus had to sail between the monster Scylla and the whirlpool Charybdis, a narrow passage usually understood as that through the Strait of Messina, which divide Sicily from Italy proper.
5. The Roman name for Persephone, who is believed to have been seized by Hades as she gathered flowers near the town of Enna in central Sicily.

"No, no; I should have stayed."

"Well," said Ralph, "if that's what we are both up to, I don't see where Sicily comes in!"

His companion was silent; he sat staring at the fire. At last, looking up, "I say, tell me this," he broke out; "did you really mean to go to Sicily when we started?"

"Ah, *vous m'en demandez trop!*[6] Let me put a question first. Did you come with me quite—platonically?"

"I don't know what you mean by that. I wanted to come abroad."

"I suspect we've each been playing our little game."

"Speak for yourself. I made no secret whatever of my desiring to be here a while."

"Yes, I remember you said you wished to see the Minister of Foreign Affairs."

"I've seen him three times. He's very amusing."

"I think you've forgotten what you came for," said Ralph.

"Perhaps I have," his companion answered rather gravely.

These two were gentlemen of a race which is not distinguished by the absence of reserve, and they had travelled together from London to Rome without an allusion to matters that were uppermost in the mind of each. There was an old subject they had once discussed, but it had lost its recognised place in their attention, and even after their arrival in Rome, where many things led back to it, they had kept the same half-diffident, half-confident silence.

"I recommend you to get the doctor's consent, all the same," Lord Warburton went on, abruptly, after an interval.

"The doctor's consent will spoil it. I never have it when I can help it."

"What then does Mrs. Osmond think?" Ralph's friend demanded.

"I've not told her. She'll probably say that Rome's too cold and even offer to go with me to Catania. She's capable of that."

"In your place I should like it."

"Her husband won't like it."

"Ah well, I can fancy that; though it seems to me you're not bound to mind his likings. They're his affair."

"I don't want to make any more trouble between them," said Ralph.

"Is there so much already?"

"There's complete preparation for it. Her going off with me would make the explosion. Osmond isn't fond of his wife's cousin."

"Then of course he'd make a row. But won't he make a row if you stop here?"

"That's what I want to see. He made one the last time I was in Rome, and then I thought it my duty to disappear. Now I think it's my duty to stop and defend her."

"My dear Touchett, your defensive powers—!" Lord Warburton began with a smile. But he saw something in his companion's face that checked him. "Your duty, in these premises, seems to me rather a nice question," he observed instead.

Ralph for a short time answered nothing. "It's true that my defensive powers are small," he returned at last; "but as my aggressive ones are still

6. You ask too much! (French).

smaller Osmond may after all not think me worth his gunpowder. At any rate," he added, "there are things I'm curious to see."

"You're sacrificing your health to your curiosity then?"

"I'm not much interested in my health, and I'm deeply interested in Mrs. Osmond."

"So am I. But not as I once was," Lord Warburton added quickly. This was one of the allusions he had not hitherto found occasion to make.

"Does she strike you as very happy?" Ralph enquired, emboldened by this confidence.

"Well, I don't know; I've hardly thought. She told me the other night she was happy."

"Ah, she told *you*, of course," Ralph exclaimed, smiling.

"I don't know that. It seems to me I was rather the sort of person she might have complained to."

"Complained? She'll never complain. She has done it—what she *has* done—and she knows it. She'll complain to you least of all. She's very careful."

"She needn't be. I don't mean to make love to her again."

"I'm delighted to hear it. There can be no doubt at least of *your* duty."

"Ah no," said Lord Warburton gravely; "none!"

"Permit me to ask," Ralph went on, "whether it's to bring out the fact that you don't mean to make love to her that you're so very civil to the little girl?"

Lord Warburton gave a slight start; he got up and stood before the fire, looking at it hard. "Does that strike you as very ridiculous?"

"Ridiculous? Not in the least, if you really like her."

"I think her a delightful little person. I don't know when a girl of that age has pleased me more."

"She's a charming creature. Ah, she at least is genuine."

"Of course there's the difference in our ages—more than twenty years."

"My dear Warburton," said Ralph, "are you serious?"

"Perfectly serious—as far as I've got."

"I'm very glad. And, heaven help us," cried Ralph, "how cheered-up old Osmond will be!"

His companion frowned. "I say, don't spoil it. I shouldn't propose for his daughter to please *him*."

"He'll have the perversity to be pleased all the same."

"He's not so fond of me as that," said his lordship.

"As that? My dear Warburton, the drawback of your position is that people needn't be fond of you at all to wish to be connected with you. Now, with me in such a case, I should have the happy confidence that they loved me."

Lord Warburton seemed scarcely in the mood for doing justice to general axioms—he was thinking of a special case. "Do you judge she'll be pleased?"

"The girl herself? Delighted, surely."

"No, no; I mean Mrs. Osmond."

Ralph looked at him a moment. "My dear fellow, what has she to do with it?"

"Whatever she chooses. She's very fond of Pansy."

"Very true—very true." And Ralph slowly got up. "It's an interesting question—how far her fondness for Pansy will carry her." He stood there a moment with his hands in his pockets and rather a clouded brow. "I hope, you know, that you're very—very sure. The deuce!" he broke off. "I don't know how to say it."

"Yes, you do; you know how to say everything."

"Well, it's awkward. I hope you're sure that among Miss Osmond's merits her being—a—so near her stepmother isn't a leading one?"

"Good heavens, Touchett!" cried Lord Warburton angrily, "for what do you take me?"

Chapter XL

Isabel had not seen much of Madame Merle since her marriage, this lady having indulged in frequent absences from Rome. At one time she had spent six months in England; at another she had passed a portion of a winter in Paris. She had made numerous visits to distant friends and gave countenance to the idea that for the future she should be a less inveterate Roman than in the past. As she had been inveterate in the past only in the sense of constantly having an apartment in one of the sunniest niches of the Pincian[1]—an apartment which often stood empty—this suggested a prospect of almost constant absence; a danger which Isabel at one period had been much inclined to deplore. Familiarity had modified in some degree her first impression of Madame Merle, but it had not essentially altered it; there was still much wonder of admiration in it. That personage was armed at all points; it was a pleasure to see a character so completely equipped for the social battle. She carried her flag discreetly, but her weapons were polished steel, and she used them with a skill which struck Isabel as more and more that of a veteran. She was never weary, never overcome with disgust; she never appeared to need rest or consolation. She had her own ideas; she had of old exposed a great many of them to Isabel, who knew also that under an appearance of extreme self-control her highly-cultivated friend concealed a rich sensibility. But her will was mistress of her life; there was something gallant in the way she kept going. It was as if she had learned the secret of it—as if the art of life were some clever trick she had guessed. Isabel, as she herself grew older, became acquainted with revulsions, with disgusts; there were days when the world looked black and she asked herself with some sharpness what it was that she was pretending to live for. Her old habit had been to live by enthusiasm, to fall in love with suddenly-perceived possibilities, with the idea of some new adventure. As a younger person she had been used to proceed from one little exaltation to the other: there were scarcely any dull places between. But Madame Merle had suppressed enthusiasm; she fell in love now-a-days with nothing; she lived entirely by reason and by wisdom. There were hours when Isabel would have given anything for lessons in this art; if her brilliant friend had been near she would have made an appeal

---

1. The Pincian Hill, in the city's northeast, can be climbed from either the Piazza del Popolo or the Spanish Steps, and from its top one can also access the Villa Borghese. A favorite promenade in nineteenth-century Rome, it figures in "Daisy Miller" and was a part of what was known as the "Strangers' Quarter"—that is, those parts of the city favored as a residence by foreign visitors. The Osmonds' Palazzo Roccanera lies, in contrast, in a more purely Roman quarter.

to her. She had become aware more than before of the advantage of being like that—of having made one's self a firm surface, a sort of corselet of silver.

But, as I say, it was not till the winter during which we lately renewed acquaintance with our heroine that the personage in question made again a continuous stay in Rome. Isabel now saw more of her than she had done since her marriage; but by this time Isabel's needs and inclinations had considerably changed. It was not at present to Madame Merle that she would have applied for instruction; she had lost the desire to know this lady's clever trick. If she had troubles she must keep them to herself, and if life was difficult it would not make it easier to confess herself beaten. Madame Merle was doubtless of great use to herself and an ornament to any circle; but was she—would she be—of use to others in periods of refined embarrassment? The best way to profit by her friend—this indeed Isabel had always thought—was to imitate her, to be as firm and bright as she. She recognised no embarrassments, and Isabel, considering this fact, determined for the fiftieth time to brush aside her own. It seemed to her too, on the renewal of an intercourse which had virtually been interrupted, that her old ally was different, was almost detached—pushing to the extreme a certain rather artifical fear of being indiscreet. Ralph Touchett, we know, had been of the opinion that she was prone to exaggeration, to forcing the note—was apt, in the vulgar phrase, to overdo it. Isabel had never admitted this charge—had never indeed quite understood it; Madame Merle's conduct, to her perception, always bore the stamp of good taste, was always "quiet." But in this matter of not wishing to intrude upon the inner life of the Osmond family it at last occurred to our young woman that she overdid a little. That of course was not the best taste; that was rather violent. She remembered too much that Isabel was married; that she had now other interests; that though she, Madame Merle, had known Gilbert Osmond and his little Pansy very well, better almost than any one, she was not after all of the inner circle. She was on her guard; she never spoke of their affairs till she was asked, even pressed—as when her opinion was wanted; she had a dread of seeming to meddle. Madame Merle was as candid as we know, and one day she candidly expressed this dread to Isabel.

"I *must* be on my guard," she said; "I might so easily, without suspecting it, offend you. You would be right to be offended, even if my intention should have been of the purest. I must not forget that I knew your husband long before you did; I must not let that betray me. If you were a silly woman you might be jealous. You're not a silly woman; I know that perfectly. But neither am I; therefore I'm determined not to get into trouble. A little harm's very soon done; a mistake's made before one knows it. Of course if I had wished to make love to your husband I had ten years to do it in, and nothing to prevent; so it isn't likely I shall begin to-day, when I'm so much less attractive than I was. But if I were to annoy you by seeming to take a place that doesn't belong to me, you wouldn't make that reflection, you'd simply say I was forgetting certain differences. I'm determined not to forget them. Certainly a good friend isn't always thinking of that; one doesn't suspect one's friends of injustice. I don't suspect you, my dear, in the least; but I suspect human nature. Don't think I make myself uncomfortable; I'm not always watching myself. I think I sufficiently prove it in talking to you as I do now. All I wish to say is, however, that if you were to be jealous—that's the form it would take—I should be sure to think it was a little my fault. It certainly wouldn't be your husband's."

Isabel had had three years to think over Mrs. Touchett's theory that Madame Merle had made Gilbert Osmond's marriage. We know how she had at first received it. Madame Merle might have made Gilbert Osmond's marriage, but she certainly had not made Isabel Archer's. That was the work of—Isabel scarcely knew what: of nature, providence, fortune, of the eternal mystery of things. It was true her aunt's complaint had been not so much of Madame Merle's activity as of her duplicity: she had brought about the strange event and then she had denied her guilt. Such a guilt would not have been great, to Isabel's mind; she couldn't make a crime of Madame Merle's having been the producing cause of the most important friendship she had ever formed. This had occurred to her just before her marriage, after her little discussion with her aunt and at a time when she was still capable of that large inward reference, the tone almost of the philosophic historian, to her scant young annals. If Madame Merle had desired her change of state she could only say it had been a very happy thought. With her, moreover, she had been perfectly straightforward; she had never concealed her high opinion of Gilbert Osmond. After their union Isabel discovered that her husband took a less convenient view of the matter; he seldom consented to finger, in talk, this roundest and smoothest bead of their social rosary.

"Don't you like Madame Merle?" Isabel had once said to him. "She thinks a great deal of you."

"I'll tell you once for all," Osmond had answered. "I liked her once better than I do to-day. I'm tired of her, and I'm rather ashamed of it. She's so almost unnaturally good! I'm glad she's not in Italy; it makes for relaxation—for a sort of moral *détente*. Don't talk of her too much; it seems to bring her back. She'll come back in plenty of time."

Madame Merle, in fact, had come back before it was too late—too late, I mean, to recover whatever advantage she might have lost. But meantime, if, as I have said, she was sensibly different, Isabel's feelings were also not quite the same. Her consciousness of the situation was as acute as of old, but it was much less satisfying. A dissatisfied mind, whatever else it may miss, is rarely in want of reasons; they bloom as thick as buttercups in June. The fact of Madame Merle's having had a hand in Gilbert Osmond's marriage ceased to be one of her titles to consideration; it might have been written, after all, that there was not so much to thank her for. As time went on there was less and less, and Isabel once said to herself that perhaps without her these things would not have been. That reflection indeed was instantly stifled; she knew an immediate horror at having made it. "Whatever happens to me let me not be unjust," she said; "let me bear my burdens myself and not shift them upon others!" This disposition was tested, eventually, by that ingenious apology for her present conduct which Madame Merle saw fit to make and of which I have given a sketch; for there was something irritating—there was almost an air of mockery—in her neat discriminations and clear convictions. In Isabel's mind to-day there was nothing clear; there was a confusion of regrets, a complication of fears. She felt helpless as she turned away from her friend, who had just made the statements I have quoted: Madame Merle knew so little what she was thinking of! She was herself moreover so unable to explain. Jealous of her—jealous of her with Gilbert? The idea just then suggested no near reality. She almost wished jealousy had been possible; it would have made in a manner for refreshment. Wasn't it in a manner one of the symptoms of happiness? Madame Merle, however, was wise, so wise that she might have been pretending to know Isabel better than Isabel knew herself. This young woman had always been fertile in resolutions—many of them of an elevated character; but at no period had they flourished (in the privacy of her heart) more richly than to-day. It is true that they all had a family likeness; they might have been summed up in the determination that if she was to be unhappy it should not be by a fault of her own. Her poor winged spirit had always had a great desire to do its best, and it had not as yet been seriously discouraged. It wished, therefore, to hold fast to justice—not to pay itself by petty revenges. To associate Madame Merle with its disappointment would be a petty revenge—especially as the pleasure to be derived from that would be perfectly insincere. It might feed her sense of bitterness, but it would not loosen her bonds. It was impossible to pretend that she had not acted with her eyes open; if ever a girl was a free agent she had been. A girl in love was doubtless not a free agent; but the sole source of her mistake had been within herself. There had been no plot, no snare; she had looked and considered and chosen. When a woman had made such a mistake, there was only one way to repair it—just immensely (oh, with the highest grandeur!) to accept it. One folly was enough, especially when it was to last for ever; a second one would not much set it off. In this vow of reticence there was a certain nobleness which kept Isabel going; but Madame Merle had been right, for all that, in taking her precautions.

One day about a month after Ralph Touchett's arrival in Rome Isabel came back from a walk with Pansy. It was not only a part of her general determination to be just that she was at present very thankful for Pansy—it was also a part of her tenderness for things that were pure and weak. Pansy was dear to her, and there was nothing else in her life that had the rightness of the young creature's attachment or the sweetness of her own clearness about it. It was like a soft presence—like a small hand in her own; on Pansy's part it was more than an affection—it was a kind of ardent coercive faith. On her own side her sense of the girl's dependence was more than a pleasure; it operated as a definite reason when motives threatened to fail her. She had said to herself that we must take our duty where we find it, and that we must look for it as much as possible. Pansy's sympathy was a direct admonition; it seemed to say that here was an opportunity, not eminent perhaps, but unmistakable. Yet an opportunity for what Isabel could hardly have said; in general, to be more for the child than the child was able to be for herself. Isabel could have smiled, in these days, to remember that her little companion had once been ambiguous, for she now perceived that Pansy's ambiguities were simply her own grossness of vision. She had been unable to believe any one could care so much—so extraordinarily much—to please. But since then she had seen this delicate faculty in operation, and now she knew what to think of it. It was the whole creature—it was a sort of genius. Pansy had no pride to interfere with it, and though she was constantly extending her conquests she took no credit for them. The two were constantly together; Mrs. Osmond was rarely seen without her stepdaughter. Isabel liked her company; it had the effect of one's carrying a nosegay composed all of the same flower. And then not to neglect Pansy, not under any provocation to neglect her—this she had made an article of religion. The young girl had every appearance of being happier in Isabel's society than in that of any one save her father, whom she admired with an intensity justified by the fact that, as paternity was an exquisite pleasure to Gilbert Osmond, he had always been luxuriously mild. Isabel knew how Pansy liked to be with her and how she studied the means of pleasing her. She had decided that the best way of pleasing her was negative, and consisted in not giving her trouble—a conviction which certainly could have had no reference to trouble already existing. She was therefore ingeniously passive and almost imaginatively docile; she was careful even to moderate the eagerness with which she assented to Isabel's propositions and which might have implied that she could have thought otherwise. She never interrupted, never asked social questions, and though she delighted in approbation, to the point of turning pale when it came to her, never held out her hand for it. She only looked toward it wistfully—an attitude which, as she grew older, made her eyes the prettiest in the world. When during the second winter at Palazzo Roccanera she began to go to parties, to dances, she always, at a reasonable hour, lest Mrs. Osmond should be tired, was the first to propose departure. Isabel appreciated the sacrifice of the late dances, for she knew her little companion had a passionate pleasure in this exercise, taking her steps to the music like a conscientious fairy. Society, moreover, had no drawbacks for her; she liked even the tiresome parts—the heat of ballrooms, the dulness of dinners, the crush at the door, the awkward waiting for the carriage. During the day, in this vehicle, beside her stepmother, she sat in a small fixed, appreciative posture, bending forward and faintly smiling, as if she had been taken to drive for the first time.

On the day I speak of they had been driven out of one of the gates of the city and at the end of half an hour had left the carriage to await them by the roadside while they walked away over the short grass of the Campagna, which even in the winter months is sprinkled with delicate flowers. This was almost a daily habit with Isabel, who was fond of a walk and had a swift length of step, though not so swift a one as on her first coming to Europe. It was not the form of exercise that Pansy loved best, but she liked it, because she liked everything; and she moved with a shorter undulation beside her father's wife, who afterwards, on their return to Rome, paid a tribute to her preferences by making the circuit of the Pincian or the Villa Borghese. She had gathered a handful of flowers in a sunny hollow, far from the walls of Rome, and on reaching Palazzo Roccanera she went straight to her room, to put them into water. Isabel passed into the drawing-room, the one she herself usually occupied, the second in order from the large ante-chamber which was entered from the staircase and in which even Gilbert Osmond's rich devices had not been able to correct a look of rather grand nudity. Just beyond the threshold of the drawing-room she stopped short, the reason for her doing so being that she had received an impression. The impression had, in strictness, nothing unprecedented; but she felt it as something new, and the soundlessness of her step gave her time to take in the scene before she interrupted it. Madame Merle was there in her bonnet, and Gilbert Osmond was talking to her; for a minute they were unaware she had come in. Isabel had often seen that before, certainly; but what she had not seen, or at least had not noticed, was that their colloquy had for the moment converted itself into a sort of familiar silence, from which she instantly perceived that her entrance would startle them. Madame Merle was standing on the rug, a little way from the fire; Osmond was in a deep chair, leaning back and looking at her. Her head was erect, as usual, but her eyes were bent on his. What struck Isabel first was that he was sitting while Madame Merle stood; there was an anomaly in this that arrested her. Then she perceived that they had arrived at a desultory pause in their exchange of ideas and were musing, face to face, with the freedom of old friends who sometimes exchange ideas without uttering them. There was nothing to shock in this; they were old friends in fact. But the thing made an image, lasting only a moment, like a sudden flicker of light. Their relative positions, their absorbed mutual gaze, struck her as something detected. But it was all over by the time she had fairly seen it. Madame Merle had seen her and had welcomed her without moving; her husband, on the other hand, had instantly jumped up. He presently murmured something about wanting a walk and, after having asked their visitor to excuse him, left the room.

"I came to see you, thinking you would have come in; and as you hadn't I waited for you," Madame Merle said.

"Didn't he ask you to sit down?" Isabel asked with a smile.

Madame Merle looked about her. "Ah, it's very true; I was going away."

"You must stay now."

"Certainly. I came for a reason; I've something on my mind."

"I've told you that before," Isabel said—"that it takes something extraordinary to bring you to this house."

"And you know what I've told *you*; that whether I come or whether I stay away, I've always the same motive—the affection I bear you."

"Yes, you've told me that."

"You look just now as if you didn't believe it," said Madame Merle.

"Ah," Isabel answered, "the profundity of your motives, that's the last thing I doubt!"

"You doubt sooner of the sincerity of my words."

Isabel shook her head gravely. "I know you've always been kind to me."

"As often as you would let me. You don't always take it; then one has to let you alone. It's not to do you a kindness, however, that I've come today; it's quite another affair. I've come to get rid of a trouble of my own—to make it over to you. I've been talking to your husband about it."

"I'm surprised at that; he doesn't like troubles."

"Especially other people's; I know very well. But neither do you, I suppose. At any rate, whether you do or not, you must help me. It's about poor Mr. Rosier."

"Ah," said Isabel reflectively, "it's his trouble then, not yours."

"He has succeeded in saddling me with it. He comes to see me ten times a week, to talk about Pansy."

"Yes, he wants to marry her. I know all about it."

Madame Merle hesitated. "I gathered from your husband that perhaps you didn't."

"How should he know what I know? He has never spoken to me of the matter."

"It's probably because he doesn't know how to speak of it."

"It's nevertheless the sort of question in which he's rarely at fault."

"Yes, because as a general thing he knows perfectly well what to think. To-day he doesn't."

"Haven't you been telling him?" Isabel asked.

Madame Merle gave a bright, voluntary smile. "Do you know you're a little dry?"

"Yes; I can't help it. Mr. Rosier has also talked to me."

"In that there's some reason. You're so near the child."

"Ah," said Isabel, "for all the comfort I've given him! If you think me dry, I wonder what *he* thinks."

"I believe he thinks you can do more than you have done."

"I can do nothing."

"You can do more at least than I. I don't know what mysterious connection he may have discovered between me and Pansy; but he came to me from the first, as if I held his fortune in my hand. Now he keeps coming back, to spur me up, to know what hope there is, to pour out his feelings."

"He's very much in love," said Isabel.

"Very much—for him."

"Very much for Pansy, you might say as well."

Madame Merle dropped her eyes a moment. "Don't you think she's attractive?"

"The dearest little person possible—but very limited."

"She ought to be all the easier for Mr. Rosier to love. Mr. Rosier's not unlimited."

"No," said Isabel, "he has about the extent of one's pocket-handkerchief—the small ones with lace borders." Her humour had lately turned a good deal to sarcasm, but in a moment she was ashamed of exercising it on so innocent an object as Pansy's suitor. "He's very kind, very honest," she presently added; "and he's not such a fool as he seems."

"He assures me that she delights in him," said Madame Merle.

"I don't know; I've not asked her."

"You've never sounded her a little?"

"It's not my place; it's her father's."

"Ah, you're too literal!" said Madame Merle.

"I must judge for myself."

Madame Merle gave her smile again. "It isn't easy to help you."

"To help me?" said Isabel very seriously. "What do you mean?"

"It's easy to displease you. Don't you see how wise I am to be careful? I notify you, at any rate, as I notified Osmond, that I wash my hands of the love-affairs of Miss Pansy and Mr. Edward Rosier. *Je n'y peux rien, moi!*[2] I can't talk to Pansy about him. Especially," added Madame Merle, "as I don't think him a paragon of husbands."

Isabel reflected a little; after which, with a smile, "You don't wash your hands then!" she said. After which again she added in another tone: "You can't—you're too much interested."

2. There's nothing I can do about it myself (French).

Madame Merle slowly rose; she had given Isabel a look as rapid as the intimation that had gleamed before our heroine a few moments before. Only this time the latter saw nothing. "Ask him the next time, and you'll see."

"I can't ask him; he has ceased to come to the house. Gilbert has let him know that he's not welcome."

"Ah yes," said Madame Merle, "I forgot that—though it's the burden of his lamentation. He says Osmond has insulted him. All the same," she went on, "Osmond doesn't dislike him so much as he thinks." She had got up as if to close the conversation, but she lingered, looking about her, and had evidently more to say. Isabel perceived this and even saw the point she had in view; but Isabel also had her own reasons for not opening the way.

"That must have pleased him, if you've told him," she answered, smiling.

"Certainly I've told him; as far as that goes I've encouraged him. I've preached patience, have said that his case isn't desperate if he'll only hold his tongue and be quiet. Unfortunately he has taken it into his head to be jealous."

"Jealous?"

"Jealous of Lord Warburton, who, he says, is always here."

Isabel, who was tired, had remained sitting; but at this she also rose. "Ah!" she exclaimed simply, moving slowly to the fireplace. Madame Merle observed her as she passed and while she stood a moment before the mantel-glass and pushed into its place a wandering tress of hair.

"Poor Mr. Rosier keeps saying there's nothing impossible in Lord Warburton's falling in love with Pansy," Madame Merle went on.

Isabel was silent a little; she turned away from the glass. "It's true—there's nothing impossible," she returned at last, gravely and more gently.

"So I've had to admit to Mr. Rosier. So, too, your husband thinks."

"That I don't know."

"Ask him and you'll see."

"I shall not ask him," said Isabel.

"Pardon me; I forgot you had pointed that out. Of course," Madame Merle added, "you've had infinitely more observation of Lord Warburton's behaviour than I."

"I see no reason why I shouldn't tell you that he likes my stepdaughter very much."

Madame Merle gave one of her quick looks again. "Likes her, you mean—as Mr. Rosier means?"

"I don't know how Mr. Rosier means; but Lord Warburton has let me know that he's charmed with Pansy."

"And you've never told Osmond?" This observation was immediate, precipitate; it almost burst from Madame Merle's lips.

Isabel's eyes rested on her. "I suppose he'll know in time; Lord Warburton has a tongue and knows how to express himself."

Madame Merle instantly became conscious that she had spoken more quickly than usual, and the reflection brought the colour to her cheek. She gave the treacherous impulse time to subside and then said as if she had been thinking it over a little: "That would be better than marrying poor Mr. Rosier."

"Much better, I think."

"It would be very delightful; it would be a great marriage. It's really very kind of him."

"Very kind of him?"

"To drop his eyes on a simple little girl."

"I don't see that."

"It's very good of you. But after all, Pansy Osmond—"

"After all, Pansy Osmond's the most attractive person he has ever known!" Isabel exclaimed.

Madame Merle stared, and indeed she was justly bewildered. "Ah, a moment ago I thought you seemed rather to disparage her."

"I said she was limited. And so she is. And so's Lord Warburton."

"So are we all, if you come to that. If it's no more than Pansy deserves, all the better. But if she fixes her affections on Mr. Rosier I won't admit that she deserves it. That will be too perverse."

"Mr. Rosier's a nuisance!" Isabel cried abruptly.

"I quite agree with you, and I'm delighted to know that I'm not expected to feed his flame. For the future, when he calls on me, my door shall be closed to him." And gathering her mantle together Madame Merle prepared to depart. She was checked, however, on her progress to the door, by an inconsequent request from Isabel.

"All the same, you know, be kind to him."

She lifted her shoulders and eyebrows and stood looking at her friend. "I don't understand your contradictions! Decidedly I shan't be kind to him, for it will be a false kindness. I want to see her married to Lord Warburton."

"You had better wait till he asks her."

"If what you say's true, he'll ask her. Especially," said Madame Merle in a moment, "if you make him."

"If I make him?"

"It's quite in your power. You've great influence with him."

Isabel frowned a little. "Where did you learn that?"

"Mrs. Touchett told me. Not you—never!" said Madame Merle, smiling.

"I certainly never told you anything of the sort."

"You *might* have done so—so far as opportunity went—when we were by way of being confidential with each other. But you really told me very little; I've often thought so since."

Isabel had thought so too, and sometimes with a certain satisfaction. But she didn't admit it now—perhaps because she wished not to appear to exult in it. "You seem to have had an excellent informant in my aunt," she simply returned.

"She let me know you had declined an offer of marriage from Lord Warburton, because she was greatly vexed and was full of the subject. Of course I think you've done better in doing as you did. But if you wouldn't marry Lord Warburton yourself, make him the reparation of helping him to marry some one else."

Isabel listened to this with a face that persisted in not reflecting the bright expressiveness of Madame Merle's. But in a moment she said, reasonably and gently enough: "I should be very glad indeed if, as regards Pansy, it could be arranged." Upon which her companion, who seemed to regard this as a speech of good omen, embraced her more tenderly than might have been expected and triumphantly withdrew.

Chapter XLI

Osmond touched on this matter that evening for the first time; coming very late into the drawing-room, where she was sitting alone. They had spent the evening at home, and Pansy had gone to bed; he himself had been sitting since dinner in a small apartment in which he had arranged his books and which he called his study. At ten o'clock Lord Warburton had come in, as he always did when he knew from Isabel that she was to be at home; he was going somewhere else and he sat for half an hour. Isabel, after asking him for news of Ralph, said very little to him, on purpose; she wished him to talk with her stepdaughter. She pretended to read; she even went after a little to the piano; she asked herself if she mightn't leave the room. She had come little by little to think well of the idea of Pansy's becoming the wife of the master of beautiful Lockleigh, though at first it had not presented itself in a manner to excite her enthusiasm. Madame Merle, that afternoon, had applied the match to an accumulation of inflammable material. When Isabel was unhappy she always looked about her—partly from impulse and partly by theory—for some form of positive exertion. She could never rid herself of the sense that unhappiness was a state of disease—of suffering as opposed to doing. To "do"—it hardly mattered what—would therefore be an escape, perhaps in some degree a remedy. Besides, she wished to convince herself that she had done everything possible to content her husband; she was determined not to be haunted by visions of his wife's limpness under appeal. It would please him greatly to see Pansy married to an English nobleman, and justly please him, since this nobleman was so sound a character. It seemed to Isabel that if she could make it her duty to bring about such an event she should play the part of a good wife. She wanted to be that; she wanted to be able to believe sincerely, and with proof of it, that she had been that. Then such an undertaking had other recommendations. It would occupy her, and she desired occupation. It would even amuse her, and if she could really amuse herself she perhaps might be saved. Lastly, it would be a service to Lord Warburton, who evidently pleased himself greatly with the charming girl. It was a little "weird" he should—being what he was; but there was no accounting for such impressions. Pansy might captivate any one—any one at least but Lord Warburton. Isabel would have thought her too small, too slight, perhaps even too artificial for that. There was always a little of the doll about her, and that was not what he had been looking for. Still who could say what men ever were looking for? They looked for what they found; they knew what pleased them only when they saw it. No theory was valid in such matters, and nothing was more unaccountable or more natural than anything else. If he had cared for *her* it might seem odd he should care for Pansy, who was so different; but he had not cared for her so much as he had supposed. Or if he had, he had completely got over it, and it was natural that, as that affair had failed, he should think something of quite another sort might succeed. Enthusiasm, as I say, had not come at first to Isabel, but it came to-day and made her feel almost happy. It was astonishing what happiness she could still find in the idea of procuring a pleasure for her husband. It was a pity, however, that Edward Rosier had crossed their path!

At this reflection the light that had suddenly gleamed upon that path lost something of its brightness. Isabel was unfortunately as sure that

Pansy thought Mr. Rosier the nicest of all the young men—as sure as if she had held an interview with her on the subject. It was very tiresome she should be so sure, when she had carefully abstained from informing herself; almost as tiresome as that poor Mr. Rosier should have taken it into his own head. He was certainly very inferior to Lord Warburton. It was not the difference in fortune so much as the difference in the men; the young American was really so light a weight. He was much more of the type of the useless fine gentleman than the English nobleman. It was true that there was no particular reason why Pansy should marry a statesman; still, if a statesman admired her, that was his affair, and she would make a perfect little pearl of a peeress.

It may seem to the reader that Mrs. Osmond had grown of a sudden strangely cynical, for she ended by saying to herself that this difficulty could probably be arranged. An impediment that was embodied in poor Rosier could not anyhow present itself as a dangerous one; there were always means of levelling secondary obstacles. Isabel was perfectly aware that she had not taken the measure of Pansy's tenacity, which might prove to be inconveniently great; but she inclined to see her as rather letting go, under suggestion, than as clutching under deprecation—since she had certainly the faculty of assent developed in a very much higher degree than that of protest. She would cling, yes, she would cling; but it really mattered to her very little what she clung to. Lord Warburton would do as well as Mr. Rosier—especially as she seemed quite to like him; she had expressed this sentiment to Isabel without a single reservation; she had said she thought his conversation most interesting—he had told her all about India. His manner to Pansy had been of the rightest and easiest— Isabel noticed that for herself, as she also observed that he talked to her not in the least in a patronising way, reminding himself of her youth and simplicity, but quite as if she understood his subjects with that sufficiency with which she followed those of the fashionable operas. This went far enough for attention to the music and the barytone. He was careful only to be kind—he was as kind as he had been to another fluttered young chit at Gardencourt. A girl might well be touched by that; she remembered how she herself had been touched, and said to herself that if she had been as simple as Pansy the impression would have been deeper still. She had not been simple when she refused him; that operation had been as complicated as, later, her acceptance of Osmond had been. Pansy, however, in spite of *her* simplicity, really did understand, and was glad that Lord Warburton should talk to her, not about her partners and bouquets, but about the state of Italy, the condition of the peasantry, the famous grist-tax, the *pellagra*,[1] his impressions of Roman society. She looked at him, as she drew her needle through her tapestry, with sweet submissive eyes, and when she lowered them she gave little quiet oblique glances at his person, his hands, his feet, his clothes, as if she were considering him. Even his person, Isabel might have reminded her, was better than Mr. Rosier's. But Isabel contented herself at such moments with wondering where this gentleman

---

1. In 1868 the new government of a united Italy introduced a tax on the grinding of grains meant for food; wildly unpopular, it weighed especially heavily on the poor, and was repealed in 1883. Pellagra was caused by a vitamin deficiency brought on by an overreliance on polenta, made from cornmeal, as a staple food. Its many consequences ranged from rough skin (*polle agra*) to diarrhea and dementia.

was; he came no more at all to Palazzo Roccanera. It was surprising, as I say, the hold it had taken of her—the idea of assisting her husband to be pleased. It was surprising for a variety of reasons which I shall presently touch upon. On the evening I speak of, while Lord Warburton sat there, she had been on the point of taking the great step of going out of the room and leaving her companions alone. I say the great step, because it was in this light that Gilbert Osmond would have regarded it, and Isabel was trying as much as possible to take her husband's view. She succeeded after a fashion, but she fell short of the point I mention. After all she couldn't rise to it; something held her and made this impossible. It was not exactly that it would be base or insidious; for women as a general thing practise such manœuvres with a perfectly good conscience, and Isabel was instinctively much more true than false to the common genius of her sex. There was a vague doubt that interposed—a sense that she was not quite sure. So she remained in the drawing-room, and after a while Lord Warburton went on to his party, of which he promised to give Pansy a full account on the morrow. After he had gone she wondered if she had prevented something which would have happened if she had absented herself for a quarter of an hour; and then she pronounced—always mentally—that when their distinguished visitor should wish her to go away he would easily find means to let her know it. Pansy said nothing whatever about him after he had gone, and Isabel studiously said nothing, as she had taken a vow of reserve until after he should have declared himself. He was a little longer in coming to this than might seem to accord with the description he had given Isabel of his feelings. Pansy went to bed, and Isabel had to admit that she could not now guess what her stepdaughter was thinking of. Her transparent little companion was for the moment not to be seen through.

She remained alone, looking at the fire, until, at the end of half an hour, her husband came in. He moved about a while in silence and then sat down; he looked at the fire like herself. But she now had transferred her eyes from the flickering flame in the chimney to Osmond's face, and she watched him while he kept his silence. Covert observation had become a habit with her; an instinct, of which it is not an exaggeration to say that it was allied to that of self-defence, had made it habitual. She wished as much as possible to know his thoughts, to know what he would say, beforehand, so that she might prepare her answer. Preparing answers had not been her strong point of old; she had rarely in this respect got further than thinking afterwards of clever things she might have said. But she had learned caution—learned it in a measure from her husband's very countenance. It was the same face she had looked into with eyes equally earnest perhaps, but less penetrating, on the terrace of a Florentine villa; except that Osmond had grown slightly stouter since his marriage. He still, however, might strike one as very distinguished.

"Has Lord Warburton been here?" he presently asked.

"Yes, he stayed half an hour."

"Did he see Pansy?"

"Yes; he sat on the sofa beside her."

"Did he talk with her much?"

"He talked almost only to her."

"It seems to me he's attentive. Isn't that what you call it?"

"I don't call it anything," said Isabel; "I've waited for you to give it a name."

"That's a consideration you don't always show," Osmond answered after a moment.

"I've determined, this time, to try and act as you'd like. I've so often failed of that."

Osmond turned his head slowly, looking at her. "Are you trying to quarrel with me?"

"No, I'm trying to live at peace."

"Nothing's more easy; you know I don't quarrel myself."

"What do you call it when you try to make me angry?" Isabel asked.

"I don't try; if I've done so it has been the most natural thing in the world. Moreover I'm not in the least trying now."

Isabel smiled. "It doesn't matter. I've determined never to be angry again."

"That's an excellent resolve. Your temper isn't good."

"No—it's not good." She pushed away the book she had been reading and took up the band of tapestry Pansy had left on the table.

"That's partly why I've not spoken to you about this business of my daughter's," Osmond said, designating Pansy in the manner that was most frequent with him. "I was afraid I should encounter opposition—that you too would have views on the subject. I've sent little Rosier about his business."

"You were afraid I'd plead for Mr. Rosier? Haven't you noticed that I've never spoken to you of him?"

"I've never given you a chance. We've so little conversation in these days. I know he was an old friend of yours."

"Yes; he's an old friend of mine." Isabel cared little more for him than for the tapestry that she held in her hand; but it was true that he was an old friend and that with her husband she felt a desire not to extenuate such ties. He had a way of expressing contempt for them which fortified her loyalty to them, even when, as in the present case, they were in themselves insignificant. She sometimes felt a sort of passion of tenderness for memories which had no other merit than that they belonged to her unmarried life. "But as regards Pansy," she added in a moment, "I've given him no encouragement."

"That's fortunate," Osmond observed.

"Fortunate for me, I suppose you mean. For him it matters little."

"There's no use talking of him," Osmond said. "As I tell you, I've turned him out."

"Yes; but a lover outside's always a lover. He's sometimes even more of one. Mr. Rosier still has hope."

"He's welcome to the comfort of it! My daughter has only to sit perfectly quiet to become Lady Warburton."

"Should you like that?" Isabel asked with a simplicity which was not so affected as it may appear. She was resolved to assume nothing, for Osmond had a way of unexpectedly turning her assumptions against her. The intensity with which he would like his daughter to become Lady Warburton had been the very basis of her own recent reflections. But that was for herself; she would recognise nothing until Osmond should have put it into words; she would not take for granted with him that he thought Lord

Warburton a prize worth an amount of effort that was unusual among the Osmonds. It was Gilbert's constant intimation that for him nothing in life was a prize; that he treated as from equal to equal with the most distinguished people in the world, and that his daughter had only to look about her to pick out a prince. It cost him therefore a lapse from consistency to say explicitly that he yearned for Lord Warburton and that if this nobleman should escape his equivalent might not be found; with which moreover it was another of his customary implications that he was never inconsistent. He would have liked his wife to glide over the point. But strangely enough, now that she was face to face with him and although an hour before she had almost invented a scheme for pleasing him, Isabel was not accommodating, would not glide. And yet she knew exactly the effect on his mind of her question: it would operate as an humiliation. Never mind; he was terribly capable of humiliating *her*—all the more so that he was also capable of waiting for great opportunities and of showing sometimes an almost unaccountable indifference to small ones. Isabel perhaps took a small opportunity because she would not have availed herself of a great one.

Osmond at present acquitted himself very honourably. "I should like it extremely; it would be a great marriage. And then Lord Warburton has another advantage: he's an old friend of yours. It would be pleasant for him to come into the family. It's very odd Pansy's admirers should all be your old friends."

"It's natural that they should come to see me. In coming to see me they see Pansy. Seeing her it's natural they should fall in love with her."

"So I think. But you're not bound to do so."

"If she should marry Lord Warburton I should be very glad," Isabel went on frankly. "He's an excellent man. You say, however, that she has only to sit perfectly still. Perhaps she won't sit perfectly still. If she loses Mr. Rosier she may jump up!"

Osmond appeared to give no heed to this; he sat gazing at the fire. "Pansy would like to be a great lady," he remarked in a moment with a certain tenderness of tone. "She wishes above all to please," he added.

"To please Mr. Rosier, perhaps."

"No, to please me."

"Me too a little, I think," said Isabel.

"Yes, she has a great opinion of you. But she'll do what I like."

"If you're sure of that, it's very well," she went on.

"Meantime," said Osmond, "I should like our distinguished visitor to speak."

"He has spoken—to me. He has told me it would be a great pleasure to him to believe she could care for him."

Osmond turned his head quickly, but at first he said nothing. Then, "Why didn't you tell me that?" he asked sharply.

"There was no opportunity. You know how we live. I've taken the first chance that has offered."

"Did you speak to him of Rosier?"

"Oh yes, a little."

"That was hardly necessary."

"I thought it best he should know, so that, so that—" And Isabel paused.

"So that what?"

"So that he might act accordingly."

"So that he might back out, do you mean?"

"No, so that he might advance while there's yet time."

"That's not the effect it seems to have had."

"You should have patience," said Isabel. "You know Englishmen are shy."

"This one's not. He was not when he made love to *you*."

She had been afraid Osmond would speak of that; it was disagreeable to her. "I beg your pardon; he was extremely so," she returned.

He answered nothing for some time; he took up a book and fingered the pages while she sat silent and occupied herself with Pansy's tapestry. "You must have a great deal of influence with him," Osmond went on at last. "The moment you really wish it you can bring him to the point."

This was more offensive still; but she felt the great naturalness of his saying it, and it was after all extremely like what she had said to herself. "Why should I have influence?" she asked. "What have I ever done to put him under an obligation to me?"

"You refused to marry him," said Osmond with his eyes on his book.

"I must not presume too much on that," she replied.

He threw down the book presently and got up, standing before the fire with his hands behind him. "Well, I hold that it lies in your hands. I shall leave it there. With a little good-will you may manage it. Think that over and remember how much I count on you." He waited a little, to give her time to answer; but she answered nothing, and he presently strolled out of the room.

Chapter XLII

She had answered nothing because his words had put the situation before her and she was absorbed in looking at it. There was something in them that suddenly made vibrations deep, so that she had been afraid to trust herself to speak. After he had gone she leaned back in her chair and closed her eyes; and for a long time, far into the night and still further, she sat in the still drawing-room, given up to her meditation. A servant came in to attend to the fire, and she bade him bring fresh candles and then go to bed. Osmond had told her to think of what he had said; and she did so indeed, and of many other things. The suggestion from another that she had a definite influence on Lord Warburton—this had given her the start that accompanies unexpected recognition. Was it true that there was something still between them that might be a handle to make him declare himself to Pansy—a susceptibility, on his part, to approval, a desire to do what would please her? Isabel had hitherto not asked herself the question, because she had not been forced; but now that it was directly presented to her she saw the answer, and the answer frightened her. Yes, there was something—something on Lord Warburton's part. When he had first come to Rome she believed the link that united them to be completely snapped; but little by little she had been reminded that it had yet a palpable existence. It was as thin as a hair, but there were moments when she seemed to hear it vibrate. For herself nothing was changed; what she once thought of him she always thought; it was needless this feeling should change; it seemed to her in fact a better feeling than ever. But he? had he still the idea that she might be more to him than other women? Had he the wish

to profit by the memory of the few moments of intimacy through which
they had once passed? Isabel knew she had read some of the signs of such
a disposition. But what were his hopes, his pretensions, and in what strange
way were they mingled with his evidently very sincere appreciation of poor
Pansy? Was he in love with Gilbert Osmond's wife, and if so what comfort did he expect to derive from it? If he was in love with Pansy he was
not in love with her stepmother, and if he was in love with her stepmother
he was not in love with Pansy. Was she to cultivate the advantage she possessed in order to make him commit himself to Pansy, knowing he would
do so for her sake and not for the small creature's own—was this the service her husband had asked of her? This at any rate was the duty with
which she found herself confronted—from the moment she admitted to
herself that her old friend had still an uneradicated predilection for her
society. It was not an agreeable task; it was in fact a repulsive one. She
asked herself with dismay whether Lord Warburton were pretending to
be in love with Pansy in order to cultivate another satisfaction and what
might be called other chances. Of this refinement of duplicity she presently acquitted him; she preferred to believe him in perfect good faith.
But if his admiration for Pansy were a delusion this was scarcely better
than its being an affectation. Isabel wandered among these ugly possibilities until she had completely lost her way; some of them, as she suddenly
encountered them, seemed ugly enough. Then she broke out of the labyrinth, rubbing her eyes, and declared that her imagination surely did her
little honour and that her husband's did him even less. Lord Warburton
was as disinterested as he need be, and she was no more to him than she
need wish. She would rest upon this till the contrary should be proved;
proved more effectually than by a cynical intimation of Osmond's.

Such a resolution, however, brought her this evening but little peace,
for her soul was haunted with terrors which crowded to the foreground of
thought as quickly as a place was made for them. What had suddenly set
them into livelier motion she hardly knew, unless it were the strange
impression she had received in the afternoon of her husband's being in
more direct communication with Madame Merle than she suspected. That
impression came back to her from time to time, and now she wondered it
had never come before. Besides this, her short interview with Osmond half
an hour ago was a striking example of his faculty for making everything
wither that he touched, spoiling everything for her that he looked at. It
was very well to undertake to give him a proof of loyalty; the real fact was
that the knowledge of his expecting a thing raised a presumption against
it. It was as if he had had the evil eye; as if his presence were a blight and
his favour a misfortune. Was the fault in himself, or only in the deep
mistrust she had conceived for him? This mistrust was now the clearest
result of their short married life; a gulf had opened between them over
which they looked at each other with eyes that were on either side a declaration of the deception suffered. It was a strange opposition, of the like
of which she had never dreamed—an opposition in which the vital principle
of the one was a thing of contempt to the other. It was not her fault—she
had practised no deception; she had only admired and believed. She had
taken all the first steps in the purest confidence, and then she had suddenly found the infinite vista of a multiplied life to be a dark, narrow
alley with a dead wall at the end. Instead of leading to the high places of

happiness, from which the world would seem to lie below one, so that one could look down with a sense of exaltation and advantage, and judge and choose and pity, it led rather downward and earthward, into realms of restriction and depression where the sound of other lives, easier and freer, was heard as from above, and where it served to deepen the feeling of failure. It was her deep distrust of her husband—this was what darkened the world. That is a sentiment easily indicated, but not so easily explained, and so composite in its character that much time and still more suffering had been needed to bring it to its actual perfection. Suffering, with Isabel, was an active condition; it was not a chill, a stupor, a despair; it was a passion of thought, of speculation, of response to every pressure. She flattered herself that she had kept her failing faith to herself, however— that no one suspected it but Osmond. Oh, he knew it, and there were times when she thought he enjoyed it. It had come gradually—it was not till the first year of their life together, so admirably intimate at first, had closed that she had taken the alarm. Then the shadows had begun to gather; it was as if Osmond deliberately, almost malignantly, had put the lights out one by one.[1] The dusk at first was vague and thin, and she could still see her way in it. But it steadily deepened, and if now and again it had occasionally lifted there were certain corners of her prospect that were impenetrably black. These shadows were not an emanation from her own mind: she was very sure of that; she had done her best to be just and temperate, to see only the truth. They were a part, they were a kind of creation and consequence, of her husband's very presence. They were not his misdeeds, his turpitudes; she accused him of nothing—that is but of one thing, which was *not* a crime. She knew of no wrong he had done; he was not violent, he was not cruel: she simply believed he hated her. That was all she accused him of, and the miserable part of it was precisely that it was not a crime, for against a crime she might have found redress. He had discovered that she was so different, that she was not what he had believed she would prove to be. He had thought at first he could change her, and she had done her best to be what he would like. But she was, after all, herself—she couldn't help that; and now there was no use pretending, wearing a mask or a dress, for he knew her and had made up his mind. She was not afraid of him; she had no apprehension he would hurt her; for the ill-will he bore her was not of that sort. He would if possible never give her a pretext, never put himself in the wrong. Isabel, scanning the future with dry, fixed eyes, saw that he would have the better of her there. She would give him many pretexts, she would often put herself in the wrong. There were times when she almost pitied him; for if she had not deceived him in intention she understood how completely she must have done so in fact. She had effaced herself when he first knew her; she had made herself small, pretending there was less of her than there really was. It was because she had been under the extraordinary charm that he, on his side, had taken pains to put forth. He was not changed; he had not disguised himself, during the year of his courtship, any more than she. But she had seen only half his nature then, as one saw the disk of the moon when it was partly masked by the shadow of the earth. She saw the full moon now—she saw the whole man. She had

---

1. Cf. Othello's words as he prepares to strangle Desdemona, "Put out the light, and then put out the light. . . ." *Othello* V.ii.7.

kept still, as it were, so that he should have a free field, and yet in spite of this she had mistaken a part for the whole.

Ah, she had been immensely under the charm! It had not passed away; it was there still: she still knew perfectly what it was that made Osmond delightful when he chose to be. He had wished to be when he made love to her, and as she had wished to be charmed it was not wonderful he had succeeded. He had succeeded because he had been sincere; it never occurred to her now to deny him that. He admired her—he had told her why: because she was the most imaginative woman he had known. It might very well have been true; for during those months she had imagined a world of things that had no substance. She had had a more wondrous vision of him, fed through charmed senses and oh such a stirred fancy!—she had not read him right. A certain combination of features had touched her, and in them she had seen the most striking of figures. That he was poor and lonely and yet that somehow he was noble—that was what had interested her and seemed to give her her opportunity. There had been an indefinable beauty about him—in his situation, in his mind, in his face. She had felt at the same time that he was helpless and ineffectual, but the feeling had taken the form of a tenderness which was the very flower of respect. He was like a sceptical voyager strolling on the beach while he waited for the tide, looking seaward yet not putting to sea. It was in all this she had found her occasion. She would launch his boat for him; she would be his providence; it would be a good thing to love him. And she had loved him, she had so anxiously and yet so ardently given herself—a good deal for what she found in him, but a good deal also for what she brought him and what might enrich the gift. As she looked back at the passion of those full weeks she perceived in it a kind of maternal strain—the happiness of a woman who felt that she was a contributor, that she came with charged hands. But for her money, as she saw to-day, she would never have done it. And then her mind wandered off to poor Mr. Touchett, sleeping under English turf, the beneficent author of infinite woe! For this was the fantastic fact. At bottom her money had been a burden, had been on her mind, which was filled with the desire to transfer the weight of it to some other conscience, to some more prepared receptacle. What would lighten her own conscience more effectually than to make it over to the man with the best taste in the world? Unless she should have given it to a hospital there would have been nothing better she could do with it; and there was no charitable institution in which she had been as much interested as in Gilbert Osmond. He would use her fortune in a way that would make her think better of it and rub off a certain grossness attaching to the good luck of an unexpected inheritance. There had been nothing very delicate in inheriting seventy thousand pounds; the delicacy had been all in Mr. Touchett's leaving them to her. But to marry Gilbert Osmond and bring him such a portion—in that there would be delicacy for her as well. There would be less for him—that was true; but that was his affair, and if he loved her he wouldn't object to her being rich. Had he not had the courage to say he was glad she was rich?

Isabel's cheek burned when she asked herself if she had really married on a factitious theory, in order to do something finely appreciable with her money. But she was able to answer quickly enough that this was only half the story. It was because a certain ardour took possession of her—a sense of the earnestness of his affection and a delight in his personal qualities. He was better than any one else. This supreme conviction had filled her life for months, and enough of it still remained to prove to her that she could not have done otherwise. The finest—in the sense of being the subtlest—manly organism she had ever known had become her property, and the recognition of her having but to put out her hands and take it had been originally a sort of act of devotion. She had not been mistaken about the beauty of his mind; she knew that organ perfectly now. She had lived with it, she had lived *in* it almost—it appeared to have become her habitation. If she had been captured it had taken a firm hand to seize her; that reflection perhaps had some worth. A mind more ingenious, more pliant, more cultivated, more trained to admirable exercises, she had not encountered; and it was this exquisite instrument she had now to reckon with. She lost herself in infinite dismay when she thought of the magnitude of *his* deception. It was a wonder, perhaps, in view of this, that he didn't hate her more. She remembered perfectly the first sign he had given of it—it had been like the bell that was to ring up the curtain upon the real drama of their life. He said to her one day that she had too many ideas and that she must get rid of them. He had told her that already, before their marriage; but then she had not noticed it: it had come back to her only afterwards. This time she might well have noticed it, because he had really meant it. The words had been nothing superficially; but when in the light of deepening experience she had looked into them they had then appeared portentous. He had really meant it—he would have liked her to have nothing of her own but her pretty appearance. She had known she had too many ideas; she had more even than he had supposed, many more than she had expressed to him when he had asked her to marry him. Yes, she *had* been hypocritical; she had liked him so much. She had too many ideas for herself; but that was just what one married for, to share them with some one else. One couldn't pluck them up by the roots, though of course one might suppress them, be careful not to utter them. It had not been this, however, his objecting to her opinions; this had been nothing. She had no opinions—none that she would not have been eager to sacrifice in the satisfaction of feeling herself loved for it. What he had meant had been the whole thing—her character, the way she felt, the way she judged. This was what she had kept in reserve; this was what he had not known until he had found himself—with the door closed behind, as it were—set down face to face with it. She had a certain way of looking at life which he took as a personal offence. Heaven knew that now at least it was a very humble, accommodating way! The strange thing was that she should not have suspected from the first that his own had been so different. She had thought it so large, so enlightened, so perfectly that of an honest man and a gentleman. Hadn't he assured her that he had no superstitions, no dull limitations, no prejudices that had lost their freshness? Hadn't he all the appearance of a man living in the open air of the world, indifferent to small considerations, caring only for truth and knowledge and believing that two intelligent people ought to look for them together and, whether they found them or not, find at least some happiness in the search? He had told her he loved the conventional, but there was a sense in which this seemed a noble declaration. In that sense, that of the love of harmony and order and decency and of all the stately offices of life, she went with him freely, and his warning had contained nothing ominous. But when, as the months had elapsed, she had followed him further and he had led her into the mansion of his own habitation, then, *then* she had seen where she really was.

She could live it over again, the incredulous terror with which she had taken the measure of her dwelling. Between those four walls she had lived ever since; they were to surround her for the rest of her life. It was the house of darkness, the house of dumbness, the house of suffocation. Osmond's beautiful mind gave it neither light nor air; Osmond's beautiful mind indeed seemed to peep down from a small high window and mock at her. Of course it had not been physical suffering; for physical suffering there might have been a remedy. She could come and go; she had her liberty; her husband was perfectly polite. He took himself so seriously; it was something appalling. Under all his culture, his cleverness, his amenity, under his good-nature, his facility, his knowledge of life, his egotism lay hidden like a serpent in a bank of flowers. She had taken him seriously, but she had not taken him so seriously as that. How could she— especially when she had known him better? She was to think of him as he thought of himself—as the first gentleman in Europe. So it was that she had thought of him at first, and that indeed was the reason she had married him. But when she began to see what it implied she drew back; there was more in the bond than she had meant to put her name to. It implied a sovereign contempt for every one but some three or four very exalted people whom he envied, and for everything in the world but half a dozen ideas of his own. That was very well; she would have gone with him even there a long distance; for he pointed out to her so much of the baseness and shabbiness of life, opened her eyes so wide to the stupidity, the depravity, the ignorance of mankind, that she had been properly impressed with the infinite vulgarity of things and of the virtue of keeping one's self unspotted by it. But this base, ignoble world, it appeared, was after all what one was to live for; one was to keep it for ever in one's eye, in order not to enlighten or convert or redeem it, but to extract from it some recognition of one's own superiority. On the one hand it was despicable, but on the other it afforded a standard. Osmond had talked to Isabel about his renunciation, his indifference, the ease with which he dispensed with the usual aids to success; and all this had seemed to her admirable. She had thought it a grand indifference, an exquisite independence. But indifference was really the last of his qualities; she had never seen any one who thought so much of others. For herself, avowedly, the world had always interested her and the study of her fellow creatures been her constant passion. She would have been willing, however, to renounce all her curiosities and sympathies for the sake of a personal life, if the person concerned had only been able to make her believe it was a gain! This at least was her present conviction; and the thing certainly would have been easier than to care for society as Osmond cared for it.

He was unable to live without it, and she saw that he had never really done so; he had looked at it out of his window even when he appeared to be most detached from it. He had his ideal, just as she had tried to have hers; only it was strange that people should seek for justice in such different quarters. His ideal was a conception of high prosperity and propriety, of the aristocratic life, which she now saw that he deemed himself always, in essence at least, to have led. He had never lapsed from it for an hour; he would never have recovered from the shame of doing so. That again was very well; here too she would have agreed; but they attached such different ideas, such different associations and desires, to the same formulas. Her notion of the aristocratic life was simply the union of great knowledge with great liberty; the knowledge would give one a sense of duty and the liberty a sense of enjoyment. But for Osmond it was altogether a thing of forms, a conscious, calculated attitude. He was fond of the old, the consecrated, the transmitted; so was she, but she pretended to do what she chose with it. He had an immense esteem for tradition; he had told her once that the best thing in the world was to have it, but that if one was so unfortunate as not to have it one must immediately proceed to make it. She knew that he meant by this that she hadn't it, but that he was better off; though from what source he had derived his traditions she never learned. He had a very large collection of them, however; that was very certain, and after a little she began to see. The great thing was to act in accordance with them; the great thing not only for him but for her. Isabel had an undefined conviction that to serve for another person than their proprietor traditions must be of a thoroughly superior kind; but she nevertheless assented to this intimation that she too must march to the stately music that floated down from unknown periods in her husband's past; she who of old had been so free of step, so desultory, so devious, so much the reverse of processional. There were certain things they must do, a certain posture they must take, certain people they must know and not know. When she saw this rigid system close about her, draped though it was in pictured tapestries, that sense of darkness and suffocation of which I have spoken took possession of her; she seemed shut up with an odour of mould and decay. She had resisted of course; at first very humorously, ironically, tenderly; then, as the situation grew more serious, eagerly, passionately, pleadingly. She had pleaded the cause of freedom, of doing as they chose, of not caring for the aspect and denomination of their life—the cause of other instincts and longings, of quite another ideal.

Then it was that her husband's personality, touched as it never had been, stepped forth and stood erect. The things she had said were answered only by his scorn, and she could see he was ineffably ashamed of her. What did he think of her—that she was base, vulgar, ignoble? He at least knew now that she had no traditions! It had not been in his prevision of things that she should reveal such flatness; her sentiments were worthy of a radical newspaper or a Unitarian preacher.[2] The real offence, as she ultimately perceived, was her having a mind of her own at all. Her mind was to be his—attached to his own like a small garden-plot to a deer-park. He would rake the soil gently and water the flowers; he would weed the beds and gather an occasional nosegay. It would be a pretty piece of property for a proprietor already far-reaching. He didn't wish her to be stupid. On the contrary, it was because she was clever that she had pleased him. But he expected her intelligence to operate altogether in his favour, and so far from desiring her mind to be a blank he had flattered himself that it would

2. Unitarianism developed as a dissenting sect of Protestantism in the seventeenth century; it denied the existence of the Trinity and affirmed the unity of God. By the nineteenth century it was known, in New England especially, as a liberal and egalitarian faith devoted to social reform, much indeed as it is today.

be richly receptive. He had expected his wife to feel with him and for him, to enter into his opinions, his ambitions, his preferences; and Isabel was obliged to confess that this was no great insolence on the part of a man so accomplished and a husband originally at least so tender. But there were certain things she could never take in. To begin with, they were hideously unclean. She was not a daughter of the Puritans, but for all that she believed in such a thing as chastity and even as decency. It would appear that Osmond was far from doing anything of the sort; some of his traditions made her push back her skirts. Did all women have lovers? Did they all lie and even the best have their price? Were there only three or four that didn't deceive their husbands? When Isabel heard such things she felt a greater scorn for them than for the gossip of a village parlour—a scorn that kept its freshness in a very tainted air. There was the taint of her sister-in-law: did her husband judge only by the Countess Gemini? This lady very often lied, and she practised deceptions that were not simply verbal. It was enough to find these facts assumed among Osmond's traditions—it was enough without giving them such a general extension. It was her scorn of his assumptions, it was this that made him draw himself up. He had plenty of contempt, and it was proper his wife should be as well furnished; but that she should turn the hot light of her disdain upon his own conception of things—this was a danger he had not allowed for. He believed he should have regulated her emotions before she came to it; and Isabel could easily imagine how his ears had scorched on his discovering he had been too confident. When one had a wife who gave one that sensation there was nothing left but to hate her.

She was morally certain now that this feeling of hatred, which at first had been a refuge and a refreshment, had become the occupation and comfort of his life. The feeling was deep, because it was sincere; he had had the revelation that she could after all dispense with him. If to herself the idea was startling, if it presented itself at first as a kind of infidelity, a capacity for pollution, what infinite effect might it not be expected to have had upon *him*? It was very simple; he despised her; she had no traditions and the moral horizon of a Unitarian minister. Poor Isabel, who had never been able to understand Unitarianism! This was the certitude she had been living with now for a time that she had ceased to measure. What was coming—what was before them? That was her constant question. What would he do—what ought *she* to do? When a man hated his wife what did it lead to? She didn't hate him, that she was sure of, for every little while she felt a passionate wish to give him a pleasant surprise. Very often, however, she felt afraid, and it used to come over her, as I have intimated, that she had deceived him at the very first. They were strangely married, at all events, and it was a horrible life. Until that morning he had scarcely spoken to her for a week; his manner was as dry as a burned-out fire. She knew there was a special reason; he was displeased at Ralph Touchett's staying on in Rome. He thought she saw too much of her cousin—he had told her a week before it was indecent she should go to him at his hotel. He would have said more than this if Ralph's invalid state had not appeared to make it brutal to denounce him; but having had to contain himself had only deepened his disgust. Isabel read all this as she would have read the hour on the clock-face; she was as perfectly aware that the sight of her interest in her cousin stirred her husband's rage as if Osmond had locked

her into her room—which she was sure was what he wanted to do. It was
her honest belief that on the whole she was not defiant, but she certainly
couldn't pretend to be indifferent to Ralph. She believed he was dying at
last and that she should never see him again, and this gave her a tenderness for him that she had never known before. Nothing was a pleasure to
her now; how could anything be a pleasure to a woman who knew that
she had thrown away her life? There was an everlasting weight on her
heart—there was a livid light on everything. But Ralph's little visit was
a lamp in the darkness; for the hour that she sat with him her ache for
herself became somehow her ache for *him*. She felt to-day as if he had
been her brother. She had never had a brother, but if she had and she
were in trouble and he were dying, he would be dear to her as Ralph was.
Ah yes, if Gilbert was jealous of her there was perhaps some reason; it
didn't make Gilbert look better to sit for half an hour with Ralph. It was
not that they talked of him—it was not that she complained. His name
was never uttered between them. It was simply that Ralph was generous
and that her husband was not. There was something in Ralph's talk, in
his smile, in the mere fact of his being in Rome, that made the blasted
circle round which she walked more spacious. He made her feel the good
of the world; he made her feel what might have been. He was after all as
intelligent as Osmond—quite apart from his being better. And thus it
seemed to her an act of devotion to conceal her misery from him. She
concealed it elaborately; she was perpetually, in their talk, hanging out
curtains and arranging screens. It lived before her again—it had never
had time to die—that morning in the garden at Florence when he had
warned her against Osmond. She had only to close her eyes to see the
place, to hear his voice, to feel the warm, sweet air. How could he have
known? What a mystery, what a wonder of wisdom! As intelligent as Gilbert? He was much more intelligent—to arrive at such a judgement as that.
Gilbert had never been so deep, so just. She had told him then that from
her at least he should never know if he was right; and this was what she
was taking care of now. It gave her plenty to do; there was passion, exaltation, religion in it. Women find their religion sometimes in strange exercises, and Isabel at present, in playing a part before her cousin, had an
idea that she was doing him a kindness. It would have been a kindness
perhaps if he had been for a single instant a dupe. As it was, the kindness
consisted mainly in trying to make him believe that he had once wounded
her greatly and that the event had put him to shame, but that, as she was
very generous and he was so ill, she bore him no grudge and even considerately forbore to flaunt her happiness in his face. Ralph smiled to himself, as he lay on his sofa, at this extraordinary form of consideration; but
he forgave her for having forgiven him. She didn't wish him to have the
pain of knowing she was unhappy: that was the great thing, and it didn't
matter that such knowledge would rather have righted him.

For herself, she lingered in the soundless saloon long after the fire had
gone out. There was no danger of her feeling the cold; she was in a fever.
She heard the small hours strike, and then the great ones, but her vigil
took no heed of time. Her mind, assailed by visions, was in a state of extraordinary activity, and her visions might as well come to her there, where
she sat up to meet them, as on her pillow, to make a mockery of rest. As I
have said, she believed she was not defiant, and what could be a better

proof of it than that she should linger there half the night, trying to persuade herself that there was no reason why Pansy shouldn't be married as you would put a letter in the post-office? When the clock struck four she got up; she was going to bed at last, for the lamp had long since gone out and the candles burned down to their sockets. But even then she stopped again in the middle of the room and stood there gazing at a remembered vision—that of her husband and Madame Merle unconsciously and familiarly associated.

Chapter XLIII

Three nights after this she took Pansy to a great party, to which Osmond, who never went to dances, did not accompany them. Pansy was as ready for a dance as ever; she was not of a generalising turn and had not extended to other pleasures the interdict she had seen placed on those of love. If she was biding her time or hoping to circumvent her father she must have had a prevision of success. Isabel thought this unlikely; it was much more likely that Pansy had simply determined to be a good girl. She had never had such a chance, and she had a proper esteem for chances. She carried herself no less attentively than usual and kept no less anxious an eye upon her vaporous skirts; she held her bouquet very tight and counted over the flowers for the twentieth time. She made Isabel feel old; it seemed so long since she had been in a flutter about a ball. Pansy, who was greatly admired, was never in want of partners, and very soon after their arrival she gave Isabel, who was not dancing, her bouquet to hold. Isabel had rendered her this service for some minutes when she became aware of the near presence of Edward Rosier. He stood before her; he had lost his affable smile and wore a look of almost military resolution. The change in his appearance would have made Isabel smile if she had not felt his case to be at bottom a hard one: he had always smelt so much more of heliotrope than of gunpowder. He looked at her a moment somewhat fiercely, as if to notify her he was dangerous, and then dropped his eyes on her bouquet. After he had inspected it his glance softened and he said quickly: "It's all pansies; it must be hers!"

Isabel smiled kindly. "Yes, it's hers; she gave it to me to hold."

"May I hold it a little, Mrs. Osmond?" the poor young man asked.

"No, I can't trust you; I'm afraid you wouldn't give it back."

"I'm not sure that I should; I should leave the house with it instantly. But may I not at least have a single flower?"

Isabel hesitated a moment, and then, smiling still, held out the bouquet. "Choose one yourself. It's frightful what I'm doing for you."

"Ah, if you do no more than this, Mrs. Osmond!" Rosier exclaimed with his glass in one eye, carefully choosing his flower.

"Don't put it into your button-hole," she said. "Don't for the world!"

"I should like her to see it. She has refused to dance with me, but I wish to show her that I believe in her still."

"It's very well to show it to her, but it's out of place to show it to others. Her father has told her not to dance with you."

"And is that all *you* can do for me? I expected more from you, Mrs. Osmond," said the young man in a tone of fine general reference.

"You know our acquaintance goes back very far—quite into the days of our innocent childhood."

"Don't make me out too old," Isabel patiently answered. "You come back to that very often, and I've never denied it. But I must tell you that, old friends as we are, if you had done me the honour to ask me to marry you I should have refused you on the spot."

"Ah, you don't esteem me then. Say at once that you think me a mere Parisian trifler!"

"I esteem you very much, but I'm not in love with you. What I mean by that, of course, is that I'm not in love with you for Pansy."

"Very good; I see. You pity me—that's all." And Edward Rosier looked all round, inconsequently, with his single glass. It was a revelation to him that people shouldn't be more pleased; but he was at least too proud to show that the deficiency struck him as general.

Isabel for a moment said nothing. His manner and appearance had not the dignity of the deepest tragedy; his little glass, among other things, was against that. But she suddenly felt touched; her own unhappiness, after all, had something in common with his, and it came over her, more than before, that here, in recognisable, if not in romantic form, was the most affecting thing in the world—young love struggling with adversity. "Would you really be very kind to her?" she finally asked in a low tone.

He dropped his eyes devoutly and raised the little flower that he held in his fingers to his lips. Then he looked at her. "You pity me; but don't you pity *her* a little?"

"I don't know; I'm not sure. She'll always enjoy life."

"It will depend on what you call life!" Mr. Rosier effectively said. "She won't enjoy being tortured."

"There'll be nothing of that."

"I'm glad to hear it. She knows what she's about. You'll see."

"I think she does, and she'll never disobey her father. But she's coming back to me," Isabel added, "and I must beg you to go away."

Rosier lingered a moment till Pansy came in sight on the arm of her cavalier; he stood just long enough to look her in the face. Then he walked away, holding up his head; and the manner in which he achieved this sacrifice to expediency convinced Isabel he was very much in love.

Pansy, who seldom got disarranged in dancing, looking perfectly fresh and cool after this exercise, waited a moment and then took back her bouquet. Isabel watched her and saw she was counting the flowers; whereupon she said to herself that decidedly there were deeper forces at play than she had recognised. Pansy had seen Rosier turn away, but she said nothing to Isabel about him; she talked only of her partner, after he had made his bow and retired; of the music, the floor, the rare misfortune of having already torn her dress. Isabel was sure, however, she had discovered her lover to have abstracted a flower; though this knowledge was not needed to account for the dutiful grace with which she responded to the appeal of her next partner. That perfect amenity under acute constraint was part of a larger system. She was again led forth by a flushed young man, this time carrying her bouquet; and she had not been absent many minutes when Isabel saw Lord Warburton advancing through the crowd. He presently drew near and bade her good-evening; she had not seen him since

the day before. He looked about him, and then "Where's the little maid?"
he asked. It was in this manner that he had formed the harmless habit of
alluding to Miss Osmond.

"She's dancing," said Isabel. "You'll see her somewhere."

He looked among the dancers and at last caught Pansy's eye. "She sees
me, but she won't notice me," he then remarked. "Are you not dancing?"

"As you see, I'm a wall-flower."

"Won't you dance with me?"

"Thank you; I'd rather you should dance with the little maid."

"One needn't prevent the other—especially as she's engaged."

"She's not engaged for everything, and you can reserve yourself. She
dances very hard, and you'll be the fresher."

"She dances beautifully," said Lord Warburton, following her with his
eyes. "Ah, at last," he added, "she has given me a smile." He stood there
with his handsome, easy, important physiognomy; and as Isabel observed
him it came over her, as it had done before, that it was strange a man of
his mettle should take an interest in a little maid. It struck her as a great
incongruity; neither Pansy's small fascinations, nor his own kindness, his
good-nature, not even his need for amusement, which was extreme and
constant, were sufficient to account for it. "I should like to dance with
you," he went on in a moment, turning back to Isabel; "but I think I like
even better to talk with you."

"Yes, it's better, and it's more worthy of your dignity. Great statesmen
oughtn't to waltz."

"Don't be cruel. Why did you recommend me then to dance with Miss
Osmond?"

"Ah, that's different. If you danced with her it would look simply like a
piece of kindness—as if you were doing it for her amusement. If you dance
with me you'll look as if you were doing it for your own."

"And pray haven't I a right to amuse myself?"

"No, not with the affairs of the British Empire on your hands."

"The British Empire be hanged! You're always laughing at it."

"Amuse yourself with talking to me," said Isabel.

"I'm not sure it's really a recreation. You're too pointed; I've always to
be defending myself. And you strike me as more than usually dangerous
to-night. Will you absolutely not dance?"

"I can't leave my place. Pansy must find me here."

He was silent a little. "You're wonderfully good to her," he said
suddenly.

Isabel stared a little and smiled. "Can you imagine one's not being?"

"No indeed. I know how one is charmed with her. But you must have
done a great deal for her."

"I've taken her out with me," said Isabel, smiling still. "And I've seen
that she has proper clothes."

"Your society must have been a great benefit to her. You've talked to her,
advised her, helped her to develop."

"Ah yes, if she isn't the rose she has lived near it."

She laughed, and her companion did as much; but there was a certain
visible preoccupation in his face which interfered with complete hilarity.
"We all try to live as near it as we can," he said after a moment's hesitation.

Isabel turned away; Pansy was about to be restored to her, and she welcomed the diversion. We know how much she liked Lord Warburton; she thought him pleasanter even than the sum of his merits warranted; there was something in his friendship that appeared a kind of resource in case of indefinite need; it was like having a large balance at the bank. She felt happier when he was in the room; there was something reassuring in his approach; the sound of his voice reminded her of the beneficence of nature. Yet for all that it didn't suit her that he should be too near her, that he should take too much of her good-will for granted. She was afraid of that; she averted herself from it; she wished he wouldn't. She felt that if he should come too near, as it were, it might be in her to flash out and bid him keep his distance. Pansy came back to Isabel with another rent in her skirt, which was the inevitable consequence of the first and which she displayed to Isabel with serious eyes. There were too many gentlemen in uniform; they wore those dreadful spurs, which were fatal to the dresses of little maids. It hereupon became apparent that the resources of women are innumerable. Isabel devoted herself to Pansy's desecrated drapery; she fumbled for a pin and repaired the injury; she smiled and listened to her account of her adventures. Her attention, her sympathy were immediate and active; and they were in direct proportion to a sentiment with which they were in no way connected—a lively conjecture as to whether Lord Warburton might be trying to make love to her. It was not simply his words just then; it was others as well; it was the reference and the continuity. This was what she thought about while she pinned up Pansy's dress. If it were so, as she feared, he was of course unwitting; he himself had not taken account of his intention. But this made it none the more auspicious, made the situation none the less impossible. The sooner he should get back into right relations with things the better. He immediately began to talk to Pansy—on whom it was certainly mystifying to see that he dropped a smile of chastened devotion. Pansy replied, as usual, with a little air of conscientious aspiration; he had to bend toward her a good deal in conversation, and her eyes, as usual, wandered up and down his robust person as if he had offered it to her for exhibition. She always seemed a little frightened; yet her fright was not of the painful character that suggests dislike; on the contrary, she looked as if she knew that he knew she liked him. Isabel left them together a little and wandered toward a friend whom she saw near and with whom she talked till the music of the following dance began, for which she knew Pansy to be also engaged. The girl joined her presently, with a little fluttered flush, and Isabel, who scrupulously took Osmond's view of his daughter's complete dependence, consigned her, as a precious and momentary loan, to her appointed partner. About all this matter she had her own imaginations, her own reserves; there were moments when Pansy's extreme adhesiveness made each of them, to her sense, look foolish. But Osmond had given her a sort of tableau of her position as his daughter's duenna, which consisted of gracious alternations of concession and contraction; and there were directions of his which she liked to think she obeyed to the letter. Perhaps, as regards some of them, it was because her doing so appeared to reduce them to the absurd.

After Pansy had been led away, she found Lord Warburton drawing near her again. She rested her eyes on him steadily; she wished she could sound his thoughts. But he had no appearance of confusion. "She has promised to dance with me later," he said.

"I'm glad of that. I suppose you've engaged her for the cotillion."

At this he looked a little awkward. "No, I didn't ask her for that. It's a quadrille."[1]

"Ah, you're not clever!" said Isabel almost angrily. "I told her to keep the cotillion in case you should ask for it."

"Poor little maid, fancy that!" And Lord Warburton laughed frankly. "Of course I will if you like."

"If I like? Oh, if you dance with her only because I like it—!"

"I'm afraid I bore her. She seems to have a lot of young fellows on her book."

Isabel dropped her eyes, reflecting rapidly; Lord Warburton stood there looking at her and she felt his eyes on her face. She felt much inclined to ask him to remove them. She didn't do so, however; she only said to him, after a minute, with her own raised: "Please let me understand."

"Understand what?"

"You told me ten days ago that you'd like to marry my stepdaughter. You've not forgotten it!"

"Forgotten it? I wrote to Mr. Osmond about it this morning."

"Ah," said Isabel, "he didn't mention to me that he had heard from you."

Lord Warburton stammered a little. "I—I didn't send my letter."

"Perhaps you forgot *that*."

"No, I wasn't satisfied with it. It's an awkward sort of letter to write, you know. But I shall send it to-night."

"At three o'clock in the morning?"

"I mean later, in the course of the day."

"Very good. You still wish then to marry her?"

"Very much indeed."

"Aren't you afraid that you'll bore her?" And as her companion stared at this enquiry Isabel added: "If she can't dance with you for half an hour how will she be able to dance with you for life?"

"Ah," said Lord Warburton readily, "I'll let her dance with other people! About the cotillion, the fact is I thought that you—that you—"

"That I would do it with you? I told you I'd do nothing."

"Exactly; so that while it's going on I might find some quiet corner where we may sit down and talk."

"Oh," said Isabel gravely, "you're much too considerate of me."

When the cotillion came Pansy was found to have engaged herself, thinking, in perfect humility, that Lord Warburton had no intentions. Isabel recommended him to seek another partner, but he assured her that he would dance with no one but herself. As, however, she had, in spite of the remonstrances of her hostess, declined other invitations on the ground that she was not dancing at all, it was not possible for her to make an exception in Lord Warburton's favour.

"After all I don't care to dance," he said; "it's a barbarous amusement: I'd much rather talk." And he intimated that he had discovered exactly the corner he had been looking for—a quiet nook in one of the smaller

---

1. The cotillion was a line dance that allowed for more flirtation than the quadrille, a kind of square dance in which participants regularly changed partners.

rooms, where the music would come to them faintly and not interfere with conversation. Isabel had decided to let him carry out his idea; she wished to be satisfied. She wandered away from the ball-room with him, though she knew her husband desired she should not lose sight of his daughter. It was with his daughter's *prétendant*,[2] however; that would make it right for Osmond. On her way out of the ball-room she came upon Edward Rosier, who was standing in a doorway, with folded arms, looking at the dance in the attitude of a young man without illusions. She stopped a moment and asked him if he were not dancing.

"Certainly not, if I can't dance with *her!*" he answered.

"You had better go away then," said Isabel with the manner of good counsel.

"I shall not go till she does!" And he let Lord Warburton pass without giving him a look.

This nobleman, however, had noticed the melancholy youth, and he asked Isabel who her dismal friend was, remarking that he had seen him somewhere before.

"It's the young man I've told you about, who's in love with Pansy."

"Ah yes, I remember. He looks rather bad."

"He has reason. My husband won't listen to him."

"What's the matter with him?" Lord Warburton enquired. "He seems very harmless."

"He hasn't money enough, and he isn't very clever."

Lord Warburton listened with interest; he seemed struck with this account of Edward Rosier. "Dear me; he looked a well-set-up young fellow."

"So he is, but my husband's very particular."

"Oh, I see." And Lord Warburton paused a moment. "How much money has he got?" he then ventured to ask.

"Some forty thousand francs a year."

"Sixteen hundred pounds? Ah, but that's very good, you know."

"So I think. My husband, however, has larger ideas."

"Yes; I've noticed that your husband has very large ideas. Is he really an idiot, the young man?"

"An idiot? Not in the least; he's charming. When he was twelve years old I myself was in love with him."

"He doesn't look much more than twelve to-day," Lord Warburton rejoined vaguely, looking about him. Then with more point, "Don't you think we might sit here?" he asked.

"Wherever you please." The room was a sort of boudoir, pervaded by a subdued, rose-coloured light; a lady and gentleman moved out of it as our friends came in. "It's very kind of you to take such an interest in Mr. Rosier," Isabel said.

"He seems to me rather ill-treated. He had a face a yard long. I wondered what ailed him."

"You're a just man," said Isabel. "You've a kind thought even for a rival."

Lord Warburton suddenly turned with a stare. "A rival! Do you call him my rival?"

"Surely—if you both wish to marry the same person."

"Yes—but since he has no chance!"

2. Suitor (French).

"I like you, however that may be, for putting yourself in his place. It shows imagination."

"You like me for it?" And Lord Warburton looked at her with an uncertain eye. "I think you mean you're laughing at me for it."

"Yes, I'm laughing at you a little. But I like you as somebody to laugh at."

"Ah well, then, let me enter into his situation a little more. What do you suppose one could do for him?"

"Since I have been praising your imagination I'll leave you to imagine that yourself," Isabel said. "Pansy too would like you for that."

"Miss Osmond? Ah, she, I flatter myself, likes me already."

"Very much, I think."

He waited a little; he was still questioning her face. "Well then, I don't understand you. You don't mean that she cares for him?"

"Surely I've told you I thought she did."

A quick blush sprang to his brow. "You told me she would have no wish apart from her father's, and as I've gathered that he would favour me—!" He paused a little and then suggested "Don't you see?" through his blush.

"Yes, I told you she has an immense wish to please her father, and that it would probably take her very far."

"That seems to me a very proper feeling," said Lord Warburton.

"Certainly; it's a very proper feeling." Isabel remained silent for some moments; the room continued empty; the sound of the music reached them with its richness softened by the interposing apartments. Then at last she said: "But it hardly strikes me as the sort of feeling to which a man would wish to be indebted for a wife."

"I don't know; if the wife's a good one and he thinks she does well!"

"Yes, of course you must think that."

"I do; I can't help it. You call that very British, of course."

"No, I don't. I think Pansy would do wonderfully well to marry you, and I don't know who should know it better than you. But you're not in love."

"Ah, yes I am, Mrs. Osmond!"

Isabel shook her head. "You like to think you are while you sit here with me. But that's not how you strike me."

"I'm not like the young man in the doorway. I admit that. But what makes it so unnatural? Could any one in the world be more loveable than Miss Osmond?"

"No one, possibly. But love has nothing to do with good reasons."

"I don't agree with you. I'm delighted to have good reasons."

"Of course you are. If you were really in love you wouldn't care a straw for them."

"Ah, really in love—really in love!" Lord Warburton exclaimed, folding his arms, leaning back his head and stretching himself a little. "You must remember that I'm forty-two years old. I won't pretend I'm as I once was."

"Well, if you're sure," said Isabel, "it's all right."

He answered nothing; he sat there, with his head back, looking before him. Abruptly, however, he changed his position; he turned quickly to his friend. "Why are you so unwilling, so sceptical?"

She met his eyes, and for a moment they looked straight at each other. If she wished to be satisfied she saw something that satisfied her; she saw in his expression the gleam of an idea that she was uneasy on her own account—that she was perhaps even in fear. It showed a suspicion, not a hope, but such as it was it told her what she wanted to know. Not for an instant should he suspect her of detecting in his proposal of marrying her stepdaughter an implication of increased nearness to herself, or of thinking it, on such a betrayal, ominous. In that brief, extremely personal gaze, however, deeper meanings passed between them than they were conscious of at the moment.

"My dear Lord Warburton," she said, smiling, "you may do, so far as I'm concerned, whatever comes into your head."

And with this she got up and wandered into the adjoining room, where, within her companion's view, she was immediately addressed by a pair of gentlemen, high personages in the Roman world, who met her as if they had been looking for her. While she talked with them she found herself regretting she had moved; it looked a little like running away—all the more as Lord Warburton didn't follow her. She was glad of this, however, and at any rate she was satisfied. She was so well satisfied that when, in passing back into the ball-room, she found Edward Rosier still planted in the doorway, she stopped and spoke to him again. "You did right not to go away. I've some comfort for you."

"I need it," the young man softly wailed, "when I see you so awfully thick with *him!*"

"Don't speak of him; I'll do what I can for you. I'm afraid it won't be much, but what I can I'll do."

He looked at her with gloomy obliqueness. "What has suddenly brought you round?"

"The sense that you are an inconvenience in doorways!" she answered, smiling as she passed him. Half an hour later she took leave, with Pansy, and at the foot of the staircase the two ladies, with many other departing guests, waited a while for their carriage. Just as it approached Lord Warburton came out of the house and assisted them to reach their vehicle. He stood a moment at the door, asking Pansy if she had amused herself; and she, having answered him, fell back with a little air of fatigue. Then Isabel, at the window, detaining him by a movement of her finger, murmured gently: "Don't forget to send your letter to her father!"

Chapter XLIV

The Countess Gemini was often extremely bored—bored, in her own phrase, to extinction. She had not been extinguished, however, and she struggled bravely enough with her destiny, which had been to marry an unaccommodating Florentine who insisted upon living in his native town, where he enjoyed such consideration as might attach to a gentleman whose talent for losing at cards had not the merit of being incidental to an obliging disposition. The Count Gemini was not liked even by those who won from him; and he bore a name which, having a measurable value in Florence, was, like the local coin of the old Italian states, without currency in other parts of the peninsula. In Rome he was simply a very dull Florentine, and it is not remarkable that he should not have cared to pay frequent visits to a place where, to carry it off, his dulness needed more explanation than was convenient. The Countess lived with her eyes upon Rome, and it was the constant grievance of her life that she had not an habitation there. She was ashamed to say how seldom she had been allowed to visit that city; it scarcely made the matter better that there were other members of the Florentine nobility who never had been there at all. She went whenever she could; that was all she could say. Or rather not all, but all she said she could say. In fact she had much more to say about it, and had often set forth the reasons why she hated Florence and wished to end her days in the shadow of Saint Peter's. They are reasons, however, that do not closely concern us, and were usually summed up in the declaration that Rome, in short, was the Eternal City and that Florence was simply a pretty little place like any other. The Countess apparently needed to connect the idea of eternity with her amusements. She was convinced that society was infinitely more interesting in Rome, where you met celebrities all winter at evening parties. At Florence there were no celebrities; none at least that one had heard of. Since her brother's marriage her impatience had greatly increased; she was so sure his wife had a more brilliant life than herself. She was not so intellectual as Isabel, but she was intellectual enough to do justice to Rome—not to the ruins and the catacombs, not even perhaps to the monuments and museums, the church ceremonies and the scenery; but certainly to all the rest. She heard a great deal about her sister-in-law and knew perfectly that Isabel was having a beautiful time. She had indeed seen it for herself on the only occasion on which she had enjoyed the hospitality of Palazzo Roccanera. She had spent a week there during the first winter of her brother's marriage, but she had not been encouraged to renew this satisfaction. Osmond didn't want her—that she was perfectly aware of; but she would have gone all the same, for after all she didn't care two straws about Osmond. It was her husband who wouldn't let her, and the money question was always a trouble. Isabel had been very nice; the Countess, who had liked her sister-in-law from the first, had not been blinded by envy to Isabel's personal merits. She had always observed that she got on better with clever women than with silly ones like herself; the silly ones could never understand her wisdom, whereas the clever ones—the really clever ones—always understood her silliness. It appeared to her that, different as they were in appearance and general style, Isabel and she had somewhere a patch of common ground that they would set their feet upon at last. It was not very large, but it was firm, and they should both know it when once they had really touched it. And then she lived, with Mrs. Osmond, under the influence of a pleasant surprise; she was constantly expecting that Isabel would "look down" on her, and she as constantly saw this operation postponed. She asked herself when it would begin, like fire-works, or Lent, or the opera season; not that she cared much, but she wondered what kept it in abeyance. Her sister-in-law regarded her with none but level glances and expressed for the poor Countess as little contempt as admiration. In reality Isabel would as soon have thought of despising her as of passing a moral judgement on a grasshopper. She was not indifferent to her husband's sister, however; she was rather a little afraid of her. She wondered at her; she thought her very extraordinary. The Countess seemed to her to have no soul; she was like a bright rare shell, with a polished surface and a remarkably pink lip, in which something would rattle when you shook it. This rattle was apparently the Countess's spiritual principle, a little loose nut that tumbled about inside of her. She was too odd for disdain, too anomalous for comparisons. Isabel would have invited her again (there was no question of inviting the Count); but Osmond, after his marriage, had not scrupled to say frankly that Amy was a fool of the worst species—a fool whose folly had the irrepressibility of genius. He said at another time that she had no heart; and he added in a moment that she had given it all away—in small pieces, like a frosted wedding-cake. The fact of not having been asked was of course another obstacle to the Countess's going again to Rome; but at the period with which this history has now to deal she was in receipt of an invitation to spend several weeks at Palazzo Roccanera. The proposal had come from Osmond himself, who wrote to his sister that she must be prepared to be very quiet. Whether or no she found in this phrase all the meaning he had put into it I am unable to say; but she accepted the invitation on any terms. She was curious, moreover; for one of the impressions of her former visit had been that her brother had found his match. Before the marriage she had been sorry for Isabel, so sorry as to have had serious thoughts—if any of the Countess's thoughts were serious—of putting her on her guard. But she had let that pass, and after a little she was reassured. Osmond was as lofty as ever, but his wife would not be an easy victim. The Countess was not very exact at measurements, but it seemed to her that if Isabel should draw herself up she would be the taller spirit of the two. What she wanted to learn now was whether Isabel had drawn herself up; it would give her immense pleasure to see Osmond overtopped.

Several days before she was to start for Rome a servant brought her the card of a visitor—a card with the simple superscription "Henrietta C. Stackpole." The Countess pressed her finger-tips to her forehead; she didn't remember to have known any such Henrietta as that. The servant then remarked that the lady had requested him to say that if the Countess should not recognize her name she would know her well enough on seeing her. By the time she appeared before her visitor she had in fact reminded herself that there was once a literary lady at Mrs. Touchett's; the only woman of letters she had ever encountered—that is the only modern one, since she was the daughter of a defunct poetess. She recognised Miss Stackpole immediately, the more so that Miss Stackpole seemed perfectly unchanged; and the Countess, who was thoroughly good-natured, thought it rather fine to be called on by a person of that sort of distinction. She wondered if Miss Stackpole had come on account of her mother—whether she had heard of the American Corinne. Her mother was not at all like Isabel's friend; the Countess could see at a glance that this lady was much more contemporary; and she received an impression of the improvements that were taking place—chiefly in distant countries—in the character (the professional character) of literary ladies. Her mother had been used to wear a Roman scarf thrown over a pair of shoulders timorously bared of their tight black velvet (oh the old clothes!) and a gold laurel-wreath set upon a multitude of glossy ringlets. She had spoken softly and vaguely, with the accent of her "Creole" ancestors, as she always confessed; she sighed a great deal and was not at all enterprising. But Henrietta, the Countess could see, was always closely buttoned and compactly braided; there was something brisk and business-like in her appearance; her manner was almost conscientiously familiar. It was as impossible to imagine her ever vaguely sighing as to imagine a letter posted without its address. The Countess could not but feel that the correspondent of the *Interviewer* was much more in the movement than the American Corinne.

She explained that she had called on the Countess because she was the only person she knew in Florence, and that when she visited a foreign city she liked to see something more than superficial travellers. She knew Mrs. Touchett, but Mrs. Touchett was in America, and even if she had been in Florence Henrietta would not have put herself out for her, since Mrs. Touchett was not one of her admirations.

"Do you mean by that that I am?" the Countess graciously asked.

"Well, I like you better than I do her," said Miss Stackpole. "I seem to remember that when I saw you before you were very interesting. I don't know whether it was an accident or whether it's your usual style. At any rate I was a good deal struck with what you said. I made use of it afterwards in print."

"Dear me!" cried the Countess, staring and half-alarmed; "I had no idea I ever said anything remarkable! I wish I had known it at the time."

"It was about the position of woman in this city," Miss Stackpole remarked. "You threw a good deal of light upon it."

"The position of woman's very uncomfortable. Is that what you mean? And you wrote it down and published it?" the Countess went on. "Ah, do let me see it!"

"I'll write to them to send you the paper if you like," Henrietta said. "I didn't mention your name; I only said a lady of high rank. And then I quoted your views."

The Countess threw herself hastily backward, tossing up her clasped hands. "Do you know I'm rather sorry you didn't mention my name? I should have rather liked to see my name in the papers. I forget what my views were; I have so many! But I'm not ashamed of them. I'm not at all like my brother—I suppose you know my brother? He thinks it a kind of scandal to be put in the papers; if you were to quote him he'd never forgive you."

"He needn't be afraid; I shall never refer to him," said Miss Stackpole with bland dryness. "That's another reason," she added, "why I wanted to come to see you. You know Mr. Osmond married my dearest friend."

"Ah, yes; you were a friend of Isabel's. I was trying to think what I knew about you."

"I'm quite willing to be known by that," Henrietta declared. "But that isn't what your brother likes to know me by. He has tried to break up my relations with Isabel."

"Don't permit it," said the Countess.

"That's what I want to talk about. I'm going to Rome."

"So am I!" the Countess cried. "We'll go together."

"With great pleasure. And when I write about my journey I'll mention you by name as my companion."

The Countess sprang from her chair and came and sat on the sofa beside her visitor. "Ah, you must send me the paper! My husband won't like it, but he need never see it. Besides, he doesn't know how to read."

Henrietta's large eyes became immense. "Doesn't know how to read? May I put that into my letter?"

"Into your letter?"

"In the *Interviewer*. That's my paper."

"Oh yes, if you like; with his name. Are you going to stay with Isabel?"

Henrietta held up her head, gazing a little in silence at her hostess. "She has not asked me. I wrote to her I was coming, and she answered that she would engage a room for me at a *pension*.[1] She gave no reason."

The Countess listened with extreme interest. "The reason's Osmond," she pregnantly remarked.

"Isabel ought to make a stand," said Miss Stackpole. "I'm afraid she has changed a great deal. I told her she would."

"I'm sorry to hear it; I hoped she would have her own way. Why doesn't my brother like you?" the Countess ingenuously added.

"I don't know and I don't care. He's perfectly welcome not to like me; I don't want every one to like me; I should think less of myself if some people did. A journalist can't hope to do much good unless he gets a good deal hated; that's the way he knows how his work goes on. And it's just the same for a lady. But I didn't expect it of Isabel."

"Do you mean that she hates you?" the Countess enquired.

"I don't know; I want to see. That's what I'm going to Rome for."

"Dear me, what a tiresome errand!" the Countess exclaimed.

"She doesn't write to me in the same way; it's easy to see there's a difference. If you know anything," Miss Stackpole went on, "I should like to hear it beforehand, so as to decide on the line I shall take."

The Countess thrust out her under lip and gave a gradual shrug. "I know very little; I see and hear very little of Osmond. He doesn't like me any better than he appears to like you."

"Yet you're not a lady correspondent," said Henrietta pensively.

"Oh, he has plenty of reasons. Nevertheless they've invited me—I'm to stay in the house!" And the Countess smiled almost fiercely; her exultation, for the moment, took little account of Miss Stackpole's disappointment.

This lady, however, regarded it very placidly. "I shouldn't have gone if she *had* asked me. That is I think I shouldn't; and I'm glad I hadn't to make up my mind. It would have been a very difficult question. I shouldn't have liked to turn away from her, and yet I shouldn't have been happy under her roof. A *pension* will suit me very well. But that's not all."

"Rome's very good just now," said the Countess; "there are all sorts of brilliant people. Did you ever hear of Lord Warburton?"

"Hear of him? I know him very well. Do you consider him very brilliant?" Henrietta enquired.

"I don't know him, but I'm told he's extremely *grand seigneur*. He's making love to Isabel."

"Making love to her?"

"So I'm told; I don't know the details," said the Countess lightly. "But Isabel's pretty safe."

Henrietta gazed earnestly at her companion; for a moment she said nothing. "When do you go to Rome?" she enquired abruptly.

"Not for a week, I'm afraid."

"I shall go to-morrow," Henrietta said. "I think I had better not wait."

"Dear me, I'm sorry; I'm having some dresses made. I'm told Isabel receives immensely. But I shall see you there; I shall call on you at your

---

1. Essentially a B&B; a modest lodging with a limited number of rooms, offering breakfast and sometimes other meals but without the full services of a hotel. Most common in Italy and the German-speaking countries.

pension." Henrietta sat still—she was lost in thought; and suddenly the Countess cried: "Ah, but if you don't go with me you can't describe our journey!"

Miss Stackpole seemed unmoved by this consideration; she was thinking of something else and presently expressed it. "I'm not sure that I understand you about Lord Warburton."

"Understand me? I mean he's very nice, that's all."

"Do you consider it nice to make love to married women?" Henrietta enquired with unprecedented distinctness.

The Countess stared, and then with a little violent laugh: "It's certain all the nice men do it. Get married and you'll see!" she added.

"That idea would be enough to prevent me," said Miss Stackpole. "I should want my own husband; I shouldn't want any one else's. Do you mean that Isabel's guilty—guilty—?" And she paused a little, choosing her expression.

"Do I mean she's guilty? Oh dear no, not yet, I hope. I only mean that Osmond's very tiresome and that Lord Warburton, as I hear, is a great deal at the house. I'm afraid you're scandalised."

"No, I'm just anxious," Henrietta said.

"Ah, you're not very complimentary to Isabel! You should have more confidence. I'll tell you," the Countess added quickly: "if it will be a comfort to you I engage to draw him off."

Miss Stackpole answered at first only with the deeper solemnity of her gaze. "You don't understand me," she said after a while. "I haven't the idea you seem to suppose. I'm not afraid for Isabel—in that way. I'm only afraid she's unhappy—that's what I want to get at."

The Countess gave a dozen turns of the head; she looked impatient and sarcastic. "That may very well be; for my part I should like to know whether Osmond is." Miss Stackpole had begun a little to bore her.

"If she's really changed that must be at the bottom of it," Henrietta went on.

"You'll see; she'll tell you," said the Countess.

"Ah, she may *not* tell me—that's what I'm afraid of!"

"Well, if Osmond isn't amusing himself—in his own old way—I flatter myself I shall discover it," the Countess rejoined.

"I don't care for that," said Henrietta.

"I do immensely! If Isabel's unhappy I'm very sorry for her, but I can't help it. I might tell her something that would make her worse, but I can't tell her anything that would console her. What did she go and marry him for? If she had listened to me she'd have got rid of him. I'll forgive her, however, if I find she has made things hot for him! If she has simply allowed him to trample upon her I don't know that I shall even pity her. But I don't think that's very likely. I count upon finding that if she's miserable she has at least made *him* so."

Henrietta got up; these seemed to her, naturally, very dreadful expectations. She honestly believed she had no desire to see Mr. Osmond unhappy; and indeed he could not be for her the subject of a flight of fancy. She was on the whole rather disappointed in the Countess, whose mind moved in a narrower circle than she had imagined, though with a capacity for coarseness even there. "It will be better if they love each other," she said for edification.

"They can't. He can't love any one."

"I presumed that was the case. But it only aggravates my fear for Isabel. I shall positively start to-morrow."

"Isabel certainly has devotees," said the Countess, smiling very vividly. "I declare I don't pity her."

"It may be I can't assist her," Miss Stackpole pursued, as if it were well not to have illusions.

"You can have wanted to, at any rate; that's something. I believe that's what you came from America for," the Countess suddenly added.

"Yes, I wanted to look after her," Henrietta said serenely.

Her hostess stood there smiling at her with small bright eyes and an eager-looking nose; with cheeks into each of which a flush had come. "Ah, that's very pretty—*c'est bien gentil!*[2] Isn't it what they call friendship?"

"I don't know what they call it. I thought I had better come."

"She's very happy—she's very fortunate," the Countess went on. "She has others besides." And then she broke out passionately. "She's more fortunate than I! I'm as unhappy as she—I've a very bad husband; he's a great deal worse than Osmond. And I've no friends. I thought I had, but they're gone. No one, man or woman, would do for me what you've done for her."

Henrietta was touched; there was nature in this bitter effusion. She gazed at her companion a moment, and then: "Look here, Countess, I'll do anything for you that you like. I'll wait over and travel with you."

"Never mind," the Countess answered with a quick change of tone: "only describe me in the newspaper!"

Henrietta, before leaving her, however, was obliged to make her understand that she could give no fictitious representation of her journey to Rome. Miss Stackpole was a strictly veracious reporter. On quitting her she took the way to the Lung' Arno, the sunny quay beside the yellow river where the bright-faced inns familiar to tourists stand all in a row. She had learned her way before this through the streets of Florence (she was very quick in such matters), and was therefore able to turn with great decision of step out of the little square which forms the approach to the bridge of the Holy Trinity. She proceeded to the left, toward the Ponte Vecchio,[3] and stopped in front of one of the hotels which overlook that delightful structure. Here she drew forth a small pocket-book, took from it a card and a pencil and, after meditating a moment, wrote a few words. It is our privilege to look over her shoulder, and if we exercise it we may read the brief query: "Could I see you this evening for a few moments on a very important matter?" Henrietta added that she should start on the morrow for Rome. Armed with this little document she approached the porter, who now had taken up his station in the doorway, and asked if Mr. Goodwood were at home. The porter replied, as porters always reply, that he had gone out about twenty minutes before; whereupon Henrietta presented her card and begged it might be handed him on his return. She left the inn and pursued her course along the quay to the severe portico of the Uffizi, through which she presently reached the entrance of the famous gallery of paintings. Making her way in, she ascended the high staircase which leads to the upper chambers. The long corridor, glazed on one side and

2. It's really nice! (French).
3. Two of Florence's oldest bridges over the Arno. The Ponte Vecchio was lined with shops, most of them selling jewelry, and was historically the river's major crossing point; the Ponte di Santa Trinita was a few hundred yards downstream.

decorated with antique busts, which gives admission to these apartments, presented an empty vista in which the bright winter light twinkled upon the marble floor. The gallery is very cold and during the midwinter weeks but scantily visited. Miss Stackpole may appear more ardent in her quest of artistic beauty than she has hitherto struck us as being, but she had after all her preferences and admirations. One of the latter was the little Correggio of the Tribune[4]—the Virgin kneeling down before the sacred infant, who lies in a litter of straw, and clapping her hands to him while he delightedly laughs and crows. Henrietta had a special devotion to this intimate scene— she thought it the most beautiful picture in the world. On her way, at present, from New York to Rome, she was spending but three days in Florence, and yet reminded herself that they must not elapse without her paying another visit to her favourite work of art. She had a great sense of beauty in all ways, and it involved a good many intellectual obligations. She was about to turn into the Tribune when a gentleman came out of it; whereupon she gave a little exclamation and stood before Caspar Goodwood.

"I've just been at your hotel," she said. "I left a card for you."

"I'm very much honoured," Caspar Goodwood answered as if he really meant it.

"It was not to honour you I did it; I've called on you before and I know you don't like it. It was to talk to you a little about something."

He looked for a moment at the buckle in her hat. "I shall be very glad to hear what you wish to say."

"You don't like to talk with me," said Henrietta. "But I don't care for that; I don't talk for your amusement. I wrote a word to ask you to come and see me; but since I've met you here this will do as well."

"I was just going away," Goodwood stated; "but of course I'll stop." He was civil, but not enthusiastic.

Henrietta, however, never looked for great professions, and she was so much in earnest that she was thankful he would listen to her on any terms. She asked him first, none the less, if he had seen all the pictures.

"All I want to. I've been here an hour."

"I wonder if you've seen my Correggio," said Henrietta. "I came up on purpose to have a look at it." She went into the Tribune and he slowly accompanied her.

"I suppose I've seen it, but I didn't know it was yours. I don't remember pictures—especially that sort." She had pointed out her favourite work, and he asked her if it was about Correggio she wished to talk with him.

"No," said Henrietta, "it's about something less harmonious!" They had the small, brilliant room, a splendid cabinet of treasures, to themselves; there was only a custode hovering about the Medicean Venus.[5] "I want you to do me a favour," Miss Stackpole went on.

Caspar Goodwood frowned a little, but he expressed no embarrassment at the sense of not looking eager. His face was that of a much older man than our earlier friend. "I'm sure it's something I shan't like," he said rather loudly.

"No, I don't think you'll like it. If you did it would be no favour."

4. A sumptuously decorated octagonal room containing some of the Uffizi's greatest treasures; the Correggio, "Virgin Adoring the Christ Child," has been a part of its collection since the early seventeenth century.
5. A lifesize marble statue, made in the first century B.C.E. from an earlier original, of the nude Venus, who stands with a hand half-shielding her breasts.

"Well, let's hear it," he went on in the tone of a man quite conscious of his patience.

"You may say there's no particular reason why you should do me a favour. Indeed I only know of one: the fact that if you'd let me I'd gladly do *you* one." Her soft, exact tone, in which there was no attempt at effect, had an extreme sincerity; and her companion, though he presented rather a hard surface, couldn't help being touched by it. When he was touched he rarely showed it, however, by the usual signs; he neither blushed, nor looked away, nor looked conscious. He only fixed his attention more directly; he seemed to consider with added firmness. Henrietta continued therefore disinterestedly, without the sense of an advantage. "I may say now, indeed—it seems a good time—that if I've ever annoyed you (and I think sometimes I have) it's because I knew I was willing to suffer annoyance for you. I've troubled you—doubtless. But I'd *take* trouble for you."

Goodwood hesitated. "You're taking trouble now."

"Yes, I am—some. I want you to consider whether it's better on the whole that you should go to Rome."

"I thought you were going to say that!" he answered rather artlessly.

"You *have* considered it then?"

"Of course I have, very carefully. I've looked all round it. Otherwise I shouldn't have come so far as this. That's what I stayed in Paris two months for. I was thinking it over."

"I'm afraid you decided as you liked. You decided it was best because you were so much attracted."

"Best for whom, do you mean?" Goodwood demanded.

"Well, for yourself first. For Mrs. Osmond next."

"Oh, it won't do *her* any good! I don't flatter myself that."

"Won't it do her some harm?—that's the question."

"I don't see what it will matter to her. I'm nothing to Mrs. Osmond. But if you want to know, I do want to see her myself."

"Yes, and that's why you go."

"Of course it is. Could there be a better reason?"

"How will it help you?—that's what I want to know," said Miss Stackpole.

"That's just what I can't tell you. It's just what I was thinking about in Paris."

"It will make you more discontented."

"Why do you say 'more' so?" Goodwood asked rather sternly. "How do you know I'm discontented?"

"Well," said Henrietta, hesitating a little, "you seem never to have cared for another."

"How do you know what I care for?" he cried with a big blush. "Just now I care to go to Rome."

Henrietta looked at him in silence, with a sad yet luminous expression. "Well," she observed at last, "I only wanted to tell you what I think; I had it on my mind. Of course you think it's none of my business. But nothing is any one's business, on that principle."

"It's very kind of you; I'm greatly obliged to you for your interest," said Caspar Goodwood. "I shall go to Rome and I shan't hurt Mrs. Osmond."

"You won't hurt her, perhaps. But will you help her?—that's the real issue."

"Is she in need of help?" he asked slowly, with a penetrating look.

"Most women always are," said Henrietta, with conscientious evasiveness and generalising less hopefully than usual. "If you go to Rome," she added, "I hope you'll be a true friend—not a selfish one!" And she turned off and began to look at the pictures.

Caspar Goodwood let her go and stood watching her while she wandered round the room; but after a moment he rejoined her. "You've heard something about her here," he then resumed. "I should like to know what you've heard."

Henrietta had never prevaricated in her life, and, though on this occasion there might have been a fitness in doing so, she decided, after thinking some minutes, to make no superficial exception. "Yes, I've heard," she answered; "but as I don't want you to go to Rome I won't tell you."

"Just as you please. I shall see for myself," he said. Then inconsistently, for him, "You've heard she's unhappy!" he added.

"Oh, you won't see that!" Henrietta exclaimed.

"I hope not. When do you start?"

"To-morrow, by the evening train. And you?"

Goodwood hung back; he had no desire to make his journey to Rome in Miss Stackpole's company. His indifference to this advantage was not of the same character as Gilbert Osmond's, but it had at this moment an equal distinctness. It was rather a tribute to Miss Stackpole's virtues than a reference to her faults. He thought her very remarkable, very brilliant, and he had, in theory, no objection to the class to which she belonged. Lady correspondents appeared to him a part of the natural scheme of things in a progressive country, and though he never read their letters he supposed that they ministered somehow to social prosperity. But it was this very eminence of their position that made him wish Miss Stackpole didn't take so much for granted. She took for granted that he was always ready for some allusion to Mrs. Osmond; she had done so when they met in Paris, six weeks after his arrival in Europe, and she had repeated the assumption with every successive opportunity. He had no wish whatever to allude to Mrs. Osmond; he was *not* always thinking of her; he was perfectly sure of that. He was the most reserved, the least colloquial of men, and this enquiring authoress was constantly flashing her lantern into the quiet darkness of his soul. He wished she didn't care so much; he even wished, though it might seem rather brutal of him, that she would leave him alone. In spite of this, however, he just now made other reflections—which show how widely different, in effect, his ill-humour was from Gilbert Osmond's. He desired to go immediately to Rome; he would have liked to go alone, in the night-train. He hated the European railway-carriages, in which one sat for hours in a vise, knee to knee and nose to nose with a foreigner to whom one presently found one's self objecting with all the added vehemence of one's wish to have the window open; and if they were worse at night even than by day, at least at night one could sleep and dream of an American saloon-car. But he couldn't take a night-train when Miss Stackpole was starting in the morning; it struck him that this would be an insult to an unprotected woman. Nor could he wait until after she had gone unless he should wait longer than he had patience for. It wouldn't do to start the next day. She worried him; she oppressed him; the idea of spending the day in a European railway-carriage with her offered a complication of irritations. Still, she was a lady travelling alone; it was his duty to put himself out for her. There could be no two questions about that; it was a perfectly clear necessity. He looked extremely grave for some moments and then said, wholly without the flourish of gallantry but in a tone of extreme distinctness, "Of course if you're going to-morrow I'll go too, as I may be of assistance to you."

"Well, Mr. Goodwood, I should hope so!" Henrietta returned imperturbably.

Chapter XLV

I have already had reason to say that Isabel knew her husband to be displeased by the continuance of Ralph's visit to Rome. That knowledge was very present to her as she went to her cousin's hotel the day after she had invited Lord Warburton to give a tangible proof of his sincerity; and at this moment, as at others, she had a sufficient perception of the sources of Osmond's opposition. He wished her to have no freedom of mind, and he knew perfectly well that Ralph was an apostle of freedom. It was just because he was this, Isabel said to herself, that it was a refreshment to go and see him. It will be perceived that she partook of this refreshment in spite of her husband's aversion to it, that is partook of it, as she flattered herself, discreetly. She had not as yet undertaken to act in direct opposition to his wishes; he was her appointed and inscribed master; she gazed at moments with a sort of incredulous blankness at this fact. It weighed upon her imagination, however; constantly present to her mind were all the traditionary decencies and sanctities of marriage. The idea of violating them filled her with shame as well as with dread, for on giving herself away she had lost sight of this contingency in the perfect belief that her husband's intentions were as generous as her own. She seemed to see, none the less, the rapid approach of the day when she should have to take back something she had solemnly bestown. Such a ceremony would be odious and monstrous; she tried to shut her eyes to it meanwhile. Osmond would do nothing to help it by beginning first; he would put that burden upon her to the end. He had not yet formally forbidden her to call upon Ralph; but she felt sure that unless Ralph should very soon depart this prohibition would come. How could poor Ralph depart? The weather as yet made it impossible. She could perfectly understand her husband's wish for the event; she didn't, to be just, see how he *could* like her to be with her cousin. Ralph never said a word against him, but Osmond's sore, mute protest was none the less founded. If he should positively interpose, if he should put forth his authority, she would have to decide, and that wouldn't be easy. The prospect made her heart beat and her cheeks burn, as I say, in advance; there were moments when, in her wish to avoid an open rupture, she found herself wishing Ralph would start even at a risk. And it was of no use that, when catching herself in this state of mind, she called herself a feeble spirit, a coward. It was not that she loved Ralph less, but that almost anything seemed preferable to repudiating the most serious act—the single sacred act—of her life. That appeared to make the whole future hideous. To break with Osmond once would be to break for ever; any open acknowledgement of irreconcilable needs would be an admission that their whole attempt had proved a failure. For them there could be no condonement, no compromise, no easy forgetfulness, no formal readjustment. They had attempted only one thing, but that one thing was to have been exquisite. Once they missed it nothing else would do; there was no conceivable substitute for that success. For the moment, Isabel went to the Hôtel de Paris as often as she thought well; the measure of propriety was in the canon of taste, and there couldn't have been a better proof that morality was, so to speak, a matter of earnest appreciation. Isabel's application of that measure had been particularly free to-day, for in addition to the general truth that she couldn't leave Ralph to die alone she had something important to ask of him. This indeed was Gilbert's business as well as her own.

She came very soon to what she wished to speak of. "I want you to answer me a question. It's about Lord Warburton."

"I think I guess your question," Ralph answered from his armchair, out of which his thin legs protruded at greater length than ever.

"Very possibly you guess it. Please then answer it."

"Oh, I don't say I can do that."

"You're intimate with him," she said; "you've a great deal of observation of him."

"Very true. But think how he must dissimulate!"

"Why should he dissimulate? That's not his nature."

"Ah, you must remember that the circumstances are peculiar," said Ralph with an air of private amusement.

"To a certain extent—yes. But is he really in love?"

"Very much, I think. I can make that out."

"Ah!" said Isabel with a certain dryness.

Ralph looked at her as if his mild hilarity had been touched with mystification. "You say that as if you were disappointed."

Isabel got up, slowly smoothing her gloves and eyeing them thoughtfully. "It's after all no business of mine."

"You're very philosophic," said her cousin. And then in a moment: "May I enquire what you're talking about?"

Isabel stared. "I thought you knew. Lord Warburton tells me he wants, of all things in the world, to marry Pansy. I've told you that before, without eliciting a comment from you. You might risk one this morning, I think. Is it your belief that he really cares for her?"

"Ah, for Pansy, no!" cried Ralph very positively.

"But you said just now he did."

Ralph waited a moment. "That he cared for you, Mrs. Osmond."

Isabel shook her head gravely. "That's nonsense, you know."

"Of course it is. But the nonsense is Warburton's, not mine."

"That would be very tiresome." She spoke, as she flattered herself, with much subtlety.

"I ought to tell you indeed," Ralph went on, "that to me he has denied it."

"It's very good of you to talk about it together! Has he also told you that he's in love with Pansy?"

"He has spoken very well of her—very properly. He has let me know, of course, that he thinks she would do very well at Lockleigh."

"Does he really think it?"

"Ah, what Warburton really thinks—!" said Ralph.

Isabel fell to smoothing her gloves again; they were long, loose gloves on which she could freely expend herself. Soon, however, she looked up, and then, "Ah, Ralph, you give me no help!" she cried abruptly and passionately.

It was the first time she had alluded to the need for help, and the words shook her cousin with their violence. He gave a long murmur of relief, of pity, of tenderness; it seemed to him that at last the gulf between them had been bridged. It was this that made him exclaim in a moment: "How unhappy you must be!"

He had no sooner spoken than she recovered her self-possession, and the first use she made of it was to pretend she had not heard him. "When I talk of your helping me I talk great nonsense," she said with a quick smile. "The idea of my troubling you with my domestic embarrassments! The matter's very simple; Lord Warburton must get on by himself. I can't undertake to see him through."

"He ought to succeed easily," said Ralph.

Isabel debated. "Yes—but he has not always succeeded."

"Very true. You know, however, how that always surprised me. Is Miss Osmond capable of giving us a surprise?"

"It will come from him, rather. I seem to see that after all he'll let the matter drop."

"He'll do nothing dishonourable," said Ralph.

"I'm very sure of that. Nothing can be more honourable than for him to leave the poor child alone. She cares for another person, and it's cruel to attempt to bribe her by magnificent offers to give him up."

"Cruel to the other person perhaps—the one she cares for. But Warburton isn't obliged to mind that."

"No, cruel to her," said Isabel. "She would be very unhappy if she were to allow herself to be persuaded to desert poor Mr. Rosier. That idea seems to amuse you; of course you're not in love with him. He has the merit—for Pansy—of being in love with Pansy. She can see at a glance that Lord Warburton isn't."

"He'd be very good to her," said Ralph.

"He has been good to her already. Fortunately, however, he has not said a word to disturb her. He could come and bid her good-bye to-morrow with perfect propriety."

"How would your husband like that?"

"Not at all; and he may be right in not liking it. Only he must obtain satisfaction himself."

"Has he commissioned you to obtain it?" Ralph ventured to ask.

"It was natural that as an old friend of Lord Warburton's—an older friend, that is, than Gilbert—I should take an interest in his intentions."

"Take an interest in his renouncing them, you mean?"

Isabel hesitated, frowning a little. "Let me understand. Are you pleading his cause?"

"Not in the least. I'm very glad he shouldn't become your stepdaughter's husband. It makes such a very queer relation to you!" said Ralph, smiling. "But I'm rather nervous lest your husband should think you haven't pushed him enough."

Isabel found herself able to smile as well as he. "He knows me well enough not to have expected me to push. He himself has no intention of

pushing, I presume. I'm not afraid I shall not be able to justify myself!"
she said lightly.

Her mask had dropped for an instant, but she had put it on again, to
Ralph's infinite disappointment. He had caught a glimpse of her natural
face and he wished immensely to look into it. He had an almost savage
desire to hear her complain of her husband—hear her say that she should
be held accountable for Lord Warburton's defection. Ralph was certain
that this was her situation; he knew by instinct, in advance, the form that
in such an event Osmond's displeasure would take. It could only take the
meanest and cruellest. He would have liked to warn Isabel of it—to let
her see at least how he judged for her and how he knew. It little mattered
that Isabel would know much better; it was for his own satisfaction more
than for hers that he longed to show her he was not deceived. He tried
and tried again to make her betray Osmond; he felt cold-blooded, cruel,
dishonourable almost, in doing so. But it scarcely mattered, for he only
failed. What had she come for then, and why did she seem almost to offer
him a chance to violate their tacit convention? Why did she ask him his
advice if she gave him no liberty to answer her? How could they talk of
her domestic embarrassments, as it pleased her humorously to designate
them, if the principal factor was not to be mentioned? These contradictions were themselves but an indication of her trouble, and her cry for help,
just before, was the only thing he was bound to consider. "You'll be decidedly at variance, all the same," he said in a moment. And as she answered
nothing, looking as if she scarce understood, "You'll find yourselves thinking very differently," he continued.

"That may easily happen, among the most united couples!" She took up
her parasol; he saw she was nervous, afraid of what he might say. "It's a
matter we can hardly quarrel about, however," she added; "for almost all the
interest is on his side. That's very natural. Pansy's after all his daughter—not
mine." And she put out her hand to wish him good-bye.

Ralph took an inward resolution that she shouldn't leave him without his
letting her know that he knew everything: it seemed too great an opportunity to lose. "Do you know what his interest will make him say?" he asked
as he took her hand. She shook her head, rather dryly—not discouragingly—
and he went on. "It will make him say that your want of zeal is owing to
jealousy." He stopped a moment; her face made him afraid.

"To jealousy?"

"To jealousy of his daughter."

She blushed red and threw back her head. "You're not kind," she said in
a voice that he had never heard on her lips.

"Be frank with me and you'll see," he answered.

But she made no reply; she only pulled her hand out of his own, which
he tried still to hold, and rapidly withdrew from the room. She made up
her mind to speak to Pansy, and she took an occasion on the same day,
going to the girl's room before dinner. Pansy was already dressed; she was
always in advance of the time: it seemed to illustrate her pretty patience
and the graceful stillness with which she could sit and wait. At present
she was seated, in her fresh array, before the bed-room fire; she had blown
out her candles on the completion of her toilet, in accordance with the
economical habits in which she had been brought up and which she was
now more careful than ever to observe; so that the room was lighted only

by a couple of logs. The rooms in Palazzo Roccanera were as spacious as they were numerous, and Pansy's virginal bower was an immense chamber with a dark, heavily-timbered ceiling. Its diminutive mistress, in the midst of it, appeared but a speck of humanity, and as she got up, with quick deference, to welcome Isabel, the latter was more than ever struck with her shy sincerity. Isabel had a difficult task—the only thing was to perform it as simply as possible. She felt bitter and angry, but she warned herself against betraying this heat. She was afraid even of looking too grave, or at least too stern; she was afraid of causing alarm. But Pansy seemed to have guessed she had come more or less as a confessor; for after she had moved the chair in which she had been sitting a little nearer to the fire and Isabel had taken her place in it, she kneeled down on a cushion in front of her, looking up and resting her clasped hands on her stepmother's knees. What Isabel wished to do was to hear from her own lips that her mind was not occupied with Lord Warburton; but if she desired the assurance she felt herself by no means at liberty to provoke it. The girl's father would have qualified this as rank treachery; and indeed Isabel knew that if Pansy should display the smallest germ of a disposition to encourage Lord Warburton her own duty was to hold her tongue. It was difficult to interrogate without appearing to suggest; Pansy's supreme simplicity, an innocence even more complete than Isabel had yet judged it, gave to the most tentative enquiry something of the effect of an admonition. As she knelt there in the vague firelight, with her pretty dress dimly shining, her hands folded half in appeal and half in submission, her soft eyes, raised and fixed, full of the seriousness of the situation, she looked to Isabel like a childish martyr decked out for sacrifice and scarcely presuming even to hope to avert it. When Isabel said to her that she had never yet spoken to her of what might have been going on in relation to her getting married, but that her silence had not been indifference or ignorance, had only been the desire to leave her at liberty, Pansy bent forward, raised her face nearer and nearer, and with a little murmur which evidently expressed a deep longing, answered that she had greatly wished her to speak and that she begged her to advise her now.

"It's difficult for me to advise you," Isabel returned. "I don't know how I can undertake that. That's for your father; you must get his advice and, above all, you must act on it."

At this Pansy dropped her eyes; for a moment she said nothing. "I think I should like your advice better than papa's," she presently remarked.

"That's not as it should be," said Isabel coldly. "I love you very much, but your father loves you better."

"It isn't because you love me—it's because you're a lady," Pansy answered with the air of saying something very reasonable. "A lady can advise a young girl better than a man."

"I advise you then to pay the greatest respect to your father's wishes."

"Ah yes," said the child eagerly, "I must do that."

"But if I speak to you now about your getting married it's not for your own sake, it's for mine," Isabel went on. "If I try to learn from you what you expect, what you desire, it's only that I may act accordingly."

Pansy stared, and then very quickly, "Will you do everything I want?" she asked.

"Before I say yes I must know what such things are."

Pansy presently told her that the only thing she wanted in life was to marry Mr. Rosier. He had asked her and she had told him she would do so if her papa would allow it. Now her papa wouldn't allow it.

"Very well then, it's impossible," Isabel pronounced.

"Yes, it's impossible," said Pansy without a sigh and with the same extreme attention in her clear little face.

"You must think of something else then," Isabel went on; but Pansy, sighing at this, told her that she had attempted that feat without the least success.

"You think of those who think of you," she said with a faint smile. "I know Mr. Rosier thinks of me."

"He ought not to," said Isabel loftily. "Your father has expressly requested he shouldn't."

"He can't help it, because he knows I think of *him*."

"You shouldn't think of him. There's some excuse for him, perhaps; but there's none for you."

"I wish you would try to find one," the girl exclaimed as if she were praying to the Madonna.

"I should be very sorry to attempt it," said the Madonna with unusual frigidity. "If you knew some one else was thinking of you, would you think of him?"

"No one can think of me as Mr. Rosier does; no one has the right."

"Ah, but I don't admit Mr. Rosier's right!" Isabel hypocritically cried.

Pansy only gazed at her, evidently much puzzled; and Isabel, taking advantage of it, began to represent to her the wretched consequences of disobeying her father. At this Pansy stopped her with the assurance that she would never disobey him, would never marry without his consent. And she announced, in the serenest, simplest tone, that, though she might never marry Mr. Rosier, she would never cease to think of him. She appeared to have accepted the idea of eternal singleness; but Isabel of course was free to reflect that she had no conception of its meaning. She was perfectly sincere; she was prepared to give up her lover. This might seem an important step toward taking another, but for Pansy, evidently, it failed to lead in that direction. She felt no bitterness toward her father; there was no bitterness in her heart; there was only the sweetness of fidelity to Edward Rosier, and a strange, exquisite intimation that she could prove it better by remaining single than even by marrying him.

"Your father would like you to make a better marriage," said Isabel. "Mr. Rosier's fortune is not at all large."

"How do you mean better—if that would be good enough? And I have myself so little money; why should I look for a fortune?"

"Your having so little is a reason for looking for more." With which Isabel was grateful for the dimness of the room; she felt as if her face were hideously insincere. It was what she was doing for Osmond; it was what one had to do for Osmond! Pansy's solemn eyes, fixed on her own, almost embarrassed her; she was ashamed to think she had made so light of the girl's preference.

"What should you like me to do?" her companion softly demanded.

The question was a terrible one, and Isabel took refuge in timorous vagueness. "To remember all the pleasure it's in your power to give your father."

"To marry some one else, you mean—if he should ask me?"

For a moment Isabel's answer caused itself to be waited for; then she heard herself utter it in the stillness that Pansy's attention seemed to make. "Yes—to marry some one else."

The child's eyes grew more penetrating; Isabel believed she was doubting her sincerity, and the impression took force from her slowly getting up from her cushion. She stood there a moment with her small hands unclasped and then quavered out: "Well, I hope no one will ask me!"

"There has been a question of that. Some one else would have been ready to ask you."

"I don't think he can have been ready," said Pansy.

"It would appear so—if he had been sure he'd succeed."

"If he had been sure? Then he wasn't ready!"

Isabel thought this rather sharp; she also got up and stood a moment looking into the fire. "Lord Warburton has shown you great attention," she resumed; "of course you know it's of him I speak." She found herself, against her expectation, almost placed in the position of justifying herself; which led her to introduce this nobleman more crudely than she had intended.

"He has been very kind to me, and I like him very much. But if you mean that he'll propose for me I think you're mistaken."

"Perhaps I am. But your father would like it extremely."

Pansy shook her head with a little wise smile. "Lord Warburton won't propose simply to please papa."

"Your father would like you to encourage him," Isabel went on mechanically.

"How can I encourage him?"

"I don't know. Your father must tell you that."

Pansy said nothing for a moment; she only continued to smile as if she were in possession of a bright assurance. "There's no danger—no danger!" she declared at last.

There was a conviction in the way she said this, and a felicity in her believing it, which conduced to Isabel's awkwardness. She felt accused of dishonesty, and the idea was disgusting. To repair her self-respect she was on the point of saying that Lord Warburton had let her know that there *was* a danger. But she didn't; she only said—in her embarrassment rather wide of the mark—that he surely had been most kind, most friendly.

"Yes, he has been very kind," Pansy answered. "That's what I like him for."

"Why then is the difficulty so great?"

"I've always felt sure of his knowing that I don't want—what did you say I should do?—to encourage him. He knows I don't want to marry, and he wants me to know that he therefore won't trouble me. That's the meaning of his kindness. It's as if he said to me: 'I like you very much, but if it doesn't please you I'll never say it again.' I think that's very kind, very noble," Pansy went on with deepening positiveness. "That is all we've said to each other. And he doesn't care for me either. Ah no, there's no danger."

Isabel was touched with wonder at the depths of perception of which this submissive little person was capable; she felt afraid of Pansy's wisdom—began almost to retreat before it. "You must tell your father that," she remarked reservedly.

"I think I'd rather not," Pansy unreservedly answered.

"You oughtn't to let him have false hopes."

"Perhaps not; but it will be good for me that he should. So long as he believes that Lord Warburton intends anything of the kind you say, papa won't propose any one else. And that will be an advantage for me," said the child very lucidly.

There was something brilliant in her lucidity, and it made her companion draw a long breath. It relieved this friend of a heavy responsibility. Pansy had a sufficient illumination of her own, and Isabel felt that she herself just now had no light to spare from her small stock. Nevertheless it still clung to her that she must be loyal to Osmond, that she was on her honour in dealing with his daughter. Under the influence of this sentiment she threw out another suggestion before she retired—a suggestion with which it seemed to her that she should have done her utmost. "Your father takes for granted at least that you would like to marry a nobleman."

Pansy stood in the open doorway; she had drawn back the curtain for Isabel to pass. "I think Mr. Rosier looks like one!" she remarked very gravely.

Chapter XLVI

Lord Warburton was not seen in Mrs. Osmond's drawing-room for several days, and Isabel couldn't fail to observe that her husband said nothing to her about having received a letter from him. She couldn't fail to observe, either, that Osmond was in a state of expectancy and that, though it was not agreeable to him to betray it, he thought their distinguished friend kept him waiting quite too long. At the end of four days he alluded to his absence.

"What has become of Warburton? What does he mean by treating one like a tradesman with a bill?'

"I know nothing about him," Isabel said. "I saw him last Friday at the German ball. He told me then that he meant to write to you."

"He has never written to me."

"So I supposed, from your not having told me."

"He's an odd fish," said Osmond comprehensively. And on Isabel's making no rejoinder he went on to enquire whether it took his lordship five days to indite a letter. "Does he form his words with such difficulty?"

"I don't know," Isabel was reduced to replying. "I've never had a letter from him."

"Never had a letter? I had an idea that you were at one time in intimate correspondence."

She answered that this had not been the case, and let the conversation drop. On the morrow, however, coming into the drawing-room late in the afternoon, her husband took it up again.

"When Lord Warburton told you of his intention of writing what did you say to him?" he asked.

She just faltered. "I think I told him not to forget it."

"Did you believe there was a danger of that?"

"As you say, he's an odd fish."

"Apparently he has forgotten it," said Osmond. "Be so good as to remind him."

"Should you like me to write to him?" she demanded.

"I've no objection whatever."

"You expect too much of me."

"Ah yes, I expect a great deal of you."

"I'm afraid I shall disappoint you," said Isabel.

"My expectations have survived a good deal of disappointment."

"Of course I know that. Think how I must have disappointed myself! If you really wish hands laid on Lord Warburton you must lay them yourself."

For a couple of minutes Osmond answered nothing; then he said: "That won't be easy, with you working against me."

Isabel started; she felt herself beginning to tremble. He had a way of looking at her through half-closed eyelids, as if he were thinking of her but scarcely saw her, which seemed to her to have a wonderfully cruel intention. It appeared to recognise her as a disagreeable necessity of thought, but to ignore her for the time as a presence. That effect had never been so marked as now. "I think you accuse me of something very base," she returned.

"I accuse you of not being trustworthy. If he doesn't after all come forward it will be because you've kept him off. I don't know that it's base: it is the kind of thing a woman always thinks she may do. I've no doubt you've the finest ideas about it."

"I told you I would do what I could," she went on.

"Yes, that gained you time."

It came over her, after he had said this, that she had once thought him beautiful. "How much you must want to make sure of him!" she exclaimed in a moment.

She had no sooner spoken than she perceived the full reach of her words, of which she had not been conscious in uttering them. They made a comparison between Osmond and herself, recalled the fact that she had once held this coveted treasure in her hand and felt herself rich enough to let it fall. A momentary exultation took possession of her—a horrible delight in having wounded him; for his face instantly told her that none of the force of her exclamation was lost. He expressed nothing otherwise, however; he only said quickly: "Yes, I want it immensely."

At this moment a servant came in to usher a visitor, and he was followed the next by Lord Warburton, who received a visible check on seeing Osmond. He looked rapidly from the master of the house to the mistress; a movement that seemed to denote a reluctance to interrupt or even a perception of ominous conditions. Then he advanced, with his English address, in which a vague shyness seemed to offer itself as an element of good-breeding; in which the only defect was a difficulty in achieving transitions. Osmond was embarrassed; he found nothing to say; but Isabel remarked, promptly enough, that they had been in the act of talking about their visitor. Upon this her husband added that they hadn't known what was become of him—they had been afraid he had gone away. "No," he explained, smiling and looking at Osmond; "I'm only on the point of going." And then he mentioned that he found himself suddenly recalled to England: he should start on the morrow or the day after. "I'm awfully sorry to leave poor Touchett!" he ended by exclaiming.

For a moment neither of his companions spoke; Osmond only leaned back in his chair, listening. Isabel didn't look at him; she could only fancy how he looked. Her eyes were on their visitor's face, where they were the more free to rest that those of his lordship carefully avoided them. Yet Isabel was sure that had she met his glance she would have found it expressive. "You had better take poor Touchett with you," she heard her husband say, lightly enough, in a moment.

"He had better wait for warmer weather," Lord Warburton answered. "I shouldn't advise him to travel just now."

He sat there a quarter of an hour, talking as if he might not soon see them again—unless indeed they should come to England, a course he strongly recommended. Why shouldn't they come to England in the autumn?—that struck him as a very happy thought. It would give him such pleasure to do what he could for them—to have them come and spend a month with him. Osmond, by his own admission, had been to England but once; which was an absurd state of things for a man of his leisure and intelligence. It was just the country for him—he would be sure to get on well there. Then Lord Warburton asked Isabel if she remembered what a good time she had had there and if she didn't want to try it again. Didn't she want to see Gardencourt once more? Gardencourt was really very good. Touchett didn't take proper care of it, but it was the sort of place you could hardly spoil by letting it alone. Why didn't they come and pay Touchett a visit? He surely must have asked them. Hadn't asked them? What an ill-mannered wretch!—and Lord Warburton promised to give the master of Gardencourt a piece of his mind. Of course it was a mere accident; he would be delighted to have them. Spending a month with Touchett and a month with himself, and seeing all the rest of the people they must know there, they really wouldn't find it half bad. Lord Warburton added that it would amuse Miss Osmond as well, who had told him that she had never been to England and whom he had assured it was a country she deserved to see. Of course she didn't need to go to England to be admired—that was her fate everywhere; but she would be an immense success there, she certainly would, if that was any inducement. He asked if she were not at home: couldn't he say good-bye? Not that he liked good-byes—he always funked them. When he left England the other day he hadn't said good-bye to a two-legged creature. He had had half a mind to leave Rome without troubling Mrs. Osmond for a final interview. What could be more dreary than final interviews? One never said the things one wanted—one remembered them all an hour afterwards. On the other hand one usually said a lot of things one shouldn't, simply from a sense that one had to say something. Such a sense was upsetting; it muddled one's wits. He had it at present, and that was the effect it produced on him. If Mrs. Osmond didn't think he spoke as he ought she must set it down to agitation; it was no light thing to part with Mrs. Osmond. He was really very sorry to be going. He had thought of writing to her instead of calling—but he would write to her at any rate, to tell her a lot of things that would be sure to occur to him as soon as he had left the house. They must think seriously about coming to Lockleigh.

If there was anything awkward in the conditions of his visit or in the announcement of his departure it failed to come to the surface. Lord Warburton talked about his agitation; but he showed it in no other manner, and Isabel saw that since he had determined on a retreat he was capable of executing it gallantly. She was very glad for him; she liked him quite well enough to wish him to appear to carry a thing off. He would do that

on any occasion—not from impudence but simply from the habit of success; and Isabel felt it out of her husband's power to frustrate this faculty.
A complex operation, as she sat there, went on in her mind. On one side
she listened to their visitor; said what was proper to him; read, more or
less, between the lines of what he said himself; and wondered how he
would have spoken if he had found her alone. On the other she had a perfect consciousness of Osmond's emotion. She felt almost sorry for him;
he was condemned to the sharp pain of loss without the relief of cursing.
He had had a great hope, and now, as he saw it vanish into smoke, he was
obliged to sit and smile and twirl his thumbs. Not that he troubled himself to smile very brightly; he treated their friend on the whole to as vacant
a countenance as so clever a man could very well wear. It was indeed a
part of Osmond's cleverness that he could look consummately uncompro-
mised. His present appearance, however, was not a confession of disappointment; it was simply a part of Osmond's habitual system, which was
to be inexpressive exactly in proportion as he was really intent. He had
been intent on this prize from the first; but he had never allowed his eagerness to irradiate his refined face. He had treated his possible son-in-law
as he treated every one—with an air of being interested in him only for
his own advantage, not for any profit to a person already so generally, so
perfectly provided as Gilbert Osmond. He would give no sign now of an
inward rage which was the result of a vanished prospect of gain—not the
faintest nor subtlest. Isabel could be sure of that, if it was any satisfaction
to her. Strangely, very strangely, it was a satisfaction; she wished Lord Warburton to triumph before her husband, and at the same time she wished
her husband to be very superior before Lord Warburton. Osmond, in his
way, was admirable; he had, like their visitor, the advantage of an acquired
habit. It was not that of succeeding, but it was something almost as good—
that of not attempting. As he leaned back in his place, listening but vaguely
to the other's friendly offers and suppressed explanations—as if it were
only proper to assume that they were addressed essentially to his wife—
he had at least (since so little else was left him) the comfort of thinking
how well he personally had kept out of it, and how the air of indifference,
which he was now able to wear, had the added beauty of consistency. It
was something to be able to look as if the leave-taker's movements had no
relation to his own mind. The latter did well, certainly; but Osmond's
performance was in its very nature more finished. Lord Warburton's position was after all an easy one; there was no reason in the world why he
shouldn't leave Rome. He had had beneficent inclinations but they had
stopped short of fruition; he had never committed himself, and his honour was safe. Osmond appeared to take but a moderate interest in the proposal that they should go and stay with him and in his allusion to the
success Pansy might extract from their visit. He murmured a recognition,
but left Isabel to say that it was a matter requiring grave consideration.
Isabel, even while she made this remark, could see the great vista which
had suddenly opened out in her husband's mind, with Pansy's little figure
marching up the middle of it.

Lord Warburton had asked leave to bid good-bye to Pansy, but neither
Isabel nor Osmond had made any motion to send for her. He had the air
of giving out that his visit must be short; he sat on a small chair, as if it
were only for a moment, keeping his hat in his hand. But he stayed and

stayed; Isabel wondered what he was waiting for. She believed it was not to see Pansy; she had an impression that on the whole he would rather not see Pansy. It was of course to see herself alone—he had something to say to her. Isabel had no great wish to hear it, for she was afraid it would be an explanation, and she could perfectly dispense with explanations. Osmond, however, presently got up, like a man of good taste to whom it had occurred that so inveterate a visitor might wish to say just the last word of all to the ladies. "I've a letter to write before dinner," he said; "you must excuse me. I'll see if my daughter's disengaged, and if she is she shall know you're here. Of course when you come to Rome you'll always look us up. Mrs. Osmond will talk to you about the English expedition: she decides all those things."

The nod with which, instead of a hand-shake, he wound up this little speech was perhaps rather a meagre form of salutation; but on the whole it was all the occasion demanded. Isabel reflected that after he left the room Lord Warburton would have no pretext for saying, "Your husband's very angry"; which would have been extremely disagreeable to her. Nevertheless, if he had done so, she would have said: "Oh, don't be anxious. He doesn't hate *you*: it's me that he hates!"

It was only when they had been left alone together that her friend showed a certain vague awkwardness—sitting down in another chair, handling two or three of the objects that were near him. "I hope he'll make Miss Osmond come," he presently remarked. "I want very much to see her."

"I'm glad it's the last time," said Isabel.

"So am I. She doesn't care for me."

"No, she doesn't care for you."

"I don't wonder at it," he returned. Then he added with inconsequence: "You'll come to England, won't you?"

"I think we had better not."

"Ah, you owe me a visit. Don't you remember that you were to have come to Lockleigh once, and you never did?"

"Everything's changed since then," said Isabel.

"Not changed for the worse, surely—as far as we're concerned. To see you under my roof"—and he hung fire but an instant—"would be a great satisfaction."

She had feared an explanation; but that was the only one that occurred. They talked a little of Ralph, and in another moment Pansy came in, already dressed for dinner and with a little red spot in either cheek. She shook hands with Lord Warburton and stood looking up into his face with a fixed smile—a smile that Isabel knew, though his lordship probably never suspected it, to be near akin to a burst of tears.

"I'm going away," he said. "I want to bid you good-bye."

"Good-bye, Lord Warburton." Her voice perceptibly trembled.

"And I want to tell you how much I wish you may be very happy."

"Thank you, Lord Warburton," Pansy answered.

He lingered a moment and gave a glance at Isabel. "You ought to be very happy—you've got a guardian angel."

"I'm sure I shall be happy," said Pansy in the tone of a person whose certainties were always cheerful.

"Such a conviction as that will take you a great way. But if it should ever fail you, remember—remember—" And her interlocutor stammered a little. "Think of me sometimes, you know!" he said with a vague laugh. Then he shook hands with Isabel in silence, and presently he was gone.

When he had left the room she expected an effusion of tears from her stepdaughter; but Pansy in fact treated her to something very different.

"I think you *are* my guardian angel!" she exclaimed very sweetly.

Isabel shook her head. "I'm not an angel of any kind. I'm at the most your good friend."

"You're a very good friend then—to have asked papa to be gentle with me."

"I've asked your father nothing," said Isabel, wondering.

"He told me just now to come to the drawing-room, and then he gave me a very kind kiss."

"Ah," said Isabel, "that was quite his own idea!"

She recognised the idea perfectly; it was very characteristic, and she was to see a great deal more of it. Even with Pansy he couldn't put himself the least in the wrong. They were dining out that day, and after their dinner they went to another entertainment; so that it was not till late in the evening that Isabel saw him alone. When Pansy kissed him before going to bed he returned her embrace with even more than his usual munificence, and Isabel wondered if he meant it as a hint that his daughter had been injured by the machinations of her stepmother. It was a partial expression, at any rate, of what he continued to expect of his wife. She was about to follow Pansy, but he remarked that he wished she would remain; he had something to say to her. Then he walked about the drawing-room a little, while she stood waiting in her cloak.

"I don't understand what you wish to do," he said in a moment. "I should like to know—so that I may know how to act."

"Just now I wish to go to bed. I'm very tired."

"Sit down and rest; I shall not keep you long. Not there—take a comfortable place." And he arranged a multitude of cushions that were scattered in picturesque disorder upon a vast divan. This was not, however, where she seated herself; she dropped into the nearest chair. The fire had gone out; the lights in the great room were few. She drew her cloak about her; she felt mortally cold. "I think you're trying to humiliate me," Osmond went on. "It's a most absurd undertaking."

"I haven't the least idea what you mean," she returned.

"You've played a very deep game; you've managed it beautifully."

"What is it that I've managed?"

"You've not quite settled it, however; we shall see him again." And he stopped in front of her, with his hands in his pockets, looking down at her thoughtfully, in his usual way, which seemed meant to let her know that she was not an object, but only a rather disagreeable incident, of thought.

"If you mean that Lord Warburton's under an obligation to come back you're wrong," Isabel said. "He's under none whatever."

"That's just what I complain of. But when I say he'll come back I don't mean he'll come from a sense of duty."

"There's nothing else to make him. I think he has quite exhausted Rome."

"Ah no, that's a shallow judgement. Rome's inexhaustible." And Osmond began to walk about again. "However, about that perhaps there's no hurry," he added. "It's rather a good idea of his that we should go to England. If it were not for the fear of finding your cousin there I think I should try to persuade you."

"It may be that you'll not find my cousin," said Isabel.

"I should like to be sure of it. However, I shall be as sure as possible. At the same time I should like to see his house, that you told me so much about at one time: what do you call it?—Gardencourt. It must be a charming thing. And then, you know, I've a devotion to the memory of your uncle: you made me take a great fancy to him. I should like to see where he lived and died. That indeed is a detail. Your friend was right. Pansy ought to see England."

"I've no doubt she would enjoy it," said Isabel.

"But that's a long time hence; next autumn's far off," Osmond continued; "and meantime there are things that more nearly interest us. Do you think me so very proud?" he suddenly asked.

"I think you very strange."

"You don't understand me."

"No, not even when you insult me."

"I don't insult you; I'm incapable of it. I merely speak of certain facts, and if the allusion's an injury to you the fault's not mine. It's surely a fact that you have kept all this matter quite in your own hands."

"Are you going back to Lord Warburton?" Isabel asked. "I'm very tired of his name."

"You shall hear it again before we've done with it."

She had spoken of his insulting her, but it suddenly seemed to her that this ceased to be a pain. He was going down—down; the vision of such a fall made her almost giddy: that was the only pain. He was too strange, too different; he didn't touch her. Still, the working of his morbid passion was extraordinary, and she felt a rising curiosity to know in what light he saw himself justified. "I might say to you that I judge you've nothing to say to me that's worth hearing," she returned in a moment. "But I should perhaps be wrong. There's a thing that would be worth my hearing—to know in the plainest words of what it is you accuse me."

"Of having prevented Pansy's marriage to Warburton. Are those words plain enough?"

"On the contrary, I took a great interest in it. I told you so; and when you told me that you counted on me—that I think was what you said—I accepted the obligation. I was a fool to do so, but I did it."

"You pretended to do it, and you even pretended reluctance to make me more willing to trust you. Then you began to use your ingenuity to get him out of the way."

"I think I see what you mean," said Isabel.

"Where's the letter you told me he had written me?" her husband demanded.

"I haven't the least idea; I haven't asked him."

"You stopped it on the way," said Osmond.

Isabel slowly got up; standing there in her white cloak, which covered her to her feet, she might have represented the angel of disdain, first cousin to that of pity. "Oh, Gilbert, for a man who was so fine—!" she exclaimed in a long murmur.

"I was never so fine as you. You've done everything you wanted. You've got him out of the way without appearing to do so, and you've placed me in the position in which you wished to see me—that of a man who has tried to marry his daughter to a lord, but has grotesquely failed."

"Pansy doesn't care for him. She's very glad he's gone," Isabel said.

"That has nothing to do with the matter."

"And he doesn't care for Pansy."

"That won't do; you told me he did. I don't know why you wanted this particular satisfaction," Osmond continued; "you might have taken some other. It doesn't seem to me that I've been presumptuous—that I have taken too much for granted. I've been very modest about it, very quiet. The idea didn't originate with me. He began to show that he liked her before I ever thought of it. I left it all to you."

"Yes, you were very glad to leave it to me. After this you must attend to such things yourself."

He looked at her a moment; then he turned away. "I thought you were very fond of my daughter."

"I've never been more so than to-day."

"Your affection is attended with immense limitations. However, that perhaps is natural."

"Is this all you wished to say to me?" Isabel asked, taking a candle that stood on one of the tables.

"Are you satisfied? Am I sufficiently disappointed?"

"I don't think that on the whole you're disappointed. You've had another opportunity to try to stupefy me."

"It's not that. It's proved that Pansy can aim high."

"Poor little Pansy!" said Isabel as she turned away with her candle.

Chapter XLVII

It was from Henrietta Stackpole that she learned how Caspar Goodwood had come to Rome; an event that took place three days after Lord Warburton's departure. This latter fact had been preceded by an incident of some importance to Isabel—the temporary absence, once again, of Madame Merle, who had gone to Naples to stay with a friend, the happy possessor of a villa at Posilippo.[1] Madame Merle had ceased to minister to Isabel's happiness, who found herself wondering whether the most discreet of women might not also by chance be the most dangerous. Sometimes, at night, she had strange visions; she seemed to see her husband and her friend—his friend—in dim, indistinguishable combination. It seemed to her that she had not done with her; this lady had something in reserve. Isabel's imagination applied itself actively to this elusive point, but every now and then it was checked by a nameless dread, so that when the charming woman was away from Rome she had almost a consciousness of respite. She had already learned from Miss Stackpole that Caspar Goodwood was in Europe, Henrietta having written to make it known to her immediately after meeting him in Paris. He himself never wrote to Isabel, and though he was in Europe she thought it very possible he might not desire to see her. Their last interview, before her marriage, had had quite the character of a complete rupture; if she remembered rightly he had said he wished to take his last look at her. Since then he had been the most discordant survival of her earlier time—the only one in fact with

1. Now heavily overbuilt, Posillipo is a historic resort on the Bay of Naples; today a part of the city itself.

which a permanent pain was associated. He had left her that morning with
a sense of the most superfluous of shocks: it was like a collision between
vessels in broad daylight. There had been no mist, no hidden current to
excuse it, and she herself had only wished to steer wide. He had bumped
against her prow, however, while her hand was on the tiller, and—to complete the metaphor—had given the lighter vessel a strain which still occasionally betrayed itself in a faint creaking. It had been horrid to see him,
because he represented the only serious harm that (to her belief) she had
ever done in the world: he was the only person with an unsatisfied claim
on her. She had made him unhappy, she couldn't help it; and his unhappiness was a grim reality. She had cried with rage, after he had left her,
at—she hardly knew what: she tried to think it had been at his want of
consideration. He had come to her with his unhappiness when her own
bliss was so perfect; he had done his best to darken the brightness of those
pure rays. He had not been violent, and yet there had been a violence in
the impression. There had been a violence at any rate in something somewhere; perhaps it was only in her own fit of weeping and in that after-sense
of the same which had lasted three or four days.

The effect of his final appeal had in short faded away, and all the first
year of her marriage he had dropped out of her books. He was a thankless
subject of reference; it was disagreeable to have to think of a person who
was sore and sombre about you and whom you could yet do nothing to
relieve. It would have been different if she had been able to doubt, even a
little, of his unreconciled state, as she doubted of Lord Warburton's; unfortunately it was beyond question, and this aggressive, uncompromising
look of it was just what made it unattractive. She could never say to herself that here was a sufferer who had compensations, as she was able to
say in the case of her English suitor. She had no faith in Mr. Goodwood's
compensations and no esteem for them. A cotton-factory was not a compensation for anything—least of all for having failed to marry Isabel Archer.
And yet, beyond that, she hardly knew what he had—save of course his
intrinsic qualities. Oh, he was intrinsic enough; she never thought of his
even looking for artificial aids. If he extended his business—that, to the
best of her belief, was the only form exertion could take with him—it
would be because it was an enterprising thing, or good for the business;
not in the least because he might hope it would overlay the past. This
gave his figure a kind of bareness and bleakness which made the accident
of meeting it in memory or in apprehension a peculiar concussion; it was
deficient in the social drapery commonly muffling, in an overcivilized
age, the sharpness of human contacts. His perfect silence, moreover, the
fact that she never heard from him and very seldom heard any mention of
him, deepened this impression of his loneliness. She asked Lily for news
of him, from time to time; but Lily knew nothing of Boston—her imagination was all bounded on the east by Madison Avenue. As time went on
Isabel had thought of him oftener, and with fewer restrictions; she had
had more than once the idea of writing to him. She had never told her
husband about him—never let Osmond know of his visits to her in Florence; a reserve not dictated in the early period by a want of confidence in
Osmond, but simply by the consideration that the young man's disappointment was not her secret but his own. It would be wrong of her, she had

believed, to convey it to another, and Mr. Goodwood's affairs could have, after all, little interest for Gilbert. When it had come to the point she had never written to him; it seemed to her that, considering his grievance, the least she could do was to let him alone. Nevertheless she would have been glad to be in some way nearer to him. It was not that it ever occurred to her that she might have married him; even after the consequences of her actual union had grown vivid to her that particular reflection, though she indulged in so many, had not had the assurance to present itself. But on finding herself in trouble he had become a member of that circle of things with which she wished to set herself right. I have mentioned how passionately she needed to feel that her unhappiness should not have come to her through her own fault. She had no near prospect of dying, and yet she wished to make her peace with the world—to put her spiritual affairs in order. It came back to her from time to time that there was an account still to be settled with Caspar, and she saw herself disposed or able to settle it to-day on terms easier for him than ever before. Still, when she learned he was coming to Rome she felt all afraid; it would be more disagreeable for him than for any one else to make out—since he *would* make it out, as over a falsified balance-sheet or something of that sort—the intimate disarray of her affairs. Deep in her breast she believed that he had invested his all in her happiness, while the others had invested only a part. He was one more person from whom she should have to conceal her stress. She was reassured, however, after he arrived in Rome, for he spent several days without coming to see her.

Henrietta Stackpole, it may well be imagined, was much more punctual, and Isabel was largely favoured with the society of her friend. She threw herself into it, for now that she had made such a point of keeping her conscience clear, that was one way of proving she had not been superficial— the more so as the years, in their flight, had rather enriched than blighted those peculiarities which had been humorously criticised by persons less interested than Isabel, and which were still marked enough to give loyalty a spice of heroism. Henrietta was as keen and quick and fresh as ever, and as neat and bright and fair. Her remarkably open eyes, lighted like great glazed railway-stations, had put up no shutters; her attire had lost none of its crispness, her opinions none of their national reference. She was by no means quite unchanged, however; it struck Isabel she had grown vague. Of old she had never been vague; though undertaking many enquiries at once, she had managed to be entire and pointed about each. She had a reason for everything she did; she fairly bristled with motives. Formerly, when she came to Europe it was because she wished to see it, but now, having already seen it, she had no such excuse. She didn't for a moment pretend that the desire to examine decaying civilisations had anything to do with her present enterprise; her journey was rather an expression of her independence of the old world than of a sense of further obligations to it. "It's nothing to come to Europe," she said to Isabel; "it doesn't seem to me one needs so many reasons for that. It is something to stay at home; this is much more important." It was not therefore with a sense of doing anything very important that she treated herself to another pilgrimage to Rome; she had seen the place before and carefully inspected it; her present act was simply a sign of familiarity, of her knowing all about it, of her having as good a right as any one else to be there. This was all very well, and Henrietta was restless; she had a perfect right to be restless too, if one came to that. But she had after all a better reason for coming to Rome than that she cared for it so little. Her friend easily recognised it, and with it the worth of the other's fidelity. She had crossed the stormy ocean in midwinter because she had guessed that Isabel was sad. Henrietta guessed a great deal, but she had never guessed so happily as that. Isabel's satisfactions just now were few, but even if they had been more numerous there would still have been something of individual joy in her sense of being justified in having always thought highly of Henrietta. She had made large concessions with regard to her, and had yet insisted that, with all abatements, she was very valuable. It was not her own triumph, however, that she found good; it was simply the relief of confessing to this confidant, the first person to whom she had owned it, that she was not in the least at her ease. Henrietta had herself approached this point with the smallest possible delay, and had accused her to her face of being wretched. She was a woman, she was a sister, she was not Ralph, nor Lord Warburton, nor Caspar Goodwood, and Isabel could speak.

"Yes, I'm wretched," she said very mildly. She hated to hear herself say it; she tried to say it as judicially as possible.

"What does he do to you?" Henrietta asked, frowning as if she were enquiring into the operations of a quack doctor.

"He does nothing. But he doesn't like me."

"He's very hard to please!" cried Miss Stackpole. "Why don't you leave him?"

"I can't change that way," Isabel said.

"Why not, I should like to know? You won't confess that you've made a mistake. You're too proud."

"I don't know whether I'm too proud. But I can't publish my mistake. I don't think that's decent. I'd much rather die."

"You won't think so always," said Henrietta.

"I don't know what great unhappiness might bring me to; but it seems to me I shall always be ashamed. One must accept one's deeds. I married him before all the world; I was perfectly free; it was impossible to do anything more deliberate. One can't change that way," Isabel repeated.

"You *have* changed, in spite of the impossibility. I hope you don't mean to say you like him."

Isabel debated. "No, I don't like him. I can tell you, because I'm weary of my secret. But that's enough; I can't announce it on the housetops."

Henrietta gave a laugh. "Don't you think you're rather too considerate?"

"It's not of him that I'm considerate—it's of myself!" Isabel answered.

It was not surprising Gilbert Osmond should not have taken comfort in Miss Stackpole; his instinct had naturally set him in opposition to a young lady capable of advising his wife to withdraw from the conjugal roof. When she arrived in Rome he had said to Isabel that he hoped she would leave her friend the interviewer alone; and Isabel had answered that he at least had nothing to fear from her. She said to Henrietta that as Osmond didn't like her she couldn't invite her to dine, but they could easily see each other in other ways. Isabel received Miss Stackpole freely in her own sitting-room, and took her repeatedly to drive, face to face with Pansy, who, bending a little forward, on the opposite seat of the carriage, gazed at the celebrated authoress with a respectful attention which Henrietta occasionally found irritating. She complained to Isabel that Miss Osmond had a little look as if she should remember everything one said. "I don't want to be remembered that way," Miss Stackpole declared; "I consider that my conversation refers only to the moment, like the morning papers. Your stepdaughter, as she sits there, looks as if she kept all the back numbers and would bring them out some day against me." She could not teach herself to think favourably of Pansy, whose absence of initiative, of conversation, of personal claims, seemed to her, in a girl of twenty, unnatural and even uncanny. Isabel presently saw that Osmond would have liked her to urge a little the cause of her friend, insist a little upon his receiving her, so that he might appear to suffer for good manners' sake. Her immediate acceptance of his objections put him too much in the wrong—it being in effect one of the disadvantages of expressing contempt that you cannot enjoy at the same time the credit of expressing sympathy. Osmond held to his credit, and yet he held to his objections—all of which were elements difficult to reconcile. The right thing would have been that Miss Stackpole should come to dine at Palazzo Roccanera once or twice, so that (in spite of his superficial civility, always so great) she might judge for herself how little pleasure it gave him. From the moment, however, that both the ladies were so unaccommodating, there was nothing for Osmond but to wish the lady from New York would take herself off. It was surprising how little satisfaction he got from his wife's friends; he took occasion to call Isabel's attention to it.

"You're certainly not fortunate in your intimates; I wish you might make a new collection," he said to her one morning in reference to nothing visible at the moment, but in a tone of ripe reflection which deprived the remark of all brutal abruptness. "It's as if you had taken the trouble to pick out the people in the world that I have least in common with. Your cousin I have always thought a conceited ass—besides his being the most ill-favoured animal I know. Then it's insufferably tiresome that one can't tell him so; one must spare him on account of his health. His health seems to me the best part of him; it gives him privileges enjoyed by no one else. If he's so desperately ill there's only one way to prove it; but he seems to have no mind for that. I can't say much more for the great Warburton. When one really thinks of it, the cool insolence of that performance was something rare! He comes and looks at one's daughter as if she were a suite of apartments; he tries the door-handles and looks out of the windows, raps on the walls and almost thinks he'll take the place. Will you be so good as to draw up a lease? Then, on the whole, he decides that the rooms are too small; he doesn't think he could live on a third floor; he must look out for a *piano nobile*. And he goes away after having got a month's lodging in the poor little apartment for nothing. Miss Stackpole, however, is your most wonderful invention. She strikes me as a kind of monster. One hasn't a nerve in one's body that she doesn't set quivering. You know I never have admitted that she's a woman. Do you know what she reminds me of? Of a new steel pen—the most odious thing in nature. She talks as a steel pen writes; aren't her letters, by the way, on ruled paper? She thinks and moves and walks and looks exactly as she talks. You may say that she doesn't hurt me, inasmuch as I don't see her. I don't see her, but I hear her; I hear her all day long. Her voice is in my ears; I can't get rid of it. I know exactly what she says, and every inflexion of the tone in which she says it. She says charming things about me, and they give you great comfort. I don't like at all to think she talks about me—I feel as I should feel if I knew the footman were wearing my hat."

Henrietta talked about Gilbert Osmond, as his wife assured him, rather less than he suspected. She had plenty of other subjects, in two of which the reader may be supposed to be especially interested. She let her friend know that Caspar Goodwood had discovered for himself that she was unhappy, though indeed her ingenuity was unable to suggest what comfort he hoped to give her by coming to Rome and yet not calling on her. They met him twice in the street, but he had no appearance of seeing them; they were driving, and he had a habit of looking straight in front of him, as if he proposed to take in but one object at a time. Isabel could have fancied she had seen him the day before; it must have been with just that face and step that he had walked out of Mrs. Touchett's door at the close of their last interview. He was dressed just as he had been dressed on that day, Isabel remembered the colour of his cravat; and yet in spite of this familiar look there was a strangeness in his figure too, something that made her feel it afresh to be rather terrible he should have come to Rome. He looked bigger and more overtopping than of old, and in those days he certainly reached high enough. She noticed that the people whom he passed looked back after him; but he went straight forward, lifting above them a face like a February sky.

Miss Stackpole's other topic was very different; she gave Isabel the latest news about Mr. Bantling. He had been out in the United States the year before, and she was happy to say she had been able to show him considerable attention. She didn't know how much he had enjoyed it, but she would undertake to say it had done him good; he wasn't the same man when he left as he had been when he came. It had opened his eyes and shown him that England wasn't everything. He had been very much liked in most places, and thought extremely simple—more simple than the English were commonly supposed to be. There were people who had thought him affected; she didn't know whether they meant that his simplicity was an affectation. Some of his questions were too discouraging; he thought all the chambermaids were farmers' daughters—or all the farmers' daughters were chambermaids—she couldn't exactly remember which. He hadn't seemed able to grasp the great school system; it had been really too much for him. On the whole he had behaved as if there were too much of everything—as if he could only take in a small part. The part he had chosen was the hotel system and the river navigation. He had seemed really fascinated with the hotels; he had a photograph of every one he had visited. But the river steamers were his principal interest; he wanted to do nothing but sail on the big boats. They had travelled together from New York to Milwaukee, stopping at the most interesting cities on the route; and whenever they started afresh he had wanted to know if they could go by the steamer. He seemed to have no idea of geography—had an impression that Baltimore was a Western city and was perpetually expecting to arrive at the Mississippi. He appeared never to have heard of any river in

America but the Mississippi and was unprepared to recognise the existence of the Hudson, though obliged to confess at last that it was fully
equal to the Rhine. They had spent some pleasant hours in the palace-cars;
he was always ordering ice-cream from the coloured man. He could never
get used to that idea—that you could get ice-cream in the cars. Of course
you couldn't, nor fans, nor candy, nor anything in the English cars! He
found the heat quite overwhelming, and she had told him she indeed
expected it was the biggest he had ever experienced. He was now in
England, hunting—"hunting round" Henrietta called it. These amusements were those of the American red men; we had left that behind long
ago, the pleasures of the chase. It seemed to be generally believed in
England that we wore tomahawks and feathers; but such a costume was
more in keeping with English habits. Mr. Bantling would not have time
to join her in Italy, but when she should go to Paris again he expected to
come over. He wanted very much to see Versailles again; he was very fond
of the ancient *régime*.[2] They didn't agree about that, but that was what
she liked Versailles for, that you could see the ancient *régime* had been
swept away. There were no dukes and marquises there now; she remembered on the contrary one day when there were five American families,
walking all round. Mr. Bantling was very anxious that she should take up
the subject of England again, and he thought she might get on better with
it now; England had changed a good deal within two or three years. He
was determined that if she went there he should go to see his sister, Lady
Pensil, and that this time the invitation should come to her straight. The
mystery about that other one had never been explained.

Caspar Goodwood came at last to Palazzo Roccanera; he had written
Isabel a note beforehand, to ask leave. This was promptly granted; she
would be at home at six o'clock that afternoon. She spent the day wondering what he was coming for—what good he expected to get of it. He had
presented himself hitherto as a person destitute of the faculty of compromise, who would take what he had asked for or take nothing. Isabel's hospitality, however, raised no questions, and she found no great difficulty in
appearing happy enough to deceive him. It was her conviction at least that
she deceived him, made him say to himself that he had been misinformed.
But she also saw, so she believed, that he was not disappointed, as some
other men, she was sure, would have been; he had not come to Rome to
look for an opportunity. She never found out what he had come for; he offered
her no explanation; there could be none but the very simple one that he
wanted to see her. In other words he had come for his amusement. Isabel
followed up this induction with a good deal of eagerness, and was
delighted to have found a formula that would lay the ghost of this gentleman's ancient grievance. If he had come to Rome for his amusement this
was exactly what she wanted, for if he cared for amusement he had got
over his heartache. If he had got over his heartache everything was as it
should be and her responsibilities were at an end. It was true that he took
his recreation a little stiffly, but he had never been loose and easy and she
had every reason to believe he was satisfied with what he saw. Henrietta

2. A collective term for the political and social order of France, embodied in the great palace at
Versailles, before the Revolution of 1789.

was not in his confidence, though he was in hers, and Isabel consequently received no side-light upon his state of mind. He was open to little conversation on general topics; it came back to her that she had said of him once, years before, "Mr. Goodwood speaks a good deal, but he doesn't talk." He spoke a good deal now, but he talked perhaps as little as ever; considering, that is, how much there was in Rome to talk about. His arrival was not calculated to simplify her relations with her husband, for if Mr. Osmond didn't like her friends Mr. Goodwood had no claim upon his attention save as having been one of the first of them. There was nothing for her to say of him but that he was the very oldest; this rather meagre synthesis exhausted the facts. She had been obliged to introduce him to Gilbert; it was impossible she should not ask him to dinner, to her Thursday evenings, of which she had grown very weary, but to which her husband still held for the sake not so much of inviting people as of not inviting them.

To the Thursdays Mr. Goodwood came regularly, solemnly, rather early; he appeared to regard them with a good deal of gravity. Isabel every now and then had a moment of anger; there was something so literal about him; she thought he might know that she didn't know what to do with him. But she couldn't call him stupid; he was not that in the least; he was only extraordinarily honest. To be as honest as that made a man very different from most people; one had to be almost equally honest with *him*. She made this latter reflection at the very time she was flattering herself she had persuaded him that she was the most light-hearted of women. He never threw any doubt on this point, never asked her any personal questions. He got on much better with Osmond than had seemed probable. Osmond had a great dislike to being counted on; in such a case he had an irresistible need of disappointing you. It was in virtue of this principle that he gave himself the entertainment of taking a fancy to a perpendicular Bostonian whom he had been depended upon to treat with coldness. He asked Isabel if Mr. Goodwood also had wanted to marry her, and expressed surprise at her not having accepted him. It would have been an excellent thing, like living under some tall belfry which would strike all the hours and make a queer vibration in the upper air. He declared he liked to talk with the great Goodwood; it wasn't easy at first, you had to climb up an interminable steep staircase, up to the top of the tower; but when you got there you had a big view and felt a little fresh breeze. Osmond, as we know, had delightful qualities, and he gave Caspar Goodwood the benefit of them all. Isabel could see that Mr. Goodwood thought better of her husband than he had ever wished to; he had given her the impression that morning in Florence of being inaccessible to a good impression. Gilbert asked him repeatedly to dinner, and Mr. Goodwood smoked a cigar with him afterwards and even desired to be shown his collections. Gilbert said to Isabel that he was very original; he was as strong and of as good a style as an English portmanteau,—had plenty of straps and buckles which would never wear out, and a capital patent lock. Caspar Goodwood took to riding on the Campagna and devoted much time to this exercise; it was therefore mainly in the evening that Isabel saw him. She bethought herself of saying to him one day that if he were willing he could render her a service. And then she added smiling:

"I don't know, however, what right I have to ask a service of you."

"You're the person in the world who has most right," he answered. "I've given you assurances that I've never given any one else."

The service was that he should go and see her cousin Ralph, who was ill at the Hôtel de Paris, alone, and be as kind to him as possible. Mr. Goodwood had never seen him, but he would know who the poor fellow was; if she was not mistaken Ralph had once invited him to Gardencourt. Caspar remembered the invitation perfectly, and, though he was not supposed to be a man of imagination, had enough to put himself in the place of a poor gentleman who lay dying at a Roman inn. He called at the Hôtel de Paris and, on being shown into the presence of the master of Gardencourt, found Miss Stackpole sitting beside his sofa. A singular change had in fact occurred in this lady's relations with Ralph Touchett. She had not been asked by Isabel to go and see him, but on hearing that he was too ill to come out had immediately gone of her own motion. After this she had paid him a daily visit—always under the conviction that they were great enemies. "Oh yes, we're intimate enemies," Ralph used to say; and he accused her freely—as freely as the humour of it would allow—of coming to worry him to death. In reality they became excellent friends, Henrietta much wondering that she should never have liked him before. Ralph liked her exactly as much as he had always done; he had never doubted for a moment that she was an excellent fellow. They talked about everything and always differed; about everything, that is, but Isabel—a topic as to which Ralph always had a thin forefinger on his lips. Mr. Bantling on the other hand proved a great resource; Ralph was capable of discussing Mr. Bantling with Henrietta for hours. Discussion was stimulated of course by their inevitable difference of view—Ralph having amused himself with taking the ground that the genial ex-guardsman was a regular Machiavelli. Caspar Goodwood could contribute nothing to such a debate; but after he had been left alone with his host he found there were various other matters they could take up. It must be admitted that the lady who had just gone out was not one of these; Caspar granted all Miss Stackpole's merits in advance, but had no further remark to make about her. Neither, after the first allusions, did the two men expatiate upon Mrs. Osmond—a theme in which Goodwood perceived as many dangers as Ralph. He felt very sorry for that unclassable personage; he couldn't bear to see a pleasant man, so pleasant for all his queerness, so beyond anything to be done. There was always something to be done, for Goodwood, and he did it in this case by repeating several times his visit to the Hôtel de Paris. It seemed to Isabel that she had been very clever; she had artfully disposed of the superfluous Caspar. She had given him an occupation; she had converted him into a caretaker of Ralph. She had a plan of making him travel northward with her cousin as soon as the first mild weather should allow it. Lord Warburton had brought Ralph to Rome and Mr. Goodwood should take him away. There seemed a happy symmetry in this, and she was now intensely eager that Ralph should depart. She had a constant fear he would die there before her eyes and a horror of the occurrence of this event at an inn, by her door, which he had so rarely entered. Ralph must sink to his last rest in his own dear house, in one of those deep, dim chambers of Gardencourt where the dark ivy would cluster round the edges of the glimmering window. There seemed to Isabel in these days something sacred in Gardencourt; no chapter of the past was more perfectly irrecoverable. When she thought of the months she had spent there the tears rose to her eyes. She flattered herself, as I say, upon her ingenuity, but she had need of all she could muster; for several events occurred which seemed to confront and defy her. The Countess Gemini arrived from Florence—arrived with her trunks, her dresses, her chatter, her falsehoods, her frivolity, the strange, the unholy legend of the number of her lovers. Edward Rosier, who had been away somewhere,—no one, not even Pansy, knew where,— reappeared in Rome and began to write her long letters, which she never answered. Madame Merle returned from Naples and said to her with a strange smile: "What on earth did you do with Lord Warburton?" As if it were any business of hers!

Chapter XLVIII

One day, toward the end of February, Ralph Touchett made up his mind to return to England. He had his own reasons for his decision, which he was not bound to communicate; but Henrietta Stackpole, to whom he mentioned his intention, flattered herself that she guessed them. She forbore to express them, however; she only said, after a moment, as she sat by his sofa: "I suppose you know you can't go alone?"

"I've no idea of doing that," Ralph answered. "I shall have people with me."

"What do you mean by 'people'? Servants whom you pay?"

"Ah," said Ralph jocosely, "after all, they're human beings."

"Are there any women among them?" Miss Stackpole desired to know.

"You speak as if I had a dozen! No, I confess I haven't a soubrette[1] in my employment."

"Well," said Henrietta calmly, "you can't go to England that way. You must have a woman's care."

"I've had so much of yours for the past fortnight that it will last me a good while."

"You've not had enough of it yet. I guess I'll go with you," said Henrietta.

"Go with me?" Ralph slowly raised himself from his sofa.

"Yes, I know you don't like me, but I'll go with you all the same. It would be better for your health to lie down again."

Ralph looked at her a little; then he slowly relapsed. "I like you very much," he said in a moment.

Miss Stackpole gave one of her infrequent laughs. "You needn't think that by saying that you can buy me off. I'll go with you, and what is more I'll take care of you."

"You're a very good woman," said Ralph.

"Wait till I get you safely home before you say that. It won't be easy. But you had better go, all the same."

Before she left him, Ralph said to her: "Do you really mean to take care of me?"

"Well, I mean to try."

"I notify you then that I submit. Oh, I submit!" And it was perhaps a sign of submission that a few minutes after she had left him alone he burst into a loud fit of laughter. It seemed to him so inconsequent, such a

---

1. A saucy, coquettish maidservant; but the term usually refers to a stock character in farce or comic opera rather than to domestic service as such.

conclusive proof of his having abdicated all functions and renounced all exercise, that he should start on a journey across Europe under the supervision of Miss Stackpole. And the great oddity was that the prospect pleased him; he was gratefully, luxuriously passive. He felt even impatient to start; and indeed he had an immense longing to see his own house again. The end of everything was at hand; it seemed to him he could stretch out his arm and touch the goal. But he wanted to die at home; it was the only wish he had left—to extend himself in the large quiet room where he had last seen his father lie, and close his eyes upon the summer dawn.

That same day Caspar Goodwood came to see him, and he informed his visitor that Miss Stackpole had taken him up and was to conduct him back to England. "Ah then," said Caspar, "I'm afraid I shall be a fifth wheel to the coach. Mrs. Osmond has made *me* promise to go with you."

"Good heavens—it's the golden age! You're all too kind."

"The kindness on my part is to her; it's hardly to you."

"Granting that, *she's* kind," smiled Ralph.

"To get people to go with you? Yes, that's a sort of kindness," Goodwood answered without lending himself to the joke. "For myself, however," he added, "I'll go so far as to say that I would much rather travel with you and Miss Stackpole than with Miss Stackpole alone."

"And you'd rather stay here than do either," said Ralph. "There's really no need of your coming. Henrietta's extraordinarily efficient."

"I'm sure of that. But I've promised Mrs. Osmond."

"You can easily get her to let you off."

"She wouldn't let me off for the world. She wants me to look after you, but that isn't the principal thing. The principal thing is that she wants me to leave Rome."

"Ah, you see too much in it," Ralph suggested.

"I bore her," Goodwood went on; "she has nothing to say to me, so she invented that."

"Oh then, if it's a convenience to her I certainly will take you with me. Though I don't see why it should be a convenience," Ralph added in a moment.

"Well," said Caspar Goodwood simply, "she thinks I'm watching her."

"Watching her?"

"Trying to make out if she's happy."

"That's easy to make out," said Ralph. "She's the most visibly happy woman I know."

"Exactly so; I'm satisfied," Goodwood answered dryly. For all his dryness, however, he had more to say. "I've been watching her; I was an old friend and it seemed to me I had the right. She pretends to be happy; that was what she undertook to be; and I thought I should like to see for myself what it amounts to. I've seen," he continued with a harsh ring in his voice, "and I don't want to see any more. I'm now quite ready to go."

"Do you know it strikes me as about time you should?" Ralph rejoined. And this was the only conversation these gentlemen had about Isabel Osmond.

Henrietta made her preparations for departure, and among them she found it proper to say a few words to the Countess Gemini, who returned at Miss Stackpole's *pension* the visit which this lady had paid her in Florence.

"You were very wrong about Lord Warburton," she remarked to the Countess. "I think it right you should know that."

"About his making love to Isabel? My poor lady, he was at her house three times a day. He has left traces of his passage!" the Countess cried.

"He wished to marry your niece; that's why he came to the house."

The Countess stared, and then with an inconsiderate laugh: "Is that the story that Isabel tells? It isn't bad, as such things go. If he wishes to marry my niece, pray why doesn't he do it? Perhaps he has gone to buy the wedding-ring and will come back with it next month, after I'm gone."

"No, he'll not come back. Miss Osmond doesn't wish to marry him."

"She's very accommodating! I knew she was fond of Isabel, but I didn't know she carried it so far."

"I don't understand you," said Henrietta coldly, and reflecting that the Countess was unpleasantly perverse. "I really must stick to my point—that Isabel never encouraged the attentions of Lord Warburton."

"My dear friend, what do you and I know about it? All we know is that my brother's capable of everything."

"I don't know what your brother's capable of," said Henrietta with dignity.

"It's not her encouraging Warburton that I complain of; it's her sending him away. I want particularly to see him. Do you suppose she thought I would make him faithless?" the Countess continued with audacious insistence. "However, she's only keeping him, one can feel that. The house is full of him there; he's quite in the air. Oh yes, he has left traces; I'm sure I shall see him yet."

"Well," said Henrietta after a little, with one of those inspirations which had made the fortune of her letters to the *Interviewer*, "perhaps he'll be more successful with you than with Isabel!"

When she told her friend of the offer she had made Ralph Isabel replied that she could have done nothing that would have pleased her more. It had always been her faith that at bottom Ralph and this young woman were made to understand each other. "I don't care whether he understands me or not," Henrietta declared. "The great thing is that he shouldn't die in the cars."

"He won't do that," Isabel said, shaking her head with an extension of faith.

"He won't if I can help it. I see you want us all to go. I don't know what you want to do."

"I want to be alone," said Isabel.

"You won't be that so long as you've so much company at home."

"Ah, they're part of the comedy. You others are spectators."

"Do you call it a comedy, Isabel Archer?" Henrietta rather grimly asked.

"The tragedy then if you like. You're all looking at me; it makes me uncomfortable."

Henrietta engaged in this act for a while. "You're like the stricken deer, seeking the innermost shade. Oh, you do give me such a sense of helplessness!" she broke out.

"I'm not at all helpless. There are many things I mean to do."

"It's not you I'm speaking of; it's myself. It's too much, having come on purpose, to leave you just as I find you."

"You don't do that; you leave me much refreshed," Isabel said.

"Very mild refreshment—sour lemonade! I want you to promise me something."

"I can't do that. I shall never make another promise. I made such a solemn one four years ago, and I've succeeded so ill in keeping it."

"You've had no encouragement. In this case I should give you the greatest. Leave your husband before the worst comes; that's what I want you to promise."

"The worst? What do you call the worst?"

"Before your character gets spoiled."

"Do you mean my disposition? It won't get spoiled," Isabel answered, smiling. "I'm taking very good care of it. I'm extremely struck," she added, turning away, "with the off-hand way in which you speak of a woman's leaving her husband. It's easy to see you've never had one!"

"Well," said Henrietta as if she were beginning an argument, "nothing is more common in our Western cities, and it's to them, after all, that we must look in the future."[2] Her argument, however, does not concern this history, which has too many other threads to unwind. She announced to Ralph Touchett that she was ready to leave Rome by any train he might designate, and Ralph immediately pulled himself together for departure. Isabel went to see him at the last, and he made the same remark that Henrietta had made. It struck him that Isabel was uncommonly glad to get rid of them all.

For all answer to this she gently laid her hand on his, and said in a low tone, with a quick smile: "My dear Ralph—!"

It was answer enough, and he was quite contented. But he went on in the same way, jocosely, ingenuously: "I've seen less of you than I might, but it's better than nothing. And then I've heard a great deal about you."

"I don't know from whom, leading the life you've done."

"From the voices of the air! Oh, from no one else; I never let other people speak of you. They always say you're 'charming,' and that's so flat."

"I might have seen more of you certainly," Isabel said. "But when one's married one has so much occupation."

"Fortunately I'm not married. When you come to see me in England I shall be able to entertain you with all the freedom of a bachelor." He continued to talk as if they should certainly meet again, and succeeded in making the assumption appear almost just. He made no allusion to his term being near, to the probability that he should not outlast the summer. If he preferred it so, Isabel was willing enough; the reality was sufficiently distinct without their erecting finger-posts in conversation. That had been well enough for the earlier time, though about this, as about his other affairs, Ralph had never been egotistic. Isabel spoke of his journey, of the stages into which he should divide it, of the precautions he should take. "Henrietta's my greatest precaution," he went on. "The conscience of that woman's sublime."

"Certainly she'll be very conscientious."

"Will be? She has been! It's only because she thinks it's her duty that she goes with me. There's a conception of duty for you."

---

2. Divorce was illegal in Italy and difficult in Britain. But practices in the United States were easier and varied widely from state to state, with those to the West being the most permissive. In William Dean Howells's *A Modern Instance* (1882), a Bostonian goes to seek a divorce in Indiana, and the vagaries of the divorce laws would become a major theme in American fiction at the turn of the century; see Edith Wharton's *The Custom of the Country* (1913).

"Yes, it's a generous one," said Isabel, "and it makes me deeply ashamed. I ought to go with you, you know."

"Your husband wouldn't like that."

"No, he wouldn't like it. But I might go, all the same."

"I'm startled by the boldness of your imagination. Fancy my being a cause of disagreement between a lady and her husband!"

"That's why I don't go," said Isabel simply—yet not very lucidly.

Ralph understood well enough, however. "I should think so, with all those occupations you speak of."

"It isn't that. I'm afraid," said Isabel. After a pause she repeated, as if to make herself, rather than him, hear the words: "I'm afraid."

Ralph could hardly tell what her tone meant; it was so strangely deliberate—apparently so void of emotion. Did she wish to do public penance for a fault of which she had not been convicted? or were her words simply an attempt at enlightened self-analysis? However this might be, Ralph could not resist so easy an opportunity. "Afraid of your husband?"

"Afraid of myself!" she said, getting up. She stood there a moment and then added: "If I were afraid of my husband that would be simply my duty. That's what women are expected to be."

"Ah yes," laughed Ralph; "but to make up for it there's always some man awfully afraid of some woman!"

She gave no heed to this pleasantry, but suddenly took a different turn. "With Henrietta at the head of your little band," she exclaimed abruptly, "there will be nothing left for Mr. Goodwood!"

"Ah, my dear Isabel," Ralph answered, "he's used to that. There is nothing left for Mr. Goodwood."

She coloured and then observed, quickly, that she must leave him. They stood together a moment; both her hands were in both of his. "You've been my best friend," she said.

"It was for you that I wanted—that I wanted to live. But I'm of no use to you."

Then it came over her more poignantly that she should not see him again. She could not accept that; she could not part with him that way. "If you should send for me I'd come," she said at last.

"Your husband won't consent to that."

"Oh yes, I can arrange it."

"I shall keep that for my last pleasure!" said Ralph.

In answer to which she simply kissed him. It was a Thursday, and that evening Caspar Goodwood came to Palazzo Roccanera. He was among the first to arrive, and he spent some time in conversation with Gilbert Osmond, who almost always was present when his wife received. They sat down together, and Osmond, talkative, communicative, expansive, seemed possessed with a kind of intellectual gaiety. He leaned back with his legs crossed, lounging and chatting, while Goodwood, more restless, but not at all lively, shifted his position, played with his hat, made the little sofa creak beneath him. Osmond's face wore a sharp, aggressive smile; he was as a man whose perceptions have been quickened by good news. He remarked to Goodwood that he was sorry they were to lose him; he himself should particularly miss him. He saw so few intelligent men—they were surprisingly scarce in Rome. He must be sure to come back; there was something very refreshing, to an inveterate Italian like himself, in talking with a genuine outsider.

"I'm very fond of Rome, you know," Osmond said; "but there's nothing I like better than to meet people who haven't that superstition. The modern world's after all very fine. Now you're thoroughly modern and yet are not at all common. So many of the moderns we see are such very poor stuff. If they're the children of the future we're willing to die young. Of course the ancients too are often very tiresome. My wife and I like everything that's really new—not the mere pretence of it. There's nothing new, unfortunately, in ignorance and stupidity. We see plenty of that in forms that offer themselves as a revelation of progress, of light. A revelation of vulgarity! There's a certain kind of vulgarity which I believe is really new; I don't think there ever was anything like it before. Indeed I don't find vulgarity, at all, before the present century. You see a faint menace of it here and there in the last, but to-day the air has grown so dense that delicate things are literally not recognised. Now, we've *liked you*—!" With which he hesitated a moment, laying his hand gently on Goodwood's knee and smiling with a mixture of assurance and embarrassment. "I'm going to say something extremely offensive and patronising, but you must let me have the satisfaction of it. We've liked you because—because you've reconciled us a little to the future. If there are to be a certain number of people like you—*à la bonne heure!*[3] I'm talking for my wife as well as for myself, you see. She speaks for me, my wife; why shouldn't I speak for her? We're as united, you know, as the candlestick and the snuffers. Am I assuming too much when I say that I think I've understood from you that your occupations have been—a—commercial? There's a danger in that, you know; but it's the way you have escaped that strikes us. Excuse me if my little compliment seems in execrable taste; fortunately my wife doesn't hear me. What I mean is that you *might have been*—a—what I was mentioning just now. The whole American world was in a conspiracy to make you so. But you resisted, you've something about you that saved you. And yet you're so modern, so modern; the most modern man we know! We shall always be delighted to see you again."

I have said that Osmond was in good humour, and these remarks will give ample evidence of the fact. They were infinitely more personal than he usually cared to be, and if Caspar Goodwood had attended to them more closely he might have thought that the defence of delicacy was in rather odd hands. We may believe, however, that Osmond knew very well what he was about, and that if he chose to use the tone of patronage with a grossness not in his habits he had an excellent reason for the escapade. Goodwood had only a vague sense that he was laying it on somehow; he scarcely knew where the mixture was applied. Indeed he scarcely knew what Osmond was talking about; he wanted to be alone with Isabel, and that idea spoke louder to him than her husband's perfectly-pitched voice. He watched her talking with other people and wondered when she would be at liberty and whether he might ask her to go into one of the other rooms. His humour was not, like Osmond's, of the best; there was an

3. That's fine! (French).

element of dull rage in his consciousness of things. Up to this time he had not disliked Osmond personally; he had only thought him very well-informed and obliging and more than he had supposed like the person whom Isabel Archer would naturally marry. His host had won in the open field a great advantage over him, and Goodwood had too strong a sense of fair play to have been moved to underrate him on that account. He had not tried positively to think well of him; this was a flight of sentimental benevolence of which, even in the days when he came nearest to reconciling himself to what had happened, Goodwood was quite incapable. He accepted him as rather a brilliant personage of the amateurish kind, afflicted with a redundancy of leisure which it amused him to work off in little refinements of conversation. But he only half trusted him; he could never make out why the deuce Osmond should lavish refinements of any sort upon *him*. It made him suspect that he found some private entertainment in it, and it ministered to a general impression that his triumphant rival had in his composition a streak of perversity. He knew indeed that Osmond could have no reason to wish him evil; he had nothing to fear from him. He had carried off a supreme advantage and could afford to be kind to a man who had lost everything. It was true that Goodwood had at times grimly wished he were dead and would have liked to kill him; but Osmond had no means of knowing this, for practice had made the younger man perfect in the art of appearing inaccessible to-day to any violent emotion. He cultivated this art in order to deceive himself, but it was others that he deceived first. He cultivated it, moreover, with very limited success; of which there could be no better proof than the deep, dumb irritation that reigned in his soul when he heard Osmond speak of his wife's feelings as if he were commissioned to answer for them.

That was all he had had an ear for in what his host said to him this evening; he had been conscious that Osmond made more of a point even than usual of referring to the conjugal harmony prevailing at Palazzo Roccanera. He had been more careful than ever to speak as if he and his wife had all things in sweet community and it were as natural to each of them to say "we" as to say "I." In all this there was an air of intention that had puzzled and angered our poor Bostonian, who could only reflect for his comfort that Mrs. Osmond's relations with her husband were none of his business. He had no proof whatever that her husband misrepresented her, and if he judged her by the surface of things was bound to believe that she liked her life. She had never given him the faintest sign of discontent. Miss Stackpole had told him that she had lost her illusions, but writing for the papers had made Miss Stackpole sensational. She was too fond of early news. Moreover, since her arrival in Rome she had been much on her guard; she had pretty well ceased to flash her lantern at him. This indeed, it may be said for her, would have been quite against her conscience. She had now seen the reality of Isabel's situation, and it had inspired her with a just reserve. Whatever could be done to improve it the most useful form of assistance would not be to inflame her former lovers with a sense of her wrongs. Miss Stackpole continued to take a deep interest in the state of Mr. Goodwood's feelings, but she showed it at present only by sending him choice extracts, humorous and other, from the American journals, of which she received several by every post and which she

always perused with a pair of scissors in her hand. The articles she cut
out she placed in an envelope addressed to Mr. Goodwood, which she left
with her own hand at his hotel. He never asked her a question about Isabel: hadn't he come five thousand miles to see for himself? He was thus
not in the least authorised to think Mrs. Osmond unhappy; but the very
absence of authorisation operated as an irritant, ministered to the harsh-
ness with which, in spite of his theory that he had ceased to care, he now
recognised that, so far as she was concerned, the future had nothing more
for him. He had not even the satisfaction of knowing the truth; apparently
he could not even be trusted to respect her if she *were* unhappy. He was
hopeless, helpless, useless. To this last character she had called his attention by her ingenious plan for making him leave Rome. He had no objection whatever to doing what he could for her cousin, but it made him
grind his teeth to think that of all the services she might have asked of
him this was the one she had been eager to select. There had been no danger of her choosing one that would have kept him in Rome.

To-night what he was chiefly thinking of was that he was to leave her
to-morrow and that he had gained nothing by coming but the knowledge
that he was as little wanted as ever. About herself he had gained no knowledge; she was imperturbable, inscrutable, impenetrable. He felt the old
bitterness, which he had tried so hard to swallow, rise again in his throat,
and he knew there are disappointments that last as long as life. Osmond
went on talking; Goodwood was vaguely aware that he was touching again
upon his perfect intimacy with his wife. It seemed to him for a moment
that the man had a kind of demonic imagination; it was impossible that
without malice he should have selected so unusual a topic. But what did
it matter, after all, whether he were demonic or not, and whether she loved
him or hated him? She might hate him to the death without one's gaining
a straw one's self. "You travel, by the by, with Ralph Touchett," Osmond
said. "I suppose that means you'll move slowly?"

"I don't know. I shall do just as he likes."

"You're very accommodating. We're immensely obliged to you; you must
really let me say it. My wife has probably expressed to you what we feel.
Touchett has been on our minds all winter; it had looked more than once
as if he would never leave Rome. He ought never to have come; it's worse
than an imprudence for people in that state to travel; it's a kind of indeli-
cacy. I wouldn't for the world be under such an obligation to Touchett as
he has been to—to my wife and me. Other people inevitably have to look
after him, and every one isn't so generous as you."

"I've nothing else to do," Caspar said dryly.

Osmond looked at him a moment askance. "You ought to marry, and
then you'd have plenty to do. It's true that in that case you wouldn't be
quite so available for deeds of mercy."

"Do you find that as a married man you're so much occupied?" the young
man mechanically asked.

"Ah, you see, being married's in itself an occupation. It isn't always
active; it's often passive; but that takes even more attention. Then my wife
and I do so many things together. We read, we study, we make music, we
walk, we drive—we talk even, as when we first knew each other. I delight,
to this hour, in my wife's conversation. If you're ever bored take my advice

and get married. Your wife indeed may bore you, in that case; but you'll never bore yourself. You'll always have something to say to yourself—always have a subject of reflection."

"I'm not bored," said Goodwood. "I've plenty to think about and to say to myself."

"More than to say to others!" Osmond exclaimed with a light laugh. "Where shall you go next? I mean after you've consigned Touchett to his natural caretakers—I believe his mother's at last coming back to look after him. That little lady's superb; she neglects her duties with a finish—! Perhaps you'll spend the summer in England?"

"I don't know. I've no plans."

"Happy man! That's a little bleak, but it's very free."

"Oh yes, I'm very free."

"Free to come back to Rome I hope," said Osmond as he saw a group of new visitors enter the room. "Remember that when you do come we count on you!"

Goodwood had meant to go away early, but the evening elapsed without his having a chance to speak to Isabel otherwise than as one of several associated interlocutors. There was something perverse in the inveteracy with which she avoided him; his unquenchable rancour discovered an intention where there was certainly no appearance of one. There was absolutely no appearance of one. She met his eyes with her clear hospitable smile, which seemed almost to ask that he would come and help her to entertain some of her visitors. To such suggestions, however, he opposed but a stiff impatience. He wandered about and waited; he talked to the few people he knew, who found him for the first time rather self-contradictory. This was indeed rare with Caspar Goodwood, though he often contradicted others. There was often music at Palazzo Roccanera, and it was usually very good. Under cover of the music he managed to contain himself; but toward the end, when he saw the people beginning to go, he drew near to Isabel and asked her in a low tone if he might not speak to her in one of the other rooms, which he had just assured himself was empty. She smiled as if she wished to oblige him but found herself absolutely prevented. "I'm afraid it's impossible. People are saying good-night, and I must be where they can see me."

"I shall wait till they are all gone then."

She hesitated a moment. "Ah, that will be delightful!" she exclaimed.

And he waited, though it took a long time yet. There were several people, at the end, who seemed tethered to the carpet. The Countess Gemini, who was never herself till midnight, as she said, displayed no consciousness that the entertainment was over; she had still a little circle of gentlemen in front of the fire, who every now and then broke into a united laugh. Osmond had disappeared—he never bade good-bye to people; and as the Countess was extending her range, according to her custom at this period of the evening, Isabel had sent Pansy to bed. Isabel sat a little apart; she too appeared to wish her sister-in-law would sound a lower note and let the last loiterers depart in peace.

"May I not say a word to you now?" Goodwood presently asked her.

She got up immediately, smiling. "Certainly, we'll go somewhere else if you like." They went together, leaving the Countess with her little circle, and for a moment after they had crossed the threshold neither of them spoke. Isabel would not sit down; she stood in the middle of the room slowly fanning herself; she had for him the same familiar grace. She seemed to wait for him to speak. Now that he was alone with her all the passion he had never stifled surged into his senses; it hummed in his eyes and made things swim round him. The bright, empty room grew dim and blurred, and through the heaving veil he felt her hover before him with gleaming eyes and parted lips. If he had seen more distinctly he would have perceived her smile was fixed and a trifle forced—that she was frightened at what she saw in his own face. "I suppose you wish to bid me good-bye?" she said.

"Yes—but I don't like it. I don't want to leave Rome," he answered with almost plaintive honesty.

"I can well imagine. It's wonderfully good of you. I can't tell you how kind I think you."

For a moment more he said nothing. "With a few words like that you make me go."

"You must come back some day," she brightly returned.

"Some day? You mean as long a time hence as possible."

"Oh no; I don't mean all that."

"What _do_ you mean? I don't understand! But I said I'd go, and I'll go," Goodwood added.

"Come back whenever you like," said Isabel with attempted lightness.

"I don't care a straw for your cousin!" Caspar broke out.

"Is that what you wished to tell me?"

"No, no; I didn't want to tell you anything; I wanted to ask you—" he paused a moment, and then—"what have you really made of your life?" he said, in a low, quick tone. He paused again, as if for an answer; but she said nothing, and he went on; "I can't understand, I can't penetrate you! What am I to believe—what do you want me to think?" Still she said nothing; she only stood looking at him, now quite without pretending to ease. "I'm told you're unhappy, and if you are I should like to know it. That would be something for me. But you yourself say you're happy, and you're somehow so still, so smooth, so hard. You're completely changed. You conceal everything; I haven't really come near you."

"You come very near," Isabel said gently, but in a tone of warning.

"And yet I don't touch you! I want to know the truth. Have you done well?"

"You ask a great deal."

"Yes—I've always asked a great deal. Of course you won't tell me. I shall never know if you can help it. And then it's none of my business." He had spoken with a visible effort to control himself, to give a considerate form to an inconsiderate state of mind. But the sense that it was his last chance, that he loved her and had lost her, that she would think him a fool whatever he should say, suddenly gave him a lash and added a deep vibration to his low voice. "You're perfectly inscrutable, and that's what makes me think you've something to hide. I tell you I don't care a straw for your cousin, but I don't mean that I don't like him. I mean that it isn't because I like him that I go away with him. I'd go if he were an idiot and you should have asked me. If you should ask me I'd go to Siberia to-morrow. Why do you want me to leave the place? You must have some reason for that; if you were as contented as you pretend you are you wouldn't care. I'd rather know the truth about you, even if it's damnable, than have come here for nothing. That isn't what I came for. I thought I shouldn't care. I came because I wanted to assure myself that I needn't think of you any more. I haven't thought of anything else, and you're quite right to wish me to go away. But if I must go, there's no harm in my letting myself out for a single moment, is there? If you're really hurt—if *he* hurts you—nothing *I* say will hurt you. When I tell you I love you it's simply what I came for. I thought it was for something else; but it was for that. I shouldn't say it if I didn't believe I should never see you again. It's the last time—let me pluck a single flower! I've no right to say that, I know; and you've no right to listen. But you don't listen; you never listen, you're always thinking of something else. After this I must go, of course; so I shall at least have a reason. Your asking me is no reason, not a real one. I can't judge by your husband," he went on irrelevantly, almost incoherently; "I don't understand him; he tells me you adore each other. Why does he tell me that? What business is it of mine? When I say that to you, you look strange. But you always look strange. Yes, you've something to hide. It's none of my business—very true. But I love you," said Caspar Goodwood.

As he said, she looked strange. She turned her eyes to the door by which they had entered and raised her fan as if in warning. "You've behaved so well; don't spoil it," she uttered softly.

"No one hears me. It's wonderful what you tried to put me off with. I love you as I've never loved you."

"I know it. I knew it as soon as you consented to go."

"You can't help it—of course not. You would if you could, but you can't, unfortunately. Unfortunately for me, I mean. I ask nothing—nothing, that is, I shouldn't. But I do ask one sole satisfaction:—that you tell me—that you tell me—!"

"That I tell you what?"

"Whether I may pity you."

"Should you like that?" Isabel asked, trying to smile again.

"To pity you? Most assuredly! That at least would be doing something. I'd give my life to it."

She raised her fan to her face, which it covered all except her eyes. They rested a moment on his. "Don't give your life to it; but give a thought to it every now and then." And with that she went back to the Countess Gemini.

Chapter XLIX

Madame Merle had not made her appearance at Palazzo Roccanera on the evening of that Thursday of which I have narrated some of the incidents, and Isabel, though she observed her absence, was not surprised by it. Things had passed between them which added no stimulus to sociability, and to appreciate which we must glance a little backward. It has been mentioned that Madame Merle returned from Naples shortly after Lord Warburton had left Rome, and that on her first meeting with Isabel (whom, to do her justice, she came immediately to see) her first utterance had been an enquiry as to the whereabouts of this nobleman, for whom she appeared to hold her dear friend accountable.

"Please don't talk of him," said Isabel for answer; "we've heard so much of him of late."

Madame Merle bent her head on one side a little, protestingly, and smiled at the left corner of her mouth. "You've heard, yes. But you must remember that I've not, in Naples. I hoped to find him here and to be able to congratulate Pansy."

"You may congratulate Pansy still; but not on marrying Lord Warburton."

"How you say that! Don't you know I had set my heart on it?" Madame Merle asked with a great deal of spirit, but still with the intonation of good-humour.

Isabel was discomposed, but she was determined to be good-humoured too. "You shouldn't have gone to Naples then. You should have stayed here to watch the affair."

"I had too much confidence in you. But do you think it's too late?"

"You had better ask Pansy," said Isabel.

"I shall ask her what you've said to her."

These words seemed to justify the impulse of self-defence aroused on Isabel's part by her perceiving that her visitor's attitude was a critical one. Madame Merle, as we know, had been very discreet hitherto; she had never criticised; she had been markedly afraid of intermeddling. But apparently she had only reserved herself for this occasion, since she now had a dangerous quickness in her eye and an air of irritation which even her admirable ease was not able to transmute. She had suffered a disappointment which excited Isabel's surprise—our heroine having no knowledge of her zealous interest in Pansy's marriage; and she betrayed it in a manner which quickened Mrs. Osmond's alarm. More clearly than ever before Isabel heard a cold, mocking voice proceed from she knew not where, in the dim void that surrounded her, and declare that this bright, strong, definite, worldly woman, this incarnation of the practical, the personal, the immediate, was a powerful agent in her destiny. She was nearer to her than Isabel had yet discovered, and her nearness was not the charming accident she had so long supposed. The sense of accident indeed had died within her that day when she happened to be struck with the manner in which the wonderful lady and her own husband sat together in private. No definite suspicion had as yet taken its place; but it was enough to make her view this friend with a different eye, to have been led to reflect that there was more intention in her past behaviour than she had allowed for at the time. Ah yes, there had been intention, there had been intention, Isabel said to herself; and she seemed to wake from a long pernicious dream. What was it that brought home to her that Madame Merle's intention had not been good? Nothing but the mistrust which had lately taken body and which married itself now to the fruitful wonder produced by her visitor's challenge on behalf of poor Pansy. There was something in this challenge which had at the very outset excited an answering defiance; a nameless vitality which she could see to have been absent from her friend's professions of delicacy and caution. Madame Merle had been unwilling to interfere, certainly, but only so long as there was nothing to interfere with. It will perhaps seem to the reader that Isabel went fast in casting doubt, on mere suspicion, on a sincerity proved by several years of good offices. She moved quickly indeed, and with reason, for a strange truth was filtering into her soul. Madame Merle's interest was identical with Osmond's: that was enough. "I think Pansy will tell you nothing that will make you more angry," she said in answer to her companion's last remark.

"I'm not in the least angry. I've only a great desire to retrieve the situation. Do you consider that Warburton has left us for ever?"

"I can't tell you; I don't understand you. It's all over; please let it rest. Osmond has talked to me a great deal about it, and I've nothing more to say or to hear. I've no doubt," Isabel added, "that he'll be very happy to discuss the subject with you."

"I know what he thinks; he came to see me last evening."

"As soon as you had arrived? Then you know all about it and you needn't apply to me for information."

"It isn't information I want. At bottom it's sympathy. I had set my heart on that marriage; the idea did what so few things do—it satisfied the imagination."

"Your imagination, yes. But not that of the persons concerned."

"You mean by that of course that I'm not concerned. Of course not directly. But when one's such an old friend one can't help having something at stake. You forget how long I've known Pansy. You mean, of course," Madame Merle added, "that *you* are one of the persons concerned."

"No; that's the last thing I mean. I'm very weary of it all."

Madame Merle hesitated a little. "Ah yes, your work's done."

"Take care what you say," said Isabel very gravely.

"Oh, I take care; never perhaps more than when it appears least. Your husband judges you severely."

Isabel made for a moment no answer to this; she felt choked with bitterness. It was not the insolence of Madame Merle's informing her that Osmond had been taking her into his confidence as against his wife that struck her most; for she was not quick to believe that this was meant for insolence. Madame Merle was very rarely insolent, and only when it was exactly right. It was not right now, or at least it was not right yet. What touched Isabel like a drop of corrosive acid upon an open wound was the knowledge that Osmond dishonoured her in his words as well as in his thoughts. "Should you like to know how I judge *him*?" she asked at last.

"No, because you'd never tell me. And it would be painful for me to know."

There was a pause, and for the first time since she had known her Isabel thought Madame Merle disagreeable. She wished she would leave her. "Remember how attractive Pansy is, and don't despair," she said abruptly, with a desire that this should close their interview.

But Madame Merle's expansive presence underwent no contraction. She only gathered her mantle about her and, with the movement, scattered upon the air a faint, agreeable fragrance. "I don't despair; I feel encouraged. And I didn't come to scold you; I came if possible to learn the truth. I know you'll tell it if I ask you. It's an immense blessing with you that one can count upon that. No, you won't believe what a comfort I take in it."

"What truth do you speak of?" Isabel asked, wondering.

"Just this: whether Lord Warburton changed his mind quite of his own movement or because you recommended it. To please himself I mean, or to please you. Think of the confidence I must still have in you, in spite of having lost a little of it," Madame Merle continued with a smile, "to ask such a question as that!" She sat looking at her friend, to judge the effect of her words, and then went on: "Now don't be heroic, don't be unreasonable, don't take offence. It seems to me I do you an honour in speaking so. I don't know another woman to whom I would do it. I haven't the least idea that any other woman would tell me the truth. And don't you see how well it is that your husband should know it? It's true that he doesn't appear to have had any tact whatever in trying to extract it; he has indulged in gratuitous suppositions. But that doesn't alter the fact that it would make a difference in his view of his daughter's prospects to know distinctly what really occurred. If Lord Warburton simply got tired of the poor child, that's one thing, and it's a pity. If he gave her up to please you it's another. That's a pity too, but in a different way. Then, in the latter case, you'd perhaps resign yourself to not being pleased—to simply seeing your step-daughter married. Let him off—let us have him!"

Madame Merle had proceeded very deliberately, watching her companion and apparently thinking she could proceed safely. As she went on Isabel grew pale; she clasped her hands more tightly in her lap. It was not that her visitor had at last thought it the right time to be insolent; for this was not what was most apparent. It was a worse horror than that. "Who are you—what are you?" Isabel murmured. "What have you to do with my husband?" It was strange that for the moment she drew as near to him as if she had loved him.

"Ah then, you take it heroically! I'm very sorry. Don't think, however, that I shall do so."

"What have you to do with me?" Isabel went on.

Madame Merle slowly got up, stroking her muff, but not removing her eyes from Isabel's face. "Everything!" she answered.

Isabel sat there looking up at her, without rising; her face was almost a prayer to be enlightened. But the light of this woman's eyes seemed only a darkness. "Oh misery!" she murmured at last; and she fell back, covering her face with her hands. It had come over her like a high-surging wave that Mrs. Touchett was right. Madame Merle had married her. Before she uncovered her face again that lady had left the room.

Isabel took a drive alone that afternoon; she wished to be far away, under the sky, where she could descend from her carriage and tread upon the daisies. She had long before this taken old Rome into her confidence, for in a world of ruins the ruin of her happiness seemed a less unnatural catastrophe. She rested her weariness upon things that had crumbled for centuries and yet still were upright; she dropped her secret sadness into the silence of lonely places, where its very modern quality detached itself and grew objective, so that as she sat in a sun-warmed angle on a winter's day, or stood in a mouldy church to which no one came, she could almost smile at it and think of its smallness. Small it was, in the large Roman record, and her haunting sense of the continuity of the human lot easily carried her from the less to the greater. She had become deeply, tenderly acquainted with Rome; it interfused and moderated her passion. But she had grown to think of it chiefly as the place where people had suffered. This was what came to her in the starved churches, where the marble columns, transferred from pagan ruins, seemed to offer her a companionship in endurance and the musty incense to be a compound of long-unanswered prayers.

There was no gentler nor less consistent heretic than Isabel; the firmest of worshippers, gazing at dark altar-pictures or clustered candles, could not have felt more intimately the suggestiveness of these objects nor have been more liable at such moments to a spiritual visitation. Pansy, as we know, was almost always her companion, and of late the Countess Gemini, balancing a pink parasol, had lent brilliancy to their equipage; but she still occasionally found herself alone when it suited her mood and where it suited the place. On such occasions she had several resorts; the most accessible of which perhaps was a seat on the low parapet which edges the wide grassy space before the high, cold front of Saint John Lateran, whence you look across the Campagna at the far-trailing outline of the Alban Mount[1] and at that mighty plain, between, which is still so full of all that has passed from it. After the departure of her cousin and his companions she roamed more than usual; she carried her sombre spirit from one familiar shrine to the other. Even when Pansy and the Countess were with her she felt the touch of a vanished world. The carriage, leaving the walls of Rome behind, rolled through narrow lanes where the wild honeysuckle had begun to tangle itself in the hedges, or waited for her in quiet places where the fields lay near, while she strolled further and further over the flower-freckled turf, or sat on a stone that had once had a use and gazed through the veil of her personal sadness at the splendid sadness of the scene—at the dense, warm light, the far gradations and soft confusions of colour, the motionless shepherds in lonely attitudes, the hills where the cloud-shadows had the lightness of a blush.

On the afternoon I began with speaking of, she had taken a resolution not to think of Madame Merle; but the resolution proved vain, and this lady's image hovered constantly before her. She asked herself, with an almost childlike horror of the supposition, whether to this intimate friend of several years the great historical epithet of *wicked* were to be applied. She knew the idea only by the Bible and other literary works; to the best of her belief she had had no personal acquaintance with wickedness. She had desired a large acquaintance with human life, and in spite of her having flattered herself that she cultivated it with some success this elementary privilege had been denied her. Perhaps it was not wicked—in the historic sense—to be even deeply false; for that was what Madame Merle had been—deeply, deeply, deeply. Isabel's Aunt Lydia had made this discovery long before, and had mentioned it to her niece; but Isabel had flattered herself at this time that she had a much richer view of things, especially of the spontaneity of her own career and the nobleness of her own interpretations, than poor stiffly-reasoning Mrs. Touchett. Madame Merle had done what she wanted; she had brought about the union of her two friends; a reflection which could not fail to make it a matter of wonder that she should so much have desired such an event. There were people who had the match-making passion, like the votaries of art for art; but Madame Merle, great artist as she was, was scarcely one of these. She

---

1. San Giovanni in Laterano is the oldest great church in Rome, founded in the fourth century C.E. on the site of an earlier palace; it, rather than St. Peter's, is the cathedral of the Archdiocese of Rome and the church from which the papacy originally took its power. The building is an accretion of the centuries, with its façade dating from 1734. The Alban Mountains lie to the south, but the view Isabel had is now obscured by the city's growth. James's description here corresponds to the account he gives in "Roman Rides" (1873); see pp. 442–45 in this Norton Critical Edition.

thought too ill of marriage, too ill even of life; she had desired that particular marriage but had not desired others. She had therefore had a conception of gain, and Isabel asked herself where she had found her profit. It took her naturally a long time to discover, and even then her discovery was imperfect. It came back to her that Madame Merle, though she had seemed to like her from their first meeting at Gardencourt, had been doubly affectionate after Mr. Touchett's death and after learning that her young friend had been subject to the good old man's charity. She had found her profit not in the gross device of borrowing money, but in the more refined idea of introducing one of her intimates to the young woman's fresh and ingenuous fortune. She had naturally chosen her closest intimate, and it was already vivid enough to Isabel that Gilbert occupied this position. She found herself confronted in this manner with the conviction that the man in the world whom she had supposed to be the least sordid had married her, like a vulgar adventurer, for her money. Strange to say, it had never before occurred to her; if she had thought a good deal of harm of Osmond she had not done him this particular injury. This was the worst she could think of, and she had been saying to herself that the worst was still to come. A man might marry a woman for her money perfectly well; the thing was often done. But at least he should let her know. She wondered whether, since he had wanted her money, her money would now satisfy him. Would he take her money and let her go? Ah, if Mr. Touchett's great charity would but help her to-day it would be blessed indeed! It was not slow to occur to her that if Madame Merle had wished to do Gilbert a service his recognition to her of the boon must have lost its warmth. What must be his feelings to-day in regard to his too zealous benefactress, and what expression must they have found on the part of such a master of irony? It is a singular, but a characteristic, fact that before Isabel returned from her silent drive she had broken its silence by the soft exclamation: "Poor, poor Madame Merle!"

Her compassion would perhaps have been justified if on this same afternoon she had been concealed behind one of the valuable curtains of time-softened damask which dressed the interesting little *salon* of the lady to whom it referred; the carefully-arranged apartment to which we once paid a visit in company with the discreet Mr. Rosier. In that apartment, towards six o'clock, Gilbert Osmond was seated, and his hostess stood before him as Isabel had seen her stand on an occasion commemorated in this history with an emphasis appropriate not so much to its apparent as to its real importance.

"I don't believe you're unhappy; I believe you like it," said Madame Merle.

"Did I say I was unhappy?" Osmond asked with a face grave enough to suggest that he might have been.

"No, but you don't say the contrary, as you ought in common gratitude."

"Don't talk about gratitude," he returned dryly. "And don't aggravate me," he added in a moment.

Madame Merle slowly seated herself, with her arms folded and her white hands arranged as a support to one of them and an ornament, as it were, to the other. She looked exquisitely calm but impressively sad. "On your side, don't try to frighten me. I wonder if you guess some of my thoughts."

"I trouble about them no more than I can help. I've quite enough of my own."

"That's because they're so delightful."

Osmond rested his head against the back of his chair and looked at his companion with a cynical directness which seemed also partly an expression of fatigue. "You do aggravate me," he remarked in a moment. "I'm very tired."

"*Eh moi donc!*"[2] cried Madame Merle.

"With you it's because you fatigue yourself. With me it's not my own fault."

"When I fatigue myself it's for you. I've given you an interest. That's a great gift."

"Do you call it an interest?" Osmond enquired with detachment.

"Certainly, since it helps you to pass your time."

"The time has never seemed longer to me than this winter."

"You've never looked better; you've never been so agreeable, so brilliant."

"Damn my brilliancy!" he thoughtfully murmured. "How little, after all, you know me!"

"If I don't know you I know nothing," smiled Madame Merle. "You've the feeling of complete success."

"No, I shall not have that till I've made you stop judging me."

"I did that long ago. I speak from old knowledge. But you express yourself more too."

Osmond just hung fire. "I wish you'd express yourself less!"

"You wish to condemn me to silence? Remember that I've never been a chatterbox. At any rate there are three or four things I should like to say to you first. Your wife doesn't know what to do with herself," she went on with a change of tone.

"Pardon me; she knows perfectly. She has a line sharply drawn. She means to carry out her ideas."

"Her ideas to-day must be remarkable."

"Certainly they are. She has more of them than ever."

"She was unable to show me any this morning," said Madame Merle. "She seemed in a very simple, almost in a stupid, state of mind. She was completely bewildered."

"You had better say at once that she was pathetic."

"Ah no, I don't want to encourage you too much."

He still had his head against the cushion behind him; the ankle of one foot rested on the other knee. So he sat for a while. "I should like to know what's the matter with you," he said at last.

"The matter—the matter—!" And here Madame Merle stopped. Then she went on with a sudden outbreak of passion, a burst of summer thunder in a clear sky: "The matter is that I would give my right hand to be able to weep, and that I can't!"

"What good would it do you to weep?"

"It would make me feel as I felt before I knew you."

"If I've dried your tears, that's something. But I've seen you shed them."

"Oh, I believe you'll make me cry still. I mean make me howl like a wolf. I've a great hope, I've a great need, of that. I was vile this morning; I was horrid," she said.

---

2. And what about me! (French).

"If Isabel was in the stupid state of mind you mention she probably didn't perceive it," Osmond answered.

"It was precisely my deviltry that stupefied her. I couldn't help it; I was full of something bad. Perhaps it was something good; I don't know. You've not only dried up my tears; you've dried up my soul."

"It's not I then that am responsible for my wife's condition," Osmond said. "It's pleasant to think that I shall get the benefit of your influence upon her. Don't you know the soul is an immortal principle? How can it suffer alteration?"

"I don't believe at all that it's an immortal principle. I believe it can perfectly be destroyed. That's what has happened to mine, which was a very good one to start with; and it's you I have to thank for it. You're *very* bad," she added with gravity in her emphasis.

"Is this the way we're to end?" Osmond asked with the same studied coldness.

"I don't know how we're to end. I wish I did! How do bad people end?—especially as to their *common* crimes. You have made me as bad as yourself."

"I don't understand you. You seem to me quite good enough," said Osmond, his conscious indifference giving an extreme effect to the words.

Madame Merle's self-possession tended on the contrary to diminish, and she was nearer losing it than on any occasion on which we have had the pleasure of meeting her. The glow of her eye turned sombre; her smile betrayed a painful effort. "Good enough for anything that I've done with myself? I suppose that's what you mean."

"Good enough to be always charming!" Osmond exclaimed, smiling too.

"Oh God!" his companion murmured; and, sitting there in her ripe freshness, she had recourse to the same gesture she had provoked on Isabel's part in the morning: she bent her face and covered it with her hands.

"Are you going to weep after all?" Osmond asked; and on her remaining motionless he went on: "Have I ever complained to you?"

She dropped her hands quickly. "No, you've taken your revenge otherwise—you have taken it on *her*."

Osmond threw back his head further; he looked a while at the ceiling and might have been supposed to be appealing, in an informal way, to the heavenly powers. "Oh, the imagination of women! It's always vulgar, at bottom. You talk of revenge like a third-rate novelist."

"Of course you haven't complained. You've enjoyed your triumph too much."

"I'm rather curious to know what you call my triumph."

"You've made your wife afraid of you."

Osmond changed his position; he leaned forward, resting his elbows on his knees and looking a while at a beautiful old Persian rug, at his feet. He had an air of refusing to accept any one's valuation of anything, even of time, and of preferring to abide by his own; a peculiarity which made him at moments an irritating person to converse with. "Isabel's not afraid of me, and it's not what I wish," he said at last. "To what do you want to provoke me when you say such things as that?"

"I've thought over all the harm you can do me," Madame Merle answered. "Your wife was afraid of me this morning, but in me it was really you she feared."

"You may have said things that were in very bad taste; I'm not responsible for that. I didn't see the use of your going to see her at all: you're capable of acting without her. I've not made *you* afraid of me that I can see," he went on; "how then should I have made her? You're at least as brave. I can't think where you've picked up such rubbish; one might suppose you knew me by this time." He got up as he spoke and walked to the chimney, where he stood a moment bending his eye, as if he had seen them for the first time, on the delicate specimens of rare porcelain with which it was covered. He took up a small cup and held it in his hand; then, still holding it and leaning his arm on the mantel, he pursued: "You always see too much in everything; you overdo it; you lose sight of the real. I'm much simpler than you think."

"I think you're very simple." And Madame Merle kept her eye on her cup. "I've come to that with time. I judged you, as I say, of old; but it's only since your marriage that I've understood you. I've seen better what you have been to your wife than I ever saw what you were for me. Please be very careful of that precious object."

"It already has a wee bit of a tiny crack," said Osmond dryly as he put it down. "If you didn't understand me before I married it was cruelly rash of you to put me into such a box. However, I took a fancy to my box myself; I thought it would be a comfortable fit. I asked very little; I only asked that she should like me."

"That she should like you so much!"

"So much, of course; in such a case one asks the maximum. That she should adore me, if you will. Oh yes, I wanted that."

"I never adored you," said Madame Merle.

"Ah, but you pretended to!"

"It's true that you never accused me of being a comfortable fit," Madame Merle went on.

"My wife has declined—declined to do anything of the sort," said Osmond. "If you're determined to make a tragedy of that, the tragedy's hardly for her."

"The tragedy's for me!" Madame Merle exclaimed, rising with a long low sigh but having a glance at the same time for the contents of her mantel-shelf. "It appears that I'm to be severely taught the disadvantages of a false position."

"You express yourself like a sentence in a copy-book. We must look for our comfort where we can find it. If my wife doesn't like me, at least my child does. I shall look for compensations in Pansy. Fortunately I haven't a fault to find with her."

"Ah," she said softly, "if I had a child—!"

Osmond waited, and then, with a little formal air, "The children of others may be a great interest!" he announced.

"You're more like a copy-book than I. There's something after all that holds us together."

"Is it the idea of the harm I may do you?" Osmond asked.

"No; it's the idea of the good I may do for you. It's that," Madame Merle pursued, "that made me so jealous of Isabel. I want it to be my work," she added, with her face, which had grown hard and bitter, relaxing to its habit of smoothness.

Her friend took up his hat and his umbrella, and after giving the former article two or three strokes with his coat-cuff, "On the whole, I think," he said, "you had better leave it to me."

After he had left her she went, the first thing, and lifted from the mantel-shelf the attenuated coffee-cup in which he had mentioned the existence of a crack; but she looked at it rather abstractedly. "Have I been so vile all for nothing?" she vaguely wailed.

Chapter L

As the Countess Gemini was not acquainted with the ancient monuments Isabel occasionally offered to introduce her to these interesting relics and to give their afternoon drive an antiquarian aim. The Countess, who professed to think her sister-in-law a prodigy of learning, never made an objection, and gazed at masses of Roman brickwork as patiently as if they had been mounds of modern drapery. She had not the historic sense, though she had in some directions the anecdotic, and as regards herself the apologetic, but she was so delighted to be in Rome that she only desired to float with the current. She would gladly have passed an hour every day in the damp darkness of the Baths of Titus[1] if it had been a condition of her remaining at Palazzo Roccanera. Isabel, however, was not a severe cicerone; she used to visit the ruins chiefly because they offered an excuse for talking about other matters than the love-affairs of the ladies of Florence, as to which her companion was never weary of offering information. It must be added that during these visits the Countess forbade herself every form of active research; her preference was to sit in the carriage and exclaim that everything was most interesting. It was in this manner that she had hitherto examined the Coliseum, to the infinite regret of her niece, who—with all the respect that she owed her—could not see why she should not descend from the vehicle and enter the building. Pansy had so little chance to ramble that her view of the case was not wholly disinterested; it may be divined that she had a secret hope that, once inside, her parents' guest might be induced to climb to the upper tiers. There came a day when the Countess announced her willingness to undertake this feat—a mild afternoon in March when the windy month expressed itself in occasional puffs of spring. The three ladies went into the Coliseum together, but Isabel left her companions to wander over the place. She had often ascended to those desolate ledges from which the Roman crowd used to bellow applause and where now the wild flowers (when they are allowed) bloom in the deep crevices; and to-day she felt weary and disposed to sit in the despoiled arena. It made an intermission too, for the Countess often asked more from one's attention than she gave in return; and Isabel believed that when she was alone with her niece she let the dust gather for a moment on the ancient scandals of the Arnide.[2] She so remained below therefore, while Pansy guided her undiscriminating aunt to the steep brick staircase at the foot of which the custodian unlocks the tall

1. Near the Colosseum and built by the emperor of that name on the site of Nero's palace; the baths contain some of Rome's best-preserved wall paintings, and in the late nineteenth century they were in the process of excavation.
2. Probably a misprint or contraction for "Arno-side"; the edition of 1881 reads "Florence."

wooden gate. The great enclosure was half in shadow; the western sun brought out the pale red tone of the great blocks of travertine—the latent colour that is the only living element in the immense ruin. Here and there wandered a peasant or a tourist, looking up at the far sky-line where, in the clear stillness, a multitude of swallows kept circling and plunging. Isabel presently became aware that one of the other visitors, planted in the middle of the arena, had turned his attention to her own person and was looking at her with a certain little poise of the head which she had some weeks before perceived to be characteristic of baffled but indestructible purpose. Such an attitude, to-day, could belong only to Mr. Edward Rosier; and this gentleman proved in fact to have been considering the question of speaking to her. When he had assured himself that she was unaccompanied he drew near, remarking that though she would not answer his letters she would perhaps not wholly close her ears to his spoken eloquence. She replied that her stepdaughter was close at hand and that she could only give him five minutes; whereupon he took out his watch and sat down upon a broken block.

"It's very soon told," said Edward Rosier. "I've sold all my bibelots!" Isabel gave instinctively an exclamation of horror; it was if he had told her he had had all his teeth drawn. "I've sold them by auction at the Hôtel Drouot,"[3] he went on. "The sale took place three days ago, and they've telegraphed me the result. It's magnificent."

"I'm glad to hear it; but I wish you had kept your pretty things."

"I have the money instead—fifty thousand dollars. Will Mr. Osmond think me rich enough now?"

"Is it for that you did it?" Isabel asked gently.

"For what else in the world could it be? That's the only thing I think of. I went to Paris and made my arrangements. I couldn't stop for the sale; I couldn't have seen them going off; I think it would have killed me. But I put them into good hands, and they brought high prices. I should tell you I have kept my enamels. Now I have the money in my pocket, and he can't say I'm poor!" the young man exclaimed defiantly.

"He'll say now that you're not wise," said Isabel, as if Gilbert Osmond had never said this before.

Rosier gave her a sharp look. "Do you mean that without my bibelots I'm nothing? Do you mean they were the best thing about me? That's what they told me in Paris; oh they were very frank about it. But they hadn't seen *her*!"

"My dear friend, you deserve to succeed," said Isabel very kindly.

"You say that so sadly that it's the same as if you said I shouldn't." And he questioned her eyes with the clear trepidation of his own. He had the air of a man who knows he has been the talk of Paris for a week and is full half a head taller in consequence, but who also has a painful suspicion that in spite of this increase of stature one or two persons still have the perversity to think him diminutive. "I know what happened here while I was away," he went on. "What does Mr. Osmond expect after she has refused Lord Warburton?"

Isabel debated. "That she'll marry another nobleman."

"What other nobleman?"

"One that he'll pick out."

3. See p. 153, n.1.

Rosier slowly got up, putting his watch into his waistcoat-pocket. "You're laughing at some one, but this time I don't think it's at me."

"I didn't mean to laugh," said Isabel. "I laugh very seldom. Now you had better go away."

"I feel very safe!" Rosier declared without moving. This might be; but it evidently made him feel more so to make the announcement in rather a loud voice, balancing himself a little complacently on his toes and looking all round the Coliseum as if it were filled with an audience. Suddenly Isabel saw him change colour; there was more of an audience than he had suspected. She turned and perceived that her two companions had returned from their excursion. "You must really go away," she said quickly.

"Ah, my dear lady, pity me!" Edward Rosier murmured in a voice strangely at variance with the announcement I have just quoted. And then he added eagerly, like a man who in the midst of his misery is seized by a happy thought: "Is that lady the Countess Gemini? I've a great desire to be presented to her."

Isabel looked at him a moment. "She has no influence with her brother."

"Ah, what a monster you make him out!" And Rosier faced the Countess, who advanced, in front of Pansy, with an animation partly due perhaps to the fact that she perceived her sister-in-law to be engaged in conversation with a very pretty young man.

"I'm glad you've kept your enamels!" Isabel called as she left him. She went straight to Pansy, who, on seeing Edward Rosier, had stopped short, with lowered eyes. "We'll go back to the carriage," she said gently.

"Yes, it's getting late," Pansy returned more gently still. And she went on without a murmur, without faltering or glancing back.

Isabel, however, allowing herself this last liberty, saw that a meeting had immediately taken place between the Countess and Mr. Rosier. He had removed his hat and was bowing and smiling; he had evidently introduced himself, while the Countess's expressive back displayed to Isabel's eye a gracious inclination. These facts, none the less, were presently lost to sight, for Isabel and Pansy took their places again in the carriage. Pansy, who faced her stepmother, at first kept her eyes fixed on her lap; then she raised them and rested them on Isabel's. There shone out of each of them a little melancholy ray—a spark of timid passion which touched Isabel to the heart. At the same time a wave of envy passed over her soul, as she compared the tremulous longing, the definite ideal of the child with her own dry despair. "Poor little Pansy!" she affectionately said.

"Oh never mind!" Pansy answered in the tone of eager apology.

And then there was a silence; the Countess was a long time coming. "Did you show your aunt everything, and did she enjoy it?" Isabel asked at last.

"Yes, I showed her everything. I think she was very much pleased."

"And you're not tired, I hope."

"Oh no, thank you, I'm not tired."

The Countess still remained behind, so that Isabel requested the footman to go into the Coliseum and tell her they were waiting. He presently returned with the announcement that the Signora Contessa begged them not to wait—she would come home in a cab!

About a week after this lady's quick sympathies had enlisted themselves with Mr. Rosier, Isabel, going rather late to dress for dinner, found Pansy sitting in her room. The girl seemed to have been awaiting her; she got up from her low chair. "Pardon my taking the liberty," she said in a small voice. "It will be the last—for some time."

Her voice was strange, and her eyes, widely opened, had an excited, frightened look. "You're not going away!" Isabel exclaimed.

"I'm going to the convent."

"To the convent?"

Pansy drew nearer, till she was near enough to put her arms round Isabel and rest her head on her shoulder. She stood this way a moment, perfectly still; but her companion could feel her tremble. The quiver of her little body expressed everything she was unable to say. Isabel nevertheless pressed her. "Why are you going to the convent?"

"Because papa thinks it best. He says a young girl's better, every now and then, for making a little retreat. He says the world, always the world, is very bad for a young girl. This is just a chance for a little seclusion—a little reflexion." Pansy spoke in short detached sentences, as if she could scarce trust herself; and then she added with a triumph of self-control: "I think papa's right; I've been so much in the world this winter."

Her announcement had a strange effect on Isabel; it seemed to carry a larger meaning than the girl herself knew. "When was this decided?" she asked. "I've heard nothing of it."

"Papa told me half an hour ago; he thought it better it shouldn't be too much talked about in advance. Madame Catherine's to come for me at a quarter past seven, and I'm only to take two frocks. It's only for a few weeks; I'm sure it will be very good. I shall find all those ladies who used to be so kind to me, and I shall see the little girls who are being educated. I'm very fond of little girls," said Pansy with an effect of diminutive grandeur. "And I'm also very fond of Mother Catherine. I shall be very quiet and think a great deal."

Isabel listened to her, holding her breath; she was almost awe-struck. "Think of *me* sometimes."

"Ah, come and see me soon!" cried Pansy; and the cry was very different from the heroic remarks of which she had just delivered herself.

Isabel could say nothing more; she understood nothing; she only felt how little she yet knew her husband. Her answer to his daughter was a long, tender kiss.

Half an hour later she learned from her maid that Madame Catherine had arrived in a cab and had departed again with the signorina. On going to the drawing-room before dinner she found the Countess Gemini alone, and this lady characterised the incident by exclaiming, with a wonderful toss of the head, "*En violà, ma chére, une pose!*"[4] But if it was an affectation she was at a loss to see what her husband affected. She could only dimly perceive that he had more traditions than she supposed. It had become her habit to be so careful as to what she said to him that, strange as it may appear, she hesitated, for several minutes after he had come in, to allude to his daughter's sudden departure: she spoke of it only after they were seated at table. But she had forbidden herself ever to ask Osmond a question. All she could do was to make a declaration, and there was one that came very naturally. "I shall miss Pansy very much."

---

4. There it is, my dear, but what an affectation! (French).

He looked a while, with his head inclined a little, at the basket of flowers in the middle of the table. "Ah yes," he said at last, "I had thought of that. You must go and see her, you know; but not too often. I dare say you wonder why I sent her to the good sisters; but I doubt if I can make you understand. It doesn't matter; don't trouble yourself about it. That's why I had not spoken of it. I didn't believe you would enter into it. But I've always had the idea; I've always thought it a part of the education of one's daughter. One's daughter should be fresh and fair; she should be innocent and gentle. With the manners of the present time she is liable to become so dusty and crumpled. Pansy's a little dusty, a little dishevelled; she has knocked about too much. This bustling, pushing rabble that calls itself society—one should take her out of it occasionally. Convents are very quiet, very convenient, very salutary. I like to think of her there, in the old garden, under the arcade, among those tranquil virtuous women. Many of them are gentlewomen born; several of them are noble. She will have her books and her drawing, she will have her piano. I've made the most liberal arrangements. There is to be nothing ascetic; there's just to be a certain little sense of sequestration. She'll have time to think, and there's something I want her to think about." Osmond spoke deliberately, reasonably, still with his head on one side, as if he were looking at the basket of flowers. His tone, however, was that of a man not so much offering an explanation as putting a thing into words—almost into pictures—to see, himself, how it would look. He considered a while the picture he had evoked and seemed greatly pleased with it. And then he went on: "The Catholics are very wise after all. The convent is a great institution; we can't do without it; it corresponds to an essential need in families, in society. It's a school of good manners; it's a school of repose. Oh, I don't want to detach my daughter from the world," he added; "I don't want to make her fix her thoughts on any other. This one's very well, as *she* should take it, and she may think of it as much as she likes. Only she must think of it in the right way."

Isabel gave an extreme attention to this little sketch; she found it indeed intensely interesting. It seemed to show her how far her husband's desire to be effective was capable of going—to the point of playing theoretic tricks on the delicate organism of his daughter. She could not understand his purpose, no—not wholly; but she understood it better than he supposed or desired, inasmuch as she was convinced that the whole proceeding was an elaborate mystification, addressed to herself and destined to act upon her imagination. He had wanted to do something sudden and arbitrary, something unexpected and refined; to mark the difference between his sympathies and her own, and show that if he regarded his daughter as a precious work of art it was natural he should be more and more careful about the finishing touches. If he wished to be effective he had succeeded; the incident struck a chill into Isabel's heart. Pansy had known the convent in her childhood and had found a happy home there; she was fond of the good sisters, who were very fond of her, and there was therefore for the moment no definite hardship in her lot. But all the same the girl had taken fright; the impression her father desired to make would evidently be sharp enough. The old Protestant tradition had never faded from Isabel's imagination, and as her thoughts attached themselves to this striking example of her husband's genius—she sat looking, like him, at the basket of flowers—poor little Pansy became the heroine of a tragedy.

Osmond wished it to be known that he shrank from nothing, and his wife found it hard to pretend to eat her dinner. There was a certain relief presently, in hearing the high, strained voice of her sister-in-law. The Countess too, apparently, had been thinking the thing out, but had arrived at a different conclusion from Isabel.

"It's very absurd, my dear Osmond," she said, "to invent so many pretty reasons for poor Pansy's banishment. Why don't you say at once that you want to get her out of my way? Haven't you discovered that I think very well of Mr. Rosier? I do indeed; he seems to me *simpaticissimo*.[5] He has made me believe in true love; I never did before! Of course you've made up your mind that with those convictions I'm dreadful company for Pansy."

Osmond took a sip of a glass of wine; he looked perfectly good-humoured. "My dear Amy," he answered, smiling as if he were uttering a piece of gallantry, "I don't know anything about your convictions, but if I suspected that they interfere with mine it would be much simpler to banish *you*."

Chapter LI

The Countess was not banished, but she felt the insecurity of her tenure of her brother's hospitality. A week after this incident Isabel received a telegram from England, dated from Gardencourt and bearing the stamp of Mrs. Touchett's authorship. "Ralph cannot last many days," it ran, "and if convenient would like to see you. Wishes me to say that you must come only if you've not other duties. Say, for myself, that you used to talk a good deal about your duty and to wonder what it was; shall be curious to see whether you've found it out. Ralph is really dying, and there's no other company." Isabel was prepared for this news, having received from Henrietta Stackpole a detailed account of her journey to England with her appreciative patient. Ralph had arrived more dead than alive, but she had managed to convey him to Gardencourt, where he had taken to his bed, which, as Miss Stackpole wrote, he evidently would never leave again. She added that she had really had two patients on her hands instead of one, inasmuch as Mr. Goodwood, who had been of no earthly use, was quite as ailing, in a different way, as Mr. Touchett. Afterwards she wrote that she had been obliged to surrender the field to Mrs. Touchett, who had just returned from America and had promptly given her to understand that she didn't wish any interviewing at Gardencourt. Isabel had written to her aunt shortly after Ralph came to Rome, letting her know of his critical condition and suggesting that she should lose no time in returning to Europe. Mrs. Touchett had telegraphed an acknowledgement of this admonition, and the only further news Isabel received from her was the second telegram I have just quoted.

Isabel stood a moment looking at the latter missive; then, thrusting it into her pocket, she went straight to the door of her husband's study. Here she again paused an instant, after which she opened the door and went in. Osmond was seated at the table near the window with a folio volume before him, propped against a pile of books. This volume was open at a page of small coloured plates, and Isabel presently saw that he had been copying from it the drawing of an antique coin. A box of water-colours and fine brushes lay before him, and he had already transferred to a sheet

5. Nice, sympathetic, likeable (Italian), to a superlative degree.

of immaculate paper the delicate, finely-tinted disk. His back was turned toward the door, but he recognised his wife without looking round.

"Excuse me for disturbing you," she said.

"When I come to your room I always knock," he answered, going on with his work.

"I forgot; I had something else to think of. My cousin's dying."

"Ah, I don't believe that," said Osmond, looking at his drawing through a magnifying glass. "He was dying when we married; he'll outlive us all."

Isabel gave herself no time, no thought, to appreciate the careful cynicism of this declaration; she simply went on quickly, full of her intention: "My aunt has telegraphed for me; I must go to Gardencourt."

"Why must you go to Gardencourt?" Osmond asked in the tone of impartial curiosity.

"To see Ralph before he dies."

To this, for some time, he made no rejoinder; he continued to give his chief attention to his work, which was of a sort that would brook no negligence. "I don't see the need of it," he said at last. "He came to see you here. I didn't like that; I thought his being in Rome a great mistake. But I tolerated it because it was to be the last time you should see him. Now you tell me it's not to have been the last. Ah, you're not grateful!"

"What am I to be grateful for?"

Gilbert Osmond laid down his little implements, blew a speck of dust from his drawing, slowly got up, and for the first time looked at his wife. "For my not having interfered while he was here."

"Oh yes, I am. I remember perfectly how distinctly you let me know you didn't like it. I was very glad when he went away."

"Leave him alone then. Don't run after him."

Isabel turned her eyes away from him; they rested upon his little drawing. "I must go to England," she said, with a full consciousness that her tone might strike an irritable man of taste as stupidly obstinate.

"I shall not like it if you do," Osmond remarked.

"Why should I mind that? You won't like it if I don't. You like nothing I do or don't do. You pretend to think I lie."

Osmond turned slightly pale; he gave a cold smile. "That's why you must go then? Not to see your cousin, but to take a revenge on me."

"I know nothing about revenge."

"I do," said Osmond. "Don't give me an occasion."

"You're only too eager to take one. You wish immensely that I would commit some folly."

"I should be gratified in that case if you disobeyed me."

"If I disobeyed you?" said Isabel in a low tone which had the effect of mildness.

"Let it be clear. If you leave Rome to-day it will be a piece of the most deliberate, the most calculated, opposition."

"How can you call it calculated? I received my aunt's telegram but three minutes ago."

"You calculate rapidly; it's a great accomplishment. I don't see why we should prolong our discussion; you know my wish." And he stood there as if he expected to see her withdraw.

But she never moved; she couldn't move, strange as it may seem; she still wished to justify herself; he had the power, in an extraordinary degree, of making her feel this need. There was something in her imagination he could always appeal to against her judgement. "You've no reason for such a wish," said Isabel, "and I've every reason for going. I can't tell you how unjust you seem to me. But I think you know. It's your own opposition that's calculated. It's malignant."

She had never uttered her worst thought to her husband before, and the sensation of hearing it was evidently new to Osmond. But he showed no surprise, and his coolness was apparently a proof that he had believed his wife would in fact be unable to resist for ever his ingenious endeavour to draw her out. "It's all the more intense then," he answered. And he added almost as if he were giving her a friendly counsel: "This is a very important matter." She recognised that; she was fully conscious of the weight of the occasion; she knew that between them they had arrived at a crisis. Its gravity made her careful; she said nothing, and he went on. "You say I've no reason? I have the very best. I dislike, from the bottom of my soul, what you intend to do. It's dishonourable; it's indelicate; it's indecent. Your cousin is nothing whatever to me, and I'm under no obligation to make concessions to him. I've already made the very handsomest. Your relations with him, while he was here, kept me on pins and needles; but I let that pass, because from week to week I expected him to go. I've never liked him and he has never liked me. That's why you like him—because he hates me," said Osmond with a quick, barely audible tremor in his voice. "I've an ideal of what my wife should do and should not do. She should not travel across Europe alone, in defiance of my deepest desire, to sit at the bed-side of other men. Your cousin's nothing to you; he's nothing to us. You smile most expressively when I talk about *us*, but I assure you that *we*, *we*, Mrs. Osmond, is all I know. I take our marriage seriously; you appear to have found a way of not doing so. I'm not aware that we're divorced or separated; for me we're indissolubly united. You are nearer to me than any human creature, and I'm nearer to you. It may be a disagreeable proximity; it's one, at any rate, of our own deliberate making. You don't like to be reminded of that, I know; but I'm perfectly willing, because—because—" And he paused a moment, looking as if he had something to say which would be very much to the point. "Because I think we should accept the consequences of our actions, and what I value most in life is the honour of a thing!"

He spoke gravely and almost gently; the accent of sarcasm had dropped out of his tone. It had a gravity which checked his wife's quick emotion; the resolution with which she had entered the room found itself caught in a mesh of fine threads. His last words were not a command, they constituted a kind of appeal; and, though she felt that any expression of respect on his part could only be a refinement of egotism, they represented something transcendent and absolute, like the sign of the cross or the flag of one's country. He spoke in the name of something sacred and precious—the observance of a magnificent form. They were as perfectly apart in feeling as two disillusioned lovers had ever been; but they had never yet separated in act. Isabel had not changed; her old passion for justice still abode within her; and now, in the very thick of her sense of her husband's blasphemous sophistry, it began to throb to a tune which for a moment promised him the victory. It came over her that in his wish to preserve appearances he was after all sincere, and that this, as far as it went, was a merit. Ten minutes before she had felt all the joy of irreflective action—a joy to which she had so long been a stranger; but action had been suddenly changed to slow renunciation, transformed by the blight of Osmond's touch. If she must renounce, however, she would let him know she was a victim rather than a dupe. "I know you're a master of the art of mockery," she said. "How can you speak of an indissoluble union—how can you speak of your being contented? Where's our union when you accuse me of falsity? Where's your contentment when you have nothing but hideous suspicion in your heart?"

"It is in our living decently together, in spite of such drawbacks."

"We don't live decently together!" cried Isabel.

"Indeed we don't if you go to England."

"That's very little; that's nothing. I might do much more."

He raised his eyebrows and even his shoulders a little: he had lived long enough in Italy to catch this trick. "Ah, if you've come to threaten me I prefer my drawing." And he walked back to his table, where he took up the sheet of paper on which he had been working and stood studying it.

"I suppose that if I go you'll not expect me to come back," said Isabel.

He turned quickly round, and she could see this movement at least was not designed. He looked at her a little, and then, "Are you out of your mind?" he enquired.

"How can it be anything but a rupture?" she went on; "especially if all you say is true?" She was unable to see how it could be anything but a rupture; she sincerely wished to know what else it might be.

He sat down before his table. "I really can't argue with you on the hypothesis of your defying me," he said. And he took up one of his little brushes again.

She lingered but a moment longer; long enough to embrace with her eye his whole deliberately indifferent yet most expressive figure; after which she quickly left the room. Her faculties, her energy, her passion, were all dispersed again; she felt as if a cold, dark mist had suddenly encompassed her. Osmond possessed in a supreme degree the art of eliciting any weakness. On her way back to her room she found the Countess Gemini standing in the open doorway of a little parlour in which a small collection of heterogeneous books had been arranged. The Countess had an open volume in her hand; she appeared to have been glancing down a page which failed to strike her as interesting. At the sound of Isabel's step she raised her head.

"Ah my dear," she said, "you, who are so literary, do tell me some amusing book to read! Everything here's of a dreariness—! Do you think this would do me any good?"

Isabel glanced at the title of the volume she held out, but without reading or understanding it. "I'm afraid I can't advise you. I've had bad news. My cousin, Ralph Touchett, is dying."

The Countess threw down her book. "Ah, he was so simpatico. I'm awfully sorry for you."

"You would be sorrier still if you knew."

"What is there to know? You look very badly," the Countess added. "You must have been with Osmond."

Half an hour before Isabel would have listened very coldly to an intimation that she should ever feel a desire for the sympathy of her sister-in-law, and there can be no better proof of her present embarrassment than the fact that she almost clutched at this lady's fluttering attention. "I've been with Osmond," she said, while the Countess's bright eyes glittered at her.

"I'm sure then he has been odious!" the Countess cried. "Did he say he was glad poor Mr. Touchett's dying?"

"He said it's impossible I should go to England."

The Countess's mind, when her interests were concerned, was agile; she already foresaw the extinction of any further brightness in her visit to Rome. Ralph Touchett would die, Isabel would go into mourning, and then there would be no more dinner-parties. Such a prospect produced for a moment in her countenance an expressive grimace; but this rapid, picturesque play of feature was her only tribute to disappointment. After all, she reflected, the game was almost played out; she had already overstayed her invitation. And then she cared enough for Isabel's trouble to forget her own, and she saw that Isabel's trouble was deep. It seemed deeper than the mere death of a cousin, and the Countess had no hesitation in connecting her exasperating brother with the expression of her sister-in-law's eyes. Her heart beat with an almost joyous expectation, for if she had wished to see Osmond overtopped the conditions looked favourable now. Of course if Isabel should go to England she herself would immediately leave Palazzo Roccanera; nothing would induce her to remain there with Osmond. Nevertheless she felt an immense desire to hear that Isabel would go to England. "Nothing's impossible for you, my dear," she said caressingly. "Why else are you rich and clever and good?"

"Why indeed? I feel stupidly weak."

"Why does Osmond say it's impossible?" the Countess asked in a tone which sufficiently declared that she couldn't imagine.

From the moment she thus began to question her, however, Isabel drew back; she disengaged her hand, which the Countess had affectionately taken. But she answered this enquiry with frank bitterness. "Because we're so happy together that we can't separate even for a fortnight."

"Ah," cried the Countess while Isabel turned away, "when I want to make a journey my husband simply tells me I can have no money!"

Isabel went to her room, where she walked up and down for an hour. It may appear to some readers that she gave herself much trouble, and it is certain that for a woman of a high spirit she had allowed herself easily to be arrested. It seemed to her that only now she fully measured the great undertaking of matrimony. Marriage meant that in such a case as this, when one had to choose, one chose as a matter of course for one's husband. "I'm afraid—yes, I'm afraid," she said to herself more than once, stopping short in her walk. But what she was afraid of was not her husband—his displeasure, his hatred, his revenge; it was not even her own later judgement of her conduct—a consideration which had often held her in check; it was simply the violence there would be in going when Osmond wished her to remain. A gulf of difference had opened between them, but nevertheless it was his desire that she should stay, it was a horror to him that she should go. She knew the nervous fineness with which he could feel an objection. What he thought of her she knew, what he was capable of saying to her she had felt; yet they were married, for all that, and marriage meant that a woman should cleave to the man with whom, uttering tremendous vows, she had stood at the altar. She sank down on her sofa at last and buried her head in a pile of cushions.

When she raised her head again the Countess Gemini hovered before her. She had come in all unperceived; she had a strange smile on her thin lips and her whole face had grown in an hour a shining intimation. She lived assuredly, it might be said, at the window of her spirit, but now she was leaning far out. "I knocked," she began, "but you didn't answer me. So I ventured in. I've been looking at you for the last five minutes. You're very unhappy."

"Yes; but I don't think you can comfort me."

"Will you give me leave to try?" And the Countess sat down on the sofa beside her. She continued to smile, and there was something communicative and exultant in her expression. She appeared to have a deal to say, and it occurred to Isabel for the first time that her sister-in-law might say something really human. She made play with her glittering eyes, in which there was an unpleasant fascination. "After all," she soon resumed, "I must tell you, to begin with, that I don't understand your state of mind. You seem to have so many scruples, so many reasons, so many ties. When I discovered, ten years ago, that my husband's dearest wish was to make me miserable—of late he has simply let me alone—ah, it was a wonderful simplification! My poor Isabel, you're not simple enough."

"No, I'm not simple enough," said Isabel.

"There's something I want you to know," the Countess declared—"because I think you ought to know it. Perhaps you do; perhaps you've guessed it. But if you have, all I can say is that I understand still less why you shouldn't do as you like."

"What do you wish me to know?" Isabel felt a foreboding that made her heart beat faster. The Countess was about to justify herself, and this alone was portentous.

But she was nevertheless disposed to play a little with her subject. "In your place I should have guessed it ages ago. Have you never really suspected?"

"I've guessed nothing. What should I have suspected? I don't know what you mean."

"That's because you've such a beastly pure mind. I never saw a woman with such a pure mind!" cried the Countess.

Isabel slowly got up. "You're going to tell me something horrible."

"You can call it by whatever name you will!" And the Countess rose also, while her gathered perversity grew vivid and dreadful. She stood a moment in a sort of glare of intention and, as seemed to Isabel even then, of ugliness; after which she said: "My first sister-in-law had no children."

Isabel stared back at her; the announcement was an anticlimax. "Your first sister-in-law?"

"I suppose you know at least, if one may mention it, that Osmond has been married before! I've never spoken to you of his wife; I thought it mightn't be decent or respectful. But others, less particular, must have done so. The poor little woman lived hardly three years and died childless. It wasn't till after her death that Pansy arrived."

Isabel's brow had contracted to a frown; her lips were parted in pale, vague wonder. She was trying to follow; there seemed so much more to follow than she could see. "Pansy's not my husband's child then?"

"Your husband's—in perfection! But no one else's husband's. Some one else's wife's. Ah, my good Isabel," cried the Countess, "with you one must dot one's i's!"

"I don't understand. Whose wife's?" Isabel asked.

"The wife of a horrid little Swiss who died—how long?—a dozen, more than fifteen, years ago. He never recognised Miss Pansy, nor, knowing what he was about, would have anything to say to her; and there was no reason why he should. Osmond did, and that was better; though he had to fit on afterwards the whole rigmarole of his own wife's having died in childbirth, and of his having, in grief and horror, banished the little girl from his sight for as long as possible before taking her home from nurse. His wife had really died, you know, of quite another matter and in quite another place: in the Piedmontese mountains, where they had gone, one August, because her health appeared to require the air, but where she was suddenly taken worse—fatally ill. The story passed, sufficiently; it was covered by the appearances so long as nobody heeded, as nobody cared to look into it. But of course I knew—without researches," the Countess lucidly proceeded; "as also, you'll understand, without a word said between us—I mean between Osmond and me. Don't you see him looking at me, in silence, that way, to settle it?—that is to settle *me* if I should say anything. I said nothing, right or left—never a word to a creature, if you can believe that of me: on my honour, my dear, I speak of the thing to you now, after all this time, as I've never, never spoken. It was to be enough for me, from the first, that the child was my niece—from the moment she was my brother's daughter. As for her veritable mother—!" But with this Pansy's wonderful aunt dropped—as, involuntarily, from the impression of her sister-in-law's face, out of which more eyes might have seemed to look at her than she had ever had to meet.

She had spoken no name, yet Isabel could but check, on her own lips, an echo of the unspoken. She sank to her seat again, hanging her head. "Why have you told me this?" she asked in a voice the Countess hardly recognised.

"Because I've been so bored with your not knowing. I've been bored, frankly, my dear, with not having told you; as if, stupidly, all this time I couldn't have managed! *Ça me dépassé*,[1] if you don't mind my saying so, the things, all round you, that you've appeared to succeed in not knowing. It's a sort of assistance—aid to innocent ignorance—that I've always been a bad hand at rendering; and in this connexion, that of keeping quiet for my brother, my virtue has at any rate finally found itself exhausted. It's not a black lie, moreover, you know," the Countess inimitably added. "The facts are exactly what I tell you."

"I had no idea," said Isabel presently; and looked up at her in a manner that doubtless matched the apparent witlessness of this confession.

"So I believed—though it was hard to believe. Had it never occurred to you that he was for six or seven years her lover?"

"I don't know. Things *have* occurred to me, and perhaps that was what they all meant."

"She has been wonderfully clever, she has been magnificent, about Pansy!" the Countess, before all this view of it, cried.

"Oh, no idea, for me," Isabel went on, "ever *definitely* took that form." She appeared to be making out to herself what had been and what hadn't. "And as it is—I don't understand."

1. It's beyond me (French).

She spoke as one troubled and puzzled, yet the poor Countess seemed to have seen her revelation fall below its possibilities of effect. She had expected to kindle some responsive blaze, but had barely extracted a spark. Isabel showed as scarce more impressed than she might have been, as a young woman of approved imagination, with some fine sinister passage of public history. "Don't you recognise how the child could never pass for *her* husband's?—that is with M. Merle himself," her companion resumed. "They had been separated too long for that, and he had gone to some far country—I think to South America. If she had ever had children—which I'm not sure of—she had lost them. The conditions happened to make it workable, under stress (I mean at so awkward a pinch), that Osmond should acknowledge the little girl. His wife was dead—very true; but she had not been dead too long to put a certain accommodation of dates out of the question—from the moment, I mean, that suspicion wasn't started; which was what they had to take care of. What was more natural than that poor Mrs. Osmond, at a distance and for a world not troubling about trifles, should have left behind her, *poverina*,[2] the pledge of her brief happiness that had cost her her life? With the aid of a change of residence—Osmond had been living with her at Naples at the time of their stay in the Alps, and he in due course left it for ever—the whole history was successfully set going. My poor sister-in-law, in her grave, couldn't help herself, and the real mother, to save *her* skin, renounced all visible property in the child."

"Ah, poor, poor woman!" cried Isabel, who herewith burst into tears. It was a long time since she had shed any; she had suffered a high reaction from weeping. But now they flowed with an abundance in which the Countess Gemini found only another discomfiture.

"It's very kind of you to pity her!" she discordantly laughed. "Yes indeed, you have a way of your own—!"

"He must have been false to his wife—and so very soon!" said Isabel with a sudden check.

"That's all that's wanting—that you should take up *her* cause!" the Countess went on. "I quite agree with you, however, that it was much too soon."

"But to me, to me—?" And Isabel hesitated as if she had not heard; as if her question—though it was sufficiently there in her eyes—were all for herself.

"To you he has been faithful? Well, it depends, my dear, on what you call faithful. When he married you he was no longer the lover of another woman—*such* a lover as he had been, *cara mia*,[3] between their risks and their precautions, while the thing lasted! That state of affairs had passed away; the lady had repented, or at all events, for reasons of her own, drawn back: she had always had, too, a worship of appearances so intense that even Osmond himself had got bored with it. You may therefore imagine what it was—when he couldn't patch it on conveniently to *any* of those he goes in for! But the whole past was between them."

"Yes," Isabel mechanically echoed, "the whole past is between them."

"Ah, this later past is nothing. But for six or seven years, as I say, they had kept it up."

2. Poor little one (Italian).
3. My dear (Italian).

She was silent a little. "Why then did she want him to marry me?"

"Ah my dear, that's her superiority! Because you had money; and because she believed you would be good to Pansy."

"Poor woman—and Pansy who doesn't like her!" cried Isabel.

"That's the reason she wanted some one whom Pansy would like. She knows it; she knows everything."

"Will she know that you've told me this?"

"That will depend upon whether you tell her. She's prepared for it, and do you know what she counts upon for her defence? On your believing that I lie. Perhaps you do; don't make yourself uncomfortable to hide it. Only, as it happens this time, I don't. I've told plenty of little idiotic fibs, but they've never hurt any one but myself."

Isabel sat staring at her companion's story as at a bale of fantastic wares some strolling gypsy might have unpacked on the carpet at her feet. "Why did Osmond never marry her?" she finally asked.

"Because she had no money." The Countess had an answer for everything, and if she lied she lied well. "No one knows, no one has ever known, what she lives on, or how she has got all those beautiful things. I don't believe Osmond himself knows. Besides, she wouldn't have married him."

"How can she have loved him then?"

"She doesn't love him in that way. She did at first, and then, I suppose, she would have married him; but at that time her husband was living. By the time M. Merle had rejoined—I won't say his ancestors, because he never had any—her relations with Osmond had changed, and she had grown more ambitious. Besides, she has never had, about him," the Countess went on, leaving Isabel to wince for it so tragically afterwards—"she *had* never had, what you might call any illusions of *intelligence*. She hoped she might marry a great man; that has always been her idea. She has waited and watched and plotted and prayed; but she has never succeeded. I don't call Madame Merle a success, you know. I don't know what she may accomplish yet, but at present she has very little to show. The only tangible result she has ever achieved—except, of course, getting to know every one and staying with them free of expense—has been her bringing you and Osmond together. Oh, she did that, my dear; you needn't look as if you doubted it. I've watched them for years; I know everything—everything. I'm thought a great scatterbrain, but I've had enough application of mind to follow up those two. She hates me, and her way of showing it is to pretend to be for ever defending me. When people say I've had fifteen lovers she looks horrified and declares that quite half of them were never proved. She has been afraid of me for years, and she has taken great comfort in the vile, false things people have said about me. She has been afraid I'd expose her, and she threatened me one day when Osmond began to pay his court to you. It was at his house in Florence; do you remember that afternoon when she brought you there and we had tea in the garden? She let me know then that if I should tell tales two could play at that game. She pretends there's a good deal more to tell about me than about her. It would be an interesting comparison! I don't care a fig what she may say, simply because I know *you* don't care a fig. You can't trouble your head about me less than you do already. So she may take her revenge as she chooses; I don't think she'll frighten you very much. Her great idea has been to be tremendously irreproachable—a kind of full-blown lily—the incarnation of propriety. She has always worshipped that god. There should be no scandal about Cæsar's wife, you know; and, as I say, she has always hoped to marry Cæsar.[4] That was one reason she wouldn't marry Osmond; the fear that on seeing her with Pansy people would put things together— would even see a resemblance. She has had a terror lest the mother should betray herself. She has been awfully careful; the mother has never done so."

"Yes, yes, the mother has done so," said Isabel, who had listened to all this with a face more and more wan. "She betrayed herself to me the other day, though I didn't recognise her. There appeared to have been a chance of Pansy's making a great marriage, and in her disappointment at its not coming off she almost dropped the mask."

"Ah, that's where she'd dish herself!" cried the Countess. "She has failed so dreadfully that she's determined her daughter shall make it up."

Isabel started at the words "her daughter," which her guest threw off so familiarly. "It seems very wonderful," she murmured; and in this bewildering impression she had almost lost her sense of being personally touched by the story.

"Now don't go and turn against the poor innocent child!" the Countess went on. "She's very nice, in spite of her deplorable origin. I myself have liked Pansy; not, naturally, because she was *hers*, but because she had become yours."

"Yes, she has become mine. And how the poor woman must have suffered at seeing me—!" Isabel exclaimed while she flushed at the thought.

"I don't believe she has suffered; on the contrary, she has enjoyed. Osmond's marriage has given his daughter a great little lift. Before that she lived in a hole. And do you know what the mother thought? That you might take such a fancy to the child that you'd do something for her. Osmond of course could never give her a portion. Osmond was really extremely poor; but of course you know all about that. Ah, my dear," cried the Countess, "why did you ever inherit money?" She stopped a moment as if she saw something singular in Isabel's face. "Don't tell me now that you'll give her a *dot*. You're capable of that, but I would refuse to believe it. Don't try to be too good. Be a little easy and natural and nasty; feel a little wicked, for the comfort of it, once in your life!"

"It's very strange. I suppose I ought to know, but I'm sorry," Isabel said. "I'm much obliged to you."

"Yes, you seem to be!" cried the Countess with a mocking laugh. "Perhaps you are—perhaps you're not. You don't take it as I should have thought."

"How should I take it?" Isabel asked.

"Well, I should say as a woman who has been made use of." Isabel made no answer to this; she only listened, and the Countess went on. "They've always been bound to each other; they remained so even after she broke off—or *he* did. But he has always been more for her than she has been for him. When their little carnival was over they made a bargain that each should give the other complete liberty, but that each should

---

4. A proverbial phrase holds that "Caesar's wife must be above suspicion." It dates to the general's decision to divorce his wife Pompeia (ca. 62 B.C.E.) merely because she was suspected of some never-proven impropriety; the story is in Plutarch.

also do everything possible to help the other on. You may ask me how I know such a thing as that. I know it by the way they've behaved. Now see how much better women are than men! She has found a wife for Osmond, but Osmond has never lifted a little finger for *her*. She has worked for him, plotted for him, suffered for him; she has even more than once found money for him; and the end of it is that he's tired of her. She's an old habit; there are moments when he needs her, but on the whole he wouldn't miss her if she were removed. And, what's more, to-day she knows it. So you needn't be jealous!" the Countess added humorously.

Isabel rose from her sofa again; she felt bruised and scant of breath; her head was humming with new knowledge. "I'm much obliged to you," she repeated. And then she added abruptly, in quite a different tone: "How do you know all this?"

This enquiry appeared to ruffle the Countess more than Isabel's expression of gratitude pleased her. She gave her companion a bold stare, with which, "Let us assume that I've invented it!" she cried. She too, however, suddenly changed her tone and, laying her hand on Isabel's arm, said with the penetration of her sharp bright smile: "Now will you give up your journey?"

Isabel started a little; she turned away. But she felt weak and in a moment had to lay her arm upon the mantel-shelf for support. She stood a minute so, and then upon her arm she dropped her dizzy head, with closed eyes and pale lips.

"I've done wrong to speak—I've made you ill!" the Countess cried.

"Ah, I must see Ralph!" Isabel wailed; not in resentment, not in the quick passion her companion had looked for; but in a tone of far-reaching, infinite sadness.

Chapter LII

There was a train for Turin and Paris that evening; and after the Countess had left her Isabel had a rapid and decisive conference with her maid, who was discreet, devoted and active. After this she thought (except of her journey) only of one thing. She must go and see Pansy; from her she couldn't turn away. She had not seen her yet, as Osmond had given her to understand that it was too soon to begin. She drove at five o'clock to a high door in a narrow street in the quarter of the Piazza Navona,[1] and was admitted by the portress of the convent, a genial and obsequious person. Isabel had been at this institution before; she had come with Pansy to see the sisters. She knew they were good women, and she saw that the large rooms were clean and cheerful and that the well-used garden had sun for winter and shade for spring. But she disliked the place, which affronted and almost frightened her; not for the world would she have spent a night there. It produced to-day more than before the impression of a well-appointed prison; for it was not possible to pretend Pansy was free to leave it. This innocent creature had been presented to her in a new and violent light, but the secondary effect of the revelation was to make her reach out a hand.

1. One of the city's great public spaces, shaped like a long narrow ellipsis, on the site of an ancient stadium, and near the Palazzo Farnese. It is now lined with cafés, and its center is dominated by Bernini's Fountain of the Four Rivers.

The portress left her to wait in the parlour of the convent while she went to make it known that there was a visitor for the dear young lady. The parlour was a vast, cold apartment, with new-looking furniture; a large clean stove of white porcelain, unlighted, a collection of wax flowers under glass, and a series of engravings from religious pictures on the walls. On the other occasion Isabel had thought it less like Rome than like Philadelphia, but to-day she made no reflexions; the apartment only seemed to her very empty and very soundless. The portress returned at the end of some five minutes, ushering in another person. Isabel got up, expecting to see one of the ladies of the sisterhood, but to her extreme surprise found herself confronted with Madame Merle. The effect was strange, for Madame Merle was already so present to her vision that her appearance in the flesh was like suddenly, and rather awfully, seeing a painted picture move. Isabel had been thinking all day of her falsity, her audacity, her ability, her probable suffering; and these dark things seemed to flash with a sudden light as she entered the room. Her being there at all had the character of ugly evidence, of handwritings, of profaned relics, of grim things produced in court. It made Isabel feel faint; if it had been necessary to speak on the spot she would have been quite unable. But no such necessity was distinct to her; it seemed to her indeed that she had absolutely nothing to say to Madame Merle. In one's relations with this lady, however, there were never any absolute necessities; she had a manner which carried off not only her own deficiencies but those of other people. But she was different from usual; she came in slowly, behind the portress, and Isabel instantly perceived that she was not likely to depend upon her habitual resources. For her too the occasion was exceptional, and she had undertaken to treat it by the light of the moment. This gave her a peculiar gravity; she pretended not even to smile, and though Isabel saw that she was more than ever playing a part it seemed to her that on the whole the wonderful woman had never been so natural. She looked at her young friend from head to foot, but not harshly nor defiantly; with a cold gentleness rather, and an absence of any air of allusion to their last meeting. It was as if she had wished to mark a distinction. She had been irritated then, she was reconciled now.

"You can leave us alone," she said to the portress; "in five minutes this lady will ring for you." And then she turned to Isabel, who, after noting what has just been mentioned, had ceased to notice and had let her eyes wander as far as the limits of the room would allow. She wished never to look at Madame Merle again. "You're surprised to find me here, and I'm afraid you're not pleased," this lady went on. "You don't see why I should have come; it's as if I had anticipated you. I confess I've been rather indiscreet—I ought to have asked your permission." There was none of the oblique movement of irony in this; it was said simply and mildly; but Isabel, far afloat on a sea of wonder and pain, could not have told herself with what intention it was uttered. "But I've not been sitting long," Madame Merle continued; "that is I've not been long with Pansy. I came to see her because it occurred to me this afternoon that she must be rather lonely and perhaps even a little miserable. It may be good for a small girl; I know so little about small girls; I can't tell. At any rate it's a little dismal. Therefore I came—on the chance. I knew of course that you'd come, and her father as well; still, I had not been told other visitors were forbidden. The good woman—what's her name? Madame Catherine—made no objection whatever. I stayed twenty minutes with Pansy; she has a charming little room, not in the least conventual, with a piano and flowers. She has arranged it delightfully; she has so much taste. Of course it's all none of my business, but I feel happier since I've seen her. She may even have a maid if she likes; but of course she has no occasion to dress. She wears a little black frock; she looks so charming. I went afterwards to see Mother Catherine, who has a very good room too; I assure you I don't find the poor sisters at all monastic. Mother Catherine has a most coquettish little toilet-table, with something that looked uncommonly like a bottle of eau-de-Cologne. She speaks delightfully of Pansy; says it's a great happiness for them to have her. She's a little saint of heaven and a model to the oldest of them. Just as I was leaving Madame Catherine the portress came to say to her that there was a lady for the signorina. Of course I knew it must be you, and I asked her to let me go and receive you in her place. She demurred greatly—I must tell you that—and said it was her duty to notify the Mother Superior; it was of such high importance that you should be treated with respect. I requested her to let the Mother Superior alone and asked her how she supposed I would treat you!"

So Madame Merle went on, with much of the brilliancy of a woman who had long been a mistress of the art of conversation. But there were phases and gradations in her speech, not one of which was lost upon Isabel's ear, though her eyes were absent from her companion's face. She had not proceeded far before Isabel noted a sudden break in her voice, a lapse in her continuity, which was in itself a complete drama. This subtle modulation marked a momentous discovery—the perception of an entirely new attitude on the part of her listener. Madame Merle had guessed in the space of an instant that everything was at end between them, and in the space of another instant she had guessed the reason why. The person who stood there was not the same one she had seen hitherto, but was a very different person—a person who knew her secret. This discovery was tremendous, and from the moment she made it the most accomplished of women faltered and lost her courage. But only for that moment. Then the conscious stream of her perfect manner gathered itself again and flowed on as smoothly as might be to the end. But it was only because she had the end in view that she was able to proceed. She had been touched with a point that made her quiver, and she needed all the alertness of her will to repress her agitation. Her only safety was in her not betraying herself. She resisted this, but the startled quality of her voice refused to improve—she couldn't help it—while she heard herself say she hardly knew what. The tide of her confidence ebbed, and she was able only just to glide into port, faintly grazing the bottom.

Isabel saw it all as distinctly as if it had been reflected in a large clear glass. It might have been a great moment for her, for it might have been a moment of triumph. That Madame Merle had lost her pluck and saw before her the phantom of exposure—this in itself was a revenge, this in itself was almost the promise of a brighter day. And for a moment during which she stood apparently looking out of the window, with her back half-turned, Isabel enjoyed that knowledge. On the other side of the window lay the garden of the convent; but this is not what she saw; she saw nothing of the budding plants and the glowing afternoon. She saw, in the crude light of that revelation which had already become a part of experience and to which the very frailty of the vessel in which it had been offered her only gave an intrinsic price, the dry staring fact that she had been an applied handled hung-up tool, as senseless and convenient as mere shaped wood and iron. All the bitterness of this knowledge surged into her soul again; it was as if she felt on her lips the taste of dishonour. There was a moment during which, if she had turned and spoken, she would have said something that would hiss like a lash. But she closed her eyes, and then the hideous vision dropped. What remained was the cleverest woman in the world standing there within a few feet of her and knowing as little what to think as the meanest. Isabel's only revenge was to be silent still—to leave Madame Merle in this unprecedented situation. She left her there for a period that must have seemed long to this lady, who at last seated herself with a movement which was in itself a confession of helplessness. Then Isabel turned slow eyes, looking down at her. Madame Merle was very pale; her own eyes covered Isabel's face. She might see what she would, but her danger was over. Isabel would never accuse her, never reproach her; perhaps because she never would give her the opportunity to defend herself.

"I'm come to bid Pansy good-bye," our young woman said at last. "I go to England to-night."

"Go to England to-night!" Madame Merle repeated sitting there and looking up at her.

"I'm going to Gardencourt. Ralph Touchett's dying."

"Ah, you'll feel that." Madame Merle recovered herself; she had a chance to express sympathy. "Do you go alone?"

"Yes; without my husband."

Madame Merle gave a low vague murmur; a sort of recognition of the general sadness of things. "Mr. Touchett never liked me, but I'm sorry he's dying. Shall you see his mother?"

"Yes; she has returned from America."

"She used to be very kind to me; but she has changed. Others too have changed," said Madame Merle with a quiet noble pathos. She paused a moment, then added: "And you'll see dear old Gardencourt again!"

"I shall not enjoy it much," Isabel answered.

"Naturally—in your grief. But it's on the whole, of all the houses I know, and I know many, the one I should have liked best to live in. I don't venture to send a message to the people," Madame Merle added; "but I should like to give my love to the place."

Isabel turned away. "I had better go to Pansy. I've not much time."

While she looked about her for the proper egress, the door opened and admitted one of the ladies of the house, who advanced with a discreet smile, gently rubbing, under her long loose sleeves, a pair of plump white hands. Isabel recognised Madame Catherine, whose acquaintance she had already made, and begged that she would immediately let her see Miss Osmond. Madame Catherine looked doubly discreet, but smiled very blandly and said: "It will be good for her to see you. I'll take you to her myself." Then she directed her pleased guarded vision to Madame Merle.

"Will you let me remain a little?" this lady asked. "It's so good to be here."

"You may remain always if you like!" And the good sister gave a knowing laugh.

She led Isabel out of the room, through several corridors, and up a long staircase. All these departments were solid and bare, light and clean; so thought Isabel, are the great penal establishments. Madame Catherine gently pushed open the door of Pansy's room and ushered in the visitor; then stood smiling with folded hands while the two others met and embraced.

"She's glad to see you," she repeated; "it will do her good." And she placed the best chair carefully for Isabel. But she made no movement to seat herself; she seemed ready to retire. "How does this dear child look?" she asked of Isabel, lingering a moment.

"She looks pale," Isabel answered.

"That's the pleasure of seeing you. She's very happy. *Elle éclaire la maison*,"[2] said the good sister.

Pansy wore, as Madame Merle had said, a little black dress, it was perhaps this that made her look pale. "They're very good to me—they think of everything!" she exclaimed with all her customary eagerness to accommodate.

"We think of you always—you're a precious charge," Madame Catherine remarked in the tone of a woman with whom benevolence was a habit and whose conception of duty was the acceptance of every care. It fell with a leaden weight on Isabel's ears; it seemed to represent the surrender of a personality, the authority of the Church.

When Madame Catherine had left them together Pansy kneeled down and hid her head in her stepmother's lap. So she remained some moments, while Isabel gently stroked her hair. Then she got up, averting her face and looking about the room. "Don't you think I've arranged it well? I've everything I have at home."

"It's very pretty; you're very comfortable." Isabel scarcely knew what she could say to her. On the one hand she couldn't let her think she had come to pity her, and on the other it would be a dull mockery to pretend to rejoice with her. So she simply added after a moment: "I've come to bid you good-bye. I'm going to England."

Pansy's white little face turned red. "To England! Not to come back?"

"I don't know when I shall come back."

"Ah, I'm sorry," Pansy breathed with faintness. She spoke as if she had no right to criticise; but her tone expressed a depth of disappointment.

"My cousin, Mr. Touchett, is very ill; he'll probably die. I wish to see him," Isabel said.

"Ah yes; you told me he would die. Of course you must go. And will papa go?"

"No; I shall go alone."

For a moment the girl said nothing. Isabel had often wondered what she thought of the apparent relations of her father with his wife; but never by a glance, by an intimation, had she let it be seen that she deemed them deficient in an air of intimacy. She made her reflexions, Isabel was sure; and she must have had a conviction that there were husbands and wives who were more intimate than that. But Pansy was not indiscreet even in thought; she would as little have ventured to judge her gentle stepmother as to criticise her magnificent father. Her heart may have stood almost as

---

2. She brightens the place (French).

still as it would have done had she seen two of the saints in the great picture in the convent-chapel turn their painted heads and shake them at
each other. But as in this latter case she would (for very solemnity's sake)
never have mentioned the awful phenomenon, so she put away all knowledge of the secrets of larger lives than her own. "You'll be very far away," she
presently went on.

"Yes; I shall be far away. But it will scarcely matter," Isabel explained;
"since so long as you're here I can't be called near you."

"Yes, but you can come and see me; though you've not come very often."

"I've not come because your father forbade it. To-day I bring nothing
with me. I can't amuse you."

"I'm not to be amused. That's not what papa wishes."

"Then it hardly matters whether I'm in Rome or in England."

"You're not happy, Mrs. Osmond," said Pansy.

"Not very. But it doesn't matter."

"That's what I say to myself. What does it matter? But I should like to
come out."

"I wish indeed you might."

"Don't leave me here," Pansy went on gently.

Isabel said nothing for a minute; her heart beat fast. "Will you come
away with me now?" she asked.

Pansy looked at her pleadingly. "Did papa tell you to bring me?"

"No; it's my own proposal."

"I think I had better wait then. Did papa send me no message?"

"I don't think he knew I was coming."

"He thinks I've not had enough," said Pansy. "But I have. The ladies are
very kind to me and the little girls come to see me. There are some very
little ones—such charming children. Then my room—you can see for
yourself. All that's very delightful. But I've had enough. Papa wished me
to think a little—and I've thought a great deal."

"What have you thought?"

"Well, that I must never displease papa."

"You knew that before."

"Yes; but I know it better. I'll do anything—I'll do anything," said Pansy.
Then, as she heard her own words, a deep, pure blush came into her
face. Isabel read the meaning of it; she saw the poor girl had been vanquished. It was well that Mr. Edward Rosier had kept his enamels! Isabel
looked into her eyes and saw there mainly a prayer to be treated easily. She
laid her hand on Pansy's as if to let her know that her look conveyed no
diminution of esteem; for the collapse of the girl's momentary resistance
(mute and modest though it had been) seemed only her tribute to the truth
of things. She didn't presume to judge others, but she had judged herself;
she had seen the reality. She had no vocation for struggling with combina-
tions; in the solemnity of sequestration there was something that overwhelmed her. She bowed her pretty head to authority and only asked of
authority to be merciful. Yes; it was very well that Edward Rosier had
reserved a few articles!

Isabel got up; her time was rapidly shortening. "Good-bye then. I leave
Rome to-night."

Pansy took hold of her dress; there was a sudden change in the child's
face. "You look strange; you frighten me."

"Oh, I'm very harmless," said Isabel.

"Perhaps you won't come back?"

"Perhaps not. I can't tell."

"Ah, Mrs. Osmond, you won't leave me!"

Isabel now saw she had guessed everything. "My dear child, what can I do for you?" she asked.

"I don't know—but I'm happier when I think of you."

"You can always think of me."

"Not when you're so far. I'm a little afraid," said Pansy.

"What are you afraid of?"

"Of papa—a little. And of Madame Merle. She has just been to see me."

"You must not say that," Isabel observed.

"Oh, I'll do everything they want. Only if you're here I shall do it more easily."

Isabel considered. "I won't desert you," she said at last. "Good-bye, my child."

Then they held each other a moment in a silent embrace, like two sisters; and afterwards Pansy walked along the corridor with her visitor to the top of the staircase. "Madame Merle has been here," she remarked as they went; and as Isabel answered nothing she added abruptly: "I don't like Madame Merle!"

Isabel hesitated, then stopped. "You must never say that—that you don't like Madame Merle."

Pansy looked at her in wonder; but wonder with Pansy had never been a reason for non-compliance. "I never will again," she said with exquisite gentleness. At the top of the staircase they had to separate, as it appeared to be part of the mild but very definite discipline under which Pansy lived that she should not go down. Isabel descended, and when she reached the bottom the girl was standing above. "You'll come back?" she called out in a voice that Isabel remembered afterwards.

"Yes—I'll come back."

Madame Catherine met Mrs. Osmond below and conducted her to the door of the parlour, outside of which the two stood talking a minute. "I won't go in," said the good sister. "Madame Merle's waiting for you."

At this announcement Isabel stiffened; she was on the point of asking if there were no other egress from the convent. But a moment's reflexion assured her that she would do well not to betray to the worthy nun her desire to avoid Pansy's other friend. Her companion grasped her arm very gently and, fixing her a moment with wise, benevolent eyes, said in French and almost familiarly: *"Eh bien, chère Madame, qu'en pensez-vous?"*[3]

"About my stepdaughter? Oh, it would take long to tell you."

"We think it's enough," Madame Catherine distinctly observed. And she pushed open the door of the parlour.

Madame Merle was sitting just as Isabel had left her, like a woman so absorbed in thought that she had not moved a little finger. As Madame Catherine closed the door she got up, and Isabel saw that she had been thinking to some purpose. She had recovered her balance; she was in full possession of her resources. "I found I wished to wait for you," she said urbanely. "But it's not to talk about Pansy."

_____

3. Well, my dear lady, what do you think of it? (French).

Isabel wondered what it could be to talk about, and in spite of Madame Merle's declaration she answered after a moment: "Madame Catherine says it's enough."

"Yes; it also seems to me enough. I wanted to ask you another word about poor Mr. Touchett," Madame Merle added. "Have you reason to believe that he's really at his last?"

"I've no information but a telegram. Unfortunately it only confirms a probability."

"I'm going to ask you a strange question," said Madame Merle. "Are you very fond of your cousin?" And she gave a smile as strange as her utterance.

"Yes, I'm very fond of him. But I don't understand you."

She just hung fire. "It's rather hard to explain. Something has occurred to me which may not have occurred to you, and I give you the benefit of my idea. Your cousin did you once a great service. Have you never guessed it?"

"He has done me many services."

"Yes; but one was much above the rest. He made you a rich woman."

"*He* made me—?"

Madame Merle appearing to see herself successful, she went on more triumphantly: "He imparted to you that extra lustre which was required to make you a brilliant match. At bottom it's him you've to thank." She stopped; there was something in Isabel's eyes.

"I don't understand you. It was my uncle's money."

"Yes; it was your uncle's money, but it was your cousin's idea. He brought his father over to it. Ah, my dear, the sum was large!"

Isabel stood staring; she seemed to-day to live in a world illumined by lurid flashes. "I don't know why you say such things. I don't know what you know."

"I know nothing but what I've guessed. But I've guessed that."

Isabel went to the door and, when she had opened it, stood a moment with her hand on the latch. Then she said—it was her only revenge: "I believed it was you I had to thank!"

Madame Merle dropped her eyes; she stood there in a kind of proud penance. "You're very unhappy, I know. But I'm more so."

"Yes; I can believe that. I think I should like never to see you again."

Madame Merle raised her eyes. "I shall go to America," she quietly remarked while Isabel passed out.

Chapter LIII

It was not with surprise, it was with a feeling which in other circumstances would have had much of the effect of joy, that as Isabel descended from the Paris Mail at Charing Cross[1] she stepped into the arms, as it were—or at any rate into the hands—of Henrietta Stackpole. She had telegraphed to her friend from Turin, and though she had not definitely said to herself that Henrietta would meet her, she had felt her telegram would produce some helpful result. On her long journey from Rome her mind had been given up to vagueness; she was unable to question the future. She

---

1. A major railway station, near Trafalgar Square. The terminus of the South Eastern Railway, it was the London destination for trains from the Channel crossing between Calais and Dover.

performed this journey with sightless eyes and took little pleasure in the countries she traversed, decked out though they were in the richest freshness of spring. Her thoughts followed their course through other countries—strange-looking, dimly-lighted, pathless lands, in which there was no change of seasons, but only, as it seemed, a perpetual dreariness of winter. She had plenty to think about; but it was neither reflexion nor conscious purpose that filled her mind. Disconnected visions passed through it, and sudden dull gleams of memory, of expectation. The past and the future came and went at their will, but she saw them only in fitful images, which rose and fell by a logic of their own. It was extraordinary the things she remembered. Now that she was in the secret, now that she knew something that so much concerned her and the eclipse of which had made life resemble an attempt to play whist with an imperfect pack of cards, the truth of things, their mutual relations, their meaning, and for the most part their horror, rose before her with a kind of architectural vastness. She remembered a thousand trifles; they started to life with the spontaneity of a shiver. She had thought them trifles at the time; now she saw that they had been weighted with lead. Yet even now they were trifles after all, for of what use was it to her to understand them? Nothing seemed of use to her to-day. All purpose, all intention, was suspended; all desire too save the single desire to reach her much-embracing refuge. Gardencourt had been her starting-point, and to those muffled chambers it was at least a temporary solution to return. She had gone forth in her strength; she would come back in her weakness, and if the place had been a rest to her before, it would be a sanctuary now. She envied Ralph his dying, for if one were thinking of rest that was the most perfect of all. To cease utterly, to give it all up and not know anything more—this idea was as sweet as the vision of a cool bath in a marble tank, in a darkened chamber, in a hot land.

She had moments indeed in her journey from Rome which were almost as good as being dead. She sat in her corner, so motionless, so passive, simply with the sense of being carried, so detached from hope and regret, that she recalled to herself one of those Etruscan figures couched upon the receptacle of their ashes. There was nothing to regret now—that was all over. Not only the time of her folly, but the time of her repentance was far. The only thing to regret was that Madame Merle had been so—well, so unimaginable. Just here her intelligence dropped, from literal inability to say what it was that Madame Merle had been. Whatever it was it was for Madame Merle herself to regret it; and doubtless she would do so in America, where she had announced she was going. It concerned Isabel no more; she only had an impression that she should never again see Madame Merle. This impression carried her into the future, of which from time to time she had a mutilated glimpse. She saw herself, in the distant years, still in the attitude of a woman who had her life to live, and these intimations contradicted the spirit of the present hour. It might be desirable to get quite away, really away, further away than little grey-green England, but this privilege was evidently to be denied her. Deep in her soul—deeper than any appetite for renunciation—was the sense that life would be her business for a long time to come. And at moments there was something inspiring, almost enlivening, in the conviction. It was a proof of strength—it was a proof she should some day be happy again. It couldn't be she was to live only to suffer;

she was still young, after all, and a great many things might happen to her yet. To live only to suffer—only to feel the injury of life repeated and enlarged—it seemed to her she was too valuable, too capable, for that. Then she wondered if it were vain and stupid to think so well of herself. When had it ever been a guarantee to be valuable? Wasn't all history full of the destruction of precious things? Wasn't it much more probable that if one were fine one would suffer? It involved then perhaps an admission that one had a certain grossness; but Isabel recognised, as it passed before her eyes, the quick vague shadow of a long future. She should never escape; she should last to the end. Then the middle years[2] wrapped her about again and the grey curtain of her indifference closed her in.

Henrietta kissed her, as Henrietta usually kissed, as if she were afraid she should be caught doing it; and then Isabel stood there in the crowd, looking about her, looking for her servant. She asked nothing; she wished to wait. She had a sudden perception that she should be helped. She rejoiced Henrietta had come; there was something terrible in an arrival in London. The dusky, smoky, far-arching vault of the station, the strange, livid light, the dense, dark, pushing crowd, filled her with a nervous fear and made her put her arm into her friend's. She remembered she had once liked these things; they seemed part of a mighty spectacle in which there was something that touched her. She remembered how she walked away from Euston, in the winter dusk, in the crowded streets, five years before. She could not have done that to-day, and the incident came before her as the deed of another person.

"It's too beautiful that you should have come," said Henrietta, looking at her as if she thought Isabel might be prepared to challenge the proposition. "If you hadn't—if you hadn't; well, I don't know," remarked Miss Stackpole, hinting ominously at her powers of disapproval.

Isabel looked about without seeing her maid. Her eyes rested on another figure, however, which she felt she had seen before; and in a moment she recognised the genial countenance of Mr. Bantling. He stood a little apart, and it was not in the power of the multitude that pressed about him to make him yield an inch of the ground he had taken—that of abstracting himself discreetly while the two ladies performed their embraces.

"There's Mr. Bantling," said Isabel, gently, irrelevantly, scarcely caring much now whether she should find her maid or not.

"Oh yes, he goes everywhere with me. Come here, Mr. Bantling!" Henrietta exclaimed. Whereupon the gallant bachelor advanced with a smile—a smile tempered, however, by the gravity of the occasion. "Isn't it lovely she has come?" Henrietta asked. "He knows all about it," she added; "we had quite a discussion. He said you wouldn't, I said you would."

"I thought you always agreed," Isabel smiled in return. She felt she could smile now; she had seen in an instant, in Mr. Bantling's brave eyes, that he had good news for her. They seemed to say he wished her to remember he was an old friend of her cousin—that he understood, that it was all right. Isabel gave him her hand; she thought of him, extravagantly, as a beautiful blameless knight.

"Oh, I always agree," said Mr. Bantling. "But she doesn't, you know."

---

2. Isabel is hardly yet middle aged, but James liked the phrase and used it as the title for an 1893 short story as well as for the third and unfinished volume of his autobiography (1917).

"Didn't I tell you that a maid was a nuisance?" Henrietta enquired. "Your young lady has probably remained at Calais."

"I don't care," said Isabel, looking at Mr. Bantling, whom she had never found so interesting.

"Stay with her while I go and see," Henrietta commanded, leaving the two for a moment together.

They stood there at first in silence, and then Mr. Bantling asked Isabel how it had been on the Channel.

"Very fine. No, I believe it was very rough," she said, to her companion's obvious surprise. After which she added: "You've been to Gardencourt, I know."

"Now how do you know that?"

"I can't tell you—except that you look like a person who has been to Gardencourt."

"Do you think I look awfully sad? It's awfully sad there, you know."

"I don't believe you ever look awfully sad. You look awfully kind," said Isabel with a breadth that cost her no effort. It seemed to her she should never again feel a superficial embarrassment.

Poor Mr. Bantling, however, was still in this inferior stage. He blushed a good deal and laughed, he assured her that he was often very blue, and that when he was blue he was awfully fierce. "You can ask Miss Stackpole, you know. I was at Gardencourt two days ago."

"Did you see my cousin?"

"Only for a little. But he had been seeing people; Warburton had been there the day before. Ralph was just the same as usual, except that he was in bed and that he looks tremendously ill and that he can't speak," Mr. Bantling pursued. "He was awfully jolly and funny all the same. He was just as clever as ever. It's awfully wretched."

Even in the crowded, noisy station this simple picture was vivid. "Was that late in the day?"

"Yes; I went on purpose. We thought you'd like to know."

"I'm greatly obliged to you. Can I go down to-night?"

"Ah, I don't think *she'll* let you go," said Mr. Bantling. "She wants you to stop with her. I made Touchett's man promise to telegraph me to-day, and I found the telegram an hour ago at my club. 'Quiet and easy,' that's what it says, and it's dated two o'clock. So you see you can wait till to-morrow. You must be awfully tired."

"Yes, I'm awfully tired. And I thank you again."

"Oh," said Mr. Bantling, "we were certain you would like the last news." On which Isabel vaguely noted that he and Henrietta seemed after all to agree. Miss Stackpole came back with Isabel's maid, whom she had caught in the act of proving her utility. This excellent person, instead of losing herself in the crowd, had simply attended to her mistress's luggage, so that the latter was now at liberty to leave the station. "You know you're not to think of going to the country to-night," Henrietta remarked to her. "It doesn't matter whether there's a train or not. You're to come straight to me in Wimpole Street.[3] There isn't a corner to be had in London, but I've got you one all the same. It isn't a Roman palace, but it will do for a night."

3. In Marylebone, running north and perpendicular to Oxford Street, toward Regent's Park; a very solid bourgeois address.

"I'll do whatever you wish," Isabel said.

"You'll come and answer a few questions; that's what I wish."

"She doesn't say anything about dinner, does she, Mrs. Osmond?" Mr. Bantling enquired jocosely.

Henrietta fixed him a moment with her speculative gaze. "I see you're in a great hurry to get your own. You'll be at the Paddington Station[4] to-morrow morning at ten."

"Don't come for my sake, Mr. Bantling," said Isabel.

"He'll come for mine," Henrietta declared as she ushered her friend into a cab. And later, in a large dusky parlour in Wimpole Street—to do her justice there had been dinner enough—she asked those questions to which she had alluded at the station. "Did your husband make you a scene about your coming?" That was Miss Stackpole's first enquiry.

"No; I can't say he made a scene."

"He didn't object then?"

"Yes, he objected very much. But it was not what you'd call a scene."

"What was it then?"

"It was a very quiet conversation."

Henrietta for a moment regarded her guest. "It must have been hell-ish," she then remarked. And Isabel didn't deny that it had been hellish. But she confined herself to answering Henrietta's questions, which was easy, as they were tolerably definite. For the present she offered her no new information. "Well," said Miss Stackpole at last, "I've only one criti-cism to make. I don't see why you promised little Miss Osmond to go back."

"I'm not sure I myself see now," Isabel replied. "But I did then."

"If you've forgotten your reason perhaps you won't return."

Isabel waited a moment. "Perhaps I shall find another."

"You'll certainly never find a good one."

"In default of a better my having promised will do," Isabel suggested.

"Yes; that's why I hate it."

"Don't speak of it now. I've a little time. Coming away was a complica-tion, but what will going back be?"

"You must remember, after all, that he won't make you a scene!" said Henrietta with much intention.

"He will, though," Isabel answered gravely. "It won't be the scene of a moment; it will be a scene of the rest of my life."

For some minutes the two women sat and considered this remainder, and then Miss Stackpole, to change the subject, as Isabel had requested, announced abruptly: "I've been to stay with Lady Pensil!"

"Ah, the invitation came at last!"

"Yes; it took five years. But this time she wanted to see me."

"Naturally enough."

"It was more natural than I think you know," said Henrietta, who fixed her eyes on a distant point. And then she added, turning suddenly: "Isa-bel Archer, I beg your pardon. You don't know why? Because I criticised you, and yet I've gone further than you. Mr. Osmond, at least, was born on the other side!"

---

4. Terminus of the Great Western Railway; the point of origin for trains for both Gardencourt and its original (see p. 419 of this edition), Hardwick, as well as for Oxford.

It was a moment before Isabel grasped her meaning; this sense was so modestly, or at least so ingeniously, veiled. Isabel's mind was not possessed at present with the comicality of things; but she greeted with a quick laugh the image that her companion had raised. She immediately recovered herself, however, and with the right excess of intensity, "Henrietta Stackpole," she asked, "are you going to give up your country?"

"Yes, my poor Isabel, I am. I won't pretend to deny it; I look the fact in the face. I'm going to marry Mr. Bantling and locate right here in London."

"It seems very strange," said Isabel, smiling now.

"Well yes, I suppose it does. I've come to it little by little. I think I know what I'm doing; but I don't know as I can explain."

"One can't explain one's marriage," Isabel answered. "And yours doesn't need to be explained. Mr. Bantling isn't a riddle."

"No, he isn't a bad pun—or even a high flight of American humour. He has a beautiful nature," Henrietta went on. "I've studied him for many years and I see right through him. He's as clear as the style of a good prospectus. He's not intellectual, but he appreciates intellect. On the other hand he doesn't exaggerate its claims. I sometimes think we do in the United States."

"Ah," said Isabel, "you're changed indeed! It's the first time I've ever heard you say anything against your native land."

"I only say that we're too infatuated with mere brain-power; that, after all, isn't a vulgar fault. But I *am* changed; a woman has to change a good deal to marry."

"I hope you'll be very happy. You will at last—over here—see something of the inner life."

Henrietta gave a little significant sigh. "That's the key to the mystery, I believe. I couldn't endure to be kept off. Now I've as good a right as any one!" she added with artless elation.

Isabel was duly diverted, but there was a certain melancholy in her view. Henrietta, after all, had confessed herself human and feminine, Henrietta whom she had hitherto regarded as a light keen flame, a disembodied voice. It was a disappointment to find she had personal susceptibilities, that she was subject to common passions, and that her intimacy with Mr. Bantling had not been completely original. There was a want of originality in her marrying him—there was even a kind of stupidity; and for a moment, to Isabel's sense, the dreariness of the world took on a deeper tinge. A little later indeed she reflected that Mr. Bantling himself at least was original. But she didn't see how Henrietta could give up her country. She herself had relaxed her hold of it, but it had never been her country as it had been Henrietta's. She presently asked her if she had enjoyed her visit to Lady Pensil.

"Oh yes," said Henrietta, "she didn't know what to make of me."

"And was that very enjoyable?"

"Very much so, because she's supposed to be a master mind. She thinks she knows everything; but she doesn't understand a woman of my modern type. It would be so much easier for her if I were only a little better or a little worse. She's so puzzled; I believe she thinks it's my duty to go and do something immoral. She thinks it's immoral that I should marry her

brother; but, after all, that isn't immoral enough. And she'll never understand my mixture—never!"

"She's not so intelligent as her brother then," said Isabel. "He appears
to have understood."

"Oh no, he hasn't!" cried Miss Stackpole with decision. "I really believe
that's what he wants to marry me for—just to find out the mystery and
the proportions of it. That's a fixed idea—a kind of fascination."

"It's very good in you to humour it."

"Oh well," said Henrietta, "I've something to find out too!" And Isabel
saw that she had not renounced an allegiance, but planned an attack. She
was at last about to grapple in earnest with England.

Isabel also perceived, however, on the morrow, at the Paddington Station, where she found herself, at ten o'clock, in the company both of Miss
Stackpole and Mr. Bantling, that the gentleman bore his perplexities
lightly. If he had not found out everything he had found out at least the
great point—that Miss Stackpole would not be wanting in initiative. It was
evident that in the selection of a wife he had been on his guard against
this deficiency.

"Henrietta has told me, and I'm very glad," Isabel said as she gave him
her hand.

"I dare say you think it awfully odd," Mr. Bantling replied, resting on
his neat umbrella.

"Yes, I think it awfully odd."

"You can't think it so awfully odd as I do. But I've always rather liked
striking out a line," said Mr. Bantling serenely.

Chapter LIV

Isabel's arrival at Gardencourt on this second occasion was even quieter
than it had been on the first. Ralph Touchett kept but a small household,
and to the new servants Mrs. Osmond was a stranger; so that instead of
being conducted to her own apartment she was coldly shown into the
drawing-room and left to wait while her name was carried up to her aunt.
She waited a long time; Mrs. Touchett appeared in no hurry to come to
her. She grew impatient at last; she grew nervous and scared—as scared
as if the objects about her had begun to show for conscious things, watching her trouble with grotesque grimaces. The day was dark and cold; the
dusk was thick in the corners of the wide brown rooms. The house was
perfectly still—with a stillness that Isabel remembered; it had filled all
the place for days before the death of her uncle. She left the drawing-room
and wandered about—strolled into the library and along the gallery of pictures, where, in the deep silence, her footstep made an echo. Nothing
was changed; she recognised everything she had seen years before; it might
have been only yesterday she had stood there. She envied the security of
valuable "pieces" which change by no hair's breadth, only grow in value,
while their owners lose inch by inch youth, happiness, beauty; and she
became aware that she was walking about as her aunt had done on the day
she had come to see her in Albany. She was changed enough since then—
that had been the beginning. It suddenly struck her that if her Aunt Lydia
had not come that day in just that way and found her alone, everything

might have been different. She might have had another life and she might have been a woman more blest. She stopped in the gallery in front of a small picture—a charming and precious Bonington[1]—upon which her eyes rested a long time. But she was not looking at the picture; she was wondering whether if her aunt had not come that day in Albany she would have married Caspar Goodwood.

Mrs. Touchett appeared at last, just after Isabel had returned to the big uninhabited drawing-room. She looked a good deal older, but her eye was as bright as ever and her head as erect; her thin lips seemed a repository of latent meanings. She wore a little grey dress of the most undecorated fashion, and Isabel wondered, as she had wondered the first time, if her remarkable kinswoman resembled more a queen-regent or the matron of a gaol. Her lips felt very thin indeed on Isabel's hot cheek.

"I've kept you waiting because I've been sitting with Ralph," Mrs. Touchett said. "The nurse had gone to luncheon and I had taken her place. He has a man who's supposed to look after him, but the man's good for nothing; he's always looking out of the window—as if there were anything to see! I didn't wish to move, because Ralph seemed to be sleeping and I was afraid the sound would disturb him. I waited till the nurse came back; I remembered you knew the house."

"I find I know it better even than I thought; I've been walking everywhere," Isabel answered. And then she asked if Ralph slept much.

"He lies with his eyes closed; he doesn't move. But I'm not sure that it's always sleep."

"Will he see me? Can he speak to me?"

Mrs. Touchett declined the office of saying. "You can try him," was the limit of her extravagance. And then she offered to conduct Isabel to her room. "I thought they had taken you there; but it's not my house, it's Ralph's; and I don't know what they do. They must at least have taken your luggage; I don't suppose you've brought much. Not that I care, however. I believe they've given you the same room you had before; when Ralph heard you were coming he said you must have that one."

"Did he say anything else?"

"Ah, my dear, he doesn't chatter as he used!" cried Mrs. Touchett as she preceded her niece up the staircase.

It was the same room, and something told Isabel it had not been slept in since she occupied it. Her luggage was there and was not voluminous; Mrs. Touchett sat down a moment with her eyes upon it. "Is there really no hope?" our young woman asked as she stood before her.

"None whatever. There never has been. It has not been a successful life."

"No—it has only been a beautiful one." Isabel found herself already contradicting her aunt; she was irritated by her dryness.

"I don't know what you mean by that; there's no beauty without health. That is a very odd dress to travel in."

Isabel glanced at her garment. "I left Rome at an hour's notice; I took the first that came."

"Your sisters, in America, wished to know how you dress. That seemed to be their principal interest. I wasn't able to tell them—but they seemed

---

1. Richard Parkes Bonington (1801–1828), English landscape painter who built his career in France and died young, like Ralph, of tuberculosis.

to have the right idea: that you never wear anything less than black brocade."

"They think I'm more brilliant than I am; I'm afraid to tell them the truth," said Isabel. "Lily wrote me you had dined with her."

"She invited me four times, and I went once. After the second time she should have let me alone. The dinner was very good; it must have been expensive. Her husband has a very bad manner. Did I enjoy my visit to America? Why should I have enjoyed it? I didn't go for my pleasure."

These were interesting items, but Mrs. Touchett soon left her niece, whom she was to meet in half an hour at the midday meal. For this repast the two ladies faced each other at an abbreviated table in the melancholy dining-room. Here, after a little, Isabel saw her aunt not to be so dry as she appeared, and her old pity for the poor woman's inexpressiveness, her want of regret, of disappointment, came back to her. Unmistakeably she would have found it a blessing to-day to be able to feel a defeat, a mistake, even a shame or two. She wondered if she were not even missing those enrichments of consciousness and privately trying—reaching out for some aftertaste of life, dregs of the banquet; the testimony of pain or the cold recreation of remorse. On the other hand perhaps she was afraid; if she should begin to know remorse at all it might take her too far. Isabel could perceive, however, how it had come over her dimly that she had failed of something, that she saw herself in the future as an old woman without memories. Her little sharp face looked tragical. She told her niece that Ralph had as yet not moved, but that he probably would be able to see her before dinner. And then in a moment she added that he had seen Lord Warburton the day before; an announcement which startled Isabel a little, as it seemed an intimation that this personage was in the neighbourhood and that an accident might bring them together. Such an accident would not be happy; she had not come to England to struggle again with Lord Warburton. She none the less presently said to her aunt that he had been very kind to Ralph; she had seen something of that in Rome.

"He has something else to think of now," Mrs. Touchett returned. And she paused with a gaze like a gimlet.

Isabel saw she meant something, and instantly guessed what she meant. But her reply concealed her guess; her heart beat faster and she wished to gain a moment. "Ah yes—the House of Lords and all that."

"He's not thinking of the Lords; he's thinking of the ladies. At least he's thinking of one of them; he told Ralph he's engaged to be married."

"Ah, to be married!" Isabel mildly exclaimed.

"Unless he breaks it off. He seemed to think Ralph would like to know. Poor Ralph can't go to the wedding, though I believe it's to take place very soon."

"And who's the young lady?"

"A member of the aristocracy; Lady Flora, Lady Felicia—something of that sort."

"I'm very glad," Isabel said. "It must be a sudden decision."

"Sudden enough, I believe; a courtship of three weeks. It has only just been made public."

"I'm very glad," Isabel repeated with a larger emphasis. She knew her aunt was watching her—looking for the signs of some imputed soreness, and the desire to prevent her companion from seeing anything of this kind enabled her to speak in the tone of quick satisfaction, the tone almost of relief. Mrs. Touchett of course followed the tradition that ladies, even married ones, regard the marriage of their old lovers as an offence to themselves. Isabel's first care therefore was to show that however that might be in general she was not offended now. But meanwhile, as I say, her heart beat faster; and if she sat for some moments thoughtful—she presently forgot Mrs. Touchett's observation—it was not because she had lost an admirer. Her imagination had traversed half Europe; it halted, panting, and even trembling a little, in the city of Rome. She figured herself announcing to her husband that Lord Warburton was to lead a bride to the altar, and she was of course not aware how extremely wan she must have looked while she made this intellectual effort. But at last she collected herself and said to her aunt: "He was sure to do it some time or other."

Mrs. Touchett was silent; then she gave a sharp little shake of the head. "Ah, my dear, you're beyond me!" she cried suddenly. They went on with their luncheon in silence; Isabel felt as if she had heard of Lord Warburton's death. She had known him only as a suitor, and now that was all over. He was dead for poor Pansy; by Pansy he might have lived. A servant had been hovering about; at last Mrs. Touchett requested him to leave them alone. She had finished her meal; she sat with her hands folded on the edge of the table. "I should like to ask you three questions," she observed when the servant had gone.

"Three are a great many."

"I can't do with less; I've been thinking. They're all very good ones."

"That's what I'm afraid of. The best questions are the worst," Isabel answered. Mrs. Touchett had pushed back her chair, and as her niece left the table and walked, rather consciously, to one of the deep windows, she felt herself followed by her eyes.

"Have you ever been sorry you didn't marry Lord Warburton?" Mrs. Touchett enquired.

Isabel shook her head slowly, but not heavily. "No, dear aunt."

"Good. I ought to tell you that I propose to believe what you say."

"Your believing me's an immense temptation," she declared, smiling still.

"A temptation to lie? I don't recommend you to do that, for when I'm misinformed I'm as dangerous as a poisoned rat. I don't mean to crow over you."

"It's my husband who doesn't get on with me," said Isabel.

"I could have told him he wouldn't. I don't call that crowing over *you*," Mrs. Touchett. "Do you still like Serena Merle?" she went on.

"Not as I once did. But it doesn't matter, for she's going to America."

"To America? She must have done something very bad."

"Yes—very bad."

"May I ask what it is?"

"She made a convenience of me."

"Ah," cried Mrs. Touchett, "so she did of me! She does of every one."

"She'll make a convenience of America," said Isabel, smiling again and glad that her aunt's questions were over.

It was not till the evening that she was able to see Ralph. He had been dozing all day; at least he had been lying unconscious. The doctor was there, but after a while went away—the local doctor, who had attended his father and whom Ralph liked. He came three or four times a day; he was deeply interested in his patient. Ralph had had Sir Matthew Hope, but he had got tired of this celebrated man, to whom he had asked his mother to send word he was now dead and was therefore without further need of medical advice. Mrs. Touchett had simply written to Sir Matthew that her son disliked him. On the day of Isabel's arrival Ralph gave no sign, as I have related, for many hours; but toward evening he raised himself and said he knew that she had come. How he knew was not apparent, inasmuch as for fear of exciting him no one had offered the information. Isabel came in and sat by his bed in the dim light; there was only a shaded candle in a corner of the room. She told the nurse she might go—she herself would sit with him for the rest of the evening. He had opened his eyes and recognised her, and had moved his hand, which lay helpless beside him, so that she might take it. But he was unable to speak; he closed his eyes again and remained perfectly still, only keeping her hand in his own. She sat with him a long time—till the nurse came back; but he gave no further sign. He might have passed away while she looked at him; he was already the figure and pattern of death. She had thought him far gone in Rome, and this was worse; there was but one change possible now. There was a strange tranquillity in his face; it was as still as the lid of a box. With this he was a mere lattice of bones; when he opened his eyes to greet her it was as if she were looking into immeasurable space. It was not till midnight that the nurse came back; but the hours, to Isabel, had not seemed long; it was exactly what she had come for. If she had come simply to wait she found ample occasion, for he lay three days in a kind of grateful silence. He recognised her and at moments seemed to wish to speak; but he found no voice. Then he closed his eyes again, as if he too were waiting for something—for something that certainly would come. He was so absolutely quiet that it seemed to her what was coming had already arrived; and yet she never lost the sense that they were still together. But they were not always together; there were other hours that she passed in wandering through the empty house and listening for a voice that was not poor Ralph's. She had a constant fear; she thought it possible her husband would write to her. But he remained silent, and she only got a letter from Florence and from the Countess Gemini. Ralph, however, spoke at last—on the evening of the third day.

"I feel better to-night," he murmured, abruptly, in the soundless dimness of her vigil; "I think I can say something." She sank upon her knees beside his pillow; took his thin hand in her own; begged him not to make an effort—not to tire himself. His face was of necessity serious—it was incapable of the muscular play of a smile; but its owner apparently had not lost a perception of incongruities. "What does it matter if I'm tired when I've all eternity to rest? There's no harm in making an effort when it's the very last of all. Don't people always feel better just before the end? I've often heard of that; it's what I was waiting for. Ever since you've been here I thought it would come. I tried two or three times; I was afraid you'd get tired of sitting there." He spoke slowly, with painful breaks and long pauses; his voice seemed to come from a distance. When he ceased he lay with his face turned to Isabel and his large unwinking eyes open into her own. "It was very good of you to come," he went on. "I thought you would; but I wasn't sure."

"I was not sure either till I came," said Isabel.

"You've been like an angel beside my bed. You know they talk about the angel of death. It's the most beautiful of all. You've been like that; as if you were waiting for me."

"I was not waiting for your death; I was waiting for—for this. This is not death, dear Ralph."

"Not for you—no. There's nothing makes us feel so much alive as to see others die. That's the sensation of life—the sense that we remain. I've had it—even I. But now I'm of no use but to give it to others. With me it's all over." And then he paused. Isabel bowed her head further, till it rested on the two hands that were clasped upon his own. She couldn't see him now; but his far-away voice was close to her ear. "Isabel," he went on suddenly, "I wish it were over for you." She answered nothing; she had burst into sobs; she remained so, with her buried face. He lay silent, listening to her sobs; at last he gave a long groan. "Ah, what is it you have done for me?"

"What is it you did for me?" she cried, her now extreme agitation half smothered by her attitude. She had lost all her shame, all wish to hide things. Now he must know; she wished him to know, for it brought them supremely together, and he was beyond the reach of pain. "You did something once—you know it. O Ralph, you've been everything! What have I done for you—what can I do to-day? I would die if you could live. But I don't wish you to live; I would die myself, not to lose you." Her voice was as broken as his own and full of tears and anguish.

"You won't lose me—you'll keep me. Keep me in your heart; I shall be nearer to you than I've ever been. Dear Isabel, life is better; for in life there's love. Death is good—but there's no love."

"I never thanked you—I never spoke—I never was what I should be!" Isabel went on. She felt a passionate need to cry out and accuse herself, to let her sorrow possess her. All her troubles, for the moment, became single and melted together into this present pain. "What must you have thought of me? Yet how could I know? I never knew, and I only know to-day because there are people less stupid than I."

"Don't mind people," said Ralph. "I think I'm glad to leave people."

She raised her head and her clasped hands; she seemed for a moment to pray to him. "Is it true—is it true?" she asked.

"True that you've been stupid? Oh no," said Ralph with a sensible intention of wit.

"That you made me rich—that all I have is yours?"

He turned away his head, and for some time said nothing. Then at last: "Ah, don't speak of that—that was not happy." Slowly he moved his face toward her again, and they once more saw each other. "But for that—but for that—!" And he paused. "I believe I ruined you," he wailed.

She was full of the sense that he was beyond the reach of pain; he seemed already so little of this world. But even if she had not had it she would still have spoken, for nothing mattered now but the only knowledge that was not pure anguish—the knowledge that they were looking at the truth together. "He married me for the money," she said. She wished to say everything; she was afraid he might die before she had done so.

He gazed at her a little, and for the first time his fixed eyes lowered their lids. But he raised them in a moment, and then, "He was greatly in love with you," he answered.

"Yes, he was in love with me. But he wouldn't have married me if I had been poor. I don't hurt you in saying that. How can I? I only want you to understand. I always tried to keep you from understanding; but that's all over."

"I always understood," said Ralph.

"I thought you did, and I didn't like it. But now I like it."

"You don't hurt me—you make me very happy." And as Ralph said this there was an extraordinary gladness in his voice. She bent her head again, and pressed her lips to the back of his hand. "I always understood," he continued, "though it was so strange—so pitiful. You wanted to look at life for yourself—but you were not allowed; you were punished for your wish. You were ground in the very mill of the conventional!"

"Oh yes, I've been punished," Isabel sobbed.

He listened to her a little, and then continued: "Was he very bad about your coming?"

"He made it very hard for me. But I don't care."

"It is all over then between you?"

"Oh no; I don't think anything's over."

"Are you going back to him?" Ralph gasped.

"I don't know—I can't tell. I shall stay here as long as I may. I don't want to think—I needn't think. I don't care for anything but you, and that's enough for the present. It will last a little yet. Here on my knees, with you dying in my arms, I'm happier than I have been for a long time. And I want you to be happy—not to think of anything sad; only to feel that I'm near you and I love you. Why should there be pain? In such hours as this what have we to do with pain? That's not the deepest thing; there's something deeper."

Ralph evidently found from moment to moment greater difficulty in speaking; he had to wait longer to collect himself. At first he appeared to make no response to these last words; he let a long time elapse. Then he murmured simply: "You must stay here."

"I should like to stay—as long as seems right."

"As seems right—as seems right?" He repeated her words. "Yes, you think a great deal about that."

"Of course one must. You're very tired," said Isabel.

"I'm very tired. You said just now that pain's not the deepest thing. No— no. But it's very deep. If I could stay—"

"For me you'll always be here," she softly interrupted. It was easy to interrupt him.

But he went on, after a moment: "It passes, after all; it's passing now. But love remains. I don't know why we should suffer so much. Perhaps I shall find out. There are many things in life. You're very young."

"I feel very old," said Isabel.

"You'll grow young again. That's how I see you. I don't believe—I don't believe—" But he stopped again; his strength failed him.

She begged him to be quiet now, "We needn't speak to understand each other," she said.

"I don't believe that such a generous mistake as yours can hurt you for more than a little."

"Oh Ralph, I'm very happy now," she cried through her tears.

"And remember this," he continued, "that if you've been hated you've also been loved. Ah but, Isabel—*adored*!" he just audibly and lingeringly breathed.

"Oh my brother!" she cried with a movement of still deeper prostration.

Chapter LV

He had told her, the first evening she ever spent at Gardencourt, that if she should live to suffer enough she might some day see the ghost with which the old house was duly provided. She apparently had fulfilled the necessary condition; for the next morning, in the cold, faint dawn, she knew that a spirit was standing by her bed. She had lain down without undressing, it being her belief that Ralph would not outlast the night. She had no inclination to sleep; she was waiting, and such waiting was wakeful. But she closed her eyes; she believed that as the night wore on she should hear a knock at her door. She heard no knock, but at the time the darkness began vaguely to grow grey she started up from her pillow as abruptly as if she had received a summons. It seemed to her for an instant that he was standing there—a vague, hovering figure in the vagueness of the room. She stared a moment; she saw his white face—his kind eyes; then she saw there was nothing. She was not afraid; she was only sure. She quitted the place and in her certainty passed through dark corridors and down a flight of oaken steps that shone in the vague light of a hall-window. Outside Ralph's door she stopped a moment, listening, but she seemed to hear only the hush that filled it. She opened the door with a hand as gentle as if she were lifting a veil from the face of the dead, and saw Mrs. Touchett sitting motionless and upright beside the couch of her son, with one of his hands in her own. The doctor was on the other side, with poor Ralph's further wrist resting in his professional fingers. The two nurses were at the foot between them. Mrs. Touchett took no notice of Isabel, but the doctor looked at her very hard; then he gently placed Ralph's hand in a proper position, close beside him. The nurse looked at her very hard too, and no one said a word; but Isabel only looked at what she had come to see. It was fairer than Ralph had ever been in life, and there was a strange resemblance to the face of his father, which, six years before, she had seen lying on the same pillow. She went to her aunt and put her arm around her; and Mrs. Touchett, who as a general thing neither invited nor enjoyed caresses, submitted for a moment to this one, rising, as might be, to take it. But she was stiff and dry-eyed; her acute white face was terrible.

"Dear Aunt Lydia," Isabel murmured.

"Go and thank God you've no child," said Mrs. Touchett, disengaging herself.

Three days after this a considerable number of people found time, at the height of the London "season," to take a morning train down to a quiet station in Berkshire and spend half an hour in a small grey church which stood within an easy walk. It was in the green burial-place of this edifice that Mrs. Touchett consigned her son to earth. She stood herself at the edge of the grave, and Isabel stood beside her; the sexton himself had not a more practical interest in the scene than Mrs. Touchett. It was a solemn occasion, but neither a harsh nor a heavy one; there was a certain geniality in the appearance of things. The weather had changed to fair; the day, one of the last of the treacherous May-time, was warm and windless, and the air had the brightness of the hawthorn and the blackbird. If it was sad to think of poor Touchett, it was not too sad, since death, for him, had had no violence. He had been dying so long; he was so ready; everything had been so expected and prepared. There were tears in Isabel's eyes, but they were not tears that blinded. She looked through them at the beauty of the day, the splendour of nature, the sweetness of the old English churchyard, the bowed heads of good friends. Lord Warburton was there, and a group of gentlemen all unknown to her, several of whom, as she afterwards learned, were connected with the bank; and there were others whom she knew. Miss Stackpole was among the first, with honest Mr. Bantling beside her; and Caspar Goodwood, lifting his head higher than the rest—bowing it rather less. During much of the time Isabel was conscious of Mr. Goodwood's gaze; he looked at her somewhat harder than he usually looked in public, while the others had fixed their eyes upon the churchyard turf. But she never let him see that she saw him; she thought of him only to wonder that he was still in England. She found she had taken for granted that after accompanying Ralph to Gardencourt he had gone away; she remembered how little it was a country that pleased him. He was there, however, very distinctly there; and something in his attitude seemed to say that he was there with a complex intention. She wouldn't meet his eyes, though there was doubtless sympathy in them; he made her rather uneasy. With the dispersal of the little group he disappeared, and the only person who came to speak to her—though several spoke to Mrs. Touchett—was Henrietta Stackpole. Henrietta had been crying.

Ralph had said to Isabel that he hoped she would remain at Gardencourt, and she made no immediate motion to leave the place. She said to herself that it was but common charity to stay a little with her aunt. It was fortunate she had so good a formula; otherwise she might have been greatly in want of one. Her errand was over; she had done what she had left her husband to do. She had a husband in a foreign city, counting the hours of her absence; in such a case one needed an excellent motive. He was not one of the best husbands, but that didn't alter the case. Certain obligations were involved in the very fact of marriage, and were quite independent of the quantity of enjoyment extracted from it. Isabel thought of her husband as little as might be; but now that she was at a distance, beyond its spell, she thought with a kind of spiritual shudder of Rome. There was a penetrating chill in the image, and she drew back into the deepest shade of Gardencourt. She lived from day to day, postponing, closing her eyes, trying not to think. She knew she must decide, but she decided nothing; her coming itself had not been a decision. On that occasion she had simply started. Osmond gave no sound and now evidently would give none; he would leave it all to her. From Pansy she heard nothing, but that was very simple: her father had told her not to write.

Mrs. Touchett accepted Isabel's company, but offered her no assistance; she appeared to be absorbed in considering, without enthusiasm but with perfect lucidity, the new conveniences of her own situation. Mrs. Touchett was not an optimist, but even from painful occurrences she managed to extract a certain utility. This consisted in the reflexion that, after all, such things happened to other people and not to herself. Death was disagreeable, but in this case it was her son's death, not her own; she had never flattered herself that her own would be disagreeable to any one but Mrs. Touchett. She was better off than poor Ralph, who had left all the commodities of life behind him, and indeed all the security; since the worst of dying was, to Mrs. Touchett's mind, that it exposed one to be taken advantage of. For herself she was on the spot; there was nothing so good as that. She made known to Isabel very punctually—it was the evening her son was buried—several of Ralph's testamentary arrangements. He had told her everything, had consulted her about everything. He left her no money; of course she had no need of money. He left her the furniture of Gardencourt, exclusive of the pictures and books and the use of the place for a year; after which it was to be sold. The money produced by the sale was to constitute an endowment for a hospital for poor persons suffering from the malady of which he died; and of this portion of the will Lord Warburton was appointed executor. The rest of his property, which was to be withdrawn from the bank, was disposed of in various bequests, several of them to those cousins in Vermont to whom his father had already been so bountiful. Then there were a number of small legacies.

"Some of them are extremely peculiar," said Mrs. Touchett; "he has left considerable sums to persons I never heard of. He gave me a list, and I asked then who some of them were, and he told me they were people who at various times had seemed to like him. Apparently he thought you didn't like him, for he hasn't left you a penny. It was his opinion that you had been handsomely treated by his father, which I'm bound to say I think you were—though I don't mean that I ever heard him complain of it. The pictures are to be dispersed; he has distributed them about, one by one, as little keepsakes. The most valuable of the collection goes to Lord Warburton. And what do you think he has done with his library? It sounds like a practical joke. He has left it to your friend Miss Stackpole—'in recognition of her services to literature.' Does he mean her following him up from Rome? Was that a service to literature? It contains a great many rare and valuable books, and as she can't carry it about the world in her trunk he recommends her to sell it at auction. She will sell it of course at Christie's,[1] and with the proceeds she'll set up a newspaper. Will that be a service to literature?"

This question Isabel forbore to answer, as it exceeded the little interrogatory to which she had deemed it necessary to submit on her arrival. Besides, she had never been less interested in literature than to-day, as she found when she occasionally took down from the shelf one of the rare and valuable volumes of which Mrs. Touchett had spoken. She was quite unable to read; her attention had never been so little at her command. One afternoon, in the library, about a week after the ceremony in the churchyard, she was trying to fix it for an hour; but her eyes often wandered from the book in her hand to the open window, which looked down the long avenue. It was in this way that she saw a modest vehicle approach the door and perceived Lord Warburton sitting, in rather an uncomfortable attitude, in

---

1. London auction house, founded in 1766. Rare books are still an important part of its trade, but unlike its rival Sotheby's, it was not first established to sell them.

a corner of it. He had always had a high standard of courtesy, and it was therefore not remarkable, under the circumstances, that he should have taken the trouble to come down from London to call on Mrs. Touchett. It was of course Mrs. Touchett he had come to see, and not Mrs. Osmond; and to prove to herself the validity of this thesis Isabel presently stepped out of the house and wandered away into the park. Since her arrival at Gardencourt she had been but little out of doors, the weather being unfavourable for visiting the grounds. This evening, however, was fine, and at first it struck her as a happy thought to have come out. The theory I have just mentioned was plausible enough, but it brought her little rest, and if you had seen her pacing about you would have said she had a bad conscience. She was not pacified when at the end of a quarter of an hour, finding herself in view of the house, she saw Mrs. Touchett emerge from the portico accompanied by her visitor. Her aunt had evidently proposed to Lord Warburton that they should come in search of her. She was in no humour for visitors and, if she had had a chance, would have drawn back behind one of the great trees. But she saw she had been seen and that nothing was left her but to advance. As the lawn at Gardencourt was a vast expanse this took some time; during which she observed that, as he walked beside his hostess, Lord Warburton kept his hands rather stiffly behind him and his eyes upon the ground. Both persons apparently were silent; but Mrs. Touchett's thin little glance, as she directed it toward Isabel, had even at a distance an expression. It seemed to say with cutting sharpness: "Here's the eminently amenable nobleman you might have married!" When Lord Warburton lifted his own eyes, however, that was not what they said. They only said "This is rather awkward, you know, and I depend upon you to help me." He was very grave, very proper and, for the first time since Isabel had known him, greeted her without a smile. Even in his days of distress he had always begun with a smile. He looked extremely self-conscious.

"Lord Warburton has been so good as to come out to see me," said Mrs. Touchett. "He tells me he didn't know you were still here. I know he's an old friend of yours, and as I was told you were not in the house I brought him out to see for himself."

"Oh, I saw there was a good train at 6:40, that would get me back in time for dinner," Mrs. Touchett's companion rather irrelevantly explained. "I'm so glad to find you've not gone."

"I'm not here for long, you know," Isabel said with a certain eagerness.

"I suppose not; but I hope it's for some weeks. You came to England sooner than—a—than you thought?"

"Yes, I came very suddenly."

Mrs. Touchett turned away as if she were looking at the condition of the grounds, which indeed was not what it should be, while Lord Warburton hesitated a little. Isabel fancied he had been on the point of asking about her husband—rather confusedly—and then had checked himself. He continued immitigably grave, either because he thought it becoming in a place over which death had just passed, or for more personal reasons. If he was conscious of personal reasons it was very fortunate that he had the cover of the former motive; he could make the most of that. Isabel thought of all this. It was not that his face was sad, for that was another matter; but it was strangely inexpressive.

"My sisters would have been so glad to come if they had known you were still here—if they had thought you would see them," Lord Warburton went on. "Do kindly let them see you before you leave England."

"It would give me great pleasure; I have such a friendly recollection of them."

"I don't know whether you would come to Lockleigh for a day or two? You know there's always that old promise." And his lordship coloured a little as he made this suggestion, which gave his face a somewhat more familiar air. "Perhaps I'm not right in saying that just now; of course you're not thinking of visiting. But I meant what would hardly be a visit. My sisters are to be at Lockleigh at Whitsuntide for five days; and if you could come then—as you say you're not to be very long in England—I would see that there should be literally no one else."

Isabel wondered if not even the young lady he was to marry would be there with her mamma; but she did not express this idea. "Thank you extremely," she contented herself with saying; "I'm afraid I hardly know about Whitsuntide."

"But I have your promise—haven't I?—for some other time."

There was an interrogation in this; but Isabel let it pass. She looked at her interlocutor a moment, and the result of her observation was that—as had happened before—she felt sorry for him. "Take care you don't miss your train," she said. And then she added: "I wish you every happiness."

He blushed again, more than before, and he looked at his watch. "Ah yes, 6.40; I haven't much time, but I've a fly at the door. Thank you very much." It was not apparent whether the thanks applied to her having reminded him of his train or to the more sentimental remark. "Good-bye, Mrs. Osmond; good-bye." He shook hands with her, without meeting her eyes, and then he turned to Mrs. Touchett, who had wandered back to them. With her his parting was equally brief; and in a moment the two ladies saw him move with long steps across the lawn.

"Are you very sure he's to be married?" Isabel asked of her aunt.

"I can't be surer than he; but he seems sure. I congratulated him, and he accepted it."

"Ah," said Isabel, "I give it up!"—while her aunt returned to the house and to those avocations which the visitor had interrupted.

She gave it up, but she still thought of it—thought of it while she strolled again under the great oaks whose shadows were long upon the acres of turf. At the end of a few minutes she found herself near a rustic bench, which, a moment after she had looked at it, struck her as an object recognised. It was not simply that she had seen it before, nor even that she had sat upon it; it was that on this spot something important had happened to her—that the place had an air of association. Then she remembered that she had been sitting there, six years before, when a servant brought her from the house the letter in which Caspar Goodwood informed her that he had followed her to Europe; and that when she had read the letter she looked up to hear Lord Warburton announcing that he should like to marry her. It was indeed an historical, an interesting, bench; she stood and looked at it as if it might have something to say to her. She wouldn't sit down on it now—she felt rather afraid of it. She only stood before it, and while she stood the past came back to her in one of those rushing waves of emotion by which persons of sensibility are visited at odd hours. The effect of this agitation was a sudden sense of being very tired, under the influence of which she overcame her scruples and sank into the rustic seat. I have said that she was restless and unable to occupy herself; and whether or no, if you had seen her there, you would have admired the justice of the former epithet, you would at least have allowed that at this moment she was the image of a victim of idleness. Her attitude had a singular absence of purpose; her hands, hanging at her sides, lost themselves in the folds of her black dress; her eyes gazed vaguely before her. There was nothing to recall her to the house; the two ladies, in their seclusion, dined early and had tea at an indefinite hour. How long she had sat in this position she could not have told you; but the twilight had grown thick when she became aware that she was not alone. She quickly straightened herself, glancing about, and then saw what had become of her solitude. She was sharing it with Caspar Goodwood, who stood looking at her, a few yards off, and whose footfall on the unresonant turf, as he came near, she had not heard. It occurred to her in the midst of this that it was just so Lord Warburton had surprised her of old.

She instantly rose, and as soon as Goodwood saw he was seen he started forward. She had had time only to rise when, with a motion that looked like violence, but felt like—she knew not what, he grasped her by the wrist and made her sink again into the seat. She closed her eyes; he had not hurt her; it was only a touch, which she had obeyed. But there was something in his face that she wished not to see. That was the way he had looked at her the other day in the churchyard; only at present it was worse. He said nothing at first; she only felt him close to her—beside her on the bench and pressingly turned to her. It almost seemed to her that no one had ever been so close to her as that. All this, however, took but an instant, at the end of which she had disengaged her wrist, turning her eyes upon her visitant. "You've frightened me," she said.

"I didn't mean to," he answered, "but if I did a little, no matter. I came from London a while ago by the train, but I couldn't come here directly. There was a man at the station who got ahead of me. He took a fly that was there, and I heard him give the order to drive here. I don't know who he was, but I didn't want to come with him; I wanted to see you alone. So I've been waiting and walking about. I've walked all over, and I was just coming to the house when I saw you here. There was a keeper, or some one, who met me; but that was all right, because I had made his acquaintance when I came here with your cousin. Is that gentleman gone? Are you really alone? I want to speak to you." Goodwood spoke very fast; he was as excited as when they had parted in Rome. Isabel had hoped that condition would subside; and she shrank into herself as she perceived that, on the contrary, he had only let out sail. She had a new sensation; he had never produced it before; it was a feeling of danger. There was indeed something really formidable in his resolution. She gazed straight before her; he, with a hand on each knee, leaned forward, looking deeply into her face. The twilight seemed to darken round them. "I want to speak to you," he repeated; "I've something particular to say. I don't want to trouble you—as I did the other day in Rome. That was of no use; it only distressed you. I couldn't help it; I knew I was wrong. But I'm not wrong now;

please don't think I am," he went on with his hard, deep voice melting a moment into entreaty. "I came here to-day for a purpose. It's very different. It was vain for me to speak to you then; but now I can help you."

She couldn't have told you whether it was because she was afraid, or because such a voice in the darkness seemed of necessity a boon; but she listened to him as she had never listened before; his words dropped deep into her soul. They produced a sort of stillness in all her being; and it was with an effort, in a moment, that she answered him. "How can you help me?" she asked in a low tone, as if she were taking what he had said seriously enough to make the enquiry in confidence.

"By inducing you to trust me. Now I know—to-day I know. Do you remember what I asked you in Rome? Then I was quite in the dark. But to-day I know on good authority; everything's clear to me to-day. It was a good thing when you made me come away with your cousin. He was a good man, a fine man, one of the best; he told me how the case stands for you. He explained everything; he guessed my sentiments. He was a member of your family and he left you—so long as you should be in England—to my care," said Goodwood as if he were making a great point. "Do you know what he said to me the last time I saw him—as he lay there where he died? He said: 'Do everything you can for her; do everything she'll let you.'"

Isabel suddenly got up. "You had no business to talk about me!"

"Why not—why not, when we talked in that way?" he demanded, following her fast. "And he was dying—when a man's dying it's different." She checked the movement she had made to leave him; she was listening more than ever; it was true that he was not the same as that last time. That had been aimless, fruitless passion, but at present he had an idea, which she scented in all her being. "But it doesn't matter!" he exclaimed, pressing her still harder, though now without touching a hem of her garment. "If Touchett had never opened his mouth I should have known all the same. I had only to look at you at your cousin's funeral to see what's the matter with you. You can't deceive me any more; for God's sake be honest with a man who's so honest with you. You're the most unhappy of women, and your husband's the deadliest of fiends."

She turned on him as if he had struck her. "Are you mad?" she cried.

"I've never been so sane; I see the whole thing. Don't think it's necessary to defend him. But I won't say another word against him; I'll speak only of you," Goodwood added quickly. "How can you pretend you're not heart-broken? You don't know what to do—you don't know where to turn. It's too late to play a part; didn't you leave all that behind you in Rome? Touchett knew all about it, and I knew it too—what it would cost you to come here. It will have cost you your life? Say it will"—and he flared almost into anger: "give me one word of truth! When I know such a horror as that, how can I keep myself from wishing to save you? What would you think of me if I should stand still and see you go back to your reward? 'It's awful, what she'll have to pay for it!'—that's what Touchett said to me. I may tell you that, mayn't I? He was such a near relation!" cried Goodwood, making his queer grim point again. "I'd sooner have been shot than let another man say those things to me; but he was different; he seemed to me to have the right. It was after he got home—when he saw he was dying, and when I saw it too. I understand all about it: you're afraid to go back. You're perfectly alone; you don't know where to turn. You can't turn anywhere; you know that perfectly. Now it is therefore that I want you to think of *me*."

"To think of 'you'?" Isabel said, standing before him in the dusk. The idea of which she had caught a glimpse a few moments before now loomed large. She threw back her head a little; she stared at it as if it had been a comet in the sky.

"You don't know where to turn. Turn straight to *me*. I want to persuade you to trust me," Goodwood repeated. And then he paused with his shining eyes. "Why should you go back—why should you go through that ghastly form?"

"To get away from *you*!" she answered. But this expressed only a little of what she felt. The rest was that she had never been loved before. She had believed it, but this was different; this was the hot wind of the desert, at the approach of which the others dropped dead, like mere sweet airs of the garden. It wrapped her about; it lifted her off her feet, while the very taste of it, as of something potent, acrid and strange, forced open her set teeth.

At first, in rejoinder to what she had said, it seemed to her that he would break out into greater violence. But after an instant he was perfectly quiet; he wished to prove he was sane, that he had reasoned it all out. "I want to prevent that, and I think I may, if you'll only for once listen to me. It's too monstrous of you to think of sinking back into that misery, of going to open your mouth to that poisoned air. It's you that are out of your mind. Trust me as if I had the care of you. Why shouldn't we be happy—when it's here before us, when it's so easy? I'm yours for ever—for ever and ever. Here I stand; I'm as firm as a rock. What have you to care about? You've no children; that perhaps would be an obstacle. As it is you've nothing to consider. You must save what you can of your life; you mustn't lose it all simply because you've lost a part. It would be an insult to you to assume that you care for the look of the thing, for what people will say, for the bottomless idiocy of the world. We've nothing to do with all that; we're quite out of it; we look at things as they are. You took the great step in coming away; the next is nothing; it's the natural one. I swear, as I stand here, that a woman deliberately made to suffer is justified in anything in life—in going down into the streets if that will help her! I know how you suffer, and that's why I'm here. We can do absolutely as we please; to whom under the sun do we owe anything? What is it that holds us, what is it that has the smallest right to interfere in such a question as this? Such a question is between ourselves—and to say that is to settle it! Were we born to rot in our misery—were we born to be afraid? I never knew *you* afraid! If you'll only trust me, how little you will be disappointed! The world's all before us—and the world's very big. I know something about that."[2]

Isabel gave a long murmur, like a creature in pain; it was as if he were pressing something that hurt her. "The world's very small," she said at random; she had an immense desire to appear to resist. She said it at random, to hear herself say something; but it was not what she meant. The

---

2. The novel's second echo of the conclusion to *Paradise Lost* (see p. 224). Edith Wharton alludes to this moment in chapter 19 of *The Age of Innocence* (1920).

world, in truth, had never seemed so large; it seemed to open out, all round her, to take the form of a mighty sea, where she floated in fathomless waters. She had wanted help, and here was help; it had come in a rushing torrent. I know not whether she believed everything he said; but she believed just then that to let him take her in his arms would be the next best thing to her dying. This belief, for a moment, was a kind of rapture, in which she felt herself sink and sink. In the movement she seemed to beat with her feet, in order to catch herself, to feel something to rest on.

"Ah, be mine as I'm yours!" she heard her companion cry. He had suddenly given up argument, and his voice seemed to come, harsh and terrible, through a confusion of vaguer sounds.

This however, of course, was but a subjective fact, as the metaphysicians say; the confusion, the noise of waters, all the rest of it, were in her own swimming head. In an instant she became aware of this. "Do me the greatest kindness of all," she panted. "I beseech you to go away!"

"Ah, don't say that. Don't kill me!" he cried.

She clasped her hands; her eyes were streaming with tears. "As you love me, as you pity me, leave me alone!"

He glared at her a moment through the dusk, and the next instant she felt his arms about her and his lips on her own lips. His kiss was like white lightning, a flash that spread, and spread again, and stayed; and it was extraordinarily as if, while she took it, she felt each thing in his hard manhood that had least pleased her, each aggressive fact of his face, his figure, his presence, justified of its intense identity and made one with this act of possession.[3] So had she heard of those wrecked and under water following a train of images before they sink. But when darkness returned she was free. She never looked about her; she only darted from the spot. There were lights in the windows of the house; they shone far across the lawn. In an extraordinarily short time—for the distance was considerable— she had moved through the darkness (for she saw nothing) and reached the door. Here only she paused. She looked all about her; she listened a little; then she put her hand on the latch. She had not known where to turn; but she knew now. There was a very straight path.

Two days afterwards Caspar Goodwood knocked at the door of the house in Wimpole Street in which Henrietta Stackpole occupied furnished lodgings. He hardly removed his hand from the knocker when the door was opened and Miss Stackpole herself stood before him. She had on her hat and jacket; she was on the point of going out. "Oh, good-morning," he said, "I was in hopes I should find Mrs. Osmond."

Henrietta kept him waiting a moment for her reply; but there was a good deal of expression about Miss Stackpole even when she was silent. "Pray what led you to suppose she was here?"

"I went down to Gardencourt this morning, and the servant told me she had come to London. He believed she was to come to you."

Again Miss Stackpole held him—with an intention of perfect kindness— in suspense. "She came here yesterday, and spent the night. But this morning she started for Rome."

---

3. This passage is one of the most heavily revised parts of the New York Edition; see the articles by Anthony J. Mazzella and Tessa Hadley in this Norton Critical Edition, p. 499 and p. 613 for a comparison with the 1882 edition.

Caspar Goodwood was not looking at her; his eyes were fastened on the doorstep. "Oh, she started—?" he stammered. And without finishing his phrase or looking up he stiffly averted himself. But he couldn't otherwise move.

Henrietta had come out, closing the door behind her, and now she put out her hand and grasped his arm. "Look here, Mr. Goodwood," she said; "just you wait!"

On which he looked up at her—but only to guess, from her face, with a revulsion, that she simply meant he was young. She stood shining at him with that cheap comfort, and it added, on the spot, thirty years to his life. She walked him away with her, however, as if she had given him now the key to patience.

BACKGROUNDS AND CONTEXTS

The Writer and His Work

We first hear of what became *The Portrait of a Lady* in a letter James sent from Paris to William Dean Howells on October 24, 1876. He was, he wrote, planning a companion piece to *The American,* then being serialized under Howells's editorship in the *Atlantic Monthly.* The protagonist of that novel was called Christopher Newman, and the new book would be the tale of "an *Americana*—the adventures in Europe of a female Newman, who of course equally triumphs over the insolent foreigner."[1] That description has its irony; Newman's own triumph is at best a moral one, and this *Americana* might well come away with nothing at all. James hoped that *Scribner's* would take it for serialization, but the deal didn't come off, and a few months later he offered it to Howells, describing it as "the portrait of the character and recital of the adventures of a woman—a great swell, psychologically; a *grande nature*—accompanied with many 'developments.'"[2] The *Atlantic* could not, however, start on another of his novels so soon after *The American* had finished its run, and James put the project aside. He does write in his New York Edition preface of having taken up an old beginning when he finally set to work on the book in the spring of 1880, but the manuscript doesn't survive and we have no sense of how far he had earlier gotten, of what this ur-*Portrait* may have been like.

The letters in the first part of this section pick up the story in the summer of 1879, when James approached his publishers once more, and this time on both sides of the ocean. He wanted a success—a material as well as an artistic success—and therefore took special care with his negotiations. By arranging for the book's simultaneous serialization in the English *Macmillan's Magazine* as well as the American *Atlantic* he could guard against piracy and ensure his copyright in both Britain and the United States. That required each journal to adjust its schedule to the other's, and they also had to take account of what else of his was appearing and where; *Washington Square* was running in London's *Cornhill* during the summer and fall of 1880, and James didn't want to compete with himself. *Macmillan's* bought the novel's British serial rights for £250, or a bit more than $1,200; in America he got $250 per installment, a figure that over its fourteen-month course came to $3,000. James's income from magazines almost always exceeded his royalties on the finished book itself, and the *Portrait* was no exception. Yet though his sales were small in comparison with Mark Twain's or even with Howells's, the novel's American edition did run through six printings in less than a year, and over time it proved both the most popular, and the most lucrative, of his full-length novels.

Most of the letters here concentrate on such arrangements, but two of them call for special attention. The first chapters of the *Portrait* were in print long before James had finished writing; a common practice in the period. He doesn't

---

1. Michael Anesko's invaluable *Letters, Fictions, Lives: Henry James and William Dean Howells* (Oxford University Press, 1977) collects the surviving correspondence between the two writers, along with the essays they each wrote on the other, and provides as well a detailed account of their friendship. The letter quoted here is on pp. 122–23.
2. Letter of Febuary 2, 1877. In *Letters, Fictions, Lives*, p. 125.

appear to have had any trouble in meeting his deadlines, and yet in a July 1881 letter to the *Atlantic*'s owners, the Boston publishing house of Houghton Mifflin, he writes that he will need an extra month in the magazine to bring the work to an end. Dickens always knew in advance just how many parts he would require; so did George Eliot with *Middlemarch*. James did not, and in fact had first projected a serial of somewhere between eight and twelve installments; so the novel grew into its form, rather than having to fit itself into some already determined shape. The second letter comes from a quarter of a century on, a 1906 note to his agent, J. B. Pinker. In it James arranges for a photographic frontispiece for the first volume of the novel in the New York Edition, and identifies Hardwick Court in Oxfordshire as the model for Gardencourt, the English country house at which the book begins. That frontispiece, by Alvin Langdon Coburn, is reproduced along with that to the novel's second volume on pp. 417–18 of this Norton Critical Edition.

The letter to Pinker brings the novel closer to James's own family history. He was always open about the imaginative place he gave to the life and death of his cousin Mary "Minny" Temple, who died at twenty-four of tuberculosis. She became his type of the fearless questioning American girl, the model for both Isabel and Milly Theale in *The Wings of the Dove* (1902). James was her first cousin on her mother's side. And the Canadian-born Charles Rose, the owner of Hardwick Court, was her first cousin on her father's; his own father, the financier Sir John Rose, was the uncle-by-marriage whom Minny would have visited in England if she had ever been able to travel, just as Isabel stays with old Daniel Touchett. I've reprinted here a letter James wrote from England in 1870. Addressed to his mother, it describes his initial reactions to Minny's death; it could be supplemented with another written a few days later to his brother William, which reiterates and amplifies its sentiments.[3] These letters show that the young writer was already turning Minny's life into a story. Her unlived years went on in his head, a process also suggested by an 1881 letter to his friend, Grace Norton, who had spotted Minny's presence in Isabel as she read the *Portrait*'s opening chapters.

James returned to his memories of Minny in *Notes of a Son and Brother* (1914), the second volume of his autobiography. There he included a number of her letters, altering some of her sentences in the process to make them fit his own ideas of good prose. Some scholars have charged him with suppressing Minny's voice,[4] but by this point James had long been what he called a "fingerer of style,"[5] and he did the same thing to his brother William's letters as well. I have chosen more purely descriptive passages to reprint here. My selection from the autobiography also includes an account of the Florentine villa on which James modeled Gilbert Osmond's, and of the American friends who had an apartment there.

These things all form a part of what, in his preface to *The Ambassadors*, James called "the story of one's story,"[6] and so too are the selections here from his notebooks. For much of his life he kept a journal in which he jotted down ideas for future work—bits of conversation, scraps of gossip, even potential names for his characters. Some of these notebook entries show him working up an entire story in a few rapid moments, canvassing possibilities, rejecting some ideas and embracing others, as though his pages were thinking aloud. In the only surviving entry for the *Portrait* he works his way through the novel's

3. See *Henry James Letters I*, ed. Leon Edel (Cambridge: The Belknap Press, 1974), pp. 223–29.
4. See, for example, Alfred Habegger, *Henry James and the "Woman Business"* (Cambridge University Press, 1989) or Lyndall Gordon, *A Private Life of Henry James* (W. W. Norton, 1999).
5. The phrase comes from James's 1893 story "The Middle Years." See *Complete Stories 1892–1898* (New York: Library of America, 1996), p. 344.
6. Henry James, *Literary Criticism II: European Writers and the Prefaces* (New York: Library of America, 1984), p. 1309.

twenty-odd last chapters. He spots the difficulties in what he's already done and sketches his way around them; he plots out just how to reveal the novel's final secrets, and traces the implications of its open ending.

I've accompanied this with an excerpt from the very different notebook that James kept in the fall and winter of 1881–82. With the *Portrait* completed, he sailed for the United States that October, returning for the first time since he left for Paris at the end of 1875. He carried with him a sense of confidence in his achievement, of mastery; he saw his family in Cambridge and his friends in Washington and New York, and began to plan his next steps. At the end of January his mother died, unexpectedly, and he didn't get back to Britain until May. But early in his visit he sat down in a Boston hotel room and wrote out a chronicle of his professional life so far; an account that, in retrospect, defines the myth he made out of the choices that shaped his career, his expatriation above all. The *American Journal* includes the most detailed account we have of the *Portrait*'s composition, and in particular of James's movements during the months he spent upon it, from its 1880 beginning in a hotel room over the Arno to its virtual completion in Venice the following year.

Much of the novel was written in Italy, and most of it is set there. Scenery in the *Portrait* is never simply a set piece, never just an inert block of description. It always serves some dramatic purpose, and yet what it tells us about the characters' perceptions and desires depends on the fact that James had already mastered it *as* scenery in the series of brilliant travel essays he wrote in the 1870s. The selections here all concentrate on the built environment. From "Recent Florence" I've taken a description of the villas around Florence, which offers a glancing elliptical account of that city's expatriate life. That's followed by two evocations of Rome. My selection from "A Roman Holiday" concentrates on the city's great churches; that from "Roman Rides" details James's experience of the Campagna. Taken together they testify to what he calls the "unbroken continuity" of Roman life, to a world that "you can never flatter yourself you have discovered." Someone else has always been there before you; in her unhappy Roman marriage, Isabel Archer will find herself sustained by that very sense of continuity.

LETTERS ON THE PUBLICATION OF *THE PORTRAIT OF A LADY*

To Frederick Macmillan[†]

Reform Club.
Pall Mall. S.W.
July 22*d* [1879]

My dear Macmillan

I write you a line to day [*sic*], in hopes it may catch you in Cheshire. I think that *November 1880* would be too early a date for me to attempt to begin a novel in *Macmillan*, & that January of the following year is the first moment at which I ought to undertake it. If you have a story for the gap after the termination of Mrs. O. [Oliphant], I will undertake to begin

---

† From *The Correspondence of Henry James and the House of Macmillan, 1877–1914*, ed. Rayburn S. Moore (Baton Rouge: Louisiana State University Press, 1993), p. 38. Reprinted by permission of Palgrave Macmillan. Macmillan was James's first London publisher; Frederick Macmillan (1851–1936) was the firm's junior partner.

in *January 1881—unless* you are disposed to assent to a scheme which occurred to me this morning. I am to furnish Howells a story for the last half of 1880, & the *Atlantic* has always objected to "simultaneity" with the English magazines. But as he has, (as I told you,) just written to me to propose simultaneity with *Macmillan* or the *Cornhill* for his own forthcoming novel, I suppose he wouldn't raise his prohibition as to mine. In that case you would of course be welcome to begin my story at the same time he does—I suppose at midsummer. If you don't like this, & prefer an *exclusive* novel, then, as I say I will begin in January of the following year. The latter scheme I think I like as well as the former, & if you will let me know your disposition I will abide by what you say. * * *

Yours ever
H. James Jr.

To William Dean Howells[†]

My address is always here.
3, BOLTON STREET,
PICCADILLY. W.
Aug. 19th [1879]

My dear Howells—

Without waiting for your answer to my letter of some time since (I forget exactly when,) I think it better to write to you again. Shortly after I wrote before, the Macmillans came down upon me with the assurance that they hold me definitely pledged to furnish them a serial for next year. They are perfectly willing to *simultane*, & if you can be brought to do so, the thing can easily be settled. Your note to me about "simultaning" your own next novel has led me to believe that you might be so brought. (You will let me hear by the way, I hope, what has come of my visit to Leslie Stephen[1]—he himself has left town.) With my chance here & my chance at home, it is very difficult for me not to wish to bring out in both places at once, & escape the bad economy of lavishing a valuable fiction upon a single public. If objection to simultaneous publication is a matter of dignity with the *Atlantic*, there is no reason why it should be more difficult than Blackwood, Fraser, the *Cornhill* & Macmillan. I hope it won't, as this will, in this case & all others to come, greatly simplify the producing question with me—I can always be your novelist if I can publish here also Try & think I am worth it—worth having on those terms. If you will see it so I engage to produce the most immortal & fortune-making (all round) works. Will you kindly let me know about this as soon as possible—I am

---

† The following letters to Howells are from *Letters, Fictions, Lives: Henry James and William Dean Howells*, ed. Michael Anesko (New York: Oxford University Press, 1997), pp. 138–39. Reprinted by permission of Oxford University Press. Notes are by the editor of this Norton Critical Edition. William Dean Howells (1837–1920) was the editor of the *Atlantic Monthly* from 1871 to 1881. He and James first met in the mid-1860s, and became friends for life. His own novels include *The Rise of Silas Lapham* (1885) and *A Hazard of New Fortunes* (1890). James's letters here are devoted to sorting out the details of the *Portrait's* simultaneous serialization on both sides of the Atlantic.
1. A prolific man of letters (1832–1904), editor of the *Cornhill*, one of Britain's leading monthly magazines, and first editor of the *Dictionary of National Biography*, he is now best known as the father of Virginia Woolf.

spending this cold, wet, dismal summer, as you see, in this big, empty wilderness of paving stones. It's horribly un-rural & little natural, but I go abroad (to Paris) for the autumn, on Sept. 1st. I have lately seen several times our friend Clemens,[2] on his way back to Hartford. He seemed to me a most excellent pleasant fellow—& what they call here very "quaint." Quaint he is! & his two ladies charming.

Yours ever faithfully—
H. James jr

To William Dean Howells

August 23 [1879]
REFORM CLUB,
PALL MALL. S. W.

Dear Howells,—

If I had only kept over my letter of three or four days since, 24 hours, I should have written it, to better purpose, with yours of the 8th before me. I earn by this, to my satisfaction, that you are willing, with regard to my projected serial, to entertain the idea of simultaneity, & I hasten to be explicit, as you say, in respect to my terms in this case. Considering that the instalments are to be long ones, & the thing is to appear nearly a year hence, by which time I hope to have achieved a surcease of reputation, I don't see how I can ask less than $250 a number—the same price that was paid for the *Europeans*, & that Scribner pays me for the *Confidence*, which is in short instalments. I hope this will suit Osgood, & that you will find yourselves able to consent to the simultaneity of appearance with Macmillan of which I treated in my letter of three days ago. I dwelt so on this in that letter, that it doesn't seem to me worthwhile to say at present anything about terms for exclusive publication, as in case the simultaneous business doesn't suit you I fear I should have to postpone writing a novel for the *Atlantic* alone. But I trust it will suit. I don't pretend to fix the *number* of instalments, more than to say, *probably* not less than six, & more than eight. Also it *may* be that I shall have to ask you to begin in *June*: but this I shall know later. I don't know that there is anything else to settle or to touch upon. I think I told you that my title would (probably) be "The Portrait of a lady." But on this meanwhile please observe complete silence. And do let me hear from you at your 1st commodity.

* * *

Yours
H. J. jr

---

2. Otherwise known as Mark Twain (1835–1910). The two men did not like each other's work and rarely met, but they always got on well when they did.

To Frederick Macmillan[†]

Paris.
42 Rue Cambon.
28*th* September [1879]

Dear Mr. Macmillan

In answering your note in regard to the proposed serial for next year in the Magazine, just before I left London, about a month ago, I promised you that I would let you know definitively about the matter as soon as I shld. have heard from the *Atlantic Monthly,* in which my plan was to publish the novel simultaneously with *Macmillan.* I have only just heard; but apparently the project can be carried out. There is a point which differs from your proposal, but I imagine that you will be able to accede to it: viz: that the novel begin in *July* rather than in *June.* This would be more convenient both to the *Atlantic* & to me. I should also mention that the monthly parts are to be pretty long—24 or 25 pages—; there will be, I suppose, *about eight* of them. I don't think there will be less than eight, and there may be *nine.* I wrote to you that your terms—£250—were agreeable to me, & if these details are not inconvenient to you, I suppose we may consider the matter settled. My novel is *probably* to be called "The Portrait of a Lady"; but upon this I observe the Silence of death!

* * *Very truly yours

H. James Jr.

To William Dean Howells[‡]

Florence, April 18th [1880]

Carino Amico—

The most caressing epithets of a caressing language are not out of place in regard to the particular motive of my writing to you. My imagination seeks eagerly for anything that will ease me off a little & rob my letter of its sting. This sting resides, brutally speaking, in my earnest wish that you may find it not fatally inconvenient to begin my promised serial in *October* instead of *August!* A postponement of two whole months!—the thing will probably have to you an impudent sound. But I throw myself on your mercy & urge upon your attention that the story shall be a 100 per cent better by each day that you have to wait. My motives for this petition are twofold. In the first place I withdrew a month ago from London & its uproar, its distractions & interruptions, in order to concentrate myself upon my work. But if London is uproarious, Italy is insidious, perfidious, fertile in pretexts for one's haunting its lovely sights & scenes rather than one's writing-table; so that, in respect to my novel, it has been a month lost rather than gained. In

---

† From *The Correspondence of Henry James and the House of Macmillan, 1877–1914,* ed. Rayburn S. Moore (Baton Rouge: Louisiana State University Press, 1993), p. 42. Reprinted by permission of Palgrave Macmillan.

‡ The following letters to Howells are from *Letters, Fictions, Lives: Henry James and William Dean Howells,* ed. Michael Anesko (New York: Oxford University Press, 1997), pp. 148–49, 151, 156–58. Reprinted by permission of Oxford University Press. Notes are by the editor of this Norton Critical Edition.

the second place I think I wrote you before that I lately finished a serial tale for the *Cornhill*.[1] This has proved by the editor's measurement longer than by my own, so that instead of running through 4 numbers, it will extend to *six*. As it begins in *June* this will make it terminate in *November*; & it will be agreeable to *Macmillan* that the novel for them & you, shall not begin till the thing in the *Cornhill* is virtually leaving the scene. Behold, dear Howells, my reasons; I trust they will seem to you worthy of a compatriot & a Christian, & that the delay won't cause you any material discomfort. It will leave me a chance to get forward a good deal further than I should otherwise do, before beginning to publish. I shall assume that I have touched you by this appeal, & shall proceed in consequence; but a line in answer (to 3 Bolton St. Piccadilly,) will nevertheless be very welcome.

—Come back to Italy as soon as you can: but don't come with a masterpiece suspended in the air by the tenderest portions of its texture; or else forbid yourself the pleasure of paying your proper respects to this land of loveliness.—I have just come back from a ten days' run to Rome & Naples, & shall be in this place for the longer or shorter time that I remain absent from England. Florence is delightful, as usual, but I am lacerated with the effort of tearing myself away from Rome, where I feared I shouldn't do much work, but which is, to Florence, as sunlight unto moonlight.—* * *

your devotissimo—
H. James jr

To William Dean Howells

3, BOLTON STREET,
PICCADILLY. W.
July 20th [1880]

Dear Howells.

I send you to day 48 printed pages of my novel—which should have gone to you five days since, but that just as I received the sheets from the printer I was taken with a sharp attack of illness which kept me in bed for three days, unable to use a pen. This is the first moment I have got my wits about me again. (I had a terrible siege of neuralgic pain in my head, to which, I am sorry to say, I am wofully liable.)

What you have herewith are the sheets of Macmillan containing the 1st part (number) of the story & the greater portion of the second number. You shall have in two or three days the rest of the second & the whole of the third. After that the sequel will flow freely. You will see that the 1st part is *very* long (26¼ pages of *Macmillan*) (which will make, I shld. say, just about the same of the *Atlantic*.) The following numbers will, as a general thing, probably be shorter by two or three pages. I wrote you that *October* was the month fixed for beginning here; but I am afraid I did not make as clear to you as I ought (as I was indeed myself rather inattentive to the fact at the time) that for the *Atlantic* this must mean the NOVEMBER number. It is only by your publishing a fortnight after Macmillan, rather than a fortnight before, that I can secure the English copyright:

---

1. *Washington Square*.

an indispensable boon. This is what Harper is doing with my little *Washington Square*, which beginning in the *Cornhill* in *June*, began in Harper in July. Don't worry about the *P. of a L.* being stolen in the few days interval of time that may elapse between the October *Macmillan* arriving in New York, & the *Atlantic* coming out: for Houghton & Mifflin will please immediately have the thing copyrighted for me, & each number of Macmillan will contain (as the current *Cornhills* do) a footnote duly setting forth that I have taken out the American copyright & will have my pound of flesh from whomsoever infringes it. In *November* then I look for you to begin. I feel as if I had done nothing but delay & disappoint you with regard to this production; but you see what it is to have given me a boundless faith in your *bonté*. Prove it once more.

* * *

Ever yours
H. *James* jr

To William Dean Howells

Dec. 5*th* [1880]
3, BOLTON STREET,
PICCADILLY. W.

Dear Howells.

I didn't mean to put the screw on you to the extent of *two* volumes of native fiction, & am much obliged to you for your generosity.[1] I shall not attempt to read the books just now, but keep them for the larger leisure of a journey abroad, later in the winter. Dizzy's "Endymion",[2] which is the actuality of the hour here, has almost fatally disgusted me with the literary form to which it pretends to belong. Can the novel be a thing of virtue, when such a contemptibly bad novel as that is capable of being written—& read? Perhaps, however, Aldrich & the Grandissimo will reconcile me to this branch of art. I asked you about the latter because I had observed one or two notices of him which seemed to indicate (in superlative terms) that the G.A.N.[3] had at last arrived; but from the moment that public opinion had not forced him on your own perusal, I was willing to give the G.A.N. another chance.—Your strictures on my own story seem to me well-founded (don't say that I don't take criticism like an angel.) The girl is over-analysed, & her journalistic friend *seems* (whether she is or not) over drawn. But in defense of the former fault I will say that I intended to make a young woman about whom there should be a great deal to tell & as to whom such telling should be interesting; & also that I think she is analysed once for all in the early part of the book & doesn't turn herself inside out quite so much afterwards. (So at least it seems to me—perhaps you will not agree with me). Miss

1. Howells had sent James two recent novels: Thomas Bailey Aldrich's *The Stillwater Tragedy*, and George Washington Cable's *The Grandissimes*.
2. Benjamin Disraeli (1804–1881), the flamboyant former Conservative prime minister; *Endymion* (1880), a romance of political life, was the last novel he completed.
3. The Great American Novel, a phrase first coined by the novelist John W. DeForest (1826–1906) in an 1868 essay for the *Nation*. As young writers Howells and James joked repeatedly about the idea.

Stackpole is not I think really exaggerated—but 99 readers out of a 100 will think her so: which amounts to the same thing. She is the result of an impression made upon me by a variety of encounters & acquaintances made during the last few years; an impression which I had often said to myself could not be exaggerated. But one must have received the impression, & the home-staying American doubtless does not do so as strongly as the expatriated; it is over here that it offers itself in its utmost relief.—That you think well of Lord W. makes me regret more than I already do that he is after all but a secondary figure. I have made rather too much of his radicalism in the beginning—there is no particular use for it later.—I must have been strangely vague as to *all* the conditions of my story when I first corresponded with you about it, & I am glad to have wrung from you the confession that you expected it to be in six numbers, for this will teach me to be more explicit in future. I certainly supposed I had been so in this case—the great feature of my projected tale being that it was to be long—longer than its predecessors. Six months, for a regular novel, is a very small allowance—I mean for dealing with a long period of time & introducing a number of figures. You make your own stories fit into it, but it is only by contracting the duration of the action to a few weeks. Has not this been the case in all of them? Write one that covers a longer stretch of months or years, and I think you will see that it will immediately take more of the magazine. I believed that in this case you positively desired something voluminous & I believed equally that I had announced my voluminosity well in advance. I am afraid that it will be a characteristic of my future productions (in, I hope, a reasonable measure;) but I will be careful to put the points on my i's * * *

faithfully yours
H. *James jr*

To Houghton Mifflin and Co.[†]

3 Bolton St.
July 13*th* [1881]

Dear Sirs.
On my return from the continent last night I find your note of June 23d. I was on the point of writing to you with reference to the eventual issue of the *Portrait*. I am afraid you will be a little alarmed to learn that I have had to ask from Messrs. Macmillan *one additional month* of their magazine, and I shall have therefore to beg the same favour of you. The story is to terminate in the NOVEMBER Macmillan, instead of the October, as first intended, and will have run therefore through *fourteen numbers!* The last three instalments, however, are to be considerably shorter than the others: September and October twenty pages, and November about fifteen. My story is so portentously long that I am very sorry to stretch it out further; but I have suffered myself to get overcrowded at the end. I hope this change will not make you, or the *Atlantic*, too uncomfortable. I do not think that as a book it will seem too long—that is, to be read with interest. It may be

† From *Henry James Letters II*, ed. Leon Edel (Cambridge: The Belknap Press, 1975), pp. 356–57. Copyright © 1975 by Leon Edel, editorial. Copyright © 1975 by Alexander R. James, James copyright material. Reprinted by permission. Note is by the editor of this Norton Critical Edition.

however impossible to put it into a single *readable* volume (let alone a hand-some one), and I should think it would be: but of this I must leave you judges, acting on your discretion. The idea of a volume of seven or eight hundred pages *does* alarm me. I prefer that you should print the book from *revised* sheets of the *Atlantic*, which I will immediately send you. As the extension of the thing in Macmillan gives you more time, I don't suppose you will be inconvenienced by a slight delay. (The revisions are not numer-ous, but such as they are I should like them observed.) I must of course remind you that the book should not be issued in America before it is pub-lished here, as in that case I lose my English copyright. I am unable to say today just when it will appear in London, but I shall ascertain in a day or two, and will then let you know. But there is no probability that you will wish to be ready before my publishers here.

I beg to thank you for your cheque on London for $250 in payment for the July *portion* of my story—which I have just received. And I also beg to inquire whether a cheque for *June* was sent me in the usual course—or whether it was by accident overlooked? No cheque for June has reached me. I should have written about it sooner, but I thought it had perhaps been forgotten, and would be included in July. I now see there has been some accident and should like you to help me know *where* it has been. As you are very regular in your missives, I am afraid it has been lost on the way. Will you kindly let me know whether I thereby lose my cheque altogether, or whether there is any remedy? Don't you sometimes send duplicates? I should be thankful to have my mind relieved on this point at your earliest conve-nience. I send to Mr. Aldrich[1] today the copy of my serial for October.

Believe me very truly yours
H. James Jr.

To James B. Pinker[†]

Lamb House, Rye
14*th* June 1906

Dear Mr. Pinker.

Your letter this morning received, on the questions of illustrations, re-animates and inspires me. It isn't that I don't see what an ornament a thor-oughly good one to each volume will be to the series, but only that I have been rather frightened and flustered at the thought of having to give time to the invention and preparation of them—in addition to providing (which, however, I *shall* enjoy!) some sixteen or seventeen perfect Introductions. The prospect clears beautifully if you will kindly write to our friends in New York that I will gladly aid and abet them with suggestion and sympathy on

---

1. Thomas Bailey Aldrich (1836–1907) had just replaced Howells as the *Atlantic*'s editor.
† From *Henry James Letters IV*, ed Leon Edel (Cambridge: The Belknap Press 1984), pp. 409–10. Copyright © 1984 by Leon Edel, editorial. Copyright © 1984 by Alexander R. James, James copy-right material. Reprinted by permission. Note is by the editor of this Norton Critical Edition. Pinker (1863–1922) was one of Britain's first professional literary agents, and began representing James in 1898; his other clients included Joseph Conrad, H. G. Wells, George Bernard Shaw, and many more. James wrote of his dislike for illustrated editions of his work in the New York Edition preface to *The Golden Bowl*, but did agree to a single photographic frontispiece for each volume, all of them taken by the young American photographer Alvin Langdon Coburn (1882–1966).

The English Home (ca. 1907), by Alvin Langdon Coburn (1882–1966). Gelatin silver print, 23.8×28.1 cm. Frontispiece to the first volume of *The Portrait of a Lady* in the New York Edition. Courtesy of The George Eastman Museum and The Universal Order.

The Roman Bridge (ca. 1907), by Alvin Langdon Coburn (1882–1966).
Gelatin silver print, 23×28.2 cm. Frontispiece to second volume of
The Portrait of a Lady in the New York Edition. Courtesy of The George
Eastman Museum and The Universal Order.

this ground, if they see their way to taking over, themselves, the *procuring* and, as it were, working out of the pictures. When I spoke of the little villa-panel subject, by the way, in writing both to you and to New York a couple of days ago I had a stupid confusion of mind about its being wanted for *Roderick*. Of course it isn't, for that one volume, but if it's a practicable pro-duction, artistically speaking, it will serve excellently for one of the volumes of *The Portrait*, where a Florentine villa is again closely involved. Therefore, if I have my photograph for Volume I of the series, and the little villa-panel does successfully lend itself, there are two subjects secured to start with. Also, I think I can, beyond doubt, get a pleasing and artistic thing of this house, from the garden, and also procure a good reproduceable, slightly nebulous view of the English country house (Hardwicke, near Pangbourne, on the Thames) which I had vaguely and approximately in mind, years ago, for the opening of the *Portrait* (the place belongs to Charles D. Rose, M.P[1] with whom I had then been staying there, and I can easily write to them about it). These things I will set my young American photographer upon, as soon as I have received from him the result of our second and probably much more successful portrait attempt. All thanks, I repeat, for your offer to communicate to the Scribners my full assent to their occupying them-selves with the illustrations as far as ever they can. Please say to them, with this, that I will willingly, as far as possible, and as ingeniously contribute. I only recoil in terror from undertaking *too much.*

You shall receive for forwarding upwards of 350 pages of the *Portrait* as soon as I myself receive from town the last of the considerable num-ber of fully-retyped pages of which said copy partly consists. Yours very truly

Henry James

From Notes of a Son and Brother[†]

*   *   *

Immediately, at any rate, the Albany cousins, or a particular group of them, began again to be intensely in question for us; coloured in due course with reflections of the War as their lives, not less than our own, were to become—and coloured as well too, for all sorts of notation and apprecia-tion, from irrepressible private founts. Mrs. Edmund Tweedy, bereft of her own young children, had at the time I speak of opened her existence, with the amplest hospitality, to her four orphaned nieces, who were also our father's and among whom the second in age, Mary Temple the younger,[1]

---

1. Sir Charles Day Rose (1847–1913), created 1st Baronet (a hereditary knighthood) in 1909. A Canadian-born banker and financier, he was a family connection of James's by marriage, and the owner of Hardwick House in Oxfordshire, the model for the novel's Gardencourt.

† From *Notes of a Son and Brother* (New York: Charles Scribner's Sons, 1914), pp. 76–79, 457–58, 460–62, 475–83. Notes are by the editor of this Norton Critical Edition.

1. Called "Minny" by her friends and family, Mary Temple (1845–1870) was James's first cousin on his father's side; her mother had been a James. She was one of four siblings orphaned by their parents' death from tuberculosis, the disease that would kill her. After their parents' death they lived with their aunt, Mary Tweedy née Temple. Minny is the acknowledged model for Isabel, and indeed for the mixture of fearlessness and spontaneity that marks James's (often doomed) American girls from the eponymous Daisy Miller (1878) to Milly Theale of *The Wings of the Dove* (1902).

about in her seventeenth year when she thus renewed her appearance to our view, shone with vividest lustre, an essence that preserves her still, more than half a century from the date of her death, in a memory or two where many a relic once sacred has comparatively yielded to time. Most of those who knew and loved, I was going to say adored, her have also yielded—which is a reason the more why thus much of her, faint echo from too far off though it prove, should be tenderly saved. If I have spoken of the elements and presences round about us that "counted," Mary Temple was to count, and in more lives than can now be named, to an extraordinary degree; count as a young and shining apparition, a creature who owed to the charm of her every aspect (her aspects were so many!) and the originality, vivacity, audacity, generosity, of her spirit, an indescribable grace and weight—if one might impute weight to a being so imponderable in common scales. Whatever other values on our scene might, as I have hinted, appear to fail, she was one of the first order, in the sense of the immediacy of the impression she produced, and produced altogether as by the play of her own light spontaneity and curiosity—not, that is, as through a sense of such a pressure and such a motive, or through a care for them, in others. "Natural" to an effect of perfect felicity that we were never to see surpassed is what I have already praised all the Albany *cousinage* of those years for being; but in none of the company was the note so clear as in this rarest, though at the same time symptomatically or ominously palest, flower of the stem; who was natural at more points and about more things, with a greater range of freedom and ease and reach of horizon than any of the others dreamed of. They had that way, delightfully, with the small, after all, and the common matters—while she had it with those too, but with the great and rare ones over and above; so that she was to remain for us the very figure and image of a felt interest in life, an interest as magnanimously far-spread, or as familiarly and exquisitely fixed, as her splendid shifting sensibility, moral, personal, nervous, and having at once such noble flights and such touchingly discouraged drops, such graces of indifference and inconsequence, might at any moment determine. She was really to remain, for our appreciation, the supreme case of a taste for life as life, as personal living; of an endlessly active and yet somehow a careless, an illusionless, a sublimely forewarned curiosity about it: something that made her, slim and fair and quick, all straightness and charming tossed head, with long light and yet almost sliding steps and a large light postponing, renouncing laugh, the very muse or amateur priestess of rash speculation. To express her in the mere terms of her restless young mind, one felt from the first, was to place her, by a perversion of the truth, under the shadow of female "earnestness"—for which she was much too unliteral and too ironic; so that, superlatively personal and yet as independent, as "off" into higher spaces, at a touch, as all the breadth of her sympathy and her courage could send her, she made it impossible to say whether she was just the most moving of maidens or a disengaged and dancing flame of thought. No one to come after her could easily seem to show either a quick inward life or a brave, or even a bright, outward, either a consistent contempt for social squalors or a very marked genius for moral reactions. She had in her brief passage the enthusiasm of humanity—more, assuredly, than any charming girl who ever circled, and would fain have continued to circle, round a ballroom. This kept her indeed for a time more interested in the individual, the immediate human, than in the race or the social order at large; but that, on the other hand, made her ever so restlessly, or quite inappeasably, "psychologic." The psychology of others, in her shadow—I mean their general resort to it—could only for a long time seem weak and flat and dim, above all not at all amusing. She burned herself out; she died at twenty-four.

*   *   *

"North Conway"[2] in the foregoing has almost the force for me of a wizard's wand; the figures spring up again and move in a harmony that is not of the fierce present; the sense in particular of the August of '65 shuts me in to its blest unawarenesses not less than to all that was then exquisite in its current certainties and felicities; the fraternising, endlessly conversing group of us gather under the rustling pines—and I admire, precisely, the arrival, the bright revelation as I recover it, of the so handsome young man, marked with military distinction but already, with our light American promptitude, addressed to that high art of peace in which a greater eminence awaited him, of whom this most attaching member of the circle was to make four years later so wise and steady a confidant.[3] Our circle I fondly call it, and doubtless then called it, because in the light of that description I could most rejoice in it, and I think of it now as having formed a little world of easy and happy interchange, of unrestricted and yet all so instinctively sane and secure association and conversation, with all its liberties and delicacies, all its mirth and its earnestness protected and directed so much more from within than from without, that I ask myself, perhaps too fatuously, whether any such right conditions for the play of young intelligence and young friendship, the reading of Matthew Arnold and Browning,[4] the discussion of a hundred human and personal things, the sense of the splendid American summer drawn out to its last generosity, survives to this more complicated age. * * * If drama we could indeed feel this as being, I hasten to add, we owed it most of all to our just having such a heroine that everything else inevitably came. Mary Temple was beautifully and indescribably *that*—in the technical or logical as distinguished from the pompous or romantic sense of the word; wholly without effort or desire on her part—for never was a girl less consciously or consentingly or vulgarly dominant—everything that took place around her took place as if primarily in relation to her and in her interest: that is in the interest of drawing her out and displaying her the more. This too without her in the least caring, as I say—in the deep, the morally nostalgic indifferences that were the most finally characteristic thing about her—whether such an effect took place or not; she liked nothing in the world so much as to see others fairly exhibited; not as they might best please her by being, but as they might most fully reveal themselves, their stuff and their truth: which was the only

2. In New Hampshire's White Mountains; then a summer and now a winter resort.

3. John Chipman Gray (1839–1915); after the Civil War a Boston lawyer, Harvard professor, and eventually dean of Harvard Law School. He was accompanied on this North Conway summer by another young war veteran and Boston lawyer, the future Supreme Court justice Oliver Wendell Holmes (1841–1935).

4. Robert Browning (1812–1889), English poet whose greatest works are almost all dramatic monologues: *Men and Women* (1855), *The Ring and the Book* (1868–69). Matthew Arnold (1822–1888), English poet and critic; his works include *Culture and Anarchy* (1869). James later met both men, and Browning became a friend.

thing that, after any first flutter for the superficial air or grace in an acquaintance, could in the least fix her attention. She had beyond any equally young creature I have known a sense for verity of character and play of life in others, for their acting out of their force or their weakness, whatever either might be, at no matter what cost to herself; and it was this instinct that made her care so for life in general, just as it was her being thereby so engaged in that tangle that made her, as I have expressed it, ever the heroine of the scene. Life claimed her and used her and beset her— made her range in her groping, her naturally immature and unlighted way from end to end of the scale. No one felt more the charm of the actual—only the actual comprised for her kinds of reality (those to which her letters perhaps most of all testify), that she saw treated round her for the most part either as irrelevant or as unpleasant. She was absolutely afraid of noth- ing she might come to by living with enough sincerity and enough wonder; and I think it is because one was to see her launched on that adventure in such bedimmed, such almost tragically compromised conditions that one is caught by her title to the heroic and pathetic mark. It is always difficult for us after the fact not to see young things who were soon to be lost to us as already distinguished by their fate; this particular victim of it at all events might well have made the near witness ask within himself how her restlessness of spirit, the finest reckless impatience, was to be assuaged or "met" by the common lot.

*   *   *

These are great recognitions, but how can I slight for them a mention that has again and again all but broken through in my pages?—that of Francis Boott and his daughter (she to become later on Mrs. Frank Duve- neck and to yield to the same dismal decree of death before her time that rested on so many of the friends of our youth).[5] When I turn in thought to the happiness that our kinswoman was still to have known in her short life, for all her disaster, Elizabeth Boott, delightful, devoted and infinitely under the charm, at once hovers for me; this all the more, I hasten to add, that we too on our side, and not least Mary Temple herself, were under the charm, and that *that* charm, if less immediately pointed, affected all our young collective sensibility as a wondrous composite thing. There was the charm for us—if I must not again speak in assurance but for myself—that "Europe," the irrepressible even as the *ewig Weibliche*[6] of literary allusion was irre- pressible, had more than anything else to do with; and then there was the other that, strange to say (strange as I, once more, found myself feeling it) owed nothing of its authority to anything so markedly out of the picture. The spell to which I in any case most piously sacrificed, most cultivated the sense of, was ever of this second cast—and for the simple reason that the other, serene in its virtue, fairly insolent in its pride, needed no rites and no care. It must be allowed that there was nothing composite in any

5. Francis Boott (1813–1904) was an amateur composer who lived on the proceeds of a Lowell tex- tile factory. A widower, he had moved with his daughter Elizabeth (1846–1888) to Italy at mid- century, where he lived in the Villa Castellani, on the hill of Bellosguardo just outside the old walls of Florence. See James's description of it in "Recent Florence," p. 437 of this Norton Criti- cal Edition. Elizabeth Boott was a serious and accomplished painter, and in 1886 married her former teacher, the American artist Frank Duveneck (1846–1919). The young James first met them in Newport, Rhode Island, where Elizabeth Boott also became a friend of Minny Temple.
6. The eternal feminine; from the very end of Goethe's *Faust, Part II* (1832).

spell proceeding, whether directly or indirectly, from the great Albany connection: this form of the agreeable, through whatever appeals, could certainly not have been more of a piece, as we say—more of a single superfused complexion, an element or principle that we could in the usual case ever so easily and pleasantly account for. The case of that one in the large number of my cousins whom we have seen to be so incomparably the most interesting was of course anything but the usual; yet the Albany origin, the wood-note wild, sounded out even amid her various voices and kept her true, in her way, to something we could only have called local, or perhaps family, type. Essentially, however, she had been a free incalculable product, a vivid exception to rules and precedents; so far as she had at all the value of the "composite" it was on her own lines altogether—the composition was of things that had lain nearest to hand. It mattered enormously for such a pair as the Bootts, intimately associated father and daughter, that what had lain nearest *their* hand, or at least that of conspiring nature and fortune in preparing them for our consumption, had been the things of old Italy, of the inconceivable Tuscany, that of the but lately expropriated Grand Dukes in particular, and that when originally alighting among us *en plein* Newport they had seemed fairly to reek with a saturation, esthetic, historic, romantic, that everything roundabout made precious. I was to apprehend in due course, and not without dismay, that what they really most reeked with was the delight of finding us ourselves exactly as we were; they fell so into the wondrous class of inverted romantics, several other odd flowers of which I was later on to have anxiously to deal with: we and our large crude scene of barbaric plenty, as it might have been called, beguiled them to appreciations such as made our tribute to themselves excite at moments their impatience and strike them as almost silly. It was *our* conditions that were picturesque, and I had to make the best of a time when they themselves appeared to consent to remain so but by the beautiful gaiety of their preference. This, I remember well, I found disconcerting, so that my main affectionate business with them became, under amusement by the way, that of keeping them true to type. What above all contributed was that they really couldn't help their case, try as they would to shake off the old infection; they were of "old world" production through steps it was too late to retrace; and they were in the practical way and in the course of the very next years to plead as guilty to this as the highest proper standard for them could have prescribed. They "went back," and again and again, with a charming, smiling, pleading inconsequence—any pretext but the real one, the fact that the prime poison was in their veins, serving them at need; so that, as the case turned, all my own earlier sense, on the spot, of Florence and Rome was to mix itself with their delightfully rueful presence there. I could then perfectly put up with that flame of passion for Boston and Newport in them which still left so perfect their adaptability to Italian installations that would have been impossible save for subtle Italian reasons.

I speak of course but of the whole original view: time brings strange revenges and contradictions, and all the later history was to be a chapter by itself and of the fullest. We had been all alike accessible in the first instance to the call of those references which played through their walk and conversation with an effect that their qualifying ironies and amusing reactions, where such memories were concerned, couldn't in the least abate; for nothing in fact lent them a happier colour than just this ability to afford so carelessly to cheapen the certain treasure of their past. They had enough of that treasure to give it perpetually away—in our subsequently to be more determined, our present, sense; in short we had the fondest use for their leavings even when they themselves hadn't. Mary Temple, with her own fine quality so far from composite, rejoiced in the perception, however unassisted by any sort of experience, of what their background had "meant"; she would have liked to be able to know just that for herself, as I have already hinted, and I actually find her image most touching perhaps by its so speaking of what she with a peculiar naturalness dreamed of and missed. Of clear old English stock on her father's side, her sense for what was English in life—so we used to simplify—was an intimate part of her, little chance as it enjoyed for happy verifications. In the Bootts, despite their still ampler and more recently attested share in that racial strain, the foreign tradition had exceedingly damped the English, which didn't however in the least prevent her being caught up by it as it had stamped itself upon the admirable, the infinitely civilised and sympathetic, the markedly *produced* Lizzie. This delightful girl, educated, cultivated, accomplished, toned above all, as from steeping in a rich old medium, to a degree of the rarest among her coevals "on our side," had the further, the supreme grace that she melted into American opportunities of friendship— and small blame to her, given such as she then met—with the glee of a sudden scarce believing discoverer. Tuscany could only swoon away under comparison of its starved sociabilities and complacent puerilities, the stress of which her previous years had so known, with the multiplied welcomes and freedoms, the exquisite and easy fellowships that glorified to her the home scene. Into not the least of these quick affinities had her prompt acquaintance with Mary Temple confidently ripened; and with no one in the aftertime, so long as that too escaped the waiting shears, was I to find it more a blest and sacred rite, guarded by no stiff approaches, to celebrate my cousin's memory. That really is my apology for this evocation—which might under straighter connections have let me in still deeper; since if I have glanced on another page of the present miscellany at the traps too often successfully set for my wandering feet my reader will doubtless here recognise a perfect illustration of our danger and will accuse me of treating an inch of canvas to an acre of embroidery. Let the poor canvas figure time and the embroidery figure consciousness—the proportion will perhaps then not strike us as so wrong. Consciousness accordingly still grips me to the point of a felt pressure of interest in such a matter as the recoverable history—history in the esthetic connection at least—of its insistent dealings with a given case. How in the course of time for instance was it not insistently to deal, for a purpose of application, with the fine prime image deposited all unwittingly by the "picturesque" (as I absolutely required to feel it) Boott situation or Boott *data*? The direct or vital value of these last, in so many ways, was experiential, a stored and assimilated thing; but the seed of suggestion proved after long years to have kept itself apart in order that it should develop under a particular breath. A not other than lonely and bereft American, addicted to the arts and endowed for them, housed to an effect of long expatriation in a massive old Florentine villa with a treasured and tended little daughter by his side, *that* was the germ which for reasons beyond my sounding the case of Frank Boott had been appointed to plant deep down in my vision of things.

So lodged it waited, but the special instance, as I say, had lodged it, and it lost no vitality—on the contrary it acquired every patience—by the fact that little by little each of its connections above ground, so to speak, was successively cut. Then at last after years it raised its own head into the air and found its full use for the imagination. An Italianate bereft American with a little moulded daughter in the setting of a massive old Tuscan residence was at the end of years exactly what was required by a situation of my own—conceived in the light of the Novel; and I *had* it there, in the authenticated way, with its essential fund of truth, at once all the more because my admirable old friend had given it to me and none the less because he had no single note of character or temper, not a grain of the non-essential, in common with my Gilbert Osmond. This combination of facts has its shy interest, I think, in the general imaginative or reproductive connection—testifying as it so happens to do on that whole question of the "putting of people into books" as to which any ineptitude of judgment appears always in order. I probably shouldn't have had the Gilbert Osmonds at all without the early "form" of the Frank Bootts, but I still more certainly shouldn't have had them with the *sense* of my old inspirers. The form had to be disembarrassed of that sense and to take in a thoroughly other; thanks to which account of the matter I am left feeling that I scarce know whether most to admire, for support of one's beautiful business of the picture of life, the relation of "people" to art or the relation of art to people. * * *

* * *

Letter to Mary James[†]

Great Malvern[1], March 26, 1870.

Dearest Mother,

I received this morning your letter with father's note, telling me of Minny's death—news more strong and painful that I can find words to express. Your last mention of her condition had been very far from preparing me for this. The event suggests such a host of thoughts—that it seems vain to attempt to utter them. You can imagine all I feel. Minny seemed such a breathing immortal reality that the mere statement of her death conveys little meaning; really to comprehend it I must wait—we must all wait—till time brings with it the poignant sense of loss and irremediable absence. I have been spending the morning letting the awakened swarm of old recollections and associations flow into my mind—almost *enjoying* the exquisite pain they provoke. Wherever I turn in all the recent years of my life I find Minny somehow present, directly or indirectly—and with all that wonderful ethereal brightness of presence which was so peculiarly her own. And now to sit down to the idea of her *death*! As much as a human creature

---

† From *Henry James Letters I*, ed. Leon Edel (Cambridge: The Belknap Press, 1974), pp. 218–19, 221–23. Copyright © 1974 by Leon Edel, editorial. Copyright © 1974 by Alexander R. James, James copyright material. Reprinted with permission. Note is by the editor of this Norton Critical Edition.
1. James was on his first adult trip to Europe when his cousin Minny Temple died. He received the news at the English spa town of Great Malvern; this is one of several letters he wrote from there in response to her death.

may, I fancy, she will survive in the unspeakably tender memory of her friends. No attitude of the heart seems tender and generous enough not to do her some unwilling hurt—now that she has melted away into such a dimmer image of sweetness and weakness! Oh dearest Mother! oh poor struggling suffering *dying* creature! But who complains that she's gone or would have her back to die more painfully? She certainly never seemed to have come into this world for her own happiness—as that of others—or as anything but as a sort of divine reminder and quickness—a transcendent protest against our acquiescence in its grossness. To have known her is certainly an immense gain, but who would have wished her to live longer on such a footing—unless he had felt within him (what I felt little enough!) some irresistible mission to reconcile her to a world to which she was essentially hostile. There is absolute balm in the thought of poor Minny and *rest*—rest and immortal absence!

But viewed in a simple human light, by the eager spirit that insists upon its own—her death is full of overflowing sadness. It comes home to me with irresistible power, the sense of how much I knew her and how much I loved her. As I look back upon the past, from the time I was old enough to feel and perceive, her friendship seems literally to fill it—with proportions magnified doubtless by the mist of tears. I am very glad to have seen so little of her suffering and decline—but nevertheless every word in which you allude to the pleasantness of that last visit has a kind of heartbreaking force. "Dear bright little Minny" as you most happily say: what an impulse one feels to sum up her rich little life in some simple compound of tenderness and awe. Time for you at home will have begun to melt away the hardness of the thought of her being in future a simple memory of the mind—a mere pulsation of the heart: to me as yet it seems perfectly inadmissible. I wish I were at home to hear and talk about her: I feel immensely curious for all the small facts and details of her last week. Write me any gossip that comes to your head. By the time it reaches me it will be very cheerful reading. Try and remember anything she may have said and done. I have been raking up all my recent memories of her and her rare personality seems to shine out with absolute defiant reality. Immortal peace to her memory! I think of her gladly as unchained from suffering and embalmed forever in all our hearts and lives. Twenty years hence what a pure eloquent vision she will be.

But I revert in spite of myself to the hard truth that she is *dead*—silent—absent forever—she the very heroine of our common scene. If you remember any talk of hers about me—any kind of reference or message—pray let me know of it. I wish very much father were able to write me a little more in detail concerning the funeral and anything he heard there. I feel absolutely *vulgarly* eager for any fact whatever. Dear bright little Minny—God bless you dear Mother, for the words. What a pregnant reference in future years—what a secret from those who never knew her! In her last letter to me she spoke of having had a very good photograph taken, which she would send. It has never come. Can you get one—or if you have only the house copy can you have it repeated or copied? I should very much like to have it—for the day when to think of her will be nothing but pure blessedness. Pray, as far as possible, attend to this. Farewell. I am melted down to such an ocean of love that you may be sure you all come in for your share.

Evening. I have had a long walk this afternoon and feel already strangely familiar with the idea of Minny's death. But I can't help wishing that I had been in closer relation with her during her during her last hours—and find a solid comfort at all events in thinking of that long never-to-be-answered letter I wrote to her from Florence. If ever my good genius prompted me, it was then. It is no surprise to me to find that I felt for her an affection as deep as the foundations of my being, for I always knew it; but I now become sensible how her image, softened and sweetened by suffering and sitting patient and yet expectant, so far away from the great world with which so many of her old dreams and impulses were associated, has operated in my mind as a gentle incentive to action and enterprise. There have been so many things I have thought of telling her, so many stories by which I had a fancy to make up her lack to her,—as if she were going to linger on as a graceful invalid to listen to my stories! It was only the other day, however, that I dreamed of meeting her somewhere this summer with Mrs. Post. Poor Minny! how much she was not to see! It's hard to believe that she is not seeing greater things now. On the dramatic fitness—as one may call it—of her early death it seems almost idle to dwell. No one who ever knew her can have failed to look at her future as a sadly insoluble problem—and we almost all had imagination enough to say, to murmur at least, that life—poor narrow life—contained no place for her. How all her conduct and character seem to have pointed to this conclusion—how profoundly inconsequential, in her history, continued life would have been! Every happy pleasant hour in all the long course of our friendship seems to return to me, vivid and eloquent with the light of the present. I think of Newport as with its air vocal with her accents, alive with her movements. But I have written quite enough—more than I expected. I couldn't help thinking this afternoon how strange it is for me to be pondering her death in the midst of this vast indifferent England which she fancied she would have liked. Perhaps! There was no answering in the cold bright landscape for the loss of her liking. Let me think that her eyes are resting on greener pastures than even England's. But how much—how long—we have got to live without her! It's no more than a just penalty to pay, though, for the privilege of having been young with her. It will count in old age, when we live more than now, in reflection, to have had such a figure in our youth.

But I must say farewell. Let me beg you once more to send me any possible talk of reminiscences—no matter how commonplace. I only want to make up for not having seen her—I resent their having buried her in New Rochelle. She ought to be among her own people. Good night. My letter doesn't read over-wise, but I have written off my unreason. You promise me soon a letter from Alice—the sooner the better. Willy I trust will also be writing. Good night, dearest Mother,

Your loving son,
H. James

Write me who was at the funeral and I shall write next from here—then possibly from London.

Letter to Grace Norton[†]

Dec 28*th* 1880[1]

* * *

* * * I am glad you are reading my long story—though that is not the way to read it. My theory is (it may be my conceit again) that it will bear reading again as a whole. It is much the best thing I have done—though not the best I shall do. You are both right and wrong about Minny Temple. I had her in mind and there is in the heroine a considerable infusion of my impression of her remarkable nature. But the thing is not a portrait. Poor Minny was essentially *incomplete* and I have attempted to make my young woman more rounded, more finished. In truth everyone, in life, is incomplete, and it is [in] the work of art that in reproducing them one feels the desire to fill them out, to justify them, as it were. I am delighted if I interest you; I think I shall to the end. * * *

Ever yours
H. James Jr.

From The Notebooks[‡]

Names. Osmond.—Rosier.—Mr. & Mrs. Match.—Name for husband in P. of L.:—*Gilbert Osmond.*—Raymond Gyves.—Mrs. Gift.—Name in *Times*: Lucky Da Costa. Name in Knightsbridge: Tagus Shout. Other names.—Couch.—Bonnycastle.—Theory.—Cridge.—Arrant.—Mrs Tippett.—Noad.

P. of an L. After Isabel's marriage there are *five* more instalments, and the success of the whole story greatly depends upon this portion being well conducted or not.[1] Let me then make the most of it—let me imagine the best. There has been a want of action in the earlier part, and it may be made up here. The elements that remain are, in themselves, I think, very interesting, and they only need to be strongly and happily combined. The weakness of the whole story is that it is too exclusively psychological—that it depends to[o] little on incident; but the complete unfolding of the situation that is established by Isabel's marriage may nonetheless be quite sufficiently dramatic. The idea of the whole thing is that the poor girl, who

† From *Henry James Letters II*, ed. Leon Edel (Cambridge: The Belknap Press, 1975), pp. 323–24. Copyright © 1975 by Leon Edel, editorial. Copyright © 1975 by Alexander R. James, James copyright material. Reprinted by permission. Note is by the editor of this Norton Critical Edition.
1. A Cambridge friend (1834–1926) of the James family, and recipient of many of the novelist's best letters. She had known Minny, and in 1870 James had written to her about his cousin's death.
‡ The text for this excerpt from the first volume of James's *Notebooks* has been established by Philip Horne, working from and newly transcribing the manuscripts held at Harvard University's Houghton Library; this is MS Am 1094 (222la v.1). It will appear in a forthcoming edition of the novelist's complete notebooks from Cambridge University Press as part of their ongoing *Complete Fiction of Henry James*, and is printed in this Norton Critical Edition by permission. James's undated sketch for the long concluding section of *The Portrait of a Lady* was most probably written at the end of December 1880 or just after the turn of the year; the list of names that precedes it dates from some months before.
1. There in fact would be six further installments, not five.

has dreamed of freedom and nobleness, who has done, as she believes, a generous, natural, clear-sighted thing, finds herself in reality ground in the very mill of the conventional. After a year or two of marriage the antagonism between her nature and Osmond's comes out—the open opposition of a noble character and a narrow one. There is a great deal to do here in a small compass; every word, therefore, must tell—every touch must count. If the last five parts of the story appear crowded, this will be rather a good defect in consideration of the perhaps too great diffuseness of the earlier portion. Isabel awakes from her sweet delusion—oh, the art required for making this delusion natural!—and finds herself face to face with a husband who has ended by conceiving a hatred for her own larger qualities. These facts, however, are not in themselves sufficient; the situation must be marked by important events. Such an event is the discovery of the relation that has existed between Osmond and Madame Merle—the discovery that she has married Madame Merle's lover. Madame Merle, in a word, is the mother of Pansy. Edward Rosier comes to Rome, falls in love with Pansy and wants to marry her; but Osmond opposes the marriage, on the ground of Rosier's insufficient means. Isabel favours Pansy—she sees that Rosier would make her an excellent husband, be tenderly devoted and kind to her—but Osmond absolutely forbids the idea. Lord Warburton comes to Rome, sees Isabel again and declares to her that he is resigned, that he has succeeded in accepting the fact of her marriage and that he is now disposed, himself, to marry. He makes the acquaintance of Pansy, is charmed with her, and at last tells Isabel that he should like to make her his wife. Isabel is almost shocked, for she distrusts this sentiment of Lord Warburton's; and the reader must feel that she mistrusts it justly. This same sentiment is a very ticklish business. It is honest up to a certain point; but at bottom, without knowing it, Lord W.'s real motive is the desire to be near Isabel, whom he sees, now, to be a disappointed, and unhappy woman. This is what Isabel has perceived; she feels that it would [be] cruel to Pansy, dangerous to herself, to allow such a marriage—for which however there are such great material inducements that she cannot well oppose it. Her position is a most difficult one, for by begging Lord Warburton to desist she only betrays her apprehension of him—which is precisely what she wishes not to do. Besides, she is afraid of doing a wrong to Pansy. Madame Merle, meanwhile, has caught a glimpse of Warburton's state of mind and eagerly takes up the idea of his marrying the girl. Pansy is very much in love with Rosier—she has no wish to marry Lord W. Isabel is so convinced at last of this that she feels absolved from considering her prospects with Lord W. and treats the latter with such coldness that he feels the vanity of hope and withdraws from the field, having indeed not paid any direct attention to Pansy, whom he cannot in the least be accused of jilting. Madame Merle, very angry at his withdrawal, accuses Isabel of having dissuaded him out of jealousy, because of his having been an old lover of hers and her wishing to keep him for herself; and she still opposes the marriage with Rosier, because she has been made to believe by Lord Warburton's attentions that Pansy may do something much more brilliant. Isabel resents Madame Merle's interference, demands of her what she has to do with Pansy. Whereupon Madame Merle, in whose breast the suppressed feeling of maternity has long been rankling, and who is passionately jealous of Isabel's influence over Pansy, breaks out with the cry that she alone has a right—that Pansy is her daughter. (To be settled later whether this revelation is to be made by Mme Merle herself, or by the Countess Gemini. Better on many grounds that it should be the latter; and yet in that way I lose the "great scene" between Madame Merle and Isabel.) In any event this whole matter of Mme Merle is (like Lord W.'s state of mind about Pansy) a very ticklish one—very delicate and difficult to handle. To make it natural that she should have brought about Isabel's marriage to her old lover—this is in itself a supreme difficulty. It is not, however, an impossibility, for I honestly believe it rests upon nature. Her old interest in Osmond remains in a modified form; she wishes to do something for him, and she does it through another rather than by herself. That, I think, is perfectly natural. As regards Pansy the strangeness of her conduct is greater; but we must remember that we see only its surface—we don't see her reasoning. Isabel has money, and Mme Merle has great confidence in her benevolence, in her generosity; she has no fear that she will be a harsh stepmother, and she believes she will push the fortunes of the child she herself is unable to avow and afraid openly to patronize. In all this Osmond sinks a little into the background—but one must get the sense of Isabel's exquisitely miserable revulsion. Three years have passed—time enough for it to have taken place. His worldliness, his deep snobbishness, his want of generosity, etc.; his hatred of her when he finds that she judges him, that she morally protests at so much that surrounds her. The uncleanness of the air; the Countess Gemini's lovers, etc. Caspar Goodwood of course must reappear, and Ralph, and Henrietta; Mrs. Touchett, too, for a moment. Ralph's helpless observation of Isabel's deep misery; her determination to show him nothing, and his inability to help her. This to be a strong feature in the situation. Pansy is sent back to the convent, to be kept from Rosier. Caspar Goodwood comes to Rome, because he has heard from Henrietta that Isabel is unhappy, and Isabel sends him away. She hears from Ralph, at Gardencourt, that he is ill there (Ralph, himself), that indeed he is dying. (The letter to come from Mrs. Touchett who is with him; or even it would be well that it should be a telegram; it expresses Ralph's wish to see her.) Isabel tells Osmond she wishes to go; Osmond, jealously and nastily, forbids it; and Isabel, deeply distressed and embarrassed, hesitates. Then Madame Merle, who wishes her to make a *coup de tête*, to leave Osmond, so that she may be away from Pansy, reveals to her her belief that it was Ralph who induced his father to leave her the £70,000. Isabel, then, violently affected and overcome, starts directly for England. She reaches Ralph at Gardencourt, and finds Caspar Goodwood and Henrietta also there: i.e., in London. Ralph's death, Isabel's return to London, and interview with Caspar G.— his passionate outbreak; he beseeches her to return with him to America. She is greatly moved, she feels the full force of his devotion—to which she has never done justice; but she refuses. She starts again for Italy—and her departure is the climax and termination of the story.

With strong handling it seems to me that it may all be very true, very powerful, very touching. The obvious criticism of course will be that it is not finished—that I have not seen the heroine to the end of her situation—that I have left her *en l'air.*—This is both true and false. The *whole* of anything is never told; you can only take what groups together. What I have done has that unity—it groups together. It is complete in itself—and the rest may be taken up or not, later.

[*In a darker ink, so written some time later: beginning with a long dash*]

————I am not sure that it would not be best that the exposure of Mme Merle should never be complete, and above all that she should not denounce herself. This would injure very much the impression I have wished to give of her profundity, her self-control, her regard for appearances. It may be enough that Isabel should believe the fact in question—in consequence of what the Countess Gemini has told her. Then, when Madame Merle tells her of what Ralph has done for her of old,—tells it with the view I have mentioned of precipitating her defiance of Osmond—Isabel may charge her with the Countess G.'s secret. This Madame Merle will deny—but deny in such a way that Isabel knows she lies; and then Isabel may depart.—The last (October) instalment to take place wholly in England. At the very last Caspar Goodwood goes to Pratt's hotel, and is told that Mrs. Osmond has left it the night before. Later in the day he sees Henrietta who has the last word—utters the last line of the story: a characteristic characterization of Isabel.

* * *

From The American Journal, 1881–82[†]

Brunswick Hotel, Boston.[1]
November 25th 1881.

If I should write here all that I might write, I should speedily fill this as yet unspotted blank-book, bought in London six months ago, but hitherto unopened. It is so long since I have kept any notes, taken any memoranda, written down my current reflections, taken a sheet of paper, as it were, into my confidence! Meanwhile so much has come and gone, so much that it is now too late to catch, to reproduce, to preserve. I have lost too much by losing, or rather by not having acquired, the note-taking habit. It might be of great profit to me; & now that I am older, that I have more time, that the labour of writing is less onerous to me, & I can work more at my leisure, I ought to endeavour to keep, to a certain extent, a record of passing impressions, of all that comes, that goes, that I see, & feel, & observe. To catch and keep something of life—that's what I mean. Here I am back in America, for instance, after six years of absence, & likely while here to see and learn a great deal that ought not to become mere waste material. Here I am, *da vero,*[2] and here I am likely to be for the next five months. I am glad I have come—it was a wise thing to do. I needed to see again *les*

† From *Henry James: Autobiographies,* ed. Philip Horne (New York: Library of America, 2016), pp. 635–36, 642–46. Notes are by the editor of this Norton Critical Edition.
1. On the corner of Clarendon and Boylston streets.
2. In truth (Italian).

miens,[3] to revive my relations with them, and my sense of the consequences that these relations entail. Such relations, such consequences, are a part of one's life, and the best life, the most complete, is the one that takes full account of such things. One can only do this by seeing one's people from time to time, by being with them, by entering into their lives. Apart from this I hold it was not necessary I should come to this country. I am 37 years old,[4] I have made my choice, & God knows that I have now no time to waste. My choice is the old world—my choice, my need, my life. There is no need for me to-day to argue about this; it is an inestimable blessing to me, and a rare good fortune, that the problem was settled long ago, & that I have now nothing to do but to act on the settlement.—My impressions here are exactly what I expected they would be, & I scarcely see the place, and feel the manners, the race, the tone of things, now that I am on the spot, more vividly than I did while I was still in Europe. My work lies there—and with this vast new world, je n'ai que faire.[5] One can't do both— one must choose. No European writer is called upon to assume that terrible burden, and it seems hard that I should be. The burden is necessarily greater for an American—for he *must* deal, more or less, even if only by implication, with Europe; whereas no European is obliged to deal in the least with America. No one dreams of calling him less complete for not doing so. (I speak of course of people who do the sort of work that I do; not of economists, of social science people.) The painter of manners who neglects America is not thereby incomplete as yet; but a hundred years hence—fifty years hence perhaps—he will doubtless be accounted so. My impressions of America, however, I shall after all, not write here. I don't need to write them (at least not àpropos of Boston;) I know too well what they are. In many ways they are extremely pleasant; but, heaven forgive me! I feel as if my time were terribly wasted here!

* * * In the spring I went to Italy—partly to escape the "Season", which had become a terror to me. I couldn't keep out of it (I had become a highly-developed diner-out, &c,) & its interruptions, its repetitions, its fatigues, were horribly wearisome, & made work extremely difficult. I went to Florence and spent a couple of months, during which I took a short run down to Rome and to Naples, where I had not been since my first visit to Italy, in 1869. I spent three days with Paul Joukowsky[6] at Posilippo, and a couple of days alone at Sorrento. Florence was divine, as usual, and I was a great deal with the Bootts, at that exquisite Bellosguardo.[7] At the Hotel de l'Arno, in a room in that deep recess, in the front, I began the *Portrait of a Lady*—that is I took up, and worked over, an old beginning, made long before. I returned to London to meet William, who came out in the early part of June, & spent a month with me in Bolton St, before going to the

---

3. Mine, my own; i.e., his family (French).

4. He was in fact 38.

5. I have nothing to do (French).

6. James had met the Russian-born Paul Zhukovsky (1845–1912) in Paris and wrote to his family in Cambridge that the two had sworn an "eternal friendship." But in writing of Zhukovsky elsewhere in the *American Journal* James quotes a line from Dante: "*Non ragioniam di lui—ma guarda e passa*" (or in English, "Let's not talk about him; just look and move on"), and the suggestion of James's biographers has been that he was both frightened by and drawn to the Russian's open homosexuality. In Posillipo Zhukovsky was part of the circle around Richard Wagner; he designed the sets for the composer's last opera, *Parsifal* (1882).

7. See n. 5 on p. 422 of this Norton Critical Edition.

continent. That summer and autumn I worked, tant bien que mal,[8] at my novel which began to appear in *Macmillan* in October (1880.) I got away from London more or less—to Brighton, detestable in August, to Folkestone, Dover, St. Leonard's &c. I tried to work hard, and I paid very few visits. I had a plan of coming to America for the winter, and even took my passage; but I gave it up. William came back from abroad & was with me again for a few days, before sailing for home. I spent November & December quietly in London, getting on with the *Portrait*, which went steadily, but very slowly, every part being written twice. About Xmas I went down into Cornwall. * * * I came back to London for a few weeks, and then, again, I went abroad. I wished to get away from the London crowd, the London hubbub, all the entanglements & interruptions of London life; and to quietly bring my novel to a close. So I planned to betake myself to Venice. I started about February 10th and I came back the middle of July following. I have always to pay toll in Paris—it's impossible to pass through. I was there for a fortnight, which I didn't much enjoy. Then I travelled down through France, to Avignon, Marseilles, Nice, Mentone & San Remo, in which latter place I spent three charming weeks, during most of which time I had the genial society of Mrs. Lombard & Fanny L.[9] who came over from Nice for a fortnight. I worked there capitally, and it made me very happy. I used in the morning, to take a walk among the olives, over the hills, behind the queer little black, steep town. Those old paved roads that rise behind and above San Remo, and climb and wander through the dusky light of the olives, have an extraordinary sweetness. Below and beyond, were the deep ravines, on whose sides old villages were perched, and the blue sea, glittering through the grey foliage. Fanny L. used to go with me—enjoying it so much that it was a pleasure to take her. I went back to the inn to breakfast (that is, lunch) and scribbled for 3 or 4 hours in the afternoon. Then, in the fading light, I took another stroll, before dinner. We went to bed early, but I used to read late. I went with the Lombards, one lovely day, on an enchanting drive—to the strange little old mountain town of Ceriana. I shall never forget that; it was one of the things one remembers; the grand clear hills, among which we wound higher and higher; the long valleys, swimming seaward, far away beneath; the bright Mediterranean, growing paler and paler as we rose above it; the splendid stillness, the infinite light, the clumps of olives, the brown villages, pierced by the carriage road, where the vehicle bumped against opposite doorposts. I spent ten days at Milan after that, working at my tale & scarcely speaking to a soul; Milan was cold, dull, & less attractive than it had been to me before. Thence I went straight to Venice, where I remained till the last of June—between three and four months. It would take long to go into that now; and yet I can't simply pass it by. It was a charming time; one of those things that don't repeat themselves; I seemed to myself to grow young again. The lovely Venetian spring came and went, and brought with it an infinitude of impressions, of delightful hours. I became passionately fond of the place, of the life, of the people, of the habits. I asked myself at times whether it wouldn't be a happy thought to

8. More or less; for better or worse (French).
9. Mother and daughter; Cambridge friends of the James family.

take a little pied-à-terre there, which one might keep forever. I looked at
unfurnished apartments; I fancied myself coming back every year. I *shall*
go back; but not every year. Herbert Pratt was there for a month, and I
saw him tolerably often; he used to talk to me about Spain, about the East,
about Tripoli, Persia, Damascus; till it seemed to me that life would be
manquée[1] altogether if one shouldn't have some of that knowledge. He was
a most singular, a most interesting type, and I shall certainly put him into
a novel.[2] I shall even make the portrait close, and he won't mind. Seeing
picturesque lands, simply for their own sake, and without making any use
of it—that, with him, is a passion—a passion of which if one lives with
him a little (a little, I say; not too much) one feels the contagion. He gave
me the nostalgia of the sun, of the south, of colour, of freedom, of being
one's own master, and doing absolutely what one pleases. He used to say
"I know such a sunny corner, under the South wall of old Toledo. There's
a wild fig growing there; I have lain on the grass, with my guitar. There
was a musical muleteer, &c." I remember one evening when he took me to
a queer little wine shop, haunted only by gondoliers & facchini,[3] in an out
of the way corner of Venice. We had some excellent muscat wine; he had
discovered the place and made himself quite at home there. Another evening I went with him to his rooms—far down on the Grand Canal, overlooking the Rialto. It was a hot night; the cry of the gondoliers came up
from the Canal. He took out a couple of Persian books and read me extracts
from Firdausi and Saadi.[4] A good deal might be done with Herbert Pratt.
He, however, was but a small part of my Venice. I lodged on the Riva, 4161
4^0 p^0. The view from my windows was "una bellezza;"[5] the far-shining
lagoon, the pink walls of San Giorgio, the downward curve of the Riva,
the distant islands, the movement of the quay, the gondolas in profile. Here
I wrote, diligently every day & finished, or virtually finished, my novel. As
I say, it was a charming life; it seemed to me at times, too improbable, too
festive. I went out in the morning—first to Florian's, to breakfast; then to
my bath, at the Stabilimento Chitarin; then I wandered about, looking at
pictures, street life &c, till noon, when I went for my real breakfast to the
Café Quadri.[6] After this I went home and worked till six o'clock—& sometimes only till five. In this latter case I had time for an hour or two en
gondole before dinner. The evenings I strolled about, went to Florian's,
listened to the music in the Piazza, & two or three nights a week went to
Mrs. Bronson's. That was a resource—but the milieu was too American.
Late in the spring came Mrs. V. R.,[7] from Rome, who was an even greater
resource. I went with her one day to Torcello, & Burano; where we took
our lunch and ate it on a lovely canal at the former place. Toward the last

1. Lacking (French).
2. He did; Herbert Pratt (1841–1915), a Cambridge friend of William James, became the endlessly talkative Gabriel Nash in *The Tragic Muse* (1890).
3. Porters.
4. Abu l'Qasim Ferdowsi Tusi (c. 940–1020), Persian poet, author of the Shanameh or Book of
Kings; Saadi Shirazi (c. 1210–c. 1291), Persian poet, aphorist, and moralist.
5. The Riva degli Schiavoni is the great waterfront esplanade that begins where the Grand Canal
opens out into the Venetian lagoon. James's rooms were on the fourth floor, and his view was a
beauty: the sixteenth-century San Giorgio Maggiore, built to designs by Palladio, sits on a
small island across the lagoon.
6. Florian's and the Café Quadri are the oldest and grandest cafes in the Piazza San Marco, and
still very much in business.
7. Katherine De Kay Bronson (1834–1901), originally from New York, owned a small house, the
Casa Alvisi, on the Grand Canal, that was a center of the city's expatriate life; *Italian Hours*
contains a memorial essay to her. Mrs. V. R. was probably Anne Van Rensselaer.

of April I went down to Rome and spent a fortnight—during part of which I was laid up with one of those terrible attacks in my head. But Rome was very lovely; I saw a great deal of Mrs. V. R.: had (with her) several beautiful drives. One in particular I remember; out beyond the Ponte Normentano, a splendid Sunday. We left the carriage & wandered into the fields, where we sat down for some time. The exquisite stillness, the divine horizon, brought back to me out of the buried past all that ineffable, incomparable impression of Rome. (1869, 1873.) I returned to Venice by Ancona and Rimini. From Ancona I drove to Loreto, and, on the same occasion, to Recanati, to see the house of Giacomo Leopardi,[8] whose infinitely touching letters I had been reading while in Rome. The day was lovely and the excursion picturesque; but I was not allowed to enter Leopardi's house. I saw, however, the dreary little hill-town where he passed so much of his life, with its enchanting beauty of site, and its strange, bright loneliness. I saw the streets—I saw the views he looked upon. . . . Very little can have changed. I spent only an evening at Rimini, where I made the acquaintance of a most obliging officer, who seemed delighted to converse with a forestiero,[9] and who walked me (it was a Sunday evening) all over the place. I passed near *Urbino*: that is I passed a station, where I might have descended to spend the night, to drive to Urbino the next day. But I didn't stop! If I had been told that a month before, I should have repelled the foul insinuation. But my reason was strong. I was so nervous about my interrupted work that every day I lost was a misery, and I hurried back to Venice and to my MS. But I made another short absence, in June—a 5 days' giro to Vicenza, Bassano, Padua. At Vicenza I spent 3 of these days—it was wonderfully sweet; old Italy, and the old feeling of it. Vivid in my memory is the afternoon I arrived, when I wandered into the Piazza and sat there in the warm shade, before a caffè, with the smooth slabs of the old pavement around me, the big palace & the tall campanile opposite, &c. It was so soft, so mellow, so quiet, so genial, so Italian; very little movement, only the waning of the bright day, the approach of the summer night. Before I left Venice the heat became intense, the days and nights alike impossible. I left it at last, and closed a singularly happy episode; but I took much away with me.

I went straight to the Lake of Como and over the Splügen spent only a lovely evening (with the next morning) at Cadenabbia. I mounted the Splügen under a splendid sky, and I shall never forget the sensation of rising, as night came (I walked incessantly, after we began to ascend) into that cool pure Alpine air, out of the stifling *calidarium* of Italy. I shall always remember a certain glass of fresh milk which I drank that evening, in the gloaming, far up, (a woman at a wayside hostel had it fetched from the cow) as the most heavenly draft that ever passed my lips. I went straight to Lucerne, to see Mrs. Kemble,[1] who had already gone to Engelberg. I spent a day on the lake, making the giro; it was a splendid day, & Switzerland looked more sympathetic than I had ventured to hope. I went up to Engelberg, & spent nearly a week with Mrs. Kemble & Miss Butler, in that grim, ragged, rather vacuous, but by no means absolutely unbeautiful valley.

8. Giacomo Leopardi (1798–1837), Italian poet, essayist, aphorist, and thinker.
9. Foreigner (Italian).
1. Fanny Kemble (1809–1893), English actress, memoirist, and raconteur from whom James got many of his best anecdotes.

Recent Florence[†]

I have never known Florence more charming than I found her for a week in this brilliant October. She sat in the sunshine beside her yellow river like the little treasure-city that she has always seemed, without commerce, without other industry than the manufacture of mosaic paper-weights and alabaster Cupids, without actuality, or energy, or earnestness, or any of those rugged virtues which in most cases are deemed indispensable for civic robustness; with nothing but the little unaugmented stock of her mediæval memories, her tender-colored mountains, her churches and palaces, pictures and statues. There were very few strangers; one's detested fellow sight-seer was infrequent; the native population itself seemed scanty; the sound of wheels in the streets was but occasional; by eight o'clock at night, apparently, every one had gone to bed, and the wandering tourist, still wandering, had the place to himself,—had the thick shadow-masses of the great palaces, and the shafts of moonlight striking the polygonal paving-stones, and the empty bridges, and the silvered yellow of the Arno, and the stillness broken only by a homeward step, accompanied by a snatch of song from a warm Italian voice. My room at the inn looked out on the river, and was flooded all day with sunshine. There was an absurd orange-colored paper on the walls; the Arno, of a hue not altogether different, flowed beneath, and on the other side of it rose a line of sallow-fronted houses, of extreme antiquity, crumbling and moldering, bulging and protruding over the stream. (I talk of their fronts; but what I saw was their shabby backs, which were exposed to the cheerful flicker of the river, while the fronts stood forever in the deep, damp shadow of a narrow medæval street.) All this brightness and yellowness was a perpetual delight; it was a part of that indefinably charming color which Florence always seems to wear as you look up and down at it from the river, from the bridges and quays. This is a kind of grave brilliancy—a harmony of high tints—which I am at a loss to describe. There are yellow walls and green blinds and red roofs, and intervals of brilliant brown and natural-looking blue; but the picture is not spotty or gaudy, thanks to the colors being distributed in large and comfortable masses, and to its being washed over, as it were, by I cannot say what happy softness of sunshine. The river-front of Florence is, in short, a delightful composition. Part of its charm comes, of course, from the generous aspect of those high-based old Tusean palaces which a renewal of acquaintance with them has again commended to me as the most dignified dwellings in the world. Nothing can be finer than that look of giving up the whole immense area and elevation of the ground-floor to simple purposes of vestibule and staircase, of court and high-arched entrance; as if this were all but a massive pedestal for the real habitation, and people were not properly housed unless, to begin with, they should be lifted fifty feet above the pavement. The great blocks of the basement, the great intervals, horizontally and vertically, from window to window (telling of the height and breadth of the rooms within); the armorial

† From "Recent Florence," *Atlantic Monthly* 41.247 (May 1878): 586–88.

shield hung forward at one of the angles; the wide-brimmed roof, over-shadowing the narrow street; the rich old browns and yellows of the walls,—these simple elements are put together with admirable art.

Take one of these noble structures out of its oblique situation in town; call it no longer a palace, but a villa; set it down upon a terrace, on one of the hills that encircle Florence, with a row of high-waisted cypresses beside it, a grassy court-yard, and a view of the Florentine towers and the valley of the Arno, and you will think it perhaps even more impressive and pic-turesque. It was a Sunday noon, and brilliantly warm, when I arrived in Florence; and after I had looked from my windows awhile at that quietly-basking river-front I have spoken of, I took my way across one of the bridges and then out of one of the gates,—that immensely tall old Roman Gate, whereof the space from the top of the arch to the cornice (except that there is scarcely a cornice, it is all a plain, massive piece of wall) is as great (or seems to be) as that from the ground to the former point. Then I climbed a steep and winding way—much of it a little dull, if one likes, being bounded by mottled, mossy garden walls—to a villa on a hill-top, where I found various things that seemed to resolve my journey into a sort of pil-grimage of admiration and envy.[1] Seeing them again, often, for a week, both by sunlight and moonshine, I never quite learned not to covet them; not to feel that not being a part of them was somehow to miss a particular little chance of felicity. What a tranquil, contented life it seemed, with exquisite beauty as a part of its daily texture!—the sunny terrace, with its tangled *podere*[2] beneath it; the bright gray olives against the bright blue sky; the long, serene, horizontal lines of other villas, flanked by their upward cypresses, disposed upon the neighboring hills; the richest little city in the world in a softly-scooped hollow at one's feet, and beyond it the most beautiful of views, changing color, shifting shadows, and through all its changes remaining grandly familiar. Within the villa was a great love of art and a painting-room full of successful work, so that if human life there seemed very tranquil, the tranquillity meant simply contentment and devoted occupation. A beautiful occupation in that beautiful position, what could possibly be better? That is what I spoke just now of envying, a way of life that is not afraid of a little isolation and tolerably quiet days. When such a life presents itself in a dull or an ugly place, we esteem it, we admire it, but we do not feel it to be the ideal of good fortune. When, however, the people who lead it move as figures in an ancient, noble land-scape, and their walks and contemplations are like a turning of the leaves of history, we seem to be witnessing an admirable case of virtue made easy; meaning here by virtue, contentment and concentration, the love of privacy and of study. One need not be exacting if one lives among local conditions that are of themselves constantly suggestive. It is true, indeed, that I might, after a certain time, grow weary of a regular afternoon stroll among the Florentine lanes; of the sitting on low parapets, in intervals of flower-topped wall, and looking across at Fiesole, or down the rich-hued valley of the Arno towards Pisa and the sea; of pausing at the open gates of villas and wondering at the height of cypresses and the depth of loggias; of walking home in the fading light and noting on a dozen westward-looking

1. See the note on p. 422 of this Norton Critical Edition.
2. Farm (Italian).

surfaces the glow of the opposite sunset. But for a week or so all this was a charming entertainment. The villas are innumerable, and, if one is a stranger, half the talk is about villas. This one has a story; that one has another; they all look as if they had stories. Most of them are offered to rent (many of them for sale) at prices unnaturally low; you may have a tower and a garden, a chapel and a stretch of thirty windows, for three or four hundred dollars a year. In imagination, you hire three or four; you take possession, and settle, and live there. About the finest there is something very grave and stately; about two or three of the best there is something even solemn and tragic. From what does this latter impression come? You gather it as you stand there in the early dusk, looking at the long, pale-brown façade, the enormous windows, the iron cages fastened upon the lower ones. Part of the sadness of aspect of these great houses comes, even when they have not fallen into decay, from their look of having outlived their original use. Their extraordinary largeness and massiveness are a satire upon their present fate. They were not built with such a thickness of wall and depth of embrasure, such a solidity of staircase and superfluity of stone, simply to afford an economical winter residence to English and American families. I don't know whether it was the appearance of these strong old villas, which seemed so dumbly conscious of a change of manners, that threw a tinge of melancholy over the general prospect; certain it is that, having always found this plaintive note in the beautiful harmony of the view, it seemed to me now particularly distinct. "Lovely, lovely, but oh, how sad!" the fanciful stranger could not but murmur to himself as, in the late afternoon, he looked at the view from over one of the low parapets, and then, with his hands in his pockets, turned away indoors to candles and dinner.

* * *

A Roman Holiday[†]

* * *

If you stop, however, to observe everything worthy of your water-colors, you will never reach the Lateran.[1] My business was much less with the interior of St. John Lateran, which I have never found peculiarly interesting, than with certain charming features of its surrounding precinct,—the crooked old court beside it, which admits you to the Baptistery and to a delightful rear-view of the queer architectural odds and ends which in Rome may compose a florid ecclesiastical façade. There are more of these, a stranger jumble of chance detail, of lurking recesses and wanton projections and inexplicable windows, than I have memory or phrases for; but

---

† From "A Roman Holiday," *Atlantic Monthly* 32.189 (July 1873): 6–11.
1. St. John Lateran. See the note on p. 354 of this Norton Critical Edition. "A Roman Holiday" is studded with allusions to and descriptions of the city's archaeological and architectural features, and James's all-too-knowing style depends on the assumption that the reader will recognize his references. Many of them have already been noted in the text of *The Portrait of a Lady* itself; of those that are not, the most important is the Basilica of Santa Maria Maggiore, built in the fifth century and notable for both its mosaics and the marble columns taken from earlier classical buildings that support its nave.

the gem of the collection is the oddly perched peaked turret, with its yellow travertine welded upon the rusty brick-work, which was not meant to be suspected, and the brick-work retreating beneath and leaving it in the odd position of a tower *under* which you may see the sky. As to the great front of the church overlooking the Porta San Giovanni, you are not admitted behind the scenes; the phrase is quite in keeping, for the architecture has a vastly theatrical air. It is extremely imposing,—that of St. Peter's alone is more so; and when from far off on the Campagna you see the colossal images of the mitred saints along the top standing distinct against the sky, you forget their coarse construction and their breezy draperies. The view from the great space which stretches from the church steps to the city wall is the very prince of views. Just beside you, beyond the great portico of mosaics, is the Scala Santa, the marble staircase on which (says the legend) Christ descended under the weight of Pilate's judgment, and which all Christians must forever ascend on their knees; before you is the city gate which opens upon the Via Appia Nuova, the long gaunt file of arches of the Claudian aqueduct, their jagged ridge stretching away like the vertebral column of some monstrous, mouldering skeleton, and upon the blooming brown and purple flats and dells of the Campagna and the glaring blue of the Alban Mountains, spotted with their white, high-nestling towns, all beautifully named,—Grotta Ferrata, Rocca di Papa, Castel Gandolfo, Albano, Palestrina; and to your left is the great grassy space lined with dwarfish mulberry-trees, which stretches across to the damp little sister-basilica of Santa Croce in Gerusalemme. During a former visit to Rome I lost my heart to this idle tract, and wasted much time in sitting on the steps of the church and watching certain white-cowled friars who were sure to be passing there for the delight of my eyes. There are fewer friars now, and there are a great many of the king's recruits who inhabit the ex-conventual barracks adjoining Santa Croce, and are led forward to practise their goose-step on the sunny turf. Here, too, the poor old cardinals who are no longer to be seen on the Pincio, descend from their mourning-coaches and relax their venerable knees. These members alone still testify to the traditional splendor of the princes of the Church; for as they advance, the lifted black petticoat reveals a flash of scarlet stockings, and makes you groan at the victory of civilization over color.

If St. John Lateran disappoints you internally, you have an easy compensation in traversing the long lane which connects it with Santa Maria Maggiore and entering the singularly perfect nave of that most delightful of churches. The first day of my stay in Rome, under the old dispensation, I spent in wandering at random through the city, with accident for my *valet de place*. It served me to perfection and introduced me to the best things, among others to Santa Maria Maggiore. First impressions, memorable impressions, are generally irrecoverable; they often leave one the wiser, but they rarely return in the same form. I remember of my coming uninformed and unprepared into Santa Maria Maggiore, only that I sat for half an hour on the edge of the base of one of the marble columns of the beautiful nave and enjoyed a perfect feast of fancy. The place seemed to me so endlessly suggestive that perception became a sort of throbbing confusion of images, and I departed with a sense of knowing a good deal that is not set down in Murray.[2] I have sat down more than once at the base of the same column again; but you live your life but once, the parts as well as the whole. The obvious charm of the church is the elegant grandeur of the nave,—its perfect shapeliness and its rich simplicity, its long double row of white marble columns and its high flat roof, embossed with intricate gildings and mouldings. It opens into a choir of an extraordinary splendor of effect, which I recommend you to visit of a fine afternoon. At such a time, the glowing western light, entering the high windows of the tribune, kindles the scattered masses of color into sombre brightness, scintillates on the great solemn mosaic of the vault, touches the porphyry columns of the superb *baldachino* with ruby lights, and buries its glaring shafts in the deep-toned shadows which cluster over frescos and sculptures and mouldings. The deeper charm to me, however, is the social atmosphere of the church, as I must call it for want of a better term,—the sense it gives you, in common with most of the Roman churches and more than any of them, of having been prayed in for several centuries by a singularly complicated and picturesque society. It takes no great shrewdness to perceive that the social *rôle* of the Church in Italy is terribly shrunken nowadays; but also as little, perhaps, to feel that, as they stand, these deserted temples were produced by a society leavened through and through by ecclesiastical manners, and that they formed for ages the constant background of the human drama. They are, as one may say, the *churchiest* churches in Europe,—the fullest of gathered detail and clustering association. There is not a figure that I have read of in history, fiction, or poetry pertaining to Italy,—and dreamed of in consequence,—that I cannot imagine in its proper place kneeling before the lamp-decked Confession beneath the altar of Santa Maria Maggiore. One sees after all, however, even among the most palpable realities, very much what one's capricious intellect projects there; and I present my remarks simply as a reminder that one's constant excursions into churches are not the least interesting episodes of one's walks in Rome.

*　*　*

I owe the reader amends for writing either of Roman churches or of Roman walks, without an allusion to St. Peter's. I go there often on rainy days, with prosaic intentions of "exercise," and carry them out, body and mind. As a mere *promenade*, St. Peter's is unequalled. It is better than the Boulevards, than Piccadilly or Broadway, and if it were not the most beautiful place in the world, it would be the most entertaining. Few great works of art last longer to one's curiosity. You think you have taken its measure; but it expands again, and leaves your vision shrunken. I never let the ponderous leather curtain bang down behind me, without feeling as if all former visits were but a vague prevision, and this the first crossing of the threshold. Tourists will never cease to be asked, I suppose, if they have not been disappointed in the size of St. Peter's; but a few modest spirits, here and there, I hope, will never cease to say No. It seemed to me from the first the hugest thing conceivable,—a real exaltation of one's idea of space; so that one's entrance, even from the great empty square, glaring beneath the deep blue sky, or cool in the far-cast shadow of the immense

2. See p. 201 of this Norton Critical Edition.

façade, seems not so much a going in somewhere as a going out. I should confidently recommend a first glimpse of the interior to a man of pleasure in quest of new sensations, as one of the strongest the world affords. There are days when the vast nave looks vaster than at others, and the gorgeous baldachino a longer journey beyond the far-spreading tesselated plain of the pavement, when the light has a quality which lets things look their largest, and the scattered figures mark happily the scale of certain details. Then you have only to stroll and stroll, and gaze and gaze, and watch the baldachino lift its bronze architecture, like a temple within a temple, and feel yourself, at the bottom of the abysmal shaft of the dome, dwindle to a crawling dot. Much of the beauty of St. Peter's resides, I think, in the fact that it is all *general* beauty, that you are appealed to by no specific details, that the details indeed, when you observe them, are often poor and sometimes ridiculous. The sculptures, with the sole exception of Michael Angelo's admirable *Pietà*, which lurks obscurely in a dusky chapel, are either bad or indifferent; and the universal incrustation of marble, though sumptuous enough, has a less brilliant effect than much later work of the same sort,—that, for instance, of St. Paul's without the Walls. The supreme beauty of the church is its magnificently sustained simplicity. It seems—as it is—a realization of the happiest mood of a colossal imagination. The happiest mood, I say, because this is the only one of Michael Angelo's works in the presence of which you venture to be cheerful. You may smile in St. Peter's without a sense of sacrilege, which you can hardly do, if you have a tender conscience, in Westminster Abbey or Notre Dame. The abundance of enclosed light has much to do with your smile. There are no shadows, to speak of, no marked effects of shade; but effects of light innumerable,—points at which the light seems to mass itself in airy density, and scatter itself in enchanting gradations and cadences. It performs the office of shadow in Gothic churches; hangs like a rolling mist along the gilded vault of the nave, melts into bright interfusion the mosaic scintillations of the dome, clings and clusters and lingers and vivifies the whole vast atmosphere. A good Catholic, I suppose, is a Catholic anywhere, in the grandest as well as in the humblest churches; but to a traveller not especially pledged to be devout, St. Peter's speaks more of contentment than of aspiration. The mind seems to expand there immensely, but on its own level, as we may say. It marvels at the reach of the human imagination and the vastness of our earthly means. This is heaven enough, we say: what it lacks in beauty it makes up in certainty. And yet if one's half-hours at St. Peter's are not actually spent on one's knees, the mind reverts to its tremendous presence with an ardor deeply akin to a passionate effusion of faith. When you are weary of the swarming democracy of your fellow-tourists, of the unremunerative aspects of human nature on the Corso and Pincio, of the oppressively frequent combination of coronets on carriage panels and stupid faces in carriages, of addled brains and lacquered boots, of ruin and dirt and decay, of priests and beggars and the myriad tokens of a halting civilization, the image of the great temple depresses the balance of your doubts and seems to refute the invasive vulgarity of things, and assure you that nothing great is impossible. It is a comfort, in other words, to feel that there is nothing but a cab-fare between your discontent and one of the greatest of human achievements.

* * *

Roman Rides[†]

ROME, last of April.
I shall always remember the first I took: out of the Porta del Popolo[1] to where the Ponte Molle, whose single arch sustains a weight of historic tradition, compels the sallow Tiber to flow between its four great *mannered* ecclesiastical statues, over the crest of the hill, and along the old posting-road to Florence. It was mild midwinter, the season, peculiarly, of color on the Roman Campagna; and the light was full of that mellow purple glow, that tempered intensity, which haunts the after-visions of those who have known Rome like the memory of some supremely irresponsible pleasure. An hour away, I pulled up, and stood for some time at the edge of a meadow, gazing away into remoter distances. Then and there, it seemed to me, I measured the deep delight of knowing the Campagna. But I saw more things in it than it is easy to repeat. The country rolled away around me into slopes and dells of enchanting contour, checkered with purple and blue and blooming brown. The lights and shadows were at play on the Sabine Mountains,—an alternation of tones so exquisite that you can indicate them only by some fantastic comparison to sapphire and amber. In the foreground a *contadino*,[2] in his cloak and peaked hat, was jogging solitary on his ass; and here and there in the distance, among blue undulations, some white village, some gray tower, helped deliciously to make the scene the typical "Italian landscape" of old-fashioned art. It was so bright and yet so sad, so still, and yet so charged, to the supersensuous ear, with the murmur of an extinguished life, that you could only say it was intensely and deliciously strange, and that the Roman Campagna is the most suggestive place in the world. To ride once, under these circumstances, is of course to ride again, and to allot to the Campagna a generous share of the time one spends in Rome.

It is a pleasure that doubles one's horizon, and one can scarcely say whether it enlarges or limits one's impression of the city proper. It certainly makes St. Peter's seem a trifle smaller, and blunts the edge of one's curiosity in the Forum. If you have ridden much, to think of Rome afterwards will be, I imagine, to think still respectfully and regretfully enough of the Vatican and the Pincio, the streets and the duskily picturesque street-life; but it will be even more to wonder, with an irrepressible contraction of the heart, when again you shall feel yourself bounding over the flower-smothered turf, or pass from one framed picture to another beside the open arches of the crumbling aqueducts. You look at Rome so often from some grassy hill-top—hugely compact within its walls, with St. Peter's overtopping all things and yet seeming small, and the vast girdle of marsh and meadow receding on all sides to the mountains and the sea—that you come to remember it at last as hardly more than a large detail in an

---

† From "Roman Rides," *Atlantic Monthly* 32.190 (August 1873): 190–91, 193–94, 196–98.
1. This ancient gate was, until the arrival of the railroad, the traditional point of departure for travelers heading to the north of Italy, and of course the storied point of arrival for those arriving from that direction; see Goethe's account of his entrance through it into "the hub of the world" in his *Italian Journey*. In James's day an Englishman named Jarrett kept a livery stable in the nearby Piazza del Popolo, from which the novelist rented his horse.
2. Peasant (Italian).

impressive landscape. And within the walls you think of your intended ride as a sort of romantic possibility; of the Campagna generally as an illimitable experience. One's rides certainly make Rome a richer place to live in than most others. To dwell in a city which, much as you grumble at it, is, after all, very fairly a modern city; with crowds, and shops, and theatres, and *cafés*, and balls, and receptions, and dinner-parties, and all the modern confusion of social pleasures and pains; to have at your door the good and evil of it all; and yet to be able in half an hour to gallop away and leave it a hundred miles, a hundred years, behind, and to look at the tufted broom glowing on a lonely tower-top in the still blue air, and the pale pink asphodels trembling none the less for the stillness, and the shaggy-legged shepherds leaning on their sticks in motionless brotherhood, with the heaps of ruin and the scrambling goats and staggering little kids treading out wild desert smells from the top of hollow-sounding mounds; and then to come back through one of the great gates, and, a couple of hours later, find yourself in the "world," dressed, introduced, entertained, inquisitive, talking about *Middlemarch*[3] to a young English lady, or listening to Neapolitan songs from a gentleman in a very low-cut shirt,—all this is to lead a sort of double life, and to gather from the hurrying hours more impressions than a mind of modest capacity quite knows how to dispose of. * * *

The Campagna differs greatly on the two sides of the Tiber; and it is hard to say which, for the rider, has the greater charm. The half-dozen rides you may take from the Porta San Giovanni possess the perfection of traditional Roman interest, and lead you through a far-strewn wilderness of ruins,—a scattered maze of tombs and towers and nameless fragments of antique masonry. The landscape here has two great features; close before you on one side is the long, gentle swell of the Alban Mountains, deeply, fantastically blue in most weathers, and marbled with the vague white masses of their scattered towns and villas. It is hard to fancy a softer curve than that with which the mountain sweeps down from Albano to the plain; it is a perfect example of the classic beauty of line in the Italian landscape,—that beauty which, when it fills the background of a picture, makes us look in the foreground for a broken column bedded in flowers, and a shepherd piping to dancing nymphs. At your side, constantly, you have the broken line of the Claudian Aqueduct carrying its broad arches far away into the plain. The meadows along which it lies are not the smoothest in the world for a gallop, but there is no pleasure greater than to wander over it. It stands knee-deep in the flower-strewn grass, and its rugged piers are hung with ivy, as the columns of a church are draped for a *festa*. Every archway is a picture, massively framed, of the distance beyond,—of the snow-tipped Sabines and lonely Soracte. As the spring advances, the whole Campagna smiles and waves with flowers; but I think they are nowhere more rank and lovely than in the shifting shadow of the aqueducts, where they muffle the feet of the columns and smother the half-dozen brooks which wander in and out like silver meshes between the legs of a file of giants. They make a niche for themselves, too, in every crevice and tremble on the vault of the empty conduits. The ivy hereabouts, in the

---

3. Novel by George Eliot, first published as a serial in 1871–72. James's review of it appeared in *Galaxy*, an American monthly, in March 1873.

springtime, is peculiarly brilliant and delicate; and though it cloaks and muffles these Roman fragments far less closely than the castles and abbeys of England, it hangs with the light elegance of all Italian vegetation. It is partly, doubtless, because their mighty outlines are still unsoftened that the aqueducts are so impressive. They seem the very source of the solitude in which they stand; they look like architectural spectres, and loom through the light mists of their grassy desert, as you recede along the line, with the same insubstantial vastness as if they rose out of Egyptian sands.[4] It is a great neighborhood of ruins, many of which, it must be confessed, you have applauded in many an album. But station a peasant with sheepskin coat and bandaged legs in the shadow of the tomb or tower best known to drawing-room art, and scatter a dozen goats on the mound above him, and the picture has a charm which has not yet been sketched away.

* * *

This unbroken continuity of impressions which I have tried to indicate is an excellent example of the intellectual background of all enjoyment in Rome. It effectually prevents pleasure from becoming vulgar, for your sensation rarely begins and ends with itself; it never berates; it recalls, commemorates, resuscitates something else. At least half the merit of everything you enjoy must be that it suits you absolutely; but the larger half, here, is generally that it has suited some one else, and that you can never flatter yourself you have discovered it. It is historic, literary, suggestive; it has played some other part than it is just then playing to your eyes. It was an admission of this truth that my discriminating friend who showed me the Claudes[5] found it impossible to designate a certain delightful region which you enter at the end of an hour's riding from the Porta Cavalleggieri as anything but Arcadia. The exquisite correspondence of the term in this case altogether revived its faded bloom; here veritably the oaten pipe must have stirred the windless air, and the satyrs have laughed among the brookside reeds. Three or four long grassy dells stretch away in a chain between low hills over which slender trees are so discreetly scattered that each one is a resting-place for a shepherd. The elements of the scene are simple enough, but the composition has extraordinary refinement. By one of those happy chances which keep observation, in Italy, always in her best humor, a shepherd had thrown himself down under one of the trees in the very attitude of Melibœus.[6] He had been washing his feet, I suppose, in the neighboring brook, and had found it pleasant afterwards to roll his short breeches well up on his thighs. Lying thus in the shade, on his elbow, with his naked legs stretched out on the turf, and his soft peaked hat over his long hair crushed back like the veritable bonnet of Arcady, he was exactly the figure for the background of this happy valley. The poor fellow, lying there in rustic weariness and ignorance, little fancied that he was a symbol of Old World meanings to New World eyes. Such eyes may find as great a store of picturesque meanings in the corkwoods of Monte Mario, tenderly loved of all equestrians. These are less severely pastoral

4. Cf. Percy Bysshe Shelley, "Ozymandias" (1818).
5. Claude Lorrain (ca. 1600–1682), French painter who made his career in Rome. He is celebrated for his landscapes, which draw on the features of the Roman Campagna or countryside to produce an image of eternity.
6. A herdsman; one of the speakers in the first of the ten pastoral poems that make up Virgil's *Eclogues* (ca. 39–38 B.C.E.).

than our Arcadia, and you might more properly lodge there a damsel of Ariosto than a nymph of Theocritus.[7] Among them is strewn a lovely wilderness of flowers and shrubs, and the whole place has such a charming woodland air, that, casting about me the other day for a compliment, I declared that it reminded me of New Hampshire. My compliment had a double edge, and I had no sooner uttered it than I smiled—or sighed—to perceive in all the undiscriminated botany about me the wealth of detail, the idle elegance and grace of Italy alone,—the natural stamp of the land which has the singular privilege of making one love her unsanctified beauty all but as well as those features of one's own country toward which nature's small allowance doubles that of one's own affection. In this matter of suggestiveness, no rides are more profitable than those you take in the Villa Doria or the Villa Borghese;[8] or do not take, possibly, if you prefer to reserve these particular regions (the latter in especial) for your walking-hours. People do ride, however, in both villas, which deserve honorable mention in this regard. The Villa Doria, with its noble site, its lovely views, its great groups of stone-pines, so clustered and yet so individual, its lawns and flowers and fountains, its altogether princely disposition, is a place where one may pace, well mounted, of a brilliant day, with an agreeable sense of its being a rather more elegant pastime to balance in one's stirrups than to trudge on even the smoothest gravel. But at the Villa Borghese the walkers have the best of it; for they are free of those delicious, outlying corners and bosky byways which the rumble of barouches never reaches. Early in March it becomes a perfect epitome of the spring. You cease to care much for the melancholy greenness of the disfeatured statues which has been your chief winter's intimation of verdure; and before you are quite conscious of the tender streaks and patches in the great, quaint, grassy arena round which the Propaganda[9] students, in their long skirts, wander slowly, like dusky seraphs revolving the gossip of Paradise, you spy the brave little violets uncapping their azure brows beneath the high-stemmed. One's walks, here, would take us too far, and one's pauses detain us too long, when, in the quiet parts, under the wall, one comes across a group of certain charming little scholars in full-dress suits and white cravats, shouting over their play in clear Italian, while a grave young priest, under a tree, watches them over the top of his book. I have wished only to say a word for one's rides,—to suggest that they give one, not only exercise, but memories.

---

7. Ariosto, Italian poet of *Orlando Furioso* (1516). Theocritus, Greek poet of the third century B.C.E., commonly taken as the inventor of pastoral poetry.
8. Not simply villas but great parks adjacent to Rome itself, and named for the princely families that once owned them.
9. Otherwise known as the Sacred Congregation for the Propagation of the Faith, the missionary arm of the papacy.

Contemporary Responses

James never had an entirely easy time with his reviewers. His stories had run in the *Atlantic* and elsewhere for a decade by the time he published his first book, *A Passionate Pilgrim and Other Tales* (1875), and he had gained a small but appreciative audience. Yet his work always met with reservations. Critics admitted the brilliance of his prose, and in an anonymous piece on *The American* (1877), the *New York Tribune* suggested that he had "a diction so rich and pure, so fluent and copious, so finely shaded yet capable of such varied service, that it is, in itself, a form of genius." But the same review complained that the novel lacked the "profound and universal human sympathy" it needed to temper its "scientific apprehension" of its characters.[1] James was too coolly dispassionate, too disengaged; many readers thought his people were like bits of marble, beautifully carved but inanimate. His protagonists were often unsympathetic, he made no clear division between villains and heroes, and he refused the accustomed pleasures of closure. At the *Atlantic* his friend and editor William Dean Howells tried to persuade him to provide the happy endings he thought their readers wanted; in response James wrote *The Europeans* (1878), which finishes with a handful of marriages but refuses to let the most interesting of its possible unions come off. To some people he simply seemed to ask too much, and that would only increase with the years.

Still, he couldn't be ignored; for one thing, he was far too prolific. *A Passionate Pilgrim* may have been his first book, but by the end of the year he had released two more, *Transatlantic Sketches*, a collection of essays, and a long novel called *Roderick Hudson*. And then there was "Daisy Miller" (1878). That story of a New York girl's indiscretions in Europe was first published in Britain, after a Philadelphia magazine rejected it as a libel on American femininity; for Daisy dies in Rome, of malaria and a compromised reputation alike, after she is seen out walking with an Italian. Most readers loved it, though, and the behavior of the title character was discussed and argued about as though she were real. James himself eventually dismissed the tale as slight, but it gave him his first taste of fame and ensured that every reader of the major British and American magazines would recognize his byline. What it didn't provide was money. In those days before international copyright the tale was immediately pirated in America, and James got almost nothing from its quickly sold 20,000 copies; all he could do was to follow it with a few briskly written comedies about the social relations of America and Europe, like "An International Episode" and "The Pension Beaurepas." Yet success brought troubles of its own. His strictures on the provinciality of American life made him suspect to a public still anxious about its place in the world, and so did his place of residence, for in the winter of 1876–77 James had settled himself in London. He no longer had an American home, and soon became a fixture in Britain's social and literary worlds alike.

1. *New York Tribune*, May 8, 1877.

The Portrait of a Lady was reviewed on both sides of the ocean as the work of an important writer, and the selection of contemporary responses below could easily be multiplied. Some critics suggested that James had become a figure with whom any serious reader needed to contend; in the *Atlantic* Horace E. Scudder wrote that his "method" was by now so firmly established that one had "better accept . . . and measure it than complain of it."[2] In summarizing the novel's monthly serial installments the *Nation's* anonymous critic thought it "considerably the most important"[3] book James had yet written, and noted what remains even now a source of his appeal: a prose so nuanced that "the reader feels irresistibly flattered at the homage paid to his perceptive powers."[4] Though not everyone liked it: the *Athenaeum* thought it "dull"[5] and the *New York Times* suggested that most readers would "resent its length."[6]

This section reprints three reviews, along with two later comments. In his piece for the *Nation*, where James had long been a contributor, W. C. Brownell suggests what's new about the *Portrait*, reading with an intelligence that shows why he later became one of the period's leading book editors. Two British reviews are more skeptical. R. H. Hutton argues that Isabel's own portrait lacks definition, and emphasizes the novel's "agnosticism": not just the absence of a religious consciousness but that of any explicit moral commentary or judgment. Margaret Oliphant admires the book's intelligence along with its minor characters. But she finds it ponderous, and is moreover disturbed by its open ending, which leaves Isabel's fate uncertain; so for that matter is Hutton uneasy with the ending. The last two pieces in this section are by close friends. James burned most of his correspondence, and so we've little sense of what his contemporaries said to him about his work. The letter here from Constance Fenimore Woolson is an exception, one he received during an 1882 visit to America and left behind when he returned to Britain. It contains the period's shrewdest account of the *Portrait's* place in his developing career and reputation. And finally, Howells provides an overview of that career in terms that now seem unexceptionable but which at the time proved inflammatory. He wrote that the novel had become "a finer art in our day than it was with Dickens and Thackeray"; meaning not that James was a greater novelist but rather that his artistic process was in some sense more refined. It still provoked a reaction, with Oliphant depicting American literature as engaged in a hostile takeover of the English language.[7] Other British critics followed her lead, and though James told his friend that "the indictment [was] rubbish,"[8] attacks on the two of them remained as "thick as blackberries."[9] Those attacks did, however, have one happy consequence: they led James to write his "Art of Fiction" (1884), the century's most perceptive and quotable account of the nature of the novel itself.

2. Horace Scudder, *Atlantic Monthly,* January 1882.
3. *The Nation,* March 24, 1881.
4. *The Nation,* November 18, 1880.
5. *The Athenaeum,* November 1881.
6. *New York Times,* November 27, 1881.
7. See her essay in *Blackwood's Edinburgh Magazine,* January 1883.
8. Letter of November 27, 1882, in Michael Anesko, ed. *Letters, Fictions, Lives: Henry James and William Dean Howells,* (Oxford University Press, 1997), p. 236.
9. Letter of March 20, 1883; in *Letters, Fictions, Lives,* p. 240.

R. H. HUTTON

From *The Spectator*†

If Mr. Henry James had called this book "The Portrait of Two Gentlemen," we might have admitted the aptness of the description, for the real power of the book consists in the wonderful pictures given of Ralph Touchett and Mr. Osmond, which have rarely been equalled in fiction for the skill and delicacy of the painting. But as for Isabel Archer—or Mrs. Osmond, as she afterwards becomes—who is the lady of whom the portrait is taken, we venture to say that the reader never sees her, or realises what she is, from the beginning of the book to the close. She is the one lady of whom no portrait is given, though she is studied till the reader is weary of the study. We have a very admirable portrait of Mrs. Touchett, a brilliant one of the Countess Gemini, a very clever one of Madame Merle, a most finished and attractive one of poor little Pansy Osmond, a very humorous one of Henrietta Stackpole; but of Isabel Archer one has no portrait at all, but only an interminable and laborious effort to paint one, an effort which is entirely in vain. One knows that she is pretty, that she loves freedom, that she loves experience, that she has endless day-dreams, that she is compassionate to the helpless, that she is grateful for goodness, and proud, not to say defiant, towards those who are not good to her; but beyond that, one knows nothing about her. Apparently, she has no faith whatever, no fixed standard even of inward life and motive, though she is always chasing ideals with no particular substance, or even uniformity, in them. Why she is so much fascinated by a man so utterly destitute of anything that is large in mind or heart, as Mr. Osmond, so made up, indeed, of fastidious selfishness,—unless it be for the artistic deference of his manner towards her, it is impossible to say. He says of himself, "No, I am not conventional, I am convention itself;" and, indeed, after one great breach of convention, sedulously concealed, he appears to have accepted convention, as distinguished from any of the moral or spiritual grounds of convention, as the whole aim of his life. So far as the reader has been prepared by the very elaborate studies of Isabel which precede the acquaintance with Mr. Osmond, one would have said that such a character as his could not have had any true fascination for her, and it remains one of the problems of the story why it ever had such a fascination,—a problem that it is all the more difficult to solve, since the reader, though fully understanding the rather feline character of Mr. Osmond's love of convention, is never really let into the confidence of his wife. It is this which, together with Mr. Henry James's very agnostic view of Art, spoils the book. The effect of the picture as a whole is this,—that while all the subsidiary painting is most lucid and delicate, the central figure remains shrouded in mist. Where the strongest light and the most definite impression should be, there is nothing but haze, nothing but a laborious riddle. Nevertheless, Mr. Henry James shows something more than his habitual skill,—and how

---

† From *The Spectator* (November 26, 1881): 1504–06. Richard Holt Hutton (1826–1897) was the magazine's coeditor; he wrote often on theological issues, but was also one of the age's most perceptive critics, writing on George Eliot in particular.

great that is, in our opinion, we have often had occasion to state,—in the wonderful picture of Mr. Osmond's temporary transfiguration during the few scenes in which he is presented to us as a suitor for Isabel. There one does, at least for a moment, understand that there might be some illusion about him,—not an illusion as to largeness of character, for he has not even a shadow of it, but as to the reverence and sweetness of his nature, of which he has really nothing but the outside, and yet so good an outside of it, that it is difficult for a moment to doubt that there is not something more behind. * * * As a set-off against this disagreeable picture is that of Ralph Touchett, the humorous, Anglo-American invalid,—who throughout the book is dying slowly of consumption,—and who shuffles about with his hands in his pockets and a shrewd eye always fixed on the life about him, eliciting all its characteristic features, in love with Isabel himself, though without ever thinking of sacrificing her, and indeed generously forgetting his own future in the desire to add to his cousin Isabel's happiness. Ralph Touchett is a very powerful picture, and a fine pendant to that of Osmond, the delicately-enamelled idolator of his own tastes and dignity, for whom Ralph's improvident generosity to his cousin unfortunately set a trap, by endowing her with wealth to which she had no claim, and which proves to her a pure misfortune. Such are the two leading characters of the book,—as powerfully drawn as Isabel's is feebly and faintly drawn,—companion pictures of niggardness of soul, on the one side, and magnanimity, of an unpretending type, on the other. Besides these, there are, as we have said, plenty of side-figures, many of them exhibiting Mr. Henry James's best insight and highest humour. As regards the latter quality, the relations of Henrietta Stackpole and Captain Bantling are painted with a finer humour than anything we remember in our author's work.

But the cloven foot of Mr. Henry James's agnosticism,—as artist no less than as thinker,—is shown at the close of his tale, with even more nakedness than he has ever shown it yet. That he always likes to end his tales with a failure of anything like the old poetic justice, we all know. That perplexing relations should ravel themselves, rather than unravel themselves, and end, so far as there is an ending at all, in something worse than they began in, is one of Mr. Henry James's canons of art. The tendency of life, he holds, is to result in a general failure of the moral and spiritual hopes it raises. If you let your story land itself in a wreck, or fade away into a blank and pallid apathy,—that is true art to this author. But never before has he closed a novel by setting up quite so cynical a sign-post into the abyss, as he sets up at the close of this book. He ends his *Portrait of a Lady*, if we do not wholly misinterpret the rather covert, not to say almost cowardly, hints of his last page, by calmly indicating that this ideal lady of his, whose belief in purity has done so much to alienate her from her husband, in that it had made him smart under her contempt for his estimates of the world, saw a "straight path" to a liaison with her rejected lover. And worse still, it is apparently intended that this is the course sanctioned both by her high-minded friend, Miss Stackpole, and by the dying cousin whose misfortune it had been to endow her with wealth that proved fatal to her happiness. The close of *The Portrait of a Lady* throws a strange light on the results to be expected from pure agnosticism in its relation to Art. Mr. Henry James long ago rejected the idea that real life is intelligible and significant, even so far as this—that the artistic presentation of it ought to satisfy the mind and heart, as the greater dramatists and novelists have always endeavoured to satisfy the mind and heart. But he has never till now ventured to indicate that the natural end of a noble nature, after it has wrecked itself by a great mistake, is ignoble surrender to selfish passion. Yet it is quite true that pure agnosticism is most likely to lead hither. Isabel is painted as trusting to nothing to keep her right in life but vague, generous aspirations, without compass and without clue; and for such a one, it is natural enough that, at the last pinch, all morality should seem nothing but convention, and the "straight path" a mere descent to selfish indulgence. We can hardly speak too highly of the skill and genius shown in many parts of *The Portrait of a Lady*. We can hardly speak too depreciatingly of the painting of that portrait itself, or of the moral collapse into which the original of the portrait is made to full. After all, even if it had been provided that Isabel should have attained her ideal, the result we certainly expected, we should not have cared much for a young lady made up of such extremely vague aspirations. As it is, we are filled with wonder that agnostic Art should have got so far as to place a great blot in the centre of a carefully-painted picture, without seeing that agnostic Art has, as Art, committed suicide in so doing.

W. C. BROWNELL

From *The Nation*[†]

Mr. James's novel, which caused each number of the *Atlantic Monthly* to be awaited with impatience last year, gains in its complete presentation, and, like most novels of any pretensions, is most readable when read consecutively. Unlike most novels, however, whose fate (and the fortune of whose authors) it is to appear serially, the reason for this does not consist in the condensation which the reader is thus enabled to make in spite of the author, but in the fact that it is a work of art of which the whole is equal to no fewer than all of its parts, and of which there is a certain "tendency," to lose which is to miss one of the main features of the book. In other words, 'The Portrait of a Lady' is an important work, the most important Mr. James has thus far written, and worthy of far more than mere perusal—worthy of study, one is inclined to say. It is in fact a little too important—to express by a paradox the chief criticism to be made upon it—or, at all events, the only impression left by it which is not altogether agreeable. For the first two or three hundred pages one is beguiled by a kind of entertainment always of a high order—the dissection of an interesting character by a clever and scrupulous demonstrator. After that, though it would be misleading to say that the interest flags—the interest being throughout the book remarkable for its evenness—the feeling supervenes that to be still entertained argues a happy aptitude for most serious and "intellectual" delectation. Most persons will recall some experience

† From *The Nation* 34.866 (February 2, 1882): 102–03. William Crary Brownell (1851–1928), American critic and later an editor at Charles Scribner's Sons, where he worked with Edith Wharton, among others.

of the same sensation in first becoming acquainted with undisguisedly philosophical writings—such as the writings of Emerson or Burke. To others it may be indicated by saying that it is just the sensation Carlyle missed in finding the works of George Eliot "dool—just dool." In America, it is well known, we do not find George Eliot dull, and it is upon our appetite for this sort of provender that Mr. James doubtless relies, and undoubtedly does well to rely. Nevertheless, it is possible to feel what Carlyle meant without agreeing with it; and though maintaining firmly the absorbing interest of 'The Portrait of a Lady,' we are ready to admit that once or twice we have laid aside the book for a season, with the exhilaration which Mr. Howells has somewhere observed to be coincident with giving up a difficult task. One of the happiest of the many happy remarks made in 'The Portrait of a Lady' is in Miss Stackpole's characterization of her *fiancé*: "He's as clear as glass; there's no mystery about him. He is not intellectual, but he appreciates intellect. On the other hand, he doesn't exaggerate its claim. *I sometimes think we do in the United States.*" The person of whom this is said naturally cuts a smaller figure in the novel than the more complex organizations, in dealing with which Mr. James is most at home; and it is the inference from this circumstance that we have in mind. For not only are the simpler though perennial elements of human nature in general eschewed by Mr. James, but his true distinction—that is to say, his strength and weakness also—consists in his attempt to dispense with all the ordinary machinery of the novelist except the study of subtle shades of character. In other words, his masterpiece, as 'The Portrait of a Lady' must be called, is not only outside of the category of the old romance of which 'Tom Jones,' for example, may stand as the type, but also dispenses with the dramatic movement and passionate interest upon which the later novelists, from Thackeray to Thomas Hardy, have relied. In a sense, and to a certain extent, Turgeneff may be said to be Mr. James's master, but even a sketch or a study by Turgeneff is turbulence itself beside the elaborate placidity of these 519 pages. This involves the necessity of the utmost care in presenting the material, and accordingly we have that squaring of the elbows and minute painstaking which not only result inevitably in occasional lumbering movement, but which lend the work an air of seeming more important than any book whatever could possibly be; so that it is perhaps fortunate for its popularity (which, by the way, we believe is extraordinary) that we exaggerate the claims of intellect occasionally in the United States.

Even this measure of fault-finding, however, seems a little ungracious, not to say hypercritical, in view of the distinguished success of Mr. James's experiment in applying the development theory to novel-writing, so to speak. We have ourselves followed the succession of his stories since 'Roderick Hudson' [1875] appeared with mingled interest and regret, because he has seemed to be getting further and further away from very safe ground, where he was very strong, and into the uncertainties of an unfamiliar region of which it was impossible to tell whether its novelty or its real merit gave it its interest. The elemental characters and dramatic situations of the novel just mentioned were strongly handled, and the work being, comparatively speaking, a youthful one, its promise seemed even greater than its actual qualities. But, almost as if he had been an amateur dipping into another branch of effort after having demonstrated his ability in one, Mr. James immediately abandoned the field of imaginative romance as it is generally understood. He at once made clear his faculty for his new choice, and the field he entered on with 'The American,' and continued with the shorter stories illustrative of American types, became immediately popular. 'Daisy Miller' [1878] may almost be said to mark an era in the mental progress of many persons who exaggerate the claims of intellect occasionally; it is wearisome to recall the "discussions" it occasioned in drawing-rooms and in print. There was, to be sure, a Chauvinist view, so to speak, taken of this and its associated sketches, by persons who omitted to perceive that Mr. James had not only made the current mechanical speculations about "the coming American novel" an anachronism, but had also displayed his patriotism and the national genius by inventing a new variety of literature. But naturally Mr. James might be expected to heed rather those of his readers who appreciated and enjoyed his motives and rejoiced in his discovery of romantic sociology. And this seemed his real danger; for though to these readers this reading conveyed a peculiarly refined pleasure, on account both of its novelty and the cleverness of its execution, there was no certainty that this pleasure was not a rather temporary mood, and likely to pass away after the novelty had worn off. Instead, however, of avoiding this danger by a return to the perennially interesting material with which he first dealt, Mr. James has conquered it, *vi et armis*, by a persistence that at one time seemed a little wilful. No one can now pretend, whatever his own literary likes and dislikes may be, that romantic sociology, exploited as Mr. James has shown it capable of being, is not a thoroughly serious field of literature, whose interest is permanent and dignified.

'The Portrait of a Lady' is a modest title, though an apt one. The portrait of the lady in question is indeed the theme of the book, and it is elaborated with a minuteness so great that when finally one begins to find it confusing it becomes evident that the ordinary point of view must be changed, and the last detail awaited—as in a professedly scientific work—before the whole can appear. Miss Isabel Archer is an orphan to whom her aunt gives an opportunity of seeing the world, and to whom her aunt's husband leaves a large fortune, at the instance of his son, who is unselfishly and romantically interested to see what his cousin will make of her life when nothing prevents her from doing as she wishes. The reader at once assumes the position of this young man, and with more or less (less in our own case, we confess) sympathy, watches the progress of the drama which he has set going. At the climax the heroine discovers that she has wrecked her life most miserably. The spiritual transition from the Isabel Archer of Albany to the Mrs. Osmond of Rome is of course accomplished in part by natural disposition and in part by the influence of the numerous characters which surround her. The way in which this influence is exhibited is a marked feature of the book. If George Eliot was the first to make of this important moral phenomenon a distinct study, Mr. James has here, in our opinion, quite surpassed her. Any one can judge by comparing the reciprocal effect upon the development of each other's characters of the Lydgates in 'Middlemarch' with that of the Osmonds here. The other characters are treated with a microscopy hardly inferior. Osmond himself is one of the most palpable of those figures in fiction which are to be called subtle. Madame Merle, his former mistress, mother of his child, who makes the marriage between him and his poverty and Isabel and her wealth, and who, up to the climax of the book, is Isabel's ideal, is, if anything, even better done. There is something almost uncanny in the perfection with which these secretive natures are turned inside out for the reader's inspection. As for the heroine, the American girl *par excellence*, it seems as if, scientifically speaking, Mr. James had said the last word on this subject; at any rate till the model herself is still further developed. For example: "She never looked so charming as when, in the genial heat of discussion, she received a crushing blow full in the face and brushed it away as a feather." There are pages as good.

It has long been evident that Mr. James's powers of observation are not only remarkably keen, but sleepless as well. But 'The Portrait of a Lady' would not be what it is if it did not possess a *fonds*[1] of moral seriousness, in addition to and underlying its extraordinary interest of purely intellectual curiosity. There is a specific lesson for the American girl in the first place; there are others, more general, which accompany every imaginative work of large importance. That these are nowhere distinctly stated is now nothing new in fiction even of a distinctly moral purpose. But Mr. James has carried suggestiveness in this regard further than any rival novelist, and though, unless one has ears to hear, it is entirely possible to miss the undertone of his book, to an appreciative sense there is something exquisite in the refinement with which it is conveyed. Refinement in this respect cannot be carried too far. In strictly literary matters Mr. James's fastidiousness may be objected to, perhaps, if one chooses; he has carried the method of the essayist into the domain of romance: its light touch, its reliance on suggestiveness, its weakness for indirect statement, its flattering presupposition of the reader's perceptiveness, its low tones, its polish. Upon occasion, where the circumstances really seem to warrant a little fervor, you only get from the author of 'The Portrait of a Lady' irreproachability. Objection to this may easily be carried too far, however; and those who do thus carry it too far, and argue that no people ever spoke and acted with the elegance and precision of the personages here portrayed, must of necessity pay the penalty of ultra-literalness and miss the secret of Mr. James's success. To characterize this secret with adequate fulness would require far more than the space at our disposal; but it may be sufficiently indicated by calling it the imaginative treatment of reality. In this unquestionably lies Mr. James's truly original excellence. 'The Portrait of a Lady' is the most eminent example we have thus far had of realistic art in fiction *à outrance*,[2] because its substance is thoroughly, and at times profoundly, real, and at the same time its presentation is imaginative. On the one hand, wilfulness and fantasticality are avoided, and on the other, prose and flatness. One may even go further, and say that the book succeeds in the difficult problem of combining a scientific value with romantic interest and artistic merit.

1. Depth, bottom, ground (French).
2. To an extreme; at the outer limits (French).

MARGARET OLIPHANT

From *Blackwood's*[†]

* * * This gentleman's work in the world seems to be a peculiar one. It is to record and set fully before us the predominance of the great American race, and the manner in which it has overrun and conquered the Old World. All, or almost all, of his social studies have their scene laid on the Continent, or in this island. It is true there are occasional interludes of America, but it is not in these that he seems most at home. The manner in which the heir of time—in the shape of the cultivated and accomplished son, or, still more, daughter of the West—dominates the old-fashioned scenery of countries which were, as old people say, great and powerful before America was ever heard of, is both amusing and impressive. Italy and France and Old England have lived their lives and had their reverses, and built their old castles and towns, and even arranged their landscapes— for him. The chief use of their old families is to furnish victims, in the shape of elder sons, for those delicate beauties who come conquering and to conquer from the fashionable circles of New York or the exotic plains of California. They inspect our antiquities as Germans criticise Hamlet, with the view of showing that we ourselves are unable to appreciate, and take comparatively little interest in, either the Tower or the Poet; and they patronise our institutions, most frequently from the high aristocratic side of the question, and object to our reforms, as the Solomons of the earth—who have tried all that man can do in that direction and found it naught—have perhaps some right to do. In short, they overshadow alto- gether the background against which they pose, and make London and Paris and Rome into Western settlements, with the most easy conscious- ness that they are lords of all. In some of M. Tourgenieff's books the same position is tacitly claimed, more or less, for the Russian; but then it is only world-playgrounds (which, if we remember rightly, is the dignified title by which some philosophers on our own side honour Switzerland[1]) which are represented as in the possession of the Muscovite. English performances of the same kind are of a more modest description. We do indeed plant our little colonies of pleasure all about, yet we give them, when we can, some relation to the "natives," and love to show our respect for that society into which, we are humbly aware, we are but sparely admitted. But Mr. James shows us his countrymen in the attitude of conquerors, dominating, not intruding, upon the foreign world about them.

* * *

The one thing which the book is not, is what it calls itself. There are several portraits of subordinate ladies—of Mrs. Touchett and Miss Stackpole, for example, both of which are admirable pictures; but of the

---

[†] From *Blackwood's Edinburgh Magazine* (March 1882): 374–83. The Scottish-born Margaret Oliphant (1828–1897) was a prolific novelist and exceptionally tough critic; she is best known today for her ghost stories and for The Chronicles of Carlingford (1863–76), a loose series of novels about the social and religious life of an English town.
[1]. Cf. Leslie Stephen, *The Playground of Europe* (1871), an account of mountain climbing in the Swiss Alps.

heroine, upon whom the greatest pains have been expended, and to whom endless space is afforded for the setting forth of her characteristics, we have no portrait, nor, even with the enormous amount of material supplied by Mr. James, do we find it easy to put together anything which will serve to supply the defect. We doubt much whether, in all the historical records that exist, we have as much material for the construction, let us say, of a recognisable portrait of Queen Elizabeth—no insignificant figure—as we have for that of Isabel Archer, the young lady who suddenly appears in the doorway of an old English country-house, inhabited like most other desirable places by American tenants—in this case her uncle and her cousin—fresh from her native country, prepared to take instant possession of her birthright as the explorer, discoverer, and conqueror of the old country,—and, in fact, reducing the gentlemen who meet her into instant subjection in the course of half an hour. How she does so, except by being very pretty, as we are told she is, we do not know; though the gentlemen in question are too experienced and clever in their own persons to be immediately subjugated by simple beauty. "Her head was erect, her eye brilliant, her flexible figure turned itself lightly this way and that, in sympathy with the alertness with which she evidently caught impressions. Her impressions were numerous, and they were all reflected in a clear, still smile," is Mr. James's description of his heroine; and it is about the clearest view we get of the young lady. For once in a way he is outside of her: but as he goes on he gets more and more within the circle of this irresistible young woman's personality; and we have to receive both herself and her immediate surroundings, not so much as they actually are, but as they are seen through her eyes. This is always confusing; for self-knowledge at its closest has many limitations, and the most impartial student of his own mind will probably get more light upon it by overhearing one sharp characterisation from outside than by weeks of self-examination. Isabel's aspect from outside is conveyed to us only in the raptures of her adorers; for all the men she encounters fall in love with her: first, her cousin Ralph Touchett, then Lord Warburton, then Osmond, whom she marries: besides a persistent Boston man, who makes nothing of crossing the Atlantic to get a glimpse of her, and turns up again and again with a sort of dogged inappropriateness at every new stage of her career.

There is but little vicissitude, however, in her career; she comes to "Europe" with something of the intention which Mr. James illustrated with, we think, a great deal more power, though less of the extremely refined and cultivated skill of which he is now master, in 'The American' [1877] the first work by which he was known in England; that is, to get everything she can out of her life and its opportunities,—all the sensation, the information, the variety of experience which it is possible it can convey. There is this difference between the young and visionary girl and the mature man, that whereas Mr. James's first hero wanted practical satisfaction for his desires, and to get possession of all that was best, including, as the most indispensable article of all, the fairest and most costly flower of womanhood which was to be found or purchased anyhow,— Isabel prefers not to have anything but the sense of having—the wealth of spiritual possession. For this reason she likes to retain a hold upon the lovers whom she will not marry. The English lord with all his fine qualities—and it cannot be said that our American author and heroine do not do full justice to these qualities with a refined sense of the admirableness of the position, and the importance which attaches to so curious and desirable a specimen of humanity—gives her the most agreeable consciousness of power, though all his advantages do not tempt her to marry him, and she is sorry for vexing him—almost as sorry as she is agreeably excited by the incident altogether. Indeed it would appear that this accompaniment of homage is natural to the young American woman, and that she would feel herself to be treated unfairly if at least one English lord, besides innumerable other candidates of different descriptions, did not attest her power. This is very different from the more vulgar development of the American young woman, who is bent on securing a title for herself. Mr. James's young ladies never do this. * * * Their curiosity about the English aristocrat is fresh and eager. They contemplate him attentively as the greatest novelty within their reach, and like and admire him as one of the wonders of the world; but they do not care to go any further. Isabel Archer passes through this phase very serenely, liking the new interest it puts into her life. But as a matter of fact she does not care for anything much except new interests. The adventures, or rather encounters, through which we are permitted to accompany her, are in reality but a small part of her career. There are gaps in which she travels far and wide—rapidly, eagerly, arduously. "She was like a thirsty person draining cup after cup," but always coming back again to the old investigation—the earnest study of all new phenomena—the consideration of how everything affected herself. Her desire for new experiences never fails, even when she gets into the dead block in which, as is natural, her perpetually increasing circle of moral enlightenment and sensation ends. * * *

It was inevitable that such a heroine should end unhappily—even if it were not inevitable that all Mr. James's books should break off with a sharp cut of arbitrary conclusion, leaving all the questions they so skilfully raise unsolved. Isabel, through the means of a wonderful woman whom she meets in her aunt's house, and who is a sort of symbol of unusual experience, as the younger woman is of the craving for it, falls under the fascinations of a certain aesthetic and beauty-loving American, Gilbert Osmond by name, who lives on one of the heights which surround Florence, a poor yet elegant *dilettante* life, "picking up" rarities of all kinds, making amateur drawings, surrounded by the faded silks and crafty embellishments of a collector, with a pretty little Dresden shepherdess of a daughter, newly returned from the convent, whose perfect conventional simplicity, freshness, and submission, afford Mr. James the means of making one of his most finished and perfect sketches. We confess to being quite unable to understand how it is that Isabel falls into Osmond's toils, unless it is because so elaborate and self-conscious a personality recoils instinctively, even though full of an abstract admiration for truth, from the downright and veracious, and finds in the complications of an elaborately conventional mind something that has the air of being larger and richer than the true. The reader is never for a moment taken in by the superiority of this most carefully dressed and posed figure, whose being altogether is mysterious, and of whom, notwithstanding the author's elaborate descriptions, we never penetrate the *fin mot*.

"Success," says Mr. James, "for Gilbert Osmond, would be to make himself felt; that was the only success to which he could now pretend. It is not a kind of distinction that is officially recognised, unless, indeed, the operation be performed upon multitudes of men. Osmond's life would be to impress himself not largely but deeply—a distinction of the most private sort: a single character might offer the whole measure of it. The clear and sensitive nature of a generous girl would make space for the record."

It is to be supposed, therefore, that this refined and philosophical *dilettante*, secluding himself among his faded silks and aesthetic ornaments, in his villa on Bellosguardo, is like a spider in his web awaiting the arrival of the fly which it shall be worth his while to capture. But, after all, these elaborate preparations were scarcely necessary for the capture of a young lady who was only Miss Archer, with a fortune of sixty thousand pounds. Had a Grand Duchess been his aim, it would have been comprehensible. There is far too great an effort for an insufficient result; and the almost immediate failure of their after relations is confusing and unaccountable. Something of the same curious failure we remember to have found in "Daniel Deronda,"[2] where Gwendolen and her husband, after their elaborate drawing together, fly asunder the moment they are married, with a suddenness and bitterness—brutality on the man's part, and misery on the woman's—for which we find no adequate motive, since there was neither passion between them to die out, nor motive enough beforehand to force a union which was to end so abruptly. That Isabel should discover her husband to be, as he describes himself, not only conventional, but convention itself, when she believed him to be nobly superior to the world, is one thing; but that she should discover him to hate her is quite another; and his jealousy and tyranny in the one development seem out of character with his easy gracefulness and gentlemanliness in the other.

The last volume is full of the complete and utter failure to which the heroine's hopes and high desires have come; but it cannot be said that she acquits herself with the dignity that might have been expected of her under the disappointment. Not only does she allow her wretchedness to be taken for granted by all her friends, but it would almost seem as if, in the utter collapse of the world about her, this most abstract and intellectual of heroines is driven at last to the conclusion that the only good in life is to make a snatch at happiness anyhow—to take what is offered her at last in utter relinquishment of any better hope. She has left her husband to watch at the deathbed of the devoted cousin Ralph, who has loved her all through, and has been her best and most faithful friend; and when all is over, is suddenly brought face to face with the true American, the violent lover, with all the ardour and practical force of the New World, of whom, among the rest of her sensations, she has always been a little afraid. No trace of love for Caspar has ever appeared in her before; but he comes upon her suddenly, when she is weak with grief for Ralph, and contemplating with horror her return to the bitter round of her duties with Osmond. The American not only pours forth his passion, but proposes to her to fly with him from the wretchedness of her fate. "Why shouldn't we be happy?" he says; "the world is all before us, and the world is large," as—we are obliged to remind Mr. James—a great many gentlemen in Mr. Caspar Goodwood's

---

2. By George Eliot (1876); James refers to that novel in his preface to the *Portrait*, and critics have often taken Eliot's account of the relation between Gwendolen Harleth and Grandcourt as a model for that between Isabel and Osmond.

position have said to a great many unhappy wives in the pages of fiction before.

> Isabel gave a long murmur like a creature in pain: it was as if he were pressing something that hurt her. "The world is very small," she said at random; she had an immense desire to appear to resist. She said it at random to hear herself say something; but it was not what she meant. The world in truth had never seemed so large; it seemed to open out all around her, to take the form of a mighty sea, where she floated in fathomless waters. She had wanted help, and here was help; it had come in a rushing torrent. I know not whether she believed anything that he said; but she believed that to let him take her in his arms would be the next best thing to dying. This belief for the moment was a kind of rapture in which she felt herself sinking and sinking. In the movement she seemed to beat with her feet, in order to catch herself, to feel something to rest upon.

She does not yield, it is needless to say: our author could not have so far forgotten himself. But when this impetuous lover, by no means despairing of success, finds that she has returned to her home, he is consoled by her friend Miss Stackpole, with the significant words—the last in the book—"Look here, Mr. Goodwood," she said; "just you wait!"

It is not very long since a respectable and gifted writer in another work of fiction permitted a young man of the highest virtue and honour to propose to a pure and honourable girl, utterly unprotected, that she should go away with him and be happy in a world which was large enough to conceal them, in much the same way; prefacing his proposal by the compliment that he knew she was not one of the prejudiced people who would be shocked by such a proposal: and so far was that spotless maiden from being shocked, that she took herself severely to task for her cruelty in refusing to make to her lover—poor fellow—the little sacrifice he asked.[3] What do these gentlemen mean, we wonder? Isabel, so far as she has any body at all, is as free from fleshly stain as the purest imagination could desire. Is it only that in her search after experience her author felt it necessary that she should taste also the excitement of an unlawful passion? or is it his mind to preach that the world being so hollow and miserable, and devoid of hope, the best thing we can do is to eat and drink, for to-morrow we die? Anyhow, it is a most equivocal if not debasing conclusion, and brings us up sharp with a discord instead of the symphony of harmonising chords with which it has been the habit of art to accompany the end of every story. As a rule Mr. James rejects symphonies, and attempts no harmonising conclusions. He leaves us usually tantalised, half angry with an end which is left to our imagination. But this is not a way of leaving matters to the imagination which we can at all consent to take from his hand. Abstract as is his heroine, a congeries of thoughts and questions rather than a woman, we cannot endure the possibility, even, of a future stain for her. It is a sort of insult to his own art, which is altogether out of accord with any such harsh effects. Let smaller workmen avail themselves of these easy means of startling the reader; from him we have a right to expect better things.

---

3. Oliphant probably has in mind George Meredith's *The Tragic Comedians* (1880).

In following out the chief thread of this elaborate work, we have in reality neglected the best of it, which is to be found in the characters which are secondary. Mrs. Touchett the aunt, who introduces Isabel to all the dangers of Europe,—the little dry independent woman, whose correspondence with her family is by curt telegrams—who consults her own independent fancy in all she does, asks little, and gives little in the way of affection, yet is by no means destitute of kindness,—is a curiously individual figure, so real and so odd that she must, we suspect, come from the life—that shelter of all eccentricities. Her son Ralph Touchett is by far the most lovable character in the book. The easy spectator position which his bad health and his temperament alike made natural; the smiling renunciation of life and all individual hopes which he has made without a word, without the sympathy or support of any consoler; his shuffle of easy contemplative indolence; the mild half-pathetic fun which he gets out of every incident,—go to our heart from the first appearance he makes on the scene. His love and care for his father; his profound tenderness and half-amused watch over his cousin, changing towards the end into a melancholy sense that his own act in securing her possession of a fortune has been her ruin; his unfailing courage and sweetness of temper,—make his appearance always delightful. If he did not smile in the face of fate, and turn off his worst pangs with a jest, we know and he knows that there would be in the world no more melancholy spectacle than this gradual going down of youth and hope and intelligence into the grave, imbittered by the sense that his weakness makes him powerless to help the being he loves best, and that his death will leave her to fight alone with a thousand troubles. He is conscious of all this, yet is amused with the vagaries of existence to the last, and keeps sorrow at arm's-length—keenly though he is aware of its presence. Miss Stackpole, too, is delightful in her genial Americanisms. We feel, indeed, that this lady—the correspondent of the 'Interviewer,' who comes to Europe half with the intention of watching over her friend, and more than half with the determination to fathom the inner life of England, especially in the homes of the great—is a concession on Mr. James's part to the British public,—a somewhat defiant proof that he is not afraid to take up even the conventional American of commonplace satire and make her captivate and charm the unbelieving. Her perfect boldness, combined with a modesty and purity so complete, that we are ashamed even of the thought that it is necessary to give her credit for qualities so innate and self-evident, are made delightfully comical by Henrietta's own unconsciousness of anything odd in her perfectly dauntless proceedings—her roamings about the world with Mr. Bantling in attendance—her free movements and still more free speech. Her speech, however, is free only in the way of interrogation and advice, in which her self-confidence is absolute—as is also, whenever there is any call for it, her kindness and devotion. Mr. James is not so successful with the personages who are not American. Lord Warburton is a very careful study of a fair big Englishman of rank and every heroic quality—but the author has too much the air of walking round and round the typical figure he admires so much, and pointing out his proportion—the size and nobility, the unconscious and easy grace of the aristocrat who puts his aristocracy so little forward, and is so modest and genial. And perhaps his contrast of the inanimate and submissive young ladies, who are Lord Warburton's sisters, as of the perfect little Pansy—the convent child of French and Italian breeding,—with his all-fascinating and all-intelligent American young woman, is not a very fair proceeding. This, however, we leave to his own conscience.

The book altogether is one of the most remarkable specimens of literary skill which the critic could lay his hand upon. It is far too long, infinitely ponderous, and pulled out of all proportion by the elaboration of every detail; but there is scarcely a page in it that is not worked out with the utmost skill and refinement, or which the reader will pass over without leaving something to regret—that is, if he has leisure for the kind of reading which is delightful for its own sake in complete independence of its subject. The conversation in it is an art by itself. To give an appearance of actualness and spontaneity to an artificial production so careful, refined, and elaborate, must have required a prodigious effort. We have heard it characterised very cleverly as resembling one of those games in which one of the party has to go out while the others task their ingenuity in devising how to puzzle him. When he returns with his mind on the full strain, the ingenious succession of questions and answers which are struck out by a party accustomed to the art may approach, if it is very well done, the perfection of the endless pages in which Mr. James carries on his word-fence with the most curious *vraisemblance* and air of being real. But nothing so elaborate ever could be real, and the dazzle sometimes fatigues, though the effect is one which cannot be contemplated without admiration.

CONSTANCE FENIMORE WOOLSON

Letter to Henry James[†]

12 February 1882

* * *

Thanks for the *Portrait*. I have seen quite a number of the criticisms that have appeared, and have been interested in them because of one point.

But first—what a splendid success for a book of that grade—a book of such delicately fine workmanship—to have every journal, from the London dailies down through all the magazines to the newspapers of Ohio, bringing out a notice of it as an important event of the day. No other novelist has this but you. (It is true that you do not appreciate the newspapers of Ohio.) You know what I think of the rank of your work; it entertains me much to watch the careless public advancing towards my opinion.

† From *Henry James Letters III*, ed. Leon Edel (Cambridge: The Belknap Press, 1980), pp. 529–35. Copyright © 1980 by Leon Edel, editorial. Copyright © 1980 by Alexander R. James, James copyright material. Reprinted by permission. The American writer Constance Fenimore Woolson (1840–1894) first met James in 1880 in Florence, just as he was beginning work on *The Portrait of a Lady*. She had long admired his work, and they became good friends, even sharing a villa on Bellosguardo in the spring of 1887. Woolson committed suicide in Venice in 1894, after a period of depression; James acted as her de facto executor and burned many of her papers, including his letters to her. Her novels include *Anne* (1881) and *For the Major* (1883), but she is best known for her superb short stories; a recent selection is available as *Miss Grief and Other Stories*, ed. Anne Boyd Rioux (New York: W. W. Norton, 2016). Rioux has also written the most recent biography, *Constance Fenimore Woolson: Portrait of a Lady Novelist* (New York: W. W. Norton, 2016).

The point I note is—that, over the *Portrait*, our American critics have come to an entirely new, and this time I think permanent, tone about you. Their first tone was unmitigated praise. I do'nt think you appreciated, over there among the chimney-pots, the laudation your books received in America, as they came out one by one. * * * It was but human, however, that this laudation should not go on forever. In addition—as you were all the time advancing—it began to occur to these critics that you were going by even their encouragement; that possibly too you did not estimate at its true worth the importance of their help and sympathy. They began, in short, to be jealous. Your *Hawthorne* [1879] gave them their opportunity; your *Washington Square* [1880] did not decrease it. That was their second tone.—The *Portrait* has now brought them to a third. The first—flattering as it was—was never without the accompanying chord that you were a young fellow; your talent, your style, your this and that, were marvelous *in* a young fellow etc. They looked forward "confidently" to your "future." But, after all, they would have preferred to continue looking forward. It gave a pleasant sense of patronage. But—in the *Portrait*—this future is more than suspected to have become the present. They see it and cannot deny it. They do'nt like it. The whole tone is different. With ill humor here and there according to their tempers—with more or less clearness according to their powers of perception, they are virtually acknowledging, one and all, in these criticisms, that you are no longer the coming man, but that (whether for good or for ill) you have "arrived." To acknowledge this has been for some of them like little Rosier's selling his bibelots, or rather as that sacrifice of his struck Isabel—"as if he had had all his teeth drawn." One or two remark, gloomily, that you have founded a new school of novel-writing, and get out of it in that way; because they are free, of course, to not admire the school.

* * *

I have come slowly to the conclusion that the *Portrait is* the finest novel you have written. "Slowly," because I so much like the others, and hate to desert old friends. I did'nt completely yield until I had read the last two chapters. Then I had to. The scene between Goodwood and Isabel at the end is, in my opinion, by far the strongest scene of the kind you have given to the public. It has the naturalness which all you write possesses, but it has in addition a force (which real life does contain, I think)—a force which you have rather held back—at least the expression of it—in your other books; purposely—as I have always supposed. I wanted to see it let out a trifle. And here it is let out. I did'nt want much. But that little I did want. Now, I am satisfied.

* * *

I think you were mistaken in the judgment of the story you gave me, briefly, in Rome—mistaken in two points. One is Madame Merle. You thought that in the beginning she was too much described—that it gave the impression that she was to be more prominent than she really becomes. I do not agree with you. She looms up in the latter part of the story so darkly and powerfully—powerfully although always in a sort of haze—that for the time being she overshadows Isabel, and one cares more for her than for the younger woman. The touch that does it is given when the Countess says—"And the end of it is that he is tired of her. And what is more, today she knows it." Life holds no deeper tragedy than that. I have never believed that bad people suffered any the less because they were bad.—And, beside Osmond, Mme Merle is almost good! Who can help feeling for her when she buries her face in her hands after Osmond's horrible—"You seem to me quite good enough," and—"Good enough to be always charming" (49th chapter). It is tragic. Yet Mme Merle herself is not tragic. The combination marks your skill.

The other point is Osmond. You said you saw him distinctly yourself, but that you doubted whether he would be distinct to your readers. Rest easy (only you are always easy!); he is. He is a more finished creation even than Grandcourt (*Daniel Deronda*); as distinct; more finely detestable; and haunting, and suffocating than George Eliot's Englishman, and overtopping him by not being emphasized by a violent death. It is real life in all its unavenging cold monotony that Osmond should go on living; and that point shows by how much you are the finer artist. But George Eliot could'nt stand it; she had to kill off her Englishman. A woman, after all, can never be a complete artist.

Such a character as Osmond's is an entirely new one in literature. Yet one sees at once that he is completely possible. What a combination to be fine, and fastidious, and without heart! I have known one or two persons who were cultivated, and fastidious, and without heart; but they also had a brutal side—which Osmond has not. Save in the thought, which underlies his words. The whole of the 42d chapter is a masterpiece.

I have a good deal to say about Isabel (I wo'nt say it all). With no character of yours have I ever felt myself so much in sympathy. I watched with much curiosity your Christina, Mme de Cintré, the Baroness, Mme de Mauves, and others,—I looked on with interest as Gertrude and Charlotte, Mary Garland, Bessie Alden, Angela, Catherine, poor Daisy[1] and the rest, came and went. But with Isabel it has been quite different. I found myself judging her and thinking of her with a perfect sympathy, and comprehension, and a complete acquaintance as it were; everything she did and said I judged from a personal standpoint. I never said to myself as I did about Christina, for instance—"I do'nt know;—it may be so." I always knew exactly all about Isabel. (Of course I only mean that it has seemed so. Very likely you will say that my fancied knowledge is not correct.)

Poor Isabel! poor idealizing imaginative girls the world over—sure, absolutely sure to be terribly unhappy. And the worst of it is that it cannot be prevented. One would suppose that a father and mother might do something. But, strangely enough, a mother is often the last person to understand her daughter; she understands her as her child, but not as the woman. And the father, if he really loves his child, does not welcome the thought that she may love some one else; he puts it as far from him as possible, and only accepts it, when it must be accepted, as a dose to be swallowed with as good a grace as he can summon. He never wants to talk about it beforehand! And thus the poor Isabels go believingly to their ruin.

---

1. These are all names of James's female protagonists, from the title character of "Mme de Mauves" (1874), his first great story, to Catherine Sloper of *Washington Square*, among others.

One gets hopeless enough sometimes (while watching them) to think that a duller mind, a more commonplace character, is the better gift. Simple goodness, and a gentle affectionate unjudging nature, seem the high prizes for a woman to gain in this lottery of life.

The Isabels—your Isabel—are always so sure! She *knows* she is right. She cannot say so openly, because it presupposes the superior fineness of her own comprehension and intelligence over that of her friends and relatives. And this is the fatal pitfall; because, if she could talk it over frankly with someone, she might be saved. But she never can. She sees her Osmond in a certain light; the different light in which others see him, is only their own coarser vision. And being always self-conceited—poor Isabel!—she at heart rather prefers this state of things. And so she moves onward proudly, securely, and often nobly according to her light—to the miserable end.

How you know her! In chapter 14, for instance, where she begins a half-explanation, saying that she can't escape—escape by separating herself—and the rest of it—that is a wonderful and true bit of portraiture. Again in the latter part of the 21st chapter, where she sees that she might even like the limitations of Goodwood, some day far in the future—that they might then be like "a clear and quiet harbor, enclosed by a fine granite breakwater"—that is also a perfect divination. Because that is the peculiarity of such a temperament—there is no end to the visions, the imaginations. It is like the spirit which the fisherman let out of the vial—it grows into a great mist and fills the whole sky.

Poor Isabel!—(I am afraid I shall be beginning every paragraph with that)—what a cameo-like picture of her, and her sure mistake, is that visit with Mme Merle to Osmond's villa on Bellosguardo. His method of beginning to interest her; his assumed half-embarrassment yet desire to please; his asking her how she likes his sister; his leading with him his little daughter, in her short white frock—everything so exquisitely designed and carried out to produce a certain impression—nothing underscored, all so delicately moderate.

* * *

My last criticism is that you do not let us see, with any distinctness, whether Isabel really loved Osmond. She tells Mrs. Touchett that she does'nt love Lord Warburton; but she does'nt tell her or anybody (if my memory serves me) that she does love Gilbert Osmond. You do'nt let her even tell Osmond himself—at least with the public *entiers*. We are therefore left to a choice between two beliefs. One is that she never really loved Osmond; it is her imagination, not her love, which has been led captive. He fills an ideal. No one else did that. She *thinks* she loves him; but as she does not, the absence of heart-breaking, insupportable, killing griefs in her heart and life, after she finds out what he really is, is explained, and quite natural.

The other hypothesis is that she did love him. But that a distinct expression of it, and of the following agony, is left to the imagination of the reader, as things easily to be supplied;—according to the time-honored method of Mr. Henry James.

Personally, you know, I would rather not have it "left." But I add, with willingness, that probably you know best.

How did you ever dare write a portrait of a lady? Fancy any woman's attempting a portrait of a gentleman! Would'nt there be a storm of ridicule! Every clerk on the Maumee river would know more about it than a George Eliot. For my own part, in my small writings, I never dare put down what men are thinking, but confine myself simply to what they do and say. For, long experience has taught me that whatever I suppose them to be thinking at any especial time, that is sure to be exactly what they are *not* thinking. What they *are* thinking, however, nobody but a ghost could know.

WILLIAM DEAN HOWELLS

Henry James, Jr.†

The events of Mr. James's life—as we agree to understand events—may be told in a very few words. His race is Irish on his father's side and Scotch on his mother's, to which mingled strains the generalizer may attribute, if he likes, that union of vivid expression and dispassionate analysis which has characterized his work from the first. There are none of those early struggles with poverty, which render the lives of so many distinguished Americans monotonous reading, to record in his case: the cabin hearth-fire did not light him to the youthful pursuit of literature; he had from the start all those advantages which, when they go too far, become limitations.

He was born in New York city in the year 1843, and his first lessons in life and letters were the best which the metropolis—so small in the perspective diminishing to that date—could afford. In his twelfth year his family went abroad, and after some stay in England made a long sojourn in France and Switzerland. They returned to America in 1860, placing themselves at Newport, and for a year or two Mr. James was at the Harvard Law School, where, perhaps, he did not study a great deal of law. His father removed from Newport to Cambridge in 1866, and there Mr. James remained till he went abroad, three years later, for the residence in England and Italy which, with infrequent visits home, has continued ever since.[1]

It was during these three years of his Cambridge life that I became acquainted with his work. He had already printed a tale—"The Story of a Year" [1865]—in the "Atlantic Monthly," when I was asked to be Mr. Fields's[2] assistant in the management, and it was my fortune to read Mr. James's second contribution in manuscript. "Would you take it?" asked

† From *Century Magazine* 25.1 (November 1882): 25–29. For Howells, see p. 410 of this Norton Critical Edition. With its bold claims about the degree to which fiction has "become a finer art in our day than it was with Dickens and Thackeray," this essay sparked a series of attacks in British periodicals. Margaret Oliphant was an especially fierce respondent, suggesting that American literature was engaged in a hostile takeover of the English language; other critics compared the dense plotting of Dickens and Thackeray to James's relative paucity of "incident" and argued that for the Americans "the best novelist is he who has no story to tell." James wrote to Howells that the two of them seemed "daily immolated on the altar" of the English classics, but the controversy had one benefit: it led, in 1884, to James's own essay on "The Art of Fiction," one of the central statements in the history of Anglo-American criticism.

1. Howells's account here is severely telescoped; see the Chronology on pp. 641–44 of this Norton Critical Edition for a more accurate summary of James's movements.
2. James T. Fields (1817–1881), partner in the Boston firm of Ticknor and Fields, which published Hawthorne, among others; the firm bought the *Atlantic* in 1861, and Fields served as its editor until 1871, when Howells became his successor.

my chief. "Yes, and all the stories you can get from the writer." One is
much securer of one's judgment at twenty-nine than, say, at forty-five; but
if this was a mistake of mine I am not yet old enough to regret it. The
story was called "Poor Richard," [1867] and it dealt with the conscience
of a man very much in love with a woman who loved his rival. He told this
rival a lie, which sent him away to his death on the field,—in that day
nearly every fictitious personage had something to do with the war,—but
Poor Richard's lie did not win him his love. It still seems to me that the
situation was strongly and finely felt. One's pity went, as it should, with
the liar; but the whole story had a pathos which lingers in my mind equally
with a sense of the new literary qualities which gave me such delight in it.
I admired, as we must in all that Mr. James has written, the finished workmanship in which there is no loss of vigor; the luminous and uncommon
use of words, the originality of phrase, the whole clear and beautiful style,
which I confess I weakly liked the better for the occasional gallicisms
remaining from an inveterate habit of French. Those who know the writings of Mr. Henry James[3] will recognize the inherited felicity of diction
which is so striking in the writings of Mr. Henry James, Jr. The son's diction is not so racy as the father's; it lacks its daring, but it is as fortunate
and graphic; and I cannot give it greater praise than this, though it has,
when he will, a splendor and state which is wholly its own.

Mr. James is now so universally recognized that I shall seem to be making an unwarrantable claim when I express my belief that the popularity
of his stories was once largely confined to Mr. Fields's assistant. They had
characteristics which forbade any editor to refuse them; and there are no
anecdotes of thrice-rejected manuscripts finally printed to tell of him; his
work was at once successful with all the magazines. But with the readers
of "The Atlantic," of "Harper's," of "Lippincott's," of "The Galaxy," of "The
Century," it was another affair. The flavor was so strange, that, with rare
exceptions, they had to "learn to like" it. Probably few writers have in
the same degree compelled the liking of their readers. He was reluctantly
accepted, partly through a mistake as to his attitude—through the confusion of his point of view with his private opinion—in the reader's mind.
This confusion caused the tears of rage which bedewed our continent in
behalf of the "average American girl" supposed to be satirized in Daisy
Miller, and prevented the perception of the fact that, so far as the average
American girl was studied at all in Daisy Miller, her indestructible innocence, her invulnerable new-worldliness, had never been so delicately
appreciated. It was so plain that Mr. James disliked her vulgar conditions,
that the very people to whom he revealed her essential sweetness and light
were furious that he should have seemed not to see what existed through
him. In other words, they would have liked him better if he had been a
worse artist—if he had been a little more confidential.

But that artistic impartiality which puzzled so many in the treatment
of Daisy Miller is one of the qualities most valuable in the eyes of those
who care how things are done, and I am not sure that it is not Mr. James's
most characteristic quality. As "frost performs the effect of fire," this

---

3. Henry James, Sr. (1811–1882) wrote widely on religious issues, but though he had a marked
    gift for aphorism, his many self-published books found virtually no audience.

impartiality comes at last to the same result as sympathy. We may be quite sure that Mr. James does not like the peculiar phase of our civilization typified in Henrietta Stackpole; but he treats her with such exquisite justice that he lets *us* like her. It is an extreme case, but I confidently allege it in proof.

His impartiality is part of the reserve with which he works in most respects, and which at first glance makes us say that he is wanting in humor. But I feel pretty certain that Mr. James has not been able to disinherit himself to this degree. We Americans are terribly in earnest about making ourselves, individually and collectively; but I fancy that our prevailing mood in the face of all problems is that of an abiding faith which can afford to be funny. He has himself indicated that we have, as a nation, as a people, our joke, and every one of us is in the joke more or less. We may, some of us, dislike it extremely, disapprove it wholly, and even abhor it, but we are in the joke all the same, and no one of us is safe from becoming the great American humorist at any given moment.[4] The danger is not apparent in Mr. James's case, and I confess that I read him with a relief in the comparative immunity that he affords from the national facetiousness. Many of his people are humorously imagined, or rather humorously *seen*, like Daisy Miller's mother, but these do not give a dominant color; the business in hand is commonly serious, and the droll people are subordinated. They abound, nevertheless, and many of them are perfectly new finds, like Mr. Tristram in "The American," [1877] the bill-paying father in the "Pension Beaurepas," [1879] the anxiously Europeanizing mother in the same story, the amusing little Madame de Bellegarde, Henrietta Stackpole, and even Newman himself.[5] But though Mr. James portrays the humorous in character, he is decidedly not on humorous terms with his reader; he ignores rather than recognizes the fact that they are both in the joke.

If we take him at all we must take him on his own ground, for clearly he will not come to ours. We must make concessions to him, not in this respect only, but in several others, chief among which is the motive for reading fiction. By example, at least, he teaches that it is the pursuit and not the end which should give us pleasure; for he often prefers to leave us to our own conjectures in regard to the fate of the people in whom he has interested us. There is no question, of course, but he could tell the story of Isabel in "The Portrait of a Lady" to the end, yet he does not tell it. We must agree, then, to take what seems a fragment instead of a whole, and to find, when we can, a name for this new kind in fiction. Evidently it is the character, not the fate, of his people which occupies him; when he has fully developed their character he leaves them to what destiny the reader pleases.

The analytic tendency seems to have increased with him as his work has gone on. Some of the earlier tales were very dramatic: "A Passionate Pilgrim," [1871] which I should rank above all his other short stories, and

---

4. Howells alludes here to one of James's most celebrated—and controversial—critical passages. In *Hawthorne* (1879) he summarizes all the things a European might take for granted that are missing in American life, a list that runs for half a page from cathedrals to "Epsom [and] Ascot." He then adds, "The American knows that a good deal remains; what it is that remains— that is his secret, his joke, as one may say." But few enough of his readers were in on that joke. See *Henry James: Literary Criticism*, vol. 1, ed. Leon Edel (New York: Library of America, 1984), pp. 351–52.

5. Mme de Bellegarde and Christopher Newman are characters in *The American*.

for certain rich poetical qualities, above everything else that he has done, is eminently dramatic. But I do not find much that I should call dramatic in "The Portrait of a Lady," while I do find in it an amount of analysis which I should call superabundance if it were not all such good literature. The novelist's main business is to possess his reader with a due conception of his characters and the situations in which they find themselves. If he does more or less than this he equally fails. I have sometimes thought that Mr. James's danger was to do more, but when I have been ready to declare this excess an error of his method I have hesitated. Could anything be superfluous that had given me so much pleasure as I read? Certainly from only one point of view, and this a rather narrow, technical one. It seems to me that an enlightened criticism will recognize in Mr. James's fiction a metaphysical genius working to æsthetic results, and will not be disposed to deny it any method it chooses to employ. No other novelist, except George Eliot, has dealt so largely in analysis of motive, has so fully explained and commented upon the springs of action in the persons of the drama, both before and after the facts. These novelists are more alike than any others in their processes, but with George Eliot an ethical purpose is dominant, and with Mr. James an artistic purpose. I do not know just how it should be stated of two such noble and generous types of character as Dorothea[6] and Isabel Archer, but I think that we sympathize with the former in grand aims that chiefly concern others, and with the latter in beautiful dreams that primarily concern herself. Both are unselfish and devoted women, sublimely true to a mistaken ideal in their marriages; but, though they come to this common martyrdom, the original difference in them remains. Isabel has her great weaknesses, as Dorothea had, but these seem to me, on the whole, the most nobly imagined and the most nobly intentioned women in modern fiction; and I think Isabel is the more subtly divined of the two. If we speak of mere characterization, we must not fail to acknowledge the perfection of Gilbert Osmond. It was a profound stroke to make him an American by birth. No European could realize so fully in his own life the ideal of a European *dilettante* in all the meaning of that cheapened word; as no European could so deeply and tenderly feel the sweetness and loveliness of the English past as the sick American, Searle, in "The Passionate Pilgrim."

What is called the international novel is popularly dated from the publication of "Daisy Miller," [1878] though "Roderick Hudson" [1875] and "The American" had gone before; but it really began in the beautiful story which I have just named. Mr. James, who invented this species in fiction, first contrasted in the "Passionate Pilgrim" the New World and Old World moods, ideals, and prejudices, and he did it there with a richness of poetic effect which he has since never equalled. I own that I regret the loss of the poetry, but you cannot ask a man to keep on being a poet for you; it is hardly for him to choose; yet I compare rather discontentedly in my own mind such impassioned creations as Searle and the painter in "The Madonna of the Future" [1873] with "Daisy Miller," of whose slight, thin personality I also feel the indefinable charm, and of the tragedy of whose innocence I recognize the delicate pathos. Looking back to those early stories, where Mr. James stood at the dividing ways of the novel and the

6. The heroine of George Eliot's *Middlemarch* (1871–72).

romance,[7] I am sometimes sorry that he declared even superficially for the former. His best efforts seem to me those of romance; his best types have an ideal development, like Isabel and Claire Belgarde and Bessy Alden and poor Daisy and even Newman. But, doubtless, he has chosen wisely; perhaps the romance is an outworn form, and would not lend itself to the reproduction of even the ideality of modern life. I myself waver somewhat in my preference—if it is a preference—when I think of such people as Lord Warburton and the Touchetts, whom I take to be all decidedly of this world. The first of these especially interested me as a probable type of the English nobleman, who amiably accepts the existing situation with all its possibilities of political and social change, and insists not at all upon the surviving feudalities, but means to be a manly and simple gentleman in any event. An American is not able to pronounce as to the verity of the type; I only know that it seems probable and that it is charming. It makes one wish that it were in Mr. James's way to paint in some story the present phase of change in England. A titled personage is still mainly an inconceivable being to us; he is like a goblin or a fairy in a story-book. How does he comport himself in the face of all the changes and modifications that have taken place and that still impend? We can hardly imagine a lord taking his nobility seriously; it is some hint of the conditional frame of Lord Warburton's mind that makes him imaginable and delightful to us.

It is not my purpose here to review any of Mr. James's books; I like better to speak of his people than of the conduct of his novels, and I wish to recognize the fineness with which he has touched-in the pretty primness of Osmond's daughter and the mild devotedness of Mr. Rosier. A masterly hand is as often manifest in the treatment of such subordinate figures as in that of the principal persons, and Mr. James does them unerringly. This is felt in the more important character of Valentin Belgarde, a fascinating character in spite of its defects,—perhaps on account of them—and a sort of French Lord Warburton, but wittier, and not so good. "These are my ideas," says his sister-in-law, at the end of a number of inanities. "Ah, you call them ideas!" he returns, which is delicious and makes you love him. He, too, has his moments of misgiving, apparently in regard to his nobility, and his acceptance of Newman on the basis of something like "manhood suffrage" is very charming. It is of course difficult for a remote plebeian to verify the pictures of legitimist society in "The American," but there is the probable suggestion in them of conditions and principles, and want of principles, of which we get glimpses in our travels abroad; at any rate, they reveal another and not impossible world, and it is fine to have Newman discover that the opinions and criticisms of our world are so absolutely valueless in that sphere that his knowledge of the infamous crime of the mother and brother of his betrothed will have no effect whatever upon them in their own circle if he explodes it there. This seems like aristocracy indeed! and one admires, almost respects, its survival in our day. But I always regretted that Newman's discovery seemed the precursor of his magnanimous resolution not to avenge himself; it weakened the effect of this, with which it had really nothing to do. Upon the whole,

7. The classic distinction between these two forms of fiction, which mattered more and seemed more distinct to Victorian readers than it does today, can be found in Richard Chase, *The American Novel and Its Tradition* (1957; rpt. Baltimore: Johns Hopkins University Press, 1980), pp. 12–13.

however, Newman is an adequate and satisfying representative of Americanism, with his generous matrimonial ambition, his vast good-nature, and his thorough good sense and right feeling. We must be very hard to please if we are not pleased with him. He is not the "cultivated American" who redeems us from time to time in the eyes of Europe; but he is unquestionably more national, and it is observable that his unaffected fellow-countrymen and women fare very well at Mr. James's hands always; it is the Europeanizing sort like the critical little Bostonian in the "Bundle of Letters," [1878] the ladies shocked at Daisy Miller, the mother in the "Pension Beaurepas" who goes about trying to be of the "native" world everywhere, Madame Merle and Gilbert Osmond, Miss Light and her mother, who have reason to complain, if any one has. Doubtless Mr. James does not mean to satirize such Americans, but it is interesting to note how they strike such a keen observer. We are certainly not allowed to like them, and the other sort find somehow a place in our affections along with his good Europeans. It is a little odd, by the way, that in all the printed talk about Mr. James—and there has been no end of it—his power of engaging your preference for certain of his people has been so little commented on. Perhaps it is because he makes no obvious appeal for them; but one likes such men as Lord Warburton, Newman, Valentin, the artistic brother in "The Europeans," [1878] and Ralph Touchett, and such women as Isabel, Claire Belgarde, Mrs. Tristram, and certain others, with a thoroughness that is one of the best testimonies to their vitality. This comes about through their own qualities, and is not affected by insinuation or by downright *petting*, such as we find in Dickens nearly always and in Thackeray too often.

The art of fiction has, in fact, become a finer art in our day than it was with Dickens and Thackeray. We could not suffer the confidential attitude of the latter now, nor the mannerism of the former, any more than we could endure the prolixity of Richardson or the coarseness of Fielding. These great men are of the past—they and their methods and interests; even Trollope and Reade are not of the present. The new school derives from Hawthorne and George Eliot rather than any others; but it studies human nature much more in its wonted aspects, and finds its ethical and dramatic examples in the operation of lighter but not really less vital motives. The moving accident is certainly not its trade; and it prefers to avoid all manner of dire catastrophes. It is largely influenced by French fiction in form; but it is the realism of Daudet rather than the realism of Zola[8] that prevails with it, and it has a soul of its own which is above the business of recording the rather brutish pursuit of a woman by a man, which seems to be the chief end of the French novelist. This school, which is so largely of the future as well as the present, finds its chief exemplar in Mr. James; it is he who is shaping and directing American fiction, at least. It is the ambition of the younger contributors to write like him; he has his following more distinctly recognizable than that of any other English-writing novelist. Whether he will so far control this following as

---

8. Alphonse Daudet (1840–1897), now best known for *Lettres de mon Moulin* (1866), but in the nineteenth century famous too for his realistic novels, including *Jack* (1878) and *Numa Roumestan* (1881). Émile Zola (1840–1902), author of *L'Assommoir* (1877), *Nana* (1880), *Germinal* (1885), and many other novels that provided a comprehensive account of French life under the Second Empire. James knew both men; he liked Daudet, and saw Zola's naturalism as the chief competitor to his own aesthetic.

to decide the nature of the novel with us remains to be seen. Will the reader be content to accept a novel which is an analytic study rather than a story, which is apt to leave him arbiter of the destiny of the author's creations? Will he find his account in the unflagging interest of their development? Mr. James's growing popularity seems to suggest that this may be the case; but the work of Mr. James's imitators will have much to do with the final result.

In the meantime it is not surprising that he has his imitators. Whatever exceptions we take to his methods or his results, we cannot deny him a very great literary genius. To me there is a perpetual delight in his way of saying things, and I cannot wonder that younger men try to catch the trick of it. The disappointing thing for them is that it is not a trick, but an inherent virtue. His style is, upon the whole, better than that of any other novelist I know; it is always easy, without being trivial, and it is often stately, without being stiff; it gives a charm to everything he writes; and he has written so much and in such various directions, that we should be judging him very incompletely if we considered him only as a novelist. His book of European sketches[9] must rank him with the most enlightened and agreeable travelers; and it might be fitly supplemented from his uncollected papers with a volume of American sketches. In his essays on modern French writers he indicates his critical range and grasp;[1] but he scarcely does more, as his criticisms in "The Atlantic" and "The Nation" and elsewhere could abundantly testify.

There are indeed those who insist that criticism is his true vocation, and are impatient of his devotion to fiction; but I suspect that these admirers are mistaken. A novelist he is not, after the old fashion, or after any fashion but his own; yet since he has finally made his public in his own way of story-telling—or call it character-painting if you prefer,—it must be conceded that he has chosen best for himself and his readers in choosing the form of fiction for what he has to say. It is, after all, what a writer has to say rather than what he has to tell that we care for nowadays. In one manner or other the stories were all told long ago; and now we want merely to know what the novelist thinks about persons and situations. Mr. James gratifies this philosophic desire. If he sometimes forbears to tell us what he thinks of the last state of his people, it is perhaps because that does not interest him, and a large-minded criticism might well insist that it was childish to demand that it must interest him.

I am not sure that my criticism is sufficiently large-minded for this. I own that I like a finished story; but then also I like those which Mr. James seems not to finish. This is probably the position of most of his readers, who cannot very logically account for either preference. We can only make sure that we have here an annalist, or analyst, as we choose, who fascinates us from his first page to his last, whose narrative or whose comment may enter into any minuteness of detail without fatiguing us, and can only truly grieve us when it ceases.

9. *Transatlantic Sketches* (1875).
1. *French Poets and Novelists* (1878).

The Novel in Revision

The New York Edition took James four years of steady work, and toward the end he sat at his desk with an ever-increasing sense of exhaustion; ever-increasing even though the revisions on such late volumes as *The Ambassadors* were far lighter than they had been on his first ones. *The Portrait of a Lady* became the third novel in the series, after *Roderick Hudson* and *The American*. He began to go over it in the spring of 1906 and finished at the end of July, and though he altered every page and indeed almost every paragraph, the job itself went smoothly. Other books gave him far more trouble. With *The American*, for example, James found that he could no longer accept the logic of its plot. Only he couldn't now change it, and struggled to mask its improbabilities as much as he could; the *Portrait*'s structure, in contrast, had been sound from the start.

James did his revisions to the *Portrait* on a set of specially prepared pages. His agent, J. B. Pinker, took two copies of the novel and cut their bindings, slicing each leaf free, and then had each one pasted onto a larger piece of paper. That gave James a single unbound copy with a few inches of white space on all sides in which to scrawl. Now held at Harvard's Houghton Library, these pages look like a textual maze, full of word balloons, strike-outs, and phrases interpolated between the lines; an example can be seen on p. 483 of this Norton Critical Edition. James's handwriting had never been clear, and sometimes he changed so much that his quarto sheet became an illegible tangle of lines and arrows. The compositors, he knew, would complain about such pages, and so he put the especially muddy ones aside to be typed.

He hoped that the New York Edition would stand as his monument, and so it does; but he did not live to see it recognized as such. The initial critical response was muted. Many readers resented any alteration to the books they had known for years; others read his great prefaces and turned his frank assessment of his own weaknesses against him. Moreover, it proved a financial failure: the edition's low sales barely covered the cost of the permissions fees demanded by the different publishers who held his rights. Then in 1934 the critic R. P. Blackmur collected James's prefaces into a single volume that he called *The Art of the Novel*. Blackmur's own introduction overstated their theoretical coherence; nevertheless he established them, and the work of revision from which they grew, as the supreme achievement of the novelist's last years. Our concern, however, lies not with that larger story but with the alterations to the *Portrait* itself. I've chosen five essays about James's revisions to reprint here, ones that go beyond the comparison of textual details to substantive questions of interpretation. But before introducing them I want to offer a sample of his work, presenting it without commentary but putting the changes in bold. The passage comes from James's initial description of Gilbert Osmond, and here it is in the novel's 1882 version:

> He was a man of forty, with a well-shaped head, upon which the hair, still dense, but prematurely grizzled, had been cropped close. He had a thin, delicate, sharply-cut face, of which the only fault was that it looked too pointed; an appearance to which the shape of his beard contributed not a

little. This beard, cut in the manner of the portraits of the sixteenth century and surmounted by a fair moustache, of which the ends had a picturesque upward flourish, gave its wearer a somewhat foreign, traditionary look, and suggested that he was a gentleman who studied effect. His luminous intelligent eye, an eye which expressed both softness and keenness—the nature of the observer as well as of the dreamer—would have assured you, however, that he studied it only within well-chosen limits, and that in so far as he sought it he found it. You would have been much at a loss to determine his nationality; he had none of the superficial signs that usually render the answer to this question an insipidly easy one. If he had English blood in his veins, it had probably received some French or Italian commixture; he was one of those persons who, in the matter of race, may, as the phrase is, pass for anything. He had a light, lean, lazy-looking figure, and was apparently neither tall nor short. He was dressed as a man dresses who takes little trouble about it.[1]

And here it is in the New York Edition as reprinted in this volume:

He was a man of forty, with a **high but** well-shaped head, **on** which the hair, still dense, but prematurely grizzled, had been cropped close. He had **a fine, narrow, extremely modeled and composed face, of which the only fault was just this effect of its running a trifle too much to points**; an appearance to which the shape of **the** beard contributed not a little. This beard, cut in the manner of the portraits of the sixteenth century and surmounted by a fair moustache, of which the ends had a **romantic** upward flourish, gave its wearer a foreign, traditionary look and suggested that he was a gentleman who studied **style. His conscious, curious eyes, however, eyes at once vague and penetrating, intelligent and hard, expressive of** the observer as well as of the dreamer, would have assured you **that** he studied it only within well-chosen limits, and that in so far as he sought it he found it. You would have been much at a loss to determine his **original clime and country**; he had none of the superficial signs that usually render the answer to this question an insipidly easy one. If he had English blood in his veins it had probably received some French or Italian commixture; **but he suggested, fine gold coin as he was, no stamp nor emblem of the common mintage that provides for general circulation; he was the elegant complicated medal struck off for a special occasion**. He had a light, lean, **rather languid-looking** figure, and was apparently neither tall nor short. He was dressed as a man dresses who takes little **other trouble about it than to have no vulgar things**. (162)

Some changes are but a single word; others add whole clauses, and in one case, James cuts a word rather than adding or changing one. No sentence here goes unaltered, and yet my example isn't especially notable. Many passages have revisions on this scale, and in some ways it's more interesting to note the moments James left pretty much alone, such as the wonderful description, in chapter 49, of Isabel's drive through Rome, where "in a world of ruins the ruin of her happiness seemed a less unnatural catastrophe."

An earlier Norton Critical Edition of this novel (1995) included a large textual apparatus that went through these changes page by page. I've decided against doing that here. This volume uses the text of the New York Edition. That's the one from which I teach, and I think it is in all ways stronger than the 1882 version. In writing about the *Portrait*, though, I do often turn to that earlier text, especially in reconstructing the story of James's artistic process. Any full

---

1. In *Henry James: Novels 1881–1886* (New York: Library of America, 1985), p. 425.

consideration of the novel requires constant comparison, with both editions open on your desk; fortunately they are each in print and easy to find. For many years textual scholars—and not just those at work on James—emphasized the last state of a given work, as representing the author's final intentions. Some critics today, however, rely instead on a book's initial version, the one that shaped its original reception: a shift that reflects our current emphasis on seeing works in their historical context, rather than as self-contained verbal icons. And in James's case there's an extra impetus for that preference. He left some important books out of the New York Edition, and in using a work's first iteration one does at least have a consistent principle of selection in moving from novel to novel. That, for example, is the choice the Library of America has made in its edition of James's work, and anyone who wants to compare the *Portrait*'s two texts will find the 1882 version included in their volume called *Henry James: Novels 1881–1886*.

The older James told friends that he was always astonished at how "filthily"[2] he used to write, and his secretary, Theodora Bosanquet, noted in her memoir of him, partially reprinted here, that he believed his early books all needed to be redone before they were "fit for appearance in the company" of his later ones; that was true even with the *Portrait*, successful though it had been, and the revised novel differs in thousands of particulars from the version his readers had known for a quarter of a century. Yet he meant those revisions to do more than to kick his early style into line. He also wanted, in Bosanquet's words, to uncover the "values implicit in his early works, the retrieval of neglected opportunities," and her two statements point in effect to different things. Both suggest James's sense of his work's inadequacies, but the one stresses its problems and the other its potentialities, the things the old writer might do that the younger one could not.

The revisions to the *Portrait* speak above all to his sense of its potential. The novel's style was already rich enough to sustain the brocade of his later manner. Many of its revisions seem inconsequential, substituting a proper name for a pronoun, or making a character "hint" instead of "intimate." Others are substantial, and as the example above shows, James took additional care in establishing his people. But the largest changes occur in his account of Isabel, and they have a special importance in the last pages of the novel's last chapter. Let me look at one of them, unimportant in itself, as a way to illustrate their burden. When she arrives at Gardencourt at the end of the novel the new servants make her wait while her name is brought up to her aunt. She waits a long time, and in the book's first version James had written that "she grew impatient at last; she grew nervous and even frightened."[3] The words say enough, but by 1906 he wanted to say something more, and now Isabel grows "nervous and scared—as scared as if the objects about her had begun to show for conscious things, watching her trouble with grotesque grimaces" (387).

That revision does two things. James now shows us the shape of Isabel's fears in a way that takes us far more deeply into her mind, and he figures that interior plunge in physical terms. The very furniture of these "wide brown rooms"[4] now glows with malicious life, as though the material world were responsive to the terms of her inner being, and many of the changes in James's account of her do put an additional weight on the imagistic workings of her mind. Few of them will register on even a careful reader as he or she moves from line to line. Yet they have great cumulative force, and that additional access of interiority does align the work's second version with James's last novels. Yet it's too simple to say that he has simply revised the *Portrait* in the light of his own later interests; for

2. Letter to Brander Matthews, March 24, 1915. In *Henry James Letters IV*, ed. Leon Edel (Harvard University Press, 1988), p. 744.
3. *Novels 1881–1886*, p. 777.
4. Ibid.

even in its first version it isn't finally about such things as the relations of America and Europe, or a young woman's choice of a husband. It was even then a drama of perception, and one that hangs upon the point of view of its protagonist.

No, there's something more complicated happening here, and we can best understand it by looking at the different ways in which James's prefaces define the act of revision. Sometimes he saw his books as if they were organic beings: living things that were capable of growth and change, children that could be trained up into a presentable maturity. More often he described them in pictorial terms, as if he were putting each piece back up on the easel, and asking himself what "time and the weather"[5] had done to it. Some had faded, and no varnish could bring them back. Other seemed to contain "a few buried secrets,"[6] and could be made to flush into color. An expression could be heightened, a pose adjusted, and yet he saw himself as working on what was already implicitly present. That's what Bosanquet meant in speaking of the New York Edition as a recovery of the chances he'd missed. But James says other things about revision as well, and in the preface to *The Golden Bowl* writes that in going back over his early work he has tried to close the gap between "the march of my present attention . . . [and] the march of my original expression."[7] I see the *Portrait*'s second version as a fulfillment of its first; as if the novel, like a person, had grown up while remaining in essence the same. To some readers, though, that statement will in fact suggest he's done something more to the book than simply retouch it, that the concerns of his later career are now dominant.

In their different ways the essays reprinted here each explore the terms of that debate. The first of them comes from a small volume published by the Hogarth Press in 1924. Theodora Bosanquet was James's secretary during the last decade of his life, taking down his dictation at her Remington typewriter but also doing much more, including finding him his last London apartment and organizing attendance at his 1916 deathbed. Her *Henry James at Work* provides an invaluable record of the old writer's habits of mind, and the pages included here contain the best evidence we have, outside of his own essays, of the way he saw the act of revision itself. Bosanquet does not, however, offer a close account of the difference those revisions make to interpretation. That process started with a 1944 essay by the Harvard critic F. O. Matthiessen. The article grew out of a class in which his students worked through a comparison of the two editions, and in its attention to the difference made by individual words it remains a central text for anyone interested in James's style. Many of his revisions, Matthiessen argues, work to emphasize the operations of Isabel's own consciousness as such, and often substitute that word for others. So when she first meets Osmond, she is no longer merely "entertained," as she was in 1882, but has "a private thrill in the consciousness of a new relation."

A new relation—or perhaps a new novel. Anthony J. Mazella's study suggests that Isabel isn't the same character in the New York Edition as she was in the novel's initial version. The revisions in essence remake her, in part by assigning a different set of motives for her actions. Nina Baym pushes such a reading further, arguing that it's not only Isabel that's new; the later text is a fundamentally different book. The first version stands for her as the product of its historical moment, a social novel written against the background of an ever-increasing discussion of women's rights and opportunities. The revisions, in contrast, turn it into an interior drama, a modernist look into Isabel's

---

5. Henry James, *Literary Criticism II: European Writers and the Prefaces* (New York: Library of America, 1984), p. 1045. The prefaces to *Roderick Hudson* and *The Golden Bowl*—the first and last novels in the edition, respectively—contain the fullest account of James's process.
6. Ibid., p. 1046.
7. Ibid., p. 1329.

understanding of her own situation. I would challenge Baym's position, for when in chapter 42 James set Isabel in motionless activity before the fire he discovered both the formal and the thematic preoccupations of his later career. His revisions don't change the novel so much as they make its opening chapters fit the book that it had, by its last ones, become. But the point is worth arguing, and her essay provides a necessary reminder of the way in which the *Portrait* stands as a book of its time, even as it also transformed that time. And, finally, Philip Horne's *Henry James and Revision* offers the most comprehensive account of the whole question to date, considering revision not simply in terms of the textual changes to the New York Edition but as a feature of James's creative life as a whole. One book revises another, a later character grows out of an earlier one, and Horne demonstrates that James's changes to the *Portrait* in particular amount to a conscious mediation "between the beginnings of his career and its later consummations."

THEODORA BOSANQUET

From Henry James at Work[†]

* * *

IV

In the autumn of 1907, when I began to tap the Remington typewriter at Henry James's dictation[1], he was engaged on the arduous task of preparing his Novels and Tales for the definitive New York edition, published in 1909. Since it was only between breakfast and luncheon that he undertook what he called "inventive" work, he gave the hours from half-past ten to half-past one to the composition of the prefaces which are so interesting a feature of the edition. In the evenings he read over again the work of former years, treating the printed pages like so many proof-sheets of extremely corrupt text. The revision was a task he had seen in advance as formidable. He had cultivated the habit of forgetting past achievements almost to the pitch of a sincere conviction that nothing he had written before about 1890 could come with any shred of credit through the ordeal of a critical inspection. On a morning when he was obliged to give time to the selection of a set of tales for a forthcoming volume, he confessed that the difficulty of selection was mainly the difficulty of reading them at all. "They seem," he said, "so bad until I *have* read them that I can't force myself to go through them except with a pen in my hand, altering as I go the crudities and ineptitudes that to my sense deform each page." Unfamiliarity and adverse prejudice are rare advantages for a writer to bring to the task of choosing among his works. For Henry James the prejudice might give way to half reluctant appreciation as the unfamiliarity passed into recognition, but it must be clear to every reader of the prefaces that he never lost the sense of being paternally responsible for two distinct families. For the earlier brood, acknowledged fruit of his alliance

---

† From *Henry James at Work* (1928; rpt. New York: Library of America, 2016), pp. 732–38. Notes are by the editor of this Norton Critical Edition. Bosanquet (1880–1961) became James's secretary in 1907 and remained with him until his death in 1916. Her memoir of him was first published by Leonard and Virginia Woolf at the Hogarth Press.
1. James suffered from writer's cramp and at some point during the composition of *What Maisie Knew* (1897) had begun to dictate his work.

with Romance, he claimed indulgence on the ground of their youthful spontaneity, their confident assurance, their rather touching good faith. One catches echoes of a plea that these elderly youngsters may not be too closely compared, to their inevitable disadvantage, with the richly endowed, the carefully bred, the highly civilized and sensitized children of his second marriage, contracted with that wealthy bride, Experience. Attentive readers of the novels may perhaps find the distinction between these two groups less remarkable than it seemed to their writer. They may even wonder whether the second marriage was not rather a silver wedding, with the old romantic mistress cleverly disguised as a woman of the world. The different note was possibly due more to the substitution of dictation for pen and ink than to any profound change of heart. But whatever the reason, their author certainly found it necessary to spend a good deal of time working on the earlier tales before he considered them fit for appearance in the company of those composed later. Some members of the elder family he entirely cast off, not counting them worth the expense of completely new clothes. Others he left in their place more from a necessary, though deprecated, respect for the declared taste of the reading public than because he loved them for their own sake. It would, for instance, have been difficult to exclude *Daisy Miller* from any representative collection of his work, yet the popularity of the tale had become almost a grievance. To be acclaimed as the author of *Daisy Miller* by persons blandly unconscious of *The Wings of the Dove* or *The Golden Bowl* was a reason among many for Henry James's despair of intelligent comprehension. Confronted repeatedly with *Daisy*, he felt himself rather in the position of some *grande dame* who, with a jewel-case of sparkling diamonds, is constrained by her admirers always to appear in the simple string of moonstones worn at her first dance.

From the moment he began to read over the earlier tales, he found himself involved in a highly practical examination of the scope and limits of permissible revision. Poets, as he pointed out, have often revised their verse with good effect. Why should the novelist not have equal license? The only sound reason for not altering anything is a conviction that it cannot be improved. It was Henry James's profound conviction that he could improve his early writing in nearly every sentence. Not to revise would have been to confess to a loss of faith in himself, and it was not likely that the writer who had fasted for forty years in the wilderness of British and American misconceptions without yielding a scrap of intellectual integrity to editorial or publishing tempters should have lost faith in himself. But he was well aware that the game of revision must be played with a due observance of the rules. He knew that no novelist can safely afford to repudiate his fundamental understanding with his readers that the tale he has to tell is at least as true as history and the figures he has set in motion at least as independently alive as the people we see in offices and motorcars. He allowed himself few freedoms with any recorded appearances or actions, although occasionally the temptation to correct a false gesture, to make it "right," was too strong to be resisted. We have a pleasant instance of this correction in the second version of *The American*. At her first appearance, the old Marquise de Bellegarde had acknowledged the introduction of Newman by returning his handshake "with a sort of British positiveness which reminded him that she was the daughter of the

Earl of St. Dunstan's." In the later edition she behaves differently. "Newman came sufficiently near to the old lady by the fire to take in that she would offer him no hand-shake. . . . Madame de Bellegarde looked hard at him and refused what she did refuse with a sort of British positiveness which reminded him that she was the daughter of the Earl of St. Dunstan's." There were good reasons why the Marquise should have denied Newman a welcoming handshake. Her attitude throughout the book was to be consistently hostile and should never have been compromised by the significantly British grip. Yet it is almost shocking to see her snatching back her first card after playing it for so many years. She was to perform less credible actions than shaking hands with an innocent American, as her progenitor knew very well. He invited his readers, in the preface to *The American*, to observe the impossible behaviour of the noble Bellegarde family, but he realized that since they had been begotten in absurdity the Bellegardes could under no stress of revision achieve a very solid humanity. The best he could do for them was to let a faint consciousness flush the mind of Valentin, the only detached member of the family. In the first edition Valentin warned his friend of the Bellegarde peculiarities with the easy good faith of the younger Henry James under the spell of the magic word "Europe." "My mother is strange, my brother is strange, and I verily believe I am stranger than either. Old trees have queer cracks, old races have odd secrets." To this statement he added in the revised version: "We're fit for a museum or a Balzac novel." A comparable growth of ironic perception was allowed to Roderick Hudson, whose comment on Rowland's admission of his heroically silent passion for Mary Garland, "It's like something in a novel," was altered to: "It's like something in a bad novel."

V

But the legitimate business of revision was, for Henry James, neither substitution nor re-arrangement. It was the demonstration of values implicit in the earlier work, the retrieval of neglected opportunities for adequate "renderings." "It was," as he explained in his final preface, "all sensibly, as if the clear matter being still there, even as a shining expanse of snow spread over a plain, my exploring tread, for application to it, had quite unlearned the old pace and found itself naturally falling into another, which might sometimes more or less agree with the original tracks, but might most often, or very nearly, break the surface at other places. What was thus predominantly interesting to note, at all events, was the high spontaneity of these deviations and differences, which become thus things not of choice but of immediate and perfect necessity: necessity to the end of dealing with the quantities in question at all." On every page the act of re-reading became automatically one with the act of re-writing, and the revised parts are just "those rigid conditions of re-perusal, registered; so many close notes, as who should say, on the particular vision of the matter itself that experience had at last made the only possible one." These are words written with the clear confidence of the artist who, in complete possession of his "faculties," had no need to bother himself with doubts as to his ability to write better at the end of a lifetime of hard work and varied experience than at the beginning. He knew he could write better. His readers have not always agreed with his own view. They have denounced the multiplication of qualifying clauses, the imposition of a system of punctuation which, although rigid and orderly, occasionally fails to act as a guide to immediate comprehension of the writer's intention, and the increasing passion for adverbial interpositions. "Adjectives are the sugar of literature and adverbs the salt," was Henry James's reply to a criticism which once came to his ears.

It must be admitted that the case for the revised version relies on other merits than simplicity or elegance to make its claim good. It is not so smooth, nor so easy, nor, on the whole, so pretty as the older form. But it is nearly always richer and more alive. Abstractions give place to sharp definite images, loose vague phrases to close-locked significances. We can find a fair example of this in *The Madonna of the Future*, a tale first published in 1879.[2] In the original version one of the sentences runs: "His professions, somehow, were all half professions, and his allusions to his work and circumstances left something dimly ambiguous in the background." In the New York Edition this has become: "His professions were practically somehow, all masks and screens, and his personal allusions as to his ambiguous background mere wavings of the dim lantern." In some passages it would be hard to deny a gain of beauty as well as of significance. There is, for instance, a sentence in the earlier account of Newman's silent renunciation of his meditated revenge, in the Cathedral of Notre Dame: "He sat a long time; he heard far-away bells chiming off, at long intervals, to the rest of the world." In the definitive edition of *The American* the passage has become: "He sat a long time; he heard far-away bells chiming off into space, at long intervals, the big bronze syllables of the Word."

A paragraph from *Four Meetings*, a tale worked over with extreme care, will give a fair idea of the general effect of the revision. It records a moment of the final Meeting, when the helplessly indignant narrator is watching poor Caroline ministering to the vulgar French cocotte who has imposed herself on the hospitality of the innocent little New Englander.

"At this moment," runs the passage of 1879, "Caroline Spencer came out of the house bearing a coffee pot on a little tray. I noticed that on her way from the door to the table she gave me a single quick vaguely appealing glance. I wondered what it signified; I felt that it signified a sort of half-frightened longing to know what, as a man of the world who had been in France, I thought of the Countess. It made me extremely uncomfortable. I could not tell her that the Countess was very possibly the runaway wife of a little hairdresser. I tried, suddenly, on the contrary, to show a high consideration for her."

The "particular vision" registered on re-perusal reveals states of mind much more definite than these wonderings and longings and vague appeals.

"Our hostess moreover at this moment came out of the house, bearing a coffee-pot and three cups on a neat little tray. I took from her eyes, as she approached us, a brief but intense appeal—the mute expression, as I felt, conveyed in the hardest little look she had yet addressed me, of her longing to know what as a man of the world in general and of the French world in particular, I thought of these allied forces now so encamped on

---

2. Actually in 1873. But 1879 was the date of its first appearance in Britain, as the title story of a volume published by Macmillan.

the stricken field of her life. I could only 'act,' however, as they said at North Verona, quite impenetrably—only make no answering sign. I couldn't intimate, much less could I frankly utter, my inward sense of the Countess's probable past, with its measure of her virtue, value and accomplishments, and of the limits of consideration to which she could properly pretend. I couldn't give my friend a hint of how I myself personally 'saw' her interesting pensioner—whether as the runaway wife of a too-jealous hair-dresser or of a too-morose pastry-cook, say; whether as a very small bourgeoise, in fine, who had vitiated her case beyond patching up, or even some character of the nomadic sort, less edifying still. I couldn't let in, by the jog of a shutter, as it were, a hard informing ray and then, washing my hands of the business, turn my back for ever. I could on the contrary but save the situation, my own at least, for the moment, by pulling myself together with a master hand and appearing to ignore everything but that the dreadful person between us *was* a 'grande dame.'"

Anyone genuinely interested in "the how and the whence and the why these intenser lights of experience come into being and insist on shining," will find it a profitable exercise to read and compare the old and the new versions of any of the novels or tales first published during the 'seventies or 'eighties. Such a reader will be qualified to decide for himself between the opinion of a bold young critic that "all the works have been subjected to a revision which in several cases, notably *Daisy Miller* and *Four Meetings*, amounts to their ruin," and their writer's confidence that "I shouldn't have breathed upon the old catastrophes and accidents, the old wounds and mutilations and disfigurements wholly in vain. . . . I have prayed that the finer air of the better form may sufficiently seem to hang about them and gild them over—at least for readers, however few, at all *curious* of questions of air and form."

* * *

F. O. MATTHIESSEN

The Painter's Sponge and Varnish Bottle[†]

I

One sign of how little technical analysis James has received is the virtual neglect of his revisions. Beyond Theodora Bosanquet's sensitive remarks in 'Henry James at Work' and occasional citation to annotate the elaborations of his later manner, they have been passed by. The only detailed exception is an essay on *Roderick Hudson* wherein the writer held that James' additions had largely served to spoil the clean outlines of its style.[1]

---

† From *Henry James: The Major Phase*, ed. F. O. Matthiessen (London and New York: Oxford University Press, 1944) pp. 152–86. Reprinted by permission of Oxford University Press. Matthiessen (1902–1950) taught for many years at Harvard and was one of the founding figures in the then-new discipline of American Studies; his *American Renaissance* (1941) set the canon of mid-nineteenth-century American literature for several generations. He committed suicide after a period of depression brought on both by the death of his partner, Russell Cheney, and by inquiries from the House Un-American Activities Committee.

1. Hélène Harvitt, 'How Henry James Revised *Roderick Hudson*: A Study in Style,' PMLA (March 1924), 203–227.

Yet James made these revisions at the plentitude of his powers, and they constituted a *re-seeing* of the problems of his craft. He knew that it would be folly to try to recast the structure of any of his works. In the first preface that he wrote, that to *Roderick Hudson*, he developed an analogy for his aims in the way his fellow-craftsman on canvas went about to freshen his surfaces, to restore faded values, to bring out 'buried secrets.' He undertook, in particular, a minute verbal reconsideration of the three early novels that he chose to re-publish.

My reason for singling out *The Portrait of a Lady* is that it is a much richer book than either of the two others. *Roderick Hudson* is full of interest for James' development, since the two halves of his nature, the creator and the critic, are in a sense projected in Roderick and Rowland. Moreover, he there first tried out his device of having his narrative interpreted by the detached observer. But the book as a whole remains apprentice work. The revision of *The American*—the most extensive of all—might tell us, among other things, how James tried to repair what he had himself come to consider the falsely romantic aspects of his denouement. But *The Portrait of a Lady* is his first unquestioned masterpiece. By considering all the issues that the revisions raise, we may see it with renewed clarity.[2]

Larger changes are very few. A page of conversation between Ralph Touchett and Lord Warburton (at the very end of Chapter XXVII) was recast in a way that shows James' more mature sense of a dramatic scene. What had been two pages of psychological scrutiny of Osmond just before his proposal to Isabel (Chapter XXIX) were felt by James to be otiose, and were cut to ten lines—an item of interest for the conventional view that the older James always worked the other way. But, with two important exceptions later to be looked into, we are to be concerned here with the tiniest brush strokes. What must be kept constantly in mind, therefore, is the design of the canvas as a whole. If that is done, we may have the intimate profit of watching the artist at his easel and of gaining insight into his principles of composition.

The writer's equivalent for the single flake of pigment is the individual word; and two words which James felt to be in need of consistent readjustment—'picturesque' and 'romantic'—form in themselves an index to his aims. He had begun the book in Florence and had finished it in Venice. He had been at the time still strongly under the spell of Italian art, which, as he wrote William, had first taught him 'what the picturesque is.' He had consequently used the word freely as a kind of aesthetic catch-all, too loosely as he came to feel, for he struck it out in almost every case. He had applied it to Gardencourt, to Isabel's grandmother's house in Albany, to Osmond's *objets d'art*; he changed it in the first case

2. James had developed early the habit of touching up his texts wherever possible; and he even made a few slight alterations in the *Portrait* between its appearance in *The Atlantic Monthly* (November 1880–December 1881) and in volume form. For instance, Madame Merle's first name was changed from Geraldine to Serena. But the changes that can instruct us in the evolution of his technique are naturally those he introduced when returning to the book after more than a quarter of a century.

James' copies of both *The American* and *The Portrait of a Lady*, containing his innumerable revisions in longhand on the margins and in inserted pages of typescript, are now in the Houghton Library at Harvard.

I want to thank again the group of Harvard and Radcliffe students with whom I read through Henry James in the winter of 1943, since they did most of the spade work for this essay.

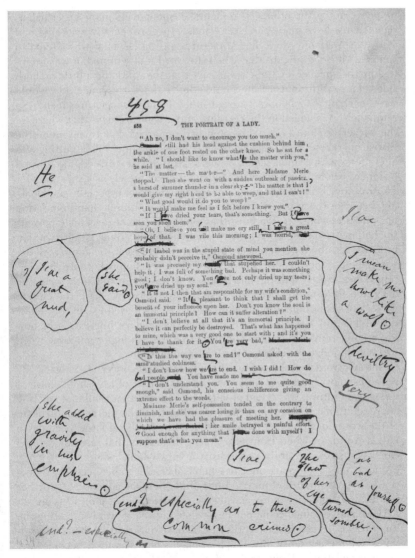

A sample page of James's revision to the New York Edition of *The Portrait of a Lady*. MS Am 1237.17, Houghton Library, Harvard University. For the final version, see p. 356–57 in this Norton Critical Edition.

to 'pictorial,' in the others to 'romantic.'[3] Some of its many other occurrences must have made the later James wince, especially where he had said that Madame Merle had 'a picturesque smile.' That was altered to 'amused.' It is significant that when the word was retained, it was qualified by the speaker, by Isabel, who says that she would be a little on both sides of a revolution, that she would admire the Tories since they would have 'a chance to behave so exquisitely. I mean so picturesquely.' 'So exquisitely' was added in the revision, and it is no accident that where, in the earlier version, Lord Warburton had remarked that Isabel found the British 'picturesque,' he was later made to say '"quaint."' That putting into quotation marks underscores Isabel's attitude, as, indeed, do several instances where James introduced 'romantic' not merely as a substitute for 'picturesque.' Isabel's first judgment of Caspar as 'not especially good looking' becomes 'he was not romantically, rather obscurely handsome'; and her initial response to Warburton as 'one of the most delectable persons she had met' is made much firmer—she judges him, 'though quite without luridity—as a hero of romance.' And when we find that she doesn't tell her sister about either his or Osmond's proposal, not simply because 'it entertained her to say nothing' but because 'it was more romantic,' and she delighted in 'drinking deep, in secret, of romance,' we have the clue to what James is building up through his greatly increased use of this adjective and noun. He is bound to sharpen the reader's impression of how incorrigibly romantic Isabel's approach to life is, an important issue when we come to judge the effect of the book's conclusion.

Another word that shows the drift of James' later concern is 'vulgar.' One of James' most limiting weaknesses, characteristic of his whole phase of American culture, was dread of vulgarity, a dread that inhibited any free approach to natural human coarseness. But here the increased intrusion of the word does no great damage. When 'the public at large' becomes 'a vulgar world,' or when Henrietta Stackpole asserts that our exaggerated American stress on brain power 'isn't a vulgar fault' (she had originally pronounced it a 'glorious' one), or when Isabel adds to her accruing reflections that Osmond had married her, 'like a vulgar adventurer,' for her money, we simply see more sharply the negative pole of James' vision.

His positive values come out in a whole cluster of words affecting the inner life of his characters, words in which we may read all the chief attributes of Jamesian sensibility. Ralph's 'delights of observation' become 'joys of contemplation.' Warburton's sisters' 'want of vivacity' is sharpened to 'want of play of mind,' just as Isabel's 'fine freedom of composition' becomes 'free play of intelligence.' On the other hand, Warburton, in Ralph's description, is toned down from 'a man of imagination' to 'a man of a good deal of charming taste,' in accordance with the high demands that James came to put upon the imagination as the discerner of truth. It is equally characteristic that Isabel's 'feelings' become her 'consciousness,' and that her 'absorbing happiness' in her first impressions of England becomes 'her fine, full consciousness.' She no longer feels that she is 'being entertained' by Osmond's conversation; rather she has 'what always gave her a very

3. I have included all the detailed references to both editions in the version of this essay that appeared in *The American Bookman* (Winter 1944). To avoid spotting these pages with unnecessary footnotes, I refer to that periodical any reader who is interested in following out the comparison for himself.

private thrill, the consciousness of a new relation.' Relations, intelligence, contemplation, consciousness—we are accumulating the words that define the Jamesian drama. No wonder that James came to feel that it had been flat to say that Isabel was fond 'of psychological problems.' As he rewrote it, she became fond, as he was, 'ever, of the question of character and quality, of sounding, as who should say, the deep personal mystery.'

II

To progress from single words to questions of style, we note at once the pervasive colloquialization. The younger James had used the conventional forms, 'cannot' and 'she would'; in his revised conversation these always appear as 'can't and 'she'd.' Of more interest is his handling of the 'he said—she said' problem, upon which the older James could well take pride for his ingenuity. Isabel 'answered, smiling' becomes Isabel 'smiled in return' or Isabel 'gaily engaged.' Osmond 'hesitated a moment' becomes that Jamesian favorite, Osmond 'just hung fire.' And for one more out of a dozen other evasions of the obvious, the Countess Gemini no longer 'cried . . . with a laugh'; her sound and manner are condensed into one word, 'piped.'

James' humor has often been lost sight of in discussion of the solemnities of his mandarin style. But he didn't lose it himself. His original thumbnail characterization of Isabel's sister was descriptive: 'Lily knew nothing about Boston; her imagination was confined within the limits of Manhattan.' A graphic twist brings that to life with a laugh: 'her imagination was all bounded on the east by Madison Avenue.'

The later James was more concrete. He had also learned what a source of life inheres in verbal movement. 'Their multifarious colloquies' is heavily abstract, whereas 'their plunge . . . into the deeps of talk' takes us right into the action. So too with the diverse ways in which James launched his characters into motion, as when Henrietta 'was very well dressed' became 'she rustled, she shimmered'; or when the Countess, instead of entering the room 'with a great deal of expression,' did it 'with a flutter through the air.' Such movement means that James was envisaging his scenes more dramatically; and, in the passage where Isabel has just been introduced to Osmond, we can see how natural it had become for the novelist to heighten any theatrical detail. Where he had formerly written that Isabel sat listening to Osmond and Madame Merle 'as an impartial auditor of their brilliant discourse,' he now substituted 'as if she had been at the play and had paid even a large sum for her place.' And as this scene advances, instead of saying that Madame Merle 'referred everything' to Isabel, James wrote that she 'appealed to her as if she had been on the stage, but she could ignore any learnt cue without spoiling the scene.'

Operating more pervasively, here as always, upon James' imagination, were analogies with pictures rather than with the stage. When he wanted to enrich his bare statement that the Countess 'delivered herself of a hundred remarks from which I offer the reader but a brief selection,' he said that she 'began to talk very much as if, seated brush in hand before an easel, she were applying a series of considered touches to a composition of figures already sketched in.' A phrase that shows us James' very process is when Isabel, instead of 'examining the idea' (of Warburton's 'being a personage'), is made to examine 'the image so conveyed.' The growth from ideas to images is what James had been fumbling for in his earlier preoccupation with the picturesque. The word might now embarrass him, but not the secret he had learned through it. He had originally opened the first of the chapters to be laid in Osmond's villa by remarking that 'a picturesque little group' was gathered there. What he meant to imply was made much more explicit in the revision: 'a small group that might have been described by a painter as composing well.'

That concern with composition grew from the conviction which he voiced in the preface to *Roderick Hudson*, that the novelist's subject, no less than the painter's, consisted ever in 'the related state, to each other, of certain figures and things.' And characters, he came to believe, could be best put into such relations when they were realized as visually, as lambently, as possible. This belief led him into one of his most recurrent types of revision, into endowing his *dramatis personae* with characterizing images. He had concluded his initial account of Ralph's ill health by remarking, 'The truth was that he had simply accepted the situation.' In place of that James was to introduce the poignancy that is Ralph's special note: 'His serenity was but the array of wild flowers niched in his ruin.' In comparable fashion, James added to his first description of Osmond, with no parallel in the original, an image that embodies the complex nature we are to find in him: 'He suggested, fine gold coin as he was, no stamp nor emblem of the common mintage that provides for general circulation; he was the elegant complicated medal struck off for a special occasion.'

Such elaborate images, more than any other aspect of James' later style, show his delight in virtuosity. Occasionally they seem to have been added purely because his eye fell on a dull patch of canvas, and he set out to brighten it up. Warburton's dim sisters don't contribute much in the original beyond 'the kindest eyes in the world.' But, in revising, James let himself go: their eyes are now 'like the balanced basins, the circles of "ornamental water," set, in parterres, among the geraniums.' In that image any functional intention may seem lost in the rococo flourish; but such was not usually the case. Take one very typical instance in the first detailed description of Caspar Goodwood—and it is significant of James' matured intentions that he introduced characterizing images of his chief figures at such important points. We are told in the first version that Caspar had undergone the usual gentleman athlete's education at Harvard, but that 'later, he had become reconciled to culture.' In the revision James conveyed much more of Caspar's energetic drive by means of a muscular image: 'later on he had learned that the finer intelligence too could vault and pull and strain.'

The full effect that James was trying for in such images might be instanced by the chapter which introduces Henrietta. Here we might follow James in the process of enlivening his sketch by a dozen fresh touches. The most interesting of these bring out Henrietta's character by the device of interrelating her appearance with her career. He did not rest content with saying that 'she was scrupulously, fastidiously neat. From top to toe she carried not an ink-stain.' He changed this into: 'she was as crisp and new and comprehensive as a first issue before the folding. From top to toe she had probably no misprint.' In spite of the loudness of her voice (which caused James to alter Henrietta 'murmured' to Henrietta 'rang out'), Ralph was originally surprised to find that she was not 'an abundant talker.' But in the revision the detailed glance at her profession is sustained, and he finds her not 'in the large type, the type of horrid "headlines."' Yet she still remains fairly terrifying to Ralph, and, a few pages farther on, James emphasized that by another kind of image. To point up the fact that 'she was brave,' he added, 'she went into cages, she flourished lashes, like a spangled lion-tamer.' With that as a springboard James could rise to the final sentence of this chapter. Originally Ralph had concluded, 'Henrietta, however, is fragrant—Henrietta is decidedly fragrant!' But this became a punch line: 'Henrietta, however, does smell of the Future—it almost knocks one down!'

James remarked in his preface that he had given the reader 'indubitably too much' of Henrietta—a thing that could be said of most of his *ficelles*; but in retouching he had at least done what he could to brighten every inch. In relation to her we may note another phase of his revision, his addition of epithets to characterize the world of which she is part. In Rome she is struck by the analogy between the ancient chariot ruts and 'the iron grooves which mark the course of the American horse-car.' These become more up to date: 'the overjangled iron grooves which express the intensity of American life.' Where James had written 'the nineteenth century,' he was later to call it 'the age of advertisement'; and glancing, not at America but at Europe, he named it 'an overcivilized age.' But it was Henrietta's realm he was thinking of again when, instead of having Madame Merle remark that 'it's scandalous, how little I know about the land of my birth,' he had her call it rather, in his most revelatory addition of this type: 'that splendid, dreadful, funny country—surely the greatest and drollest of them all.'

III

So far I have avoided the question that is usually raised first about James' revisions. Didn't he sometimes overwrite to no purpose as a mere occupational disease? Occasionally, without doubt, it is the older James talking instead of a character, as when Pansy, instead of saying, 'I have no voice—just a little thread,' is made to transform this into '. . . just a small sound like the squeak of a slate-pencil making flourishes.' But look at another sample where at first it would appear as though James had taken twice as many words to say the same thing, where 'Marriage meant that a woman should abide with her husband' became 'Marriage meant that a woman should cleave to the man with whom, uttering tremendous vows, she had stood at the altar.' In its context we can at least see what James was after. This passage is part of Isabel's reflections, and both its fuller rhythm and density are meant to increase its *inner* relevance. The best way, therefore, to judge the final value of James' rewriting is to relate it in each case to the character involved, an obligatory proceeding in dealing with the writer who asked, in *The Art of Fiction*: 'What is a picture or a novel that is *not* of character?'

The diverse types of revision demanded by the different characters may also remind us that we have in this book the most interestingly variegated group that James ever created. The center of attention is always Isabel, and the changes devoted to her may be read as a brief outline of the interpretation which James hoped we should give to his heroine. A few involve her looks. Whereas acquaintances of the Archer girls used to refer to her as 'the thin one,' James' tenderness for her was later to make this sound less invidious: 'the willowy one.' From his initial description of her in the house at Albany, he wanted to emphasize that she was less mistress of her fate than she fondly believed. He pointed this up by changing 'young girl' to 'creature of conditions.' He also, as a past master of what could be gained by the specific notation, changed the conditioning of her taste from 'a glimpse of contemporary aesthetics' to 'the music of Gounod, the poetry of Browning, the prose of George Eliot'—a change which recalls that these were also Minny Temple's tastes.

But James' chief interest in his heroine is revealed through another type of change. Warburton's belief that she is 'a thoroughly interesting woman' is made more intimate—'a really interesting little figure.' And a few lines below, when Ralph concludes that a character like hers 'is the finest thing in nature,' he says more precisely what he means by adding, in the revision, that she is 'a real little passionate force.' James devoted many of his later brush strokes to bringing her out as exactly that. Instead of passively wanting 'to be delighted,' she now wants 'to hurl herself into the fray.' It is equally symptomatic of her conduct that she refuses Warburton, not because such a marriage fails 'to correspond to any vision of happiness that she had hitherto entertained,' but because it fails 'to support any enlightened prejudice in favour of the free exploration of life.' The Isabel whom the later James saw with so much lucidity is a daughter of the transcendental afterglow, far less concerned about happiness than about enlightenment and freedom.

Another addition indicates that what is most required to make her respond is 'a bait to her imagination.' That is exactly why she is caught by Osmond. Mrs. Touchett originally said that Isabel was capable of marrying him 'for his opinions'; but she heightens this with more of the girl's romanticism in saying 'for the beauty of his opinions or for his autograph of Michael Angelo.' And that is how we see Isabel reacting to him. His 'things of a deep interest' become 'objects, subjects, contacts . . . of a rich association.' She reads into them also, in a favorite phrase of the later James, 'histories within histories.' When she defends him to Ralph, the revision makes her grounds much more explicit by adding to her question, 'What do you know against him?'—'What's the matter with Mr. Osmond's type, if it be one? His being so independent, so individual, is what I most see in him.' And again, instead of saying 'Mr. Osmond is simply a man— he is not a proprietor,' she expands this with her feeling, 'Mr. Osmond's simply a very lonely, a very cultivated and a very honest man—he's not a prodigious proprietor.'

This is the Isabel of whom James felt it no longer adequate just to say, 'she was an excitable creature, and now she was much excited.' He transformed that into an image: 'Vibration was easy to her, was in fact too constant with her, and she found herself now humming like a smitten harp.' Such vibrations are intrinsic to the rhythm of her thought. She no longer reflects merely that 'she had loved him,' but extends that reflection with 'she had so anxiously and yet so ardently given herself.' It is not padding, therefore, when, upon discovering how wrong she has been about Osmond, she does not conclude, 'There was only one way to repair it—to accept it,' but adds '. . . just immensely (oh, with the highest grandeur!) to accept it.'

The revisions affecting Osmond are of a very different sort. Far more of them relate to his appearance, to the polished, elegant and slightly ambiguous surface which James wants the reader to study more fully. His 'sharply-cut face' becomes 'extremely modelled and composed.' James' description of his eyes is far more careful. They are no longer 'luminous' and 'intelligent' expressing 'both softness and keenness,' but 'conscious, curious eyes . . . at once vague and penetrating, intelligent and hard.' This is quite in keeping with his smile, which is now his 'cool' smile, and with his voice, of which it is now said that, though fine, it 'somehow wasn't sweet.' He does not speak 'with feeling' but 'beautifully'; and his laugh, instead of being 'not ill-natured,' has now 'a finer patience.' James has done an expert job of heightening Osmond's thoroughly studied effect. He underscores the fact that Osmond's taste was his only law by saying, not that he lived 'in a serene, impersonal way,' but 'in a sorted, sifted, arranged world,' where his 'superior qualities' become 'standards and touchstones other than the vulgar.'

Osmond is entirely devoted to forms, and to accent this trait, James introduces one of his most interesting later devices: he interrelates Osmond's character with his surroundings in a way that shows again how much the novelist had learned from the plastic arts.[4] On the first occasion that Osmond entertains Isabel, James wants her to be impressed with the rare distinction of the collector's villa. Osmond's footboy is now made deliberately picturesque: instead of remaining merely 'the shabby footboy,' he becomes 'tarnished as to livery and quaint as to type,' and, with a fine added flourish, James tells us that he might 'have issued from some stray sketch of old-time manners, been "put in" by the brush of a Longhi or a Goya.' James also added in the revision that Osmond was marked for Isabel 'as by one of those signs of the highly curious that he was showing her on the underside of old plates and in the corner of sixteenth-century drawings.' As Isabel thinks over this visit afterwards, she reflects that his care for beauty 'had been the main occupation of a lifetime of which the arid places were watered with the sweet sense of a quaint, half-anxious, half-helpless fatherhood.' In the revision these thoughts rise from her impression of how she had seen him: his preoccupation with beauty made his life 'stretch beneath it in the disposed vistas and with the ranges of steps and terraces and fountains of a formal Italian garden—allowing only for arid places freshened by the natural dews,' and so on.

In building up the reasons why she took her romantic view of him, James also embarked on an extended flight:

> What continued to please this young lady was his extraordinary subtlety. There was such a fine intellectual intention in what he said, and the movement of his wit was like that of a quick-flashing blade.

> What continued to please this young woman was that while he talked so for amusement he didn't talk, as she had heard people, for 'effect.' He uttered his ideas as if, odd as they often appeared, he were used to them and had lived with them; old polished knobs and heads and handles, of precious substance, that could be fitted if necessary

---

4. I have given further instances from his earlier works in "Henry James and the Plastic Arts," *The Kenyon Review* (Autumn 1943).

to new walking-sticks—not switches plucked in destitution from the common tree and then too elegantly waved about.

The new passage stresses, if in oblique ways and with some needless verbiage, Osmond's utter dependence on art rather than on nature. The 'old polished knobs,' like the 'complicated medal' to which he is compared, make him indisseverable from his collector's items. It is not surprising that such a deliberately shaped work of art as he is 'mystified' Isabel. (In the first version he had merely 'puzzled' her.) It is fitting too that, as she comes under his fascination, she should feel not merely 'a good deal older than she had done a year before,' but also 'as if she were "worth more" for it, like some curious piece in an antiquary's collection.' For, in ways that her inexperience cannot possibly fathom, that is precisely how Osmond proposes to treat her. She appeals to him, not for being 'as bright and soft as an April cloud,' but in one of James' most functional revisions, 'as smooth to his general need of her as handled ivory to the palm.'

The mystification is only Isabel's, the ambiguity is all in what Osmond concealed, not in any doubts that James entertained about him. The revision increases his 'lost' quality. His 'peculiarities' are called his 'perversities,' and where it was remarked that he consulted his taste alone, James now adds 'as a sick man consciously incurable consults at last only his lawyer.' The reader accepts entirely Ralph's judgment of Osmond as a sterile dilettante; but his quality is deepened when Ralph recognizes the futility of trying to persuade Isabel, not that the man is 'a humbug,' but rather that there is something 'sordid or sinister' in him. With that deepening even Osmond becomes poignant: his 'keen, expressive, emphatic' face becomes 'firm, refined, slightly ravaged'—a far more telling portrait.

The character in this book around whom ambiguity gathers most is Madame Merle, since she has to play a double rôle throughout. James' changes involving her are chiefly of two sorts. He decided, for one thing, that her surface should be less transparent to Isabel. And so it is when Isabel asks her if she has not suffered that her 'picturesque smile' is elaborated into 'the amused smile of a person seated at a game of guesses.' She is also called 'smooth' instead of 'plump.' When Madame Merle introduced her to Osmond, Isabel wondered about 'the nature of the tie that united them. She was inclined to imagine that Madame Merle's ties were peculiar.' As James looked over that, it seemed to strike too close to the actual liaison, which he didn't want Isabel to suspect for a long time yet. So he toned it up to 'the nature of the tie binding these superior spirits. She felt that Madame Merle's ties always somehow had histories.'

But in the other type of change for Madame Merle, James felt, as he did with Osmond, that he must make her character unmistakable to the reader. So he no longer endowed her with 'a certain nobleness,' but with 'a certain courage'; not with 'geniality' but with 'grace.' Even in changing the music that Isabel overhead her playing from 'something of Beethoven's' to 'something of Schubert's,' James must have felt that he was bringing it more within Madame Merle's emotional compass. When Isabel finally comes to know her secret, the girl reflects, not just that her friend was 'false,' but 'even deeply false . . . deeply, deeply, deeply.' And Madame

Merle's guilt is spoken of, not in terms 'of vivid proof,' but 'of ugly evidence . . . of grim things produced in court.'

Such details—of which there are many more—are important in allaying the usual suspicion that James' ambiguity is unintentional, the obscurantism of a man who couldn't make up his own mind. When the writing becomes denser, as it frequently does in the revision, this is owing rather to James' gradual development of one of his special gifts, the ability so to handle a conversation that he keeps in the air not merely what is said, but what isn't—the passage of thoughts without words. The situation here which challenged most this skill of the later James was when Warburton turned up again after Isabel's marriage. What she had to decide was whether, despite his honorable pretensions, he was still in love with her. Their interplay is made more subtle. To judge the value of this kind of rewriting you must follow the whole chapter, but one series of slight changes may show what James was about.

As they met again, in the first version, Isabel 'hardly knew whether she were glad or not.' Warburton, however, 'was plainly very well pleased.' In the revision his feelings are not given to us so explicitly: he 'was plainly quite sure of his own sense of the matter.' Only as the conversation advances do Isabel—and the reader—gain the evidence she is after. In a moment or two, he remarks how charming a place she has to live in. In the original he said this, 'brightly, looking about him.' But this became: 'with a look, round him, at her established home, in which he might have caught the dim ghost of his old ruefulness.' That reveals to Isabel nearly all she needs, and her impression is clinched, when, instead of turning upon her 'an eye that gradually became more serious,' he gives her, in addition, 'the deeper, the deepest consciousness of his look.' From that moment Isabel knows how unwise it would be for him to marry her stepdaughter Pansy, no matter how much Osmond wants the match.

If such a situation caused James thus to weave the texture of his style more complexly, the changes that relate to Pansy and to Ralph, though equally slight, may reveal another significant quality. In the scale of emotional vibrations James is more impressive in striking the note of tenderness than that of passion. We can observe this in the way he heightened some of his most moving passages. How utterly Pansy is at the mercy of her father's will is underlined by several details. Consider, for instance, her smile, in connection with which we can note again James' extraordinary care to bring out every revelatory phase of his characters' looks. At the moment of Pansy's first appearance in the narrative, James remarked that her 'natural and usual expression seemed to be a smile of perfect sweetness.' But the point about Pansy is that she has had so little chance to be natural or spontaneous, and so James revised this: her face was 'painted with a fixed and intensely sweet smile.' So too with the characterizing image that he created for her. Instead of saying that Pansy entertained Isabel 'like a little lady,' James wrote that she 'rose to the occasion as the small, winged fairy in the pantomime soars by the aid of the dissimulated wire.' Thus Pansy's trapped state is suggested to us from the outset, and on the occasion when Isabel tells her that she is going to marry her father, James made two additions that show how he had learned to handle irony. Originally Isabel had said, 'My good little Pansy, I shall be very kind to you.' But to that James added: 'A vague, inconsequent vision of her coming in some odd way to need it had intervened with the effect of a chill.' And when Pansy answered, 'Very well then; I have nothing to fear,' James no longer had her declare that 'lightly,' but 'with her note of prepared promptitude.' And he also added, as part of Isabel's reflection: 'What teaching she had had, it seemed to suggest—or what penalties for non-performance she dreaded!'

We can read, in these extensions, the same thing that we have observed in the major characters, James' deepening of emotional tones. The most affecting passage in the book is the death of Ralph, for there James is expressing the tenderness of pure devotion, disencumbered of any worldly aims. The characterizing image noted above was designed to increase our sense of Ralph's precarious hold on life. To increase also our sense of his devotion to Isabel, 'his cousin' was twice changed to 'the person in the world in whom he was most interested.' The scene between these two, as he lies dying, is very short, and the only significant change is in Ralph's last speech. In the original this read: '"And remember this," he continued, "that if you have been hated, you have also been loved."' To that James added: '"Ah, but, Isabel—*adored!*" he just audibly and lingeringly breathed.' There it may become a debatable matter of taste whether the simpler form is not more moving; but the later James felt impelled to a more high-keyed emotional register. Both Ralph and Isabel, instead of 'murmuring' or 'adding softly' are made to 'wail.'[5] It is difficult to keep such tones from becoming sentimental, but how little James was inclined to sentimentalize can be seen in his handling of Ralph's funeral. Originally James pronounced it 'not a disagreeable one'; but he made his later statement stronger: it was 'neither a harsh nor a heavy one.'

IV

The two most extensive passages of rewriting are yet to be looked at. One relates to the Countess Gemini, and the other to Caspar Goodwood. Both can give us insight into how James conceived dramatic structure, and how he also felt that the climax of this book needed strengthening.

In comparing the two versions, it is notable that the sequence of chapters which James pronounced, in the preface, as being the best in the book—the sequence that extends from Isabel's glimpse of the two together, with Osmond seated while Madame Merle is standing, through the long vigil in which Isabel gradually pieces together her situation—that these three chapters (XL–XLII), with their important issues, were left substantially unchanged. So too with the fateful interview between Osmond and Isabel (Chapter XLVI) which shows how hopelessly far apart they have grown. But the scene with the Countess (Chapter LI), in which Isabel's suspicions are first given explicit names, was greatly recast. Some of the reasons for this are suggested by what James wrote in his notebook at the time when the novel had begun to appear in *The Atlantic* and he was trying to see his way clear to his conclusion: 'After Isabel's marriage there are five more instalments, and the success of the whole story greatly

---

5. This is also true in the other most directly emotional scene, the death of Ralph's father:
"My father died an hour ago."
"Ah, my poor Ralph!" the girl murmured, putting out her hand to him.
"My dear father died an hour ago."
"Ah, my poor Ralph!" she gently wailed, putting out her two hands to him.

depends upon this portion being well conducted or not. Let me then make the most of it—let me imagine the best. There has been a want of action in the earlier part, and it may be made up here. The elements that remain are in themselves, I think, very interesting, and they are only to be strongly and happily combined. The weakness of the whole story is that it is too exclusively psychological—that it depends too little on incident; but the complete unfolding of the situation that is established by Isabel's marriage may nonetheless be quite sufficiently dramatic. The idea of the whole thing is that the poor girl, who has dreamed of freedom and nobleness, who has done, as she believes, a generous, natural, clear-sighted thing, finds herself in reality ground in the very mill of the conventional. After a year or two of marriage the antagonism between her nature and Osmond's comes out—the open opposition of a noble character and a narrow one. There is a great deal to do here in a small compass; every word, therefore, must tell—every touch must count. If the last five parts of the story appear crowded, this will be rather a good defect in consideration of the perhaps too great diffuseness of the earlier portion.'

As James went on outlining his intentions, he was still undecided whether the revelation of Pansy's parentage should come through Madame Merle herself or through the Countess: 'Better on many grounds that it should be the latter; and yet in that way I lose the "great scene" between Madame Merle and Isabel.' Twenty-five years later he was still bothered by what he had lost. In the passage of deadly quietness between Isabel and Osmond, and, subsequently, between Isabel and Madame Merle, he seems to have felt that his drama was too inward, that he needed a more emotional scene. And so he rewrote nearly all the lines in which the Countess told Isabel of the liaison.

He had already given considerable attention to making the Countess' character a more lively mixture. Ralph's first description of her was changed from 'rather wicked' to 'rather impossible'; and in her own disarming self-characterization, instead of saying, 'I am only rather light,' she pronounced herself 'only rather an idiot and a bore.' James had originally said that her expression was 'by no means disagreeable'; but here he particularized: it was made up of 'various intensities of emphasis and wonder, of horror and joy.' Also, to a quite astonishing degree, by recurring to a bird-image for her, he sustained her in a whir. For example, in her first meeting with Isabel, she delivered her remarks 'with a variety of little jerks and glances.' But the bird-motif gave these the momentum of 'little jerks and pecks, of roulades of shrillness,' with the result that James was stimulated to a further flight of his own, and added that her accent was 'as some fond recall of good English, or rather of good American, in adversity.'

This kind of a character had dramatic possibilities, and, in his revision, James exploited them to the full. He did everything he could to make her revelations to Isabel into the 'great scene' he had missed. Isabel is alone, thinking of what will happen if, in defiance of Osmond's wishes, she goes to England to see Ralph before he dies. Then, suddenly, the Countess 'stood before her.' Thus the original, but in the rewriting the Countess 'hovered before her.' And to give us an intimation that something is coming, James added that the Countess 'lived assuredly, it might be said, at the window of her spirit, but now she was leaning far out.' As Lawrence Leighton, who first drew my attention to the importance of this scene for James' structure, remarked, this is like 'an extra blast from the trumpets' to announce the herald. It occurs to Isabel for the first time that her sister-in-law might say something, not 'important,' but 'really human.'

In what follows much subtle attention was paid to the Countess' diction. James endowed her with a more characteristic colloquial patter, with such epithets as 'poverina' and 'cara mia.' Instead of saying that Madame Merle had wanted 'to save her reputation,' she says, 'to save her skin'; and, in her view, Isabel has not merely 'such a pure mind'—she calls it 'beastly pure,' as such a woman would. Her speeches are considerably increased in length, one of them by almost a page. There is hardly any addition to her ideas, but as Mr. Leighton also observed, 'James wanted a good harangue, the sort of speech an actress could get her teeth into.' Her quality is melodramatic, but it is effectively more baleful than in the first version.

James has also built up the contrast between her and Isabel. The Countess expected—and hoped—that the girl would burst out with a denunciation of Osmond. But instead she is filled with pity for Madame Merle. She thinks even of Osmond's first wife, that 'he must have been false' to her—'and so very soon!' That last phrase is an addition that emphasizes Isabel's incurable innocence, despite all the experience through which she is passing. It glances ironically also at her own situation. When she goes on to reflect that at least Osmond has been faithful to her, the Countess says it depends on what you call faithful: 'When he married you he was no longer the lover of another woman—*such* a lover as he had been, *cara mia*, between their risks and their precautions, while the thing lasted!' Everything after the dash is added, and we can hear the Countess smacking her lips over such details, while Isabel recoils into herself. Where the first version had remarked that she 'hesitated, though there was a question in her eyes,' the utter cleavage between her and her gossipy interlocutress is now brought out: she 'hesitated as if she had not heard; as if her question—though it was sufficiently there in her eyes—were all for herself.' When, a moment or two later, Isabel wondered why Madame Merle never wanted to marry Osmond, the Countess had originally contented herself with saying that Madame Merle 'had grown more ambitious.' But to that James added: '"besides, she has never had, about him," the Countess went on, leaving Isabel to wince for it so tragically afterwards—"she *had* never had, what you might call any illusions of *intelligence*."' The Countess is happy to get in a dig at her brother, but for Isabel and for the reader there is the irony that Isabel herself had been fooled by just such illusions. That gives the final twist to the knife.

After this scene there remain only four chapters. There is the brief final encounter with Madame Merle, who sees in an instant that Isabel now knows everything. Isabel then says good-bye to Pansy, but promises that she won't desert her. The rest of the book is taken up with Isabel's trip to England, with her farewell to Ralph, and with Caspar's return to her. The last chapter is largely her struggle with him, and James' significant additions are led up to by the emphases that he has given to Caspar's character earlier in the book. He has introduced many details that sharpen the impression of Caspar's indomitable energy. When Isabel first compares him with Warburton, she feels that there is 'something too forcible, something oppressive and restrictive' about him. But this was made more concrete: 'a disagreeably strong push, a kind of hardness of presence.' A revelatory image was introduced to contrast Isabel's feeling about Warburton: instead of refusing to 'lend a receptive ear' to his suit, she now 'resists conquest' at his 'large quiet hands.' But Caspar is 'a kind of fate,' now, indeed, 'a kind of grim fate.' He himself gives fuller expression to the tension between them when he has first pursued her to London. Instead of saying, 'Apparently it was disagreeable to you even to write,' he makes it 'repugnant.' And he remarks bitterly, not that his insistence on his suit 'displeases' her, but that it 'disgusts.' As the best means of characterizing him, James developed a recurrent image of armor. In his first account he had merely remarked that Caspar was 'the strongest man' Isabel had ever known; but to this he added: 'she saw the different fitted parts of him as she had seen, in museums and portraits, the different fitted parts of armoured warriors—in plates of steel handsomely inlaid with gold.' Later on, his eyes, instead of wearing 'an expression of ardent remonstrance,' seemed 'to shine through the vizard of a helmet.' And when Isabel tries to measure his possible suffering, she no longer reflects that 'he had a sound consititution,' but that 'he was naturally plated and steeled, armed essentially for aggression.'

He follows her to Italy to object strenuously to her engagement to Osmond: 'Where does he come from? Where does he belong?' That second question was added in the revision, as was also Isabel's thought, 'She had never been so little pleased with the way he said "belawng."' But, in spite of everything, Isabel cannot escape feeling Caspar's power; and in rewriting their final scene, James made an incisive analysis of his mixed repulsion and attraction for her. She is alone under the trees at Gardencourt, when Caspar suddenly appears—just as Warburton had surprised her there once before. In what follows we are made to feel her overpowering sensation of his physical presence, from the moment that James adds that he was 'beside her on the bench and pressingly turned to her.' As he insists that her husband is 'the deadliest of fiends,' and that he, Caspar, is determined to prevent her from the 'horror' of returning to him (both 'deadliest' and 'horror' were additions), Isabel realizes that 'she had never been loved before,' To that realization the original had added: 'It wrapped her about; it lifted her off her feet.' But now James wrote: 'She had believed it, but this was different; this was the hot wind of the desert, at the approach of which the others dropped dead, like mere sweet airs of the garden. It wrapped her about; it lifted her off her feet, while the very taste of it, as of something potent, acrid, and strange, forced open her set teeth.'

That image takes her as far away from her surroundings and the gentlemanly devotion of a Warburton as it does from the decadent egotism of an Osmond. For a moment she is completely overpowered. Caspar's voice, saying, 'Be mine, as I'm yours,' comes to her, not merely 'through a confusion of sound,' but 'harsh and terrible, through a confusion of vaguer sounds.' He takes her in his arms, and, in the first version, the climax is reached with: 'His kiss was like a flash of lightning; when it was dark again she was free.' But now James felt it necessary to say far more: 'His kiss was like white lightning, a flash that spread, and spread again, and stayed; and it was extraordinarily as if, while she took it, she felt each thing in his hard manhood that had least pleased her, each agressive fact of his face, his figure, his presence, justified of its intense identity and made one with this act of possession. So had she heard of those wrecked and under water following a train of images before they sink. But when darkness returned she was free.'

That conveys James' awareness of how Isabel, in spite of her marriage, has remained essentially virginal, and of how her resistance and her flight from Caspar are partly fear of sexual possession. But the fierce attraction she also feels in this passage would inevitably operate likewise for a girl of her temperament, in making her do what she conceived to be her duty, and sending her back to her husband.

v

That brings us to the ending of the book, which has seldom been rightly interpreted. The difference between the two versions is one of the few of James' revisions that is generally known. Henrietta has told Caspar that Isabel has gone back to Rome:

> 'Look here, Mr. Goodwood,' she said; 'just you wait.' On which he looked up at her.

Thus the final lines in the original. But to these James added:

> —but only to guess, from her face, with a revulsion, that she simply meant he was young. She stood shining at him with that cheap comfort, and it added, on the spot, thirty years to his life. She walked him away with her, however, as if she had given him now the key to patience.

Many critics have held this difference to mean that James had changed his mind, that in the original he had given Caspar more hope. But he seems rather to have made unmistakably explicit what he had always intended to imply. He had said in his notebook outline that Isabel was to be greatly moved by Caspar's 'passionate outbreak': 'she feels the full force of his devotion—to which she has never done justice; but she refuses. She starts again for Italy—and her departure is the climax and termination of the story.' James had also observed there that Henrietta was to have 'the last word,' to utter 'a characteristic characterization of Isabel.' But he must have felt in revising that he had been too brief, that he had failed to drive home to the reader that what was being expressed was no sure promise about Isabel, but rather Henrietta's optimism, which refuses to accept defeat.

The end of Isabel's career is not yet in sight. That fact raises a critical issue about James' way of rounding off his narratives. He was keenly aware of what his method involved. As he wrote in his notebook, upon concluding his detailed project: 'With strong handling it seems to me that it may all be very true, very powerful, very touching. The obvious criticism of course will be that it is not finished—that it has not seen the heroine to the end of her situation—that I have left her *en l'air*. This is both true and false. The *whole* of anything is never told; you can only take what groups together. What I have done has that unity—it groups together. It is complete in itself—and the rest may be taken up or not, later.'

This throws a great deal of light—perhaps more than any single passage of his published work—on how James conceived of structure. He recounted in the preface to the *Portrait* how Turgenieff had encouraged him in his belief that the important thing to start with was not an air-tight plot, but rather a character or group of characters who are so living that the main question becomes to 'invent and select' the complications that such characters 'would be most likely to produce and to feel.'

Years before the *Portrait*, William James had commented on the effect of such a method, as it struck him in *A Most Extraordinary Case* (1868), one of the first half dozen stories that Henry had printed. William felt that here he understood for the first time what Henry was aiming for: 'to give an impression like that we often get of people in life: Their orbits come out of space and lay themselves for a short time along of ours, and then off they whirl again into the unknown, leaving us with little more than an impression of their reality and a feeling of baffled curiosity as to the mystery of the beginning and the end of their being,' William thought such a method difficult to make succeed, but 'with a deep justification in nature.' He was to grow somewhat less sure of its efficacy, as can be read in his tone about *The Tragic Muse*: 'the final winding up is, as usual with you, rather a losing of the story in the sand, yet that is the way in which things lose themselves in real life.' Henry, on the other hand, grew steadily to have more confidence in what he was doing, until he declared, in the preface to *Roderick Hudson*: 'Really, universally, relations stop nowhere, and the exquisite problem of the artist is eternally but to draw, by a geometry of his own, the circle within which they shall happily *appear* to do so.' That gives his essential conception of the kind of wholeness that form imposes.

He had been particularly concerned in the *Portrait* with launching Isabel Archer into action, with presenting her so vividly that his narrative would compose itself around the primary question, 'Well, what will she *do*?' It has recently been assumed that James believed entirely in the rightness of his heroine's conduct, and that since our age no longer feels as he—and she—did about the strictness of the marriage vow, we can no longer respond to the book except as to a period piece. But that is to misread not merely the ending, but all of James' own 'characteristic characterization' of Isabel. He could hardly have made a more lucid summary of the weaknesses that she exposed to Europe: 'her meagre knowledge, her inflated ideals, her confidence at once innocent and dogmatic, her temper at once exacting and indulgent'—that whole passage of analysis on the evening after her arrival at Gardencourt, a passage untouched in the revision, is meant to have our closest scrutiny.

As Isabel embarks on her 'free exploration' of life, Henrietta is outspoken in declaring that she is drifting rather to 'some great mistake,' that she is not enough 'in contact with reality,' with the 'toiling, striving' world. Ralph tells her that she has 'too much conscience'—a peculiarly American complication in the romantic temperament. Although all her diverse friends are united in their disapproval of Osmond, she proceeds to do the wrong thing for the right reasons. She has a special pride in marrying him, since she feels that she is not only 'taking,' but also 'giving'; she feels too the release of transferring some of the burden of her inheritance to another's conscience—James' way of commenting on how harm was done to her by her money. But once she discerns what Osmond is really like, and how he has trapped her, she is by no means supine in his toils. She stands up to him with dignity, she even asks Pansy, 'Will you come away with me now?' Yet Isabel knows that is impossible; she knows, even as she leaves, that she will have to return to Rome for Pansy's sake.

But much more is involved than that—James' whole conception of the discipline of suffering. It is notable that his kinship here to Hawthorne becomes far more palpable in the final version. Take the instance when, at the time of Ralph's death, Isabel realizes how Mrs. Touchett has missed the essence of life by her inability to feel. It seemed to Isabel that Ralph's mother 'would find it a blessing today to be able to indulge a regret. She wondered whether Mrs. Touchett were not trying, whether she had not a desire for the recreation of grief.' James made this much fuller, particularly the latter portion. Isabel wondered if Mrs. Touchett 'were not even missing those enrichments of consciousness and privately trying—reaching out for some aftertaste of life, dregs of the banquet; the testimony of pain or the cold recreation of remorse.' The view of suffering adumbrated there, even the phrasing, recalls Hawthorne's *The Christmas Banquet*, where the most miserable fate is that of the man whose inability to feel bars him out even from the common bond of woe.

The common bond of sin, so central to Hawthorne's thought, was also accentuated through James' retouching. When Madame Merle finally foresees what is ahead, she says to Osmond in the original, 'How do bad people end? You have made me bad.' But James extended this with a new italicized emphasis, 'How do bad people end?—especially as to their *common* crimes. You have made me as bad as yourself.' Isabel's link with humanity, if not through sin—unless her willful spirit counts as such—is through her acceptance of suffering. The inevitability of her lot is made more binding in the revision. Her reflection that 'she should not escape, she should last,' becomes 'she should never escape, she should last to the end.' She takes on heightened stature when James no longer says that, while she sat with Ralph, 'her spirit rose,' but that 'her ache for herself became somehow her ache for *him*.' The pathos of her situation is also intensified in proportion to her greater knowledge of what is involved. 'She reflected that things change but little, while people change so much' is far less affecting than 'she envied the security of valuable "pieces" which change by no hair's breadth, only grow in value, while their owners lose inch by inch, youth, happiness, beauty.'

In both the original and the revision Isabel lays the most scrupulous emphasis upon the sacredness of a promise. Despite all her eagerness for culture, hers is no speculative spirit. Osmond comes to despise her for having 'the moral horizon' of a Unitarian minister—'poor Isabel, who had never been able to understand Unitarianism!' But whether she understands it or not, she is a firm granddaughter of the Puritans, not in her thought but in her moral integrity. In portraying her character and her fate, James was also writing an essay on the interplay of free will and determinism. Isabel's own view is that she was 'perfectly free,' that she married Osmond of her most deliberate choice, and that, however miserable one may be, one must accept the consequences of one's acts. James knew how little she was free, other than to follow to an impulsive extreme everything she had been made by her environment and background.

Thus he leaves her to confront her future, and is satisfied if he has endowed his endowed his characters with so much 'felt life' that the reader must weigh for himself what is what is likely to lie ahead in her relation with Osmond. It may be that, as Isabel herself conjectures, he may finally 'take her money and let her go.' It may be that once she has found a husband for Pansy, she will feel that she no longer has to remain in Rome. James believed that the arbitrary circle of art should stimulate such speculations beyond its confines, and thus create also the illusion of wider life. He had about Isabel a tragic sense, but he did not write a tragedy, as he was to do in *The Wings of the Dove*, since this earlier drama was lacking in the finality of purgation and judgment. But his view of his material was not at all ambiguous. He knew how romantic Isabel was, how little experienced she was in mature social behavior. He had shown that she was completely mistaken in believing that 'the world lay before her—she could do whatever she chose.' But James also knew the meaning and the value of renunciation. The American life of his day, in its reckless plunge to outer expansiveness and inner defeat, had taught him that as his leading spiritual theme. Through Isabel Archer he gave one of his fullest and freshest expressions of inner reliance in the face of adversity. It is no wonder that, after enumerating her weaknesses, he had concluded: 'she would be an easy victim of scientific criticism if she were not intended to awaken on the reader's part an impulse more tender . . .'

ANTHONY J. MAZZELLA

The New Isabel[†]

A careful analysis of the revision of *The Portrait of a Lady* will reveal that there are two *Portraits*, not one, and that each is a different literary experience. The Isabel Archer who faces her destiny is not the same young woman in both versions, nor is the quality of her destiny the same. She may travel the same road in each case, and meet people with the same names; but the road has different landmarks and the people are different travelers—more keenly felt, more sharply there, more fully realized—and other than what they were. The sense of her destiny is transmuted by a deeper range of images, while the destiny itself is peopled with characters who have lived other lives and gone different ways. The road she now follows has sudden drops and altered vistas and intriguing byways. And overriding all, perhaps, is the fuller identity of her creator.

James had completed arrangements with Charles Scribner's Sons for publication of the New York Edition toward the end of 1905.[1] By mid-May, 1906, he had revised enough of the *Portrait* to write James B. Pinker, his literary agent, that he estimated the typed revisions, "the most intricate" pages, represented "about half the whole" of his output.[2] Several times in 1906, during the demanding process of revising the first three works for the New York Edition (*Roderick Hudson, The American,* and *The Portrait of a Lady*), James communicated his progress to Pinker, declaring on one

---

[†] From *The Portrait of a Lady: A Norton Critical Edition*, ed. Robert D. Bamberg (New York: W. W. Norton, 1975). Written for the first Norton Critical Edition of this novel and based on a 1970 Columbia University doctoral dissertation, "The Revised *Portrait of a Lady*: Text and Commentary."

1. Sydney J. Krause, *Henry James's Revisions of The Portrait of a Lady* (Ph.D. dissertation, Columbia University, 1956), p. 21.

2. Quoted in Krause, p. 20.

occasion that "when the difficult business of working over those 3 first novels will be ended, the rest of the business will go infinitely faster."[3]

By mid-June, 1906, he had revised some 350 pages of the *Portrait*. By the end of July, he had completed his revisions, or certainly the first stages (more was to be altered before the final version appeared in the New York Edition), for he had advised Pinker to deliver his marked copy of the 1881 American Edition to H. O. Houghton and Company, Cambridge, Massachusetts, the printers who were to supply his proof sheets.[4] The new *Portrait of a Lady* published in 1908 was now a changed *Portrait*.

Of the thousands of changes, the most significant concern characterization, and of the characters, the most significant is Isabel. Whenever James introduced an important character for the first time, his revisions multiplied. Any examination of such introductions will easily verify this; that of Mrs. Touchett, for example, in Chapter 3, or of Madame Merle in Chapter 18. But no one received more continuous attention than Isabel, either as the subject of revision herself or as one responsible for alteration in James's conception of other characters. The point is that the original characters exist differently in the revision. And we are responding in a new way to new characters in a new work.

A major element in the refinement of Isabel into another character is an emphasis on her freedom and vulnerability. Her destiny, in the revision, becomes one that is at once unlimited and fraught with peril. The primary literary means James uses to effect this emphasis on freedom is imagistic: a use of the conventional free bird and an introduction of the image of a greyhound. James increases the effectiveness of this latter image by incorporating it in a miniature drama in which Isabel's plain sister Lilian yearns for other possibilities:

> "I have never felt like Isabel's sister, and I am sure I never shall," she had said to an intimate friend; a declaration which made it all the more creditable that she had been prolific in sisterly offices. / "I've never kept up with Isabel—it would have taken *all* my time," she had often remarked; in spite of which, however, she held her rather wistfully in sight; watching her as a motherly spaniel might watch a free greyhound. (220/31)[5]

In addition to the greyhound image there is a bird image amplified initially in the revised version to include an aspect of freedom and later introduced in this new fullness in another revised passage. Isabel, in the first instance, had recently arrived at Pratt's Hotel for her stay in London when, one evening, she was startled by a visit from Caspar Goodwood. It is in his revised response to her peroration on independence that a somewhat Victorian bird becomes free: "To his mind she had always had wings, and this was but the flutter of those stainless pinions." / "He had never supposed she hadn't wings and the need of beautiful free movements . . ." (356/117). Later, when Mrs. Touchett began her journey from

---

3. Ibid., p. 21.
4. Ibid.
5. Page references throughout are given first for the novel's 1882 version, as available in the Library of America edition (New York: Library of America, 1985), and then for the New York Edition, as printed in this Norton Critical Edition [*Editor*].

Paris to Italy, she made it clear to her niece that it was Isabel's decision to come along:

> "Now, of course, you are completely your own mistress," she said. / "Now, of course, you're completely your own mistress and are as free as the bird on the bough. . . ." (416/156)

This new emphasis on freedom is struck early in the novel when in Chapter 3 James revises the account of Isabel's youth. Of her primary school in the earlier version, Isabel "had expressed great disgust with the place . . . ." But in the later version, she "had protested against its laws . . ." (214/27). She had earlier elected to meet Mrs. Touchett in 'the office,' "the most joyless chamber" in the house at Albany. Later, this meeting-place is called "the most depressed of its scenes" (215/28), a revision which suggests, in effect, limited as well as melancholy vistas.

The element of freedom is also emphasized negatively as a limitation. In one instance, in a possible echo of the earlier greyhound image but more likely as a result of a more immediate revision—Isabel's sister, once "popular," is now "fetching" (224/34)—this negative aspect of freedom is expressed in canine image:

> Isabel could have no illusions . . . as to the moderate character of her own triumphs. / Isabel could have no illusions . . . as to the limits of her own power to frisk and jump and shriek—above all with rightness of effect. (224/34)

In this revision, Isabel becomes also a character who is more conscious of the effect of her actions.

In another instance, after Isabel has refused Lord Warburton's proposal of marriage, the revision of her reflection becomes more precise, less conventional, and indicative of her dislike of limitation:

> the idea [of marriage to Lord Warburton] failed to correspond to any vision of happiness . . . . / the idea failed to support any enlightened prejudice in favour of the free exploration of life. . . . (304/84)

And just a little later, she fears that a limitation of her freedom might mean almost a literal paralysis:

> the situation might . . . contain elements that would displease her . . . / might . . . contain oppressive, might contain narrowing elements, might prove really but a stupefying anodyne. . . . (304/84)

Related to her fear of limitation are her altered response to Madame Merle and James's slightly different conception of minor characters. In both instances, the change stresses various aspects of freedom. When, in Chapter 18, Isabel first meets Madame Merle and notices her face, she responds to a new suggestiveness which reinforces the rightness of her attraction to this woman because it is related to her sense of freedom: "It was a face that told of a rich nature and of quick and liberal impulses . . ." / "It was a face that told of an amplitude of nature and of quick and free motions. . . ." (370/126)

Early in the novel, when we meet Daniel Touchett, the reference to his money is altered to stress the value money will come to have for Isabel—the freedom that money can bring. Lord Warburton and Daniel Touchett are engaged in lively banter about wealth when Warburton remarks that Touchett should not chide him for being rich because, in the first version, "'you are so ridiculously wealthy,'" and in the revision, because "'you have—haven't you?—such unlimited means'" (199/19).

Also early in the novel, when Isabel and her uncle are discussing the reality of fictional heroines, Daniel Touchett criticizes a lady-novelist friend of Ralph's first for being unreliable and for having "'Too much imagination . . .'" and then for having "'Too free a fancy . . .'" (247/49). This minor change repeats the stress on freedom and comments subtly on Isabel's conception of freedom as having its roots not in life but in fiction.

And finally, the refinement of Isabel's freedom is strengthened by having another character respond to this element in her nature. The rejected Lord Warburton is walking with Isabel in the gallery of Gardencourt in Chapter 14 when she stops to examine a picture. In the first version, "there was something young and flexible in her movement, which her companion noticed." But in the revision, "there was something so young and free in her movement that her very pliancy seemed to mock at him" (325/97).

Besides this emphasis on Isabel's freedom, there is in the revision a heightened sense of the danger she faces in the future. This sense of danger in Isabel's destiny begins with cosmic overtones, is visible at times in subtle ways, and eventually comes to include Pansy's fate as well. It is related to her ideas on marriage, to the conventional proposals of marriage she receives from her three suitors, and to the fatality of money. But as events in both novels move toward the area of basic sexual responses, this sense of danger in the revised version becomes a fear of a special kind of annihilation: that of the mind by the erotic. And it is this fear, as we shall see, that ultimately influences the new Isabel's major decisions.

Sitting alone in her grandmother's house in Albany on a rainy afternoon, Isabel in the first version responds with neutrality to the coming of spring: "the spring-time presented itself as a questionable improvement. Isabel, however, gave as little attention as possible to the incongruities of the season. . . ." But in the revision there is an awareness of danger and ugliness on a cosmic scale: "the spring-time was indeed an appeal—and it seemed a cynical, insincere appeal—to patience. Isabel, however, gave as little heed as possible to cosmic treacheries" (215/28).

Much later, in Chapter 21, Isabel considers, with a new emphasis which subtly links her fate with bruises, a person's relationship with Mrs. Touchett: "you knew exactly where to find her, and were never liable to chance encounters with her." / 'you knew exactly where to find her and were never liable to chance encounters and concussions" (417/157). Also in this chapter, she considers with a slight shift in emphasis achieved through the introduction of martial imagery, the fateful implications of her Italian sojourn:

> She was glad to pause, however, on the edge of this larger knowledge; the stillness of these soft weeks seemed good to her. They were a peaceful interlude in a career which she had little warrant as yet for regarding as agitated . . . / She was glad to pause, however, on the edge of this larger adventure; there was such a thrill even in the preliminary hovering. It affected her moreover as a peaceful interlude, as a hush of the drum and fife in a career which she had little warrant as yet for regarding as agitated . . . (420/159)

Later, in Chapter 29, after she has met Osmond, she comes to link her visit to Rome with time past, using an image that contains a disturbing mixture of pleasant joy and ominous suffocation and protection:

> the pleasantest incident of her life—so it pleased her to qualify her little visit to Rome—was coming to an end. / . . . so it pleased her to qualify these too few days in Rome, which she might musingly have likened to the figure of some small princess of one of the ages of dress overmuffled in a mantle of state and dragging a train that it took pages or historians to hold up—that this felicity was coming to an end. (508/215)

Also in this chapter, she responds differently to Osmond's proposal, this time charging it with the ambiguous tug of fate:

> The tears came into Isabel's eyes—they were caused by an intenser throb of that pleasant pain I spoke of a moment ago. / The tears came into her eyes: this time they obeyed the sharpness of the pang that suggested to her somehow the slipping of a fine bolt—backward, forward, she couldn't have said which. (509/216)

The image of the bolt as conceived by the later Isabel is ambiguously a freeing and an enslaving mechanism—a sense of unknown fate.

Before her marriage, she comes to sense danger even in Pansy's future. In the early version hers is a "moral" appreciation of Pansy's innocence, but in the revision it is "anxiously moral" (555/245). And at their meeting just before her marriage, Isabel comes to have an unsettling vision of Pansy's destiny:

> "My good little Pansy," said Isabel, gently, "I shall be very kind to you." / . . . "I shall be ever so kind to you." A vague, inconsequent vision of her coming in some odd way to need it had intervened with the effect of a chill. (557/246)

This sense of an ominous future and a dangerous destiny is partly, induced by the inclination of the revised Isabel to view marriage as a destructive element and as perilous. Early in the novel, in Chapter 6, the 1908 Isabel felt that few men she knew were worth "a ruinous expenditure." The 1881 Isabel objected merely to "an expenditure of imagination" (244/246). Furthermore, the earlier Isabel's thoughts on marriage usually "ended by frightening her." For the later Isabel, the process ended slightly more ominously, "in alarms" (244/46).

When she encounters Caspar Goodwood at Pratt's Hotel in London and he insists that she will marry, the 1881 Isabel impatiently rejoins: "'Very well, I will then.'" The 1908 Isabel redefines the situation as threatening: "'Very well then. We'll put it that I'm not safe'" (352/115). Goodwood's response to her attitude also heightens the sense of danger: he sees her in the earlier version as acting as if she were "'going to commit a crime'"; but in the later version, the crime becomes "'some atrocity'" (357/118).

The later Isabel's sense of the danger surrounding marriage is reinforced by two additional revisions. In the first, her protestations to Madame Merle of ease in the presence of men is belied by the brutality of the image she uses: "'I am not afraid of them'" / "'Why, I'm not afraid of them—I'm as used to them as the cook to the butcher-boys'" (443/173). And in the second, she is discussing with Ralph the possibility of falling in love with Osmond: [She:] "'The more information one has about a person the better.'" [He:] "'I don't agree to that.'" / '"The more information one has about one's dangers the better.' I don't agree to that—it may make them dangers'" (447/176).

The ominous note is detailed, further, in the later Isabel's relationship with each of her suitors. Before Lord Warburton's influence becomes strong, the early Isabel is encouraged to explore English society and promises "to be delighted." The later Isabel views the prospect more violently, for she promises "to hurl herself into the fray" (256/54).

When Warburton proposes, the later Isabel, unlike the earlier one, has a sense of being trapped: "though she was lost in admiration of her opportunity she managed to move back into the deepest shade of it, even as some wild, caught creature in a vast cage" (82). And when she considers confiding Warburton's proposal to her cousin, she, unlike the early Isabel, conceives eliminating the possibility in highly negative terms: "she would have had to do herself violence to air this special secret to Ralph" (85). In addition, the later Isabel's rejection of Warburton becomes sullied through her particular cast of mind:

> . . . she had just given a sort of personal accent to her independence by making up her mind to refuse Lord Warburton. / . . . she had just given a sort of personal accent to her independence by looking so straight at Lord Warburton's big bribe and yet turning away from it. (309/87)

For both the Warburton and the Isabel of the revision, "unhappiness" becomes ominously "a life of misery" (326/98). Finally, her recollection for Ralph at Pratt's Hotel of her rejection of Warburton's suit becomes imagistically compelling in its chilling note of finality:

> . . . she took no pleasure in recalling Lord Warburton's magnanimous disappointment. / . . . when she felt again in her face, as from a recurrent wave, the cold breath of her last suitor's surprise, she could only muffle her head till the air cleared. (336/104)

The later Caspar Goodwood received similar treatment. When he is first introduced; in Chapter 4, Isabel has just been reviewing her life after her aunt's visit in Albany and has no desire to see him. The early Isabel delays seeing him and paces "the room with a certain feeling of embarrassment." The later Isabel is not embarrassed but distressed: "she moved about the room with a new sense of complications" (226/35).

In Chapter 13, after telling her uncle of her rejection of Warburton, the early Isabel finds herself thinking of Goodwood's influence on her freedom and is "haunted at moments by the image of his disapproval" of what she has done. But the later Isabel, ominously placed, is haunted "by the image, by the danger, of his disapproval" (309/86). And in the same chapter, his having followed her to Europe makes him for the early Isabel "a kind of fate"; for the later Isabel, "a kind of grim fate" (309/87).

In Chapter 16, when Goodwood surprises her at Pratt's Hotel and declares his love, the 1881 Isabel merely "felt the force of it!" The 1908 Isabel felt more, felt a trap, "felt it thrown off, into the vast of truth and poetry, as practically a bait to her imagination" (351/114). And when Goodwood leaves her trembling at the beginning of Chapter 17, the early Isabel is excited; the later Isabel wants to withdraw to refuge and to safety:

She was an excitable creature, and now she was much excited; but she wished to resist excitement, and the attitude of prayer . . . seemed to help her to be still. / Vibration was easy to her, was in fact too constant with her, and she found herself now humming like a smitten harp. She only asked, however, to put on the cover, to case herself again in brown holland, but she wished to resist excitement, and the attitude of devotion . . . seemed to help her to be still. (359/119)

A sense of being trapped is also present more emphatically for the later Isabel when she first meets Gilbert Osmond at his hillside villa outside Florence:

There was something rather severe about the place; it looked somehow as if, once you were in, it would not be easy to get out. / There was something grave and strong in the place; it looked somehow as if, once you were in, you would need an act of an energy to get out. (451/179)

And the concern of the later Isabel not to commit an esthetic error in his presence is presented as a state of helplessness which does not occur to the early Isabel:

It would have annoyed her . . . to pass by something at which the truly initiated mind would arrest itself. She was very careful . . . / It would have annoyed her . . . to pass by something at which the truly initiated mind would arrest itself. She had no wish to fall into that grotesqueness—in which she had seen women (and it was a warning) serenely, yet ignobly, flounder. She was very careful . . . (461/185)

Finally, the response of the later Isabel to her inheritance completes the sense of danger which she, but not the early Isabel, conceives as an integral part of "affronting her destiny." When, in Chapter 20, the early Isabel learns of her fortune, the narrator elects not "to enter into her meditations or to explain why it was that some of them were of a rather pessimistic cast." But the narrator who tells the later Isabel's story declines "to explain exactly why her new consciousness was at first oppressive" (407/150). And when, in the same chapter, she meets Henrietta Stackpole in Paris and they discuss the possibilities of her wealth, the early Isabel gazes "upon this vivid but dusky picture of her future," while the later Isabel is confronted by a "lurid scene" (413/154). Even the later Henrietta sees Isabel's future life not as "reality" as does the early Henrietta, but as "grim reality" (413/154).

One aspect of personal reality not recognized by the early Isabel caps what is perhaps the single most important area of response in the later Isabel and is crucial as a preliminary factor in understanding her conduct and her sense of a dangerous destiny. This aspect of her being, almost mutely recognized only by the later Isabel, is a fear of sexual possession. The later Isabel is shown as being afraid of the erotic and, at the end of the revised Chapter 12, this fear is made virtually explicit. The early Isabel is going to reject Warburton and wonders only "whether she were not a cold, hard girl." But the later Isabel senses more; she wonders "whether she were not a cold, hard, priggish person" (305/84). This priggishness is obliquely echoed later, in the next chapter in her letter of rejection to Warburton. While the first Isabel in refusing Warburton could see him in the implied erotic terms of a husband, the later Isabel could not:

". . . I do not find myself able to regard you in the light of a husband . . ."
/ ". . . I am not, I am really and truly not, able to regard you in the
light of a companion for life . . ." (312/88)

Although this fear of the erotic rests primarily in Isabel, there is a disturbing erotic ambience which pervades the revised novel and communicates itself to the reader of that version. In this area of the erotic, James
extensively revised his treatment of minor objects and secondary characters, and especially Isabel's relationship to Warburton and Goodwood. In
the former relationship there is both an increase and a decrease of sexual
connotation and awareness, and in the latter there is a vivid expression of
male physicality.

A small cluster of changes early in the work begins the new emphasis
on the erotic. It is significant that the later Isabel will recall a childhood
neighbor though a bedroom reference while the early Isabel does not, and
that a bedroom reference present in the early version but not related to
Isabel will be removed from the later version:

> . . . the Dutch house . . . was occupied by a primary school for
> children . . . kept in an amateurish manner by a demonstrative lady,
> of whom Isabel's chief recollection was that her hair was puffed out
> very much at the temples . . . / . . . Isabel's chief recollection of her
> was that her hair was fastened with strange bedroomy combs at the
> temples . . . (213–14/27)

> . . . her sister's words must have prompted a remark that she made
> to her husband in the conjugal chamber as the two were getting ready
> to go to the hotel. / . . . her sister's words had doubtless prompted a
> word spoken to her husband as the two were making ready for their
> visit. (221/32)

The third of these early revisions which contribute to the sexual ambience of the 1908 version is the most powerful, for it occurs as part of the
texture of the novel and is unrelated to Isabel. Isabel's sister Lilian, in the
first version, is the mistress of a sedate establishment, "a house which presented a narrowness of new brown stone to Fifty-third Street . . ." But the
change in the revision is staggering for its unexpectedness: this house is
now "a wedge of brown stone violently driven into Fifty-third Street . . ."
(220/31). The sexual connotation, very evident here, is reinforced through
countless other revisions in the novel's presentation of objects, characters,
actions, and responses:

> [the boys Isabel knew]: local youth / suspicious swains (225/35)

> [Ralph observing her]: bending his eyes . . . on her figure / . . . on her
> presence (236/42)

> [her egotism]: she was often reminded that there were other gardens
> in the world than those of her virginal soul . . . / . . . of her remark-
> able soul . . . (244/46)

> [Ralph speaking to Isabel of Warburton's health]: ". . . he's detest-
> ably robust." / ". . . he's detestably sound." (262/58)

> [Ralph under the penetrating gaze of Henrietta Stackpole]: . . . there
> was something in Miss Stackpole's gaze that made him . . . feel

vaguely embarrassed and uncomfortable. / . . . there was something . . . that made him . . . feel vaguely embarrassed—less inviolate, more dishonoured, than he liked. (276/66)

[Ralph and Isabel discussing Henrietta]: . . . "I did think she was trying to attract me. Excuse my superficiality." / ". . . Forgive my depravity." (284/72)

[Henrietta relative to Ralph]: . . . her relations with him / . . . her
renewed contact with him (286/73)

[Isabel's opinion of Goodwood's arrival]: The feeling was oppressive
/ The feeling pressed upon her (292/76)

[Goodwood's letter about England]: "If I like this country at present, it
is only because you are here." / ". . . only because it holds you." (293/77)

[Henrietta and Mr. Bantling]: harmless confederates / groping celibates (155)

[Ned Rosier gazing into a room at the Palazzo Roccanera]: . . . through
the open door it looked very pretty. / . . . through the open door it
looked the very temple of authorised love. (573/256)

It is the largely negative aspects of physical love that are visible in the
above examples. The boys Isabel knew are no longer sexually neutral but
erotically dangerous; Ralph, conversely, looks upon not a physical Isabel
(figure), but an almost metaphysical Isabel (presence); her soul is intellectually rendered rather than physically described (remarkable, not virginal); Warburton loses some of his physicality in the revision (sound
instead of robust), but squirms in mutely sexual terms under Henrietta's
gaze (no longer uncomfortable, but now less inviolate and more dishonoured); Ralph considers it depraved and not superficial that he should have
felt Henrietta was trying to attract him; Isabel is no longer oppressed by
Goodwood's visit, but pressed upon; Goodwood's preference for England
is expressed not in neutral but in tactile terms (you are here/it holds you);
Henrietta and Bantling are portrayed as amusingly pathetic sexual adven-
turers (groping celibates); and Rosier's vision becomes an erotic one as a
pretty room becomes a temple of love.

If these elements suggest that James was increasingly concerned with
the erotic in his conception of the new Isabel, his revision of her relationships, first with Warburton and then with Goodwood, confirm it.

Warburton, at the outset, is made to consider himself anew in physical
terms. As the early Warburton speaks to Isabel at Gardencourt in Chapter 12, he asserts: "'I am a very judicious fellow.'" The later Warburton is
more earthy: "'I am a very judicious animal'" (299/80). James has Isabel
notice the change: the early Isabel saw him "looking at her with eyes that
shone with the light of . . . passion." The later Isabel sees "eyes charged
with the light of . . . passion" (80).

The later Isabel then becomes aware of a physical Warburton that never
existed for her 1881 predecessor. He offers her the world:

These words were uttered with a tender eagerness which went to Isabel's heart . . . / These words were uttered with a breadth of candour
that was like the embrace of strong arms—that was like the fragrance
straight in her face, and by his clean, breathing lips, of she knew not
what strange gardens, what charged airs. (302/82)

And when he kisses her hand he bends not "his head" but, in a hint of nakedness, "his handsome bared head" (304/84).

When the early Isabel resists him, she does not feel "warranted in lending a receptive ear to her English suitor," a view that suggests little physicality and no anxiety. But when the later Isabel resists, there is a suggestion of a delicate rape avoided: she "resisted conquest at her English suitor's large quiet hands" (308/86).

After her rejection of him, there are revisions which more accurately describe the situation between Isabel and Lord Warburton as one in which she is largely afraid of his masculinity. Toward the end of Chapter 21, as Isabel walks along the Mediterranean shore, she thinks again of Warburton. The earlier Isabel refers to him as a lover; the later Isabel is more careful:

> She had so definitely undertaken to forget him, as a lover, that a corresponding effort on his own part would be eminently proper. / She had so definitely undertaken to preserve no record of what had passed between them that a corresponding effort on his own part would be eminently just. (421/160).

On the other hand, he continues to be present in physical terms to other characters. In Chapter 26, for example, the 1881 Mrs. Touchett thinks of Isabel as "a young lady for whom Lord Warburton had not been up to the mark." For the later Mrs. Touchett, however, she is someone "with whom Lord Warburton had not successfully wrestled" (473/192).

In Chapter 27 Isabel and Warburton meet unexpectedly at the Roman Forum. While the early Isabel merely looks at a bashful figure, the later Isabel experiences at once a sense of fear and near nakedness:

> . . . he stood there, smiling a little, blushing a good deal, and raising his hat. / . . . he stood there baring his head to her perceptibly pale surprise. (487/202).

When Isabel objects to Warburton's advances in 1881, he vows to remain silent. But the later Warburton makes a comment which for erotic innuendo in context rivals those of *Watch and Ward*: "'I'll keep it down. I'll keep it down always'" (205). (In addition, the next substantive reference is appropriately to an excavation.)

The revised Warburton's newly physical and erotic presence is minor, however, when compared with that of the revised Caspar Goodwood; his erotic presence is detailed and explicit. And the later Isabel's final decision in the novel has as a principal motivation a deep fear of Goodwood's eroticism. For her, Goodwood achieves compelling existence solely in phallic terms, a factor embodied in his very name from the beginning.

After informing her uncle, in Chapter 13, of her refusal of Warburton, she muses on the presence of Caspar Goodwood. He represents a threat to her sense of freedom. For the early Isabel, this threat is merely oppressive and restrictive. The later Isabel thinks similarly, but her words reveal a far deeper anxiety:

> There was something too forcible, something oppressive and restrictive, in the manner in which he presented himself. / There was a disagreeably strong push, a kind of hardness of presence, in his way of rising before her. (308–09/86)

As each continues to muse, this division in their concern is reinforced. The early Isabel objects to him because "there was something very strong about him"; the later, because "he insisted, ever, with his whole weight and force" (309/86).

Each continues to register objections and each continues to reveal the hidden basis of her concern: for the early Isabel it is a dislike of personal aggression; for the later Isabel it is a fear that her freedom will be lost through erotic possession. The later Isabel fears a limitation of her freedom in yielding to Goodwood because, as the revisions reveal, she feels that she would yield to him fully as she would to no one else. When the early Isabel objects to Goodwood's showing his "seriousness too simply," the later Isabel tellingly objects on a sensual level to the manifestation of his "appetites and designs" (311/88).

Even after the experience of marriage to Osmond and childbirth and the revelations of Countess Gemini, the later Isabel will continue to look at Goodwood as an erotic threat to freedom, and more so when she is apparently least free.

In the final chapter, Goodwood returns to unsettle and utimately to galvanize Isabel who rises from a bench at Gardencourt where Warburton had surprised her six years before. The scene, in the revision, becomes a stark metaphor for all the fearful erotic ambience pervading the revised novel, an eroticism which at last becomes almost a tangible fear.

Goodwood arrives in silence and forces her to sit again. To the early Isabel, "He said nothing at first; she only felt him close to her." The later Isabel felt more: he was "beside her on the bench and pressingly turned to her" (795/399). While he argues that she has no good reason to return to Rome, the 1908 Isabel is struggling to control the disturbing impact of his erotic presence; and her subsequent words may best be viewed as the visible product of this inner anxiety. Each Isabel, continuing to confront Goodwood, says that she is going back to get away from him. But what the 1881 Isabel means, she acknowledges, is that "she had never been loved before. It wrapped her about; it lifted her off her feet." This response is almost uneventful in its brevity. The response of the later Isabel, however, reveals a desperate struggle to resist violation, physical and total:

> . . . she had never been loved before. She had believed it, but this was different; this was the hot wind of the desert, at the approach of which the others dropped dead, like mere sweet airs of the garden. It wrapped her about; it lifted her off her feet, while the very taste of it, as of something potent, acrid and strange, forced open her set teeth. (797/401)

When the early Isabel beseeched Goodwood to go away, she merely said it. The later, more distressed, more anguished Isabel "panted" (799/402).

And finally, fear and eroticism become a visible force in the famous kiss. The kiss is a sudden explosion for the early Isabel, nothing more: "His kiss was like a flash of lightning; when it was dark again she was free." But the kiss is so much more for the later Isabel, for in the revised version we finally begin to see *why* Isabel is afraid of the erotic:

> His kiss was like white lightning, a flash that spread, and spread again, and stayed; and it was extraordinarily as if, while she took it, she felt each thing in his hard manhood that had least pleased her,

each aggressive fact of his face, his figure, his presence, justified of its intense identity and made one with this act of possession. So had she heard of those wrecked and under water following a train of images before they sink. But when darkness returned she was free. (799/402)

We have seen, through an analysis of the revisions concerning the erotic, that Isabel fears sexual possession as it affects freedom, but James had not made clear why Isabel was thus afraid. In this passage (but more so in the next sequence of revisions discussed below) he does. James suggests that, at heart, what Isabel fears is a loss through the erotic of a special freedom—the freedom of the mind to function unimpeded. And he suggests that it is essentially for this reason that she must return to Rome. She is not afraid merely of the erotic experience itself but rather its tendency to diminish the life of the mind. Goodwood threatens not so much her body as that annihilation of consciousness which comes with the intensely erotic; which would mean her "death," because for Isabel consciousness is the real center of her being. She exists supremely on the level of pure mind, and the erotic would destroy that existence.

The most extraordinary thing about the revised kiss is not the new inclusion of erotic detail but the fact that the later Isabel is operating at optimum consciousness throughout, struggling to maintain the mind's control in the midst of, for her, destructive emotion. The kiss catches up the phallic motif that surrounded Goodwood, makes it almost concrete, and then dissipates it through Isabel's control of consciousness. The fearful white lightning that threatened annihilation is itself annihilated by a conscious awareness of death. The kiss means possession, and by a mental fiat Isabel induces a scene of archetypal drowning. It is through this induced death of eroticism that Isabel secures her release and makes her decision to return to Rome.

Because the kiss meant none of this to the early Isabel, her decision to return to Rome seemed to some incomprehensible. For the later Isabel, the kiss crystallized her fears and made imminent the annihilation of the mind by the erotic. The decision to return to Rome, absurd to some for the early Isabel, is inevitable for the later Isabel, coming as it does from fear of control by the erotic of the mind's power to operate. Considered from this perspective Isabel's return to Rome in the New York Edition becomes almost positive and challenging, for in that constricting environment only the mind has intense and wide freedom of movement, and Isabel, it seems, is to be engaged in a difficult struggle with Osmond to counter his intransigence and relieve Pansy's plight. Thoreau's comments in "Civil Disobedience," as he wryly observed his captors, may be instructive here: "I could not but smile to see how industriously they locked the door on my meditations, which followed them out again without let or hindrance, and *they* were really all that was dangerous."

The danger for Isabel then, as the later James conceived it, was not what sex might do to her body but what it might do to her mind, for James went to great lengths to have the 1908 Isabel exist primarily on the level of consciousness at the same time that he was emphasizing her freedom (i.e., freedom of the mind to act fully), linking it to the "felt life," and developing the erotic as a threat to the mind's activity through displacing, diminishing, or weakening it.

In Jamesian terms, therefore, the single most important attribute distinguishing the second Isabel from the first is that the new Isabel experiences life through a significantly expanded consciousness. For her, life becomes preeminently a life of the mind. Of the revisions that demonstrate this emphasis on the mind's centrality, some are obvious, others are subtle, but all are immeasureably illuminating.

For example, whereas the first Isabel looks with "quick perception," the second Isabel sees with "clear perception" (205/22), an emphasis not on speed but on the mind's lucidity. While the first "narrowly scrutinized her companions" at Gardencourt; the second, engaged in a survey of the grounds, "had also made room in it for her companions" (207/24), a suggestion of mind expansiveness. And if the first looked at Lord Warburton with "startled eyes," the second "rested her wider eyes on him" (209/25), an indication not only of greater control and less the fluttered girl, but also of deeper probing and absorption.

The most significant revision, however, implies an equation of the very act of living with consciousness. Early in Chapter 12, the narrator, describing his first heroine, speaks of her "vision of a completed life" and talks of her "soul." But when he describes his second heroine, he notes her "visions of a completed consciousness" and refers to her "sublime soul" (296/78). In the revision, then, life becomes consciousness and Isabel grows sublime because more conscious. Earlier in the novel occurs another revision which reinforces this idea. Isabel is swept up by the beauty of Gardencourt when she suddenly thinks of those less fortunate than herself, and this momentary thought makes the first Isabel's "absorbing happiness appear to her a kind of immodesty." The second Isabel has a similar thought but it made 'her fine, full consciousness appear a kind of immodesty" (244/47). Thus, happiness too, by implication, is equated with consciousness, and the entire spectrum of the second Isabel's experience reaches apotheosis in and through her consciousness. And finally, later in the novel, after she has met Gilbert Osmond, she responds to him in a way that makes human relations a matter of the mind's life:

> . . . she felt that she was being entertained. / . . . she had what always gave her a very private thrill, the consciousness of a new relation. (457/183)

A further refinement of the new Isabel's consciousness appears through the introduction of a uniquely Jamesian word—"fine." Lord Warburton impresses both Isabels, but with an essential difference: he made a vivid impression on the "mind" of the first; but he sharply registered himself on the "fine sense" of the second (256/54).—a revision that implies James's high estimate of the mind. This revision occurs in Chapter 7. Very late in the novel, in Chapter 53, Isabel asks a question about the fate of a woman of sensitivity. But the phrasing of each question is significant. The first Isabel asks, "Was it not much more probable that if one were delicate one would suffer?" The second Isabel wonders whether "if one were fine one would suffer" (770/383), a phrase carrying with it the suggestiveness that to be fine is to be the best that one can be.

An adjunct to the expanded consciousness of the new Isabel is a clarification of her way of looking at the world: she sees it through the pages of a book. In Chapter 7, the Isabels have spent an evening with Lord Warburton. The first "thought him quite one of the most delectable persons she had met," a response whose frame of reference is everyday life. The second, however, "scarce fell short of seeing him—though quite without luridity—as a hero of romance" (257/55). Here the frame of reference is the imagination. This frame of reference is echoed in Chapter 31 when Isabel tells her sister Lily absolutely nothing about the offers from Warburton and Osmond. The difference in the two versions is the difference between a person engaged chiefly in a general and public reality and a consciousness absorbed in a private world of romance:

> It entertained her more to say nothing, and she had no idea of asking poor Lily's advice. / It was more romantic to say nothing, and, drinking deep, in secret, of romance, she was as little disposed to ask poor Lily's advice as she would have been to close that rare volume forever. (521/223)

The Isabel of the romance consciousness has also a consciousness that expands in other, less noticeable ways: she is aware of nuances, she responds more fully, her mind is more striking, her range of interest more broad. When strolling through Gardencourt with Ralph in Chapter 5, the first Isabel prefers "not to talk about herself," while the second, suggesting there is more to say, would rather not "dilate just yet on herself" (236/42). The second also changes her locus of attention in Lord Warburton from person to mind. While she walks with him at Gardencourt in Chapter 12, she deems him incapable of being not "a frivolous person" but "a loose thinker" (298/80). He, in turn, is more alert to her mental activity: the first Warburton is afraid of her "mind"; the second, of her "remarkable mind" (303/83). And when she rejects his proposal at the end of Chapter 12, she does so for logical and not amorous reasons:

> If it were pride that interfered with her accepting Lord Warburton, it was singularly misplaced; and she was so conscious of liking him that she ventured to assure herself it was not. She liked him too much to marry him, that was the point; something told her that she should not be satisfied . . . / If it had been pride that interfered with her accepting Lord Warburton such a *bétise* was singularly misplaced; and she was so conscious of liking him that she ventured to assure herself it was the very softness, and the fine intelligence, of sympathy. She liked him too much to marry him, that was the truth; something assured her there was a fallacy somewhere in the glowing logic of the proposition—as *he* saw it—even though she mightn't put her very finest finger-point on it . . . (305/84)

The details of this revision—the words "intelligence," "truth," and "logic"; the foreign phrase; the delicate image of her fingertip—all transform the response of the woman to the sphere of the cerebral.

The second Isabel responds to London in a somewhat similar manner, so that the emphasis is slightly more on the mind than on the senses: whereas the first was "constantly interested and often excited," the second was "full of premises, conclusions, emotions" (334/103).

The response of the second Isabel to Madame Merle is also more finely intellectual: when Madame Merle discussed Mrs. Touchett, the first Isabel "agreed with her." The second, however, more alert to nuances, "rose eagerly to the sense of her shades" (391/140).

Her response to money, on the other hand, becomes strangely sensuous. In Chapter 20, the first Isabel, in responding to her inheritance, finds she has the "leisure to contemplate the windfall"; but her counterpart discovers she has the "leisure to measure and weigh and otherwise handle" the legacy (407/150).

Gilbert Osmond, quite understandably, sets more chords of consciousness vibrating in the second Isabel than in the first:

> . . . [his] personal points struck our observant young lady as the signs of unusual sensibility. / . . . [his] personal points struck our sensitive young woman as signs of quality, of intensity, somehow as promises of interest. (459/184)

And while the first could marry him "for his opinions," the second was looking for more: "the beauty of his opinions or . . . his autograph of Michael Angelo" (473/193).

At the end of the novel, during her long journey from Rome to Gardencourt, she muses on the question of Madame Merle. The revision offers a subtle shift from creative contemplation (imagination) to pure mind (intelligence):

> The only thing to regret was that Madame Merle had been so—so strange. Just here Isabel's imagination paused, from literal inability to say what it was Madame Merle had been. / The only thing to regret was that Madame Merle had been so—well, so unimaginable. Just here her intelligence dropped, from literal inability to say what it was that Madame Merle had been. (769/382)

Even more subtle is the refinement in the revised version of the technique of one character getting inside the mind of another, so that the reader grows aware of a greater consciousness at play. This unique ability for cerebral penetration centers, not surprisingly, in Isabel, and highlights what had grown to become a striking focal point in the later James: intense personal closeness occurs not on the level of the emotions and physical intercourse but on the level of consciousness and the interpenetration of minds.

An extraordinary example of this penetration occurs near the very end of the novel, in Chapter 54. When Mrs. Touchett speaks to the 1881 Isabel, we see her and we see Isabel; but when she speaks to the 1908 Isabel, we get inside Isabel in order to become conscious of her aunt:

> Mrs. Touchett had pushed back her chair, and Isabel left the table and walked, rather consciously, to one of the deep windows, while her aunt followed her with her eyes. / Mrs. Touchett had pushed back her chair, and as her niece left the table and walked, rather consciously, to one of the deep windows, she felt herself followed by her eyes. (781/390)

Indeed, the whole of Chapter 54 exhibits a cluster of such penetrations. When Isabel arrives at Gardencourt and is kept waiting, the first becomes "nervous and even frightened." But the fears of the second take on palpable shape as she begins to penetrate the objects around her:

> . . . she grew nervous and scared—as scared as if the objects about
> her had begun to show for conscious things, watching her trouble
> with grotesque grimaces. (777/387)

Her acute awareness, unlike that of her counterpart, begins to probe
incisively the quality of human life:

> She reflected that things change but little, while people change so
> much . . . / She envied the security of valuable "pieces" which change
> by no hair's breadth, only grow in value, while their owners lose inch
> by inch youth, happiness, beauty . . . (777/387)

When her aunt finally arrives, she is kissed by Isabel, who senses her
lips. In the revision, her aunt kisses her and we sense Isabel:

> Her lips felt very thin indeed as Isabel kissed her. / Her lips felt very
> thin indeed on Isabel's hot cheek. (778/388)

And later the second Isabel speculates on the nature of her aunt's grief
in a revision which, unlike the former version, demonstrates an act of consciousness rather than an expression of sentimentality:

> She wondered whether Mrs. Touchett were not trying [to indulge
> regret], whether she had not a desire for the recreation of grief. / She
> wondered if she were not even missing those enrichments of con-
> sciousness and privately trying—reaching out for some after-taste of
> life, dregs of the banquet; the testimony of pain or the cold recreation
> of remorse. (779/389)

Also noteworthy are the increased degrees of consciousness elsewhere in
the novel, which, in the revision, achieves fullness and becomes highly
meaningful as a remarkable adventure of the mind—with its attendant tragedy for the person possessing that mind. The Isabel in the first version seems
capricious; the Isabel in the second is possessed of a unique, ultimately
fascinating—and, more important, comprehensible—consciousness.

When, at the start of Chapter 27, she is impressed by Rome, it is her
consciousness that operates and not her feelings:

> The sense of the mighty human past was heavy upon her, but it was
> interfused in the strangest, suddenest, most capricious way, with the
> fresh, cool breath of the future. Her feelings were so mingled that
> she scarcely knew whither any of them would lead her . . . / The
> sense of the terrible human past was heavy to her, but that of some-
> thing altogether contemporary would suddenly give it wings that it
> could wave in the blue. Her consciousness was so mixed that she
> scarcely knew where the different parts of it would lead her . . .
> (485/201)

And when Warburton surprises her at the Forum, we get her mental activity instead of merely a view of him:

> . . . he stood there, smiling a little, blushing a good deal, and raising
> his hat. / . . . he stood there baring his head to her perceptibly pale
> surprise. (487/202)

The silence that follows their talk moves from the plane of the trite communication to the level of the mute exchange of minds. At his silence, the

first Isabel "knew what he was thinking of. His eyes were fixed on the ground; but at last he raised them and said gravely—'I have written to you several times.'" But his silence for the second Isabel "said so much more than either had said that it scarce needed his final words. 'I've written you several times'" (488/203).

This exchange of minds continues in the revision when she asks pointedly if he plans to stay in Rome as long as she does:

> Lord Warburton looked at her a moment, with an uncomfortable smile. / His flushed smile, for a little, seemed to sound her. (490/205)

A more remarkable communication of minds, or, more accurately, Isabel's expectation of such a communication, occurs in Chapter 30 when she longs to ask Pansy for information about her father but checks herself for this intrusion. The first Isabel is concerned that her curiosity might be discovered; the second, in a more completely gendered image, fears that Osmond's sensibility may become aware of her interest:

> . . . her imagination was hushed with the horror at the idea of taking advantage of the little girl—it was of this she would have accused herself—and of leaving an audible trace of her emotion behind. / . . . her imagination was hushed with the horror of taking advantage of the little girl—it was of this she would have accused herself—and of exhaling into the air where he might still have a subtle sense for it any breath of her charmed state. (517/221)

The revision of Isabel's love for Osmond is particularly revealing. While the first Isabel is made to "feel that there was after all something very invidious in being in love; much as the sentiment was theoretically approved of," the second Isabel, more pointedly, is made "conscious, almost with awe, of the invidious and remorseless tide of the charmed and possessed condition, great as was the traditional honour and imputed virtue of being in love" (552/243). Thus, entering into the second Isabel's consciousness is the awareness of being helpless when possessed by another and of losing one's freedom of mind when "charmed" or bewitched. But Isabel does marry Osmond, and one may ask how she reconciles this marriage with the retention of an untrammeled life of the mind. She does so, James seems to suggest in a later revision, by viewing life with Osmond as life for consciousness:

> Osmond had the attachment of old acquaintance, and Isabel the stimulus of new, which seemed to assure her a future of beautiful hours. / Osmond had the attachment of old acquaintance and Isabel the stimulus of new, which seemed to assure her a future at a high level of consciousness of the beautiful. (554/244)

In Chapter 38, when Warburton visits Isabel at her palazzo, an exchange of minds again becomes apparent in the revision. In the first version, we view him; in the second, we accompany Isabel as *she* penetratingly views him. He has just observed, "brightly, looking about him," that her place is charming. In the revision he states that her place is charming, "with a look, round him, at her established home, in which she might have caught the dim ghost of his old ruefulness" (584/263).

The first Isabel makes an ordinary recovery from the jolt of seeing him again; for the second the recovery is remarkable and made interiorly:

> "I have heard of you from time to time," said Isabel, who had now completely recovered her self-possession. / "I've heard of you from time to time," said Isabel, who had already, with her rare capacity for such inward feats, taken the measure of what meeting him again meant for her. (584/264)

The second Warburton reacts in kind. When Osmond leaves them alone together, the first Warburton merely stands there; the second mentally penetrates:

> He stood a moment, looking at Isabel with an eye that gradually became more serious. "I am really very glad to see you." / Then the visitor turned on Isabel the deeper, the deepest, consciousness of his look, which gradually became more serious. "I'm really very glad to see you." (584/264)

When, in Chapter 41, she considers having failed Osmond, the second Isabel places herself inside his mind; the first does not; the first "was determined not to be haunted by images of a flat want of zeal." Her counterpart, with the slightest but most significantly rendered difference, "was determined not to be haunted by visions of his wife's limpness under appeal" (618/286).

Continuing, in the next chapter, her fireside musings on the value of her relationship with Gilbert Osmond, the second Isabel demonstrates, unlike her predecessor, a quality of mind that is noteworthy in its presentation of the paradox of her spiritual materialism and her intellectual eroticism. The first Isabel believes simply that the "finest individual she had ever known was hers; the simple knowledge was a sort of act of devotion." But the second considers with complexity: "The finest—in the sense of being the subtlest—manly organism she had ever known had become her property, and the recognition of her having but to put out her hands and take it had been originally a sort of act of devotion" (632/295).

Finally, in her relations with the Countess Gemini, the second Isabel is made to demonstrate two further examples of her mind's awareness—this time in the realm of memory. In the first instance, the Countess delivers one of her revelations. The early Isabel takes it passively; but the second responds, and her response reveals that the event has long remained with her:

> . . . the Countess rose also, while the sharp animation of her bright, capricious face emitted a kind of flash. She stood a moment looking at Isabel, and then said—"My first sister-in-law had no children!" / . . . the Countess rose also, while her gathered perversity grew vivid and dreadful. She stood a moment in a sort of glare of intention and, as seemed to Isabel even then, of ugliness; after which she said: "My first sister-in-law had no children!" (749/369)

In the second instance, the two are discussing Madame Merle, and again the idea that Isabel will remember painfully is made clear. Madame Merle, according to the first Countess, did not care to marry Osmond merely because "she had grown more ambitious." The second Countess goes further:

". . . she had grown more ambitious. Besides, she has never had, about him," the Countess went on, leaving Isabel to wince for it so tragically afterwards—"she *had* never had, what you might call any illusions of *intelligence*. . . ." (752/372)

A revision, earlier in the novel, serves easily as a means of establishing the essential difference between the two Isabels: the first exists without much complexity; the second embraces multiple levels of existence. It is in Chapter 46 that Warburton comes to announce his departure for England, thereby dooming irrevocably Osmond's plans for his daughter and precipitating the rupture between Isabel and Osmond. But before these events can occur, Isabel is sitting seemingly between the two men and probing the minds of each. For the first Isabel, this activity is "a double operation"; for the second Isabel, the Isabel of the mind, it is "a complex operation" (683/327); and the difference between "double" and "complex" partly expresses the difference between the Isabel of 1881 and the Isabel of 1908.

Not merely a matter of heightened consciousness, however, separates the two Isabels. They are disunited by the degree of freedom and vulnerability possessed by the later Isabel who, in addition, tends to view her vulnerability more clearly as an adjunct of marriage but who is only dimly aware—unlike the first Isabel who is not aware at all—that the basis of her anxiety is a fear that the freedom constituted by the clear conduct of her consciousness may be annihilated by sexual possession. We have, then, in the later Isabel a presence of fears which emanate from, and return to, her remarkable consciousness, thus making the act of "affronting her destiny" a study—sometimes tragic and ironic—of the life of the mind for the later Isabel whereas it was frequently an uneven portrait of a girl's caprice for her predecessor. Because she exists on a compelling level of mind, the later Isabel does what she does. But her distant predecessor does what she does for reasons perhaps best ascribed to the folly of her youth and the esthetics of her incompleteness.

NINA BAYM

Revision and Thematic Change in
The Portrait of a Lady†

When Henry James revised *The Portrait of a Lady* for the New York edition he made thousands of changes in the wording of the text. (*The Portrait of a Lady* was originally serialized in twelve installments[1] in *Macmillan's Magazine* beginning in October 1880 and in the *Atlantic Monthly* beginning one month later. First editions were separately published in England and America in 1881. The first edition shows a few hundred minor revisions in wording from the serialized version. The New York edition, a selection of James's writing, appeared from 1907 to 1909, the extensively reworded text of *The Portrait* being published in 1908.) The revised version is stylistically and thematically closer to his later interests than the early one had been. Its

† From *Modern Fiction Studies* 22.2 (Summer 1976): 183–200. Copyright © 1976 by the Purdue Research Foundation, West Lafayette, Indiana. Reprinted by permission of The Johns Hopkins University Press.
1. Actually fourteen [*Editor*].

writing is more complex, mannered, and metaphorical. It is thematically less timely and realistic, for its main concern is the private consciousness. In the 1908 version, Isabel Archer's inner life is the center of the character and of the novel's reality. In the early version the inner life is only one aspect of character, which is defined by behavior in a social context.

Owing to the prestige of the New York edition, the novel of 1881 has largely been ignored by readers and critics, with a resulting loss in our sense of the early James as opposed to the later. In particular we do not see how topical and timely *The Portrait of a Lady* was. The 1881 novel was one of an increasing number of works about "the woman question." The heroine, an appealing young American, wants to live an independent and meaningful life; but she is thwarted. Unlike many works of the period on this theme, *The Portrait* did not depict Isabel's desire as unnatural and misguidedly unfeminine, nor did it employ the standard formula of saving her from this delusion by love and marriage. On the contrary, the novel sympathized with her aim to the point of calling both love and marriage into question. Moreover, it judged Isabel as limited by those inner qualities that, together with external obstacles, prevented her from pursuing and realizing her wish.

The changes of 1908, transforming the story into a drama of consciousness, overlaid and in places obliterated the coherence of the 1881 version. Omissions and additions altered all the characters significantly. Finally, James wrote a preface for the new work which announced that the story centered in the heroine's consciousness and that its action was the development of her perception and awareness. The preface instructed the reader in how to interpret, what to admire, and what to deplore in the work. This preface is significant because it has largely controlled the critical readings of *The Portrait*. Since its interpretation works for 1908 but not so well for 1881, readers turning to the early version with the preface in mind naturally find an imperfect approximation of the revision. In case after case, passages which figure importantly in criticism of *The Portrait* occur in 1908 only. Strong arguments for Isabel's spiritual transcendence, and equally strong arguments for her hypocritical egotism, derive from that text. But the version of 1881 is a different work. Early James was a masterful writer with his own interests. Once recovered, the 1881 story with its topical focus on the "new woman" and its skillful use of fictional formulae may prove to be just as interesting as the version of 1908.

The most extensive revisions concern Isabel Archer. She appears on almost every page of the book, and virtually every page about her undergoes change. Although some of these are only excisions or substitutions of single words, the cumulative effect is considerable. The chief intent of these changes is to endow her with the acute, subtle consciousness required for a late James work, which the early Isabel lacks. At the same time that James gives her a rich mental life in 1908, he effaces the original main quality of her character, emotional responsiveness. Her intellectual agility is greatly extended at the expense of her emotional nature.

From this basic change, others follow. Early Isabel is trapped by her simplicity; late Isabel must be the dupe of her subtlety. Victimized by an appeal to her highest faculties, she is less a fool than a saint. There is a corresponding change of tone to treat this more remarkable being. For example, "brilliant and noble" in 1881 becomes "high and splendid . . . and yet oh so radiantly gentle!" in 1908, while "a bright spirit" is rewritten as "a 'lustre' beyond any recorded losing or rediscovering" (chap. 37). As Isabel is exalted, other characters are degraded. Madame Merle and Osmond are thoroughly blackened, and many supporting figures are flattened and undercut by exaggerated comic treatment. The change in the two villains enhances the pathos in the situation of the trapped sensibility—Isabel Archer as redrawn is much more like Milly Theale than like the original Isabel Archer—while the minor characters lose their function as independent centers of judgment and awareness in the novel. When he is through, James has left nothing solid for the reader except the boundless imagination of Isabel. But in 1881 a limited imagination is her greatest shortcoming.

In 1881, Isabel is an intelligent, sensitive, perceptive, idealistic girl with a ready interest in life. Her imagination, however is conventionally romantic (like that of many other heroines of fiction), the natural expression of a youthful spirit limited in education and experience. Unfortunately, this imaginativeness is mistaken by Isabel and those who surround her as some sort of brilliance. Isabel's overestimation of herself is a fault, but her real wish to be morally and spiritually fine is extremely attractive. Endowing her with a real, rather than a fancied, imaginative superiority in 1908, James takes away the aspiring quality of her character which is so endearing. Making her live intensely in her mind rather than her feelings, he deprives her of some of the appealing spontaneity, vivacity, and activity in the 1881 character.

Let us note some of the changes which make her more observant and less active, more intellectual and less emotional. In chapter 2, "quick" perception becomes "clear," "startled" eyes merely "widen," and "brilliant" eyes are toned down to "lighted." In chapter 3, Isabel finds the rainy springtime "a questionable improvement" over winter; this is sophisticated in 1908 to "an appeal—and it seemed a cynical, insincere appeal—to patience," just as "the incongruities of the season" become "cosmic treacheries." "Fresh impressions" of her "entertaining" Aunt Lydia become "a matter of high but easy irony, or comedy," which "so held" her, and Mrs. Touchett's "deeply interesting" conversation changes to "food for deep reflexion." Vague impulses of feeling are replaced by more precise thoughts, and ordinary ideas become more intense and extravagant.

This process continues even in indirect changes like the alteration of Isabel's wish not to "take a nap" in 1881 to a disinclination for "dozing forgetfulness" in 1908. Taking a nap is a simple physical action; dozing forgetfulness shows that for Isabel sleep means a sacrifice of intellectual activity. In the same chapter (chap. 4) Isabel's "heart" is changed to her "soul" and her having "gone so far as to forgive" becomes "committed the conscious solecism of forgiving." Similarly, "a certain feeling of embarrassment" becomes "a new sense of complications." The emotion of uneasiness is regularly replaced in 1908 by this sense of complication; another example occurs in chapter 27 when Lord Warburton's appearance in the first version "made her vaguely uneasy" but in 1908 "affected her as a complication of the wrong sort—she liked so complications of the right." In chapter 6, James removes the characterizing word "impulsively," and revises "absorbing happiness" to "fine, full consciousness" and "artless" to "prompt." In chapter 9, he replaces "coquetry" with "the calculation of her effect" and in chapter 11 "a fine freedom of composition" with "a free play of intelligence." James is recreating the heroine as a person who is continually "reading" her environment and is consequently less active in it.

James brings this out clearly in changing her responses toward her suitors from feeling and impulse to reflection and analysis. She judges their offers in 1908 according to whether life with them will support imaginative freedom. Visions of a "completed life" with Lord Warburton in 1881 change to "completed consciousness" in 1908; instead of possibly being "an incumbrance" Lord Warburton may represent "a complication of every hour"; an offer that "failed to correspond to any vision of happiness" in 1881 "failed to support any enlightened prejudice in favour of the free exploration of life" in 1908; and "elements that would displease her" became "narrowing elements . . . a stupefying anodyne" (chap. 12). As for Caspar Goodwood, his "limitations" became "impediments to the finer respiration" (chap. 21). Isabel in 1881 is much more ordinary, so to speak, in that she wants happiness and pleasure from a relationship with a man; in 1908, her requirements are more ascetic and aesthetic.

James also rewrote passages describing her responses to Europe. Her "impressions" change to a "fulness" of "response" and her "feelings" of Rome predictably become her "consciousness" of the city. St. Peter's is no longer just a "church" to her, but "the greatest of human temples" (chap. 27). In this context, the image of Osmond on his hilltop (chap. 26) which "happened to take her fancy particularly" in 1881 is revised in 1908 to "put on for her a particular harmony with other supposed and divined things, histories within histories." Isabel's awareness replaces her faculty of feeling in 1908; she responds with her mind rather than her emotions. In 1881 Isabel's emotions, besides being quick, are also rather imprecise. The 1908 responses are more intellectual and also more specific. But imprecision in 1881 is not a stylistic fault; it conveys an important aspect of Isabel's character. She respects herself partly as a person of sensibility, and rightly so, but the vagueness of her feelings leads directly to many of her mistakes. (James tells us all this in the long analytic passages of chapter 6, but much of what he says no longer seems applicable in 1908.) Because she values her feelings she permits, even encourages, them to guide her. But good and true feelings can be as treacherous as bad ones. This point is important for the theme of The Portrait in 1881 and for James's handling of Isabel in love. Love is necessarily quite different in the two versions. In 1881 James makes Isabel genuinely in love with Osmond, shows that this real feeling is untrustworthy, and demonstrates thereby how the desire for independence can be subverted by true love.

In 1908, love is complicated by the heroine's self-awareness. She is not a character likely to get swept away on a wave of feeling. The question of her attraction to Osmond is a major interpretive problem in the 1908 version. One example will demonstrate the nature of James's changes. In 1881, when Osmond declares his love, Isabel feels dread. "What made her dread great was precisely the force which, as it would seem, ought to have banished all dread—the consciousness of what was in her own heart. It was terrible to have to surrender herself to that" (chap. 29). Here is a conventional maidenly response to the first sensation of sexual passion. The feeling is there and though she will eventually surrender to it, it frightens her as it should frighten a pure and decorous Victorian girl. But in 1908,

James attributes her dread to "the sense of something within herself, deep down, that she supposed to be inspired and trustful passion. It was there like a large sum stored in a bank—which there was a terror in having to begin to spend. If she touched it, it would all come out."

This major change adds much that was not there, even implicitly, in 1881. Dozens of critical essays have quoted the "money in the bank" metaphor to impute corrupt or at least disagreeable qualities to Isabel. That she thinks of her feelings as hoarded money, and of love as disbursement, clearly puts obstacles in the way of reading the character as purely admirable and generous. For our purposes, the phrasing "which she supposed to be inspired and trustful passion" is especially baffling. Does James mean that love founded on misperception is not really love, and that therefore Isabel does not love Osmond? Or that she has mistaken not Osmond but her own feelings toward him, and feels not love but some other, more devious, emotion? The cagey phrasing of the revision has opened the door to many theories, some of great sensitivity and perception, about Isabel's feelings. But her feelings in 1881 present no difficulties and require no theories.

The change of Isabel's sphere from emotional to intellectual has reverberations for other aspects of the book. How can so acute and subtle a mind be so seriously wrong about her surroundings? It is easy to comprehend how the Isabel of 1881 might be taken in. But for Isabel in 1908, as for late James characters in general, only a profound, complete, accomplished conspiracy in the outer world can keep her from seeing what is there. This is the reason why, in the revision, Madame Merle and Osmond lose such good qualities as they possess in the original, and are turned into wholly devious and shallow people. Their modicum of natural warmth and their substantial capacities disappear; both become mere swindlers.

Madame Merle when introduced in chapter 18 is originally said to be playing the piano with the touch of an artist, but she is reduced to a performer with skill and feeling in 1908. As [F. O.] Matthiessen has observed, she plays Beethoven in 1881 and Schubert in 1908, which Matthiessen feels is "more within Madame Merle's compass." But of course her compass is defined partly by what she plays! Her "fine, frank smile" in the first version becomes "a sort of world-wide smile, a thing that overreached frontiers," while her "ardent" impulses become only "strong" and, in a later chapter, her "sagacity" is reduced to "tact." For Matthiessen, these changes make "her character unmistakable to the reader," but their evident result is not to clarify, but to change the 1881 character by eliminating frankness, warmth, and spontaneity.

Her artificial and exploitative nature is stressed at every turn. "A brilliant fugitive from Brooklyn" in 1881, she is called (chap. 19) a "perverted product of their common soil" in 1908. She tells Isabel in 1881 that the English "were the finest people in the world" but in 1908 that they are "the most convenient in the world to live with" (chap. 19). The idea that she is always something of a "foreigner" in the original, i.e., that she has an uncomprehended private side, is changed in the revision to the idea that she is always "something of a public performer, condemned to emerge only in character and in costume" (chap. 31), which means that she has no private side.

The image of a character constructed entirely for effect is even more extensively developed in Osmond. James intensifies parts of the 1881 chapter while excising aspects suggesting naturalness and warmth. Osmond in

1881 is a selfish, spoiled, failed, and snobbish man. Nevertheless, there is sincerity in his nature. Rewriting passages about him, James changes his "luminous and intelligent" eyes which express "softness and keenness" to "conscious, curious eyes . . . at once vague and penetrating, intelligent and hard" (chap. 22). Osmond responds "with feeling" in 1881 but "beautifully" in 1908 (chap. 24). The other characters think much less of him, as indeed they ought, in 1908 than in 1881. Ralph compares him in 1881 to a prince who has abdicated in a fit of "magnanimity," but this word becomes "fastidiousness" in 1908 (chap. 23). Mrs. Touchett, who had originally "liked" him because "she thought him so much of a gentleman," now simply "had from far back found a place on her scant list for this gentleman, though wondering dimly by what art and what process—so negative and wise as they were—he had everywhere effectively imposed himself" (chap. 26).

The most substantial change James makes in this character involves a two-page cut—the largest single excision by far in the revision. He takes out a lengthy analysis of Osmond and his motives in chapter 29, but not (as Matthiessen has it) because it is "otiose." The cut considerably changes his interpretation of the character. In the original, Osmond is explained as a selfish man who wanted more than anything in life to succeed. When he falls in love with Isabel, he determines that her admiration will be success enough: "Osmond's line would be to impress himself not largely but deeply; a distinction of the most private sort. A single character might offer the whole measure of it; the clear and sensitive nature of a generous girl would make space for the record." It is true that Osmond sees Isabel only as an admiring audience for his performance, but it is also true that he is content to perform for her alone and that he recognizes her intrinsic qualities.

As he closes up that gap made by the cut, James begins by changing "the desire to succeed greatly—in something or other" to "the desire to have something or other to show for his 'parts'" and concludes by substituting, for Osmond's idea of Isabel as his audience, a more exploitative idea of her as a kind of publicity agent. "His 'style' was what the girl had discovered with a little help; and now, beside herself enjoying it, she should publish it to the world without his having any of the trouble. She would do the thing *for* him, and he would not have waited in vain." He thinks of Isabel only in terms of what she can do for him. She is without intrinsic value, no longer "bright and soft as an April cloud" but "smooth to his general need of her as handled ivory to the palm."

Even though Isabel is a simple character in 1881, the fact that Madame Merle and Osmond are better people means that in an important way she is less taken in by them than is the revised character. Some of the good things that the early Isabel perceives in them are really there. But the finer intelligence of 1908 demands a finer trap, and Merle and Osmond must put on a better show. This requires that they become more complete performers. Because the revisions to this effect deprive them of substance and transform them into empty shells, the heroine of 1908, even though she is so subtle, is paradoxically much more superficial and dense than the Isabel of 1881. She is certainly a worse judge of people, and since she is alone in 1908 in her uncritical evaluation of this pair, she is more stiff and self-righteous in her mistake. This peculiar combination has not struck all readers as attractive, and has given many students of the revised novel a good deal of trouble. This trouble exists to a much smaller degree, if at all, in the early version.

Besides making Osmond and Madame Merle more vicious, James touches almost all of the other characters to reduce them as independent centers of value and judgment. It is as though the younger James had cared for all his characters and tried to give them an illusion of life and depth, while in 1908 only Isabel was real to him. The one character who is not played down is Ralph, in whom James brings out the victimized but transcendent consciousness more than in 1881. Ralph's affinity with Isabel is more pronounced in 1908 than his curiosity or affection. In 1881, his intervention in her life is largely a substitute for an undeclarable love, while in 1908 Isabel is more like an alter ego. He cannot realize his dreams, but possibly she will do it for him. The great moment of the 1908 novel is his death scene—much sentimentalized in the rewriting—when for an instant he and Isabel look at the truth together. This is the union of two consciousnesses. The development of Ralph in 1908 heightens the consciousness theme, and since Ralph's view of Isabel is so uncritical, it also supports the adulatory approach to her character.

The other personalities, however, are flattened and made less genial. Lily (Isabel's sister), Mrs. Touchett, Countess Gemini, and Henrietta—all the other women in the book, in sum—are treated more harshly. An example concerning Lily is worth some examination because it shows the details of James's method. In 1881 (chap. 31), the sisters "had come to Paris, a city beloved by Lily, but less appreciated by Isabel, who in those days was constantly thinking of Rome." In 1908, they "reached the French capital, which was worshipped, and with costly ceremonies, by Lily, but thought of as noisily vacant by Isabel, who in these days made use of her memory of Rome as she might have done, in a hot and crowded room, of a phial of something pungent hidden in her handkerchief." This revision exalts Isabel at the expense of Lily and Paris. The original sentence is mainly informational. It judges neither Paris nor Lily, and by telling us that Isabel was unable to forget Rome lets us know that she is in love with Osmond. The new version makes Paris vulgar and Lily's feelings materialistic, while Isabel's preference for Rome is a sign of aesthetic discrimination. In 1881 she cannot help remembering Rome, but in 1908, on the contrary, memories of Rome are consciously resorted to.

The changes in Countess Gemini alter her nature thoroughly; many of James's revisions seem quite cruel. Presenting her in chapter 24, James changes her "very human and feminine expression . . . by no means disagreeable" to one which, "thanks to various intensities of emphasis and wonder, of horror and joy, was not inhuman." In 1881, she "presented no appearance of wickedness" but in 1908 she "revealed no depths." Her "greeting" to Isabel, than which nothing could have been "kinder or more innocent" in 1881, becomes her "demonstrations" which suggested "the violent waving of some flag of general truce" in 1908. The grotesque exaggerations destroy the character's humanity. When she finally tells Isabel about Merle and Osmond, it is not inappropriate for Isabel, who surmises in 1881 only that the Countess is going to say something "important," to think in 1908 that for the first time she is going to say something "really human." It is difficult to be sure why James discredited the character, but in doing so he certainly nullifies the weight of any of her judgments and opinions. Most particularly, he thoroughly undercuts the many bitter statements she makes about the married woman's lot, statements which have thematic import in the original *Portrait*.

The most important set of changes of this kind result in the systematic vulgarization of Henrietta Stackpole in the 1908 version. Her friend, Bantling, a comic character from the first, becomes sillier in 1908, a change less important in itself than for the way it reflects on her. He is her companion, after all, and to the extent that he is more vulgar, so is she. The relationship is crudely treated: "frank allies" in 1881, they are "groping celibates" in 1908 (chap. 20). Dozens of revisions make Henrietta harsher, more unpleasant, and more stupid. This is important, because Isabel thinks of her in both versions as an "example of useful activity" and takes her for "a model" (chap. 6). In 1881 Isabel is partly measured by her inability to emulate her model; but in 1908 the character is so belittled that the idea of Henrietta as a model is simply absurd. For one thing, James adopts a newly patronizing tone toward her journalistic talents and writings, satirizing aspects of the character which were more respectfully treated in 1881. Though very much a "journalist" and hence not very profound in 1881, she is nevertheless highly talented and thoroughly professional. Quite possibly in later years James became more conservative on such issues as woman's equality, but more likely his growing absorption with the inner life made a character who was engrossed in the world of work and action appear inconsequential.

In chapter 10, her first appearance, Henrietta is no longer "decidedly pretty" but only "delicately . . . fair." James removes the approving phrases "very well dressed" and "scrupulously, fastidiously neat," substituting for the latter phrase "crisp and new and comprehensive as a first issue before the folding." In 1881 she "carried not an ink-stain" while in 1908 she "had probably no misprint." The point of the 1881 description is to demonstrate that Henrietta is not a stereotyped female journalist, unsexed and unkempt. She is pretty, decorous, and ladylike. The later images stress her modernity and brashness, turning her into a different cliché—the tough, efficient career girl. Removing the element of softness and personal understatement from Henrietta's character, James makes her loud, overbearing, and obnoxious.

The process extends to very fine details. An 1881 image of her eyes as large polished buttons (chap. 10) expands in 1908 to "buttons that might have fixed the elastic loops of some tense receptacle," introducing tension into a previously serene character. The originally "brave" Henrietta "went into cages" and "flourished lashes, like a spangled lion-tamer" in revision. The spangles are out of keeping with her earlier sartorial decorum, and the flourished lashes bring a new image of aggressiveness to the depiction. When he changes "Miss Stackpole's brilliant eyes expanded still further" to "ocular surfaces" which "unwinkingly caught the sun," he is certainly making her more machine-like, and when Ralph's comment that she is "decidedly fragrant" is altered to "Henrietta, however, does smell of the Future—it almost knocks one down!" an image of subtlety is replaced by its opposite. Matthiessen notes some of these changes approvingly, pointing out how James has "brightened every inch" of his portrait; but it is precisely the brightening operation that cheapens the character.

It is odd to read in James's preface to the New York edition the author's apology for Henrietta—as exemplifying "in her superabundance not an element of my plan, but only an excess of my zeal. . . . Henrietta must have been at that time a part of my wonderful notion of the lively"—when one is aware that much of the liveliness was in fact put into the treatment by the revisions. When Henrietta comes to Rome after Isabel has married, we read originally that "her eye had lost none of its serenity" but in the revision that "her remarkably open eyes, lighted like great glazed railway-stations, had put up no shutters" (chap. 47). And the final sentences of the book, which have her "shining" at Caspar Goodwood with "cheap comfort," were also added in 1908.

These revisions are thematically crucial; as I have suggested, Henrietta is originally presented as a partial touchstone for Isabel. In 1881 the two women are more like one another than in 1908, and their stories are both germane to the issue of women's independence. As some critics have observed with surprise, Henrietta is the one character in the novel to achieve a successful and meaningful life. Moreover, she advances many of the most perceptive comments about Isabel, which are constantly being utilized by critics even as they belittle the speaker of them. Henrietta exemplifies a realized independence; she suggests what the "new woman" has and what she lacks, what she gains and what she sacrifices. Finally, she shows clearly by contrast that Isabel is not a new woman despite the goals she sets for herself. The contrast between Henrietta's sense and Isabel's sensibility recalls Jane Austen, and although Henrietta never has importance in the novel comparable to Isabel's, their stories are balanced to a certain extent. She is not merely a *ficelle* in 1881, but has independent function.

It is hardly surprising that twenty-seven busy years after he wrote *The Portrait* James would be unable to reproduce the context from which the work had originally been created. One never steps twice into the same river, and no changing artist can write the same work twice. We can recapture the context of *The Portrait of a Lady* in 1881 to some extent ourselves by so simple a historical exercise as reading the serialization in the *Atlantic Monthly* from November 1880 through December 1881, amidst many fictional and essayistic treatments of the new American girl. "What is this curious product of today, the American girl or woman?" began Kate Gannet Wells in an essay entitled "The Transitional American Woman," which appeared in December 1881 along with the second installment of *The Portrait*. "Does the heroine of any American novel fitly stand as a type of what she is? And, furthermore, is it possible for any novel, within the next fifty years, truly to depict her as a finality, when she is still emerging from new conditions in a comparatively old civilization, when she does not yet understand herself, and when her actions are often the awkward results of motives, complex in their character, unconsciously [sic] to herself?"

To this contemporary question James's story at once seems to offer a response. A certain fictional formula, too, had already developed for the new American girl; indeed it seems to have developed simultaneously with the obvious and widespread change in feminine aspirations epitomized by (though by no means confined to) the woman's movement. The formula was both a conservative answer to, and a literary exploitation of, the new woman's situation—a modern version of the essential feminine fable, the rescue story. An intelligent and attractive young girl, who is independent and wishes to remain so, is "rescued" from this false conception of an appropriate feminine life, by love and marriage. When she falls in love, the natural impulses denied by her desire for independence assert themselves. She finds independence incompatible with a woman's way of living. But this is a happy discovery, for the traditional feminine life fulfills her, and she learns the error of her earlier aspirations. An interesting example of the formula appeared concurrently with *The Portrait* in the *Atlantic Monthly* from June through November of 1881. This was William D. Howells's brief novel, *Dr. Breen's Practice*. In this rather weak story, the heroine is a young doctor who gives up her career after her first patient because she becomes conscious of her psychological unfitness for professional pressure and responsibility. As the wife of a mill owner she will use her traditional medical training in an acceptable feminine way by tending the children of the workers.

This "marriage versus independence" formula is now the most common plot in stories about women. James's use of it can be traced from *Washington Square*, a beautiful and bitter little work which immediately preceded *The Portrait* in composition (and has much in common with it), on to *The Bostonians* in 1886 and *The Tragic Muse* in 1890. It can be associated only with his early phase, when his fiction often dealt with current social material. That the original *Portrait* is controlled by the dynamics of the formal can be seen in the first few chapters, which introduce Isabel amidst conversation about Lord Warburton's need to marry an interesting woman and define her mainly by her fondness for her independence. A reader following the story for the first time would certainly expect Isabel eventually to be brought back into her proper sphere by happy love and see the plot propelled by the question of which suitor could succeed in effecting her rescue. But, as she resists the offers of lovers who believe that they are giving her great opportunities, the embattled Isabel becomes increasingly sympathetic, and when she is finally "saved" from her independence, the event is no rescue but a capture. That is, James uses the popular formula while rejecting its assumptions, so that his form and theme reach beyond formulaic simplification.

Since both Warburton and Goodwood are highly eligible as husbands, the reader may feel that Isabel's solution would have been a different marriage rather than none at all. Critics have mostly believed that Isabel ought to have married and take her severely to task for failing to fall in love with one or the other, dividing into camps according to whom they favor. But the formula proposes love as invariably saving by making young women invariably love wisely, and this is one falsehood James is exposing. Moreover, to assume that Isabel ought to marry because she is female is to beg one of the major questions raised by her story—and, indeed, by the stories of all the other women in *The Portrait*, Henrietta excepted. Many of the critics have just the attitude that disturbs Isabel in her suitors: the presumption that because an offer has been made, she is obligated to accept it or to have an excellent reason for turning it down. Neither Warburton nor Goodwood can accept the idea that she refuses them because she is unwilling to accept any mode of existence that is not self-expressive. But this is Isabel's good transcendental reason (as Quentin Anderson and others have stressed)—this and the unimpeachable emotional truth that she doesn't love either of them.

Warburton "had conceived the design of drawing her into the system in which he lived and moved. A certain instinct, not imperious, but persuasive, told her to resist—it murmured to her that virtually she had a system and an orbit of her own" (chap. 12). It does not matter that the forms of Goodwood's and Warburton's lives are good, and that a woman might live happily and usefully within them. They require the woman to be a satellite in someone else's solar system, and Isabel claims the right to be her own sun. If we define her by membership in the human race rather than the female sex, her claim is admirable. This is how James regards her. He shows it clearly by the fact that Isabel's rejection of Lord Warburton leads Ralph directly to his decision to give her money. The rejection convinces Ralph that her wish for independence is serious and that she is worthy of achieving it. Her wish is thus treated with great respect, not in the least as an aberration.

Ralph is also convinced—wrongly, as it turns out—that a woman could not be strong enough to refuse Lord Warburton unless she had an alternate vision of an independent life. But here Isabel's femaleness does play an important part—brought up female, she has no idea what she might "do" to be independent. The word does not translate into action. This is a terrible limitation, and although James traces its awful consequences, he does not blame her for it. The actual condition of feminine independence, rare as it is, comes about (as Henrietta's story demonstrates) less by choice than necessity, is expressed in unremitting commitment and hard work, and requires fortitude and ability in unusual degree. For these tough requirements Isabel is unfitted by her protected and insulated background, by her lack of training and discipline, and by a "romantic" temperament encouraged by her circumstances.

Here is a subtlety in James's consideration of the theme: modern as it seems, the desire for independence in a young woman may well represent an old-fashioned feminine ignorance of the real world. Consequently, Ralph's gift is no boon to Isabel, and the covert bequest deprives her of one option she has hitherto successfully employed in threatening situations: the choice of turning it down. The fortune imposes on her a necessity to act for which she is hopelessly unprepared. It is no wonder that her first reactions are depression and restlessness and that, startled into premature action, she becomes conventional and traditional.

Basically, she wants to get rid of the fortune and escape the burdens it imposes on her. Because of this special need she is vulnerable to Osmond in a way that she would not have been were she poor (quite apart from the fact that, then, he would not have been interested in her). Older and wiser than she, he will know how to use the money. His apparent lifelong resistance to commitment corresponds to a negative idea of freedom which now, under the pressure of Isabel's need, transforms itself into a positive goal. Because Osmond is less obviously a product of environment than Goodwood and Warburton, Isabel thinks him more free. More important, no clear shape defines itself for the existence of Osmond's putative wife, and therefore Isabel imagines that as Mrs. Osmond she can shape her own life. Although running from independence by reverting to the traditional pattern of love and marriage, Isabel does so in a way that permits her the illusion that she is still seeking freedom. Thus, though the cage she runs into is much smaller than she anticipated, there is no denying that her first free action was to put herself into it. James's point is not that the desire to be independent is dangerous in itself, but that such a desire when its substance is all romantic is no different from any other romantic dream, and will meet the same defeat in real life.

Yet surely he could have established this point without making Osmond and Merle so treacherous. The melodrama of Isabel's later situation certainly detracts from the novel's social realism, and makes her story more specialized, less universal, than it appeared at first. But there is a reason for the many ugly interactions and dreadful revelations of the last third of the book. They push Isabel to the inevitable point of leaving Osmond. This eventuality is much on her mind. As a conventional woman with no more idea than before of how she might live independently, Isabel shrinks from the possibility but cannot see how it can finally be avoided. "She seemed to see, however, the rapid approach of the day when she would have to take back something that she had solemnly given. Such a ceremony would be odious and monstrous; she tried to shut her eyes to it meanwhile" (chap. 45). The later events in the book force her to defy Osmond, and she increasingly realizes the groundlessness of all the reasons she can advance to stay with him. The conspiracy against her is necessary for the plot line because her learning of it destroys her last illusion—that she had married Osmond with her eyes open. Since Isabel did not freely choose him but was manipulated into the marriage, she is absolved from the moral obligation to suffer the results of her own decision. Therefore, if she remains with Osmond, it will be for the same kinds of reasons that originally drew her to him—his promise of an escape from independence and its implications.

Thus the question of whether Isabel will leave Osmond, which propels the story in the last third of the novel, continues the theme of female independence beyond Isabel's marriage. Because James has not followed the popular formula into its apotheosis of love and marriage, he is logically pushed to consider the aftermath of a bad union. Though not part of the formula—which did not and is only now beginning to accept divorce as a part of the texture of human social life—the issue of divorce was from the beginning implicated in questions of female independence and had been debated as a separate question since at least the late 1830s. Henry James, Sr., had taken part in an exchange of letters about it in the *Tribune* and declared himself in favor of "freely legitimating divorce, within the limits of a complete guarantee to society against the support of offspring." Thus it is by no means true that only vulgar or profligate people were associated with the cause of liberalizing the divorce laws.

The senior James's remark also explains why Isabel, having been given a child, was made to lose it. As Goodwood says, in his passionate exhortation, "What have you to care about? You have no children; that perhaps would be an obstacle. As it is, you have nothing to consider" (chap. 55). So even this matter is plotted to give Isabel free rein to leave Osmond. And if Isabel cannot bring herself to the modern American solution of divorce—it is so advanced by Henrietta—she can certainly simply separate from Osmond. Obviously, separation carries no social stricture in the world of the novel. Mrs. Touchett is an apostle of propriety, but lives apart from her husband for no reason except that she prefers to. In fact James is not writing about the abstract right or wrong of divorce, and this judgment does not control his plotting. He is considering what a certain kind of character would do in given circumstances. He concludes that Isabel would come very close to breaking with Osmond, but would recoil at the last.

The agent of recoil is Caspar Goodwood, but we must remember that Isabel's alternatives are not all subsumed in the choice between him and Osmond. She has still the alternative of going her own way, but in fact is less able than before to translate this idea into action. If, as a "free" woman, her greatest independent gesture had been to walk alone from Euston Station to her hotel (chap. 31), she realizes when she returns to London that even this motion is beyond her now. "She remembered how she walked away from Euston, in the winter dusk, in the crowded streets, five years before. She could not have done that to-day, and the incident came before her as the deed of another person" (chap. 53).

In contrast, James gives us Henrietta, crossing continents and oceans without flutter. In Henrietta, too, we have evidence that James does not want to say that independence is metaphysically incompatible with love and marriage. Despite the rather cynical portrayal of love and marriage in most of his fiction, he does not go so far as this in *The Portrait*. The independent spirits in the book—Henrietta and Bantling—fall in love and plan to marry, and this is presented as a happy event. Isabel's disappointment in her friend for showing such weakness is only an extension of her own disillusionment. James's idea, however, seems almost to be that the real possibilities of love and marriage are to be experienced only by those who do not depend on them to give life meaning.

James sympathizes with Isabel's ideals, deplores the external obstacles that thwart them, and still objectively shows how much the obstacles are internal, in Isabel's inadequate preparation for and understanding of the life she thinks she has chosen. He also appears to suggest that those whose romantic idealism may most attract them to this "modern" goal may be the least fitted to achieve it because romantic idealism is other-worldly. His own attraction to the romantic idealist as a type enabled him to bind all this into a single structure with an appropriate tone.

The text of 1908 is not sufficiently revised to transform the work into a late James piece, but is enough changed to cloud the original dynamics of the story. It is a baffling and problematical work, much more so than the text of 1881. The changes created many of the problems. They override the social theme of the work and partly erase it. The matrix of values which radiates out from "independence" in 1881 centers in "awareness" in 1908, with attendant dislocations of emphasis. Awareness in 1881 is a means toward the end of an independent life; in 1908 the independent life is attained only in awareness—the two things are almost identical. The only possible independence is the independence of perfect enlightenment. Consequently, Isabel is no longer perceived as having failed, and, not having failed, she has no limitations or shortcomings of thematic consequence.

PHILIP HORNE

From Perspectives in *The Portrait of a Lady*[†]

* * *

Great Scenes

When planning in his notebook the revelation that Madame Merle is Pansy's mother, James at first imagines a direct confrontation between Isabel and her older friend on the subject of their rights over the girl.

> Isabel resents Madame Merle's interference, demands of her what she has to do with Pansy. Whereupon Madame Merle, in whose breast the suppressed feeling of maternity has long been rankling, and who is passionately jealous of Isabel's influence over Pansy, breaks out with the cry that she alone has a right—that Pansy is her daughter [429–30].

But immediately, as if this passionate cry rang melodramatically false to the cageyness established as characteristic of Madame Merle, James steps back into a questioning parenthesis:

> (To be settled later whether this revelation is to be made by Mme Merle herself, or by the Countess Gemini. Better on many grounds that it should be the latter; and yet in that way I lose the 'great scene' between Madame Merle and Isabel.) [430]

Having said this, James continues to sketch the plot up to the end of the novel; after an interval, indicated by crosses; he gives himself his well-known justification for ending *en l'air*—that 'The *whole* of anything is never told; you can only take what groups together' [431]; and then after leaving another space he returns to the question of the maternity-revelation.

> I am not sure that it would not be best that the exposure of Mme Merle should never be complete, and above all that she should not denounce herself. This would injure very much the impression I have wished to give of her profundity, her self-control, her regard for appearances. It may be enough that Isabel should believe the fact in question—in consequence of what the Countess Gemini has told her. Then, when Madame Merle tells her of what Ralph has done for her of old—tells it with the view I have mentioned to precipitating her defiance of Osmond—Isabel may charge her with the Countess G.'s secret. This Madame Merle will deny—but deny in such a way that Isabel knows she lies; and *then* Isabel may depart [431].

The consideration that 'above all . . . she should not denounce herself' is a familiar one for readers of *The Wings of the Dove*, where the conspiring Densher stifles in conversation with Milly the exclamation that 'I know what one would do for Kate!' because 'resisting the impulse to break out was what he *was* doing for Kate'.[1] The same fear of exposure pervades *The*

---

† From *Henry James and Revision: The New York Edition* (Oxford: The Clarendon Press, 1990), pp. 209–27. Reprinted by permission of Oxford University Press. The author's notes have been edited and renumbered. Page numbers in square brackets refer to this Norton Critical Edition; those in parentheses to the *Portrait* in *Henry James: Novels 1881–1886* (New York: Library of America, 1985).

1. *The Wings of the Dove*, in *Henry James: Novels 1901–1902* (New York: Library of America, 2006), p. 474 [*Editor*].

Golden Bowl, where the confronted Prince is puzzled into a momentary lapse of dignity which makes Maggie feel, 'as in a flash, how such a consequence, a foredoomed infelicity, partaking of the ridiculous even in one of the cleverest, might be of the very essence of the penalty of wrong-doing'.[2] In these late works people don't *deliberately* give themselves away, because of the 'regard for appearances' which they share with Madame Merle and Osmond.

The notebook debate of 1880 or 1881 fascinatingly shows us James revising his intentions in the process of thinking out the action—revising impulses towards melodrama and explicit confrontation which are lively in the works of the 1870s and channelling them into potent indirections which anticipate those he was master of two and three decades later. Thus 'Isabel may charge her with the Countess G.'s secret' is a resurfacing of the urge for moral statements and the making of 'scenes', recalling Newman's charge of the Bellegardes with Mrs Bread's secret in *The American*; but it is an urge which does not get into, or rather does not get acted upon in, the 1882 scene with Madame Merle. Like Newman but at an earlier stage, Isabel experiences the bitterness of a desire for revenge only for it to pass over: 'There was a moment during which, if she had turned and spoken, she would have said something that would hiss like a lash. But she closed her eyes, and then the hideous vision died away' (759). 'Hiss like a lash' *has* the lurid pigment of a melodramatic 'great scene'—only fended off to the conditional—and the 'hideous vision' is only that, a vision. A moment later 'Isabel's only revenge was to be silent still', moreover; and we can recall how Maggie Verver, the exemplary manipulator of loaded silences, might fairly, as James comments, 'have yearned for it, for the straight vindictive view, the rights of resentment, the rages of jealousy, the protests of passion, as for something she had been cheated of not least'; a conventionally alliterating repertoire of strong affects figured, to distance the bombastic, as 'nothing nearer to experience than a wild eastern caravan, looming into view with crude colours in the sun, fierce pipes in the air, high spears against the sky, all a thrill, a natural joy to mingle with, but turning off short before it reached her and plunging into other defiles'.[3] The abnegation of the vindictive as remotely romantic has a different basis from that in *The American*, where Newman seriously contemplates exacting revenge and then mysteriously and impressively refrains; for it is as 'her husband's wife' and 'her father's daughter' that Maggie finds the self-righteous mode inconceivable. She has unlike Newman a set of family responsibilities, imposed by her great 'love' for the others, which prevents any such horrified flight from the domestic complexities of her situation. It may be that the loved and fragile Pansy performs the same function for Isabel, humanly representing the necessity of limiting any damage to be done.

The undeclarative passage between Isabel and Madame Merle at Pansy's convent belies James's notebook worry that 'in that way I lose the "great scene" between Madame Merle and Isabel'. The scene works by keeping Isabel in pained silence while her betrayer puts up a monologue which is supposed to cover herself; and then having the monologue falter: 'She had

2. *The Golden Bowl*, in *Henry James: Novels 1903–1911* (New York: Library of America, 2010), p. 862 [*Editor*].
3. Ibid., p. 892.

not proceeded far before Isabel noted a sudden rupture in her voice, which was in itself a complete drama' (758). The *NYE* makes this 'a sudden break in her voice, a lapse in her continuity, which was in itself a complete drama' [376]. Both early and revised texts draw attention to the inferential excitement to be derived from the small crack in her consistency, 'a complete drama' making a strong claim for the dramatic potency of unspoken transactions when much is at stake. James is venturing an experiment here, and immediately glosses the moment with a polemical insistence to make clear that Madame Merle has guessed that Isabel knows, explaining just how 'This subtle modulation marked a momentous discovery.' The equivalent moment in *The Golden Bowl* again has the young heroine listening to a monologue by her treacherous friend and picking out the troubled consciousness denoted by the quality of her voice. Charlotte Stant, here, loudly acting as a guide for visitors to Fawns, does not have an actual vocal 'lapse': rather, 'The high voice went on; its quaver was doubtless for conscious ears only, but there were verily thirty seconds during which it sounded, for our young woman, like the shriek of a soul in pain'.[4] 'Doubtless . . . only, but . . . verily' produces less explicitly *The Portrait*'s combination of the 'subtle' and the 'momentous'. Maggie is brought to tears by a quavering rather than an interruption in her rival's speech; which is a reflection of the fact that whereas in *The Portrait* a certainty is attained through intuition ('Madame Merle had guessed in the space of an instant that everything was at an end between them'), in *The Golden Bowl* Charlotte's suffering is a torment of uncertainty: she is deprived of any sense of what others know, and is thus socially and emotionally disabled. The claim entered in *The Portrait* for 'a complete drama' in a broken voice, and the registered possibility of a remark that would hiss like a lash, recognizably anticipate the acuteness with which 'it sounded, for our young woman, like the shriek of a soul in pain'. In both cases the psychological punishment is conveyed by a violent, hellish metaphor; though the crucial insight of *The Golden Bowl*, that the punishment is all the crueller for not being applied from the outside, distinguishes it from the earlier work. At all events we can see the innovative changes of mind about the structure and treatment of this climactic scene in *The Portrait*, which James's notebooks permit us to trace, as steps in an evolution towards the formal and thematic preoccupations of his 'major phase'; an evolution more *evident*, at least, in this scene than in the preceding one, that of the revelations by the Countess Gemini, which repeats patterns familiar from *Roderick Hudson* and *The American*—though doing so with an ulterior motive.

   The chapter above on *Roderick Hudson* drew attention to James's problems in the 1870s with the plausible conveyance of plot information between his characters and especially with the final revelation of secrets. Coleridge's Ancient Mariner, his 'glittering eye' indicating a compulsion to speak out about a crime (and spoil the fun of a marriage, incidentally), serves James again in *The Portrait*, in the scene between Isabel and the Countess Gemini which prepares us for the confrontation with Madame Merle at the convent. In 1882 the Countess, confronting Isabel with something to say, 'had a strange smile on her thin lips, and a still stranger glitter in her small dark eye' (748). But the *NYE* seems to want to put this quite

4. Ibid., p. 930.

otherwise: 'she had a strange smile on her thin lips and her whole face had grown in an hour a shining intimation. She lived assuredly, it might be said, at the window of her spirit, but now she was leaning far out' [369]. In the Houghton Library manuscript of the revision, though, we can see that 'a shining' begins as 'a living'; while 'assuredly' is an insertion, a further thought. The reference to light in 'glitter', that is, at first gets suppressed but then returns in 'shining' as the idea of 'living' is transferred and expanded into the sentence about leaning out, which alerts us to a departure in the Countess from her habitual angle of inclination. But if the Ancient Mariner is here submerged, he comes back a dozen lines later in a revision, more explicitly than in his 1882 form. The earlier version reads:

> She appeared to have something to say, and it occurred to Isabel for the first time that her sister-in-law might say something important. She fixed her brilliant eyes upon Isabel, who found at last a disagreeable fascination in her gaze (748).

The *NYE* gives this an enlivening turn or two:

> She appeared to have a deal to say, and it occurred to Isabel for the first time that her sister-in-law might say something really human. She made play with her glittering eyes, in which there was an unpleasant fascination [369].

'Really human' makes Isabel's scepticism till now about the Countess seem a matter of course rather than of pride (since she has been 'not really human' rather than 'unimportant'), and gives an emphasis which dramatically enlarges our sense of what she may say. 'Made play' suggests an expressive motion the reverse of 'fixed', and prepares us for the theatricality of her recital; while the allusion in 'her glittering eyes' intimates not only her need to speak but also the auditor's reluctance.

If the basic format of the scene is melodramatic or romantic, though, both in 1882 and in the much-amplified *NYE* version, the melodramatic or romantic element is there just in order to be discarded—in favour of the movement, in the following scene with Madame Merle, towards a complex play of silences and understandings. The combination of the Madame Merle and Countess Gemini scenes as a pair is a crucial step on from the first notebook idea of them as alternatives ('in that way I lose the "great scene" between Madame Merle and Isabel'). F. O. Matthiessen, in his pioneering piece on the revisions of *The Portrait*, comments on the Countess's 'dramatic possibilities' which James 'in his revision . . . exploited to the full'; and he quotes Lawrence Leighton observing that 'James wanted a good harangue, the sort of speech an actress could get her teeth into'.[5] He then remarks, subsequently and separately, on the way in which 'James has also built up the contrast between her and Isabel',[6] by making the young American's reactions more unexpected by her.

But there is a relation between the Countess's values—which don't have currency with Isabel—and her melodramatic presentation, one which we can see as complicating Matthiessen's claim that here James 'did everything he could to make her revelations to Isabel into the "great scene" he

---

5. F. O. Matthiessen, ed., *Henry James: The Major Phase* (Oxford New York and London: University Press, 1944) pp. 175–76. [See p. 493/494 in this Norton Critical Edition—*Editor*.]
6. *The Major Phase*, p. 176. [See p. 494 in this Norton Critical Edition—*Editor*.]

had missed'.[7] The Countess's revelation is not a *self*-denunciation, nor an unmotivated spilling of the beans, but a polemical denunciation of her resented brother and Madame Merle from the point of view of a partisan hostility to marriage and with a particular intention for the effect to be made on her hearer. We can be prompted by the revisions to see the Countess, already in 1882, as an artistic figure choosing her means for producing intended effects by her revelation; like James, shown by the notebooks consciously deciding how to bring about what is also *his* revelation. Once the words have been spoken, in 1882, Isabel, who has at first found 'the announcement . . . an anti-climax' (749), says she doesn't understand.

> She spoke in a low, thoughtful tone, and the poor Countess was equally surprised and disappointed at the effect of her revelation. She had expected to kindle a conflagration, and as yet she had barely extracted a spark. Isabel seemed more awe-stricken than anything else (750).

In the *NYE*, the account is pointed to give first a sharper sense of the Countess's failure as artistic, and then of Isabel's peculiar reaction which registers the failure.

> She spoke as one troubled and puzzled, yet the poor Countess seemed to have seen her revelation fall below its possibilities of effect. She had expected to kindle some responsive blaze, but had barely extracted a spark. Isabel showed as scarce more impressed than she might have been, as a young woman of approved imagination, with some fine sinister passage of public history [371].

The raising of the question of '*possibilities* of effect' can point us back to the critical calculations in the notebooks: 'effect' in 1882 might simply have meant 'result of a cause', where in the *NYE*, differently placed, it suggests a rhetorical idea of audience manipulation. 'Conflagration' in 1882 has the Countess an emotional arsonist, with 'in flagrante delicto' behind it, but as if any kind of fire would do. 'Some responsive blaze' in the *NYE* spells out the desired sympathy in indignation which is too faintly suggested by the 'con-' in 'conflagration'; the Countess wants Isabel to feel as fierce as she does.

The *NYE*'s last sentence establishes a clearer syntactic balance of values: '*scarce* more impressed than' takes us in a clearer direction than 'more awe-stricken than'; while the strong adjectival pointing of the quantities introduced—approved imagination' and 'fine sinister passage of public history'—establishes something detached and 'scarce more than' blandly impersonal in Isabel's appreciation of the news. '*Public* history', particularly, conveys her instinctive unwillingness to associate such calculating duplicities with her own life; and the *NYE*'s near-simile here ('scarce more than') recalls that from *The Golden Bowl* quoted above where Maggie feels the vindictive view as 'nothing nearer to experience than a wild eastern caravan . . . turning off short before it reached her'. Maggie, no more inflammable than Isabel, has in the same passage been unable to 'give herself . . . to the vulgar heat of her wrong'.

---

7. *The Major Phase*, p. 175. [See p. 493 in this Norton Critical Edition—*Editor*.]

In *The Golden Bowl* the revelation to Maggie of the deception and adultery comes through the unlikely agency of the little man in the Bloomsbury shop, without benefit even of the preparatory characterization we have in *The Portrait* for the Countess; and a comparable revelation is made by the vindictive Lord Mark in *The Wings of the Dove*; but these scenes, confrontations consisting of plain statements of facts previously suppressed, are not—that is are only indirectly—presented. The stress on the 'anti-climax' of the Countess Gemini's fully staged revelation can be seen as offering a rationale for these later elisions: in the Countess's view it is a genre scene, grandly operatic, with a conventional lively delivery and a conventional passionate response (the repertoire of attitudes listed by Maggie)—but as we have noted, this is not the kind of scene in which James's American heroines, coming from another world, feel they can participate. Isabel's pitiful tears signal her refusal to accept the terms in which the Countess presents the material, and her insertion of the events narrated into a quite different sort of story. James's remark that Isabel was to be 'an *Americana*—a female counterpart to Newman' is germane to this: like Newman, only without delay, she rejects the proffered European ethic of revenge in favour of conduct more enlightened and less brutally selfish, and does so in a way related to her distance from the European conventions (attitudes struck and scenes made) in which the unacceptable values are enshrined.

James's handling of point of view in the Countess's revelation scene corresponds to the play of values thus dramatized. The scene begins from Isabel's point of view, and keeps to it from her initial sense of the revelation as 'an anti-climax' up to her stunned absorption of its main implications, at which point she nearly speaks the name of Madame Merle. Then '"Why have you told me this?" she asked, in a voice which the Countess hardly recognised' (750). It is the *Countess's* cognitive process that is offered here, for the first time in the scene, at a moment of traumatic strangeness for Isabel; we seem to have a withdrawal from the central character's consciousness into that of the person attempting to produce a special effect in her. Straight after this Isabel says she doesn't understand and we get the paragraph discussed above, where 'the poor Countess *was* equally surprised and disappointed at the effect of her revelation' while 'Isabel *seemed* more awe-stricken than anything else' (my emphases). After which James begins to present the dialogue as a sensitive spectator would write of a piece of theatrical action, without assuming special insight into the characters' thoughts. We are left in some doubt about Isabel's internal processes. When she bursts into tears we are authorially informed that 'It was a long time since she had shed any' (751); 'suddenly controlling herself' is an uncontroversial inference to draw from appearances, but even so is revised to the more superficial 'with a sudden check' in the NYE [371]. In the NYE when Isabel asks if Osmond has been faithful 'To me—', she does so '*as if* her question . . . were all for herself' [371; my emphasis]. On the next page 'Isabel sat staring at her companion's story as at a bale of fantastic wares that some strolling gypsy might have unpacked on the carpet at her feet' [372]; which is a novelized stage direction, not an entry into her consciousness. We don't get the Countess's view either, but a comment on her which need not be directly Isabel's: 'if she lied she lied well' [372]. It is not till [the next page] that Isabel's feelings return to the text with the reference to Pansy as 'her daughter'—Madame Merle's; and even here it is in an account of their numb state which, in the *NYE*, has been *prepared* by the revision two pages before about 'public history': '"It seems very wonderful", she murmured; and in this bewildering impression she had almost lost her sense of being personally touched by the story.' Then Isabel flushes 'at the thought' (the reader's minor insight) of Madame Merle's pain at seeing her own successful step-motherhood; but even so for another three-quarters of a page she and the Countess are rendered from the outside: when the Countess cries 'Why did you ever inherit money?', 'She stopped a moment, *as if* she saw something singular in Isabel's face.' Finally 'Isabel rose from her sofa again; *she felt* bruised and short of breath; her head was humming with new knowledge'; and '*she felt* weak' [373; my emphases].

We come back to Isabel, then, though not very conclusively, after what we could think of as an experimental abstention from explicit authorial insight, one which allows a suspense to build up about the nature of the heroine's response to such shattering news, and about how far her code of values will be tenable and sustaining in face of it. Such a suspense gives a go with the whip to the European vindictive view; there are occasions when we are with the Countess looking at Isabel. The scene is a test of Isabel's moral imagination, which has to come up with an alternative relation to circumstances it has not been prepared to contemplate. The complete withdrawal from the point of view of Milly Theale at the comparable juncture (Lord Mark's brutal divulging of the plot) in *The Wings of the Dove* seems to be James's furthest extension of this practice or principle: with Densher's subsequent burning of Milly's letter it asks the reader to supply imaginatively the heroine's possibilities of response at a moment of ethical and emotional crisis. Even in *The Portrait*, however, where Isabel's point of view is re-entered, the authorial privilege of 'going behind', of detailing and accounting for her thoughts and feelings, is considerably limited from this point on, in the technique of 'gradual authorial withdrawal':[8] a ready proof being the controversy surrounding the novel's ending, which so many have differed about, or found frustratingly ambiguous.

In the Sequel

The Portrait ends equivocally; James in his notebook anticipates the criticism that Isabel is left *en l'air*, and confidently equivocates: 'This is both true and false.' He goes on, explaining,

> The *whole* of anything is never told; you can only take what groups together. What I have done has that unity—it groups together. It is complete in itself—and the rest may be taken up or not, later [431].

Which kind of wholeness of telling is being referred to here, temporal or philosophical—or both? What will happen when Isabel returns to Rome and Osmond is something we care about and are deprived of; the nature of Isabel's decision to return, which does fall within the temporal compass of the book, is another thing about which we care and yet are left without details. She leaves as she has entered, 'in motion and, so to speak, in transit'

8. Ora Segal, *The Lucid Reflector: The Observer in Henry James's Fiction* (New Haven: Yale University Press, 1959), p. 55.

[7], as James says in the Preface. She does so 'all tormentingly', for Casper Goodwood at least. Yet in the sense that the final section of the work has shown Isabel adrift and emotionally exhausted, unable to reach a decision, we can feel some finality in her having now decided, and a double propriety, to which we may have ambivalent reactions, in her thus fulfilling her promise to Pansy to return at the same time as going back to Osmond (in some sense) and thus not 'repudiating the most serious act—the single sacred act—of her life' (668). The strength of the marriage bond as a consideration for Isabel has been intensified in the NYE—though before the Countess Gemini's revelations: 'marriage meant that a woman should abide with her husband' (748), 'should cleave to the man with whom, uttering tremendous vows, she had stood at the altar' [368]. And the promise to Pansy has been acknowledged by Henrietta—reluctantly but without qualification—as in itself a sufficient reason to go back (773). We are not put in a position definitively to arbitrate between the force of these two promises in Isabel's decision, though the stress placed by James throughout on the importance of the relation to Pansy ought to correct any interpretation of Isabel's return as merely a capitulation to Osmond's marital power and his cult of respectable appearances.

Under the influence of Freud and perhaps of some of James's own NYE revisions to the penultimate scene, many critics have read Isabel's return as really motivated by something different from either of these ties, as a flight from sexual passion and the 'hard manhood' of Caspar Goodwood [402]. Richard Poirier, apparently with a Lawrentian idea of fullness in mind, puts the point persuasively as an inadequacy in James's intentions: 'even his most cherished value, the idea of individual freedom from social restriction, begins to look suspiciously like an abstract rationalization by which Isabel makes her fear of sex into an ideal of conduct'[9]—a point which presumably applies as much to the quitting of Caspar Goodwood at the end as to the refusal of her suitors in the beginning. Poirier argues that James strongly endorses Isabel's principled decision: 'in talking about her return we should be talking about a novel, not about a person, about the relation of her act to James's whole intention, more than about its revelation of her individual psychology'.[1] But he sees the novel as less good for thus relegating the matter of individual psychology. In *The Portrait*, according to Poirier, James 'had reached a point of crisis in his capacity to imagine a character in all its fullness and yet to present her as an object of more ideological than psychological interest'.[2] That is, Poirier reads Isabel as a figure mistakenly presented for ideological admiration (sticking to her word *vis-à-vis* Pansy and Osmond) but in fact striking the reader as psychologically—sexually—flawed. James in this view is on the point of discovering—or artistically accepting—that psychology underlies and redefines ideology (what's shown in the action of *The Bostonians*, his next novel). Poirier sees James as insufficiently true to his insights:

> James does give us, however, a very tentative suggestion about Isabel which, if developed in conjunction with all that is fully achieved,

9. Richard Poirier, *The Comic Sense of Henry James: A Study of the Early Novels* (New York and London: Oxford University Press, 1960), p. 150.
1. Ibid., p. 244.
2. Ibid., p. 252.

would have, for me at least, made the novel a greater work than it is. I refer to the implication that there can be no such thing as the 'freedom' which Isabel wants and which Ralph and James want for her, simply for the reason that regardless of opportunity in the world outside, there are in everyone the flaws, the fears, the neuroses that fix and confine and stifle.[3]

The 'tentative suggestion' runs counter to what Poirier sees as the damagingly 'glamorous' movement of the book,[4] its poetic sympathy with the future-fancying of its heroine, which is said to embody James's romantically excessive 'reverence for impractical aspiration'.[5]

Anthony J. Mazzella in his essay on 'The New Isabel' takes a more sympathetic view than Poirier of essentially the same interpretation: he brings together the Osmond–Pansy promises and the rejection of Goodwood as twin aspects of a highly abstract value: the rejection is construed as coming 'from fear of control by the erotic of the mind's power to operate', while the return to Rome is 'almost' a 'positive' challenge, 'for in that constricting environment only the mind has intense and wide freedom of movement'.[6] Mazzella, that is, accepts the reading that Isabel is afraid of sex, but makes it mindless sex she fears so that her final decision can be approved by reference to the high principle of 'mind' and its freedom.

It is not necessary, however, to see James's intentions as so unambivalently ideological: we can understand the ending perfectly well as deliberately engaging our uncertainty about what frame of reference to apply to Isabel's final movement, the ideological (in which it can be noble and ethically uplifting) or the psychological (in which it can be a repressively aim-inhibited transference of sexual urges on to other ground). Such a deliberate solicitation of ambiguity need not signify reprehensible uncertainty on James's part: it puts a valuable question to the reader about the relation between the realm of ethics and the 'deeper psychology', about the roots of noble actions and the capacity of human beings for sincere selflessness. In real life there is no certainty or consensus about the status and origins of high-minded actions, so those who perform them often have to go through with them psychologically 'blind', and we have to watch the process with some mixture of scepticism and generosity. Events *may* show whether the motives were pure (or sufficiently so)—but they also may happen *not* to show this, and to leave us in doubt.

We can find something chillingly lofty about Isabel's return, as about the conduct of the comparably placed Euphemia de Mauves in the 1874 story *Madame de Mauves*, where the betrayed wife behaves so impeccably ('She was stone, she was ice') that she drives her European husband to blow out his brains. The suitor in that case, Longmore, ends like Goodwood, waiting; but the delay is of his own making: 'in the midst of all the ardent tenderness of his memory of Mme. de Mauves, he has become conscious of a singular feeling, for which awe would be hardly too strong a

---

3. Ibid., p. 207.
4. Ibid., p. 223.
5. Ibid., p. 249.
6. Anthony J. Mazzella, "The New Isabel" [p. 510 in this Norton Critical Edition—*Editor*].

name'.[7] Yet such a chill, while accompanied with a due scepticism about the springs of virtuous behaviour, does not prevent the spectator's appreciation of the awe-inspiring acts of self-abnegation which provoke it. If Isabel can save Pansy from Osmond's manipulation she will have done real good, even if she is partly driven to keep her promise by her pride, and even if her pride is intimately associated with her capacity for error.

James's attitude at the end, veiled as it then is, presumably corresponds to his proleptic authorial statement early on, unaltered in the *NYE*, 'that, later, she became consistently wise only at the cost of an amount of folly which will constitute almost a direct appeal to charity' (297). When this statement is made (after the surprising rejection of Warburton's proposal), the emphasis falls on the folly and the charity needed; but 'consistently wise', when we recall it at the conclusion, seems to approve the final decision without qualification—though sardonic ingenuity could extend the lessons of folly and defer 'later' till *after* the novel's end, to make her return to Rome itself the 'amount of folly' so costly as a course of education; a view to suit Caspar Goodwood, whose hopes are put off into some belated future.

What is to happen 'later' is variously important for the poised and weighted ending of *The Portrait*: as James said to himself in the notebook, 'the rest may be taken up or not, later'. Consideration of the novel is haunted by calculations as to what may happen in the sequel, whether metaphorically or in a literal volume taking up and pushing on the old story. The idea of a continuation was enough in the air to receive a denial as late as 1898, when James was pleased by A. C. Benson's praise, but stated that 'I shall never write a sequel to the *P. of an L.* . . . . It's all too faint and far away—too ghostly and ghastly—and I have bloodier things *en tête*. I can do better than that!'.[8] In the event, though, it was not to Isabel Osmond that James turned later in the 1880s when he came to write the novel which was his nearest approach to a sequel, but to the Princess Casamassima, a figure who had ended *Roderick Hudson* in a state so far from 'consistently wise'. In a general sense *The Princess Casamassima* repeats the action of *Roderick Hudson* (Christina again fascinates and reduces to suicidal despair a sensitive young hero); and the Balzacian reappearance of a triangle of characters (Christina, Madame Grandoni, and the Prince), though the setting and the *central* concern are so different, creates resonances between texts that matter more to the meaning of the new work than those produced in *The Ambassadors* by the recurrence of Gloriani from *Roderick Hudson* twenty-six years before, or those in *The Golden Bowl* by the location of the crucial adulterous exploit at Matcham, mentioned as Lord Mark's destination in Chapter 37 of *The Wings of the Dove*. The contrast between the two women's final characters and situations vitally influences James's choice of Christina rather than Isabel for an extension of career. Christina is trapped in a loveless marriage and is

---

7. "Madame de Mauves," in *Henry James: Complete Stories 1864–1874* (New York: Library of America, 1999), p. 903 [*Editor*].
8. These words are echoed in an unpublished letter from HJ to his niece Peggy on 19 June 1913, responding to the Minny Temple letters she had sent him for the autobiography: 'what an infinitely pathetic faraway little ghostly voice it seems' (Berkeley TS transcript). [The Benson letter appears in Philip Horne, *Henry James: A Life in Letters* (New York: Viking, 1999), p. 298—*Editor*.]

romantically desperate for fulfilment and escape, and is thus a figure established as passionately uncomfortable within social rules and divisions, a ready source of plots; whereas Isabel has made her mistake and faced it, resisting Goodwood's summons to romantic flight and finding an honourable duty in her step-maternal relation to Pansy. From the vista of 'pathless lands' she dismally looked over from the train to London (382), she comes, on leaving Goodwood, to a clear view: 'She had not known where to turn; but she knew now. There was a very straight path' (402). Christina, that is, still represents aimless potentiality at the end of *Roderick Hudson*; Isabel has found direction and resolve.

At the beginning of this chapter I dealt briefly with the sense in which Isabel Archer is a creative extension and continuation of Minny Temple; and the end of *The Portrait* presents a conclusive aspect of the process. 'Minny was essentially incomplete', James wrote to Grace Norton; whereas Isabel's *Portrait* 'is complete in itself'. Whereas Isabel moves through 'pathless lands' to a vision of the 'very straight path' before her, James's last impression of Minny, recorded later in *Notes of a Son and Brother*, was 'as of a child struggling with her ignorance in a sort of pathless desert of the genial and the casual'.[9] Matthiessen, discussing *The Portrait*, quotes William James in a letter commenting relevantly on *The Tragic Muse*: 'the final winding up is, as usual with you, rather a losing of the story in the sand, yet that is the way in which things lose themselves in real life'.[1] Minny's real life story gets lost in the sand, the pathless desert, incomplete in a way that causes lamentation, and needs imaginative restoration. In *Notes of a Son and Brother*, alive to the pain of her life, James comes to the end of Minny's letters 'with a sigh of supreme relief for an end intimately felt as at hand';[2] back on 29 March 1870, writing to William, he had thought of 'the very heroine of our common scene', as he called her three days before to his mother, as 'the helpless victim and toy of her own intelligence—so that there is positive relief in thinking of her being removed from her own heroic treatment and placed in kinder hands'.[3] The relief of ending as such is denied Isabel, whose 'amount of folly' has from the start taken the form of quixotically hoping for a crisis: 'Sometimes she went so far as to wish that she should find herself some day in a difficult position, so that she might have the pleasure of being as heroic as the occasion demanded' (242). The marriage to Osmond which ultimately offers this chance more immediately gives her a challenge to meet from Ralph, and he sees her 'having caught a glimpse, as she thought, of the heroic line, and desiring to advance in that direction' (545).

These earlier moments cannot necessarily be applied with any directness of irony to the actual ending, since the 'pleasure' as such of her return to Rome may well be minimal, while 'the heroic line' here involves defending Osmond from Ralph—a line she entirely abandons in the death-bed scene, where 'nothing mattered now but the only knowledge that was not pure anguish—the knowledge that they were looking at the truth together'

9. *Henry James: Autobiographies*, ed. Philip Horne (New York: Library of America, 2016), p. 541 [Editor].
1. *The Major Phase*, p. 182. [See p. 497 in this Norton Critical Edition—Editor.]
2. *Henry James: Autobiographies*, p. 561 [Editor].
3. *Henry James Letters I*, ed. Leon Edel (Cambridge: The Belknap Press, 1974), p. 223. [See p. 426 in this Norton Critical Edition—Editor.]

(785). The ironic or awestruck remark that 'Women find their religion sometimes in strange exercises' (639) applies to Isabel's attempts to deceive Ralph about her suffering, which she equally drops at the close. The heroism of the ending is, at least in great part, presented as purged of its folly; 'the heroic line' is not the same as the 'very straight path' and the seeing of Ralph's spectre connotes a serious change of state, a passage through suffering to consistent wisdom. Isabel's promise to Pansy that 'I will come back' (765) is an engagement she would have to betray to go off with Caspar Goodwood, and no reader has a right to *demand* that she break it, whatever the dismay with which her last action is regarded. Isabel can be seen as more 'complete' than Minny partly in finding a path, a worthwhile aim; and having married in the summer of 1873 at twenty-four, the age at which Minny was removed by death in 1870 from her own heroic treatment, she is very possibly by the spring of 1877, when the novel ends, 'filled out' and 'justified', in the words of the letter to Grace Norton.

We could certainly see Isabel's return to Gardencourt near the end of the novel as drawing attention to a new elegiac wisdom acquired since her first visit there. In the passage whose manuscript revisions are reproduced as the frontispiece of this book, the pictures in the gallery make her movingly conscious of the cruel contrast between human beings, who decay, and works of art, which seem so permanent—in a way which anticipates Milly Theale's tears before the Bronzino portrait in *The Wings of the Dove.*

> Nothing was changed; she recognised everything that she had seen years before; it might have been only yesterday that she stood there. She reflected that things change but little, while people change so much (777).

In the *NYE* James, recognizing everything that he had seen years before, makes a change in *his* work of art, one which shows Isabel realizing a sad dissimilarity between things and people that she has wishfully ignored earlier in the action. After her travels, we recall, 'she only felt older—ever so much, and as if she were "worth more" for it, like some curious piece in an antiquary's collection'; a feeling which corresponds to her susceptibility to Osmond. Now, at Gardencourt, James expands the second sentence to give it a more disturbing pathos:

> She envied the security of valuable 'pieces' which change by no hair's breadth, only grow in value, while their owners lose inch by inch youth, happiness, beauty . . . [387].

James, changing his valued 'piece' by more than a 'hair's breadth', may take some consolation from his continuing grasp of the action; but poor Isabel, who now knows herself a 'piece' *not* 'valuable' to Osmond, is unrelievedly stuck with her human mutability, and the dying Ralph's. This tragic consciousness of failure and loss seems to be the pre-condition of her closing movement towards an uncertain but more truly perceived future.

Eleven days after Minny Temple's death, when James, in Great Malvern, had still not heard the news, he wrote to his father that 'something tells me that there is somehow too much Minny to disappear for some time yet—more life than she has yet lived out'.[4] The end of *The Portrait*, itself

---

4. Ibid., p. 214 [*Editor*].

a reflection of Minny's continuing life in James's imagination, is full of very similar references to the life in Isabel's future. On the visionary journey to England she deeply senses how 'life would be her business for a long time to come' (769). And her intuition that 'she should last' (770), becomes twenty-six years later 'she should last to the end' [383], grimly foreseeing a bound on her seeing of life and invoking an 'end' not that of the novel. When the dying Ralph asks if all is over between her and Osmond, Isabel replies, 'Oh no; I don't think anything is over' (785). *The Portrait* makes itself felt as an act of selection, of framing, which doesn't pretend to exhaust its subject when *it* is over but rather indicates how much lies outside its scope, in a way which relies on the connection it is alleging between its imaginative world and the conditions of real life. Its '"artistic" idea', to take James's polemical terms from 'The Art of Fiction' three years later, does in a special sense 'render any ending at all impossible',[5] by not including for representation what subsequently happens to Osmond and Pansy and Isabel herself. There is a mysterious life after the close of the book, and it is explicitly invoked in the conclusion, an act of reference to a larger and underlying reality behind and beyond the work of art. The conjured set of pseudo-historical data available for consultation and allusion—the imaginative world which the novelist draws up and then draws material from—shows forcefully here at the very edge of the book in James's purposeful abbreviation of the text.

The last pages of *The Portrait* formally parallel and significantly inflect two scenes from immediately previous works by James. The scene in the dark English garden with Caspar Goodwood echoes in its excitement at potential liberation the scene in the dark Genevan garden of *The Pension Beaurepas* (April 1878), whence the trapped heroine Aurora Church nearly flees with the hesitant narrator from the Europeanizing tyranny of her awful mother: 'It seemed to me, for a moment, that to pass out of that gate with this yearning, straining young creature would be to pass into some mysterious felicity. If I were only a hero of romance, I would offer, myself, to take her to America'.[6] Caspar Goodwood unhesitantly offers, himself, to take Isabel to America, and we could say tempts Isabel with the possibility of passionate surrender to him as 'a hero of romance'. We could see the point of these scenes as the resistance of a temptation to leave behind the oppressive constraints, already vividly demonstrated in both stories, of convention and duty corruptly defined (by Mrs Church and Osmond).

The closing scene between Caspar Goodwood and Henrietta Stackpole, which immediately follows, looks back to the last moments of *Washington Square* (1881), which in England first appeared in a volume together with *The Pension Beaurepas*. The heroine Catherine Sloper has taken her resolve and turned down her suitor Morris Townsend, who, implausibly encouraged by his supporter Mrs Penniman but unyieldingly dejected, sees only a bleak future for himself. Mrs Penniman asks,

> 'But you will not despair—you will come back?'
> 'Come back? Damnation!' And Morris Townsend strode out of the house, leaving Mrs. Penniman staring.

5. *Henry James, Literary Criticism I* (New York: Library of America, 1984), p. 48 [*Editor*].
6. *Henry James: Complete Stories 1874–1884* (New York: Library of America, 1999), p. 449 [*Editor*].

Catherine, meanwhile, in the parlor, picking up her morsel of fancy-work, had seated herself with it again—for life, as it were.[7]

The depressingly bland encouragement and the disconsolate reaction recur with a more humane and less satirical point in *The Portrait*—where, though, the heroine's future, having already been evoked on the previous page ('There was a very straight path'), is not mentioned. Henrietta grasps Goodwood's arm.

'Look here, Mr. Goodwood, she said; 'just you wait!'
On which he looked up at her (800).

1882 thus leaves the reader to provide expressions for Goodwood's (to us blank) face and mind in this gnomic final notation. The *NYE* amplifies, with an appended paragraph, the unhappiness of this ending for him:

On which he looked up at her—but only to guess, from her face, with a revulsion, that she simply meant he was young. She stood shining at him with that cheap comfort, and it added, on the spot, thirty years to his life. She walked him away with her, however, as if she had given him now the key to patience [403].

This revision occurs almost 'thirty years' after *1882*, and seems to call on its own temporal distance from the first composition to imagine a life sentence of disappointment (an 'addition to' which is really a subtraction from his life). Caspar knows, we are aware, that 'there are disappointments which last as long as life' (713). The view into Goodwood's future here includes Isabel's by imagining no end to his unsuccessful persistence with her. In both *The Portrait* and *Washington Square* the prospect is 'for life', and the statement of that is a way of propelling the action presented in the book forward to echo into the silence and emptiness after its final words. The *NYE*'s 'but' in 'but only to guess' quasi-pugnaciously jumps to correct any reading of this as a purely cheerful termination, and clarifies the ambiguity of *1882*'s half-line (he may look up thinking things are promising, *or* in immediate disgust) into a small narrative of hope followed by disappointment. The revision carries us a few moments and a few steps further into the hitherto blank future that begins with the words 'The End', as if to demonstrate James's continuing grasp of its substance; and these appended moments make the exchange between Isabel's friends more amply evoke things to come. The emblematic exchange of speech-less views between the two, she 'shining' and he presumably glowering, is fixed as a tableau 'on the spot' and metaphorically borne into the future by the hyperbolic figure which packs into it thirty years of aroused impa-tience. With the long-term future thus newly spun out of a brief confron-tation, James beautifully takes advantage of the fact a few lines above in *1882* that Henrietta is dressed ready to go out, and balances Caspar's pas-sive immobility with her cheerful pushiness by having her 'walk him away with her', in a construction which leaves intact our sense of him as still really frozen, emotionally out of action. They physically leave the scene, justifying James's final scene-break with a more convincingly natural rhythm than in the abrupter and more disconcertingly authorial 'cut' of

7. *Washington Square, The Pension Beaurepas, A Bundle of Letters*, 2 vols. (London: Macmillan & Co. 1881) i. 266.

1882. The *NYE* makes it truer, we can feel, that 'it groups together', gives us as readers more of a 'key to patience'. From the static long perspective of the previous sentence we move out of the book with a brisk return to the short term; the crystallizing 'now', which pulls together the sentence around Henrietta's sense of a provisionally satisfactory ending, is a manuscript insertion on a last page typed for the *NYE*—maybe James's final, pointedly immediate revision in a work consciously mediating between the beginnings of his career and its later consummations.

CRITICISM

James had admirers in the years immediately after his death, such as Percy Lubbock in his now-undervalued *The Craft of Fiction* (1921), but detailed accounts of individual works were at first rare. That began to change in the 1930s. R. P. Blackmur collected James's prefaces to the New York Edition into a volume called *The Art of the Novel* (1934), and the American New Critics found themselves increasingly drawn to a fiction that could be read as closely as a poem. James's work also proved inescapable for the writers associated with two very different journals: the Cambridge quarterly *Scrutiny*, under the editorship of F. R. Leavis, who in *The Great Tradition* (1948) put James at the heart of the novel's history; and the *Partisan Review*, where the critics known as the New York Intellectuals were clustered. In the years after World War II, James's work was increasingly taught in universities, and the conjunction of the paperback revolution and the course syllabus only added to his standing. Colleges needed lots of cheap editions, and many of them now came with authoritative prefaces by figures like Blackmur or Lionel Trilling. Still, James's reputation required one final thing to become permanent. He had asked that no biography be written, but in 1953 (thirty-seven years after his death) the first of Leon Edel's eventual five volumes appeared, volumes that Edel accompanied with one collection after another of James's stories, essays, and letters.

A few titles can suggest the burden of that midcentury criticism. *The Pilgrimage of Henry James, The Complex Fate, The Conquest of London*[1]—these all stressed James's expatriation, emphasizing the biographical drama to which his own *American Journal* bears witness. That was accompanied, however, by books with titles like *The Expense of Vision, The Imagination of Disaster*, or *The Ordeal of Consciousness*,[2] ones that put their weight on a sense of artistic struggle, on defining the strenuous relation between the aesthetic and moral. They valued irony and renunciation, and idealized what Dorothea Krook called "James' high conscience as an artist."[3] One could easily fill a collection with superb accounts of *The Portrait of a Lady* drawn from the first decades after World War II. I've chosen just two of them, though, and have taken Dorothy Van Ghent's essay from *The English Novel: Form and Function* as a normative reading, the sort of piece everyone should look at before moving on to more recent and often more idiosyncratic criticism. Other accounts could play this role as well, and some of them are listed in the annotated bibliography at the end of this Norton Critical Edition. I've supplemented the Van Ghent with William Gass's assessment of the ethical stakes in the way James's characters treat each other, a statement by an academic philosopher who is also a major American novelist.

My selection of later criticism concentrates on the last thirty years, during which James has received more scholarly attention than any American writer except Faulkner. Much of that scholarship has considered specific contextual

---

1. By, respectively, Van Wyck Brooks (1925), Marius Bewley (1952), and Leon Edel (1962).
2. Laurence Holland (1964), J. A. Ward (1961), and Dorothea Krook (1962).
3. Dorothea Krook, *The Ordeal of Consciousness in Henry James* (Cambridge: Cambridge University Press, 1962), p. 53.

or historical points; superb articles have measured the exact scale of Isabel's fortune, or asked how the period's divorce laws might affect her thinking about her marriage. I've decided, however, to focus on formalist accounts that speak either to the work as a whole or to particular cruxes in the critical tradition, as well as on pieces accessible to students, reserving those on more limited aspects of the novel, along with some highly theoretical approaches, for the bibliography. Jonathan Freedman's reading of James's relation to British aestheticism puts the novelist at the center of late Victorian debates about the nature of art and the relation of that art to life itself. James kept his distance from figures like Walter Pater and Oscar Wilde, but their work had much in common; and Freedman approaches their connection by looking at Gilbert Osmond: the *Portrait*'s villain, but also someone whose tastes and beliefs tell us a great deal about the period. Millicent Bell's study of the novel's heroine is drawn from her magisterial *Meaning in Henry James* (1991), a book in the grand tradition of those I've mentioned above, and yet one marked by a narratological sophistication that allows it to evade one of the New Criticism's great weaknesses: its inability to read for the plot.

Robert Weisbuch's 1998 essay offers a version of an argument first made in his now-classic *Atlantic Double-Cross: American Literature and British Influence in the Age of Emerson* (1986). Its examination of James as an American writer in Europe returns us to some of the earliest questions about the nature of his achievements, and then goes further. For in exploring James's debt to Milton he writes rather of good and evil in a world where those terms aren't finally determined by geography. Tessa Hadley has herself become a prominent novelist in the years since she published *Henry James and the Imagination of Pleasure* (2002), with its shrewd and measured account of the novel's conclusion, one that disturbed James's contemporaries by being both open and unhappy at once. No reader can avoid thinking about the connection between Caspar Goodwood's kiss and Isabel's decision to return to Rome, and Hadley's essay stands as our best recent account of the issue. And finally, my own "The Rocccanera" looks at the moment James singled out as the best thing in the book: chapter 42, in which Isabel sits for hours, motionless in front of the fire, does nothing, and sees everything. His representation of her inner life in those pages provides an early version of what his brother William called "the stream of consciousness," and in doing so looks forward to the modernist fiction of the next century.

DOROTHY VAN GHENT

On *The Portrait of a Lady*†

To go from Hardy's *Tess* [1892] to James's *The Portrait of a Lady* is to go from Stonehenge to St. Peter's and from a frozen northern turnip field, eyed hungrily by polar birds, to the Cascine gardens where nightingales sing. Though both books concern the "campaign" of a young woman—a campaign that, expressed most simply, is a campaign *to live*—a greater difference of atmosphere could scarcely be imagined nor of articulation of what it means *to live*. The gaunt arctic birds in Tess have witnessed, with

---

† From *The English Novel: Form and Function* (New York: Holt, Rinehart & Winston, 1953), pp. 211–28. Copyright © 1953 South-Western, a part of Cengage Learning, Inc. Reproduced by permission. Page numbers in square brackets refer to this Norton Critical Edition.

their "tragical eyes," cataclysms that no human eye might see, but of which they retain no memory. The birds offer a symbol of Tess's world: a world inimical to consciousness, where one should have no memory (Tess's fatal error is to remember her own past), where the eye of the mind should remain blank, where aesthetic and moral perceptivity is traumatic. The nightingales that sing to Isabel Archer and her lover in the "grey Italian shade" also offer a symbol of a world: they are the very voice of memory, of an imperishable consciousness at once recreating and transcending its ancient, all-human knowledge. It is to the tutelage of the European memory that Isabel Archer passionately surrenders herself in her campaign *to live*, that is, to become conscious; for, in James's world, the highest affirmation of life is the development of the subtlest and most various consciousness. In doing so, she must—like the girl in the barbarous legend of the nightingale, who, likewise in a foreign land, read an obscene crime in the weaving of a tapestry—come into knowledge of an evil which, in its own civilized kind, is as corrupting and implacable as that in the old tale. But consciousness here, as an activity nourished by knowledge, transcends the knowledge which is its content: and this too is in analogy with the ancient symbolic tale, where knowledge of evil is transcended, in the very doom of its reiteration, by the bird's immortal song.

The Portrait is not, like *Tess*, a tragedy, but it is as deeply informed with the tragic view of life: that tragic view whose essence is contained in the words, "He who loses his life shall find it," and "Except a corn of wheat fall into the ground and die, it abideth alone: but if it die, it bringeth forth much fruit." We associate tragic seriousness of import in a character's destiny with tension between the power of willing (which is "free") and the power of circumstances ("necessity") binding and limiting the will; and if either term of the tension seems lacking, seriousness of import fails. Apparently, no two authors could be at further antipodes than James and Hardy in the respective emphases they place on these terms. In Hardy, the protagonist's volition founders at every move on a universally mechanical, mysteriously hostile necessity; it is only in Tess's last acts, of blood sacrifice and renunciation of life, that her will appallingly asserts its freedom and that she gains her tragic greatness. In James's *Portrait*, and in his other novels as well, the protagonist appears to have an extraordinarily unhampered play of volition. This appearance of extraordinary freedom from the pressure of circumstances is largely due to the "immense deal of money" (the phrase is taken from an early page of *The Portrait*) with which James endows his world—for, in an acquisitive culture, money is the chief symbol of freedom. The vague rich gleams of money are on every cornice and sift through every vista of the world of *The Portrait*, like the muted gold backgrounds of old Persian illuminations; and the human correlative of the money is a type of character fully privileged with easy mobility upon the face of the earth and with magnificent opportunities for the cultivation of aesthetic and intellectual refinements. It is by visualizing with the greatest clarity the lustrously moneyed tones of the James universe that we make ourselves able to see the more clearly what grave, somber shapes of illusion and guilt he organizes in this novel. The tension between circumstances and volition, "necessity" and "freedom," is demonstrated at the uppermost levels of material opportunity where, presumably, there is most freedom and where therefore freedom becomes most threatening—and where necessity wears its most insidious disguise, the disguise of freedom.

In following the previous studies, the reader will perhaps have been impressed with the fact that the novel as a genre has shown, from *Don Quixote* on, a constant concern with the institutions created by the circulation of money and with the fantasies arising from the having of it, or, more especially, the not having it; a concern not always so direct as that of *Moll Flanders* and *Vanity Fair*,[1] but almost inevitably implicit at least, expressed in indirect forms of aspiration and encitement to passion. As the definitively middle-class literary genre, the novel purchased its roots in a money-conscious social imagination. The wealth shining on the James world is a kind of apogee of the novel's historical concern with money, showing itself, in *The Portrait*, as a grandly sweeping postulate of possession: as if to say, "Here, now, is all the beautiful money, in the most liberating quantities: what ambition, what temptation, what errors of the will, what evil, what suffering, what salvation still denote the proclivities of the human even in a world so bountifully endowed?"

The "international myth"[2] that operates broadly in James's work, and that appears, in this novel, in the typical confrontation of American innocence and moral rigor with the tortuosities of an older civilization, gives its own and special dimension to the moneyed prospect. James came to maturity in a post–Civil War America euphoric with material achievement. In terms of the Jamesian "myth," American wealth is now able to buy up the whole museum of Europe, all its visible "point" of art objects and culture prestige, to take back home and set up in the front yard (we need look no further, for historical objectification of this aspect of the "myth," than to William Randolph Hearst's epic importation of various priceless chunks of Europe to California). If the shadows of the physically dispossessed—the sweat and the bone-weariness and the manifold anonymous deprivation in which this culture-buying power had its source— are excluded from James's money-gilded canvas, the shadow of spiritual dispossession is the somber shape under the money outline. We are not allowed to forget the aesthetic and moral impoverishment that spread its gross vacuum at the core of the American acquisitive dream—the greed, the obtuse or rapacious presumption, the disvaluation of values that kept pace to pace with material expansion. James's characteristic thematic contrasts, here as in other novels, are those of surface against depth, inspection against experience, buying power against living power, the American tourist's cultural balcony against the European abyss of history and memory and involved motive where he perilously or callously teeters. In *The Portrait*, the American heroine's pilgrimage in Europe becomes a fatally serious spiritual investment, an investment of the "free" self in and with the circumstantial and binding past, a discovery of the relations of the self with history, and a moral renovation of history in the freedom of the individual conscience. It is a growing of more delicate and deeper-reaching

---

1. *Moll Flanders* (1722), by Daniel Defoe; *Vanity Fair* (1847–48), by William Makepeace Thackeray. These novels are, along with Thomas Hardy's *Tess of the d'Urbervilles* (1892) and Cervantes' *Don Quixote* (1605), the subjects of earlier chapters in Van Ghent's book [*Editor*].
2. Discussion of James's "international myth" will be found in *The Question of Henry James*, edited by F. W. Dupee (New York: Henry Holt & Company, Inc., 1945), and Philip Rahv's *Image and Idea* (New York: New Directions, 1949).

roots and a nourishment of a more complex, more troubled, more creative personal humanity. It is, in short, what is ideally meant by "civilization," as that word refers to a process that can take place in an individual.

The postulate of wealth and privilege is, in revised terms, that of the second chapter of Genesis (the story of Adam in the garden)—that of the optimum conditions which will leave the innocent soul at liberty to develop its potentialities—and, as in the archetype of the Fall of Man, the postulate is significant not as excluding knowledge of good and evil, but as presenting a rare opportunity for such knowledge. It is the bounty poured on Isabel Archer (significantly, the man who gives her the symbolical investiture of money is a man who is fatally ill; significantly, also, she is under an illusion as to the giver) that makes her "free" to determine her choice of action, and thus morally most responsible for her choice; but it is the very bounty of her fortune, also, that activates at once, as if chemically, the proclivity to evil in the world of privilege that her wealth allows her to enter—it is her money that draws Madame Merle and Osmond to her; so that her "freedom" is actualized as imprisonment, in a peculiarly ashen and claustral, because peculiarly refined, suburb of hell. Isabel's quest had, at the earliest, been a quest for happiness—the naïvely egoistic American quest; it converts into a problem of spiritual salvation, that is, into a quest of "life"; and again the Biblical archetype shadows forth the problem. After eating of the fruit of the tree of knowledge of good and evil, how is one to regain access to the tree of life?

The great fairy tales and saints' legends have identified life with knowledge. For the fairy-tale hero, the fruit of the tree of life that is the guerdon of kingdom is the golden fleece or the golden apples that his wicked stepmother or usurping uncle have sent him in quest of; and to achieve the guerdon he must go through all tormenting knowledge—of serpents, floods, fire, ogres, enchantment, and even of his own lusts and murderous capacities. The ordeal of the heroes of saints' legends is also an ordeal of knowledge of evil, and the guerdon is life. As do these ancient tales, *The Portrait* identifies life with the most probing, dangerous, responsible awareness—identifies, as it were, the two "trees," the tree of the Fall and the tree of the Resurrection. The heroine's voluntary search for fuller consciousness leads her, in an illusion of perfect freedom to choose only "the best" in experience, to choose an evil; but it is this that, by providing insight through suffering and guilt, provides also access to life—to the fructification of consciousness that is a knowledge of human bondedness. At the very end of the book, Caspar Goodwood gives passionate voice to the illusion of special privileges of choice and of a good to be had by exclusion and separateness: he says to Isabel,

> "It would be an insult to you to assume that you care for . . . the bottomless idiocy of the world. We've nothing to do with all that; we're quite out of it . . . We can do absolutely as we please; to whom under the sun do we owe anything? What is it that holds us, what is it that has the smallest right to interfere . . . The world's all before us—and the world's very big." [401]

Isabel answers at random, "The world's very small." What attitude of mind takes her back to Rome, back to old evil and old servitude, is not described; we know only that she does go back. But it is evident that she does so because the "small" necessitous world has received an extension, not in the horizontal direction of imperial mobility that Caspar Goodwood suggests, but an invisible extension in depth, within her own mind—an extension into the freedom of personal renunciation and inexhaustible responsibility. The knowledge she has acquired has been tragic knowledge, but her story does not stop here, as it would if it were a tragedy—it goes on out of the pages of the book, to Rome, where we cannot follow it; for the knowledge has been the means to "life," and having learned to live, she must "live long," as she says. It is only the process of the learning that the portrait frame itself holds.

The title, *The Portrait*, asks the eye to see. And the handling of the book is in terms of seeing. The informing and strengthening of the eye of the mind is the theme—the ultimate knowledge, the thing finally "seen," having only the contingent importance of stimulating a more subtle and various activity of perception. The dramatization is deliberately "scenic," moving in a series of recognition scenes that are slight and low-keyed at first, or blurred and erroneous, in proportion both to the innocence of the heroine and others' skill in refined disguises and obliquities; then, toward the end, proceeding in swift and livid flashes. For in adopting as his compositional center the growth of a consciousness, James was able to use the bafflements and illusions of ignorance for his "complications," as he was able to use, more consistently than any other novelist, "recognitions" for his crises. Further, this action, moving through errors and illuminations of the inward eye, is set in a symbolic construct of things to be seen by the physical eye—paintings and sculptures, old coins and porcelain and lace and tapestries, most of all buildings: the aesthetic riches of Europe, pregnant with memory, with "histories within histories" of skills and motivations, temptations and suffering. The context of particulars offered to physical sight (and these may be settings, like English country houses or Roman ruins, or objects in the setting, like a porcelain cup or a piece of old lace draped on a mantel, or a person's face or a group of people—and the emphasis on the visual is most constant and notable not in these particulars, extensive as they are, but in the figurative language of the book, in metaphors using visual images as their vehicle) intensifies the meaning of "recognition" in those scenes where *sight* is *insight*, and provides a concrete embodiement of the ambiguities of "seeing."

In James's handling of the richly qualitative setting, it is characteristically significant that he suggests visual or scenic traits almost always in such a way that the emphasis is on *modulations of perception in the observer*. The "look" of things is a response of consciousness and varies with the observer; the "look" of things has thus the double duty of representing external stimuli, by indirection in their passage through consciousness, and of representing the observer himself. For instance, when Ralph takes Isabel through the picture gallery in the Touchett home, the "imperfect" but "genial" light of the bracketed lamps shows the pictures as "vague squares of rich colour," and the look of the pictures is Isabel's state at the moment—her eager and innately gifted sensibility and her almost complete ignorance, her conscious orientation toward an unknown "rich" mode of being that is beautiful but indeterminate. Let us take another example from late in the book. Directly after that conversation with

Madame Merle when Isabel learns, with the full force of evil revelation, Madame Merle's part in her marriage, she goes out for a drive alone.

> She had long before this taken old Rome into her confidence, for in a world of ruins the ruin of her happiness seemed a less unnatural catastrophe. She rested her weariness upon things that had crumbled for centuries and yet still were upright; she dropped her secret sadness into the silence of lonely places, where its very modern quality detached itself and grew objective, so that as she sat in a sun-warmed angle on a winter's day, or stood in a mouldy church to which no one came, she could almost smile at it and think of its smallness. Small it was, in the large Roman record, and her haunting sense of the continuity of the human lot easily carried her from the less to the greater. She had become deeply, tenderly acquainted with Rome: it interfused and moderated her passion. But she had grown to think of it chiefly as the place where people had suffered. This was what came to her in the starved churches, where the marble columns, transferred from pagan ruins, seemed to offer her a companionship in endurance and the musty incense to be a compound of long-unanswered prayers. [353]

Here the definition of visible setting—churches and marble columns and ruins, and comprehending all these, Rome—though it is full, is vague and diffuse, in the external sense of the "seen"; but in the sense that it is a setting evoked by Isabel's own deepened consciousness, it is exactly and clearly focused. It is Rome *felt*, felt as an immensity of human time, as a great human continuum of sadness and loneliness and passion and aspiration and patience; and it has this definition by virtue of Isabel's personal ordeal and her perception of its meaning. The "vague squares of rich colour" have become determinate.

The theme of "seeing" (the theme of the developing consciousness) is fertile with ironies and ambiguities that arise from the natural symbolism of the act of seeing, upon which so vastly many of human responses and decisions are dependent. The eye, as it registers surfaces, is an organ of aesthetic experience, in the etymological sense of the word "aesthetic," which is a word deriving from a Greek verb meaning "to perceive"—to perceive through the senses. James provides his world with innumerable fine surfaces for this kind of perception; it is a world endowed with the finest selective opportunities for the act of "seeing," for aesthetic cultivation. But our biological dependence upon the eye has made it a symbol of intellectual and moral and spiritual perception, forms of perception which are—by the makers of dictionaries—discriminated radically from aesthetic perception. Much of James's work is an exploration of the profound identity of the aesthetic and the moral. (In this he is at variance with the makers of dictionaries, but he has the companionship of Socrates' teacher Diotima, as her teaching is represented by Plato in the *Symposium*. Diotima taught that the way to spiritual good lay through the hierarchies of the "beautiful," that is, through graduations from one form of aesthetic experience to another.) Aesthetic experience proper, since it is acquired through the senses, is an experience of *feeling*. But so also moral experience, when it is not sheerly nominal and ritualistic, is an experience of *feeling*. Neither one has reality—has psychological depth—unless it is "felt" (hence

James's so frequent use of phrases such as "felt life" and "the very *taste* of life," phrases that insist on the feeling-base of complete and integrated living). Furthermore, both aesthetic and moral experience are nonutilitarian. The first distinction that aestheticians usually make, in defining the aesthetic, is its distinction from the useful; when the aesthetic is converted to utility, it becomes something else, its value designation is different—as when a beautiful bowl becomes valuable not for its beauty but for its capacity to hold soup. So also the moral, when it is converted to utility, becomes something else than the moral—becomes even immoral, a parody of or a blasphemy against the moral life (in our richest cultural heritage, both Hellenic and Christian, the moral life is symbolically associated with utter loss of utility goods and even with loss of physical life—as in the Gospel passage, "Leave all that thou hast and follow me," or as in the career of Socrates, or as in Sophocles' *Antigone*). Moral and aesthetic experience have then in common their foundation in feeling and their distinction from the useful. The identity that James explores is their identity in the most capacious and most integrated—the most "civilized"—consciousness, whose sense relationships (aesthetic relationships) with the external world of scenes and objects have the same quality and the same spiritual determination as its relationships with people (moral relationships). But his exploration of that ideal identity involves cognizance of failed integration, cognizance of the many varieties of one-sidedness or one-eyedness or blindness that go by the name of the moral or the aesthetic, and of the destructive potentialities of the human consciousness when it is one-sided either way. His ironies revolve on the ideal concept of a spacious integrity of feeling: feeling, ideally is *one*—and there is ironic situation when feeling is split into the "moral" and the "aesthetic," each denying the other and each posing as *all*.

There is comic irony in Henrietta Stackpole's moral busybodyness as she flutters and sputters through Europe obtaining feature materials for her home-town newspaper, "featuring" largely the morally culpable unAmericanism of Europeans to serve her readers as a flattering warning against indulgence in the aesthetic. Henrietta is a stock James comedy character, and she is essential. Without Henrietta's relative incapacity to "see" more than literal surfaces, the significant contrast between surface and depth, between outward and inward "seeing," between undeveloped and developed consciousness, would lose a needed demonstration. (But let us say for Henrietta that, like Horatio in *Hamlet*, she is employed by the dramatist for as many sorts of purposes as his scenes happen to demand; when a foil of obtuseness is wanted, Henrietta is there, and when a foil of good interpretive intelligence or plain charitable generosity is wanted, Henrietta is also there. She is the type of what James technically called the *ficelle*, a wholly subordinate character immensely useful to take in confidences from the principals and to serve other functions of "relief"— "relief" in that sense in which the lower level of a relievo provides perspective for the carved projections.) In Mrs. Touchett, what appears at first as the comic irony of absolute aesthetic insensitivity accompanied by a rugged moral dogmatism ("she had a little moral account-book—with columns unerringly ruled and a sharp steel clasp—which she kept with exemplary neatness") becomes at the end of the book, with her son's death, the tragic irony of that kind of ambiguous misery which is an inability to acknowledge or realize one's own suffering, when suffering is real but the channels of feeling have become nearly atrophied by lack of use. At the midday meal, when Isabel and Mrs. Touchett come together after the night of Ralph's death,

> Isabel saw her aunt not to be so dry as she appeared, and her old pity for the poor woman's inexpressiveness, her want of regret, of disappointment, came back to her. Unmistakably she would have found it a blessing to-day to be able to feel a defeat, a mistake, even a shame or two. [Isabel] wondered if [her aunt] were not even missing those enrichments of consciousness and privately trying—reaching out for some aftertaste of life, dregs of the banquet; the testimony of pain or the cold recreation of remorse. On the other hand perhaps she was afraid; if she should begin to know remorse at all it might take her too far. Isabel could perceive, however, how it had come over her dimly that she had failed of something, that she saw herself in the future as an old woman without memories. Her little sharp face looked tragical. [389]

Mrs. Touchett's habitual moralistic denial of feeling as an aesthetic indulgence has left her deserted even by herself, even by her love of her son, even by memory, even by suffering. She is stranded in a morality that is tragically without meaning.

In Madame Merle and Osmond the ironies intrinsic to James's theme receive another turn. Madame Merle first appeals to Isabel's admiration by her capacity for "feeling"—for that kind of feeling to which the term "aesthetic" has been specially adapted in common modern use: feeling for the arts, the sensuous perceptivity underlying the arts, and, by extension, feeling for the finer conventions of manners as "arts of living." (Madame Merle "knew how to feel . . . This was indeed Madame Merle's great talent, her most perfect gift.") At Gardencourt, when she is not engaged in writing letters, she paints (she "made no more of brushing in a sketch than of pulling off her gloves") or she plays the piano (she "was a brave musician") or she is "employed upon wonderful tasks of rich embroidery." (The presentation is just a bit insidious, not only because of Madame Merle's so very great plasticity in going from one art to another, but also in the style of the phrases: the suggestion of conventional fluidity in the comparison of her ease in painting with the ease of "pulling off her gloves," the word "brave"—an honorific word in certain places, but carrying here the faintest note of bravado—and the word "employed," suggesting, as it reverberates, Madame Merle's not disinterested professional aestheticism.) Her senses are active and acute: walking in the English rain, she says,

> "It never wets you and it always smells good." She declared that in England the pleasures of smell were great . . . and she used to lift the sleeve of her British overcoat and bury her nose in it, inhaling the clear, fine scent of the wool. [135–36]

Just how acute her perceptions are is shown never more clearly than in that scene in which she learns of the distribution of property after Mr. Touchett's death, occurring in Chapter XX of Volume I. Mrs. Touchett has just told her that Ralph, because of the state of his health, had hurried away from England before the reading of the will, in which Isabel had been left half of the fortune accruing to him. With this news, Madame

Merle "remained thoughtful a moment, her eyes bent on the floor," and when Isabel enters the room, Madame Merle kisses her—this being "the only allusion the visitor, in her great good taste, made . . . to her young friend's inheritance." There are no other signs than these (and the episode is typical of James's minor "recognition scenes") of just how quickly and acutely Madame Merle's senses—her perception, her intuition—have functioned in apprising her of the possibilities of exploitation now opened, and in apprising her also of the fact that Ralph is the real donor of Isabel's fortune, a fact of which Isabel herself remains ignorant until Madame Merle viciously informs her. Madame Merle's feeling for situation is so subtly educated that she needs but the slightest of tokens in order to respond. And yet, with a sensitivity educated so exquisitely and working at such high tension she is morally insensible—or almost so; not quite—for, unlike Osmond, whose damnation is in ice where the moral faculty is quite frozen, she still has the spiritual capacity of those whose damnation is in fire, the capacity to know that she is damned.

Madame Merle and Osmond use their cultivated aestheticism for utility purposes—Madame Merle, to further her ambition for place and power; Osmond, to make himself separate and envied. Their debasement of the meaning of the aesthetic becomes symbolically vicious when it shows itself in their relationships with people—with Isabel, for instance, who is for them an object of virtu that differs from other objects of virtu in that it bestows money rather than costs it. This is the evil referred to by Kant in his second Categorical Imperative: the use of persons as means—an evil to which perhaps all evil human relationships reduces. In the case of Madame Merle and Osmond, it has a peculiar and blasphemous ugliness, inasmuch as the atmosphere of beauty in which they live—beauty of surroundings and of manners—represents the finest, freest product of civilization and is such, ideally, as to induce the most reverential feeling for people as well as for things. Isabel first appeals to Osmond as being "as smooth to his general need of her as handled ivory to the palm": it is an "aesthetic" image suggesting his fastidiousness but, ironically, suggesting at the same time his coarseness—for while ivory, like pearls, may be the more beautiful for handling, "handled ivory" might also be the head of a walking stick, and it is in some sort as a walking stick that he uses Isabel. An extension at the same figure, without the aesthetic and with only the utilitarian connotation, indicates Osmond's real degeneracy: Isabel finally realizes that she has been for him "an applied handled hung-up tool, as senseless and convenient as mere wood and iron." But the evil is not one that can be isolated or confined; it is automatically proliferative. Morally dead himself, incapable of reverence for the human quality in others, Osmond necessarily tries to duplicate his death in them, for it is by killing their volition that he can make them useful; dead, they are alone "beautiful." He urges upon Isabel the obscene suggestion that she, in turn, "use" Lord Warburton by exploiting Warburton's old love for herself in order to get him to marry Pansy; and Osmond can find no excuse for her refusal except that she has her private designs for "using" the Englishman. But it is in Osmond's use of Pansy, his daughter, that he is most subtly and horribly effective. He has made her into a work of art, the modeling materials being the least artful of childish qualities—her innocence and gentleness; and he has almost succeeded in reducing her will to an echo of his own. The quaint figure of Pansy, always only on the edge of scenes, is of great structural importance in the latter half of the book; for she shows the full measure of the abuse that Isabel resists, and it is to nourish in her whatever small germ of creative volition may remain—to salvage, really, a life—that Isabel returns to Rome and to Osmond's paralyzing ambiance.

The moral question that is raised by every character in the book is a question of the "amount of felt life" that each is able to experience, a question of how many and how various are the relationships each can, with integrity, enter into. Or, to put the matter in its basic metaphor, it is a question of how much each person is able to "see," and not only to see but to compose into creative order. The moral question, since it involves vision, feeling, and composition, is an aesthetic one as well. Madame Merle and Osmond are blind to certain relations: "I don't pretend to know what people are meant for," Madame Merle says, ". . . I only know what I can do with them." Mrs. Touchett is blind to certain others. Let us stop for a moment with Henrietta Stackpole's comic crudity of vision, for the "eye" is all-important, and the ranges of vision really begin with an eye like that of Henrietta, and the ranges of vision really begin with an eye like that of Henrietta. It is "a peculiarly open, surprised-looking eye." "The most striking point in her appearance was the remarkable fixedness of this organ."

> She fixed her eyes on [Ralph], and there was something in their character that reminded him of large polished buttons—buttons that might have fixed the elastic loops of some tense receptacle: he seemed to see the reflection of surrounding objects on the pupil. The expression of a button is not usually deemed human, but there was something in Miss Stackpole's gaze that made him, a very modest man, feel vaguely embarrassed—less inviolate, more dishonoured, than he liked. [66]

Henrietta, with her gregariously refractive button-sight, has also "clearcut views on most subjects . . . she knew perfectly in advance what her opinions would be." Henrietta's is the made-up consciousness, the pseudo consciousness, that is not a process but a content hopelessly once and for all given, able to refract light but not to take it in. (We can understand Henrietta's importance, caricatural as she is, by the fact that she is the primitive form of the pseudo consciousness which Madame Merle and Osmond, in their so much more sophisticated was, exhibit: theirs too is the made-up consciousness, a rigidified content, impervious and uncreative.) The Misses Molyneux, Lord Warburton's sisters, have "eyes like the balanced basins, the circles of 'ornamental water,' set, in parterres, among the geraniums." Let us note that the figure is drawn from an "aesthetic" arrangement, that of formal gardens—and in this sense has directly opposite associations to those of Henrietta's buttons (presumably very American, very *useful* buttons). The Misses Molyneux's eyes, like Henrietta's, also merely reflect surrounding objects, and reflect more limitedly, far less mobily; but the image is significant of certain kinds of feeling, of "seeing," that Henrietta is incapable of, and that have derived from ancient disciplines in human relationships—contemplative feeling, reverence, feeling for privacy and for grace. Extremely minor figures such as these, of the bottoms and the basins, are pregnant with the extraordinarily rich, extraordinarily subtle potentialities of the theme of "seeing" as an infinitely graduated cognizance of relations between self and world.

In this book, the great range of structural significance through figurative language is due to the fact that whatever image vehicle a figure may have—even when the image is not itself a visual one—the general context is so deeply and consistently characterized by acts of "seeing" that every metaphor has this other implied extension of meaning. For example, a very intricate and extensive symbolic construct is built on a metaphor of opening doors. Henrietta, Ralph says, "walks in without knocking at the door." "She's too personal," he adds. As her eyes indiscriminately take in everything that is literally to be seen, so she walks in without knocking at the door of personality: "she thinks one's door should stand ajar." The correspondence of eyes and doors lies in the publicity Henrietta assumes (she is a journalist): her eye is public like a button, and responds as if everything else were public, as if there were no doors, as if there were nothing to be seen but what the public (the American newspaper public) might see without effort and without discomfort. In James's thematic system of surfaces and depths, "sight" is something achieved and not given, achieved in the loneliness of the individual soul and in the lucidity of darkness suffered; privacy is its necessary stamp, and it cannot be loaned or broadcast any more than can the loneliness or the suffering. "I keep a band of music in my anteroom," Ralph tells Isabel.

> "It has orders to play without stopping; it renders me two excellent services. It keeps the sounds of the world from reaching the private apartments, and it makes the world think that dancing's going on within." [51]

The notation has its pathos through Ralph's illness. Isabel "would have liked to pass through the ante-room . . . and enter the private apartments." It is only at the end, through her own revelations of remorse and loss, that those doors open to her.

The ironic force of the metaphor of doors, as it combines with the metaphor of "seeing," has a different direction in the crucial scene in Chapter LI of the second volume—one of the major "recognition scenes" in the book, where Isabel sees Osmond's full malignancy, a malignancy the more blighting as it takes, and sincerely takes, the form of honor, and where Osmond sees unequivocally the vivid, mysterious resistance of a life that he has not been able to convert into a tool. Isabel comes to tell him that Ralph is dying and that she must go to England. She opens the door of her husband's study without knocking.

> "Excuse me for disturbing you," she said.
> "When I come to your room I always knock," he answered going on with his work.
> "I forgot; I had something else to think of. My cousin's dying."
> "Ah, I don't believe that," said Osmond, looking at his drawing through a magnifying glass. "He was dying when we married; he'll outlive us all." [365]

Osmond is here engaged in an activity representative of a man of taste and a "collector"—he is making traced copies of ancient coins (the fact that it is an act of tracing, of copying, has its own significance, as has the object of his attention: coins). What he "sees" in the situation that Isabel describes to him is quite exactly what he sees in the fact that she has opened the door without knocking; a transgression of convention; and what he does not see is the right of another human being to feel, to love, to will individually. Further, what he appallingly does not see is his dependence, for the fortune Isabel has brought him, on the selfless imagination of the dying man, Ralph; or, even more appallingly (for one can scarcely suppose that Madame Merle had left him ignorant of the source of Isabel's wealth), what he does not see is any reason for the moral responsibility implied by "gratitude," a defect of vision that gives a special and hideous bleakness to his use of the word "grateful," when he tells Isabel that she has not been "grateful" for his tolerance of her esteem for Ralph. The metaphor of the "doors" thus goes through its changes, each associated with a depth or shallowness, a straightness or obliquity of vision, from Henrietta's aggressive myopia, to Ralph's reticence and insight, to Osmond's refined conventionalism and moral astigmatism.

Let us consider in certain other examples this reciprocity between theme and metaphor, insight and sight, image and eye. Isabel's native choice is creativity, a "free exploration of life," but exploration is conducted constantly—vision is amplified constantly—at the cost of renunciations. It is in the "grey depths" of the eyes of the elder Miss Molyneux, those eyes like the balanced basins of water set in parterres, that Isabel recognizes what she has had to reject in rejecting Lord Warburton: "the peace, the kindness, the honour, the possessions, a deep security and a great exclusion." Caspar Goodwood has eyes that "seemed to shine through the vizard of a helmet." He appears always as an armorman: "she saw the different fitted parts of him as she had seen, in museums and portraits, the different fitted parts of armoured warriors—in plates of steel handsomely inlaid with gold." "He might have ridden, on a plunging steed, the whirlwind of a great war." The image is one of virility, but of passion without relation, aggressive energy without responsibility. The exclusions implied by Caspar's steel-plated embrace are as great as those implied by the honor and the peace that Lord Warburton offers; and yet Isabel's final refusal of Caspar and of sexual possession is tragic, for it is to a sterile marriage that she returns.

Architectural images, and metaphors whose vehicle (like doors and windows) is associated with architecture, subtend the most various and complex of the book's meanings; and the reason for their particular richness of significance seems to be that, of all forms that are offered to sight and interpretation, builders are the most natural symbols of civilized life, the most diverse also as to what their fronts and interiors can imply of man's relations with himself and with the outer world. Osmond's house in Florence has an "imposing front" of a "somewhat incommunicative character."

> It was the mask, not the face of the house. It had heavy lids, but no eyes; the house in reality looked another way—looked off behind. . . . The windows of the ground-floor, as you saw them from the piazza, were, in their noble proportions, extremely architectural; but their function seemed less to offer communication with the world than to defy the world to look in. [161]

(One notes again here the characteristic insistence on *eyes* and *looking*.) The description, perfectly fitting an old and noble Florentine villa, exactly equates with Osmond himself, and not only Isabel's first illusional impression of him—when it is his renunciatory reserve that attracts her, an appearance suggesting those "deeper rhythms of life" that she seeks—but also her later painful knowledge of the face behind the mask, which, like the house, is affected with an obliquity of vision, "looked another way—looked off behind." The interior is full of artful images; the group of people gathered there "might have been described by a painter as composing well"; even the footboy "might, tarnished as to livery and quaint as to type, have issued from some stray sketch of old-time manners, been 'put in' by the brush of a Longhi or a Goya"; the face of little Pansy is "painted" with a "fixed and intensely sweet smile." Osmond's world, contained within his eyeless house, is "sorted, sifted, arranged" for the eye; even his daughter is one of his arrangements. It is a world bred of ancient disciplines modulating through time, selection and composition, to the purest aesthetic form.

> [Isabel] carried away an image from her visit to his hill-top . . . which put on for her a particular harmony with other supposed and divined things, histories within histories . . . It spoke of the kind of personal issue that touched her most nearly; of the choice between objects, subjects, contacts—what might she call them?—of a thin and those of a rich association . . . of a care for beauty and perfection so natural and so cultivated together that the career appeared to stretch beneath it in the disposed vistas and with the ranges of steps and terraces and fountains of a formal Italian garden . . . [195]

The illusion is one of a depth and spaciousness and delicacy of relationships, an illusion of the civilized consciousness.

But while Osmond's world suggests depth, it is, ironically, a world of surfaces only, for Osmond has merely borrowed it. The architectural metaphor shifts significantly in the passage in which Isabel takes the full measure of her dwelling. "It was the house of darkness, the house of dumbness, the house of suffocation."

> She had taken all the first steps in the purest confidence, and then she had suddenly found the infinite vista of a multiplied life to be a dark, narrow alley with a dead wall at the end. Instead of leading to the high places of happiness . . . it led rather downward and earthward, into realms of restriction and depression where the sound of other lives, easier and freer, was heard as from above . . . [292–93]

"When she saw this rigid system close about her, draped though it was in pictured tapestries . . . she seemed shut up with an odour of mould and decay." Again the architectural image changes its shape in that passage (quoted earlier in this essay) where Isabel takes her knowledge and her sorrow into Rome, a Rome of architectural ruins. Here also are depth of human time, "histories within histories," aesthetic form, but not "arranged," not borrowable, not to be "collected"—only to be *lived* in the creative recognitions brought to them by a soul itself alive. The image that accompanies Ralph through the book—"his serenity was but the array of wild flowers niched in his ruin"—gains meaning from the architectural images so frequent in the Roman scenes (as, for instance, from this:

[Isabel] had often ascended to those desolate ledges from which the Roman crowd used to bellow applause and where now the wild flowers . . . bloom in the deep crevices). [359]

Whereas Osmond's forced "arrangements" of history and art and people are without racination, blighting and lifeless, Ralph's "array of wild flowers" is rooted, even if precariously rooted in a ruin; it is a life *grown*, grown in history, fertilized in the crevices of a difficult experience. The metaphor is another version of St. John's "Except a corn of wheat fall into the ground and die, it abideth alone; but if it die, it bringeth forth much fruit." Isabel, still seeking that freedom which is growth, goes back to Osmond's claustral house, for it is there, in the ruin where Pansy has been left, that she has placed roots, found a crevice in which to grow straightly and freshly, found a fertilizing, civilizing relationship between consciousness and circumstances.

WILLIAM H. GASS

The High Brutality of Good Intentions[†]

*   *   *

It is the particular achievement of Henry James that he was able to transform the moral color of his personal vision into the hues of his famous figure in the carpet; that he found a form for his awareness of moral issues, an awareness that was so pervasive it invaded furniture and walls and ornamental gardens and perched upon the shoulders of his people a dove for spirit, beating its wings with the violence of all Protestant history; so that of this feeling, of the moving wing itself, he could make a *style*. This endeavor was both aided and hindered by the fact that, for James, art and morality were so closely twined, and by the fact that no theory of either art or morality had footing unless, previous to it, the terrible difficulties of vision and knowledge, of personal construction and actual fact, of, in short, the relation of reality to appearance had been thoroughly overcome. James's style is a result of his effort to master, at the level of his craft, these difficulties, and his effort, quite apart from any measure of its actual success with these things, brought to the form of the novel in English an order of art never even, before him, envisioned by it.

Both Henry James and his brother were consumed by a form of The Moral Passion. Both struggled to find in the plural world of practice a vantage for spirit. But William was fatally enmeshed in the commercial. How well he speaks for the best in his age. He pursues the saint; he probes the spiritual disorders of the soul; he commiserates with the world-weary and encourages the strong; he investigates the nature of God, His relation to the world, His code; he defends the possible immortality of the soul and the right to believe: and does all so skillfully, with a nature so sensitive, temperate and generous, that it is deeply disappointing to discover, as one soon

† From *Accent* 18 (Winter 1958): 62–71. © 1958 by *Accent*. Reprinted by permission of the author.

must, that the lenses of his mind are monetary, his open hand is open for the coin, and that the more he struggles to understand, appreciate, and rise, the more instead he misses, debases, and destroys.

> In the religion of the once-born the world is a sort of rectilinear or one-storied affair, whose accounts are kept in one denomination, whose parts have just the values which naturally they appear to have, and of which a simple algebraic sum of pluses and minuses will give the total worth. Happiness and religious peace consist in living on the plus side of the account. In the religion of the twice-born, on the other hand, the world is a double-storied mystery. Peace cannot be reached by the simple addition of pluses and elimination of minuses from life. Natural good is not simply insufficient in amount and transient, there lurks a falsity in its very being. Cancelled as it all is by death if not by earlier enemies, it gives no final balance, and can never be the thing intended for our lasting worship.[1]

Even when William, in a passage not obviously composed with the book-keeper's pen, makes a literary allusion, as here:

> Like the single drops which sparkle in the sun as they are flung far ahead of the advancing edge of a wave-crest or of a flood, they show the way and are forerunners. The world is not yet with them, so they often seem in the midst of the world's affairs to be preposterous . . . [2]

it turns out to be a covert reference to "getting and spending."

Henry James was certainly aware that one is always on the market, but as he grew as an artist he grew as a moralist and his use of the commercial matrix of analogy[3] became markedly satirical or ironic and his investigation of the human trade more self-conscious and profound until in nearly all the works of his maturity his theme is the evil of human manipulation, a theme best summarized by the second formulation of Kant's[4] categorical imperative:

> So act as to treat humanity, whether in thine own person or in that of any other, in every case as an end withal, never as a means only.

Nothing further from pragmatism can be imagined, and if we first entertain the aphorism that though William was the superior thinker, Henry had the superior thought, we may be led to consider the final effect of their rivalry,[5] for the novels and stories of Henry James constitute the most searching criticism available of the pragmatic ideal of the proper treatment

1. William James, *The Varieties of Religious Experience*, Modern Library, New York, p. 163. God does a wholesale not a retail business, p. 484. The world is a banking house, p. 120. Catholic confession is a method of periodically auditing and squaring accounts, p. 126. Examples could be multiplied endlessly, not only in *The Varieties* but in all his work. In *The Varieties* alone consult pages: 28, 38, 39, 133, 134, 135, 138, 330, 331, 333, 340, 347, 429fn, 481, 842.
2. Ibid., p. 450.
3. Mark Schorer's expression, "Fiction and the Matrix of Analogy," *The Kenyon Review*, XI, No. 4 (1949). The commercial metaphor pervades James's work and has been remarked so frequently that it scarcely requires documentation.
4. Immanuel Kant (1724–1804), German philosopher who wrote foundational works, such as *Critique of Pure Reason* (1781), in virtually all aspects of the discipline. The idea of the categorical imperative was introduced in his *Groundwork of the Metaphysics of Morals* (1785) [Editor].
5. Leon Edel develops this theme in the first volume of his biography, *Henry James: The Untried Years, 1834–1870*.

and ultimate worth of man. That this criticism was embodied in Henry James's style, William James was one of the first to recognize. "Your methods and my ideals seem the reverse, the one of the other," he wrote to Henry in a letter complaining about the "interminable elaboration" of *The Golden Bowl*. Couldn't we have, he asks, a "book with no twilight or mustiness in the plot, with great vigour and decisiveness in the action, no fencing in the dialogue, no psychological commentaries, and absolute straightness in the style?"[6] Henry would rather have gone, he replies, to a dishonored grave.

The Portrait of a Lady is James's first fully exposed case of human manipulation; his first full-dress investigation, at the level of what Plato called "right opinion," of what it means to be a consumer of persons, and of what it means to be a person consumed. The population of James's fictional society is composed, as populations commonly are, of purchasers and their purchases, of the handlers and the handled, of the users and the used. Sometimes actual objects, like Mrs. Gereth's spoils,[7] are involved in the transaction, but their involvement is symbolic of a buying and a being sold which is on the level of human worth (where the quality of the product is measured in terms of its responsiveness to the purchaser's "finest feelings," and its ability to sound the buyer's taste discreetly aloud), and it is for this reason that James never chooses to center his interest upon objects which can, by use, be visibly consumed. In nearly all of the later novels and stories, it is a human being, not an object, it is first Isabel Archer, then Pansy, who is the spoil, and it is by no means true that only the "villains" fall upon her and try to carry her off; nor is it easy to discover just who the villains really are.

Kant's imperative governs by its absence—as the hollow center. It is not that some characters, the "good" people, are busy being the moral legislators of mankind and that the others, the "bad" people, are committed to a crass and shallow pragmatism or a trifling estheticism; for were that the case *The Portrait* would be just another skillful novel of manners and James would be distinctly visible, outside the work, nodding or shaking his head at the behavior of the animals in his moral fable. He would have managed no advance in the art of English fiction. James's examination of the methods of human consumption goes too deep. He is concerned with all of the ways in which men may be reduced to the status of objects and because James pursues his subject so diligently, satisfying himself only when he has unravelled every thread, and because he is so intent on avoiding in himself what he has revealed as evil in his characters and exemplifying rather what he praises in Hawthorne who, he says, "never intermeddled,"[8] the moral problem of *The Portrait* becomes an esthetic problem, a problem of form, the scope and course of the action, the nature of the characters, the content of dialogue, the shape and dress of setting, the points-of-view, the figures of speech, the very turn and tumble of the sentences themselves directed by the problem's looked-for solution, and there is consequently no suggestion that one should choose up sides or take to heart his criticism of a certain society nor any invitation to

---

6. Quoted by R. B. Perry, *The Thought and Character of William James*, 2 vols., Boston (1935), Vol. I, p. 424.
7. The famously undescribed furniture of James's *The Spoils of Poynton* (1897).
8. *The American Essays of Henry James.* ed. by Leon Edel, Vintage, New York (1956), "Nathaniel Hawthorne," p. 23.

discuss the moral motivations of his characters *as if* they were surrogates for the real.

The moral problem, moreover, merges with the esthetic. It is possible to be an artist, James sees, in more than paint and language, and in *The Portrait*, as it is so often in his other work, Isabel Archer becomes the unworked medium through which, like benevolent Svengali,[9] the shapes and admirers of beautifully brought out persons express their artistry and themselves. The result is very often lovely, but it is invariably sad. James has the feeling, furthermore, and it is a distinctly magical feeling, that the novelist takes possession of his subject through his words; that the artist is a puppeteer; his works are the works of a god. He constantly endeavors to shift the obligation and the blame, if there be any, to another: his reflector, his reverberator, his sensitive gong. In *The Portrait* James begins his movement toward the theory of the point-of-view. The phrase itself occurs incessantly. Its acceptance as a canon of method means the loss of a single, universally objective reality. He is committed, henceforth, to a standpoint philosophy, and it would seem, then, that the best world would be that observed from the most sensitive, catholic, yet discriminating standpoint. In this way, the esthetic problem reaches out to the metaphysical. This marvelous observer: what is it he observes? Does he see the world as it really is, palpitating with delicious signs of the internal, or does he merely fling out the self-capturing net? James struggles with this question most obviously in *The Sacred Fount* but it is always before him. So many of his characters are "perceptive." They understand the value of the unmolded clay. They feel they know, as artists, what will be best for their human medium. They will *take up* the young lady (for so it usually is). They will *bring* her *out*. They will do for her; *make something* of her. She will be *beautiful* and *fine*, in short, she will inspire *interest*, *amusement*, and *wonder*. And their pursuit of the ideally refractive medium parallels perfectly Henry James's own, except he is aware that his selected lens dare not be perfect else he will have embodied a god again, and far more obnoxious must this god seem in the body of a character than he did in the nib of the author's pen; but more than this, James knows, as his creations so often do not, that this manipulation is the essence, the ultimate germ, of the evil the whole of his work condemns, and it is nowhere more brutal than when fronted by the kindest regard and backed by a benevolent will.

The Portrait of a Lady, for one who is familiar with James, opens on rich sounds. None of his major motifs is missing. The talk at tea provides us with five, the composition of the company constitutes a sixth, and his treatment of the setting satisfies the full and holy seven. The talk moves in a desultory fashion ("desultory" is the repetitive word) and in joking tones ("That's a sort of joke" is the repetitive phrase) from health and illness, and the ambiguity of its value, to boredom, considered as a kind of sickness,

---

9. A sinister hypnotist in George Du Maurier's best-selling *Trilby* (1894) who seduces, manipulates, and exploits the title character, in the process transforming her into a great singer; now a byword. Du Maurier (1834–1896) was for much of his life best known as a graphic artist, working mostly for *Punch* but also illustrating the magazine versions of James's *Washington Square*. He in fact offered *Trilby*'s plot to James, and then at the American's insistence wrote it himself [Editor].

and the ambiguity of its production.[1] Wealth is suggested as a cause of boredom, then marriage is proposed as a cure. The elder Touchett warns Lord
Warburton not to fall in love with his niece, a young lady recently captured
by his wife to be exhibited abroad. The questions about her are: has she
money? is she interesting? The jokes are: is she marriageable? is she
engaged? Isabel is the fifth thing, then—the young, spirited material. Lord
Warburton is English, of course, while the Touchetts are Americans.
Isabel's coming will sharpen the contrast, dramatize the confrontation.
Lastly, James dwells lovingly on the ancient red brick house, emphasizing
its esthetic appeal, its traditions, its status as a work of art. In describing the
grounds he indicates, too, what an American man of money may do: fall in
love with a history not his own and allow it, slowly, to civilize him, draw him
into Europe. Lord Warburton is said to be bored. It is suggested that he is
trying to fall in love. Ralph is described as cynical, without belief, a condition ascribed to his illness by his father. "He seems to feel as if he had never
had a chance." But the best of the ladies will save us, the elder Touchett
says, a remark made improbable by his own lack of success.

The structure of the talk of this astonishing first chapter foreshadows
everything. All jests turn earnest, and in them, as in the aimless pattern
of the jesters' leisure, lies plain the essential evil, for the evil cannot be
blinked even though it may not be so immediately irritating to the eye as
the evil of Madame Merle or Gilbert Osmond. There is in Isabel herself a
certain willingness to be employed, a desire to be taken up and fancied, if
only because that very enslavement, on other terms, makes her more free.
She refuses Warburton, not because he seeks his own salvation in her,
his cure by "interest," but rather because marriage to him would not satisfy her greed for experience, her freedom to see and feel and do. Neither
Warburton nor Goodwood appeals as a person to Isabel's vanity. She is a
great subject. She will make a great portrait. She knows it. Nevertheless
Isabel's ambitions are at first naive and inarticulate. It is Ralph who sees
the chance, in her, for the really fine thing; who sees in her his own chance,
too, the chance at life denied him. It is Ralph, finally, who empowers her
flight and in doing so draws the attention of the hunters.

Ralph and Osmond represent two types of the artist. Osmond regards
Isabel as an opportunity to create a work which will flatter himself and
be the best testimony to his taste. Her intelligence is a silver plate he will
heap with fruits to decorate his table. Her talk will be for him "a sort
of served dessert." He will rap her with his knuckle. She will ring. As
Osmond's wife, Isabel recognizes that she is a piece of property; her mind
is attached to his like a small garden-plot to a deer park. But Ralph obeys
the strictures *The Art of Fiction* was later to lay down. He works rather
with the medium itself and respects the given. His desire is to exhibit it,
make it whole, refulgent, round. He wants, in short, to make an image or
to see one made—a portrait. He demands of the work only that it be "interesting." He effaces himself. The "case" is his concern. *The Portrait's* crucial scene, in this regard, is that between Ralph and his dying father. Ralph

1. Illness, in James's novels, either signifies the beautiful thing (the Minny Temple theme) or it
provides the excuse for spectatorship and withdrawal, the opportunity to develop the esthetic
sense (the Henry James theme).

cannot love Isabel. His illness prevents him. He feels it would be wrong. Nevertheless, he takes, he says, "a great interest" in his cousin although he has no real influence over her.

> "But I should like to do something for her . . . I should like to put a little wind in her sails . . . I should like to put it into her power to do some of the things she wants. She wants to see the world for instance. I should like to put money in her purse. [131–132]

The language is unmistakable. It is the language of Iago. Ralph wants her rich.

> "I call people rich when they're able to meet the requirements of their imagination. Isabel has a great deal of imagination." [132]

With money she will not have to marry for it. Money will make her free. It is a curious faith. Mr. Touchett says, "You speak as if it were for your mere amusement," and Ralph replies, "So it is, a good deal." Mr. Touchett's objections are serenely met. Isabel will be extravagant but she will come to her senses in time. And, Ralph says,

> ". . . it would be very painful to me to think of her coming to the consciousness of a lot of wants she should be unable to satisfy. . . ."
> "Well, I don't know . . . I don't think I enter into your spirit. It seems to me immoral."
> "Immoral, dear daddy?"
> "Well, I don't know that it's right to make everything so easy for a person."[2]
> "It surely depends upon the person. When the person's good, your making things easy is all to the credit of virtue. To facilitate the execution of good impulses, what can be a nobler act? . . ."
> "Isabel's a sweet young thing; but do you think she's so good as that?"
> "She's as good as her best opportunities . . ."
> "Doesn't it occur to you that a young lady with sixty thousand pounds may fall a victim to the fortune-hunters?"
> "She'll hardly fall a victim to more than one."
> "Well, one's too many."
> "Decidedly. That's a risk, and it has entered into my calculation. I think it's appreciable, but I think it's small, and I'm prepared to take it . . ."
> "But I don't see what good you're to get of it. . . ."
> "I shall get just the good I said a few moments ago I wished to put into Isabel's reach—that of having met the requirements of my imagination. . . ."

The differences between Gilbert Osmond and Ralph Touchett are vast, but they are also thin.

Isabel Archer is thus free to try her wings. She is thrown upon the world. She becomes the friend of Madame Merle, "the great round world herself": polished, perfect, beautiful without a fault, mysterious, exciting,

---

2. A remark characteristic of the self-made man. In the first chapter, Mr. Touchett attributes Warburton's "boredom" to idleness. "You wouldn't be bored if you had something to do; but all you young men are too idle. You think too much of your pleasure. You're too fastidious, and too indolent, and too rich." Caspar Goodwood is the industrious suitor.

treacherous, repellent, and at bottom, like Isabel, identically betrayed; like Isabel again, seeking out of her own ruin to protect Pansy, the new subject, "the blank page," from that same round world that is herself. It is irony of the profoundest sort that "good" and "evil" in their paths should pass so closely. The dark ambitions of Serena Merle are lightened by a pathetic bulb, and it is only those whose eyes are fascinated and convinced by surface who can put their confident finger on the "really good." Ralph Touchett, and we are not meant to miss the appropriateness of his name, has not only failed to respect Isabel Archer as an end, he has failed to calculate correctly the qualities of his object. Isabel is a sweet, young thing. She is not yet, at any rate, as good as her best opportunities. The sensitive eye was at the acute point blind. Ralph has unwittingly put his bird in a cage. In a later interview, Isabel tells him she has given up all desire for a general view of life. Now she prefers corners. It is a corner she's been driven to. Time after time the "better" people curse the future they wish to save with their bequests. Longdon of *The Awkward Age* and Milly Theale of *The Wings of the Dove* come immediately to mind. Time after time the better artists fail because their point-of-view is ultimately only *theirs*, and because they have brought the esthetic relation too grandly, too completely into life.

In the portrait of Fleda Vetch of *The Spoils of Poynton* James has rendered an ideally considerate soul. Fleda, a person of modest means and background, possesses nevertheless the true sense of beauty. She is drawn by her friend Mrs. Gereth into the full exercise of that sense and to an appreciation of the ripe contemplative life which otherwise might have been denied her. Yet Fleda so little awards the palm to mere cleverness or sensibility that she falls in love with the slow, confused, and indecisive Owen Gereth. Fleda furthermore separates her moral and her esthetic ideals. Not only does she refuse to manipulate others, she refuses, herself, to be manipulated. The moral lines she feels are delicate. She takes all into her hands. Everyone has absolute worth. Scruples beset and surround her and not even Mrs. Gereth's righteousness, the warmth of her remembered wrongs, can melt them through. The impatience which James generates in the reader and expresses through Mrs. Gereth is the impatience, precisely, of his brother: for Fleda to act, to break from the net of scruple and seize the chance. It would be for the good of the good. It would save the spoils, save Owen, save Mrs. Gereth, save love for herself; but Fleda Vetch understands, as few people in Henry James ever do, the high brutality of such good intentions. She cannot accept happiness on the condition of moral compromise, for that would be to betray the ground on which, ideally, happiness ought to rest. Indeed it would betray happiness itself, and love, and the people and their possessions that have precipitated the problem and suggested the attractive and fatal price.

It is not simply in the organization of character, dialogue, and action that Henry James reveals The Moral Passion, nor is it reflected further only in his treatment of surroundings[3] but it represents itself and its ideal

3. When, for instance, in *The Portrait* Gilbert Osmond proposed to Isabel, the furnishings of the room in which their talk takes place seem to Osmond himself "ugly to distress" and "the false colours, the sham splendour . . . like vulgar, bragging, lying talk"—an obvious commentary by the setting on the action.

in the increasing scrupulosity of the style: precision of definition, respect for nuance, tone, the multiplying presence of enveloping metaphors, the winding around the tender center of ritual lines; like the approach of the devout and worshipful to the altar, these circumlocutions at once protecting the subject and slowing the advance so that the mere utility of the core is despaired of and it is valued solely in the contemplative sight. The value of life lies ultimately in the experienced quality of it, in the integrity of the given not in the usefulness of the taken. Henry James does not peer through experience to the future, through this future to the future futures, endlessly down the infinite tube. He does not find in today only what is needful for tomorrow. His aim is rather to appreciate and to respect the things of his experience and to set them, finally, free.

JONATHAN FREEDMAN

From Professions of Taste: Henry James, British Aestheticism, and Commodity Culture†

Portrait of an Aesthete: Gilbert Osmond and the Satire of Aestheticism

Like *Roderick Hudson* [1875], *Portrait of a Lady* inscribes a historically specific response to aestheticism. It is important to remember that when James arrived in London in 1880 to finish the novel, the aesthetic craze was at its height. Aestheticism had at that very moment moved from a coterie concern to a public sensation. Oscar Wilde's[1] notoriety had reached its apogee: having come down from Oxford some two years previously, Wilde threw himself into the round of dinner parties and soirees, enthralling many and shocking the rest with his calculated outrageousness. His fame, and that of his set, extended beyond the range of dinner-party gossip. No fewer than three plays brought aestheticism to the attention of the West End public. James Albery's inept *Where's the Cat?*, a more successful farce, *The Colonel*, by the mediocre but prolific Frank Burnand, and, of course, Gilbert and Sullivan's *Patience* all opened in 1881, the latter two to spectacular public response. And, seemingly every week, *Punch* launched satirical lampoons at the aesthetes, sometimes in prose, sometimes in cartoons, most from the hand of George Du Maurier.

Aestheticism thus formed the subject matter of the plays James was seeing, the newspapers and periodicals he was reading, and, undoubtedly, the parties he was attending. It was becoming part of his professional life as well. James met Du Maurier when the latter's lampoons of the aesthetes were at their peak of popularity, and entered into protracted negotiations

---

† From *Professions of Taste: Henry James, British Aestheticism, and Commodity Culture* (Palo Alto: Stanford University Press, 1990), pp. 146–66. Copyright © 1990 by the Board of Trustees of the Leland Stanford Junior University. Reprinted by permission of the publisher. Page references to the novel are to the 1882 edition as printed in *Henry James: Novels 1881–1886* (New York: Library of America, 1985). Freedman's notes have been edited to provide complete bibliographic information.

1. Irish writer (1854–1900), known as a personality long before he wrote anything of permanent value. His works include "The Decay of Lying" (1889), *The Picture of Dorian Gray* (1890), and *The Importance of Being Earnest* (1895). Wilde was arrested in 1895 for sodomy, convicted of "gross indecency," and sentenced to two years of hard labor. *De Profundis*, a prison letter to his former lover, Lord Alfred Douglas, was published posthumously (1905) [*Editor*].

with him over the illustrations to *Washington Square*. And the issue of *Macmillan's* in which *Portrait* was first published was preceded immediately by one containing a venomous attack on aestheticism, entitled "The New Renaissance; or, The Gospel of Intensity," by the conservative art critic Harry Quilter; the novel's second installment was followed immediately by William Michael Rossetti's response to Quilter's assault.

It is not surprising, therefore, that aestheticism was also becoming part of James's own novel, largely through the vehicle of the malevolent Gilbert Osmond. Indeed, the representation of Osmond is thoroughly grounded in this historical moment—far more thoroughly than critics have acknowledged. Osmond resembles not only the idle American expatriate connoisseurs in Italy—of whom there were certainly enough by 1881, as James learned on his journeys there—but also the English aesthetes he was meeting, gossiping about, seeing at the theater. "What is life but an art? Pater has said that so well, somewhere" says a fatuous young American named Louis Leverett in James's 1879 story, *A Bundle of Letters*; so does Gilbert Osmond, when he tells Isabel that one "ought to make one's life a work of art" (507). Osmond's taste for Japanese china and his collection of bric-a-brac place him directly in the context of the "aesthetic craze" of the late 1870's, since it was precisely these objects that the aesthetic movement prized and that its members (especially Rossetti and Whistler) collected. To nail down the association and understand its point, we need turn only to Lord Warburton's comment on what Isabel bitterly calls Osmond's "genius for upholstery"—"there is a great rage for that sort of thing now": Osmond, as collector and interior designer alike is identified with the rage or mania whose apotheosis James was witnessing in London (588). Moreover, as Richard Ellmann has reminded us, James slyly signals the connection between Osmond and the epigone of aestheticism, Oscar Wilde: the poem Osmond sends to Isabel as part of his perverse courtship, *Rome Revisited*, subtly alludes to Wilde's *Rome Unvisited*—published, along with the rest of Wilde's poems, in 1881, to a chorus of critical catcalls.

Noting the precision with which Osmond's historical provenance is established helps us appreciate what James called in *The Art of Fiction* the novel's "solidity of specification," but it does something more important as well. It helps us understand not only that Osmond is partially composed in response to the aesthetes whose careers James was witnessing as he wrote the novel, but also that he is depicted along the satirical lines James was reading in magazines or seeing at the theater. Indeed, far more than being a reflection of the "real" Oscar Wilde or any of the other "real" aesthetes James knew, the representation of Osmond mirrors and mimics the satirical attacks on these aesthetes launched largely, but not exclusively, by Du Maurier and the rest of the *Punch* coterie. Their satirical portraits of the aesthete focused formulaically, even obsessively, on a limited number of issues, and James follows out the lines of this satire quite faithfully. As represented by the *Punch* satirists, the aesthete is, above all else, indolent. He is languid, weary, enervated, bored; he prefers inaction to action, passivity to assertion, all things decaying to those robust and healthy. His very demeanor implies his enervation: the characteristic pose of a Du Maurier aesthete is a cultivated slouch, and even the sunflowers and pansies he holds in his hands droop. Moreover, the aesthete believes in his own enervation. Extending Pater's praise for "*being* as distinct from *doing*—a certain disposition of the mind" as the ground of value, the Du Maurier aesthete establishes his moral superiority on the basis of his perfected being and being alone, and urges others to imitate his self-satisfied indolence. In the cartoon *Maudle on the Choice of a Profession* (1881), for example, Du Maurier's aesthete Maudle (who had come to look, as of 1881, exactly like Oscar Wilde) slouches in the direction of Mrs. Brown, "a Philistine from the country," to drawl his appreciation of her would-be artist son. "*Why* should he be an artist?" asks Maudle. "Well, he must be *something!*" replies Mrs. Brown. "Why should he *be* anything?" responds Maudle. "Why not let him remain for ever content to *exist beautifully?*"[2]

Snobbery is the basis as well of the second ground of satire: the aesthete is a creature of inexplicable enthusiasms and eccentric tastes whose values the aesthete and the aesthete alone is capable of identifying while asserting them to be transcendentally valid. Chinoiserie, medieval Italian painting, peacock's feathers, and dadoes: all are objects of delight to the aesthete and of confusion to the other members of his world, since the qualities that make such objects "aesthetic" are impossible to define except in vague, and thus ultimately absurd, terms. As Bunthorne, in Gilbert's *Patience*, says:

> If you're anxious for to shine in the high aesthetic
>   line as a man of culture rare,
> You must get up all the germs of the transcendental
>   terms, and plant them everywhere.
> You must lie upon the daisies and discourse in novel phrases of your
>   complicated state of mind,
> The meaning doesn't matter if it's only idle chatter of a
>   transcendental kind.
>   And every one will say
>   As you walk your mystic way,
> "If this young man expresses himself in terms too deep for *me*,
> Why, what a very singularly deep young man this deep young
>   man must be!"[3]

The aesthete's exaltation of taste, in other words, represents an expression of his or her will to power; and, in the terms of the social struggle in which these characters are frequently engaged, will to social power—a means of intimidating their gullible audience with recondite enthusiasms and dilettantish predilections. Moreover, there is something unnatural or perverse in the aesthete's tastes. He or she is, literally, a commodity fetishist; libidinal energies are deflected from healthy and normal outlets onto art objects, which are thus worshipped in a perverse and unhealthy manner. The most famous example of this habit of thought is Du Maurier's famous cartoon, *The Six-Mark Teapot* (1880). There, an "aesthetic bridegroom" and an "intense bride"—the term "intense" served in these satires, as it did for Quilter, as a virtual synonym for "aesthetic"—gaze reverently at a blue china teapot: "It is quite consummate, is it not?" asks the leering male (it is difficult to tell whether he is leering at the teapot or

---

2. *Punch* 80 (Feb. 12, 1881): 62.
3. W. S. Gilbert, *Plays and Poems* (New York: Random House, 1923), pp. 199–200. Further citations to Gilbert's works in the text will refer to this edition.

the bride); "It is, indeed! Oh, Algernon, let us live up to it!" replies his bride, a look of rapt aesthetic devotion on her face.[4]

Finally, as far as the satirists are concerned, the aesthete is a phony, a fraud, a mountebank. Some ulterior motive was necessary to explain their bizarre affectations, their mysterious enthusiasms. Such a motive was not hard to find: self-promotion, self-advancement, and pecuniary self-aggrandizement, particularly the self-aggrandizing attempts of those who by birth or wealth or both are excluded from high society to make their way into its confines. Streyke, in *The Colonel*, worms his way into the good graces of the Forester family in order to marry off his cousin and make his own fortune; when he is unmasked, we learn that the nephew is really an apothecary's assistant, not a struggling young artist, and that "the gifted master, Lambert Streyke" himself is really an accountant turned confidence man. The applications of aestheticism's valorization of the pose to the fine art of social climbing were no less obvious to Du Maurier. Throughout this period, Du Maurier's cartoons consistently portrayed aesthetes as *parvenus* seeking to climb the social ladder. In 1880, for example, his aesthete Postlethwaite avers that "the Lily had carried me through my first season, the Primrose through my second . . . what Flower of Flowers is to carry me through my next?" In 1876, one Swellington Spiff expresses the hope that his china collection will help him meet a duke.[5] Some of the more gullible members of Du Maurier's high society may be fooled by these aesthetes, but the social act Du Maurier's cartoons inscribe is that of the public revelation of their hypocrisy and fraudulence. Indeed, in one of the final cartoons in the Du Maurier aesthete series, Maudle and Postlethwaite and their favorite hostess, the *parvenue* Mrs. Cimabue Brown, learn that their fame is due to *Punch* and *Punch* alone; the title of the cartoon, and the act it seeks to perform, is "Frustrated Social Ambition."

The representation of Osmond conforms to these outlines with striking accuracy. In the first description of Osmond, James not only emphasizes the artifice of his appearance—his "thin, delicate, sharply-cut face," the "beard, cut in the manner of the portraits of the sixteenth century"—but also his resemblance to one of Du Maurier's cartoon figures. The description of Osmond he offers here is strikingly similar to the thin, pale, and indolent "aesthetic bachelors" Du Maurier drew: "he had a light, lean, lazy-looking figure, and was apparently neither tall nor short" (425). Throughout this scene, it is precisely Osmond's aestheticist languor that is emphasized:

> "What epithet would properly describe me?" [Osmond asks Madame Merle].
> "You are indolent. For me that is your worst fault."
> "I am afraid it is really my best."
> "You don't care," said Madame Merle, gravely.
> "No; I don't think I care much. What sort of fault do you call that?" (435)

We can note here not only that Osmond's indolence places him in the aestheticist tradition, but that the rhetoric he uses to announce it does so as

---

4. *Punch* 79 (Oct. 30, 1880): 194.
5. These examples were suggested to me by Leonée Ormond, *George Du Maurier* (Routledge, 1969), p. 307.

well. The paradoxical reversal of terms of value—"I am afraid it is really my best"—is, of course, a recognizable characteristic of Oscar Wilde's epi-grammatic wit; and Osmond's paradoxical praise for his own capacities of indolence anticipates almost precisely Wilde's assertion that "to do nothing at all is the most difficult thing in the world, the most difficult and the most intellectual."[6]

The representation of Osmond shares other direct affinities with popu-lar satires on aestheticism. Like Maudle, Osmond proclaims himself to be a creature beyond the mere exigencies of vocational choice: "I could do nothing. I had no prospects, I was poor, and I was not a man of genius . . . I was simply the most fastidious young gentleman living" (463). Osmond's career, of course, *is* his fastidiousness; he is solely a creature of taste, "the incarnation of taste," as Ralph Touchett puts it—partially the tastes of the aesthetic era, although not exclusively so; moreover, further like Du Maurier or Gilbert, the novel demystifies his fine taste, viewing it as nothing more than a form of affected pretension (547). As in Du Mau-rier's satires, it is only the naive characters who see Osmond's taste as rich, rare, and extraordinary. Osmond may be, as Isabel believes early in their courtship, "the man who had the best taste in the world," but those with greater sophistication think otherwise (631). Lord Warburton, as we have already seen, identifies Osmond's taste as a product of the more ephem-eral sort of fashion; Ned Rosier is even more unsparing. "It's papa's taste; he has so much," Pansy tells him; "he had a good deal, Rosier thought; but some of it was bad" (574). As indeed it is: when Rosier walks his way through Osmond's collection, he notes for us, through the delicate modu-lations of the *style indiret libre*, the aesthetic gaucherie represented by the "big cold Empire clock" in Gilbert's living room, the diminished imagina-tion registered by his collection of miniatures (574). As the novel progresses, Osmond's taste becomes progressively, even incrementally, diminished. When the reader first encounters him, Osmond is sketching the Alps and expressing quiet contentment over his "discovering . . . a sketch by Coreg-gio on a panel daubed over by some inspired idiot"; by the end of the novel, having been endowed with the greatest possible acquisitive scope by Isa-bel's wealth, he realizes the requirements of his imagination by collecting miniatures and sketching a gold coin (463). Osmond is finally attacked by the novel on the same ground on which Oscar Wilde was attacked by his critics: he is nothing more than an "aesthetic sham," or, in Ralph's words, a "sterile dilettante" (547).

More than the critique of his taste links Osmond to the satirical por-traits of the aesthetes. He, like them, is finally portrayed by the novel as being nothing more than a social climber, a parvenu—even an American!—who seeks to use his aesthetic sensibilities, particularly as manifested in his choice of a wife, to mount the social ladder. Like Du Maurier's aes-thetes, his stance of fastidious disdain for the social milieu is finally revealed to be only a highly developed form of hypocrisy. Ralph Touchett puts the revelation of Gilbert's worldliness for us most eloquently when, late in the novel, he realizes that

---

6. Oscar Wilde, *The Artist as Critic: Critical Writings of Oscar Wilde*, ed. Richard Ellmann (New York: Random House, 1968), pp. 233, 381 [*Editor*].

under the guise of caring only for intrinsic values, Osmond lived exclusively for the world. Far from being its master, as he pretended to be, he was its very humble servant, and the degree of its attention was his only measure of success. He lived with his eye on it, from morning till night, and the world was so stupid it never suspected the trick. Everything he did was *pose*—*pose* so deeply calculated that if one were not on the lookout one mistook it for impulse. Ralph had never met a man who lived so much in the land of calculation. His tastes, his studies, his accomplishments, his collections, were all for a purpose. His life on his hill-top in Florence had been a *pose* of years. His solitude, his ennui, his love for his daughter, his good manners, his bad manners, were so many features of a mental image constantly present to him as a model of impertinence and mystification. His ambition was not to please the world, but to please himself by excit- ing the world's curiosity and then declining to satisfy it. It made him feel great to play the world a trick. (597–98)

Indeed, Ralph's critique repeats precisely the terms of denigration employed by the popular satirists of aestheticism. For them, too, the aesthete's bizarre "tastes, his studies, his accomplishments, his collections" serve only a "social purpose." Gilbert's Bunthorne, whose "medievalism's affectation / Born of a morbid love of admiration" (199), or the Du Maurier aesthetes who attempt to crash high society by means of their aesthetic refinement are all shown to possess the combination of indifference and obsessive con- sideration for the social sphere Osmond displays. "What is it to be an Aes- thete?" asked Frederic Harrison, who then proceeds to give a virtual paraphrase of Ralph's condemnation of Osmond. "Is it not to air one's zeal for Art, not out of genuine love of beauty, but out of fashion and love of display, in order to be like our neighbours or to be unlike our neighbours, in the wantonness of a noisy life and a full pocket?"[7] Gilbert and Du Maurier and Harrison would all agree that the most galling feature of the aesthete was the curious admixture of "impertinence and mystification" Ralph defines as the essence of Osmondism. All join Ralph and, by extension, James, in the satirical rejection of the aesthete, in his expulsion from the social and moral community he seeks to join.

I don't mean to stress the satirized side of Osmond's character at the expense of its other components, particularly that aspect critics have tended to focus on: his massive egotism, his manipulative coldness— those qualities in Osmond that cause Isabel to think of him as possessing "the evil eye," the "faculty for making everything wither that he touched," the qualities that make Osmond resemble the villain of a Gothic romance (629, 628). But I also think that it is an aspect of James's representational strategy we should not ignore. That the novel also invites us to view Osmond satirically has consequences not otherwise graspable if we view him in terms of the Gothic (or even Hawthornean) romance paradigm. For it brings Osmond into a recognizably social world. Instead of asking us to view Osmond and Osmondism as representing a nearly supernatural form of evil (James's version of "motiveless malignity"), or as a psychological

---

7. Harrison, "The Aesthete," reprinted in *The Choice of Books and Other Literary Pieces* (London: Macmillan, 1896), p. 291. Harrison's representative aesthete—whom he dubs Young Osric, an obvious thrust at Wilde—is also recognizably Osmondian.

allegory of the causes and consequences of such evil, it invites us to understand the social dimensions of his behavior: to understand its role in the
power games of the human community, to understand the ubiquity, even
the banality of such games. Instead of asking us to view his character in
isolation, James's satire demands that we view the links between Osmond's
form of behavior and that of the other characters in the novel. The notorious ambivalence of satire, its tendency to break down precisely the moral
boundaries it has sought to establish, affects this novel as well. As we are
asked to view Osmond as a vehicle of malevolence, we are also led to notice
the form of behavior he so spectacularly exemplifies in all the characters
who surround him—even, or especially, those characters at whose expense
he is satirized. In this, James uses satire for ends precisely the opposite of
those for which we saw it deployed in *Roderick Hudson*. Instead of seeking
to discriminate between an aesthete and those with whom he is surrounded, James here uses a satirized aestheticism to complicate these relations: in this novel aestheticism is understood as being an endemic—indeed
epidemic—contagion, ultimately infecting even the author himself.

Ralph, Isabel, James: The Ubiquity of Aestheticism

We see this contagion most clearly in the novel's portrayal of Ralph
Touchett. As virtually all critics of the novel have noted, there are numerous troubling similarities between Isabel's benefactor and her bane, and
their common connoisseurship is at the center of them. R. P. Blackmur
puts the matter with his customary suavity when he writes that "everyone
tampers with Isabel, and it is hard to say whether her cousin Ralph
Touchett, who had arranged the bequest, or the Prince, Gilbert Osmond,
who marries her because of it, tampers the more deeply."[8] The link between
the two inheres in more than just their common "tampering," however: it
extends to the very perceptual systems that underlie such acts. Gilbert
views Isabel, as he views everyone in his narrow world, as an objet d'art,
a potential "figure in his collection of choice objects" (501). Osmond's particular form of what we might call the aestheticizing vision is marked
both by the distance of the contemplative observer, coolly evaluating the
people he encounters with an assumed—if fraudulent—disinterestedness,
and by the ruthlessness with which he seeks to make them into testimonies to his taste. Such a vision carries with it an implicit notion of both
self and other. In Gilbert's form of vision, the self is understood to be a
smug, observing entity, a private and self-satisfied "point of view," while
all others are treated as objects of this contemplative vision, to be either
appreciated or rejected but always transformed into signs of the supreme
taste of the observer. Gilbert's aestheticizing vision, in other words, might
also be said to be a reifying vision. Despite the nobility of his rhetoric,
Osmond perceives all the others he encounters as detached, deadened
objects of his purely passive perception, and seeks to make those who
refuse to be so into such beautiful objects. And when Ralph first meets
Isabel, he first resists, and then succumbs to a similar impulse:

8. Blackmur, "*The Portrait of a Lady*," in *Studies in Henry James* (New York: New Directions,
   1983), p. 193.

If his cousin were to be nothing more than an entertainment to him, Ralph was conscious that she was an entertainment of a high order. "A character like that," he said to himself, "is the finest thing in nature. It is finer than the finest work of art—than a Greek bas-relief, than a great Titian, than a Gothic cathedral. It is very pleasant to be so well treated where one least looked for it. I had never been more blue, more bored, than for a week before she came; I had never expected less that something agreeable would happen. Suddenly, I receive a Titian, by the post, to hang on my wall—a Greek bas-relief to stick over my chimney piece. The key of a beautiful edifice is thrust into my hand, and I am told to walk in and admire." (254)

At first, Ralph sees Isabel as a character of pure "nature" who possesses a vital energy of her own, whose "play" transcends that of any work of art. Isabel transcends all the mental structures Ralph erects to define her, all the images he conjures up to describe her. But he is not able to sustain this vision of Isabel for long. Soon, he subtly but unmistakably metamorphoses her into that which he had previously claimed she transcended—a work of art. By so doing, he begins inadvertently to show Osmondian characteristics. Having defined the mystery that is Isabel as a painting or bas-relief, he attempts imaginatively to collect her. For after he has mentally transformed Isabel into a particularly beautiful but nevertheless static portrait of a lady, the next logical step is to hang her on the wall of his mental portrait gallery. To translate from the novel's metaphorical language back into the grammar of its plot: Ralph endows Isabel with a fortune (much as one would endow an art museum) in order to continue to contemplate her—to "gratif[y] my imagination" (382).

I mention these well-known passages not to inculpate Ralph, but rather to suggest how unwittingly he falls into Gilbert's aestheticizing vision. This judgment must be calibrated rather delicately, for many critics fall into the traps of wholly idealizing Ralph (as we are clearly meant to do, up to a certain point) or condemning him (as we are also meant to do, but again only up to a certain point). Neither approval nor condemnation, however, does justice to the tragic machine James creates out of the inevitability and the insidiousness of the process of aestheticization. Such acts are inevitable for Ralph because they are a cognitive necessity. It is impossible for even so subtle a consciousness as Ralph's to tolerate a phenomenon like Isabel, which remains so resolutely resistant to definition. Despite his own desire to do otherwise, Ralph is forced by the very structure of his perception to reify and then aestheticize Isabel, to treat her with the detached but appreciative vision of the discerning connoisseur. The novel clearly demonstrates the negative consequences of such an aestheticizing vision—even so generous a vision as one that compares Isabel to a Titian. Ralph thinks he can respond to Isabel as he would to a work of art, with energetic detachment and consummate disinterestedness. But he is forced to discover that this is impossible, for she is neither a painting nor a bas-relief but only an extremely naive human being—prey, like all humans, to making ill-considered decisions. Isabel challenges his disinterestedness by doing what paintings cannot: by growing and changing along the idiosyncratic lines of her own character. And—in one of the bitterest ironies of this endlessly ironic book—she will exercise this freedom by marrying the one man who attempts what Ralph only imagines: to turn her into a beautiful but static and immobile work of art.

For Isabel suffers precisely the same kind of aestheticist contagion as Ralph. She, too, shares a good many of the more problematic qualities of Osmond's aestheticism, albeit in a more benign shape, and it is precisely these qualities that cause her to fall under his control. Isabel's aestheticism is signaled by James through the application of much of the characteristic language of the British aesthetic movement to his descriptions of Isabel, particularly those early in the novel. Indeed, James runs through most of the famous, if not notorious, catchphrases of the Conclusion to *The Renaissance* in depicting her. We learn that Isabel possesses a "delicate . . . flame-like spirit"; that she responds to Lord Warburton with a "quickened consciousness"; that she enjoys a number of aesthetic "pulsations" in St. Peter's; and, late in the novel, that she muses over the "infinite vista of a multiplied life" with which she first encountered Osmond (242, 257, 485, 629). To a certain extent, James employs this language to describe the eagerness with which the young Isabel partakes of the Paterian endeavor of "drain[ing] the cup of experience," a propensity Osmond appeals to in his protracted seduction: "Go everywhere," he said at last, in a low, kind voice, "do everything; get everything out of life" (345, 508). But as in the case of Ralph, Isabel's aestheticism is more deeply ingrained, and more ultimately problematic, than it appears at first glance. Isabel possesses an aestheticizing vision of her own and, as with Ralph, this vision is understood as something of a cognitive necessity. For when Isabel first meets Osmond, her reaction to him, as was Ralph's to her, is one of utter confusion:

> His pictures, his carvings and tapestries were interesting; but after a while Isabel became conscious that the owner was more interesting still. He resembled no one she had ever seen; most of the people she knew might be divided into groups of half-a-dozen specimens. There were one or two exceptions to this; she could think, for instance, of no group that would contain her Aunt Lydia. There were other people who were, relatively speaking, original—original, as one might say, by courtesy—such as Mr. Goodwood, as her cousin Ralph, as Henrietta Stackpole, as Lord Warburton, as Madame Merle. But in essentials, when one came to look at them, these individuals belonged to types which were already present to her mind. Her mind contained no class which offered a natural place to Mr. Osmond—he was a specimen apart. (458–59)

As in the case of Ralph, Isabel's cognitive difficulties are caused by Osmond's failure to conform to any of her preexisting mental categories. But Isabel's mistakes are even more extensive. What Isabel fails to realize is that Gilbert's ambiguousness is a result of his limitations, not a sign of the subtlety or fineness of his character. She cannot see that her failure to place Osmond is utterly appropriate: that, having no positive qualities of his own, he can only be defined in terms of negation. This is how virtually every character in the book defines Gilbert. Madame Merle introduces him to Isabel in the language of negation: "No career, no name, no position, no fortune, no past, no future, no anything" (393). After meeting Osmond for the first time in Rome, Ralph identifies him to Warburton by

name. "What is he besides?" Warburton asks. "Nothing at all," Ralph
replies (495). Gilbert himself proposes to Isabel with a declaration that,
like all of Gilbert's statements, is at once literally true and deeply false: "I
have neither fortune, nor fame, nor extrinsic advantages of any kind. So I
offer nothing" (509–10).

Isabel commits the error of mistaking Gilbert's passivity for mystery, his
fastidiousness for subtlety, his indifference for reserve. And she responds
to the mystery of his poverty in the same way as Ralph responded to that
of her plentitude: by mentally transforming him into a work of art that
could meet the requirements of her imagination. This process, again like
the one Ralph undertakes with her, reaches a climax in a moment of
mental *ekphrasis*, a moment at which she imagines Osmond as a finely
drawn "picture":

> She had carried away an image from her visit to his hill-top which
> her subsequent knowledge of him did nothing to efface and which
> happened to take her fancy particularly—the image of a quiet, clever,
> sensitive, distinguished man, strolling on a moss-grown terrace above
> the sweet Val d'Arno, and holding by the hand a little girl whose sym-
> pathetic docility gave a new aspect to childhood. The picture was
> not brilliant, but she liked its lowness of tone, and the atmosphere of
> summer twilight that pervaded it. (476)

Indeed, there is even a greater portion of aestheticism in Isabel's
response to her mental picture than in Ralph's to his. She explicitly adopts
the attitude he unconsciously falls into, that of the connoisseur, for she
stands back from her image of Osmond to nod her approval of its "lowness of tone" and the "atmosphere of summer twilight that pervaded it."
Her subsequent actions extend this incipient Osmondism. Having so
appreciated her own mental image of this "specimen apart," Isabel proceeds to try to add it to her own collection. Just as the greatest triumph of
Gilbert's career as a collector was "discovering . . . a sketch by Coreggio
on a panel daubed over by some inspired idiot," so Isabel fancies that she
alone is capable of identifying the true value of the artwork that is Osmond
(463). The result, needless to say, is disastrous. Her unwittingly Osmondian tendency to see Osmond as he sees himself—as a rare and fine work
of art—leads to her equally unwitting Osmondian attempt to collect
Osmond. By seeking to marry "the man who had the best taste in the
world" for what she sees as "an indefinable beauty about him—in his situation, in his mind, in his face," Isabel finds herself transformed into a
mere extension of that taste, an object for cultivated appreciation possessing "nothing of her own but her pretty appearance" (631, 632). Seeking to
collect a collector, she finds herself collected.

My purpose in stressing these parallels is not merely to inculpate Isabel, but rather to suggest the universality of aestheticism in the novel. Aestheticism of one sort or another is a donnée of *The Portrait of a Lady*, a
piece of perceptual equipment James issues each of his characters. In
doing so, he suggests how a "sterile dilettante" like Osmond can exert so
powerful a force. The plot of the novel is so constructed that Osmond's
aestheticism causes Isabel's and Ralph's to rebound against them. We have
seen this effect in the way that Osmond's designs on Isabel force Ralph to
face the consequences of his own disingenuously disinterested vision of

her; Osmond confronts Ralph with a grotesque parody of his own attempt to achieve a detached, aestheticized vision of Isabel and blatantly enacts the appropriating reification delicately implicit in Ralph's perception. We may see it even more clearly in Isabel's marriage, in which Osmond's aestheticism corresponds to her naive aestheticist propensities in just enough ways to trap her irrevocably.

Through the first two-thirds of the book, then, we witness a movement that seeks to include all characters—even (or especially) the most sensitive and richly aware characters—in a form of belief and behavior that is satirized, but not expunged, by Osmond. This movement reaches a climax at the beginning of chapter 37, when we see through the eyes of yet another aesthete, Ned Rosier, Isabel "framed in the gilded doorway . . . the picture of a gracious lady" (570). Ned sees Isabel as Ralph had unconsciously seen her and as Osmond consciously wishes to see her: a static, reified art object. But at this moment, the problematic powers of aestheticism seem to have extended even further. For by reminding us that Isabel has been converted, or has converted herself, into a person whose "function" is to "represent" her husband, James is also reminding us of the affinities between aestheticism and his own representational endeavor (597). For insofar as the novel claims to be a "portrait of a lady"—a detached, objective account of Isabel's experience—it aligns itself with the possibilities it has thoroughly criticized: with the purely disinterested aestheticizing vision of Ralph, and the ironic detachment and masked will to power of Osmond. Indeed, it would seem that Gilbert, not Ralph, would most successfully figure James's own authorial aestheticism, since Ralph's irony is qualified by deep imaginative sympathy and since his stance of disinterested observation is abandoned as early as chapter 22, and since Gilbert, not Ralph, is most intensely interested in transforming Isabel into a representation of himself.

The exploration of the problematic dimension of aestheticism reaches its climax, then, with Rosier's identification of Isabel as a portrait of a lady. At this moment, it appears that all the novel's characters and even its author are somehow implicated in one form or another of Gilbert's malevolent aestheticism, just as Roderick and Rowland were in *Roderick Hudson* and just as all the characters of *The Author of Beltraffio* will be. But this same moment also initiates a countermovement. If in the first two-thirds of the novel James is interested in linking divergent characters to Osmond, in its final part, he attempts to differentiate between them and Gilbert. If the novel suggests that even the most noble, if naive, examples of the aestheticizing vision are fatally flawed, then James's alternatives are clear: either he needs to abandon or alter his fictional project entirely, or he needs to find a way to repurify the aesthetic itself, to demonstrate that perceptual and experiential responses like intense observation and the aestheticizing vision might prove redeemable, if not redemptive. And, needless to say, it is this latter path that he chooses.

Aestheticism and the Gospel of Freedom

We may observe the first step in this process by noting the increasing interest the novel gives to discriminating between Osmond and the other characters. The most spectacular instance of this discrimination is its portrayal of the relation between Osmond and Madame Merle. During the first two-thirds of the novel, we have been asked to note their commonality: we have witnessed their combined interest in acquiring a fortune for Gilbert and a mother for Pansy by marrying Osmond to Isabel. More important, we have encountered the view of the world that can make such plots possible. Madame Merle, like Osmond, perceives herself and all those around her as things to be arranged or manipulated, and is thus able to adjust her own appearances the better to shape the actions of others in order to achieve her ends. But in the last third of the novel we discover that the two can—indeed, must—be distinguished from each other. Gilbert is finally the only character who can fully exemplify the reified self that Madame Merle so eloquently defines. This discovery opens the way to more of the novel's ironies, for, just as Gilbert uses the implicit aestheticism of Isabel Archer against her, so he employs Madame Merle's reified vision of the self to reify Madame Merle herself.

The kinds of identifications and discriminations we are asked to make between these two characters are among the subtlest and most complicated in the novel. To cite but one example, Gilbert and Madame Merle are initially united, but ultimately distinguished, by their concern for appearances. We have seen the deep duplicity of this concern throughout the novel, for we have witnessed the ways they present Mrs. Touchett, Isabel, and society at large with artfully arranged poses: Madame Merle as disinterested friend and "the cleverest woman in the world"; Osmond as devoted father and aloof aesthete who cares nothing for the opinion of the world (759). But as soon as we understand the "horror" (as Madame Merle calls it) these facades are constructed to conceal, we are asked to distinguish between their desires (389). Gilbert's concern for propriety and love of convention is shown to be one small part of his obsessive concern for "the world" and that world's opinion of him. Madame Merle's concern, while superficially similar, is ultimately antithetical to his. Her "worship of appearances" is motivated not by her love of convention or her concern for propriety but rather by her fear of the discovery of her adulterous secret. Further, this divergence between Madame Merle and her former lover provides the grounds for the final break in their relation. For, as the Countess Gemini informs Isabel, Madame Merle's "worship of appearances" became "so intense that even Osmond himself got tired of it" (751). In other words, the very ground on which stands the relation she seeks so desperately to conceal is ultimately destroyed by the tenacity with which she is compelled to conceal it.

Just as we are asked to discriminate between the attitudes of Osmond and Madame Merle toward "the world," we are also asked to differentiate between their values and perceptions throughout the rest of the novel. We are initially inclined to grant Madame Merle a stature that is denied Osmond. For one thing, Madame Merle is ultimately distinguished from the reifying aestheticism with which she has been associated for much of the novel, and Osmond alone is left to bear its taint. This particular discrimination is suggested in a number of ways throughout the last third of *Portrait*, but one of the more important is made by Isabel herself. Late in the novel, just after her ride on the Campagna, Isabel broods over Madame Merle's role in arranging her marriage, and she remembers "the wonder" of her strong "desire" for the "event." "There were people who had the match-making passion, like the votaries of art for art," Isabel reflects, "but Madame Merle, great artist as she was, was scarcely one of these" (725). This passage, of course, reflects Isabel's increasingly bitter view of Madame Merle; after all, she has just applied "the great historical epithet of *wicked*" to her "false" friend (725). And the identification of Madame Merle as a "great artist" associates art with the sinister manipulation of others. But Isabel's observation reminds us that Madame Merle does indeed seem to be granted some of the less equivocal powers of the artist, and that her qualities are therefore to be distinguished from Osmond's sterile aestheticism. Madame Merle possesses in abundance the positive qualities James habitually associated with the artist—a rich sensibility, a subtlety, a complex and ultimately tragic capacity for deep emotion—along with the admittedly less positive side of the Jamesian artist—the ability to manipulate poses and create surfaces to achieve equivocal ends. As a result of this identification, Madame Merle's stature seems to increase. We are led to view her, along with Isabel, as someone who has been trapped and betrayed by circumstance and convention, and who has therefore been forced to employ even (especially) her most positive qualities for mere manipulation—and failed manipulation at that.

Sympathetic as the novel asks us to be toward Madame Merle, however, we also acknowledge that in the final divergence between her and Osmond it traps her in its own relentlessly ironic logic. She may transcend her own definition of the self as a mere collection of reified qualities, but Gilbert does not, and his amoral aestheticism finally punishes her in a chillingly appropriate manner. If Madame Merle, along with Gilbert, has turned Isabel into a deadened object of her will—in Isabel's own words, into "a dull, un-reverenced tool"—so Madame Merle finally discovers, she too has been used by Osmond as a mere tool, to be discarded when she is no longer useful to him (759). This dimension of their relation becomes clear in their final scene together, in which a cracked cup becomes horrifically emblematic of their relations. Madame Merle's "precious object" is established as a symbol of their relation when Gilbert sunders that relation at the same moment as he discovers "a small crack" in the cup (730). By the end of the scene, when Madame Merle turns again to her own object, it takes on an even more resonant meaning: "After he had left her, Madame Merle went and lifted from the mantel-shelf the attenuated coffee-cup in which he had mentioned the existence of a crack; but she looked at it rather abstractedly. 'Have I been so vile all for nothing?' she murmured to herself" (731).

The scene is delicate and subtle, and, as many critics have noted, it adumbrates the symbolistic later James, the James of *The Golden Bowl*. But it is important to observe that the scene is also savagely satiric, and that its satire here too is again cognate with that of popular satires on aestheticism. The notion of representing human relations in terms of crockery is one which, as we have seen, exercised the moral indignation of the *Punch* satirists from the time of Du Maurier's famous 1880 cartoon on the subject of living up to one's teapot. Here, too, the aesthete's propensity to reify his relations in trivializing terms is imaged by these satiric means. But the calculated whimsy of this early cartoon is replaced in James's text by an unsparing irony: the aesthete not only demonstrates his reifying vision, but also the aesthetic flaws of the object of his contemplation. In doing so, the development of James's satire and that of Du Maurier parallel each other with uncanny accuracy. On May 14, 1881, there appeared in *Punch* a mordant sketch, probably by Du Maurier, entitled *Philistia Defiant*, "in which aestheticism, assisted by a Teapot, is the cause of a division between friends."[9] In the sketch, a Mrs. Vamp invites a friend, Betsinda Grig, to her "High-Art boudoir in South Kensington," in order to appreciate, admire, adore, and ultimately "live up to" a newly acquired antique teapot, with a small crack in it. After a long speech in praise of the teapot, Betsinda replies, "with drawlingly deliberate acerbity, 'It's dreadfully cracked, and horribly ugly; if *that's* what you mean by Unutterably Utter and all the rest of it. And, upon my word, Sara, I think you must be living up—or down—to it, for you seem to get more decidedly cracked and more utterly ugly every day.'"

My point in mentioning this sketch is not to point to a "source" for James's scene, but rather to suggest how in this scene he finds his satirical energies developing along lines parallel to those of Du Maurier. Indeed, James outdoes the increasing acidulousness of Du Maurier's satire. In James's hands, a "deliberate acerbity" works to punish not only the reifying aesthete, but his reified victim as well. It is precisely Madame Merle's own reified vision of the self as a collection of things that is turned against her, for she has become to Gilbert nothing more than the appurtenance she believes the self to be. She is of no more consequence to him than an exquisite cup, to be discarded if and when flaws are discovered in it. And, to complete the irony, we realize in her moment of self-discovery, at her own "murmured" threnody to her love for Gilbert and her lament for what she has done in the name of that love, that Osmond rejects her for precisely the passionate emotion and keen intelligence she displays in her moment of horrified recognition. In short, all the qualities that make her more than a mere object are precisely those that cause Osmond to discard her as one.

The most important discrimination established in the last third of the novel, however, is that between Isabel and Osmond. For as Isabel grasps the flaws of her aestheticizing vision and begins to move beyond this form of apprehension, she progresses into a heightened and purified form of aestheticism—a form of aestheticism superficially similar to, but ultimately distinguishable from, the reifying aestheticism of an Osmond. It's true that Osmondian language tends to be associated with the representation of her own thought processes—as, for example, when she too rejects Madame Merle. The effect of Madame Merle's unexpectedly appearing at Pansy's convent is compared by Isabel to a "sort of reduplication"; this hint of an aestheticizing temper is carried further when Isabel sees Madame Merle's uncertainty "as distinctly as if it had been a picture on the wall" (756–57, 759). Indeed, Isabel might be said to approach Osmondism here—however justifiably—since her action in this scene, like Osmond's throughout the novel, is to withdraw, to retreat into being "silent still—leav[ing] Madame Merle in this unprecedented situation" (759). But Isabel's aestheticizing imagination leads her in a wholly different direction than does Osmond's. In this scene, her refusal directly to confront Madame Merle still grants her an essential otherness, still allows her her

9. *Punch* 80 (May 14, 1881): 221.

own scope of action—grants Madame Merle the opportunity to judge herself, to do "a kind of proud penance" (767).

What is true of Isabel's behavior in this scene is true of her perceptual apparatus as well. As her aestheticizing vision moves beyond the reifying aestheticism so thoroughly implicated in Osmondism, it progresses to a higher form of aestheticism—if "aesthetic" is understood as informed by the original sense of *aesthesis*, as a heightening or perfection of the act of perception. The most extended exercise in such heightened vision is provided in the most famous moment in the novel—the moment James claimed to have been most proud of—Isabel's silent reverie in chapter 42. That chapter is of the utmost importance for our endeavor, for it provides an example of a form of perception structurally different from that we have seen associated with Gilbert throughout the novel and in which we can implicate every other character. Isabel's visions in this scene are important because they are so intense and because they are so personal. Like Osmond's aestheticizing vision, they are fully grounded in the self, but they are ultimately antithetical to Osmond's. Her flickering visions in chapter 42 do not partake of Osmond's narcissistic attempt to force the objects in the world to serve as objects for his detached contemplation. Rather, unlike Osmond, Isabel achieves a moment of her own vision experienced in, of, and for itself; a moment of vision that is fully detached from the world of objects but that helps her to understand the nature of that world. And, I would suggest, the homology between Isabel's vision and that of Paterian *aesthesis* may be seen more clearly when we juxtapose chapter 42 with the Conclusion to *The Renaissance*. Both Pater and James privilege a special moment at which, under conditions of high intensity, "a quickened, multiplied consciousness" comes into powerful visionary being. It is quite true that there are significant dissimilarities between the circumstances under which such an intense vision may come into being and the uses to which it can be put. For James, the "quickened consciousness" is (as it is always for James) attached to high emotional drama, while for Pater such a consciousness is activated through many forms of intense experience—"great passions" including, among others, both the "ecstasy and sorrow of love" and (first among equals) "the poetic passion, the desire of beauty, the love of art for art's sake".[1] But my point here is that for both James and Pater the moment at which consciousness exercises itself in heightened vision is valuable in and of itself—is the ultimate end, the perfect end. Pater's aesthete and James's heroine both achieve a perfect moment of intense vision which, for their authors, is the highest—perhaps the only—consummation possible in a world shadowed over by death and human failure.

This valorization of *aesthesis*, of what James calls in the Preface to the novel "the mere still lucidity" of Isabel's mental vision, suggests one way that the novel recuperates a form of aestheticism.[2] But it is precisely by means of this recuperation that critics have taken James to task for being an aesthete in the negative sense of the word. Here, the achievement of a form of transcendence by means of consciousness and consciousness alone

---

1. Walter Pater, *The Works of Walter Pater*, 8 vols. (London: Macmillan, 1900–01) 1: 238, 239 [*Editor*].
2. See p. 13 in this Norton Critical Edition [*Editor*].

would seem, at the very best, to associate James with a naive form of reification, and at the very worst to identify him as an arrogant connoisseur
of consciousness. For this moment seems to define the transcendent self
as fundamentally contemplative, passive, inert, to remove that self from
any real contact with others, from any possibility of action, indeed, from
history itself; it would thus seem to imprison Isabel in the prison house
of consciousness as thoroughly as Osmond imprisons her in the Palazzo
Roccanera. Isabel, Michael Gilmore writes, "chooses a freedom that is
mental rather than experiential, a freedom uncontaminated by sensuous
engagement with the world." James, he adds ominously, "makes a similar choice for his art."[3]

James, however, anticipates—and sidesteps—this critique. For there is
another moment in the novel at which the aestheticizing vision is deployed,
and to ends that are different from either those we see with Osmond or
those we see in chapter 42. I am referring to the scene, a few chapters
later, of Isabel's lonely ride on the Campagna. For we encounter in this
passage yet another variant of the mode of perception Isabel shares with
Osmond. As a tourist, as an observing traveler, Isabel would seem to fall
into the detached, contemplative mode of Osmond; moreover she seems
to perform the Osmondian task of aestheticizing the natural world she
encounters, of responding to it as to a work of art:

> The carriage, passing out of the walls of Rome, rolled through nar-
> row lanes, where the wild honeysuckle had begun to tangle itself in
> the hedges, or waited for her in quiet places where the fields lay near,
> while she strolled further and further over the flower-freckled turf,
> or sat on a stone that had once had a use, and gazed through the veil
> of her personal sadness at the splendid sadness of the scene—at the
> dense, warm light, the far gradations and soft confusions of colour,
> the motionless shepherds in lonely attitudes, the hills where the cloud-
> shadows had the lightness of a blush. (724)

While this exercise of the aestheticizing vision may seem superficially
similar to Gilbert's, it is ultimately antithetical to his vision and value system alike. Isabel may sit in Osmond's position of the detached aesthetic
observer, viewing the Campagna spread out before her like a painted
landscape—all motion arrested, its figures fixed in "lonely attitudes," its
colors and gradations displayed in the rich muted colors of an artist's
palette—but she does not seek to detach herself from that scene. For the
"profound sympathy" between Isabel's perception and the objects she
encounters is repeatedly suggested in this passage, often by verbal repetition or by transfer of qualities from the Campagna to Isabel's life; "the
sadness of landscape" reflecting her "sadness of mood," the "lonely attitudes" of the shepherds reflecting her own sense of loneliness and betrayal.
As she "rest[s] her weariness upon things that had crumbled for centuries,"
as she "drop[s] her secret sadness into the silence of lonely places," Isabel
comes to recognize the "haunting sense of the continuity of the human
lot" (723–24). Having learned from Rome, a "place where people had suffered," of the commonality of her own suffering, she rejoins the human

---

3. Gilmore, "The Commodity World of *The Portrait of a Lady*," *New England Quarterly* 59 (1986):
    p. 73 [*Editor*].

community—not the corrupt community of Roman society that Gilbert and Madame Merle inhabit, but a more fully human community of shared suffering (724). Rather than possessing a reifying vision of landscape as irrevocably other, as alien and mute objects unconnected to human emotions and events and coldly to be appreciated as such, Isabel achieves at this moment a humanizing vision in which her individual "sadness" and the sadness of the scene connect to form an image of commonality and community, not one of alienation and superiority. If in chapter 42 Isabel moves beyond her superficial Paterian aestheticism into the more valuable mode of Paterian *aesthesis*, so here she moves beyond a superficial form of aestheticizing vision into a richer, more meaningful one: one that emphasizes her own embeddedness in historical process, her own participation in the human community—in short, the very "sensuous engagement with the world" whose absence Gilmore decries.

It is this version of the aestheticist vision that provides James with his most deeply treasured, and most arduously won, triumph. For this moment of detached yet meaningful perception provides a way out of the artistic impasse James has created for himself. Isabel's vision provides a more positive model for the stance of the detached author than does Osmond's, one that can lead to a sense of communion, not solipsism; to sympathy, not superiority. James signals this, I think, by the very abstemiousness with which he treats Isabel's dilemma at the end of the novel. If James is like Osmond in enmeshing Isabel in a plot whose goal is to aestheticize her, to transform her into a static, frozen portrait of a lady (the literary equivalent of the murderous aestheticization performed by the Duke in Browning's *My Last Duchess*), he can demonstrate himself to be a non-Osmondian author only by opening up the plot: by refusing the consolation of closure, whether comic, ironic, or tragic. It is in response to this problematic, I am suggesting, that James ends his novel with an interpretive mystery— and one of the most famous cruxes in American literature: the question of Isabel's mysteriously motivated return to Osmond. Certainly, the novel supplies by implication many reasons for this return: her loyalty to Pansy, her affirmation of convention and of social forms, her affirmation of the value of renunciation. But the novel carefully refuses to choose between these various explanations. Further, it ends without giving any further indication of the success or failure of Isabel's course of action, thereby precluding any final judgment of the wisdom or folly of her choice.

It is this narrative silence that provides the final repudiation of the reifying aestheticism associated with Osmond and of the narrative problematics it initiates. James's narrative voice here may be detached, but it is hardly unsympathetic. Indeed, its failure to pass any final judgment on Isabel may be taken as an acknowledgment of James's authorial sympathy rather than as an indication of his ironic distance. For by this silence, James reminds the reader of the values that Osmond's reifying aestheticism ignores: a respect for the fundamentally mysterious otherness of human beings. The mystery with which the novel concludes indicates James's authorial acknowledgement of the otherness of others, for this gesture acknowledges Isabel's ability to transcend any one vision that tries to fix or define her—even the author's own ostensibly omniscient vision. By granting Isabel such resonant ambiguity, in other words, James endows Isabel with the powers Rossetti endows Jenny or—more relevantly—those

Isabel grants Madame Merle. For the effect of this conclusion is to enable Isabel to step beyond the narrative frame within which she is enclosed, to move out of the "Portrait of a Lady"; it is—in a phrase James added to Isabel's final vision of Madame Merle in the New York edition—"like suddenly, and rather awfully, seeing a painted picture move."[4]

MILLICENT BELL

Isabel Archer and the Affronting of Plot[†]

In James's succession of heroines Isabel Archer sums up and goes beyond Daisy Miller and Catherine Sloper[1] as the one who most profoundly explores the policy of resistance to social and narrational expectations— the conventions of character which the culture would impose upon her, the role which life, as well as literature, seems to insist must be the outcome of her selfhood. James spoke of her in his 1908 preface as "affronting her destiny"[7], and his peculiar choice of word has not been sufficiently remarked upon; he did not mean simply that she *con*fronted or faced up to her destiny but that she hostilely defied it, slapped it in the face. Yet she is a more interesting figure than Daisy or Catherine, whose silent, immobile tenacity of pure being is all they have. As they are victimized by—yet resist—the story-making of others, so is and does she; but she is, in addition, the victim of her own romantic expectation of some unforeseeable state when all that she feels herself to be might find adequate outcome. Fortified against a commonplace, foreseeable future, she still does not succeed in finding the enactment, the history that would bring this finer state about. This failure makes her more tragic than the earlier heroines, who suffer only at the hands—or minds—of others.

It is possible to think of her as a character in search of its plot. We can thus identify her in a primary way with the writer, who conceived her, he recalled, as a "detached character." His novel had not originated in a suggestion of events for which he imagined the actors.

> I see that it must have consisted not at all in any conceit of a "plot," nefarious name, in any flash, upon the fancy, of a set of relations, or in any one of those situations that, by a logic of their own, immediately fall, for the fabulist, into movement, into a march or a rush, a patter of quick steps; but altogether in the sense of a single character, the character and aspect of a particular engaging young woman, to which the usual elements of a "subject," certainly of a setting, were to be superadded. [4]

That plot should be "nefarious" is as peculiar, perhaps, as the idea that a character should "affront" its destiny. As he recalls the way his novel grew from its "germ" of character, how he sought out its plot, as the imagined person herself would do, James seems to think of plot as threatening as

---

4. See p. 375 in this Norton Critical Edition [*Editor*].
† From *Meaning in Henry James* (Cambridge: Harvard University Press, 1991), pp. 80–82, 83–86, 94–106, 108–17. Copyright © 1991 by the President and Fellows of Harvard College. Reprinted by permission. Page numbers in square brackets refer to this Norton Critical Edition.
1. The protagonist of the 1881 *Washington Square; Daisy Miller*: the heroine of James's most famous eponymous tale (1878) [*Editor*].

well as promising fulfillment of that first conception. Turgenev had told James that his own stories always originated in

> the vision of some person or persons, who hovered before him, soliciting him, as the active or passive figure, interesting him and appealing to him just as they were and by what they were. He saw them, in that fashion, as *disponibles*, saw them subject to the chances, the complications of existence, and saw them vividly, but then had to find for them the right relations, those that would most bring them out; to imagine, to invent and select and piece together the situations most useful and favourable to the sense of the creatures themselves, the complications they would be most likely to produce and to feel. [4–5]

The result of such an effort, Turgenev had admitted, was still that he was "often accused of not having 'story' enough." Yet he protested, James remembered, by saying,

> I seem to myself to have as much as I need—to show my people, to exhibit their relations with each other; for that is all my measure. If I watch them long enough I see them come together, I see them *placed*, I see them engaged in this or that act and in this or that difficulty. How they look and move and speak and behave, always in the setting I have found for them, is my account of them—of which I dare say, alas, *que cela manque souvent d'architecture*. [5]

James claims to take "higher warrant" from Turgenev for his own habit of being, as he said, "so much more antecedently conscious of my figures than of their setting . . . I might envy, though I couldn't emulate, the imaginative writer so constituted as to see his fable first and to make out its agents afterwards" [5]. One might suspect some disingenuousness here. A good many of James's stories, as his notebooks show, started from an anecdote, a whisp of *plot*, for which he then had to imagine the actors. But the idea of a discrepancy between character and story—a technical problem on the one hand—is profoundly thematic also. It is related to the way James conceives the experience of his heroine, but also to the way in which he finds himself forced to look at all human attempts to bring into relation the claim of personal essence and a design of life which validates it to itself and to the world. From one point of view the result of the author's search for a story that will fully express such a heroine is only in part successful, as her search for the role is also frustrated, and even self-frustrated. At the same time, the negativity that marks her career, her profound distrust of offered roles, is both an acceptance of personal defeat and the writer's renunciation of story in its traditional sense.

* * *

"The novel is of its very nature an 'ado,'" James wrote—using another odd word, his substitute for the "nefarious" word "plot"—"an ado about something, and the larger the form it takes the greater of course the ado. Therefore, consciously, that was what one was in for—for positively organizing an ado about Isabel Archer" [8]. The ado—motion of some sort, if not the relentlessly forward motion implied by "plot"—would arise from her relations with others as perceived from her own viewpoint. "Place the centre of the subject in the young woman's own consciousness and you get as interesting and as beautiful a difficulty as you could wish . . . Make her only interested enough, at the same time, in the things that are not herself, and this relation needn't fear to be too limited" [9]. And James concludes, making his ambiguous term for action, "doing" (already compromised by his "ado"), take a third sense, that of the artist's own efforts: "To depend upon her and her little concerns wholly to see you through will necessitate, remember, your really 'doing' her" [10]. The "ado" about Isabel and also the artist's "doing"—plot and the art of narrative—will begin with the question, as he sees, of "What will she *do*?" [10].

The novelist himself will begin by giving his character motion, however, by that initial act which had started off American characters in earlier fictions—*Roderick Hudson, The American,* "Daisy Miller." "The first thing she'll do will be to come to Europe." But this will be movement mental as well as physical. As a perceptive young pilgrim, James had found his own high adventure of the mind in the encounter with Europe. It might seem as much adventure for Isabel as all those traditional narrative excitements she is denied. He uses the word "independence"—Isabel's most frequently noted attribute—to remark upon her "independence of flood and field, of the moving accident, of battle and murder and sudden death" [12]; her independence, in other words, from the old plots of physical action.

Making her story an adventure of perception would allow his feminine protagonist to enter into the realm of the novel. *The Portrait of a Lady* does not employ the services of the distant observer-narrator who tells the tale in "Daisy Miller" and *Washington Square,* an impartial, ironic presence, positioned well outside the consciousness of the heroine. The "Daisy Miller" narrator is content to participate, with reservations, in the limited perceptions of Winterbourne, knowing no more than this observer about Daisy's inner being. The Jamesian persona who tells Catherine Sloper's story is a historian of manners whose own masculine sophistication so exceeds the simplicity of her mind that he can only treat it by coming perilously close to her father's condescension. But the "ado" about Isabel Archer involves a sympathetic though urbane participation in her thoughts; she is by nature and intelligence closer to her maker than those earlier heroines, as though his sense of the artist's special empathy with the condition of women is now more conscious. It was precisely this discovery that made him proud of this work's advance of design upon his previous efforts, "a structure reared with an 'architectural' competence, as Turgenieff would have said, that makes it, to the author's own sense, the most proportioned of his productions after 'The Ambassadors'" [10].

James exaggerates the consistency of his centering—the traditional self-conscious narrator who stands well away from his favorite character is not banished altogether. The narrative consciousness still seems, as previously in his fiction, to be male, and to resemble the author himself more than Isabel. And not only does he often reveal his separation from the heroine, he participates in the inner thoughts of others—particularly Ralph Touchett, who may be closer to his own viewpoint, being also a tolerant and affectionate, as well as richly perceiving, sponsor of her development. While Isabel *is* the center, she is so not only because she is seen from within her own consciousness but because she is the object of observation by the other characters as well—who either try to understand or to manipulate her, like generous or tyrannic novelists. As a result, the social uncertainty of female selfhood is reflected in the novel's formal irresolution, its subjection to relativism. James's compensatory conversion of the inner life into a substitute field of action for his inactive protagonist is haunted by the knowledge that she is excluded from action in its physical and social sense as men are not (unless, like Ralph, they are invalids).

Isabel is always a subject for a portrait—the occasion for the effort of perception—rather than the portrait promised in the title. Perhaps the title simply declares that the novel's subject is the *effort* to achieve such a portrait, such a single view, and it asks to the last, "Who is Isabel, what is she?" All the other characters, along with the narrator and the reader, as well as Isabel herself, are engaged in the *attempt* to define her, but no fixed image emerges from this play of perceptions—though in the end, it may be said, she does for a moment become something else than herself, the generic type she has resisted, the "portrait of *a* lady." And yet, though James argues that Isabel's encounters make a drama of perception and feeling, it is not, of course, only perception and feeling that are brought into play at her entrance into Gardencourt or her first meeting with Madame Merle—the examples he offers. On these occasions she also enters the domain of plot in the sense he disdains, entrained in a story with plenty of motion. The heroine will be loved by four men and marry the worst; she will be victimized by both a well-intentioned secret plot to endow her with money and a wicked one to marry her for that money; the belated revelations of both designs and of the concealed prehistory of her false friends, and various subsidiary actions, all make for melodrama, plot at its most egregious. But these events are not the doing of a heroine whose drama, James would insist, is not what happens to her but how she takes it.

That Isabel is the victim rather than the perpetrator of "plot"—those plots of action to which her "motionless seeing" is opposed—has, exactly, a double sense. In showing how such a narrative is a menace to the "free" character, James gives us reason to reflect on the cause of that ambiguity in language which makes us look with suspicion on the very act of structuring implied in the general sense of "plot," essential though such structuring, whether of temporal or other phenomena, may be to human thought. One is reminded that such words as "design" and "scheme" and "contrive" carry, also, the suggestion of malicious intent. And even the neutral "doing," the word we have heard so much of from James, gains a sinister meaning as it reverberates from the moment Ralph asks his mother, "What do you want to do with her?" [39], to the later occasion of Madame Merle's remark to Osmond, "I don't pretend to know what people are meant for, I only know what I can do with them" [170].

So, she is plotted against—in the sense of the word that is certainly "nefarious"; the novel invokes the meaning of plot as machination enforcing some undesired end in the spring laid for the innocent maiden by dark conspirators who take advantage of her good nature to rob her of her fortune and imprison her in the dungeon of marriage. But—more important—she is the victim of narrative ideas of what she will be and do, which others seek to impose upon her. The example of their own lives and personalities, to which she finds herself attracted, will press upon her alternate possibilities of development, of projected life stories. In their place she will only have her own aching sense of potential brilliance, her undenotable personal utopianism. In rejecting the marriage-plot of early nineteenth-century fiction she will become, unwittingly, a character in the plot of conspiracy as her false friend and her hypocritical Gothic suitor "make" her marriage after all. In this struggle the two senses of "plot" conflate; both plots are schemes of entrapment, though it is from only the unconcealed and seemingly unthreatening marriage-plot that she (vainly) tries to escape.

*   *   *

James's statement that the first thing he will make Isabel "do" is come to Europe has a certain disingenuousness about it, for this initial act is nearly suppressed out of the narrative. Not until the third chapter do we get a brief view of that moment when Mrs. Touchett descends upon Isabel in her grandmother's Albany house. The house is described in a curiously detailed way. Some of these details are autobiographical, corresponding to James's recollections—set down long afterward in *A Small Boy and Others*—including the adjoining primary school and the taste "of accessible garden peaches"[2] associated with his own grandmother's house in Albany. As tokens of an infantine time, which James remembered as also an age of innocence in American culture, the description must have functioned in the writer's mind in a symbolic way, and does so for the uncommon modern reader who happens to recall certain pages of the autobiography, which was published thirty years after the novel. There are a few more bits of the past of Isabel-James, farther on—her (his) father's "aversion" to unpleasantness, and the educational theories which had induced him to transport his daughters (sons) three times across the Atlantic before Isabel-James was fourteen. And when we read that, as a girl, Isabel had "an immense curiosity about life and was constantly staring and wondering" [34], we are reminded of the way James describes himself as a boy who was always "gaping." * * * As a glimpse of Isabel's own childhood it signals James's secret identification with her, something which reinforces his concentration upon her consciousness, making for an authorial attachment more intimate and tender than his fleeting, skeptical identification with Winterbourne in "Daisy Miller."

But these associations, to which one is helped by adding to the text something unavailable to the contemporary reader, are hardly enough to give either Isabel's earlier history or the culture that has produced her a dramatic presence in the novel. The fact that she is an orphan, responsible to no one but herself, completes the severance from her antecedents. She herself feels that her situation makes her belong "quite to the independent class"—that is, the class of those "independent" of customary plots—when she insists to Casper Goodwood that she is disqualified for the role which conducts the heroine to the marriage-ending. "I'm not in my first youth—I can do what I choose . . . I've neither father nor mother; I'm poor and of a serious disposition; I'm not pretty. I therefore am not bound to be timid and conventional; indeed I can't afford such luxuries. Besides, I try to judge things for myself; to judge wrong, I think, is more honourable than not to judge at all. I don't wish to be a mere sheep in the flock; I wish to choose my fate and know something of human affairs

2. Henry James, *Autobiography*, ed. Frederick W. Dupee (New York: Criterion Books, 1956), pp. 4–5.

beyond what other people think it compatible with propriety to tell me" [117].

Merely as a reminder of influences or models which Isabel rejects, James permits us the briefest of backward glances at her two sisters, her only surviving relatives, now remotely behind her across the sea—one married, not brilliantly, to an Army officer posted "in the unfashionable West," the oldest, Lilian, the mother of two "peremptory little boys," to a lawyer in New York, where she is "the mistress of a wedge of brown stone violently driven into Fifty-third Street" [31]. James's crisp phrases express the finality of these fates, and Lilian's view of Isabel's own necessary consummation might have been uttered at the opening of one of Austen's novels: "I want to see her safely married—that's what I want to see" [32]. It is clear that James understands the exact nature of this expectation when he summarizes in the most compact way all Isabel's preparation. Like his own sister Alice, who paced the cliffs of Newport and dreamed of an inaccessible life of action during the Civil War, Isabel is said to have "passed months of this long period in a state of almost passionate excitement, in which she felt herself at times (to her extreme confusion) stirred almost indiscriminately by the valour of either army." James's empathetic feminist irony is felt in the comment which follows almost directly: "she had had everything a girl could have: kindness, admiration, bonbons, bouquets, the sense of exclusion from none of the privileges of the world she lived in, abundant opportunity for dancing, plenty of new dresses, the London *Spectator*, the latest publications, the music of Gounod, the poetry of Browning, the prose of George Eliot" [35].

Isabel's developmental possibilities are not ones Lilian or her husband can imagine, however; her "originality" bewilders them. "I've never kept up with Isabel—it would have taken *all* my time" [31] says this sister. Her husband "hope(s) she isn't going to develop anymore" [32], and observes, exactly as though she is a novel, that he cannot read her, she's "written in a foreign tongue" [32]; the kind of story she might figure in is quite beyond him. James thus introduces but brings into doubt the naturalist scheme of prediction as well as the traditional marriage-plot model, letting the reader know that his heroine is not to be "explained" by her class, type, upbringing, and, above all, by her past. In effect, she has no past and her future is obscure.

She herself accepts her aunt's invitation with "a desire to leave the past behind her and, as she said to herself, to begin afresh" [33]. And much later, when she is about to meet Osmond, she still considers that the past has no hold upon her: "It was in her disposition at all times to lose faith in the reality of absent things . . . The past was apt to look dead" [159]. Her attitude toward others, too, is to assume that they have no past, or to prefer not to inquire about it. This must explain her lack of curiosity about the previous relationship of Ralph and Madame Merle—which is hinted at, but which we never learn about. "With all her love of knowledge," we are told, "she had a natural shrinking from raising curtains and looking into unlighted corners. The love of knowledge coexisted in her mind with the finest capacity for ignorance" [142]. More dangerously for herself, she is incurious about Osmond's past: "His life had been mingled with other lives more than he admitted . . . For the present she refrained from provoking further revelations" [187]. And so she never really understands what would seem obvious until, as the Countess Gemini says, the i's are dotted for her—"*ça me dépasse,* if you don't mind my saying so, the things, all round you, that you've appeared to succeed in not knowing" [370].

Isabel's gap of beginning is one of the functions of the international situation which, in so many of James's fictions, introduces a lately landed American whose qualities are to be tested in the European world. She seems newborn when she steps onto the lawn of Gardencourt in the opening chapter. And even before she appears, Mrs. Touchett's telegram has attached to her that description, "independent," which she soon uses of herself. In a paradoxical sense, of course, this also makes her the symbolic representative of her nation's ideals—her own declarations never cease to echo the language of the American Declaration. But in its absolute sense independence means the right to be free even of a culture committed to freedom. When Isabel wonders at the fact that her aunt's own point of view doesn't seem particularly American (it is one of the moments when she sounds like her friend Henrietta), Mrs. Touchett exclaims, "My point of view, thank God, is personal!"—which Isabel thinks "a tolerable description of her own manner of judging" [50].

Isabel's independence might, for a moment, be thought of as a hereditarily determined as well as determining quality, for Mr. Touchett immediately recognizes it as a "family trait," which Isabel shares with his wife. This is hardly implied, however—the resemblance between the two is something else. It is a hypothetical prediction of a destiny that Isabel's very rejection of models implies. We learn just enough about Mrs. Touchett herself to be provided with a glimpse of the history of someone who is so "fond of her own way," as Mr. Touchett says, or who, as her son adds, "likes to do everything for herself and has no belief in anyone's power to help her" [21]. At their meeting in Albany, the older woman seems to recognize the kinship when her niece refuses to promise to do everything she is told. Mrs. Touchett then responds, "You're fond of your own way; but it's not for me to blame you" [30].

Another term applied to both women by Ralph is "natural" [40]. * * * Implying a certain freedom from the modes and manners of ordered society, it signifies freedom from those deterministic "natural" laws which make the idea of the natural seem the very reverse of free in later nineteenth-century thinking. The "nature" referred to is not Darwin's but the Nature of Emerson's essay. Such a concept belongs especially to American culture before 1850 but is persistently American, a dream we have never entirely surrendered to naturalistic determinism. The one fault Isabel was to find with Madame Merle in the time of her great admiration for that accomplished woman was, "she was not natural—she had rid herself of every remnant of that tonic wildness which we may assume to have belonged even to the most amiable persons in the ages before country-house life was the fashion"[137]. This is an unmistakable reference to Thoreau, who says in *Walden*: "We need the tonic of wildness."[3]

Of course, there is nothing very wild about the elderly Mrs. Touchett, who holds Isabel to a stricter propriety than the girl is used to when she wishes to linger downstairs with the gentlemen after her aunt has retired.

---

3. Henry David Thoreau, "Walden," *The Writings of Henry David Thoreau.* 20 vols. (Boston and New York: Houghton Mifflin Company, 1893.) 2:350.

Mrs. Touchett extends her benevolent sponsorship to Isabel only for the most conventional of enterprises—acquisition of European culture and of a husband—her viewpoint being exactly the same as Mrs. Ludlow's; she is openly disappointed when Isabel rejects that great *parti*, Lord Warburton. Yet she is in her own person, nevertheless, a warning. In the old woman's sterile eccentricity, her wandering which knows no resting place, and her emotional distance from the husband and son who have not seen her for a year, we are given the outcome of Mrs. Touchett's independence. It is an exhibition of what might even be Isabel's fate, an alternative of existence embedded in the text as one anticipation of the outcome of her views and qualities. Since she must marry, as everyone but she feels, she would only be able to preserve her independence by becoming someone like her aunt. In the end, this does not seem impossible if her marriage to Osmond should remain an undissolved formal connection in the years to be imagined for her beyond the closing pages. As unlike her dry, elderly aunt as she seems, the reader should not forget that Isabel reminds Mr. Touchett of his wife as a young girl.

This method of presenting Isabel's alterity is one James extends to most of the other characters, who are not only independent forces acting upon her but represent other lives she might live. Ironically, since it is her determination to resist models as much as she can, James expresses through the characters that surround his heroine the idea that a life is a path with many forkings; in traveling past these we have only the illusion of treading a single, inevitable course. Forecasting in the novel may be admonitory or optative as well as predictive. It is only after her marriage that Isabel feels that her alterity is exhausted. As she broods before the fire upon the mistake the marriage has been, she reflects, "She had taken all the first steps in the purest confidence, and then she had suddenly found the infinite vista of a multiplied life to be a dark, narrow alley with a dead wall at the end" [292].

Two representatives of her American origins follow her to Europe and continue to exhibit that side of herself which is unmodified by foreign experience. Henrietta Stackpole is Isabel without her grace and superior intelligence but with something of her freshness and American insistence upon self-determination. There will be moments, as already noted, when the two friends sound very much alike. Henrietta's alterity to Isabel is that she has achieved her "independence" without modifying these qualities. She is an example of an alternative to marriage, which is not the role of the old maid dependent of Victorian families, but the working woman's proud self-support. That it is Henrietta who does, after all, marry an English gentleman while Isabella refuses one, is James's joke played on a "new woman" about whom he had mixed feelings. Another joke is the fact that this free American is the very representative of categorical thinking. She is always looking for "types" to figure in her articles for the newspapers and insists on the niceness of national distinctions; Ralph annoys her by not being clearly either English or American—but she decides he is a type, after all, "the alienated American," of which he is "a beautiful specimen" [68].

Casper Goodwood also represents something important in Isabel's past, but James does his best to repress it from view. His name is not even spoken in the early description of Albany, though he is unquestionably the "person from whom she was looking for a visit" when she hears her aunt's footstep outside her door. We know nothing at all about him until Henrietta mentions in Chapter II that he has come over in the steamer with her—and charges Isabel with being "faithless" [75]. Whether the charge has foundation, however—what exactly has been the previous history of her relations with Goodwood—we are never told, though her relations with Lord Warburton and Osmond, his rivals, are given to us from their beginnings—and this shutting off of any backward view of him is still another index of that suppression of beginning which has kept most of Isabel's American past over the horizon. The character of Casper is treated somewhat summarily by James, who does not seem to want to remember, any more than does Isabel, just what Casper has been to her. Yet, in another novel, he might be a hero—someone not unlike Christopher Newman—a resistant American masculinity. He, also, is a "new man," having made a fortune in industrial America, and also comes to Europe with the view that he can have what he wants—in this case, Isabel.

Neither Henrietta nor Casper, who are allied, succeeds in modifying Isabel's history. Yet Casper's pursuit is nearly successful. His urgency is answered to powerfully in Isabel's nature. This may be interpreted sexually—and her evasion of his suit put down to sexual fear. But it may be more in harmony with James's intention to see that the American "freedom" Casper offers her is only another design which she strives against—though one that is closely related to her own desire for freedom from old forms. He resembles her (is one version of her) in his very American self-sufficiency, being the "self-made man" in material terms as she would be a self-made personality, owing nothing to others. When he tells her at the last that the world is very large, and asks, "To whom under the sun do we owe anything?" [401], he seems to be voicing her own principles—as well as the proud solvency of the successful entrepreneur—though by this time she has come to understand the limitations of the independence she was once so proud of. Still, marriage with this suitor remains potential in the narrative like so many other potentialities, and the narrator remarks that there were moments when she said to herself that "she might evade him for a time, but that she must make terms with him at last." Though she has rejected him as well as Lord Warburton she still feels, toward the end of the first volume, that she "might really . . . come to the end of things that were not Casper (even though there appeared so many of them), and find rest in those very elements of his presence which struck her now as impediments to the finer respiration. It was conceivable that these impediments should some day prove a sort of blessing in disguise—a clear and quiet harbor enclosed by a brave granite breakwater" [160].

This is so powerfully put—with the image of the granite breakwater representing Casper's restrictive yet, protective nature—that one may, if one is distressed by such a misleading implication of the outcome, protest that the writer does not seem to know how his novel will end. One answer is that we are in the mind, after all, of Isabel, who does *not* know what happens in the next chapter—that she meets Osmond. But another is that James wishes to keep all possibilities open even against the logic of a plot that seems to be reducing them one by one. Casper's persistence in her life will continue to suggest an alternate outcome. He does not succeed,

within the bounds of the novel, in doing what he wishes—uniting himself with Isabel—yet it is representative of his nature as well as hers that
he believes in an unquenchable futurity in himself and others, and presses
his suit to the end. It is typical of him that he even seems to think that
Ralph's death from tuberculosis can be prevented when he visits him in
Rome after Isabel's marriage: "He couldn't bear to see a pleasant man, so
pleasant for all his queerness, so beyond anything to be done. There was
always something to be done, for Goodwood, and he did it in this case by
repeating several times his visit to the Hôtel de Paris" [339]. Isabel is left
"free" after his electric kiss, finally. Henrietta's last encouragement to
Casper, "Just you wait!" implies a closure beyond the last page of the 1882
text, but James subdued this ambiguity in the New York Edition, and the
revised ending maintains the openness of the novel, its gap of ending, and
is in harmony with Casper's own stubborn refusal of finality. In the later
version, James added, "but only to guess from her face, with a revulsion,
that she simply meant he was young. She stood shining at him with that
cheap comfort, and it added, on the spot, thirty years to his life. She walked
him away with her, however, as if she had given him now the key to
patience" [403].

Madame Merle is another possible outcome for an Isabel who might
remain poor, growing older in Europe, and come to the point of having to
say, in her turn, "My dreams were so great—so preposterous." Madame
Merle also says, "the dreams of one's youth, why they were enchanting,
they were divine! Who had ever seen such things come to pass?" [143]. She,
too, we must remember, is an American, and "the breezy freedom of the
stars and stripes might have shed an influence upon the attitude she there
took towards life" [127]. She seems, at first, also to be without a past, having had a husband who is never mentioned by her and of whom Ralph only
says that he "would be likely to pass away" [128]. She has had time to
acquire a significant history, in fact; it has changed her, and remains present in her life in Pansy, but this history is quite invisible to Isabel.

What Madame Merle seems to be—however arrived at—stirs the younger
woman to a passion of emulation. Something of this attitude is shared by
Mrs. Touchett, of whom Ralph says that "if she were not herself (which she
after all much prefers) she would like to be Madame Merle" [127–28]. As
their acquaintance continues, Isabel's fascination with Madame Merle's
accomplishments and charms increases, and she finds herself "desiring to
emulate them, and in twenty such ways this lady presented herself as a
model. 'I should like awfully to be so!' Isabel secretly exclaimed, more than
once, as one after another of her friend's fine aspects caught the light" [136].
The one flaw Isabel finds in her, as I have said, is that she seems to be without "naturalness"—the American quality which Isabel herself possesses and
prizes. But, in fact, it may be one of the novel's numerous potentialities that
although she discovers this admired model to be someone who has decep-
tively plotted against her, Isabel may be nevertheless (as Leo Bersani has
suggested) in the process of absorbing the example of Madame Merle in the
end—that is, mastering the art of appearances.[4]

---

4. "James has to recuperate Madame Merle morally by incorporating her into Isabel—that is by
creating a character whose intentions coincide exactly with his or her fictions," Leo Bersani,
"The Jamesian Lie," *Partisan Review* 36. 1 (Winter 1969): 62.

Even Pansy is a variant Isabel, another female innocent upon whom others work their designs, though her innocence is that of Nature, from which all tonic wildness has been bred out in a convent garden. In the final move to the role of sponsor and protector of Pansy—by which she assumes Ralph's role in relation to herself—Isabel acts to recover possibility for a younger self. Pansy's story provides, in the novel's late stages, a doubling back to her stepmother's own early condition, and gives one the feeling that the possibilities latent then have not, after all, disappeared; Pansy's promise of happiness keeps Isabel's alterity alive. In enacting Ralph's role toward herself in her own relationship with Pansy, Isabel again confirms her identity with him. She shares with him the imaginative qualities which make possible a donation of one's own expectations to another, a surrogateship both generous and fatal. His donation to Isabel—not merely of money but of personal expectations—is duplicated not only in her relationship with Pansy but in her earlier relationship with Osmond himself.

This implied cyclicity also threatens the expectation that Pansy may turn out to be happier than her sponsor, multiplying for us even further the alternatives which vibrate beyond the novel's final page. As we remember the fatality of Ralph's gift we see the darker side of his spectatorship, which links him unexpectedly to such a character as Dr. Sloper, who watches Catherine as though she were a character in a play and wonders whether she will show him some surprises in the next act. Ralph, we are told, is kept alive at the end by the fact that Isabel's drama is still not played out: "He was determined to sit out the performance" [273]. But when Isabel first meets Pansy, she too is a playgoer; Pansy strikes her as "an *ingénue* in a French play" or "the ideal *jeune fille* of foreign fiction" [195].

Ralph's superior mental and emotional qualities would seem to make him the only one among the men who love Isabel who is her true mate. But the relationship is closer still. It is worth pondering that James has made Ralph unable to offer her physical passion. Ralph cannot act in any way except by furthering someone else's history, though he is sometimes reminded "that the finest of pleasures is the rush of action." There is something deadly, a stillness of exhaustion, that marks Gardencourt, that beautiful garden place where if one life begins, two others are ending—the lives of the dying father and the mortally ill son who wait for Isabel in that "little eternity" of tea-time, when time has seemed to stop on the great lawn. The money of one man and the love of the other produce their intended gift of expanded life to Isabel. But the legacy is infected with their deaths.

Isabel herself is not only like the Touchetts, but like James, the motionless see-er who is an affectionate, spectatorial witness of his characters' efforts as he gives them their lives, their plots. I have referred earlier to James's recognition of his own identity with female life in a society which kept both women and the artist at the periphery of social power. Ralph, the man with the artistic sensibility, enacts a classically female abnegation. The free Isabel, who once scorned the idea that she had to marry at all, now accepts the most conventional of female plots in the abnegation of wifehood; women, *typically*, must act through men. So, it is Osmond, as I have said, in whose life Isabel first dreams of making herself potent, sponsoring the expression of *his* supposed free nature as she has been sponsored. Ralph was right in accusing her, in the beginning, of not wanting to touch or taste life. She would rather act through delegation, by marrying. Osmond will do her doing for her. If he is guilty of regarding her as an object, she is guilty, also, of thinking of him as an instrument. And James, the artist, identifies with this delegation. The "rush of action" which Ralph misses may be understood not only as that of the battlefield or of sexual intercourse but in a literary sense as the "doing" of the novel, which is James's own substitute for living action—a doing which is, in this case, an affirmation of not-doing. Just as Isabel had been seen by her Albany relatives as a book "written in a foreign tongue," so Ralph (for whom the ordinary plots of manhood are inapplicable) sees himself as "a good book in a poor translation—a meagre entertainment for a young man who felt that he might have been an excellent linquist" [38].

Osmond, the person most inimical to Isabel, is thus also related to her as the means by which her money can be translated into action—as she had been the intended translation of the Touchett money. The image by which she conceives of her role in relation to Osmond is exactly the same as that used by Ralph when he tells his father that he would like to "put a little wind in her sails" [132]: "She would launch his boat for him; she would be his providence" [294]. Her benevolence, like Ralph's, results from her own incapacity to use money directly. This incapacity is literal; as a woman she has no way to make money "work," since women of her type and time are only consumers. Less literally it represents her reluctance to seek that "doing" which closes down her potentiality.

Osmond appeals to her precisely because he seems another self. Repeatedly the comment is made by others that he has *done* nothing. Madame Merle characterizes him as "Gilbert Osmond—he lives in Italy; that's all one can say about him or make of him. He's exceedingly clever, a man made to be distinguished; but, as I tell you, you exhaust the description when you say he's Mr. Osmond who lives *tout bêtement* in Italy. No career, no name no position, no fortune, no past, no future, no anything" [141]. When Madame Merle observes to the Countess Gemini that her brother "is one of the cleverest of men," his sister says, "I've heard you say that before but I haven't yet discovered what he has done." Madame Merle, who at last sees some possibility for action in Osmond's case—his marriage to Isabel—replies merely, "He has done nothing that has had to be undone. And he has known how to wait" [191–192]. Osmond himself, we are told, feels that by his marriage his unexpressed self can find tongue. "The desire to have something or other to show for his 'parts'—to show somehow or other—had been the dream of his youth; but as the years went on the conditions attached to any marked proof of rarity had affected him more and more as gross and detestable; like the swallowing of mugs of beer to advertise what one could 'stand.'" Now, like Isabel, he expects to find manifestation through another: "She should do the thing *for* him, and he would not have waited in vain" [214].

Unappealing as Osmond's negativity might seem, it is the very reason Isabel finds him more attractive than anyone she has known. "What has he ever done?" challenges Goodwood when he hears that she intends to marry this man, and she declares with pride, for it echoes her own abstention, "Nothing at all" [229]. His virtues, for her, are a list of negatives: "No property, no title, no honours, no houses, nor lands, nor position, nor reputation, nor brilliant belongings of any sort. It's the total absence of these things that pleases me" [241], she tells Ralph.

Of course, one will say that Isabel is wrong to see this extreme Emersonianism in Osmond. Though Osmond declines the manifestations of action, he is a collector of objects and a cultivator of appearances; he is intensely aware, in truth, of his effect in the world—and imposes this awareness on Isabel after they are married. The most Emersonian of her wooers, despite his cotton mills, is Goodwood; "to whom under the world do we owe anything?" are nearly his last words to her. "Oh, he was intrinsic enough; she never thought of his even looking for artificial aids," Isabel reflects when Goodwood comes to see her in Rome after her marriage. His figure, she observes, had "a kind of bareness and bleakness which made the accident of meeting in memory or apprehension a peculiar concussion; it was deficient in the social drapery commonly muffling, in an overcivilized age, the sharpness of human contacts" [332].

But, then, she has defined herself as "independent" of all these things in the same negative way. One recalls, again, her declaration to Madame Merle concerning a hypothetical wooer—that nothing he possessed would matter to her, just as nothing that belonged to her was any measure of herself [144]. It is such a self, sequestered from expression in outer things or acts, that she has cherished in herself and thinks she recognizes in Osmond, the ideal lover of whom she had spoken. He actually admits to her that he has had no "natural indifference" to outward show and that his life has exhibited his "studied, wilful renunciation"—a mock enactment of the giving-up which is the heroic gesture of so many Jamesian idealists. Isabel, however, does not understand that his "renunciation" is no more than an attitude. James remarks that in her characteristic way, she had "invented a fine theory about Gilbert Osmond, she loved him not for what he really possessed, but for his very poverties dressed out as honors" [241]. Her imagination, writing its own story, had seen him as another character than the actual one: "she had had a more wondrous vision of him, fed through charmed senses and oh such a stirred fancy! She had not read him right" [294], she later realizes.

Yet her instinct for a resemblance which makes him her ultimate and most humiliating alter-ego is not altogether mistaken. In his fastidious disdain for vulgar effort he is, again, a version of her own resistance to action; his aesthetic connoisseurship is a possibility latent in her own interest in the collection of fine sensations. He is not wrong when, after stating his personal view that "one ought to make one's life a work of art" [215], he tells her that this is exactly what he believed she herself was trying to do. In what seems to be his successful fusion of American independence of spirit, disdain for "accoutrements," and European appreciation of the heritage of Western culture, he appears to represent what she aspires to. In the multitude of her potentialities even Gilbert Osmond is latent.

* * *

It is in relation to these others who propose her development that Isabel tries to define those terms which are her spiritual watchwords. When she rejects Goodwood upon his first arrival in Europe, she declares, "I like my liberty too much. If there's one thing in the world I'm fond of it's my personal independence." Bemused, the free American man protests, "Who would wish less to curtail your liberty than I? What can give me greater pleasure than to see you perfectly independent—doing whatever you like? It's to make you independent, that I want to marry you." Isabel calls his statement a "beautiful sophism." She must suspect that his idea of independence is in large part the material one—he will marry her and free her of material concerns—but the implication that money is freedom has social truth. Goodwood is correct in saying that an unmarried woman in Isabel's time and place isn't actually socially "independent" but "hampered at every step" [117]. Marriage, especially marriage to someone with money, would give her the social role without which her selfhood cannot compose itself. Isabel's reply to Goodwood, that *because* she is poor, among other things, she can reject this definition of selfhood (it is the same, after all, as Madame Merle's), is one that cannot stand the test of social reality.

Ralph's role is ambiguous. On the one hand, he appreciates her character. It is he who raises the artist's question, almost as James put it in the preface: "It was a fine free nature; but what was she going to do with herself?" He reminds himself that his question about "doing" is "irregular, for with most women one had no occasion to ask it. Most women did with themselves nothing at all; they waited, in attitudes more or less gracefully passive, for a man to come that way and furnish them with a destiny" [53]. Ralph does not know, any more than Isabel, what new plot might be written for her; he has the attitude of the literary experimenter who shares her hope of discarding stale plots and finding a new one. Yet his sense of how to put "wind in her sails" is less abstract than hers. The economic sense of "independent" is never far from the text, entering in that first ambiguous use of the word in Mrs. Touchett's telegram, over which the gentlemen on the lawn at Gardencourt ponder, uncertain whether she means that her niece is "well off" or "fond of (her) own way" [21]. Ralph decides to see that she has money so that she will be able to express this fondness for her own way *because* she is well off—the two senses of the term exhibiting their hidden connection. He explicitly links money and imagination when he tells his father that he wants to make Isabel rich, explaining, "I call people rich when they're able to meet the requirements of their imagination" [132].

Yet he is as vague as she will be when it comes to defining what she will be able to "do with herself." Money, after all, is itself an abstract potentiality, which does not shape the exact futurity of its possessor. He is only able to think of what money will *prevent* her from doing. "If she has an easy income she'll never have to marry for a support. That's what I want cannily to prevent. She wishes to be free, and your bequest will make her free" [132]. Aside from this, the seventy thousand pounds are to "facilitate the execution of [her] good impulses," in which Ralph shares her faith. Her goodness itself, he understands, is only what she will "do"; "she's as good as her best opportunities" [133].

When she is rich, Isabel herself—it is one of her contradictions—accepts the idea that riches make one more free than penniless idealism, though she is filled with a certain amount of fear. "A large fortune means freedom, and I'm afraid of that. It's such a fine thing, and one should make such a good use of it . . . I'm not sure it's not a greater happiness to be powerless" [158]. But as time passes, her imagination of freedom recovers, and she pictures her future "by the light of her hopes, her fears, her fancies, her ambitions, her predilections . . . She lost herself in a maze of visions; the fine things to be done by a rich, independent, generous girl who took a large human view of occasions and obligations were sublime in the mass" [159]. The money increases her sense of a great potential for some still unchosen action, but one which escapes the plot of femalehood; she "made up her mind that to be rich was a virtue because it was to be able to do and to do could only be sweet. It was a graceful contrary of the stupid side of weakness—especially the feminine variety" [150].

Goodwood, as we have seen, had thought she simply wanted to see the world a bit and offered to help her do so, but she told him he could only help her by putting the sea between them. When he then protested, "One would think you were going to commit some atrocity," she retorted, "Perhaps I am. I wish to be free even to do that if the fancy takes me" [118]. Yes, even an "atrocity" must be included in her freely conceivable choice of lives. And "choice," of course, is another of her watchwords. The act of choice is more important than the thing chosen. One recalls the scene at Gardencourt when, following the discussion about remaining downstairs alone with the young men, her aunt says, "You're too fond of your own ways": "Yes, I think I'm very fond of them. But I always want to know the things one shouldn't do." "So as to do them?" asks her aunt. "So as to choose" [56], said Isabel.

Such declarations make Isabel sound like a flaming rebel—except that we know that she has never done an improper thing in her life. It is the theoretical right of choice that she cherishes—to the point, indeed, of making no choice, and so preserving choice still longer. Yet she begins to see that her abstention from choice, her withholding from action, may be an evasion of life. Osmond is successfully wooing her by describing himself as someone who has always rejected action, yet he correctly identifies his rule of life as "negative," as "wilful renunciation." At the end of the novel's first volume, as she is already, unconsciously, preparing to break out of her resistance to marriage, she admits to changing her plans and projects every day. "It seems frivolous," she says, "One ought to choose something very deliberately, and be faithful to that" [186].

As for Isabel's visions themselves, they remain unspecified from first to last. James stresses her determination to be more responsive to her own imagination than to anything else. "Her imagination," we are told, "was by habit ridiculously active; when the door was not open it jumped out of the window" [33]. The energetic motion of the image points up the paradox that imagination is, after all, "motionless," and does not of itself produce action. Yet her fine imagination is crowded with images drawn from literary models. In the beginning, Isabel agrees with Ralph that she brings romance with her, and has "brought it to the right place" [42]. When introduced to Lord Warburton she childishly exclaims. "Oh, I hoped there would be a lord; it's just like a novel!" [23]. So one of Austen's marriageable heroines—or her mother—might have fluttered at the approach of an attractive, titled gentleman in quest of a wife, "hoping to fall in love," as Warburton is supposed to be. Isabel "scarce fell short of seeing him—though quite without luridity—as a hero of romance" [55]. But this does not turn out to mean that she will figure in a tale in which a portionless girl marries a Darcy, though Lord Warburton, proposing to her, knows what role he is playing: "It was at first sight, as the novels say; I know now that's not a fancy phrase, and I shall think better of novels for evermore" [80]. She also expects to find a ghost in Gardencourt—an appropriate item for romance—but though this will eventually make its appearance in her story, it will come in a symbolic way. As the reader listens to these remarks in the novel's fifth chapter, he cannot yet tell what he is in for— and hears the music of various plots begin to sound. The novelist himself may be entertaining the idea of all of them.

Yet Isabel's vagueness, her reluctance to objectify her feelings by action, seems an inhibition of creative decision. We can look critically, again, at some of those declarations she makes on behalf of her "freedom." Her cousin senses her antideterministic personality: "I don't believe you allow things to be settled for you." She replies, "Oh, yes; if they're settled as I like them" [25]. This suggests, misleadingly, that she knows clearly what she wants. She was "always planning her own development." But we have no glimpse of these plans. She herself wonders as she rejects Lord Warburton, "What view of life, what design upon fate, what conception of happiness, had she that pretended to be larger than these large, these fabulous occasions? If she wouldn't do such a thing as that then she must do great things, she must do something greater" [84]. But what are these greater things?

In fact, it is never at all clear what she expects of life. She wants knowledge, but is it that mythic knowledge that is the fruit of suffering? From literature, again, she has learned "that the unpleasant had been even too absent from her knowledge, for she had gathered from her acquaintance with literature that it was a source of interest and even instruction" [33]. When she refuses Lord Warburton, she explains that in marrying him she would be trying to escape "the usual chances and dangers . . . what most people know and suffer" [98]. Her desire not to be exempted from experience is not, as one might think, a religious or a moral one—though it seems to resemble that acceptance of the whole mortal condition which is an imitation of Christ—an association that does press forward in the case of James's later heroine, Milly Theale. Isabel's is an intellectual or aesthetic interest—which is what Ralph accuses her of when he suspects that she really is not prepared to experience life fully, but wants simply to "see . . . not to feel." Though she bridles, and responds that seeing and feeling cannot be distinguished for "a sentient being," his challenge has point. Yet she seems to contradict herself when she admits that she does not suffer easily, and protests, "It's not absolutely necessary to suffer; we were not made for that"—and declares that she has come to Europe "to be as happy as possible" [43]. Certainly she does not choose the suffering she brings upon herself unwittingly. Rather, she will, like most people, try to be happy and fail.

If one is tempted to call her flighty and superficial on this as on other occasions, one is missing the opportunity of sharing the plausibility of each of these attitudes—to entertain them, successively, as she does. As James's narrator says, "Isabel Archer was a young person of many theories" [44]. Rather than condemning her for their numerousness or incompatibility, James embraces the variety of possibilities which, as novelist, *he* entertains. And that openness to experience which she claims for herself, even if it is suspected to be a desire to see rather than to feel, is precisely the artist's own. In chapter 6 when he summarizes some of her virtues and defects the narrator observes, "her errors and delusions were frequently such as a biographer interested in preserving the dignity of his subject must shrink from specifying" [44]. Yet he insists: "with her meagre knowledge, her inflated ideals, her confidence at once innocent and dogmatic, her temper at once exacting and indulgent, her mixture of curiosity and fastidiousness, of vivacity and indifference, her desire to look very well and to be if possible even better, her determination to see, to try, to know, her combination of the delicate, desultory, flame-like spirit and the eager and personal creature of conditions: she would be an easy victim of scientific criticism if she were not intended to awaken on the reader's part an impulse more tender and more purely expectant" [45]. Expectancy is what we are required to have because she herself is conceived as always expectant, always ready for new realizations.

As I have been suggesting, her inability to forecast her own future, to anticipate the shape of her peculiar fate, is understandable if we remember that in discarding a conventional life pattern or any of the conventional plots of the novel, she asks for a definition lying outside of the stock of available selfhoods. James does not know any more than she how she might live as herself in another way than by choosing one of the fates that are offered her. Her "maze of visions" will turn out to have very little to do with her destiny except to lead her to make the most mistaken of choices, to do an "atrocity" in marrying Gilbert Osmond.

It is perfectly true that it is money, her "independence," that makes something happen when she accepts his proposal, as though it is the spring mechanism which puts this doll into motion at last. She herself is not so much choosing as chosen, but it is the money that has given her a fate. The plot, which has been virtually stationary for most of the first half of the novel—consisting simply of repeated considerations of Isabel by means of her confrontations with others—now moves under the stimulus of her money. In a society based on a money economy, governed by the compulsions of the market, nothing, indeed, does happen except by the application of this source of all motion. And so here—Ralph had been right in thinking that money would give Isabel a plot. She is motivated to marry Osmond by the desire to make her money do something in the world, while the plot to marry her for her money—as conceived by Madame Merle and Osmond—has only been set in motion by those seventy thousand pounds.

But with her engagement early in the second volume, she may be said to have at last embraced the marriage-plot she has resisted so long. James had misgivings, as he worked on the novel, that there had been "a want of action in the earlier part," which he hoped would be made up in the chapters following his heroine's marriage. He thought of the matter technically: "The weakness of the whole story is that it is too exclusively psychological—that it depends too little on incident," but he hoped that "the complete unfolding of the situation that is established by Isabel's marriage may nonetheless be sufficiently dramatic."[5] The novel's structure, however, justifies itself thematically if it is seen that the nonprogressive character of the early half is a representation of Isabel's own deferral of action.

She now reminds Casper that she had warned him that she would do as she chose, but he reminds her that she had told him to doubt any rumor

5. See pp. 428–29 in this Norton Critical Edition [*Editor*].

of her engagement. Has she changed with this definitive step? Ralph says, "You must have changed immensely. A year ago you valued your liberty beyond everything." Isabel seems, indeed, at this moment of her greatest happiness, to turn her back on that principle, for she answers, "It doesn't look to me now, I admit, such an inviting expanse" [237]. Continuing to explain his particular objections to Osmond, Ralph invokes once more those images of the free sail before the wind with which he had associated her: "You seemed to me to be soaring far up in the blue—to be, sailing in the bright light, over the heads of men." But "poor Isabel . . . wandering into the didactic," as James says, only replies, "I've never moved on a higher plane that I'm moving on now. There's nothing higher for a girl than to marry—a person she likes" [239]. That others dislike Osmond only confirms her conviction that she has "married to please herself"— and so preserved her liberty [242].

The structure of the text continues to preserve this liberty, however, by making it seem that Isabel has not acted at all, has not broken the barrier that separates her potentiality from its limiting expression. Though the scene of Osmond's initial declaration of love to Isabel is presented dramatically in chapter 29, her acceptance of him, months later, is elided between chapters 31 and 32. Her momentous moment of *choice*—so long delayed—is thus a virtual blank, permitting us to feel that her potentiality is still intact. And not only the scene of her acceptance of Osmond and the wedding itself (described in one sentence in a later chapter [269]), but all that happened during the succeeding time to change Isabel far more, one might imagine, than she had changed at the time of her engagement is virtually nonexistent. The major ellipsis of the novel is, of course, the three or four years following her wedding, which fall between chapters 35 and 36. Yet this omitted stretch of life has included the virtual breakdown of her marriage, her disillusion in Osmond, the death of her infant. That her marriage has broken down, of course, is itself a defeat of the marriage-plot as a closure of female destiny. The ellipsis in the text must be explained by the breakdown of this narrative structure as well as by the breakdown of Isabel's literal marriage. We do not need to know the details of Osmond's depravities or cruelties to know that her project for the exfoliation of the free self has had no realization.

She herself insists, indeed, that she has acted once and for all. When she contemplates an open rupture with Osmond if he forbids her to visit Ralph's sickroom in Rome, she tells herself that "almost anything seemed preferable to repudiating the most serious act—the single sacred act—of her life" [317], and still later she tells Henrietta, who advises her to leave Osmond, "One must accept one's deeds. I married him before all the world; I was perfectly free; it was impossible to do anything more deliberate" [334]. Osmond himself invokes the same principle in his attempt to prevent her journey to Gardencourt to the dying Ralph. He reminds her that their marriage was "of our own deliberate making . . . we should accept the consequences of our actions" [366].

But Osmond's argument is dishonest since he knows, as Isabel does not yet, how little the marriage was her act, after all. The effect created by the ellipsis is justified for this reason, also. Though she had believed in "the spontaneity of her own career" [354], she had not chosen but been chosen. "What have you to do with my husband . . . What have you to do with me?" she comes to the point of desperately asking Madame Merle, who replies, "Everything." She realizes, then, "that Mrs. Touchett was right. Madame Merle had married her" [353]. Yet later still, Madame Merle has her own disclosure to make, that Isabel's marriage is not so much this false friend's act as Ralph's. It is Isabel's last epiphany: "He made you a rich woman. He imparted to you that extra lustre which was required to make you a brilliant match. At bottom it's him you've to thank" [381].

Isabel has resisted the coercion of formula by resisting Osmond's desire to obliterate her independent personality. But what (nearly unimaginable) form has that resistance taken? Even this element, insofar as it might represent a struggling Isabel, is more absent than present in the text. The details of her marital unhappiness, the actual incidents, remain, even in retrospective reference, abstract or obscure. His vices appear to her as negatives, just as his virtues once had done—he is a more desolating parody, now, of her own self-definition by not doing. "What does he do to you?" Henrietta asks, and Isabel responds, "He does nothing. But he doesn't like me" [334]. Even her solitary recollections in the famous vigil of chapter 42 are metaphor rather than drama. Osmond has "put the lights out one by one." But what exactly were the "shadows" that emanated from him? "They were not his misdeeds, his turpitudes; she accused him of nothing . . . She knew of no wrong he had done; he was not violent, he was not cruel: she simply believed he hated her" [293]. He had discovered one day that she had "too many ideas" and disliked her for them, while she had discovered in him a "sovereign contempt for every one but some three or four very exalted people whom he envied, and for everything in the world but half a dozen ideas of his own." He pretended indifference but lived for the recognition of society; he was the soul of convention, while she "had pleaded the cause of freedom, of doing as they chose, of not caring for the aspect and denomination of their life" [297]. The remarkable ruminative essay consists almost entirely of summary statements such as these. It has been justly praised—by James himself to begin with—but it must be recognized for what it is—a denial of presentation, a sleight of hand to cover the wide gap of Isabel's marriage, her single action and its aftermath. James claimed for it the virtue of dramatized thought, but as memory it is peculiarly unevocative of specific past action.

Perhaps this ellipsis is an ellipsis of the element of sexual union, the "act" which lies outside the terminus of the conventional marriage-plot. Since Isabel's marriage occurs at the center rather than at the end of the story, we are forced to consider the nature of the relation that has proved so disappointing to her, knowing her already as someone who once asserted that "a woman ought to be able to live to herself, in the absence of exceptional flimsiness, and that it was perfectly possible to be happy without the society of a more or less coarse-minded person of another sex" [46]. James subtly but sufficiently suggests her sexual timidity, especially in the language almost invariably used to describe her responses to Casper. One may guess, on this plane, that her choice of Osmond is partly dictated by the fact that he appeals most to her *ideas*. That she later finds that some of his ideas are "unclean" may reflect a revelation of his sexuality, which she had not anticipated.

But despite the pertinency of these hints it is more important, I think, to see Isabel's sexual history, insofar as it is implied, as representing a more general encounter with experience. Plot itself, it may be said, is describable in sexual terms. The arousal of tension, the achievement of climax, the attainment of pleasure, and the dissolution of desire itself in the subsidence to quiescence—these phrases describe the trajectory of a story. Isabel both desires and fears a story as much as she both desires and fears sexual union; both threaten the pure potentiality of the unaroused personality, which only subsists in itself. It is in this subtle way, I think, that we must at the last explain her rejection, made with such a mixture of response and terror, of Casper. The marriage closure is rejected just as the marriage to Osmond in the center of the novel has been unrealizable. Casper's kiss, the ritual gesture which ends so many novels, is present in all its power on the final page only to reveal its inability to provide an ending to the story of Isabel Archer.

* * *

ROBERT WEISBUCH

Henry James and the Idea of Evil[†]

Henry James needed an imagination of Evil; it was a requirement of his artistic vocation as well as his personal identity. He had a huge ambition not only for his own fiction, but for the novel generally, which in his moment was still an adolescent inhabiting the outskirts of cultural respectability, where film (or "the movies") lived twenty years ago. James worked as a propagandist for the genre, playing a kind of shell game by worrying in his essays or prefaces over various aspects of fictional composition, as though one could simply assume for it the serious stature of lyric, epic, and dramatic poetry. But when in his own work he wanted to connect allusively to these established literary traditions, the problem of Evil became his chief conduit. I want here to examine this process in * * * *The Portrait of a Lady*, to question why Evil so dominates his imagination when the very concept had, by his own estimation, become creaky, suspect, lame.

The greatness of the novel depended for James on subtlety and scope, the fineness of his work that everyone acknowledges, and the breadth, which James-haters miss. For fiction to be serious it had to be subtle, had to capture the essential tone of a moment or render the complexity of an attitude or situation in its subtlest shade. Characters in fiction seem never to have thought, really thought, until James; indeed, James invents interpersonal thinking, as his characters respond with the utmost consequence to each other's verbal and physical nuances to the point where a kind of mystical telepathy without the mysticism gets created. One such sentence in *Portrait of a Lady* reads "Not for an instant should he suspect her of detecting in his proposal of marrying her step-daughter an implication of increased nearness to herself, or of thinking it, on such a betrayal,

† From *The Cambridge Companion to Henry James*, ed. Jonathan Freedman (Cambridge and New York: Cambridge University Press, 1998), pp. 102–105, 112–19. Copyright © 1998 Cambridge University Press. Reprinted with the permission of Cambridge University Press. Page numbers in square brackets are to the New York Edition version of the novel, as printed in this Norton Critical Edition. A discussion of "Daisy Miller" and "The Turn of the Screw" has been cut.

ominous" [307]. I promise—or threaten—to return to that sentence in its surrounding context, but here it exemplifies James's unrepentant stretching of the limits of language and syntax to render a complex situation exactly.

To make this project work, and to connect his finework of wrought intelligence with a human breadth, James required not so much the large social canvas of his Victorian contemporaries and predecessors but the great themes: and the greatest of all, from the earliest epics through Dante's *Inferno* and Milton's *Paradise Lost*, has been provided by the question of Evil. But James also knows not only that he requires this grand theme, but that it is an anachronism. When he brings his heroine in *Portrait* to the realization that her great friend and mentor has sold her like a mere thing into a loveless marriage, Isabel Archer does not simply ask herself whether Madame Merle is evil. Rather, James has her question "whether to this intimate friend of several years the great historical epithet of *wicked* were to be applied." And the epithet is introduced as strikingly second-hand, as if Evil is fustian, unreal: "She knew the idea only by the Bible and other literary works" [354]. This belatedness of Evil, this understanding of it as a matter of texts and letters, ultimately became James's great contribution to the imagination of Evil. It leads James to the strategy of reasserting its importance by questioning it, challenging it actively, not asserting flatly its existence but making it a competitor in a world acknowledged to be skeptical of it.

James's strikingly original strategy, then, is—paradoxically—one of restoration: he renews the consequence of Evil by problematizing its reality. * * * And he gained the freedom to do so because he had recourse not only to the Bible or to "literary works," but to another imaginary of Evil: a New World of Evil. If James freely "picks and chooses" in his allusions to Evil, he does so in a strikingly American context. Those diminishings of Evil we might locate in the British eighteenth and nineteenth centuries— where the grand supernatural Evil that Milton made the subject of his epic became gothicized, parodied, attenuated, or psychologized in fiction and poetry alike—do not happen in the literature of the United States of the same period. In fact, the snobbish disdain that Britain, as a former imperial power, has toward its lost colony adds a postcolonial piquancy to the notion of Evil. When the British argue that Americans have no literature because America lacks a history, writers like Charles Brockden Brown and Hawthorne respond by invoking an American Puritan past with all its emphasis on negativity and evil. The didactic theological ideas of the Puritans will not be accepted by American writers two centuries later, but they will continue to excite their imaginations, and never quite get disowned even when they are transformed into more secular and psychological versions of themselves. And again, in response to an associated British taunt that America lacked a sufficiently complex society to be worthy of literary treatment or even human interest, Americans could argue that the very lack of a historically rich social configuration freed them to think largely about the permanent aspects of the human estate. Emerson proclaimed that every individual "can live all history in his own person," that "all facts of history preexist the mind as laws," and Thoreau saw whole past cultures recapitulated in our momentary moods—"the history which we read is only a fainter memory of events which have happened in our own experience."[1] Freed of the clutter of history and an intricately corrupt social arrangement of classes and experience, these Americans argued, we can contemplate Self, Other, and God in an open field.

Admittedly, Henry James is not about to chase Melville's white whale— aside from his temperamental limits—it is a few very packed American decades too late. Yet, in accepting whole cloth the great theme of British fiction, courtship, and marriage, and its famous arena of domestic inter- personal language, conversation, James never forgoes his own dictum, "it's a complex fate, being an American," and one of its responsibilities is fight- ing a mystified valuation of Europe. At age 21, with an American's pride in epistemological enterprise, he writes, "Mr. Dickens is a great observer and a great humorist, but nothing of a philosopher," and much later he will relegate George Eliot to the occupation of a historian and Anthony Trollope to that of an undisciplined windbag.[2] It is by reinvoking mystery and metaphysics that James stakes out his postcolonial claim as an Amer- ican writer: the great issue of Evil, the one that fixed the gaze of Dante and Milton, would provide the American tone in the British fictional ter- ritory James occupies.

One more problem faces this project, however: the new American tra- dition in literature also provides James with his opposition, a great mind that did not contain the notion of Evil. "Our young people are diseased with the theological problems of original sin, origin of evil, predestina- tion and the like," wrote Ralph Waldo Emerson. "They never presented a practical difficulty to any man,—never darkened across any man's road who did not go out of his way to seek them. They are the soul's mumps and measles, and whooping coughs."[3] Sometimes Emerson can sound the more orthodox note of Evil as "merely privative, not absolute; . . . like cold which is the privation of heat."[4] Elsewhere, more rebelliously proclaim- ing, "I unsettle all things," "no evil is pure, nor hell itself without its extreme satisfactions,"[5] James puts on a face of astonishment in relation to these notions in his essays and letters, where he famously speaks of Emerson's "ripe unconsciousness of evil."[6] In his fiction, he creates a whit- tled, more naive version of that figure, where he serves as a model for the innocent Americans who visit Europe. In the passage I cited above, he attributes Emerson's naiveté to the "plain, God-fearing, practical society which surrounded him," and wonders at the fact that Emerson thrice jour- neyed to Europe, "a more complicated world," without changing his "spirit, his moral taste, as it were [, which] abode always within the undec- orated walls of his youth. There he could dwell with that ripe uncon- sciousness." Characters like Isabel Archer and Daisy Miller were versions

1. Ralph Waldo Emerson, *Collected Works*, Centenary Edition, ed. Edward Waldo Emerson (Bos- ton and New York: Houghton Mifflin, 1903–4), Vol. 2, pp. 6, 3; Thoreau, *A Week on the Con- cord and Merrimack Rivers* (Boston: Houghton Mifflin, 1961), p. 323.
2. Quoted in Cornelia P. Kelley, *The Early Development of Henry James* (Urbana: University of Illinois Press, 1930), p. 53.
3. "Spiritual Laws," in *The Portable Emerson*, revised ed., ed. Carl Bode in collaboration with Malcolm Bradbury (New York: Viking Penguin, 1981), p. 199.
4. "The Divinity School Address," in *The Portable Emerson*, p. 75.
5. "Circles," in *The Portable Emerson*, p. 238.
6. Review of *A Memoir of Ralph Waldo Emerson*, in *The Critical Muse: Selected Literary Criticism*, ed. Roger Gard (London: Penguin, 1987), p. 213.

of Emerson on the move, making the same journey from the same beginning place of ideas that does not include Evil; and each of them is tested by whether they can grow beyond their youths as Emerson cannot. But, to complete the dilemma, Emerson must also be retained, or at least part of him: staying Emerson may lead to disaster, but losing him, as expatriates who seek to shed their American identities lose him, means losing one's soul and perpetrating "the dark, the foul, the base" that James's Emerson did not even acknowledge to exist (Gard, p. 227).

Now for the fun of seeing what James can do with his clunky Satanic subject. We know that James needs to doubt the wicked even as he insists on its plausibility, that he must establish some allusive networks that relate spiritual absolutes to social living while not allowing them to encourage a reductive escape from thinking of people in their complexities and not as mere representations of a single idea. We know that he is going to make his characters travel for that expansion of intelligence that eluded Emerson and that they must grow beyond but not out of who they have been. But we do not know yet, until we enter the fabric of the fiction, how terrible it can be.

* * *

Daisy Miller's late-night conversings with men scandalize Rome, or at least the false Rome of the American expatriates. When Isabel Archer considers remaining in conversation with a man after other members of the household have retired, her aunt warns her against "taking what seems to me too much liberty." Isabel, thanking her, insists that she always wants to know the conventions of "things one shouldn't do." Mrs. Touchett responds, "So as to do them?" and Isabel, shooting ahead of Daisy, replies, "So as to choose" [56]. Like Daisy Miller and like Christopher Newman in *The American*, Isabel Archer is an Emerson on the road, a young woman who reads German Idealist philosophy in the locked office at Albany that occludes a view of the street; an overly theoretic, though wonderfully fresh and earnest self-realizer. She is not merely a typical American—in this novel Henrietta Stackpole, a flattened version of Margaret Fuller in her role as a correspondent for the *New York Herald*, full of prefabricated attitudes toward Europe and immune to growth, exists to be that. But the novel's title, *The Portrait of a Lady*, implies by the word "Lady" an achieved maturity, the goal that James held for an America in need of cultural growing-up, just as a "portrait" suggests a cultural maturity in acknowledging the world of art. Unlike Daisy Miller Isabel Archer is booked to grow up, and on that development James stakes his epic attempt to write a novel that will be a great work of art.

It is probably just a coincidence that the initials of the main words in the title of James's novel are those of Milton's epic *Paradise Lost*, but one is tempted to call it an accident made in Heaven, for Milton's epic is very much the basis for James's attempt. Eventually we will examine the multitude of allusions and their meanings, but here it is enough to say that this is a novel of *felix culpa*, the fortunate fall, much like the Genesis story and even more like Milton's rewriting of it. But just as in Milton's poem, everything is pointed toward a defining of freedom. The novel certainly concerns the unexpectedly far-reaching consequences of a character's inadequacies of perception, and in that it is wholly reminiscent of ["Daisy Miller"] and ["The Turn of the screen"]. But here alone we have a full development of necessity and freedom, circumstance and free will, in which each, bewilderingly, may take on the appearance of the other. And here alone, perhaps, until James's very last works will this freedom be achieved, precisely because a character will learn the deep comprehension of necessity.

That necessity is insisted upon in the first three words of the novel—"Under certain circumstances"—which acknowledge the reality of a world not created by the self but independent and sometimes governing. And we are introduced to the Edenic Gardencourt before we are introduced to Isabel for the plain reason that England and Europe exist, individually and culturally, before the American girl does; it is the world that by its priority of time—the world into which she and America are born—becomes her circumstance, hard lesson as it is to an Emersonian young woman. But this part of the preordained is indeed lovely, as the very name Gardencourt implies the best merging of ordered nature and noble civilization; and, as two of the three figures in this "peculiarly English picture I have attempted to sketch" [15] are American—though Americans who retain their national identities while acclimating wonderfully to their British surroundings—Gardencourt suggests the best merging of England and America. But it is a declining, drowsy Eden. It is a lovely dusk, but night will fall. Mr. Touchett is dying, his son Ralph is deathly ill as well and living under a sure sentence of premature death, and their visitor the handsome Lord Warburton is a member of a British aristocracy that no longer knows what to do with itself. (Later Warburton will be posed in Rome standing on a cracked pavement by the portrait of "The Dying Gladiator.") The moment Isabel enters, the dog barks, she scoops it up, and the place begins to move. That is why the two younger men will fall in love with her and the older one will dower her: she renews the vitality of this fatigued Eden. But for Isabel herself, once she struggles to an understanding of Gardencourt's high values, she will have to transform the lost place into an aspect of her spirit and have it inform her actions in a world where even civilized Edens are always being lost. For James, the new American frontier is eastward, reintegrating the Old World; but what happens to Gardencourt is what happens to the frontier of writers like Twain. It remains available at all only if it is internalized, for it is going, going, gone.

As for Isabel, within moments her rejoinder to learning the identity of Lord Warburton—"Oh, I hoped there would be a lord; it's just like a novel!" [23]—puts her in a league with Jane Austen's Catherine Morland and the entire tradition of heroines in the British realistic novel, all of them remarkable but self-deluded, in need of an encounter with the real. The carefully delineated linear time scheme—broken only, if brilliantly, by a gap of several years in the middle of the book, during which all is changed utterly for Isabel—and the tone of the patience-demanding narrator create a link to the British tradition as well. But Elizabeth Bennet and Dorothea Brooke never had to deal with anyone like Gilbert Osmond or Madame Merle. They never, that is, had to deal with that wickedness we defined earlier as personified Evil that is the special realm of American romance. But it is most Osmond who moves the novel's self-definition away from England into the mid-Atlantic.

To say that Osmond is James's personification of aspects of Evil is to put it with too much cold logic; Osmond is the name for what James hates. Some commentators have associated Osmond and Isabel's wonderful cousin Ralph as art-substituting-for-life ghouls, but, in fact, it is the distinction between them that makes Osmond a ghoul indeed and Ralph an avatar for James himself. At one point Isabel compares the two. For both, "life was a matter of connoisseurship," but she makes the distinction that "in Ralph it was an anomaly, a kind of humorous excrescence, whereas in Mr. Osmond it was the keynote and everything was in harmony with it" [184]. This is almost true—not everything in Osmond's life will turn out to be in harmony with a principle of beauty—and yet it is awful, because Isabel thinks the distinction is to Osmond's advantage. Ralph compares Isabel's arrival to receiving "a Titian by post, to hang on my wall," but he quickly notes that the young woman's "passionate force" is "finer than the finest work of art—than a Greek bas-relief, than a great Titian, than a Gothic cathedral" [53]. Art is to serve life, which surpasses it. Osmond's desire, "to make one's life a work of art," is an aestheticism to make the skin crawl. If Osmond's duplicitous life—he has had an affair while married, has advertised the child as his dead wife's, marries Isabel for her money and because she turns down the proposal of an English lord, and so on—fulfills his aim, that is only because (and this is James's great laugh) his taste in art is itself poor. In the words of the young man in love with Osmond's daughter, Ned Rosier—another, rosier, aesthete, physically healthier than Ralph and morally healthier than Osmond—his taste is atrocious.

And Isabel falls in love with him. And then, even after she learns all about his evil, she returns to him. This is how the novel is structured. In both cases, Isabel will make a decision that will surprise and disappoint any reader of spirit. This is James's daring, to have Isabel choose in a way that might appear wholly at odds with our sense of her, but which in each case, on closer examination, is completely, even lavishly, prepared for by what James has told us of her. And that is the point, the demand for closer examination. It is what is required of Isabel within the novel and of us without, as the narrator abjures us not to judge too quickly and then almost punishes us by our surprise at Isabel's two major decisions. James makes us aware of the barbarisms of perceptions to which we as well as Isabel are prone—the same doubling of character and reader's predicament we found in the tales, an epistemological problem made as warm as life's heartbeat.

For when we look back to comprehend Isabel's choice, we learn her character as if for the first time. The motives are shockingly multiple. "Isabel had in the depths of her nature an . . . unquenchable desire to please" [34]; Osmond, with his judgmental reserve, encourages this desire in Isabel as her other suitors, falling over themselves, have not. Osmond appears wonderfully unconditioned—as Merle describes him, "No career, no name, no position, no fortune, no past, no future, no anything" [141], a string of negatives that reminds one of Emerson's definition of evil as "merely privative." But Madame Merle, pimping toward the marriage she desires, desiring it after all for the good of her daughter and her lover, counts rightly upon Isabel's fear of constriction. And she is also playing upon another of Isabel's facets, her "certain nobleness of imagination which rendered her a good many services and played her a great many tricks" [45], in Osmond and in Europe on her tour, "seeing often in the things she looked at a great deal more than was there, and yet not seeing many of the items enumerated in her Murray." Thus, when she hears Osmond exulting over an art find, "her imagination supplied the human element which she was sure had not been wanting" [187]. Yet, even without her mixture of imaginative generosity, careless perception, and cultural insecurity, Isabel would find Osmond's "studies, my willful resignation" attractive, as confirming her own decisions against marriage to Goodwood or Warburton. She can give herself completely, yet safely, to this paragon of the Nothing.

Isabel's final choice, to return to her marriage, is her triumph, as this choice to marry in the first place is her utter defeat; and that intelligent readers wish to deny this simply underscores the difficult logic of any fortunate fall. If, then, Isabel had been led by that "deepest thing" of giving herself completely, now "Deep in her soul—deeper than any appetite for renunciation—was the sense that life would be her business for a long time to come" [46]. The new formulation of the deep thing is a huge advance, no longer self-referential, but acknowledging a world in which the self participates. Many American novels end with a new quest just defined, and Isabel's notion of life "business" to transact suggests that this is another such one. Her decision, then, has nothing to do with resignation nor with duty. She returns not at all to save Osmond; indeed, she could ruin him, given her knowledge. Though she never will do that and he may never even know that she could, the power in this marriage has shifted. Nor does she return simply to save her stepdaughter, though Pansy does have something to do with it. Isabel instead follows the words of Osmond, redeeming them from his emptiness, giving them meaning for the first and only time: "I think we should accept the consequences of our actions, that what I value most in life is the honour of a thing," says the most dishonorable of men [366].

James is daring here in giving his villain something of the truth to state. It is not a matter of honor but of acknowledging the self, albeit a self understood, with Hawthorne and against Emerson, as a result of accumulated experience. Isabel must return to Osmond, as Hawthorne's Hester finally must return to the Boston that victimized her, to affirm her identity. This is where her life has taken place, and anywhere else would mark not a fresh start but a dissolution. If she is to see her earlier decision to marry Osmond as solely the result of the deceptions of others—and she has reason to do so—then she defines herself as Osmond's creature indeed. If she instead affirms that she was complicit in this terrible decision, that confession allows her to retain a sense of her earlier choice as free. By returning to Osmond, Isabel thus literally defeats his freedom-killing powers and affirms herself, then and now.

And with this return come a cluster of Miltonic allusions, turned on themselves. "The world lay before her—she could do whatever she chose" and she lost her way, "almost on purpose, in order to get more sensations" [224]. Now, after Goodwood's white-lightning kiss (which does not, as the "frigid" theory argues, frighten her back to Osmond—rather this "act of possession" reminds her that she is right to desire a self-determining life), Isabel discovers "a very straight path" [402], home to her struggle, her "business," her life. Earlier, a dismal Isabel had envied Ralph his dying and wished "to cease utterly," seeing death as "sweet as the vision of a cool bath in a marble tank, in a darkened chamber, in a hot land" [382], while Goodwood's passion had made her see a train of images akin to "those wrecked and under water . . . before they sink," dying in the sense of giving control of her life to her American suitor. Such a return to her initial state, to the America of her emigration, would be a return to a false Eden now, a regressive doubling, a death. Instead Isabel chooses to make her world.

This choice thereby *rewrites* the Miltonic epic it invokes, and it gains expanding resonance by James's dealings with this equally allusive progenitor. The echoes occur on almost every page. Gardencourt is a civilized Eden and Isabel's "nature had, in her conceit, a certain garden-like quality." But Isabel is a prideful Eve, "very liable," the narrator playfully admits, "to the sin of self-esteem" [44]; and like Eve, she bears a "general disposition to elude any obligation to take a restricted view" [82]. She wishes to look upon "the cup of experience" without touching it [110]. Mr. Touchett, with his "unlimited means," is something of a god with whom Ralph as a sort of Christ intervenes on behalf of Isabel, who in this sense plays the role of humanity. In her confusion, Isabel mistakes this god and his free gift of money (which is tantamount to free will) for Satan, naming him "the beneficent author of infinite woe" [294], like Quint to the Governess.[7] And Ralph, like Christ, heals Isabel by his dying.

Osmond, of course, takes the money Mr. Touchett and Ralph had provided for Isabel—just as Satan takes the free will provided for humankind by God and Christ. Goodwood says Osmond possesses "a kind of demonic imagination" [347]. Like Satan, he corrupts the Church, not only by his fantasy of becoming pope (surely he would take the name Innocent), but more by sending Pansy to a convent, converting it to a prison. "His egotism lay hidden like a serpent in a bank of flowers" [296] and, like Satan, he is a disappointed, envious revenger. He has, as his faithful assistant Merle says, enacted his revenge on Isabel, who mistook the devil for an instrument for expanding freedom: "Instead of leading to the high places of happiness, . . . it led rather downward and earthward, into realms of restriction and depression where the sound of other lives, easier and freer, was heard from above, and where it served to deepen the feeling of failure" [292–93]. Life with Osmond is Hell.

Ashamed and with "infinite dismay," Isabel cannot confess her unhappiness to Ralph, much as "he made her feel the good of the world." She hides her reality from him as Adam and Eve, fallen, hide from the Angel, but then "women find their religion sometimes in strange exercises" [299]. But this antireligion gives way: In "a tone of far-reaching, infinite sadness" (the counter to her "infinite dismay" earlier), Isabel must visit the dying Ralph. He "spoke at last—on the evening of the third day" [391] recalling the Resurrection. And Ralph, who earlier, in recognizing Isabel's hidden misery, "feels as if I had fallen myself," releases Isabel's sorrow in a theologically tinged emotion: "'Oh my brother!' she cried with a movement of still deeper prostration" as Ralph tells her that "if you've been hated, you've also been loved. Ah but, Isabel—*adored!*" [394]. Her confession that she has suffered wins her, the next morning, a witnessing of the ghost of

7. In "The Turn of the Screw" [*Editor*].

Gardencourt, a holy rather than a gothic ghost as Ralph's spirit and the suffering-achieved higher innocence of a ruined but persisting Gardencourt become hers.

Yet, in that final interview, which is one of the greatest scenes in literature, Ralph tells Isabel never to wish for death. "Dear Isabel, life is better; for in life there's love. Death is good—but there's no love" [392]. This is not a particularly Miltonic view; and, in fact, James employs all of the Miltonic allusions so tellingly yet without urging us to obey their spirit entirely. Indeed, in the passage I noted in the first part of this essay, where Isabel considers whether Madame Merle is evil, "wicked," James pins Isabel's salvation on refusing that mode of understanding. Of course, Merle requires that epithet if that is to be our mode of understanding: Merle, who cannot shed tears, who is beyond redemption, who is in Ralph's description "the great round world itself," constitutes with Osmond the world in their false appearings, the flesh in their illicit relations, the devil in their forfeiture of the free will of others. But that is not where Isabel's thought takes her, even as she is recognizing Merle's calumny for the first time. The long paragraph that begins with Isabel questioning whether the great historical epithet fits, ends with Isabel imagining how Osmond must be punishing Merle for procuring him a marriage so little to his liking: "What must be his feelings to-day in regard to his too-zealous benefactress, and what expression must they have found on the part of such a master of irony?" Even this vision recalls Milton's Satan, in his hateful encounter with his antifamily of Sin and Death; and yet Isabel's thoughts proceed to a far more lovely secular vale. James writes, "It is a singular, but a characteristic, fact that before Isabel returned from her silent drive she had broken its silence by the soft exclamation: 'Poor, poor Madame Merle'" [355].

The biblical and Miltonic lexicon is insufficiently flexible, too impoverishing of a full and empathizing consciousness, a complete recognition of self and other, which is Jamesian salvation. And even earlier, once Isabel is alerted to how deep in Hell she lives by Osmond's plea to her to marry off Pansy to Warburton, we see in action that same imagination that will save Isabel. You will recall that nearly impossible sentence that I mentioned toward the beginning of this essay. It occurs when Isabel is speaking with Warburton, and she is hoping to warn him that his desire for Pansy is neither really healthy nor legitimate, that it is, in fact, a substitute for his feelings for Isabel and thus not very kind in regard to Pansy. But what we read is, "Not for an instant should he suspect her of detecting in his proposal of marrying her step-daughter an implication of increased nearness to herself, or of thinking it, on such a betrayal, ominous." That is, she discovers a way to say to him by an undertone, a glance, an air, "I trust you, so do look to your motives and I give you perfect freedom to do as you will knowing you will do rightly." Meanwhile she spares him all the pain of a direct confrontation. Asked by Osmond to manipulate crudely, as do he and Merle, Isabel employs a tender half-manipulation, not to enslave Warburton as Osmond would do, nor to brand or moralize upon him as Milton might, but to free him into his best self, his generously thinking self. And Isabel accomplishes this by her own act of generous and intensely subtle thinking, thinking that is beautiful and self-expelling. This is Jamesian Good.

Isabel is no goody. She never really accepts the Countess Gemini's suggestion to be a little wicked and take revenge, but she does exult in noting to Osmond, "How much you must want to make sure of him!" [325] in regard to Warburton; a "horrible delight" precedes for a moment her exclamation of pity for Merle, and Isabel does say enough to banish Merle back to her native, and hated, Brooklyn. Yet Isabel really does not take the real revenge that a moral condemnation would bring. She chooses, with her eyes painfully open, not to live in a world of moral absolutes or to act upon others as if moral epithets could sum them. It is not so much that such a revenge would make her like her enemies, always the paradox in revenge, but that it would be based on a reduction of experience that would rob the self. She accepts the challenge of excruciatingly careful and self-aware perception that is James's answer in this undoctrinaire time for ridding our new freedom of the horror it holds for those who * * * cannot substitute this rigor of the heart's intelligence for imposed dogma. The world is now truly all before Isabel and all before us, we who have been shorn of the comforting simplifications, and who must live now by our wits and by our love.

TESSA HADLEY

'Just you wait!': Reflections on the Last Chapters of *The Portrait of a Lady*†

Critics (and presumably readers) have been tripping up on and debating the ending of *The Portrait of a Lady* since the novel first appeared in 1881; in those early days with unsophisticated perplexity and often impatience. Even the very sympathetic review by James's friend W. D. Howells in *Century* balks at James's leaving us 'to our own conjectures in regard to the fate of the people in whom he has interested us' before submitting to swallowing his treatment meekly: 'We must agree, then, to take what seems a fragment instead of a whole, and to find, when we can, a name for this new kind in fiction' [467].

In *The Portrait* James has constructed his *impasse*: the spirited Isabel in an impossible marriage, having made what feels like a terminal rupture in disobeying her husband and coming to England to be with her dying cousin, tempted momentarily by the renewed importunity of Caspar Goodwood. But he does not seem to have left us all the instructions for how we get out of it. Does Isabel have to return to her hated husband and his punishments for her defection ('It will not be the scene of a moment; it will be a scene of the rest of my life', [385])? What other possible futures does the novel allow us to envisage for her? *Is* Caspar a solution? These speculations sound very like Isabel's own, in her railway

† From *Henry James and the Imagination of Pleasure* (Cambridge and New York: Cambridge University Press, 2002), pp. 23–39, 182–84. Copyright © 2002 Tessa Hadley. Reprinted with the permission of Cambridge University Press. The argument in this essay depends on examining the exact terms with which James first described Isabel's situation, therefore page references incorporated in the text are of two kinds. Those indicated by the letter L are to the 1882 text of the novel as included in *Henry James: Novels, 1882–1886* (New York: Library of America, 1985). Those without prefix and in square brackets are to the New York Edition text of the novel, or to other materials, as printed in this Norton Critical Edition. Notes have been renumbered.

carriage crossing Europe on her way to Ralph (although she has not calculated yet on Caspar's offer), and she too feels that the 'middle years', the years ahead, the immediate question of what she will *do*, are wrapped from her in a 'grey curtain', she only has a 'mutilated glimpse' of any future (382–83).

These days we are more sophisticatedly perplexed. The problem is not simply one of James 'frustrating the reader's curiosity' about a handful of 'characters'.[1] As readers—or at least as critics—we are irreversibly committed to the idea that a serious novel will have moved beyond '"objectively realistic representation" to a stage of reading the significations that lie behind or within reality'.[2] What James means us to understand Isabel might do at the end of his novel *matters*, because James is elaborating a crucial moment in the development of that theme of marriage and adultery which, it has been argued, is one of the fundamentals to the whole novel 'project', from the beginnings of the theme in *La Nouvelle Héloise*, *Elective Affinities*, and so on.[3]

One of the energies driving the nineteenth-century development of the novel is that head of steam built up by the contradiction between the form's tendency on the one hand towards a resolution in adaptation to social forms and norms (its inbuilt drive, for example, towards happy endings in marriages); and on the other hand, its narratives rooted in a subjective individualism that cannot always square with resolution, that cannot but register individual reluctance, resistance, *differentness*, and raise unanswerable protests against the 'contract'. In Tony Tanner's elegant formulation, it is the 'tension between law and sympathy which holds the great bourgeois novel together'.[4] The *impasse* James has engineered at the end of *The Portrait of a Lady*, between submission to the form of marriage and commitment to the individual pursuit of happiness and freedom, is a place the English-language novel has visited numerous times already by 1881.

The 'solutions', or resolutions, for Dorothea Casaubon and Gwendolen Grandcourt (and for that matter for Jane Eyre) come from offstage, in the form of convenient demises; but we know already from something in the texture of *The Portrait of a Lady*—partly to do with just how very self-consciously it inscribes itself into that tradition of novels structured around strained marriage contracts—that James is pressing the development of the tradition to a new point where that kind of formal manipulation will not answer. An authorial rescue (Osmond falling out of a small high window at the Palazzo Roccanera?) would intrude here like an outmoded piece of theatre.

James introduces the possibility of another way out of the *impasse*—also traditional, even if traditionally (in the English-language novel) outlawed—in the shape of Caspar Goodwood offering himself in defiance of all convention and all contract. The offer opens up under Isabel's feet—abyss, escape—but in her first panicking recognition of it she flies, away from

---

1. November 1882. In *Henry James: The Critical Heritage*, ed. Roger Gard (London: Routledge and Kegan Paul, 1968), pp. 126–34. [From an unsigned review, *Saturday Review*, December 1881—*Editor*.]
2. I have borrowed this formulation from J. M. Coetzee, in *White Writing: On the Culture of Letters in South Africa* (New Haven: Yale University Press, 1988), p. 113.
3. Notably of course in Tony Tanner's *Adultery in the Novel: Contract and Transgression* (Baltimore: Johns Hopkins University Press, 1979).
4. Tanner, *Adultery in the Novel*, p. 14.

the lover and back to the security of the lighted house. Has James proposed the third ingredient of the classic adulterous triangle—the 'other man'—only in order to eliminate him from the equation? It is difficult now to read the 1881 ending of the novel as if we did not know the New York Edition revisions, but originally it finished with Henrietta's injunction to Caspar:

> "Look here, Mr Goodwood," she said; "just you wait!"
> On which he looked up at her. (L800).

Taking that by itself, it does not seem ridiculous to interpret it as a reviewer in the *Spectator* did in 1881, relishingly appalled at what he calls James's 'pure agnosticism':

> never before has he closed a novel by setting up so cynical a sign-post into the abyss, as he sets up at the close of this book. He ends his *Portrait of a Lady*, if we do not wholly misinterpret the rather covert, not to say almost cowardly, hints of his last page, by calmly indicating that this ideal lady of his, whose belief in purity has done so much to alienate her from her husband, in that it had made him smart under her contempt for his estimates of the world, saw a 'straight path' to a liaison with her rejected lover. [450]

Most contemporary reviewers, after some puzzled hesitation, saw that Isabel's 'straight path' was away from and not into the arms of Caspar Goodwood, but their hesitation was understandable. Without the New York Edition underscoring, Henrietta's injunction and Caspar's look are deeply equivocal: *uninterpretable*, surely? How could we read them and *be sure* Caspar has nothing to hope for? Although when James added his final sentence in 1905[5] (the year he worked on the revisions for the New York Edition) he may have imagined he was making obvious what insensitive readers had only too densely missed, he was in fact tipping into definiteness a 'close' which, intriguingly, had closed nothing, had hovered on the brink of a future which it did not offer to make out any better than Isabel could herself in her 'mutilated glimpse'. In the 1881 edition Isabel is sent back to Rome, but we only have an unclear idea as to *what for*, and what could happen next: we can only piece together into a guess all the fragments of Isabel's own and her friends' speculation. In the New York Edition at least we are made sure that what could happen next cannot be Caspar:

> "Look here, Mr Goodwood," she said; "just you wait!"
> On which he looked up at her—but only to guess, from her face, with a revulsion, that she simply meant he was young. She stood shining at him with that cheap comfort, and it added, on the spot, thirty years to his life. She walked him away with her, however, as if she had given him now the key to patience. [403]

It makes for a neatly ironic measure of cultural shift that the language used in the *Spectator* to deplore James's 'agnosticism'—'the tendency of life, he holds, is to result in a general failure of the moral and spiritual hopes it raises'—sounds remarkably like a strain of late twentieth-century disapproval of James's conclusion to *The Portrait*. Only where the *Spectator* reviewer upbraided James for giving Isabel to her lover we are now

---

5. Actually 1906 [*Editor*].

outraged (with some better justification perhaps) that he seems to be giving her back to her husband. It is of course no mere accident of narrative that it is *Rome* Isabel returns to. The city cannot help standing for the weight of past empire and the constraints of tradition, for 'law' against 'sympathy'; although James is too complex a writer to labour this value one-sidedly, and the novel is rich with the consolations as well as the constraints for Isabel of Rome's and Europe's pastness. (When she sits looking from St John Lateran across the Campagna, she registers the 'endurance' as well as the 'splendid sadness' of the old ruins: 'she leaned her weariness upon things that had crumbled for centuries and yet still were upright', [353].) The argument, though, that the ending of *The Portrait of a Lady* represents a willed conservatism on James's part, a sort of resistance in the spirit but submission to the letter of the law, needs to be met; and is seminal to an interpretation of James's attitude to pleasure and to the proprieties in his later novels.[6]

Before we can justly decide what order of gesture James's is at the end of *The Portrait of a Lady*, and whether he is cutting away at a stroke all the equivocation of the second half of the novel in a resort to a transcendent and absolute value—'the traditionary decencies and sanctities of marriage' (L667)—we need to penetrate further back, to see how that equivocation—that *impasse*—is constructed in the first place. Significantly, most interpretations of the ending as a conservative return of Isabel to her husband (whether sympathetic or unsympathetic to James's gesture) depend upon a reading in which James has constructed Isabel as flawed; as committing, out of hubris or lack of self-knowledge, some fatal punishable error, or exhibiting—the psychoanalytic sin—some 'inner damage'. In other words, the logic of the conservative ending is perceived as being that if James feels justified in punishing her, he must have had her do something to be punished for (even if he / we perceive her punishment as tragic).

This is the retributive model of fictional structure. Interestingly, from the evidence of contemporary reviews of *The Portrait*, literary criticism of our 'agnostic' twenty-first century is more prone to the retributive model than James's contemporary and relatively unsophisticated reader. The reader in 1881 might require Isabel to be punished, certainly, if she reneged on her marriage; but he (occasionally she) does not require it because Isabel has 'an inability to extend her imagination beyond the superficial, the conventional' or because she 'refuses to let the "light" of her own sexuality shine'.[7] Here and there in 1881 (the American reviewers like her—and believe in her—more often than the English reviewers) she gets a most sympathetic reading:

6. As Alfred Habegger puts it: 'The freedom that interests James is the internal kind, where the manacles do not get taken off the hands but the spirit—somehow—spreads its wings'. *Henry James and the 'Woman Business'* (Cambridge University Press, 1989), p. 180.
7. Fred Kaplan, *Henry James: The Imagination of Genius* (London: Hodder and Stoughton, 1992), p. 239; Bonnie L. Heron, 'Substantive Sexuality, Henry James constructs Isabel Archer as a Complete Woman in his Revised Version of Portrait of a Lady', *Henry James Review* 16.2 (1995), 139. F.R. Leavis seems to think James does not punish Isabel *enough*: 'that she shouldn't be led by their unanimity to question her own valuation convicts her of a notable lack of sense, not to say extremely unintelligent obstinacy . . . but James doesn't let us suppose that he shares this view'. *The Great Tradition* (London: Chatto and Windus, 1948), p. 127.

The fine purpose of her freedom, the resolution with which she seeks to be the maker of her destiny, the subtle weakness into which all this betrays her, the apparent helplessness of her ultimate position, and the conjectured escape only through patient forbearance—what are these, if not attributes of womanly life expended under current conditions?[8]

The open-endedness of this reading—its absence of fictional determinism—surely approximates more closely to the experience of reading the character than any punitive closed system. 'Under current conditions'—with the sharpness of contemporaneity—the woman struggling between her personal unhappiness and her ideal of loyalty in marriage evoked, not astonished psychopathology (there must be something the matter), but (at best) tact and respect.

Rather than having worked from the idea of a closed, predetermined psychology, James has in fact taken the risk in *Portrait of a Lady* of inhabiting a psychology in flux, still in formation, full of the potential for surprises. Searching through the treatment of Isabel's advancing disenchantment to discover what she has it in her to do in her *impasse*, what we come away with is an Isabel whose consciousness and experience are not single and unified but made up of bewilderingly contradictory elements; intuitions and ideals, fragments learned and instinctual, obstinacies and vanities and self-doubt. She convinces herself, and us, both that she cannot co-exist with Osmond and that she cannot leave him. She literally voices both possibilities, gives in the words that visit her brooding reflections *both* values their weight and power: the 'traditionary decencies and sanctities of marriage' (L667), 'the violence there would be in going when Osmond wished her to remain' (L748), as well as 'the rapid approach of a day when she should have to take back something that she had solemnly given' (L667) and her worry that she does not know 'what great unhappiness might bring me to' (L694).

As well as what Isabel consciously reflects on, James gives us in tangible fact the deep instinctual resistance of her spirit to Osmond that goes on at a level below consciousness, in the comedy of how helplessly, provokingly defiant she is with him even as she believes herself most to be conforming to the letter of his law. When he tells her to sit on the sofa she chooses the chair. How fiercely, staunchly, she resists him in argument (compared, say, to Dorothea with Casaubon): 'There is a thing that would be worth my hearing—to know in the plainest words of what it is you accuse me' (L688). And how *adequate* to him, intellectually, verbally, her defiance is (compared, say, to Gwendolen's): 'I don't think that on the whole you are disappointed. You have had another opportunity to try and bewilder me' (L689). She cannot help (James knows uncannily the operations of married conflict) the very punctiliousness of her obedience becoming a twisted critique of what he commandeers her obedience for.

Incidentally, there is some comedy, too, in Isabel's believing she keeps the secret of her unhappiness so effectively. She proclaims it in fact at every pore, surely, for anyone attuned to her (for example when she replies

8. H. E. Scudder, from an unsigned review, *Atlantic* 49 (1882). In Gard (ed.), *Critical Heritage*, pp. 126–30.

to Lord Warburton's remarking her husband must be very clever that he 'has a genius for upholstery' [266]): not because she wants to be pitied, or even because she wants them to know, but simply because she does not have the faculty of pretence.

Osmond's response to his wife's galling rectitude-with-reservation is not to dissimulate the inequity of his conventional, obligating advantage over her ('he was her appointed and inscribed master', [317]) but simply to invoke it. (Again, uncanny insight into that spiralling married refusal of one another's terms of reference: if she accuses him of being tyrannous, he'll answer with exaggerated tyranny.) Isabel in the subtlety of her psychological flux, in which conventional obligations have long been entangled with the filmy stuff of an intuitive and personal value-system, has come up against the brute archaic power-fact still, for all its different dressing up, inherent in nineteenth-century marriage. It is no mere incidental joke that the Countess, after Isabel tells her Osmond has forbidden her to travel to England, says, 'when I want to make a journey my husband simply tells me I can have no money!' (L747). What is someone made of subtler stuff to *do* with brute fact?

It is the nature of the irony that plays around the portrait of Isabel which is at issue in deciding how retributive or open-ended James's 'solution' is, and what his attitude is, finally, to her 'formlessness', her psychology in flux. In the later dialogically structured novels James dispenses with an omniscient narrator capable of commenting, for example, that Isabel 'was probably very liable to the sin of self-esteem' (L241), or that she *flattered herself* that she had gathered a rich experience' (L519). Here in *The Portrait of a Lady* he is still employing that conventional apparatus of discursive commentary which it is easy to interpret as some kind of directional inscription, or 'last word', on the primary illusionistic fabric of the novel. Yet when James informs us from his superior vantage that Isabel has 'an unquenchable desire to think well of herself' (L241) that trajectory of comprehension could hardly produce the illusion of life by itself: the commentary has to be carried into conviction on the back of a wave of other 'experiences' of Isabel—her talk, her situation, her appearance, her adventures, and, by the second half of the novel, her *own* insistent self-commentating narrative and analysis which almost replaces the intrusive authorial one. The illusion, finally, overspills the circumscription; an explicit commentary can be contained within a novel which is by no means circumscribed by that commentary.

Alfred Habegger suggests that the 'pattern' for Isabel's story comes from James's ironic reading of contemporary American women novelists: in numerous early reviews for *The Nation*, *The North American Review* and others James expressed his exasperation with so many 'middle-aged lovers' who spent their time 'breaking the hearts and wills of demure little schoolgirls', those same schoolgirls who had most passionately professed desires for freedom and self-sufficiency. It seems very plausible that James should have made this anomaly—a much-reiterated high value on personal freedom going along with a profound unacknowledged desire to submit to a suspiciously paternal-seeming master—a hidden ingredient in the psychological baggage of an Isabel formed, after all, in the same America as Anne Moncure Crane and Elizabeth Stoddard (the novelists Habegger

makes reference to). No doubt it is closely tied up with Isabel's 'unquenchable desire to please' (L224) and her 'infinite hope that she should never
do anything wrong' (L241); and it is probably connected too with one very
characteristic movement of Isabel's thought, out of complacency and into
a painful and hurriedly repressed self-doubt. It happens, for example, just
after she has refused Lord Warburton:

> Who was she, what was she, that she should hold herself superior?
> What view of life, what design upon fate, what conception of happi-
> ness, had she, that pretended to be larger than this large occasion? . . .
> she was wondering whether she was not a cold, hard girl; and when
> at last she got up and rather quickly went back to the house, it was
> because, as she had said to Lord Warburton, she was really fright-
> ened at herself. (L304–05)

That fear at herself is reiterated throughout the novel, particularly in the
last sections as she contemplates, having no idea what she will do next, the
crisis in her marriage: 'I am afraid . . . Afraid of myself! If I were afraid of
my husband, that would simply be my duty. That is what women are
expected to be' (L709); and, 'constantly present to her mind were all the
traditional decencies and sanctities of marriage. The idea of violating
them filled her with shame as well as dread' (L667). 'Marriage meant that in
such a case as this, when one had to choose, one chose as a matter of course
for one's husband. "I am afraid—yes, I am afraid," she said to herself' (L748).

   These are all James's representations, no doubt, of the operations of
what Habegger calls Isabel's 'hidden internal bondage': they are easy for
us to recognise, now, as part of an especially feminine equipment, results
of a cultural patterning at the deepest and most unconscious level.[9] Habegger is plausible, too, when he suggests James might be ironising, even,
qualities of Isabel's dignity in suffering at the Palazzo Roccanera: the
'noble nickel-plated mask worn by so many women's heroines of the time'
is also part of the cultural equipment, and part of Isabel's 'unquenchable
desire to think well of herself'.[1] James's irony, though, is simply a compo-
nent in a whole movement that opens up a generous space for imagining
Isabel, one that is much larger than her own ideas about herself, or, for
that matter, James's 'ideas' about her. He recognises a treacherous double
bind in contemporary imaging of the female, and describes how the individual fluid consciousness finds its stumbling and inevitably incomplete
account in and through and around those images.

   If James is at pains to register this 'pathology' of a feminine ideal, it
would be misrepresenting the overall effect of *The Portrait*, however, not
to stress how he also registers in Isabel a resilience, an energy, a self-
confidence, all independent of the outcome of her idealistic experiments.
(It is in fact the irresistible surging of that self-confidence that causes some
of her moments of self-doubt in the first part of the novel: how *dare* she
be so sure she does not want to marry Lord Warburton?) We know this
resilience of hers is independent of her early optimistic rhetoric because
we have one of the strongest expressions of it at one of her worst moments,
when she is travelling across Europe back to Ralph:

9. Habegger, *The 'Woman Business'*, p. 156.
1. Habegger, *The 'Woman Business'*, p. 157.

This impression carried her into the future, of which from time to time she had a mutilated glimpse. She saw herself, in the distant years, still in the attitude of a woman who had her life to live, and these intimations contradicted the spirit of the present hour. It might be desirable to die; but this privilege was evidently to be denied her. Deep in her soul—deeper than any appetite for renunciation—was the sense that life would be her business for a long time to come. And at moments there was something inspiring, almost exhilarating, in the conviction. It was a proof of strength—it was a proof that she should some day be happy again. It couldn't be that she was to live only to suffer—only to feel the injury of life repeated and enlarged—it seemed to her that she was too valuable, too capable, for that. Then she wondered whether it were vain and stupid to think so well of herself. When had it ever been a guarantee to be valuable? . . . Was it not much more probable that if one were delicate one would suffer? It involved then, perhaps, an admission that one had a certain grossness; but Isabel recognised, as it passed before her eyes, the quick, vague shadow of a long future. (L769–70)

In Isabel's self-interrogation here, she passes in review several major items in the Victorian female agenda. Are not delicate things supposed to suffer? Is not renunciation a key gesture in the feminine repertoire? Faced with the insoluble contradiction of her unhappy marriage, would not the delicate thing to do be to pale away and die? If so, then delicacy (that prime ingredient of Victorian femininity) is not for Isabel: *cannot be*, because life surges in her from somewhere deeper than the Victorian ideal, and if that convicts her of a certain 'grossness', by Victorian standards, then so be it. She is learning all the time, and knows now to let this ideal past her with a shrug. It is James's creation of this energetic field around her rather than her specific utterances that engages us with the youthfully presumptuous Isabel at the opening of the novel; the presumption of youth borrows at any given cultural moment whatever rhetoric is current to express reach and appetite and potential. And it is Isabel's energies that Osmond had not counted on when he planned his cultural manipulations, her mind 'attached to his own like a small garden-plot to a deer-park', where he would 'rake the soil gently and water the flowers; he would weed the beds and gather an occasional nosegay' (L636). Instead among the carefully tended hybrid blooms he calls honour and decency thrust the rank weeds of Isabel's 'pure mind': 'We don't live decently together!' she cries (L745).

If we do not believe that James is interested in punishing Isabel for her presumption or for the inadequacy of her ideas, by invoking at his ending a sacrifice to law in returning her to Rome and to her husband, then we are left with a novel in which the tension between law and sympathy is unresolved at its close. We understand from her return that she still feels herself answerable to law, to what 'seems right' (Ralph says, 'As seems right—as seems right? . . . Yes, you think a great deal about that', (L786)). We know, too, that Isabel's return is partly for Pansy, who figures as the sister / daughter left behind in the very mill of the conventional, helpless to resist it because she does not have Isabel's energy; so that the return certainly has its aspect as a gesture of female solidarity. 'I don't think anything is over', Isabel says (L785).

But the return to Rome also feels provisional. She has, after all, made her first crucial gesture of disobedience to Osmond, which alters everything; they have acknowledged to one another that any such disobedience will be irrevocable.

> To break with Osmond once would be to break for ever; any open acknowledgement of irreconcilable needs would be an admission that their whole attempt would prove a failure. For them there could be no condonement, no compromise, no easy forgetfulness, no formal readjustment. (L668)

We have a novel that ends poised on the brink of something, balanced over a choice it does not—with any finality—actually *make*. In so far as a choice is made—albeit a provisional, opaque, equivocal one—it is a choice against Caspar Goodwood, and it is Isabel's. She saves herself, by flying from England: the loss of control, the wave of sudden new passionate—erotic— sensation she experienced in Caspar's arms is not what she wants, now, as a solution to her marriage. She wants to stand on her feet. ('In the movement she seemed to beat with her feet, in order to catch herself, to feel something to rest on' (L799).) The flight from drowning sends her back for that confrontation with her marriage which lingering in England only postponed. The involuntary helplessness of passion is the alibi classically offered wives exiting their unsatisfactory marriages: and Isabel wants none of it. She wants a clear head.

The function of Caspar's intervention, though, draws our attention to just how *Portrait of a Lady* is *not*, in fact, composed around the classic adulterous triangle; James's interrogation of the law as represented by the traditionary sanctities and decencies of marriage is not to consist in this novel of testing it primarily against the pressures of passion, of abandonment, of ecstasy. The conflict is all within the civilised temple, around an internal moral contradiction and opposed conceptions of honour, one outward and conventional, one personal and instinctive: between versions, in fact, of what is *right*. When Caspar does offer himself, and for a moment—in spite of the fact that the actual words of his appeal to Isabel are in the spirit of the most enlightened New World rationalism—the novel opens to a glimpse of that other, Dionysiac thing, a 'comet in the sky', 'the hot wind of the desert', 'something potent, acrid, strange' [401], it can only come in the context of the rest of the novel as a sidelight, a surprise, something Isabel has left out of count and cannot make space for suddenly. If she is 'natural', then her nature is something straight and sunlit; it is instructive to compare her English churchyard at Ralph's funeral ('the air had the brightness of the hawthorn and the blackbird', [395]) with the lusty paganism of Charlotte's and the Prince's Matcham in *The Golden Bowl* ('sunny, gusty, lusty English April, all panting and heaving with impatience, or kicking and crying . . . like some infant Hercules who wouldn't be dressed').[2]

Readers complain of a sexual numbness in the novel, and it is true that one of the ways in which James fails to convince us of the likelihood of an Isabel choosing an Osmond is in failing to create for us his sexual

2. Henry James, *The Golden Bowl* (1904; rpt. New York: Library of America, 2010), p. 679 [*Editor*].

attractiveness for her; although Habegger's clues about Isabel's search for the dream-father and his quotation from Constance Fenimore Woolston's astonished recognition of how James had 'divined' something in female fantasy do help.[3] (Creating convincingly the sexual attractiveness of men for women is to be one of James's distinctive achievements in the late period, from the vacillating Sir Claude through the fatal Vanderbank to Merton Densher and Chad and the Prince.) It is impossible for us to imagine reading an Isabel who says *yes* to Caspar; the whole dynamic of *The Portrait* runs against it. Yet at that late moment his offer is suddenly almost overwhelmingly tempting. It is not the open-air fresh reasonableness of his arguments that tempts Isabel, but an erotic she has never opened to before; it reaches her now perhaps just because she is broken down and in extremity.

Revising the novel in 1905, James is careful to specify that this sex which tempts her is bodily, animal, participatory ('the very taste of it, as of something potent, acrid, and strange, forced open her set teeth', [401]); not the etherised swoonings Yellow Book seducees were prone to. She is afraid of Caspar—he is 'dangerous'—for the first time, as she takes in 'each thing in his hard manhood that had least pleased her, each aggressive fact of his face, his figure, his presence' [402]. There is a thundering recognition in that '*had* least pleased her': in retrospect the whole callowness of her maiden reading of him appears, her treating him as her conquest to be wound in and out on her silver thread, to be exasperated with, to be pitied. Now the very hardness of him that had seemed—to her maidenliness—repellent and awkward, is revealed as dangerous and desirable. It is in fact the 'maidenliness' of Isabel that is under threat and collapsing in this scene, the persisting 'virginity' of her type even into marriage and motherhood: and as she speeds her 'straight path' to the lighted house we can both appreciate the consistency of the Diana-like flight and survival intact (she is Isabel *Archer*, after all), and regret the sexual womanliness she has not tasted: is not, perhaps, ever to taste. She makes her enigmatic pause at the door to look around her: why? Is it in an unacknowledged hope that he has followed her and will prevent her going in? But even Caspar is too much of a gentleman for that.

In 1905 James no doubt had a different perspective—having written into his late novels such different, non-virginal women as Kate, Mme de Vionnet and Charlotte—on just *what* he had created in Isabel: her type, its maidenliness, its essential chastity. (Perhaps he felt more certain that from Isabel's type there *was* no hope, ever, for Caspar; and hence his addition of the determining last sentence.) His comment on the type in his later novels is more ironic, their fate less straight, more twisted. Nanda in *The Awkward Age* would have abased herself in order to get Van, and weeps bitter tears at retiring to her nunnery at Mr Longdon's. Fleda in *The Spoils of Poynton* travelling to fetch the trophy of her sacrifice of her lover to decent conduct, the Maltese cross to treasure secretly into a maiden-auntish old age, finds the whole fine thing gone up in dirty smoke. We fear that the Isabels of one generation, making their sacrifices to their ideals of honour, become the Lady Julias (in *The Awkward Age*) of another;

3. Habegger, *The 'Woman Business'*, p. 153.

the treasures of their refusals, their abstentions, are an equivocal legacy for their hungry and curious grand-daughters.

What James has finely understood in 1881, in Isabel's scene with Caspar, is the actual operation, in behaviour and language, of this 'virginal' cultural ideal of womanhood; 'good' girls profoundly impressed with the need to 'please' and not to do 'wrong'. What the erotic threatens here is not simply a social form. As Thomas Mann wrote about *Anna Karenina*:

> Custom and morality, how far are they distinguishable, how far are they—in effect—one and the same, how far do they coincide in the heart of the socially circumscribed human being? The question hovers unanswered over the whole novel. But such a work is not compelled to answer questions. Its task is to bring them out, to enrich the emotions, to give them the highest and most painful degree of questionableness.[4]

A cultural ideal of womanhood is enmeshed tentacularly, tenaciously, at the very roots of the construction of literary femininity. We watch the rehearsal of a familiar literary pattern: man presses woman to give herself to him; woman is overcome by the desire to give in to him, but a cultural overvoice that judges against herself never remits its condemnatory commentary. 'What bliss?' says Anna Karenina with disgust and horror. For Mme de Renal in *Le Rouge et le Noir*, 'all at once that terrible word: adulteress, came to her'. 'It's wrong', says Chekhov's lady with a lapdog, 'You'll be the first not to respect me now.'[5] And we seem to see that pattern in operation *within* the psychological flux and fluidity of a 'real' woman, within Isabel's personality and selfhood (illusion overspills circumscription again). Isabel has no language in which she can say yes; her language says no for her, rehearses in her own mouth a familiar protest, attempts to circumscribe in thin conventional words the inchoate flood of her actual experience.

> '. . . The world's all before us—and the world's very big. I know something about that.'
> Isabel gave a long murmur, like a creature in pain; it was as if he were pressing something that hurt her. 'The world's very small,' she said at random; she had an immense desire to appear to resist. She said it at random, to hear herself say something; but it was not what she meant. The world, in truth, had never seemed so large; it seemed to open out, all round her, to take the form of a mighty sea, where she floated in fathomless waters. (L798)

> 'Ah, be mine as I'm yours!' she heard her companion cry. He had suddenly given up argument, and his voice seemed to come through a confusion of sound.

> This however, of course, was but a subjective fact, as the metaphysicians say; the confusion, the noise of waters, and all the rest of it, were in her own head. In an instant she became aware of this. 'Do me the greatest kindness of all,' she panted. 'I beseech you to go away!'

4. Mann, *Essays of Three Decades*, trans. H. Lowe-Porter (London: Secker and Warburg, n.d.), p. 184.
5. *Anna Karenina*, trans. Aylmer Maude (Oxford University Press, 1965), p. 169; *Le Rouge et le Noir* (Paris: Garnier-Flammarion, 1964), p. 93 (my translation); *Lady with a Lapdog*, trans. David Magarshack (Harmondsworth: Penguin, 1970), p. 268.

'Ah, don't say that.' Don't kill me!' he cried.
She clasped her hands; her eyes were streaming with tears.
'As you love me, as you pity me, leave me alone!' (L799)

Isabel *cannot speak* what Caspar can, that 'the world is very big'; even though that is, for a moment, her actual experience. She is in pain 'as though he were pressing something that hurt her', she can only answer that 'the world is very small', as if the utterance came from an infinitely lesser space of possibility. She says to him, 'Are you mad?', although at that moment it is she who is experiencing sensations like madness, a confusion of sound and noise of waters in her own head. When she begs him, 'As you love me, as you pity me, leave me alone!', she offers the archetypal virtuous compromise with sexual temptation, inviting the desired profanation—the kiss—and admitting her incapacity to resist even while articulating the still predominant desire *not* to succumb, to be honourable, to be *good*. A still predominant honour is helpless none the less—because femininely weak—in the path of the onrush of desire.

It is a compromise convenient for literature, crushing for the female subjectivity that finds its account there. However ambivalent we may feel about Isabel's Diana-like chastity, we cannot want her to succumb to the compromise, to act *yes* while still only able clearly to articulate *no*. Edith Wharton's stories, even though written out of very divorced and extra-marital *fin-de-siècle* New York, are full of women more or less broken in that particular double bind: distinct from, of course, though not unrelated to, the double bind that has freedom-loving girls in search of a master to submit to.[6] (Wharton is also very good, in connection with Mann's remarks, on the impossibility of disentangling within the individual subjectivity social verdict and self-condemnation.)

In *Anna Karenina, Le Rouge et le Noir* and "Lady with a Lapdog," it goes without saying that the 'consciousness' of the fiction inhabits a much more open space than can be filled by the rehearsal of dismayed feminine virtue by Anna Karenina, Mme de Renal or Anna Sergeyevna. In all these cases, the enveloping 'larger' space around the female moralising feels specifically male; the male author / narrator may value and admire or even count on this female will-to-chastity (Chekhov's Gurov finds it boring), but he knows it co-exists with a world of other sexual varieties. The male consciousness has an advantage of worldliness it may even deplore (Tolstoy, for example, who throws so much weight behind Anna's 'intuition' of her own transgressiveness) but cannot wish away.

What is distinctive in the rehearsal of the pattern at the end of *The Portrait of a Lady* is how James's account of it stands within and not outside the troubled self-contradicting female subjectivity. This has partly to do, of course, with his writing in the English / American and not the 'improper' European tradition: the English fictional space was precisely *supposed* to be co-existent with a 'female' virtue (we remember what a mess this makes of the end of *The Mill on the Floss*). But behind James's position lies all his saturation in that European tradition, and his scorn, sometimes, for the 'soap and water' of English fictional 'propriety':

6. See, for example, 'Souls Belated' and 'Autres Temps', reprinted in *Roman Fever* (London: Virago Modern Classics, 1983).

I have been seeing something of Daudet, Goncourt, and Zola; and there is nothing more interesting to me now than the effort and experiment of this little group, with its truly infernal intelligence of art, form, manner—its intense artistic life. They do the only kind of work, today, that I respect; and in spite of their ferocious pessimism and their handling of unclean things, they are at least serious and honest. The floods of tepid soap and water which under the name of novels are being vomited forth in England, seem to me, by contrast, to do little honour to our race.[7]

James treats the scene from within Isabel's subjectivity not because he cannot imagine or approve of other perspectives, but because he wants and needs to engage in an interrogation of 'propriety' from within. (Possibly this makes his love scene read as somewhat 'maidenly', alongside its European counterparts.) But the danger with a male enveloping worldliness and how it fictionalises female 'virtue' is that the treatment can verge on 'connoisseurship', on relishing the 'piquancy' of a less evolved consciousness than the narrative's own. We have no reason to wish to see Mme de Renal liberated from her conventional notions of the wickedness of adultery: they are, on the contrary, intrinsic to her charm, not because *Stendhal* believes in the least that she ought to be faithful to Monsieur—after all, this is the writer who later in the same novel creates relishingly, and without a trace of squeamishness, a Mathilde de la Mole!—but because the fact *she* thinks she ought to speaks an innocence the male narrative can only yearn for and never return to. And because Mme de Renal is conventionally 'moral', Julien's conquest of her is all the more piquant. Purity—'goodness'—can still have a 'value' (in the connoisseur's sense) even for a palette that has long entertained all the other colours.

James's interrogation of the value of 'traditionary decencies and sanctities', though, is sited at the very point where convention focuses: in the 'goodness' of 'good' women themselves. James has committed himself enthusiastically to that tradition in English fiction of siting narratives within female consciousness; but he is also to commit himself progressively to broadening the scope of that female consciousness to include the big unchaste world of European fiction. An image crops up on Isabel's journey to Ralph which not only seems to suggest in embryo the imagery James uses to express in *The Golden Bowl* Maggie Verver's slow process of uncovering the real beneath the innocent-seeming surface, but also could serve as an account of the whole drive behind the renewal and development in James's writing from *What Maisie Knew* onwards.

> She had plenty to think about; but it was not reflection, or conscious purpose, that filled her mind. Disconnected visions passed through it, and sudden dull gleams of memory, of expectation. The past and the future alternated at their will, but she saw them only in fitful images, which came and went by a logic of their own. It was extraordinary the things she remembered. Now that she was in the secret, now that she knew something that so much concerned her, and the eclipse of which had made life resemble an attempt to play whist with an imperfect pack of cards, the truth of things, their mutual relations,

7. To W. D. Howells (1884). *Henry James Letters III*, ed. Leon Edel (Cambridge: The Belknap Press, 1980), p. 29.

their meaning, and for the most part their horror, rose before her with a kind of architectural vastness. (L768)

The architectural vastness could be Maggie's pagoda, the whist game looks forward to the bridge game Maggie prowls around, at once excluded and controlling. The intuition of vast secret structures of behaviours underlying surface proprieties suggests the problems of 'knowledge' for the heroines of *Maisie* and *The Awkward Age*, as well as Milly Theale's vulnerability and Woollett's obtuseness.

Meanwhile back at the end of *The Portrait of a Lady* Isabel, having been plunged dizzyingly under the surface by her discoveries about her husband and by Caspar's kiss, scrambles back out onto the dry land of her belief in herself, leaving us with the sensation of an opaque and not entirely fulfilling ending to the novel. The novel tests out 'traditional decencies and sanctities' on their own terms and ends in an impasse: Isabel has taken the first steps out onto a bridge which as yet only reaches into the air and has no dry land the other side to come down on. The 'proprieties' are ironised in the novel—even tragically; and James has accurately recorded the inbuilt constraints, the double binds, in a 'good' woman's psychology and in her language; but he has not found another voice for his woman yet. She thinks and feels beyond the conventional, but she cannot say or act: he cannot imagine it for her. She does not have a language to override what 'seems right', nor to say yes to that erotic that opens up for her late, and frighteningly.

The challenge Isabel's unfulfilment sets for the development of this theme in James's writing—the formal / conventional stretched and tested by the subjective / affective—is to create a language for womanliness which is not anchored in goodness, or chastity, or unsexuality. James of course was not in any vanguard in English-language fiction in terms of his subject matter: heroines were flying from husbands to lovers in their throngs, long before James dreamed up Kate or Mme de Vionnet or Charlotte. Yet what so many 'daring' novels testify to is the linguistic and ideological persistence of ideals of 'goodness' long beyond the fact. (For example, again, Edith Wharton's troubled adulteress in 'Souls Belated'; and of course Sue Bridehead in *Jude the Obscure*.) What is really a radical development in late James is the convincing creation of a space and language in fiction for a womanhood liberated to kick over the traces with no more ado than a man. If Charlotte is destroyed at the end of *The Golden Bowl* it is not because of the operations of her own conscience. If Merton makes a judgement against Kate at the end of *The Wings of the Dove*, it is not because she came to his room: on the contrary, that was his sign of her good faith. If Mme de Vionnet is unhappy, it is not because she thinks she is sinful, but because she knows she cannot keep Chad.

Perhaps in the end the bridge is never built to bring Isabel safely down on another side: perhaps the sort of development James has to make out of her impasse is more like a leap, a free fall. Certainly the women of the later novels inhabit a space where it is no easy matter—where it is in fact wishful thinking—to find footholds and control as Isabel sturdily insists. And although those women may have the sexual fulfilment she eschews, there are no certainties in their universe to match that real centre of

Portrait of a Lady, more pivotal in fact than Caspar's kiss, when Isabel and Ralph finally—on his deathbed—share the truth about her marriage in a transcendent scene of mutual enlightened intelligence:

> nothing mattered now but the only knowledge that was not pure anguish—the knowledge that they were looking at the truth together . . .

> '. . . You said just now that pain is not the deepest thing, No—no. But it is very deep. If I could stay—'
> 'For me you will always be here,' she softly interrupted. It was easy to interrupt him.
> But he went on, after a moment—
> 'It passes, after all; it's passing now. But love remains . . .'

> 'And remember this,' he continued, 'that if you have been hated, you have also been loved.'
> 'Ah, my brother!' she cried, with a movement of still deeper prostration. (L785–86)

There is plenty of mutual enlightened intelligence in the late novels, but transcendent it is not; it is contingent, vulnerable, temporary. (What becomes, for example, of the exceptional mutuality of Kate and Merton at the opening of *The Wings of the Dove*, described as if they found themselves face to face at the top of a pair of ladders looking over their respective garden walls?) With new freedoms for James's heroines comes a loss of certainty; a free fall intimately related, of course, to the developments in James's form, where whatever was left of the controlling intrusive narrator and his containing ironies is sunk in the opaque subjective dialogic medium of the late fiction.

MICHAEL GORRA

The Roccanera[†]

The door belongs to Madame Merle, and the young man with his finger on the bell is named Edward Rosier.[1] James writes that we "will perhaps not have forgotten" (559) him, but we have met this character just once before and readers of the *Atlantic* would have had four months in which to lose track of him. He is a childhood friend of Isabel's, with an inherited income of £1,600 a year, and so thoroughly Frenchified that he sometimes has to hunt for the right English word. He hunts, and fails to find it; referring to Isabel, for example, not as Pansy's stepmother, but as her *belle-mère*. For that is how he sees her now, as the stepmother of the

---

† From *Portrait of a Novel: Henry James and the Making of an American Masterpiece* (New York: Liveright, 2012), pp. 222–38, 356, 357. Copyright © 2012 by Michael Gorra. Used by permission of Liveright Publishing Corporation. Page numbers in parentheses are to the 1882 text of the novel as printed in *Henry James: Novels 1881–1886* (New York: Library of America, 1985).
1. This book's previous chapter examines the novel's serialization, and ends by noting that its ninth installment had begun as follows: "One afternoon, toward dusk, in the autumn of 1876, a young man of pleasing appearance rang at the door of a small apartment on the third floor of an old Roman house." (559). This is the only date James gives us for the novel's action [*Editor*].

perfect young girl he has met that summer in Switzerland. Ned Rosier has never in his life done anything indiscreet, but he does follow the Osmonds down to Rome, where they have lived since their marriage, and after a month he has learned two things. He knows that Osmond doesn't think he's rich enough, and that Madame Merle has some unexplained pull with Pansy's family. So he rings, and hopes she'll help him.

This is the second of the novel's great ellipses. The first, as we have seen, came just before Isabel's marriage, when James skipped over the year that ended with Osmond's successful proposal, and presented us with a *fait accompli*. We didn't even know she was engaged until the novelist made Caspar Goodwood cross the ocean simply to express his outrage. Now he has jumped again, a gap in time that corresponds to a gap in our knowledge of his heroine, and new readers inevitably find it disorienting; they may even feel cheated. We have not been to Isabel's wedding; we have not witnessed the start of her life in marriage; all we know is that she has settled in Rome and that her stepdaughter has met a boy. We don't even know how much time has passed, and then James knocks the wind out of us. Madame Merle tells Rosier that Isabel will probably favor his suit "if her husband does not" (562). Nothing more, not yet, but it's enough to show us that the marriage has broken down even before we have seen it begin. We may not have trusted Osmond, but we knew that Isabel did and hoped that Ralph was wrong about him. Instead, we have gone from promise to ruin in the space of three pages, and it is as if our hopes have been drowned.

Three pages, and three years. We can work out the time from something else Madame Merle tells us. Isabel has had a son, "who died two years ago, six months after his birth" (564–65). Those details allow us to date the novel's every scene. We will be told that her wedding was in June, and Rosier appears at the door at the start of December 1876. So we can place the marriage in 1873, and can even say that she conceived later that summer. But the child is dead, and in truth it's hard to make very much of him. James does not connect that death to whatever has blighted the Osmonds' marriage, and when Isabel later thinks back over its failure she will not spare the infant a thought. James gives her a child because it's both the most efficient and least explicit way he has of telling us that the marriage has been consummated, and yet motherhood itself has no part in his conception of Isabel's future. She believes that in marrying Osmond she has acted freely, and at the end of the novel she will need that liberty once more. She will need to choose with a freedom that she would not have in a child's presence.

That baby aside, James refuses here to give us any direct knowledge of the inner life of Isabel's marriage, and as a reader I'm split between my frustration at his refusal to take us over the brink and my admiration at the skill with which he switches his lens and approaches her through a hitherto-forgotten character. Still, that change does signal a larger change in mood, and perhaps a loss of *brio*. No scene after Isabel's marriage offers the expansive delight of the book's early chapters, the feeling of enchanted discovery with which she enters her European life. She no longer has decisions to make but must learn to live with the one she did, and the book shifts to a minor key, less exhilarating but with a new gravity and indeed nobility, whose force increases with each chapter.

At first, however, James's decision to present Isabel indirectly can seem bewildering. He shows her through Rosier's eyes and Rosier's story, shows us only her social self, and it will take him sixty pages to open the closed door of her private life. We need something to do while we wait, however, and he uses the question of Pansy's suitors and possible marriage to delay and distract us. Another American girl will have to choose. Madame Merle promises to help Rosier as much she can, and then she immediately tells Osmond. The news is disturbing—so disturbing, in fact, that Osmond signals his disapproval by offering the young man his *left* hand at the next of Isabel's regular Thursday evening receptions. Rosier has no choice. He has to take it, but he turns away as soon as he can, and then finds himself face-to-face with Isabel once more.

She stands framed in a doorway, as at Gardencourt, and again she is dressed in black. The repetition is unobtrusive, but James means us to notice it and it serves to mark a difference; almost as if her story were starting over. She no longer wears the traveling dress of a girl in mourning, but is gowned in black velvet instead, and we don't need to imagine the clinging stuff of Sargent's scandalous and contemporaneous *Madame X* to see her as bare-armed and décolleté. At Gardencourt she had stood in the door of an ivy-covered house, gazing onto a green lawn, and then stepped out into the world before her. Here, however, the door that encloses her is smothered in gold leaf, and she looks only from one interior space to another, a receding vista of rooms enfilade. Isabel waits for others to approach, a hostess who appears to Rosier as the very picture of a lady, a woman whom the "years had touched . . . only to enrich" (570). But Rosier has never been to Gardencourt, and the reader will see a greater change. This portrait allows for a fourth dimension.

We need to pause over that doorway, over the setting that James has provided for her. Money went far in Rome. Servants and food, horses and houses—all of them were cheaper in Italy than in London, and with the painted ceilings thrown in for free. Isabel lives with a magnificence that even her substantial fortune would not have allowed in Britain, and as he walks through her rooms, Rosier finds himself admitting that "these people were very strong in *bibelots*" (567), in the beautiful decorative objects that he himself most covets. But the sensibility behind it all belongs to Osmond alone. Isabel has had nothing to do with furnishing their house and claims to have no taste of her own; her husband, in contrast, has what she calls a "genius for upholstery" (588). The place is his, an assertion of his will, of the self he wants to project. It is an old "high house in the very heart of Rome; a dark and massive structure overlooking a sunny *piazzetta* in the neighbourhood of the Farnese Palace" (566). Rome may be bright, but the building itself is called the Palazzo Roccanera, the Black Rock, and to Rosier its darkness matters. For it seems to him as if Pansy's home is a kind of fortress, a place in which she might easily be locked up.

James describes it as marked with a "stern old Roman name, which smelt . . . of crime and craft and violence" (566), a place mentioned in guidebooks and visited by tourists. It has been most reliably identified with the Palazzo Antici-Mattei, a complex of sixteenth- and seventeenth-century buildings whose austere façade was built to designs by Carlo Maderno, and where the rooms on the *piano nobile* have ceilings by Domenichino and Pietro da Cortona among others.[2] James masked the original just a bit by giving it some frescoes by Caravaggio instead. That makes one start. The Victorians did not admire the painter we call by that name, and he gets just two one-line references in *Italian Hours*; nor is he known to have worked in fresco. Still, the Mattei family did own a few of his canvases.[3] They had made their fortune buying up real estate after the city was sacked in 1527, and quickly became one of the most powerful clans in Rome; three centuries later they were still turning out cardinals. The building now houses the Centro Studi Americani, and many visiting lecturers have found themselves in the rooms that were in some sense once Isabel's. Nevertheless, the palazzo remains forbidding indeed, darkened by age and with barred windows on the ground floor. Inside, the courtyard walls are encrusted with fragments of ancient statuary, and the loggia overlooking it is lined with "a row of mutilated statues and dusty urns" (566–67), just as James described it. But there are many palaces in Rome, and I suspect that what drew him to this one wasn't just its architecture or its atmospheric history, but rather its particular location in the city itself.

It lies indeed in the heart of the town, and not that far from the Palazzo Farnese. It is closer, however, to both the church of the Gesù and the Capitol, and closer still to the Palazzo Cenci, itself associated with crime and craft and violence. Every literate Victorian knew Shelley's play about Beatrice Cenci, who at the end of the sixteenth century was executed for killing the father who had raped her.[4] It is closest of all to the Ghetto, whose walls lay just a few paces off and which was abolished only with the final unification of Italy in 1870. The quarter is ancient and aristocratic, and was in Osmond's period decayed; a neighborhood beyond all question of fashion, a place of squalid streets and private interior splendor. Which makes it a very good address indeed—a good *Roman* address, and about as far as possible from the American colony that gathered around the Spanish Steps. That's where Madame Merle lives, but Osmond detests the modern city of hotels and English bankers. Not everyone is invited to their Thursday evenings, and even those who are might discover that the house isn't easy to find, buried as it is in the narrow twisting streets of history itself. Its location stands as both a sign of his originality and a mark of his "traditionary" (425) pose. This part of Rome may lie on level ground, but so far as the *stranieri* are concerned, the Roccanera is a Roman equivalent of Osmond's Tuscan hilltop.

One unexpected caller does, however, find his way to them, an Englishman whom Osmond doesn't at first recognize. Lord Warburton has come south with Ralph, whose consumption has grown worse each year and who now thinks of wintering in Sicily. But the journey has worn him out. He cannot move from their hotel, and one reason for Warburton's visit is simply to announce their arrival. For Isabel has had no advance word, and to us that's the truly startling thing: the cousins have fallen so far

---

2. See Charles S. Anderson, *Person, Place, and Thing in Henry James's Novels* (Durham, NC: Duke University Pres, 1977), 292. See also Harry Brewster, *A Cosmopolite's Journey* (London: Radcliffe Press, 1998), 182, a memoir by an expatriate of another generation who spent a part of his childhood there.

3. On their ownership of work by Michelangelo Merisi da Caravaggio, see Jonathan Harr, *The Lost Painting* (New York: Random House, 2005).

4. Percy Bysshe Shelley (1792–1822), English poet who drowned sailing off the Tuscan coast; he wrote *The Cenci* (1819), about noblewoman Beatrice Cenci (1577–1599) [*Editor*].

apart that they're no longer in regular touch. James writes that the "reflective reader" (592) shouldn't find this surprising, given Ralph's view of Isabel's marriage, and we are told something similar about each of her old friends. Mrs. Touchett has faded from her life, and even Madame Merle has grown distant. Until this winter she has preferred England to Rome, and she now tells Isabel, a bit too often, that she doesn't want to presume on the fact that she's known Osmond for so long. Marriage often does attenuate old friendships, and yet the novel insists that we notice it, reminding us of it each time that the author brings back an old name.

James has a difficult task here. The chapters after Isabel's marriage do not introduce a single new character, and he needs instead, as the novel starts over again, to catch us up on all his old ones after a gap in years if not in pages. He keeps both Henrietta Stackpole and Caspar Goodwood alive in our minds by bringing them down to Rome, and there is a special brilliance in his retrospective account of Ralph in particular. Ralph has come to Rome only once since Isabel's marriage and quickly realized that his very presence made Osmond so unaccountably nervous that he in turn made it uncomfortable for his wife. Now he has returned, close to death and yet kept alive by his belief that his cousin's story isn't yet over, and James dives down into the character's memory and then swims up to breast the novel's present. It fuses these years into a single image of Ralph's estrangement from her, a verbal equivalent of a medieval miniature in which several incidents share the same space. But let me put it a different way. There is a prismatic quality to these chapters. James doesn't let us look at the white light of Isabel's being directly, but instead refracts it through the differently shaded impressions of his other characters. Once he has done that, however, once he has reintroduced his cast, James needs to move forward into the new relations created by her marriage, and at this point the novel becomes thick with plot in every sense of the word.

The most important element in that plotting concerns Warburton's surprising interest in Pansy. He finds her charming, at once polished and ingenuous, and comes repeatedly to sit with her at the Roccanera, even as he worries that Isabel won't be pleased by his interest. For of course, as he tells Ralph, "there's the difference in our ages." It's the most roundabout way to suggest that he's thinking of marriage, and the idea so startles the invalid that it makes him risk Warburton's anger. "I hope," Ralph says, "you are sure that among Miss Osmond's merits her being a—so near her stepmother isn't a leading one?" (603–04). Nor is Ralph the only one who has noticed Warburton's attentions. Rosier has, and grown jealous. And Osmond has seen it too, and seen deep. He has seen what Ralph fears, and decided he can use it.

Isabel herself has seen something else. James hasn't yet defined the precise contours of her marital troubles, but one day she returns home from a drive and stops short at the entrance to the drawing room. For she has, James writes, "received an impression" (611), and must pause to take it in. She has found Madame Merle standing while Osmond remains sunk in his chair, two old friends caught in a moment of ruminant silence. There's nothing particularly unusual in that silence, but the image does offer her a flicker of perception, albeit one that's gone before she can read it. What catches her is their physical posture—the gentleman sitting while the lady, his guest, stands. In fact, Madame Merle herself recognizes its oddity, and after Osmond leaves the room, explains that she herself was just about to go away. Now she stays to talk, however, to muse over Rosier's jealousy and the odd fact that Warburton seems to have fallen in love with Pansy. Isabel too has spotted the Englishman's interest but hasn't discussed it with her husband, and the subject makes her impatient. So their conversation grows snappish, and becomes only more so when Madame Merle alludes to something that Isabel has never told her. For the older woman knows of Warburton's proposal at Gardencourt, and hopes that she will now "make him the reparation of helping him to marry some one else" (617).

Indeed, Isabel wants to—wants anyway to try. She believes that to give her husband this personage as a son-in-law would be to "play the part of a good wife. She wanted to be that; she wanted to be able to believe, sincerely, that she had been that" (618). Still, she finds Warburton's attachment strange. Pansy seems to her so small, so limited, but she does try to talk herself into it; then she remembers Rosier and admits that the girl prefers the young American. That night Isabel is sitting by herself in the drawing room when her husband comes in. It's the first time James has shown them together and alone since their marriage, and Osmond now tells her that he wants their visitor to declare his intentions. That admission costs him something. He's so used to acting as if none of the world's prizes are ever worth an effort, and his words make Isabel recognize how intensely he wants to see his daughter at Lockleigh. Still, the girl can't make it happen on her own; any proposal will depend upon Isabel's willingness to use the influence he knows she still has. "The moment you really wish it, you can bring him to the point" (625), he says, and his words mean exactly what Ralph had earlier suggested. Osmond may speak of loving his daughter, but he knows that her chief merit in Warburton's eyes can only be her nearness to her stepmother.

"It lies in your hands" (626), he tells her, and then walks out, while Isabel remains by the fire. What she sees as she sits there will produce a moment of reverie that lasts the full length of a night, a chapter that stands as one of James's greatest achievements and a turning point in the history of the novel.

Isabel will sit long that night, until the oil lamps have burned out and the candles have guttered down to their sockets. She will sit and think, motionless, while her mind moves over the whole history of her married life. Nothing happens in the *Portrait*'s famous forty-second chapter, and yet her meditation "has all the vivacity of incident,"[5] as James put it in the novel's preface, a reverie that throws the novel's action forward by returning her to her past. And she begins by working through the situation that Osmond's words have put before her. Those words make her see that Warburton does indeed want to please her, and she wonders if he believes even now that she might be something more to him than a friend. Still, she cannot quite square the idea with the evident sincerity of his fondness for Pansy. That fondness may be a delusion, but she immediately acquits him of pretending to be in love with the girl as a way of pursuing her instead. In fact, Warburton himself has been genuinely startled by Ralph's earlier

5. See p. 13 of this Norton Critical Edition [*Editor*].

suggestion; a few chapters on he will look at it squarely and take himself back to England. But to acquit Warburton is not to acquit Osmond, and with each minute the "service her husband had asked of her" (628) seems more and more repugnant. He wants her to flirt—but that puts it too mildly. He wants her to use what sexual hold she has over Warburton as a means to her stepdaughter's marriage; as though she were bait. He's pimping her, and she knows it. So her recognition of the Englishman's innocence brings her no peace, and as she sits through the night, she finds herself "haunted with terrors" (628), among them the curious sensation of seeing her friend and her husband together.

On this night Isabel will think, more than ever before, about just why she married, and what made it go wrong. She—we—will feel the continued power of Osmond's charm, and we will understand just how her distrust of her husband has grown. Neither of them is the partner the other one expected, though at first he had believed "he could change her, and she had done her best to be what he would like" (630). We will get the explanation that James refused us when the novel resumed after Isabel's marriage and at the end of these dozen pages will know almost everything of importance about the early years of their union. That ellipsis will be closed. James's work here offers a new way of presenting the interior life, a new kind of fiction, and yet the chapter gives us more than an early example of what William James would soon name the "stream of consciousness."[6] It will of course give us that, and in a moment we will see how. But it also has a structural task to perform in the novel as a whole.

James either could not or chose not to dramatize the week-by-week dissolution of trust that is the Osmond's marriage. He offers us Isabel's retrospective understanding of its failure but doesn't depict the process of that failure itself, and I do not think it possible to define with any precision the complex of psychological and technical reasons that made him refuse such scenes. So let's presume instead that such a depiction was never his purpose, that his interest lies elsewhere, in Isabel's understanding of the consequences of her marital choice. Still, we do need to know why it's the wrong choice, and at this point George Eliot can help us. Though not in the obvious way. She writes brilliantly about marriages going wrong in both *Middlemarch* (1872) and *Daniel Deronda* (1876), and that of Gwendolen Harleth and Henleigh Grandcourt in the latter novel is in some ways a model for Isabel's own. Another aspect of *Daniel Deronda* seems to me equally important, however, and far less often remarked upon.

We're now accustomed to novels marked by narrative disjunctions, books predicated on flashbacks or memory that seem to glide back and forth in time; books in which the order of events and the order of their telling are at odds. We have read Conrad and Faulkner, Proust and Woolf, and know how to piece a chronology out of a story's discontinuous shards. But the readers of James's day were not nearly so used to such structures. Most novels of the period relied on a linear narrative, and though they might allow themselves brief moments of retrospection, the story thrust always forward. *Daniel Deronda* is different. George Eliot liked the opportunities that the massive serial parts of *Middlemarch* had given her, and she returned to that form in the later book, once more dividing it into eight

---

6. William James, *Writings 1878–1899* (New York: Library of America, 1992), p. 152.

parts of about 100 pages each. This time, however, she did something more than use that architecture as a way to ease her movement from plot to plot. She also used those large blocks of narrative to disrupt chronology in a way that a more conventional serial novelist like Dickens could not. The epigraph to her first chapter suggests that any such opening is but the "make-believe of a beginning"; all starting points are arbitrary, and "no retrospect" ever takes us back to the true origin of things. Narrative form isn't given by the calendar, but must instead be made, and so, after a dramatic opening scene at a German casino, George Eliot falls back in time for 200 pages in order to show how her characters got there. The opening chapters hold us—an English girl losing at roulette. We want to know why she plays with such abandon. And what about the man who returns the necklace she pawns?

Of course, George Eliot wasn't the first to begin in the middle; her structure has one of the grandest of all pedigrees in the *Odyssey* and the *Aeneid*. Very few Victorian novels used that gambit, however, and none so successfully. Nevertheless, such breaks in sequence would have an incalculable effect on later fiction, beginning with *The Portrait of a Lady* itself. Not that James appears, at first, to disrupt chronology as such. The jump that puts young Rosier at Madame Merle's door is not in itself a violation of narrative order. But it does create a gap. It puts us into a situation we don't fully understand, and here James found an elective affinity with his predecessor's experiment in time. George Eliot presents her own retrospective in an omniscient third person that's indistinguishable from that in the rest of her narrative, fully dramatizing each stage in the process that has brought her main characters to the casino. James's narratological problem is more complicated. In the preface to *The Golden Bowl* he described his own inveterate preference for an "oblique view of my presented action"—not an impersonal God-like account of the affair, but rather one "of somebody's impression of it."[7] And so it is at this crucial moment in the *Portrait*. The middle of Isabel's marriage lies itself in the middle of the novel, and James needs to fill us in, not as George Eliot does on what happens before the book "begins," but instead on the events of its unwritten center. He closes the gap by breaking chronology, allowing Isabel's memory to stitch over the tear in the novel that is the moment of her marriage itself: a chapter of interior monologue in which there is no physical action beyond the burning of a candle.

Still, a full understanding of just how this chapter covers—or perhaps recovers—the past will require a closer look, and before proceeding we had better get the taste of it in our mouths:

> He had told her that he loved the conventional; but there was a sense in which this seemed a noble declaration. In that sense, the love of harmony, and order, and decency, and all the stately offices of life, she went with him freely, and his warning had contained nothing ominous. But when, as the months elapsed, she followed him further and he led her into the mansion of his own habitation, then, then she had seen where she really was. She could live it over again, the incredulous terror with which she had taken the measure of her dwelling. Between those four walls she had lived ever since; they were to

7. In Henry James, *Literary Criticism II* (New York: Library of America, 1984), p. 1322 [*Editor*].

surround her for the rest of her life. It was the house of darkness, the house of dumbness, the house of suffocation. Osmond's beautiful mind gave neither light nor air; Osmond's beautiful mind, indeed, seemed to peep down from a small high window and mock at her. Of course it was not physical suffering; for physical suffering there might have been a remedy. She could come and go; she had her liberty; her husband was perfectly polite. He took himself so seriously; it was something appalling. (633–34)

In some ways there's nothing particularly difficult about this passage, and its first readers had few problems in comprehending it. It provides an example of the free indirect discourse that most of James's contemporaries used in depicting their characters' inner lives.[8] He allows Isabel's own particular idiom—her vocabulary and biases and ways of understanding—to percolate through his own narration, and the language provides a series of tip-offs that tells us we've been put inside the character's mind: the verb "seemed" in the first sentence, the reiterated "then, then" with which James suggests Isabel's incredulity, the afterthoughts represented by all those semicolons. We come particularly close to her in the passage's last words— "something appalling"—which offer a colloquial summation of Osmond's character. Yet though Isabel's notes do infiltrate James's voice, they don't undermine it. His own tones are muffled, but they remain very much in place, and he maintains the distinction between author and character. So we see through her eyes, and at the same time look at those eyes; we have just enough distance on her to mix our sympathy with judgment.

All this is conventional enough, and yet there is indeed something different about the way Isabel's mind works here. Her language is intensely visual, and while the imagery in this passage runs to the domestic, in other places it refers to the garden or the seashore or the vista of a "dark, narrow alley" (629). Those images are, however, all metaphors; the four walls that surround her are not precisely those of the Palazzo Roccanera. Osmond may seem as if he had "deliberately, almost malignantly . . . put the lights out one by one" (629), and yet the shadow in which she now lives belongs to a moral and not a physical climate. Very little in this chapter points to a particular moment in Isabel's married life, to the individual events of those missing three years: an account, say, of her first dinner with Osmond after the death of their child; or an argument over his belief that even the best of women all eventually take lovers. That's not the kind of thing she remembers. Instead, she allows her mind to slip from one generalized moment of perception to another, collapsing those years into a sense of the "everlasting weight upon her heart" (638). But that sense, like the rest of the chapter's richly imagistic language, remains untethered to an account of any one incident, and even as James fills the gap in his narrative, the actual events of her life go undramatized.[9]

In this, his account of Isabel's reverie differs markedly from his predecessors' accounts of their own characters' inner lives. One example must

---

8. See, for starters, Dorrit Cohn, *Transparent Minds: Narrative Modes for Presenting Consciousness in Fiction* (Princeton: Princeton University Press, 1978); Franco Moretti, "Serious Century," in *The Novel*, vol. 1 (Princeton: Princeton University Press, 2006); James Wood, *How Fiction Works* (New York: Farrar, Straus & Giroux, 2008).
9. See Millicent Bell, "Isabel Archer and the Affronting of Plot" in this Norton Critical Edition, pp. 603–04 [*Editor*].

serve for many. Near the end of *Middlemarch*, Dorothea Brooke sobs herself to sleep on the floor, believing that her hopes of happiness are now forever gone. When she wakes, however, she forces herself to relive the shattering events of the previous day and to weigh the role of other people in the scene that has so broken her. She thinks consecutively, she asks herself questions and answers them, she comes to a final understanding and determines to act upon it. It takes about a page, and similar moments could be found in Austen or Trollope, Thackeray or Howells. Isabel's night before the fire occupies a much greater space in the novel, a much longer time in the reader's experience, and part of its originality lies in the simple fact of duration. Her meditation is long enough to provide its own justification. It doesn't have to lead to any course of action, and it ends without her having reached a conclusion of any kind. Yet there is a greater originality in what the chapter *doesn't* do, in its refusal to fill those missing years with what James called "solidity of specification."[1] For Isabel's mind, ordinarily so hampered by Osmond's mocking egotism, here seems to float free. She roams, she wanders, unconfined by reference to any particular moment, and it is no accident that her mind is most active when she sits most perfectly still, as though consciousness itself were briefly disembodied.

We can get a richer appreciation of James's work here by looking at something his brother wrote just a few years later. William James spent the 1880s at work on his own first book: a massive project, intended as a college text, which he turned in ten years late and that finally appeared as the *Principles of Psychology* in 1890. Early versions of some of its chapters did, however, come out along the way, and in 1884 he published an essay called "On Some Omissions of Introspective Psychology" in *Mind*, then as now one of the most important of all journals in the academic study of philosophy. There he coined a phrase that has, for better or worse, become central to our understanding of modern fiction. William James argued that what first strikes us about what he called the stream of consciousness is its absence of uniformity, "the different *pace* of its different portions."[2] It pools and it flows, spreads wide and runs deep, but its activity never ceases and there is no part of our mental life that does not belong to it. In putting it that way he underlined his difference from earlier thinkers, who conceived of consciousness "like one who should say a river consists of nothing but pailsful, spoonsful, quartpotsful, barrelsful, and other moulded forms of water. [Yet] Even were the pails and the pots all actually standing in the stream, still between them the free water would continue to flow."[3] That, in fact, is what George Eliot had done with Dorothea—she had drawn out a few buckets of interiority, and stood them in a row. But for William James consciousness wasn't a set of propositions or conclusions. It was a process, unbounded, and his essay provides an exceptionally rigorous account of how, in the years to come, the novel would describe that inner life. It is a kind of crib sheet for modernism itself.

Except that Henry had gotten there first. His 1906 preface to the *Portrait* is the product of memory, and maybe we should be skeptical when he depicts his younger self as saying that he wanted to focus upon "the

1. Henry James, *Literary Criticism I* (New York: Library of America, 1984), p. 53.
2. William James, ibid., p. 987.
3. Ibid., p. 164.

young woman's own consiousness," that he would make the story one of "her relation to herself."[4] But if any single chapter of the *Portrait* does embody those ambitions, it is this one, and it stands as an ever more central part of his *oeuvre*. He wrote to William in the spring of 1884 that the essay in *Mind* had "defeated"[5] him, and yet some lines in that year's "Art of Fiction" do seem to echo it. For him consciousness isn't a stream but a "chamber,"[6] and our sensibilities are like a spider's web suspended within it, capturing everything that comes within reach of its filaments. Forty years later Virginia Woolf—he had known her from birth, he had dined with her parents—would describe that consciousness as a "luminous halo, a semi-transparent envelope."[7] The metaphor changes but the phenomenon remains, and what James does in this chapter is much closer to Woolf's own achievement in *To the Lighthouse* than it is to Eliot's *Middlemarch*. Of course, Woolf's very sentences gave her contemporaries trouble, as at this period James's own did not. In some ways the *Portrait*'s might seem but to extend what other writers had already done, to differ from them only in degree. Yet in his avoidance of buckets, in the inconclusive and associative flow of Isabel's thoughts, and even in his sheer ability to sustain his account of those thoughts, James here goes so much further than his predecessors that it amounts to a difference in kind. No writer in English had yet offered so full an account of the inner life, and in remembering this chapter for his preface he allowed himself, for once, to make an unqualified judgement—"It is obviously the best thing in the book."[8]

Probably it is; but best or not, it is clearly the most important. Yet nothing in James's plans for the novel seemed to anticipate it. The notes in which he blocked out the book's last stages make no mention of Isabel's motionless vigil, and though he does write of needing to characterize her estrangement from Osmond, he gives himself no suggestions as to how he might do it. I suspect that the idea for this chapter came to him late. Only when he was at last upon it did he discover the technique that would allow him to handle her revulsion. Only then did James find a method, at once expansive and abbreviated, with which to define Isabel's marriage. Whatever the history of its composition, however, there is no doubt that this chapter marks a turning point. James's earlier work had often substituted a character's impression of an event for the event itself. These pages do more—they change our very sense of what counts as an event in fiction. Sitting still counts; thinking, doing nothing, not moving. Emotions count, and the activity of perception as well. James would write many kinds of fiction over the next twenty-five years, but from this point on the central events of his characters' lives increasingly take place, not in the social world, but within; interior acts of interpretation or understanding. Chapter 42 marks the point at which James stopped being just an important American writer with a special knowledge of Europe on the one hand and the predicament of young women on the other. It marks the point at which his own work became Jamesian: the point at which he began to

---

4. See p. 9 in this Norton Critical Edition [*Editor*].
5. Letter of April 21, 1884, in *Henry James Letters III*, ed. Leon Edel (Cambridge: The Belknap Press, 1980), p. 41.
6. In *Literary Criticism I*, p. 52.
7. Virginia Woolf, "Modern Fiction," in *The Common Reader* (New York: Harcourt, Brace, 1925), 154.
8. See p. 13 in this Norton Critical Edition [*Editor*].

shape the future, a writer whose books made other books possible, a central figure in the history of the novel itself.

James closes the gap in his story only when it becomes dramatically necessary to do so. Osmond has left the Warburton business in Isabel's hands, and at this point we can't fully understand either that request or her reaction to it without some fuller understanding of their marriage. So the requirements of the present produce a return to the past, a break in sequence in which both Isabel's mind and the novel itself rove back in time, working to fill the hole in our knowledge. Later writers would take this further, would violate chronology with a recklessness that James himself could not imagine. Conrad would make a career out of retrospection; Faulkner would seem to freeze time itself in its place. In some ways James remained a Victorian, and when in *The Golden Bowl* Maggie Verver brings Isabel's kind of freely moving intelligence to bear on her own marriage, she directs it toward the present and not the past. She thinks her way through a situation that she wants not simply to understand but to shape. By that time James was willing and able to write about the inner life of a marriage, indeed about passion itself. And perhaps both the *Portrait's* great ellipsis and the idea of consciousness that he developed to deal with it did indeed allow him to evade a difficulty.

That indirection is inseparable from the fact that he asks us to see the failure of that marriage in broadly sexual terms: to remember Isabel's earlier fears of surrendering her very self, and to think of them now as realized. Not in any crude or even precisely physical way. James made few substantive revisions to this chapter for the New York Edition, but one of them does suggest the nature and presence of Isabel's own desire. There may indeed be things she doesn't want to hear, forms of knowledge from which she wants to protect herself, but where in 1881 she had merely "loved" Osmond, in the later version she "anxiously and yet so ardently"[9] gave herself to him. That shift clarifies; it lets us know that what's gone wrong isn't some insurmountable reticence or dysfunction. James also tells us—and in the first edition—that Isabel "was not a daughter of the Puritans" (636) and writes too that Osmond has committed no crime, no moment of violence or cruelty. What's gone wrong isn't a question of some particular action, and perhaps it isn't even sex itself but rather some aspect of Osmond's being for which James finds a sexual language. For we cannot miss the charge with which he writes that at a certain point the man's "personality, touched as it never had been, stepped forth and stood erect" (636). It stands up, makes itself visible, its presence felt. The image is there in 1881 and unchanged in the later edition, and though the metaphor could if necessary be disowned, it does define Osmond's threat, the force with which he assaults her very sense of self. Her "real offence . . . was her having a mind of her own at all" (636), and he wants to knock it out of her. He wants to treat her mind as an annex of his, and furnished only with his tastes and opinions. He has not counted on her resistance, however, and at every obstacle his hatred grows.

Isabel resists both because she must and because she finds Osmond's own beliefs so entirely repugnant; above all, his claim that life is a matter

9. See p. 294 in this Norton Critical Edition [*Editor*].

of prescribed forms and not freedoms. We will learn much more as she thinks through the night, will learn everything we need to know. She will meditate on Osmond's contempt for everyone in the world except the handful of people he envies instead, and of his desire to extract from the world some acknowledgment of his own superiority. She will contemplate his claim that it's somehow "indecent" (637) for her to visit Ralph at his hotel. And in thinking about Ralph's invalid life Isabel will at last understand his attempt to warn her off this marriage. She will recognize that his generosity is in itself a form of intelligence and one her husband lacks. So she sits quietly on as the candles burn down, her mind a cauldron of activity. But at last she rises, and then stops, her memory caught, in the chapter's last words, by that afternoon's impression of "her husband and Madame Merle, grouped unconsciously and familiarly" (639).

Henry James: A Chronology

Henry James had a long and busy life. He traveled widely, published more than any comparably significant novelist of his day, and could count almost all the great writers of his period, from England, France, and the United States, among his friends and acquaintances. This chronology makes no claim to be comprehensive; it includes James's changes of country or house and the dates of many of his books, but few social details. Interested readers should consult Edgar F. Harden's A *Henry James Chronology* (Palgrave Macmillan, 2005), which offers a month-by-month tracking of both his life and his work, or one of the standard biographies.

1843 Henry James is born April 15 in New York City, second son of Henry and Mary Robertson James; Henry Sr. has an inherited income of approximately $10,000 a year and will never work for a living. There will eventually be five children: William (1841), Garth Wilkinson (1845), Robertson (1846), and Alice (1848). Later that year Henry James Sr. takes his young family to England and then France.

1845 Family returns to America after two years in Europe, settling briefly in Albany and then (1847) in New York City.

1851 Henry and William start school, moving frequently from one institution to another in accordance with their father's whims.

1855 Henry Sr. moves his family to Europe, where they live mostly in Switzerland and France. Children attend a series of schools, but their education is experimental and often interrupted.

1858–59 The Jameses return to America; they live briefly in Newport, Rhode Island, before Henry Sr., dissatisfied with American education, takes them back to Europe; Henry studies in Geneva and Bonn. Family returns to Newport.

1860 In Newport Henry renews acquaintance with his orphaned Temple cousins, and especially with Mary Temple, known as "Minny."

1861 Injures his back while helping extinguish a fire in a stable. This "obscure hurt," now usually thought to be a slipped disc, keeps him out of the Civil War, and has marked physical and psychological effects alike. William enrolls at the Lawrence Scientific School at Harvard.

1862–63 Briefly studies at Harvard Law School. Younger brothers "Wilky" and "Bob" enlist in the Union Army, serving as officers in regiments of black enlisted men. Wilky is badly wounded in the 1863 assault of the 54th Massachusetts on Fort Wagner in South Carolina.

1864	First publications: a story, "A Tragedy of Error," anonymously in *Continental Monthly*, and a book review in the *North American Review*. Henry Sr. moves the family to Cambridge.
1865	First fiction under his own name: "The Story of a Year," in the *Atlantic Monthly*. Over the next few years he will publish both fiction and criticism with increasing frequency, writing especially for the *Atlantic* and the newly established *Nation*. Growing friendship (1866 on) with William Dean Howells.
1869–70	First independent trip to Europe, from February 1869 to May the following year. Meets George Eliot in London; late spring and summer in Paris and Switzerland; autumn in Italy. Travels north at the new year and is in England when he learns that his cousin Minny has died of tuberculosis. Returns to Cambridge, where he lives at his father's house and cannot yet settle into a career.
1872–74	Accompanies his sister Alice on her own tour of Europe, May through October 1872. Stays on after her return until September 1874, spending both winters in Italy. Writes travel pieces and works on *Roderick Hudson,* his first long novel.
1874–75	Lives in New York while missing Europe. First book, *A Passionate Pilgrim and Other Tales*, followed soon by *Transatlantic Sketches*. *Roderick Hudson* is serialized in the *Atlantic* and published in book form at the end of the year. Now determined to make an expatriate life, sails for France in October.
1875–76	Settles in Paris that November, soon meets Ivan Turgenev and is then introduced to Gustave Flaubert, Émile Zola, and others. Friendship with Russian émigré Paul Zhukovsky. In December 1876 moves to London, where at 3 Bolton Street, Piccadilly, he will live for the next decade.
1877	*The American.*
1878–79	Now fully immersed in English society, and a frequent guest at country houses and smart dinner tables. "Daisy Miller" published in the *Cornhill* (1878) and makes him a celebrity; English edition of selected stories, *The Madonna of the Future* (1879), and *Hawthorne* (1879).
1880–81	*Washington Square.* In March travels to Florence where he begins work on *The Portrait of a Lady*; serialization starts that fall in *Macmillan's Magazine* (UK) and the *Atlantic*. First meeting, in Florence, with Constance Fenimore Woolson. In February 1881 leaves London for Paris and then Venice, where he brings the novel near its close. Returns to America in October, his first visit in six years. *The Portrait of a Lady* published as book, though with 1882 on the title page of its American edition.
1882	Mary James dies in January, and Henry helps settle his father and sister in a new house. Returns to England in May, and then back to America in December, where Henry Sr. dies just before his arrival.
1884–86	Alice James moves to England. *The Bostonians* and *The Princess Casamassima* (both 1886). Moves to 34 De Vere Gardens in South Kensington.

1886–87   In December leaves for extended stay in Italy, mostly in Florence and Venice. Lives in Woolson's Florentine villa; writes "The Aspern Papers" and many other tales.

1890   *The Tragic Muse.* Disappointed by his sales, decides to write plays rather than novels; his stage adaptation of *The American* (1891) has a modest success. Continues to write short fiction but will not publish another novel until 1896.

1892   Alice James dies of breast cancer.

1894   Constance Fenimore Woolson commits suicide in Venice. He travels there to help her relatives dispose of her effects; burns his correspondence with her.

1895   His hopes for theatrical success rest on *Guy Domville*, which premieres January 5; he is booed when he takes a bow at the end of the performance, and he determines to abandon the stage. "The Altar of the Dead."

1896   *The Other House.*

1897   Suffering from writer's cramp, hires a stenographer and begins dictating his work. Signs lease for Lamb House in Rye, on the Sussex coast, which he will buy in 1899. *The Spoils of Poynton* and *What Maisie Knew.*

1898   "The Turn of the Screw."

1899   *The Awkward Age.* Friendship with young Norwegian-American sculptor Hendrik Andersen. William James visits Lamb House, their first meeting in six years.

1900   Begins *The Ambassadors*; the start of what will be called his "Major Phase."

1902   *The Wings of the Dove.*

1903   *The Ambassadors*; *William Wetmore Story and His Friends*, a biographical study of American expatriate life in Italy; and *The Better Sort* (tales). Start of friendship with Edith Wharton.

1904–05   *The Golden Bowl.* In August sails for America, his first visit in more than twenty years. Lectures all along the eastern seaboard and then across the country, even visiting California. Forms plans with Scribner's for the New York Edition of his novels and tales. Returns to Britain in July and begins writing a travel book, *The American Scene* (1907).

1906–08   Revises *The Portrait of a Lady* and writes its preface for the New York Edition; in all he will write eighteen prefaces for that edition. Writes "The Jolly Corner" in the summer of 1906; in 1907 hires Theodora Bosanquet as his typist. First volumes of the New York Edition published; its commercial failure is quickly apparent.

1909–10   *Italian Hours.* Late in the year burns forty years of letters and papers. Growing depression. In spring 1910 William James comes with his wife, Alice, despite his own heart troubles, to give him support. James returns with him to America that August; William dies.

1911   Returns to England, and while working on his autobiography begins to write his way out of depression. Takes London flat at 21 Carlyle Mansions, Cheyne Walk, in Chelsea.

1913–14   *A Small Boy and Others*, first volume of autobiography, followed by *Notes of a Son and Brother* (1914). For his seventieth birthday his admirers commission John Singer Sargent to paint his portrait; one of Sargent's greatest, it now hangs in London's National Portrait Gallery. Increasingly unwell, and depressed by the start of the Great War.

1915   Appalled by American neutrality, becomes a British citizen. That December suffers the first of a series of strokes.

1916   Awarded the Order of Merit by King George V. Dies February 28, in London; his ashes are later buried in the family plot in the Cambridge Cemetery, where his epitaph reads "Novelist, citizen of two nations, interpreter of his generation on both sides of the sea."

Suggestions for Further Reading

The literature on Henry James is vast, helpful, provocative, and ever chang-ing; the documentary evidence pertaining to his life, his work, and his world can seem unending. I have not listed here those scholarly books and articles excerpted in this Norton Critical Edition; what remains will daunt even a dedicated reader, and yet represents only a fraction of what's available. The standard biography is still Leon Edel's, published in five volumes (Lippincott, 1953–72); a one-volume redaction that's more open about James's sexual identity appeared in 1985. Fred Kaplan's *Henry James: The Imagination of Genius* (Morrow, 1992) does a better job than Edel on the money side of James's professional world. Lyndall Gordon's *A Private Life of Henry James* (W. W. Norton, 1999) considers his relations with his cousin Minny Temple and his friend Constance Fenimore Woolson; its thesis is arguable, but it has a fine eye for the details of daily life. R. W. B. Lewis's *The James Family* (Far-rar, Straus & Giroux, 1991) offers a highly readable chronicle of the novelist's relations with his parents and siblings.

James's 10,000 extant letters are one of the main sources—and pleasures— for anyone interested in him. Edel put together a four-volume selection (1974–84) for The Belknap Press of Harvard University Press, but that's begun to be superseded by the *The Complete Letters of Henry James*, ed. Greg W. Zacharias and Pierre A. Walker (University of Nebraska Press, 2006, 2009); almost a dozen heavily annotated volumes have appeared to date, but the story is only up to the time of *The Portrait of a Lady* itself. Philip Horne's *Henry James: A Life in Letters* (Viking, 1999) offers a superb one-volume edi-tion with linking commentary. Over the years there have also appeared spe-cialized volumes devoted to James's correspondence with his brother William, or with such friends as Henry Adams and Edith Wharton. Michael Anesko's *Letters, Fictions, Lives: Henry James and William Dean Howells* (Oxford University Press, 1997) provides a compelling record of a literary collaboration and friendship.

The Library of America has released sixteen volumes of James's work: six of his novels and five containing his complete tales, two each of his criticism and travel essays, and most recently (2016) one of his autobiographical writ-ings. All can be recommended, but those devoted to his criticism, the pref-aces included, have no equal. Cambridge University Press is now in the process of publishing a complete edition of James's fiction, which will include his notebooks and prefaces. The notebooks are currently available in *The Complete Notebooks of Henry James*, ed. Edel and Powers (Oxford University Press, 1987).

Van Wyck Brooks's *New England: Indian Summer 1865–1915* (Dutton, 1940) remains an extraordinarily readable account of the literary world from which James emerged. See also Alex Zwerdling's *Improvised Europeans: American Literary Expatriates and the Siege of London* (Basic Books, 1998), while James's own *William Wetmore Story and His Friends* (1903) offers a fascinating look at what he called the "precursors," the generation of Ameri-cans before his own who made their life in Europe.

Reviews of James's work are collected in both *Henry James: The Contemporary Reviews*, ed. Kevin J. Hayes (Cambridge University Press, 1996) and *Henry James: The Critical Heritage*, ed. Roger Gard (Routledge, 1968). *Perspectives on James's* The Portrait of a Lady, ed. William T. Stafford (New York University Press, 1967) collects many of the most interesting articles on the novel to that date. But see also Laurence Holland, *The Expense of Vision: Essays on the Craft of Henry James* (Princeton University Press, 1964); Dorothea Krook, *The Ordeal of Consciousness in Henry James* (Cambridge University Press, 1962), Richard Poirer, *The Comic Sense of Henry James* (Oxford University Press, 1967), and R. W. Stallman, *The House that James Built* (Michigan State University Press, 1961).

All current students of James are indebted to the shrewd archival work of Michael Anesko; see *Friction with the Market: Henry James and the Profession of Authorship* (Oxford University Press, 1986) and *Monopolizing the Master: Henry James and the Politics of Modern Literary Scholarship* (Stanford University Press, 2012). Paul B. Armstrong's *The Phenomenology of Henry James* (University of North Carolina Press, 1983) offers a demanding reading of *The Portrait of a Lady* in terms of twentieth-century Continental philosophy. *New Essays on* The Portrait of a Lady, ed. Joel Porte (Cambridge University Press, 1990) includes several useful articles; see especially Donatella Izzo's "*The Portrait of a Lady* and Modern Narrative" and Alfred Habegger's polemical "The Fatherless Heroine and the Filial Son: Deep Background for *The Portrait of a Lady*." Peter Brooks's *Henry James Goes to Paris* (Princeton University Press, 2007) provides an elegant account of the influence of the French capital, and of French fiction, on James's work. *Henry James' New York Edition: The Construction of Authorship*, ed. David McWhirter (Stanford University Press, 1995) contains a series of specially commissioned essays on that late edition by a number of important scholars.

On *The Portrait of a Lady* itself, interesting chapters can be found in recent books by Sigi Jöttkandt, *Acting Beautifully: Henry James and the Ethical Aesthetic* (State University of New York Press, 2005); J. Hillis Miller, *Literature as Conduct: Speech Acts in Henry James* (Fordham University Press, 2005); and Hilary M. Schor, *Curious Subjects: Women and the Trials of Realism* (Oxford University Press, 2013). I have also learned from these articles: Nancy Bentley, "Conscious Observation: Jane Campion's *Portrait of a Lady*," on the 1996 film, in Susan M. Griffin, *Henry James Goes to the Movies* (University Press of Kentucky, 2002); Sarah Blackwood, "Isabel Archer's Body," *The Henry James Review* 31.3 (2010); Melissa J. Ganz, "'A Strange Opposition': *The Portrait of a Lady* and the Divorce Debates," *Henry James Review* 27.2 (2006); Clair Hughes, "The Color of Life: The Significance of Dress in *The Portrait of a Lady*," *Henry James Review* 18.1 (1997); Adrian Poole, "Dying Before the End: The Reader in *The Portrait of a Lady*," *The Yearbook of English Studies* 26 (1996); Lee Clark Mitchell, "Beyond the Frame of *The Portrait of a Lady*," *Raritan* 17.3 (1998); Elliot M. Schrero, "How Rich was Isabel Archer?" *Henry James Review* 20.1 (1999); Phyllis Van Slyck, "Isabel Archer's 'Delicious Pain': Charting Lacanian Desire in *The Portrait of a Lady*," *American Imago* 70.4 (2013); and Sandra A. Zagarell, "*The Portrait of a Lady*: 'No Intention of Deamericanising,'" *Henry James Review* 35.1 (2014).

In recent years a number of companion volumes to James's work have appeared, each containing essays or entries by many different hands. Some of these function largely as works of reference; the most useful either synthesize current scholarship or lay out new lines of argument. Two of the best are Greg W. Zacharias, *A Companion to Henry James* (Blackwell, 2008), and David McWhirter, *Henry James in Context* (Cambridge University Press, 2010.) The journal of record in the field is *The Henry James Review*, published by Johns Hopkins University Press and edited by Susan M. Griffin at the University of Louisville; it is a publication unusual in the ranks of single-author journals for the breadth and sophistication of its theoretical and historical interests, as well as for the skeptical eye it often turns upon its subject. The two best websites are the Henry James Scholar's Guide to Web Sites at www2.newpaltz.edu/~hathaway and that of Creighton University's Center for Henry James Studies at centerforhenryjamesstudies.weebly.com.